THE OXFORD

GENDER AND POLITICS

THE OXFORD HANDBOOK OF

....

GENDER AND POLITICS

....

Edited by

GEORGINA WAYLEN
KAREN CELIS
JOHANNA KANTOLA
and
S. LAUREL WELDON

OXFORD
UNIVERSITY PRESS

OXFORD
UNIVERSITY PRESS

Oxford University Press is a department of the University of Oxford.
It furthers the University's objective of excellence in research, scholarship,
and education by publishing worldwide.

Oxford   New York
Auckland   Cape Town   Dar es Salaam   Hong Kong   Karachi
Kuala Lumpur   Madrid   Melbourne   Mexico City   Nairobi
New Delhi   Shanghai   Taipei   Toronto

With offices in
Argentina   Austria   Brazil   Chile   Czech Republic   France   Greece
Guatemala   Hungary   Italy   Japan   Poland   Portugal   Singapore
South Korea   Switzerland   Thailand   Turkey   Ukraine   Vietnam

Oxford is a registered trademark of Oxford University Press
in the UK and certain other countries.

Published in the United States of America by
Oxford University Press
198 Madison Avenue, New York, NY 10016

Library of Congress Cataloging-in-Publication Data
The Oxford handbook of gender and politics / edited by Georgina Waylen... [et al.].
p. cm.
ISBN 978-0-19-975145-7 (hardcover : alk. paper); 978-0-19-046191-1 (paperback : alk. paper)
1. Women—Political activity.   2. Feminism.   3. Women—Government policy.
I. Waylen, Georgina.
HQ1236.O99 2013
305.42—dc23
2012013313

ISBN 978-0-19-046191-1

CONTENTS

....

Contributors

....

Brooke Ackerly is associate professor of political science at Vanderbilt University.

Kate Bedford is reader in law at the University of Kent.

Karen Beckwith is the Flora Stone Mather Professor in the Department of Political Science at Case Western Reserve University.

Merike Blofield is associate professor of political science at the University of Miami.

Louise Chappell is professor and former Australian Research Council Future Fellow in the School of Social Sciences at the University of New South Wales.

Karen Celis is research professor in the Department of Political Science at the Vrije Universiteit Brussel.

Valerie Chepp is assistant professor of sociology at Hamline University.

Sarah Childs is professor of politics and gender at the University of Bristol.

Rachel Cichowski is associate professor for the Law, Societies, and Justice program in the Department of Political Science at the University of Washington.

Patricia Hill Collins is Distinguished University Professor at the University of Maryland, College Park, and professor emeritus of Africana studies and sociology at the University of Cincinnati.

Diana Coole is professor of political and social theory at Birkbeck, University of London.

Rita Kaur Dhamoon is assistant professor of political science at the University of Victoria.

R. Amy Elman is professor of political science and William Weber chair of social science at Kalamazoo College.

Christina Ewig is associate professor of gender and women's studies and political science at the University of Wisconsin, Madison.

Lucy Ferguson is an independent researcher and consultant based in Madrid and a former honorary research fellow in politics at the University of Sheffield.

MYRA MARX FERREE is the Alice H. Cook Professor of Sociology and director of the European Union Center of Excellence at the University of Wisconsin, Madison.

LIESL HAAS is associate professor of political science at California State University, Long Beach.

LENE HANSEN is Project Director of Images and International Security and professor of international relations in the Department of Political Science at the University of Copenhagen.

MARY HAWKESWORTH is Distinguished Professor of Political Science and Women's and Gender Studies at Rutgers University.

JUTTA JOACHIM is associate professor of political science at the Leibniz University Hannover.

JOHANNA KANTOLA is Academy research fellow and senior lecturer of gender studies at the University of Helsinki.

MIKI CAUL KITTILSON is associate professor of political science at Arizona State University.

KELSY KRETSCHMER is assistant professor at Southern Illinois University, Carbondale.

MONA LENA KROOK is associate professor of political science at Rutgers University.

AMY LIND is Mary Ellen Heintz Endowed Chair and Professor of Women's, Gender, and Sexuality Studies at the University of Cincinnati.

MOYA LLOYD is professor of political theory at Loughborough University.

EMANUELA LOMBARDO is lecturer in political science at Madrid Complutense University.

JONI LOVENDUSKI is Anniversary Professor of Politics at Birkbeck College, University of London.

AMY G. MAZUR is professor in the Department of Political Science at Washington State University.

DOROTHY E. MCBRIDE is emeritus professor of political science at Florida Atlantic University.

PETRA MEIER is professor of politics at the University of Antwerp.

DAVID S. MEYER is professor of sociology, political science, and planning, policy, and design at the University of California, Irvine.

VÉRONIQUE MOTTIER is fellow and director of studies in social and political sciences at Jesus College, Cambridge, and professor in sociology at the University of Lausanne.

BAUKJE PRINS holds a chair in citizenship and diversity at the The Hague University of Applied Sciences.

SHIRIN M. RAI is professor in the Department of Politics and International Studies at the University of Warwick.

SHAHRA RAZAVI is chief of reserch and data at United Nations Women.

SAWITRI SAHARSO is professor of intercultural governance at the University of Twente and associate professor of sociology at VU University.

DIANE SAINSBURY is professor emerita in the Department of Political Science at Stockholm University.

LESLIE SCHWINDT-BAYER is associate professor of political science at Rice University.

BIRTE SIIM is professor of gender research in social sciences in the Department of Culture and Global Studies at Aalborg University.

JUDITH SQUIRES is professor of political theory at the University of Bristol.

DARA Z. STROLOVITCH is associate professor of political science at Princeton University.

SURUCHI THAPAR-BJÖRKERT is senior lecturer in the Department of Government at the University of Uppsala.

ERICA TOWNSEND-BELL is assistant professor of political science at Oklahoma State University.

AILI MARI TRIPP is professor of political science and gender and women's studies and director of the Center for Research on Gender and Women at the University of Wisconsin, Madison.

JACQUI TRUE is professor of politics and international relations and Australian Research Council Future Fellow at Monash University.

MIEKE VERLOO is professor of comparative politics and inequality issues at Radboud University Nijmegen and scientific director of the Quality in Gender and Equality Policies (QUING) project at the Institute for Human Sciences.

GEORGINA WAYLEN is professor of politics at the University of Manchester.

S. LAUREL WELDON is Distinguished Professor of political science and director of the Center for Research on Diversity and Inclusion at Purdue University.

THE OXFORD HANDBOOK OF

GENDER AND POLITICS

INTRODUCTION

GENDER AND POLITICS: A GENDERED WORLD, A GENDERED DISCIPLINE

KAREN CELIS, JOHANNA KANTOLA,
GEORGINA WAYLEN, AND
S. LAUREL WELDON

POLITICS as a real-world phenomenon and political science as an academic discipline are gendered. This introduction and this volume aim to explain what this means and why it is important. People all over the world find that the basic conditions of their lives—their safety, health, education, work, as well as access to markets, public space, and free expression—are fundamentally shaped by their identification as belonging to particular sex or gender groups. Individual bodies may be typed as male or female, masculine or feminine, heterosexual or homosexual, transgendered or nongendered in a dizzying variety of ways across cultures and over time. However, these social practices of gender often appear natural and unproblematic, even biological and therefore impossible to change, in the social contexts in which they occur. But a cursory review of the literature on the biological basis of sex, taking into account the wide variety of the number and content of gender categories across social contexts, reveals a world far more complex than this simplistic male–female dichotomy would suggest (Butler 1990; Dreger 1998; Fausto-Sterling 2000). Gender is never just about sex but varies by race, ethnicity, nation, class, and a variety of other dimensions of social life.

Indeed, the persistent, dichotomous sex-typing characteristic of many institutions of the modern world would be a matter of intellectual curiosity if the consequences of being identified with a particular sex were not so dire. Across the globe, gender determines who goes hungry and who gets adequate nutrition and water, who can vote, run for office, marry, or have rights to children, who commands authority and respect and who is denigrated and dismissed, and who is most vulnerable to violence and abuse in their own homes and intimate relationships (see, e.g., World Health Organization and London School of Hygiene and Tropical Medicine 2010; Htun 2003; Htun and Weldon 2011). These norms shape more than personal and family relationships or career paths, though they certainly shape those: they shape religious practice and the structure of markets and processes of governance (Charrad 2010; Brettell and Sargeant 2001; Lamphere 2001).

Let's examine a few concrete examples. If we look at some of the key issues that constitute the partisan divide between political parties in the United States—whether it is reproductive rights or same-sex marriage—we can see that many of the "culture wars" issues are fundamentally questions about which sexual and intimate behaviors of men and women should be accepted and supported by the society at large (Wolbrecht 2000; Inglehart and Norris 2003; but see also Sanbonmatsu 2002). In the Philippines, income from domestic worker care work is the number one export and the largest source of foreign currency, while Lim (1998) estimates that income from sex work comprises between 2 and 11 percent of the gross domestic product of Thailand. And, finally, since 2008 the global economic crisis has had a very differentiated impact in terms of the resulting spending cuts and austerity programs. It is clear that some groups are affected far more adversely than others, and many women—who make up a large proportion of state and public sector employees and the majority of single parents and the poor—have been particularly hard hit and affected in different ways from men (Waylen 2012). Perhaps most profoundly, gender influences the very ways we organize and think about the world and our way of knowing about the world.

In such a context, it is hardly surprising that political science as a discipline is also gendered and fundamentally shaped by these social norms about sex and sexuality. The canonical definitions of politics that have delineated the boundaries of the discipline have been read to exclude many of the topics covered in this handbook. As we will see, the study of politics has now broadened beyond the narrow focus on those holding formal office and the politics of distribution. It now encompasses many new groups espousing "gender trouble" as well as new ideas about masculinity and femininity across a range of contexts, from house and home to the houses of Parliament. Yet, despite the vibrancy of the gender and politics scholarship shown in this handbook and a long history of gender activism, gender is still ignored in much academic political science.

In contrast to this omission, this handbook makes gender the point of departure for thinking about political science, taking it, in the words of bell hooks (1984), from margin to center. In doing so, it attempts a number of things. First, it challenges existing political science in terms of its concepts, subject matter, and even its methods. Second, it demonstrates the diversity of the gender and politics scholarship, embracing interdisciplinarity and a plurality of methods and approaches in ways that are unusual in political science. And finally, it shows that much of the gender and politics scholarship has close links with the practice of politics, and feminism in particular, which again is unusual within most political science. As a result, although the categories of analysis overlap with other handbooks to some degree (with chapters on institutions, social movements, interest groups, and multiculturalism), there are also categories such as sexual violence, reproductive rights, or sexuality and the body more generally not found (or less salient) in the other handbooks,. More importantly, the organization of the chapters, and the priority given to these topics, is different from the handbooks that overlook gender.

In this introduction, we map some of the changes that form the backdrop to this handbook, and we locate the gender and politics scholarship by delineating its relationship to the discipline of political science as it is conventionally understood and to politics as a practice. We cannot do full justice to the complexity and sophistication of the wealth of gender and politics scholarship that now exists, as what we can present here is limited and inevitably involves some oversimplification. But we argue that gender is centrally important to politics and that inequalities are embedded in both the study and practice of politics. We also show that many scholars, influenced by feminism in its various different forms, see their work as challenging these inequalities and use standard methods and approaches as well as those that are more experimental or innovative.

As such, we do not discuss the different chapters but give you instead some context within which to locate them and an understanding of the development of the gender and politics subfield. We end by outlining some of the challenges that remain before giving a very brief outline of the handbook. For in-depth analyses of key concepts such as gender, intersectionality, reproductive rights, and ones more familiar to political scientists such as citizenship, the state, and representation—all central to the gender and politics scholarship—we direct readers to the individual chapters.

AN "INCOMPLETE REVOLUTION"?

Our starting point is to recognize the big changes that have taken place both in politics as practice and political science as a discipline over the last century. We do not adhere to a standard metanarrative, often seen in political science and other disciplines, of a uniformly patriarchal world that began to be transformed when feminism (depicted as originating in the West in the 1960s) spread to the rest of the world. However, it is remarkable that in 1950 the vast majority of the world's legislators were male and that family law in most places had come to privilege men in areas from property rights (including inheritance rights and rights to children) to sexual rights (Interparliamentary Union (IPU); Htun and Weldon 2011): Male dominance in formal, decision-making positions had come to seem natural and uncontestable, and male authority in the family was seen as a biological necessity and mark of civilization since colonial times.

Feminist activists and scholars have, of course, contextualized and questioned these patterns of male domination, pointing out that male domination is neither natural nor desirable. Anthropologists have documented the wide variety of family forms and modes of social organization around the world, defying any effort to theorize a universal public–private split or form of male dominance (Lamphere 2001). For example, in Indonesia, trading in the market was seen as the domain of women (Brenner 2001). And the Oneida (a First Nations group) in North America traditionally saw formal politics (making collective decisions) as women's domain (Sunseri 2011). So women's exclusion from the public sphere (defined as positions of leadership in community decision-making and economic affairs) cannot be seen as continuous throughout history or as universal.

Research similarly shows the bankruptcy of the notion of the supposedly universal patriarchal family form. Historical and current family forms range widely from polyandry (one wife, many husbands) to polygyny (one husband, many wives) and includes matrifocal and matrilineal structures (where inheritance and kinship structures pass through women) (Menon 2001). None of these modes of organization necessarily preclude male dominance, but they caution us against universalizing stories of public and private and common gender roles. So the idea that the world was characterized by a uniform, patriarchal structure until the 1970s does not comport with the anthropological or historical record (Brettell and Sargeant 2001; Jolly and Macintyre 1989).

Nor is it correct to see feminism as a Western invention or recent idea. As Jayawardena (1986, 2) notes, "Debates on women's rights and education were held in 18th-century China, and there were movements for women's social emancipation in early 19th-century India;...feminist struggles originated between 60–80 years ago in many countries of Asia...the fact that such movements flourished in several non-European countries during this period has been 'hidden from history.'" Even in the West, feminism did not begin in the 1960s. Enlightenment thinkers such as Mary Wollstonecraft and John Stuart Mill were writing in favor of women's emancipation, with Wollstonecraft writing *A Vindication of the Rights of Women* as early as 1792 and Mill *The Subjection of Women* in 1789.

However, as a result of women's activism over the last century, in every region of the world we have seen dramatic changes in attitudes about sexuality and gender as well as a transformation of laws and policies on a wide range of issues from violence against women, family law, women's access to political power and work, the criminalization of homosexuality, and maternity and parental leave (though these changes have by no means been uniform or uncontested) (Weldon 2002a; Htun 2003; Krook 2009; Charrad 2010; Htun and Weldon 2011). Women have organized to demand their rights in virtually every country in the world, though with varying degrees of success (Htun and Weldon 2012). Feminist activists have used a wide array of tactics, from street theater to petitions and lobbying, to demand these rights.

The numbers of women who are prominent politicians and heads of state and international bodies in Europe, Africa, and Latin America have increased. Since 1980, more than 30 national leaders have been women. In this decade alone, Hillary Clinton has been the U.S. secretary of state (the third woman to hold the position in the last three administrations), and Michele Bachelet, Cristina Fernandez de Kirchner, and Dilma Roussef were elected as presidents in Chile, Argentina, and Brazil, respectively. Ellen Johnson Sirleaf was elected president of Liberia, and Christine Lagarde became the first female director at the International Monetary Fund (IMF) in 2011. The parity cabinet (2004–2008) of Zapatero's socialist government in Spain contained equal numbers of male and female ministers and outraged the defense establishment with the appointment of a visibly pregnant woman as defense minister (Waylen 2012, 25). And in November 2011, the lower houses of government in Rwanda and Andorra were composed of at least 50 percent women.

The discipline of political science has also been transformed. There are now more women involved in the academic study of politics. By 2002, 35 percent of assistant professors in the United States were women (APSA 2004). There have also been some very distinguished and influential women political scientists (in 2009 the political scientist Elinor Ostrom became the first woman to win the Nobel prize for economics). And the academy as a whole has recently made some concerted efforts to create more of a level playing field with regard to women. So it would be impossible to deny that there have been significant efforts and achievements, both in terms of increasing women's political representation and improving the opportunities for women scholars in the academy in general (Waylen 2012, 25).

But both the world and the disciplines are still male dominated even today. The global average for women in the lower house of legislatures was still only 20 percent in November 2011, a figure that conceals some big variations ranging from an average of 42.3 percent in the Nordic Countries to 12.9 percent in the Pacific region (Inter-Parliamentary Union). At the United Nations, only 6 of 37 under-secretary generals (16 percent) were women. And international business remains perhaps the most male-dominated of these spheres of power; women comprise only 1.4 percent of chief executive officers of Fortune 500 companies. On a day-to-day basis, women still struggle to improve the conditions of their lives. A woman dies in childbirth every minute, and 99 percent of these maternal deaths take place in the third world. Women make up a majority of the world's poor and are disproportionately illiterate. The revolution in academia is similarly unfinished, with only 22 percent of academic political scientists in United States and United Kingdom in 2002 and even fewer women at the highest ranks and the most prestigious research universities (APSA 2004).

Gender and politics scholars argue that the roots of this enduring male domination in both politics and the political science academy are complex and profound. Challenging this deep-seated domination is more than simply a problem of adding women or increasing the "sheer numbers" in public office (Beckwith and Cowell-Meyers 2003). While important, it is not enough in itself. More significant change is needed both to politics as a practice and to political science as a discipline to make them gender equitable. To facilitate this, we need to understand what is it about politics as an academic discipline and politics as a practice and the ways the two interact that results in this overrepresentation of men and a profound gender blindness.

If we first think about the nature of politics and political science as an academic discipline, several interconnected factors jump out. First, as Virginia Sapiro (1981) suggests, part of the reason for the discipline's gender blindness lies in the low numbers of women in the discipline. For her, the structural position of women reproduces the androcentric biases of the discipline. Second, and perhaps more importantly, the discipline's categories and methods were developed by privileged men to consider those issues of concern to them. This domination is reflected in the very narrow and ideological definitions of what counts as politics on which the Anglo-American disciplines have traditionally been based. Politics, narrowly construed, is the activity of government or governing. Indeed, the word *politics* in the original Greek was used by Aristotle to connote those questions that pertained to the operation of the *polis*, the political community. The distinctive feature of politics is its public or general nature, the way it affects the community as a whole as distinct from private matters (Arendt 1958; Wolin 1960). Politics is also seen as the study of power, and sometimes by extension the study of the powerful. But some broader definitions of politics have also had a long provenance in political science: Dahl (1984, 9–10) defined politics as relating to power and political systems as "any persistent pattern of human relationships that involves, to a significant extent, control, influence, power or authority." Others connect politics fundamentally to distributions, as in "who gets what, where, when and how" or the authoritative allocation of value (Easton 1953).

The traditional focus on politics as the study of the machinery of government and electoral politics or on political elites and formal institutions rendered women and gender invisible in spite of their foundational importance for building the welfare state and for constructing postcolonial nations, for the conduct of war and terrorism, and for maintaining social and economic privilege more generally. The roots of these core assumptions about what constitutes *politics* in the Anglo-American tradition can be traced to the work of political theorists like John Locke, who based many of their ideas on the analytical separation of the public and the private spheres. The Anglo-American disciplines took up this widely accepted (if mistaken) view of the transcultural and transhistorical universality of the public–private split, namely, that citizens or heads of household (for which one should read men) were the ones who were active (and who should be active) in the public sphere. This subsumed women (and also children) into the household or family within a private sphere where "every man's home is his castle" and in which he can do as he pleases free from the interference of the state (Pateman 1983). This analytical exclusion of women from the public sphere created politics as a male sphere from which women were legitimately excluded as political subjects. In turn, at least when it came to women, the private sphere was seen as lying outside the political arena and therefore did not form part of the legitimate subject matter of the discipline. But regulation of women's access to abortion, sexuality, and male violence against female relatives in the family was then, as now, seen as a legitimate area of action for governments, revealing the inconsistency and gender bias that undergirds the ideology of *separate spheres*.

The notion of a separation of the public and private spheres persists today. Its reflection (even if it remains partial and contested) in many legal systems around the world is remarkable given the range of family and societal forms that characterize the world's cultures. In many places, assumptions about women and men and their respective roles in the public and private spheres still affect issues, from who governs to who decides intimate matters such as sexuality and childbearing. It affects the ways economies are structured and economic value—seen as created in the productive public sphere and not in the reproductive private sphere—is calculated. It also continues to affect what counts as politics and the political, still predominantly *high politics* in the public sphere; who is seen as a suitable person to be involved in politics; and what are appropriate issues—often narrowly defined—that exclude certain activities and actors and embody particular notions of masculinity and femininity. These ideas have again affected what has been deemed suitable subject matter for the academic discipline of politics.

Even though some of the conventional definitions of politics would seem to allow for the study of a broader range of phenomena, it was feminists who pushed for a definition of politics that encompassed the personal and the private. Indeed, a rallying cry for many feminists has been that the personal is the political. In *Sexual Politics*, Kate Millett (1968, 23) defines politics as "power structured relationships, arrangements whereby one group of persons is controlled by another." Enloe (1996) points out that study of power must include not only those perceived as the "powerful" but also all those involved in the realization of power and influence for those at the top. The powerful (whether bureaucratically, economically, or socially powerful) depend on the everyday, regularized activities of others to make their decisions (or nondecisions) realities. And

Young (1990) critiques these analytic approaches that focus on distributions, arguing that they obscure the power dynamics that produce these distributions, thereby depoliticizing them. So feminists brought the personal and the private into the study of the political, and they have also drawn attention to the politics of knowledge production (and structures of production and reproduction more generally), meaning, and identity.

Feminists have highlighted how the discipline has been gendered in its approach to the valuation of knowledge. Political scientists have often assumed researchers to be disembodied and objective. Today, many political scientists (including some feminists) consider themselves *positivists*, often meaning that they use statistical methods (not actually seen as feature of positivism in most accounts of the term—see Deising 1992) or avoid "normative" or value-laden analysis, sticking only to "the facts." Some feminist scholars have joined critical theorists and postmodernists in challenging this so-called positivist approach, forcing a wider awareness of epistemological issues and a better acquaintance with philosophy of science more generally. Feminists have called for greater epistemological sophistication and nuance, introducing political scientists to a range of epistemological approaches from pragmatism and postmodernism to standpoint epistemology and hermeneutics. This diversity of approaches and methods is a strength of feminist scholarship and a model for the field.

More generally, feminist methodology reveals how gender fundamentally structures science, shaping more than the choice of methods (or tools) or methodology (approach to the use of such tools) in that it determines the questions that scholars ask and the areas of inquiry (Harding 1987). Feminists have also shown that seemingly neutral research tools produce different results when used by female social scientists or social scientists of color. Survey respondents give different responses to interlocutors of different identities; participant observation produces different opportunities and results for men and women. Some feminist scholars have revealed how social power structures knowledge so that the way we define and value knowledge reinforces patterns of class, race, and gender inequality.

The legacy of these assumptions—the artificial analytical separation of the public and private, the privileging of high politics, and the adoption of certain models of the individual researcher and the research process—remains a source of resistance to efforts to change the discipline and make it more inclusive and equitable. And if we turn to politics as practice, we see that these underlying assumptions have also impacted how politics is practiced. For example, Lovenduski and Norris's (1995) ground-breaking research documented how in the mid-1990s British Conservative party candidate selection committees unashamedly looked askance at women aspiring to be candidates—accusing them of neglecting their homes and husbands. Similarly, in many countries domestic violence has been considered something with which the police should not interfere, lying outside state jurisdiction in the realm of the private.

THE GENDER AND POLITICS SCHOLARSHIP

Feminism as a form of *theory* and *practice* has remained important to scholars and to the research carried out in the field of gender and politics. For many gender scholars, therefore, the "personal is political"—their academic interests have been inseparable from their political commitment. Their endeavor is therefore one of "critical scholarship" with an explicitly normative dimension. And from the late 1960s, women academics also began to organize inside the discipline. The women's caucus of the American Political Science Association was established in 1969, the International Political Science Association created a Study Group on Sex Roles and Politics in 1976, and in 1986 the Standing Group on Women and Politics was created within the European Consortium for Political Research. Debates about separate gender sections and panels on women and politics—seen by some as separatist—linked to broader questions about women's political participation, such as whether women should organize within established structures (political parties, trade unions) or autonomously (Dahlerup 2010). Scholars pressing alternative sexualities pushed further, sometimes arguing for a destabilization of analytic as well as social categories (e.g., Butler 1990). The development of much academic work on gender and politics was shaped by this broader context of feminist and lesbian, gay, bisexual, transgender, and queer (LGBTQ) activism.

Thus, the burgeoning gender and politics scholarship has looked at a range of themes using a diversity of approaches. Much has focused on women—first on including women in the current categories and analyses of political science—thereby gendering the classic "units of analysis" such as citizens, voters, legislators, parties, legislatures, states, and nations. A second strand on women has examined political activities in arenas traditionally seen as outside political science. A third strand has looked at gender as a structure of social organization. Finally, mirroring struggles within the broader feminist movement, women of color (women of marginalized races and ethnicities), women in the developing world, postcolonial feminists, and LGBTQ scholars pressed for a place in the study of gender politics, sometimes finding a degree of accommodation and sometimes, frustrated with resistance, founding their own scholarly institutions and threads of research. We briefly describe these developments next.

The Inclusion Project: The Difference Women Make (or Not)

The inclusion project, as Squires (1999) named it, aims to expose the absence of women, to reveal the degree to which that leads to partial, shallow, and biased knowledge, and to integrate women into the theories, institutions, and practices from which they had been excluded (Sapiro 1994; Zerilli 2006, 106–107). It examines women and politics in a more traditional sense, for example, electoral institutions, political parties, and political behavior, showing where women fit and what their impact is (Lovenduski 1981; Randall 1982; Lovenduski and Norris 1995). It seeks to uncover sameness and difference between women and men—without seeing women as somehow a deviant version of the male norm—and to assess whether "gender-blind" theories also apply to women, in different ways or not at all.

Scholars challenged the widely held stereotypes about women's political activity and behavior in the conventional political arena (Bourque and Grossholtz 1974). The classic early gender work on voting behavior, for example, demonstrated that when education, age, and background are controlled for, men and women vote at same rates, thereby disproving earlier beliefs that women's rate was lower than men's (Duverger 1995). Similarly, work in the United States finds that when women run they are just as likely as men to get elected and just as able as men to raise money. However, scholars also showed that women and men do often exhibit differences in their political attitudes and behavior, but not necessarily in the ways that had been assumed (e.g., it was long thought that women were inherently more right wing than men). Men and women do tend to line up on issues in different ways—but not necessarily on a straight-forward left–right split (such as on law and order). In 2011, while 52 percent of British men initially supported bombing of Libya, only 35 percent of British women did (Waylen 2012, 28). This gender gap is often found in voting behav-ior. At the last U.K. general election, the Conservatives had an 18 percent lead among 25–34-year-old men, whereas the Labour Party had an 11 percent lead among women of the same age (Waylen 2012, 28.

As part of the "inclusion project," gender scholars have studied women's presence in parties and governments, focusing on the differing numerical levels of their representation (descriptive representation), particularly in legislatures. They have argued for more women in politics and have discussed strategies, such as party and electoral quotas, to increase numbers of women in legisla-tures (Dahlerup 2006; Krook 2009). More recently, in part reflecting real-world changes, women in executives have been analyzed both comparatively and in single case studies (Jalazai 2008; Annesley and Gains 2010; Franceschet and Thomas 2011).

Interest in descriptive representation was partly due to a concern with its links to *substantive representation*: do women represent women's interests and change political style and culture? The question of if and how women legislators enhance women's substantive representation—"do more women make a difference?"—is an important one. Those advocating a politics of presence claimed that women's expe-riences generate knowledge about women's problems and their solutions and that women prioritize such issues (Phillips 1995). And some studies confirmed that the presence of women did change decision-making and policies (Wängnerud 2000; Swers 2002; Celis 2006; Kittilson 2008; Schwindt-Bayer 2011).

However, studies also highlight obstacles on the route from descriptive to substantive representation. Not all women legislators want to represent women (at least not in a feminist fashion), and not all women representatives who might want to can do so because of the parties they belong to, their institutional context, and the districts they are elected in, namely, "presence without empowerment" (Swers 2002; Celis 2008; Htun and Piscopo 2010). Related to this, the so-called critical mass debate explored whether a certain minimum proportion of women is needed to change the institutions and enable women to act for women (Dahlerup 1988). But empirical research has found little support for the critical mass thesis (Childs and Krook 2006). These critiques demonstrate the limits of descriptive representation as a mechanism for political transformation (with implications for the relationship between quotas and women's substantive representation) (Franceschet and Piscopo 2008; Franceschet et al. 2012; Weldon 2002, 2011). Some now argue that scholars interested in women's substantive representation should inductively investigate "critical actors" for women and how different actors in various political sites define and construct women's issues and interests (Celis et al. 2008; Childs and Krook 2006; Reingold and Swers 2011).

However, some feminist scholars have also criticized the "add women and stir" scholarship that seeks to include women in political science by asking traditional questions and using traditional methods. How far it can radically alter the discipline is disputed. Its advocates argue that it destabilizes and challenges existing categories. Goertz and Mazur (2008, 7) claim that "the 'add women and stir' metaphor suggests that the result of the addition of gender is only minor. However, the key issue is what happens to the mix after stirring: if the mixture blows up, then the addition of gender is of importance." Pamela Paxton (2008), for example, demonstrates that adding women's suffrage as a variable to the categorization of democratic systems drastically changes regime classifications. But critics argue that problems including women in political science will remain because, as we have seen, many mainstream theories, categories, concepts, and practices are based on initial exclusion of women (Zerilli 2006, 107). Hence, it is based on narrow notions of how discrimination and structural inequalities work and cannot theorize the broader societal processes behind gender inequalities. Moreover, the narrow focus on women and sex differences often reflects an unexamined assumption that *women* constitute a unified category who are stable and coherent subjects with identifiable, shared interests. Only recently, for example, has research on the impact of quotas also looked at the impact on ethnic minority women (Hughes 2011). The inclusion project therefore remains unfinished and the discipline still has a great deal to learn about women in conventional politics.

The Study of Women on Their Own Terms

Taking a different point of departure, other gender scholars have examined women in politics on their own terms. They are less concerned with sameness and difference between women and men within traditional political institutions and analyze women's political activities and legal reform, institutions, and policy of concern to women *as women*, thereby bringing new areas of study into the discipline. One important body of work examines the diverse activities and ideas that are often thought of as feminist but has also studied women's movements and organizations broadly construed. It demonstrates how feminist movements put important issues on to the political agenda and documents the diverse forms women's organizations take and the wide range of issues they engage with (Katzenstein and Mueller 1987; Ferree and Martin 1995). This includes women's organizing in developing countries (Basu 1994; Waylen 1996) as well as in Europe (Lovenduski and Randall 1993; Gelb 1996; Kaplan 1992). Examples of such research includes analyses of organizations like the National Organization of Women (NOW), which operated nationally throughout the United States to campaign for women's equality from 1966 onward (Barakso 2004) or studies of the way gender, race, and class worked together to structure the civil rights movement (Simien 2011).

This strand of research goes beyond the study of feminist movements, however, also covering women in racist (Blee 1991, 2002) and conservative movements (Schreiber 2008). The research looks at movements that were more specifically focused around certain issues such as the women's peace movement, epitomized, for example, by the women's peace camp at Greenham Common, which was attempting to prevent the United States from siting cruise missiles at one of its airbases in the United Kingdom in the 1980s, and also at the widespread campaigns around abortion and reproductive choice and pornography.

There is also a wealth of research on the political impact of these activities, from changing identities and culture to changing policy (Weldon 2002; Banaszak, Beckwith, and Rucht 2005). Feminists have launched highly successful campaigns to get reform in areas from violence against women to quotas to maternity leave and family law and have demanded institutional reforms such as the creation of women's commissions and women's policy agencies (McBride Stetson and Mazur 1995; Elman 1996; Mazur 2002). Autonomous organizations also provided important services such as women's refuges and rape crisis centers (Ferree and Martin 1995).

Women's organizing has also been important for processes of democratization. Although initially ignored by democratization scholars, women's movements played an important part in the breakdown of some nondemocratic regimes—often bringing about the "end of fear" (Alvarez 1990, Waylen 1994). Some of these women were the first protestors on the streets; perhaps the best known are human rights protesters such as the Madres of the Plaza de Mayo in Argentina, who, at great personal risk, demonstrated publicly to demand the return of their missing children (and in some cases grandchildren) who had been 'disappeared' by the repressive military regime. These movements also included feminist organizations. Feminists in Chile, for example, held one of the first demonstrations against the Pinochet regime to celebrate international women's day in 1983 and campaigned using the slogan "democracy in the home and in the country" (Jaquette 1994).

In addition to their important role in the broader opposition movements against dictatorship, organized women also tried to ensure that the outcomes of some transitions would bring positive change for women, such as increased political representation and the provision of greater rights in the post transition period (Waylen 2007). In both the Chilean and South African transitions women organized in an attempt to influence the developing political processes but with varying results (Hassim 2005; Waylen 2010). And in 2011 we have seen some similar efforts in Tunisia and Egypt as part of the Arab Spring. Egyptian women organized after only one women was appointed as part of the transitional government and a clause was inserted in the draft constitution that appeared to preclude women from becoming president.

Although not successful everywhere, women's movements have changed international norms—enabling on a global level the recognition of women's rights as human rights and anti-violence against women measures (Friedman 1995, 2009; Weldon 2006). A raft of equality measures has been introduced. Electoral quotas are now widespread (adopted in roughly half the world's parliaments); though they are controversial, if they are well designed, actually implemented, and enforced (unlike in France and Brazil), they are one of the most effective ways to "fast track" increases in women's representation (Dahlerup 2006; Krook 2009). Equality legislation, gender mainstreaming, and women's policy agencies (WPAs) have also been established in most of the world and endorsed by international and regional bodies like the European Union and the United Nations (Squires 2007; Kantola 2010). Gender equality policies and policies of importance to women are defined not only by feminism, women's movement organizations, and women's policy agencies but also by issues; the extent that women's organizations are included in policy-making processes has shown to be highly issue specific (Krizsán et al. 2010; McBride and Mazur 2010; Verloo 2011, 7). Htun and Weldon (2010) showed that feminist policy change depends on whether issues are doctrinal; about the status of women predominantly; or also strongly about class. As a consequence of this research, then, we now know a lot about women's movements and the impact of women activists in a wide array of political arenas.

The Study of Gender Regimes, Gendered States, and Institutions

Another strand of research focuses on broader societal patterns, examining regimes rather than specific policies and studying the state rather than particular laws. A distinct literature examines how particular institutional structures shape family, society, and polity. MacKinnon (1989, 161) perhaps most famously argued that "the state is male in the feminist sense: It sees and treats women the way men see and treat women." Some argued the state was a "male protection racket" (Rubin 2004), whereas others argued that finding the man in the state was more complex than identifying dominant men (Brown 1995), necessitating examination of bureaucratic structures and broader processes of knowledge production (Kantola 2006).

The strength of this research has been to move beyond specific women and men to look at the bigger picture, examining historical legacies and how policies and activities combine to create larger effects. In welfare state studies, this examination of the state structure has generated a wide variety of typologies on regimes, gender contracts, and worlds of welfare (Duncan 1995, 1996; Connell 2002). The literature on gender regimes generated typologies of nations according to whether they promoted male breadwinners or dual-income families (Lewis 1993) and later developed models on what might follow the demise of male breadwinner regimes: the universal breadwinner, the caregiver parity, and the universal caregiver models (Fraser 1997). Comparative studies of, for example, the social and employment policies of different countries on the basis of these models generated insights into the ways these social structures either challenged or reproduced gender inequalities. The study of welfare states and of the ways that institutional structures undergird social organization is an important and continuing field of research. Sylvia Walby's (2009) system theory explaining change in inequality, in turn, takes multiple equality regimes (gender, class, and race/ethnicity) and domains (the economy, the polity, civil society, and violence) into account and explains how regimes and domains impact each other in a nonpredictable way, thus defining the evolution of inequality.

Gender Trouble: Intersectionality, Sexuality, and Poststructuralism

A persistent critique of the universalizing approach of feminist scholarship has cut across all these areas, culminating in a fundamental critique of the concept of gender from a variety of quarters. From 1980 onward, important moves were made to deconstruct the category of gender (Butler 1990; Scott 1999). Using the feminist strategy of *displacement* in relation to politics—namely, destabilizing existing categories, binaries, and oppositions—scholars argued that as the gendered categories and concepts legitimated the exclusion of women, they had to be radically rethought, examining, for example, how gendered power relationships construct citizenship and the nation, the state, and bureaucracy (Lister 1997; Yuval-Davis 1997; Squires 1999; Kantola 2006). The focus shifts from women's presence in and exclusion from different institutions to understanding gendered structures of those institutions and how to transform them. Institutions and structures are not just gendered but also gendering: they produce the very gendered subjects of politics. Power here is understood as productive, not just repressive (Foucault 1980), and this kind of power is most effective when it lures us to fulfill the standards of normative femininities and masculinities.

Gender has multiple meanings and analyses that include the production of sexuality, masculinities, and femininities that had hitherto been downplayed in the gender and politics scholarship. The increasing fragmentation of feminism has resulted in feminisms in the plural and the problematization of women as a coherent and unified category, which adds greater analytical complexity particularly once race, class, and sexuality are fully analyzed. This work also posed important challenges to concepts such as objective knowledge and the role of researcher and researched. It has required self-reflexivity about feminism's hegemonic discourses and exclusions. Feminists who are of color, working class, postcolonial, and lesbian, argue that failure to consider the distinctive and sometimes conflicting interests among women has created a bias toward the experience of white middle-class women (hooks 1984; Lorde 1984; Collins 1990; Smooth 2011). Queer theorists and lesbian feminists also have critiqued what they call the *heteronormativity* (taking heterosexuality for granted) of much of the feminist work on gender.

Scholars of gender and race in the United States have critiqued the examination of gender and race apart from one other; these two concepts are not separable like pop-beads on a necklace (Spelman 1988). Harris (1990) argues that conceptualizing women of color as having "more of" the problems of white women and black men is an inadequate way to analyze the experience of women of color. Crenshaw (1993) shows how critical dimensions of women of color's experience of violence are missed when we fail to examine their distinctive sources of vulnerability: women of minority ethnicity have been excluded from the already scarce spaces in women's shelters in the United States because they do not speak English; women of color have been unable to get action on violence in their own communities because of sensitivities about criticizing one's own group (Richie and Kahuna 2000). These arguments have prompted feminists of color to develop the concept of intersectionality to get at the complex interrelationship between gender and race (Hancock 2007; Smooth 2011). For example, disaggregating the gender gap in voting in the United States by race reveals that the gender gap emerged earlier among African Americans and is today larger there.

REMAINING CHALLENGES AND FUTURE DIRECTIONS

Big challenges remain within politics as it is both practiced and studied. Contestation has increased around issues associated with gender equality, demonstrating its political character and the ways practices surrounding it are embedded in broader societal and political processes. Neoliberalism, the financial crisis, and various processes of de-democratization (Verloo 2011) are fundamentally shaping the political context and the austerity measures are having a very differentiated impact by gender (as well as by race, class, and disability). On one hand, women's and feminist movements and organizations are also embedded in these changes. According to Fraser (2009), the once emancipatory feminist critiques of the economy, androcentrism, and the state have been redirected to serve to legitimate neoliberal capitalism. On the other hand, an increasingly sexualized culture, with issues of violence, rape, street harassment, and pornography, may also be impacting a popularly vaunted decline in feminism. Interest in feminism has resurged, particularly among younger women, using new forms of activism, such as blogs, demonstrations, and technologies such as social media (Banyard 2010). SlutWalks, which began in Toronto and later spread all over the world to cities as far apart as London, Singapore, Berlin, Buenos Aires, Mexico City, and New York in summer 2011 following remarks made by a senior police officer to Canadian law students, are further evidence of this.

In this context, a number of important challenges remain for gender scholarship. First, as many have argued, too little attention is still given to issues of intersectionality (Collins 1990; Hancock 2007; Weldon 2008). As we have seen, much of the pioneering gender scholarship was primarily focused on the issues and concerns of white middle-class women. Scholars were then forced to pay more attention to race, class, sexuality, and disability by vocal black, working-class, lesbian, and postcolonial feminists. Gender and politics scholars are now increasingly exploring what Kimberlé Crenshaw (1993) termed *political intersectionality*, (i.e., how intersectionality is relevant to political strategies and policies) and are examining how political institutions and practices, such as laws and equality institutions, produce intersectionality policies and either aid or hamper feminist goals (Ferree 2009; Kantola and Nousiainen 2009; Krizsan, Skjeie, and Squires 2012). Others are exploring how identity groups can be constituted within—rather than prior to—inequality policies (Cooper 2004, 49–51). Intersectionality can therefore appear to have disciplinary functions as a governmental discourse that produces more identities (Grabham 2009, 199).

Intersectionality will undoubtedly bring fundamental changes to the conceptual, methodological, and normative paradigm of the gender and politics scholarship. It requires sophisticated methods and research designs able to deal with complexity without particularism. Most importantly, intersectionality also challenges existing theories and begs for new normative standards. For instance, the radical acknowledgment that change "for women" can have multiple desirable directions depending on the groups of women taken into account and that key values like *feminism* and *gender equality* are defined in multiple and possibly even conflicting ways cannot help but cause major shifts in the scholarship, which until now has predominantly used a singular version of such values.

More generally, having established the multidimensionality of gender, scholars need to continue to theorize the nature of and relationship between these distinct dimensions. For example, theorists of gender have delineated dimensions of nation, heteronormativity, hierarchies of power, and divisions of labor as dimensions of gender (Young 2005; see also Connell 2002). Turning to the analysis of law and policy making, some have suggested a distinction between market or class-related or redistributive policies and those that are focused on status or rights (Htun and Weldon 2010; Blofield and Haas 2005). More work theorizing and analyzing these distinctive dimensions is needed.

Second, and again this is not a new insight, it is recognized that more attention needs to be given to men and masculinities, although this lack is understandable given the early focus on "putting women back in." Building on the pioneering work that has already been undertaken, men and masculinities need to be problematized more in gender and politics (Hooper 2001; Connell 2002; Bjarnegard 2010). This exhortation provokes an anxiety among some feminists that having finally developed a context in which we can study women, we will be back to studying men and their concerns again. Nevertheless, the study of men and masculinity is critical to moving the field of gender politics forward. Third, the gender scholarship has sometimes been too narrowly focused on the formulation of gender equality policies and the workings of gender equality bodies (Waylen 2012). This is not to deny the excellent work that has been done on women's policy agencies and equality measures, but this has sometimes been at the expense of examining how wider policies and institutions are gendered and the implications of this.

Last, we need to continue to develop theoretical accounts of politics that better link structure, action, and ideas. Early work was overly focused on actors. No one would deny that actors, and certain actors in particular, are hugely important in both the conventional and nonconventional political arenas. But sometimes the research has been overly concerned with counting the numbers of women ("descriptive representation") first in legislatures and now in some of the recent work on women in executives. In common with much social science, there has been an "institutional turn" in gender and politics. Feminist institutionalists are developing a wider understanding of institutions as gendered structures and an improved understanding of how they operate in gendered ways (Mackay and Waylen 2009; Krook and Mackay 2011). Underlying this development is a belief that if we understand institutions as rules, norms, and practices, then we need to know how formal and informal rules, norms, and practices are gendered (Chappell and Waylen 2013). And in particular one of the key questions for all institutionalists, including feminists, is how to explain institutional change. How and why does change occur (or not occur)? And linked to that, how is it that institutions can remain the same? We need to explain institutional continuity or more accurately institutional reproduction. How do institutions actually sustain and reproduce themselves (Waylen 2012)? This can help us to understand why attempts to change institutions do not have the desired results or why the creation of new institutions do not always fulfill the hopes of their designers.

There is also a need for more research that focuses on discourses and ideas as well as actors and structures, examining, for example, the role that discourses and ideas about gender and sexuality play in constituting political actors and structures in the global economy (Bedford 2009; Lind 2010), violence (Kantola, Norocel, and Repo 2011), and gender equality policies (Lombardo and Forest 2012). Recent research looks not only at how and why gender inequality occurs or persists but also how and why gender difference is constructed and gender inequality reproduced through institutions and policies (Prügl 2007). Particular notions of politics reproduce particular kinds of gendered subject positions and agents and result in particular performances of gender (cf. Butler 1990). Reflecting this insight, emphasis has shifted from studying women's substantive representation to "the constitutive representation of gender"—the ways that women and men as political subjects, their femininities and masculinities as well as their "interests", are produced as part of the representative process (Saward 2010; Childs and Webb 2012). More robust analyses of structural change and feminist and women's agency require that we need to integrate accounts of regimes, institutions, and other structural dimensions of gender and politics on one hand with issues such as identity, self-understanding, and other subjective, micro-level phenomena on the other hand.

THE STRUCTURE OF THE HANDBOOK

This handbook takes up many of these themes and issues in its seven substantive sections. It recognizes the complexity and multidimensionality of gender. As demonstrated already, gender is not just about sexuality, the body, work, motherhood, or violence, as some scholars have claimed. Rather gender operates along many, interrelated dimensions, including sex and sexuality, family, race and nation, work, and institutionalized relations of power and violence. We have organized these chapters to highlight the political nature of these phenomena and also to show they structure nations, states, markets, and civil society. These latter concepts are more traditional categories of political analysis that nonetheless are also critical for the study of politics and gender.

We hope that this handbook will be accessible to all starting and established political and social scientists, so we begin in the first section by explaining some key concepts and how they relate to each other and also by explaining the variety of and contributions to method and methodology in the field. The chapters cover two families of concepts: (1) sex, gender, feminism, and intersectionality; and (2) power, politics, domination, and oppression. We then turn to examine various dimensions of gender politics and the ways they condition state, market, and civil society. In the second section, we begin with body politics—the political importance of the body, sexuality, reproduction, and violence—overcoming the public–private distinction and showing how power relations shape not only the "public" sphere but also the "private" sphere that then becomes "political." In the next section on political economy, the focus widens to look at the politics of social reproduction, the family and the household, and how the gendered individual and the family or household interacts with the wider economy and markets at the national and global levels. In the next section we investigate various forms and contexts of gendered organizing by women and men—including feminist, nonfeminist, antifeminist, and transnational movements by women and men as well as civil society as a realm of gendered political action more generally.

The subsequent two sections consider the relationship between gender and a range of more traditional political institutions, systems, and structures. First, we look at gendered praxes of participation and representation in various political systems, political parties, electoral systems, judicial politics, and courts. The next section focuses on the gendered nature of the state, governance, and policy making, and the actors and processes involved. The final section focuses on the debates and the puzzles surrounding equality, citizenship, identity, multiculturalism, nations, and security. As a whole, this handbook aims to illustrate the evolution, establishment, and institutionalization of the field of gender and politics. Its chapters also show the diversity and pluralism of this field and illustrate some of the clear lines of agreement and disagreement in the field of politics and gender. Each section has its own introduction highlighting the developments, the old and new debates, and future challenges for the key themes within that section as well as linking it to the rest of the handbook and discipline.

The Oxford Handbook on Gender and Politics is therefore premised on the belief that it is vitally important that we improve our understanding of how both politics as a practice and political science as a discipline are gendered; this will help us to change both the practice and the discipline of politics for the better.

References

Alvarez, Sonia. 1990. *Engendering democracy in Brazil*. Princeton, NJ: Princeton University Press.

Annesley, Claire, and Francesca Gains. 2010. "The core executive: Gender, power and change. *Political Studies* 58(5): 909–929.

American Political Science Association (APSA). 2004. APSA report on the advancement of women in political science. Washington, DC: Author.

Arendt, Hannah. 1958. *The human condition*. Chicago: University of Chicago Press.

Banaszak, Lee-Ann, Karen Beckwith, and Dieter Rucht (Eds.). 2003. *Women's movements face the reconfigured state*. Cambridge, UK: Cambridge University Press.

Banyard, Kat. 2010. *The equality illusion: The truth about women & men today*. London: Faber & Faber.

Barakso, Maryann. 2004. Governing now: Grassroots activism in the National Organization for Women. Ithaca, NY: Cornell University Press.

Basu, Amrita (Ed.). 1994. *The challenge of local feminisms: Women's movements in global perspective.* Boulder, CO: Westview.

Beckwith, Karen, and Kimberley Cowell-Meyers. 2003. "Sheer numbers." Paper presented at the annual meeting of the American Political Science Association, Philadelphia, August 31–September 3.

Bedford, Kate. 2009. *Developing partnerships: Gender, sexuality and the reformed World Bank.* Minneapolis: University of Minnesota Press.

Bjarnegard, Elin. 2010. "Men in politics: Revising patterns of gendered parliamentary representation in Thailand and beyond." PhD dissertation, University of Uppsala.

Blee, Kathleen. 1991. *Women of the Klan: Racism and gender in the 1920s.* Berkeley: University of California Press.

Blee, Kathleen. 2002. *Inside organized racism: Women in the hate movement.* Berkeley: University of California Press.

Blofield, Merike, and Liesl Haas. 2005. "Defining a democracy: Reforming the laws on women's rights in Chile, 1990–2002." *Latin American Politics and Society* 47(3): 35–68.

Bourque, Susan C., and Jean Grosssholtz. 1974. "Politics an unnatural practice: Political science looks at female participation." *Politics and Society* 4: 225–266.

Brenner, Suzanne. 2001. "Why women rule the roost: Rethinking Javanese ideologies of gender and self-control." In Caroline Brettell and Carolyn Sargeant, eds., *Gender in cross-cultural perspective.* Upper Saddle River, NJ: Prentice-Hall.

Brettell, Caroline, and Carolyn Sargeant. 2001. *Gender in cross-cultural perspective.* Upper Saddle River, NJ: Prentice-Hall.

Brown, Wendy. 1995. *States of injury: Power and freedom in late modernity.* Princeton, NJ: Princeton University Press.

Butler, Judith. 1990. *Gender trouble: Feminism and the subversion of identity.* New York: Routledge.

Celis, K. 2006. "Substantive representation of women: The representation of women's interests and the impact of descriptive representation in the Belgian parliament (1900–1979)." *Journal of Women, Politics and Policy* 28(2): 85–114.

Celis, K. 2008. "Studying women's substantive representation in legislatures: When representative acts, contexts and women's interests become important." *Representation* 44(2): 111–123.

Celis, K., S. Childs, J. Kantola, and M.L. Krook. 2008. "Rethinking women's substantive representation." *Representation* 44(2): 99–110.

Chappell, Louise, and Georgina Waylen. 2013. "Gender and the Hidden Life of Institutions." *Public Administration.* Forthcoming.

Charrad, Mounira. 2010. "Kinship, Islam or oil? Culprits of gender inequality." *Politics & Gender.* 5(4): 546–553.

Childs, Sarah, and Mona Lena Krook. 2006. "Should feminists give up on critical mass? A contingent yes." *Politics & Gender* 2(4): 522–530.

Childs, Sarah, and Paul Webb. 2012. *Sex, gender and the conservative party.* Basingstoke, UK: Palgrave Macmillan.

Connell, Robert. 2002. *Gender.* Cambridge, UK: Polity Press.

Cooper, Davina. 2004. *Challenging diversity: Rethinking equality and the value of difference.* Cambridge, UK: Cambridge University Press.

Collins, Patricia Hill. 1990. *Black feminist thought: Knowledge, consciousness, and the politics of empowerment.* Boston: Unwin Hyman.

Crenshaw, Kimberle. 1993. "Demarginalizing the intersection of race and sex." In D. Kelly Weisberg, ed., *Feminist legal theory: Foundations, vol. 1.* Philadelphia: Temple University Press.

Dahl, Robert. 1984. *Modern political analysis.* Upper Saddle River, NJ: Prentice-Hall.

Dahlerup, Drude. 1988. "From a small to a large minority: Women in Scandinavian politics." *Scandinavian Political Studies* 11(4): 275–298.

Dahlerup, Drude (Ed.). 2006. *Women, quotas and politics.* London: Routledge.

Dahlerup, Drude. 2010. "The development of gender and politics as a new research field within the framework of the ECPR." *European Political Science* 9: 85–98.

Deising, Paul. 1992. *How social science works.* Pittsburgh: University of Pittsburgh Press.

Dreger, Alice. 1998. *Hermaphrodites and the medical invention of sex.* Cambridge, MA: Harvard University Press.

Duncan, Simon. 1995. "Theorizing European gender systems." *Journal of European Social Policy* 5(4): 263–284.

Duncan, Simon. 1996. "The diverse worlds of European patriarchy." In Maria Dolors Garcia-Ramon and Janice Monk, eds., *Women of the European Union: the politics of work and daily life.* New York: Routledge, pp. 74–110.

Easton, David. 1953. *The political system: An inquiry into the state of political science.* New York: Knopf.

Elman, R. Amy. 1996. *Sexual subordination and state intervention: Comparing Sweden and the United States.* Oxford: Berghahn Books.

Enloe, Cynthia. 1996. "Margins, silences and bottom rungs: How to overcome the underestimation of power in the study of international relations." In Steve Smith, Ken Booth, and Maryisa Zalewski, eds., *International theory: Positivism and beyond.* Cambridge, UK: Cambridge University Press, pp. 11–46.

Fausto-Sterling, Ann. 2000. *Sexing the body: Gender politics and the construction of sexuality.* Basic Books.

Ferree, Myra Marx. 2009. "Inequality, intersectionality, and the politics of discourse: Framing feminist alliances." In Emanuela Lombardo, Petra Meier, and Mieke Verloo, eds., *The discursive politics of gender equality: Stretching, bending and policy-making.* London: Routledge, 86–104.

Ferree, Myra Marx, and Patricia Yancey Martin. 1995. *Feminist organizations: Harvest of the new women's movement.* Philadelphia: Temple University Press.

Foucault, Michel. 1980. *Power/knowledge: Selected interviews and other writings 1972–1977.* London: Prentice Hall.

Franceschet, Susan, Mona Lena Krook and Jennifer M. Piscopo (Eds). 2012. The Impact of Gender Quotas. New York: Oxford University Press, 2012.

Franceschet, Susan, and Jennifer M. Piscopo. 2008. "Gender quotas and women's substantive representation: Lessons from Argentina." *Politics & Gender* 4(3): 393–425.

Franceschet, Susan, and Thomas Gwynn. 2011. "Gender and Executive Office: Analysing parity cabinets in Chile and Spain." Paper presented at the European Conference for Political Research (ECPR) General Conference, Reykjavik, August 23–26.

Fraser, Nancy. 1997. *Justice interruptus: Critical reflections on the "postsocialist" conditions.* London: Routledge.

Fraser, Nancy. 2009. Feminism, capitalism and the cunning of history. *New Left Review* 56: 97–117.

Friedman, Elisabeth. 1995. "Women's human rights: The emergence of a movement." In Julie Peters and Andrea Wolper, eds., *Women's rights, human rights.* London: Routledge, pp. 18–35.

Friedman, Elisabeth Jay. 2009. Re(gion)alizing women's human rights in Latin America. *Politics & Gender* 5: 349–375.

Gelb, Joyce. 1989. *Feminism and politics: A comparative perspective.* Berkeley: University of California Press.

Goertz, Garry, and Amy Mazur (Eds.). 2008. *Politics, gender, and concepts: Theory and methodology.* Cambridge, UK: Cambridge University Press.

Grabham, Emily. 2009. "Intersectionality: Traumatic impressions." in Emily Grabham, Davina Cooper, Jane Krishnadas, and Didi Herman, eds., *Intersectionality and beyond: Law, power and the politics of location.* Abingdon: Routledge-Cavendish, pp. 183–201.

Hancock, Ange-Marie. 2007. "When multiplication doesn't equal quick addition: Examining intersectionality as a research paradigm." *Perspectives on Politics* 5(1): 63–79.

Harding, Sandra. 1987. "Introduction: Is there a feminist method?" in Sandra Harding, ed., *The science question in feminism.* Ithaca, NY: Cornell University Press, pp. 1–14.

Harris, Angela. 1990. "Race and essentialism in feminist legal theory." *Stanford Law Review* 42: 581.

Hassim, Shireen. 2005. *Women's organizations and democracy in South Africa: Contesting authority.* Madison: University of Wisconsin Press.

hooks, bell. 1984/2000. *Feminist theory: From margin to center.* Cambridge, MA: South End Press.

Hooper, Charlotte. 2001. *Manly states: Masculinities, international relations and gender politics.* New York: Columbia University Press.

Htun, Mala. 2003. *Sex and the state: Abortion, divorce and the family under Latin American dictatorships and democracy.* New York: Cambridge University Press.

Htun, Mala, and Jennifer Piscopo. 2010. "Presence without empowerment?" Paper presented at the Conflict Prevention and Peace Forum, December. http://webarchive.ssrc.org/pdfs/Mala_Htun_and_Jennifer_M._Piscopo-Presence_without_Empowerment_CPPF_Briefing_Paper_Dec_2010_f.pdf.

Htun, Mala, and Laurel Weldon. 2010. "When do governments promote women's rights? A framework for the comparative analysis of sex equality policy." *Perspectives on Politics* 8(1): 207–216.

Htun, Mala, and Weldon, S. Laurel. 2011."State power, religion, and women's rights: A comparative analysis of family law." *Indiana Journal of Global Legal Studies.* 18(1) (Winter): 145–165.

Htun, Mala, and Weldon, S. Laurel. 2012. "The civic origins of progressive policy change: A comparative analysis of policies on violence against women." *American Political Science Review,* 106(3) (August.).

Hughes, M. 2011. Intersectionality, quotas, and minority women's political representation worldwide. *American Political Science Review* 105(3): 604–620.

Inglehart, Ronald, and Pippa Norris. 2003. *Rising tide: Gender equality and cultural change.* Cambridge, UK: Cambridge University Press.

Lim, Lin Lean (Ed.). 1998. *The sex sector: The economic and social bases of prostitution in Southeast Asia.* Geneva: International Labour Organization.

Jalazai, F. 2008. "Women rule." *Politics and Gender* 4(3): 305–331.

Jaquette, Jane (Ed.). 1994. *The women's movement in Latin America: Participation and democracy.* Boulder, CO: Westview Press.

Jayawardena, Kumari. 1986. *Feminism and nationalism in the third world.* London, UK: Zed Books.

Jolly, Margaret, and Macintyre, Martha.eds. 1989. *Family and gender in the Pacific: Domestic contradictions and the colonial impact.* Cambridge UK: Cambridge University Press.

Kantola, Johanna. 2006. *Feminists theorize the state.* Basingstoke, UK: Palgrave Macmillan.

Kantola, Johanna. 2010. *Gender and the European Union.* Basingstoke, UK: Palgrave Macmillan.

Kantola, Johanna, Cristian Norocel, and Jemima Repo. 2011. "Gendering violence in school shootings in Finland." *European Journal of Women's Studies* 18(2): 183–198.

Kantola, Johanna, and Kevät Nousiainen. 2009. "Institutionalizing intersectionality in Europe: Introducing the theme." *International Feminist Journal of Politics* 11(4): 459–477.

Kaplan, Gisela. 1992. *Contemporary Western European feminism.* New York: New York University Press.

Katzenstein, Mary, and Carol Mueller (Eds.). 1987. *The women's movements of the United States and Western Europe.* Philadelphia: Temple University Press.

Kittilson, Miki Caul. 2008. "Representing women: The adoption of family leave in comparative perspective." *Journal of Politics* 70(2): 323–334.

Krizsán, Andrea, Tamás Dombos, Erika Kispéter, Linda Szabó, Jasminka Dedic, Martin Jaigma, Roman Kuhar, Ana Frank, Birgit Sauer, and Mieke Verloo. 2010. "Framing gender equality in the European Union and its current and future member states." Final LARG report QUING. http://www.quing.eu.

Krizsán, Andrea, Hege Skeije, and Judith Squires. 2012. *Institutionalizing intersectionality: The changing nature of European equality regimes.* Basingstoke, UK: Palgrave Macmillan.

Krook, Mona L. 2009. *Quotas for women in politics: Gender and candidate selection reform worldwide.* Oxford: Oxford University Press.

Krook Mona L., and Fiona Mackay (Eds.). 2011. *Gender, politics and institutions: Towards a feminist institutionalism.* Basingstoke, UK: Palgrave.

Lamphere, Louise. 2001. "The domestic sphere of women and the public world of men: The strengths and limits of an anthropological dichotomy." In Caroline Brettel and Carolyn Sargeant, eds., *Gender in cross-cultural perspective.* Upper Saddle River, NJ: Prentice-Hall, pp. 100–109.

Lewis, Jane (Ed.). 1993. *Women and social policies in Europe: Work, family and the state.* Brookfield, VT: Edward Elgar.

Lind, Amy (Ed.). 2010. *Development, sexual rights and global governance.* London: Routledge.

Lister, Ruth. 1997. *Citizenship: feminist perspectives.* Basingstoke, UK: Macmillan.

Lombardo, Emanuela, and Maxime Forest (Eds.). 2012. *The Europeanization of gender equality policies: A discursive-sociological approach.* Basingstoke, UK: Palgrave Macmillan.

Lorde, Audre. 1984. *Sister outsider: Chapters and speeches.* Berkeley, CA: Crossing Press.

Lovenduski, Joni. 1981. "Toward the emasculation of political science." In Dale Spender, ed., *Men's studies modified: The impact of feminism on academic disciplines.* Oxford: Pergamon.

Lovenduski, Joni, and Pippa Norris. 1995. *Political recruitment: Gender, race and class in British parliament.* Cambridge, UK: Cambridge University Press.

Lovenduski, Joni, and Vicky Randall. 1993. *Contemporary feminist politics: Women and power in Britain.* Oxford: Oxford University Press.

Mackay, Fiona, and Georgina Waylen. 2009. Critical perspectives on feminist institutionalism. *Politics & Gender* 5(2): 237–280.

Shanti Menon. 2001. Male authority and female autonomy: A study of the matrilineal nayars of Kerala, South India. In Caroline B. Brettell and Carolyn F. Sargent, eds., *Gender in cross-cultural perspective.* Upper Saddle River: Prentice Hall, 352–361.

Mackinnon, Catharine. 1989. *Towards a feminist theory of the state.* Cambridge, MA: Harvard University Press.

Mazur, Amy. 2002 *Theorizing feminist policy.* Oxford: Oxford University Press.

McBride, Dorothy E., and Amy G. Mazur. 2010. *The politics of state feminism: Innovation in comparative research.* Philadelphia: Temple University Press.

McBride Stetson, Dorothy, and Amy G. Mazur, eds. 1995. *Comparative State Feminism.* Thousand Oaks: Sage Publications.

Millett, Kate. 1968. *Sexual politics.* Boston: New England Free Press.

Pateman, Carole. 1983. "Feminist critiques of the public/private dichotomy." In S. L. Benn and G. F. Gauss, eds., *Public and private in social life.* London: Croom Helm.

Paxton, Pamela. 2008. "Gendering democracy." In Garry Goertz and Amy Mazur, eds., *Politics, gender, and concepts: Theory and methodology.* Cambridge, UK: Cambridge University Press.

Phillips, Anne. 1995. *The politics of presence.* Oxford: Clarendon Press.

Prügl, Elisabeth. 2007. "Gender and EU Politics." In Knud Erik Jørgensen, Mark A. Pollack, and Ben Rosamond, eds., *The handbook of European Union politics.* London: SAGE.

Randall, Vicky. 1982. *Women and politics: An international perspective.* New York: Macmillan.

Reingold, Beth, and Michele Swers. 2011. An endogenous approach to women's interests: When interests are interesting in and of themselves. *Politics & Gender* 7(3): 429–435.

Richie, Beth, and Kanuha. 2000. "Battered women of color." In Anne Minas, ed., *Gender basics: Feminist perspectives on women and men,* 2nd ed. Belmont, CA: Wadsworth, 213–220.

Rubin, Gayle. 2004. "The traffic in women." In Julie Rivkin and Michael Ryan, *Literary theory: An anthology,* 2nd ed. Malden, MA: Blackwell, 770–794.

Sanbonmatsu, Kira. 2002. *Democrats/Republicans and the politics of women's place.* Ann Arbor: University of Michigan Press.

Sapiro, Virginia. 1981. "When are interests interesting? The problem of political representation of women." *American Political Science Review* 75(3): 701–716.

Sapiro, Virginia. 1994. *Women in American society: An introduction to women's studies.* Mountain View, CA: Mayfield.

Saward, Michael. 2010. *The representative claim.* Oxford: Oxford University Press.

Schreiber, R. 2008. *Righting feminism.* Oxford: Oxford University Press.

Schwindt-Bayer, Leslie. 2011. *Political power and women's representation in Latin America.* Oxford: Oxford University Press.

Scott, Joan. 1999. "Some reflections on gender and politics." In Myra Marx Ferree, Judith Lorber, and Beth B. Hess, eds., *Revisioning gender.* London: SAGE, pp. 70–98.

Simien, Evelyn M. (Ed.). 2011. *Gender and lynching: The politics of memory.* New York: Palgrave/Macmillan.

Smooth, Wendy. 2011. "Standing for women? Which women? The substantive representation of women's interests and the research imperative of intersectionality." *Politics & Gender* 7(3): 436–441.

Spelman, Elizabeth. 1988. *Inessential woman.* Boston: Beacon Press.

Squires, Judith. 1999. *Gender in political theory.* Cambridge, UK: Polity Press.

Squires, Judith. 2007. *The new politics of gender equality.* Basingstoke, UK: Palgrave Macmillan.

Sunseri, Lina. 2011. *Being again of one mind: Oneida women and the struggle for decolonization.* Vancouver: UBC Press.

Swers, Michele L. 2002. *The difference women make: The policy impact of women in Congress.* Chicago: University of Chicago Press.

Verloo, Mieke. 2011. "Gender equality policies as interventions in a changing world." Keynote lecture at the second gender and politics European Consortium for Political Research (ECPR) conference, Budapest, January 13. http://www.ecprnet. eu/sg/ecpg/documents/keyNotes/Gender_equality_policies_as_interventions_in_a_ changing_world.pdf consulted on 20 February 2011.

Walby, Sylvia. 2009. *Globalization and inequalities: Complexity and contested modernities.* London: SAGE.

Wängnerud, Lena. 2000. "Testing the politics of presence: Women's representation in the Swedish Riksdag." *Scandinavian Political Studies* 23(1): 67–91.

Waylen, Georgina. 1994. "Women and democratization: Conceptualizing gender relations in transition politics." *World Politics* 46(3): 573–588.

Waylen, Georgina. 1996. *Gender in third world politics.* Boulder, CO: Lynn Rienner.

Waylen, Georgina. 2007. *Engendering transitions: Women's mobilization, institutions and gender outcomes.* Oxford: Oxford University Press.

Waylen, Georgina. 2010. "Gendering policy and politics in transitions to democracy: Chile and South Africa." *Policy and Politics* 8(1): 337–352.

Waylen, Georgina. 2012. "Gender matters in politics." *The Political Quarterly* 38(4): 24–32.

Weldon, S. L. 2002a. *Protest, policy and the problem of violence against women: A cross-national comparison.* Pittsburgh: University of Pittsburgh Press.

Weldon, S. L. 2002b. "Beyond bodies: Institutional sources of representation for women." *Journal of Politics* 64(4): 1153–1174.

Weldon, S. L. 2006. "Inclusion, solidarity and social movements: The global movement on gender violence." *Perspectives on Politics* 4(1): 55–74.

Weldon, S. L. 2008. "The concept of intersectionality." In Amy G. Mazur and Gary Goertz, eds., *Gender and concepts.* Cambridge, UK: Cambridge University Press.

Weldon. S. L. 2011. *When protest makes policy: How social movements represent disadvantaged groups.* Ann Arbor: University of Michigan Press.

Wolbrecht, Christina. 2000. *The politics of women's rights: Parties, position and change.* Princeton, NJ: Princeton University Press.

Wolin, Sheldon S. 1960. *Politics and vision: Continuity and innovation in Western political thought.* Boston: Little Brown.

World Health Organization and London School of Hygiene and Tropical Medicine. 2010. *Preventing intimate partner and sexual violence against women: Taking action and generating evidence.* Geneva: World Health Organization.

Young, Iris. 1990. *Justice and the politics of difference.* New Haven, CT: Princeton University Press.

Young, Iris Marion. 2005. *On female body experience: "Throwing like a girl" and other chapters.* Oxford: Oxford University Press.

Yuval-Davis, Nira. 1997. *Gender and nation.* London: SAGE.

Zerilli, Linda. 2006. "Feminist theory and the canon of political thought." In John Dryzek, Bonnie Honig, and Anne Phillips, eds., *The Oxford handbook on political theory.* Oxford: Oxford University Press, pp. 106–124.

PART I

GENDER AND
POLITICS: CONCEPTS
AND METHODS

IDENTIFYING a set of substantive categories and an array of approaches, this volume implicitly delineates the boundaries of the field of politics and gender. In a field as diverse and diffuse as gender politics, the result is necessarily incomplete, representing our collective "mobilization of bias" or our sense of what had to be included. In this section, the chapters provide a conceptual basis for evaluating this array and hopefully will spark ideas in the reader for new ways and areas of study not envisioned here.

The complex concepts that are central for contemporary study of gender—sex, sexuality, heteronormativity, intersectionality, and feminism as well as gender itself—are subject to sustained discussion and analysis. Introductory feminist texts used to say that gender was the social meaning of sex. But feminists have increasingly come to eschew such biological foundationalism and to agree that sex itself is a social construct. In the contemporary world, we might say that gender is a form of social organization that exalts the masculine and denigrates and dismisses the feminine. But contemporary feminists have also begun to theorize subordinated masculinities and intersectional privilege and marginalization. Definitions of *gender* tend to reflect the theoretical approach of the analyst. Some ways of thinking about gender, or gender–race, are inextricably linked to these other concepts, such as intersectionality or sexuality. Feminism is a concept that is in some ways even more fraught, having clear connections to political action and actors and serving as an ideal for many scholars and activists. Feminism is at once a research agenda, a political program, and an ideal. In some ways, we can say that it is a term that potentially embraces all of the worlds women and men, so we should not expect it to be simple to define or unidimensional in its content.

Thus, the account of what gender is, what sex is, what sexuality and race are, and how they are all interrelated is constantly contested and developing. The essays in this section cannot make these complex matters simple, though we hope the essays provide valuable guides to the debates about and main approaches to these concepts. Collectively, though, these essays do lay out the ways that contemporary gender politics has embraced the exploration of these meanings and relationships as a theoretical and empirical area of study, and the subsequent sections take up aspects of these questions—from body to nation to market to state—showing how gender shapes politics (and vice versa) across these dimensions.

No less tricky is the definition of politics, which we discuss to some degree in the introduction to the handbook. The political has sometimes been defined rather narrowly as pertaining to the activities of governing, to the formal institutions of government. Gender scholars have much to say about governing and governance but cast a wider net, as do many mainstream scholars as well. Politics, understood as "the authoritative allocation of value" (in David Easton's classic formulation) or as the working of systems of power and authority, has a much wider purview. Systems of power work, gender scholars show, not only through elections and militaries but also through processes of normalization and social construction by recognizing some families and bodies as acceptable and others as deviant, powerless, or properly marginalized. Systems of power allow some to speak while others are silenced; these powerful discourses elevate some identities and ideas and suppress or ridicule others. These broader definitions, then, are centrally about identifying the complex ways that power and authority suffuse polity, economy, and society.

Both feminists and mainstream political theorists put power at the center of a definition of politics, but more scholars talk about power than define it or explain what it means and how it works. Mainstream scholars, beginning with Robert Dahl, write about distinctive faces of power; Dahl's work is generally the basis for distinguishing the first (and perhaps most intuitive) face of power (when one person has power over another, getting that person to do things they would not otherwise do). The second face of power, generally associated with Peter Bachrach and Morton Baratz, is power that results from particular forms of organization and categories—the mobilization of bias—and that obscures some issues and questions and prevents their discussion. This face of power is thought of as the power to set the agenda. The third face of power, usually traced to the work of Stephen Lukes, is to persuade people that their interests are such that they ought not question the organization of categories or try to do certain things in the first place.

This mainstream discussion of power, however, has been unconnected with feminist discussions of power, which focus more on power as a structural relationship (following Michel Foucault) and on acting together, in concert, in a voluntary way, to achieve positive ends as a kind of power (following Hannah Arendt), often called empowerment. Feminist critiques of domination and power as a social relation inform both moves and have much to say to traditional discussions of power. Feminist international relations theorists such as Cynthia Enloe, Elisabeth Prugl, and Brigit Locher have shown how feminist notions of power are important for political science. In fact, one might see in current work by Kathryn Sikkink and others on the way so-called soft power of norms and persuasion, civil society modes of influence, and the connections between identity and such norms as examples of the importance of collective empowerment and of power as a way to construct identities and interests. The important role that norms or "informal institutions" play in the current exercise of bureaucratic authority or power might also demonstrate the way that power is incorporated into particular discourses. Thus, political scientists interested in power should read not only the essay in this section on power but also the essays in other sections on institutions, norms, and global governance, and the section on civil society.

Feminism as a research paradigm not only provides an expanded set of subjects for political scientists but also brings some additional tools to the discussion of methods, methodology, and epistemology. Although no specific method or research tool is the most feminist choice in all circumstances (e.g., participant observation and regression analysis are equally feminist in the abstract), some specific features of feminist research guide decisions about method, methodology, and theory. These distinctive features reflect an epistemology that explores and acknowledges the role of politics in the production of knowledge itself and seeks to take account of the political dimensions of science. Thus, the realm of gender and politics potentially includes the study of political science or, even more broadly, social science.

In her essay titled "Sex, Gender, and Sexuality: From Naturalized Presumption to Analytical Categories," Mary Hawkesworth explicates the concepts of sex, gender, and sexuality. She reviews the multiplicity of ways the concept of gender is understood. She relates it to both sex and sexuality, showing how gender, sexuality, and even the seemingly foundational biological category of sex are socially constructed.

The second essay, "Intersectionality" by Valerie Chepp and Patricia Hill Collins, presents an overview of some of the main ideas of intersectionality. The chapter approaches the burgeoning field of studies of intersectionality as a distinctive knowledge project that has shaped the social sciences, summarizes its core ideas, and discusses selected specific contributions of the field. The chapter outlines the consequences from the identification of intersectionality research with women's studies and gender scholarship. In this essay, the meaning of intersectionality throughout some of its applications to political phenomena of American democracy from legislatures to hip-hop.

The third essay, "Feminism," by Rita Dhamoon reviews debates among feminists about what feminism means, considering different ways of understanding feminism, its central features, and methods of inquiry deployed by feminists. These debates concern whether feminists should aim for equality or difference, whether differences among women force us to abandon the concept of gender, and whether "women" can be thought of as a group with agency or identity or whether we should focus our energies on destabilizing and deconstructing gender.

In the fourth essay, titled "Power, Politics, Domination, and Oppression," Moya Lloyd points out that feminist and mainstream discussions of power have proceeded with little cross-fertilization. And although there is no single way to characterize feminist discussions of power, a number of different currents in feminist thinking can be discerned about power and politics. Lloyd discusses four such currents: power as a resource; power as a capacity; power as domination, or *power-over*; and power as productive.

The last essay in this section, by Brooke Ackerly and Jacqui True, reviews debates about methods and methodologies in gender and politics. The chapter shows how feminist social scientists adapt and refine a range of methods for feminist questions and feminist purposes. This distinctive methodological process, rather than any single research design or analytical method, defines feminist approaches to methods. The reasons for these methodological developments are explained, and some concrete examples of these methodological processes and approaches are given from the contemporary study of gender and politics.

CHAPTER 1

....

SEX, GENDER, AND SEXUALITY: FROM NATURALIZED PRESUMPTION TO ANALYTICAL CATEGORIES

....

MARY HAWKESWORTH

IN the social sciences and in the popular imagination, sex, like race, is typically construed as a biological or physical characteristic. Taken as given or natural, sex is deemed to exist outside of politics and culture. Indeed, for many it is deemed to be fixed and immutable, altogether beyond the reach of the state. Yet that is far from the whole story. Sex is also a political category and a legal status that determines citizenship rights, educational and employment opportunities, levels of income and wealth, and access to prestige and power. In most parts of the world, babies are assigned a sex before they are given a name, and that designation carries legal weight that haunts the individual from cradle to grave (Matambanadzo 2005, 214). Affixed to birth certificates, passports, drivers' licenses, draft cards, credit applications, marriage licenses, and death certificates, legal sex sculpts the contours of individual freedom and belonging in ways that ensure that domination and subordination are thoroughly corporeal.

Demonstrating that embodiment is profoundly political is one of the most distinctive contributions of feminist scholarship. Across a wide array of disciplines, feminist scholars have contested the pervasive assumption that "sexual dimorphism"—the belief that there are two and only two sexes—mandates a particular political order. They have conceptualized racialization and gendering as political processes that create and sustain divisions of labor, social stratifications, modes of subjection, and structures of desire. And they have traced the historical emergence of—and the political work done by—beliefs concerning biological determinism.

This chapter provides an overview of the complex debates within feminist scholarship concerning sex, gender, and sexuality as lived experiences and as analytical categories. It begins by exploring the vocabulary feminist scholars have developed to denaturalize embodiment and to demonstrate how physical capacities have been consolidated into national orders of finely honed hierarchies of difference. It traces efforts to differentiate sex from gender and sexuality while also illuminating the power dimensions embedded in all three concepts. It then examines competing accounts of gender as a cultural mechanism devised to connect dichotomous constructions of sex to heterosexual desire. The final sections of the chapter explore various deployments of sex, gender, and sexuality as intersecting analytical categories, mapping some of intricate national, transnational, and global power dynamics made visible by feminist attention to the politics of embodiment.

FROM EMBODIMENT TO ANALYTIC CATEGORY

In every day usage, there are multiple meanings of the terms *sex* and *gender*, but the two are often conflated and understood to be inseparably tied to physical embodiment. According to Harold Garfinkel (1967), the natural attitude encompasses a series of unquestionable axioms that tie gender irrevocably to sex. These axioms include the belief that there are two and only two sexes or genders; the belief that sex–gender is invariant; the belief that genitals are the essential sign of sex–gender; the belief that the male–female dichotomy is natural; the belief that being masculine or feminine is natural and not a matter of choice; and the belief that all individuals can (and must) be classified as male or female—any deviation from such a classification being either a joke or a pathology. Garfinkel pointed out that for most people the beliefs constituting the natural attitude are "incorrigible;" they are held with such conviction that it is near impossible to challenge their validity (122–128).

Despite the difficulty of the task, feminist scholarship challenges the convictions constitutive of the natural attitude. Through empirical and theoretical studies, feminist researchers have demonstrated that widely held presumptions about sexed embodiment and gender identity are wrong, that sex and gender are political constructs rather than natural givens, and that they vary cross-culturally and from one historical era to another. Feminist scholars have also shown that the natural attitude toward sex and gender has an intricate history tied to modernity, construed as a Western hegemonic project. To challenge the natural attitude, feminist scholars have begun by taking issue with a host of assumptions about sex, gender, and sexuality.

SEX

Since the eighteenth century, sex has typically been understood as the anatomical division of the human species into male and female. As Thomas Laqueur (1990) so carefully documented, however, sexual dimorphism is intimately tied to the politics of modernity. As natural science displaced theology in Enlightenment metaphysics, the one-sex model of embodiment that had dominated European political thought and practice for nearly two millennia gave way to a two-sex model that posited men and women as incommensurate opposites rather than as embodied souls ordered along a continuum on the basis of proximity to the divine. Although corporeal differences carried political and social consequence in earlier eras, the relevant markers of difference prior to the eighteenth century were not lodged in the genitalia or reproductive organs. "Penis/vagina, testicles/ovaries, female menstruation and the absence of monthly bleeding in men" were not taken "as self-evident marks of opposition....Instead each element of these was understood as a version of the other in accord with a metaphysically given relationship: women were less perfect men whose respective anatomy and physiology reflected this order" (Laqueur 2012, 803). In the eighteenth century, the emerging "natural philosophy" proposed that human biology should be understood in terms of sexual dimorphism, "a fixed oppositeness, that was somehow foundational and beyond culture," providing a "natural foundation" for differentiated social roles and responsibilities, legal status, as well as divisions of power and opportunity (806).

In the midst of Enlightenment proclamations of universal rights derived from the self-evident truth that all men are created equal, political theorists and republican revolutionaries in both the United States and France extrapolated from the new biological dimorphism grounds for excluding women from membership in the political community. Asserting that reproductive physiology

determines individual character and political capacity, republican revolutionaries on both sides of the Atlantic adopted the notion that sexual difference
dictates proper political status and behavior, insisting that any transgressions
of the gendered political order threatened the very basis of society and civilization. To shore up women's supposed biological incapacity for politics, male lawmakers passed legislation barring women from participation in political clubs,
political organizations, and political parties and from political office (Landes
1988, 1998; Cody 2001, 2005).

Over the course of the nineteenth century, male lawmakers in nations across
the globe replicated the republican practice of using the law to bar women from
politics and restrict them to the private sphere. As Ann Towns (2009, 2010)
demonstrates, exclusion was embraced in Europe as an indication of more
advanced civilization and was then imposed as a civilizing measure on colonies
in Africa and Asia as European nations expanded their colonial empires. These
colonial impositions displaced earlier indigenous forms of women's political
authority (Okonjo 1994, Oyewumi 1997).

Despite the overt political means by which these exclusions and restrictions were enacted, the growing authority of science afforded them a "natural"
justification: disparate male and female anatomies carried "natural" mandates
for social roles—mandates implicated in the very survival of the species. As
biological determinist frames gained ascendency, the political work involved in
the subordination of women was rendered invisible and replaced with fictive
pasts accredited by evolutionary theories that posited male dominance as natural and universal.

Within the version of biological dimorphism cultivated over the twentieth century, male and female are construed as natural kinds, distinguished
by unique configurations of chromosomes (xy–xx), hormones (androgens-
estrogens), gonads (reproductive organs such as testes and ovaries), internal
morphology (seminal vesicles and prostate as opposed to vagina, uterus, and
fallopian tubes), external genitalia (penis and scrotum, clitoris and labia), as
well as secondary sex characteristics (body hair, facial hair, breasts). Feminist
scholars have shown, however, that none of the typical correlates of biological
sex conform to the demands of a classification as natural kinds. Within philosophical discourses, a natural kind refers to a category that exists independent
of the observer and that can be defined in terms of an essence, a set of properties common to all members of the kind. Feminist scholarship has repudiated
the notion of any sexual essence precisely because "there are no behavioral or
physical characteristics that always and without exception are true only of one
gender" (Kessler and McKenna 1978, 1). Chromosomes, hormones, sperm production, and egg production all fail to differentiate all men from all women
or to provide a common core within each sex. "No matter how detailed an
investigation science has thus far made, it is still not possible to draw a clear
dividing line even between male and female" (Devor 1989, 1). Indeed, both men
and women have testosterone and estrogen in their systems and the human

X chromosome, wantonly mischaracterized as the female chromosome, is not only common to both men and women but also carries a large collection of male sperm genes (Richardson 2012). Even the insistence that there are two and only two sexes is mistaken. As biologist Ann Fausto-Sterling (1993) points out, using strictly biological criteria, there are not two but five sexes in nature. In addition to males and females, there are multiple modes of intersexuals—*herms* (persons born with both a testis and an ovary), *merms* (persons born with testes and some aspect of female genitalia), and *ferms* (persons who have ovaries combined with some forms of male genitalia).

The social sciences have done no better than the natural sciences in their efforts to identify behavioral differences that conform to the definition of a natural kind. Attitudinal and behavioral "sex differences" reflect social attributions that have nothing to do with natural differences. Within social science research, indicators of "biologically based femininity" typically include interest in weddings and marriage, preference for marriage over career, interest in infants and children, and enjoyment of childhood play with dolls, whereas indicators of "biologically based masculinity" include high activity levels, self-assurance, and a preference for career over marriage (Devor 1989, 11–15). Psychological inventories of masculinity and femininity manifest the misogynist tendency to define socially valued traits as male (logical, self-confident, ambitious, decisive, knows way around world) and less valued characteristics as female (talkative, gentle, sensitive to others' feelings, interested in appearance, strong need for security) (32). Yet, even with all the cultural bias built into such indicators, empirical studies have not been able to clearly differentiate men and women in the cultures that produced them. "'Normal femininity' of the psychological test variety may actually be a rare commodity. In one study of college-aged females, only 15 percent of the heterosexual sample tested as feminine on a widely accepted sex role inventory. The remaining 85 percent scored as either masculine or as some combination of masculine and feminine" (15). Differences cast in terms of averages, tendencies, and percentages do not meet the criteria of a natural kind.

Rather than being given in nature, sexual dimorphism is imposed by human beings who are trying to make sense of the natural world. As Suzanne Kessler and Wendy McKenna (1978, 163) note, this imposition is as characteristic of scientific inquiry as it is of everyday observation:

> Scientists construct dimorphism where there is continuity. Hormones, behavior, physical characteristics, developmental processes, chromosomes, and psychological qualities have all been fitted into dichotomous categories. Scientific knowledge does not inform the answer to the question, "What makes a person a man or a woman?" Rather it justifies (and appears to give grounds for) the already existing conviction that a person is either a man or a woman and that there is no problem differentiating between the two. Biological, psychological, and social differences do not lead to our seeing two genders. Our seeing two genders leads to the "discovery" of biological, psychological, and social differences.

Gender

To break the hold of biological reductionism, that is, the belief that anatomy dictates disposition and social role, feminist scholars adopted the concept of *gender* to designate culturally specific characteristics associated with masculinity and femininity. In early feminist works, gender was used to demonstrate the wide range of variation in cultural constructions of femininity and masculinity and in social roles assigned to men and women historically and cross-culturally. In subsequent works, gender was used to analyze the social organization of relationships between men and women (Rubin 1975; Barrett 1980; MacKinnon 1987), to investigate the reification of human differences (Vetterling-Braggin 1982; Hawkesworth 1990; Shanley and Pateman 1991), to conceptualize the semiotics of the body, sex, and sexuality (Suleiman 1985; de Lauretis 1984; Doane 1987; Silverman 1988), to explain the distribution of burdens and benefits in society (Walby 1986; Connell 1987; Boneparth and Stoper 1988), to illustrate the microtechniques of power (de Lauretis 1987; Bartky 1988; Sawicki 1991), to illuminate the structure of the psyche (Chodorow 1978), and to account for individual identity and aspiration (Epperson 1988; Butler 1990).

Interdisciplinary feminist scholars have used the concept of gender in markedly different ways, however. Gender has been analyzed as an attribute of individuals (Bem 1974, 1983), as an interpersonal relation (Spelman 1988), and as a mode of social organization (Firestone 1970; Eisenstein 1979). Gender has been defined in terms of status (Lopata and Thorne 1978), sex roles (Amundsen 1971; Epstein 1971; Janeway 1971), and sexual stereotypes (Friedan 1963; Anderson 1983). It has been conceived as a structure of consciousness (Rowbotham 1973), as triangulated psyche (Chodorow 1978), and as internalized ideology (Barrett 1980; Grant 1993). It has been discussed as a product of attribution (Kessler and McKenna 1978), socialization (Ruddick 1980; Gilligan 1982), disciplinary practices (Butler 1990; Singer 1993), and accustomed stance (Devor 1989). Gender has been depicted as an effect of language (Daly 1978; Spender 1980); a matter of behavioral conformity (Amundsen 1971; Epstein 1971); a structural feature of labor, power, and cathexis (Connell, 1987); a "doing" or performance (West and Zimmerman 1987; Butler 1990); and a mode of perception (Kessler and McKenna 1978; Bem 1993). Gender has been cast in terms of a binary opposition, variable and varying continua, and in terms of a layering of personality. It has been characterized as difference (Irigaray 1985a, 1985b) and as relations of power manifested in domination and subordination (MacKinnon 1987; Gordon 1988). It has been construed in the passive mode of seriality (Young 1994) and in the active mode as a process creating interdependence (Levi-Strauss 1969, 1971; Smith 1992) or as an instrument of segregation and exclusion (Davis 1981; Collins 1990). Gender has been denounced as a prisonhouse (Cornell and Thurschwell 1986) and embraced as inherently liberating (Irigaray 1985b; Smith 1992). It has been identified as a universal phenomenon (Lerner 1986) and as a historically specific consequence of modernity's increasing sexualization of women (Riley 1988; Laqueur 1990).

As the interpretations of gender proliferated in feminist scholarship, a number of feminist scholars raised questions about the utility of gender as an analytical category. Susan Bordo (1993, 216) identified two currents fueling the emergence of "gender skepticism." One current flows from the experiences of women of color and lesbian feminists who suggested that the multiple-jeopardy characteristic of their lives raises serious questions about the validity of gender generalizations. If gender is always mediated by race, class, ethnicity, and sexual orientation, then an analytical framework that isolates gender or construes gender in terms of an additive model is seriously flawed and may serve only to mask the numerous privileges of white, middle-class, heterosexual feminists who have the luxury of experiencing only one mode of oppression (King 1988; Spelman 1988; Higginbotham 1992). The second current flows from postmodern criticism, which depicts gender narratives as totalizing fictions that create a false unity out of heterogeneous elements. In addition to calling into question the binary opposition that fixes men and women in permanent relations of domination and subordination, postmodern critics also challenged the ground of the sex–gender distinction. If gender was devised to illuminate the social construction of masculinity and femininity and naively took the sexed body as given, then it has little to offer in a postmodern world that understands the body, sex, and sexuality as socially constructed (Butler 1990, 1993, 2004).

SEXUALITY

Variously characterized as an instinctual urge, a species imperative, the means of procreation, a site of pleasure and desire, and a primitive elemental force that all societies seek to control (Rubin 1993), sexuality has also been subject to critical investigation by feminist scholars. Whether celebrated as a source of physical delight or denounced as a temptation to sin, traditional depictions of sexuality were often cast as the scene of the first sexual division of labor. In Aristotle's vivid terminology, the male was defined as he who mounts and the female as she who is mounted, inscribing both a presumption of heterosexuality and an active–passive dichotomy at the core of putatively natural erotic practices (*On the Generation of Animals*, Book I, 2). Noting the power differentials embedded in such a construction of natural urges, early feminist scholars suggested that it is a mistake to construe sexuality solely in terms of desire, pleasure, and procreation, for it is also a system of domination.

In an early radical feminist analysis, Shulamith Firestone (1970) characterized eroticism as a subspecies of romanticism, a cultural tool of male power that channels women's desire for love into genital sex. Castigating Freud's invention of the myth of vaginal orgasm, Anne Koedt (1970) suggested that this perverse construction of "mature sexuality" defined women's pleasure exclusively in terms of what pleases men. Far from being a space for the free play of desire, radical feminist theorists conceived heterosexuality as a political relation of domination and subordination that puts men first and maintains male supremacy (MacKinnon 1987), a social institution of violence that places women in perpetual servitude to men (Wittig 1979), a cosmogony that envisions men and women as complementary because they "fit together" while masking asymmetrical power relations (Delphy 1993), and a compulsory system that assures men the right of access (physical, emotional, and economic) to women while requiring that lesbians be invisible in contemporary societies and written out of history (Rich 1980).

By situating heterosexuality in relation to larger structures of male power, early feminist thinkers suggested a strong affinity between lesbianism and feminism. Charlotte Bunch (1972), for example, depicted lesbianism as a political choice and as a revolt against white male power by women-identified women who act together to end sexual and political domination. Similarly, Monique Wittig (1979) characterized lesbianism as an escape from the class of women and from servitude to men. Differentiating lesbianism from male homosexuality, Adrienne Rich (1980) envisioned a lesbian continuum, which encompassed a political stance that entails commitment to the value of feminism and freedom of women as a group, a form of primary emotional intensity among women, bonding against male tyranny, marriage resistance, conscious desire for erotic experience with women, and the strength to break taboos and reject compulsory sexual subordination.

In a pathbreaking book that helped launch the field of queer theory, *Epistemology of the Closet*, Eve Sedgwick (1990, 27) questioned the tendency in many feminist works to conflate sex, gender, and sexuality, suggesting the need for greater analytical differentiation of these concepts: "The study of sexuality is not coextensive with the study of gender; correspondingly the study of anti-homophobic inquiry is not coextensive with feminist inquiry. But we can't know in advance how they will be different." In a related move, Cheshire Calhoun (1994) challenged the conflation of lesbianism and feminism, calling for a clear distinction between patriarchy (or structures of male domination) and heterosexuality. According to Calhoun, feminist theorists had failed to recognize that heterosexuality is a political structure of domination distinct from patriarchy; heterosexuality divides heterosexuals and nonheterosexuals into different groups with different rights and opportunities, creating privilege for some while systematically excluding others. Echoing Audre Lorde's (1985) insight that heterosexism is the belief in the inherent superiority of one form of loving, Calhoun defined *heterosexualism* as a political system that supports both male privilege and heterosexual privilege. It enshrines the man–woman dyad as the basic unit of society; privileges reproduction as a heterosexual domain; and produces gender dimorphism, sexual divisions of labor, and occupational and legal arrangements that privilege heterosexuals.

Audre Lorde (1985) also pointed out that homophobia, which encompasses both a terror of love for the same sex and a hatred of those who are gay and lesbian, is a powerful mechanism of social control. Homophobia drives a wedge between gay and straight while also deploying the coercive powers of hetero-sexuality to keep gays and lesbians closeted. To be outed is to risk losing one's biological children in a custody battle, being denied the possibility of adopt-ing children, losing one's job, being punished for public displays of affection, facing housing discrimination, being harassed by neighbors, being subjected to "normalizing" therapies, being excluded from representations of love, being denied the right to marry, and being subject to physical violence and death at the hands of virulent homophobes (Calhoun 1994; Pharr 1997). Linking these forms of coercion to microtechniques of power that produce normalized and disciplined bodies, Michael Warner (1991) theorized heteronormativity as encompassing intricate expectations, demands, and constraints that sustain hierarchies of difference grounded on the presumed naturalness of heterosexual-ity. Heteronormativity is systemic, pervading cultural production, occupational structures, legal and political institutions, medical practices, and immigration protocols as well as religious, philosophical, and scientific discourses, deni-grating and marginalizing those who refuse the strictures of heterosexuality. Indeed, heteronormativity is so pervasive that it has been assimilated within gay and lesbian communities in the form of homonormativity (Duggan 2003), a system of values that privileges homosexuals who mimic heterosexual norms of monogamy, marriage, and family while pathologizing dissident forms of queer existence.

DIFFERENTIATING SEX, GENDER, AND SEXUALITY

With the growth of feminist and queer scholarship over the past four decades, there has been continuing debate about how best to theorize the complex rela-tions among sex, gender, and sexuality in relation to the politics of embodiment. Within these debates, particular attention has been given to the examination of sex, gender, and sexuality as lived experience and to their deployment as analytical categories. Although scholars disagree about the meaning and util-ity of these concepts, they have cultivated an analytical vocabulary that distin-guishes sex, sexuality, sexual identity, gender identity, gender role, and gender role identity. Virtually all scholars working in gender and sexualities studies employ some of these distinctions, although all do not use the terms in the same way. Sex, for example, can refer to biological features such as chromo-somes, hormones, internal and external sexual and reproductive organs, or acts romantically characterized as lovemaking. Gender identity typically refers to individuals' feeling of being a man or a woman, but this feeling may be defined in a rudimentary sense as having a conviction that their sex assignment at birth was "anatomically and psychologically correct" (Stoller 1985, 11), more expansively as a patterned subjectivity that bears some relation to cultural conceptions of masculinity–femininity or more critically as a "refiguring of flesh in ways that adhere to normative gender codes...making it abide by preexisting gender laws" (Stryker 2006, 247). *Identity* can also mean markedly different things: a psychological sense of "who I am"; a sociological notion of a person qua agent prior to assuming specific social roles; a Foucauldian concept that captures an array of regulatory practices that produce the internal coherence of the subject; a philosophical concern with the individuation and unity of a person in the face of change; a narrative construction individuals develop to make sense of their lives; or a political identification with a group or collective, often produced in and through exclusionary political processes and state policies.

Although usage varies from text to text, most feminist scholars would grant that there are important conceptual differences between sex construed in biological terms or in relation to the materiality of the body; sexuality understood to encompass sexual practices and erotic behavior; sexual identity referring to designations such as heterosexual, homosexual, gay, lesbian, queer, bisexual, or asexual; gender identity as a psychological sense of oneself as a man or a woman, a sense that need not be tied to physical embodiment as transgender and transsexual activism have made clear; gender role as a set of prescriptive, culture-specific expectations about what is appropriate for men and women; and gender role identity, a concept devised to capture the extent to which persons approve of and participate in feelings and behaviors deemed to be appropriate to their culturally constituted gender (Kessler and McKenna 1978, 7–11; Barrett 1980, 42–79).

This analytic vocabulary provides distinctions that are critical to feminist efforts to challenge the natural attitude. The distinction between gender identity and gender role identity, for example, opens the possibility that one can have a clear sense of oneself as a woman (or a man) while being thoroughly disaffected from and refusing participation in prevailing conceptions of femininity (or masculinity). This distinction breaks any connection between masculinity–femininity and sexed bodies, interpreting masculinity and femininity as culture-specific abstractions that mark a chasm between romanticized ideal and lived experience, attributed and actual, propaganda and practice.

Once conceptual distinctions that differentiate sex, sexuality, sexual identity, gender identity, gender role, and gender role identity are delineated, then critical questions emerge: What do these phenomena have to do with one another? How are they related? How do their complex interrelations pertain to gender as lived experience or to gender as a power relation?

The natural attitude postulates sex as the determinant of gender identity that flows naturally into a particular mode of (hetero)sexuality and mandates certain rational gender roles embraced happily by individuals with uniformly positive gender role identities (that is, a person born with a uterus naturally develops a nurturing personality, craves association with a member of the "opposite" sex, engages in heterosexual intercourse, gives birth, happily assumes the responsibilities of childrearing, and defines meaningful existence in relation to mothering). Feminist scholars have challenged each of these posited relations. Drawing upon linguistics, historical analysis, structuralism, deconstruction, Freudian, Kleinian, and Lacanian psychoanalysis, phenomenology, existential and cognitive psychology, as well as dialectical materialism, feminist scholars have advanced various accounts of the relations that obtain among sex, gender, sexuality, and identity and have investigated how such complex social processes are naturalized, masking political agendas that inform them.

Exploring the Connections among Sex, Gender, and Sexuality

Operating within the confines of the natural attitude, sociobiologists, evolutionary psychologists, and physical anthropologists have no difficulty explaining putative connections between sex, gender, and sexuality, claiming that they are dictated by the demands of species survival. Defining men as sperm producers and women as egg producers, they suggest sexual dimorphism exists to foster diversity, providing richer opportunities for genetic variation than asexual modes of reproduction and thereby affording survival advantages for particular gene pools. Sociobiologists, for example, characterize heterosexual intercourse as a form of cooperation to produce zygotes, yet they also suggest that species survival mandates different sexual practices for men and women. Because, they claim, sperm are cheap—males supposedly produce 100 million sperm per ejaculation—sexual promiscuity affords advantages for the promotion of male genes. Eggs, on the other hand, are costly—females produce only 20 to 30 viable eggs over the course of a lifetime—therefore, females are more inclined toward fidelity and monogamy as strategies to promote the survival of their gene pool. The putative adaptive advantages afforded by sex-specific sexual practices are claimed to generate distinctive traits associated with masculinity (aggressiveness) and femininity (coyness) (Milam 2012). Gendered divisions of labor—from fictive accounts of man-the-hunter, women-the-gatherer to contemporary claims about men's overrepresentation and women's underrepresentation in positions of power, wealth, and prestige—are similarly explained in terms of the survival advantages (Wilson 1975, 1978). Rooting their claims in neuroscience, genetics, and evolutionary psychology, best-selling authors such as Simon Baron Cohen (2004) and Steven Pinker (2002) have reinvigorated old debates about innate sexual differences, supposedly hard-wired in the brain that affect cognitive abilities, communication skills, and the capacity to perform a host of social and political roles.

Critics have pointed out pervasive and systemic flaws in the sociobiological account of gender. At a methodological level, sociobiology falls prey to circular reasoning that violates the norms of scientific inquiry. Because they assume that existing traits are genetic adaptations, sociobiologists offer no empirical evidence to demonstrate that particular traits or behaviors are "heritable." They advance purportedly universal claims about sex differences drawn primarily from observations of baboons but offer no justification for their selection bias. Research on some 200 other primate species provides no credible evidence to support sociobiological claims. In particular, claims about costly eggs and cheap sperm that undergird claims about sex-specific sexual practices have been found invalid and unwarranted. In addition, the notion advanced by sociobiologists that the rich and vast domains of culture are genetically based mistakenly assigns responsibility to nature for the design of human institutions (Gould 1980; Fausto-Sterling 1986; Fedigan 1992; Tang-Martinez 1997). Unable to provide scientific evidence to support their unwarranted claims, sociobiologists proffer a defense of a narrow range of male-privileging, heteronormative behaviors by attributing survival advantage to them. Although "scientific" claims about sex differences in the brain are enormously popular, gaining widespread media attention, they too are seriously flawed. Rebecca Jordan-Young (2010) has provided systematic evidence that studies treating the brain as an "accessory reproductive organ" suffer from a host of methodological flaws. Her detailed examination of the quasi-experiments and proxy variables deployed in brain organization studies demonstrate not only that it is impossible to identify any hard-wired male-typical or female-typical behavior but also that particular studies are riddled with inconsistencies, ambiguities, and contradictions.

Despite their patent inadequacy as accounts of embodiment, sexuality, or gendered social practices, biological reductionist arguments surface regularly in popular culture and in feminist discourses. Following noted anthropologist Claude Levi-Strauss (1969, 1971), many accept a conception of culture as an elaborate mechanism devised to create interdependence and cooperation in the reproduction of the species. Stephen Smith (1992), for example, suggests that species reproduction requires sexual differentiation and therefore that culture creates that differentiation through processes of gendering to ensure the perpetuation of the species but masks its role by attributing the original difference to sex itself. "Since men and women have significantly different reproductive risks and opportunities in evolutionary terms, their guiding sex-related emotions must be sex-differentiated, that is, there must be different female and male sexual natures" (124). Defining gender as a "conventional formation of a plastic humanity" (15), Smith suggests that culture shapes what is perceived as a body. Through "embodiment," "the community stipulates what counts as a male/ female body, what life will be like in a male/female body in relation to other bodies, what norms (and latitudes) of character and conduct are associated with these bodies, and who is male and female" (91). When culture takes up the task of molding human nature, then, its aim is to enhance its own *construction* of what is naturally given, marking sex differentiations through language, character, and social roles. According to Smith, "Heterosexuality's postulated union of male and female specializations is the basic premise of the gender system" (80). Indeed, he suggests that "confronting sex differences makes me realize that I need a partner to reproduce...A gendered being teams with other gendered beings" (71). Echoing sociobiological presumptions, Smith suggests that the cultural creation of gender complementarity serves the larger purpose of species survival.

Smith's (1992) account operates within the confines of a "base/superstructure" model of the sex–gender distinction (Connell 1987, 50; Laqueur 1990, 124). Within this model, the body is assumed to provide the raw material that culture can refine in various but limited ways. Thus, gender is assumed to be hard-wired, at least, in part. The presumed naturalness of gender, its purported emergence in the absence of force or coercion, turns on a presumption of hard-wiring. When nature is imagined as the ground of cultural constructions of gender, discussions of gender seldom move far beyond presuppositions concerning inherent sex differences. R. W. Connell explained this recurrent problem in feminist accounts of gender by suggesting that in our culture "the notion of natural sex difference forms a limit beyond which thought cannot go" (66). Similarly, Holly Devor (1989, 45–46) described biological determinism as the dominant cognitive schema in North America, that is, as the conceptual structure that organizes social experience on the basis of shared understandings. Mary Poovey (1988), Ludmilla Jordanova (1989), and Thomas Laqueur (1990) provided fascinating accounts of the emergence of the base–superstructure model of gender since the seventeenth century. According to Laqueur, "It is a sign of modernity to ask for a single, consistent biology as the source or foundation for masculinity and femininity" (61). Whatever the cause of this tendency toward biological determinism, it is a troubled ground for feminist accounts of sex, gender, and sexuality. As Smith's account makes clear, appeal to a biological ground traps gender in the ideology of procreation, which construes sexuality and erotic practices in relation only to reproduction (Barrett 1980, 62–77), according women an essential maternal role mandated by culture and nature—a role undifferentiated by race, ethnicity, nationality, age, class, sexual orientation, or any mode of individuality.

Judith Butler's (1990) influential work, *Gender Trouble*, set out to disrupt the hold of biological determinism by explaining how the naturalness of sex, sexuality, and gender are "constituted through discursively constrained performative acts that produce the body through and within the categories of sex" (x). She cautioned at the outset that "'being' a sex or a gender" is fundamentally impossible" (18). The binary oppositions male–female and masculine–feminine are incompatible with the continuous variability of human characteristics, constructing a false opposition between the sexes and an artificial coherence within each term of the binary. Stereotypical genders, then, must be understood as "ontological locales that are fundamentally uninhabitable" (146). Rejecting the "old dream of symmetry," Butler argues that gender must be understood not as a noun, nor as a set of attributes but as a "doing," a performative that constitutes the identity that it purports to be (24).

According to Butler (1990), gender is the process that constructs the internal coherence of sex, (hetero)sexual desire, and (hetero)sexual practice within the modern subject. It is the mechanism that produces a notion of a presocial body shaped by culture. And it provides the standard of intelligibility for persons that informs both the naturalistic paradigm and the authentic-expressive paradigm of the self. "Gender is the discursive/cultural means by which 'sexed nature' or 'a natural sex' is produced and established as 'prediscursive,' prior to culture, a politically neutral surface on which culture acts" (7). Gender performs this work of naturalization through the "stylized repetition of actions through time" (141). The natural attitude is produced through the repetition of words, acts, and gestures. The sheer weight of these repetitions leads the actor to believe in and act in the mode of belief. Gender functions, then, as a regulatory fiction, "a fabrication, a fantasy instituted and inscribed on the surface of bodies" (136). Becoming gendered is a laborious process, and bringing the self into belief in the natural attitude is arduous; however, the intensity of effort and the power relations that produce this effect are hidden by the very "naturalization" at the core of the gendering process.

Butler's (1990) account reverses the direction of causality presumed by the natural attitude. Rather than sex structuring the parameters of two genders, "gender designates the apparatus of production whereby sexes are established" (7). But Butler insists that gender itself is the effect of specific formations of power, institutions, practices, and discourses that establish and regulate its shape and meaning. She identifies phallogocentrism and compulsory heterosexuality as the discursive sites that produce gender. "The heterosexualization of desire *requires* and *institutes* the production of discrete and asymmetrical oppositions between 'feminine' and 'masculine' understood as expressive attributes of 'female' and 'male'" (17, emphasis added). Thus, in a surprising twist Butler, like Smith (1992), appeals to the cultural creation of heterosexuality as the explanation of gender. In Butler's analysis, gender as performativity becomes the cultural force that produces belief in the naturalness of heterosexuality. The effect of compulsory heterosexuality, gender reproduces a natural heterosexual world even as it produces a body experienced as natural fact.

Becoming a gender is becoming naturalized as a man or a woman. According to Butler (1990), this involves a complex psychological process that eroticizes the body. The taboo against homosexuality in conjunction with the taboo against incest differentiate bodily parts and pleasures on the basis of gendered meanings, as melancholia deadens some organs to pleasure and brings others to life (68–70). This deadening is far from complete, however. Rather than generating a fixed identity, gender performances give rise to "multiple and coexisting identifications [that] produce conflicts, convergences, and innovative dissonances within gender configurations, which contest the fixity of masculine and feminine placements with respect to the paternal law" (67).

The very possibility of such multiple identifications is central to Butler's (1990) strategy for confounding gender. In contrast to Smith's (1992) affirmation of gender as a heteronormative project, Butler denounced the modes of power that produce homosexuality as necessary yet prohibited, as within culture yet marginalized. Arguing that power can never be escaped, only redeployed, Butler endorsed parody as a tactic designed to subvert the real or the sexually factic. Strategies of subversive repetition can dispel belief in the illusions of the natural body, desire, or sexuality, thereby rendering gender incredible (141, 146). Interpreting gender in terms of the cultural production of heterosexual desire and psychoanalytic production of gender identity, Butler's account makes gender a matter of the self—a self that appears peculiarly unmarked by race, class, ethnicity, or nationality. Her conceptualization privatizes gender, offering little prospect for addressing gender structures beyond the psyche.

In *Gender and Power*, Connell (1987) advanced a "systematic social theory of gender" that strives to account for the historicity of gender, the dynamic role of gender in economic, political, sexual and psychological domains, the relation between personal agency and social structure in gender formation and reproduction, as well as the turbulence and contradictions pertaining to gender as lived experience. Attuned to the problems associated with conceptions of gender that construe women as perennial victims, Connell developed a practice-based theory of gender attentive to both the constraining power of gender and the myriad struggles people engage against those constraints. Providing a cogent critique of all modes of biological determinism, Connell notes that the body is never experienced without cultural mediation and defines gender in terms of the cognitive and interpretive practices that "create, appropriate, and recreate reproductive biology" (79).

Connell (1987) rejects all theories that attempt to derive gender from natural differences, biological reproduction, the functional needs of society, or the imperatives of social reproduction, insisting that functionalist arguments must be viewed with extreme suspicion. They serve only to mask the power underlying these cultural symbolizations and thereby justify inequitable distributions of social burdens and benefits. Connell suggests that the social practices

constituting gender bear no direct relation to what might be considered functional for human reproduction. The patterns of posture, movement, dress,
adornment, body shape, body image, sexuality, intonation, speech, skilling, and
deskilling associated with cultural constructions of masculinity and femininity may not be at all conducive to reproduction. Connell also notes that gender as a social practice is more than a mere marking of the human body; "it
is the weaving of a structure of symbols which exaggerate and distort human
potential" (79). Far more than an attribute of an individual or a characteristic
of a social collectivity, gender is the active process that reduces people to, and
conceives social life in terms of, reproductive function, thereby constraining
individual potential (97, 140, 245). Indeed, gender constrains specific structures
tied to particular social practices of labor, power, and cathexis.

According to Connell (1987), as a constraint upon labor, gender structures
the allocation of particular types of work, the organization of domestic activity, the division of paid versus unpaid labor, the segregation of labor markets,
patterns of production and consumption, wage levels, opportunities for employment and promotion, and even the conditions and terms of labor exchange.
Within the domain of power, gender structures authority, control, and coercion:
it establishes hierarchies in public and private sectors, creates a virtual male
monopoly of institutional and interpersonal violence, and promotes particular
domestic and sexual asymmetries. Defining cathexis in terms of practices constructing emotionally-charged relations with others, Connell notes that gender
structures identities of desiring subjects and designation of desirable objects,
patterns of desire, sexual practices, as well as, terms and conditions for sexual
exchange.

Despite the enormous complexity of Connell's (1987) account of gender
and despite repeated cautions against functionalist explanation, Connell, too,
turns to notions of gender complementarity to explain why gender persists.
"There is a logic to paradoxes such as gross exaggerations of difference by
social practices of dress....They are part of a continuing effort to sustain the
social definition of gender, an effort that is necessary precisely because the
biological logic...cannot sustain gender categories" (81). According to Connell,
this logic is linked to the heterosexualization of desire. "The solidarity of the
heterosexual couple is formed on the basis of some kind of reciprocity rather
than on the basis of common situation or experience...Sexual difference is in
large part what gives erotic flavor to relationships. It is emphasized as a means
of heightening and intensifying pleasure, hence, the systematic exaggeration of
gender differences" (113).

Although Connell (1987) explicitly tried to avoid heterosexism in discussing
gender as a mode of constraint, the notion that "sexual difference" heightens
erotic pleasure depends on heterosexist presuppositions. Sedgwick (1990) points
out that the heterosexual–homosexual opposition allows equivocation in the
meaning imputed to "homo"/sexual. As one moves from notions of one sex to
same sex to self-same to sameness, an enormous range of differences is elided.

And this elision sustains Connell's assumption that there is greater difference, hence greater potential erotic pleasure, across genders than within genders. "The new calculus of homo/hetero...owes its sleekly utilitarian feel to the linguistically unappealable classification of anyone who shares one's gender as the 'same' as oneself, and anyone who does not share one's gender as Other" (160). But Sedgwick notes that even the most cursory examination of human beings will reveal that being of the same gender cannot guarantee "similarity" anymore than being of "opposite" genders can guarantee difference. Moreover, the belief that the gender of one's sexual partner is the crucial difference determining pleasure (rather than differences pertaining to, e.g., positions, acts, techniques, zones or sensations, physical types, emotional and symbolic investments, relations of power) will not withstand serious scrutiny. Thus, there appears to be a suppressed procreationist premise in Connell's allusion to the best means to heighten erotic pleasure. Once again, a procreationist agenda surfaces in an explanation of gender.

Despite important differences in their approaches to and conceptions of gender as lived experience, the accounts of Butler (1990), Connell (1987), and Smith (1992) implicate gender in the ideology of procreation, a conception of sexuality that reduces the erotic to reproduction (Barrett 1980, 62–77). In so doing, these texts incorporate presuppositions that replicate rather than undermine the natural attitude (Hawkesworth 1997).

Gender as an Analytic Category

In addition to trying to explain the intricate connections between sex, gender, and sexuality as lived experience, feminist scholars have devoted considerable attention to theorizing and deploying gender as an analytic category within discipline-based and interdisciplinary research. Within the philosophy of science, an analytic category is understood as a heuristic device that performs both positive and negative functions in a research program (Lakatos 1970). As a positive heuristic, gender as an analytic category illuminates an area of inquiry, framing a set of questions for investigation, such as how power operates in the production of sex, gender, and sexuality within specific racial, ethnic, and national contexts. As an analytic category, gender need not involve any explicit methodological commitment, merely identifying puzzles or problems in need of exploration or clarification, but it does provide concepts, definitions, and hypotheses to guide research. Lakatos's notion of a negative heuristic also suggests shared assumptions so central to a mode of analysis that they cannot be jettisoned (132).

In an important and influential essay, Joan Scott (1986) suggested that gender is a useful category for historical analysis because it illuminates

aspects of power embedded in social organization missed by traditional historiography. "Gender is a constitutive element of social relationships based
on perceived differences between the sexes, and gender is a primary way of
signifying relationships of power" (1067). In explicating gender as a constitutive element of social relationships, Scott emphasizes that gender operates in multiple fields, including culturally available symbols that surface
in multiple representations and contexts, normative concepts that set forth
interpretations of the meanings of symbols, social institutions and organizations, and subjective identities (1067–1068). According to Scott, gender
analysis "provides a way to decode meaning and to understand the complex
connections among various forms of human interaction" (1070). Noting that
gender is always contextually defined and repeatedly constructed, Scott cautions that gender analysts must not replicate the mistakes of early feminist
accounts that credited gender as a universal causal force. On the contrary,
gender analysts must seek a "genuine historicization and deconstruction of
the terms of sexual difference" (1065). Scott demonstrates that problematic
theoretical assumptions informing radical feminism, Marxist feminism, and
psychoanalytic feminism gave rise to various misapplications of gender as an
analytic category, resulting in ahistorical analyses, oversimplified and reductive explanations, universal generalizations impervious to change in history,
exclusive fixation on the subject, and restrictive foci on the family or the
household. Such flaws need not be endemic to gender analysis, however.
Indeed, Scott argues that a self-critical deployment of gender analysis could
provide meaningful explanations of historically and culturally specific relations obtaining between individual subjects and modes of social organization. If feminist scholars examine "how things happened in order to find out
why they happened" (1067), their analytical investigations will enable them
to reverse and displace the binary and hierarchical construction of gender,
refuting the naive belief that gender "is real or self-evident or in the nature
of things" (1066).

Sandra Harding (1986) also advanced a highly influential conception
of gender as an analytic category. "The fact that there are class, race, and
cultural differences between women and between men is not, as some have
thought, a reason to find gender difference either theoretically unimportant
or politically irrelevant. In virtually every culture, gender difference is a pivotal way in which humans identify themselves as persons, organize social
relations, and symbolize meaningful natural and social events and processes"
(18). The very pervasiveness of gender requires systematic feminist analysis.
Thus, Harding argues that feminists must theorize gender, conceiving it as
"an analytic category within which humans think about and organize their
social activity rather than as a natural consequence of sex difference, or even
merely as a social variable assigned to individual people in different ways
from culture to culture" (17). Recognizing that gender appears only in culturally specific forms in no way mitigates the force of gender analysis. On the

contrary, gender as an analytic category illuminates crucial cultural processes. "Gendered social life is produced through three distinct processes: it is the result of assigning dualistic gender metaphors to various perceived dichotomies that rarely have anything to do with sex differences (gender symbolism); it is the consequence of appealing to these gender dualisms to organize social activity, dividing necessary social activities between different groups of humans (gender structure); it is a form of socially constructed individual identity only imperfectly correlated with either the reality or the perception of sex differences (individual gender)" (17–18). According to Harding, feminist investigations of gender symbolism, gender structure, and individual gender challenge the basic presuppositions of the natural attitude, thereby helping to dispel essentialized identities while creating the possibility of a politics grounded in solidarities that cross the divisions of race, class, age, ethnicity, and sexual orientation.

The conception of gender as an analytic category advanced by Scott and Harding laid the groundwork for research investigating how gender is used to provide a coherent account of the intricate connections linking psyche to social organization, social roles to cultural symbols, normative beliefs to "the experience" of the body and sexuality. Illuminating a range of questions for feminist investigation that challenge androcentric and heteronormative assumptions, gender as an analytical tool has been used by feminist scholars to identify important issues pertaining to social institutions, relations and symbols, as well as individual identities, which can be investigated within particular cultures and subcultures at particular historical moments. Scott and Harding also identify a negative heuristic of gender analysis. As formulated by Donna Haraway (1991, 131), as an analytical category, gender "contest[s] the naturalization of sex differences in multiple arenas of struggle."

The cogent critiques of black feminist theorists, critical race theorists, and postcolonial theorists further elaborated the negative heuristic of gender and sexualities studies: sex, gender, and sexuality cannot be studied in isolation. Whether framed in terms of a concept of intersectionality (Crenshaw 1989; McCall 2005), "hybridity" (Anzaldua 1987, Bhabha 1994, Friedman 1998), "articulation" (Hall 1980a, 1980b) or "assemblage" (Deleuze and Guattari 1987; Puar 2007), feminist scholarship seeks to investigate the mutually constitutive and structuring power of race, gender, class, ethnicity, sexuality, and nationality in social relations. Illuminating how hierarchies of difference are created, sustained, and reproduced through the intricate interplay of concrete social practices, feminist scholars construe racialization, gendering, and heterosexualization as interlocking processes that produce not simply difference but also political asymmetries and social hierarchies, simultaneously creating the dominant and the subordinate. By moving beyond additive approaches to investigate mutual constitution, feminist scholars have identified research questions that are not possible within the parameters of mainstream social science.

Innovative Approaches to Sex, Gender, and Sexuality in Gender and Politics Research

....

Within the field of gender and politics research, feminist scholars have challenged naturalized views of race, sex, and sexuality, calling attention to processes of racialization, gendering, heteronormativity, and homonormativity through which relations of power and forms of inequality are constructed within the nation-state, shaping the identities of individuals as well as institutional practices. Through detailed studies of laws, norms, and organizational processes, they have demonstrated how enforced segregation and separate spheres produce men and women of particular races, sexualities, classes, and ethnicities as beings who have been not only accorded a place in a sociopolitical order but also taught to know their place. Rather than situating ability and interest within the aptitude of the individual, feminist scholars have shown how imputed natural interests and abilities of women and men of various races, sexualities, classes, and ethnicities are the result of state-prescribed limitations in education, occupation, immigration, citizenship, and office-holding (Siltanen 1994; Haney Lopez 1996; Flammang 1997; Ngai 2005; Hawkesworth 2012).

Racialization, gendering, and heteronormativity are part of the daily operations of state power, deployed as means for particular states to realize their visions of national identity and national order (Stevens 1999). Raced-gendered-sexualized patterns of skilling and deskilling, differences in political rights and economic opportunities, and modes of political visibility and invisibility structure the identities, self-understandings, and life-prospects of citizens. Rather than succumb to mythic constructions of the nation that emphasize ties of blood and ancestry, feminist scholars have traced how political decisions have produced physical characteristics associated with particular nations. Immigration policies, antimiscegenation laws, and eugenic practices, for example, produce the distinctive physical appearance of a nation's population by constraining reproductive partners and choices. Laws, court decisions, and census categories define who counts as the privileged cohort (e.g., *white Americans, Aryans,* or *heterosexuals*) for citizenship purposes and who counts as disadvantaged (e.g., *non-whites, blacks, Asians, Jews,* or *homosexuals*) for purposes of exclusion, ascribing racialized meanings to physical features and ancestry (Haney Lopez 1996, 14–15; Yanow 2003). Laws and policies also produce certain behaviors and attitudes associated with inferiority through exclusions from citizenship, educational and professional opportunities, and office holding; through the legalization of unequal treatment; and through differential access to public speech, civil rights, and political visibility (Fraser 1989; Haney Lopez 1996; Phelan 2001; Lehring 2003).

Power and disadvantage related to race, class, gender, and sexuality are created and maintained not only through law but also through institutional processes, practices, images, ideologies, and distributional mechanisms (Acker 1990, 1992; Kenney 1996; Steinberg 1992). Organizational practices, standard operating procedures, institutional rules and regulations play a central role in creating and entrenching hierarchies associated with particular modes of embodiment. Violence, coerced divisions of labor, formal and informal policing of modes of dress, adornment, deportment, stylizations of the body, voice intonations and inflections, erotic practices, skilling or deskilling, and complex regimes of visibility and invisibility are part of the micropolitics of racialization, gendering, and heterosexualization.

Mainstream political scientists often depict the state as a collection of impartial institutions, governed by neutral and rational procedures, designed to foster formal equality before the law, equal rights of participation, and practicable mechanisms of accountability. By contrast, women and politics scholars suggest that the state is better understood as a raced and gendered institution. Over the past several decades, feminist scholars have documented in specific contexts how raced and gendered norms operate within particular political, social, and economic institutions and practices to construct and maintain power dynamics that favor men of the dominant race or ethnicity (Hawkesworth 2003, 2006).

Beyond making women's lives and contributions visible, feminist scholars have used sex, gender, and sexuality as analytical categories to develop alternative research practices that further feminist, queer, and antiracist goals of social transformation. Central to this effort is a unique way of attending to and theorizing structures of power that operate by demarcating certain domains as natural, accidental, or prepolitical and, as such, beyond the reach of social intervention. By theorizing power relations that encompass embodiment, sexuality, and oppressive structures that permeate everyday life—whether they gain their purchase from culture, tradition, or changing local, national, transnational and global practices—feminist scholarship renders the politics of difference and the politics of knowledge intelligible and actionable.

Troubling both false universals and confining stereotypes, feminist analysis tracks complex operations of power by resisting overgeneralization, recognizing the roots of particular judgments, and actively engaging multiple theoretical frames and cultural perspectives. Grounded in particularity and attentive to specificity, feminist scholarship cultivates reflective comparisons that illuminate the visible and the invisible—modes of embodiment, facets of desire, dynamics of social existence, categories that structure perception and action, intended and unintended consequences of action and inaction, macro and micro structures that constrain. By interrogating processes of representation, racialization, gendering, and heterosexualization, feminist research investigates dimensions of social, cultural, political, economic, national, and transnational life that go undetected in mainstream discourses. Advancing new ways to comprehend the politics of difference, this scholarship demonstrates how hierarchies are produced, sustained, challenged, and transformed through cultural production and regimes of visuality as well as through economic restructuring and the practices of international governmental and financial institutions and the laws, norms, and policies of nation-states, communities, workplaces, and households. In deploying race, sex, gender, and sexuality as intersecting categories of analysis, feminist scholarship demonstrates conclusively that the politics of embodiment is epistemically, morally, and substantively relevant to academic research.

REFERENCES

Acker, Joan. 1990. "Hierarchies, job bodies: A theory of gendered organizations." *Gender and Society* 4(2): 139–158.

Acker, Joan. 1992. "Gendered institutions: From sex roles to gendered institutions." *Contemporary Sociology* 21(5): 565–569.

Amundsen, Kirsten. 1971. *The silenced majority.* Englewood Cliffs, NJ: Prentice Hall.

Anderson, Margaret. 1983. *Thinking about women.* New York: Macmillan.

Anzaldua, Gloria. 1987. *Borderlands/La Frontera: The new mestiza.* San Francisco: Spinsters/Aunt Lute.

Barrett, Michele. 1980. *Women's oppression today.* London: Verso.

Bartky, Sandra. 1988. "Foucault, femininity and the modernization of patriarchal power." In Irene Diamond and Lee Quinby, eds., *Feminism and Foucault.* Boston: Northeastern University Press.

Bem, Sandra. 1974. "The measurement of psychological androgyny." *Journal of Clinical and Consulting Psychology* 42: 155–162.

Bem, Sandra. 1983. "Gender schematic theory and its implications for child development." *Signs: Journal of Women in Culture and Society* 8: 598–616.

Bem, Sandra. 1993. *Lenses of gender.* New Haven, CT: Yale University Press.

Bhabha, Homi K. 1994. *The location of culture.* London: Routledge.

Boneparth, Ellen, and Emily Stoper, eds. 1988. *Women power and policy: Towards the year 2000.* New York: Pergamon.

Bordo, Susan. 1993. *Unbearable weight: Feminism, Western culture and the body.* Berkeley: University of California Press.

Bunch, Charlotte. 1972. "Lesbians in revolt." *The Furies:* Lesbian/Feminist Monthly 1(January): 8–9. Available online at http://library.duke.edu/rubenstein/ scriptorium/wlm/furies/.

Butler, Judith. 1990. *Gender trouble.* New York: Routledge.

Butler, Judith. 1993. *Bodies that matter.* New York: Routledge.

Butler, Judith. 2004. *Undoing gender.* New York: Routledge.

Calhoun, Cheshire. 1994. "Separating lesbian theory from feminist theory." *Ethics* 104(3): 558–581.

Chodorow, Nancy. 1978. *The reproduction of mothering.* Berkeley: University of California Press.

Cody, Lisa Forman. 2001. "Sex, civility, and the self: Du Coudray, D'Eon, and eighteenth-century conceptions of gendered, national and psychological identity." *French Historical Studies* 24(3): 379–407.

Cody, Lisa Forman. 2005. *Birthing the nation: Sex, science, and the conception of eighteenth century Britons.* Oxford: Oxford University Press.

Cohen, Simon Baron. 2004. *The essential difference*. London: Penguin.

Collins, Patricia Hill. 1990. *Black feminist thought*. New York: Harper Collins.

Connell, R.W. 1987. *Gender and power*. Stanford: Stanford University Press.

Cornell, Drucilla, and Adam Thurschwell. 1986. "Femininity, negativity, intersubjectivity." *Praxis International* 5(4): 484–504.

Crenshaw, Kimberle. 1989. "Demarginalizing the intersection of race and sex: A black feminist critique of antidiscrimination doctrine, feminist theory and antiracist politics." *University of Chicago Legal Forum* 4: 139–167.

Daly, Mary. 1978. *GYN/ecology*. Boston: Beacon.

Davis, Angela. 1981. *Women, race and class*. New York: Random House.

de Lauretis, Theresa. 1984. *Alice doesn't: feminism, semiotics, cinema*. Bloomington: Indiana University Press.

de Lauretis, Theresa. 1987. *Technologies of gender*. Bloomington: Indiana University Press.

Deleuze, Gilles, and Felix Guattari. 1987. *A thousand plateaus*. Trans. and Foreword by Brian Massumi. Minneapolis: University of Minnesota Press.

Delphy, Christine. 1993. "Rethinking sex and gender." *Women's Studies International Forum* 16(4): 1–9.

Devor, Holly. 1989. *Gender blending: Confronting the limits of duality*. Bloomington: Indiana University Press.

Doane, Mary Ann. 1987. *The desire to desire*. Bloomington: Indiana University Press.

Duggan, Lisa. 2003. *The twilight of equality? Neoliberalism, cultural politics, and the attack on democracy*. Boston: Beacon Press.

Eisenstein, Zillah. 1979. *Capitalist patriarchy and the case for socialist feminism*. New York: Monthly Review Press.

Epperson, Sharon. 1988. "Studies link subtle sex bias in schools with women's behavior in the workplace." *Wall Street Journal*, September 16, p. 19.

Epstein, Cynthia Fuchs. 1971. *Woman's place*. Berkeley: University of California Press.

Fausto-Sterling, Anne. 1986. *Myths of gender*. New York: Basic Books.

Fausto-Sterling, Anne. 1993. "The five sexes: Why male and female are not enough." *Sciences* (March–April): 20–24.

Fedigan, Linda M. 1992. *Primate paradigms*. Chicago: University of Chicago Press.

Firestone, Shulamith. 1970. *The dialectic of sex*. New York: William Morrow.

Flammang, Janet. 1997. *Women's political voice*. Philadelphia: Temple University Press.

Fraser, Nancy. 1989. "Women, welfare, and the politics of need interpretation." In *Unruly practices*. Minneapolis: University of Minnesota Press.

Friedan, Betty. 1963. *The feminine mystique*. New York: W.W. Norton.

Friedman, Susan Stanford. 1998. *Mappings: Feminism and the cultural geographies of encounter*. Princeton, NJ: Princeton University Press.

Garfinkel, Harold. 1967. *Studies in ethnomethodology*. Englewood Cliffs, NJ: Prentice Hall.

Gilligan, Carol. 1982. *In a different voice*. Cambridge, MA: Harvard University Press.

Gordon, Linda. 1988. *Heroes of their own lives: The politics and history of family violence*. New York: Viking.

Gould, Stephen J. 1980. "Sociobiology and the theory of natural selection." In G. W. Barlow and J. Silverberg, eds., *Sociobiology: Beyond nature/nurture*. Boulder, CO: Westview Press, 257–269.

Grant, Judith. 1993. *Fundamental feminism*. New York: Routledge.

Hall, Stuart. 1980a. "Cultural studies: Two paradigms." *Media, Culture, and Society* 2(1): 57–72.

Hall, Stuart. 1980b. "Encoding/decoding." In S. Hall, D. Hobson, A. Lowe, and P. Willis, eds., *Culture, media, language*. London: Hutchinson, 128–140.

Haney Lopez, Ian. 1996. *White by law*. New York: New York University Press.

Haraway, Donna. 1991. "Gender for a Marxist dictionary: The sexual politics of a word." *Simians, Cyborgs and Women*. New York: Routledge.

Harding, Sandra. 1986. *The science question in feminism*. Ithaca, NY: Cornell University Press.

Hawkesworth, Mary. 1990. "The reification of difference." *Beyond Oppression*. New York: Continuum Publishing Company.

Hawkesworth, Mary. 1997. "Confounding gender." *Signs: Journal of Women in Culture and Society* 22(3): 649–685.

Hawkesworth, Mary. 2003. "Congressional enactments of race-gender: Toward a theory of raced-gendered institutions." *American Political Science Review* 97(4):529–550.

Hawkesworth, Mary. 2006. *Feminist inquiry: From political conviction to methodological innovation*. New Brunswick, NJ: Rutgers University Press.

Hawkesworth, Mary. 2012. *Political worlds of women: Activism, advocacy, and governance in the 21st Century*. Boulder, CO: Westview/Perseus.

Higginbotham, Evelyn Brooks. 1992. "African-American women's history and the metalanguage of race." *Signs: Journal of Women in Culture and Society* 17(2): 251–274.

Irigaray, Lucy. 1985a. *Speculum of the other woman*. Trans. Gillian Gill. Ithaca, NY: Cornell University Press.

Irigaray, Lucy. 1985b. *This sex which is not one*. Trans. Catherine Porter. Ithaca, NY: Cornell University Press.

Janeway, Elizabeth. 1971. *Man's world, women's place*. New York: Delta Books.

Jordan-Young, Rebecca. 2010. *Brain storm: The flaws in the science of sex differences*. Cambridge, MA: Harvard University Press.

Jordanova, Ludmilla. 1989. *Sexual visions: Images of gender in science and medicine between the 18th and 20th centuries*. Madison: University of Wisconsin Press.

Kenney, Sally. 1996. "New research on gendered political institutions." *Political Research Quarterly* 49 (June): 445–466.

Kessler, Suzanne, and Wendy McKenna. 1978. *Gender: An ethnomethodological approach*. New York: John Wiley.

King, Deborah. 1988. "Multiple jeopardy, multiple consciousness: The context of black feminist ideology." *Signs: Journal of Women in Culture and Society* 14(1): 42–72.

Koedt, Anne. 1970. "The myth of the vaginal orgasm." *Notes from the first year*. New York: New York Radical Women. Available online at http://www.uic.edu/orgs/cwluherstory/CWLUArchive/vaginalmyth.html.

Lakatos, Imre. 1970. "Falsification and the methodology of scientific research programmes." In Imre Lakatos and Alan Musgrave, eds., *Criticism and the growth of knowledge*. Cambridge, UK: Cambridge University Press.

Landes, Joan. 1988. *Women and the public sphere in the age of the French revolution*. Ithaca, NY: Cornell University Press.

Landes, Joan. 1998. *Feminism, the public and the private*. New York: Oxford University Press.

Laqueur, Thomas. 1990. *Making sex: Body and gender from the Greeks to Freud*. Cambridge, MA: Harvard University Press.

Laqueur, Thomas. 2012. "The rise of sex in the eighteenth century: Historical context and historiographical implications." *Signs: Journal of Women in Culture and Society* 37(4): 802–813.

Lehring, Gary. 2003. *Officially gay: The political construction of sexuality in the U.S. military.* Philadelphia: Temple University Press.

Lerner, Gerda. 1986. *The creation of patriarchy.* New York: Oxford University Press.

Levi-Strauss, Claude. 1969. *The elementary structures of kinship.* Boston: Beacon Press.

Levi-Strauss, Claude. 1971. "The family." In H. Shapire, ed., *Man, culture and society.* London: Oxford University Press.

Lopata, Helene, and Barrie Thorne. 1978. "On the term, 'sex roles.'" *Signs: Journal of Women in Culture and Society* 3(3): 718–721.

Lorde, Audre. 1985. *I am your sister: Black women organizing across sexualities.* New York: Women of Color Press.

MacKinnon, Catharine. 1987. *Feminism unmodified.* Cambridge, MA: Harvard University Press.

Matambanadzo, Saru. 2005. "Engendering sex: birth certificates, biology, and the body in Anglo-American law." *Cardozo Women's Law Journal* 11: 213–246.

McCall, Leslie. 2005. "The complexity of intersectionality." *Signs: Journal of Women in Culture and Society* 30(3): 1771–1800.

Milam, Erika Lorraine. 2012. "Making males aggressive and females coy: Gender across the animal-human boundary." *Signs: Journal of Women in Culture and Society* 37 (4): 935–960.

Okonjo, Kamene. 1994. "Women and the evolution of a Ghanian political synthesis." In Barbara Nelson and Najma Chowdhury, eds., *Women and politics worldwide.* New Haven, CT: Yale University Press, 285–297.

Oyewumi, Oyeronke. 1997. *The invention of women: Making an African sense of Western gender discourses.* Minneapolis: University of Minnesota Press.

Ngai, Mae M. 2005. *Impossible subjects: Illegal aliens and the making of modern America.* Princeton, NJ: Princeton University Press.

Pharr, Suzanne. 1997. *Homophobia: Weapon of sexism.* Berkeley, CA: Chardon Press.

Phelan, Shane. 2001. *Sexual strangers: Gays, lesbians, and dilemmas of citizenship.* Philadelphia: Temple University Press.

Pinker, Steven. 2002. *The blank slate: The modern denial of human nature.* New York: Viking.

Poovey, Mary. 1988. *Uneven developments.* Chicago: University of Chicago Press.

Puar, Jasbir. 2007. *Terrorist assemblage: Homonationalism in queer times.* Chapel Hill, NC: Duke University Press.

Rich, Adrienne. 1980. "Compulsory heterosexuality and lesbian existence." *Signs: Journal of Women in Culture and Society* 5(4): 631–660.

Richardson, Sara. 2012. "Sexing the x: How the x became the 'female chromosome.'" *Signs: Journal of Women in Culture and Society,* 37(4): 909–933.

Riley, Denise. 1988. *Am I that name? Feminism and the category of "women" in history.* Minneapolis: University of Minnesota Press.

Rowbotham, Sheila. 1973. *Women's consciousness, man's world.* London: Penguin.

Rubin, Gayle. 1975. "The traffic in women: Notes on the political economy of sex." In Rayner Reiter, ed., *Toward an Anthropology of Women.* New York: Monthly Review Press.

Rubin, Lillian. 1993. "The sexual dilemma." In Alison Jaggar and Paula Rothenberg, eds., *Feminist frameworks,* 3d ed. New York: McGraw Hill.

Ruddick, Sara. 1980. "Maternal thinking." *Feminist Studies* 6(2): 342–367.

Sawicki, Jana. 1991. "Foucault and feminism: Toward a politics of difference." In Mary Shanley and Carole Pateman, eds., *Feminist interpretations and political theory.* University Park: University of Pennsylvania Press.

Scott, Joan. 1986. "Gender: A useful category for historical analysis." *American Historical Review* 91: 1053–1075.

Sedgwick, Eve. 1990. *Epistemology of the closet.* Berkeley: University of California Press.

Shanley, Mary, and Carole Pateman, eds. 1991. *Feminist interpretations and political theory.* University Park: Pennsylvania State University Press.

Siltanen, Janet. 1994. *Locating gender: Occupational segregation, wages and domestic responsibilities.* London: UCL Press.

Silverman, Kaja. 1988. *The acoustic mirror.* Bloomington: Indiana University Press.

Singer, Linda. 1993. *Erotic welfare: Sexual theory and politics in the age of epidemic.* New York: Routledge.

Smith, Steven G. 1992. *Gender thinking.* Philadelphia: Temple University Press.

Spelman, Elizabeth. 1988. *Inessential woman.* Boston: Beacon Press.

Spender, Dale. 1980. *Man made language.* London: Routledge.

Stevens, Jacqueline. 1999. *Reproducing the state.* Princeton, NJ: Princeton University Press.

Stoller, Robert. 1985. *Presentations of gender.* New Haven, CT: Yale University Press.

Stryker, Susan. 2006. "My words to Victor Frankenstein above the village of Chamounix: Performing transgender rage." In Susan Stryker and Stephen Whittle, eds., *The transgender reader.* New York: Routledge, 244–256.

Suleiman, Susan Rubin, ed. 1985. *The female body and Western culture.* Cambridge, MA: Harvard University Press.

Tang-Martinez, Zuleyma. 1997. "The curious courtship of sociobiology and feminism: A case of irreconcilable differences." In Patricia Adair Gawaty, ed., *Feminism and evolutionary biology.* New York: Chapman Hall, 116–150.

Towns, Ann. 2009. "The status of women as a standard of 'civilization.'" *European Journal of International Relations* 15(4): 681–706.

Towns, Ann. 2010. *Women and states: Norms and hierarchies in international society.* Cambridge and New York: Cambridge University Press.

Vetterling-Braggin, Mary, ed. 1982. *"Femininity," "masculinity," and "androgyny."* Totowa, NJ: Littlefield Adams.

Walby, Sylvia. 1986. *Patriarchy at work.* Minneapolis: University of Minnesota Press.

Warner, Michael. 1991. "Introduction: Fear of a queer planet." *Social Text* 9(4): 3–17.

West, Candace, and Don Zimmerman. 1987. "Doing gender." *Gender and Society* 1(2): 125–151.

Wilson, Edward O. 1975. *Sociobiology: The new synthesis.* Cambridge, MA: Harvard University Press.

Wilson, Edward O. 1978. *On human nature.* Cambridge, MA: Harvard University Press.

Wittig, Monique. 1979. "One is not born a woman." In *Proceedings of the Second Sex Conference.* New York: Institute for the Humanities. Available online at http://www.oocities.org/saidyoungman/wittig01.htm.

Yanow, Dvora. 2003. *Constructing "race" and "ethnicity" in America: Category-making in public policy and administration.* Armonk, NY: M.E. Sharpe.

Young, Iris. 1994. "Gender as seriality: Thinking about women as a social collective." *Signs: Journal of Women in Culture and Society* 19(3): 713–738.

CHAPTER 2

INTERSECTIONALITY

PATRICIA HILL COLLINS AND VALERIE CHEPP

INTRODUCTION

The idea of intersectionality has gained considerable visibility within the early twenty-first century academy. Currently housed within a broad and interdisciplinary body of scholarship, the idea of intersectionality weaves across multiple disciplines, garnering increasing acceptance within social science fields as diverse as sociology (Collins 2007), psychology (Mahalingam, Balan, and Haritatos 2008; Warner 2008), economics (Ruwanpura 2008), and political science (Hancock 2007a; Simien 2007; Ackerly and True 2008; Weldon 2008). Fields that have been oriented to public practice have shown a special affinity for intersectionality. For example, intersectionality's close affinity with legal scholarship, specifically critical race theory and LatCrit theory, highlights the ways intersectional insights have been cultivated in an intellectual context explicitly devoted to social action and change (Matua 2010). Similarly, public policy finds utility in intersectional analyses for understanding how intersectional social locations impact life choices (Manuel 2006). Intersectionality has also made significant contributions to the field of public health, where social determinants of health disparities are increasingly approached from intersectional perspectives (Dworkin 2005; Schulz and Mullings 2006; Weber and Fore 2007).[1]

Given intersectionality's growing acceptance, remarkably little consensus exists on its definition. Inconsistency and ambiguity surround the term (Phoenix and Pattynama 2006; Davis 2008), hallmarks of an emerging construct. Intersectionality has been described as a theory (Manuel 2006; Steinbugler, Press, and Dias 2006; Phoenix and Pattynama 2006; Hancock 2007b; Bowleg 2008; Nash 2008, 2009), a theory of identity (Nash 2008), a theoretical contribution (McCall 2005), and a theoretical paradigm (Hancock 2007b). Intersectionality has also been approached conceptually, as a perspective (Browne and Misra 2003; Steinbugler et al. 2006), a concept (Knapp 2005), and a type of analysis (Yuval-Davis 2006; Nash 2009). Other scholars seem more focused on intersectionality's placement in the research process, with some approaching intersectionality as a methodological approach (Yuval-Davis 2006; Steinbugler et al. 2006), an analytic perspective (Steinbugler et al. 2006), a research paradigm (Hancock 2007b; Bowleg 2008), a measurable variable (Bowleg 2008), and a type of data (Bowleg 2008). Finally, there is a category of intersectionality as something we personally "experience" (Bowleg 2008), opening the door to the many narrative works such as autobiographies, autoethnographies, and ethnographies that are inspired in some fashion by intersectionality. While this ambiguity and inconsistency likely result from a well-intentioned effort on the part of scholars to advance the promise of intersectionality,[2] the slippage in terminology can feel imprecise and foster uneven outcomes.

One way of approaching this ambiguity lies in examining how practitioners in the field of race, class, and gender studies, a field that catalyzed current expressions of intersectionality, describe its distinguishing features. In 2001, sociologist Bonnie Thornton Dill surveyed seventy faculty members from seventeen colleges and universities in the United States, many of whom had helped launch race, class, and gender studies itself, on their perceptions of the core features and status of the field. Dill's study provides an important starting point for examining how practitioners of race, class, and gender studies understand intersectionality. As Dill points out, "What I take from these interviews is that work 'at the intersections' is an analytical strategy, an approach to understanding human life and behavior rooted in the experiences and struggles of marginalized people. It is also an important tool linking theory with practice that can aid in the empowerment of communities and individuals. Finally, it is a theoretical perspective that insists on examining the multi-dimensionality of human experience" (2002, 6).

In this chapter, we engage one core question: how do we make sense of intersectionality as a construct that is so widespread and visible yet simultaneously loosely defined and paradoxical? For the purposes of this volume's focus on intersectionality, gender, and politics, we build on Dill's (2002) insight that "working at the intersections" (or intersectionality) encompasses an analytical strategy that insists on examining the multidimensionality of human experience that might aid in the empowerment of individuals and communities. As a working definition, we suggest that intersectionality consists of an assemblage of ideas and practices that maintain that gender, race, class, sexuality, age, ethnicity, ability, and similar phenomena cannot be analytically understood in isolation from one another; instead, these constructs signal an intersecting constellation of power relationships that produce unequal material realities and distinctive social experiences for individuals and groups positioned within them. This insight creates analytic space for a more robust understanding of the privileges and penalties associated with intersecting systems of oppression as well as a multifaceted conception of standpoint epistemologies and knowledges.[3] Yet because a comprehensive response to this question merits a deeper analysis than this working definition, this essay will sketch out some of the broad contours of the kinds of themes that might be considered in making sense of intersectionality.

We approach our overarching question through a chapter in two parts. The first half presents an overview of some of the main ideas of intersectionality by summarizing its core ideas and examining selected specific contributions of the field thus far. We place this overview within a sociology of knowledge framework, conceptualizing intersectionality as a *knowledge project* whose umbrella is broad enough to encompass the ambiguities, contradictions, and questions discussed in the introduction. In the second half, we examine two contemporary sites that have been differentially affected by the trajectory of intersectionality: (1) the close ties that intersectionality has with women's studies and gender scholarship; and (2) the wider American political arena, with special attention to the implications of intersectionality for democracy.

INTERSECTIONALITY: A CONCEPTUAL FRAMEWORK

Intersectionality is a term that has been increasingly applied to knowledge projects whose purpose is to understand all dimensions of power relations, including race, class, gender, and sexuality. Intersectional knowledge projects have reconceptualized these phenomena as mutually constructing systems of power. Yet a sociology of knowledge framework suggests that knowledge—including knowledge aimed at better understanding intersectionality—is socially constructed and transmitted, legitimated, and reproduced by social mechanisms deeply intertwined with (intersecting) social systems of power.[4] As such, we do not view intersectionality as a finished construct (i.e., as a theory of power relations), as a methodology to be used in studying social phenomena, or as a construct that can be examined. Many current debates about intersectionality lie in this space of defining what kind of knowledge or political project it is and might be (see, e.g., Walby 2007; Nash 2008). Given these debates, here we use the term intersectionality to refer to a dynamic constellation of ideas and practices that are sensitive to and compatible with insights gleaned from the sociology of knowledge. Stated differently, we approach intersectionality as a knowledge project or, more accurately, as a constellation of knowledge projects.

This understanding of intersectionality through the framework of knowledge projects enables us to identify several important, emerging core themes of intersectional analyses that collectively constitute distinguishing features of intersectional scholarship. These themes are not all present in a given work, and each theme is not unique to intersectionality. Rather, the varying combinations of these themes can be seen as distinguishing features of a range of intersectional knowledge projects, all of which are positioned in some direct relation to these themes.

The first core idea of intersectional knowledge projects stresses that systems of power (e.g., race, gender, class, sexuality, ability, age, country of origin, citizenship status) cannot be understood in isolation from one another; instead, systems of power intersect and coproduce one another to result in unequal material realities and the distinctive social experiences that characterize them. Stated differently, racism, sexism, class exploitation, and similar oppressions mutually construct one another, drawing upon similar practices and forms of organization (Acker 1999). Intersectional knowledge projects acknowledge the ways political and economic structural arrangements such as modernity, patriarchal rule, and capitalism operate in constellation with one another (Knapp 2005). For any given social context, collectively, these social domains constitute a specific matrix of domination that reflects the particularities of a given time and place (Collins 2000).[5]

Second, intersectional knowledge projects acknowledge that the distinctive social locations of individuals and groups within intersecting power relations have important epistemological implications. This insight suggests that knowledge cannot be separated from the power relations in which it participates and which shape it (Foucault 1980; Collins 1986). All knowledge is constructed within and helps to construct intersecting power relations; notably, this includes the construct of intersectionality itself. Stoetzler and Yuval-Davis (2002, 316) discuss the situated imagination as a crucial component of feminist standpoint theory, pointing to the ways social positioning shapes knowledge as well as the imagination. This approach yields two unique insights: (1) individuals and groups are differently positioned in a distinctive matrix of domination, which has implications for how we experience society including *what we know and can imagine*, and the material realities that accompany this experience; and (2) individuals and groups can *simultaneously* experience privilege and disadvantage (Crenshaw 1991).

A third core idea that characterizes many intersectional knowledge projects is an attention to relationality and relational processes (Collins 2000; Stoetzler and Yuval-Davis 2002; Phoenix and Pattynama 2006,187). This emphasis on relationality highlights the ways race, gender, class, and other systems of power are constituted and maintained through relational processes (Anderson 1996; Glenn 1998; Acker 1999; Yuval-Davis 2006).[6] The analytic importance of relationality in intersectional scholarship demonstrates how various social positions (occupied by actors, systems, and political and economic structural arrangements) necessarily acquire meaning and power (or a lack thereof) in relationship to other social positions. This highlights the intersecting and coconstructing nature of social systems and structures organized around power and inequality. For example, Collins (2010) addresses the political implications of intersectionality's conceptualization of social groups as fundamentally characterized by interrelationships across power differences. Indeed, the very prefix given to the term intersectionality marks an important departure away from binary Western thinking that classifies idea systems and eras according to pre- and post- (e.g., premodern, poststructuralism); instead, prefixes such as inter- and trans- reflect the interrelated nature of social power relations that are increasingly recognized in social and political theory as well as in intersectionality (Emirbayer 1997; Collins 2010, 28, fn. 13).

A fourth and related core idea of intersectional knowledge projects concerns the contours of the different standpoints, epistemologies, and knowledges that accompany multiple social locations. Not only are actual social relations relational, but also the worldviews that they catalyze are necessarily relational. Epistemologically, intersectionality highlights the various standpoints that intersocial (i.e., not dichotomous) locations occupy; these alternative standpoints challenge Enlightenment understandings of truth that are often purported by those in the center. Intersectionality's ability to draw attention to and account for intersocial locations—including those on the margins (Crenshaw 1991)—challenges binary thinking, shifting the analytic focus on the fluidity among, interrelationships between, and coproduction of various categories and systems of power (Collins 1993). While the second core theme described demonstrates that power shapes knowledge and different social locations result in different epistemological worldviews, this fourth core theme recognizes that standpoints—and not just social relations—are relational (and thus coconstructing). This core insight of intersectional knowledge projects destabilizes claims to truth, thereby acknowledging the presence of alternative truths in intersocial locations (Collins 2000).

This attention to material, social, and epistemological relationality leads to a fifth prominent theme emerging out of the literature on intersectionality, namely, the significance of boundaries. An awareness of the analytic significance of boundaries underscores intersectional knowledge projects' claims about the multifaceted nature of intersecting social phenomena, for example, individual and group identities, and social issues as constructed at the intersection of multiple agendas. This attention to boundaries within intersectional scholarship can be understood as part of a larger tradition and recent trend within humanities and social scientific scholarship that uses the concept of boundaries to make sense of various relational processes (Lamont and Molnár 2002). Within this context, a simplified or one-dimensional understanding of identity politics fails to account for those social locations on the margins, borders, and boundaries of identity categories (Anzaldúa 1987; Crenshaw 1991). This attention to boundaries has also included a recognition of the ability for intersectional knowledge projects to transcend boundaries, particularly the disciplinary boundaries endemic to the academy (Nash 2009).

A final dimension of intersectional knowledge projects involves a concern with complexity (Dhamoon 2011). For example, scholars suggest that using intersectionality as an analytical strategy compels us to grapple with the complexity of the world (Davis 2008, 79). In her efforts to highlight social class as an important feature of intersectional knowledge projects, Acker (1999, 52) argues that systems of power are "complexly interrelated at a multiplicity of sites within particular historical developments." McCall (2005) explores the relationship between complexity and intersectionality in her article "The Complexity of Intersectionality," in which she describes three methodological approaches scholars of intersectionality use when making sense of analytic categories (e.g., race, class, gender); each approach treats the complexity of such categories differently. While *anticategorical* analyses deconstruct categorical boundaries by exposing their socially constructed nature, *intercategorical* complexity strategically assumes the reality of such categories in an effort to document social inequalities between different categorical groups. The third approach, *intracategorical* complexity, adopts analytic features of anti- and intercategorical complexity by deconstructing categories while strategically accepting their existence in an effort to document social inequalities within a master category. McCall points to the work of Crenshaw (1991) and other feminists of color as working within this intracategorical register of analysis (1779).[7] Walby (2007) also recognizes the connection between complexity and intersectionality, applying complexity theory to intersecting systems of social inequality in an effort to theoretically link a structural analysis to an analysis of social relations and change, demonstrating how these two sets of overlapping (not nested) social systems work together.[8]

These distinguishing features of intersectional knowledge projects have had several noteworthy influences on contemporary scholarship across a range of disciplines as well as within interdisciplinary initiatives. For one, take, for example, how ideas emerging from intersectional knowledge projects significantly contribute to our understanding of culture. By introducing ideas about the intersecting nature of racial, gender, class, and other systems of power in various cultural meaning-making processes, intersectional knowledge projects bring additional levels of sophistication to emerging models of cultural theory (see, e.g., Lamont 2000). Intersectionality's contribution to theories of culture spotlights the ways cultural fields are heterogeneous and incoherent (Smelser 1992), necessarily characterized by multiple systems of intersecting and coconstitutive power relationships that fundamentally gain meaning through complex relational processes. Indeed, cultural theories seek to highlight the fluidity and subjective nature of previously assumed fixed dichotomies, demonstrating how these dualities coproduce one another by relying on binary thinking for meaning (Bourdieu 1990). (Thus, for example, there is no understanding of man without a parallel yet "opposite" understanding of woman.) As such, intersectional knowledge projects not only call into question single sets of dichotomous concepts but also offer an analysis for how all these sets or systems of dichotomous thinking intersect to produce a culturally specific context of meaning making characterized by unique social phenomena and unequal material circumstances. Take, for instance, the case of eugenics. Intersectional knowledge projects help to make sense of this cultural phenomenon by showing how the intersections of different constructs, such as race, rationality, and disability, might result in a social movement that seeks to "purify" the human race through a meaning-making process of eugenics. Intersectional knowledge projects illustrate how the dichotomies of white–nonwhite, rational–irrational (or feeble-minded), and able-bodied–disable-bodied intersect to produce a circumstance where nonwhite, irrational or feeble-minded, and disabled all become meaningfully coherent targets of a eugenics movement (Galton 1904; Roberts 1997; Carey 2003).

Moreover, intersectional knowledge projects have the potential to shape existing theoretical understandings of culture as well. Take, for example, how intersectionality affects understandings of Pierre Bourdieu's classic concept of *cultural fields*. Bourdieu (1984, 1990) theorizes fields as particular social spaces governed by an internal logic, composed of individuals positioned within a set of social relations with varying amounts and types of capital, each of whom are vying for social power, status, and wealth. While the boundaries of a field are always imprecise and changing (definable only by empirical research), examples of social fields can include politics, education, employment, land, lifestyle—basically any social arena where social actors are struggling to maintain or improve their position according to the field's defining capital (economic, cultural, symbolic, and social) (Jenkins 1992). Fields, in addition to habitus and capital, are three interrelated concepts Bourdieu (1984) develops to show how culture serves as a site of social conflict and class domination. While Bourdieu (1984) echoes insights from intersectionality (e.g., relationality, boundaries, unique social locations, and unequal material realities), his work focuses primarily on a system of class domination and therefore is limited by its lack of an intersectional analysis. Thus, intersectional knowledge projects build upon (and improve) previous theories of culture such as Bourdieu's.

A second influence of intersectional knowledge projects concerns their ability to catalyze new questions and areas of investigation within existing academic disciplines, especially in fields that focus on the interconnectedness of the academy and some aspect of the general public (i.e., academic traditions that have a history of praxis). Tracing the patterns of incorporation of race, class, and gender studies generally, and intersectionality in particular, within the discipline of sociology provides a closer look at how intersectionality as a knowledge project can energize prevailing practices (Collins 2007). Intersectionality holds a special place within the discipline of sociology, particularly its history of praxis in the form of public sociology, where academic sociologists place their academic labor in conversation with a general public (Burawoy 2005). If, however, public sociology "represents the interests of humanity—interests in keeping at bay both state despotism and market tyranny" (ibid., 24), insights from intersectionality are central to a successful public sociology enterprise since public sociologists must recognize how these state and market systems operate in constellation with one another.

Thus, via its overlap with public sociology, intersectional scholarship potentially contributes much to the field of sociology. Yet one key feature of this knowledge project has had particular significance for the discipline: intersectionality's unique and novel analysis of power and inequality. Prior to the ubiquity of intersectional knowledge projects within the discipline, sociological analyses of power were less nuanced in that the concept of power itself was a largely taken-for-granted concept; that is, one either had or did not have power. However, as intersectional frameworks have been more prominent within sociological research, sociologists have come to produce more theoretically sophisticated concepts of power, locating power relationally and complexly across multiple intersecting systems of domination (e.g., race, class, gender; Dill 1983) and operating within different domains of social organization (i.e., structural, cultural, disciplinary, and interpersonal; Collins 2009). Such a conceptualization allows for more robust analyses of power and inequality, as an intersectional framework enables sociologists to account for social experiences located outside and between social boundaries; these include those marginal experiences that might otherwise "fall through the cracks" when power is analyzed along single and independent axes (see, e.g., Harvey Wingfield 2009). This increased emphasis on relationality, multiplicity, complexity, and boundaries in sociological analyses of power and inequality reflects a larger recognition within the discipline of the theoretical importance of such concepts (Emirbayer 1997; Lamont and Molnár 2002; Walby 2007).

In this way, intersectional knowledge projects might be understood as catalyzing a paradigm shift within the discipline of sociology (Kuhn [1962]1996), thereby revolutionizing the way contemporary sociologists discuss and come to understand relations of power and inequality. Therefore, a third important influence of intersectional knowledge projects consists of their efficacy in encouraging existing fields to rethink their main assumptions and paradigms. While established paradigms may have already begun to shift in the discipline of sociology and related areas of study, intersectional knowledge projects' ability to catalyze new questions are seemingly more recent within other social science disciplines, such as political science (Simien 2007; Simien and Hancock 2011). Dhamoon's (2011) effort to highlight key considerations involved in mainstreaming intersectional knowledge in political science research is a prime example of how intersectional knowledge projects can catalyze new areas of investigation in existing fields, eventually leading long-standing academic traditions to rethink central tenets. Often this influence stems from intersectional knowledge projects' epistemological recognition that a field's dominant assumptions and paradigms are produced within a context of power relations, where white, middle-class, heterosexual, male, able-bodied experiences are taken as the (invisible) norm. Take gender for example. Recognizing that much of the canonical scholarship on gender was produced largely by male scholars, intersectional knowledge projects have interrogated the basic epistemological assumptions embedded in classic gender scholarship. For example, Williams's (2000) concept of the ideal worker norm illuminates the ways workplaces are structured around an imagined ideal worker, which assumes workers have male bodies and men's social experiences. Highlighting how this assumption is embedded not only in workplace structures but also implicitly in previous scholarship on gender, work, and family, Williams demonstrates how the ideal worker norm excludes women from equally participating in the workplace.

Intersectionality's focus on relationality, multiplicity, complexity, and social boundaries has helped to recast gender beyond narrow definitions of *woman* and has shifted attention to the complex, relational boundaries that construct our understandings of masculinity and femininity. Here, scholars have pointed to the ways the parameters (i.e., boundaries) around masculinity get defined in relationship to, and draw power from, constructions around femininity (Connell 1987; Kimmel 1994). In doing so, scholars have unveiled masculinity and male domination as visible social experiences that result in unequal material realities. In fact, we might consider the ways intersectional knowledge projects have recast the main ideas of inequality studies more broadly. While previous research on inequality focused largely on those bearing the brunt of inequality (e.g., women, minorities, the poor), intersectionality's emphasis on the complex and coconstructing relationship between domination systems highlights the importance of researching the privileged as well as the disadvantaged to more fully address the complex and multifaceted dynamics of inequality (Choo and Ferree 2010). This contribution to studies of inequality has not only resulted in the growing attention to men and masculinity within gender studies but has also provided a backdrop against which we have seen the emergence of whiteness studies and research on the economic elite.[9]

INTERSECTIONALITY, GENDER, AND POLITICS

Here we revisit the core question that motivates this essay: how do we make sense of intersectionality as a construct that is so widespread, visible, yet simultaneously loosely defined and paradoxical? Approaching intersectionality as a knowledge project allows us to explore how the distinguishing features of intersectionality as described already did not emerge fully formed. Rather, these same ideas reappear across many social locations yet remain invisible, in part, because they have not yet been connected as part of one broader knowledge project. At the same time, a prevailing narrative does dominate intersectionality's told emergence. Often, scholars geographically locate intersectionality's genesis in the United States, emerging largely from African American women's (and other U.S. women of color) experiences in the social movements of the 1950s, 1960s, and 1970s (see, e.g., Nash 2008; Weldon 2008). This narrative acknowledges intersectional knowledge projects' ties with U.S. black feminist politics in the 1960s and 1970s, followed by its travels into academic settings in the 1980s and 1990s. In essence, this narrative ties intersectionality to themes of gender and politics.

The acceptance of this taken-for-granted narrative about intersectionality's ostensible origins sheds light on our overarching question. We suggest that intersectional knowledge projects are deeply implicated in late twentieth and early twenty-first century politics and that the travels of such projects into academic settings heightened some aspects of intersectional knowledge projects while suppressing others. This leads us to take a closer look at the connections between intersectionality as a knowledge project and understandings of power and politics that emerged both in academic settings and wider political arenas. Here, we examine two contemporary sites that have been differentially affected by intersectional knowledge projects: (1) the significance of the close ties that intersectionality has had with women's studies and gender scholarship; and (2) the effects, if any, of intersectional knowledge projects on the wider American political arena. Our first site traces the close ties that intersectionality has with women's studies and gender scholarship, raising the question of how power relations affected intersectionality's ability to travel into the center of this area of inquiry (at least in feminist theory), and the political implications of this trajectory. For our second site, we explore varying patterns of visibility and invisibility within the wider American political arena, with special attention to the implications of intersectionality for democracy.

Intersectionality, Women's Studies, and Gender Scholarship

Today, intersectionality occupies significant space and status within women's studies and gender scholarship, evidenced by its reach into scholars' research agendas, departments' infrastructures, topics of articles, books and key journals, special journal issues, conference themes, course syllabi components, and full courses designated entirely to intersectionality. Thus, it is commonplace today to see scholars list intersectionality as a research interest or area of expertise on their academic websites or university homepages. Intersectional language frequently describes departmental or disciplinary aims or serves as a core component of departmental curriculum and syllabi.[10] Moreover, intersectionality occupies a significant space in the content of articles appearing in some of the field's most prominent journals,[11] and several gender studies journals have dedicated entire issues to the topic, such as the *International Feminist Journal of Politics* issue titled "Institutionalizing Intersectionality" (2009, vol. 11, no. 4), the *European Journal of Women's Studies* issue on "Intersectionality" (2006, vol. 13, no. 3), the symposium on intersectionality in *Politics & Gender* (2007, vol. 3, no. 2), and *Sex Roles'* special issue on intersectional approaches to empirical research on gender (2008, vol. 59, no. 5–6). A plethora of books have been written about intersectionality,[12] and publishers have dedicated entire book series to the topic, such as Routledge's "Advances in Feminist Studies and Intersectionality" and Palgrave Macmillan's series "The Politics of Intersectionality." Intersectionality has also served as an organizing theme for various academic conferences.[13]

Intersectionality's extensive influence, perhaps even dominance, in contemporary women's studies and gender scholarship raises key questions from a sociology of knowledge standpoint: what are the implications of intersectionality's extensive travels into these particular fields of knowledge production? Why have women's studies scholars initially and gender studies scholars now, both within interdisciplinary women's studies units and traditional disciplinary units, been so receptive to this idea of intersectionality? Who are these people? What theoretical and empirical challenges do they face that intersectionality helps to address? By illustrating the dialectical relationship between knowledge production and politics, we offer a preliminary answer to these questions.

African American women are prominent within the origin stories of intersectionality as connected to feminist politics of the 1960s and 1970s because, as a collectivity, they were uniquely positioned to have multiple angles of vision and experiential knowledge on social inequalities in U.S. society as well as on the political action strategies needed to address them. In the struggle for civil rights, African American women saw how racism worked to economically exploit African Americans as a collectivity. With African American men, they were positioned to see how racism and class exploitation operated within U.S. society. The civil rights movement aimed to address the political disenfranchisement and the economic poverty of African Americans and similarly placed racial minorities. At the same time, African American women could also see how sexism shaped their opportunities and experiences as women—for example, their confinement to low-paying, dead-end jobs reserved for women, and the oppression they experienced from men within the civil rights movement who largely prioritized the fight against racism at the expense of fighting gender inequality. Subsequently in the women's movement, African American women experienced racism at the hands of white women who advocated for an idea of a universal sisterhood yet failed to acknowledge the white, middle-class biases implicit in their model, thereby excluding the experiences and concerns of women of color. For example, while the women's movement chose to focus on abortion rights as the centerpiece of their reproductive rights political platform, women of color struggled to draw attention within the movement to the extensive sterilization practices being performed on various women of color, including blacks, Native Americans, and Chicanas. Women of color's experiences with sterilization abuse were largely marginalized within the feminist movement's agenda for reproductive freedom while abortion rights, an issue more pertinent to the lives of white women, took center stage (Roberts 1997). Sexuality also formed an important part of an emerging black feminist movement, initiated by African American lesbians and bisexual women who highlighted the ways sexuality operated as a system of power through such mechanisms as heteronormativity (Combahee River Collective [1977]1995). The constellation of African American women's experiences with race, class, gender, and sexual oppression, often in the context of social movement politics of the 1950s, 1960s, and 1970s, catalyzed African American women to call for new approaches to analyses of oppression and social inequality (Davis 1983; Dill 1983; Lorde 1984; Collins 1993).

During this same period, scholars and activists in other social locations also began to examine how their specific experiences at intersections of race, class, gender, and sexuality produced the patterns of privilege and disadvantage that shaped their individual and group experiences. For example, Latinas and Asian American women followed similar paths in developing feminist projects that took the specificity of cultural and ethnic differences into account, for example, religiosity, language, and citizenship status (Roth 2004). Although black feminists were prominent in the articulation of and visibility afforded to intersectionality in the late twentieth-century U.S. context, other groups of women advanced similar knowledge claims from a variety of social locations, including works from Native American, Chicana, and Chinese American perspectives by scholars such as Paula Gunn Allen, Cherríe Moraga, Gloria Anzaldúa, and Maxine Hong Kingston as well as by working-class, Marxist, and queer women (Combahee River Collective [1977]1995; Davis 1983; Lorde 1984; Rich 1986; Jordan 2002). Collectively, a series of social actors began to theorize the core ideas and epistemologies that eventually became associated with the intersectional approach, arguing that socially constructed categories of difference and inequality interact—simultaneously—with other systems of power (Collins 1993). Such a theoretical framework recognizes how social actors or groups might concurrently experience oppression and privilege, and it considers how race, class, gender, and sexuality function in the structural bases of domination and subordination and therefore how these systems of power get institutionalized in society. As such, women working both inside and outside the black feminist context offered fresh analyses of inequality that considered the intersecting nature of race, gender, sexuality, class, religion, ethnicity, language status, citizenship status, and other systems of power, yet such contributions from these other social locations are often omitted from intersectionality's stock narrative.

The case of the U.S. women's movement, the visibility of intersectional knowledge projects, and the emergence of women's studies within the academy underscores the interrelationship between knowledge production and political possibilities, thereby offering insight into intersectionality's unique travel trajectory in the academy. Stated differently, the case of intersectionality in this particular historical and intellectual context illustrates the ways knowledge production can shape politics and, similarly, the ways politics can shape knowledge production. Intersectionality as a recognizable analytical strategy came on the heels of a U.S. feminist movement that moved in two directions. On one hand, it moved into a phase of unobtrusive mobilization, a movement that shifted to focus to getting rules and regulations changed in ways that fostered gender equity. In this organizational mode, the women's movement has experienced considerable success, for example, the passage of Title IX. On the other hand, the broad social agenda of an overtly feminist movement was politically derailed, in part, because of its failure to grapple with differences among women's unique social experiences and unequal material realities in the context of the backlash leveled at the national movement.

This historical event reveals two features of the interrelationship between knowledge production and political possibilities that can account for intersectional knowledge projects' travels in the academy, including an explanation for how these projects became so closely aligned with women's studies and gender scholarship. First, despite the fact that the grassroots U.S. women's movement showed considerable promise, such movements were stifled in part due to the tremendous resistance to feminism launched by political figures and by the popular press. The knowledge developed in local settings as a constellation of grassroots organizations that worked across differences of race, class, and sexuality remained local and didn't travel. For example, Anne Valk's (2008) study of grassroots organizations in Washington, D.C., provides a provocative glimpse of how women who were committed to diverse political projects struggled with one another in fashioning a feminist movement that could be called "intersectional." In contrast to the richness of ideas advanced by women on the front line of the women's movement, dominant gender analyses—or published knowledge—of the time was ill-equipped to theorize the era's political needs. The politically galvanizing gender knowledge projects that garnered national attention—perhaps most notably Betty Friedan's (1963) *The Feminine Mystique*—offered an analysis of gender oppression that largely assumed a similar experience among women: white, middle-class, suburban, heterosexual, homemaker. Despite the pivotal role played by women of color in catalyzing and maintaining the movement (Roth 2004), the media routinely painted feminism as "white." Moreover, white movement leaders inadvertently or intentionally marginalized women of color's voices and political needs by organizing a feminist politics according to the type of gender oppression offered by the most visibly prevailing (i.e., published) gender knowledge projects of the time. Given that a knowledge project's visibility is always shaped by the dominant power relationships of a particular social, historical, and intellectual context, the knowledge project represented in Friedan's highly influential book helped to set the agenda for a very narrow type of feminist politics. In this way, we can see how knowledge shapes politics, creating political possibilities but also political pitfalls.

Second, the interrelationship between knowledge and politics is evident in that the political victories of the women's movement, notably the establishment of women's studies programs at universities across the country, had significant implications for knowledge production. For the first time, institutionalized intellectual spaces were created to produce knowledge about women's experiences. The scholars and activists operating in these newly created intellectual spaces continued to struggle with the unresolved contradictions of the women's movement regarding race, class, and sexuality yet lacked access to the rich record of actual feminist politics suggested in Valk's (2008) work. It is important to remember that women of color who had been involved in the women's movement also moved into the academy during the period of the formation of women's studies, albeit in much smaller numbers than white women and not necessarily into programs dedicated specifically to women's studies. As a knowledge paradigm of praxis, intersectional knowledge projects offered feminist scholars and activists alike a theoretical template (but not an actual politics) for addressing the unresolved issues from the feminist movement. Intersectionality may have been especially appealing to gender scholars within women's studies programs because it satisfied a theoretical need during a time when women's studies scholarship had not yet rigidly adapted a paradigmatic approach to the study of women's complex experiences. The legacy of this historical convergence, revealed by the dialectical relationship between knowledge production and politics, is evident in intersectionality's present-day command of gender scholarship. Once a knowledge paradigm takes hold, it becomes difficult to shift (Kuhn [1962]1996).

Yet while this account might explain in part why intersectionality initially became and continues to be so closely aligned with gender scholarship, the question still left unanswered is: what are the implications of having intersectionality so closely associated with gender? One implication seems to be that intersectionality has come to be characterized as a feminist theory (or some other tool for feminist scholarship, such as a feminist research paradigm). Characterizing intersectionality as a feminist theory presents two challenges: (1) intersectionality becomes synonymous with or a derivative of feminist theory; and (2) our ability to recognize other intellectual traditions that exhibit key features of intersectional thought is limited. These are challenges for intersectional knowledge projects in that they might misrepresent what is really going on in this field of knowledge production by overstating intersectional knowledge projects' affinities with feminist theory and understating convergences with other sites of knowledge production. In the first case, intersectionality's close association with gender scholarship has resulted in scholars naming (or defining) intersectionality as a feminist theory. Perhaps most notably, Kathy Davis's (2008) characterization of intersectionality as a successful feminist theory places intersectionality in the pantheon of feminist theories.[14] Such a move presents a second challenge in that, by defining intersectionality as a feminist theory, other sites of intersectional knowledge production are at risk of getting overlooked. One such site might be American pragmatism, which shares many of the core ideas of intersectional knowledge projects outlined in the first part of the chapter. Namely, pragmatic knowledge projects reject dichotomous thinking and embrace an understanding of the world grounded in relational processes, they acknowledge the complexity of human experiences and destabilize claims to truth by highlighting individual and group experiences as a form of evidence and epistemological insight, and they advocate for a brand of theory that is rooted in practice (Rochberg-Halton 1987; Seigfried 1993). Notably, pragmatism's affinities with feminist theory have been acknowledged (Seigfried 1993). Such work raises questions around the potential to overlook intersectional knowledge project's affinities with other sites of knowledge production. The case of American pragmatism might be particularly significant when we consider questions around political change and action and pragmatism's reputation for "getting things done" alongside the erasure of social action and praxis from self-identified intersectional knowledge projects inside the academy. Does the recognition of such affinities reveal that core features of intersectional knowledge projects did not get erased but rather are expressed in alternative knowledge traditions? In the same way Jennifer Nash suggests decoupling intersectionality from black feminism, perhaps intersectional scholars should seek to loosen, or at least broaden, intersectional knowledge projects' affinity with feminist theorizing to open this unique knowledge project's insights to fields of research beyond gender studies.[15]

Another implication of having intersectionality so closely aligned with gender is that gender scholars become intersectionality's major advocates in the academy. This presents its own challenges, as studies of gender are almost required to be intersectional, and intersectional studies become tightly connoted with analyses of gender. Such a tight affinity might blind us to other avenues of knowledge production in that knowledge simply gets recycled through the disciplines. Andrew Abbott's (2001) work on the evolution and organization of knowledge in the social sciences points to the ways fractal (or dichotomous) thinking operates to produce narrow avenues of academic inquiry and discovery. By tightly linking intersectionality to gender scholarship, gender scholars occupy a potentially confining position whereby they are unable to entertain—or even see—research questions that fall outside the parameters of an intersectional framework. This is due to the fractal logic governing knowledge production once a research tradition becomes tightly aligned with a discipline of study (Abbott 2001).

Another implication of having intersectional knowledge projects so closely aligned with gender concerns the ways initiating intersectional arguments within the parameters of gender essentially shape subsequent intersectional scholarship. Specifically, intersectionality can be reduced to one variation of feminist theory or practice, thus subordinating intersectionality to feminist agendas. If gender scholarship and its conventions become the starting point for intersectional knowledge projects, then all intersectional scholarship may be inflected by these point-of-origin concerns. Valerie Smith's (1998) analysis of literary sources illustrates how the sequencing of identity categories and systems of power affected subsequent intersectional analyses, such as starting with race and then incorporating gender, yields different accounts of social phenomena than accounts that start with gender and incorporate race. In essence, what appear to be intersectional arguments are, in actuality, patterns of incorporation of additional categories into a master category. In the case of intersectional knowledge projects' association with gender scholarship, we see the more politically powerful category of gender serving as the master category.

Such an arrangement leads us to ask: what does intersectionality look like without gender? Similarly, given its close affinity with black feminist and women of color studies, what does intersectionality look like without race? Can we take the major intellectual contributions of intersectionality and apply them to other sites of analysis? Detaching intersectionality from studies of gender might lead to other productive sites of inquiry of intersecting systems of power. Importantly, scholars are beginning to push intersectional knowledge projects in this direction, evidenced by, for instance, the "Under-Examined Intersectionalities" workshop at the 2010 University of California, Los Angeles, intersectionality conference, which featured intersectional analyses of less traditional topics such as the built environment and religion as well as new work in the field of disability studies.[16] In this way, gender scholars' "ownership" of the intersectionality paradigm might blind gender scholars and nongender scholars alike, as it ushers gender scholars to apply intersectional analyses almost robotically, and it might prevent nongender scholars from considering insights from intersectionality that are germane to their areas of expertise.

Intersectionality and Democratic Politics

Another site where the main ideas of intersectionality have made uneven progress concerns varying patterns of visibility and invisibility within the wider American political arena. In what ways, if any, have intersectional knowledge projects influenced broader political processes? There are no definitive answers to this question, only suggestive arguments for how and where intersectional knowledge projects appear in American politics. To explore this question further, and in a way that cuts across disciplinary boundaries, we engage a standard and more expansive definition of *the political*.

One way to examine how and where intersectional knowledge projects appear in American politics is to begin with a standard definition, where politics is understood to mean the processes, philosophies, behaviors, and systems of organization that relate to state governance. This understanding of the political is especially pervasive in political science intersectional research. For example, several authors have looked at the intersectional conditions under which members of specific intersectional communities are silenced or burdened, particularly in legislative elections and the U.S. Congress (Bratton and Haynie 1999; Hawkesworth 2003; Smooth 2006).[17] Others have sought to integrate intersectional analyses into public policy making and leadership (Manuel 2006; Hankivsky and Cormier 2011). Such scholarship points to some specific and productive ways intersectional knowledge projects have begun to enter into the U.S. democratic political arena, where the political is conceptualized as phenomena related to state governance.

A more expansive definition of the political also helps to highlight the varying patterns of visibility and invisibility that intersectional knowledge projects have made in U.S. democratic politics. This more expansive definition recognizes the multiple ways politics, and specifically democratic politics, get discussed. Similar to the Greek *politikos*, an expansive understanding of the political "involves the negotiations of a pluralist world, people of different views, interests, and backgrounds interacting in order to accomplish some task" (Boyte 2004, xi–xii). This includes various interpretations of "everyday politics" (see, e.g., Scott 1985, 1990; Kelley 1994; Cohen 2004; Harris-Lacewell 2004), which are typically enacted in citizen-created spaces by political "amateurs" rather than experts (Boyte 2004), often outside official political institutions (Fraser 1989). Rather than conceptualizing politics specifically as state power, an expansive understanding of politics refers to power more generally. An example is Collins's (2004) understanding of black sexual politics, which examines the different ways racism, sexism, and heterosexism intersect as systems of power; although Collins takes state-level processes into account, her conceptualization of black sexual politics encompasses social processes beyond the state. In this chapter, we work in both registers of the political, recognizing the tension between knowledge projects that understand politics as state governance and ones that conceptualize politics as power writ large. Feminists have made similar claims in their move to define "the personal is political," pointing to the numerous ways systems of power operate outside formal political institutions, shaping even the most intimate and personal domains of our social experiences and material realities. Our following examples around U.S. democratic politics and popular culture work at the intersection of this tension between standard and more expansive definitions of the political, with an eye toward the emancipatory potential of intersectional knowledge projects rooted in a commitment to praxis and social justice.

Recall that for the purposes of this volume's focus on intersectionality, gender, and politics, we identified Dill's (2002) insight that "working at the intersections" (or intersectionality) encompasses an analytical strategy that insists on examining the multidimensionality of human experience that might aid in the empowerment of individuals and communities. The race, class, and gender practitioners in Dill's study approached intersectionality not simply as an academic knowledge project, the implicit focus of much contemporary gender scholarship, but also as "an important tool linking theory with practice that can aid in the empowerment of communities and individuals" (Dill 2002, 6). This understanding of praxis as linked to social justice agendas suggests that understandings of intersectionality within the context of black feminist and similar social movement politics also had an eye on the broader theme of democratic politics. The shift from the race/class/gender/sexuality politics associated with social movement politics and praxis of the 1950s–1970s changed during the period of incorporation into the academy in the 1980s and 1990s. We suggest that intersectionality (or at least its ideas) had a more "bridging" character during the 1980s, straddling academic and political arenas when the term intersectionality became incorporated into academic norms and practices. This shift fostered a narrowing of vision, reducing the social justice ethos that initially animated intersectional knowledge projects.

We propose that a similar redefinition occurred when social justice initiatives of race/class/gender/sexuality emerging from social movement politics became recast as diversity agendas. Having implications for American democratic politics, diversity agendas advance a limited politics of monocategorical thinking that results in binaries of blacks–whites, men–women, race–gender, and the like. Moreover, diversity agendas suggest a strategy of tolerance, of learning to be sensitive to the differences of others rather than challenging and reforming the very categories themselves that create categorical differences. In essence, the construct of diversity stands as the public face of the conceptual framework of intersectionality, a face that, like intersectionality, has moved farther away from its moorings in social movement politics.

Here we examine two major sites of contemporary politics where these phenomena can be observed. U.S. electoral politics constitutes one important site for examining the workings of intersectional knowledge projects. The 2008 presidential election provided a provocative example of how ideas about intersectionality have penetrated the political arena (see, e.g., Hancock 2009; Junn 2009). In that historic democratic primary, despite the fact that all candidates had both racial and gendered identities, mass media routinely emphasized Barack Obama's race and Hillary Clinton's gender. Depicting the candidates in this fashion fostered media coverage of African American women who were asked to "pick" between their race and their gender as a way to predict their voting patterns in the election. Moreover, the social class of the candidates remained a background yet ever-present factor in the campaign, though it never rose to the level of visibility granted race and gender. Once the primaries were over and the campaign for the general election ensued, the electorate was once again ushered into a narrow conceptual framework in which they were to choose between Obama's race and Sarah Palin's gender, yet this time social class did enter the debate, as Obama was casted as an Ivy League educated, out-of-touch elite and Palin was portrayed as an intellectually unsophisticated nonelite. Yet these ideas about race, gender, and class as they were discussed in the mass media were hardly put in dialogue with one another. For example, it was assumed that Palin's identity (notably, the media discussed these as identity categories rather than systems of power) would attract the female electorate and the working-class electorate, though her candidacy, motivated by a logic of simple identity politics, was never really deployed to pull in the votes of poor women. Intersectional knowledge projects eschew the kind of monocategorical thinking that characterized the 2008 presidential election. Overall, the thirty years of academic scholarship touting the intersectional nature of race, class, and gender in shaping individual identities, as well as the opportunity structures that individuals encounter, seemingly made little headway in influencing mass media coverage of the election.

The 2010 midterm elections provided more evidence that the main ideas of intersectional knowledge projects have made little headway in shaping outcomes in actual political arenas. U.S. electoral politics witnessed an unprecedented number of conservative women candidates, all white, several of whom were endorsed by the emerging Tea Party movement. Either–or thinking (and, once again, simple identity politics) suggests that *women* and *nonelite* (which was the platform on which many were running) candidates would lead to support for policies that help women and working- and middle-class people; however, in the November 2010 elections, this was not the case. How were we to make sense of these nonelite, white women's support for policies that appear, at least at first glance, not in their best interests? Insights from intersectional knowledge paradigms would lead us to think about these women's complex and multifaceted relationships with privilege and power to make sense of their advocacy for policies that overwhelmingly favor rich men. Yet intersectionality's inability to penetrate U.S. electoral politics left many Americans, perhaps specifically those with feminist sensibilities, conflicted by the women's presence. Were feminists to celebrate or denounce these young, nonelite, nonincumbent insurgent women's campaigns? Lacking easy access to intersectional analyses, commentators, and participants of U.S. electoral politics were unnecessarily ill-equipped to make sense of the political spectacle.

Politics do not occur exclusively within the realm of formal political institutions. Popular culture is also an important site of politics, in that the ideas and frames of mass media have the ability to shape political beliefs and behaviors. Moreover, popular culture constitutes a site of political action itself (Iton 2008). Examples from contemporary popular culture provide additional evidence that intersectional knowledge projects have an uneven effect in political spheres. Specific attention to performances of diversity in popular culture (as a substitute for richness of the conceptual framework associated with intersectionality) further demonstrates how these substitutions enable neoliberal social policies to persist.

A look at hip-hop music provides one highly visible, contemporary example where we can see the ways popular culture becomes a site for shaping political beliefs and mobilizing political action. While hip-hop culture, and specifically rap music, has had a political bent from its inception (Chepp 2011), contemporary rap artists and audiences continue to use the pop cultural phenomenon as a platform for raising political awareness and staging action for social change. One high-profile example of this is visible in rapper Nelly's 2004 planned visit to Spelman College in support of a bone marrow drive being sponsored by his foundation *4Sho4Kids*. Nelly dedicated himself to the cause after his sister was diagnosed with leukemia. However, the women of Spelman did not immediately embrace Nelly's announced visit. Having access to a comprehensive university curriculum around intersectionality and faculty support, Spelman students took action and sought to hold Nelly accountable for the images portrayed in his music videos, which largely degraded women of color. They suggested that Nelly hold the bone marrow drive but then participate in a campus dialogue about the depictions of women in hip-hop. The protest organized by the women at Spelman received national attention, and Nelly and his foundation ultimately pulled out of the event. Consistent with other intersectional knowledge projects, the students of Spelman demonstrated a sophisticated understanding of the complicated and multifaceted power relations at work. The president of Spelman's Student Government Association, Asha Jennings, said, "Nelly wants us to help his sister...but he's degrading hundreds of us" (cited in Neal 2006, 140). Jennings articulates the links between gender and racial oppression, complex and unequal relationships between and among groups—such as Nelly's sister, millions of other women of color, and male rappers, and a commitment to social justice. McCall (2005) might classify Spelman students' intersectional approach as *intracategorical complexity*, in which the students sought to highlight social inequalities within a master category, in this case, inequalities within a racial group. The protest at Spelman points to the uneven progress of intersectional analyses at work in popular culture. On one hand, Jennings and her fellow students at Spelman College successfully deploy intersectional ideas and practices in their efforts to use popular culture (hip-hop videos) as a platform and target for staging political action. At the same time, scores of pop cultural figures such as Nelly lack an intersectional perspective around how their public relations commitments to political and philanthropic issues cannot be detached from the complicated and multifaceted power relationships intertwined in their own artistic and cultural work. Too often pop stars, like Nelly, will opt out of opportunities for real engagement with intersectional knowledge projects that have the potential to lead to dialogue and social change.

CHALLENGES THAT CONFRONT CONTEMPORARY INTERSECTIONAL KNOWLEDGE PROJECTS

Within the academy, and especially within gender scholarship, intersectionality's seemingly fluid boundaries, focus on relationality, and attentiveness to complex and multifaceted power relations via a sustained reflexivity about its own practice makes for a particularly dynamic field of study. Indeed, these features might be responsible for intersectionality's success and adaptability across disciplines as described earlier (Davis 2008; Nash 2009). At the same time, the fact that intersectional knowledge projects are practiced by so many people in so many different ways suggests that this same ambiguity and open-endedness may be potential conceptual weaknesses of intersectional knowledge projects. Thus, its ostensible popularity within the academy when coupled with its virtual invisibility within nonacademic, broader political arenas suggest that intersectionality faces several unique challenges in the early twenty-first century.

One challenge is the seemingly shifting terrain that characterizes intersectional knowledge projects, where various projects might look considerably different across assorted knowledge-producing locations. In part, this is likely due to intersectionality's travels into traditional disciplines that already have an established set of discursive and methodological practices. The contours of intersectionality, which might be uniquely malleable (Davis 2008), get shaped to fit the existing rules, routines, and overarching questions of a given discipline. Here, we might consider how intersectional knowledge projects change shape as they travel to different disciplines, adapting to disciplinary conventions as they move. While this adaptability may have contributed to intersectionality's success in the academy (Davis 2008), it poses a challenge in that intersectional knowledge projects can become unrecognizable to scholars across disciplines, fostering an environment where intersectional knowledge becomes atomized, and a single linear narrative about intersectional knowledge projects' key aims and practitioners is reiterated. The failure to recognize intersectional knowledge projects across disciplinary locations contributes to the subjugated nature of some intersectional knowledge projects (e.g., American pragmatism) at the expense of the hypervisibility of others (e.g., the intellectual work of black feminists). This lack of a clear message might also contribute to the virtual absence of intersectionality in broader political arenas.

A second challenge facing contemporary intersectional knowledge projects concerns the changing nature of its relationship with the social justice traditions of oppressed groups and whether this association inhibits intersectionality's ability to secure a position of legitimacy within the academy. That is, can intersectional knowledge projects become more powerful by disassociating from the less powerful? Historically, decontextualization has been a way of enhancing a theory's status within the academy. Here we might think of postmodernism, a knowledge project known for its abstraction, decontextualization, and over-all disassociation from the social conditions of groups and individuals on the ground. Yet postmodern knowledge projects have attracted substantial power and attention within the academy. For example, in their sociological theory textbook, Ritzer and Goodman (2004, 594) assert that "it is abundantly clear that postmodernism has become the most important development not only in sociological theory but in a wide range of academic and nonacademic fields." Applying insights from the sociology of science, Davis (2008) points to intersec-tionality's appeal to generalists and specialists alike, a key feature of successful social theories. This logic highlights the importance and power of decontextu-alization. Can intersectionality follow this path to enhance its own power and privilege? Some scholars wish to leave the origins behind, arguing that intersec-tionality is more than voices from the margin. Nash (2008, 10) refers to this as an "unresolved theoretical dispute" within intersectional scholarship, in which it is "unclear whether intersectionality is a theory of marginalized subjectivity or a generalized theory of identity." While intersectional knowledge projects' current associations with the political agendas of the oppressed may limit their potential reach within the academy, decontextualizing intersectional knowledge projects and linking them to a grand theoretical tradition can address this challenge.

Travelling into traditional disciplines and becoming decontextualized from actual social conditions can have some unintended consequences for intersec-tionality. Intersectional analyses get attached to projects that look at, for exam-ple, nonmale bodies, nonwhite people, nonheterosexuals, and nonmiddle-class families. That is, scholars tend to call their work intersectional by claiming to look at race when doing work on nonwhite populations or gender so long as they are looking at women. Such assumptions renormalize and make invisible whiteness, masculinity, heterosexuality, and "able" bodies, among other hegem-onic systems. And herein lies a critical paradox within intersectional knowledge projects. Intersectional scholarship has expanded the boundaries of inequality studies by drawing attention to the relational, multifaceted, and complex proc-esses between systems of power, pointing to the ways, for example, construc-tions of masculinity, whiteness, and heterosexuality derive meaning and power from corresponding (i.e., presumed "opposite") socially constructed categories and from each other. However, intersectional scholarship inadvertently rein-scribes these systems of privilege by rendering them nongendered, nonraced, and sexually nonremarkable, in other words, "normal." This renormalization results in research that approaches these categories as unmarked and, as such, uninterrogated (Choo and Ferree 2010).

The challenge that confronts intersectionality as a sociology of knowledge project is that, because it is inherently dynamic, specifying its symbolic and structural boundaries is difficult (Lamont and Molnár 2002). Specifically, what type of theoretical character does it exhibit, traditional or critical? Whether contemporary intersectional knowledge projects can be understood as theories fundamentally grounded in practice is debatable. However, intersectional knowledge projects continue to be deployed as having the potential to effecting positive social change in people's lives (Manuel 2006). While some might argue that intersectionality's affinity to social praxis is simply a function of its close association with feminist theory, one might draw attention to its affinities with other theoretical traditions that are grounded in a set of lived practices, such as critical race theory or American pragmatism (Rochberg-Halton 1987; Seigfried 1993). To fully engage such questions, we must consider who intersectionality's main practitioners are (i.e., people who create and sustain structural locations for it, within and outside the academy, and within the academy, within traditional disciplines, in interdisciplinary areas, and as transdisciplinary endeavors). This is the creative tension between stasis and change, played out in the field of contemporary politics.

A final challenge concerns the continued salience of social justice as part of intersectionality as a knowledge project. Given the challenges in electoral politics and popular culture, how might attending to the conceptual framework of intersectionality foster democratic ideals? Democratic societies have long expressed a belief in the importance of communities to the civil society and the strength of U.S. political institutions. Yet democratic possibilities have been facilitated or hindered by the kinds of communities people have in mind. Democratic societies also require a new kind of identity, one grounded in multiplicity and complexity and with new understandings of relationality. How might we build an argument concerning the specific ways that a conceptual framework of intersectionality might foster both the vibrant communities and a robust identity politics that is vital for democratic societies?

In essence, democratic societies require new kinds of communities that ensure participation and that can grapple with legacies of oppression and resulting social and material inequalities. Market-based, individualistic conceptions of exchange relations must be replaced with robust understandings of community as a foundational construct for politics. Collins (2010) suggests that the construct of *community* might be uniquely well positioned to politically situate social groups that are increasingly recognized, thanks to insights from intersectionality, as diverse and crosscutting (Cohen 1999).

Democratic societies also require new forms of identity that take into account the complex, multifaceted, and relational nature of contemporary social realities. Recasting social groups to reflect intersectional premises requires a more robust identity politics than those put forth during the U.S. social movements of the mid-twentieth century. For example, Cohen (1997, 480) understands queer identities, broadly defined, as political locations and lived experiences around which to organize, based upon "their similar positions, as marginalized subjects relative to the state." By reconceptualizing identity in this way (i.e., as a complex, multifaceted relationship to state power), Cohen argues that we can understand, for example, how gay HIV/AIDS activists and heterosexual black women on welfare who are single parents can serve as useful political allies to one another. Both sets of queer identities challenge state definitions of what constitutes "normal" and "respectable" sexuality, and both face material penalties from the state as a result of their unique social locations relative to the state.

When combined, these shifts in understandings of community, identity, and politics have important implications for coalition building in the political landscape. These new conceptions of identities and communities can broaden our understanding of political allies and effective political partnerships. Rather than organizing along single systems of power (e.g., either gender or racial oppression) or single issues (e.g., either HIV/AIDS activism or welfare reform) or on behalf of a single community (e.g., either gay activists or single mothers), intersectional approaches to coalition building enhance democratic possibilities by expanding definitions of political allies, political identities, and political communities. Moreover, an intersectional conceptual approach to coalition building not only offers a way to organize across difference but also enables democratic actors to highlight less-than-immediately obvious similarities across individuals, interests, and groups (Cole 2008). To place this in the context of the previously cited example, an intersectional conceptual approach to coalition building provides queer communities and poor single mothers not only a framework for organizing across their differences but also an intersectional approach to coalition politics for identifying their less-than-immediate similarities. In this case, Cohen (1997) might point out their similarly marginalized positions to state power. Such a robust approach to power and politics in the United States would facilitate democratic ideals and encourage more meaningful democratic victories in that coalitions could avoid the pitfalls of unidimensional coalition politics, organized along a single axis of power or identity. Instead, intersectional frameworks allow democratic actors to build alliances organized around complex, multifaceted, and relational points of commonality, difference, and political purpose.

Notes

1. Fields more closely associated with the humanities and the arts also show patterns of embracing intersectionality. In this chapter, we focus on the social sciences, primarily in response to the focus of this handbook. We are aware that we rely on sociology more heavily than other social science disciplines. Our goal is not to survey the intersectionality scholarship in all social science fields; rather, we encourage readers across disciplines to take the themes introduced in this chapter and apply them to their own scholarly fields. Although we draw largely from sociological scholarship, we are writing to a broad audience, not just sociologists. Indeed, the field of intersectionality assumes you read broadly and across disciplines.

2. For example, the recent literature on intersectionality, methodology, and empirical validity (see, e.g., Hancock 2007a, 2007b; Bowleg 2008) is likely a response to the critique that intersectionality scholarship lacks a precise (Nash 2008) and diverse (McCall 2005) methodological approach.

3. In this essay, we use *oppression* to refer to specific systems of power such as racial oppression or gender oppression. Social inequalities typically stem from systems of oppression, yet they need not do so. For example, small children and adults are not "equal," yet this form of social inequality may not be an accurate measure of age oppression. In contrast, systems of power organized around ideas of race, class, gender, sexuality, ethnicity, age, and ability that violate norms of social justice constitute systems of oppression that catalyze characteristic forms of social organization. Social inequality and social justice can coexist. For a useful discussion of issues of oppression, see Young (1990, 66–95). In this essay, we use the term *social inequality* to reference systems of oppression.

4. The sociology of knowledge is a subfield of sociology explicitly concerned with the socially constructed nature of knowledge production and legitimation. This perspective maintains there is no one social truth; rather, via interaction with one another, we decide what "counts" as truth. This socially determined truth or knowledge gets legitimated by those in authoritative expert positions (Berger and Luckmann 1966). Michel Foucault, among others, illustrates how knowledge production and legitimation go hand in hand with relations of power and domination (Foucault 1980; Lyotard 1979/1984).

5. These intersecting systems of power are organized in different social domains (Collins 2000). Collins (2009) outlines four different domains of power that serve as locations where intersecting systems of power and the social inequalities associated with them are organized: structural, disciplinary, cultural, and interpersonal.

6. The development of this thinking went through several iterations, including the (1) *separate and different approach* (the idea that racial oppression can be compared to gender oppression but they are seen as separate influences) and the (2) *additive approach* (which "adds together" the effects of each system of oppression as static, equal parts of a whole). Collins (1993) argues that although this additive framework recognizes an important *element* of interaction that is absent from the separate and different approach, the additive approach is ultimately too simplistic in that it depends on dichotomous thinking (i.e., you are either oppressor or oppressed) and assumes that dichotomies can be ranked (i.e., assumes some groups are more oppressed than others). Collins argues that we need to ask new questions—ones that take relationality into account—if we are going reconceptualize how structures of domination and oppression are maintained.

7. Notably, McCall (2005, 1774) recognizes that different intersectional knowledge projects are shaped by the type of methodological approach employed.

8. Critiquing previous systems theory grounded in the social sciences (e.g., the work of Niklas Luhmann, Talcott Parsons, or Émile Durkheim), Walby (2007) turns to complexity theory, which is more rooted in the natural sciences, as a way to develop a systems theory where systems do not operate in a static functionalist way (e.g., Parsons). While complexity theory has very little to say about social inequality, Walby suggests that it might offer a very useful contribution to intersectionality if we adapt complexity concepts such as the systems–environment distinction (allowing for the nonsaturation of a system

in the environment that it occupies, thereby accounting for multiple systems of inequality as well as for the potentially nonnested, nonreducible nature of systems) and path dependency as mechanisms for understanding nonlinear changes along multiple axes of inequality. Walby suggests that such complexity insights make for a more flexible understanding of systems and their interaction with other systems, a very valuable feature to any theory of intersecting systems of social inequality.

9. The scholarship on the social construction of whiteness and its relationship to privilege is vast. For an early example of this work emerging out of the critical race studies legal tradition see Harris (1993). For examples of recent attention given to scholarship on the economic elite, see McCall's (forthcoming) book, *The Un/deserving Rich: American Beliefs about Inequality, Opportunity, and Redistribution*, as well as the first Elites Research Network conference held at Columbia University in October 2010.

10. In 2011, the website for Indiana University's department of gender studies described itself as "a transdisciplinary department engaging students in the study of gender and the intersection of gender with other substantive categories of analysis and identity, including race, sexuality, class, disability, and nationality" (http://www.indiana.edu/~gender/). Similarly, the website for the program of feminist studies at the University of California, Santa Barbara, describes feminist studies as "research and teaching [that] focus on the ways that relations of gender, intersecting with race, class, ethnicity, sexuality, nation, ability, and other differences, affect every aspect of society" (http://www.femst.ucsb.edu/who_we_are.html). The department of gender, women & sexuality studies at the University of Washington states on its homepage: "Intersectional and transnational analyses foreground our studies of race and ethnicity in U.S. and global contexts, as we analyze how these social formations intersect with gender, women, and sexuality in specific times and places" (http://depts.washington.edu/webwomen/).

11. A survey of articles appearing in the following selection of women's studies and feminist academic journals between January 2000 and December 2010 yields the following results (the numbers in the parentheses signify how many entries during this date range included the term *intersectionality* in an article's text): *Gender & Society* (54), *Sex Roles* (40), *Feminist Formations* (previously *NWSA Journal*) (37), *Signs* (33), *Women's Studies International Forum* (25), *Feminist Studies* (17), and *Feminist Theory* (9). Note that these search results might include, in addition to full articles that focus on intersectionality, articles that simply mention the term or book reviews or other types of publications aside from full articles. Nonetheless, the search results point to the ubiquity of the term within the field.

12. Such books include *Gender, Race, Class and Health: Intersectional Approaches* (Schulz and Mullings 2005), *Intersectionality and Politics: Recent Research on Gender, Race, and Political Representation in the United States* (Hardy-Fanta 2007), *Gender Relations: Intersectionality and Beyond* by (Siltanen and Doucet 2008), *The Intersectional Approach: Transforming the Academy through Race, Class, and Gender* (Berger and Guidroz 2009), *Emerging Intersections: Race, Class, and Gender in Theory, Policy, and Practice* (Dill and Zambrana 2009), *Theorizing Intersectionality and Sexuality* (Taylor, Hines, and Casey 2010), and *Framing Intersectionality: Debates on a Multi-Faceted Concept in Gender Studies* (Lutz, Vivar, and Supik 2011).

13. Academic conferences organized around the theme of intersectionality include the 2004 National Women's Studies Association conference, "Women in the Middle: Borders, Barriers, Intersections," the 2006 European Science Foundation conference "Intersectionality, Identity and Power: Interdisciplinary Perspectives on Intersectionality Studies," the 2008 Nordic Conference on "Gender, Intersectionality and Regional Development" in Sweden, the 2009 international conference in Frankfurt "Celebrating Intersectionality? Debates on a Multi-Faceted Concept in Gender Studies," the 2010 Critical Race Studies Symposium on "Intersectionality: Challenging Theory, Reframing Politics, Transforming Movements" sponsored by the University of California, Los Angeles, School of Law, and the 2011 Eastern Sociological Society conference on "Intersectionalities and Complex Inequalities."

14. Davis's article has been widely cited and read; for example, Sage Journals Online lists Davis's article as the most read of all *Feminist Theory* articles in October 2010, a full year and a half after its publication in April 2008.

15. Nash presented this argument at the UCLA Critical Race Studies Symposium: *Intersectionality: Challenging Theory, Reframing Politics, Transforming Movements* in a session entitled, "As Intersectionality Crosses Disciplines: Understanding Our Pasts and Continuing Our Futures" (March 12, 2010).

16. At the time of writing this chapter, *Research in Social Science and Disability* is accepting manuscript submissions for an upcoming volume, "Intersectionality Revisited," arguing that "it is necessary to update our theories of disability, incorporate intersectionality theories which ignore disability, update theories of intersectionality to include disability, and use newer data to produce more relevant results" (cited from the CFP). The volume is scheduled for publication in August 2012.

17. Our appreciation goes to the anonymous reviewer who suggested these empirical works.

References

Abbott, Andrew. 2001. *Chaos of disciplines*. Chicago: University of Chicago Press.

Acker, Joan. 1999. "Rewriting class, race, and gender: Problems in feminist rethinking." In Myra M. Ferree, Judith Lorber, and Beth B. Hess, eds., *Revisioning gender*. Thousand Oaks, CA: SAGE, 44–69.

Ackerly, Brooke, and Jacqui True. 2008. "An intersectional analysis of international relations: Recasting the discipline." *Politics & Gender* 4: 156–173.

Anderson, Cynthia D. 1996. "Understanding the inequality problematic: From scholarly rhetoric to theoretical reconstruction." *Gender & Society* 10: 729–746.

Anzaldúa, Gloria. 1987. *Borderlands/La frontera: The new mestiza*. San Francisco: Spinsters/Aunt Lute Books.

Berger, Peter, and Thomas Luckmann. 1966. *The social construction of reality*. Garden City, NJ: Doubleday.

Bourdieu, Pierre. [1979] 1984. *Distinction: A social critique of the judgment of taste*. Trans. Richard Nice. Cambridge, MA: Harvard University Press.

Bourdieu, Pierre. [1980] 1990. *The logic of practice*. Trans. Richard Nice. Stanford: Stanford University Press.

Bowleg, Lisa. 2008. "When black + lesbian + woman (does not equal) black lesbian woman: The methodological challenges of qualitative and quantitative intersectionality research." *Sex Roles* 59 (Sept.): 312–325.

Boyte, Harry C. 2004. *Everyday politics: Reconnecting citizens and public life.* Philadelphia: University of Pennsylvania Press.

Bratton, Kathleen A., and Kerry L. Haynie. 1999. "Agenda-setting and legislative success in state legislatures: The effects of gender and race." *Journal of Politics* 61: 658–679.

Browne, Irene, and Joya Misra. 2003. "The intersection of gender and race in the labor market." *Annual Review of Sociology* 29: 487–513.

Burawoy, Michael. 2005. "For public sociology." *American Sociological Review* 70: 4–28.

Carey, Allison C. 2003. "Beyond the medical model: A reconsideration of 'feeblemindedness,' citizenship, and eugenic restrictions." *Disability & Society* 18: 411–430.

Chepp, Valerie. 2011. "Rap music." In Stephen M. Caliendo and Charlton D. McIlwain, eds., *The Routledge companion to race and ethnicity.* New York: Routledge, 213–215.

Choo, Hae Yeon, and Myra Marx Ferree. 2010. "Practicing intersectionality in sociological research: A critical analysis of inclusions, interactions, and institutions in the study of inequalities." *Sociological Theory* 28: 129–149.

Cohen, Cathy J. 1997. "Punks, bulldaggers, and welfare queens: The radical potential of queer politics?" *GLQ: A Journal of Lesbian & Gay Studies* 3: 437–465.

Cohen, Cathy J. 1999. *The boundaries of blackness: AIDS and the breakdown of black politics.* Chicago: University of Chicago Press.

Cohen, Cathy J. 2004. "Deviance as resistance: A new research agenda for the study of black politics." *Du Bois Review: Social Science Research on Race* 1: 27–45.

Cole, Elizabeth R. 2008. "Coalitions as a model for intersectionality: From practice to theory." *Sex Roles* 59: 443–453.

Collins, Patricia Hill. 1986. "Learning from the outsider within: The sociological significance of black feminist thought." *Social Problems* 33: S14–S32.

Collins, Patricia Hill. 1993. "Toward a new vision: Race, class, and gender as categories of analysis and connection." *Race, Sex & Class* 1: 25–45.

Collins, Patricia Hill. 2000. *Black feminist thought: Knowledge, consciousness, and the politics of empowerment,* 2d ed. New York: Routledge.

Collins, Patricia Hill. 2004. *Black sexual politics: African Americans, gender and the new racism.* New York: Routledge.

Collins, Patricia Hill. 2007. "Pushing the boundaries or business as usual? Race, class and gender studies and sociological inquiry." In Craig Calhoun, ed., *Sociology in America: A history.* Chicago: University of Chicago Press, 572–604.

Collins, Patricia Hill. 2009. *Another kind of public education: Race, schools, the media, and democratic possibilities.* Boston: Beacon Press.

Collins, Patricia Hill. 2010. The new politics of community. *American Sociological Review* 75: 7–30.

Combahee River Collective. [1977]1995. A black feminist statement. In Beverly Guy-Sheftall, ed., *Words of fire: An anthology of African-American feminist thought.* New York: New Press, 232–240.

Connell, R. W. 1987. *Gender and power.* Stanford: Stanford University Press.

Crenshaw, Kimberlé W. 1991. "Mapping the margins: Intersectionality, identity politics, and violence against women of color." *Stanford Law Review* 43: 1241–1299.

Davis, Angela. 1983. *Women, race, and class.* New York: Vintage.

Davis, Kathy. 2008. "Intersectionality as a buzzword: A sociology of science perspective on what makes a feminist theory successful." *Feminist Theory* 9: 67–85.

Dhamoon, Rita Kaur. 2011. "Considerations on mainstreaming intersectionality." *Political Research Quarterly* 64: 230–243.

Dill, Bonnie Thornton. 1983. "Race, class, and gender: Prospects for an all-inclusive sisterhood." *Feminist Studies* 9: 131–150.

Dill, Bonnie Thornton. 2002 (Fall). "Work at the intersections of race, gender, ethnicity, and other dimensions of difference in higher education." *Connections: Newsletter of the consortium on race, gender, and ethnicity*, University of Maryland, College Park, 5–7.

Dworkin, Shari L. 2005. "Who is epidemiologically fathomable in the HIV/AIDS epidemic? Gender, sexuality, and intersectionality in public health." *Culture, Health & Sexuality* 7: 615–623.

Emirbayer, Mustafa. 1997. "Manifesto for a relational sociology." *American Journal of Sociology* 103: 281–317.

Foucault, Michel. 1980. *Power/knowledge: Selected interviews and other writings by Michel Foucault.* Ed. Colin Gordon. New York: Pantheon.

Fraser, Nancy. 1989. *Unruly practices: Power, discourse and gender in contemporary social theory.* Minneapolis: University of Minnesota Press.

Friedan, Betty. 1963. *The feminine mystique.* New York: W. W. Norton & Company.

Galton, Francis. 1904. "Eugenics: Its definition, scope, and aims." *American Journal of Sociology* 10: 1–25.

Glenn, Evelyn N. 1998. "Gender, race, and class: Bridging the language-structure divide." *Social Science History* 22: 29–38.

Hancock, Ange-Marie. 2007a. "Intersectionality as a normative and empirical paradigm." *Politics & Gender* 3: 248–254.

Hancock, Ange-Marie. 2007b. "When multiplication doesn't equal quick addition: Examining intersectionality as a research paradigm." *Perspectives on Politics* 5: 63–79.

Hancock, Ange-Marie. 2009. "An untraditional intersectional analysis of the 2008 election." *Politics & Gender* 5: 96–105.

Hankivsky, Olena, and Renee Cormier. 2011. "Intersectionality and public policy: Some lessons from existing models." *Political Research Quarterly* 64: 217–229.

Harris, Cheryl L. 1993. "Whiteness as property." *Harvard Law Review* 106: 1707–1791.

Harris-Lacewell, Melissa. 2004. *Barbershops, bibles, and BET: Everyday talk and black political thought.* Princeton, NJ: Princeton University Press.

Harvey Wingfield, Adia. 2009. "Racializing the glass escalator: Reconsidering men's experiences with women's work." *Gender & Society* 23: 5–26.

Hawkesworth, Mary. 2003. "Congressional enactments of race-gender: Toward a theory of raced-gendered institutions." *American Political Science Review* 97: 529–550.

Iton, Richard. 2008. *In search of the black fantastic: Politics and popular culture in the post-civil rights era.* New York: Oxford University Press.

Jenkins, Richard. 1992. *Pierre Bourdieu.* London: Routledge.

Jordan, June. 2002. *Some of us did not die: New and selected essays of June Jordan.* New York: Basic Books.

Junn, Jane. 2009. "Making room for women of color: Race and gender categories in the 2008 U.S. presidential election." *Politics & Gender* 5: 105–110.

Kelley, Robin D. G. 1994. *Race rebels: Culture, politics and the black working class.* New York: Free Press.

Kimmel, Michael S. 1994. "Masculinity as homophobia: Fear, shame, and silence in the construction of gender identity." In Harry Brod and Michael Kaufman, eds., *Theorizing masculinities.* Thousand Oaks, CA: SAGE, 119–141.

Knapp, Gudrun-Alexi. 2005. "Race, class, gender: Reclaiming baggage in fast travelling theories." *European Journal of Women's Studies* 12: 249–265.

Kuhn, Thomas S. [1962]1996. *The structure of scientific revolutions*, 3d ed. Chicago: University of Chicago.

Lamont, Michèle. 2000. *The dignity of working men: Morality and the boundaries of race, class, and immigration.* New York: Russell Sage Foundation.

Lamont, Michèle, and Virág Molnár. 2002. "The study of boundaries in the social sciences." *Annual Review of Sociology* 28: 167–195.

Lorde, Audre. 1984. *Sister outsider: Essays and speeches.* Freedom: Crossing Press.

Lyotard, Jean-François. [1979]1984. *The postmodern condition: A report on knowledge.* Minneapolis: University of Minnesota Press.

Mahalingam, Ramaswami, Sundari Balan, and Jana Haritatos. 2008. "Engendering immigrant psychology: An intersectionality perspective." *Sex Roles* 59: 326–336.

Manuel, Tiffany. 2006. "Envisioning the possibilities for a good life: Exploring the public policy implications of intersectionality theory." *Journal of Women, Politics and Policy* 28(3–4): 173–203.

Matua, Athena D. 2010. "Law, critical race theory and related scholarship." In Patricia Hill Collins and John Solomos, eds., *The Sage Handbook of Race and Ethnic Studies.* London: SAGE, 275–305.

McCall, Leslie. 2005. "The complexity of intersectionality." *Signs* 30: 1771–1800.

Nash, Jennifer C. 2008. "Re-thinking intersectionality." *Feminist Review* 89: 1–15.

Nash, Jennifer C. 2009. "Un-disciplining intersectionality." *International Feminist Journal of Politics* 11: 587–593.

Neal, Mark Anthony. 2006. *New black man.* New York: Routledge.

Phoenix, Ann, and Pamela Pattynama. 2006. "Intersectionality." *European Journal of Women's Studies* 13: 187–192.

Rich, Adrienne. 1986. "Compulsory heterosexuality and lesbian existence." In *Blood, bread, and poetry: Selected prose 1979–1985.* New York: W.W. Norton & Company, 23–75.

Ritzer, George, and Douglas J. Goodman. 2004. *Sociological theory*, 6th ed. New York: McGraw-Hill.

Roberts, Dorothy. 1997. *Killing the black body: Race, reproduction, and the meaning of liberty.* New York: Vintage Books.

Rochberg-Halton, Eugene. 1987. "Why pragmatism now?" *Sociological Theory* 5: 194–200.

Roth, Benita. 2004. *Separate roads to feminism: Black, Chicana, and white feminist movements in America's second wave.* New York: Cambridge University Press.

Ruwanpura, Kanchana N. 2008. "Multiple identities, multiple-discrimination: A critical review." *Feminist Economics* 14: 77–105.

Schulz, Amy J., and Leith Mullings (Eds.). 2006. *Gender, race, class, & health: Intersectional approaches.* San Francisco: Jossey-Bass.

Scott, James C. 1985. *Weapons of the weak: Everyday forms of peasant resistance.* New Haven, CT: Yale University Press.

Scott, James C. 1990. *Domination and the arts of resistance: Hidden transcripts.* New Haven, CT: Yale University Press.

Seigfried, Charlene H. 1993. "Shared communities of interest: Feminism and pragmatism." *Hypatia* 8: 1–14.

Simien, Evelyn M. 2007. "Doing intersectionality research: From conceptual issues to practical examples." *Politics & Gender* 3: 264–271.

Simien, Evelyn M., and Ange-Marie Hancock. 2011. "Mini-symposium: Intersectionality research." *Political Research Quarterly* 64: 185–186.

Smelser, Neil. 1992. "Culture: Coherent or incoherent." In Richard Münch and Neil Smelser, eds., *Theory of culture.* Berkeley: University of California Press, 3–28.

Smith, Valerie. 1998. *Not just race, not just gender: Black feminist readings.* New York: Routledge.

Smooth, Wendy. 2006. "Intersectionality in electoral politics: A mess worth making." *Politics & Gender* 2: 400–414.

Steinbugler, Amy C., Julie E. Press, and Janice Johnson Dias. 2006. "Gender, race, and affirmative action: Operationalizing intersectionality in survey research." *Gender & Society* 20: 805–825.

Stoetzler, Marcel, and Nira Yuval-Davis. 2002. "Standpoint theory, situated knowledge and the situated imagination." *Feminist Theory* 3: 315–333.

Valk, Anne M. 2008. *Radical sisters: Second-wave feminism and black liberation in Washington, D.C.* Urbana: University of Illinois Press.

Walby, Sylvia. 2007. "Complexity theory, systems theory, and multiple intersecting social inequalities." *Philosophy of the Social Sciences* 37: 449–470.

Warner, Leah. 2008. "A best practices guide to intersectional approaches in psychological research." *Sex Roles* 59: 454–463.

Weber, Lynn, and M. Elizabeth Fore. 2007. "Race, ethnicity, and health: An intersectional approach." In Hernán Vera and Joe R. Feagin, eds., *Handbook of the sociology of racial and ethnic relations.* New York: Springer, 191–218.

Weldon, Laurel S. 2008. "Intersectionality." In Gary Goertz and Amy G. Mazur, eds., *Politics, gender, and concepts: Theory and methodology.* New York: Cambridge University Press, 193–218.

Williams, Joan. 2000. *Unbending gender: Why family and work conflict and what to do about it.* New York: Oxford University Press.

Young, Iris Marion. 1990. *Justice and the politics of difference.* Princeton, NJ: Princeton University Press.

Yuval-Davis, Nira. 2006. "Intersectionality and feminist politics." *European Journal of Women's Studies* 13: 193–209.

CHAPTER 3

·····

FEMINISMS

·····

RITA KAUR DHAMOON

THE TERRAIN OF FEMINISM

·····

How feminists explain, define, and historicize feminism is itself contested and subject to interpretation. Rather than viewing this contestation as a problem about unity or coherence, this chapter starts from the premise that debates among feminists demonstrate plurality and openness to further reflection, clarification, and inquiry. We will briefly consider different ways of understanding feminism, its central features, and methods of inquiry deployed by feminists. The bulk of the chapter will deal with contemporary debates among feminists as a way to outline some of the contestations and key contributions of feminist scholars to the study of politics.

While the term *feminism* first appeared in France in the 1880s, Great Britain in the 1890s, and the United States in 1910, ideas around woman-centered political action has long existed across the globe, even if the term was not used. Different historical and geopolitical genealogies indicate that there are many forms of *feminism* rather than one formation. In the West, these variations are often described in terms of three waves of feminism. The first wave, typically described as the period from the 1700s to the 1960s, is characterized by expanding women's education and civil rights as well as including women in formal politics and the public sphere; the second wave, from the 1960s to 1980s, is presented as the era of formalizing equality rights for women through the law and public policy and increased attention to differences among women; and the third wave, from the 1990s onward, is typically represented as diverse, antifoundationalist, pro-sex, celebratory of everyday action over theory, and amorphous and unregulated (Walker 1995; Heywood and Drake 1997). Yet the narrative of the three waves, which has had much play in feminist circles, tends to overdetermine the differences between generations of feminism, even while there are various contexts and tactics across different strands of feminism (Snyder 2008). Moreover, the notion of three waves has a presumed a Western European and Anglo-American backdrop and is premised on a narrow source base, namely, Eurocentric written texts, which exclude oral narratives, sharing circles, and non-Western texts and epistemologies. Indeed, as a brown woman of Sikh-Punjabi origin born in the United Kingdom and with a Western education, my own interpretations of feminism are shaped by my shifting locations of insider–outsider and the limitations of my Eurocentric training. A chapter on feminism written from other standpoints would reflect differing interpretations.

The work of feminism can also be understood in other ways. Feminism is simultaneously (1) a research paradigm that examines the form and character of gendered life (ontology), investigates what can be known (epistemology), and develops and deploys gender-centered tools of analysis (methods); (2) an ideology that contains a system of general beliefs and values that explains how and why gender oppression occurs, and that prescribes a vision of society and government based on liberation and change in gender roles, whereby the forms of action and guiding principles are contested; and (3) a set of social movements that seek to address unequal relations of power, which has in some instances included men.

While feminism is varied, since at least the 1960s, it has been characterized by a number of key aspects that regularly feature in the contemporary feminist debates discussed below. First, central to all brands of feminism is the drive for social justice. Put differently, feminism is a form of social critique (Dhamoon 2009). Second, feminists center power, both as an organizing device that represses and produces gender relations and as a site of transformation. Third, sex and gender are central categories of analysis, and the relationship and substance of these categories is contested (Butler 1999; Firestone 1997). Fourth, feminism has identified and debated the culture–nature divide, specifically to examine whether subjects have natural affinities to particular roles and sexual desires or to unpack socially constructed meanings related to gender (Arneil 1999). Fifth, feminist analyses of the public–private divide have illuminated the patriarchal framework that generates and assigns traditional gender roles and in doing so have expanded an understanding of *the political* beyond the traditional focus on the state and government and centered the idea that "the personal is political" (Millet 1970; Hankivsky 2004). Sixth, while feminism has varied in scope, it is distinct from many other approaches in that it links theory and practice and, in doing so, highlights the significance of personal narratives, lived experience, subjectivity, and political praxis (hooks 2000). Finally, feminism is characterized by distinct and varied interests, such that feminists do not share a universal conception of the social world or a universal project; indeed, it is precisely the possibility of theorizing and practicing feminism in various ways that gives it global appeal.

Feminist inquiry entails a wide range of methods that draw on and expand existing social science tools of quantitative and qualitative analysis (Hawkesworth 2006; see also chapter 5). This includes various positivist methods that are based on studying static, categorical, error-free variables such as surveys, regression modeling, and statistical data analysis of particular groups of women in legislatures. Feminist methods also draw on and develop interpretativism and critical theory whereby realities and knowledge are treated as complex, fluid, subjective, discursive, socially constructed, products of and productive of power, and subject to individual and social action. Interpretativist and critical theory tools include standpoint theory, interview analysis, ethnographic studies and autoethnography, studies of lived experience, discourse analysis, a social determinants approach, narrative-based studies, participatory action, and community-based research. Some feminist methods of analysis—especially the use of oral traditions, narratives, storytelling, biography, and personal testimony—are criticized by mainstream social sciences because they are not seen as positivist, rigorous, theoretical, or scholarly enough. Yet much feminism seeks to challenge conventional views on epistemology, to emphasize interdisciplinarity, and to offer innovative tools of analysis and political action.

CONTEMPORARY FEMINIST THEMES AND DEBATES

While sometimes it seems that feminism has become fractured since the 1970s and therefore unsustainable as a large-scale movement, feminism has always included divisions and differing visions. There has never been a single feminist vision of the world, and indeed even within a single national context feminism has varied. In the contemporary era, three debates have characterized Western feminist political theories and practices:

- Equality as difference or sameness—where are the women?
- Differences among women—which women?
- The relationship between sex and gender—what work does the category of woman do in feminist thought and in broader sociopolitical life?

Whereas the first debate tends to assume a stable binary of man–woman, the other debates center on challenging the universality and stability of the category of *woman* and in doing so put into question the conventional foundations of feminism-as-women and raise questions about the unity of feminism. The rest of the chapter will explore these debates and the ensuing implications for the study of gender and politics.

Equality as Sameness or Difference: "Where Are the Women?"

Early feminist critiques of political study, especially the Western canon, were centered on tracking the absence of women in the core texts of the Western tradition (Zerilli 2006, 108). Among others, Jean Bethke Elshtain (1981), Susan Moller Okin (1979), and Carole Pateman (1988) traced the ways Western canonical texts restricted women to the private realm of the household and justified their exclusion from the public realm on the basis of naturalized conceptions of sex and gender, the sexual division of labor, and citizenship. For example, Okin (1989) criticized John Rawls's theory of liberalism because it could not account for injustices entrenched in familial relations. While some feminists argued that the canon was bankrupt, others aimed to integrate women into existing canonical understandings of the political; yet others aimed to transform key concepts such as democracy, citizenship, freedom, equality, and rights by centering gender as a constitutive category of politics (Zerilli 2006, 110–111). A major theme that emerged from questioning the Western canon was a fundamental challenge to the idea that biology was destiny, which had positioned women as a naturally inferior class. As Simone de Beauvoir ([1949]1973, 267) famously said, "One is not born a woman, but becomes a woman." Since at least the 1960s, various schools of feminism emerged as a response to this idea of socially constructed gender roles to ask, "Where are the women?" In exploring this question, some argue that equality means that men and women should be treated the same, others that equality means recognition of differences between men and women, and others still that move beyond the equality/difference debate to reject the idea of measuring women against male norms.

Echoing earlier arguments made by Mary Wollstonecraft (1792) and John Stuart Mill ([1869]1999), *liberal feminism* emerged as a way to integrate women into existing frameworks on the premise that men and women should be treated equally. This school of feminism drew on classical liberal ideas regarding the state, individual autonomy, progress, rationality and reason, and legal rights to argue that women's exclusion in the public sphere was unjustified. As well as extending existing liberal ideas to women and applying these to issues of employment discrimination, pay equity, and representation in government, liberal feminists also challenged the public–private divide to argue that issues such accessible and universal childcare were matters for the state rather than just concerns about private–domestic life. This challenge to the public–private divide has led to a field of study known as *ethics of care*. Ethic of care feminists demonstrate that care is publicly and politically relevant, dependent on relationships and networks of human interdependency that require a shift in the values adopted by the state when developing public policies (Tronto 1994; Chakraborti 2006). As Olena Hankivsky (2004, 1) notes, "An ethic of care has brought to the fore public dimensions of our lives that have been largely uninvestigated...The values [of an ethic of care] can be considered essential to living a worthwhile, fulfilling, and balanced life." Other feminists, such as Wendy Brown (1995), while supportive of care ethics, question the capacity of the liberal-democratic state to adequately address feminist concerns even if the state is (a limited and regulatory) site of change.

Like liberal feminism, *socialist and Marxist feminism* also acknowledges physiological differences between men and women and develops the idea that women should be treated the same as men. However, reflecting their ideological roots, socialist and Marxist feminists develop their analyses on the basis of class divisions and social structures rather than the autonomous individual and attitudes. While socialist feminists are more apt to favor peaceful and piecemeal change and are more willing to make changes within the existing system (e.g., have unions represent the interests of working women), Marxist feminists favor revolutionary transformation. Both, however, are critical of capitalism and the division of labor in public and private spheres because it creates exploitation and economic dependence of women. Both are also critical of liberal feminism because it is too easily co-opted by the "malestream" and overly focused on equality of opportunity rather than equality of outcome. These feminists argue that class and gender relations are formed through one another. An understanding of *patriarchal capitalism* allows these forms of feminism to challenge the masculinist character of the family wage, unions, unpaid household work, low wages for women (Hartmann 1997, 104), and international division of labor that creates racialized-gendered workers in the so-called third world (Mohanty 2003).

Unlike liberal feminism and socialist feminism, *radical feminism* starts from the premise that women and men are different and that there is no need for them to the same. This is the school of feminism that is often deemed to be antimale, in part because it calls for separateness between men and women and alternate social arrangements rather than an expansion or modification of the existing system. And because feminism is often represented as radical by the mainstream, it sometimes is referred to as "the F word"—that which is unspeakable. Yet through consciousness-raising groups and other forms of organizing, radical feminism importantly informs public discourses on reproductive freedom, violence against women, pornography, sexual harassment (Dworkin and MacKinnon 1997), homophobia and compulsory heterosexuality (see the chapter by Lind in this volume), the rights of sex trade workers, and rape. As well, radical feminists such as Kate Millet (1970) developed theories that expanded meanings of politics to include personal and sexual relationships and demonstrated that the study of patriarchy was intrinsically linked to *power*, a key concept in politics. Contrary to the aforementioned schools of thought, early radical feminists like Shulamith Firestone (1997) argued that sex class sprang directly from biological reality, specifically the reproductive functions of the traditional family; in short, there was a knowable essence to *woman*. Female dependence on men arose because of patriarchy and oppression of the female body. While acknowledging the importance of a material-economic analysis, radical feminists also emphasize that the original division of labor (i.e., child-bearing) is also psychosexual in that women are falsely made to believe that sex with men is compulsory and pleasurable. As a result, radical feminists want a revolution that eliminates not only male privilege but also the "dialectic of sex," namely, the sex distinction itself, whereby "genital differences between human beings would no longer matter culturally" (Firestone 1997, 25). This, some argue, would occur in part through new technologies that would provide more reproductive freedom for women, erase the categories of homosexuality and heterosexuality, and foster female-based relationships.

Over the past three decades, feminist contentions and theories have moved beyond the ideological terms of *liberal, socialist,* and *radical* and are now shaped by inventive combinations of numerous forms of critique that include these but also extend to critical theory, discourse ethics, analytic philosophy, hermeneutics, structuralism, existentialism, phenomenology, deconstruction, postcolonial theory, psychology, and neo-Marxism (Dietz 2003, 400).

This hybridization informs *male feminism* (or profeminism). Male feminism is radical in that seeks to address the roots of patriarchy but differs from the school of radical feminism in that it is not premised on eliminating the sex distinction. Male feminists specifically challenge antifeminist men's rights movements that blame women for divorce and custody laws that supposedly favor women; often, antifeminists oppose women's rights and changes in the traditional family structure on the basis of religious and cultural norms. As well as challenging such ideas, male feminists criticize the masculinist position, which holds that the traditional masculine ideal is threatened by the feminization of society. Drawing on the established feminist idea that gender is socially constructed, male feminists argue that because gender roles are learned they can be relearned differently, and as such feminism can serve men's interests (Brod 1998). And indeed, various strands of men's and masculinity studies have emerged that aim to be consistent with antisexist and antiheteronormative ideologies. David Kahane (1998, 213–215), however, also notes that male feminism is intrinsically an oxymoron, because while men are capable of deepening their understanding of their own roles in sexist privilege and oppression and operationalizing this knowledge, they are still part of the problem since they cannot fully know or transcend the advantages conferred to them. As a result, male feminists must be willing to develop ambiguous understandings of the self because they are implicated in patriarchy, to be open to criticism and self-criticism, and to engage in activist friendships to negotiate courses of action.

In a similar vein to some of the previously mentioned forms of feminism, *ecofeminism* also aims to reconcile differences between binaries, in this case between masculinity and femininity and nature versus man. Drawing from poststructuralism, postcolonialism, neo-Marxism, and other frameworks, different strands of ecofeminism maintain that a strong parallel exists between men's dominance over women and the violation of nature by men and masculinist attitudes and methods that construct women as passive and economic development above nature (Mies and Shiva 2005; Ress 2006; Schaefer 2006). Anti-globalization activist-scholar Vandana Shiva (1989) argues that women's liberation is dependent on ecological liberation (especially in the context of the color line that constitutes the Global South), and on the adoption of the *feminine principle*, which men can also adopt to create life-enhancing societies, not life-reducing or life-threatening conditions. For some ecofeminists, capitalist and patriarchal systems intersect with neocolonial and racist structures, in which ecological breakdown and social inequality are intrinsically related to the dominant development paradigm that puts profiteering man against and above nature and women. For these feminists, productivity can be reconceptualized outside the domain of capital accumulation and destruction and in terms of sustainability, valued women's work, harmony between nature and men and women, and local indigenous and diverse knowledge. As such, men are not situated as the standard for evaluating humanity and political life.

"Which Women?" Differences among Women

While the first set of debates assumes stable binary categories of woman–man, the second takes up differences among women through feminist standpoint and in terms of subjectivity rather than a unified category of women. While some issues are continuous across feminist debates (e.g., the body), at times the focus on differences among women has collapsed into a form of identity politics that has been criticized by some feminists, especially for displacing issues of class (Fraser 1997). Yet one of the major political insights of analyzing differences among women is that everyone's life is composed of multiple, intersecting discourses of power that are irreducible to a single dimension, such as gender. Intersecting differences, or intersectionality—which is discussed more specifically later and also in Chapter 2 of this volume—have become increasingly significant to feminism because they challenge the idea of a universal notion of sisterhood and women's experiences.

Since at least the mid- to late 1800s in the United States, figures such as Sojourner Truth advocated for women's rights and fought against slavery and spoke to the struggles facing black men and women (King 1988, 42–43); these U.S.-based black women challenged the racism of white suffragists who were then fighting for the right of particular women to vote without adequately addressing slavery. Further, Tharu and Lalita's (1991) landmark collection traces women's writings in India across eleven different languages from as early as 600 BC, demonstrating the abundance of ideas about gender construction and norms. Indeed, Maitrayee Chaudhuri (2005) rejects the claim that feminism in India is a Western import, yet also notes that the tentacles of colonialism have meant that Western feminism can choose whether to engage with non-Western thought and praxis, whereas this is not the case for those working in the peripheries.

Chandra Mohanty (2003, 17–24) offers a form of *third world feminism*, sometimes called *postcolonial feminism*, in which she centers the intersections of race, class, and gender discourses. She critically deploys the term *third world* to refuse Western feminist frameworks that assume and privilege an ethnocentric and homogenized conception of feminism and patriarchy; this is because the average third world woman is often constructed as sexually constrained, ignorant, poor, uneducated, tradition bound, passive, and family oriented, and this image is juxtaposed with the supposed educated, modern, autonomous, family-free, sexually liberated Western woman. Through discursive and historical materialist analysis, Mohanty (2003, 34–36) warns against universalizing women's experiences because this decontextualizes the specific historical and local ways reproduction, the sexual division of labor, families, marriage, and households are arranged. With the intention of building noncolonizing feminist solidarity within national borders and across borders, Mohanty draws attention to the micropolitics of context, subjectivity, and struggle as well as to the macropolitics of global economic and political systems and processes.

Third world feminism is very much shaped by historical shifts within nationalist movements, which have occurred in the form of anti-colonial/anti-imperial struggles, national modernization reform movements, state exploitation of women, and religious-cultural nationalist revivalisms (Heng 1997). In India, Dalit women, for instance, have been critical of feminists both within and outside of the country who frame women's rights related to employment and land claims without considerations of caste and class (Rege 2006) and who separate feminist theorizing from political organizing. Building on the work of feminists like Mohanty and Li Xiaojiang (1989) in China, Feng Xu (2009, 197) explores the heterogeneity of Chinese feminism in relation to Maoist ideas, the reform era, and UN-based international feminism to highlight that "meaningful debates about Chinese feminisms do occur within China itself, rather than always and only in dialogue with Western and Japanese interlocutors." In the context of Nigeria, Ayesha M. Iman (1997) makes the case for local feminism that has developed in the context of the post-oil boom and military regimes that have dominated since British colonial rule. Palestinian feminist movements are heavily shaped by the ongoing occupation that creates oppression and not just formal gender equality rights between men and women (Kawar 1996). These feminists emphasize the specificities of history, nation, and power.

In the United States, *black feminists* such as bell hooks (2000), Audre Lorde (1984), Patricia Hill Collins (1990, 2000), and Evelyn Simien (2006) have also refused universalizing assumptions about sisterhood. hooks, for example, examines white privilege, classism, and sexism in the work of Betty Friedan, who hooks argued made synonymous the plight of white and nonwhite women. hooks did not question that women were oppressed but argued instead that sexism varied in content and form; accordingly, her work as a black feminist has emphasized the value of examining patriarchal white supremacist capitalism. As well as challenging the erasures of racialization, sexual desire, and class by white feminists, black feminism centers the specialized knowledge created and lived by African American women, which clarifies a standpoint of and for those women, who themselves are differently and differentially situated. Importantly, the issues facing African American women in the United States and black women in other parts of the world including those in other settler states and different nations in Africa or the Caribbean may overlap but cannot be conflated.

Chicana feminism has as many different meanings as there are different Chicanas. In general, this form of feminism refers to a critical framework that centers the relationship between discourses of race, class, gender, and sexuality inequality as they affect women of Mexican descent in the United States. Cherrie Moraga (1981, 52–53) approaches Chicana feminism as "a theory in the flesh [which] means one where the physical realities of our lives—our skin color, the land or concrete we grew up on, our sexual longings—all fuse to create a politic born out of necessity. Here, we attempt to bridge the contradictions in our experience. We are the colored in a white feminist movement. We are the feminists among the people of our culture. We are often the lesbians among the straight. We do this bridging by naming ourselves and by telling our stories in our own words." Gloria Anzaldúa (1999) conceptualizes such differences in terms of psychological, sexual, spiritual and physical borderlands, hybridity, and *mestiza* identity—all of which have become relevant to feminism beyond Chicana contexts. Edwina Barvosa (2009) argues that the ambivalences, hybridities, and contradictions are important components of self-crafted identity formation. Importantly, Cristina Beltran (2004) warns that while theories of hybrid and mestiza identity have generated social justice agendas, some have also collapsed into unifying discourses that suffer from the same dreams of homogeneity, unity, authenticity, and idealized experiential knowledge that plague unreflective streams of identity politics. As such, like other kinds of feminism, Chicana feminism is constantly reflecting on its own borders and hegemonies.

In settler societies like Canada, the United States, and Australia and New Zealand, *indigenous feminists* like Cheryl Suzack et al. (2011), Andrea Smith (2005, 2006), Joyce Green (2000, 2007), and Linda Tuhiwai Smith (1999) have identified the impact of genocide and continuing forms of colonialism by addressing such issues as the disproportionate rates of violence against indigenous women, indigenous methodologies, and indigenous women's resistance. Drawing on specific instances of racism and sexism outside of their communities as well as sexism within their communities, indigenous feminists have argued that patriarchy cannot be eliminated without addressing colonialism. This is because laws implemented colonialism by regulating and attempting to eradicate indigenous women's bodies and knowledge and dispossessing all Indigenous peoples from their land. For indigenous feminists, resistance against such tactics is grounded in connections with other women and also in terms of their specific nation (e.g., Métis, Cree, Mohawk, Dene) and relationship to the land. This entails collective action with indigenous men, regenerating indigenous epistemologies and cultures in all spheres of life (including decolonizing feminism), and centering the role of women as respected decision makers. Some view political change within the nation-state, while others propose a turn away from the state and toward indigenous communities and epistemologies.

Grounded in activist work, *antiracist feminism* (which can include black and indigenous feminism) exposes the ways sexism operates within nonwhite communities, and how white supremacist discourses in Western nations interweave with patriarchal and capitalism. Before and since the events of September 11, 2001, antiracist feminists have challenged, for example, sexist Eurocentric and Islamophobic representations of the veil, which are overly determined to be inherently oppressive. As well as challenging hegemonic modes of Othering that exclude nonwhite women from mainstream society, antiracist feminists have also resisted other feminist analyses that pit one form of difference against another. Susan Moller Okin's (1999) essay "Is Multiculturalism Bad for Women?" for example, has prompted much debate about cultural rights versus sex equality rights (Nussbaum 2000; Phillips and Dustin 2004; Arneil et al. 2007; Song 2007). Liberal feminists like Okin claim that cultural accommodation of group rights undermines individual women's rights, contravenes the values of a secular state, and fails to address how most cultures and religions and especially non-Western cultures and religions are oppressive. Antiracist feminists show that such arguments merely replicate conservative positions on the veiling of women, homogenize Islamic cultures as barbaric, sustain moral panic about "an invasion" of Islam, uncritically rely on the state to protect secularism and individual rights, and perpetuate a rescue script whereby European states and men are supposedly saving imperiled Muslim women from dangerous Muslim men (Thobani 2007; Razack 2008). Resembling Gayatri Chakravorty Spivak's (1988) essay "Can the Subaltern Speak?" these feminists identify the closures and openings for marginalized women by centering the interactions between racism, patriarchy, and imperialism.

Importantly, anti-racist feminists have reflected on the fissures and connections between them. Bonita Lawrence and Enaskhi Dua (2005), for instance, note that not all nonwhite peoples are equally socially situated and that, as such, political liberation strategies need to reflect this. In particular, they examine the ways indigenous experiences, knowledge, and perspectives get overshadowed in antiracist work. To counter this, they argue it is necessary to decolonize antiracism.

Related to antiracism feminism is the form of feminism that has emerged from critical whiteness studies. Like nonwhite feminists, Peggy McIntosh (1995) argues that issues of racism and sexism are about not just the disadvantages of others but also the privilege of some. In particular, she examines white privilege among white feminists using the metaphor of an invisible weightless knapsack that carries special provisions, assurances, tools, maps, guides, codebooks, passports, visas, clothes, compass, emergency gear, and blank checks that enable white women and white feminists to appear neutral, normal, and the universally referent point (77). Ruth Frankenberg (2000) follows McIntosh, in that she too analyzes the ways race discourses privilege white women because whiteness is a location of structural advantage, a set of usually unmarked and unnamed cultural practices that are co-constructed through norms of gender, class, and dis/ability. In drawing attention to white privilege, this school of feminism foregrounds the structural racism of privilege and penalty.

Another school of feminism that has become more prominent over recent decades is called *critical feminist disability studies*. Scholars like Parin Dossa (2009) and Rosemarie Garland-Thomson (2002) show not only that disability studies need to better engage with feminist theory but also that feminist theories of reproductive technology, bodily differences, ethics of care, and immigration need to integrate a disability analysis. This is in part because, like gender, disability is a socially fabricated idea rather than a biomedical condition that demarcates disability in terms of otherness. Feminist disability theories are aimed not only at integrating marginalized subjects into mainstream society but also at transforming society, expanding and deepening feminist theory, and centering ability and disability systems as ideological rather than biological markers of the body. These theories examine gendered subjectivity in terms of constructs of disability and also compulsory systems of ablebodiedness that normalize and preserve advantaged designations of autonomy, wholeness, independence, competence, intelligence, and value. For example, women's breasts are typically sexualized, except if removed or medically scarred, thereby affecting sexual status and self-esteem and causing marginalization; state-led policies of forced sterilization of those deemed physically or mentally incapable and selective abortions to get rid of fetuses with disabilities are feminist concerns; and racialized women with disabilities are redefining the parameters of their social worlds. In short, these issues are about reproductive freedom, codes of sexual desire, and intersections of marginalization and resistance affecting differently positioned women.

Sex and Gender Debates: What Is *Woman*?

Whereas the first debate centers on bringing women into the male-dominated political realm and the second challenges universalizing conceptions of woman by centering differences, the third debate puts into question the very idea of a pregiven feminine subject with a set of assigned interests that arise from bodily and social experiences of being a woman, even if differentially situated.

In particular, this more recent debate centers on the relationship between sex and gender (see also the chapter by Hawkesworth in this volume). Whereas earlier feminists often assumed that *sex* was a biological category and *gender* referred to the socially constructed meanings attached to a sexed body, more recently feminist critics question the normalized binary structure of the biological (and not only social) representations of male–female, man–woman, and masculinity–femininity. This is because these binaries maintain the idea of a natural relationship between a biological body and a social identity. Feminist critics do not question that cultural meanings are socially produced or that intersecting differences matter, but they do challenge grand narratives, including the underlying assumption that identity politics (whether a single identity or multiple intersecting identities) is the basis of feminism because it reifies the body (Butler 1990; Brown 1995). Indeed, feminists are divided on how to respond to issues related to the body and sexuality, including "how to create gender equality when women enjoy female objectification (pornography), claim the right to make money servicing male sexual needs (prostitution), and eroticize relationships of inequality (sadomasochism)" (Snyder 2008, 189).

One brand of feminism that has grown out of the critique against a sex-equals-gender approach is *poststructural feminism*, which has also shaped debates about differences among women. This brand of feminism draws on Michel Foucault's conception of power, whereby power is a productive force that constitutes the subject in and through disciplinary power and biopolitics. While poststructural feminism accepts the notion that gender is not naturally but socially signified, it also challenges the assumption that sex is natural rather than also constructed through language. In short, sex does not lead to gender, but it is gender—'sex' too is socially made. Accordingly, the constitution of the modern subject (e.g., the female subject, the male subject, the black lesbian subject) through systems of meaning making that produce and organize sex must also be deconstructed. Drawing from psychoanalytic, Foucaultian, and feminist theories, Judith Butler (1990, 1993), for example, does not seek to include women in the category of the rational autonomous agent (a key goal of liberal feminism) but instead advances a deconstructive and genealogical approach to critique the conditions through which subjects become particular kinds of sexed, sexualized, and gendered bodies. Butler insists that gender is the effect of specific formations of power and practices of phallogocentrism and compulsory heterosexuality.

Butler (1990) offers the notion of performativity to foreground the idea that woman is not something that subjects are but rather something subjects do within already existing terms: "gender is the repeated stylization of the body, a set of repeated acts within a highly rigid regulatory frame that congeal over time and produce the appearance of substance, of a natural sort of being" (25). Performativity is not a performance by an actor or subject who preexists; rather, it a process by which gender identities are constructed through language, meaning that there is no gender identity that precedes language (the doctor who delivers a baby declares "it's a boy" or "it's a girl," for example). Following from this, Butler questions the coherence of a subject. Even the categories of man and woman, she argues, are performatively produced through repetition as if they are original, true, and authentic (Butler 1997, 304); correspondingly, compulsory heterosexuality is also constructed and regulated through repetition.

Gender categories and sexual desires, in other words, are neither essentially stable nor fully knowable, for they are produced in the process of imitating their own idealizations. This is why "there is no 'proper' gender, a gender proper to one sex rather than another, which is in some sense that sex's cultural property. Where that notion of the 'proper' operates, it is always and only improperly installed as the effect of compulsory system" (ibid., 306). In effect, Butler rejects the sex–gender distinction (thus pushing against other forms of feminism that assume that man–woman maps easily onto masculine–feminine) and concludes that the materiality of the body can be understood only through specified and contextualized cultural interpretation and discourse.

While Butler has been criticized by other feminists because her early work downplayed the material body and omitted an analysis of transgenderism, transsexuality, and racialized sexualities—issues she has since addressed (Butler 1993, 1999)—her work has importantly shown that identity categories tend to be instruments of regulatory regimes and as such need to be persistently troubled and subject to reinterpretation. Moreover, Butler's work, among others, has importantly prompted the development of such fields of inquiry as queer studies or queer theory, which grew out of and is integral to feminist studies (as well as lesbian and gay studies). Queer theory, which emerged in the 1990s, builds on the feminist idea that gender is a constitutive feature of political life and that sexual orientations and identities are shaped by social forces. In the U.S. context, queer theory also emerged in response to political practices, specifically homophobic responses to AIDS. But further to feminist work (and lesbian and gay studies), queer theory expands the focus to include any kind of sexual activities or identities that are deemed to be deviant and offers a critique of traditional identity politics that consolidates categories like women, gay, and lesbian.

The open-endedness of social categories is also characteristic of *transfeminism*, an outgrowth of feminist, lesbian and gay, and queer studies. While seemingly more prominent since the 1990s, transfeminism has been in existence for much longer, routinely addressing issues related to the loss of family, housing and employment discrimination, social stigma, and high rates of violence and also confronting transphobia within some feminist circles (Stryker 2008, 101–111). Transfeminism is not simply about blending feminism and transgenderism but about disrupting the idea of a binary (male–female mapped onto man–woman) and reconceptualizing gender in terms of a continuum. This is in part because the very meaning of *transgender* is in a constant state of becoming. Currah, Juang, and Minter (2006, xiv) remark that since 1995, 'transgender' is "generally used to refer to individuals whose gender identity or expression does not conform to the social expectations for their assigned sex birth. At the same time, related terms used to describe particular identities within that broader category have continued to evolve and multiply." Although the terminology of transgenderism may be insufficiently inclusive in some instances and imprecise in others, it has come to also include the social category of transsexuality (Namaste 2005, 2). Bobby Noble (2006, 3) sees the terms *trans-sexual* and *transgender* as essentially contested and free-floating but adds that "at its most provocative, *trans-* and the space it references refuses the medical and psychological categorical imperatives through which it has always been forced to confess." Various related terms (e.g., transvestite, cross-dresser, trans, female-to-male, male-to-female, boyz) recode identity language, such that the category of transgender has expansive and contested meanings, although these too are subject to various kinds of normalizing processes of meaning making; these normalizing processes are especially apparent in discussions about who is really trans and whether intersex should be included in the definitions of transgender and transsexuality (Currah et al. 2006. xv; Greenberg 2006; Stryker 2008, 9).

The history of peoples who challenge socially, medically, and legally imposed gender boundaries is wide-ranging (Stryker 2008). Some indigenous peoples use the term *two-spirited people* to refer to the spiritual identity of those who embody masculine and feminine spirits or genders within the same body. Importantly, the language of two-spirited is contested and tends to be universalizing of different indigenous traditions (Lang 1998), and there is too often a presumed link between two-spiritedness and transgenderism. The distinctiveness of indigenous non-normative genders lies in the link to the role of visionaries and healers who do not view sexuality and gender as separable from other aspects of life. But because indigenous epistemologies still remain on the margins, including in much feminist political thought, more understanding is needed on how indigenous peoples describe genders and sexualities that fall outside mainstream binary system of governmentality and how to interpret non-Western categories in ways that adequately represent differing indigenous meanings.

The similarities and differences between meanings can also be found in East Asian and Western understandings of key feminist terms. While it is important to examine the widening gulf between rich and poor nations in terms of first world–third world or north–south (as feminist debates about differences among women illuminate), this often excludes the diversity of East Asian feminism, which is neither Western nor from the Global South (Jackson, Jieyu, and Juhyun 2008). East Asian feminists have pointed out that meanings of sex, gender, and sexuality vary according to language and cultural specificity. Gender and sexuality, for example, have no preexisting equivalents in Asian languages and do not translate very well but have still been taken up and also reinvented by East Asian scholars (ibid., 2). Moreover, it is not clear how the mix of individualism and traditional collective will in places like Taiwan, China, and Korea differently affects the stability or deconstruction of conventional binaries of man–woman (ibid., 19). The point here is that even critiques of (feminine, masculine, trans) subjectivity will vary according to cultural and historical context.

Overall, the third debate about the meaning of woman destabilizes a binary-based understanding of female and male biological bodies that neatly map onto conventional feminine and masculine social bodies. In other words, this approach to gender politics rejects the idea that sex equals biology and gender equals culture. Not only can female biological bodies be men and socially masculine, but the spectrum of possible gender identities transcends the conventional binary of male–female that dominates the various schools of feminism discussed in early sections. Ultimately this gender trouble is a challenge to the naturalized coherency of sex, gender, sexual desires, and woman—categories often presumed to be stable among feminists discussed in earlier sections.

Is the Subject of Woman Dead in Feminism? Is Feminism Dead without the Subject of Woman?

In sum, feminism has been shaped and invigorated by critiques against the idea that the traditional feminine subject, woman, is the basis of feminist politics: namely, that the category of woman is isolated from or prioritized over other categories; that the designation of women as a single, coherent, already constituted group has the effect of signifying all women equally as powerless and without agency; and that the very process of definitively defining *gender* excludes and devalues some bodies and practices while normalizing others.

These critiques raise a prickly issue in feminist thinking, which is dubbed by Seyla Benhabib (1995) as "the death of the subject." Benhabib asks, if the subject is a fiction, a performative process of becoming or socially made body that refuses sex–gender binaries, what is the basis of feminism or womanhood? If there is no knowable subject, what drives feminist movements and in whose name are liberation claims being made? These questions have sometimes been framed in terms of essentialism versus antiessentialism and social constructivism, whereby it is argued that essentialist readings of identity assume too much (i.e., that there is a fixed and permanent social group identity of women), and constructivist interpretations do not assume enough (i.e., that there is no such thing as a social group of women).

One kind of response from feminists to this essentialism versus antiessentialism tension has been to develop what has come to be known as *intersectionality* (also see the chapter by Hill Collins and Chepp in this volume). While there is a burgeoning literature on intersectionality among feminists, it remains a marginalized lens of analysis in mainstream political study. Intersectionality is a contested term and framework of analysis, but as an umbrella term it can be generally defined as "the complex, irreducible, varied, and variable effects which ensue when multiple axes of differentiation—economic, political cultural, psychic, subjective and experiential—intersect in historically specific contexts"

(Brah and Phoenix 2004, 76). Ange-Marie Hancock (2007, 64) specifies that intersectionality is based on the idea that more than one category should be analyzed, that categories matters equally and that the relationship between categories is an open empirical question, that there exists a dynamic interaction between individual and institutional factors, that members within a category are diverse, that analysis of a set of individuals is integrated with institutional analysis, and that empirical and theoretical claims are both possible and necessary.

The term intersectionality was specifically coined and developed by American critical race scholar Kimberle Crenshaw (1989, 1991) as a way to address legal doctrinal issues and to work both within and against the law. Crenshaw used the metaphor of intersecting roads to describe and explain the unique ways racial and gender discrimination compounded each other. Crenshaw's formulation of intersectionality opened up a conceptual space through which to study how a combination of various oppressions work together to produce something unique and distinct from any one form of discrimination standing alone. Building on the idea of intersectionality, feminists have developed (sometimes conflicting) concepts and theories of interlocking oppressions (Razack 1998, 18), multiple jeopardy (King 1988), discrimination-within-discrimination (Kirkness 1987–88), multiple consciousness (Matsuda 1992), multiplex epistemologies (Phoenix and Pattynama 2006), translocational positionality (Anthias 2001), interconnectivities (Valdes 1995), synthesis (Ehrenreich 2002), positional and discursive intersectionality (Yuval-Davis 2006), and assemblages (Puar 2007). What these differing ideas all share is the need to move beyond a single-axis approach that presents the category of woman as stable and undifferentiated.

A number of other feminists have attempted to attend to the critiques of 'woman' by theorizing gender as an analytic category rather than a natural identity (Harding 1986; Beckwith 2005). Hawkesworth (1997, 681) notes that gender as category advances theories about "the cultural production of heterosexual desire, the psychoanalytic production of individual identity, the power asymmetries in social life, or the structure of perception." While recognizing these as improvements to conventional feminist notions of sex equals gender, Hawkesworth argues that even in these instances gender is presented as a universal explanan, whereby "it covertly invokes the very biological ground it set out to repudiate .... [It] operates within the confines of a base/superstructure" (662). To counter this naturalizing trend she warns against collapsing diverse notions of sexed embodiedness, sexuality, sexual and gender identity, gendered divisions of labor, gendered social relations, and gender symbolism into the single term gender.

While Butler is a severe critic of fixed and stable subject formations, she also recognizes that politically marginalized peoples may want to or have to insist on deploying categories like lesbian or gay because they are threatened. There is no question that some subjects (like lesbians and gays) are under threats of obliteration, and these threats end up dictating the terms of political resistance (Butler 1997, 304). Nonetheless, these categories, she maintains, are injurious in that they reinstall a call for essence, when in fact it is crucial to ask which version of lesbian or gay identity is being deployed, by whom, and what benefits and exclusions are subsequently produced. While any consolidation of identity requires some set of differentiations and exclusions, there is no way of controlling how that identity will be used, and if it becomes permanent and rigid it forecloses "futural significations." As such, echoing Spivak's (1988) call for "strategic essentialism" in which alliances are developed as contingent and temporary formations, Butler (1997, 305) calls for "strategic provisionality," whereby identities are approached as sites of contestation, revision, and rearticulation.

Young (1994) argues that a pragmatic feminist category of woman is important because it maintains a point of view outside of liberal individualism and gives feminist social movements their specificity. Drawing from Jean Paul Sartre, Young offers the notion of *gender as seriality*. As opposed to a group that presupposes that a collection of persons recognize themselves and one another in a unified relation, Young says a series enables an understanding of a social collective whose members are unified passively by objects around them (e.g., rules about the body, menstruation, pregnancy, sexual desire, language, clothes, division of labor). Because women have different attitudes toward these objects, there is an unorganized gender existence, members are only passively unified and isolated from one another, and the series is blurry and shifting. Young argues that gender as seriality avoids the assumption that women are a passive social collective with common attributes and situations; refuses the idea that a person's gender identity defines them singly, whether psychologically or politically, links gender to other serialities such as race; and is distinct even while it is mapped onto sex as a series.

Integrating the critique that not all women share the same biology or the same experiences, Michaele Ferguson (2007) reconceptualizes identity in terms of *practices of doing* as opposed to objects that have intrinsic meaning. She rejects identity-as-object because "when we conceive of identity as something we can know and get right, we end up with a choice between two undesirable options: either we continue searching in the vain hope that we will succeed where others have not and discover true essence our identity, or we resign ourselves to the incoherence of the subject of democratic and feminist politics. Neither choice is compelling" (35). Drawing on the work of Linda Zerilli (2006), she develops an account of collective gender identity in terms of inherited systems of beliefs rather than knowledge about all members, how the category of woman gains meaning through complex social practices rather than presumed commonalties, and political exchanges rather than truth claims. A theory of gender, Ferguson concludes, must acknowledge an infinite contestability about its own terms, engage in continuous self-critique, and refuse to settle the question of who "we" are.

Rather than posing a problem for feminism, continuous critical questioning of concepts and categories that seem foundational (such as woman) opens up the possibilities of imaging and reimagining differences in alternative and new kinds of ways (Dhamoon 2009). Accordingly, the subject of woman need be neither dead nor revered but persistently critiqued even when it is deployed; and feminism does not die without the subject of woman because this would assume that both feminism and organizing concepts are unidimensional, unconditional, stable, and permanent. Put differently, the making of woman is itself an activity of politics.

FUTURES OF FEMINISM

Different feminisms have already corrected omissions and distortions that permeate political science, illuminated social and political relations neglected by mainstream accounts, and advanced alternate explanations for political life (Hawkesworth 2005, 141) and alternate ways of organizing and living. As this field of study continues to develop, it is important to keep in mind that when feminism becomes singular and is narrowly defined and when particular centers are universalized as the referent points (e.g., white women, Western feminism, heterosexual women, lesbians), much is missed about history, difference, and political organizing.

The vast spectrum and depth of feminism is testament to its wide appeal and global application. This diversity may raise the question of what, if anything, links different strands of feminism together in practice (however loosely or tightly), if not the biological female body or the socially constructed shared sense of womanhood? This depends on coalitions and alliances between different kinds of feminist worldviews, experiences, and practices—coalitions driven by social justice concerns rather than unified conceptions of identity or common experiences. Different types of feminism already envision ways of making social change, including the following: inclusion into mainstreams; working with or against state institutions; turning away from the state entirely and toward local communities; reformulating major institutions such as the traditional family; closing the separation between men and women; engaging in new reproductive technologies; offering discursive deconstructions that produce category crises; and generating decolonized, cross-border feminist communities. While many of these agendas may conflict, the possibility of alliances and coalitions lies in critiquing and therefore disrupting the work of power—what Chela Sandoval (2000, 61–63) refers to as confrontation with difference and an "ethical commitment to egalitarian social relations." Inevitably, many of these alliances and coalitions will be temporary and context specific because the sites of power and transformative capacities of power will be differently understood. But what cuts across all feminisms is a critique of the forces and relations of power. It is this work of critiquing power that will continue to be delineated by feminists from differing vantage points, and that has led to a shift among feminists from a politics based on sisterhood to one based on solidarity among differences.

REFERENCES

Anthias, Floya. 2001. "Beyond feminism and multiculturalism: Locating difference and the politics of location." *Women's Studies International Forum* 25(3): 275–286.

Anzaldúa, Gloria. 1999. *Borderlands/la frontera: The new mestiza.* San Francisco: Spinsters/Aunt Lute.

Arneil, Barbara. 1999. *Politics and feminism.* Oxford: Blackwell Publishers.

Arneil, Barbara, Monique Deveaux, Rita Dhamoon, and Avigail Eisenberg (Eds.). 2007. *Sexual justice/cultural justice: Critical perspectives in theory and practice.* London: Routledge.

Barvosa, Edwina. 2009. *Wealth of selves: Multiple identities, mestiza consciousness and the subject of politics.* College Station: Texas A&M University Press.

Beauvoir, Simone de. [1949] 1973. *The second sex.* Trans. E. M. Parshley. New York: Vintage.

Beckwith, Karen. 2005. "A common language of gender?" *Politics and Gender* 1(1): 128–137.

Beltran, Cristina. 2004. "Patrolling borders: Hybrids, hierarchies, and the challenge of mestizaje." *Political Research Quarterly* 57(4): 595–607.

Benhabib, Seyla. 1995. "Feminism and postmodernism." In S. Benhabib, ed., *Feminist contentions: A philosophical exchange.* New York: Routledge, 17–34.

Brah, Avtar, and Ann Phoenix. 2004. "Ain't I a woman? Revisiting intersectionality." *Journal of International Women's Studies* 5(3): 75–86.

Brod, Harry. 1998. "To be a man, or not to be a man—That is the feminist question." In T. Digby, ed., *Men doing feminism.* New York: Routledge, 197–212.

Brown, Wendy. 1995. *States of injury: Power and freedom in late modernity.* Princeton, NJ: Princeton University Press.

Butler, Judith. 1990. *Gender trouble: Feminism and the subversion of identity.* New York: Routledge.

Butler, Judith. 1993. *Bodies that matter.* New York: Routledge.

Butler, Judith. 1997. "Imitation and gender insubordination." In L. Nicholson, ed., *The second wave: A reader in feminist theory.* New York: Routledge.

Butler, Judith. 1999. *Gender trouble: Feminism and the subversion of identity.* New York: Routledge, 300–315.

Chakraborti, Chhanda. 2006. "Ethics of care and HIV: A case for rural women in India." *Developing World Biopolitics* 6(2): 89–94.

Chaudhuri, Maitrayee (Ed.). 2005. *Feminism in India.* London: Zed Books.

Collins, Patricia Hill. 1990. *Black feminist thought: Knowledge, consciousness, and the politics of empowerment.* Boston: Unwin Hyman.

Collins, Patricia Hill. 2000. *Black feminist thought: Knowledge, consciousness and the politics of empowerment.* New York: Routledge.

Crenshaw, Kimberle. 1989. "Demarginalizing the intersection of race and sex: A black feminist critique of antidiscrimination doctrine, feminist theory and antiracist politics." *University of Chicago Legal Forum:* 139–167.

Crenshaw, Kimberle. 1991. "Mapping the margins: Intersectionality, identity politics, and violence against women of color." *Stanford Law Review* 43: 1241–1299.

Currah, Paisley, Richard M. Juang, and Shannon Price Minter. 2006. "Introduction." In P. Currah, R. M. Juang and S. P. Minter, eds., *Transgender rights.* Minneapolis: University of Minnesota Press, I–XIV.

Dhamoon, Rita. 2009. *Identity/difference politics: How difference is produced and why it matters.* Vancouver: University of British Columbia Press.

Dietz, Mary G. 2003. "Current controversies in feminist theory." *Annual Review of Political Science* 6: 399–431.

Dossa, Parin. 2009. *Racialized bodies, disabling worlds.* Toronto: University of Toronto Press.

Dworkin, Andrea, and Catharine MacKinnon (Eds.). 1997. *In harm's way: The pornography civil right's hearings.* Cambridge, MA: Harvard University Press.

Ehrenreich, Nancy. 2002. "Subordination and symbiosis: Mechanisms of mutual support between subordinating systems." *University of Missouri–Kansas City Law Review* 71: 251–324.

Elshtain, Jean Bethke. 1981. *Public man, private woman: Women in social and political thought.* Princeton, NJ: Princeton University Press.

Ferguson, Michaele L. 2007. "Sharing without knowing: Collective identity in feminist and democratic theory." *Hypatia* 22(4): 30–45.

Firestone, Shulamith. 1997. "The dialectic of sex." In L. Nicholson, ed., *The second wave: A reader in feminist theory.* New York: Routledge, 19–26.

Frankenberg, Ruth. 2000. "White women, race matters: The social construction of whiteness." In L. Back and J. Solomos, eds., *Theories of race and racism: A reader.* London: Routledge, 447–461.

Fraser, Nancy. 1997. *Justice interruptus: Critical reflections on the "postsocialist" condition.* New York: Routledge Press.

Garland-Thomson, Rosemarie. 2002. "Integrating disability, transforming feminist theory." *NWSA Journal* 14(3): 1–32.

Green, Joyce. 2000. "The difference debate: Reducing rights to cultural flavours." *Canadian Journal of Political Science* 33(1): 133–144.

Green, Joyce. 2007. "Taking account of Aboriginal feminism." In J. Green, ed., *Making space for indigenous feminism.* Black Point, Nova Scotia: Fernwood Publishing, 20–32.

Greenberg, Julie A. 2006. "The roads less traveled: The problem with binary sex categories." In P. Currah, R. M. Juang, and S. P. Minter, eds., *Transgender rights.* Minneapolis: University of Minnesota Press, 51–73.

Hancock, Ange-Marie. 2007. "When multiplication doesn't equal quick addition: Examining intersectionality as a research paradigm." *Perspectives on Politics* 5(1): 63–79.

Hankivsky, Olena. 2004. *Social policy and the ethics of care.* Vancouver: UBC Press.

Harding, Sandra. 1986. *The science question in feminism.* Ithaca, NY: Cornell University Press.

Hartmann, Heidi. 1997. "The unhappy marriage of Marxism and feminism." In L. Nicholson, ed., *The second wave: A reader in feminist theory.* New York: Routledge, 97–122.

Hawkesworth, Mary. 1997. "Confounding gender." *Signs* 22(3): 649–685.

Hawkesworth, Mary. 2005. "Engendering political science: An immodest proposal." *Politics & Gender* 1(1): 141–156.

Hawkesworth, Mary. 2006. *Feminist inquiry: From political conviction to methodological innovation.* New Brunswick, NJ: Rutgers University Press.

Heng, Geraldine. 1997. "'A great way to fly': Nationalism, the state & varieties of third world feminism." In M. J. Alexander and C. T. Mohanty, eds., *Feminist genealogies, colonial legacies, democratic futures.* New York: Routledge, 35–45.

Heywood, Leslie, and Jennifer Drake. 1997. "Introduction." In L. Heywood and J. Drake, eds., *Third wave agenda: Being feminist, doing feminism*. Minneapolis: University of Minnesota Press, 1–20.

hooks, bell. 2000. *Feminist theory: From margin to center*. Boston: South End Press.

Iman, Ayesha M. 1997. "The dynamic of winning: An analysis of women in Nigeria." In M. J. Alexander and C. T. Mohanty, eds., *Feminist genealogies, colonial legacies, democratic futures*. New York: Routledge, 280–307.

Jackson, Stevi, Liu Jieyu, and Woo Juhyun. 2008. "Introduction." In S. Jackson, L. Jieyu and W. Juhyun, eds., *East Asian sexualities: Modernity, gender, and new sexual cultures*. New York: Zed Books, 1–32.

Kahane, David. 1998. "Male feminism as oxymoron." In T. Digby, ed., *Men doing feminism*. New York: Routledge, 213–236.

Kawar, Amal. 1996. *Daughters of Palestine: Leading women of the Palestinian national movement*. Albany: State University of New York Press.

King, Deborah K. 1988. "Multiple jeopardy, multiple consciousness: The context of a black feminist ideology." *Signs* 14(1): 42–72.

Kirkness, Verna. 1987–88. "Emerging native women." *Canadian Journal of Women and Law* 2(2): 408–415.

Lang, Sabine. 1998. *Men as women, women as men: Changing gender in Native American cultures*. Trans. J. L. Vantine. Austin: University of Texas Press.

Lawrence, Bonita, and Enakshi Dua. 2005. "Decolonizing antiracism." *Social Justice* 32(4): 120–143.

Li, Xiaojiang. 1989. *Xinggou [sex gap]*. Beijing: Sanlian Press.

Lorde, Audre. 1984. *Sister outsider*. New York: Crossing Press.

Matsuda, Mari J. 1992. "When the first quail calls: Multiple consciousness as juriprudential method." *Women's Rights Law Reporter* 14: 297–300.

McIntosh, Peggy. 1995. "White privilege and male privilege: A personal account of coming to see correspondence through work in women's studies." In M. Anderson and P. H. Collins, eds., *Race, class and gender: An anthology*. London: Wadsworth Publishing Co, 70–81.

Mies, Maria, and Vandava Shiva. 2005. *Ecofeminism*. Halifax: Fernwood Publications.

Mill, John Stuart. [1869]1999. *The subjection of women*. Pennsylvania: The Pennsylvania State University.

Millet, Kate. 1970. *Sexual politics*. New York: Doubleday.

Mohanty, Chandra Talpade. 2003. *Feminism without borders: Decolonizing theory, practicing solidarity*. Durham, NC: Duke University Press.

Moraga, Cherrie. 1981. "Chicana feminism as 'theory in the flesh'." In C. Moraga and G. Anzaldua, eds., *This bridge called my back: Writings by radical women of colour*. San Francisco: Aunt Lute Press.

Namaste, Viviane. 2005. *Sex change, social change: Reflections on identity, institutions, and imperialism*. Toronto: Women's Press.

Noble, Jean Bobby. 2006. *Sons of the movement: FtM's risking incoherence on a post-queer cultural landscape*. Toronto: Women's Press.

Nussbaum, Martha. 2000. *Women and human development: The human capabilities approach*. Cambridge: Cambridge University Press.

Okin, Susan Moller. 1979. *Women in Western political thought*. Princeton, NJ: Princeton University Press.

Okin, Susan Moller. 1989. *Justice, gender and the family*. New York: Basic Books.

Okin, Susan Moller. 1999. "Is multiculturalism bad for women?" In J. Cohen, M. Howard, and M. C. Nussbaum, eds., *Is multiculturalism bad for women?*. Princeton, NJ: Princeton University Press, 7–25.

Pateman, Carole. 1988. *The sexual contract*. Stanford, CA: Stanford University Press.

Phillips, Anne, and Moira Dustin. 2004. "UK initiatives on forced marriage: Regulation, dialogue and exit." *Political Studies* 52(3): 531–551.

Phoenix, Ann, and Pamela Pattynama. 2006. "Editorial." *European Journal of Women's Studies* 13(3): 187–192.

Puar, Jasbir. 2007. *Terrorist assemblages: Homonationalism in queer times*. Durham, NC: Duke University Press.

Razack, Sherene. 1998. *Looking white people in the eye: Gender, race, and culture in courtrooms and classrooms*. Toronto: University of Toronto Press.

Razack, Sherene. 2008. *Casting out: The eviction of Muslims from Western law and politics*. Toronto: University of Toronto Press.

Rege, Sharmila (Ed.). 2006. *Writing caste/writing gender: Narrating Dalit women's testimonies*. New Delhi: Zubaan Books.

Ress, Mary Judith. 2006. *Ecofeminism in Latin America*. New York: Orbis Books.

Sandoval, Chela. 2000. *Methodology of the oppressed*. Minneapolis: University of Minnesota.

Schaefer, Carol. 2006. *Grandmothers counsel the world: Women elders offer their vision for our planet*. Boston: Trumpter.

Shiva, Vandana. 1989. *Staying alive: Women, ecology & development*. London: Zed Books Ltd.

Simien, Evelyn M. 2006. *Black feminist voices in politics*. Albany: State University of New York Press.

Smith, Andrea. 2005. "Native American feminism, sovereignty, and social change." *Feminist Studies* 31(1): 116–132.

Smith, Andrea. 2006. "Heteropatriarchy and the three pillars of white supremacy." In Incite!, ed., *Color of violence: the incite! anthology*. Cambridge, MA: South End Press, 68–73.

Smith, Linda Tuhiwai. 1999. *Decolonising methodologies: Research and indigneous peoples*. London: Zed Books Ltd.

Snyder, R. Claire. 2008. "What is third-wave feminism? A new directions essay." *Signs* 34(1): 175–196.

Song, Sarah. 2007. *Justice, gender, and the politics of multiculturalism*. Cambridge, UK: Cambridge University Press.

Spivak, Gayatri Chakravorty. 1988. "Can the subaltern speak?" In C. Nelson and L. Grossberg, eds., *Marxism and the interpretation of culture*. Urbana: University of Illinois Press, 271–315.

Stryker, Susan. 2008. *Transgender history*. Berkeley, CA: Seal Press.

Suzack, Cheryl and Shari Huhndorf, Jeanne Perreault and Jean Barman. 2011. *Indigenous Women and Feminism: Politics, Activism, Culture*. Vancouver: UBC Press.

Tharu, Susie, and K. Lalita (Eds.). 1991. *Women writing in India volume 1: 600 BC to the early twentieth century*. Oxford: Oxford University Press.

Thobani, Sunera. 2007. *Exalted subjects: Studies in the making of race and nation in Canada*. Toronto: University of Toronto Press.

Tronto, Joan. 1994. *Moral boundaries: A political argument for an ethic of care*. New York: Routledge.

Valdes, Francisco. 1995. "Sex and race in queer legal culture: Ruminations on identities and inter-connectivities." *California Law Review* 5 (25): 25–71.

Walker, Rebecca (Ed.). 1995. *To be real: Telling the truth and changing the face of feminism.* New York: Anchor Books.

Wollstonecraft, Mary. 1792. *A vindication of the rights of woman with structures on moral and political subjects.* London: Joseph Johnson.

Xu, Feng. 2009. "Chinese feminisms encounter international feminisms: Identity, power and knowledge production." *International Feminist Journal of Politics* 11(2): 196–215.

Young, Iris Marion. 1994. "Gender as seriality: Thinking about women as a social collective." *Signs: A Journal for Women in Culture and Society* 19(3): 713–738.

Yuval-Davis, Nira. 2006. "Intersectionality and feminist politics." *European Journal of Women's Studies* 13(3): 193–209.

Zerilli, Linda. 2006. "Feminist theory and the canon of political thought." In J. S. Dryzek, B. Honig, and A. Phillips, eds., *The Oxford handbook of political theory.* Oxford: Oxford University Press, 106–124.

CHAPTER 4

POWER, POLITICS, DOMINATION, AND OPPRESSION

MOYA LLOYD

IT should come as no surprise to discover that, from the late 1960s onward, second-wave feminists, searching for ways to make sense of women's oppression, turned their attention to the topic of power. Although few feminist writers focused exclusively on power, many more engaged with it as part of their overall discussions. A few of these turned for inspiration to existing conceptualizations of power (Komter 1991; Meyer 1991). Some, however, were more wary, pointing out the limitations of such conceptualizations from the perspective of gender (Elshtain 1992). Others concentrated, instead, on producing alternative theorizations of power more applicable to women's lives. These alternative theorizations were themselves frequently the subject of criticism within feminism, leading either to their modification or refinement or, just as commonly, to the development of alternative and, arguably, more nuanced accounts of power. One feature that many feminist accounts of power share, however, is the conviction that power and gender are interrelated. Although some writers limited themselves to examining power's operations on women, partly as a result of changing considerations within feminism (to do with how best to address the differences between women) and partly because of the development of the fields of sexuality studies and men's studies, increasingly attention shifted toward a concern with gender relations in the widest sense (incorporating femininities and masculinities in the plural). Multiple ways of understanding difference, sexuality and gender, for example, through the lens of intersectionality, have all had an important impact (for further discussions of sexuality, gender, and intersectionality, see the chapters by Hawkesworth, Collins and Valerie Chepp, and Lind in this volume). The net result of all of this is that there is no single, unified, feminist, or gendered theory of power but simply a number of different currents, four of which will be sketched in this chapter.

The first, normally advanced by liberal feminists treats power as a resource that is unequally distributed throughout society, with men the primary beneficiaries of this uneven distribution. The second approach, associated mostly with radical and materialist feminism, focuses specifically on men's power over women. It is notable for introducing the concept of patriarchy to denote a system of male power and for conceptualizing power as domination. Certain versions of this account are important in an additional way: they introduce the idea that men and women understand power in different ways. This leads to the third position covered in this chapter, again mainly connected with radical and materialist feminisms: the notion of a specifically female, if not feminist, understanding of power as *capacity* (sometimes referred to as *power to* or *empowerment*, though care needs to be taken with the usage of the latter term in particular). The final understanding of power considered here is that of power as *productive*. Taken up by those with a particular interest in gender, here gender in its multiple forms and, in some cases, sex and sexuality are argued to be effects of power.[1]

Power as "Resource"

"The words women have chosen to express their condition—inequality, oppression, subordination—all have their implications," writes Anne Phillips (1987, 2), "for each carries its own version of the problem it describes." Each, we might add, also has implications for the understanding of power it deploys. The language of inequality is typically associated with liberal feminism, where it refers to the claim that women are discriminated against on the basis of their sex. The kind of equality at stake here is not primarily formal equality (women's equal rights with men) but rather equality of opportunity. (Like most liberals, liberal feminists usually assume that some inequality of outcome is inevitable in society, given individual differences in ability, talent, and application.) Liberal feminism's concern is that women's opportunities to succeed (as individual women) are impeded by particular barriers or restrictions that limit their access to the freedoms, institutions, resources, goods, and, in some cases, rights that men have. This produces inequality and discrimination and is where power becomes relevant.

A particular problem with attempting to evaluate liberal feminist conceptions of power is that they are often implied rather than made explicit. Amy Allen (2005, n.p.) suggests, however, that some "liberal feminist approaches" to power equate with the idea of *power as resource*. Normally, when writers talk of power as a resource, they mean that power is something people have that enables them either to do things directly or to get others to do things for them. Moreover, power as resource is often tied to questions of distribution or, in some liberal feminist cases, of access to particular (state) institutions.

The link between power and distribution—that power is something men have but women do not—may be seen in the writing of Susan Moller Okin. She notes, "When we look seriously at the distribution between husbands and wives of such critical social goods as...power...we find socially constructed inequalities between them" (1989, 136). This, Okin surmises, is a result of the division of labor in the family that sees women largely responsible for child-rearing and domestic work while men engage in paid work outside the home. The goal of feminist politics, as she sees it, is to eliminate the inequalities that "stem from the division of labour and the resultant division of power within it" (ibid., 168; see also Allen 1999, 9). For liberal feminists like Okin, it is not power per se that is the problem; indeed, Okin calls it a "social good," which suggests that power is generally perceived in gender-neutral terms. Rather, sexual inequality arises from the fact that power is distributed in a way that disadvantages women as a group, without any consideration for the talents, abilities, or desires of individual women.

Okin's (1989) focus, when discussing power, is the family; other liberal feminists, however, focused on different institutions. For many liberal feminists, especially in the early years of second-wave feminism, sex discriminatory legislation—such as past laws restricting women's voting rights and their working hours and excluding them from various forms of employment or limiting their educational options—was one of the main ways (though certainly not the only one) that sexual inequality was perpetuated. To secure equality of opportunity with men, therefore, discriminatory laws needed to be overturned and new legislation (regarding, for instance, sex equality or equal pay) introduced.[2] If women were to be able to determine their own futures in the way men could, then, as Betty Friedan, author of the liberal feminist classic *The Feminine Mystique* (1963), wrote in 1968 (discussing the Equal Rights Amendment) they "need *political power*" (454, emphasis in original), by which Friedan meant access to political institutions (such as national legislatures).

From a feminist perspective, the liberal feminist understanding of power was not particularly innovative: it simply took an existing idea of power (as a resource) and applied it to the case of women. Feminist critics argued that it was also flawed. To understand power as an unequally distributed resource implies that power is something held by individuals or groups. Iris Young, however, suggests that a distinction needs to be drawn between power and resources. Resources such as money, time, or military hardware may be necessary to the exercise of power, but they are not the same as power (Young 1990a, 31; see also Allen 1999, 10). Indeed, for Young, power is not a "thing" at all; rather, and this is what liberal feminism appeared to miss—power is relational (ibid., 31; see also Cooper 1995, 9). Men, that is, do not possess power independently of women. Instead, power consists in the relationship between men and women, a relationship that accords men certain powers over women.

Second, the idea that power was merely poorly diffused was also criticized for overlooking the structural basis of domination: in particular, how relations of domination, in this case between men and women, are constructed and sustained; how specific institutions historically came to be controlled by men rather than women; and how, in short, women's subordination (rather than inequality) has been systematically secured (Hartsock [1983] 1985, 254–255; see also Hartsock 1996; Young 1990a).

Next, as Allen (1999) points out the assumption that sexual inequality could be resolved by a redistribution of power is problematic. If women lack power then "how," she asks, "are they to wield the power needed to change social relationships" (10)? If they are able to alter such relationships, it would suggest they already have power, thus undermining the liberal feminist case that they do not. If, however, it is assumed that women do not possess power and are reliant on legal reform to gain access to it, then as Allen notes, following Anna Yeatman (1997), this leaves liberal feminists in the awkward position of "depending on the state to grant women equal access to power" (11). This has a number of consequences. For Yeatman it results in a conception of *power as protection* that posits women as victims who lack agency (because, that is, they need the help of the state to protect them against men). As Zillah Eisenstein (1986) and others have pointed out, such a view overlooks the involvement of the state in the oppression of women (223). Moreover, "when power is perceived in terms of access to social, economic, or political institutions," such as political power or the state, "other possibilities," Mary Dietz (1998) suggests, "(including the radical one that power has nothing to do with access to institutions at all) are left out" (383).

To try to understand how men were able systematically to oppress women, therefore, an alternative account of power was developed. This is the idea of *power as domination* or *power as coercion* (Yeatman 1997), also known as *power over*. Linking domination (or coercion) to the idea of power over is not itself particularly original; political theorists had already made that connection. It is the association of this understanding of power with the development of some of feminism's most important ideas that is noteworthy.

POWER AS DOMINATION OR POWER OVER

Where power as resource was associated with problems of inequality and discrimination, power as domination describes the problem of women's oppression. It has tended to be deployed predominantly, that is, by those who regard oppression as the result of a system of economic, political, and ideological factors working in tandem to subordinate women.

The main characteristic of this system is that of male domination over women. The concept deployed to describe this phenomenon is patriarchy. Although widely used in radical and materialist feminism, the latter including both socialist and Marxist variants, as well as in some feminist psychoanalysis (Mitchell 1974; see also Beechey 1979), the meaning different writers attach to patriarchy varies. Where most radical feminists focus exclusively on patriarchy as a system of male power, materialist feminists, by contrast, are more interested in the relationship between patriarchy and capitalism (as a mode of production) and its class relations. What all share, however, is a sense that the theory of patriarchy can usefully illuminate the basis of women's subordination as women.

In *Sexual Politics*, Kate Millett (1977) offers one of the first systematic accounts of women's oppression. "Sexual dominion," she argues, is "perhaps the most pervasive ideology of our culture and provides its most fundamental concept of power" (25), men's dominion over women, which Millett represents as the primary and most fundamental form of oppression in existence. The evidence that contemporary society is a patriarchy can be seen, she argues, in the fact that "the military, industry, technology, universities, science, political office, and finance—in short every avenue of power within the society, including the coercive force of the police, is entirely in male hands" (25). Since politics is concerned with power, patriarchy as a system of power is political through and through. Moreover, for all its local variation, patriarchy is a universal phenomenon with a wide range of tools at its disposal: an ideology of male supremacy that governs how the sexes are socialized (males to aggression, force, and efficacy and females to passivity, virtue, and obedience); the family, patriarchy's basic unit of government under the rule of a male head, which operates as one of the main sites of such socialization; economically, through women's unpaid labor; the use of force and intimidation (including forms of sexual violence) to keep women in their place; and the work that myth and religion do in perpetuating the idea of women's inferiority (ibid.).

Patriarchal power is conceptualized by Millett (1977) as dyadic, based on a relationship of domination (power over) and subordination, with men ranged on the former side and women on the latter. This dyadic, relational view is echoed by the authors (one of whom was Shulamith Firestone) of the *Redstockings Manifesto* (1969), who observe that "all power structures throughout history have been male-dominated and male oriented. Men...have used their power to keep women in an inferior position...*All men* have oppressed women" (127). Likewise, in *Feminism Unmodified*, Catharine MacKinnon (1987) stresses the dualistic nature of patriarchal power, noting that the "social relation between the sexes is organized so that men may dominate and women must submit (3)," speculating later on in the book that "power/powerlessness *is* the sex difference" (123, emphasis in original).

In the *Sexual Contract*, Carole Pateman (1988) contends that the meaning of sexual difference rests on a master–subject model. To be a woman under patriarchy is to be subject sexually to an individual man, who is, in essence, her master. The patriarchal sexual contract thus defines masculinity in terms of freedom, domination, and command while defining femininity in terms of subjection, subordination, and obedience. Importantly for Pateman, evidence of the sexual contract not only may be discerned in the writings of the classic social contract theorists (Thomas Hobbes, John Locke, and Jean-Jacques Rousseau) or their modern-day contemporaries (John Rawls) but also underpins all contractual relations, including marriage, prostitution, surrogacy, and wage labor, all of which Pateman reads as entailing subordination understood, as Nancy Fraser (1993, 174) observes, as "subjection to a master's command."

Although Millett's (1977) account of patriarchy was widely lauded for detailing the systematic nature of women's oppression, she was (rightly or wrongly) criticized for failing to identify the origins of the relations of subordination and domination she describes (Beechey 1979, 69). Other writers, however, in different ways, did precisely that. Pateman (1988, 2), for example, argues that patriarchy originates out of a social-sexual contract that establishes what she calls, following Adrienne Rich (1980), the "law of male sex-right." This both inaugurates men's political right over women and allows them regulated access to their bodies (through, for instance, conjugal rights). Firestone (1970, 19), by contrast, suggests that the "sex class system derives from "the natural reproductive difference between the sexes"; in particular, from women's biology (menstruation, pregnancy, childbirth, and care of infants) that, prior to the introduction of birth control, rendered them reliant on men for their physical survival. Marilyn French (1985, 1994) posits that patriarchy emerged initially as a means to ensure community survival, when in response to an expanding population and food shortages, man invented horticulture; as a system of male dominance, however, patriarchy rests on men's fear of women and their feeling of inadequacy in the face of women's capacity to give birth. Alternatively, Susan Brownmiller (1975) identifies women's physical capacity to be raped as the basis of male power, whereas Juliet Mitchell (1974), in an account that endeavors to link a discussion of patriarchy grounded in psychoanalysis with a Marxist account of capitalism, surmises that male power derives from the exchange of women by men arising from the incest taboo (see also Rubin 1975).

In each case, power is regarded in negative terms—as *domination, coercion,* or *power over*—and not as a benign good or resource as some liberal feminists suggest. Many radical and materialist feminists took the view that power over was, furthermore, an essentially male or virile form of power. Take, for instance, MacKinnon (1987, 53), who in an interview suggests that in a male-dominated society "female power" is "a contradiction in terms...a misnomer." This is because power, which is "hierarchical...dominant...authoritative," is essentially "male power" (ibid., 52). Although women in a male-dominated society may be able to exercise such power in certain circumstances, the form of power they are exercising, even though they are female, is still male (or patriarchal) power.

Materialist feminist Nancy Hartsock ([1983] 1985) makes a parallel argument in *Money, Sex and Power*, one of the few feminist texts focusing explicitly on power per se. She too suggests that power relations structured by a domination–subordination dynamic are gender specific. This is why for her in a male-dominated society "the gender carried by power" leads to sexual violence, social conflict, death and the control both of other persons and of nature (210) because power over (power as domination) is, quite simply, a masculine form of power. It arises out of the specific life experiences men have; it thus has an historical materialist basis. Where MacKinnon (1987) elects not to pursue the idea of female power, Hartsock suggests that women's "life activity" gives rise to "an alternative tradition" for understanding power: one that rests, as we will see in the next section, on power as "energy, capacity, and potential" (210) and within which lies the possibility of "an understanding of power that points in more liberatory directions" (226) than the current oppressive male variant.

Understanding patriarchal power as systemic and all pervasive has important implications for feminist conceptualizations of politics. One of the most significant developments of second-wave feminism, alongside the concept of patriarchy, was the idea that the personal is political, a formulation that sought to challenge the belief that women's personal problems were private ones by demonstrating instead that they were the direct result of patriarchal power. The essence of politics, Millett (1977) and others contend, is that it is based on power relationships. A political institution, according to this line of reasoning, is "any structured activity that perpetuate[s] male domination" (Grant 1993, 34). As a result, all such institutions constitute appropriate topics both for political analysis (Jaggar 1983, 101) and for feminist action. This includes sexuality (for example, the presumption that heterosexuality is normal), sexual practices (such as prostitution or rape), intimate relations (ideas about sexual intercourse and orgasm), and family life (marriage, child-rearing, and domestic labor)— precisely the issues that concerned women.

Rethinking the nature of politics like this, as essentially about power relations, resonates in a number of ways. It challenges mainstream understandings of politics as focused on the public realm and the institutions (such as state or government) operating there. Instead, it seeks to demonstrate the political nature of a whole "set of experiences—neglected because usually allocated to the domestic realm and defined as private, non-political or even anti-political" (Mansbridge 1998a, 149). It suggests that far from requiring piecemeal reform and a simple redistribution of power, as some liberal feminists have suggested, because patriarchy is a "total system" (Jaggar 1983, 283) women's emancipation requires a more radical or revolutionary political solution to end gender domination, namely, patriarchy's overthrow. At a more mundane level, instead of legal reform, therefore, radical feminists favor direct action, including activities

such as consciousness raising (designed to counter patriarchal ideology), demonstrations, protests against acts of legislation deemed to be oppressive to
women, and the provision of particular forms of support by women for women
(rape crises centers and domestic violence shelters, to name but two).

This approach to power emerged at a time when feminism was specifically concerned with the similarities between women—the experiences or
qualities that all women shared, which separated them from men. Questions
quickly began to be raised, however, about the adequacy of understanding
power in such dichotomous terms and, in particular, about how patriarchy
was being conceptualized. Radical feminists were criticized for their presentation of women's oppression as the primary and most fundamental form of
oppression, particularly since this often meant that other forms of oppression
(racial or class) were treated simply as by-products of it. This, it was charged,
results in a failure to deal with the intersections of class, gender, and racial
oppressions (see Crenshaw 1991). Even though Marxist feminists had always
addressed the question of class (though not race), the dual systems approach
adopted by many of them was nevertheless criticized for treating women's
oppression as arising from "two distinct and relatively autonomous systems"
(Young 1990b, 21), patriarchy and capitalism, rather than from a single system
integrating both.

Objections were also leveled at conceptualizations of patriarchy that presented it as a unified, monolithic system with global reach: operating in essentially the same way at all times and in all places. This, it was charged, failed to
describe women's oppression, the primary criticism being that because earlier
radical and materialist feminists based their analyses on their own experiences
as middle-class white women (a process sometimes labeled *white solipsism*)
they were inattentive to the impact that race, class, and sexuality had on how
oppression was experienced by other groups of women (women of color, lesbians of color, poor women, and so on) (for the classic version of this critique,
see Spelman 1990).

In response, in the 1990s materialist feminists such as Teresa Ebert (1993,
1995) and Rosemary Hennessy (1993) sought to develop more nuanced accounts
of gender oppression, attentive to variations in patriarchy. Ebert (1993, 21) argues
that patriarchy is best conceived of as a "totality in process," unified by the fact
that women are invariably the oppressed sex but internally differentiated as a
result of the level of economic development of a particular society. A woman in
a late capitalist patriarchy will experience oppression in a manner different from
a woman in a feudal state, while within the same context women of different
races and classes will experience their oppression in diverse ways. Nevertheless,
for Ebert and Hennessy, gender oppression appears to remain the most basic
form of oppression, whereas oppression on the basis of race and/or sexuality
are treated as secondary forms of oppression (see Lloyd 2005, 79–83). Possibly
as a consequence of the difficulties of developing an account of patriarchy able
to deal adequately with differences of race, class, and so on, a number of writ-

ers began instead to focus on other ways of understanding gendered power relations, including emphasizing presumptive heterosexuality.

Although understanding power as domination appeared to be an advance over the liberal feminist conception insofar as it appeared to recognize the relationality of power, concerns were raised that the subordination–domination dyad was too simplistic. First, it appeared, once again, to cast women as the passive victims of power. In this case, the "oppressed group model," as Kathleen Jones refers to it (cited in Elshtain 1992, 110), casts women as "uniformly and universally downtrodden, demeaned, infantilized and coerced"; in other words, as "powerless" (ibid.). As such, it fails to recognize the kinds of power, both personal and political, that women have. Not only that, but as Fraser (1993, 180) remarks, focusing on dyadic relations of domination and subordination neglects the "more impersonal structural mechanisms" underpinning "gender inequality" (see also Young 1990a, 31–32), one effect of which is that women are no longer directly under men's control in ways they might once have been historically.

Next, as Jessica Benjamin (1988, 9) points out, understanding power in simple dualistic terms results in a tendency to construe "the problem of domination as a drama of female vulnerability victimized by male aggression." This overlooks women's (psychological) participation in their own submission by failing to examine why individuals (and not just women) submit to authority. It also fails to address a tendency implicit in such approaches, typical of radical feminism, simply to reverse the male–female binary by exalting the feminine, by for instance, valorizing female forms of power over male forms (a theme picked up in the next section).[3]

Furthermore, according to Yeatman (1997), the tendency of feminists to reduce all power to domination and to present domination (or power over) in entirely negative terms, thus as necessarily problematic, disallows the possibility of democratic uses of domination; power over that operates to "extend or even constitute the powers of its subjects" (145). What is needed, therefore, she suggests, is a more nuanced understanding both of power in general and of domination in particular.

While many of the criticisms are concerned with some of the shortcomings of power over as it relates to women or to the relation between men and women, gender theorists and writers such as bell hooks also point to the fact that the operation of patriarchal power vis-à-vis men is more complicated than some feminist accounts assume. Robert (now Raewyn) Connell (1987, 109), for instance, highlights that while "the power structure of gender is the general connection of authority with men" that this association is "immediately complicated" or "partly contradicted" by the "denial of authority to some groups of men." His suggestion that masculinity comes in different forms ("hegemonic," "conservative," and "subordinated"; Connell 1987, 110) complicates not only how patriarchy is understood but also the assumption that it operates dyadically: that men dominate and women are subordinated.

The term *hegemony* derives from the work of Antonio Gramsci, the Italian Marxist thinker, where it is used to refer, as Connell (1995, 77) puts it, "to the cultural dynamic by which a group claims and sustains a leading position in social life." *Hegemonic masculinity*, therefore, is the form of masculinity that is culturally privileged at any one time. In particular, it refers to the set of practices, not just roles or identities, that helps to perpetuate men's dominance over women (Connell and Messerschmidt 2005, 832). Importantly, hegemonic masculinity applies not only to gender hierarchies between men and women but also to hierarchical relations between groups of men, for instance, the cultural ascendancy of heterosexual men over gay men or of white males over black males. In this respect, this understanding of masculinity converges with the views of feminists of color such as bell hooks about how issues of race and class impact differentially on the experience of men, not all of whom are in the same privileged position of power as white, middle-class, heterosexual men. (For criticisms of the concept of hegemonic masculinity, see Whitehead 2002, 92–93.)

POWER AS CAPACITY OR POWER TO

One of the limitations of understanding power as domination or power over for some feminists was, as already noted, that it led to women being perpetually characterized as powerless. Reacting to this, feminists from across the theoretical spectrum, but particularly radical and lesbian feminists, began to elaborate distinctively female or feminist theories of power to counterbalance the masculinist or virile form of power as domination that underpinned this claim. Their diversity aside, what these accounts generally share is an understanding of female or feminist power as the capacity to act, a form of *power to*; this is often regarded as a superior creative form of power to the destructive power over (see, for instance, French 1985, 1994).

Two of the first women writers to differentiate power as capacity from power as domination, according to Allen (2005), were organizational theorist Mary Parker Follett, whose ideas on power directly shaped the thinking of philosopher Dorothy Emmet (1953–4), and political theorist Hannah Arendt. Follett ([1925] 1942) distinguishes between a noncoercive form of power (power with) and a coercive form (power over),[4] while Arendt (1958, 1970) redefines power away from its association with domination and violence to power as action in concert. Both thus shift the emphasis away from a conflict-based model of power, where particular persons or groups hold power over others, toward what Follett ([1925] 1942) helpfully describes as coactive power or what might be thought of as a community-based model of empowerment. According to Hartsock ([1983] 1985, chapter 9), knowingly or not, writers such as Arendt and Emmet—she makes no mention of Follett in this respect—are articulating what she calls "an alternative tradition" of power, a female or "woman-centred" (Radtke and Stam 1994, 7) theory that stresses an appreciation of power as "energy, capacity, and potential" (Hartsock, 210).[5]

Hartsock ([1983] 1985) explains the appearance of this alternative tradition in terms of the distinctive life experiences that women have compared to men, which means that they understand power differently. Such work is not feminist, however because it is not the product of "the systematic pulling together and working out of the liberatory possibilities present in that experience" (259). A theory of power, for Hartsock, is feminist only when it is the outcome of a critique of "the phallocratic institutions and ideology that constitute the capitalist form of patriarchy" (231). A feminist theory of power, then, is not just power as women understand it currently; for Hartsock, it is power as women understand it once they have undergone a process of consciousness raising that enables them to see beneath the surface operations of patriarchy to its inner workings. It is thus a theory of power that has an epistemological dimension. (Hartsock refers to this as a standpoint epistemology.)

The particular life experiences that Hartsock regards as pivotal to a feminist conceptualization of power center on the sexual division of labor and relate in particular to activities of subsistence and reproduction. Other advocates of feminist theories of power stress different experiences: several focus on either women's capacity for birth (French, 1985, 1994) or their experiences of mothering (Rich 1977; Ruddick 1990; Elshtain 1981). For instance, Virginia Held (1993, 136) argues against assuming that political life must be organized around "men's conception of power," preferring instead to focus on more developmental approaches (175), such as that encapsulated in the relation between "mothering parent" and child and where the "mothering person seeks to empower the child to act responsibly" (209; see also Mansbridge 1998a, 149).

This association of mothering with empowerment is also alluded to by Lisa Leghorn and Katherine Parker, who construe "matriarchal" power as having "more to do with creativity and cooperation, the power to change that comes from the caring for others" (cited in Douglas 1990, 224) than with control or coercion. As critics have pointed out, however, matriarchal power does not necessarily suggest a nondominative form of power since the word *matriarchy* actually implies rule by mothers (ibid.), which might logically entail a form of power over (see also Allen 1999, 21–23). Even though not tying empowerment directly to the experience of mothering, radical and lesbian feminists such as Mary Daly (1978, 1984), Marilyn French (1985), and Sarah Lucia Hoagland (1988) have also been keen to stress female power's creative rather than privative dimensions.

The idea of women's power as power to is also advanced by the feminist psychologist Jean Baker Miller. Power, she argues in *Towards a New Psychology of Women*, has conventionally implied "the ability to advance oneself and, simultaneously, to control, limit, and, if possible, destroy the power of others." It has thus entailed two aspects: "power *for* oneself and power *over* others" (Miller 1986, 116, emphasis in original). This traditionally has presented a problem for women who "do not come from a background of membership in a group that believed it needed subordinates" (ibid.) and thus have struggled to exercise power competitively over others. In practice, women's ways of operating have tended toward greater cooperation with others. As such, Miller concludes, women do not need power that hinders the development of others; power that contributes to the maintenance of a "dominant–subordinate" system (117). They need, rather, "the power to make full development possible" (ibid.). In later work, Miller (2008) extends her discussion by clarifying what she means by power to—namely, "the ability to make a change in any situation, large or small, i.e. the ability to move anything from point A to point B without the connotation of restricting or forcing anyone else" (147). This is a mode of power with the potential, she speculates, to entail "mutual empowerment" whereby people other than oneself are simultaneously empowered by a particular course of action.

Although Miller (2008) emphasizes the appropriateness of power to for women, unlike some other feminist writers, she appears not to regard power over as an exclusively masculine form of power. Rather, power over, she observes, usually results from a structural situation where a particular group has greater resources and privileges and, consequently, is able to force or control another. To illustrate, she gives the example of the African American woman supervisor who in the workplace is able to exert power over a white male worker (147) as a function of her structural situation but who does not have this power outside that context. By implication, she suggests also, that power to may be the form of power needed by all those in subordinate positions, not only women.

Anglo-American feminists were not alone in repudiating the idea of masculine or "phallic" forms of power, however; so did French feminist writers Hélène Cixous and Luce Irigaray. Cixous, for instance, distinguishes between power understood as "the will to supremacy," which is always a "power over others" and one that she rejects as despotic, and a more heterogeneous notion of "woman's powers," defined as "a *question of power over oneself*" (cited in Moi 1985, 125). Likewise, Irigaray (1985), discussing what is necessary for a women's politics, notes that when women merely seek a redistribution of existing power (perhaps of the sort envisaged by liberal feminists) they not only leave the "power structure" intact but also "resubject…themselves, deliberately or not, to a phallocratic order," one that is where "power of the masculine type" prevails (81; see also 135). This possibly suggests that Irigaray also envisages if not a form of feminine power then at least a transformed understanding of power (Allen 2005; for an alternative reading see Moi 1985, 148).

One of the issues arising from such accounts is precisely what is meant by empowerment since this is often taken to be a consequence of power to or power as capacity. Iris Young (1994) suggests two alternatives. The first focuses on the development of *individual* autonomy, confidence, and self-control in the context of "caring and supportive relationships" (49). This resonates not just with Miller's sense of power for oneself (power as enhancing the possibilities of self-development) but also with, for instance, Held's (1993) ideas about "mothering" as a way to empower others.

The second alternative is that empowerment refers to "the development of a sense of collective influence over the social conditions of one's life" (Young 1994, 48). It entails individuals engaging with others, who are similarly situated, to identify (via a practice like consciousness raising) both why they are oppressed and what they need to do to act *collectively* to change matters. This form of empowerment thus involves dialogue with others, setting up or joining organizations to bring about social change, and group solidarity that results from working collectively; it is thus a more recognizably political and democratic form of empowerment than is the first more therapeutic version. It is perhaps in this sense that Radtke and Stam (1994, 7) talk of power as capacity as representing women as "active participants in their social world."

Particularly for radical and lesbian feminists, and particularly in the earlier years of the women's movement, enabling the transformative, life-affirming power of women to flourish required a radical political solution: separatism—separate communities, that is, for women and for men. For some of them, women-only spaces or organizations (parties, women's groups) were sufficient to satisfy this requirement since this is where women would be able to learn collectively how to empower themselves; others, however, favored separation from men in all aspects of life, whether as an interim measure before integration with men in a society where sex differentiation no longer occurs (the kind of androgynous society envisioned by Millett, for instance) or as a longer-term, even permanent solution (see Douglas 1990 for further discussion).

To construe power as a capacity, however, is not necessarily to conceptualize it in nondyadic terms. Instead of (male) domination versus (female) subordination, in this instance, the operative dyad is usually male power (power over) versus female power (power to). Nor is the representation of female power as creative, life affirming, and unequivocally of benefit to others (be that the wider community, other women, or children) necessarily any less monolithic a conceptualization of power than the accounts of patriarchal power considered in the previous section. They were criticized for failing to acknowledge the power differentials between men and for not addressing questions of race and class. Here the criticism is that assuming that the power exercised by women is power to masks the fact that some women (as Miller (2008) observes), in certain circumstances, are structurally positioned to exert power over others (including men). As bell hooks (1989, 20) puts it, the observation that men have greater authority than women, although significant, "should not obscure the reality that women can and do participate in politics of domination, as perpetrators as well as victims—that we dominate and are dominated." This reality needs to be recognized, she continues, if women are to "assume responsibility for transforming ourselves and our society" (ibid.; see also Elshtain 1981).

None of the previous accounts of power, however, satisfied the increasing number of writers who were convinced that power operates in a more differentiated fashion. The final version of power explored in this chapter, therefore, is one that focuses less on gendered forms of power than on the role power relations play in producing and regulating gendered subjects—power, in other words, that genders.

POWER AS PRODUCTIVE

An understanding of the link between gender and power is undeniably central to feminist concepts of patriarchy and of power as capacity; however, the focal point of feminist writings tends to be on the impact of patriarchy on women. Little attention is paid, by contrast, to questions of men and masculinity per se. Within the gay liberation movement, as Connell (2009, 77) notes, writers have been exploring such questions; in particular, they have been concerned with how gay men are oppressed, an argument that Connell suggests "laid the foundation for the analysis of gendered power relations among men" (ibid.).

Connell's (1987) book *Gender and Power* has done much to extend the way that gender is conceptualized by emphasizing the existence of plural gender identities. This includes both different forms of masculinity as well as "emphasized femininity"—"the pattern of femininity which is given the most cultural and ideological support at present" (187)—and other forms of femininity marginalized by it. The point for Connell is that although social power is concentrated in male hands, not all men benefit from this in the same way, for hegemonic masculinity is constructed not only in relation to women but, as we saw already, also in relation to subordinate forms of masculinity.

Importantly too, for Connell (1987), gender relations are historically specific and variable. At any one time, different forms of masculinity will be vying for ascendancy (i.e., to become hegemonic); changes in the balance of forces between different groups or different ideals will produce a shift in gender patterns, as might challenges to the hegemonic form of masculinity by particular groups (male or female).[6] Moreover, although most institutions (from the family to the state) are affected by gender relations, the degree of their importance within those institutions will vary. So the "gender order," as it is called by Connell, defines possibilities for action. Connell's approach to power is, consequently, a practice-based one. It focuses on what people do by way of producing the gendered social relations they inhabit, such as attempting to attain an idealized sense of masculinity by participating in competitive sport (85). What individuals do is not chosen entirely voluntarily—the gender order sets certain constraints on action—but neither is it fully determined. This is why change in the gender order is possible (see also Connell 2009).

Not only masculinity theorists, however, rejected the accounts of power outlined in earlier sections of this paper; so, too, did feminists, several of whom turned for inspiration to the work of Michel Foucault and in particular to his ideas about the productivity of power and about normalization. In a series of analyses, Foucault identified what he contends are the characteristics of modern power (sometimes described as *disciplinary power* and at other times *capillary power*): it is productive rather than repressive; it "comes from below" rather than being exercised from above; and it "is not something that is acquired, seized or shared" (not a possession or a resource) (Foucault 1978, 94) but rather is exercised throughout the social body (hence his description of it as microphysical). It is, in short, a network of ever-shifting relations. All in all, this is a view of power as productive that challenges many of the assumptions underpinning feminist accounts of domination.

When Foucault (1978) describes power as productive, he means that it generates identities, subject positions, forms of life, and behavioral habits in accordance with particular norms. Within feminism, Susan Bordo (1993) and Sandra Bartky (1988), for instance, draw on Foucault's ideas about the "docile body" (Foucault 1977)—the body constituted by disciplinary power—in their respective explorations of the politics of appearance, specifically, how disciplines such as exercise, diet, and makeup sustain and reproduce the norms of femininity (see also Allen 2005, n.p.).

Unlike forms of (male) control that rest on the use of physical restraint, coercion or terror, women, as Bordo (1993) observes, are "willing (often, enthusiastic) participants in cultural practices [e.g., diet] that objectify and sexualize" them (28). They appear complicit in their subordination. The issue is why. The answer for both Bordo and Bartky (1988) is that power (understood as productive) genders bodies and subjects by shaping women's desires as well as their understanding of what it is to be feminine. It trains them "in docility and obedience to cultural demands" (Bordo, 27). Women, in other words, internalize the norms that define what it is to be feminine and set them to work on themselves. "The woman who checks her makeup half a dozen times a day to see if her foundation has caked," suggests Bartky, or "who, feeling fat, monitors everything she eats, has become…a self-policing subject, a self committed to a relentless self-surveillance" (81; see also Lloyd 1996, 92; Allen 2005, n.p.). There is no need for anyone—male or female—to coerce her into exercising or applying her makeup; knowing she is "under surveillance" (Bartky, 81), she regulates herself.

Perhaps the most influential discussion of this conception of power in relation to gender appears, however, in the work of Judith Butler, particularly in her book *Gender Trouble* (1990). In *Gender and Power*, Connell (1987, 64) comments, "The main reason why it has been difficult to grasp the historicity of gender relations is the persistent assumption that a transhistorical structure is built into gender by the sexual dichotomy of bodies." In other words, although gender might change, sex as a natural entity is unchanging and thus ahistorical.

In *Gender Trouble*, however, Butler proposes that sex, gender, and sexuality are all effects of power and discourse.

Up to this point, feminists had largely operated with the assumption that sex refers to the biological differences between male and female whereas gender refers to the social, cultural, and psychological characteristics ascribed to men and women. What distinguishes Butler's (1990) approach is that she challenges this distinction by contesting the idea that biological sex is a natural category (see also Wittig 1992; Delphy 1993). It is, she argues, actually a gendered category. Gender, that is, is the "discursive/cultural means" though which sex is produced as natural (Butler 1990, 7). Just as for Bordo (1993) and Bartky (1988) there are practices and discourses that constitute femininity, so for Butler there are discourses and practices that constitute binary sex—that produce it as an effect of a set of power relations that establish heterosexuality as the norm.

The heterosexual matrix, as Butler (1990) calls it in *Gender Trouble*, controls the production of sexed and gendered bodies by positing that biological sex (femaleness) naturally gives rise to a gendered identity (femininity), both of which naturally lead to sexual desire for a person of the opposite sex (a male). It thus normalizes heterosexuality. This, in turn, entails certain consequences for those who deviate from these norms: for instance, designating nonheterosexual forms of sexuality as deviant and governing them accordingly (by, say, withholding particular rights that are routinely distributed to heterosexual couples, such as the right to marry); or treating anomalously sexed bodies (for instance, the bodies of those with intersex) as ones in need of "corrective" surgery to "normalize" them (see Butler 2004a). Binary sex, in this sense, "not only functions as a norm, but is part of a regulatory practice that produces the bodies it governs, that is, whose regulatory force is made clear as a kind of productive power" (Butler 1993, 1). Power, in this sense, is not gendered; rather, it genders—and it does so according to certain norms.

A common theme in this literature is that power understood in this way is paradoxical (Bartky 1988; Bordo 1993; Butler 1997; Sawicki 1991), both constraining and enabling. As Cressida Heyes (2007, vi) puts it, "While the normalizing system of gender makes suffering victims of many of us, that's not all it does: it enables capacities and insights that can be recruited back into the service of oppression or turned in a different direction to make use feisty, rebellious, empowered or joyful." Although normalizing power certainly subjects those over whom it is exercised (disciplining and regulating them), at the same time "if, following Foucault, we understand power as *forming* the subject as well...then power," Butler (1997) surmises, "is not simply what we oppose but also, in a strong sense, what we depend on for our existence..." (2). In other words, it is also opens up possibilities. Submitting to power is, thus, the means by which people are subordinated, but it is also the way they are produced as a subject with a particular identity.

As Stephen Whitehead (2002) notes, "The [male] subject is both *subjected to masculinity*," understood as the material and symbolic practices by which it is constituted, "and *endorsed as an individual by masculinity*" (111, emphasis in original). Similarly, as Margaret McLaren (2004, 221) suggests, "The Mothers of the Plaza de Mayo in Argentina used the gender norm of virtuous motherhood to their advantage as a form of resistance," a norm that in other circumstances operated as a constraint. Likewise, the very practices that discipline women's bodies might also enable them to resist. The muscles a woman acquires through exercise might, as Bordo (1993, 28) remarks, empower her to "assert herself more forcefully at work."

Contrary to the assumption made by several critics of Foucault that construing subjects as the effect of power means they are denied agency and are thus unable to challenge the conditions of their subordination, these writers regard political agency as an effect of power and see power relations themselves as open to reconfiguration in ways that might transform or modify them. As such, productive power is not conceptualized in opposition either to freedom or to agency (as it is, for example, with power over). Rather, it is conceived as more ambivalent, giving rise to normative regimes that discriminate between those whose lives are seen to have value (to be livable, as Butler [2004a, 2004b] puts it) and those whose lives do not, as well as opening up possibilities for political contestation.

According to Butler (1990, 1993), the capacity to contest gender norms, in particular, has to do with the performativity of gender: the way particular bodily gestures, acts, and movements produce the effect of a gender identity, with gender, in other words, apprehended as a form of "doing." The man who performs femininity convincingly—by, for instance, dressing and acting like a woman—might in the right circumstances help to denaturalize the idea that biological sex determines gender identity (see Butler 1990, 1993 for her shifting views on drag). Or the lesbian couple that has a child by artificial insemination and sets up home together might begin to contest the heteronormative assumptions underpinning the family—that it requires a heterosexual male, a heterosexual female, and the children they conceive together. Instead of revolution or legislative reform, gender politics here equates with subverting or denaturalizing heteronormativity and with resignifying existing practices. As such, it has been highly influential in the development of queer theory and politics.

The idea that power is productive has not been without criticism. Its advocates intimate that this approach allows for a more fine-grained analysis of the diverse operations of gendered power at the microphysical level through practices such as diet and grooming, the organization of intimate relations, and how people move, gesture, and communicate. There is, however, a difference between claiming that power per se is productive and contending this conception of power is useful for analyzing gendered power relations. The former merely describes a capacity of modern power (that it is constitutive), while the latter (gendered power relations) refers to a particular regime of power, made up of different elements, where (at its simplest) women are subordinate to men. The worry expressed by even sympathetic critics, such as Zillah Eisenstein

(1988, 18), is that although good at illuminating the minute workings of power, a Foucauldian approach "carries deconstruction too far" (see also Hennessy 1993, 21–22). It cannot explain how dispersed manifestations of power connect and support one another in a "hierarchical system" (Eisenstein 1988, 19). Or, as Hartsock (1996, 38) charges, "systematically unequal relations of power ultimately vanish from Foucault's account of power," thus rendering the theory of little use to feminists interested in explicating women's oppression (for an alternative reading see Lloyd 2005).

Most feminist or gender theorists drawn to Foucault's analytic of power, however, tend not to rely exclusively on his work as Hartsock (1996), for example, seems to suggest. Rather, they combine insights drawn from that work with other ideas, be it an account of patriarchal domination (Bartky 1988, Bordo 1993) or the notion of heteronormativity or compulsory heterosexuality (Butler 1990, 1993). It might be suggested, therefore, that they manage to avoid (some of) the previously identified problems. Not all agree, however. Teresa Ebert (1993, 1995) describes all feminist work drawing on Foucauldian analytics of power, including that of Butler, as "ludic" and postpolitical: ludic because, among other things, it overfocuses on the body and, as such, pays insufficient attention to the material reality of oppression (that is, its relation to production); and postpolitical because it emphasizes a plurality of sites of resistance rather than the need for collectively organized sociopolitical transformation. As such, it is also postemancipatory; it denies the possibility of ever emancipating women from their oppression, which makes it an ineffective theory from a feminist perspective.

CONCLUSION

In this chapter, I have set out four broad approaches to power found in feminism and gender studies: power as resource, as domination, as capacity, and as productive. Any such attempt to map feminist or gendered accounts of power, however, encounters a number of difficulties. Firstly, power is a dynamic and evolving field of inquiry within both feminism and gender studies. Many of the accounts surveyed here were responses to particular debates taking place within feminism and elsewhere at a specific historical point in time, as, for instance, was the attempt to generate a more nuanced understanding of patriarchy attentive to issues of intersectionality or the way that power impacted on different groups of men differently. Some, though important historically in terms of how feminist views of power developed (say, the idea of power as resource), no longer feature prominently in current discussions though power itself continues to be very much a "live" concern in debates on sex and gender. Others (for instance, power as both domination and as capacity) have, as

Yeatman (1995, 155) suggests, coexisted somewhat uneasily, even contradictorily, within the same species of feminism.

Second, the sheer volume of material available means that the choice of what has been covered has been necessarily selective. There has been, for instance, relatively little discussion here about how power, as an "institutionalized feature of social life" (Petersen, cited in Locher and Prügl 2001, 115), works through people by situating them in relations of sub- and superordination organized not only around gender but also around class, race, and other axes such as sexuality. Here, as Young (1990a, 31) puts it, men and women may be agents of power without possessing power; this is because power and its attendant privileges are a function of social location or institutional position and not "some kind of stuff that can be traded, exchanged or distributed" (see also Frye 1983; Locher and Prügl 2001).[7] This type of approach is often informed by the view that power is productive. Instead, however, of focusing on the normalizing operations of power, this current concentrates on developing a structural understanding of gendered power relations.

Next, in grouping different accounts together into broad approaches, there is a risk of imposing unwarranted homogeneity onto what are essentially quite diverse positions. This is perhaps most likely to occur when two or more writers use the same term, for example power over, but do so in quite distinctive ways as do MacKinnon (1987), for whom it means an exclusively male form of power, and Miller (2008), for whom it does not. Of course, this problem is only compounded when feminist or gender theoretical discussions of power are examined alongside mainstream political science or political theory approaches where, as in this example, power over has yet other connotations. It is important, therefore, to acknowledge both the differences between approaches and those within them.

Finally, feminist and gender-based discussions of power have often (though not exclusively) operated in isolation from the debates on power taking place within the discipline of politics more broadly. Much of this latter work has centered on conceptualizing power, which has usually entailed, inter alia, the following: identifying the essential features of power, whether, for instance, it should be understood as a relation, disposition, capacity, or possession; examining how it is exercised, whether, for instance, through decision making (Dahl 1961), agenda setting (Bachrach and Baratz 1970), or shaping people's interests (Lukes 1974); classifying the different forms power takes, such as authority, persuasion, and coercion (see, e.g., Wrong 1979); exploring its relation to other concepts, such as autonomy, freedom, and responsibility; and specifying what William Connolly (1983) calls its scope, magnitude, and range. Although feminist accounts of power have not entirely ignored these considerations—as noted already, a few feminists have drawn on such work—on the whole these have not been the primary ones driving second wave feminist inquiries into power. This has meant that important debates in political science and theory relating to power, concerning its relation to freedom or agency for example, have often been overlooked by those working on gender-based or feminist accounts of power, with the result that, potentially at least, these latter theories have been impoverished as a result. The vice versa, of course, is also true: political science and political theory discussions of power have often disregarded debates within feminism and gender studies and with a similar consequence.

NOTES

1. A similar typology of power is offered by Allen (1999, 2005), while alternative typologies are offered by Squires (1999) and Yeatman (1997).
2. Although published in 1983, Alison Jaggar's *Feminist Politics and Human Nature* still offers one of the best discussions both of the central ideas of liberal feminism, including its understanding of discrimination and its limitations.
3. In response to this, Benjamin, drawing on Hegel's idea of the master–slave dialectic as well as on Freudian psychoanalysis, suggests that what is required to understand better what is meant by power as domination is a fully relational—or intersubjective—account of power centered on recognition.
4. It is important to point out, however, that the accounts developed by Arendt and Follett are, in many ways, significantly different from those advanced by the second-wave feminists who are the focus of this section. For a discussion of the place of Follett's work in the development of feminist theories of power see Mansbridge 1998b.
5. The point for Hartsock about the work of Arendt, Emmet, and perhaps by extension Follett, is that they developed understandings of power that were distinct from those of their male counterparts because, crudely put, they were women.
6. For Connell, power is only one of the three structures that determine gender inequality; the other two are labor and cathexis.
7. Locher and Prügl, for instance, develop their discussion in relation to international relations. Frye focuses on oppression.

REFERENCES

Allen, Amy. 1999. *The power of feminist theory.* Boulder, CO: Westview Press.
Allen, Amy. 2005. "Feminist perspectives on power." In Edward N. Zalta, ed., *The Stanford encyclopedia of philosophy (winter 2005 ed.)* . http://plato.stanford.edu/archives/win2005/entries/feminist-power.
Arendt, Hannah. 1958. *The human condition.* Chicago: University of Chicago Press.
Arendt, Hannah. 1970. *On violence.* New York: Harcourt, Inc.
Bachrach, P., and M. S. Baratz. 1970. *Power and poverty: Theory and practice.* New York: Oxford University Press.
Bartky, Sandra Lee. 1988. "Foucault, femininity, and the modernization of patriarchal power." In Irene Diamond and Lee Quinby, eds., *Feminism and Foucault: Reflections on resistance.* Boston: Northeastern Press, 61–86.
Beechey, Veronica. 1979. "On patriarchy." *Feminist Review* 3: 66–82.

Benjamin, Jessica. 1988. *The bonds of love: Psychoanalysis, feminism and the problem of domination.* London: Virago.

Bordo, Susan. 1993. *Unbearable weight: Feminism, Western culture and the body.* Berkeley: University of California Press.

Brownmiller, Susan. 1975. *Against our will: Men, women, and rape.* Harmondsworth, UK: Penguin.

Butler, Judith. 1990. *Gender trouble: Feminism and the subversion of identity.* London: Routledge.

Butler, Judith. 1993. *Bodies that matter: On the discursive limits of "sex."* London: Routledge.

Butler, Judith. 1995. "For a careful reading." In Seyla Benhabib, Judith Butler, Drucilla Cornell, and Nancy Fraser, eds., *Feminist contentions: A philosophical exchange (thinking gender).* London: Routledge, 127–143.

Butler, Judith. 1997. *The psychic life of power: Theories in subjection.* Stanford, CA: Stanford University Press.

Butler, Judith. 2004a. *Undoing gender.* London: Routledge.

Butler, Judith. 2004b. *Precarious life: The powers of mourning and violence.* London: Verso.

Connell, Robert. 1987. *Gender and power.* Oxford: Blackwell.

Connell, Robert. 1995. *Masculinities.* Cambridge, UK: Polity.

Connell, Raewyn. 2009. *Gender,* 2nd ed. Cambridge, UK: Polity.

Connell, Robert, and James Messerschmidt. 2005. "Hegemonic masculinity: Rethinking the concept." *Gender and Society* 19(6): 829–859.

Connolly, William. 1983. *The terms of political discourse,* 2nd ed. Oxford: Martin Robertson and Co. Ltd.

Cooper, Davina. 1995. *Power in struggle: Feminism, sexuality and the state.* Buckingham: Open University Press.

Crenshaw, Kimberle. 1991. "Mapping the margins: Intersectionality, identity politics, and violence against women of color." *Stanford Law Review* 43(6): 1241–1299.

Dahl, Robert. 1961. *Who governs? Democracy and power in an American city.* New Haven, CT: Yale University Press.

Daly, Mary. 1978. *Gyn/ecology: The metaethics of radical feminism.* London: The Women's Press.

Daly, Mary. 1984. *Pure lust: Elemental feminist philosophy.* Boston: Beacon Press.

Delphy, Christine. 1993. "Rethinking sex and gender." *Women's Studies International Forum* 16(1): 1–9.

Dietz, Mary. [1987]1998. "Context is all: Feminism and theories of citizenship." In Anne Phillips, ed., *Feminism and politics.* Oxford: Oxford University Press, 378–400.

Douglas, Carol Anne. 1990. *Love and politics: Radical feminist and lesbian theories.* San Francisco: Ism Press.

Ebert, Teresa. 1993. "Ludic feminism, the body, performance, and labor: Bringing *materialism* back into feminist cultural studies." *Cultural Critique* 23: 5–50.

Ebert, Teresa. 1995. *Ludic feminism and after: Postmodernism, desire and labor in late capitalism.* Michigan: University of Michigan Press.

Eisenstein, Zillah. 1986. *The radical future of liberal feminism.* Boston: Northeastern University Press.

Eisenstein, Zillah. 1988. *The female body and the law.* Berkeley: University of California Press.

Elshtain, Jean Bethke. 1981. *Public man, private woman.* Princeton, NJ: Princeton University Press.

Elshtain, Jean Bethke. 1992. "The power and powerlessness of women." In Gisela
    Bock and Susan James, eds., *Beyond equality and difference: Citizenship, feminist
    politics, female subjectivity.* London: Routledge, 110–125.

Emmet, Dorothy. 1953–4. "The concept of power: The presidential address".
    Proceedings of the Aristotelian Society 54: 1–26.

Firestone, Shulamith. 1970. *The dialectic of sex: The case for feminist revolution.*
    London: The Women's Press.

Follett, Mary Parker. [1925] 1942. "Power". In Henry C. Metcalf and L. Urwick eds.,
    Dynamic administration: The collected papers of Mary Parker Follett. New York:
    Harper, 72–95.

Foucault, Michel. 1977. *Discipline and punish: The birth of the prison.* Trans. Alan
    Sheridan. Harmondsworth, UK: Penguin.

Foucault, Michel. 1978. *History of sexuality,* vol. 1. Trans. Robert Hurley.
    Harmondsworth, UK: Penguin.

Fraser, Nancy. 1993. "Beyond the master/subject model: Reflections on Carole
    Pateman's sexual contract." *Social Text* 37: 173–181.

French, Marilyn. 1985. *Beyond power: On women, men and morals.* New York: Summit
    Books.

French, Marilyn. 1994. "Power/sex." In H. Lorraine Radtke and Henderikus Stam,
    eds., *Power/gender: Social relations in theory and practice.* London: SAGE, 15–35.

Friedan, Betty. 1963. *The feminine mystique.* Harmondsworth, UK: Penguin.

Friedan, Betty. 1968. "Our revolution is unique." In Kenneth M. Dolbeare and Michael
    S. Cummings, eds., *American political thought,* 5th ed. Washington, DC: CQ
    Press, 450–455.

Frye, Marilyn. 1983."Oppression and the use of definition." In Marilyn Frye, ed., *The
    politics of reality: Essays in feminist theory.* New York: Crossing Press, 1–16.

Grant, Judith. 1993. *Fundamental feminism: Contesting the core concepts of feminist
    theory.* New York: Routledge.

Hartsock, Nancy. [1983]1985. *Money, sex and power: Towards a feminist historical
    materialism.* Boston: Northeastern University Press.

Hartsock Nancy. 1996. "Community/sexuality/gender: Rethinking power." In Nancy
    J. Hirschmann and Christine Di Stefano, eds., *Revisioning the political: Feminist
    reconstructions of traditional concepts in Western political theory.* Boulder, CO:
    Westview Press, 27–49.

Held, Virginia. 1993. *Feminist morality: Transforming culture, society and politics.*
    Chicago: University of Chicago Press.

Hennessy, Rosemary. 1993. *Materialist feminism and the politics of discourse.* New York:
    Routledge.

Heyes, Cressida. 2007. *Self-transformations: Foucault, ethics, and normalized bodies.*
    Oxford: Oxford University Press.

Hoagland, Sarah Lucia. 1988. *Lesbian ethics: Toward a new value.* Palo Alto, CA:
    Institute of Lesbian Studies.

hooks, bell. 1989. *Talking back: Thinking feminist—thinking black.* Boston: Sheba
    Feminist Publishers.

Irigaray, Luce. 1985. *The sex which is not one.* New York: Cornell University Press.

Jaggar, Alison. 1983. *Feminist politics and human nature.* Brighton: Harvester
    Wheatsheaf.

Komter, Aafke. 1991. "Gender, power and feminist theory." In Kathy Davis, Monique
    Leijenaar, and Jantine Oldersma, eds., *The gender of power.* Thousand Oaks, CA:
    SAGE, 42–62.

Lloyd, Moya. 1996. "Feminism, aerobics and the politics of the body." *Body and Society* 2(2): 79–98.

Lloyd, Moya. 2005. *Beyond identity politics: Feminism, power and politics.* London: SAGE.

Locher, Birgit, and Elisabeth Prügl. 2001. "Feminism and constructivism: Worlds apart or sharing the middle ground?" *International Studies Quarterly* 45: 111–129.

Lukes, Steven. 1974. *Power: A radical view.* London: Macmillan.

MacKinnon, Catharine. 1987. *Feminism unmodified: Discourses on life and law.* Cambridge, MA: Harvard University Press.

Mansbridge, Jane. 1998a. "Feminism and democracy." In Anne Phillips, ed., *Feminism and politics.* Oxford: Oxford University Press, 142–158.

Mansbridge, Jane. [1918] 1998b. "Mary Parker Follett: Feminist and negotiator. A foreword." In Mary Parker Follett, ed.,, *The new state: Group organization the solution of popular government.* University Park, PA: Penn State University Press, xvii–xxviii.

McLaren, Margaret. 2004. "Foucault and feminism: Power, resistance, freedom." In Dianna Taylor and Karen Vintges, eds., *Feminism and the final Foucault.* Urbana: University of Illinois Press, 214–234.

Meyer, Joan. 1991. "Power and love: Conflicting conceptual schemata." In Kathy Davis, Monique Leijenaar, and Jantine Oldersma, eds., *The gender of power.* Thousand Oaks, CA: SAGE, 21–41.

Miller, Jean Baker. 1986. *Toward a new psychology of women*, 2nd ed. Harmondsworth, UK: Penguin.

Miller, Jean Baker. 2008. "Telling the truth about power." *Women & Therapy* 31(2–4): 145–161.

Millett, Kate. [1970]1977. *Sexual politics.* London: Virago.

Mitchell, Juliet. 1974. *Psychoanalysis and feminism.* London: Allen Lane.

Moi, Toril. 1985. *Sexual/textual politics: Feminist literary theory.* London: Routledge.

Okin, Susan Moller. 1989. *Justice, gender and the family.* New York: Basic Books.

Pateman, Carole. 1988. *The sexual contract.* Cambridge, UK: Polity Press.

Phillips, Anne (Ed.). 1987. *Feminism and equality.* Oxford: Blackwell.

Radtke, H. Lorraine, and Henderikus Stam (Eds.). 1994. *Power/gender: Social relations in theory and practice.* London: SAGE.

"Redstockings manifesto." 1969. In Miriam Schneir, ed., *The vintage book of feminism: The essential writings of the contemporary women's movement.* London: Vintage, 125–129.

Rich, Adrienne. 1977. *Of woman born: Motherhood as experience and institution.* London: Virago.

Rich, Adrienne. 1980. "Compulsory heterosexuality and lesbian experience". *Signs* 5(4): 631–660.

Rubin, Gayle. [1975]1998. "The traffic in women: notes on the 'political economy' of sex." In Julie Rivkin and Michael Ryan, eds., *Literary theory: An anthology.* Oxford: Blackwell, 533–560.

Ruddick, Sara. 1990. *Maternal thinking: Towards a politics of peace.* London: The Women's Press.

Sawicki, Jana. 1991. *Disciplining Foucault.* New York: Routledge.

Spelman, Elizabeth. 1990. *Inessential woman: Problems of exclusion in feminist theory.* London: The Women's Press.

Squires, Judith. 1999. *Gender in political theory.* Cambridge, UK: Polity Press.

Whitehead, Stephen. 2002. *Men and masculinities.* Cambridge, UK: Polity Press.

Wittig, Monique. 1992. *The straight mind and other essays.* Boston: Beacon Press.

Wrong, Dennis. 1979. *Power: Its forms, bases and uses.* Oxford: Basil Blackwell.

Yeatman, Anna. 1997. "Feminism and power." In Mary Lyndon Shanley and Uma Narayan, eds., *Reconstructing political theory: Feminist perspectives.* Cambridge, UK: Polity Press, 144–157.

Young, Iris Marion. 1990a. *Justice and the politics of difference.* Princeton, NJ: Princeton University Press.

Young, Iris Marion. 1990b. *Throwing like a girl and other essays in feminist philosophy and social theory.* Bloomington: Indiana University Press.

Young, Iris Marion. 1994. "Punishment, treatment, empowerment: Three approaches to policy for pregnant addicts." *Feminist Studies* 1: 33–57.

CHAPTER 5

METHODS AND METHODOLOGIES

BROOKE ACKERLY AND
JACQUI TRUE

INTRODUCTION: DEFINING FEMINIST
METHODOLOGY AND METHODS

There are no distinct feminist methodologies or methods for studying gender and politics, but feminist methodological reflection is central to the development of the field of gender and politics. In this chapter we argue that feminist methodology is a process of adapting and refining a whole range of methods for feminist questions and feminist purposes. Although the field is evolving, today this feminist methodological *process*, not any single research design or analytical method, defines feminist approaches to methods in gender and politics. Within this field feminist scholars have adopted and adapted a diverse range of conventional methods from mainstream political studies, other social sciences, and the humanities that are suited to revealing concealed power dynamics. This chapter sets out the research-driven reasons for these methodological developments and illustrates their use across a range of questions in the study of politics and gender.

The word "methodology" has come to be a catchall that includes theoretical approaches to research, research design, approaches to gathering and producing data, and approaches to analyzing data. Therefore, even though the authors of this chapter have a precise understanding of methodology and method, and the relationship between them, we expect the reader of an essay on methods and methodologies to be interested in theoretical approaches to research, research design, approaches to gathering and producing data, and approaches to analyzing data as well.

We roughly follow Sandra Harding (1987), whose definitions have become standard in the field: epistemology is a "theory of knowledge"; a methodology is "a theory and analysis of how research does or should proceed"; and methods are techniques for gathering, producing, and analyzing evidence (2–3). Some methods entail a kind of data, a way of gathering the data, and a way of analyzing the data. Ethnography, grounded theory, and participatory action research are all ways of doing research in which the processes of developing the research question and the techniques for developing and analyzing the data are deeply interdependent. For example, in ethnography the researcher uses observations and interviews over a long period of time to provide a rich mapping of the people, processes, and power dynamics of her subject of study. Other methods of data collection, like interviews, can be analyzed with a range of analytical methods. This chapter is too brief to survey all methods of data collection and analysis. Instead we focus on the methodological demands of the study of gender and politics and how feminist scholars have met these demands in their research.

In a feminist epistemology, "knowledge is power" and therefore research—using any methods—is a political act, whether the researcher understands the politics of her research or not.

As we argue in *Doing Feminist Research* (Ackerly and True 2010b, 6), a *feminist methodology* reflects on the ethical and political import and consequences of the research; this is not a claim that all scholars of gender and politics make. Some would argue like mainstream political scientists that gender and politics research should ultimately be judged by the originality and validity of its findings rather than the process through which they were generated or their normative meaning and impact. From a feminist perspective, methodology is a theoretical approach that does not require a set of lock-step rules for research like a protocol. Rather, it entails a commitment to use, and a process for using, any constellation of methods reflectively and critically. For us, this commitment has four aspects involving attentiveness to (1) unequal power relations, (2) to relationships, (3) to boundaries of inclusion-exclusion and forms of marginalization, and (4) to situating the researcher in the research process.

"Methods" refers to the specific approaches or tools we use to either collect or analyze our data in any given research project. Among feminist scholars of politics and gender we see many methods—some for collecting data such as ethnography, participant observation, semistructured interviews, and survey research—and others for analyzing data such as qualitative comparative analysis, discourse analysis, and statistical analysis. All these methods may be carried out in more or less feminist ways depending on the degree of critical reflection throughout the research process.

In the first part of the chapter we set gender and politics methodologies and methods in the context of the research questions they address. Feminist methodologies are not a political license for using *particular* methods no matter the question. Rather, they guide decisions made at various stages during the research process and provide a rigorous defense of those decisions to academic peers. Such a defense may be more necessary for feminist work because of the explicitly political understanding of theories of knowledge. While all knowledge claims are a form of political power, the feminist scholar makes those claims visible and the subject of research. Some may confuse the feminist desire to be transparent about the politics of research as itself evidence that feminist research is more political than any other knowledge claims. While such confusion may have the effect of rendering less respected explicitly feminist scholarship, this confusion also provides evidence of how difficult it is to attend to theories of knowledge once they have become normalized in academic discourse.

The second part of the chapter reviews feminist theoretical developments and methodological debates that have influenced how we understand feminist methodology as a field. These developments were informed by both the tension with dominant norms in political science research and the concern that some approaches to gender and politics research were not adequately reflective of these norms or of norms that were emerging in feminist research. Through these debates certain camps emerged within feminist research. Thus, in this section we will discuss some of the cleavages among feminist researchers with respect to feminist empiricist, standpoint, and poststructuralist epistemologies that conceive different bases for knowledge claims.

As they worked through these debates, feminists used insights from feminist normative theory in their empirical research. Normative theory has implications for determining not just the particular methods we use, but also how we study gender and politics throughout the research process. We argue that feminist theory provides the conceptual foundation for gender and politics research. Engaging with that feminist theoretical literature, either by challenging or extending it, is part of sound feminist methodology in this field, just as learning from empirical insights is essential to feminist theory (Ackerly 2009). It may be possible to research *aspects* of gender and politics without the guidance of feminist theoretical reflection on research questions, concepts, design, and methods (see Carpenter 2002). However, such research would lack the theoretical resources to connect itself to the collective endeavor of feminist scholarship on politics and gender. Later the chapter introduces three ways of thinking about feminist research that enable empiricists to apply the normative insights of feminist theory to empirical research: (1) a feminist research ethic; (2) gender analysis; and (3) intersectional analysis.

Finally, the chapter discusses some particular methods feminists have used and illustrates their use with examples from gender and politics research. These examples show how feminist scholars face the methodological challenges and decisions involved in researching gender and politics. In our exposition of this chapter we have chosen to emphasize the tools for adopting and adapting various methods rather than providing a more thorough exposition of the full range of methods. This choice reflects our focus on methodology as guiding method. Returning to Harding's (1987) framing definitions we need to be clear about our theory of research in order to adopt and adapt any method appropriately for our research question.

What Are Feminist and Gender and Politics Questions?

Our choice of research question is almost always shaped by the power relations and political considerations in the world within which we research generally and our disciplinary and institutional contexts specifically. In the study of politics, it would be oxymoronic not to consider these politics. For feminist researchers the choice to pursue some research questions over other research questions raises significant ethical and normative issues. Feminists have shown their research interest in the political and economic inequalities within countries that contribute to terrorist mobilization, in the constructions of masculinity in Western and non-Western contexts that contribute to global insecurity, and gender-based violence, not merely state-sanctioned violence (see Bunch 2003; Agathangelou and Ling 2004; Reid and Walker 2005; Kaufman-Osborn 2006; Ackerly and True 2008). Feminists are interested in these topics and in the politics of the relative emphasis of research on certain topics (Enloe 2004; Finnemore and Sikkink 1998).

Attentive to the politics of research, gender and politics researchers often use gender analysis to generate new research questions as well as to interrogate established questions. Feminist-informed researchers are led to analyze how masculinity and femininity shape politics and ask gender-sensitive research questions by observing that something is missing from existing accounts of social and political reality. Sometimes, as Kathleen Dolan (1997, 1998) shows in the U.S. context, the question is about the lack of political support for women candidates. Sometimes the "something" that is missing until recently in political institutions is women themselves (see Childs 2002). In Mala Htun's (2005, 162) words, we engage in "gender analysis because women are not there." Sometimes the something that is missing is an account of the political activity of less powerful political actors such as human rights and other social movement activists (Keck and Sikkink 1998; Eschle and Maiguashca 2010). Given their near historical absence from formal politics, studying women in politics has led to studying the ways in which gender norms and structures constrain political representation and participation and require the development of alternative political strategies and organization across, below, "inside," and "outside" states (McBride-Stetson and Mazur 1995, 2010; Chappell 2002; Weldon 2003; Sawer and Grey 2008).

The study of gender and politics thus seeks to reveal, understand and explain gender inequalities in power within and across states, markets, and civil society. Significant research has involved documenting major gender inequalities in political representation and gender differences in types of political participation (Burns, Schlozman, and Verba 2001). But feminist research has also explored the gendered construction of citizenship, democracy, and security built upon the male-as-norm individual, thus excluding or silencing women's experiences. For example, feminist political scientists and activists alike ask, "Can there be democracy without women?" (Posadskaya 1994; Paxton 2000; Waylen 2007).

Reexamining the coding schemes of the dataset used for the quantitative study of democracy, Pamela Paxton (2000) questions the coding of states without women's suffrage as "democratic." Feminists have also studied the role of women and women's movements in democratization processes using qualitative tools (Baldez 2002; Htun 2003). For example, using combined methods of ethnographic fieldwork, elite interviews, and archival work, Elisabeth Friedman (2000) finds that antiauthoritarian democratization movements opened up opportunities for women's political participation and for getting women's issues on the political agenda, but that democratic transition and consolidation did not create similar opportunities (cf True 2003; Waylen 2007).

Similarly, scholars of gender and international relations (IR) have analyzed violence and conflict from a gender perspective, asking whether international peace and security proffered by states brings security for women as well as men (Tickner 1992; Shepherd 2008; Wibben 2011). These scholars examine the effects of war, military intervention, and peace building on women's agency, rights, and well-being (Caprioli and Douglass 2008; Al-Ali and Pratt 2009; True 2012). Their research contributed to revealing the pervasive and systemic purpose of sexual violence, especially rape, in historical and contemporary warfare because it asked questions about women's security specifically.

In the afore mentioned research questions, the focus is on women, but we can also learn much about key concepts of politics like democracy, war, and nation building starting from "the women question" (see Goldstein 2001). For example, Bina D'Costa's (2006, 2010) study of rape as a weapon of war during the wars of the partition of India and the Independence of Bangladesh reveals the gendered construction of the nation-state during nation-building moments. Lombardo, Meier, and Verloo (2009, 8–9) show how policies designed to increase women's political participation themselves construct gendered representations and concepts of politics. For example, the predominant framing of the issue of gender inequality in European politics as 'women's political under-representation' suffers from the 'benchmarking fallacy' of women in political decision-making. When the dominant focus of a gender equality issue is on increasing women's numerical representation there is a risk of de-politicising the issue, by suggesting that gender equality is a matter of achieving some target figures rather than transforming power relations between men and women. Lombardo et al. ask what happens to the concept of gender equality during processes in which policy actors engage in conceptual disputes to assign meanings to concepts or in discursive activities that have the same effect.

In sum, feminist researchers "open innovative areas of research by asking new questions and reframing old problems" (Ackerly and True 2010b, 60). These create roughly three kinds of methodological dilemmas for researchers corresponding to (1) questions that create new terrain and don't have established methodologies, (2) questions that are related to existing terrain and for which there has been some methodological infrastructure developed, and (3) questions that are relatively more familiar and for which the field has tried and true approaches and methods that can be applied to analyze new data.

In whichever of these terrains a question is developed, feminist study of gender and politics questions makes particular demands on theoretical conceptualization, research design, and methods in part because of the newness of the field in its theoretical development and in terms of the empirical data that has so far been collected. Concepts need to be defined. Definitions need to be operationalized, and these operationalizations need to be measured. New measures need new data. New data may require new forms of analysis to explore new hypotheses and so on. Existing scholarship and methods often enable the exploration of nonfeminist questions or questions about politics that are not attentive to gender. The study of women or of gendered power in this context is not merely a matter of finding or creating an additional data set, which itself may be hard to do (Caprioli 2009; Parisi 2009). It is also a matter of interrogating the models of inquiry, potentially revealing "the normative commitments sustained by established hypotheses" and the modes of studying them (Ackerly and True 2010b, 62).

Feminist research is question-driven research. Consequently, feminists deploy both methods familiar to a broad range of political scientists. They use statistical analysis to study institutions (True and Mintrom 2001), gendered impacts of natural disaster (Neumayer and Plümper 2007), and gender equality and state human rights abuse (Melander 2005). They use elite interviews and archival work to reveal hidden histories of political movements for democracy (Friedman 2000; True 2003) and for voice for marginalized groups within democracy like African American women in the United States (Cole and Guy-Sheftall 2003), war crimes, and nation building (D'Costa 2010).

This broad range of research questions has also pushed gender and politics scholars sometimes to adapt existing methods and sometimes to innovate with tools more common in sociological and anthropological research such as narrative analysis and ethnography (Stern 2005; Wibben 2011). In an example of newly adopted methods for research in IR, Maria Eriksson Baaz and Maria Stern (2009) analyzed the discourses soldiers use to explain the sexualized violence they commit. They found that soldier's justifications for "why do soldiers rape?" were "crafted out of statist norms around heterosexuality and masculinity produced within their society's military institutions and armed forces" (2009: 514). They reveal how militarized masculinities in the Congo are constructed against femininity and use degrading, sexualized images of women (507).

In this section we have focused on the question-driven nature of these challenges. Whether one's research question creates new terrain, expands existing terrain, or asks new questions in familiar terrain, the methodological challenges associated with conceptualization, operationalization, generating data, and analysis must be confronted, and the researcher must address these challenges with theoretically grounded arguments. In the next we discuss selected highlights in the developments and debates in how to do feminist inquiry.

KEY DEVELOPMENTS AND DEBATES

Just as feminist theorists developed different schools of thought depending on the particular puzzles they found most compelling (Jaggar 1983; Tong 1998; Dietz 2003; Chowdhury 2009), feminists methodologists also have had debates about how to do feminist empirical research (Ackerly and Attanasi 2009). But the debates in feminist methodology do not map onto the debates of feminist theorists and instead have their own contours (see Ackerly and True 2010a).

Feminist scholars across social and political sciences in the 1970s analyzed the everyday contexts in which knowledge was generated (Stasz Stoll 1973; Bourque and Grossholtz 1974; Andersen 1975; Elshtain 1975; Rowbotham 1976). On the basis of that detailed analysis they developed a methodological perspective that views the research process as central to any account of feminist research and as itself part of the research findings that should be subject to critical evaluation (Oakley 1972; Bristow and Esper 1984). Thus, from the outset feminist scholars, including scholars of gender and politics, have been attuned to the power and authority to define what is knowledge and the boundaries of fields of knowledge such as politics or political science (Hawkesworth 2006). Early studies analyzed women's subordination in the private sphere juxtaposed to men's dominance of the public sphere of politics and community (Bourque and Grossholtz 1974; Pateman 1988; Okin 1989). Some studies linked that oppression to broader capitalist exploitation of economic inequalities in the context of race (Baker and Cooke 1935) and colonial and postcolonial exploitation (Benería and Sen 1982). These studies exemplified a feminist empiricist epistemology (Harding 1987). While they ranged in theoretical perspectives—from liberalism to Marxist historical materialism—they used analysis, scant statistical data, and their own fieldwork to fill in gaps in mainstream understanding of politics.

By the mid-1980s some feminist sociologists and political scientists began to question an approach that filled in gaps and instead challenged the framing of what was "political." That is, not only was the mainstream field of politics as it was defined incomplete, but the domain of political inquiry was broader than the field had been defining it. Feminist inquiry provoked ontological reflection. An historical material analysis of women's position, inspired by Marxism, revealed a feminist "standpoint" that explained why men and women were differently able to know about women's oppression based on their experience (Hartsock 1983). Observing that women similarly positioned to men did not experience the same privileges as men in those positions—that is, women with the same education as men did not have the same opportunities or that women with the same jobs as men did not have the same salaries—scholars theorized that women and minority women had different knowledge of privilege and power based on the ways their experiences differed in privilege from those of white men (Hill Collins 1990). Feminist standpoint theory starts from the expectation that women's experience of gender oppression is different from men's experience of gender oppression: women experience it as oppression and men experience it as privilege. This theoretical articulation of a standpoint epistemology—a position from which a particular experience of the world provides a different knowledge about oppression—was inspiring and challenging for feminist empiricists.

Although for feminist theorists standpoint epistemology causes all sorts of theoretical problems related to essentializing about the experience of categories of women based on the experiences of some women who are taken to define the category (Mohanty 1992), it presents new and interesting empirically testable hypothesis about how we know. This work was pioneered by feminists in education (Gilligan 1982, Belenky 1986) and generated a lot of methodological controversy. Today the premise seems much less controversial. Martin, Reynolds, and Keith (2002) tried to test whether such a standpoint epistemology—where those who experience oppression, such as women, are more able to recognize oppression of others, including women but also other excluded groups—existed among of U.S. judges and attorneys. Using data collected for the Florida's Gender Bias Study of attorneys and judges, which gathered data in 1988 from attorneys who were members of the Florida Bar and from all Florida judges at the time, they asked "if women and men legal professionals are similarly conscious of gender inequality and similarly observant of the gender-biased processes that produce [gender inequality]" (667). They found that women were aware of having experienced more gender bias than the men and that women and African American men were more able to recognize gender bias experienced by others.

Martin et al. (2002) used familiar statistical techniques to ask a feminist question about how we know about oppression or injustice. This approach requires using existing politicized categories of women and men, white and

African American (in the U.S. context). Another methodological development challenged the usefulness of framing political questions from within such categories as such framing contributes to the normalization of such categories including sex–gender and does not challenge our thinking about them. Postmodern critical scholars of gender and politics challenged the epistemological foundations of the category of woman—that women or women's interests could be uncovered through empirical scientific methods that relied on those same categories (Sapiro 1981; Scott 1992; Sylvester 1994). They argued that the political science discipline had been socially constructed around men's experiences in the public realm and that women could not be merely added to this research agenda (Sapiro 1998). They also questioned the ontological status of women as a group and subject of politics given significant cross-cutting differences among women in terms of race, ethnicity, sexuality, nationality, and so on.

In this section we argued that some feminist empiricists came to the study of gender to explain the absence or marginalization of women from some forms of politics and their presence in other forms of politics. Postmodern methodology turns us to the study of gender rather than women in politics to avoid universalizing women's experiences across different groups and analyze gender in relation to other identity groups or categories of oppression. Both approaches make visible the power relations, which could explain women's marginalization in politics.

Methodological diversity in the field of gender and politics, as we illustrate in the next parts of this chapter, stems from these different feminist epistemologies. However, epistemological differences among scholars of politics and gender are not primarily geographical, generational, or even theoretical. Rather, they are intrinsic to the sociological development of the subfields of political science. For example, in the study of national or comparative politics, the emergence of women representatives and women's movements participating at the level of the state (McBride-Stetson and Mazur ed. 1995, 2010) allowed the empirical field of women and politics to grow using conventional methods, whereas women were all but invisible at the time (Enloe [1989]1990). Feminist theorists draw on qualitative and quantitative data and analysis from other disciplines (Okin 1991; Nussbaum, Glover, and World Institute for Development Economics Research 1995) and their own fieldwork.

The methodological diversity of the gender and politics field can leave a scholar new to the field wondering how to evaluate the methods in any given piece of scholarship (Caprioli 2007). This has been the motivation behind scholarship making explicit feminist methodological principles and guidelines (Ackerly and Attanasi 2009; Ackerly and True 2010b). In the next section, we introduce these foundational tools that can be used across research questions and are useful in adopting and adapting particular methods to a particular research question. In the subsequent section we illustrate those finer particularities.

Broadly Applicable Tools of Methodology and Methods for the Study of Gender and Politics

Given the diversity of feminist questions and theoretical perspectives on the study of gender and politics, it would be a fruitful but long journey to survey all those methodologies and methods that feminists have used. Instead, we discuss these in two ways. We focus on methodologies that feminist scholars of politics have pioneered and that are generally useful across research questions and contexts: a research ethic, gender analysis, and intersectional analysis. The scholarship on these three methodologies is rich. Consequently, feminists can hold each other to account for how well they use these in their research. The first—a feminist research ethic—was developed by us first in international relations to describe and proscribe feminist research practice (Ackerly and True 2006, 2010b) and reflects our broader observations of good feminist scholarship. The other two are methodological tools that are broadly recognized as essential feminist tools and are likewise useful across research questions.

Feminist Research Ethic

The feminist research ethic is foundational to feminist research as a set of methodological guidelines and principles. In *Doing Feminist Research* we argue that it is "a methodological commitment to any set of research practices that reflect on the power of epistemology, boundaries, relationships, and the multiple dimensions of the researcher's location throughout the entirety of the research process..." as well as "to a normative commitment to transforming the social order that is under scrutiny if it is unjust" (Ackerly and True 2010b, 2).

The feminist research ethic requires that we use critical reflection as a work ethic during research. It also guides us to recognize and account for the provisional and contingent nature of data, the necessary construction of knowledge by way of boundaries and categories, and the need to relate to these categories and boundaries in non-essentialist and transformative ways (Ackerly and True 2010b, 2). A feminist research ethic is a background tool that many feminists use as they critically reflect on their decisions made and paths taken throughout their research process. All research into the nature of power can benefit from this feminist methodology of critical reflection. As we study the complex ways in which power works through people and institutions, we also need to consider how power operates through ideas and research practices including one's own. Feminist political scientists are interested in power relations that manifest in daily practice and in the practice of institutions often in covert, hidden ways. These include relations of gender, race, ethnicity, class, empire, neocolonialism, and heteronormativity, which are all forms of power that are able to conceal their own exercise through political, economic, and sociocultural structures. For example, the power of gender and race is such that we do not question the whiteness of a political leader or typically his masculine gender. The next two forms of generally applicable tools we discuss are gender analysis and intersectional analysis. Like a feminist research ethic, these have been developed to illuminate not only the exercise but also the pervasiveness of certain forms of power.

Gender Analysis

"Gender" is the concept that feminists developed to enable us to discuss the political meaning that different communities give to masculinity and femininity. It is often contrasted with sex, which we typically use to refer to the biological attributes of—or differences between—male and female bodies (for further elaboration of the debates around sex, gender, and sexuality see the chapter by Hawkesworth in this volume). The attempt to distinguish gender from sex is a dualism that some feminists have found useful in revealing the sociocultural construction of masculinity and femininity in a wide range of political studies. For example, gender and politics scholars might study the effect of socially constructed gender-biased stereotypes on the evaluation of gay and lesbian candidates for political office in the United States (Doan and Haider-Markel 2010). Gender analysis may also be able to explain why development initiatives fail when they focus on household units without paying attention to the power dynamics and the differences between men and women's allocation of paid and unpaid labor time and their use of resources within households (Dwyer and Bruce 1988; Tinker 1990). For example, in a context in which women are the processors of rice, increased access to credit with which the husband typically purchases unprocessed rice for processing and resale at the market increases the time burden on women (Ackerly 1995, 1997).

As the previous example shows, gender analysis can be used to understand the differences between men and women's experiences of a public policy or political environment. Gender analysis can also be used to show the ways in which the state itself is gendered (Kaplan, Alarcón, and Moallem 1999; Dhruvarajan and Vickers 2002; D'Costa 2010). Gender analysis does not mean that when doing research on gender we re-label the "sex" variable "gender." For some projects, for instance involving demographic census data, this may be the right choice. We cannot assume that it is, and it is never a substitute for gender analysis. Rather, gender analysis forces us to think about the way in which all social and political categories are constructed in relation to gender. In some contexts gender analysis may open up the study of the diversity of meanings of gender across and within race, class, ethnic, national, and sexual categories. Gender and politics researchers need to conceptualize gender in ways meaningful to a given project.

Gender analysis opens up a whole landscape of new research questions for gender and politics and is an important tool for many of the research questions identified in the previous section, including questions about representation, participation, democratization, social movements, state behavior, and global politics. Given the pervasiveness of gender norms and structures across societies, gender as an analytic category can illuminate new areas of inquiry, can frame research questions or puzzles in need of exploration, and can "provide concepts, definitions and hypotheses to guide research" (Hawkesworth 2005, 144). It can also help us to analyze data, observations, and interpretations.

Intersectional Analysis

In U.S. scholarship, black feminist theorists developed intersectional analysis through critical dialogue with antiracist African American men and antisexist white feminists (see the chapter on intersectionality in this volume as well as hooks [1984] 2000; Spelman 1988; Crenshaw 1989, 196; Collins [1990] 1991, 347; Ackerly and McDermott 2012). Intersectional analysis has become a critical way of thinking about political contexts in which multiple forces limit the effectiveness of approaches to injustice that focus on one group category—such as class, race, gender, sexuality, or immigrant status (Ackerly and True 2008). Theoretical work reveals that the familiar ways of grouping humans for activism against oppression and particularly for political analysis of oppression oversimplifies the experience of oppression (Young 1990, 1997). In people's experience, structural forces are complex. Intersectional analyses reveal the complexity of these forces (McCall 2005; Weldon 2006; Yuval-Davis 2006). As Laurel Weldon summarizes the insight of black feminist theorists about the central importance of intersectional analysis: "certain aspects of social inequality, certain social problems and injustices, will not be visible as long as we focus on gender, race and class separately" (Weldon 2006, 239).

Intersectional analysis was first used in US scholarship to reveal the challenges African American women face seeking legal remedy for employment discrimination in the United States (Crenshaw 1989) and racist sexism in other aspects of national and international public policy related to violence against women (Crenshaw 1991). Now it is a tool used to study a broad range of intersecting political dynamics and the injustices underexamined in mainstream political analysis. For example, we have used intersectional analysis to study the ways in which theoretical interests and national hegemonies affect the visibility of critical and feminist international relations scholarship (Ackerly and True 2008). However, scholars need to make sure that our use of intersectionality does not mask the injustices against African American women—or any other particular group—when we apply the tool in other contexts (Alexander-Floyd 2010).

Like a feminist research ethic and gender analysis, intersectional analysis is a tool for guiding thinking. It does not offer specific guidelines. The general guidelines for intersectional analysis are that the researcher identifies the complexity of forces at work in any given context. Attentive to that complexity, the researcher makes choices about how to study it. Reflections on diversity and the complexity of differences of oppression may lead some feminists to advocate intersectional analysis but shy away from doing it themselves. Yet it is important to look for ways in which political forces can function in intersecting ways. In her admiration of the work of D'Costa (2004) and Kavita Panjabi (2005), Elora Chowdhury (2009) argues that feminist scholarship can see similarities in the influence of colonial legacy on women's oppression and therefore women's movements, recognizing the ways in which gender norms, colonial control, and national liberation create the context of South Asian women's struggles (see particularly D'Costa 2010). In this case the scholar is using intersectional analysis to understand the political context of women's activism. However, we could also use intersectional analysis to frame the inquiry. For example, when studying women's human rights activist organizations, Ackerly (2011) asks how do *they* understand the complex intersections of power dynamics—perhaps localized versions of capitalism, patriarchy, and militarism—in the context of their work.

Like a feminist research ethic and gender analysis, intersectional analysis is a tool that can be used in concert with the full range of methods that feminists have adopted and adapted for studying questions of politics and gender. In the next section, we discuss a sample of particular methods in order to illustrate some of these particular adoptions and adaptations.

Methods for the Study of
Gender and Politics

Gender and politics research often uses innovative and nonmainstream methods for collecting and analyzing relevant data (as well as adapting familiar methods) due to the nature of gender and politics research questions, the methodological debates about how best to study them, and the methodological demands of deploying a feminist research ethic, gender analysis, and intersectional analysis. The success of any method depends on the overall research design, which determines the scope and nature of the study, its key concepts or variables, and the relationship between them. For example, gender and politics scholars may use discourse analysis as an approach to scrutinize the patterns and underlying gendered meanings in textual data. But this approach makes sense only within a research design in which discourse is theoretically conceptualized as a social structure relative to other structures and agents and where specific textual forms and examples of these are selected for theoretical reasons. Thus, "discourse analysis" as a method, per se, cannot stand apart from discourse theory as a methodology that foregrounds the power of epistemologies.

The three broadly applicable tools of feminist methodology discussed in the previous section—a feminist research ethic, gender analysis, and intersectional analysis—guide the researcher's adopting and adapting of existing techniques or innovating with new research methods. In this section, we provide some examples of gender and politics research to show how scholars do this. These examples are intended to be illustrative not definitive of feminist inquiry. For expository purposes, we discuss one tool, the interview, that is used across many research designs, and we review two research designs, comparative case studies and inferential statistical studies. Of course, interviews are not the only method for gathering data on gender and politics, just as comparative case studies and inferential statistical studies are not the only research designs. Moreover, the details of how we manage our relationships during the research process—with research collaborators, with the people who help inform our research, and with audiences for example—are just as important for research as reflection about your research design or particular methods. For a more extensive exposition on all of these questions see *Doing Feminist Research in Political and Social Science* (Ackerly and True 2010b).

Using Interview Data in Gender and Politics Research

Research that seeks to explore new puzzles often relies on interviews with key actors. For example, in the study of the rape of Bengali women by Pakistani soldiers during the 1971 Bangladesh War of Independence and the way in which the Bangladesh government treated such rape survivors after the war, D'Costa (2010) interviewed a doctor who conducted abortions after the war as well as women who survived those rapes and abortions. From the perspective of a feminist research ethic, both the doctor and the women interviewees are not "informants"; rather, they are subject-participants. They are "subjects" who provide information or "data;" however, in so doing they also are participants in the research, and as such the researcher must attend to the relationship of the researcher to these people. A feminist research ethic requires the researcher to reflect on her relationships with all those connected to the research (Ackerly and True 2010b: 3, 32, 187, 222). Here we focus on what that reflection looks like when conducting, analyzing, and contextualizing interviews.

Even before the interview, the researcher uses a feminist research ethic, gender analysis, and intersectional analysis to attend to, for example, the power dynamics between researcher and subject-participant, needing to be attentive to what these may mean for how the interview is structured, how the data are stored, what identifying data are collected, and where the interview takes place (for more detail see Ackerly and True 2010b, chapter 12 on methods for data management and field research). To address the power dynamic in the analysis of interview data some gender and politics researchers have adopted narrative analysis that explicitly recognizes the researcher-subject-participant's coconstruction of interview data (e.g., Chin 1998; Stern 2005; Wibben 2011).

Interview data are often analyzed in the context of other data. For example, interview data are often used in studying new or relatively unexplored terrain by focusing on a single case in all of its complexity so as to generate new theoretical hypotheses about the dynamics of such cases that might be relevant to other cases or to related issues. The methods used in single case studies are often multiple, allowing for triangulation of data and sources. For example, Sylvia Tamale (1999) designed a project that enabled her to study the impact of affirmative action policies to promote women's political representation and participation. She chose Uganda, her home country. Although not a liberal democracy, Uganda had a global reputation, or at least a reputation in Africa, for experimenting with such policies in a comprehensive way, including constitutional reform, legislative gender quotas, an institutional policy machinery for women, and support for women's nongovernmental organizations (NGOs) and advocacy.

Tamale (1999) approached this single case study using several qualitative methods including "elite" interviews with female and male legislators, participant observation of parliamentary debates and recording of decisions by gender, committee meetings, and women's caucuses organized for women parliamentarians by women's NGOs; interviews with leaders of prominent women's NGOs and grassroots rural women; and a constituency visit with a prominent woman parliamentarian. With attention to power, boundaries, and relationships, these qualitative field research methods of data collection enabled Tamale to glean from several angles how women political actors conceived of their own empowerment and how they were viewed by their male colleagues in Parliament and other positions of power. She supplemented this data with an extensive gender analysis of historical and contemporary documentary sources such as Hansard, Constituent Assembly proceedings, media reports, as well as a review of secondary literature on women and politics. She did not consider the data generated through her single case study and qualitative methods to be representative of all women's political activity. Rather, she argued, they constituted an "entry point" for mapping the intersections "between gender, class, ethnicity, religion, imperialism and neocolonialism ... especially pertinent for an analysis of gender relations in the African context" (3). In the book of her study *Hens Do Crow*, Tamale was crucially interested in probing the impact of the presence of women in formal politics on broader societal gender equity. Gender analysis enabled her to explore how women political actors might adapt their strategies in a particular social and historical context marked by patriarchal relations.

There are many such cases of "gender quota" reform we could choose to study, but it would be impossible to analyze all of them in any depth without an already worked out theoretical framework to guide such a global or comparative study. The phenomenon Tamale studied is so vast that her Ugandan study can only incrementally build an understanding, contributing to the collective scholarship on gender and politics. Her findings are not representative of the impact of political reforms for women all over the world but rather a piece of the picture, a picture that together gender and politics scholars will fill in over time. The single-case study research design is one way of confronting the challenge of studying a puzzle that has yet to be approached by scholars.

Interviews can be important to such projects, but the single-case research design isn't the only context in which they are useful. We chose to include a discussion of interviews rather than other methods for creating data because interviewing is common to so many research designs.

Comparative Case Study Design in Gender and Politics

When an area of gender and politics inquiry has been opened up, as with the case of gender quotas after Tamale and other's single country studies, it may be possible to generate hypotheses about patterns that we expect to see, following certain conditions or in certain contexts. Questions of patterns across time, conditions, or context cannot be understood by looking at one point in time, one context or one case alone. Questions related to gender differences in political participation, descriptive and substantive representation, leadership, social movement mobilization, questions related to the effect of gender inequalities and differences on policies, institutional or state behavior, and questions related to the relationship between women's movements, the state, and international politics (NGOs and international organizations) generally require exploration across contexts. However, because so many dimensions need to be studied in research on these topics, researchers typically compare a relatively small number of contexts or cases. We say that this is a "small" number of cases relative to the vast number of contexts in which the issue might be explored (McBride-Stetson and Mazur eds. 1995; Ackerly and True 2010b).

Case selection is very important to these projects. Examples include Georgina Waylen's (2007) study of democratic transitions and Laurel Weldon's study of state policies on violence against women (Weldon 2002). We illustrate a version of the methodology with discussion of Mona Lena Krook's (2009) *Quotas for Women in Politics: Gender and Candidate Selection Worldwide.* Having the benefit of Tamale's (1999) and other's single-country case studies of gender quotas, Krook develops a comparative study to build a common theoretical framework explaining the considerable variation worldwide in

both the origins and the impact of such reforms to increase women's political representation. Gender equality in politics is increasingly being advanced
in contexts where women have by no means achieved social and economic
equality with men (such equality is typically seen as a precursor for wom-
en's political empowerment—see following discussion of Tremblay 2007), and
where they experience the intersection of other forms of inequality as well
with respect to ethnicity, religion, neocolonialism, and empire. Krook stresses
the importance of studying these reforms comparatively given their spread
across more than one hundred countries in a relatively short period of time.
First, she asks why quotas are adopted, including why political actors support or oppose quota measures. Second, she questions whether quotas can
affect transformation in the political representation of women or whether
such transformation requires other political and institutional factors to be
present.

Despite the diversity in the origins and the impact of "gender quotas" highlighted by Krook (2009) and other scholars of gender and politics, Krook's comparative case study approach highlights both the specificity within individual
cases and the patterns and international connections across these cases. Her
study accomplishes this through the qualitative comparative analysis method
(QCA) (Ragin 1987). Krook analyzes paired comparisons of country cases where
"similar"—in one of three types of—gender quota reform (reserve seats, party
quotas, and legislative quotas) have been adopted with varying or "most different" outcomes (Pakistan and India, the United Kingdom and Sweden, Argentina
and France). Through this method she is able to identify a combination of key
actors, strategies, and contexts for each type of quota reform that affected the
outcomes of these reforms. These factors not only explain which quotas are
successful, and in what context, in increasing women's political representation,
but also allow us to deduce some policy prescriptions for expanding women's
political representation taking into account different political, institutional, and
historical contexts.

The comparative method and design allow Mona Lena Krook (2010) to
challenge dominant gender and politics theories, particularly those aimed
solely at domestic politics explanations for changes to political representation. They also allow her to seek out new theories including theories of
transnational politics and diffusion to understand cross-national patterns
of gender quota adoption and change (cf. True and Mintrom 2001; Paxton,
Hughes, and Green 2006). While qualitative comparative analysis is cross-
national in this study, it can also be used longitudinally, across time, as in the
Research Network on Gender Politics and the State project that analyzes the
relationship between women's policy machinery and women's movements in
seventeen postindustrial democracies across five policy areas from the 1970s
to the 2000s (Mazur 2001; Stetson 2001; Outshoorn 2004; Lovenduski 2005;
Haussman and Sawer 2007).

Inferential Statistical Methods in Gender and Politics

Where data are available, some gender and politics questions can be analyzed with inferential statistics (Apodaca 2009; Caprioli 2009; Parisi 2009). Manon Tremblay's (2007) study of women's political representation in democracies is an example of causal inference using feminist-informed statistical analysis. She draws inferences between the proportion of women in parliament and a range of factors theoretically assumed to have a causal effect on this proportion importantly the length of the democratic experiment, the voting system (proportional or majoritarian), the presence of gender quotas, attitudes to gender equality, the term limits of the legislature, and the number of political parties. Based on multiple regression analyses that test the causal impact of each factor controlling for the effects of the contending factors (or counterarguments), Tremblay infers the causes of women's political representation, noting remarkable difference between established democracies and new democracies. In countries where democracy has only recently been established, she finds the type of electoral system to be the most statistically significant cause of the proportion of women parliamentarians, whereas in well-established democracies she finds egalitarian attitudes toward gender roles to be the most powerful explanation. Tremblay notes that gender and politics scholars have pointed to the importance of women's mobilization in state and civil society as a key factor in increases in women's political representation. Interestingly, from a feminist methodological perspective, she acknowledges the limits of the statistical design and method given the difficulty of being able to translate this "factor," which scholars have documented in cross-national qualitative studies, into a numerical variable amenable to statistical modeling. Nonetheless, Tremblay's analysis is valuable for revealing a general pattern and suggesting some interesting new patterns to be explored in future research on women and elections.

Inferential statistics is a method of analysis that can be used only when adequate data exist or can be collected. The concepts of political science like "gender," "equality," "family," "representation," and "conflict" can mean many things in different contexts and are the subject of contestation both in theory and in political life. A feminist research ethic guides our careful reflection on how to measure a theoretical concept for empirical study. We call this process the operationalization of the concept. Inferential statistics—like other methods—requires careful theoretical reflection on the use of particular existing data (like fertility or vasectomy rates) as an operationalization of a concept as theoretically complicated as, say, gender equality (Caprioli 2003; Melander 2005). The desire to use inferential statistical analysis for cross-national comparison can require the creation of new data sets (True and Mintrom 2001). Gender analysis and intersectional analysis are important tools in the operationalization of any key concept in the study of politics and gender (Waylen 2008; Weldon 2008; Ackerly 2010; Goetz and Mazur 2008).

CONCLUSION

In each of the gender and politics studies discussed in this chapter, attention to the power of epistemology, relationships, especially with subject-participants, forms of exclusion, and marginalization in research and to the possible meanings of gender or equality were important parts of the research in one form or another. Reflection on the situatedness of the researcher, gender analysis, and intersectional analysis has been less universally used by gender and politics researchers. However, these tools are increasingly norms for feminist analysis and they are often the first to be deployed in a feminist evaluation of social scientific research.

Feminists will judge any social science research project that does not use these guiding tools for reflection to be weak and potentially flawed. That is because these feminist methodologies—a feminist research ethic, gender analysis, and intersectional analysis—are based on an understanding that all knowledge is provisional and somewhat limited by time, place, and context. Research on gender and politics is largely carried out with a measure of humility, demonstrating awareness of the many challenges, methodological among them, in studying the social and political world, which is always changing and of which we are a part. With feminist tools of research, however, there are always opportunities to broaden our research by turning assumptions from previous projects into new questions. As scholars turn to new questions they will sometimes stake out new terrain, sometimes extend existing terrain, and sometimes broaden the application of existing tools by asking new questions in familiar ways. Due to this diversity, the methodological tools of gender and politics questions are vast yet recognizably feminist in their rigorous commitment to being continually reflexive about research and the challenge of building a collective field of scholarship.

REFERENCES

Ackerly, Brooke A. 1995. "Testing the tools of development: Credit programs, loan involvement, and women's empowerment." *IDS Bulletin* 26(3): 56–68.

Ackerly, Brooke A. 1997. "What's in a design? The effects of NGO choices on women's empowerment and on family and social institutions in Bangladesh." In Anne Marie Goetz, ed., *Getting institutions right for women in development*. New York: Zed Books, 140–158.

Ackerly, Brooke A. 2000. *Political theory and feminist social criticism*. Cambridge, UK: Cambridge University Press.

Ackerly, Brooke A. 2008. *Universal human rights in a world of difference*. Cambridge, UK: Cambridge University Press.

Ackerly, Brooke A. 2009. "Why a feminist theorist studies methods." *Politics & Gender* 5(3): 431–436.

Ackerly, Brooke A. 2010. "Review of *Politics, gender, and concepts: Theory and methodology* edited by Gary Goertz and Amy Mazur." *Review of politics* 6 (4):639–642 .

Ackerly, Brooke A. 2011. "Human rights enjoyment in theory and activism." *Human Rights Review* 12: 221–239.

Ackerly, Brooke A., and Katy Attanasi. 2009. "Global feminisms: Theory and ethics for studying gendered injustice." *New Political Science* 31(4): 543–555.

Ackerly, Brooke A., and Rose McDermott. 2012. "Introduction." *Politics and Gender* 8(3).

Ackerly, Brooke A., and Jacqui True. 2006. "Studying the struggles and wishes of the age: Feminist theoretical methodology and feminist theoretical methods." In Brooke A. Ackerly, Maria Stern and Jacqui True, eds., *Feminist methodologies for international relations.* Cambridge, UK: Cambridge University Press, 241–260.

Ackerly, Brooke A., and Jacqui True. 2008. "An intersectional analysis of international relations: Recasting the discipline." *Politics & Gender* 4(1): 156–173.

Ackerly, Brooke A., and Jacqui True. 2008. "Reflexivity in practice: Power and ethics in feminist research on international relations." *International Studies Review* 10: 693–707.

Ackerly, Brooke A., and Jacqui True. 2010a. "Back to the future: Feminist theory, activism, and doing feminist research in an age of globalization." *Women's Studies International Forum* 33: 464–472.

Ackerly, Brooke A., and Jacqui True. 2010b. *Doing feminist research in political and social science.* New York: Palgrave Macmillan.

Agathangelou, Anna M., and L. H. M. Ling. 2004. "Power, borders, security, wealth: Lessons of violence and desire from September 11." *International Studies Quarterly* 48(3): 517–538.

Al-Ali, Nadje, and Nicola Pratt. 2009. *What kind of liberation? Women and the occupation of Iraq.* Berkeley: University of California Press.

Alexander-Floyd, Nikol G. 2010. "Critical race black feminism: A jurisprudence of resistance and the transformation of the academy." *Signs: Journal of Women in Culture and Society* 35(4): 810–820.

Andersen, Kristi. 1975. "Working women and political participation, 1952–1972." *American Journal of Political Science* 19(3): 439–453.

Apodaca, Clair. 2009. "Overcoming obstacles in quantitative feminist research." *Politics & Gender* 5(3): 419–426.

Baker, Ella, and Marvel Jackson Cooke. 1935. "The Bronx slave market." *Crisis* 42: 330–331, 340.

Baldez, Lisa. 2002. *Why women protest: women's movements in Chile.* Cambridge, UK: Cambridge University Press.

Belenky, Mary Field. 1986. *Women's ways of knowing: The development of self, voice, and mind.* New York: Basic Books.

Benería, Lourdes, and Gita Sen. 1982. "Class and gender inequalities and women's role in economic development: Theoretical and practical implications." *Feminist Studies* 8(1): 157–176.

Bourque, Susan C. and Jean Grossholtz. 1974. "Politics as unnatural practice: Political science looks at female participation." *Politics and Society* 4(, 2): 225–266.

Brady, Henry E., and David Collier (Eds.). 2004. *Rethinking social inquiry: Diverse tools, shared standards.* Boulder, CO: Rowman & Littlefield.

Bristow, Ann R., and Jody A. Esper. 1984. "A feminist research ethos." *Humanity and Society* 8: 489–496.

Bunch, Charlotte. 2003. "Feminism, peace, human rights and human security." *Canadian Woman Studies* 22(2): 6–11.

Burns, Nancy, Kay Schlozman, and Sidney Verba. 2001. *The private roots of public action: Gender equality and political participation*. Cambridge, MA: Harvard University Press.

Caprioli, Mary. 2003. "Gender equality and state aggression: The impact of domestic gender equality on state first use of force." *International Interactions* 29(3): 195–214.

Caprioli, Mary. 2007. "Feminist methodologies for international relations." *Perspectives on Politics* 5: 670–671.

Caprioli, Mary. 2009. "Making choices." *Politics & Gender* 5(3): 426–431.

Carpenter, Charli. 2002. "Gender theory in world politics: Contributions of a non-*feminist* standpoint." *International Studies Review* 4(3): 153–166.

Chappell, Louise. 2002. *Gendering government: feminist engagement with the state in Australia and Canada*. Vancouver: University of British Columbia Press.

Childs, Sarah. 2002. "Conceptions of representation and the passage of the sex discrimination (election candidates) bill." *Journal of Legislative Studies* 8(3): 90–108.

Chin, Christine. 1998. *In service and in servitude: Foreign female domestic workers and the Malaysian modernity project*. New York: Columbia University Press.

Chowdhury, Elora Halim. 2009. "Locating global feminisms elsewhere: Braiding us women of color and transnational feminisms." *Cultural Dynamics* 21(1): 51–78.

Cole, Johnnetta B., and Beverly Guy-Sheftall (Eds.). 2003. *Gender talk: The struggle for women's equality in African American communities*. New York: One World.

Crenshaw, Kimberle. 1989. "Demarginalizing the intersection of race and sex: A black feminist critique of antidiscrimination doctrine, feminist theory and antiracist politics." In David Kairys, ed., *The politics of law: A progressive critique*. New York: Pantheon, 195–217.

Crenshaw, Kimberle. 1991. "Mapping the margins: Intersectionality, identity politics, and violence against women of color." *Stanford Law Review* 43: 1241–1299.

D'Costa, Bina. "Coming to Terms with the Past in Bangladesh." In Luciana Ricciutelli, ed., *Feminist politics, activism and vision: Local and global challenges*. Toronto: Inanna Publications and Education; Zed, 227–247.

D'Costa, Bina. 2006. "Marginalized identity: New frontiers of research for IR?" In Brooke Ackerly, Maria Stern, and Jacqui True, eds., *Feminist methodologies for international relations*. Cambridge, UK: Cambridge University Press, 129–152.

D'Costa, Bina. 2010. *Nationbuilding, gender and war-crime in South Asia*. London: Routledge.

Dhruvarajan, Vanaja, and Jill Vickers (Eds.). 2002. *Gender, race, and nation: A global perspective*. Toronto: University of Toronto Press.

Dietz, Mary G. 2003. "Current controversies in feminist theory." *Annual Review of Political Science* 6: 399–431.

Doan, Alesha E., and Donald P. Haider-Markel. 2010. "The role of intersectional sterotypes on evaluations of gay and lesbian political candidates." *Politics & Gender* 6(1): 63–91.

Dolan, Kathleen. 1997. "Gender differences in support for women candidates: Is there a glass ceiling in American politics?" *Women and Politics* 17: 27–41.

Dolan, Kathleen. 1998. "Voting for women in the year of the woman." *American Journal of Political Science* 42: 272–293.

Dwyer, Daisy Hilse, and Judith Bruce. 1988. *A home divided: Women and income in the third world*. Stanford, CA: Stanford University Press.

Elshtain, Jean Bethke. 1975. "The feminist movement & the question of equality." *Polity* 7(4): 452–477.

Enloe, Cynthia H. [1989]1990. *Bananas, beaches & bases: Making feminist sense of international politics*. Berkeley: University of California Press.

Enloe, Cynthia H. 2004. *The curious feminist: Searching for women in a new age of empire*. Berkeley: University of California Press.

Eriksson Baaz, Maria, and Maria Stern. 2009. "Why do soldiers rape? Masculinity, violence, and sexuality in the armed forces in the Congo (DRC)." *International Studies Quarterly* 53(2): 495–518.

Eschle, Catherine, and Bice Maiguashca. 2010. *Making feminist sense of the global justice movement*. Lanham, MD: Rowman & Littlefield Publishers.

Fraser, Nancy. 2009. *Scales of justice: Reimagining political space in a globalizing world*. New York: Columbia University Press.

Friedman, Elisabeth J. 2000. *Unfinished transitions women and the gendered development of democracy in Venezuela, 1936–1996*. University Park: Pennsylvania State University Press.

Finnemore, M. and K. Sikkink (1998). "International norm dynamics and political change." *International Organization* 52(4): 887–917.

Gilligan, Carol. 1982. *In a different voice: Psychological theory and women's development*. Cambridge, MA: Harvard University Press.

Goetz, Gary, and Amy G. Mazur eds. 2008. *Politics, gender and concepts: Theory and methodology*. Cambridge: Cambridge University Press.

Goldstein, Joshua. 2001. *War and gender*. Cambridge, UK: Cambridge University Press.

Hartsock, Nancy C. M. 1983. *Money, sex, and power: Toward a feminist historical materialism*. New York: Longman.

Haussman, Melissa, and Birgit Sauer (Eds.). 2007. *Gendering the state in the age of globalization: Women's movements and state feminism in post industrial democracies*. Boulder, CO: Rowman & Littlefield.

Hawkesworth, Mary. 2005. "Engendering political science: An immodest proposal." *Politics & Gender* 1(1): 141–156.

Hawkesworth, Mary E. 2006. *Feminist inquiry: From political conviction to methodological innovation*. New Brunswick, NJ: Rutgers University Press.

Hill Collins, Patricia. 1990. *Black feminist thought: Knowledge, consciousness, and the politics of empowerment*. Boston: Unwin Hyman.

hooks, bell. [1984] 2000. *Feminist theory: From margin to center*. Cambridge, MA: South End Press.

Htun, Mala. 2003. *Sex and the state: Abortion, divorce, and the family under Latin American dictatorships and democracies*. Cambridge, UK: Cambridge University Press.

Htun, Mala. 2005. "What it means to study gender and the state." *Politics & Gender* 1(1): 157–166.

Jaggar, Alison M. 1983. *Feminist politics and human nature*. Totowa, NJ: Rowman & Allanheld.

Kaplan, Caren, Norma Alarcón, and Minoo Moallem. 1999. *Between woman and nation: Nationalisms, transnational feminisms, and the state*. Durham, NC: Duke University Press.

Kaufman-Osborn, T. 2006. "Gender trouble at Abu Ghraib?" *Politics & Gender* 1(4): 597–619.

Keck, Margaret E., and Kathryn Sikkink. 1998. *Activists beyond borders: Advocacy networks in international politics*. Ithaca, NY: Cornell University Press.

Krook, Mona Lena. 2009. *Quotas for Women in Politics: Gender and Candidate Selection Reform Worldwide*: Oxford University Press.

Lombardo, Emanuela, Petra Maier, and Mieke Verloo (Eds.). 2009. *The discursive politics of gender equality: Stretching, bending and policy-making*. New York: Routledge.

Lovenduski, Joni (Ed.). 2005. *State feminism and the political representation*. Cambridge, UK: Cambridge University Press.

Martin, Patricia Yancey, John R. Reynolds, and Shelley Keith. 2002. "Gender bias and feminist consciousness among judges and attorneys: A standpoint theory analysis." *Signs* 27(3): 665–701.

Mazur, Amy G. (Ed.). 2001. *State feminism, women's movements, and job training: Making democracies work in the global economy*. New York: Routledge.

McBride Stetson, Dorothy (Ed.). 2001. *Abortion politics, women's movements and the democratic state: A comparative study of state feminism*. Oxford: Oxford University Press.

McBride Stetson, Dorothy, and Amy G. Mazur (Eds.). 1995. *Comparative state feminism*. Thousand Oaks, CA: SAGE.

McCall, Leslie. 2005. "The complexity of intersectionality." *Signs: Journal of Women in Culture and Society* 30(3): 1771–1800.

Melander, Erik. 2005. "Gender equality and intrastate armed conflict." *International Studies Quarterly* 49(4): 695–714.

Mohanty, Chandra Talpade. 1992. "Feminist encounters: Locating the politics of experience." Michele Barrett and Anne Phillips, eds. In *Destabilizing theory*, p. 74-92, Stanford, CA: Stanford University Press.

Neumayer, Eric, and Thomas Plümper. 2007. "The gendered nature of natural disasters: The impact of catastrophic events on the gender gap in life expectancy, 1981–2002." *Annals of the Association of American Geographers* 97(3): 551–566.

Nussbaum, Martha Craven, Jonathan Glover, and World Institute for Development Economics Research. 1995. *Women, culture, and development: A study of human capabilities*. Oxford: Clarendon Press.

Oakley, Ann. 1972. *Sex, gender and society*. London: Maurice Temple Smith Ltd.

Okin, Susan. 1989. *Justice, gender, and the family*. New York: Basic Books.

Outshoorn, Joyce (Ed.). 2004. *The politics of prostitution: Women's movements, democratic states and the globalisation of sex commerce*. Cambridge, UK: Cambridge University Press.

Panjabi, Kavita. 2005. *Old maps and new: Legacies of the partition: A Pakistan diary*, Culture Studies/Border Studies. Calcutta: Seagull Books, 2005.

Parisi, Laura. 2009. "The numbers do(n't) always add up: Dilemmas in using quantitative research methods in feminist IR scholarship." *Politics & Gender* 5(3): 410–419.

Pateman, Carole. 1988. *The sexual contract*. Stanford, CA: Stanford University Press.

Paxton, Pamela. 2000. "Women's suffrage in the measurement of democracy: Problems of operationalization." *Studies in Comparative International Development* 35: 92–111.

Paxton, Pamela, Melanie M. Hughes, and Jennifer L. Green.2006. "The international women's movement and women's political representation, 1893–2003." *American Sociological Review* 71(6): 898–920.

Posadskaya, Anastasia (Ed.). 1994. *Women in Russia: A new era in Russian feminism.* London: Verso Books.

Ragin, Charles C. 1987. *The Comparative Method: Moving Beyond Qualitative and Quantitative Strategies.* Berkeley: University of California Press.

Reid, Graeme, and Liz Walker. 2005. "Editorial introduction: Sex and secrecy: A focus on African sexualities." *Culture, Health & Sexuality* 7(3): 185–194.

Rowbotham, Sheila. 1976. *Hidden from history: Rediscovering women in history from the 17th century to the present.* New York: Vintage Books.

Sapiro, Virginia. 1981. "Research frontier essays: When are interests interesting? The problem of political representation of women." *American Political Science Review* 75(3): 701–716.

Sapiro, Virginia. 1998. "Feminist Studies and Political Science—and Vice Versa." In Anne Phillips, ed., *Feminism and politics.* Oxford: Oxford University Press, 67–90.

Sawer, Marian, and Sandra Grey (Eds.). 2008. *Women's movements: In abeyance or flourishing in new ways?* New York: Routledge.

Scott, Joan E., and Judith Butler (Eds.). 1992. *Feminists theorize the political.* New York: Routledge.

Shepherd, Laura. J. 2008. *Gender, violence and security: Discourse as practice.* London: Zed Books.

Spelman, Elizabeth V. 1988. *Inessential woman: Problems of exclusion in feminist thought.* Boston: Beacon Press.

Stasz Stoll, Clarice. 1973. *Sexism: Scientific debates.* Reading, MA: Addison-Wesley.

Stern, Maria. 2005. *Naming security—Constructing identity: "Mayan women" in Guatemala on the eve of "peace."* Manchester, UK: Manchester University Press.

Stetson, Dorothy M., and Amy G. Mazur (Eds.). 1995. *Comparative state feminism.* Thousand Oaks, CA: SAGE.

Stetson, Dorothy E., and Amy G. Mazur. 2010. *The politics of state feminism: Innovation in comparative research.* Philadelphia: Temple University Press.

Sylvester, Christine. 1994. *Feminist theory and international relations in a postmodern era.* Cambridge: Cambridge University Press.

Tamale, Sylvia. 2000. *When hens do crow: Gender and parliamentary politics in Uganda.* Boulder, CO: Westview Press.

Tickner, J. Ann. 1992. *Gender in international relations: Feminist perspectives on achieving global security.* New York: Columbia University Press.

Tinker, Irene. 1990. *Persistent inequalities: Women and world development.* New York: Oxford University Press.

Tong, Rosemarie. 1998. *Feminist thought: A more comprehensive introduction.* Boulder, CO: Westview Press.

Tremblay, Manon. 2007. "Democracy, representation, and women: A comparative analysis." *Democratization* 14(4): 533–553.

True, Jacqui. 2003. *Gender, globalization and postsocialism: The Czech republic after communism.* New York: Columbia University Press.

True, Jacqui. 2012. *The political economy of violence against women.* New York: Oxford University Press.

True, Jacqui, and Michael Mintrom. 2001. "Transnational networks and policy diffusion: The case of gender mainstreaming." *International Studies Quarterly* 45(1): 27–57.

Waylen, Georgina. 2007. *Engendering transitions: Women's mobilization, institutions, and gender outcomes.* Oxford: New York: Oxford University Press.

Waylen, Georgina. 2008. "Gendering governance." In Gary Goertz and Amy G. Mazur, eds., *Politics, gender, and concepts: Theory and methodology.* Cambridge, UK: Cambridge University Press..

Weldon, S. Laurel. 2002. *Protest, policy and the problem of violence against women: A cross-national comparison.* Pittsburgh: University of Pittsburgh Press.

Weldon, S. Laurel. 2006. "The structure of intersectionality: A comparative politics of gender." *Politics & Gender* 2(2): 235–248.

Weldon, S. Laurel. 2008. "Intersectionality." In Gary Goertz and Amy Mazur, eds., *Politics, gender, and concepts: Theory and methodology.* Cambridge, UK: Cambridge University Press.

Wibben, Annick. 2011. *Feminist security studies: A narrative approach.* New York: Routledge.

Young, Iris Marion. 1990. *Justice and the politics of difference.* Princeton, NJ: Princeton University Press.

Young, Iris Marion. 1997. "Unruly categories: A critique of Nancy Fraser's dual systems theory." *New Left Review* 222: 147–160.

Yuval-Davis, Nira. 2006. "Intersectionality and feminist politics." *European Journal of Women's Studies* 13(3): 193–209.

PART II

....

BODY POLITICS

....

SEEMINGLY personal issues associated with the body—such as rape, contraception, hair and clothing styles, pregnancy, or sexual harassment—were not traditionally seen as "political" and thus were seen as outside the provenance of political science. But bodies are at the core of the political order as markers of status and power. Contemporary societies tend to segregate not only access to political power but also work, religious life, domestic work, and intimate relationships according to the sex and race of the bodies they organize. Our social, economic, and political worlds are organized to reflect these habitual and legal patterns. The corridors of power are structured to accommodate the associated characteristics of male, heterosexual bodies of dominant racial and ethnic groups. Advancement requires assimilation to the norms associated with powerful bodies: women must dress like men and warehouse their babies far from the breasts at which they feed; the schedules upon which they work are not accommodative of parental responsibilities; African American women and men straighten, cut, or otherwise downplay their distinctive hair; family laws assume and restrict relations of intimacy and the structure of families according to the sex, race, and religion of bodies. In many countries female bodies may not be warriors, those perpetrators of violence, but are marked as vulnerable to violence, as women are the disproportionate victims of rape and intimate violence. Violence polices the boundaries of approved sexual relations, as deviations from normative heterosexuality, racial hierarchies, and approved modes of masculinity and femininity are punished with harassment, bullying, battering, and sexual assault. Bodies are powerful symbols and sources of social power and privilege on one hand and subordination and oppression on the other.

Bodies are sources as well as subjects of knowledge production; for example, researchers increasingly recognize that survey researchers and interviewers will get different answers from their interlocutors depending on their race, sex, sexuality, and the like in many contexts. More importantly, our bodies shape the questions we ask and the realities against which we measure the answers (sometimes called standpoint epistemology). The National Academy of Sciences, for example, has concluded that a more diverse professoriate produces more robust, objective science. More generally, some bodies are associated with authoritative knowledge and enjoy more deference and presumptions of reasonableness while "other" bodies (mostly female, racialized, classed bodies) are dismissed as overly emotional or otherwise inappropriate for serious pursuit of knowledge. As Judith Butler (1993) suggests, the hierarchy of bodies shapes and is shaped by our processes of knowledge production.

We start our discussion of gender and politics by examining body politics to emphasize how bodies are at the core of our families, economies, and social and political institutions more generally, shaping states, civil society, and citizenship. The four chapters in this section collectively illustrate how a focus on the body can transform both what we study and how we study it in political science.

Mainstream political science has tended to treat bodies as an unproblematic category stemming largely from a presumption that bodies are part of nature, hence "natural" and, furthermore, apolitical and unchanging. We now know, though, that bodies are not determined by or determinative of "human nature": there is evidence for the fluidity of sexual and racial categories, and we increasingly learn that physical features of bodies (such as brain structures) are shaped by the social context, further blurring the nature–nurture dichotomy. Ironically, popular discussions of science have continued to emphasize or even amplify the nature–culture dichotomy, pushing the category of "women" closer to the nature, equating women to their bodies, and painting them as less rational and autonomous than men. This in turn has served to justify the continued exclusion of women from the public sphere of politics.

While the chapters in this section represent different approaches and topics in relation to body politics, they share a focus on intersectionality: the way that gender intersects with race and ethnicity, sexuality, disability, age, class, religion, and other categories or axes of difference to illustrate that bodies are at intersections of different identity markers and powers. Such approaches widen the scope of what is studied in politics even further. The chapters talk about the role that contemporary debates surrounding abortion, AIDS, contraception, population control, gender-appropriate norms, and sexual rights play in politics and how bodies that are targeted by related policies are shaped. Body politics is also closely tied together with broader processes of sovereignty, empire building, citizenship regimes, Westernization, globalization, and neoliberalization.

Diana Coole's chapter on "The Body and Politics" starts the section by analyzing the history and development of feminist thought in relation to bodies.
The chapter points to the diversity within feminist thought in relation to bodies by covering phenomenological, materialist, and poststructural approaches
to bodies, among others. At the same time, it effectively illustrates that bodies
have been and continue to be a difficult topic for feminists due to the antipathy
that women's close association to bodies created. When mapping out the most
recent developments, Coole shows how theories about bodies have experienced
a postmodern turn to language and then back again to theorizing materiality
and embodiment.

Amy Lind's chapter, "Heteronormativity and Sexuality," interrogates the
concept of sexuality as a category of political analysis and a form of power.
Sexuality is of course closely related to the questions about the body: it is a
seemingly private—even apolitical—matter but in reality is fiercely regulated by
state practices and discourses. These, in turn, serve to uphold the dominance of
heterosexuality. Lind's chapter illustrates how sexuality continues to be an even
more a difficult topic for mainstream political science than the body. Yet feminist research in the field points to the amount of power that it takes to uphold
the heterosexual matrix and its attendant assumptions, for example, about sexual citizenship and the family. The chapter also makes visible the multitude of
ways sexuality shapes the workings of institutions and informs the ways people
organize.

Veronique Mottier's chapter on "Reproductive Rights" discusses yet more
political battlegrounds that relate to gendered bodies and norms. Like the
issue of violence, reproductive rights and control have been central tools for
states and international actors in governing and gendering bodies and upholding norms about appropriate femininities and masculinities. Mottier's chapter
covers a wide range of topics from eugenics, forced sterilization, and abortion
to new reproductive technologies. The deeply gendered eugenic policy making in Western Europe and the United States shows how the categories of
gender, class, race, and ethnicity intersect to subordinate some women in the
name of states reproducing nations and protecting welfare services. Political
mobilization around abortion rights and forced sterilization, in turn, illustrates how different women and feminists approach the issue from deeply
diverging perspectives. Feminist thinking and theory around the topic has
also transformed significantly as demonstrated by the issue new reproductive
technologies.

As noted, violence polices the social organization of bodies, and R. Amy
Elman's chapter focuses on the ways that violence, as well as laws and policies on violence, reflect and shape women's subordination and mobilization
against that subordination. Political action on violence preceded the study of
violence in the field of political science, demonstrating the way that the focus
on traditional subject matter has occluded our understanding of state action.
The chapter shows how research on gender violence within the field of political

science generates insights about responsiveness of states to women's movement demands, about patterns of women's political organizing around the topic and how these are shaped by processes of globalization and neoliberalization, and the role that transnational actors, such as the European Union and the United Nation, play in national contexts and vice versa. Such research both explains national variation in state policies on gender violence and also points to the role that gender violence plays in constructing nations and conducting wars.

....

CHAPTER 6

THE BODY AND POLITICS

....

DIANA COOLE

INTRODUCTION

....

There is a vital sense in which humans are their bodies. We experience their demands and are made constantly aware of how others observe their appearances and abilities. Yet the body has been widely neglected in political thought and it is a notable success of gender studies that it has retrieved the body as a significant dimension of politics. The main approaches to the body in the field of gender studies were forged by feminists, with specific emphasis on women's embodiment: a necessary but risky strategy inasmuch as women's oppression has conventionally been founded on their identification with carnality. Just how essential sexual difference is to bodies or how foundational they are for sexed or gendered identities remain contested issues. Over time the sort of approaches developed by feminist scholarship have certainly been applied more broadly to otherwise gendered bodies—masculine, transsexual, queer, hybrid, cyborg, intersectional—thus broadening the field while displacing assumptions that the gendered body is solely a feminist issue or that sex and gender are necessarily the dominant markers or experience of actual bodies.

The focus in this chapter is on theoretical questions that arise when the (sexed/gendered) body is brought into political life and discourse. An initial section summarizes some enduring questions and identifies a number of distinctive approaches. This is followed by a more detailed analysis of these approaches, principally through an examination of representative authors and texts.

Theorizing the Body: Enduring Questions, Distinctive Approaches

Some of the most enduring questions regarding the body are ontological. What is a body? Is each body, for example, a distinct biological organism, or is it more accurately understood as the accretion of general biochemical processes that are susceptible to environmental factors? To what extent are the bodies of social actors best treated as natural phenomena that society modifies, or should the focus be on imaginary and symbolic aspects of the cultural body? In addressing such questions it has proven necessary not only to consult the latest science but also to revisit some of philosophy's most enduring oppositions, such as mind–body or culture–nature. The way the body is conceptualized has far-reaching implications regarding the perceived malleability of the flesh, the contingency or duality of gender or sex, and opportunities for political intervention or personal choice in matters of individual self-expression or behavior that are more or less corporeal.

Additionally, there are deep-seated epistemological and methodological questions posed by body matters. How do we represent or express this corporeal realm inasmuch as it is a material alterity existing in a register other than that of philosophy? Are theorists condemned merely to write *about* the body in more or less imaginative ways, or does lived experience grant some clues here? Can we know, write, or intuit in ways particularly appropriate to the body's (sexed) carnality, or does theory inevitably impose upon it alien concepts that may, in turn, be structured by gendered assumptions?

Responses to these kinds of philosophical inquiry can be enormously influential in structuring scholarship on sex, gender, and the body, especially regarding the political or ethical implications of embodiment. Over recent decades, furthermore, disagreement has been played out against the backdrop of a more general trend in critical theory away from materialist political economy or empirical social science through a cultural turn where language and literary approaches have been privileged and the body is read as a text or script. Now there is evidence of a new materialist turn as ecology, biotechnology, demography, and political economy again frame issues of bodies in social contexts (Coole and Frost 2010).

For gender studies, the point of analyzing the body is to discern the power relationships that regulate, denigrate, define, or produce it as well as to identify the ways different bodies are located and constructed. The body gains political significance by being recognized alongside language or the state as a principal site where sex, gender, and power are enmeshed. An insistence on interlocutors' embodiment within conventional political activities like parliamentary debates or deliberative forums has important ramifications for political analysis. How diverse bodies are treated by policy makers and how they fare in economic systems or familial structures—say, through welfare and tax regimes—is also influenced by perceptions and constructions of the gendered body and its roles.

Political studies of embodiment have tended, however, to go well beyond this political science framework and generally define the political more widely: as a web of power relations that situate, saturate, and constitute bodies differentially. In addition to the body's role in locating individuals within a sexual division of labor, it is recognized to serve as a key index of differential experience and practices; a significant marker of identity; a vehicle for long-standing myths and rituals; a means of expression, pleasure, and agency; a target for and instrument of power; and a site of desire or vulnerability where violence and seduction occur. For those whose bodies are most exploited or denigrated—women, but also the colonized, the laboring classes, the disabled—the stakes are particularly high. The ethics of livable flesh and the politics of how bodies are treated or interpreted as well as their corporeal agency in resisting or transgressing hegemonic norms remain some of the most significant fields for feminist or queer sexual politics as well as for critical men's, race, or postcolonial studies and for the increasingly important fields of aging and disability.

A number of distinctive theoretical approaches to sexed/gendered embodiment is discernible: materialist investigations of the body's sexually differentiated roles and functions; phenomenological attention to the experience of lived corporeality; psychoanalytic emphasis on the imaginary body; poststructuralist accounts of constructed flesh. As research methodologies, these are applicable not only to women's bodies and their sex or gender but also to a range of other bodies that are socially disadvantaged and whose corporeal markers are additionally borne by women, too. Thus class, race, ethnicity, age, and ability are all manifest in and reproduced by their carnal avatars in ways that invite critical analysis and contestation.

While the various approaches often coexist, their development also reflects both external theoretical fashions and an internal dialectic of inquiry and critique. The latter imparts a certain chronology to distinctive phases, and this lends itself to narrative reconstruction. In the case of feminist analysis of the sexed/gendered body, it is worth telling this story briefly because it conveys something of the logic of its evolution.

The long prefeminist era has to be the starting point here because it is against its presuppositions that feminism reacts. The default position for Western culture has been overwhelmingly somatophobic in the sense that the body is relegated to a piece of nature and is consequently either neglected as irrelevant or denigrated as a dangerous source of unruly passions that threaten reason, political order, and civic virtue. Because of their role in reproduction women have been considered closer to nature than men and judged to remain more in thrall to the flesh and its dangerous desires. Their affinity with the body has accordingly been used to justify women's exclusion from citizenship as well as their confinement to a private realm of family values and domestic labor in which they are regarded as men's property.

Feminist analysis shows that Western culture's treatment of the body is deeply imbued with a gender bias that privileges mind or reason, in turn identified as masculine. A conceptual edifice of binary oppositions is identified here—mind–body, culture–nature, subject–object, rational–irrational, active–passive, public–private—in which the first of each pair is perceived as superior, masculine, the norm (Lloyd 1984; Prokhovnik 1999). Eliciting and deconstructing this deep structure has been regarded as a condition of retrieving living flesh and of rethinking sex and gender. For the most part, early feminist arguments still accepted traditional oppositions and thus conceded the disadvantages of female embodiment. But they also maintained that sex was not an insuperable barrier to becoming fully human nor gender a determinant of rational incapacity (Wollstonecraft 1929). By driving this wedge of contingency into what had commonly been regarded as women's natural destiny, liberal feminism opened the door to political change.

In the mid-twentieth century, second-wave feminism would radicalize this argument about contingency. Influenced by Marxism and existential phenomenology, its proponents still tended to see women's bodies as obstacles to their emancipation. But a distinction between the biological, sexed body and gender as a psychocultural construction allowed them to reject biological determinism while advocating a postgendered, androgynous ideal. Early radical feminists initially shared such views, but they would increasingly reject negative judgments about women's bodies in favor of a woman-centered theory of sexual difference (Braidotti 1994). Anglophone radical feminism and French écriture féminine both revalorized female flesh, identifying it as the site of a distinctive kind of feminine experience and desire. For some radical feminists, women's embodiment was identified with privileged access to a superior kind of knowledge or ethical capacity associated directly with the nurturing abilities of the maternal body or more indirectly with the caring roles found in mothering or the reciprocity of lesbian relationships (Rich 1979; O'Brien 1981; Ruddick 1989). For French feminists, the task was to reimagine the very topography of female flesh and its pleasures as a challenge to (masculine) Western culture as such.

By the late 1980s, these discourses of embodied sexual difference were themselves yielding to poststructuralist and postmodern approaches to the sexed/gendered body. Their exponents rejected the binary framework of sexual difference as well as the unitary one of ungendered human equality. The radical move made by poststructuralists was to present both sex and gender as culturally constructed. As a consequence, an earlier view that gender is a contingent expression of binary sexual difference lost its organic anchor to be replaced by a thoroughly cultural body. This allowed more fluid, mobile bodies to emerge in which sexual identity is multiplicitous or undecidable; gender is queered, and the body is fragmented. If the body was by now thoroughly politicized, for feminism as a political project the downplaying of women's specific corporeality and the diffusion of gendered signifiers across a range of ambiguous bodies engendered something of a crisis (Alcoff 1998). Postmodern disintegrations provoked critics like Susan Bordo (1990) to warn against a dilution and dematerializing of gender. Resisting a "postmodern imaginary of a body whose own unity has been shattered by the choreography of multiplicity," (144) she asked what "sort of body is it that is free to change its shape and location at will, that can become anyone and travel anywhere?" (145).

Since the heyday of postmodernism and radical constructivism in the 1990s, approaches to sex, gender, and the body have become more eclectic. While theory has become more pragmatic and inclusive, interest in hybrid, unclassifiable, diverse bodies has increased. This has encouraged less universalizing philosophical approaches to phenomena like sex/gender in favor of more empirical ethnographic and sociological studies of how diverse bodies are differentially located and variously manifest themselves across different social and political spaces.

ANALYSIS OF DISTINCTIVE APPROACHES TO THE BODY

This part of the chapter looks in more detail at the distinctive approaches to sex, gender, and the body by paying particular attention to representative thinkers and classic texts.

Biological Functions and Sexed Roles

Women's liberation emerged during the 1960s as a movement for emancipating women from the biological functions that render female embodiment a liability. To appreciate this feminist antipathy toward the body as well as assumptions about its biological intransigence, it is important to remember that reliable contraception was only just becoming available. Painful childbirth, unwanted pregnancy, and everyday lives dominated by natural fecundity and its concomitant family roles remained the norm for most women (as it is still for many women in developing counties). Most nations were pronatalist, with women's reproductive role often presented as a duty. While Marxist feminists argued that women's independence meant waged labor, early radical feminist demands revolved around issues of bodily integrity. Access to new reproductive technologies and legal abortion were linked to reproductive self-determination and women's control over their fertility as well as to the liberation of sexual pleasure. The objectification of female flesh as an instrument of men's pleasure, violence against women's bodies, alternatives to heterosexual and familial relationships, emancipation from unremunerated domestic drudgery, and equal pay and status for women's work were all politicized in the new feminist agenda and revolved around the deployment of female bodies. Corporeal fashions—such as short skirts, trousers, and going braless—and styles—such as the skinny or muscular form evoking androgyny—were experimented with as part of a new body aesthetic that challenged older gender norms while freeing women from the restrictions of formal dress codes. Sexual politics meant opportunities for women to escape what had previously seemed fairly intractable bodily constraints.

Such views were epitomized by Shulamith Firestone, a founder of the women's liberation movement and author of *The Dialectic of Sex*. Firestone (1979) complained that "fears of new methods of reproduction are so widespread that as of the time of writing, 1969, the subject, outside of scientific circles, is still taboo" (188–189). Questioning an allegedly natural desire of all women to procreate, she anticipated flexible, temporary households in which the biological link between women and children is broken, artificial insemination is acceptable practice, and household chores are shared.

The importance of the sex/gender distinction in denaturalizing gender was well illustrated by Kate Millett's (1977) *Sexual Politics*, another iconic text of the early 1970s. Millett recognized that prevailing views still assumed gender distinctions follow from biological difference. While conceding the existence of biogenital differences between male and female bodies, she insisted that the significance of sexual differences and gendered temperaments is entirely social. While, moreover, sex is biological, Millett argued, gender is psychocultural and the relationship between them is contingent, even arbitrary. Socialization, interiorization, and conditioning explain how gendered temperaments are produced from generic human possibilities. Patriarchy, meanwhile, relies on deeming the sex/gender link natural and hence unassailable as well as on more brutal forms of carnal violence like rape, wife beating, and pornography, which are manifestations of cultural misogyny that considers women sex objects. Millett defined women's liberation in terms of emancipation from the biological body's functions and its associated roles and gender characteristics. Patriarchy, she concluded, is not a private misfortune that individual women suffer but a public institution that sustains power relations between the sexes, thereby allowing women to be casually oppressed in private and imprisoned in roles that arrest them "at the level of biological experience," thus permitting them to develop only half their human potential (26).

In summary, feminism emerged from a materialist account of the body that emphasized women's bodily functions and roles. These were understood as prefigured by biology but overwritten by patriarchal social structures that impose a sexual division of labor. As such, female bodies are a hazard but not a fate: new technologies were available to liberate women from the principal sites of their oppression provided gendered norms of femininity could be transformed. The theoretically radical move was to insist on the distinction and contingent relationship between sex and gender.

Existential Phenomenology and Lived Corporeality

Existential phenomenology remains one of the principal approaches to embodiment. Simone de Beauvoir was the first to apply it to women, but it is still widely used to understand gendered and other kinds of corporeal experience (Grosz 1994; Weiss 1999; Ahmed 2000; Alcoff 2006). De Beauvoir's *The Second Sex* was published in France in 1949 and became very influential among feminists during the 1960s. It has become commonplace to ascribe to it the sort of sex/gender distinction espoused by Kate Millett and thus to criticize her for sustaining the nature–culture opposition it presumes. Yet this fails to appreciate the extent to which the phenomenological body is both gendered in its most visceral experiences and irremediably contingent on its social situation.

The book's most well-known claim is that "one is not born, but rather becomes, a woman." (de Beauvoir, 1972, 295). While she insists that it is "civilization" not biology that produces her, a crucial aspect of this becoming for de Beauvoir is the way the girl's relatively androgynous body matures into feminine flesh: a process she describes in exquisite detail from the viewpoint of the girl, who suffers her body's physical and symbolic transformation as an initiation into a world of gendered customs, rites, and roles that literally become incarnated in her body as she learns to exist as a feminine being-in-the-world.

Four elements of de Beauvoir's theory warrant attention inasmuch as they illustrate her phenomenological perspective. First, despite her association with Jean-Paul Sartre, it was to their friend Maurice Merleau-Ponty that she was most indebted for her account of embodiment. With its emphasis on the primacy of perception, its account of corporeal capacities for agency and the corporeal underpinnings of reason, its insistence on the contingency of the body as an emergent phenomenon always in process, and its description of embodied subjects as beings-in-the-world, Merleau-Ponty's phenomenology places the body at the center of existence. It invites the phenomenologist to explore the lived experience of differently situated bodies as an ongoing project (Kruks, 2001). In *The Second Sex* the body is understood phenomenologically as "the instrument of our grasp upon the world." Thus, to be present in the world "implies strictly that there exists a body which is at once a material thing in the world and a point of view towards this world; but nothing requires that this body have this or that structure" (39).

Second, de Beauvoir's normative framework of an existentialist ethics is more Sartrean inasmuch as its primary value is freedom, defined in terms of the subject's ongoing efforts to recreate itself. But she pays particular attention to a Hegelian sense in which asserting selfhood and gaining recognition require individuals physically to test themselves against resistant environments and hostile others. Girls' enforced passivity in confronting the world's material recalcitrance is one reason she thinks men have more readily become subjects through opportunities (like hunting, fighting, laboring, sport) for corporeal efficacy. This in turn renders women more prone to bad faith: to choosing an inauthentic life epitomized by the security and repetition of established roles and routines, in this case as dutiful daughter, wife, and mother. Women's tragedy for de Beauvoir is that the human desire for freedom is not extinguished, yet they are "biologically destined for the repetition of Life" and complicit in the gendered roles associated with it (95).

Third, existential phenomenology's attention to experience encouraged de Beauvoir to ask what it means actually to experience female embodiment: how is this lived in ordinary, everyday existence? She contends that women "know the feminine world more intimately than do the men because we have our roots in it, we grasp more immediately than do men what it means to a human being to be feminine; and we are more concerned with such knowledge" (26–27). Her aim is to describe this gendered lifeworld.

Finally, de Beauvoir adopts the existentialist idea of a situation, whose conceptual significance is twofold. On the one hand, it emphasizes the way embodied subjects are ineluctably situated within an environment to which the body orients them. Examining the wider structural circumstances of women's historical situation—how their bodies are located and categorized or observed from the outside, as objects and functions—is therefore a necessary supplement to personal experience. On the other hand, a situation is always relatively open: it is not a determined or determining condition and can always be altered. If the reproductive body is unpropitious for a life of freedom, this is because women's existential grasp on the world has historically been "more restricted" and "less rich" than men's: biological facts do "constitute an essential element in her situation." But biology is not destiny, and the social significance of biological facts is itself changeable: they are "insufficient for setting up a hierarchy of the sexes; they fail to explain why woman is the Other; they do not condemn her to remain in this subordinate role for ever" (65). It is, de Beauvoir argues, biological, psychological, and socioeconomic structures in combination that comprise women's situation, and she believed that the mid-twentieth century offered unprecedented opportunities for changing the body's significance.

The graphic account of what the reproductive function means for women is unrelenting. "Woman, like man, is her body; but her body is something other than herself" (de Beauvoir 1972, 61). De Beauvoir is eloquent regarding the alienation wrought first through sexual penetration by another's organ and then by being "tenanted by another, who batters upon her substance throughout the period of pregnancy." While the male ejaculates then resumes his individual life of freedom, she argues, the female finds herself "possessed by foreign forces" (57). Gestation and lactation take over her body, only to leave her in a condition of "maternal servitude." "From puberty to menopause woman is the theatre of a play that unfolds within her and in which she is not personally concerned" (60).

Four levels of contingency nonetheless leaven this dismal account. First, de Beauvoir argues that (binary) sexual difference and reproduction lack an a priori foundation in nature. Asexual reproduction among lower species allows us to imagine an alternative to heterosexual arrangements. Sexual reproduction itself produces a fertilized embryo that remains "androgynous germ plasm" (43) whose sex, even after it is fixed, remains merely a potential amenable to modification by the hormonal environment. Sexual differentiation even after birth may remain unclear, with many cases of intersexuality, even a "kind of mosaic" of the two sexes, transpiring (47).

Second, women are not sexually differentiated and disadvantaged by their biology throughout their life cycle. Before puberty, girls' bodily condition is little different from boys'. And after menopause, women seem free to resume human status as a "third sex" where "delivered from the servitude imposed by female nature…her vitality is unimpaired. And what is more, she is no longer the prey of overwhelming forces; she is herself, she and her body are one" (63).

Third, physiology alone is insufficient to condemn women to otherness: "It is not merely as a body, but rather as a body subject to taboos, to laws, that the subject is conscious of himself and attains fulfilment" (de Beauvoir, 1972, 69). In becoming subject to a "second nature" of custom, women's social roles and behavioral norms have been mapped onto biological functions. By breaking this apparently natural linkage women can become gendered differently.

Finally, it is again important to note the historicity of the body's situation. If initially the "bondage of reproduction was a terrible handicap in the struggle against a hostile world," modernity witnesses two revolutions that transform women's corporeal situation: industrial and reproductive. While industrialization has drawn women back into social production, with weaker female bodies no longer being disadvantaged in a world of machines, reproductive technologies allow women finally to take control of their bodies. With modern contraception "she gained mastery of her own body. Now protected in large part from the slavery of reproduction, she is in a position to assume the economic role that is offered her and will assure her of complete independence." Together with advances in obstetrics, anesthetics, and artificial insemination, birth control allows a woman "to reduce the number of her pregnancies and make them a rationally integrated part of her life, instead of being their slave" (de Beauvoir, 1972, 152). De Beauvoir does not, however, underestimate the difficulties of change. In postwar France, she observed, "the duality of the sexes" (21) was no mere theoretical abstraction but remained everywhere apparent. "Humanity is divided into two classes of individuals whose clothes, faces, bodies, smiles, gaits, interests, and occupations are manifestly different" (14–15). It is the detailed phenomenology of this stubborn gendering, achieved within the banal details of everyday corporeal life, that makes The Second Sex such an arresting account of feminine embodiment.

It is possible here to mention only in passing some of de Beauvoir's vivid descriptions as she follows the "long apprenticeship" of physical curtailment and passivity that becoming woman entails. During adolescence she finds her body reified under the male gaze while being subjected to forces beyond her control. As she feels it "getting away from her," (333) she experiences disgust

at "this too fleshy body" (337): her swelling breasts are experienced as annoy-
ing protuberances that quiver painfully when she exercises (353); the growth of
body hair "transforms her into a kind of animal or alga." (333) She is horrified
by her menstrual blood, "the stagnant odour emanating from her—an odour of
the swamp, of wilted violets," and by the shameful rituals to which her periods
condemn her (338). Her emerging sexuality confuses her. "The sensitivity of the
erogenous zones is developing, and these are so numerous in women that her
whole body may be regarded as erogenous" (343).

Yet even these visceral experiences are contingent: de Beauvoir opines
that the discomforts of menstruation are as much a psychosomatic reaction
to their gendered signs of an unwanted future as they are real; she speculates
that girls would experience puberty differently were it treated as a biological
rite of passage and not a gateway to feminine roles. Nor is there any reason carnal efficacy should not be engendered through activities like mountain climbing or swimming. There is, moreover, a residual resistance of the
young woman. As yet unreconciled to her new passivity she merely uses the
props and gestures of femininity. *Lies, masks, mimicry, enterprise, imitation,
calculation, strategy,* and *act* are some of the terms used to describe a feminine masquerade in which "make-up, false hair, girdles and 'reinforced' bras-
sieres" play a role, with clothes, smiles, eyes, lips, gestures, and comportment
lending visible expression to the conventional signs of a sexual difference to
which the young woman has not yet submitted (380). It is once she is married
that woman slips into an inauthentic life of servicing others. "Few tasks," de
Beauvoir insists, "are more like the torture of Sisyphus than housework, with
its endless repetition." (470) Motherhood is especially uncongenial to a life of
freedom: "having a child is enough to paralyze a woman's activity entirely"
(705).

Emancipation revolves for de Beauvoir around the opportunity to work and
gain financial and sexual independence. But she recognizes that even the professional woman struggles to reconcile two worlds while making her way in a
realm defined by men. She, too, may find herself masquerading as woman by
enacting unconvincing performances of feminine passivity. The new woman,
de Beauvoir laments, still "appears most often as a 'true woman' disguised as a
man, and she finds herself as ill at ease in her flesh as in her masculine garb.
She must shed her old skin and cut her own new clothes" (734). The challenge
here is not for women to deny their bodies or even their femininity but to find
creative modes of expressing them through constructing a new feminine aesthetic and ways of being-in-the-world: a new corporeal and existential stylization of gender developed within more egalitarian social roles. Sex and gender
differences would not disappear, but "new relations of flesh and sentiment" can
emerge (740). De Beauvoir acknowledges that for many men, too, becoming
free subjects and assuming norms of masculinity can be a struggle.

The Second Sex prefigures many themes gender studies would develop
subsequently. Existential phenomenology was nevertheless eclipsed during the

1970s by the rise of structuralism and poststructuralism. Accused of human-ism and subjectivism, its focus on experience was displaced by emphasis on impersonal structures (capitalism, language, the unconscious) whose power to construct bodies or subjectivities renders suspect claims to reliable knowledge derived from experience. Even so, poststructuralists like Judith Butler would increasingly find themselves drawing on phenomenological notions like bod-ily styles of comportment or Pierre Bourdieu's account of the way corporeal memories allow cultures to reproduce themselves through embodied rituals of everydayness (Butler 1997). With renewed attention to experiential subtexts of corporeal power, Pierre Bourdieu's idea of *habitus* (Bourdieu and Wacquant, 1992, 128) would be widely invoked to explain mundane ways subaltern exclu-sions are accomplished through unquestioned bodily habits (Alcoff 2006).

Iris Marion Young's work provides two examples of this more contempo-rary use of phenomenological analysis. In a context of multiculturalism, her *Justice and the Politics of Difference* (1990) explores the subtle ways corporeal modes of communication can sustain inequality through unacknowledged acts that are sedimented "in mundane contexts of interaction—in the gestures, tone of voice, movement, and reaction of others" (123). Avoiding eye contact, exhib-iting nervousness in the presence of certain others, and keeping a distance or getting too close scarcely need to register consciously to be appreciated corpo-really as gestures of exclusion. Thus, women, inter alia, may find a casual touch or stare communicating paternalism, sexual innuendo, or contempt, thereby humiliating or embarrassing them. "The behavior, comportments, images, and stereotypes that contribute to the oppression of bodily marked groups," Young argues, "are pervasive, systemic, mutually generating, and mutually reinforcing" (152). This, in short, is a politics enacted at a corporeal level.

In the second example, Young's essay "Throwing Like a Girl" amplifies de Beauvoir's account of how girls lose confidence and competence in their bodily abilities by being excluded from the more physical pursuits encouraged in boys. The result is that female bodies come to incarnate incapacity that is deemed naturally feminine, with gender difference being manifest in such everyday cor-poreal activities as standing or sitting. In her Preface to the anthology in which the essay is reprinted, *On Female Body Experience* (2005), Young reaffirms an earlier commitment to existential phenomenology. The aim "to describe embod-ied being-in-the-world through modalities of sexual and gender difference" (7) is accomplished through descriptions of "ordinary bodily experience" like preg-nancy, menstruation, and breastedness.

Écriture Féminine

The eclipse of earlier theories of sexual embodiment had nowhere been more apparent than in so-called French feminism. By the 1980s a new way of address-ing the body had emerged, with Hélène Cixous, Julia Kristeva, and Luce Irigaray collectively being categorized as exponents of *écriture féminine* or *parler-femme*. The terms' translation, writing (as) woman or speaking (as) woman, captures the ambiguous sense in which this was both a distinctive mode of expression being developed by and for women and an attempt at putting the feminine–female body into language. Its ambition was to regender the very foundations of culture and subjectivity.

The sexed body is located here within a psychoanalytic framework that describes a psychic journey from symbiosis with the maternal body to the speaking subject who enters the symbolic realm of culture and language. For the male body that is the norm, eroticism becomes concentrated in a single sexual organ whose symbolic mark is the phallus. This is also the signifier of the symbolic register. Entering the symbolic means entering a masculine, phallocentric realm predicated on repression of female flesh. The logic and syntax of the symbolic is thus condemned by French feminism as an eviscerated phallic economy of abstract signs. It bespeaks a narcissistic subject that strives to possess the woman's body as a passive instrument of male fantasies of an impossible return to uterine plenitude. Although the symbolic defines sexual difference in its own binary terms, woman as such is claimed by proponents of *écriture féminine* to be absent or other: her body is perceived as both castrated, deficient, and as a threat or promise of regressive unity. As both lack and excess it is literally unspeakable, and she is without a voice for her own desire. Irigaray (1987) maintains that confronting sexual difference on this psychic/metaphysical level means reinterpreting "the whole relationship between the subject and discourse, the subject and the world" (119) because "this subject has always been written in the masculine form, as man" (120).

The questions raised by *écriture féminine/parler-femme* are: How does woman experience this other sexual pleasure? What and where is it? How is it inscribed in her body–psyche, and how might it be expressed in writing? How might our cultural relationship to sensuality be transformed? The objective is to develop a language more redolent of women's embodied pleasure and a feminine libidinal economy.

There is nevertheless some ambiguity as to whether the aim is a counter-symbolic that speaks the language of the unrepressed/female (a return proscribed by orthodox Lacanian theory) or whether the latter is merely provoked as a transgressive force that dislocates the symbolic order through a *jouissance* uttered by subjects-in-process who never entirely renounce instinctual pleasure. For Kristeva, for example, semiotic rhythms can be heard in infantile babbling that sings the flesh or in the "genotext" of linguistic stumbling. This more visceral, instinctual language can also be accessed through borderline mental states or maternal experience and expressed by subjects in the musical or poetic cadences of avant-garde writing where desire irrupts into language (Kristeva 1981, 137; 1984, 25, 40; 1986, 91). While for her the semiotic is feminine in the sense of being a maternal space, it is also a mobility or excess that ruins binary sexual difference and that subjects of either sex may speak.

While Irigaray (1987) is sometimes charged with reifying sexual difference, sympathetic readers insist that she is referring not to the biological body but to its imaginary morphology (Whitford 1991).[1] This is a fantasized relationship to a body that invokes the plural, tactile sensuality of female flesh as an alternative to its masculine construction as lack or void. Because for Irigaray the imaginary spans the unconscious and symbolic orders, *parler-femme* equates to an experimental social imaginary: a feminine metaphysics of passion and affect (Battersby 1998). Woman's body touches and is touched by itself in the folds and moist surfaces of flesh alive with erogenous zones, intimate in the dark recesses of its mucous membranes. Her fluid, differentiated flesh is a "perpetually half-open threshold, consisting of lips that are strangers to dichotomy" (128). The image of two lips touching captures woman's capacity for auto-affection and reciprocity. Woman "has sex organs everywhere"; "she experiences pleasure everywhere" (Irigaray, 1981, 103; 1993). In writing this sexuality the feminine is imagined no longer as lack or absence but as abundance. Its language is as labile and diffuse as its desire.

What is the body–writing relationship? Kathleen Lennon (2010, 7) refers to Irigaray's "startling claim" that "the morphology of the body is reflected in that of certain thought processes." Susan Sellers (1991, 137) suggests she comes closest to outlining the form such writing would take in her discussion of the mystics. For Irigaray the topography of female flesh and the feminine imaginary can literally alter the shape and tempo of speaking. This is a language of sensation in which desire has not been surrendered to the cold logic of grammar. Like the secretions, sex organs, and pleasures of female embodiment this writing is polyvalent, mobile, unstable; it flows across boundaries and resists fixed definitions. A different economy of speaking, whose rhythms echo blood and passion, emerges. The control endemic to male sexuality and exemplified in conceptual mastery is replaced by a feminine language that speaks the repletion of woman's sexuality in generous flows of desire that do not try to control meaning or bring closure. Well-behaved discourse, indeed identity itself, is thus disrupted by meandering meanings that refuse the eviscerated aridity of reason to pulse with forbidden pleasure.

For its critics, a danger of *écriture féminine* is that identifying women's language with nonsensical utterances or sensation risks condemning them to irrationality or silence. A suspicion of biological essentialism is difficult entirely to extirpate. Butler (1990) warns that inasmuch as a "true body" or "prediscursive libidinal multiplicity" (91) is invoked, these are merely imagined constructions produced by discourses like psychoanalysis. She suspects that *écriture féminine*'s gestures to sexual difference and female embodiment perpetuate a binary way of thinking despite its disclaimers.

Poststructuralism: Genealogies and Deconstructions of the Flesh

By the 1990s, poststructuralism had swept through gender studies to challenge many of its claims. Although it embraces several critical approaches, one thing poststructuralism's exponents agreed upon was that invocations of a natural origin or foundation for identity are actually effects of discourses that sustain an illusion of the natural to put certain phenomena beyond question. Such was the case with the body as an anchor of sexual difference. The most influential thinker here was Michel Foucault, whose genealogical method yields two somewhat different genres of analysis. The first draws on earlier studies like *Discipline and Punish* (Foucault 1977) to pursue detailed investigations of the material construction of sexed/gendered bodies. The second prefers later work like *The History of Sexuality* (Foucault 1990), where sexuality emerges as the preeminent discourse or game of truth that constitutes subjectivities and identities.

Materialist Foucauldians

Practitioners of a materialist genealogy include Sandra Lee Bartky (1988), Susan Bordo (1990), and Moya Lloyd (1996). Their aim is to explain how power operates through and on bodies via detailed technologies of control. Foucault's understanding of the body has been enormously productive here. Rather than a naturally given organism, there are diffuse potentialities: capacities, pleasures, organs. These are intensified, subdued, reoriented, regulated in accordance with historical exigencies. Normalization, discipline, surveillance, and biopower are some of the modes taken by constitutive powers that work up and work over the body's most visceral properties such that flesh is always in a process of materialization and saturated with constitutive power rather than being a natural given that power merely uses or subjugates. As a consequence of minutely calibrated sanctions and inducements, bodies are constantly developing new forms, gestures, abilities, and appearances as well as repeating established habits and conventions.

Foucault argues that modernity requires a particular kind of body for its reproduction: productive and efficient but also obedient and docile. This is produced through a "political anatomy" or "mechanics" of micro-power that draws on new scientific knowledge of how bodies work (Foucault 1977, 138). Novel techniques of fine-grained power now "directly involved the body in a political field" by investing, marking, and training it. "What was then being formed was a policy of coercions that act upon the body, a calculated manipulation of its elements, its gestures, its behavior." It is, Foucault insists, "always the body that is at issue—the body and its forces, their utility and their docility, their distribution and their submission" (25). More effective than violence, modern techniques of power "circulate through progressively finer channels, gaining access to individuals themselves, to their bodies, their gestures and all their daily actions" (Foucault 1972, 151–152). Sociocultural imperatives are thereby inscribed "on our bodies and their materiality, their forces, energies, sensations and pleasures" (Foucault 1990, 155).

Although some feminists would chastise Foucault for making scant reference to women's bodies (his main concern here is the medicalization of female functions and the production of certain stereotypes like the hysteric), his account of power has obvious implications for the sexualization and gendering of the body. As Moira Gatens (1992, 127) explains, "Gender is a material effect of the way in which power takes hold of the body," not a conditioning of the mind. Discipline, normalization, and surveillance have particular salience for women's bodies inasmuch as their gendering pivots on their subjection to masculine norms and their objectification through the male gaze. The obedient, docile body is, moreover, quintessentially a feminized corpus.

Sandra Lee Bartky's (1988) essay "Foucault, Femininity, and the Modernization of Patriarchal Power" illustrates this approach. Bartky investigates the ways disciplinary practices produce a body whose comportment is recognizably feminine thanks to a repertoire of postures, movements, and display. She explains how regimes of diet and dress discipline female flesh to produce fashionable bodies and how exercise sculpts it according to gendered norms (64, 68). Expectations of smooth, hairless skin and groomed hair are met through products and gadgets that in turn require knowledge, self-discipline, and routine. Yet images of perfection promulgated by magazines, television, and advertizing ensure women inevitably fall short. Under the watch of a ubiquitous "panoptical male connoisseur" they turn to compulsive rituals that compound a sense of failure: "woman's body language speaks eloquently, though silently, of her subordinate status in a hierarchy of gender." (74) Despite formal emancipation their microregulation—where "the invasion of the body is well-night total" in regulating size, contours, appetite, conduct—is relentless (80). For Bartky this is not merely a way of sustaining sexual difference; it is also the production of a subjected body on which "inferior status has been inscribed" (71).

Such descriptions of gendered embodiment often resemble phenomenological accounts of different corporeal styles. There is, however, an important methodological distinction: gender for poststructuralists is not an expression or experience of sexuality but a variable genealogical effect of power relations. Its connection to the sexed body, and the sexed body's relation to its disparate sexual organs, is therefore considerably more tenuous and potentially diverse. The body is not a natural entity modified by socialization or merely a surface inscribed with signs of sex/gender: it is thoroughly (re)constituted flesh.

Troubling Gender: Judith Butler

Despite the value of Foucault's approach for investigating mechanisms of bodily production, his resistance to any overarching account of power was a problem for feminism. Some notion of patriarchy tended to be imported to fill this gap. This was not very satisfactory from a poststructuralist perspective, and

Butler's (1990) *Gender Trouble*, which exemplifies the second strand of genea-logical analysis, helped resolve this hiatus. Drawing on Foucault's attention to discourses of sexuality, Butler argues that the abiding interest of such discourse lies in maintaining heterosexual norms. She reinforces this argument by refer-ence to Claude Lévi-Strauss's structural anthropology, where sexual difference is located in kinship relations predicated on the incest taboo. Sex, gender, and desire are aligned, she argues, in a "heterosexual matrix": a regime of discursive power whose success relies on giving to its own constructions the appearance of being natural.

At the core of Butler's (1990) constructivist argument is a basic inversion: rather than gender being an effect caused by the body, the sexed body is a discursive effect of gendered thinking. In this account Butler accepts a broadly Foucauldian sense of the body as an indeterminate assemblage where "some parts of the body become conceivable foci of pleasure precisely because they correspond to a normative ideal of a gender-specific body" and others are cor-respondingly "deadened to pleasure" (70). She defines gender as "the repeated stylization of the body" (33). "Consider gender," she suggests, "as a corporeal style, an 'act,' as it were, which is both intentional and performative, where 'performative' suggests a dramatic and contingent construction of meaning" (139). Cultural performances constitute the apparently natural sexed body in a way that is "discursively constrained" by the categories of sexual dualism. "That the gendered body is performative suggests that it has no ontological status apart from the various acts which constitute its reality" (136). Butler is accordingly keen to distinguish "performativeness" from existentialist notions of expression (141).

The pertinent question here is: "how does language itself produce the fic-tive construction of 'sex' that supports these various regimes of power?" (Butler, 1990, viii–ix). Butler's treatment of biology is a good example of her response. Rather than looking at biological facts and their implications, as earlier femi-nists had, she looks at biology as a discipline. Her contention is that biology is a gendered discourse that classifies indeterminate biological phenomena accord-ing to the dualistic schema prescribed by heterosexual norms. As such, it con-structs normal bodies as either male or female from a range of possibilities (Fausto-Sterling, 1992, 2000). Rather than being an accurate scientific represen-tation of natural sexual difference, then, biology is a discourse framed by the binary presuppositions of gender. This is the sense in which Butler can plausi-bly present the counterintuitive argument that sex is a construction of gender and nature a product of culture. Furthermore, she maintains, this discursive construction has material effects, as when the medical establishment intervenes physically to render ambiguous infants male or female because mainstream natural science (and also the law) cannot countenance transsexual bodies as other than aberrant (Butler, 109).

A corollary of her argument is that Butler (1990) cannot claim that trans-, inter-, or queer identities are in some sense more real or authentic than their binary counterparts. She can, however, claim that since such identities are no less natural than conventional forms of sexual difference they warrant equal respect. The resulting queer theory would be seized upon by gay, lesbian, bisexual, and transgendered persons, both as an ongoing challenge to sex/gender conformity and as a self-ascribed identity. In "queering" mainstream identities and values to flaunt what is undecidable and fluid, its practitioners proclaim a role that is both transgressive in its politics and celebratory in its practices.

Cross-dressing is the example Butler (1990) offers in *Gender Trouble* as a subversive practice. Its efficacy, she argues, does not lie in confusing the gendered ascriptions of sexed bodies or merely in demonstrating their contingent relationship. Rather, its subversiveness springs from giving the naturalizing game away: sex/gender is always a masquerade: "in imitating gender, drag implicitly reveals the imitative structure of gender itself—as well as its contingency" (137). Where de Beauvoir had described the professional woman's masquerade as a subterfuge for hiding her human desire for freedom, for Butler masquerade is the performative construction of a sexual ontology, with femininity always being a masquerade rather than a mask hiding a more authentic existence (47). If it is the repetition of sex/gender norms that produces the illusion of naturalness, then a failure to repeat accurately is potentially disruptive. Acting gender, Butler concludes, creates the idea of gender and without such acts, "there would be no gender at all" (140). This is not merely game playing: failure to believe is punished by marginalization and condemnation to an unlivable life (Butler 2004). Some critics nevertheless point out that the political effects of drag are context dependent and unpredictable, while others worry that parody, like the analysis itself, remains too focused on culture, rendering sex and gender deceptively voluntaristic.

Butler (1990) concedes that the body does set limits to the imaginary meanings it can occasion and that not just any gendered possibilities are available. But because she rejects theories that present these limits as a natural grounding or cause of gender, her approach forecloses attention to them. She insists that gender remains a "complex cultural construction," the body being regarded by her as an "occasion" for, rather than the cause of, desire. A yearning for the "ostensible anatomical facticity of sex" is dismissed as melancholic heterosexuality (71). This is congruent with a poststructuralist view that power is constructive rather than prohibiting something more original. But more materially minded critics nevertheless accuse Butler of idealism, of eliminating the entire domain of corporeal experience, and of ignoring the material resilience or agency of corporeality. Nancy Fraser (1998) would complain that Butler's body is merely cultural. What gives *Gender Trouble* its rather eviscerated sense is the theoretical nature of Butler's enterprise, her focus being on discourse rather than corporeality as such and within discourse, on linguistic structures and speech acts. Her definition of the sexed/gendered body as "a signifying practice" sounds more literary than corporeal (Butler 1990, 139). Her poststructuralist suspicion of references to a "real," prediscursive body as a referent object and her resulting use of scare quotes—"'the body' is itself a construction, as are the myriad 'bodies' that constitute the domain of gendered subjects" (8)—only add to critics' doubts regarding the survival of an actual, material body (Lloyd 2007; Chambers and Carver 2008).

Butler addresses such concerns in *Bodies that Matter* (1993), where she emphasizes her commitment to exploring the body as a process of materialization. Here she insists that she does recognize certain biological facts as "'primary' and irrefutable experiences" (xi). But her radical constructivism again precludes focusing on these so-called facts, as opposed to the way they are categorized in hegemonic discourses. It is not, then, that her work dismisses the body or denies its importance. But her theoretical approach—which owes as much to Derridean deconstruction as to Foucauldian genealogy—focuses on the way embodied identities are classified and discursively constructed rather than on details of bodily discipline or experience as such. This sort of theoretical debate about methodology preoccupied a good deal of scholarship on the sexed/gendered body during the 1990s. However, as attention has shifted to yet more diverse and fluid forms of corporeal identity it has become evident that critical analysis needs to operate on several levels and to include more empirical investigations.

Otherwise Gendered Bodies

While feminist attention to the body has understandably focused on women's bodies, critical men's studies employs similar approaches to examine the male body and masculinities. These had been treated by feminists either as merely the privileged standard relative to which female bodies are deemed lacking or as instruments of aggression. But during the 1990s men's studies began to examine the ways male bodies and stereotypes of masculinity are also constructed within networks of power relations whose images, norms, and practices may be oppressive or exclusionary for many men. Like women's gendered bodies, male flesh and the identities associated with it were now recognized as susceptible to disciplinary normalization.

The male body is also recognized to have a special relationship to carnal physicality, although this is amenable to varied cultural encodings. Despite associating (white, bourgeois) masculinity with rationality, Western cultures equate some men—notably, those from lower classes—with physical strength and sexual prowess and thus with low status. Aristotle's commentary on the natural characteristics of slaves and laborers finds itself repeated in contexts of race and class. Yet the muscular body of the virile male is also idealized as a sign of his manliness. Male bodies and masculine identities perceived as weak or effeminate frequently suffer physical violence and humiliation. At the same time, male bodies are widely recognized to have become feminized inasmuch as consumer cultures construct them as objects to be looked at and adorned with the kind of products once reserved for women's bodily modification. A complicated picture of diverse masculinities thus emerges: the new man who dons an apron with babe in arms; the footballer who weeps and poses in his underpants, desired by men and women alike; the new lad whose body is constantly made over, perhaps by working out and body-building but also through dieting, tattoos, cosmetic surgery, and fashion (Shilling 2003; Gill, Henwood, and McLean 2005). In short, not all male bodies are powerful and dominating, not all men enjoy high status, and masculinity is for many a complex minefield to be negotiated.

Critical men's studies generally favors constructivist and sociological methods in its investigations. An examination of areas where the quintessentially male body is both literally constructed and highly prized, such as sport and the military, is particularly common. The idealized male body that is athletic and tough but also adept at manipulating machinery or weaponry emerges here as a norm against which real bodies and their performances are measured. Such bodies are found also to be valorized as hypersexual and heterosexual, with areas like the military being, in turn, modeled on these gendered norms of male embodiment and capacity (Tuana 2002; Mankayi 2008; Wellard 2009).

Despite ongoing explorations of the ways women's and men's sexed and gendered bodies are identified and constructed, studies of embodiment increasingly insist on more mobile, complex, and diverse bodies. This is congruent with their emphasis on bodies as markers of identity rather than on their biological functions and roles. One manifestation of this thinking is its attention to transgendered or queer bodies that express and are nurtured by a more fluid and hybrid flesh (Jay 1998). Another is the influence of postcolonial theory, whose exponents described a hybrid body as a composite corporeality that results from multiple cultural influences, with new physical, cultural, and geopolitical combinations forging novel mixed modes of subaltern or border life. These hybrid bodies and subjectivities that are always in process defy essentialist notions of race or sex (Bhabha 1994), just as the cyborgs that are a mix of human and animal or body and machine defy conventional ontological categories (Haraway 1991).

A further development in this direction is represented by intersectional theory. This criticizes the isolation or privileging of sex/gender, insisting upon the complex ways sexuality and gender intersect with other aspects of embodied identity and experience: particularly race but also ethnicity, class, age, and ability (Price and Shildrick, 1999). Feminist images of sex and gender have long been accused of generalizing white, middle-class women's experiences and identities while universalizing categories of gender and descriptions of embodiment that are not necessarily valid for other racial or ethnic groups or for working-class, lesbian, and subaltern women. From the sexualization of certain body shapes or protuberances to the division of labor and protocols of corporeal behavior, it is evident that corporeal signs and norms of sexual identity can vary significantly. What is specific to current intersectional theory is its insistence that all bodies are situated at the intersection of numerous power structures and are therefore encoded in multidimensional ways. To do justice to this complexity, its proponents argue, it is necessary to eschew the additive approach that merely adds on different indices of identification: a shortcoming that is attributed to multiculturalism or identity politics. Rather, multiple locations are recognized as reciprocally and dynamically constitutive (Crenshaw 1991; McCall 2005; Yuval-Davis 2006).

The complexity and plurality of bodies described by intersectionality are different from the fluid, fragmented bodies invoked by deconstruction or postmodernism but equally challenge universalizing notions of the sexed/gendered body since discourses pertaining to gendered classifications and sexual norms will also vary across diverse social groups. Gender will, for example, acquire different meanings and signs in different racial contexts, and racial categories will play out differently depending upon one's sex. But elderly women in different racial or ethnic contexts will also have different norms of beauty or capacity applied to them. As men's studies show, while some aspects of identity may bestow privilege others may be a source of discrimination, with identities and their bodily markers being distributed unevenly across social hierarchies. The principal approaches previously described are still relevant for investigating this dense field, but clearly they need to be applied in subtler ways while revisiting some of their own assumptions. If the intersected body is a thick, transversal plurality of corporeal styles and signs, its complexity for analytical purposes will depend upon the number of indices included (Hancock 2007). Detailed sociological or ethnographic investigations of how embodied complexities are negotiated by particular actors in specific contexts are relevant here (Puwar 2004; Coole 2007), as are macrostudies of the ways multiple axes of structural power are interwoven.

This combination of phenomenological, constructivist, and structural approaches is indicative of a more pragmatic attitude toward critical theory over recent years, with detailed studies of diverse localized experiences combining with more holistic accounts of cross-cutting structural hierarchies. Such eclecticism is indicative of the sort of rapprochement suggested by Iris Marion Young in 2005. Young's intervention is worth mentioning in closing, because it occurred in the context of returning to the vexed issue of the sex/gender relation in the wake of poststructuralism and multiculturalism. For both sex and gender, she maintains, it is the imbrication of embodied experience and impersonal structures—ranging from the sexual division of labor to heteronormativity—that is at stake (5). She was nonetheless skeptical as to whether this is still best studied within the framework of sex and gender. Young develops this part of her argument in conversation with Toril Moi, who had argued that, in light of the ensemble of identities attributed to individuals by the late twentieth century, gender might be a less useful concept than the "lived body" (Moi 2001). Raia Prokhovnik (1999, 113) had already argued that the sex/gender distinction could be replaced by a single, "porous, permeable, notion of corporeal subjectivity." Young is sympathetic to this sort of claim regarding a more flexible category of embodiment that is less susceptible to either mind–body dualism or gender essentialism, provided the body–subject is situated within broader socioeconomic as well as discursive structures. Including the sort of materialist approaches associated with Marxist and radical feminism during the 1960s and 1970s, suitably updated regarding social context, is therefore commended.

CONCLUSION

Considerations of the relationship between sex, gender, and the body have engendered a number of distinctive approaches that draw on different responses to some profound philosophical questions regarding ontology, epistemology, and ethics. These have had particular bearing on how far down sexual and gender differences go. At the same time, the overview offered here reveals certain trends within a field where feminist theory has occupied a central if diminishing role. Political strategy here has been increasingly to displace any grounding of sex, gender, or even embodiment in nature in order to expand the realm of contingency and hence opportunities for change. This has been achieved through analysis of the protean ways power operates to construct and regulate bodies, resulting in an increasing emphasis on culture, itself regarded as a constitutive political order where identities and flesh are worked over. If initially the stress on contingency was accomplished via a sex-gender distinction that emphasized the social significance of biophysical sexual difference and the role of socialization in instilling gendered temperaments, more radical forms of constructivism would describe deconstructed flesh whose visceral formation and desire is susceptible to manifold constitutive interventions.

As a corollary of these immanent theoretical trajectories, a cultural body has emerged that is thoroughly politicized yet where sex and gender are no longer specifically associated with women's bodies or privileged as the principal markers of corporeal styles or categories of oppression. This accounts for a certain displacement of feminism in a field where attention has shifted to more diffuse queer, hybrid, and intersectional bodies. This is not to dismiss the continued importance of feminism (or critical men's studies): it is indeed thanks partly to the rigor of its analysis of sexed/gendered bodies and its responsiveness to criticism that more complex incarnations of power and identity have emerged. Increased emphasis on identity has also meant bodies being read as signs and vehicles of identification rather than investigated as organic or lived phenomena, and this move has allowed considerably more variables and varieties of corporeality to be accommodated as significant. The methodological challenge of attending to these more dynamic, complex bodies is to develop a theoretically more inclusive approach capable of investigating how diverse roles, experiences, and identities are negotiated and reproduced within intersecting structures of power.

NOTE

1. The idea that the body is never known or experienced in a raw material sense because its carnality is always interwoven with imaginary relationships to the flesh is widely endorsed in feminist literature on the body. Psychoanalytic accounts of unconscious relationships are complemented here by studies of Spinoza's work on the imagination as well as by phenomenological accounts of an internal body image or body schema. See, for example, Ros Diprose (1994), Moira Gatens (1996), and Gail Weiss (1999).

REFERENCES

Ahmed, Sara. 2000. *Strange encounters: Embodied others in postcoloniality*. London: Routledge.

Alcoff, Linda. 1988. "Cultural feminism versus poststructuralism: The identity crisis of feminist theory." *Signs* 13: 405–436.

Alcoff, Linda. 2006. *Visible bodies, race, gender, and the self.* London: Oxford University Press.

Bartky, Sandra Lee. 1988. "Foucault, femininity, and the modernization of patriarchal power." In Irene Diamond and Lee Quinby, eds., *Feminism and Foucault. Reflections on resistance*. Boston: Northeastern University, 61–86.

Battersby, Christine. 1998. *The phenomenal woman: Feminist metaphysics and the patterns of identity*. Cambridge, UK: Polity Press.

Bhabha, Homi. 1994. *The location of culture*. London: Routledge.

Bourdieu, Pierre, and L. Wacquant. 1992. *An invitation to reflexive sociology*. Cambridge, UK: Polity Press.

Bordo, Susan. 1990. "Feminism, postmodernism, and gender-skepticism." In Linda Nicholson ed., *Feminism/postmodernism*. London: Routledge, 87–118.

Braidotti, Rosi. 1994. *Nomadic subjects: Embodiment and sexual difference in contemporary feminist theory*. New York: Columbia University Press.

Butler, Judith. 1990. *Gender trouble. Feminism and the subversion of identity*. New York: Routledge.

Butler, Judith. 1993. *Bodies that matter: On the discursive limits of "sex."* New York: Routledge.

Butler, Judith. 1997. *Excitable speech: A politics of the performative*. New York: Routledge.

Butler, Judith. 2004. *Undoing gender*. New York: Routledge.

Chambers, Samuel, and Terrell Carver. 2008. *Judith Butler and political theory*. New York: Routledge.

Coole, Diana. 2007. "Experiencing discourse: Gendered styles and the embodiment of power." *British Journal of Politics and International Relations* 9(3): 413–433.

Coole, Diana, and Samantha Frost. 2010. *The new materialisms: Ontology, agency, and politics*. Durham, NC: Duke University Press.

Crenshaw, Kimberlé. 1991. "Mapping the margins: Intersectionality, identity politics, and violence against women of color." *Stanford Law Review* 43(6): 1241–1299.

de Beauvoir, Simone. 1972. *The second sex*. Harmondsworth, UK: Penguin.

Diprose, Ros. 1994. *The bodies of women: Ethics, embodiment and sexual difference*. London: Routledge.

Firestone, Shulamith. 1979. *The dialectic of sex: The case for feminist revolution*. London: Women's Press.

Foucault, Michel. 1972. *Power/knowledge*. New York: Pantheon Books.

Foucault, Michel. 1977. *Discipline and punish*. Harmondsworth, UK: Penguin.

Foucault, Michel. 1990. *The history of sexuality*, vol. 1. New York: Vintage Books.

Fausto-Sterling, Anne. 1992. *Myths of gender: Biological theories about women and men*. New York: Basic Books.

Fausto-Sterling, Anne. 2000. "The five sexes: Why male and female are not enough." *Sciences* 33(2): 20–25.

Fraser, Nancy. 1998. "Heterosexism, misrecognition and capitalism: A response to Judith Butler." *New Left Review* 228: 140–150.

Gatens, Moira. 1992. "Power, bodies and difference." In Michèle Barrett and Anne Phillips, eds., *Destabilizing theory: Contemporary feminist debates*. Cambridge, UK: Polity Press, 120–137.

Gatens, Moira. 1996. *Imaginary bodies: Ethics, power, and corporeality*. London: Routledge.

Gill, Rosalind, Karen Henwood, and Carl McLean. 2005. "Body projects and the regulation of normative masculinity." London: LSE. Available at http://eprints.lse.ac.uk/archive/00000371/

Grosz, Elizabeth. 1994. *Volatile bodies: Toward a corporeal feminism*. Bloomington: Indiana University Press.

Hancock, Ange-Marie. 2007. "When multiplication doesn't equal addition: Examining intersectionality as a research paradigm." *Perspectives on Politics* 5(1): 63–79.

Haraway, Donna. 1991. *Simians, cyborgs, and women: The reinvention of nature*. London: Routledge.

Irigaray, Luce. 1981. "This sex which is not one." In Elaine Marks and Isabelle de Courtivron, eds., *New French feminisms*. Brighton: Harvester Press, 99–106.

Irigaray, Luce. 1985. "*La mystérique*." In Irigaray, ed., *Speculum of the other woman*. Ithaca, NY: Cornell University Press, 191–202.

Irigaray, Luce. 1987. "Sexual difference." In Toril Moi, ed., *French feminist thought: A reader*. Oxford: Blackwell, 118–130.

Irigaray, Luce. 1993. *An ethics of sexual difference*. Ithaca, NY: Cornell University Press.

Kristeva, Julia. 1981. *Desire in language*. Oxford: Blackwell.

Kristeva, Julia. 1984. *Revolution in poetic language*. New York: Columbia University Press.

Kristeva, Julia. 1986. "Woman's time." In Toril Moi, ed., *The Kristeva reader*. Oxford: Blackwell, 187–213.

Kruks, Sonia. 2001. *Retrieving experience: Subjectivity and recognition in feminist politics*. Ithaca, NY: Cornell University Press.

Lennon, Kathleen. 2010. "Feminist perspectives on the body." In E. N. Zalta, ed., *The Stanford encyclopedia of philosophy*. Available at http://plato.stanford.edu/archives/fall2010/entries/feminist-body/

Lloyd, Genevieve. 1984. *The man of reason: "Male" and "female" in Western philosophy*. London: Methuen.

Lloyd, Moya. 1996. "Feminism, aerobics and the politics of the body." *Body and Society* 2(2): 79–98.

Lloyd, Moya. 2007. *Judith Butler: From norms to politics*. Cambridge, UK: Polity Press.

Mankayi, Nyameka. 2008. "Masculinity, sexuality and the body of male soldiers." *PINS* 36: 24–44.

McCall, Leslie. 2005. "The complexity of intersectionality." *Signs* 30(3): 1771–1800.

Millett, Kate. 1977. *Sexual politics*. London: Virago.

Moi, Toril. 2001. "What is a woman?" In Moi, ed., *"What is a woman?" and other essays*. Oxford: Oxford University Press.

O'Brien, Mary. 1981. *The politics of reproduction*. London: Routledge.

Price, Janet, and Margit Shildrick. 1999. *Feminist theory and the body: A reader*. Edinburgh: Edinburgh University Press.

Prokhovnik, Raia. 1999. *Rational woman*. London: Routledge.

Puwar, Nirmal. 2004. *Space invaders: Race, gender and bodies out of place*. Oxford: Berg.

Rich, Adrienne. 1979. *Of woman born: Motherhood as experience and institution*. London: Virago.

Ruddick, Sara. 1989. *Maternal thinking: Toward a politics of peace*. New York: Ballantine Books.

Sellers, Susan. 1991. *Language and sexual difference: Feminist writing in France*. Basingstoke, UK: Macmillan.

Shilling, Chris. 2003. *The body and social theory*, 2nd ed. London: SAGE.

Tuana, Nancy, William Cowling, Maurice Hamington, Greg Johnson, and Terrance MacMullan (Eds.). 2002. *Revealing male bodies*. Bloomington: Indiana University Press.

Weiss, Gail. 1999. *Body images: Embodiment as intercorporeality*. London: Routledge.

Wellard, Ian. 2009. *Sport, masculinities and the body*. London: Routledge.

Whitford, Margaret. 1991. *Luce Irigaray: Philosophy in the feminine*. London: Routledge.

Wollstonecraft, Mary. 1929. *A vindication of the rights of woman*. London: Everyman.

Young, Iris. 1990. *Justice and the politics of difference*. Princeton, NJ: Princeton University Press.

Young, Iris Marion. 2005. *On female body experience: "Throwing like a girl" and other essays*. Oxford: Oxford University Press.

Yuval-Davis, Nira. 2006. "Intersectionality and feminist politics." *European Journal of Women's Studies* 13(3): 193–209.

CHAPTER 7

HETERONORMATIVITY AND SEXUALITY

AMY LIND

HISTORICALLY, scholars of politics have paid little attention to sexuality. This has changed in recent decades, however, as scholars from various fields have begun to address sexuality as a social construct, site of contestation, identity marker, and generally speaking, as a concept central to broader processes of political change. Political science as a field has been slow to address sexuality as a legitimate form of inquiry (Bedford 2004); indeed, many of the most recent insights have been made in interdisciplinary settings. Yet feminist political scientists have long addressed how women's forms of sexuality have been socially constructed and legally regulated, and many scholars have pointed out how struggles over sexuality themselves are part and parcel of broader struggles concerning, for example, national identity, citizenship, sovereignty, or human rights (e.g., Phelan 2001 Duggan 2004; Alexander 1994 Puar 2007). Likewise, lesbian, gay, bisexual, and transgender (LGBT) studies scholars have long examined the socially constructed nature of sexual practices and identities. And queer studies scholars, who sometimes coincide with and sometimes differ from LGBT studies scholars in their epistemological and methodological approaches, have provided crucial insight into how normative sexuality—namely, hegemonic heterosexuality—has been naturalized as normal or appropriate whereas same-sex forms of sexual practice and identity, along with other lesbian, gay, bisexual, transgender and queer (LGBTQ) sexualities and forms of gender expression, have been viewed as abnormal and deviant, sometimes with serious consequences. Through these discussions, the notion of heteronormativity has become central to many scholars' analysis, both of broad societal institutions and of how hegemonic heterosexuality is central to people's everyday lives, forms of expression, intimate arrangements, and forms of desire.

While scholars of gender and politics have addressed sexuality to some degree, in areas ranging from, for example, women's political participation to state policies to examinations of conflict and militarization, until recently few have systematically analyzed how heteronormativity, or the privileging of heterosexual norms over all others, shapes political institutions and processes, ultimately affecting a wide range of individuals. This historical gap in the literature is due in part to the fact that, like gender, sexuality continues to be seen as secondary to discussions concerning politics and sometimes as a private matter, one even rooted in nature, that remains "outside" the realm of public political debate or inquiry. Within the feminist scholarship, it is also due to homophobic bias or lack of understanding among some researchers, a form of bias that no doubt has diminished over time and generations. Today, the study of sexuality is a burgeoning field of its own that continues to provide important insights into the scholarship on gender and politics in general. This chapter addresses four general areas of inquiry into the relationship of sexuality to gender and politics: (1) sexuality as a category of analysis and form of power; (2) the relationship of sexuality to politics; (3) LGBTQ individuals' participation in political processes, and (4) the heteronormative dimensions of global and regional political institutions and policies. It focuses on the contributions feminist scholars have made to introducing or rethinking sexuality and heteronormativity. In so doing, it aims to introduce the reader to historical trends in scholarship and to key contemporary debates shaping the overlapping, interdisciplinary fields of sexuality, and gender and politics.

Sexuality as a Category of Analysis and Form of Power

Rather than viewing sexuality as natural or as "outside" the realm of public politics, scholars of sexuality have demonstrated how sexual identities and practices have at once been viewed as "private matters" yet regulated by public institutions (see also the chapter by Hawkesworth in this volume). Hegemonic heterosexuality is often "naturalized into invisibility" (Cooper 1995), whereas subjugated sexualities have acquired a form of hypervisibility (e.g., men who have sex with men, gay men perceived as a public health threat) yet paradoxically also sometimes a form of invisibility (e.g., lesbians who are perceived not to have health issues or not to be mothers). Thus, sexuality is itself a form of power, one that has been used both in repressive and productive ways (Cooper 1995; Phelan 2001; Bedford 2004; Duggan 2004; Lind 2010b). Recognizing sexuality as a form of power began primarily during the mid-twentieth century, as scholars began to embrace sexuality as an object of analysis, systematically charting the ways that sexuality was socially constructed (Bernstein and Schaffner 2005, xii). Much of the earlier academic scholarship, which emerged alongside gay liberation struggles in North America, Britain, and Europe, took place within the humanities and to some extent in the field of psychology, with one important aim of depathologizing homosexuality. In North America, political science as a field began to address sexuality—and even then, only marginally—in the 1980s (Blasius 2001, 5), coinciding with the declassification of homosexuality as a mental disorder by the American Psychiatric Association in 1973, the American Psychological Association in 1975, and the Canadian Psychiatric Association in 1982. By the early to mid-1980s, however, sexuality was not only analyzed by various scholars but also became an important, increasingly visible site of political and cultural struggle in North America and Europe, and gradually throughout other regions as well. Drawing upon a longer trajectory of feminist scholarship on sexuality and power, emergent scholars of sexuality, heteronormativity, and politics began to more systematically and explicitly address how heterosexuality is a social institution and how norms of heterosexuality are embedded in political institutions, theories, and practices in such a way that second-wave feminism itself could not always grasp (important exceptions include the work of Adrienne Rich, Carole Vance, and Gayle Rubin). Lauren Berlant and Michael Warner (1998, 548) define *heteronormativity* as referring to institutions, structures, and practices that help normalize dominant forms of heterosexuality as universal and morally righteous. Unlike the related notion of homophobia, typically defined as the irrational fear of or hatred toward lesbians, gay men, and bisexuals, the concept of heteronormativity speaks more broadly to how societal norms, institutions, and cultural practices contribute to institutionalizing a form of hegemonic, normative heterosexuality that is discriminatory in both material and symbolic ways.[1] Seen from this perspective, heteronormativity (and gender normativity) has been present in various kinds of scholarship and continues to inform how political observers understand family forms, LGBT people, and broader societal institutions including the state. Earlier scholarship emphasized the relationship among the so-called private and public realms of life, including how heteronormative notions of *the family* and intimate arrangements inform broader understandings of national identity and nation-states. In this regard, states are important sites of analysis, given their role in regulating sexuality and private life. As Elizabeth Bernstein and Laurie Schaffner (2005, xiii) point out, "the state serves to shape our erotic possibilities and to impart a particular normative vision. The state, in short, has a sexual agenda." Davina Cooper (1995, 7) argues that states exert "power" in both repressive and productive ways: While earlier gay and lesbian and feminist writing emphasized how states repress sexual minorities, more recent work, often drawing from Michel Foucault, emphasizes how state practices can create or generate sexual–gender identities as well: for example, through laws that define gender identity based on biology (e.g., hormones) rather than on one's chosen form of expression or through welfare policies that define the family exclusively in heteronormative terms. Thus, for Cooper a theory of power is central to understanding state practices as well as resistance to those practices.

Some scholars address how, historically, states have always regulated sexuality and people's intimate lives, from colonial times to the present, including through so-called archaic sex laws. For example, many countries have had archaic sex laws concerning sexual practices (e.g., interracial marriage, prostitution, sodomy), sexual identities (e.g., homosexuality), or appropriate gender norms (e.g., gender segregation) as a way to institutionalize a hegemonic, heteronormative moral code, to control and define their national populations, and to maintain racial and political hegemonies (e.g., Guy 1991; Smith 2006; Hoad 2007). Given that sexuality was and continues to be naturalized and essentialized (as in Darwinian arguments of sex selection), this legislation has had the effect of institutionalizing a kind of nation, state, and citizenship based on an ideal, proper heterosexual, gender-normative citizen, typically defined in white, middle-class, Eurocentric terms. Feminist scholars of color, including scholars of intersectionality, have addressed how the control of black female and male sexuality was key to maintaining slavery and racially segregated societies (e.g., Davis 1983; Hill Collins 2005) and likewise how sexual violence has been central to colonization and racial domination strategies, both in the North and South (Crenshaw 1991; Smith 2007). Postcolonial studies scholars have pointed out that in colonized territories and postcolonial nations, archaic sex laws often eroded indigenous notions of sexuality and gender that, in some cases, were much less dichotomous in nature than colonial discourse (this analysis does not necessarily preclude an analysis of inequality in precolonial contexts). Neville Hoad argues that any "African" understanding of intimacy has been eroded by colonial discourses and practices that historically coded local, indigenous same-sex sexual practices and forms of desire as "sodomy" and as abnormal and deviant, such that in the current context, sexuality in Africa "has been made in line with a vision of white Western truth" (xv). He points out that "homosexuality is definitionally nonprocreative," thus making it "difficult to convey as a metaphor of social reproduction" (xvi). At the same time, in the context of the HIV/AIDS pandemic, Hoad notes that despite the fact that the HIV transmission rate is highest amongst heterosexuals in sub-Saharan Africa, discourses, and consequently policies continue to demonize men who have sex with men (MSMs) as traitors to the nation and continent, as contributing to an unhealthy nation and as the primary source of the problem. Thus, while homosexuality is typically viewed as nonprocreative, particularly in discourses of development and poverty in the global South, the nonprocreative, sexually deviant citizens are seen as the transmitters of the disease, despite strong empirical evidence to the contrary (Hoad 2007; also see Gosine 2005).

In a similar vein, scholars have begun to examine not only how notions of homosexuality travel and inform national contexts in the global South and North but likewise how notions of homophobia and heteronormativity travel in ways that serve to create newly articulated forms of homophobia as (an often naturalized) part of national discourse. In contrast to the claim or assumption in some Western scholarship that progress toward sexual–gender justice is linked to economic and social modernity (e.g., Altman 2001), scholars such as Michael Bosia and Meredith Weiss (forthcoming) have pointed out how homophobia itself is being produced and articulated in new, modern ways that have no relationship to economic progress or cultural modernity. Rather, as they argue:

> Both where same-sex intimate behavior was previously unnoticed or accepted and where it has never been openly tolerated, the well-studied spread of "gay" identities has been followed or even preceded by new, more aggressive, and more clearly politicized forms of [homo]phobia, even where such a phobia is not clearly rooted in traditional beliefs, attitudes, or practices. (P. 1)

Thus, crucially, it is not necessarily homosexuality that is being exported by the West but rather homophobia, as in the case of the proposed death penalty for homosexuals in Uganda; a case heavily backed financially and ideologically by foreign, especially U.S.-based religious Right organizations. Furthermore, states themselves are homophobic, thereby requiring scholarly attention to the further comparative analysis of "homophobic states" and their consequences for LGBT and other nonnormative individuals (Bosia and Weiss forthcoming).

Scholars have also noted how sexuality becomes a site of contestation particularly during times of crisis and in places of conflict, both in the past and present. As Bernstein and Schaffner (2005, xiii) note, "In times of economic and cultural flux, sex may become an easy and frequent target of campaigns for state regulation." For example, Dagmar Herzog (2005) argues that rather than dismiss sexuality as an important category of analysis in Holocaust studies and German historiography, scholars must necessarily examine sexuality as central to the success of Nazism's horrific crimes and to recurrent reconstructions of the memory and meaning of Nazism in contemporary postfascist German politics. If we overlook sexuality, Dagmar argues, "we lose opportunities to comprehend the extraordinary appeal of Nazism both to those Germans who sought the restoration of conservative family values and to those who benefited from Nazism's loosening of conventional mores" (1–2).

Herzog (2005), like other scholars, uses the notion of *sexual politics* to frame her study. David Bell and Jon Binnie (2000) define sexual politics as the terrain in which contemporary actors struggle for the right to self-determination as sexual beings, freedom of sexual and gender expression, and the right to control one's own body. Sonia Correa, Rosalind Petchesky, and Richard Parker (2008) define the term as including not only the conventionally understood formal political arena but also, for example, the economic and cultural effects on sexual–gender identity of modern capitalist consumer cultures, globalization, transnational media campaigns, and neoliberalization. The increased coupling of political enfranchisement with one's market position under neoliberal capitalism is a recurring theme in the literature. This is because unlike earlier social movements (e.g., feminist, new Left) contemporary LGBT movements emerged through, and sometimes as a result of, neoliberal policies and practices, including state as well as civil society practices (Lind 2010a).

Some scholars emphasize how sexual politics often occur through ideologies of moral panic; again, in times of crisis. As Gilbert Herdt (2009, 3) states:

> Panics produce state and nonstate stigma, ostracism, and social exclusion—the opposite of what liberalism or neoliberalism has envisioned. Sexual panics, when effective, are liminal and generate images of the monstrous. In media representations...sexual panics may generate the creation of monstrous enemies—sexual scapegoats. This 'othering' dehumanizes and strips individuals and whole communities of sexual and reproductive rights, exposing fault lines of structural violence (e.g., racism, poverty, homophobia, etc.).

Contemporary sex panics surrounding abortion, AIDS, sex, homosexuality, pornography, contraception, population control, gender-appropriate norms, and sexual rights have occurred across countries and regions and often reflect broader struggles concerning sovereignty, empire, citizenship, Westernization, and globalization. Diane di Mauro and Carole Joffe address the Religious Right and the reshaping of sexual policy in the United States during the George W. Bush years (2000–2008), which had significant impacts of non-normative households and individuals both within and outside the United States. They point out that the United States has a long history of sexual conservatism that dates back to its colonial origins, at which time a "regulatory framing of moral and sexual behaviors and values" was instilled in notions of the "American Dream" and the "American way" (di Mauro and Joffe 2009, 47). More recently, as feminist and LGBT rights movements have challenged normative sexuality, a countercurrent has emerged to defend sexual conservatism. Current sex panics continue today, as increased legal rights and legitimacy are given to fetal subjectivity, whereas LGBT rights are simultaneously being acquired and repealed or blocked on a state-by-state basis. In February 2011 in the state of Ohio, a fetus was allowed to be called as a witness in a legal hearing (Wing 2011; also see Morgan and Michaels 1999); proposals are in committee in several states to define rape more narrowly and to disallow plaintiffs in rape trials to call themselves "victims" (e.g., CNN 2011); and gays, lesbians, and transgendered people continue to be victims of hate crimes in disproportionate numbers, all in the name of defending appropriate reproduction and heteronormative family ideals. But while this form of legislative power is repressive, that of LGBT social movements continues to work in a productive sense (albeit repressive at times as well), and increasingly more states are passing same-sex partner recognition laws, including same-sex marriage or civil unions. This geopolitical arena of sexual politics, like many others, necessarily calls for scholars to approach the topic of sexuality and politics from an interdisciplinary perspective, one that takes into account formal as well as informal political processes and that goes beyond single-issue politics to address a wide range of structural inequalities (e.g., sexism, racism, class oppression, homophobia).

The Relationship of Sexuality to Politics

Studies of sexuality have contributed in numerous ways to rethinking key political categories such as citizenship, nationality, and governance. This section addresses how scholars have examined *sexual citizenship* and the heteronormative underpinnings of legal and cultural discourse concerning the family and the nation (Bell and Binnie 2000; Richardson 2000; Plummer 2001). In periods of crisis, heteronormative citizen practices and state policies are often encouraged or enforced alongside conventional masculine and feminine constructions of the *good citizen* (Richardson 2000); these constructions are sometimes referred to as *hypermasculine* or *hyperfeminine* because they involve an explicit reassertion of traditional gender roles and values. In these instances, an appeal to traditional gender roles typically undergirds broader societal anxieties concerning crisis, conflict, or change. Economic practices of neoliberalism reinforce traditional interpretations of the family in similar ways, as evidenced in the appeal by some states to reinforce and strengthen the traditional family and associated parental gender roles (e.g., mother as child rearer and household caretaker; father as financial provider for the family) in welfare reform legislation (Smith 2001; Duggan 2004). Yet even in noncrises contexts, gendered constructions are central to notions of citizenship, as feminist scholars have long pointed out; what is most interesting, then, is how particular constructions are invoked in political discourse as a way to garner political support or appeal to a sense of citizenship, security, or national belonging. Yet struggles for sexual citizenship have yielded great advances for LGBTQ people as well, as witnessed in the constitutional reforms of South Africa, Ecuador, and Fiji (Lind 2010a) and as evident in several nation-states' adoption of same-sex marriage laws (Bernstein, Marshall, and Barclay 2009). Sometimes these gains coincide with feminist gains; sometimes they do not, as witnessed in "new Left" countries in Latin America where governments have adopted antidiscrimination clauses on the basis of sexual orientation yet continued to limit access to abortion (Friedman 2007; Lind 2012). Institutions of global governance also regulate sexual practices and identities, often creating complex, transnational arenas of power within which actors must necessarily operate (Bedford 2009; Lind 2010b).

To begin, debates on sexual citizenship have opened a new discursive terrain for understanding how liberal democracies are fundamentally heteronormative or are structured according to rules and norms that privilege heterosexuals over all other nonnormative individuals such as gay men, lesbians, bisexuals, transsexuals, and, generally speaking, transgendered people.[2] Since the 1980s, activists and scholars in the United Kingdom and the United States began to use the term more widely as a way to politicize the meaning of citizenship in response to both state securitization and neoliberalization and in light of developments such as the HIV/AIDS crisis and radical queer politics that emerged during that period. Whereas traditional conceptions of citizenship, pioneered by the work of T. H. Marshall (1950), emphasize the state's role in securing the welfare and rights of its citizens (the civic liberalist tradition) or the obligation of citizens to participate politically in common affairs (the civic republican tradition), contemporary feminist, poststructuralist, and queer studies scholars emphasize a broader notion of citizenship that lends itself to creating a more participatory democracy, one that includes sexual dissidents. Indeed, a central tenet of the research on sexual citizenship is that "all citizenship is sexual citizenship" (Bell and Binnie 2000, 10) and that all citizens are sexed through political discourses of the family as heteronormative and gender normative—discourses that frame many of the debates on national identity, welfare, marriage, immigration, and labor rights, to name only a few. Thus, scholars have attempted to redefine the family in policy and the law and to further scrutinize how heteronormativity is an assumed part of state practices of citizenship and very much frames who counts as a good or bad citizen (Seidman 2001).

The concept of sexual citizenship opens up the possibility for better understanding the public–private dichotomy in political theory and practice. Scholars have noted that sexual citizenship is based on a set of dichotomies, most notably the dichotomy of public versus private space (Giddens 1992; Plummer 2001; Evans 1993, 2007). The metaphor of *the closet* serves as a case in point. The closet is evoked as a metaphor of privacy and secrecy; "coming out of the closet" evokes the idea that individuals enter the realm of public life as "out" individuals, workers, and citizens. Ken Plummer (2001, 238) uses the concept of *intimate citizenship* to reframe the public–private division. He defines intimate citizenship as including the "...rights, obligations, recognitions and respect around those most intimate spheres of life—who to live with, how to raise children, how to handle one's body, how to relate as a gendered being, how to be an erotic person." In a similar vein, Mauro Cabra, A. I. Grinspan, and Paula Viturro (2006, 262) argue that sexual citizenship involves "...that which enunciates, facilitates, defends and promotes the effective access of citizens to the exercise of both sexual and reproductive rights and to a [non-heteronormative] political subjectivity." In this sense, sexual citizenship is about the right to control one's body, experience of embodiment, and (gendered and sexed) identity in the broadest sense, despite hegemonic discourse to the contrary that naturalizes gender expectations and identities into invisibility or assumes that citizens' sexual lives, identities, and intimate arrangements are "private" and therefore outside the realm of formal politics.

Central to this spatial logic is the exclusion of the homosexual from public life, in part through repressive strategies aimed at preserving the division between the "pure heterosexual" and the "polluted homosexual" (Seidman 2001, 322). Historically, laws regulating sexuality in northern, industrialized countries and in colonized territories and postcolonial nations were passed precisely to set up this division between good and bad, pure and polluted, healthy and unhealthy, legal and criminal, as many scholars have noted (Guy 1991; Seidman 2001). In postcolonial nations in Latin America, for example, sodomy, anti-prostitution, and miscegenation laws all worked hand-in-hand to construct the ideal citizen as of Spanish or *mestizo/a* origin (i.e., as "not Indian"), middle-to upper-class, respectable, and heterosexual (Clark 2001; Prieto 2004). While many of these laws have been overturned, some remain in effect and have consequences for all individuals, heterosexual or otherwise, who do not fit within the prescribed heterosexual norms of their societies. As Steven Siedman (2001, 322) points out, "...Regimes of heteronormativity not only regulate the homosexual but control heterosexual practices by creating a moral hierarchy of good and bad sexual citizens."

Immigration studies scholars have pointed out how nation-states operate in heteronormative (as well as racialized and gendered) ways to allow "good" immigrants in and keep "bad" immigrants out. Eithne Luibhéid (2002) addresses how the U.S. border has served as a site for controlling sexuality, including of pregnant women, Chinese immigrants, prostitutes, and lesbians and gay men, all of whom have been deemed as national threats at various times in history. Indeed, in many countries, immigration and political asylum claims depend much upon the broader political climate with regard to sexual politics and citizen laws (also see Luibhéid and Cantú 2005). Siobhan Somerville points out that contemporary immigration laws, framed largely in heteronormative terms, often shadow earlier miscegenation laws that banned interracial marriage (Somerville 2005). Similarly, post-9/11 processes of securitization in North America have sometimes created convivial, paradoxical relationship among queer individuals and the post-9/11 security state, as Jasbir Puar (2007) powerfully argues in *Terrorist Assemblages*. The increased securitization of states has led to new regimes of heteronormativity, which are typically racialized and often equate certain queers with terrorism while others with the national ideal. In this way, as Puar argues, new forms of homonormativities have emerged, which privilege "respectable" gays and lesbians (read: white, middle-class, gender-appropriate) against those that fall outside the realm of normative gay sexuality and gender identity (also see Aganthagelou, Bassichis, and Spira 2008). Thus, political and cultural hegemonies exist among LGBT people as well, a point that Cathy Cohen (2001) also addresses in her research on sexuality, race, and class in LGBT communities within the United States, in which she argues for a politics "where the nonnormative and marginal positions of punks, bulldaggers, and welfare queens...[be] the basis for progressive transformative coalition work" (201). And as Puar notes, the U.S. state has publicly supported the human rights of queers under some circumstances, as in the case of Iran or other nations demonized as "evil" or as "terrorist," whereas the same state works to repress queers at home, thus raising the issue of how states operate as simultaneously homophobic and repressive yet also as productive and creative of LGBT identities. In a similar vein, Anna Aganthagelou et al. (2008) argue that there has been a "homonormative turn," as part of a broader imperial logic, which "recodes 'good' forms of national kinship (monogamous, consumptive, privatized) while punishing those that fall outside them, particularly those forms of racialized and classed kinship that continue to be the target of state violence and pathology…leaving the foundational antagonisms of capitalist liberal democracy unscathed" (122). An example of this is the emphasis on same-sex (normative) marriage as the primary mainstream political strategy pursued by gay and lesbian activists in the United States and elsewhere, an emphasis that leaves the institution of marriage and additional repressive state practices, including the criminalization of other forms of legally defined "deviant" sexual practices, unexamined and intact.

Some scholars have addressed the consequences of neoliberal states practices and policies for sexual citizenship. In neoliberal contexts, the reassertion of conventional, heteronormative family forms has taken precedence in public policies and laws, as in the U.S. "welfare reform" process, which had at its core a notion of preserving the patriarchal, heterosexual, two-parented family while simultaneously demonizing single parents and nonheterosexual family forms (Smith 2001). This occurred through linking mandatory marriage education to welfare eligibility and through related fatherhood initiatives. In this context, the privatization of the economy has occurred alongside the privatization of care and family survival in such a way that nonnormative individuals do not have access even to the newly privatized points of service in the same way that married heterosexuals do; this includes lesbian, gay, and bisexual households but also single mothers and mothers deemed "unfit" to care for their children (Smith 2001). Lisa Rofel (2007) argues that in postsocialist China, neoliberal subjectivities are created through the production of various desires—material, sexual, and affective—and that it is largely through these means that people in China are imagining their identities and practicing appropriate desires for the post-Mao era. The emergence of gay and lesbian identities in this context is thus linked to the postsocialist state and to people's quest for a new kind of citizenship.

Emergent scholarship on sexual citizenship in countries that have shifted away from neoliberal development models to socialist or "post-neoliberal" models of development point toward somewhat similar conclusions, despite major shifts in economic policy. That is, heteronormativity typically remains central to post-neoliberal forms of governance. For example, particularly in Latin America's shift to the Left in the 2000s, some socialist-leaning governments continue to rely upon homophobic, heteronormative narratives of national citizenship and development; indeed, these are relics of the "old Left" past.

Venezuela President Hugo Chavez (1999–present), probably the most well-known of Latin America's "new Left" leaders, has from the start framed his Bolivarian revolution in maternalist, heteronormative terms and, despite political support from LGBTQ sectors, has blocked repeated attempts to pass pro-LGBT legislation (Friedman 2007; Adrian 2008). In contrast, post-neoliberal governments in Bolivia and Ecuador have included new legislation that provides mechanisms for nontraditional households to access state resources, thereby paving the way for a broader notion of redistribution based on a newly defined family that is not based entirely on kinship or blood-based relations (Lind and Pazmiño Arguello 2009). Thus, sexual citizenship claims depend upon the broader political climate, the historical trajectory of postcolonial nation-building, and the ways activists and other individuals and groups negotiate the terms of citizenship within the broader arena of sexual politics and politics in general.

LGBTQ Participation in Political Processes and Social Movements

One way to understand the relationship among sexuality, gender, and politics is to examine how nonnormative groups of people have made political claims and participated in political processes. This section addresses how scholars of politics understand LGBT participation in local, national, and international politics; how LGBT voter behavior and standards of living are understood, sometimes in misguided ways; how the notion of *identity politics* has been key to understanding how LGBTQ identity markers are mobilized in given contexts; the role of LGBTQ social movements in influencing decision-making processes; and how heteronormativities as well as homonormativities are produced in and through LGBT political struggles, thereby creating new hierarchies based on race, class, and nationality, even as they acquire new forms of rights for marginalized groups of people.

To begin, as scholars have observed, LGBTQ individuals participate in formal political processes like any other group of people: as voters and sometimes as candidates, policy makers, legal experts, lobbyists, or advocates. As existing research on LGBT political participation, public opinion polls, and same-sex partner recognition legislation has shown, there is still a great need for normative empirical research documenting the lives of individuals and households that do not fit the hegemonic heteronormative and gender normative ideals of their societies or nations. For example, the 2000 U.S. Census revealed some interesting information about lesbian and gay voter participation: the census reported that self-identified gays and lesbians lived in 99.3 percent of all counties in the nation. Prior to the 2000 census, some politicians did not believe that gays and lesbians existed in their districts: As noted in the Urban Institute's publication, *The Gay and Lesbian Atlas*, "When informed that 55 same-sex couples were counted in his hometown in Mississippi, Republican State Sen. Dean Kirby told *The Clarion-Leader* (Jackson, MS), 'Surely you jest. Wow! I have never met any of these people'" (Gates and Ost 2004). Thus, the most conventional form of bringing visibility to lesbian and gay lives is potentially political in and of itself. Not surprisingly, data from the 2000 census indicate that statistically, states with more gay- and lesbian-supportive laws have higher concentrations of gay and lesbian couples (Gates and Ost 2004), and that gay and lesbian voters tend to vote for the liberal Democratic rather than the conservative Republican Party, although this too depends upon location and individual ideological affiliations that go beyond narrowly defined gay and lesbian "identity politics." The Log Cabin Republicans, a gay and lesbian political arm of the Republican Party, for example, has an increasing presence in Republican and Right-leaning politics, albeit often with great resistance from other conservative individuals and groups.

Scholarly research on gay- and lesbian-supportive laws demonstrates that often, in political and cultural battles concerning the family, there is much misinformation in the media. Thus, research documenting the socioeconomic status of LGBT individuals and their related needs for access to material resources and legal rights, both in public and private sectors, has been key to developing a clearer, more accurate understanding of LGBT populations. M. V. Lee Badgett's research on the economic status of gays and lesbians in the United States is a case in point: she reports that, contrary to popular belief, gay men and lesbians are not generally in a higher-income bracket than their heterosexual counterparts. While some gay men have acquired wealth, the majority have not; this is even less so for lesbians, who continue to face structural biases in the labor market on the basis of their gender and sometimes their race or social class (Badgett 2001). This research has implications for how future federal and state public policies and laws are created, being that historically they have been based on a heteronormative notion of the family or household, which excludes poor LGBT individuals from access to state resources.

In contrast, in the Global South, postcolonial studies scholars have attempted to counter discourses of homosexuality as "foreign" to the needs, desires, and identities of individuals who do not fit within the culturally prescribed gender and sexual order within their countries. A dire amount of research exists that documents gay, lesbian, bisexual, or transgender lives in regions such as Latin America and the Caribbean, Africa, and Asia, despite the fact that major culture wars are taking place, often supported by conservative antigay transnational networks, in several countries. On one hand, some countries such as South Africa and Argentina have national same-sex marriage laws, and others have antidiscrimination clauses on the basis of sexual orientation and gender identity in their constitutions (e.g., Ecuador, South Africa, Fiji), making them among the most progressive constitutions worldwide. On the other hand, as has been widely publicized, antihomosexuality agendas have dominated political processes in some nations, such as Uganda, where gay activists have been murdered and where the state, backed in part by the U.S.-based Religious Right, nearly made homosexuality a crime punishable by death (Gettelman 2011). In other cases, such as in Egypt, the homophobic state has worked to repress gay sexualities as a way to erase any notion of same-sex desire as "Egyptian" (Human Rights Watch 2004). This raises the additional issue that "visibility," while important, is not always positive; it can be productive yet also repressive, depending upon the national context (Bosia and Weiss forthcoming).

Scholars have also conducted research on LGBT participation in social movements. Wald, Button, and Rienzo (1996, cited in Bedford 2004) found that, in the United States, variation in the expansion of legal protection for LGBT people was influenced by the strength and political mobilization of both the gay and lesbian community and Protestant fundamentalist groups, the presence of sympathetic political elites, and the existence of a political environment responsive to new claimants. David Rayside (2001) points out in his research on LGBT activism in Britain, Canada, and the United States that while activists have made important claims, particularly since the 1980s, "...elected politicians and their parties are reluctant to take unequivocal stands on sexual orientation even when they are favorably disposed to do so. In most countries, they are prone to view gay-positive measures as vote losers" and "tend to see pro-gay sentiments as strong only for gays and lesbians themselves" (24). And even when gay-positive measures are passed, Urvashi Vaid (2004, 4) points out that access to political processes and benefits from whatever favorable decisions emerge from courts, administrative agencies, and legislatures "are not evenly spread across lines of class, race, gender and region."

Some social movement scholars have addressed the nature of LGBT social movements as *new* identity-based versus *old* strategy-based movements. The long-standing *identity* versus *strategy* debate within the social movement scholarship tends to separate struggles for recognition (typically viewed as identity based) from struggles for redistribution (typically viewed as class or material based) (Cohen 1985; Fraser 1996; Gamson 2008). While LGBT movements are often framed as "identity-based" movements, much of the recent scholarship documents the multiple ways LGBT people have limited access to material resources as a result of their second-class or noncitizen status and have struggled for broader agendas that include redistribution. This, however, is a point of contention within LGBT movements as well. On one hand, movements that wish to work within the defined boundaries of liberal democracy tend to focus on single-issue politics and fight exclusively or primarily for a normative set of gay and lesbian rights. These rights often include same-sex marriage, the right to serve in the military (in countries where gays and lesbians are not allowed to openly serve), parental rights (e.g., legal guardianship, adoption), employment rights, and inheritance and property rights. Yet movements that have effectively acquired some level of sexual citizenship—as in countries where same-sex marriage laws exist—often do so without questioning the institution of marriage or democracy within which inequalities continue to exist. Thus, more radically oriented LGBT movements challenge the very institutions of marriage and democracy (among others), question why liberal LGBT supporters wish to be part of what they view as oppressive institutions, and struggle for an alternative to marriage, military, and the family as legally defined and regulated by the state and/or by religious institutions (see Aganthagelou et al. 2008). For better or for worse, these widely contrasting political strategies and ideologies are often framed in terms of LGBT versus queer politics, particularly in the U.S. context (Gamson 2008).

Yet challenges to this dualistic understanding of LGBT social movement organizing also exist, both within the United States and transnationally. In his widely cited article, "Must Identity Movements Self-Destruct? A Queer Dilemma," Joshua Gamson (1995) argues that while some segments of the LGBT movement have adopted the notion of "queer" to challenge and broaden an understanding of identity that transcends normative categories (e.g., heterosexual vs. homosexual; cisgender vs. transgender), identity-based social movements necessarily must grapple with the essentialist paradox of fixed identity categories. "Fixed identity categories are both the basis for oppression and the basis for political power," he argues, pointing out the contradictions and messiness of identity politics. Other scholars address how identity politics are derived from and also sometimes challenge the broader political context within which political identities are constructed. Jan-Willem Duyvendak (2001), for instance, argues that in France the pursuit of a specific group identity and the representation of particular desires and interests conflicts with prevailing republican notions of egalitarianism and universalism, making it difficult for the gays and lesbians to create a movement of their own, separate from neo-Marxist and other radical leftist traditions. He contrasts this with the Netherlands' historical practice of "pillarization," which existed through the 1970s and provided an organizational framework for politics and social life (parties, schools, sports associations, the media) within carefully delineated groups (usually by religious denomination). Unlike France, this historical state practice allowed for LGBT people to organize more readily as a group. Thus, despite the fact that the Netherlands has been "depillarized" since the 1970s; the social and political legacy has nonetheless allowed for LGBT movements to organize independently (Duyvendak 2001).

Miriam Smith compares LGBT organizing processes in Canada and the United States and argues that, while gay and lesbian rights claimants in the two countries have framed the issue of same-sex marriage in similar ways, the outcomes have been quite different due to how the framings have been interpreted within the broader political climate: Whereas Canada passed federal same-sex marriage legislation in 2005, the United States continues with its legacy of federal and state Defense of Marriage Acts (DOMAs); thus, activists are forced to work toward repealing DOMAs and to propose same-sex marriage legislation at the state, rather than the federal, level (Smith 2007).[3]

In the Global South, identity politics take on different sets of meanings, ones that are typically embedded in broader struggles concerning (post)colonization, Westernization, sovereignty, and imperialism. Dennis Altman (2001) addresses the "universalizing of gay identities" as a process by which new forms of sexual expression and identities emerge throughout the world alongside the broader process of globalization. In his view, gay identities are increasingly visible in countries where material progress has occurred—a view that supports John D'Emilio's earlier claim (with regard to his historical research on the United States) that gay identities have emerged, albeit paradoxically, as a result of capitalism (D'Emilio 1984; Altman 2001). Some scholars such as Ronald Ingelhart (1997) claim to find evidence of a shift from what he terms *materialist* to *postmaterialist* values in several countries. In his study, Ingelhart shows significant shifts toward a more permissive view of abortion, divorce, homosexuality, and extramarital sex in all but two of twenty countries surveyed between 1981 and 1990. The two exceptions were South Africa and Argentina, which, interestingly, are now two of a small set of countries in the global South that have same-sex marriage laws.[4]

Other scholars address the complex transnational context within which local decisions are made about sexuality. Rather than attempting to create a barometer of sexual progress, these scholars focus instead on describing and analyzing relationships among local, national, and transnational actors in the making of public discourses concerning sexuality in their home countries. These accounts allow for an understanding of how newly articulated forms of homophobia emerge in both rich and poor countries and, likewise, how some countries in the global South, despite their economic poverty as nations, have advanced more progressive legislation than some of their northern counterparts. Thus, while some patterns of LGBT-friendly legislation may exist worldwide, there are examples of social movement organizing that point the discussion in a different direction. Suparna Bhaskaran (2004), for example, addresses how the struggle in the 1990s and 2000s to repeal Section 377 of the Indian Penal Code, an antisodomy law originally passed under British colonial rule in 1860, occurred through a confluence of local and transnational networks aimed at challenging the contemporary state's usage of the code against sexual minorities. As part of social movement opposition to the penal code language, activists argued that the contemporary homophobic state was disproportionately using the code against sexual minorities. As another part of the legal argument that was constructed, activists argued that forms of same-sex desire and nonheterosexual identities have existed in India prior to colonization and that modern conceptions of homosexuality as deviant and unnatural came about only with British colonization (note that this legal argument was proposed as a way to counter the idea that homosexuality is merely a "Western import" rather than to argue necessarily that sexual hierarchies and inequalities did not exist prior to colonization). Combined, these arguments (alongside others) helped create a legal argument for the High Court of Delhi to decriminalize same-sex behavior in 2009. And Jacqui Alexander's (1991, 1994) now-classic articles linking sexuality to neoliberal state practices in the Bahamas and in Trinidad and Tobago demonstrate this as well. Among others, she argues that neoliberal economic reform relies on women's heterosexual love to pick up the slack of state cutbacks, a process that has led to the scapegoating of gays, lesbians, and sex workers as "threats" to Caribbean postcolonial nations and colonized territories (ibid.; also see Bedford 2009, xi–xix). In these Caribbean contexts, *postmaterial values* are viewed as foreign and as "outside" the nation. There is evidence in the scholarship of other examples as well that do not necessarily correspond to a country's shift to postmaterial values. For example, whereas Ecuador continues to be a Latin American country with the highest number of churchgoers (Xie and Corrales 2010), since 1997 legislation has been passed both in neoliberal and post-neoliberal contexts that defy any logic of the "march of history" as an indicator of sexual progress (Bosia and Weiss in press; Lind in press). In 1997, homosexuality was decriminalized in the country, following a widely publicized systematic, targeted beating of four transgendered individuals in Cuenca, the country's third largest city. First beaten on the streets of Cuenca, local police then arrested them and brought them to a local jail where more than one of these individuals was raped by police. This incident drew strong support from Ecuador's generally conservative national population and was the impetus needed for activists to push for legal change and recognition. Following the decriminalization of homosexuality, in 1998 the new constitution, redrafted largely by a conservative national assembly, included antidiscrimination legislation on the basis of sexual orientation. And in the 2008 constitution, redrafted under the leadership of socialist president Rafael Correa (2007–present), additional legislation was included to protect individuals on the basis of gender identity and to provide further mechanisms for sexual–gender minorities not only to receive recognition but also to access state benefits and other material resources typically reserved for heterosexual citizens, as part of heteronormative families and households (Lind in press). All of these examples demonstrate the complexity of framing sexual politics, including LGBT rights, in postcolonial contexts.

The Heteronormative Dimensions of Global Political Institutions and Public Policies

As scholars have moved away from state-centric analyses, and as the fields of postcolonial and critical development studies have grown additional attention has been paid to how heteronormativity is embedded in institutions of global and regional governance (e.g., United Nations [UN], World Bank, World Trade Organization, European Union) and in international economic and social policies and laws (e.g., gender mainstreaming, gender and development, human rights, disaster relief, trade liberalization, national security). In addition, new forms of scholarship on heteronormativity and sexuality have emerged in the fields of international relations and international political economy. Cynthia Weber's (1999) pioneering work on "queering" U.S. state hegemony draws from various fields, including not only international relations but also psychoanalytic feminist and queer theory, to address the performative nature of U.S. imperial power through an examination of foreign policy. She analyzes the U.S. invasions of Cuba, the Dominican Republic, Grenada, and Panama to understand how the U.S. state sustains its imperial superiority through gendered representations of itself as hypermasculine (hence the emphasis on the state's performative nature) and of the invaded countries as feminine and subservient. Alongside this, she introduces readers to an understanding of how hegemonic heterosexuality holds a central, rather than a marginal or nonexistent, place in international relations discourse and practice. At the time of its publication in 1996, *Faking It* was a unique and cutting-edge contribution to the field of international relations.

Scholars of international political economy IPE have also addressed how sexuality, intimacy, heteronormativities, and homonormativities shape scholarly understandings of global restructuring and international politics. J. K. Gibson-Graham (2006) argues that discourses of globalization, both those of supporters and proponents, tend to view globalization as a "rape script," in which powerful nations and corporations have extreme power over poor nations. Seen as a rape script, globalization feels "omnipresent and inevitable," but, as the authors argue, when viewed as one form of economic practice among others, we can begin to imagine alternatives to capitalist globalization. Kimberly A. Chang and L. H. M. Ling (2000) argue that globalization has an "intimate other" that serves as what Saskia Sassen calls the "underbelly" of globalization. This intimate other, which in Chang and Ling's case refers to Filipina domestic workers in Hong Kong, helps sustain (what we can now call) regimes of heteronormativity alongside political and economic forms of power. These studies provided important bases for later, more explicit examinations of heteronormativity as a form of power and social institution. Amy Lind (2011) argues that the gender and development (GAD) field is inherently heteronormative in that many GAD policies assume that poor women and their households—the typical recipients of GAD policies—are necessarily bound to heterosexual familial arrangements, an observation that Chandra Mohanty (1991) hinted at years earlier in "Under Western Eyes" and that other scholars have critiqued as well (e.g., Harcourt 2009).

Scholars have also observed how institutions of global and regional governance, like nation-states, are inherently heteronormative, in addition to being largely Eurocentric institutions. Recent research on the World Bank, the world's largest and most influential development institution, is a case in point. Andil Gosine's (2005, 2010) research on Gay, Lesbian or Bisexual Employees (GLOBE) of the World Bank demonstrates how employees' gay, lesbian, and bisexual (GLB) identities do not necessarily translate into a particular set of GLB interests or concerns. As an important institution in the global development industry, the World Bank offers perhaps the best set of domestic partner benefits to its GLB employees. At the same time, the bank is known for its conventional heteronormative policies and practices in the Global South. Gosine's findings suggest that while the Bank may have considered changing some of its policies as a result of GLB presence among its employees (most notably, with Hans Binswanger's influence in the bank funding HIV/AIDS projects in Africa and elsewhere), for the most part GLB employees themselves did not see a correlation between their own interests and those of LGBT people in the Global South, the recipients of bank policies (Gosine 2010). Kate Bedford's (2009, xii) research on World Bank policy framings aims to "look at the sexual nature of Bank gender policy…and at the sexualized politics of the Bank as a global governing body." Her study "identifies the Bank as a key global actor in forging normative arrangements of intimacy, and it links that process to international political economy." As part of her analysis, she reveals how the Bank, while it claims to have little or no business in sexuality, is always necessarily invested in and working to create or rearticulate notions of femininity, masculinity and heteronormativity as part and parcel of their broader economic modernization agenda, even in the "kinder, gentler" post-Washington Consensus era. The bank's PROFAM project, piloted in Argentina and Ecuador, which aimed to promote family strengthening among the poor, is a case in point: As Bedford argues, the project essentially asked women to "word harder" (following the long-standing liberal WID tradition of "integrating women into development") and men to "love better," as they were asked to join workshops addressing paternal responsibilities in domestic labor as a way to "make them better partners" in normative familial arrangements (xx).

Scholars have addressed heteronormativity in other institutions as well, including in the United Nations and international development agencies. Unlike the World Bank, United Nations employees who participate in United Nations Gay, Lesbian and Bisexual Employees (UNGLOBE) must comply with the laws of their countries of origin, thereby making it difficult to organize at an employee level. At the same time, "out" UN LGBT employees and their allies have made an effort to address discrimination on the basis of sexual orientation and gender identity on a global scale; in this sense, their strategy as an employee's association diverges greatly from the bank's GLOBE (Lind 2010a). Similarly, as scholars such as Gilles Kleitz (2000) point out, international development agencies generally assume that sexuality is an attribute of the wealthy: "The poor simply can't be queer, because sexual identities are seen as a rather unfortunate result of western development and are linked to being rich and privileged" (2; see also Bedford 2009; Lind 2010a).

Studies have been conducted of regional governing bodies as well. For example, European studies scholars have analyzed how the European Union (EU) has integrated gender and sexuality concerns into its regional governance agenda (Bell 2002; Kantola 2010). In fact, the first legally binding international treaty addressing discrimination on the basis of sexual orientation was the 1997 Amsterdam Treaty, approved by the then fifteen leaders of the EU member states as a way to update the EU's original 1992 Maastricht Treaty. While the provision addressing sexual orientation in the treaty does not outlaw discrimination per se, it requires member states to abide by it to acquire and maintain EU membership. Among others, the Amsterdam Treaty paved the way for the EU's Employment Equality Directive, which serves as a guide for national governments to implement nondiscrimination policies in the workplace.

International gender policies are also being analyzed in new ways by scholars of sexuality and gender studies. For example, Jauhola (2010) provides a critique of heteronormativity in gender mainstreaming (GM) policies that aim to integrate women into political and economic processes as a way to achieve gender equality. Defined in a conventional sense, gender mainstreaming also leads to the heteronormalization of societal institutions and daily life, a fact that feminist proponents of GM have not always addressed. Jauhola addresses GM policies and practices in post-tsunami Indonesia and argues that as GM documents and gender equity policies draw from heteronormative sex–gender divisions and gender binaries, they (however unwittingly) reproduce heteronormative boundaries. Thus, even in seemingly gender-neutral policy processes such as disaster relief, heteronormativity shapes the outcome of who gets access to relief and how. One important concrete outcome of this research is that whereas heterosexual women have been the "targets" of various forms of gender equity politics, these policies, which tend to overlook the social institution of heterosexuality as an important site of heteronormalization, often erase lesbian identities and livelihoods, thereby averting as well any discussion of lesbian rights or redistributive justice (Mohanty 1991; Lind and Share 2003; 2011). Likewise, these policies, even in their explicitly defined feminist variations, can overlook or erase the identities and livelihoods of heterosexual women who do not fit within a heternormative understanding of family life: this sometimes includes sex workers, single mothers, transnational migrant households, or women who do not fit within societal (including feminist) notions of respectability and are therefore overlooked, left out of policy processes, or have little or no legal recourse or access to resources.

CONCLUSION

This chapter has addressed the trajectory of scholarship on sexuality and heteronormativity as it relates to the field of gender and politics and to politics more broadly. Its aim has been to introduce the reader to four general areas of inquiry: notions of sexuality as a form of power; the relationship between sexuality and politics; LGBT political participation; and the heteronormative dimensions of state and global policies, laws, and institutions. Although scholars' emphases differ in their epistemological and methodological approaches, there are at least four central tenets that run through this interdisciplinary scholarship: First, scholars tend to agree that sexuality is socially constructed and politically contested, despite hegemonic views that sexuality remains "outside" the realm of politics or the public domain (note that this does not mean that there is no biological aspect to sexuality but rather that even biological sex is mediated through social relations). Second, this literature sheds light on how political conceptions of citizenship and governance have historically been defined in heteronormative terms, thereby rendering individuals who do not fit into culturally prescribed sexual or gender roles as second-class (or non-) citizens. Third, it reveals how political institutions reproduce heteronormative bias and are in the business of sexuality, even when they claim otherwise, as the aforementioned examples of sexual regulation reveal (e.g., fetal subjectivity laws, abortion and homosexuality laws, World Bank and other economic development policies). Finally, this scholarship calls our attention to the largely underdeveloped research on how LGBTQ individuals understand their identities, needs, and political visions and to how historically oppressed communities of color and colonized communities perceive and experience sexual regulation and regimes of heteronormativity and homonormativity as well. Seen from this angle, sexuality is clearly central to broader processes of social change and is best understood alongside and as part and parcel of other forms of inequality and struggle.

NOTES

1. As an important parallel, transphobia is defined as the irrational fear of or hatred toward gender-variant individuals and is similarly aligned with a broader notion of gender normativity that privileges traditional gender norms and expectations over all others. Indeed, gender identity bias often overlaps with and is conflated with sexual identity bias (for example, a hate crime against a perceived homosexual is sometimes based on the attacker's perception of the victim's gender identity, as in the victim being "too feminine" or "too masculine," not on his or her same-sex intimate attachments). While the two are closely related, it is important to understand them as separate forms of phobias and normativities as well. In this chapter, although I focus primarily on heteronormativity, I discuss gender normativity to the extent possible.

2. Here I am using *transgender* as an umbrella term to include several disparate groups of individuals who do not fit within culturally prescribed gender roles, including cross-dressers, biologically born males or females who do not "pass" as their medically assigned gender, nonoperative transpeople, and also transsexuals. I use this term with the caveat that because it has become almost axiomatic when used politically, it obscures important differences between these groups as well (Currah 2006, 4–5).

3. In February 2011, however, the Obama-backed U.S. Department of Justice announced that it will no longer legally defend DOMA, thus paving the way for legal challenges to the federal policy.

4. South Africa was the first country in the global south to legalize same-sex marriage in 2006, following the country's earlier passage of the 1996 post-apartheid constitution, which provided legal protections for sexual minorities and paved the way for later gay- and lesbian-supportive legislation. Argentina's same-sex marriage law went into effect in 2010.

REFERENCES

Adrian, Tamara. 2008. Personal interview, Caracas, Venezuela. August 2.

Aganthagelou, Anna M., M. Daniel Bassichis, and Tamara L. Spira. 2008. "Intimate investments: Homonormativity, global lockdown and the seductions of empire." *Radical History Review* 100: 120–142.

Alexander, M. Jacqui. 1991. "Erotic autonomy as a politics of decolonization: An anatomy of feminist state practice in the Bahamas tourist economy." In Chandra Mohanty, Ann Russo, and Lourdes Torres, eds., *Third world women and the politics of feminism*, Bloomington: Indiana University Press, 63–100.

Alexander, M. Jacqui. 1994. "Not just (any) body can be a citizen: The politics of law, sexuality, and postcoloniality in Trinidad and Tobago and the Bahamas." *Feminist Review* 48: 5–23.

Altman, Dennis. 2001. *Global sex*. Chicago: University of Chicago Press.

Badgett, M. V. Lee. 2001. *Money, myths and change: The economic lives of lesbians and gay men*. Chicago: University of Chicago Press.

Bedford, Kate. 2004. "Political science." *GLBTQ: An encyclopedia of gay, lesbian, bisexual, transgender and queer culture*. Available at http://www.glbtq.com/social-sciences/political_science.html.

Bedford, Kate. 2009. *Developing partnerships: Gender, Sexuality and the reformed World Bank*. Minneapolis: University of Minnesota Press.

Bell, David, and Jon Binnie. 2000. *The sexual citizen: Queer politics and beyond*. Malden, MA: Blackwell Publishers.

Bell, Mark. 2002. *Anti-discrimination law and the European Union*. New York: Oxford University Press.

Berlant, Lauren, and Michael Warner. 1998. "Sex in public." *Critical Inquiry* 24: 547–566.

Bernstein, Elizabeth, and Laurie Schaffner (Eds.). 2005. *Regulating sex: The politics of intimacy and identity*. New York: Routledge.

Bernstein, Mary, Anna-Maria Marshall, and Scott Barclay. 2009. "The Challenge of Law: Sexual Orientation, Gender Identity, and Social Movements." In Scott Barclay, Mary Bernstein and Anna-Maria Marshall, eds. *Queer mobilizations: LGBT activists confront the law*. New York: New York University Press, 1–17.

Bhaskaran, Suparna. 2004. *Made in India: Decolonizations, queer sexualities, trans/national projects*. New York: Palgrave MacMillan.

Blasius, Mark. 2001. "Introduction: Sexual identities, queer politics, and the status of knowledge." In Mark Blasius, ed., *Sexual identities, queer politics*. Princeton, NJ: Princeton University Press, 3–22.

Bosia, Michael, and Meredith Weiss (Eds.). In press. *The globalization of homophobia: Perspectives and debates.* Chicago: University of Illinois Press.

Cabral, Mauro, A. I. Grinspan, and Paula Viturro. 2006. "(Trans)sexual citizenship in contemporary Argentina." In Paisley Currah, Richard M. Juang, and Shannon Price Minter, eds., *Transgender rights.* Minneapolis: University of Minnesota Press, 262–273.

Chang, Kimberly A., and L. H. M Ling. 2000. "Globalization and its intimate other: Filipina domestic workers in Hong Kong." In Marianne H. Marchand and Anne Sisson Runyan, eds., *Gender and global restructuring: Sightings, sites and resistances.* London: Routledge, 30–47.

Clark, Kim. 2001. "Género, raza y nación: La protección a la infancia en el Ecuador (1910–1945)." In Gioconda Herrera, ed. *Estudios de género.* Quito: Facultad Latinoamericana de Ciencias Sociales (FLACSO)/Instituto Latinoamericano de Investigaciones Sociales (ILDIS), 183–210.

CNN. 2011. "Lawmaker proposes relabeling rape victims as 'accusers.'" Atlanta, GA: CNN, February 7. Available at http://articles.cnn.com/2011-02-07/us/georgia.rape. law_1_fraud-victims-word-victim-burglary-victims?_s=PM:US.

Cohen, Cathy. 2001. "Punks, bulldaggers, and welfare queens: The radical potential of queer politics?" In Mark Blasius, ed., *Sexual identities, queer politics.* Princeton, NJ: Princeton University Press, 200–227.

Cohen, Jean. 1985. "Strategy or identity: New theoretical paradigms and contemporary social movements." *Social Research* 52(4): 663–716.

Collins, Patricia Hill. 2005. *Black sexual politics: African Americans, gender, and the new racism.* London: Routledge.

Cooper, Davina. 1995. *Power in struggle: Feminism, sexuality and the state.* New York: New York University Press.

Correa, Sonia, Rosalind Petchesky, and Richard Parker. 2008. *Sexuality, health and human rights.* London: Routledge.

Crenshaw, Kimberlé. 1991. "Mapping the margins: Intersectionality, identity politics and violence against women of color." *Stanford Law Review* 43(6): 1241–1299.

Davis, Angela. 1983. *Women, race and class.* New York: Vintage Books.

D'Emilio, John. 1984. "Capitalism and gay identity." In Ann Snitow, Christine Stansell, and Sharan Thompson, eds., *Powers of desire: The politics of sexuality.* New York: Monthly Review Press, 100–113.

Di Mauro, Diane, and Carole Joffe. 2009. "The religious right and the reshaping of sexual policy: Reproductive rights and sexuality education during the Bush years." In Gilbert Herdt, ed., *Moral panics, sex panics: Fear and the fight over sexual rights.* New York: New York University Press, 47–103.

Duggan, Lisa. 2004. *The twilight of equality? Neoliberalism, cultural politics, and the attack on democracy.* New York: Beacon Press.

Duyvendak, Jan-Willem. 2001. "Identity politics in France and the Netherlands: The case of gay and lesbian liberation." In Mark Blasius, ed., *Sexual identities, queer politics.* Princeton, NJ: Princeton University Press, 56–72.

Evans, David T. 1993. *Sexual citizenship: The material construction of sexualities.* New York: Routledge.

Evans, David T. 2007. "Sexual citizenship." In George Ritzer, ed., *Blackwell encyclopedia of sociology.* Malden, MA: Blackwell Publishers, 4205–4209.

Fraser, Nancy. 1996. *Justice interruptus: Critical reflections on the "postsocialist" condition.* London: Routledge.

Friedman, Elisabeth. 2007. Introduction to special issue, "How pink is the pink tide? Feminist and LGBT activists challenge the left." *NACLA Report on the Americas* 40(2): 16.

Gamson, Joshua. 1995. "Must Identity Movements Self-Destruct? A Queer Dilemma," *Social Problems* 42(4): 390–406.

Gates, Gary J., and Jason Ost. 2004. *The gay and lesbian atlas.* Washington, DC: Urban Institute Press.

Gettelman, Jeffrey. 2011. "Ugandan who spoke up for gays is beaten to death." *New York Times*, January 27. Available at http://www.nytimes.com/2011/01/28/world/africa/28uganda.html.

Gibson-Graham, J. K. 2006. *The end of capitalism (as we knew it): A feminist critique of political economy,* 2nd ed. Minneapolis: University of Minnesota Press.

Giddens, Anthony. 1992. *The transformation of intimacy: Sexuality, love and eroticism in modern societies.* Cambridge, UK: Polity Press.

Gosine, Andil. 2005. "Sex for pleasure, rights to participation, and alternatives to AIDS: Placing sexual minorities and/or dissidents in development." IDS Working Paper 228, Institute for Development Studies, Brighton, England, February.

Gosine, Andil. 2010. "The World Bank's GLOBE: Queers in/queering development." In Amy Lind, ed., *Development, sexual rights and global governance.* London: Routledge, 67–85.

Guy, Donna. 1991. *Sex and danger in Buenos Aires: Prostitution, family and nation in Argentina.* Lincoln: University of Nebraska Press.

Harcourt, Wendy. 2009. *Body politics in development: Critical debates in gender and development.* London: Zed Books.

Herdt, Gilbert. 2009. "Introduction: Moral Panics, Sexual Rights, and Cultural Anger." In Gilbert Herdt, ed. *Moral panics, sex panics: Fear and the fight over sexual rights,* New York: New York University Press, 1–46.

Hoad, Neville. 2007. *African intimacies: Race, homosexuality, and globalization.* Minneapolis: University of Minnesota Press.

Human Rights Watch. 2004. *In a time of torture: The assault on justice in Egypt's crackdown on homosexual conduct.* New York: Human Rights Watch.

Ingelhart, Ronald. 1997. *Modernization and postmodernization.* Princeton, NJ: Princeton University Press.

Jauhola, Marjaana. 2010. "Building back better?—Negotiating normative boundaries of gender mainstreaming and post-tsunami reconstruction in Nanggroe Aceh Darussalam, Indonesia." *Review of International Studies* 36: 29–50.

Kantola, Johanna. 2010. *Gender and the European Union.* New York: Palgrave Macmillan.

Kleitz, Gilles. 2000. "Why is development work so straight?" Seminar paper, Brighton, Institute of Development Studies.

Lind, Amy. 2010a. "Introduction: Development, global governance and sexual subjectivities." In Amy Lind, ed., *Development, sexual rights and global governance.* London: Routledge, 1–19.

Lind, Amy (Ed.). 2010b. *Development, sexual rights and global governance.* London: Routledge.

Lind, Amy. 2011. "Querying globalization: Sexual subjectivities, development, and the governance of intimacy." In Marianne H. Marchand and Anne Sisson Runyan, eds., *Gender and global restructuring: Sightings, sites and resistances.* London: Routledge, 48–65.

Lind, Amy. 2012. "Contradictions that endure: Family norms, social reproduction, and Rafael Correa's citizen revolution in Ecuador," *Politics and Gender* 8(2): 254–261.

Lind, Amy. In press. "Sexual politics and constitutional reform in Ecuador: From neoliberalism to the *Buen Vivir.*" In Meredith L. Weiss and Michael J. Bosia, eds., *Homophobia Goes Global: States, Movements, and the Diffusion of Oppression.* Chicago: University of Illinois Press.

Lind, Amy, and Jessica Share. 2003. "Queering development: Institutionalized heterosexuality in development theory, practice and politics in Latin America." In Kum-Kum Bhavnani, John Foran, and Priya Kurian, eds., *Feminist futures: Re-imagining women, culture and development.* London: Zed Books, 55–73.

Lind, Amy, and Sofía Pazmiño Arguello. 2009. "Activismo LGBTIQ y ciudadanías sexuales en el Ecuador: un diálogo con Elizabeth Vásquez." *Íconos: revista de ciencias sociales* (special issue on sexualities and citizenship edited by Amy Lind and Sofía Pazmiño Arguello) 35: 97–101.

Luibhéid, Eithne. 2002. *Entry denied: Controlling sexuality at the border.* Minneapolis: University of Minnesota Press.

Luibhéid, Eithne, and Lionel Cantú (Eds.). 2005. *Queer migrations: Sexuality, U.S. citizenship, and border crossings.* Minneapolis: University of Minnesota Press.

Marshall, T. H. 1950. *Citizenship and social class and other essays.* Cambridge: Cambridge University Press.

Mohanty, Chandra Talpade. 1991. "Under Western eyes: Feminist scholarship and colonial discourses." In Chandra Talpade Mohanty, Ann Russo, and Lourdes Torres, eds., *Third world women and the politics of feminism.* Bloomington: Indiana University Press, 1–51.

Morgan, Lynn M., and Meredith Wilson Michaels (Eds.). 1999. *Fetal subjects, feminist positions.* Philadelphia: University of Pennsylvania Press.

Phelan, Shane. 2001. *Sexual strangers: Gays, lesbians, and dilemmas of citizenship.* Philadelphia: Temple University Press.

Plummer, Ken. 2001. "The square of intimate citizenship: Some preliminary proposals." *Citizenship Studies* 5(3): 237–253.

Prieto, Mercedes. 2004. Liberalismo y temor: imaginando los sujetos indígenas en el Ecuador postcolonial, 1895–1950. Quito: Abya-Yala.

Puar, Jasbir. 2007. *Terrorist assemblages: Homonationalism in queer times.* Durham, NC: Duke University Press.

Rayside, David. 2001. "The structuring of sexual minority activist opportunities in the political mainstream: Britain, Canada, and the United States." In Mark Blasius, ed., *Sexual identities, queer politics.* Princeton, NJ: Princeton University Press, 23–55.

Rich, Adrienne. 1979. *On lies, secrets, and silence.* New York: Norton Press.

Richardson, Diane. 2000. "Constructing sexual citizenship: Theorizing sexual rights." *Critical Social Policy* 20(1): 105–135.

Rofel, Lisa. 2007. *Desiring China: Experiments in neoliberalism, sexuality, and public culture.* Durham, NC: Duke University Press.

Seidman, Steven. 2001. "From identity to queer politics: Shifts in normative heterosexuality and the meaning of citizenship." *Citizenship Studies* 5(3): 321–328.

Smith, Andrea. 2006. "Heteropatriarchy and the three pillars of white supremacy." In Incite! Women of color against violence, *Color of violence: The Incite! anthology.* Boston: South End Press.

Smith, Anna Marie. 2001. "The politicization of marriage in contemporary American public policy: The Defense of Marriage Act and the Personal Responsibility Act." *Citizenship Studies* 5(3): 303–320.

Smith, Miriam. 2007. "Framing same-sex marriage in Canada and the United States: Goodridge, Halpern and the national boundaries of political discourse." *Social and Legal Studies* 16(1): 5–26. Available at http://sls.sagepub.com/content/16/1/5.full.pdf+html.

Somerville, Siobhan. 2005. "Sexual aliens and the racialized state: A queer reading of the 1952 U.S. Immigration and Nationality Act." In Eithne Luibhéid and Lionel Cantú, eds., *Queer migrations: Sexuality, citizenship, and border crossings.* Minneapolis: University of Minnesota Press, 75–91.

Vaid, Urvashi. 2004. *Virtual equality: The mainstreaming of gay and lesbian liberation.* New York: Anchor Books.

Weber, Cynthia. 1999. *Faking it: US hegemony in a "post-phallic" era.* Minneapolis: University of Minnesota Press.

Wing, Nick. 2011. "Fetus set to 'testify' in favor of Ohio Anti-Abortion Bill." *Huffington Post*, March 1. Available at http://www.huffingtonpost.com/2011/03/01/ohio-abortion-bill_n_829893.html.

Xie, Selena, and Javier Corrales. 2010. "LGBT rights in Ecuador's 2008 constitution." In Javier Corrales and Mario Pecheny, eds., *The politics of sexuality in Latin America.* Pittsburgh: University of Pittsburgh Press, 224–229.

CHAPTER 8

REPRODUCTIVE RIGHTS

VÉRONIQUE MOTTIER

INTRODUCTION

Simone de Beauvoir's *The Second Sex*, first published in 1949, famously blamed women's reproductive bodies and activities for their subordinate social status. Writing at a time when marriage and motherhood constituted the main horizon of female social respectability, de Beauvoir portrayed marriage, housework, and childcare as mutually reinforcing women's dependence on men. The author reserved some of her most radical language for describing the strong emotional ties linking a mother to her child as "a mutual and harmful oppression" (1976b, 389) and the fetus as "both part of her body, and a parasite which exploits her" (1976b, 349). Echoing the trope of "voluntary motherhood" promoted by earlier, first-wave women's movements, de Beauvoir called for free access to birth control and abortion as well as collective methods of childrearing.

Reproduction, understood as the production of offspring, has constituted a key theme of feminist theory and political practice both before and after de Beauvoir. Three features of reproduction explain its importance to feminist theory and praxis. First, reproduction is conventionally considered a "women's domain." Second, and consequently, as de Beauvoir and numerous other feminist pioneers have decried, normative femininity remains to a considerable extent defined in relation to reproduction and motherhood. And third, the fact that reproduction involves the engendering of future generations turns it into an object of collective interest and anxiety. In an influential edited volume exploring the global politics of reproduction, Ginsburg and Rapp (1995) accordingly argue that, given its social importance, reproduction should be placed at the center not just of feminist theory but of social theory more generally.

Reproduction has been central to a great number of the political struggles of first- and second-wave women's movements, ranging from collective mobilizations around access to contraception, abortion, and childcare to controversies triggered by developments in the field of new reproductive technologies. In the context of such struggles, a new vocabulary of reproductive rights, reproductive health, and reproductive justice has emerged in recent decades and has acquired institutional anchoring through national and international legislation. At an international level, "reproductive rights" were first recognised as a subset of basic human rights in the (non-legally binding) "Proclamation of Tehran" of the United Nations (UN) International Conference on Human Rights in 1968, where it was stated that parents should have the right "to determine freely and responsibly the number and the spacing of their children" (para.16). The (also non-binding) "Cairo Programme of Action" adopted at the UN International Conference on Population and Development in 1994 contained the first UN definition of reproductive health, including individuals' right to "have a satisfying and safe sex life and…the capability to reproduce and the freedom to decide if, when and how often to do so" (para.7.2)—notions that were further broadened at the UN 4th World Conference on Women in Beijing in 1995. Indeed, the Beijing Platform for Action stated that women's reproductive rights, part of universal and inalienable human rights, required "equal relationships between women and men in matters of sexual relations and reproduction" (para.96).

However, the notion of reproductive rights has also deeply divided global feminist theory and practice. Western feminists' calls for access to abortion have been criticized for being a "luxury" concern of privileged women by activists from those developing nations where women have been subjected to coerced sterilization or forced abortion. This has, in turn, led to semantic disagreements over whether *reproductive freedom* signifies the freedom not to procreate or the freedom to have children when wanted. Feminists have been further divided over whether female sexual freedom or the protection against practices of female and male genital mutilation should be included in notions of reproductive health and whether such inclusion constitutes a feminist gain, or another expression of Western ethnocentrism. Finally, the promotion of reproductive rights has been criticized as meaningless unless a number of social conditions are met. Provisions such as legalized abortion and contraceptives are accessible only to those who have sufficient economic resources to be able to afford them, while practices of coercion, gender violence, and racial discrimination may impede women from freely exercising such rights. As Dorothy Roberts (1997) argues, the narrow focus on abortion rights reflects the concerns of white, middle-class women about legal restraints on choices that are otherwise available to them. Integrating the particular concerns of black women, Roberts points out, "helps to expand our vision of reproductive freedom to include the full scope of what it means to have reproductive control over one's life" (300).

Such critical debates have led to the emergence of the concept of *reproductive justice*, coined by the American Black Women's Caucus in the wake of the 1994 Cairo conference. This concept problematizes the gap between legal rights and the actual usage of such rights and links reproductive rights with social justice. It thus shifts the focus from an individualist rights-based perspective to a concern with collective structures of reproductive oppression. The frame of reproductive justice has been promoted by grassroots organizations both in the United States, such as SisterSong Women of Color Reproductive Justice Collective (founded in 1997), and its member organization Asian Communities for Reproductive Justice, and elsewhere, most prominently by the Women's Global Network for Reproductive Rights, an influential worldwide organisation founded in the Netherlands in 1984 and currently based in Manila.

Against this backdrop, the next sections of this chapter will explore feminist scholarship on three areas of the politics of reproduction, using different periodizations for each of the subsections.The first section adopts primarily a top-down perspective to examine state control over citizens' procreative choices, taking eugenic population policies during the early decades of the twentieth century as a specific example. The second section adopts a bottom-up perspective, centering on feminist mobilizations around abortion and contraceptive rights from the 1970s onward. It will trace the ways reproductive rights have been pushed into the political arena by women's movements and how feminist activism has in turn been prompted, as well as strengthened, by struggles over access to safe abortion and means of birth control. The third section of the chapter examines the impact of new reproductive technologies on contemporary politics of gender and explores feminist responses to the challenges posed by recent developments in this area.

STATE CONTROL AND
REPRODUCTIVE AGENCY

The modern state intervenes in citizens' reproductive lives and bodies in many different policy arenas, ranging from public health systems, sex education in schools, and abortion and adoption laws to population policies and natalist political rhetoric. The policy frames used in these arenas articulate ways of thinking about gender and reproductive agency, which are both reflective of modern forms of state intervention and colored by specific cultural, religious, or political contexts. In policy making, public debate, and everyday life interactions, it is tacitly taken for granted that "it's women who have children." Public anxieties about under-age sex, single parenthood, or new reproductive technologies tend to center on women and their reproductive behaviors, despite the increased usage of degendered language to do so. Male reproductive agency thus often remains a discursive blind spot, not just within public understandings of reproduction but also within feminist theorizations of gender and reproduction.

In stark contrast, the ancient Greek dramatic trilogy *Oresteia*, written by Aeschylus, offers a telling illustration of how different past understandings of gender and reproductive agency were, even within Western culture. The plays were first performed at the Dionysia festival in Athens in 458 BCE, where they won first prize. The only trilogy of ancient Greek plays to have survived until modern times, the *Oresteia* tells us the tragic myth of the cursed House of Atreus. In its first play, we witness queen Clytemnestra as she awaits the return of her husband Agamemnon, King of Argos, from the Trojan war after ten years of absence. The public learns that she nurtures deep hatred for her husband, whom she blames for the death of their daughter Iphigeneia. Indeed, at the start of the war, Agamemnon had prepared the sacrifice of their daughter in an attempt to placate the gods, who had sent him unfavorable winds preventing his war ships from sailing to Troy. In the course of the preparations for her death by her father, Iphigeneia, seemingly driven by the patriotic desire to allow the Greek ships to sail or, following an alternative reading, motivated by the fear that the noblewomen of Argos would end up as victims of rape by the men of Troy if Greece were defeated, ends up sacrificing her own life. Agamemnon doesn't help matters by bringing back a souvenir from Troy: the exotic Trojan princess Cassandra, whom he has made his concubine. In a climactic, bloody scene, Clytemnestra and her lover murder Agamemnon and Cassandra, using an axe. Clytemnestra's son Orestes now faces a dilemma: he has the moral obligation to revenge the murder of his father. However, he can do so only by killing his own mother, and matricide and patricide are seen as particularly "abhorrent to the gods" in ancient Greek culture. Despite these qualms, Orestes does kill Clytemnestra and in punishment is persecuted by the Furies (deities who revenge matricide or patricide). Driven to distraction by the Furies, Orestes flees to Athens, where a trial is called to decide whether his punishment should continue or not. At the trial, the male god of reason Apollo takes Orestes's side against the Furies, and the female, celibate, virgin god of war and wisdom Athena is left to cast the deciding vote. Athena, born out of her father Zeus's thigh without any reproductive involvement of a mother, is convinced by Apollo's argument that Clytemnestra, Orestes's mother, is not really a blood relative of Orestes. Indeed, Apollo and Athena agree that Clytemnestra's body was nothing more than a vessel for Orestes's father's sperm. Therefore, the gods conclude, Orestes's blood relationship is to his father Agamemnon and not to his mother. This rhetorical twist, in turn, makes the murder of Clytemnestra morally acceptable because it is now (to borrow a modern term) an honor killing rather than a matricide.

Although the *Oresteia* narrates mythical events, it reflects prevalent views in Western antiquity in presenting the role of the mother in reproduction as only passive. Within a patriarchy that placed (free) men and fathers at the center of power relations within the family as well as wider society, parenthood was seen to be actively determined by male sperm, not by the female reproductive body. More generally, metaphors of female bodies as simple recipients or passive vessels for active male sperm survived well into early modern times within Western culture. To the contemporary eye, the *Oresteia* appears fascinating precisely because of its disconnection of reproduction from biology. Western modernity has developed contrary understandings of gender and procreative agency, conventionally portraying reproduction as primarily a "female business," biologically tied to women's bodies. In depicting a contrasting, distinctly male-centered view of reproduction, the *Oresteia* reminds us that reproduction and reproductive agency have been understood differently within different historical time periods or cultural contexts. In other words, it reminds us that reproduction is not a natural, biological, universal process but a culturally situated experience,—just as gender and sexuality are best understood as culturally constructed rather than natural, universal, biologically driven experiences.

In addition, the *Oresteia* also draws attention to other themes that have been of key interest to feminist political theory, such as the gendered body politics of citizenship. Through Cassandra's fate, it illustrates the ways women's bodies become sexual property of male victors of war and act as metaphors for national honor as the patriotic reading of Iphigeneia's self-sacrifice suggests, whereas patriotism for male citizens is measured by their willingness to sacrifice their bodies in war. In the Trojan case, these twin dynamics were illustrated particularly sharply, since the Trojan War was aimed at retrieving a Greek nobleman's wife who had eloped with a Trojan prince (adultery with a married woman being considered a more horrendous crime than rape within ancient Greece, given the risk to the woman's husband of illegitimate offspring). Finally, Orestes's story signals the shift from Argos's system of blood revenge to a system of legal trial by jury in Athens. The trilogy thus locates the mythical origins of formal systems of justice in a dispute over gender and parenthood, thereby founding embryonic state institutions upon a gendered model of reproduction that privileges male rather than female reproductive agency.

Scandinavian feminist political scientists such as Helga Hernes (1987) and Birte Siim (1988) have explored the consequences of the gendered understanding of reproductive agency for modern views of the relationship between citizens and the state. As they point out, notions of citizenship have been deeply gendered from the moment when they started to emerge and formalize in modernity (see also the chapter by Siim in this volume). The affiliation of male citizens to both the state and the nation has been historically founded upon the model of the citizen-worker and the citizen-soldier, particularly focusing on their willingness to work and to sacrifice their bodies and their lives in war (which is of course why antimilitaristic objectors have been conventionally portrayed not just as cowardly but also as unpatriotic traitors toward the nation). In contrast, women's affiliation to the national body passes via their reproductive agency:

their duty toward the national collectivity is as citizen-mothers, generating and raising the children that will form the future nation (see also Eisenstein 1983). Indeed, Adrienne Rich observed in her influential book *Of Woman Born* (1976) that terms such as *barren* or *childless* are used to suggest illegitimate female identities, whereas no equivalent terms exist for *nonfathers* (xiii-xiv). The nation is biologically replaced through reproductive sexuality, which is tacitly coded as female. As Michel Foucault (1990) famously points out, the fact that the future of our species and more specifically that of the nation is formed by reproductive sexuality has turned the latter into an arena for collective anxiety and state intervention. What Foucault failed to recognize, or at least paid insufficient theoretical and empirical attention to, however, was the deeply gendered nature of collective concerns with citizens' reproductive sexuality. Authors such as Nira Yuval-Davis (1997) and Joanne Nagel (2003) demonstrate that female reproductive sexuality historically became a particular focus of such concerns.

One of the most dramatic examples of direct intervention of the modern state on reproductive bodies and sexuality is offered by practices of coerced sterilization. For example, during its state of emergency (1975–1977), India engaged in a notorious family planning program that involved the coerced sterilization of thousands of men and women. In China, human rights activists routinely accuse the government of using coerced abortion and sterilization as part of its one-child policy program. First announced in 1978, the program constitutes a stark reversal of Chairman Mao's earlier pronatalist stance and persecution of birth control activists in the 1950s and reflects a shift of party workers' activism from production to reproduction since the 1980s (Anagnost 1995). Czechoslovakia undertook sterilization under constraints or rewarded with welfare payments of primarily Roma women in the period from 1973 to 2001.

From the late 1920s to the 1960s, several Western countries implemented coerced sterilization policies that were partly driven by eugenic concerns. Eugenics initially emerged in the late nineteenth century as a new and self-declared science, which identified the hereditary transmission of inferior physical and mental characteristics as sources of national degeneration and focused on how to encourage instead the transmission of superior qualities to the next generation. Eugenicists aimed to assist states in implementing social policies that would improve the quality of the national "breed." In opposition to the laissez-faire of political liberalism, they advocated active social engineering and state intervention in the most private areas of citizens' lives, including their reproductive sexuality. While some eugenic thinkers proposed so-called positive eugenic measures (such as eugenic education), defined as ways to encourage reproduction by those categories of the population who were deemed to be of superior quality, others promoted negative measures such as marriage bans or sterilization to prevent inferior citizens from having children. Political calls for coerced sterilization or castration to exclude unfit categories of the population from the (future) nation were thus legitimized through the authority of eugenic science, which rapidly established itself in the context of scientific disciplines such as biological anthropology, psychiatry, and sexology. Citizens had a patriotic duty, eugenic scientists argued, to contribute to the improvement of the nation through what was termed a *conscious race-culture* (Pearson 1909, 170). In France, the cofounder of the socialist French Workers' Party, Georges Vacher de Lapouge (an anthropologist who had introduced eugenic ideas in France in the final decades of the nineteenth century), promoted the idea that male citizens should perform selectionist breeding as part of a sexual service to the nation, similar to their military service. The primary focus of eugenic thinkers, however, was on women's reproductive agency, reflecting the wider association of reproduction with women's bodies.

The eugenic concern with the improvement of the national race via the surveillance of citizens' reproductive sexuality by the state generally emerged against the political backdrop of colonial rule (Levine 2010). In colonizing states such as the United Kingdom, France, and Germany, fears about the degeneracy of the national race were intertwined with anxieties about miscegenation with colonial others. In contexts such as Switzerland and the Scandinavian countries, however, eugenic policy practices developed within an entirely different political landscape. Switzerland was never a colonial state, while the Scandinavian countries no longer had colonies (with the partial exception of Denmark) by the time eugenics emerged. A collective preoccupation with the racial hygiene of the nation nevertheless also developed in these noncolonial states (Mottier 2010).

The rise of modern social policies in the course of the twentieth century offered the institutional conditions for translating eugenic ideas into practical policy making. In the United Kingdom, the strong influence of liberal political thought with its emphasis on individual rights and attendant distrust of state intervention in private life formed an ideological barrier against invasive eugenic practices. Parliamentary attempts to pass a sterilization law foundered in the 1930s due to political opposition from the Catholic Church and the labor movement, which judged the legislation to be antiworking class (King and Hansen 1999). Political conditions were more favorable elsewhere, especially in Protestant nations such as the United States, Germany, Switzerland, and the Scandinavian countries.

The emerging welfare state also added an important additional motive to the eugenic project of preventing degeneracy of the nation: limiting public expenditure. Indeed, the inferior categories of the national population were soon to become the main recipients of the expanding welfare institutions. Sterilization of indigent single mothers came to be promoted on the grounds that it was cheaper for the state than long-term financial support. In Sweden, the eugenic sterilization of citizens labeled as *work-shy* and *asocial*, such as prostitutes and vagrants, was portrayed as a way of strengthening the social-democratic welfare-state itself, by limiting the number of future welfare dependents.

Following Indiana's introduction of the first eugenic sterilization law in the world in 1907, 33 U.S. states introduced similar legislation. The majority of coerced sterilizations under eugenic statutes across the United States took place after World War 2, in the 1950s and early 1960s. By the early 1960s, the total number of recorded sterilizations had reached over 62,000, most of these performed on individuals labeled as *mentally deficient* or *mentally ill* (Largent 2008). The last known case was recorded in 1981 in Oregon, which became in 1983 the last state to repeal its sterilization law (see Kevles 1985). The Swiss canton of Vaud became the first European setting to adopt a eugenic sterilization law in 1928, a law that was officially abrogated only in 1985 (though no eugenic sterilizations have been documented since the 1960s). The Vaud law was representative of that of other countries in allowing the sterilization without consent of the mentally ill, while its 1931 criminal law included a clause allowing for eugenically motivated abortions. This is a remarkable point considering the intense political struggle to widen access to abortion several decades later. In practice, the main targets of governmental restrictions on reproduction were those categories of the population who were thought to be carriers of degenerate hereditarily transmissible characteristics: the mentally ill, the physically disabled, and those members of the underclasses whose behavior had transgressed social norms, such as unproductive "vagrants" or unmarried mothers. Denmark, Norway, Sweden, Finland, Iceland, and Estonia all passed eugenic sterilization laws in the late 1920s and early 1930s. Eugenic sterilization was applied on a particularly large scale by Nazi Germany, following the passing of the notorious 1933 Sterilization Law, which introduced compulsory sterilization on eugenic grounds. As a result, since WW2, eugenics has come to be associated with Nazism in public debate. However, eugenic state intervention found support across the political spectrum in the 1920s and 1930s. Switzerland, Sweden, and other Scandinavian countries were among the pioneers of eugenic policy making and eugenic practices in the European context, often with social-democratic as well as right-wing support.

Eugenic policy making was deeply gendered, as scholars such as Mottier (2000), Kline (2001), Schoen (2005), and Stern (2005) point out. First, the majority of those subjected to coerced sterilization were women, particularly of the underclasses. In Sweden, for example, the number of sterilizations performed on eugenic/social grounds between 1935 and 1975 is currently estimated at around 18,600, over 90 percent of which were performed on women (Broberg and Tydén 2005, 109); this is a gender proportion echoed in many other countries for which data are available. Second, eugenic policies in turn produced gender, strengthening normative models of femininity and masculinity. Indeed, it is important to emphasize that the categories of mental illness and feeblemindedness, which were mobilized in eugenic sterilization laws, were notoriously vague at the time. They could include any kind of behaviors that deviated from social norms. The narratives used to justify eugenic sterilization of women routinely portrayed them as deviating from the social norms of female respectability, in particular in terms of their sexual morality. Underclass women who had had children out of wedlock (thereby demonstrating loose sexual morals as well as the risk of welfare dependency) thus represented particular targets of coerced sterilizations in democratic states, while women whose behavior deviated from respectable femininity in other ways were also targeted on the grounds of promiscuity, nymphomania, being oversexed, disorderly house keeping, or the inability to financially support children. The numbers of men who were subjected to eugenically motivated castrations were often already institutionalized in psychiatric or penal institutions on the grounds of sexual misbehavior. Although men labeled as sexually abnormal, such as exhibitionists or homosexuals, similarly risked so-called therapeutic castration, not all of these were eugenically driven. Such interventions also reflected the therapeutic aim of moderating deviant sex drives or were accepted voluntarily (with the pressure of long-term internment offered as only alternative). In the United States, where the gender gap in the actual numbers of sterilizations was, until the early 1960s, much less pronounced than in countries such as Sweden or Switzerland, justifications used to legitimize coerced sterilizations were similarly gendered (Kline 2001, 53). More generally, the original eugenic emphasis on the prevention of the hereditary transmission of defective characteristics became diluted in wider state measures against antisocial behaviors that were not necessarily attributed to strictly hereditary factors. This further blurred the boundaries between eugenic scientific rhetoric and its translation into concrete policy measures.

In sum, eugenic sterilization policies were heavily gendered as well as raced and classed, reflecting states' concern with control over female bodies and female sexuality as reproducers of the future nation as well as the gendered dimensions of policy making more generally that have been highlighted by political scientists such as Bacchi (1999), Stetson and Mazur (1995), and Kantola (2006). Yet it would be a mistake to assume that women were only ever victims of eugenics. While underclass women were the main social group targeted by eugenic sterilizations, middle-class women were important agents in eugenic policy making. Women's political organizations such as social purity groups were instrumental in promoting eugenic ideas in the context of wider public debates on the regulation of sexuality between the 1890s and 1930s (Gerodetti 2004). By the 1930s and 1940s, bourgeois women were actively engaged in the implementation of eugenic policies, employed as doctors or as state officials in eugenic marriage advice bureaux or carrying out voluntary work in women's charitable organizations employed with the poor or in church organizations that set up homes for unmarried mothers. Recognizing the importance of gendered models of reproductive agency is not to say, therefore, that states engaging in eugenic policy making exercised male power over its female citizens in any straightforward way. Women were often important agents in the implementation of eugenic measures, while men were sometimes its victims, as we have seen. Furthermore, the picture of state coercion over female reproductive bodies is further blurred by the fact that eugenic ideas could be instrumentalized by women who actively desired sterilization or abortion at a time when few alternative methods of birth control existed, as Schoen (2005) points out. Even in arenas of extreme reproductive oppression of women such as eugenic sterilization, possibilities of subversion, resistance, and creative reappropriation of eugenic rhetoric can thus be identified.

In more recent decades, organizations defending the reproductive rights of women and men have sprung up in many countries across the world. Compensation claims and other demands for reparative justice toward past victims of coercive sterilizations have been successful in some contexts, for example, in North Carolina and Sweden, while countries such as Switzerland have rejected such demands on the rather spurious grounds that they concerned previous governments. But it is fair to say that, at least in the Western world, the most intense feminist activism has not occurred in resistance to practices of coerced sterilization but rather in defense of abortion rights.

FEMINIST MOBILIZATIONS AND REPRODUCTIVE FREEDOM

Access to abortion was a central claim of second-wave Western women's movements in the 1970s and 1980s. It was, arguably, instrumental in mobilizing such movements in the first place. First-wave feminist pioneers such as Marie Stopes in the United Kingdom, Margaret Sanger in the United States, or Alexandra Kollontai in the USSR had already defended the importance for women to freely make their reproductive choices in the 1920s and 1930s, promoting reproductive autonomy as a precondition for the social and political emancipation of women more generally. As Sanger, the founder of the American Birth Control League (which later became Planned Parenthood) wrote in 1919, "No woman can call herself free who does not own and control her body. No woman can call herself free until she can choose consciously whether she will or will not be a mother" (6). Like many birth control activists at the time (including Marie Stopes), however, she combined this stance with enthusiastic support for negative eugenics, advocating segregation, mandatory contraception, or compulsory sterilization of the "unfit."

The provision of sex education and contraceptive information had been promoted through the somewhat euphemistic slogan of *voluntary motherhood* since the 1870s in countries such as the United States, the United Kingdom, Germany, and Switzerland, though early first-wave feminists generally rejected abortion or even unnatural contraceptive devices (other than the rhythm methods) for encouraging (particularly male) promiscuity. Indeed, early birth control activists linked their claims for female bodily autonomy to a critique of male sexuality and patriarchal marriage norms more generally. Women's rights over their own bodies were primarily understood by late nineteenth-century bourgeois suffragists and sexual morality campaigners in terms of the right to refuse sexual relations with their husbands unless ensuing offspring were welcome rather than in terms of access to contraceptive devices or abortion. The right to refuse a husband's sexual demands thus became an important political claim of late nineteenth-century women's movements, in a histori-cal and legal context that promoted the sexual submission of women within marriage. Early first-wave feminists such as Victoria Woodhull or Angela Heywood attacked marriage laws for legalizing marital rape (Gordon 1999, 7). Sexual violence and the sexual slavery of married women were frequent tropes of Free Love activists, who advocated the abolition of the institution of marriage altogether. Claims for female bodily integrity were thus intertwined with views of male sexuality as aggressive and predatory, while women's sexual needs were seen as primarily driven by reproductive instincts rather than sexual lust. Both suffragists and Free Love activists developed a strong pro-motherhood rhetoric, with the latter arguing for the separation of moth-erhood and legal marriage in the interests of women as well as children (ibid., 13). Women's natural mothering instincts were thus politically instrumental-ized to argue women's moral superiority over men's natural sexual impurity. Birth control was consequently premised on temporary or indeed permanent sexual abstinence between spouses.

In stark contrast, the political mobilization around abortion rights that gal-vanized Western second-wave feminism in the 1970s (with Simone de Beauvoir playing a prominent activist role in the French context) took place in a post-sexual revolution climate that generally considered female sexual agency, rather than its absence, as natural. As in first-wave feminism, political claims around abortion continue to be intertwined with debates over sex education, moth-erhood, femininity, and female sexuality more generally today, whereas men and masculinity are little thematized in contraceptive and abortion rights controversies.

Ongoing threats to past political achievements in this area have ensured that abortion rights continue to make cyclical reappearances on feminist agendas worldwide, against the backdrop of the rise of religious fundamental-ist actors in politics since the 1980s. In the United States, abortion rights have been particularly central to recurrent attacks on political achievements in the domain of gender equality more generally by the antifeminist New Right. In reality, the identification of abortion rights with the women's movement by its opponents perhaps overstates the importance of feminist support for free-dom of choice within the U.S. legislative process. Scholars such as Joffe (1995) and Kellough (1996) suggest that the support of the medical establishment, motivated by the desire to protect itself from governmental intrusion, was in fact crucial for passing abortion reform in the early 1970s. The so-called pro-choice movement partly overlapped with the women's movement, but they were not identical. Complex alliances arose with medical groups as well as other political actors, such as the population control organizations that had sprung up in the 1950s and 1960s (Joffe 1995; Stetson 2001, 248). Such political alliances (and resulting framing strategies) were developed by self-styled pro-life as well as pro-choice groups both within and outside of the state (Lovenduski and Outshoorn 1986; Ginsburg 1998; Stetson 2001; Ferree 2003). While not denying the importance of feminist activism, Joffe and Stetson thus suggest that the policy trajectory of abortion rights reflects the specific ways feminist claims have been intertwined with other political agendas in the U.S. context (see also Bacchi 1999, 152).

The landmark case *Roe v. Wade* (1973) signaled the Supreme Court's decision to grant women the constitutional right to abortion, though this was conditional upon their physician's support (and limited to the first trimester of pregnancy). It thereby restricted the power of the state over women's reproductive choices—if only indirectly, by protecting the autonomy of doctors (who could refuse to perform abortion on the grounds of moral objections) and doctor–patient privacy (Kellough 1996). *Roe v. Wade* has been subjected to endless legal challenges in a wide variety of U.S. states since, as documented by authors such as Luker (1984) and Solinger (1998). Over the past decade, there has been a revival of increasingly vocal antiabortion activism in the United States as well as elsewhere, which has strategically employed new medical technologies for visualizing fetuses to great emotional effect, as Morgan and Michaels (1999) and Palmer (2009) demonstrate. Yet the worldwide trend has clearly been toward an extension of abortion rights since the adoption of a recommendation to reform punitive legislation of abortion at the UN 4th World Conference on Women in Beijing in 1995 (Corrêa, Petchesky, and Parker 2008, 48). Countries such as Nicaragua, El Salvador, and Poland, where access to abortion has been severely restricted in recent years, constitute exceptions that have triggered national as well as international protests.

Political mobilizations around abortion rights were central to feminist contestations of the traditional separation between *public* and *private* spheres, as expressed in the famous second-wave slogan *the personal is political*. There have been many debates within feminist scholarship about the exact meaning of this slogan. Some understood it as a call for the abolition of the family, seen as a source of women's oppression. Phillips (1998) points out that it was originally aimed at male socialist or radical activists, to remind them that their theoretical focus on capital and labor ignored the gender inequalities at home. She argues for the integration of private issues such as sexuality and reproduction into political science analyses rather than restricting the focus of the latter to conventionally public domains. Pateman (1988) calls for an end to the distinction between public and private spheres to facilitate greater politicisation of issues previously defined as private. In contrast, Elshtain (1981) vehemently rejects such collapsing of the private into the public as totalitarian, since it would leave no area of social life outside of politics. Political theorists such as Petchesky (1984), Okin (1991), and Phillips (1991) similarly use abortion rights to argue for the importance of maintaining a separation between the public and the private. They think that reproductive choices should remain part of a private sphere, based on principles of privacy and individual decisionmaking. Such principles have been central to the defense of constitutionally guaranteed individual abortion rights by liberal legal theorists such as Ronald Dworkin (1993), as well as feminist liberal political theorists. Phillips, for example, argues that whereas the public sphere has conventionally been associated with male political agency and the private sphere with childrearing, sexuality, and the family—traditionally considered a female domain—the distinction between the two spheres should be detached from gender roles and based instead on a right to privacy, itself best seen as degendered.

This position has been criticized by radical feminists, most prominently by Catherine MacKinnon (1983, 1987), who argues that the appeal to liberal notions of privacy and "a woman's right to choose" reflects male interests. Echoing Adrienne Rich's (1977) views, MacKinnon conceptualizes abortion as another sign of what she believes to be the generalized male sexual exploitation of women rather than in terms of women's reproductive control. As a feminist strategy the appeal to women's individual rights is particularly misguided, she believes, since it leaves the foundations of male violence against women unchallenged. Petchesky's ([1984]1990) influential work *Abortion and Woman's Choice* argued for a critical rethinking of the limits of principles of privacy and personal choice, which rejected MacKinnon's theorization of women as agencyless victims of male domination for its reductionism. Instead, Petchesky undertook to salvage rights-based politics around abortion by emphasizing the need to address concrete inequalities in the conditions in which different categories of women make their individual reproductive choices and by calling for state-funded social supports to help decrease such inequalities for example around race and class. Abortion rights should not be seen as individual rights, she argued, but rather as social rights, requiring a cultural revolution in our understanding of sexuality and reproductive freedom (396). From a different theoretical angle, Drucilla Cornell (1995) revisits abortion rights discourse to develop a defense of abortion rights that proposes to rethink the liberal notions of rights and privacy. Drawing on the work of John Rawls, Cornell argues that these categories should not be treated as takenforgranted or preexisting but rather as future possibilities and aspirations.

THE GENDER POLITICS OF
NEW REPRODUCTIVE TECHNOLOGIES

Whereas feminist mobilizations around abortion and contraception have generally portrayed the latter as individual technologies and their access framed in terms of women's individual rights, as we have seen, the emergence of new reproductive technologies in recent years has triggered debates questioning the scope for individual choice. New reproductive practices such as in vitro fertilization, artificial insemination, sperm and egg donation, genetic engineering, and ultrasound screening have given rise to new areas for feminist thought and practice over recent decades. In the early years of second-wave feminism, Shulamith Firestone (1970) argued that the problematic linkage of female identity to nature and especially to women's reproductive functions should, in future times, be dissolved through new technologies of artificial reproduction and contraception. For Firestone, as for de Beauvoir (to whom Firestone's book was dedicated) before her, women's biology and central role in reproductive work were largely to blame for women's subordinate position within society. Firestone's classic and influential text *The Dialectic of Sex: The Case for Feminist Revolution* called for cybernetic technologies that would release women from the burden of giving birth. Allowing for reproduction to take place in laboratory settings would free women from the "barbarity" of both childbirth and pregnancy, that "temporary deformation of the body of the individual for the sake of the species," Firestone (188) argued. To escape the constraints of motherhood, Firestone advocated the abolition of the nuclear family, proposing to raise children instead in communal settings. The utopian cybernetic communism that she outlined would require four sets of revolutionary transformations, which Firestone theorized as intricately intertwined with each other: (1) the "freeing of women from the tyranny of reproduction by every means possible, and the diffusion of the child-rearing role to the society as a whole, men as well as women" (193); (2)"political autonomy, based on economic independence, of both women and children" (194); (3)"the complete integration of women and children into society" through the abolition of institutions such as schools that bar children from adult society—instead, relationships between adults and children should become equal and intimate, based on free choice rather than material dependency (195); (4) "the sexual freedom of all women and children" (195). Indeed, reflecting the author's borrowing of Freudian views of children as inherently sexual beings, Firestone argued against sexual repression, promoting sexual freedom for women as well as children. In Firestone's protechnology, antinatalist work, the futuristic reproductive technologies that she called for were thus portrayed in positive terms as a tool for women's liberation and societal progress more generally.

However, by the time such technologies became a reality, feminist responses to the developments of reproductive (and genetic) medicine were initially characteristically suspicious. In this, they echoed early hostile reactions to the invention and distribution of the contraceptive pill in the 1960s. Rather than interpreting the pill as a tool for women's sexual liberation (which it later was blamed for being), 1960s feminist activists criticised the perceived increase in medical control over female bodies as well as the health risks involved, which at the time were indeed much stronger than today. In a similar vein, authors such as Ann Oakley (1987) feared that those in control of reproductive technologies, doctors and the state, would gain unprecedented control over women, treating them as "walking wombs," a vision that was also central to Margaret Atwood's dystopian novel *The Handmaid's Tale*, which was published in 1985 and triggered much public debate at the time. Concerns were also voiced about the political accountability of reproductive science and medicine. Andrea Dworkin (1983, 183) predicted a future of "reproductive brothels," where women's wombs would be sold by male doctors or scientists, "a new kind of pimp," in the same way as female bodies were already being sold for male sexual pleasure. "Motherhood is becoming a new branch of female prostitution," Dworkin (181) argued.

The Feminist International Network for Resistance to Reproductive and Genetic Engineering (FINRRAGE), founded in 1984, emerged as the most prominent voice in the feminist critique of reproductive technologies (and technology more generally). Regrouping authors such as Gena Corea, Renate Klein, Raymond and Robyn Rowland, Maria Mies, and Janice Raymond, FINRRAGE adopted a strongly antitechnological stance. They declared that reproductive technologies are, by definition, patriarchal and detrimental to women and aim at male control of female bodies. As Raymond (1993, xxxi) put it, "Technological reproduction is first and foremost about the appropriation of the female body," whereas Mies (1987, 43) wrote that "any woman who is prepared to have a child manufactured for her by a fame- and money-greedy biotechnician must know that in this way she is not only fulfilling herself an individual, often egoistic wish to have a baby, but also surrendering yet another part of the autonomy of the female sex over childbearing to the technopatriarchs." For Corea (1985, 303), "in controlling the female generative organs and processes, doctors are fulfilling a male need to control woman's procreative power."

The role of men as fathers received little analytic attention in FINRRAGE's writings. To the extent that fathers do appear, they are accused of sharing the general male envy of women's child-bearing capacity and of intending to use the new technologies to wrestle women's procreative power away from them (e.g, Rowland 1984; Corea 1985, 9; Raymond 1993, 29–75). As Raymond (1993, 30) put it, "Fatherhood, not motherhood, is empowered by the new reproductive techniques" that create new norms of fatherhood grounded in male gametes and genes rather than child-rearing work. Rowland used powerful language to warn that new reproductive techniques might lead to the "final solution to the woman question," rendering women "obsolete" if control over childbearing, that "last power," was wrestled away from them by men (368). In this she echoed Dworkin's (1983) warning of a new kind of holocaust, a "gynocide" where reproductive technologies such as artificial insemination and IVF, in combination with "racist programs of forced sterilization," would give men "the means to create and control the kind of women they want:...domestics, sex prostitutes and reproductive prostitutes" (188). Raymond (1993, 32) argued that surrogacy practices create a "spermocracy" in which "male potency is power, exercised politically against the real potency of women, whose far greater contribution and relationship to the child is rendered powerless." In this analysis, the new reproductive techniques thus produce a shift in gender power that puts fathers back in patriarchal control over their offspring, echoing the gendered model of procreative agency that I have highlighted as characteristic of Greek antiquity earlier in this chapter. The ensuing political economy of a "spermatic market" is ruled by men's "liquid assets," involving the creation of a "breeder class of women sanctioned by the state" (ibid., 35). FINRRAGE feared that the political power of what Raymond calls "father essentialism" and "ejaculatory fatherhood" would further increase the power of the fathers' rights movements that emerged since the 1970s, against a backdrop of controversies around child custody and family law more generally in countries such as the United Kingdom, United States, Canada, Italy, Greece, and Germany. Organizations such as *Families Need Fathers* or *Fathers 4 Justice* have engaged in increasingly vocal political activism over the past decade.

More generally, FINRRAGE theorized new reproductive technologies as male tools for propping up patriarchy, pointing at the formal or informal exclusion of single and lesbian women from practices such as artificial insemination with donor, access to which was, until recent years, often made conditional on being married. FINRRAGE thus developed a strongly binary theorization of reproductive medicine as an arena of male power over passive, female bodies, where women-hating male scientists or "pharmacrats," to borrow Corea's vocabulary, perform invasive, expensive, and risky interventions on women's bodies (see also Klein 1989). Additionally, similarly to Stanworth (1987), FINRRAGE warned that techniques such as artificial insemination represented a slippery slope toward eugenics (Finger 1984; Corea 1985; Spallone 1987; Steinberg 1987). This argument was put particularly vehemently by Corea (1985), whose book *The Mother Machine* started with an outline of the ways artificial insemination could be used in eugenic programs to improve the quality of the human race by selecting who would be allowed to reproduce. Corea warned that while sterilization and birth control had, in past times, been tools of "negative eugenics" (which aims to prevent breeding by "defective" individuals), reproductive technologies such as artificial insemination, embryo transfer, IVF, cloning and "artificial wombs" offered dangerous new possibilities for "positive eugenics" (increasing reproduction by those categories of the population that are considered superior) (Corea 1985, 20). Other authors criticized the formal or informal exclusion of disabled women from such practices (e.g., Steinberg 1987). FINRRAGE's founding resolution thus included opposition to "eugenic population policies, in particular the fabrication of 'perfect babies'" as well as the fight against the "expropriation" and "dissection" of the female body by new reproductive practices (ibid., 329).

Today, both the extreme antitechnology and antinatalist stances have faded into the backdrop in feminist thought. The role and impact of reproductive and genetic medicine on gender relations and politics of the body tend to be debated in considerably less hostile terms, despite the fact that some of the worst fears of FINRRAGE, including the commercialization of new reproductive technologies and inequalities in access to the possibilities that they offer, have long since become reality. Instead, recent scholarship explores the ways practices in these fast-moving fields are profoundly transforming ideas of parenthood, kinship, and nature and the subjective meanings that women and men who undergo fertility treatments give to their experiences (e.g., Franklin 1997, 2007; see also Edwards et al. 1993; Farquhar 1996). Whereas feminist debates on reproductive medicine in the 1980s and 1990s had tended to center on the Western contexts in which the new techniques first emerged, recent anthropological studies have done much to enrich current understandings of the ways reproductive rights and politics are subjectively experienced by citizens in non-Western as well as Western contexts and to identify interactions and negotiations between state institutions, private businesses, and religious authorities in such settings. Nowadays, the highest rate of IVF treatments in the world is found in Israel. As Susan Kahn's (2000) book *Reproducing Jews* highlights, assisted conception has been enthusiastically embraced in this country, where it is promoted by ultraorthodox and secular forces alike. New reproductive techniques have also been welcomed in various Muslim countries, as demonstrated by Marcia Inhorn's series of studies of practices of egg and sperm donation in Egypt, Iran, and Lebanon (Inhorn 2007; Inhorn et al. 2009); Irène Maffi's (2012) research on state policies around childbirth in Jordan, which discusses the ways state-promoted obstetric techniques have transformed the relationship of Jordanian women with their reproductive bodies; and Zeynep Gürtin's (2012) analysis of IVF practices in Turkey. While these authors importantly remind us of the cultural specificity of local experiences, other scholars have called for political and research strategies that explore transnational structural inequalities in the politics of reproduction, emphasizing the need to identify possibilities for global political alliances (Ginsburg and Rapp 1995).

CONCLUDING COMMENTS

To conclude, reproductive rights have been one of the central arenas in which feminists have creatively questioned conventional understandings of politics and problematized previously takenforgranted divisions between the public and the private spheres. Abortion rights in particular continue to act as a yardstick for women's rights and gender equality more generally. They consequently continue to be the target of renewed political attacks from religious fundamentalist and other conservative forces in many national settings today. Gender scholarship in this area has produced a rethinking of the boundaries of the political, emphasizing the importance of the body, sexuality, and normative models of masculinity and femininity for political theory as well as practice. Such research has demonstrated how some categories of citizens are encouraged to reproduce, while others are disempowered from doing so, in ways that reflect power relations around gender. It has also highlighted the importance of exploring what Colen (1986) calls *stratified reproduction*, that is, the ways gender power intersects with sexual identity, social class, disability, race, and other identity markers in reproductive activities. Men and (heterosexual or gay) fathers still remain somewhat of a blind spot in much theoretical and empirical research on reproductive rights and politics, however. For example, a review of anthropological research on women's reproductive agency and health carried out in 1996 identified over 150 volumes dedicated to these topics, but only very few studies of men's reproductive experiences (Inhorn 2006; see also Inhorn et al. 2009) or of gay men as fathers, caregivers, or sperm donors (but see Mosegaard 2009).

More generally, contemporary political theorists have importantly shown the implicitly male-centered bias of much of political thought (Coole 1987; Pateman 1988). Traditional political theory has relegated themes conventionally associated with femininity such as reproduction, childcare, and sexuality to the private sphere and therefore outside of the scope of both politics and political theory (see also Mottier 2004, 281). Themes such as men's procreative activities, male sexualities, or the role of men in childrearing have thus been neglected in (mainstream as well as feminist) political debate and theory, as political theorists such as Pateman (1988) and Carver (2004) point out. In this sense and despite FINRRAGE's gloomy warnings of a male war against female procreative prominence, men remain the second sex in reproduction.[1]

ACKNOWLEDGMENTS

I would like to thank Terrell Carver, Karen Celis, James Clackson, Rebecca Flemming, Sarah Franklin, Johanna Kantola, Duncan Kelly, George Owers, Georgina Waylen, Laurel Weldon and an anonymous reviewer of an earlier draft of this chapter for their very helpful comments and suggestions.

NOTE

1. I borrow this expression from Inhorn et al. (2009).

References

Anagnost, Ann. 1995. "A surfeit of bodies: population and the rationality of the state in Post-Mao China." In Faye D. Ginsburg and Rayna Rapp, eds., *Conceiving the new world order: The global politics of reproduction*. Berkeley: University of California Press, 22–41.

Atwood, Margaret. 1985. *The handmaid's tale*. Toronto: McLelland and Steward.

Bacchi, Carol Lee. 1999. *Women, policy and politics: The construction of policy problems*. London: SAGE.

Broberg, Gunnar, and Mattias Tydén. 2005. "Eugenics in Sweden: Efficient care." In Gunnar Broberg and Nils Roll-Hansen, eds., *Eugenics and the welfare state: sterilization policy in Denmark, Sweden, Norway, and Finland*. East Lansing: Michigan State University, 77–149.

Carver, Terrell. 2004. *Men in political theory*. Manchester: Manchester University Press.

Colen, Shellee. 1986. "With respect and feelings: voices of West Indian childcare and domestic workers in New York City." In Johnnetta B. Cole, ed., *All American women: Lines that divide, ties that bind*. New York: Free Press, 46–70.

Coole, Diana. 1987. *Women in political theory: From ancient misogyny to contemporary feminism*. Boulder, CO: Lynne Rienner.

Corea, Gena. 1985. *The mother machine: Reproductive technologies from artificial insemination to artificial wombs*. London: Women's Press.

Cornell, Drucilla. 1995. *The imaginary domain: Abortion, pornography and sexual harassment*. New York: Routledge.

Corrêa, Sonia, Rosalind Petchesky, and Richard Parker. 2008. *Sexuality, health and human rights*. London: Routledge.

de Beauvoir, Simone. [1949]. 1976a. *Le deuxième sexe*, vol. 1. Paris: Gallimard.

de Beauvoir, Simone. [1949] 1976b. *Le deuxième sexe*, vol. 2. Paris: Gallimard.

Dworkin, Andrea. 1983. *Right-wing women: The politics of domesticated females*. New York: Perigree Books.

Dworkin, Ronald. 1993. *Life's dominion: An argument about abortion, euthanasia and individual freedom*. New York: Albert A. Knopf.

Edwards, Jeanette, Sarah Franklin, Eric Hirsch, Frances Price, and Marilyn Strathern (Eds.). 1993. *Technologies of procreation: Kinship in the age of assisted conception*. Manchester: Manchester University Press.

Eisenstein, Zillah. 1983. "The state, the patriarchal family and working mothers." In Irene Diamond, ed., *Families, politics and public policy*. New York: Longman.

Elshtain, Jean Bethke. 1981. *Public man, private woman*. Princeton, NJ: Princeton University Press.

Farquhar, Dion. 1996. *The other machine: Discourse and reproductive technologies*. New York: Routledge.

Ferree, Myra Marx. 2003. "Resonance and radicalism: feminist framing in the abortion debates of the United States and Germany." *American Journal of Sociology* 109(2):304–344.

Finger, Anne. 1984. "Claiming *all* of our bodies: Reproductive rights and disability." In Rita Arditti, Renate Duelli Klein, and Shelley Minden, eds., *Test-tube women: What future for motherhood?* London: Pandora Press, 281–297.

Firestone, Shulamith. 1970. *The dialectic of sex: The case for feminist revolution*. New York: Bantam Books.

Foucault, Michel. 1990. *The history of sexuality, volume 1: An introduction*. New York: Random House.

Franklin, Sarah. 1997. *Embodied progress: A cultural account of assisted conception*. London: Routledge.

Franklin, Sarah. 2007. *Dolly mixtures: The remaking of genealogy*. Durham, NC: Duke University Press.

Gerodetti, Natalia. 2004. "Lay experts: Women's social purity groups and the politics of sexuality in late nineteenth and early twentienth century Switzerland." *Women's History Review* 13(4): 585–610.

Ginsburg, Faye D. (1998). *Contested lives: The abortion debate in an American community*. Berkeley: University of California Press.

Ginsburg, Faye D., and Rayna Rapp (Eds.). 1995. *Conceiving the new world order: The global politics of reproduction*. Berkeley: University of California Press.

Gordon, Linda. 1999. "Voluntary motherhood: The beginnings of feminist birth control ideas in the United States." In Judith Walzer Leavitt, ed., *Women and health in America*, 2d rev. ed. Madison: University of Wisconsin Press, 104–116.

Gürtin, Zeynep. 2012. "Assisted reproduction in secular Turkey: Regulation, rhetoric and the role of religion." In Marcia Inhorn and Soraya Tremayne, eds., *Islam and assisted reproductive technologies: Sunni and Shia perspectives*. New York: Berghahn Books.

Hernes, Helga Maria. 1987. *Welfare state and woman power: Essays in state feminism*. Oslo: Norwegian University Press.

Inhorn, Marcia. 2006. "Defining women's health: A dozen messages from more than 150 ethnographies." *Medical Anthropology Quarterly* 20(3): 345–378.

Inhorn, Marcia (Ed.). 2007. *Reproductive disruptions: Gender, technology and biopolitics in the new millenium*. New York: Berghahn Books.

Inhorn, Marcia C., Tine Tjørnhøj-Thomsen, Helene Goldberg, and Maruska La Cour Mosegaard (Eds.). 2009. *Reconceiving the second sex: Men, masculinity and reproduction*. New York: Berghahn Books.

Joffe, Carole. 1995. *Doctors of conscience: The struggle to provide abortion before and after Roe vs Wade*. Boston: Beacon Press.

Kahn, Susan Martha. 2000. *Reproducing Jews: A cultural account of assisted conception in Israel*. Durham, NC: Duke University Press.

Kantola, Johanna. 2006. *Feminists theorise the state*. London: Palgrave McMillan.

Kellough, Gail. 1996. *Aborting law: An exploration of the politics of motherhood and medicine*. Toronto: University of Toronto Press.

Kevles, Daniel. 1985. *In the name of eugenics: genetics and the uses of human heredity*. New York: Knopf.

King, Desmond, and Randall Hansen. 1999. "Experts at work: state autonomy, social learning and eugenic sterilization in 1930s Britain." *British Journal of Political Science* 29(1): 77–107.

Klein, Renate. 1989. *Infertility: Women speak out about their experiences of reproductive medicine*. Melbourne: Spinifex Press.

Kline, Wendy. 2001. *Building a better race: Gender, sexuality and eugenics from the turn of the century to the baby boom*. Berkeley: University of California Press.

Largent, Mark A. 2008. *Breeding contempt: The history of forced sterilization in the United States*. New Brunswick, NJ: Rutger's University Press.

Levine, Philippa. 2010. "Anthropology, colonialism, and eugenics." In Alison Bashford and Philippa Levine, eds., *The Oxford handbook of the history of eugenics*. Oxford: Oxford University Press, 43–61.

Lovenduski, Joni, and Joyce Outshoorn (Eds.). 1986. *The new politics of abortion.* London: SAGE.

Luker, Kristin. 1984. *Abortion and the politics of motherhood.* Berkeley: University of California Press.

Maffi, Irène. 2012. *Women, health and the state in the Middle East: The politics and culture of childbirth in Jordan.* London: I. B. Tauris.

MacKinnon, Catherine. 1983. "The male ideology of privacy: a feminist perspective on the right to abortion," *Radical America* 17: 22–35.

MacKinnon, Catherine. 1987. *Feminism unmodified.* Cambridge, MA: Harvard University Press.

Morgan, Lynn M., and Meredith W. Michaels (Eds.). 1999. *Fetal subjects, feminist positions.* Philadelphia: University of Pensylvania Press.

Mies, Maria. 1987. "Why do we need all this? A call against genetic engineering and reproductive technology." In Patricia Spallone and Deborah Lynn Steinberg, eds., *Made to order: the myth of reproductive and genetic progress.* Oxford: Pergamon Press, 34–47.

Mosegaard, Maruska LaCour. 2009. "Stories of fatherhood: Kinship in the making." In Maria C. Inhorn, Tine Tjørnhøj-Thomsen, Helene Goldberg, and Maruska La Cour Mosegaard, eds., *Reconceiving the second sex: Men, masculinity and reproduction.* New York: Berghahn Books, 349–370.

Mottier, Véronique. 2000. "Narratives of national identity: Sexuality, race, and the Swiss 'Dream of Order.'" *Swiss Journal of Sociology* 26: 533–556.

Mottier, Véronique. 2004. "Feminism and gender theory: The return of the state." In Gerald F. Gaus and Chandran Kukathas, eds., *Handbook of political theory.* London: SAGE, 277–288.

Mottier, Véronique. 2010. "Eugenics and the state: Policy-making in comparative perspective." In Alison Bashford and Philippa Levine, eds., *The Oxford handbook of the history of eugenics.* Oxford: Oxford University Press, 134–153.

Nagel, Joanne. 2003. *Race, ethnicity and sexuality: Intimate intersections, forbidden frontiers.* Oxford: Oxford University Press.

Oakley, Ann. 1987. "From walking wombs to test-tube babies." In Michelle Stanworth, ed., *Reproductive technologies: Gender, motherhood and medicine.* Cambridge, UK: Polity Press, 36–56.

Okin, Susan Moller. 1991. "Gender, the public and the private." In David Held, ed., *Political theory today.* Cambridge, UK: Polity Press, 67–90.

Palmer, Julie. 2009. "Seeing and knowing: ultrasound imagies in the contemporary abortion debate." *Feminist Theory* 10(2): 173–189.

Pateman, Carole. 1988. *The sexual contract.* Cambridge, UK: Polity Press.

Pearson, Karl. [1909]1998. "The scope and importance to the state of the science of national eugenics." In Lucy Bland and Laura Doan, eds., *Sexology uncensored: The documents of sexual science.* Cambridge, UK: Polity Press, 169–171.

Petchesky, Rosalind Pollack. [1984]1990. *Abortion and woman's choice: The state, sexuality and reproductive freedom.* Boston: Northeastern University Press.

Phillips, Anne. 1991. *Engendering democracy.* Cambridge: Polity Press.

Phillips, Anne. 1998. "Introduction." In Anne Phillips, ed., *Feminism and politics.* Oxford: Oxford University Press, 1–20.

Raymond, Janice G. 1993. *Women as wombs: Reproductive technologies and the battle over women's freedom.* San Francisco: Harper.

Rich, Adrienne. 1976. *Of woman born: Motherhood as experience and institution.* New York: Norton.

Roberts, Dorothy. 1997. *Killing the black body: Race, reproduction and the meaning of liberty.* New York: Vintage Books.

Rowland, Robyn. 1984. "Reproductive technologies: The final solution to the woman question?"In Rita Arditti, Renate Duelli Klein, and Shelley Minden, eds., *Test-tube women: What future for motherhood?* London: Pandora Press, 356–369.

Sanger, Margaret. 1919. "A parents' problem or women's?" *The Birth Control Review* (March), 6–7.

Schoen, Johanna. 2005. *Choice and coercion: Birth control, sterilization and abortion in public health and welfare.* Chapel Hill: University of North Carolina Press.

Siim, Birte. 1988. "Towards a feminist rethinking of the welfare state." In Kathleen B. Jones and Anna G. Jonasdottir, eds., *The political interests of gender.* London: SAGE, 160–186.

Solinger, Rickie (Ed.). 1998. *Abortion wars: A half-century of struggle, 1950–2000.* Berkeley: University of California Press.

Spallone, Patricia. 1987. "Reproductive technology and the state: The Warnock Report and its clones." In Patricia Spallone and Deborah Lynn Steinberg, eds., *Made to order: The myth of reproductive and genetic progress.* Oxford: Pergamon Press, 166–183.

Stanworth, Michelle. 1987. "The deconstruction of motherhood." In Michelle Stanworth, ed., *Reproductive technologies: Gender, motherhood and medicine.* Cambridge, UK: Polity Press, 10–35.

Steinberg, Deborah Lynn. 1987. "Selective breeding and social engineering: Discriminatory politics of access to artificial insemination by donor in Great Britain." In Patricia Spallone and Deborah Lynn Steinberg, eds., *Made to order: The myth of reproductive and genetic progress.* Oxford: Pergamon Press, 184–189.

Stern, Alexandra Minna. 2005. *Eugenic nation: Faults and frontiers of better breeding in modern America.* Berkeley: University of California Press.

Stetson, Dorothy McBride (Ed.). 2001. *Abortion politics, women's movements and the democratic state: A comparative study of state feminism.* Oxford: Oxford University Press.

Stetson, Dorothy McBride, and Amy Mazur (Eds.). 1995. *Comparative state feminism.* London: SAGE.

Yuval-Davis, Nira. 1997. *Gender and nation.* London: SAGE.

CHAPTER 9

....

GENDER VIOLENCE

....

R. AMY ELMAN

Introduction
....

Over the last forty years, academics have counted, categorized, and connected the violence of boys and men against women and girls with other structural injustices in an effort to end it. Their studies helped end the dominant self-deluding narrative of fill-in-the blank exceptionalism. Assertions that the problem of such violence exists elsewhere, in the past, between others—not here—are increasingly met with incredulity. These academics, like the activists they engaged, slowly undermined the seemingly exceptional character of this abuse by taking a subject once shrouded in silence and making it into one of public concern, political action, and state—if not transnational—response. As an analytical concept that pivots on power and extends across time, space, and social place, this violence lends itself to comparative political analyses, albeit ones constrained by methodological convenience and politics.

This chapter explores these constraints and recent trends as it considers this small but burgeoning subfield within political science. It opens with the discipline's indebtedness to those few feminist theorists who first politicized male violence and then offers an overview of the empirical work concerning the responsiveness of various states (and regions) to the claims of women's movements to stem it. After considering some of the often unintended consequences of this responsiveness, we shift to the global level of governance and conclude with three key developments. These include the blurred boundaries between states, movements, and global civil society, the emerging set of international norms that define male violence, and the enduring cavernous gulf between rhetorical condemnations of male violence and political reality.

Throughout this chapter, I employ an expansive definition of this violence to include female genital mutilation, battering, sexual assault, forced pregnancy, sexual exploitation (e.g., pimping), sexual harassment, lesbian bashing, and stalking. These practices, among others, represent a violent reproduction of gender that specifically functions to enforce and perpetuate female subordination. For this reason, violence against women and girls is a subset of *gender violence* (Skinner, Hester, and Malos 2005, 2–3), which also includes, but is not limited to, violence where women are perpetrators (albeit in ways that recognize that these matters are still mediated by gender), same-sex (domestic) violence, and violence against gays and lesbians. Although political scientists have begun calling for a more expansive understanding of gendered violence, most literature on the politics of gendered violence pertains to violence against women.[1]

Despite the thousands of articles and book-length assessments, political scientists have generally been latecomers to the subject—often addressing it only after states and international institutions issued express condemnations of violence against women and girls. The principal reason for this early neglect stems from the fact that a majority of our discipline's practitioners typically base their inquiries on the assumption that our "proper" subject "lies in the public world of the economy and state" (Pateman 1989, 3) and not the private realm where ordinary men and boys have historically maintained a monopoly on the legitimate exercise of violence against the women and girls in their lives. By contrast, feminist activists in the later part of the twentieth century focused largely on trying to make this abuse visible by bringing it out of the private sphere (of the family) and into the public realm (of politics) through protests, publications, and speak-outs that called for remedies that include shelters, hotlines, and legal relief.

FEMINIST THEORISTS ON VIOLENCE

The willingness of feminist theorists to interrogate the seemingly most intimate aspects of our lives (with attention to the public–private divide) may explain why this subfield produced some of the earliest and most astute work on male violence in political science. For instance, while most early analysts of male violence depicted rape as "first and foremost a crime of violence against the body, and only secondarily (though importantly) a sex crime" (Peterson 1977, 364), Catharine MacKinnon (1979, 218–219) insisted that rape is no less serious a violation for lacking violence or being sexual. Indeed, she criticized the apparent legal requirement that sexual violations seem extraordinary. She observed, "Because the inequality of the sexes is socially defined as the enjoyment of sexuality itself, gender inequality appears consensual" (MacKinnon 1987, 7), an insight that explains how (legally) rape is regulated but rarely prosecuted (ibid., 26). Carole Pateman (1988, 189–218) similarly scrutinized the limitations of "consent" to unmask the sexualized subordination and violence inherent in prostitution, a position that denies the magical property of obliterating coercion through payment for sex. A decade later, Susan Okin's (1999) suspicion about culture was reminiscent of earlier skepticism surrounding consent in that male dominance often receives absolution beneath both mantles. After wondering what should be done when cultural claims clash with the gender equality formally endorsed by liberal states, Okin reasoned that state and community leaders who condone or excuse a plethora of cultural practices such as marital rape, stoning, female genital mutilation, and honor killings must be challenged (Okin 1999).[2] In short, cultural (or traditional) defenses for male violence are indefensible, and a politics devoid of this judgment invites fundamentalists in where feminists fear to tread (Sandel 2009, 243).

More recent theoretical work has forcefully challenged the feminist impulse to stress the gender-specific character of violence. To this end, it has countered the presumed essentialism of this scholarship (see MacKinnon 2006, 50–54). Such scholarship has criticized earlier considerations of "male violence" for insufficiently problematizing gender and perpetuating the very fixed (or naturalized) understandings of masculinity and femininity that such work likely wished to undermine. Borrowing from postmodern theorists such as Michel Foucault and Judith Bulter, Laura J. Shepherd (2008) advances a poststructuralist feminist approach to gendered violence and international security, one that stresses the performative character of gendered violence.

In addition, scholars have strived to recognize the disparate impact of male violence for differentially situated women and girls. The methodological challenges associated with such intersectional analysis can render systematic assessments a Sisyphean task for researchers (see Weldon 2006b), particularly for those assessing political authorities and institutions that present various constituencies as unproblematically monolithic (e.g., "women of color" and "women with disabilities"). As a consequence, the crucial distinctions within these groups are lost in ways that help explain the limited headway made by empiricists. (For the consequences this has for women with disablities, see Elman 2005). No wonder then that Johnson (2010, 2381) notes that scholars focused on the impact of policy reforms to stem violence against women of color (long abused by police) have generated much debate but little clarity (Matthews 1994). Celeste Montoya (2013) thus applies a "critical multi-cultural feminist analysis," in which intersectionality is central, to examine whether EU policies address different groups of women in either an inclusive or exclusive manner.

Of those efforts to better grasp gendered violence at the intersections of injustice, those exploring the connections between genocide and sexual abuse may be among the most illuminating (e.g., MacKinnon 2006, 209–233). Consider, for example, analysis emanating from Croatia in the midst of Europe's most recent genocide. Natalie Nenadic and Asja Armanda demonstrated that, while women are targeted in every genocide, the genocidal atrocities by Serbian fascists against Bosnian Muslim and Croatian women constituted yet another dimension of a larger continuum of global and historical crimes against women (Nenadic 1996; Armanda and Nenadic 2011). After noting the incredulity, indifference, and then failure on the part of states throughout the world to intervene against rape death camps, Nenadic concludes, "That the world is even less ours than we thought" (Nenadic, 464).

For feminist movements and allies determined to make the world a more hospitable place by ending the violence of men and boys against women and girls, the greatest obstacle in confronting this male violence was (and sadly still may be) first proving that it existed and then convincing others it is was wrong. It is worth remembering that as battered women's shelters spread rapidly throughout Britain and captured media attention, the press in the United States rebuffed extending coverage to what it insisted was "a British problem" (Brownmiller 1999, 262). Within two years after the first shelter was established in London in 1971, several opened their doors in the United States to reveal that the problem of woman battering was no longer Britain's alone. Ironically, the British press reacted to the U.S. feminist movement against rape in a comparable manner, alleging that sexual abuse was an American problem (Brownmiller 1999, 262). As women in Britain came forward with stories of sexual abuse, the public's perception changed and this particular rebuff concerning rape was also short-lived.[3] The early establishment of Dutch shelters for battered women provides an additional example of how refuges politicized women's grievances and transformed public consciousness, which, in turn, empowered more women to speak out. By 1979, researchers there found a notable shift from regarding male violence as a misfortune to an injustice for which women were entitled to state redress (Stolk and Wouters, cited in Hagemann-White 2001, 742). Nonetheless, in still other states (like Sweden, Finland, and Slovakia) there was little discussion of male violence until at least a decade later (for Sweden, see Elman 1996a; for Finland, see Kantola 2006, 101; for Slovakia, see Wasilieski and Miller 2010).

Indeed, in the mid-1980s, many Scandinavians regarded the relative absence of assistance for abused women as evidence that it was unnecessary. In Sweden, where gender equality is an ostensible component of national identity, the persistent refusal to tackle the matter makes it harder to speak out and easier to attribute male violence to misfortune and/or foreigners, despite a decade of evidence to the contrary (Elman 2001a). In Finland, by contrast, the public often attributed male violence to alcohol abuse (Kantola 2006). As evidence mounted about the pervasiveness of abuse and incredulity waned, there were still those who persisted in attributing violence against women and girls to nearly every other structural inequality, save sexism. Thus, while leftists tried to explain men's violence by reference to class oppression, others insisted that the violence of racialized men stems from racist oppression. In addition to sidestepping the matter of male power, such explanations perpetuate the very prejudice they claimed to counter. The feminist philosopher Susanne Kappeler notes that these explanations exonerate the perpetrators for their own actions and stigmatize the broad social strata of their belonging as a hotbed of violence (Kappeler 1995, 5–23).

Bringing the State(s) In

Given the relatively recent politicization of abuse and the ensuing adoption of policies to end it, earlier empirical works provided critical historical overviews of seemingly archaic laws, feminist mobilization, and reforms that coincided with violations (e.g., rape outside marriage and battery) that states identified as *criminal* (Bush 1992; Dobash and Dobash 1992). The benefit of this approach is that it corresponds with the discipline's emphasis on the state and thus established an essential foundation for future work.

However, the circumscribed and largely criminological emphasis of this scholarship presented problems. First, it often overlooked ordinary instances of male violence (e.g., sexual harassment) while sometimes exaggerating the state's protection in those exceptional cases where it chose to intervene (e.g., "stranger rape"). Similarly, scholars sometimes depicted the most horrific abuse in exacting detail so that others would take it seriously. Yet the unintended consequences of these efforts may have been titillation and a deadening of outrage for seemingly less severe violations—a point to which we will return when we consider public information campaigns.

Additionally, because crime reports result from those who see themselves reflected in the law as persons worthy of making a grievance and likely to be heard, fewer reported incidents may reflect less the exceptionality of abuse than its pervasiveness and subsequent belief among women and girls that they do not matter. A dearth of reported incidents could also suggest limited faith in the state's capacity to rectify sexist oppression. Conversely, a higher level of reporting may indicate both a greater awareness among women and girls that their abuse is criminal and a confidence in the state to respond accordingly. Then again, a higher level of reporting may simply reflect a higher level of abuse. Given the myriad explanations for something as seemingly simple as determining levels of criminal abuse within a single state, caution is necessary. Moreover, differing conceptions and definitions of crimes (like rape) and varied record keeping methods further complicate rigorous cross-national scholarship.

Transcending a criminological emphasis may resolve some problems, but others persist. Consider, for example, the reliance of many researchers on national prevalence surveys that typically move beyond criminal records. Because most employ different survey questions, definitions (e.g., sometimes including psychological or sexual abuse, other times not), and methodologies (e.g., telephone interviews, postal surveys or computer generated questionnaires), confusion persists about the prevalence, acceptability, and severity of male violence. As a consequence, we remain unaware of the coping strategies women and girls employ and those state interventions that might effectively prevent or mitigate abuse. In the absence of consistent and comparable measures, states, international institutions and nongovernmental organizations lack a precise means for benchmarking best practice within states (Hagemann-White 2001, 741). As a result, difficulties await those attempting meaningful comparisons within and between them.

In light of these obstacles, scholars focused less on determining the effectiveness of existing policies than on the responsiveness of states to women's claims for redress and remedy (e.g., Elman 1996a; Pande 2002; Weldon 2002; Kantola 2006; Zippel 2006; Walsh 2008; Johnson 2009b; Montoya 2013). This approach entails an exploration of whether, when, and how states adopted legal reforms, educational outreach programs, and safe spaces for battered women and survivors of sexual assault, exploitation, and harassment. While most such works are either single-country case studies (e.g., Pande 2002; Walsh 2008; Johnson 2009b) or dual cross-national assessments (e.g., Dobash and Dobash 1992; Elman 1996; Kantola 2006), S. Laurel Weldon's significantly more expansive single-author study examines national policies adopted by thirty-six democratic nation-states over two decades (1974–1994), whereas Montoya explores thirty-five countries (EU member, candidate, and prospective states) over forty years (1970–2010).

In casting a wide empirical net, Montoya (2013) finds that aggregate patterns in policy adoption coincide with international–transnational advocacy and accession, yet Weldon's (2002) global study offers a more surprising conclusion. She found that "the most responsive governments include many that have very few women in government (such as the United States, Australia, and France), while some governments with a large proportion of women in government (such as Finland) have been among the least responsive" (5). This discovery contradicts a key assumption that pervades the women and politics literature—the more women in formal positions of power, the more responsive the polity.[4] Indeed, Weldon argues that the greatest predictor of a state's responsiveness rests on the existence of a strong and independently organized women's movement. She does not deny the importance of official state women's agencies but suggests they are able to enhance state responsiveness only when working alongside autonomous movements.[5]

Yet what of significantly less institutionally developed states in which women's state agencies are weaker, ineffective, or poorly funded? While there is, as yet, no wide-range multistate study of either undemocratic or newly democratized states similar to that of Weldon's (2002), we do have single-country and regional studies that begin to address this question. In looking to Latin America in general and Guatemala specifically, Shannon Drysdale Walsh (2008) suggests that it is curious that such specialized institutions even exist, and she attributes their development to changes in international and regional norms as Latin American states transitioned away from military authoritarian rule in the

1990s. She explains that activists there took advantage of this dynamic period to argue for a more robust democracy, one that addresses male violence. However, the increasingly institutionalized character of this mobilization has certainly led many activists to question whether (and to what extent) there remains a movement (52). These newly democratized states appear to have incorporated the movement through their agencies, whereas activists on contracts with non-governmental organizations (NGOs) now spend considerable time managing projects with measurable results to increase donor support. However, Walsh suggests that it is precisely the challenges wrought by this institutionalization that may also provide activists an opportunity to transform attitudes and practices throughout Latin American society. In the Middle East, Nadje Al-Ali (2003) similarly found that while foreign funding prompted some rivalry among activists, the resulting professionalization also enhanced the quality of the few projects to stem violence women's organizations offered. And, as we will note, Janet Elise Johnson (2009b) reaches comparable conclusions in her exploration of Russia, as did Katalin Fábián (2010b), whose research concerned Poland, the Czech Republic, Slovakia, Hungary, and Slovenia.

From State to Civil Society

It seems slightly paradoxical that as more scholars began considering the import of women's agencies and autonomous movements, the relationship between states and movements changed significantly—often in ways that rendered the latter nearly nonexistent. Chiefly, the success that many movements had in politicizing male violence came at a cost. Activists were frequently subjected to backlash, and many had burned out. Moreover, movement resources were stretched thin as the demands for them increased. As a result, activists who previously embraced the rhetoric of autonomy (from the state) employed moderate neoliberal rhetoric, entering states as experts and creating more formal (NGOs) organizations—often as a means of receiving modest support from retrenched states for their work (Banaszak, Beckwith, and Rucht 2003b; Elman 2003; Franceschet 2003; Walsh 2008). In turn, states seemed more permeable to civil society and its entrepreneurial demands. Indeed, governments extended (limited) funds to combat male violence—albeit with conditions attached. According to Sonia E. Alvarez (1998, 198), "NGOs that refuse to play by the rules of the game or whose discourses and practices run counter to the official orthodoxies of the day may be losing out in the gender projects market and are often silenced or marginalized from the public debate."

Not surprisingly, governments granted funding principally to those relatively more professionalized organizations that worked closely with law enforcement and concentrated on social service delivery and less on empowering women who could then organize on their own behalf. In her work on campaigns against sexual violence, Kristin Bumiller (2008, 96) observed that feminist efforts unwittingly "led to an expansion in crime control strategies and a feminized terrain of victim services" in the United States. "As a result, the feminist movement became a partner in the unforeseen growth of a criminalized society, a phenomenon with negative consequences not only for minority and immigrant groups of men but also for those women who are subject to scrutiny within the welfare state" (xii). In Latin America, feminist NGOs continued "to struggle to provide *asesoria* and promote *conscientización* (consciousness-raising) among popular women's organizations" in ways that pushed "gender policy beyond the narrow parameters of…actually existing democracies," but Alvarez (1998, 189) found "the material resources and political rewards for doing so appear to be drying up." With grassroots protest movements in decline and looking more like formal NGOs worldwide (Johnson 2009b, 11), the exhilarating age of autonomous movements (within states that had them)[6] may be an anachronism. Ending male violence became a professional career or charitable act and less a movement objective.

The subsequent blurring of boundaries between neoliberal states and civil society left professionalized women's movements and other nongovernmental actors increasingly responsible for the adoption, execution, and monitoring of reforms (Banaszak, Beckwith, and Rucht 2003a) as states authoritatively claimed success for the mere existence of initiatives. This occurred both in advanced industrialized democracies and in states that recently transitioned to democracy. For many in Central and Eastern Europe as well as Latin America, neoliberal austerity measures savaged social service sectors in ways that raised greater obstacles for women. Latinas who played central roles in opposing authoritarianism now had even less time for political activism (Franceschet 2003, 10), while women who survived communism in Central and Eastern Europe realized that the relative accessibility of past public housing was no more, which meant that it was becoming harder for victims of male violence to find shelter and leave home (Fábián 2010a, 19). Within many advanced industrialized democracies as well, cutbacks in social spending had a disproportionate effect on women and, thus, compromised their ability to mobilize (Elman 2003).

Often unable to challenge the very states on which they had come to rely, many within movements muted their frustrations and sought support from other "outside" sources (e.g., large foundations and smaller private donations). Eventually, activists and scholars tracked this trend and assessed its consequences. The U.S. collective Women of Color Against Violence attributed the decline of grassroots movements to the "non-profit industrial complex" (Incite! Women of Color Against Violence 2007). Focusing specifically on the prison industrial complex, they found that the criminal justice solutions favored by many antiviolence organizations in the United States reinforced industrialized incarceration. This development is evidenced, in part, by the increased number of antiviolence initiatives now located within police departments—a problem for radicals who long questioned the patriarchal aspect of the state in general and police personnel more specifically. While the United States is distinguished by having the highest rates of documented incarceration in the world, an increased proliferation of criminal justice and movement partnerships can be noted globally. For instance, women's police stations (first founded in Brazil in 1985) are now commonplace throughout Latin America. Despite the dearth of comprehensive comparative data and analysis, most commentators assume these are innovative projects that must be strengthened (Jubb and Izumio 2003, 33–34). Walsh (2008), however, takes a less sanguine position after finding that Guatemala's "justice" system personnel typically regard "violence against women as an appropriate method of keeping women subordinated to the will and preferences of their male partners" (54).

For activists from less affluent states, reliance on external support also frequently meant reluctant appeals for international aid and fear that organizational goals and activities at the local level would be compromised to accommodate the agenda of those with greater power (Walsh 2008, 52–53). In some cases, though, it appears that feminist movements have been able to circumvent recalcitrant states by converting international pressure into resources and leverage on local institutions (Keck and Sikkink 1998, Chapter 5). For example, EU funding afforded some movements respectability and political leverage within their member-states (Elman 2007, 110; Fábián 2010b) and facilitated transnational networks for still others (Montoya 2008, 364, 2013).

For women in Central and Eastern Europe, where funding for feminist projects was largely funneled through foreign NGOs in the aftermath of the Cold War, suspicion centered on whether this development signified a new era of imperialism, albeit in the name of women's rights (Johnson 2009a; Fábián 2010a; Montoya 2013). Indeed, academics were apprehensive about whether such funding would contribute to the kind of welfare retrenchment experienced elsewhere. Contrary to this expectation, Johnson found that, in Russia, foreign funding "provided essential economic resources for a society undergoing massive economic and social dislocation" (151). Moreover, she found Russian women were unwilling to absolve the state of its responsibility to address male violence and, instead, made powerful arguments for the resumption of old responsibilities and the addition of new ones. Johnson's study encourages us to recognize the important differences between states and their impact for the women that mobilize within and across them. Not least, she makes clear that we can no longer focus on (local) movements and states to the exclusion of their global context (see also Johnson 2010).

Yet if earlier analyses of movements that centered on politics at the local and national levels were less helpful in grasping the growing importance of global politics (e.g., international aid, international organizations, transnational actors and regional integration), it is because there was limited evidence to suggest that transnational women's networks and international organizations seriously informed women's autonomous organizing on behalf of abused women and girls through the early 1990s in advanced industrialized states (Weldon 2002, 206). Rather, international initiatives to stem male violence often followed on the heels of once autonomous movements, a factor frequently forgotten by international actors and others who inflate the importance and protection of their own (more recent) initiatives. For instance, when Anita Gradin (1999), a former European Union (EU) commissioner, appeared before the EU's first conference on "domestic" violence against women in 1999, she credited member-states with legal reform and mentioned women's "organizations" just once to say they had "been very instrumental in pointing to the necessity for legislation for the protection of women's rights" (8). The fact that feminists throughout Europe have long been ambivalent and divided about engaging some of the very authorities that may have been indifferent to or abusive to women was nowhere noted. Still, even when international conferences and resulting conventions provide local activists substantive political opportunities to press their demands on recalcitrant states and local communities (Keck and Sikkink 1998), these same actors have had to also hold powerful regional and international actors accountable for their previously stated symbolic policies and principles (Alvarez et al. 2003)—a point evidenced by the United Nations (UN) and its revised declarations addressing violence against women.

GLOBAL POLITICS

Prior to the UN's 1993 adoption of the Declaration on the Elimination of Violence against Women, there was no international human rights instrument designed exclusively to address male violence. Even the UN's (1979) Convention on the Elimination of All Forms of Discrimination against Women excluded gender-based violence under the rubric of discrimination. It was only after women's movements insisted (at the UN's third global conference on women in Nairobi in 1985) that a failure to act against this violence would slow economic and social development that the UN adopted the 1993 Declaration. It calls on states to take immediate and decisive steps to eradicate it. Two years later, in 1995, the UN held its Fourth World Conference on Women in Beijing, the largest conference the UN ever convened. It is ironic that China's authoritarianism seemed to have neither diminished the crowds nor the stature of the proceedings. Rather, attention extends to Paragraph 118 of the conference platform. It stipulates: "Violence against women is a manifestation of the historically unequal power relations between men and women which have led to domination over and discrimination against women by men and to the prevention of women's full advancement." Perhaps less known is that paragraph's assertion that "images in the media of violence against women...including

pornography, are factors contributing to the continued prevalence of such violence." Yet there is more to the declaration than this.

The 1993 Declaration on the Elimination of Violence against Women,
adopted by the General Assembly, also introduced the term *forced prostitution*
into an international text of reference for the first time—a term that continues to gain currency, particularly among supporters of the sex industry. Malka
Marcovich (2001) explains, for survivors of prostitution, this distinction shifts
the burden of proof from those who exploit them to the women themselves
who must then prove that they were "forced." Moreover, months prior, at the
World Conference on Human Rights in Austria, the UN produced the Vienna
Declaration. It codifies an atomistic perspective of human rights, one that posits that human rights are no longer universal but instead vary according to
one's "national and regional particularities and various historical, cultural and
religious backgrounds." Thus, the rights of a woman born in Saudi Arabia, for
example, are defined not by the UN's Universal Declaration but by the accepted
(patriarchal) norms of her nation, culture, and strict Wahhabist Islamic faith.
The adoption of this Vienna document renders moot any other protections on
offer through other conventions (Marcovich 2008). It also typifies the kind of
end-run around women's universal rights that concerned feminists like Susan
Okin (1999) a decade earlier.

While some scholars have scrutinized the UN's seemingly benevolent positions on violence against women (e.g., Marcovich 2001, 2008), others have
attended to the European Union's (EU) response to it and suggested that this
international body may similarly appear more progressive than it really is. The
European Commission and other EU institutions typically labored at significant remove from the more brutal aspects of women's subordination, focusing
instead on problems they recognized as directly related to equal pay and equal
treatment (Elman 1996b, 2007; Shaw 2000; Kantola 2006, 2010). As Montoya
(2009, 333) observes, "Other than the European Parliament's 1986 Resolution
on Violence against Women, the EU's initiatives aimed at combating violence
against women have occurred primarily after the mid 1990s." Thereafter, "efforts
aimed at policy reform have been in the form of soft law reports, communications and recommendations, conferences and meetings of experts, and public
awareness campaigns" (ibid.). In turning briefly to more recent efforts taken
by the Council of Europe (COE), she finds a somewhat more active body representing 47 Member countries—one that has adopted more specific guidelines,
monitoring mechanisms and an ostensibly binding 2010 convention. However,
with a majority of the COE member countries also EU member-states, she is
nonetheless concerned that the European Commission has been slow to respond
to these efforts (Montoya 2013). This wave of international action, however symbolic, was not restricted to Europe (Htun and Weldon 2010, 8).

Following the aforementioned Nairobi conference, an explosion of regional
and subregional organizing throughout the continent led to a UN-sponsored
Africa-wide conference in 1994 (Tripp 2009). That same year Latin American

activists labored in concert with the Inter-American Commission of Women, a specialized agency of the Organization of American States (OAS) to witness the adoption of the Inter-American Convention on the Prevention, Punishment and Eradication of Violence against Women. The 1994 convention was one of many that endeavored to improve the status of women, but this one focused specifically on holding member states accountable in their efforts against male violence. More importantly, "it opened new diplomatic space by shining the international spotlight on this closeted topic" (Meyer 1998, 141). Thus, as noted earlier, Latin American activists pursued male violence within the rubric of human rights long before others did (Weldon 2006a; Friedman 2009; Htun and Weldon 2010, 7), including human rights organizations such as Amnesty International and Human Rights Watch. Indeed, both NGOs kept their distance from the daily abuses endured by women and girls until well into the 1990s and, in some respects, their reluctance lingers. Consider Amnesty International. It has "yet to partner with other domestic violence organizations to draw system-atic attention to violence against women within the United States as a human rights violation" (Libal and Parekh 2009, 1484–1485). Kathryn Libal and Serena Parekh explain that counting the actions of private individuals as human rights violations remains a matter of considerable controversy because, for traditional human rights activists, "only a state or someone acting on behalf of a state could violate human rights." Moreover, "states are often reluctant to accept [violence against women as a human rights violation] because doing so would impose a large burden on them to rectify the problem" (1480). Nonetheless, in challenging activists and states to reconsider, feminists have provoked a para-digmatic shift that has helped save lives.

The relatively recent concern on the part of human rights organizations and international institutions regarding male violence helped pique the interest of political analysts, many of whom have since sought to understand the reasons for and consequences of this change. Zippel (2006) attributes the politicization of sexual harassment to the increasing visibility of women in the workplace and the public's heightened sensitivity to violence against women more gener-ally. "Surprisingly European women had their first success in passing meas-ures against sexual harassment not in their home countries but in the EU" (11). Zippel explains that the politicization of this particular abuse arose simultane-ously with the creation of gender equality offices and networks and that these like-minded actors became a driving force for social change and a changing consciousness.

In looking eastward, Johnson (2009b) similarly emphasizes the emer-gence of a "new global feminist consensus" following the demise of the Soviet Union, but instead of equality offices she finds international donors and human rights organizations networking throughout Central and European Europe and Eurasia. While in Russia, she witnessed an influx of Western (and in particular North American) feminists who, faced with backlash at home, sought and in many instances succeeded in having an impact abroad (3). Within a decade, the alliances made between Russian women and "global" feminists and large donors "led to multiple, widespread public awareness campaigns and collaborations with local activists which successfully translated global norms into the Russian vernacular" (150).

Yet not all these networks and resulting reforms to end male violence empowered Russian women; Johnson (2009b) observes that efforts to counter sex trafficking actually supported resurgent nationalism and cast Russian men as women's protectors. She writes, "Trafficking in women mattered to the Russian media and Russian politicians because they understood that the bodies of Russian women were being exploited by foreigners and because the solution involved strengthening Russia's coercive forces" (149).

Johnson's (2009b) systematic comparison of the effects of various interventions (e.g., rape, sexual harassment, domestic violence, trafficking) suggests both that not all matters of male violence are similarly politicized and that we not assume that efforts against trafficking portend progressive efforts against male violence and the promotion of women's rights and bodily integrity. There is often more to the story—and not just within Russia. In my own efforts to understand the reasons for and consequences of the EU's recent initiatives to counter violence against women and girls (Elman 2007, Chapter 7), I found that, in emphasizing its opposition to both domestic violence within its member-states and the trafficking in women and children *from outside* the community, the EU shored up support for the continued integration of its market by appealing to several competing constituencies simultaneously (see also Montoya 2013). As in Russia, policy makers throughout Europe looked to the issue of trafficking as a means of enhancing their coercive powers while appealing to an increasing number of citizens opposed to migration. Europe's politicians thus adopted a more stringent policing of the community's borders without necessarily pursuing policies to save or enhance the quality of women's lives (Goodey 2004, 32; Askola 2007). Nonetheless, for women's groups that embrace the erroneous distinction between free and forced prostitution, the community appears to have provided a measure of relief for those women and girls deemed especially vulnerable. This stance is in keeping with the dominant human rights narrative that dates from the UN's 1993 adoption of a forced versus free prostitution distinction. This discourse presumes that women within presumably affluent communities (e.g., within the EU) have rights and privileges that make their being in prostitution freely chosen, while those (nationals) external to the market (e.g., in Russia) lack these resources that render prostitution a choice.

Most importantly, the free versus forced prostitution dichotomy protects a powerful constituency—the global sex industry and its customers. By limiting the numbers of those considered as victims, the dominant discourse effectively shields both the industry and its customers from accusations of coercion. This approach has helped legitimize the sex trade (i.e., free prostitution) as a voluntary, rational, economic choice for women. Prostitution thus

becomes an option for those who comprise the most impoverished, unemployed, and physically abused segment of the (EU) market who are nonetheless (unlike third-country nationals) empowered by their Europeanness
to embrace sex work (for this position, see Kempadoo and Doezema 1998;
Wijers 2000; Kempadoo, Sanghera, and Pattanaik 2005). Indeed, in 1982, the
European Court of Justice affirmed this stance, codifying prostitution as sex
work in one of its rulings (Elman 2007, 91).

The sex industry's global triumph rests not only in its increasing profits
but also in the growing perception that pornography and organized prostitution (if not trafficking) are activities separate and distinctive from violence against women. This perspective causes considerable frustration among
many feminists who observe that whether the violence it took to make pornography is shown depends on the consumer's preference for it (MacKinnon
2006, 248). Commenting on contemporary mainstream pornography, Rebecca
Whisnant (2010, 115) finds "aggression against women is the rule rather than
the exception," and she substantiates this claim through a brief summary
of the titles readily available on any online pornography portal (e.g., *Border
Bangers, Gangland Victims, Bitchcraft, Gag on my Cock*). In turning from
pornography to the victims of trafficking, Dorchen Leidholdt (1999) reasons that those "who are targeted are the same—poor, minority, or so-called
Third World women and children, frequently with histories of physical and
sexual abuse" (51). Their customers are also the same—"men with disposable income who achieve sexual gratification by purchasing" the bodies of
women and children" (ibid). Not least, whether brothel owners or traffickers employ or threaten violence, debt, imprisonment or brainwashing, the
women's experiences of sexually transmitted diseases, substance abuse and
physical violence are the same (ibid.). Even those reluctant to take a firm
position against prostitution and trafficking nonetheless acknowledge that
those in it have nearly always suffered repeated sexual and physical abuse
(e.g., Outshoorn 2004; Askola 2007, 212).

The (apparent) invisibility of this violence has been reinforced by recent
efforts within international and domestic contexts to address some ("domestic") violence while trivializing (and legitimizing) others (i.e., pornography and
prostitution). It is not then surprising that the international community's greatest denunciations of male violence have been increasingly reserved for those
whose behaviors interfere with its labor market (e.g., harassers *at work*, bat-
terers and traffickers of third-country nationals) and not those who generate
profits within it (like pimps and pornographers).[7]

Even the EU's seemingly most progressive rhetoric proves wanting under
scrutiny. For instance, the European Parliament's 2009 resolution on violence
against women contained no mention of pornography but did once address
prostitution, noting that its "tolerance...in Europe leads to an increase in [sex]
trafficking of women into Europe." This marks a shift from its earlier soft
law policy which is much more inclusive and feminist in its stance (i.e., the

1986 and 1997 resolutions). By focusing on prostitution merely as a contributing factor to the importation of others from *outside* of Europe for sexual exploitation (i.e., sex trafficking), the resolution reifies the commission's earlier shortcoming—one that the commission itself notes. In 2000, the commission acknowledged that by not countering the trafficking of women within the member-states, a "European citizen forced into prostitution and trafficked in its [sic] own country, would be less protected than citizens of third countries" (COM 2000, 854 final, 9).[8] That the European Parliament embraced the commission's failed policy in its 2009 resolution against violence against women is ironic though not surprising given that varied European legislation (soft-law documents) contain numerous recycled and unrealized positions.

Consider, as well, the UN's equally ineffectual positions on pornography. As noted earlier, in 1995, its state members overwhelmingly agreed that pornography was a contributing factor to the continued prevalence of violence against women and girls—a position that ignores that its manufacture itself produces and documents harm. Five years later, under its International Covenant on Civil and Political Rights, the UN's Human Rights Commission held that "pornographic material which portrays women and girls as objects of violence or degrading or inhumane treatment is *likely* to promote these kinds of treatment of women and girls" (emphasis in original), a position that fails to regard the women and girls in pornography as real (i.e., live). More recently, the African Union's protocol on women's human rights urged states "to take effective legislative and administrative measures to prevent the exploitation of women in advertising and pornography." As with earlier such statements, it seems that these have had limited, if no, effect.

Many of the international community's most ardent feminist critics remain on the periphery of policy discussions, occasional rhetoric to the contrary notwithstanding. Their persistent request that the UN or European Community concentrate on trafficking and its relationship to other forms of sexual violence (i.e., sex tourism, sexual exploitation on the internet, mail-order brides, pornography, organized prostitution) has been largely ignored. Thus, like most of their member-states, these international institutions frame trafficking as separate from prostitution and countless other enterprises that trade in sex through poverty, physical abuse, and emotional coercion. This discourse rests on a separation between the innocent victims of traffickers (often third-country nationals) and (European and other Western) women who choose prostitution, a distinction that discounts the demand that prostitution generates for trafficking while ignoring the women in prostitution who have spoken out against its violence (Farley 2006).

By contrast, well-healed NGOs and particular state sectors (e.g., criminal justice and social services) reap the fiscal rewards and political prominence from rhetoric and related efforts to counter violence against women and girls while providing limited evidence of substantive redress. In contrast, the very weakened women's movements that once provided direct relief have been replaced and their criticisms of once unresponsive authorities are now subdued—often in the hope of currying favor with these elite for desperately needed funding. If local, grassroots women's movements have been less successful in capturing the public's attention to end violence against women and girls, it is because they have been replaced by others claiming to do the same. Johnson (2009b) observes, "In contrast to the consciousness-raising of Western feminist groups in the 1970s, raising awareness is typically an external process in which women's groups use the mass media or public events to distribute information about violence against women" (12). She identifies the International Day against Violence against Women and International Human Rights Day as "successful global campaigns" as hundreds of countries participate across global divides.

CONCLUSION

While public condemnations of violence against women and girls may be important, one must subject these and other policy statements, legislation, and programs to rigorous assessments that transcend our gratitude that they simply exist. This is especially crucial when one considers that the very initiatives undertaken to raise social awareness and enhance the state's response to abused women and girls may unintentionally deaden the outrage necessary to end the more subtle or ambiguous forms of violence that women and girls endure as often these fall below the threshold of cultural awareness (Lamb 1999). For example, in the mid-1990s researchers throughout Europe found that while public service announcements condemning male violence may have created the appearance of social progress and encouraged women and girls to report those who abuse them, there was no corresponding rise in either arrests or prosecutions in those areas that sponsored "Zero Tolerance" campaigns (Kelly 1995/1996, 11).

A study in the Spanish region of Cantabria confirms this point. It revealed a decrease in the percentage of women filing official complaints and was especially disquieting because the data were first collected in 1998 and again in 2000, a year prior to and then one following the EU's yearlong campaign to enhance public awareness that the physical assault of women is a crime and that authorities could be trusted to treat it as such (the Conseulo Berges Association of Separated and/or Divorced Women 2000).

Even in those instances when increasing numbers of women come forward to seek legal redress, the outcomes can prove especially disappointing. After noting that rape conviction rates were plummeting in Britain despite the increasing number of such cases brought to trial, Sue Lees (1997) sat through nearly a dozen rape trials and analyzed over fifty court records. In *Ruling Passions:*

Sexual Violence, Reputation and the Law, she reveals the paradoxical temper of the proceedings to account for this trend. She explains that women appearing in court are expected to testify to their violation by providing graphic details of their rape. Yet it is precisely this public recounting of sexuality that renders them undignified and undeserving of the justice they seek. No less important to consider is the fact that, as Lees reminds us, the contents of these trials then circulate as pornography in prisons. In all, one comes to share her conclusion that such trials are a cruel hoax.

Whether in research pertaining to Zero Tolerance and other consciousness-raising campaigns, rape trials, or international conferences, public condemnations of male violence can mask the lenience of states and other authorities. In the aftermath of the UN's 1995 Beijing conference, Marianne Hester (2005) found that foreign intervention may have inspired the development of some social services for abused women but that policy reform within China was largely superficial, a conclusion reached as well by Sally Merry (2006) in her book on China, Fiji, India, and Hong Kong.

Scholars of efforts against male violence have come to appreciate that one must not equate the adoption of laws with enforcement, the existence of progressive policies with effective implementation, or the establishment of women's agencies and NGOs with empowerment. Yet precisely because the global NGO industrialized complex may provide a powerful appearance or promise of social change (through a barrage of repetitive rhetoric) with limited evidence to suggest progress, political scholars have an important role in offering a critical exploration of the yawning gap between rhetoric and reality in the hope of highlighting best practices.

NOTES

1. To wit, of the nearly two hundred works cited in the American Political Association's list of "Recent Works Published on LGBT Politics," only Hirsch and Rollins (2007) explicitly address violence. While future literature will, no doubt, explore the gendered dimensions of self-harm and violence against gay men, bisexuals, lesbians, and others who either appear to challenge (or insist they violate) the social norms of masculinity and femininity, this chapter's central focus concerns male violence against women and girls. In focusing squarely on this harm, I neither subscribe to fixed notions of *women* and *femininity* or *men* and *masculinity* nor embrace the now common conflation of gender with women (and girls).
2. Okin's (1999) omission of pornography as a cultural practice is disappointing, particularly as the industry operates worldwide—generating profits from sexual abuse and exploitation that are often greater than all other segments of the entertainment industry combined. In 2006 alone, *reported* revenues in only sixteen states estimated returns of $97 billion (Waltman 2010, 219). Moreover, despite the well-documented injuries perpetrated in the production, dissemination, and

consumption of pornography (see ibid.), legal authorities within liberal states have explicitly reasoned that its artistic merits trump the harms it generates. MacKinnon (1987, 4) explains that while aesthetics defines and protects pornography as art, literary criticism defines and protects it as literature, and law defines and protects it as speech. By contrast, in 1982, the U.S. Supreme Court recognized that the prevention of sexual abuse of those under 18 is a "governmental objective of surpassing importance." Thus, the state is unwilling to protect the production and dissemination of child pornography as art, literature, or protected speech.

3. Nonetheless, some years later, pundits throughout Europe were as eager to dismiss sexual harassment as a uniquely American problem (Zippel 2006, ix).

4. Few examples better reveal the fragility of this position than the conviction of Pauline Nyiramasuhuko, a former Rwandan minister of family and women's affairs. In 2011, the United Nation's International Criminal Tribunal for Rwanda found Nyiramasuhuko guilty of genocide, war crimes, and crimes against humanity, including multiple rapes that she had ordered. As the first woman to be found guilty by an international tribunal of such crimes, the court reasoned she had used her ministerial position to end the lives of hundreds of Tutsi men, women, and children. Kimberly R. Carter (2010, 355) insists that the use of rape in war is so prevalent that excluding it from international relations and security studies is an inexcusable oversight that stems from viewing rape merely as a "woman's issue"—as opposed to a crime that undermines communities, states, regions, and, by extension, global security.

5. Weldon (2002, 56) also challenges other bits of conventional wisdom. For example, she finds Latin American governments slightly more responsive than European governments (e.g., Costa Rica's policies are more impressive than Sweden's). And in finding "no clear relationship between left parties and greater responsiveness to violence against women," she disputes the familiar portrait of a woman-friendly left. This last insight reinforced my earlier comparative analysis of Sweden and the United States in which I found that the more centralized, left-leaning Swedish state proved less permeable to women's claims than the more highly fragmented and seemingly less woman-friendly federalist U.S. state (Elman 1996a, xi). As well, these critical insights about the left have since been substantiated by others. Consider Merike H. Blofield and Liesl Haas's (2005) study of thirty-eight bills in Chile pertaining to women's rights, including those designed to stem sexual assault. The authors found that "the left began to defend its proposals on the basis of what was good for the family as a whole and would allow women to fulfill their traditional roles in it (often while they took on additional roles outside the home)" (47).

6. As Janet Elise Johnson (2009, 5) points out, "Feminist comparative policy studies...assume the existence of—or at least the legacy of—a broad-based women's movement that emerged in the 1960s and 1970s."

7. Over the last decade, some scholars have been especially effective at drawing attention to the connections between "domestic violence" and the labor market (Brush 2003; see also Reeves and O'Leary-Kelly 2007).

8. Still, the EU's stated concern for the protection of third country nationals is questionable (Elman 2001b). Consider, for instance, existing protections against various forms of discrimination such as the race and framework directives—neither extend to non-EU nationals.

References

Al-Ali, Nadje. 2003. "Gender and civil society in the Middle East." *International Feminist Journal of Politics* 5: 216–232.

Alvarez, Sonia E. 1998. "Advocating feminism: The Latin American Feminist NGO 'Boom.'" *International Feminist Journal of Politics* 1(2): 181–209.

Alvarez, Sonia E., Elisabeth Jay Friedman, Erika Beckman, Maylei Blackwell, Norma Stoltz Chinchilla, Nathalie Lebon, Marysa Navarro and Marcela Ríos Tobar. 2003. "Encountering Latin American and Caribbean Feminisms." *Signs: Journal of Women in Culture and Society* 28(2): 537–579.

Armanda, Asja, and Natalie Nenadic. 2011."Genocide, pornography, and the law." In Melinda Tankard Reist and Abigail Bray, eds., *Big porn inc: Exposing the harms of the global pornography industry*. North Melbourne: Spinifex.

Askola, Heli. 2007. *Legal responses to trafficking in women for sexual exploitation in the European Union*. Oxford: Hart Publishing.

Banaszak, Lee Ann, Karen Beckwith, and Dieter Rucht. 2003a. *Women's movements facing the reconfigured state*. New York: Cambridge University Press.

Banaszak, Lee Ann, Karen Beckwith, and Dieter Rucht. 2003b. "When power relocates: Interactive changes in women's movements and states." In Lee Ann Banaszak, Karen Beckwith, and Dieter Rucht, eds., *Women's movements facing the reconfigured state*. New York: Cambridge University Press, 1–29.

Blofield, Merike H., and Liesl Hass. 2005. "Defining a Democracy: Reforming the laws on women's rights in Chile, 1990–2002." *Latin American Politics and Society* 47(3): 35–68.

Brownmiller, Susan. 1999. *In our time: Memoir of a revolution*. New York: Dial Press.

Brush, Lisa D. 2003. "Effects of work on hitting and hurting." *Violence Against Women* 9(10): 1213–1230.

Bumiller, Kristin. 2008. *In an abusive state: How neoliberalism appropriated the feminist movement against sexual violence*. Durham, NC: Duke University Press.

Bush, Diane Mitsch. 1992. "Women's movements and state policy reform aimed at domestic violence against women: A comparison of the consequences of movement mobilization in the United States and India." *Gender and Society* 6(4): 587–608.

Carter, K. R. 2010. "Should international relations consider rape a weapon of war?" *Politics & Gender* 6(3): 343–371.

Conseulo Berges Association of Separated and/or Divorced Women 2000. "A Sociological Study of Women Victims of Abuse, Update, 16 November 1998–31 Diciembre 2000."

Dobash, R. Emerson, and Russell Dobash. *Women, violence, and social change*. London: Routledge.

Elman, R. Amy. 1996a. *Sexual subordination and state intervention: Comparing Sweden and the United States*. Providence, RI: Berghahn Books.

Elman, R. Amy (Ed.). 1996b. *Sexual politics and the European Union: The new feminist challenge*. Providence, RI: Berghahn Books.

Elman, R. Amy. 2001a. "Unprotected by the Swedish welfare state revisited: Assessing a decade of reforms for battered women." *Women's Studies International Forum* 24(1): 39–52.

Elman, R. Amy. 2001b. "Testing the limits of European citizenship: Ethnic hatred and male violence." *National Women's Studies Association Journal* 13(3): 49–69.

Elman, R. Amy. 2003. "Refuge in reconstructed states: Shelter movements in the United States, Britain and Sweden." In Lee Ann Banaszak, Karen Beckwith, and Dieter Rucht, eds., *Women's movements facing the reconfigured state.* New York: Cambridge University Press, 94–113.

Elman, R. Amy. 2005. "Confronting the sexual abuse of women with disabilities." *VAWnet—Applied Research Forum,* January. Available at http://www.vawnet.org/research/summary.php?doc_id=416&find_type=web_desc_AR.

Elman, R. Amy. 2007. *Sexual equality in an integrated Europe: Virtual equality.* New York: Palgrave Macmillan.

Fábián, Katalin. 2010a. "Introduction: The politics of domestic violence in postcommunist Europe and Eurasia." In Katalin Fábián, ed., *Domestic violence in postcommunist states: Local activism, national policies, and global forces.* Bloomington: Indiana University Press, 1–42.

Fábián, Katalin. 2010b. "Reframing domestic violence: Global networks and local activism in postcommunist Central and Eastern Europe." In Katalin Fábián, ed., *Domestic violence in postcommunist states: Local activism, national policies, and global forces.* Bloomington: Indiana University Press, 221–260.

Farley, Melissa. 2006. "Prostitution, trafficking, and cultural amnesia: What we must not know in order to keep the business of sexual exploitation running smoothly." *Yale Journal of Law and Feminism* 18: 109–144.

Franceschet, Susan. 2003. "'State feminism' and women's movements: The impact of Chile's Servicio Nacional de la Mujer on women's activism." *Latin American Research Review* 38(1): 9–40.

Friedman, Elisabeth Jay. 2009. "Re(gion)alizing women's human rights in Latin America." *Politics & Gender* 5: 349–375.

Goodey, Jo. 2004. "Sex trafficking in women from Central and East European countries: promoting a 'victim-centered' and 'woman-centered' approach to criminal justice." *Feminist Review* 76: 26–45.

Gradin, Anita. 1999. "Speech by Commissioner Gradin," Cologne: European Union Conference on Violence Against Women.

Hagemann-White, Carol. 2001. "European Research on the Prevalence of Violence Against Women." *Violence Against Women* 7(7): 732–759.

Hester, Marianne. 2005. "Transnational influences on domestic violence and action—Exploring developments in China and England." *Social Policy and Society* 4: 447–456.

Hirsch, N. H., and Joe Rollins. 2007. "Sexual orientation discrimination: an international perspective." In M. V. Lee Badgett and Jeff Frank, eds., *Beating up queers: Discrimination, violence, and political attitudes in sexual minority communities.* London: Routledge, 269–276.

Htun, Mala, and S. Laurel Weldon. 2010. *Violence against women: A comparative analysis of progress on women's rights.* Washington, DC: American Political Science Association.

Incite! Women of Color Against Violence. 2007. *The revolution will not be funded: beyond the non-profit industrial complex.* Cambridge, MA: South End Press.

Johnson, Janet Elise. 2009. *Gender violence in Russia: The politics of feminist intervention.* Bloomington: Indiana University Press.

Johnson, Janet Elise. 2010. "Foreign intervention and violence against women." In Robert A. Denemark, ed., *The international studies encyclopedia*. New York: Wiley-Blackwell, 2366–2383.

Jubb, Nadine, and Wânia Painato Izumio. 2003. *Women and policing in Latin America: A revised background paper*. Dallas, TX: Latin American Studies Association.

Kantola, Johanna. 2006. *Feminists theorize the state*. New York: Palgrave MacMillan.

Kantola, Johanna. 2010. *Gender and the European Union*. The European Union series. New York: Palgrave Macmillan.

Kappeler, Susanne. 1995. *The will to change: The politics of personal behavior*. New York: Teacher's College Press.

Keck, Margaret E., and Kathryn Sikkink. 1998. *Activists beyond borders: Advocacy networks in international politics*. Ithaca, NY: Cornell University Press.

Kelly, Liz. 1995/1996. "Zero commitment." *Trouble and Strife* 32: 9–16.

Kempadoo, Kamala, and Jo Doezema. 1998. *Global sex workers: Rights, resistance, and redefinition*. New York: Routledge.

Kempadoo, Kamala, Jyoti Sanghera, and Bandana Pattanaik. 2005. *Trafficking and prostitution reconsidered: New perspectives on migration, sex work, and human rights*. Boulder, CO: Paradigm Publishers.

Lamb, Sharon. 1999. *New versions of victims: Feminists struggle with the concept*. New York: New York University Press.

Lees, Sue. 1997. *Ruling passions: Sexual violence, reputation and the law*. Buckingham: Open University Press.

Leidholdt, Dorchen. 1999. "Prostitution: A form of modern slavery." In Donna Hughes, ed., *Making the harm visible: Global sexual exploitation of women and girls*. Kingston, RI: Coalition Against Trafficking in Women, 49–55.

Libal, Kathryn, and Serena Parekh, Serena. 2009. "Reframing violence against women as a human rights violation: Evan Stark's coercive control." *Violence Against Women* 15(12): 1477–1489.

MacKinnon, Catharine A. 1979. *Sexual harassment of working women: A case of sex discrimination*. New Haven, CT: Yale University Press.

MacKinnon, Catharine A. 1987. *Feminism unmodified: Discourses on life and law*. Cambridge, MA: Harvard University Press.

MacKinnon, Catharine A. 2006. *Are women human?: And other international dialogues*. Cambridge, MA: Belknap Press.

Marcovich, Malka. 2001. "Guide to the UN Convention of 1949." North Amherst, MA: Coalition Against Trafficking in Women.

Marcovich, Malka. 2008. *Les Nations Désunies: Comment l'ONU enterre les Droits de l'Homme*. Paris: Éditions Jacob-Duvernet.

Matthews, Nancy A. 1994. *Confronting rape: The feminist anti-rape movement and the state*. The International Library of Sociology. London: New York: Routledge.

Merry, Sally Engle. 2006. *Human rights and gender violence: Translating international law into local justice*. Chicago, IL: University of Chicago Press.

Meyer, Mary K. 1998. "Negotiating international norms: The Inter-American Commission of Women and the Convention on Violence against Women." *Aggressive Behavior* 24: 135–146.

Montoya, Celeste. 2008. "The European Union, capacity building, and transnational networks: Combating violence against women through the Daphne Program." *International Organization* 62(2): 359–372.

Montoya, Celeste. 2009. "International initiative and domestic reforms: European Union efforts to combat violence against women." *Politics & Gender* 5: 325–348.

Montoya, Celeste. 2013. *From global to grassroots: The European Union, transnational advocacy, and combating violence against women.* Oxford: Oxford University Press.

Nenadic, Natalie. 1996. "Femicide: A framework for understanding genocide." In Diane Bell and Renate Klein, eds., *Radically speaking: Feminism reclaimed.* North Melbourne: Spinifex Press, 456–464.

Okin, Susan Moller (Ed.). 1999. *Is multiculturalism bad for women?* Princeton, NJ: Princeton University Press.

Outshoorn, Joyce. 2004. "Introduction: Prostitution, women's movements and democratic politics." In Joyce Outshoorn, ed., *The politics of prostitution: Women's movements, democratic states, and the globalisation of sex commerce.* Cambridge, UK: Cambridge University Press, 1–20.

Pande, Rekha. 2002. "The public face of private domestic violence." *International Feminist Journal of Politics* 4(3): 342–367.

Pateman, Carole. 1988. *The sexual contract.* Stanford, CA: Stanford University Press.

Pateman, Carole. 1989. *The disorder of women: Democracy, feminism, and political theory.* Stanford, CA: Stanford University Press.

Peterson, Susan Rae. 1977. "Coercion and rape: The state as a male protection racket." In Mary Vetterling-Braggin, Frederick Elliston, and Jane English, eds., *Feminism and philosophy.* Totowa, NJ: Littlefield, Adams.

Reeves, Carol A., and Anne M. O'Leary-Kelly. 2007. "The effects and costs of intimate partner violence for work organizations." *Journal of Interpersonal Violence* 22(3): 327–344.

Sandel, Michael J. 2009. *Justice: What's the right thing to do?* New York: Farrar, Straus and Giroux.

Shaw, Jo. 2000. "Importing gender: The challenge of feminism and the analysis of the EU legal order." *Journal of European Public Policy* 7(3): 406–431.

Shepherd, Laura J. 2008. *Gender, violence and security: Discourse as practice.* London: Zed Books.

Skinner, Tina, Marianne Hester, and Ellen Malos. 2005. "Methodology, feminism, and gender violence." In Tina Skinner, Marianne Hester, and Ellen Malos, eds., *Researching gender violence.* Cullompton, UK: Willan, 1–22.

Tripp, Aili Mari. 2009. *African women's movements: Transforming political landscapes.* Cambridge, UK: Cambridge University Press.

Walsh, Shannon Drysdale. 2008. "Engendering justice: Constructing institutions to address violence against women." *Studies in Social Justice* 2(1): 48–66.

Waltman, Max. 2010. "Rethinking democracy: Legal challenges to pornography and sex inequality in Canada and the United States." *Political Research Quarterly* 63(1): 218–237.

Wasilieski, Gabriela, and Susan L. Miller. 2010. "The elephants in the room: Ethnicity and violence against women in post-communist Slovakia." *Violence Against Women* 16(1): 99–125.

Weldon, S. Laurel. 2002. *Protest, policy and the problem of violence against women: A cross-national comparison.* Pittsburgh: University of Pittsburgh Press.

Weldon, S. Laurel. 2006a. "Inclusion, solidarity and social movements: The global movement on gender violence." *Perspectives on Politics* 4(1): 55–74.

Weldon, S. Laurel. 2006b. "The structure of intersectionality: A comparative politics of gender." *Politics & Gender* 2: 235–248.

Whisnant, Rebecca. 2010. "From Jekyll to Hyde: The grooming of male pornography consumers." In Karen Boyle, ed., *Everyday pornography*. New York: Routledge, 114–133.

Wijers, Marjan. 2000. "European Union policies on trafficking in women." In Mariagrazia Rossilli, ed., *Gender policies in the European Union*. New York: Peter Lang, 209–229.

Zippel, Kathrin S. 2006. *The politics of sexual harassment: A comparative study of the United States, the European Union, and Germany*. Cambridge, UK: Cambridge University Press.

PART III

....

GENDERED
POLITICAL ECONOMY:
PRODUCTION AND
REPRODUCTION

....

PERHAPS mirroring political science more generally, political economy has long been a somewhat neglected dimension within the gender and politics scholarship. But in recent years, it has increasingly been recognized as a potentially significant and necessary element of that scholarship, and many scholars have done more to include it in their analyses. Indeed, as part of the interdisciplinarity of the gender and politics scholarship, it is not surprising that it can draw on and bring together insights from gender scholars working in a range of disciplines including development studies, economics, international relations, international political economy, sociology, and social policy as well as feminist theory and analysis more generally. But by the same token gender has also been neglected within standard political economy of all variants—liberal, critical, and Marxist—so gender scholars have also fought to have gender and feminist analysis recognized as an important dimension within political economy that gives rise to valuable new interpretations and insights.

The inclusion of a section on political economy in this handbook is premised on several assumptions. First, a political economy section provides an additional dimension to long-standing and recognized debates within gender and politics, for example, around the gendered nature of governance and women's mobilization that are recognizably *politics*, however it is defined. Second, a political economy perspective helps to place the global dimension more to the fore within the gender and politics scholarship. This work has in the past often been quite narrowly focused on the national level. So, for example, it facilitates the incorporation of gendered analyses of globalization and global restructuring as well as of global processes such as migration that impact on debates around citizenship and nation and other themes that often figure within gender and politics scholarship. Finally, the key themes of a gendered political economy, such as the necessity of looking at the profound and fundamental links between production and reproduction, have particular implications for the ways we understand important themes such as welfare, care, the family and household, employment, and the sexual division of labor. The incorporation of debates around social reproduction also give us new ways of thinking about the public–private divide and the nature of the private sphere and the role of the family within it—issues that have long preoccupied gender and politics scholars and political theorists. Of course, incorporating social reproduction into political economy and economics in general also improves the mainstream analyses that have tended to downplay its role to the detriment of their overall understanding and the policy prescriptions that emerge.

This section contains four chapters, beginning with an overview piece by Shirin Rai. She argues that gendered (international) political economy (GIPE) has much in common with feminist political economy—indeed, the terms can be used almost interchangeably. In her overview, Rai begins by introducing the concepts that are central to a gendered (international) political economy and a feminist political economy and that also inform the other three chapters. Perhaps foremost among these are the concepts of production and reproduction (and the associated notions of accumulation and consumption). Rai explores how these are inextricably linked and fundamentally gendered before turning in the rest of the chapter to examine regimes of governance at different levels— global, national, and local and the struggles for transformation in the form of challenges to the global capitalist system—all through the prism of GIPE. She argues that the critical argument made by the GIPE literature is about the subsidy that gendered domestic work, often within the household and the family, gives to the capitalist system as a whole and that this subsidy is overlooked in both economic theory and policymaking. We therefore need to highlight the impact that this neglect has not only on scholarship but also on the lives of those engaged in social reproduction.

The key themes of GPE are then explored in more detail in the subsequent three chapters. Each has a primary emphasis on a different aspect of the gendering of production, social reproduction and its attendant relationship with the associated notions of the public–private divide and the role of unpaid domestic and care work (primarily undertaken by women) in particular. Shahra Razavi focuses on social reproduction in the private sphere in terms of the family and household. Using illustrations from all over the world, she demonstrates that the particular forms that households and families take are context specific and have different meanings in different places. As a consequence, the changes to family and household forms exacerbated by processes of globalization and capitalist transformation have played out differently in different locations. Razavi ends by discussing some of the policy implications that flow from her analysis.

Diane Sainsbury also takes up the theme of social reproduction but primarily in terms of the gendering of care work and welfare provision in both the public and private spheres. She begins by discussing conceptions of care and defining the concept of care. She then goes on to deal with the care dimensions of welfare states and the variety of policy responses. The third part of the chapter examines explanations for the policy responses, concentrating on gender relations, the economics of care, and the politics of care. The final section of the chapter moves beyond nation states to examine care across borders, specifically looking at the European Union, international organizations, and global migration. In her analysis Sainsbury focuses primarily on industrialized countries with established welfare states as the context in which most of the feminist theorizing and analysis has taken place to date. Overall, Sainsbury highlights two important trends—the globalization of care and the commodification of care and their implications for the gender division of labor—arguing that the analysis of both promises to reinvigorate theorizing and empirical studies on gender, care, and welfare.

Finally Lucy Ferguson looks at paid work and the sexual division of labor, underlining again the links between the productive and reproductive spheres and the ways they are gendered. She argues that work is one of the key processes through which gender is played out in contemporary societies, influencing and disciplining the ways different actors interact between the *public* and *private* spheres. She brings together concepts from feminist economics, sociology, gendered political economy, and development to show how the gender dynamics of paid work worldwide have been radically restructured over the last fifty years at the same time as a sexual division of labor has remained. She focuses on the feminization of employment, informalization, and labor migration to demonstrate how the gender dynamics of labor markets and household arrangements have been restructured and highlighting the complexity of these processes.

Overall this section shows us how, although an often missing dimension, the insights generated by gendered political economy can enhance and improve our analyses of concepts such as intersectionality, the family, citizenship, and rights and can add new ones to make a significant contribution to the study of gender and politics.

CHAPTER 10

GENDER AND (INTERNATIONAL) POLITICAL ECONOMY

SHIRIN M. RAI

INTRODUCTION

Gender and international political economy (GIPE) is the study of gendered social relations in the context of international political economy—how women and men are situated historically, structurally, and discursively within international political economy and with what outcomes. These outcomes have been largely negative for women, although not for all women. Issues of difference are important when we examine the situatedness of women and men within the arena of politics as well as the economy. We also find that (gendered) social relations, the markets and the state, that form the substance of the study of international political economy are not separate spheres, albeit they are often considered to be so; rather, they are co-constitutive. In not paying attention to these linkages, we can get only a partial and distorted picture of the everyday worlds that we inhabit. For example, focusing our analysis of political institutions without addressing the issues of the embeddedness of these institutions in the political economy of a state or nation would mean that we cannot fully explain the challenges and opportunities that these institutions and those that work within them face. Making assessments of the successes and failures of political institutions without considering the resources that enable or constrain them—whether these are cultural, historical, or economic—can be only superficial. Similarly, economic decisions are made by people who work in institutions.

Making sense of who these people are, why they (rather than others) are in the decision-making roles and why they make certain (rather than other) decisions, and who they represent and speak for can shed light on not only the actual processes of decision making but broader issues of whether the decisions that are made are seen as legitimate in the broader society. While some feminist work has addressed this issue of embeddedness, I would argue that more needs to be done in this regard in the gender and politics literature. This essay is a contribution toward this broadening of political analysis.

Feminist political economy is an approach that critiques mainstream economic theory and policy, suggests alternative modes of analysis that put center stage both productive and reproductive economies, and develops methodologies to take forward this critique and analysis. Therefore, to make rigid distinction between feminist political economy and GIPE is not productive. In this essay I use the term GIPE to indicate a feminist political economy approach to global issues as well as those more usually associated with the national level. Together, GIPE and feminist political economy perspectives have built on the key feminist insight that challenges division between the public and the private, the productive and the reproductive, and the gendered nature of states and markets, structure, and agency. In so doing, this branch of feminist scholarship has provided support for important critiques of political institutions, public policy, and discursive modalities of mainstream politics. For example, to understand how the public and the private divide might be bridged and why this would lead to radical transformation of public policy, a core feminist politics issue, a GIPE perspective would focus on the ways the work contributions of women and men are regarded differently in the accounting of the national economy, which then justifies particular gendered discourses of work, welfare, and crisis. If domestic work is not accounted for in a nation's gross domestic product (GDP), then those engaged full-time in social reproductive work can be seen only as objects of welfare, even as women's role as mothers is celebrated as important to the reproduction of a "stable" society. This, of course, becomes a critical issue during periods of crisis when the downward pressure on wages combines with withdrawal of state support, in particular for care and affective work to create an exogenous and endogenous crisis of social reproduction (Fraser 2011).

Feminist political economy has a long and distinguished history, starting from the path-breaking book by Esther Boserup on women's role in economic development to the conceptualization of social reproduction and the contemporary burgeoning literature on a wide spectrum of issues, including the gender bias of social restructuring programs, the gendered nature of macroeconomic policy making, the analysis of globalized and gendered modes of accumulation,[1] governance, and activism in times of crises (Boserup 1970; Bakker 1994; Folbre 1994; Elson 1995; Safa 1999; Bakker and Gill 2003; Peterson 2003; Rai and Bedford 2010; Sweetman 2010). Feminist economists have challenged the rational choice model upon which much of economics is based and have developed sophisticated analyses of the family and the household as economic units

(Folbre 1986; Sen 1987; Rai 2002; Chant and MacIlwaine 2009). And they have developed theoretical as well as methodological insights to show how social reproduction underpins capitalist accumulation and how this might be made visible through accounting for social reproductive work (Waring 1988; Picchio 1990; Elson 1998). Despite this strong tradition of scholarship, GIPE continues to be marginalized in the mainstream as well as more critical approaches to the global economy. Why is this so? This question is pertinent for the issues I raised at the start of this essay—how do we bring into focus the relations between the economic and the political, between institutional decision making and the structures in dominance within which they reside? To answer these questions we need first to examine the gender and political economy literature and the challenge it poses for the study of politics and political economy as well as its limitations and how we might address these.

In this essay I will examine three areas of gender and political economy scholarship: (1) regimes of accumulation, production, and consumption—issues concerning capital accumulation, investment, and the nature of social reproduction; material and discursive production and circulation of goods, services, and knowledges; patterns of consumption within and outside the household; changing relations between states and globalized markets under global capitalism; (2) regimes of governance—both private and public, local, national, and global; and (3) struggles for reform and transformation—examinations of challenges to the global capitalist regimes, forms that these challenges take, and the strategies that they employ. Through this examination I hope to demonstrate not only the tense relationship between GIPE and IPE but also to set out the key contribution of GIPE to a more nuanced, gender-sensitive understanding of contemporary politics.

Feminist approaches to international political economy are often lumped together as one approach, obscuring the rich variety of analyses and some critical differences among feminist scholars. However, despite these important differences, they do share some common insights. First, GIPE builds on the feminist challenge to the binary of the public and the private spheres. This challenge is vital for understanding how the political economy is conceived of and measured and how this affects the valuing of both women's contribution to the economy. The concept of social reproduction is important in outlining how this binary can and must be overcome. Building on this, a second important insight is the feminist insistence that the micro- and the macroeconomic systems of production and exchange are directly and dialectically linked. GIPE has mapped the effect of the macroeconomic policies on gender relations and has also shown how globalized processes of production and exchange are constitutive of these gendered regimes (Mies 1982; Nash and Fernandez-Kelly 1983; Elson 1995; Elson and Pearson 1997; Cook, Roberts, and Waylen 2000). The gendered household is thus as much shaped by neoliberal globalization (Safri and Graham 2010) as it constitutes it by reproducing gendered discourses of what Salzinger (2003, 10) calls "the trope of productive femininity"; this allows for women's labor to be mobilized in specific ways in local spaces, which are themselves constitutive of global production and care chains (see the other chapters in this section for further discussion of these issues). Third, feminist political economists are committed to the transformation of gendered social relations to achieve equality between men and women. This "political" impulse poses interesting issues for feminist scholars—of epistemic influence, of methodological and theoretical "bias," and of social activism and political cooption. This latter common thread ties feminist concerns of analysis of structures of capitalism and the agential challenges to these structures. In the next sections I discuss how these common insights have developed a complex and sophisticated theorization as well as political engagement within the field of gender and international political economy.

SOCIAL REPRODUCTION

One of the key theoretical articulations challenging the public and private divide can be read off the concept of social reproduction, which allowed feminist scholars and activists to put center stage the social experiences of women in the analysis of political economy and social and political institutions and to illuminate the consequences for women of this divide. The gendered segregated nature of social reproduction meant that most of this work was done by women but remained unacknowledged as work. As Bakker (2007, 541) points out, the "...focus on social reproduction seeks to place its costs at the centre of an analysis of the capitalist system of accumulation as well as relating it to questions of how the surplus in such an economy is distributed" (see also Elson 1995; Katz 2001). Over the years, considerable and varied work has been done by feminists on social reproduction—what its components are and how it should be analyzed. For early Marxist feminists, social reproduction has signified the reproduction of the capitalist system and its social relations as a whole (Edholm, Harris, and Young 1978; Mackintosh 1981). Questions were then raised about whether it should be viewed as commodity production or whether the care component associated with it makes it a more complex concept. Feminist scholars also analyzed how, in times of neoliberal economic policy ascendancy and crises, social reproduction has come to fill the gap between public welfare and private market provision (Young, Wolkowitz, and McCullagh 1981; Mies etal., 1982; Picchio 1992; Elson 1998; Hoskyns and Rai 2007; Bakker 2007; Bedford and Rai, 2010) (For further discussion of these issues see also the chapters by Ferguson, Razavi and Sainsbury in this volume.)

Here, I define social reproduction in the following way: first, as biological reproduction (including reproducing labor). This carries with it the provision of the sexual, emotional and affective services that are required to maintain family and intimate relationships; second, as unpaid production in the home of both goods and services. This includes different forms of care, as well as social provisioning and voluntary work directed at meeting needs in and of the community and third, as the reproduction of culture and ideology which stabilizes (and sometimes challenges) dominant social relations (see Hoskyns and Rai 2007:300). These components are institutionalized through gendered labor, discourses of production and reproduction, of family wage, as well as the organization and regulation of everyday life (Bakker 2007; Laslett and Brenner 1989) and indeed through reproduction of social relations on a global scale wherein the increasing privatization of social reproduction is accompanied by increased mobilization of women into the labor market at times when male unemployment is increasing, with significant affect on gendered regimes of the household as well as of global production. In times of crisis, we experience not only a crisis of social reproduction, whereby "what is at stake are the sociocultural processes that supply the indispensable solidary relations, affective dispositions and horizons of value that underpin social cooperation, as well as the appropriately socialized and skilled human beings who constitute 'labor'" (Fraser, 2011), (through this dialectic between household/production) but can also perceive a problem for the reproduction of capitalism itself (Hartsock, 2006; Brodie, 2003; LeBaron and Roberts, 2010). In this sense, "[s]ocial reproduction is the fleshy, messy, and indeterminate stuff of everyday life. It is also a set of structured practices that unfold in dialectical relation with production, with which it is mutually constitutive and in tension" (Katz, 2001: 710).

The tension that a focus on social reproduction produces, opens up to scrutiny fundamental concepts such as the nature and measurement of production and exchange, the expropriation of labor and its accumulated form. It also shows how capitalist appropriation is regulated and reproduced through state governance mechanisms—by folding it in the private sphere of the household and at the same time not accounting for social reproductive work. As Waring has argued in her landmark work (1988), the non-accounting of social reproductive work towards national income leaves most of social reproductive labor outside the production boundary. This non-recognition makes it difficult to set a value on these activities, aggregate them and compensate for their effects. The invisibilizing of social reproduction has the further effect of appropriation of care work through privatizing as well as commodifying it (Razavi 2007) and folding in "female altruism at the service of the state" (Molyneux 2006, 437; see also Beneria and Feldman 1992; Bedford 2009) thus increasing the burden of women's labor without compensating for it and reshaping gender relations both within the privatized economies of the household and through the liberalized market relations (Bedford and Rai 2010). This increased burden of social reproductive work can be conceptualized through what has been termed "depletion", as the condition of loss, without necessarily implying either its measurement or a process for replenishment that might offset it (Elson 1998; Rai Hoskyns and Thomas 2011). Studying this involves identifying indicators and forms of measurement as well as developing an appropriate terminology of how depletion of physical and mental resources of those engaged in social reproductive work can be conceptualized and taken account of in order to mitigate harm and offset market subsidy that results in cheaper goods and services leading increasing consumption (ibid.). Scholars have also paid attention to how social reproduction, while carried out largely by women, is sensitive to inequities of class and race (Mohanty 2003;Fraser 1996). Social reproduction, thus, is a key feminist concept that is central to the articulations of gendered arguments about the international political economy.

Gendered Approaches to (International) Political Economy

While social reproduction is a foundational concept in GPE and shared by feminist political economists, gendered approaches to international political economy vary considerably. One of the earliest interventions in these debates was a collection of papers by socialist feminist authors, edited by Zillah Eisenstein— *Capitalist Patriarchy and the Case for Socialist Feminism* (1979). The volume sought to establish a dialectical relationship between class and gender hierarchies and to show how these are mutually reinforcing and therefore critical to the maintenance of capitalist social relations. In her introduction she argued that "The recognition of women as a sexual class lays the subversive quality of feminism for liberalism because liberalism is premised upon women's exclusion from public life on this very class basis. The demand for real equality of women with men, if taken to its logical conclusion, would dislodge the patriarchal structure necessary to a liberal society." (1979: 5). This approach built on Friedrich Engels' work on *The Origins of Family, Private Property and the State* (1972) which argued that the establishment of private property directly led to the exclusion of women from the public sphere and the world of work, increased their dependency on the "male breadwinner" and led to the state institutionalizing as "marriage" this hierarchical gender relationship and further, that capitalist accumulation needed the female "reserve army of labor" to keep wages under control and therefore gendered hierarchies were crucial for the continued exploitation of waged workers. Socialist feminists suggested that gendered social relations needed both the control of women's labor and also the ideology that went into reproducing the conditions under which this becomes possible (Beechey 1979).

Gender scholars did not just apply Marxist ideas to gender relations—they engaged with Marxism critically, particularly by pointing out that Marxist political discourse and practice continued to marginalize struggles for women's equality by valorizing class struggle and that because of this there was little integration of the important insights that were developed by Engels' work into Marxist praxis (Hartmann 1979). Socialist feminists insisted that the two aspects of capitalist production and reproduction need to be held together, in times in tension, to fully understand the gendered nature of international political economy (Walby 1990; Bruegel 1979)[2]. Finally, building on Gramscian theory and taking into account some insights developed by critical IPE scholars, some feminist interventions have recently focused on the crisis of capitalist accumulation and the stability of conditions of social reproduction, which is then being "locked" in by "new constitutional" mechanisms of governance (Bakker and Gill 2003; Brodie 2003; Rai 2008).

While socialist feminists were focused on the relationship between capitalism and patriarchy and production and social reproduction, liberal feminists were concerned about the relationship of equality between women and men. Here, the foundational text was Wollstonecraft's *A Vindication of the Rights of Women*. As far as international political economy is concerned, liberal feminists focused on how unequal gender relations affect distortions in markets and indeed about the subsidy that is provided by women to market based profits. Political and legal reform then became the focus here in order to remove institutional barriers to equal opportunity for women and men. The UN Conventions of particular concern to liberal feminist work during this period were the 1949 Convention for the Suppression of Traffic in Persons and the Exploitation of Prostitution of Others; the 1951 Equal Remuneration for Men and Women Workers for Work of Equal Value and the 1952 Convention on the Political Rights of Women (Wallace and March 1991: 1).

Most of the early work on liberal feminist political economy took place in the field of development studies and practice in the context of the First UN Decade of Women. Esther Boserup's book, *Women's Role in Economic Development* (1970) was the first liberal feminist challenge to conventional liberal approaches to development—it combined an argument for equality with efficiency and was therefore a powerful political statement in the interests of women. Boserup, and later others (Tinker 1997) argued it was not only women who would benefit from expansion of opportunity, but the development process itself would better achieve its targets. This was an appeal to efficiency as much as to a better deal for women. This analysis became the basis upon which the women in development (WID) agenda were crafted. The project was to ensure that the benefits of modernization accrued to women as well as men in the Third World (Rai 2002, 59–62; Jaquette, 1982). Building on this work, feminist development theorists focused on the gender division of labor within the home and in waged work, access to and control over resources and benefits, material and social position of women and men in different contexts (Sen 1987; Agarwal 1988). This came to be known as the gender and development (GAD) perspective on development and political economy (Moser 1993; Elson 1995).

Building on and engaging with both these approaches to political economy and development as well as taking on board insights of Amartya Sen's work on human capabilities, has been a group of feminist political economists whose work has become influential in both academic and policy circles. They have focused on two areas—women's work, and the gendered nature of structural adjustment policies of the 1980s and 1990s (Waring 1988, Elson 1995; Beneria 2003; Agarwal, Humphries, and Robeyns 2005). In disaggregating the impact of structural adjustment policies on the family and focusing on the disproportionate burden of the privatization of social welfare that women are being forced to carry in times of economic crises, this powerful critique has resulted in some important shifts within the economic discourse of international institutions.

Recently, scholars from all these different approaches have addressed the issue of globalization of political economy to demonstrate (a) the affect of globalization of production and exchange on women and men; (b) the shifts in and transformations of governance regimes and institutions that regulate the global economy and how this might be reproducing gendered hierarchies; (c) how class and the North-South divisions continue to intersect with gender as axes of privilege and exploitation and (d) how the globalization of capitalist social relations are being challenge through global women's struggles (Elson 2000; Rai 2002; Bakker and Gill 2003; Peterson 2003; Rai and Waylen 2008; Rai and Bedford 2010).

These different approaches to gender and political economy show the richness of debate among feminists on how to think about political economy in ways that would allow us to answer Cynthia Enloe's insistent question about international politics: "It is always worth asking, 'where are the women?' Answering this question reveals the dependence of most political and economic systems not just on women, but on certain kinds of relations between women and men" (1989, 133). Some of the first issues that feminist political economists addressed were those of gendered regimes of production, consumption and accumulation. In the next section, I examine some of these issues.

REGIMES OF ACCUMULATION,
PRODUCTION AND CONSUMPTION

"The conclusion that we reach is not that production, distribution, exchange and consumption are identical, but they all form members of a totality, distinctions within a unity...," wrote Marx (1973:99). Feminist work on accumulation, production and consumption sought to demonstrate the correlation between work and sex, to examine how this correlation is reproduced materially and discursively and how this is challenged and yet remains ubiquitous. In the context of the capitalist crisis of the late 1970s that was accompanied by structural adjustment policies (SAPs), which led to the liberalization of many economies of the South, feminist political economists analysed the mobilization of women into labor markets through their employment in Economic Processing Zones (EPZs) (Elson and Pearson 1981; Mies 1982 Fernandez-Kelly 1983; Elson 1995) They were concerned about conditions of work that allowed for high levels of exploitation of female labor in the context of capitalist development accompanied by increasing burdens of social reproduction in the context of the withdrawal of the state from welfare provisioning. This analysis brought into view the family and the household as a site of production, consumption and accumulation (for a more detailed discussion of these issues see the chapters by Razavi and Ferguson in this section).

One of the first analysis of shift of production from the North to the South and its gendered consequences was Elson and Pearson's "Nimble Fingers Make Cheap Workers" (1981), in which they emphasized the interpellation of gender and production regimes and showed how export oriented production is built upon the cheap labor of the developing world, wherein women's labor, structured as pliable and disciplined, "natural" and "nimble," makes for their mobilization into the circuits of production thus reinforcing rather than challenging gendered hierarchies (See also Mies 1982). In doing so, Elson and Pearson were building on the debate about gendered division of labor within GIPE, which challenges the "naturalization" of women's skills (as opposed to the learned skills that men have and which are therefore more valued) as well as viewing them as "not transferable between the household and the market" (Gardiner 1998:214) in both classical liberal economics and in the neoclassical New Home Economics. What Elson and Pearson pointed out was that this gendered division of labor is globalized in the context of export oriented production in the South consolidating hierarchies of gender as well as of race/ethnicity in the reproduction of capitalist social relations.

Linking the macro production processes of global capitalism with micro studies of export oriented production in the household Mies et al. (1982) identified women as "the last colony" and argued that primitive accumulation remained essential to capitalist growth, and that both international and national capital and state systems exploited both the Third World as well as women in its pursuit of profit. They argued that capitalist exploitation of wage labor was based upon the male monopoly of violence in a modified form; that patriarchal violence at home and in the public space was intrinsic to the lives of women and to their exploitation. They suggested that this patriarchal dominance was maintained through the agencies of the state which institutionalized the "housewifization" of women's labor within marriage and through work legislation (Mies, Bennholdt-Thomsen and von Werlhof 1988). Building on the new international division of labor paradigm, Fernandez-Kelly (1983) showed how, with the increasing mobilization of women into the maquiladores of Mexico, the anxieties about social order, sexuality and moral dissonance could lead to a greater disciplining of women within the households rather than creating new spaces for challenging gendered hierarchies in the home and the workplace. This early work laid secure foundations of feminist analyses of the international political economy as it entered the contemporary phase of neoliberal globalization (Bair 2010).

It was followed by a remarkable number of studies outlining the reproduction of capitalist social orders that saw women as "disposable" (Wright 2006), in different contingent spaces. The literature also mapped how the crisis of capitalism becomes a crisis of social reproduction as women and men leave their homes in increasing numbers as migrants and how these migratory flows also depended on gendered regimes of work—care and sexual work for women and construction and trading work for men, for example (Perrons, Plomien, and Kilkey 2010) and indeed, globalize households as well as production and care chains (Razavi 2007; Safri and Graham 2010). The production regimes were also shown to be reliant on a dialectical relationship between formal and informal work. While the previously outlined work was focused on women in formal work regimes, later work on informalization of work under contemporary capitalism showed how this insecure and unregulated work underpinned an unequal system of production (Horn 2010; Peterson 2010; see also the chapter by Ferguson in this volume). The nature of the crises of capitalism was shown to be gendered—building on Beneria's (2003) prescient observation on "the Davos Man," there were analyses of hypermasculinized modes of exchange (Ling 1997), which were valorized as necessary markers of success and shown in ethnographic accounts of the trading floor as gendered and racialized nature (McDowell and Court 1994; Knorr-Cetina and Preda 2006). The insecurity generated by the crises also hit women and men differently, especially as social welfare was restructured and, in doing so, the social landscape itself. Levels of violence, insecurity of employment, and the sharp increase in the burden of social reproduction with the slashing of welfare spending were shown to adversely affect more women than men (Truong 1999; Brodie 2003; Fawcett 2010; Fraser 2011).

If analyses and critiques of gendered international division of labor were important to GIPE, so have been arguments about how gendered accumulation under neoliberal globalization is reconstituting gender relations as well as how these changing gender regimes are constitutive of the forms that capitalist accumulation is taking. Building on Harvey's (1991) conceptualization of accumulation through dispossession involving extension of the credit system and contraction and privatization of global commons, Hartsock (2006) argued that feminized dimensions of contemporary capital accumulations are also moments of gendered political transformation. This argument rests on the view that contemporary accumulation forces privatization of social reproduction, which becomes "dialectically intertwined with new social movement's stress on accumulation by dispossession" (177; see also Federici 2004). Such analysis of labor markets could not be complete without showing how the state was implicated in regulating and stabilizing these gendered regimes of work, and finally, how women's groups were challenging these regimes of gendered exploitation through campaigning for equal pay and good conditions of work, developing alternative methodologies of accounting for work and through political activism, and lobbying at both the national and international levels.

REGIMES OF GOVERNANCE

If accumulation, production, and exchange were shown by the gender and political economy literature to be deeply gendered, then so were regimes of governance. Feminist analyses showed how gender blindness in mainstream literature skews the analysis toward certain issues, modalities, and methodologies rather than others, which means therefore that we are unable to see alternative modes of thinking about and "doing" governance.

The market, though far from a level playing field, is given the primary political space in the discourse of contemporary globalization. While mainstream critical IPE theorists have focused on the unevenness of the market arena, feminists have shown how markets are socially embedded institutions and roles "within market systems are structured by non-market criteria" (Harriss-White 1998, 201). These non-market, though clearly not non-economic, criteria lead to specific gender-based distortions in the markets (Palmer 1991; Elson 1995). Participants come to specific markets with unequal capabilities, bargaining capacities and resources as a result of and which inhere in unequal market structures, regulated and stabilized by gendered state formations, and characterized by more or less unequal power—class and gender are two bases for unequal power relations operating in the market. These critiques are important to demonstrate how the liberalization of trade has not resulted in diminishing inequalities but on the contrary has reshaped gendered inequalities that are now being stabilized through international trade regimes such as the World Trade Organization (WTO). The key question that feminist trade theorists have asked is not about competitive advantage and the interaction between tradable and nontradable sectors but about the relationship between the productive and social reproductive sectors (van Staveren et al. 2007). While much of the feminist work has been critical of neoliberal market regimes, some scholars have noted that markets have also opened up new spaces, opportunities, and social relations for women as they get absorbed into the global labor market. Development studies scholars such as Kabeer (2000), while contesting the rational choice model of decision making, cautioned against seeing Third World women in the global market place simply as victims—"young, single, cheap, docile and dispensable" rather than as women "making choices in and through market opportunities."

Markets are stabilized and institutionalized not only in the functioning of global capitalism but also through the institutions of global governance—what Gill (1995) calls the *new constitutionalism*. Whereas until the 1990s the state was the key institution of market regulation, under neoliberal globalization supr-astate institutions have an increasing role to play in economic regulation, trans-forming the Bretton Woods system as a policy hub for disciplining of economies in the South or those in crisis and creating new institutions such as the WTO as a regulator of trade in goods and services as well as intellectual property in a liberalizing global economy. The GIPE literature engages with the concept of governance at both the level of the state and international institutions.

Feminist interventions in the state debate have a long history (for a more sustained discussion see the chapter by Chappell in this volume). One of the most important insights developed by this literature is that gendered social relations are constitutive of the state while the state is crucial to the continued dominance of patriarchal relations of production and social reproduction through law, social policy, and discursive practices (Pringle and Watson 1990; Agarwal 1994; Rai 1996; Randall and Waylen 1998). There is a strong body of feminist literature on gen-der mainstreaming that has unpacked the processes through which social policy is framed and transformed within state institutions in the context of globaliza-tion (Hafner-Burton and Pollack 2002; Rai 2003; True 2003; Walby 2005) and has shown how the neoliberal disciplining of the state is reshaping entitlement rights of citizens as well as boundaries of inclusion and exclusion—discursive as well as material (Einhorn 2000; Bakker 2003; Brodie 2003; Ong 2006). Social protec-tion, in Polanyian terms, is then being undermined within state policy struc-tures, and this in turn is affecting the boundaries of social reproduction as well as the development of human capabilities (Beneria 2003; Nussbaum et al. 2003). Further, in line with Gill's (1998) conceptualization of new constitutionalism, this reshaping of the state and markets is finding new forms through legislation and the creation of new regulatory systems and institutions that reflect the new neo-liberal social order. The state is being disciplined through its inability to regulate the huge flows of capital, through challenges to security that are truly global—such as the environment, terrorism, health pandemics—and its varying ability to access the rule-making institutions at the regional and international levels. The threat of flight of capital or its holding back from investing in new political geog-raphies has resulted in a race to the bottom that is affecting policies in all sec-tors of the political economy. The state thus becomes complicit in narrowing the borders of its own competencies and in so doing depoliticizes the shifts in policy making and restructuring of social relations.

Much work has been done on deterritorialized forms of power in the period of contemporary globalization and on the institutionalized form it is taking through the expanded remit of international and regional organizations, glo-bal networks of influence, and affect (Staudt 2003; Slaughter 2004; see also the chapter by Bedford in this volume). GIPE scholars have outlined the ways it is possible to assess the nature of gendered global institutions—as based on mar-ket principles, promoting market-based solutions to social and political prob-lems and stabilizing these solutions with the support of dominant epistemic elites (Taylor 2000). As Prugl (2008) argues, "Contemporary market-making institutions proliferate neo-liberal and patriarchal ideologies and discourses that globalize markets while constructing gender." This construction of gender through global governance is taking particular forms—gendered migratory flows resulting in new household forms at a global level, for example, are not being recognized or taken account of and restructured through heteronormative insistence on the family model of social reproduction (Bedford 2009; Safri and Graham 2010); the discourse of *women's human rights* is being used to justifiy U.S.-led interventions to reshape the post-cold war international order (Cohn 2008; Bernstein 2010) and global social imaginary is being reshaped through the privatization of global commons and the individualizing of alternatives (Fraser 1996). The reproduction of gender orders thus also takes a globalized form through discursive, policy, and institutional modes of gender disciplining through both the system of policymaking and the art of governing by excluding and including certain gendered discourses, techniques, and technologies of governance (Peterson 2003; Wohl 2008).

Global governance regimes are also, inevitably, provoking challenges, which are taking global forms and are the substance of much of the GIPE literature on women's social movements.

STRUGGLES FOR REFORM AND TRANSFORMATION

Governance debates need to make a conceptual shift to embed feminist insights, developed through everyday struggle at local, state, and global levels as well as through engagements with and critiques of mainstream literature, if theories of critical governance are to fundamentally challenge the structures-in-dominance within this field (Rai and Waylen 2008).

Following from the different analyses of the global political economy, there have been different approaches to challenging the gendered nature of the regimes of accumulation and governance. However, for most involved in these struggles, the aim remains one of particular modes of transformation of gender relations. In the words of Nancy Fraser (1996, 16), "Much like class, gender justice requires transforming the political economy so as to eliminate its gender structuring. Eliminating gender-specific exploitation and deprivation requires abolishing the gender division of labor -both the gendered division between paid and unpaid labor and the gender division within paid labor. The logic of the remedy is akin to the logic with respect to class: it is to put gender out of business as such."

Putting gender out of business is no easy task, of course, as the attempts to reshape gender relations have shown. If, as so much of the gender and political economy literature has outlined, gender relations are underpinned by and constitutive of capitalist social relations, then this is unsurprising. However, women's groups have continued to address the transformation of these relations at every level as well as to speak to different aspects of governance of these relations. At the level of the state, the focus has been on shifting the boundaries of law to challenge and transform legal regimes of property, family relations and sexuality, employment and regulation of wages, and political representation in the institutions of the state (Sangari and Vaid 1993; Rai 1996; Rubery 1998; Menon 2004; Dahlerup 2005). At the level of international institutions, the challenge has been to create networks of solidarity to address issues of conditions of work in the global production and care chains and the growing disparity between the North and the South and to develop a discourse of equality that takes into account both particular histories as well as addresses the human condition in late modernity or postmodernity (Charlesworth and Chinkin 2000; Barrientos 2005; Spivak 1988; Yuval-Davis et al. 2006; Joachim 2007; Agathangelou and Ling 2009). International institutions have also been analyzed and critiqued in terms of their gender biases and the lack of women's representation in decision-making bodies (Hafner-Burton and Pollack 2000; O'Brien et al. 2000; True 2003).

The literatures on global social movements and on political engagements of women at the global level have also begun to be theorized. Ideas about inequality and responsibility have been important to this debate: "Feminist engagements with cosmopolitanism range from trenchant support for thick cosmopolitanism in the work of Martha Nussbaum, defense of a Kantian statement of global duties by Onora O'Neill and a socially situated account of the route of global obligations in the work of Iris Young"(Unterhalter 2007, 6). For Nussbaum (2000) the focus is on women's entitlements to capabilities to function—to be human is to have a set of capabilities that require a set of rights and access to resources, which are not always available at the level of the state; this behooves the international community to respond. For O'Neill (2000), the emphasis is on global duties and obligation to address the needs of the vulnerable and to abjure violence and coercion. And for Young et al. (2006, 103) the key issue is that of a "social connection model" of responsibility which means "that all agents who contribute by their actions to the structural processes that produce injustice have responsibilities to work to remedy these injustices." Despite these normative interventions, feminist theorists and activists have been cautious about wholeheartedly endorsing modes of global networking and institutional interventions, whether in the context of differences among women across the North South divide or in terms of global development strategies such as the Millennium Development Goals or peace-keeping and democratizing initiatives (Antrobus 2003; Whitworth 2004; Chant 2007). The global neoliberal discourses on rational choice, competition instead of cooperation, and rights rather than freedoms have also worried feminist scholars.

I wanted to map this rich feminist literature on international political economy to show both the breadth and the depth of this work. We can then revisit the question posed in the introduction of this essay: why, despite its sophistication, diversity, and range, is mainstream and even critical IPE scholarship not engaging with GIPE? We can only speculate. One reason for this neglect could be ignorance, which emanates from school and university curricula that continue to marginalize gendered work. What is unfamiliar during formative periods of education remains terra incognita, discouraging forays into unknown avenues of the intellectual landscape. A second reason might be the political economy of intellectual life: who publishes and where? The regimes of knowledge production are themselves gendered—mainstreaming gendered perspectives in the work of research councils, academic conferences, journals and citations, and publishers' catalogs is proving difficult. A third reason might be the methodologies of integration: how can feminist insights challenging private and the public spheres, markets, and states as constitutive of as well as constituted by gendered regimes be made integral to theorization of political economy? Whether mainstream or critical, the IPE often takes a macroanalysis approach, while feminist political economics pays close attention to the microlevel analysis or grounded theorization. Feminist theory has insisted that experiential data is as valid as any other survey, but this is discursively relegated to lower-order theorization, which allows for the neglect of feminist work to continue. There has been minor improvement; it is now the norm that there is at least one chapter addressing gender issues in an IPE book (but see Blythe 2010 for refutation of even this modest claim) or one volume in a series, but these contributions are not on the whole engaged with or incorporated within the argument of the book or the frame of the series. Where gestures are made they are often toward outcomes (the effects on women) rather than on process (how these effects come about).

Having outlined some challenges that GIPE faces from neglect of others, it is also important to outline the challenges that it faces from within—to understand what the gaps in this literature are and how these need to be addressed if a more expansive GIPE is to emerge. It has been argued that "while there now exists a growing, albeit sparse, literature on 'race' in international relations...race has yet to be included as an analytical category shaping the study and teaching of International Relations (IR)[3] in a systematic way" (Chowdhry and Rai 2009). Here I query whether mirroring critical IPE, GIPE too needs a stronger and more robust engagement with issues of *race* and gender and with postcolonial perspectives?

THE GAPS IN THE LITERATURE

Three concerns should be raised about the current state of play in gender and political economy. First, GIPE and GAD literature, with some notable exceptions, continue to run parallel. This mirrors the relationship between the IPE and Development Studies literature—in most gender and political economy literature, the focus remains on issues of work in the North—conditions of work, equality of wages, domestic work, or migrant workers in the domestic and sex industries. In most GAD literature, on the other hand, few references can be found to key questions about accumulation and social reproduction; the focus remains largely on individual states of the South as case studies for specific development issues such as food production, violence against women, or conditions of work in Export Processing Zones (EPZs). There also tends to be a more micro-approach in the GAD literature and a macro-perspective in the GIPE framework. Issues of health, education, microcredit, and the environment dominate the GAD landscape, while broad-brush discussions on accumulation, neoliberalism, and globalization form the focus of the GIPE work. At the theoretical level, again we see marked differences: the GAD literature is dominated by the human capability approach, which emerged as a critique of the structural adjustment policies and their impact, and the GIPE work is largely framed within the neo-Gramscian approach critiquing neoliberalism and its affect, limiting dialogue between the two. There are, however, emerging conversations across these lines of inquiry that we need to encourage—of analyzing the inter-connectedness, multiplicity, and specificity of issues concerning and shaping gender relations in the twenty-first century.

Second, while neglect of emotions/affect, race, and sexuality in mainstream economics is critiqued in feminist interventions, more needs to be done to integrate these insights into GIPE, which still remains largely concerned about heterosexual households and gendered relations within these. Nearly fifteen years ago Alexander (1994) identified the hetero-normative nature of much feminist political economy as a barrier to comprehensive scholarship on gender and structural adjustment and challenged feminists to interrogate the links between political economy and models of kinship from a queer and antiracist perspective. We still have to respond to this challenge. Further, while feminist IR scholars have worked to develop antiracist and postcolonial perspectives, these also need to be better integrated (as opposed to listed or recognized) into our analysis to bridge the North–South divide and centrally address how race *and* gender are co-constitutive of state, political economy, and social relations (see also the chapter by Lind in this volume). The connections among race, political economy, and culture are there to make, if only we recognize the importance of these connections. For example, Stuart Hall (1997, 48–49) outlines these connections:

> People like me who came to England in the 1950s have been there for centuries; symbolically we have been there for centuries...I am the sugar at the bottom of the English cup of tea. I am the sweet tooth, the sugar plantations that rotted generations of English children's teeth. There are thousands of others beside me that are, you know, the cup of tea itself. Because they don't grow it in Lancashire, you know. Not a single tea plantation exists within the United Kingdom. This is the symbolization of English identity—I mean, what does

anybody know about an English person except that they can't get through the day without a cup of tea? Where does it come from? Ceylon—Sri Lanka, India. That is the outside history that is inside the history of the English. There is no English history without that other history. The notion that identity has to do with people that look the same, call themselves the same is nonsense. As a process, as a narrative, as a discourse, it is always told from the position of the other.

Such a contrapuntal rather than a linear reading of histories of political economies and nations, in contrast, demonstrates "a simultaneous awareness both of metropolitan histories and of those other subjected and concealed histories against which this dominated discourse acts" (Said 1993, 59).

Third, as Fraser (2011) argues, GIPE needs to address the growing crisis of the environment as a critical separatism between the two is increasingly problematic. While some feminist development economists as well as philosophers have addressed this issue (Shiva 1989; Agarwal 1992 and 2010; Braidotti 1993), GIPE scholars need to develop a joined up framework that allows them to argue for the development of more sensitive indicators to track current well-being and long-term sustainability. Like the GIPE scholars, environmental scholars have been arguing that the failure to account for the environmental damage that accrues through capitalist regimes of production and exchange has provided a huge subsidy to business, which has helped to fuel the massive expansion of the economy in the last two decades and is now contributing to hardship and environmental crisis. Were the gender and environmental scholarship to enter into a productive conversation, issues of social reproduction and depletion could be perhaps better addressed (Rai, Hoskyns, and Thomas 2011).

CONCLUSION

If the GIPE literature makes one critical argument, it is about the subsidy that gendered domestic work gives to the maintenance of the capitalist system as a whole. This literature shows how this subsidy is overlooked at the levels of both theorization and policymaking and what impact this neglect has on the lives of those engaged in social reproduction. In doing so, GIPE knits together the micro-, meso-, and macrolevels of analysis of international political economy and weaves an argument that integrates these levels and presents evidence, both qualitative and quantitative, to demonstrate the importance of social reproduction to the capitalist system. Figure 10.1 presents a diagram, which builds on work by Diane Elson (2000), to show what the IPE might look like if the domestic sector were incorporated alongside state and market (Hoskyns and Rai 2007, 310).

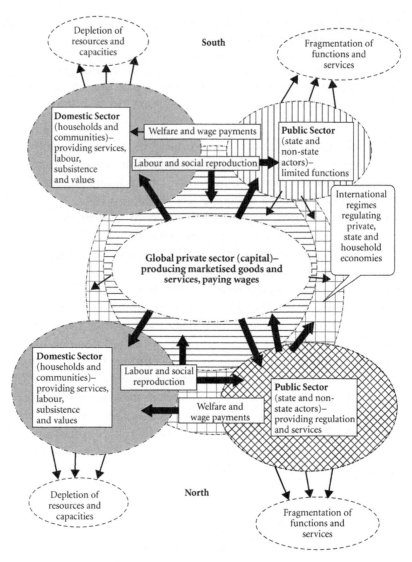

Figure 10.1 Recasting the global political economic.

The diagram shows the dominance of global private capital and shows that while the domestic sector makes a considerable input into the global market, it receives little in return for the provision of labor except through wages and some input from the state in the form of benefits and other social provision. Wages that are paid for the labor performed contribute toward accumulation of capital through processes that compensate for labor inadequately, but compensation for social reproduction is often folded into the bundle of wages and minimal welfare provisions by the state. This process is marked as depletion—when the output of social reproduction exceeds the inputs into it, which also contributes to the subsidy that social reproduction makes to private and public sectors of production. Figure 10.1 also shows that while the domestic sector is as large in the South as in the North, the input from state benefits in the South is less and overall wages are lower. This in turn subsidizes the consumption in the North, which benefits both men and women in the North at the expense of social reproductive labor in the South. Regulatory regimes, as represented in the figure, encompass the global private sector and impinge on state and households (Hoskyns and Rai 2007, 310). This diagrammatic representation of the global political economy also demonstrates how the insights developed by GIPE provide a comprehensive view of the political account, one that is sensitive to all three spheres of the economy—private, public, and domestic.

Interrogating the theoretical debates on gender and international political economy allows us to reflect upon the whether these have been able to shape policy and institutional issues, directly as well as indirectly, and if not why not. Issues of systemic and contingent elements of policy making can be analyzed, and arenas of struggle can be made visible. What this review suggests is that gender is central to the functioning and understanding of the capitalist economic system—systemically, discursively, and politically—and therefore of politics itself.

NOTES

1. This concept builds on Marxist theorizations of primitive accumulation as the origin of capital through exclusion, exploitation, and privatization and through this process the transformation of social relations under capitalism (Harvey 1991). Federici (2004) argues that this accumulation takes place through and in spheres of production and social reproduction—of public and domestic production—and the perpetuation of sex segregated social roles, the enclosure of women's bodies within the domestic sphere, and inhibition of theirmobilization as agents of change.
2. For a challenge to this view see Johnson (1996, 193), who focuses on the tensions, rather than the compatibility that exists between capitalism and patriarchy by suggesting that "the patriarchal form of the wage relation had to be fought for rather than being a foregone conclusion," although this begs the question of whether a nonpatriarchal capitalism is possible.
3. Capital letters here denote the dominant discursive modes that shape the analytics of international relations.

REFERENCES

Agarwal, Bina. 1988. *Structures of patriarchy: State, community, and the household.* New Delhi: Kali for Women.

Agarwal, Bina. 1992. "The gender and environment debate: Lessons from India." *Feminist Studies* 18(1): 119–158.

Agarwal, Bina. 1994. *A field of one's own, gender and land rights in South Asia.* Cambridge, UK: Cambridge University Press.

Agarwal, Bina, Jane Humphries, and Ingrid Robeyns (Eds.). 2005. *Amartya Sen's work and ideas: A gender perspective.* London: Routledge.

Agarwal, Bina. 2010. *Gender and Green Governance.* Oxford: Oxford University Press.

Agathangelou, Anna, and L. H. M. Ling. 2009. *Transforming world politics: From empire to multiple worlds.* London: Routledge.

Alexander, Jacqui M. 1994. "Not just (any) body can be a citizen: The politics of law, sexuality and postcoloniality in Trinidad and Tobago and the Bahamas." *Feminist Review* 48: 5–23.

Antrobus, Peggy. 2003. "MDGs—The most distracting gimmick." *Convergence* 38: 49–52.

Bair, Jennifer. 2010. "On difference and capital: Gender and the globalization of production." *Signs* 36, 1: 203–226

Bakker, Isabella. 1994. *The strategic silence: Gender and economic policy.* London: Zed Books Ltd.

Bakker, Isabella. 2003. Power, production, and social reproduction. New York: Palgrave Macmillan.

Bakker, Isabella. 2007. "Social reproduction and the constitution of a gendered political economy." *New Political Economy* 12(4): 541–556.

Bakker, Isabella, and Stephen Gill (Eds.). 2003. *Power, production and social reproduction human in/security in the global political economy.* London: Palgrave.

Barrientos, Stephanie. 2005. "The hidden ingredient: Female labour in Chilean fruit exports." *Bulletin of Latin American Research* 16(1): 71–81.

Bedford, Kate. 2009. *Developing partnerships: Gender, sexuality, and the reformed World Bank.* Minneapolis: University of Minnesota Press.

Bedford, Kate, and Shirin M. Rai. 2010. "Feminists theorize the international political economy." *Signs: Journal of Women in Culture and Society* 36(1): 1–18.

Beechey, V. 1979. "On patriarchy." *Feminist Review* 3: 66–82.

Beneria, Lourdes. 2003. *Gender, development, and globalization: Economics as if all people mattered.* London: Routledge.

Beneria, Lourdes, and Shelly Feldman. 1992. *Unequal burden: Economic crisis, persistent poverty and women's work.* Boulder, CO: Westview Press.

Bernstein, Elizabeth. 2010. "Militarized humanitarianism meets carceral feminism: The politics of sex, rights, and freedom in contemporary antitrafficking campaigns." *Signs: Journal of Women in Culture and Society* 36(1): 45–71.

Blythe, Mark. 2010. *Routledge handbook of international political economy (IPE): IPE as a global conversation.* London: Routledge.

Boserup, Esther. 1970. *Women's role in economic development.* London: George Allen and Unwin Ltd.

Braidotti, Rosi, Ewa Chrakiewicz, and Saskia Wieringa (Eds.). 1993. *Women, the environment and sustainable development: Towards a theoretical synthesis.* London: Zed Books.

Brodie, Jean. 2003. "Globalization, *in/Security* and the paradoxes of the social." In Isabella Bakker and Stephen Gill, eds., *Power, production and social reproduction human in/security in the global political economy.* New York: Palgrave Macmillan.

Bruegel, Irene. 1979. "Women as a reserve army of labour: A note on recent British experience." *Feminist Review* 3: 12–23.

Chant, Sylvia. 2007. *Gender, generation and poverty: Exploring the "feminisation of poverty" in Africa, Asia and Latin America*. Cheltenham, UK: Edward Elgar Publishers.

Chant, Sylvia, and Cathy McIlwaine. 2009. *Geographies of development in the 21st century: An introduction to the Global South*. Cheltenham, UK: Edward Elgar.

Charlesworth, Hilary, and C. M. Chinkin. 2000. *The boundaries of international law: A feminist analysis*. Manchester, UK: Manchester University Press.

Chowdhry, Geeta, and Shirin M. Rai. 2009. "The geographies of exclusion and the politics of inclusion: Race-based exclusions in the teaching of international relations." *International Studies Perspectives* 10: 84–91.

Cohn, Carol. 2008. "Mainstreaming gender in the UN security policy." In Shirin M. Rai and Georgina Waylen, eds., *Global governance: Feminist perspectives*. Basingstoke, UK: Palgrave Macmillan, 185–206.

Cook, Joanne, Jennifer Roberts and Georgina Waylen (Eds.). 2000. *Towards a gendered political economy*. Basingstoke, UK: Macmillan.

Dahlerup, Drude. 2005. *Women, quotas and politics*. London: Routledge.

Edholm, Felicity, Olivia Harris, and Kate Young (Eds.). 1978. "Conceptualising women." *Critique of Anthropology* 3: 101–130.

Einhorn, Barbara. 2000. "Gender and citizenship in the context of democratisation and economic transformation in East Central Europe." In Shirin M. Rai, ed., *International perspectives on gender and democratization*. Basingstokem UK: Palgrave, 103–124.

Eisenstein, Zillah. 1979. *Capitalist patriarchy and the case for socialist feminism*. New York: Monthly Review Press.

Elson, Diane. 1995.*Male bias in the development process*. Manchester: Manchester University Press.

Elson, Diane. 1998. "The economic, the political and the domestic: Businesses, states and households in the organisation of production." *New Political Economy* 3(2): 189–208.

Elson, Diane. 2000. "The progress of women: Empowerment and economics." In *The progress of the world's women*. New York: UNIFEM, 15–36.

Elson, Diane. 2010. "Gender and the global economic crisis in developing countries: A framework for analysis." *Gender & Development* 18(2), 201–212.

Elson, Diane, and Ruth Pearson. 1981. "'Nimble fingers make cheap workers': An analysis of women's employment in third world export manufacturing." *Feminist Review* 7: 87–107.

Elson, Diane, and Ruth Pearson. 1997. "The subordination of women and the industrialisation of factory production." In Nalini Visvanathan, Lynn Duggan, Laurie Nisonoff, and Nan Wiegersma, eds., *The women, gender and development reader*. London: Zed Books.

Engels, Frederick. 1972. *The origin of the family, private property and the state: in the light of the researches of Lewis H. Morgan*. Trans. Alick West. Introduction and notes Eleanor Burke Leacock. New York: International Pub.

Enloe, Cynthia. 1989. *Bananas, beaches and bases: Making feminist sense of international politics*. London: Pandora.

Esquivel, Valeria, Debbie Budlender, Nancy Folbre, and Indira Hirway. 2008. "Explorations: Time-use surveys in the South." *Feminist Economics* 14(3): 107–152.

Fawcett Society. 2010. "Fawcett's legal case against the budget reaches the High
    Court." Available at http://www.fawcettsociety.org.uk/index.asp?PageID=1201
Federici, Silvia. 2004. *Caliban and the witch: Women, the body and primitive
    accumulation.* New York: Autonomedia.
Folbre, N. 1986. "Hearts and spades: Paradigms of household economics." *World
    Development* 14(2): 245–255.
Folbre, N. 1994. *Who pays for the kids? Gender and the structures of constraint.*
    New York: Routledge.
Fraser, Nancy. 1996."Social justice in the age of identity politics: Redistribution,
    recognition, and participation."Paper presented at the Tanner Lectures on
    Human Values, Stanford University, April 30–May 2. Available at http://www.
    intelligenceispower.com/Important%20E-mails%20Sent%20attachments/Social%20
    Justice%20in%20the%20Age%20of%20Identity%20Politics.pdf.
Fraser, Nancy. 2011. "The wages of care: Reproductive labor as fictitious commodity."
    Paper presented at the Women's Rights in the 21st Century Lecture series,
    University of Cambridge, March 9.
Gardiner, Jean. 1998. "Beyond human capital: Households in the macroeconomy."
    New Political Economy 3(2), 209–221.
Gill, Stephen. 1995. "Globalisation, market civilisation, and disciplinary neoliberalism."
    Millennium 23(3): 399–423.
Hafner-Burton, E., and Mark A. Pollack. 2000. "Mainstreaming gender in the
    European Union." *Journal of European Public Policy* 7(3): 432–456.
Hafner-Burton, E., and Mark A. Pollack. 2002. "Mainstreaming gender in global
    governance." *European Journal of International Relations* 8: 339–373.
Hall, Stuart. 1997. "Old and new identities, old and new ethnicities." In A. D. King,
    ed., *Culture, globalization and the world system: Contemporary conditions for the
    representation of identity.* Minneapolis: University of Minnesota Press, 41–68.
Harriss-White, Barbara. 1998. "Female and male grain marketing systems, analytical
    and policy issues for West Africa and India." In Cecile Jackson and Ruth
    Pearson, eds., *Feminist Visions of Development.* Oxford: Routledge, 189–214.
Hartmann, Heidi I. 1979. "The unhappy marriage of Marxism and feminism: Towards
    a more progressive union." *Capital and Class* 3(2): 21–33.
Hartsock, Nancy. 2006. "Globalization and primitive accumulation: The contributions
    of David Harvey's dialectical materialism." In Noel Castree and Derek Gregory,
    eds., *David Harvey: A critical reader.* Malden, MA: Wiley-Blackwell, 167–190.
Harvey, David. 1991. *The condition of postmodernity: An enquiry into the origins of
    cultural change.* Malden, MA: Wiley-Blackwell.
Horn, Zoe Elena. 2010. "The effects of the global economic crisis on women in the
    informal economy: Research findings from WIEGO and the Inclusive Cities
    partners." *Gender and Development* 18(2): 263–276.
Hoskyns, Catherine, and Shirin M. Rai. 2007. "Recasting the international political
    economy: Counting women's unpaid work." *New Political Economy* 12(3):
    297–317.
Jaquette, Jane S. 1982. "Women and modernization theory: A decade of feminist
    criticism." *World Politics* 34(2): 267–284.
Joachim, Jutta M. 2007. *Agenda setting, the UN, and NGOs: Gender violence and
    reproductive rights.* Washington, DC: Georgetown University Press.
Johnson, Carol. 1996. Does capitalism really need patriarchy?: Some old issues
    reconsidered, *Women's Studies International Forum* 19(3): 193–202.

Kabeer, Naila. 2000. *The power to choose: Bangladeshi women and labour market decisions in London and Dhaka*. London: Verso.

Katz, Cindi. 2001. "Vagabond capitalism and the necessity of social reproduction." *Antipode* 33: 709–728.

Knorr-Cetina, Karin, and Alex Preda (Eds.). 2006. *The sociology of financial markets*. Oxford: Oxford University Press.

Lakhani, Nina. 2008. "Farewell to 'predictable, tiresome and dreary' women's studies." *Independent*. Available at http://www.independent.co.uk/news/education/education-news/farewell-to-predictable-tiresome-and-dreary-womens-studies-799631.html

Laslett, Barbara, and Johanna Brenner. 1989. "Gender and social reproduction: Historical perspectives." *Annual Review of Sociology* 15: 381–404.

LeBaron, Genevieve, and Adrienne Roberts. 2010. Toward a feminist political economy of capitalism and carcerality. *Signs: Journal of Women in Culture and Society* 36(1): 19–44.

Ling, L. H. M. 1997. "The other side of globalization: Hypermasculine developmentalism in East Asia." Paper presented at the International Studies Association Meeting, Toronto, March 18–22.

Mackintosh, Maureen. 1981. "Gender and economics: The sexual division of labour and the subordination of women." In Kate Young, Carol Wolkowitz, and Roselyn McCullagh, eds., *Of marriage and the market: Women's subordination in international perspective*. London: CSE Books, 1–15.

Marx, Karl. 1973. *Grundrisse: Foundations of the critique of political economy*. New York: Vintage.

McDowell, Linda, and Gillian Court. 1994. "Missing subjects: Gender, power, and sexuality in merchant banking." *Economic Geography* 70(3): 229–251.

Menon, Nivedita. 2004. *Recovering subversion: Feminist politics beyond the law*. Chicago: University of Illinois Press.

Mies Martha. 1982. *The lace makers of Narsapur: Indian housewives produce for the world market*. London: Zed Press.

Mies, Maria, Veronika Bennholdt-Thomsen, and Gaudia von Werlhof. 1988. *Women: The last colony*. London: Zed Books.

Mohanty, Chandra Talpade. 2003. *Feminism without borders: Decolonizing theory, practicing solidarity*. Chapel Hill, NC: Duke University Press.

Molyneux, Maxine. 2006. "Mothers at the service of the new poverty agenda: Progresa/Oportunidades, Mexico's conditional transfer programme." *Social Policy & Administration*, 40(4): 425–449.

Moser, Caroline O. N. 1993. *Gender planning and development: Theory, practice, and training*. New York: Routledge.

Nash, June, and Patricia Fernandez-Kelly. 1983. *Women, men, and the international division of labor*. Albany: State University of New York Press.

Nussbaum, Martha C. 2000. *Women and human development: The capabilities approach*. Cambridge, UK: Cambridge University Press.

Nussbaum, Martha, Amrita Basu, Yasmin Tambiah, and Niraja Gopal Jayal. 2003. *Essays on gender and governance*. New Delhi: United Nations Development Programme India.

O'Brien, Robert, Anne-Marie Goetz, Jan Aart Scholte, and Marc Williams. 2000. *Contesting global governance: Multilateral economic institutions and global social movements*. Cambridge, UK: Cambridge University Press.

O'Neill, Onora. 2000. *Bounds of justice*. Cambridge, UK: Cambridge University Press.

Ong, Aihwa. 2006. *Neoliberalism as exception: Mutations in citizenship and sovereignty*. Chapel Hill, NC: Duke University Press.

Palmer, Ingrid. 1991. *Gender and population in the adjustment of African economies: Planning for change*. Geneva: International Labour Organization.

Perrons, Diane, Ania Plomien, and Majella Kilkey. 2010. "Migration and uneven development within an enlarged European Union: Fathering, gender divisions and male migrant domestic services," *European Urban and Regional Studies* 17(2): 197–215.

Peterson, V. Spike. 2003. *A critical rewriting of global political economy: Reproductive, productive and virtual economies*. London: Routledge.

Peterson, V. Spike. 2010a. "A long view of globalization and crisis." *Globalizations* 7(1): 187–202.

Peterson, V. Spike. 2010b. "Informalization, inequalities and global insecurities." *International Studies Review* 12(2): 244–270.

Picchio, Antonella. 1992. *Social reproduction: The political economy of the labour market*. Cambridge, UK: Cambridge University Press.

Polanyi, Karl. 2001. *The great transformation: The political and economic origins of our time*. Boston: Beacon Press.

Pringle, Rosemary, and Sophie Watson. 1990. "Fathers, brothers, mates: The fraternal state in Australia." In Sophie Watson, ed., *Playing the state, Australian feminist interventions*. London: Verso, 229–243.

Prugl, Elizabeth. 2008. "Gender and the making of global markets: An exploration of the agricultural sector." In Shirin M. Rai and Georgina Waylen, eds., *Global governance: Feminist perspectives*. Basingstoke, UK: Palgrave Macmillan, 43–63.

Rai, Shirin M. 1996. *Women and the state: International perspectives*. London: Taylor and Francis.

Rai, Shirin M. 2002. *Gender and the political economy of development*. Cambridge, UK: Polity Press.

Rai, Shirin M. 2003. *Mainstreaming gender, democratizing the state? National machineries for the advancement of women*. Manchester, UK: Manchester University Press for the United Nations.

Rai, Shirin M. 2008. *Gender politics of development*. London: Zed Books.

Rai, Shirin M. 2008. *Global governance: Feminist perspectives*. Basingstoke: Palgrave Macmillan.

Rai, Shirin M., and Kate Bedford (Eds.). 2010. "Feminists theorize international political economy." *Signs: Journal of Women in Culture and Society* 36(1): 1–18.

Rai, Shirin M., Catherine Hoskyns, and Dania Thomas. 2011. "Depletion and social reproduction." CSGR Working Paper 247/11. Available athttp://www2.warwick.ac.uk/fac/soc/csgr/research/workingpapers/2011/27411.pdf

Rai, Shirin M., and Georgina Waylen. 2008. *Global governance: Feminist perspectives*. Basingstoke: Palgrave Macmillan.

Randall, Vicky, and Georgina Waylen (Eds.). 1998. *Gender, politics and the state*. London: Routledge.

Ravenhill, John (Ed.). 2008. *Global political economy*, 2nd ed. Oxford: Oxford University Press.

Razavi, Shahra. 2007. "The political and social economy of care in a development context." Conceptual Issues, Research Questions and Policy Options Gender and Development Programme Paper Number 3, June, United Nations Research Institute for Social Development.

Rubery, Jill. 1998. *Equal pay in Europe?: Closing the gender wage gap.* New York: St. Martin's Press.

Safa, Helen. 1999. "Free markets and the marriage market: structural adjustment, gender relations and working conditions among Dominican women workers." *Environment and Planning* 31(2): 291–304.

Safri, Maliha, and Julie Graham. 2010. "The global household: Toward a feminist postcapitalist international political economy." *Signs: Journal of Women in Culture and Society* 36(1): 99–126.

Said, Edward. 1993. *Orientalism.* New York: Pantheon.

Salzinger, L. 2003. *Genders in production: Making workers in Mexico's global factories.* Berkeley: University of California Press.Sangari, Kumkum, and Sudesh Vaid (Eds.). 1993. *Recasting women: Essays in Indian colonial history.* New Delhi: Kali for Women.

Sen, Amartya. 1987. Gender and cooperative conflicts. Helsinki, Finalnd: World Institute for Development Economics Research of the United Nations University, 1988.

Shiva, Vandana. 1989. *Staying alive: Women, ecology and development.* New Delhi: Kali for Women.

Slaughter, Anne-Marie. 2004. "Disaggregated sovereignty: Toward the public accountability of global government networks." *Government and Opposition* 39(2): 159–190.

Salzinger, Leslie. 2003. *Genders in production: Making workers in Mexico's global factories.* Berkeley: University of California Press.

Smart, Carole. 1989. *Feminism and the power of law.* London: Routledge.

Spivak, Gayatri C. 1988. "Can the subaltern speak." In Cary Nelson and Lawrence Grossberd, eds., *Marxism and the interpretation of culture.* Basingstoke, UK: Macmillan, 271–313.

Staudt, Kathleen. 2003. "Gender mainstreaming: Conceptual links to institutional machineries." In Shirin M. Rai, ed., *National machineries for the advancement of women: Mainstreaming gender, democratising the state?* Manchester, UK: Manchester University Press.

Sweetman, Caroline, and Richard King. 2010. Oxfam International Discussion Paper: Gender perspectives on the global economic crisis. Oxford: Oxfam, 1–18

Taylor, Viviene. 2000. "Marketisation of governance: Critical feminist perspectives from the south." *DAWN.* Available at http://www.DAWN.org/publications

Tinker, Irene. 1997. "The making of a Field: Advocates, practitioners and Scholars." In Nalini Visvanathan, Lynn Duggan, Laurie Nisonoff, and Nan Wiegersma (eds.), *The women, gender and development reader.* London: Zed Books.

True, Jacqui. 2003. Mainstreaming gender in global public policy. *International Feminist Journal of Politics* 5(3): 368–396.

Truong, Thanh-Dam. 1999. "The underbelly of the tiger: Gender and the demystification of the Asian miracle." *Review of International Political Economy* 6(2): 133–165.

Unterhalter, Elaine. 2007. "Cosmopolitanism, global social justice and gender equality in education." Paper presented at the HDCA conference, New York, July. Available at http://www.capabilityapproach.com/pubs/Unterhalter07.pdf

Van Staveren, Irene, Diane Elson, Nilufer Cagatay, and Caren Grown (Eds.). 2007. *The feminist economics of trade*. London: Routledge.

Walby, Sylvia. 1990. *Theorizing patriarchy*. Oxford: Basil Blackwell.

Walby, Sylvia. 2005. "Introduction: Comparative gender mainstreaming in a global era." *International Feminist Journal of Politics* 7(4): 453–470.

Wallace, Tina, and March, Candida. 1991. Changing perceptions: writing on gender and development. Oxford: Oxfam.

Waring, Marilyn. 1988. *If Women Counted*: A New Feminist Economics. Harper and Row.

Whitworth, Sandra. 2004. *Men, militarism, and UN peacekeeping: A gendered analysis*. London: Lynne Reiner.

Woehl, Stefanie. 2008. "Global governance as neoliberal governmentality." In Shirin M. Rai and Georgina Waylen, eds., *Global governance: Feminist perspectives*, 64–83. Basingstoke, UK: Palgrave Macmillan.

Women Working Worldwide. Available at http://www.women-ww.org/index.php/programmes/research

Wright, Melissa. 2006. *Disposable women and other myths of global capitalism*. London: Routledge.

Young, Iris Marion. 2006. "Responsibility and global justice, a social connection model." *Justice and Global Politics* 23: 102–130.

Young, Kate, Carol Wolkowitz, and Roslyn McCullagh (Eds.). 1981. *Of marriage and market: Women's subordination internationally and its lessons*. London: Routledge.

Yuval-Davis, Nira, Kalpana Kannabiran, and Ulrike Vieten. 2006. *The situated politics of belonging*. London: SAGE.

CHAPTER 11

HOUSEHOLDS, FAMILIES, AND SOCIAL REPRODUCTION

SHAHRA RAZAVI

INTRODUCTION

The past three decades have been marked by extensive economic reform and restructuring, commonly associated with the globalization agenda. In many contexts the new policy schema has come to be associated with growing levels of income inequality and the exacerbation of existing forms of deprivation and insecurity. Feminists, among others, have drawn attention to the strains this has brought to the day-to-day reproduction of people, families, and societies (Elson 1998)—a rupture in social reproduction.

But economic liberalization has coincided with other, more enabling processes of social and political change that have helped chip away at some of the pillars of patriarchy. This has included the articulation of more assertive agendas by social movements and civil society organizations around human rights, and women's rights more specifically. In response, many governments have taken steps to bring their laws on marriage, divorce, reproduction, and inheritance in line with the principles of equality. Responding to the new opportunities as well as the exigencies of a changing economic context, many women have taken on new breadwinning roles, while some have postponed marriage, reduced fertility, and experienced greater autonomy in their personal lives as well as more visibility and engagement in the public domain.

The privileging of rights-based agendas and the enhanced autonomy experienced by some women have also contributed to the ongoing transformation of the family as evidenced by the spread of family forms and living arrangements other than the nuclear family comprising a married couple with children. Intimate partnerships and sexuality, as well as the relationships between parents and children, seem to have moved away from the "realm of normative control and institutional regulation" (Sobotka and Toulemon 2008, 86), giving rise to the new ideal of reflexive "pure relationships" based on mutual consent (Giddens 1992). In this context some have talked about the trend away from traditional notions of the family that emphasize the role of social obligation in the reproduction of kinship systems and toward "globalizing models of family" that appear to be increasingly chosen (Padilla et al. 2007, xv)—not only in the heartlands of modernity but also across the Global South. Gays and lesbians have added their voices to those clamoring for the pluralization of relationship forms and the democratization of the private sphere, arguing for families that are chosen (Weston 1991).

But "the family" has proven to be a highly charged topic because it is imbued with politically and culturally contested ideas about "the correct or moral ways in which people should conduct their lives, and the people with whom they should conduct them" (Pine 2002, 339). One strand in the early English-speaking commentary on changes in family form and the increasing prevalence of lone parenthood resulting from high rates of cohabitation and divorce has been the perceived collapse of family values and lack of proper socialization of children; the solution being sought is in the restoration of traditional married, two-parent families and the rolling back of state support (Lewis 2006). Others have called for the reform of the heterosexual nuclear family to enhance "partnership" and gender-equitable divisions within the home to create a more solid foundation for family life (Bedford 2007). Others still have argued for a more radical democratization of the family, away from biological determinism and heteronormative assumptions and toward greater pluralism and choice.

The past three decades have therefore shown that although most political economy has ignored the contribution of the domestic to social reproduction, understanding households, families, and social reproduction and how they are gendered is a key part of political economy and politics more generally. To demonstrate this, the rest of this chapter is structured as follows. We first explain some of the terminology that is necessary to understand the key debates, before turning our attention to the political economy of social reproduction and the relations between patriarchy and capitalism. Then we provide a more empirical analysis of family change with glimpses from Western Europe, Southern Africa, and East Asia. The chapter then briefly turns to family policies that have taken center stage in many contexts and the complex objectives they seek to meet, before wrapping up with brief concluding remarks.

FAMILIES AND HOUSEHOLDS: DECENTERING BIOLOGY—RECOGNIZING PLURALITY AND DIFFERENCE

The concepts of *household* and *family* are usually distinguished by pointing out that the former is a residence group in which members' skills, capacities, and resources are combined for purposes of production, reproduction, and consumption (Goody 1972), while the latter is a more extended network of kinship relations that people may activate selectively. This kind of distinction is usually followed by noting the well-known fact that although households and families often overlap—because family is the normative way people should be recruited into households (Rapp 1991)—they are not coterminous, and do not overlap completely. Household units may include individuals who are not part of the unit comprising the conjugal couple and their children, as in the practice of child fostering, prevalent across Africa and Latin America, where children are sent to relatives so that they can be fed, clothed, and educated (Moore 1994). There are also many instances where the conjugal couple and their children do not form households. The anthropological literature of the 1960s and 1970s made frequent references to situations where the father-husband resided separately from the rest of his family, sometimes in societies that practiced polygyny or in the context of long-term migration (Bender 1967). Today there is much talk of *transnational families* as cross-border migratory flows have come to include increasing numbers of women who seek paid work across the world while their children are left behind (Ehrenreich and Hochschild 2003).

These distinctions are useful to make because they are indicative of the huge diversity of family and household forms—not only across broad cultural groupings and regional contexts but also within the same society.

We know, for example, that the nuclear household, which the modernization narrative posits as the norm, is far from universal—even in the United Kingdom, where in 2003 only 22 percent of households comprised a heterosexual couple with dependent children (ONS 2004, cited in Roseneil 2004). In Latin America such households constituted between 56 percent (in Venezuela) and 71 percent (in Paraguay) of all households (Jelin and Diaz-Munoz 2003). In South Africa only just over a third (34.5 percent) of all households conform to the nuclear norm of children living together with a middle generation, while about one-fifth (20.5 percent) of all households have three generations present (Budlender and Lund 2011).

Family forms and household structures (including their dependency ratios) also vary depending on the life stages and social strategies of their members, which can shift in response to changes in the broader socioeconomic and political context. The notion of childhood, for example, and what it should entail—financial dependence, school attendance, and being cared for by adults—are socially and historically specific. Today in many parts of the world, children in low-income strata carry out both paid and unpaid work and may receive little individual adult attention and care. Similarly, a significant life event like departure from the parental home, which is often seen as a precondition for living with a partner and becoming a parent, varies significantly, even within a relatively homogeneous geographical area like Europe. Here demographers depict wide differences in home-leaving behavior of cohorts born around 1960, with contrasting patterns prevailing in Southern Europe and in the Nordic countries (Sobotka and Toulemon 2008). Besides the availability of housing, other factors such as employment, income, and spatial distribution of universities are often important determinants of home leaving.

In the context of recurring economic crises in Latin America during the 1980s and 1990s, the proportion of extended households increased in some countries as a response to the economic privations that lower-income sectors experienced and as a means of pooling resources and meeting particular needs such as shelter (Jelin and Diaz-Munoz 2003). Similarly, household strategies, such as the tendency for women to take on paid work, the out-migration of younger and able-bodied members, or pooling and sharing of resources across extended kin networks, can change, sometimes abruptly, in response to the broader context within which these networks are embedded. This underlines the critical point that the family is neither an isolated institution (ibid.) nor autonomous. Domestic units, whatever their composition and form, are rooted in social networks that provide support and solidarity as well as being connected to the wider political economy through the flow of goods and services (Moore 1994). Later in the chapter we turn to some of the variations in family forms and explore how the broader political economy contributes to them.

Despite some recognition of diversity in family forms, it remains difficult to define precisely what sorts and range of relationships the term *family* covers, both in everyday use and in academic writing. This is because of the complex ways the term family is used and because the sets of assumptions it embraces have changed as new theories of kinship, gender, and social structure have been developed (Pine 2002). What we can say with confidence is that *families* has increasingly replaced the family as an analytic concept, and the family itself, whether singular or plural, has come to be seen less and less as a natural form of human social organization and more as a culturally specific symbolic system or ideology (ibid.).

The centrality of friendship within gay and lesbian communities, in particular, has raised fundamental questions about what constitutes kinship relations and whether families must be biologically defined. Blood or biological relations represent one possible type of kinship on the basis of which families can form. But as gay men and lesbians discovered, they too could lay claim to a distinctive type of family. "While dominant cultural representations have asserted that straight is to gay as family is to no family, at a certain point in history gay people began to contend that straight is to gay as blood family is to chosen families" (Weston 1991, 29).

As Judith Butler (2004, 26, cited in Harder 2009, 639) argues, contemporary modes of living create "relations of kinship that cross the boundaries between community and family and sometimes redefine the meaning of friendship as well. When these modes of intimate association produce sustaining webs of relationships, they constitute a breakdown of traditional kinship that displaces the presumption that biological and sexual relations structure kinship centrally." Research in the United Kingdom shows that, for many people who do not live with a partner, regardless of their lifestyles and sexualities, friendship occupies a central place in their personal lives. What this research suggests "is that social researchers have often failed to see the extent to which, often as a matter of preference, people are substituting the ties of friendship for those of blood, particularly in terms of everyday care and emotional support" (Roseneil 2004, 413).

While family relations can offer protection and love, encourage sharing and redistribution, and nurture and sustain their members, this should not obscure the extent to which they are also shaped by power differentials and conflicting interests. Nearly three decades of feminist research[1] has drawn attention to the unequal distribution of resources and burdens within households along gender and generational lines while documenting pervasive acts of violence and sexual molestation, which are often unrecognized, underreported, and even legally sanctioned in some contexts. In the past decade an emerging area of research on lesbian, gay, bisexual, and transgender families has also dealt with inequalities among partners and abusive relationships, as timidity about covering controversial issues declined (Biblarz and Savci 2010).

Much of the public concern about the family—its crisis, dysfunctionality, and imminent disintegration—tends to assume that a particular family form (married couple plus children) is the model for the family worldwide and that any deviations from this model are problematic or pathological. The phenomenon of transnational families, for example, to which reference has already been made, challenges the ideology of *family in one place*. Mothers who have migrated are often admonished and denounced by journalists and government officials for having "abandoned" their children and for causing the family to deteriorate (Parrenas 2003). There have been similar moral outcries at different points in time about "family decline" in contexts where significant numbers of children are being raised by their mothers and other family members in the absence of their biological fathers.

There is very often a normative or ideological thrust to public concerns about the family—one that tends to stigmatize those who are structurally prevented from accumulating stable resources and exercising meaningful choice in having the families they would like to have. As Rapp (1991, 210) notes with reference to the United States:

> The very poor have used their families to cement and patch tenuous relations to survival; out of their belief in "family" they have invented networks capable of making next-to-nothing go a long way...In response, they are told that

their notion of family is inadequate. It is not their notion of family that is deficient, but the relationship between household and productive resources.

The moral discourse is also sometimes in response to the dissolution of the traditional patriarchal family forms. Access to education, an independent source of income, the right to divorce, permissible forms of sexuality, as well as the emergence of new models of femininity and masculinity have helped bring about a wider range of life options and family forms. Some of the moral panic about the family is voiced by those who wish to contain the democratization of the private sphere and to reimpose a model of the family based on patriarchal moral principles which they consider to be timeless, absolute, and nonnegotiable.

SOCIAL REPRODUCTION, WOMEN'S OPPRESSION, AND CAPITALISM

Having explored how to conceptualize families and households, we are now in a position to analyze social reproduction as a sphere that is closely associated with domestic institutions (see also the chapter by Rai in this volume). Social reproduction has been defined in a variety of ways. The concept is said to include the social processes and human relations associated with the production and maintenance of people and communities on a daily and generational basis, upon which all production and exchange rest (Bakker 2003, 67; see also the chapter by Rai in this volume). It involves "the provision of food, clothing, shelter, basic safety and health care, along with the development and transmission of knowledge, social values and cultural practices and the construction of individual and collective identities" (Bezanson and Luxton 2006, 3; see also Elson 1998). The problem with these definitions is that they are too all embracing: almost everything, from factory production to unpaid work of caring for dependents to the development of national identity through immigration regimes can be included. Reflecting its functionalist moorings, the definition also tends to assume that by and large societies are recreated and perpetuated. It is not very clear how to identify moments when social relations erode and unravel.

Despite these inadequacies, the strength of the concept is that it draws attention not only to market-based activities and social relations but also to nonmarket ones. An important part of social reproduction is mediated through ties of kinship, friendship, and community. These include the performance of domestic tasks, caregiving, and a more diverse set of activities involved in building and consolidating social networks, reciprocal support relations, and community ties (social capital, as some would call it).

It is important to draw attention to these unpaid activities, because the domestic sector (families, households)—which is a key site of social reproduction—is very often taken for granted in mainstream political economy that is largely concerned with the broader economic and political processes of the macroeconomy, namely, markets and states (Elson 1998).[2] As Elson argues, "to understand the ordering (and disordering) of societies," the analytical focus was, and remains, on political and economic processes and the detailed relations between them, with little sign of interest in how "households are organised (or disorganised) both internally and in relation to economic and political structures" (189).

Elson (1998) usefully depicts the domestic sector and its interconnections with the *private sector* (markets) and the *public sector* (states) in a simple format by showing the circuits that connect them and through which flow goods, services, labor, and values (be they commercial, regulatory, or provisioning). While domestic structures can produce able-bodied and socialized worker-citizens on a daily and intergenerational basis who in turn contribute to the workings of the other sectors (both market and state), women's unpaid time is not infinitely elastic. Moreover, domestic structures rely and depend on the flow of goods, services, and values from other sectors. When these inputs are not sufficiently forthcoming, human capacities will be depleted and provisioning values destroyed.

Families, Social Reproduction, and Women's Subordination

The relations between patriarchy and capitalism and between reproduction and production have been subjects of inquiry at least since the publication of Engels's (1972) *Origins of the Family, Private Property and the State* (first published in 1884), where he attributes women's inferior social position to the institution of private property, at least among the bourgeoisie. Among proletarians, Engels argues, women were not oppressed because there was no property to be inherited.

Social reproduction was given further analytical attention within Marxist and Marxist–feminist analyses in the 1970s, which took as their starting point the fact that any mode of production also has a system of reproduction (i.e., reproduction of the people within the system) and of the system as a whole. In what became known as the domestic labor debate, the housework that women did on an unpaid basis was analyzed as a subsidy to capital that lowered the wages paid to male breadwinners. One concern with this line of reasoning was that the recourse to functionalist arguments in conceptualizing the relationship between capitalism and domestic labor had a tendency to economic reductionism and did not explain why it was *women* who did this work (Molyneux 1979). A related criticism was that by placing the focus squarely on capital and on how women's unpaid work reproduced capitalism, it had little to say about the relations between women and men. As Hartmann (1979, 5) puts it, while these analysts think that "women's work *appears* to be for men but in reality is for capital, we think that women's work in the family *really is* for men—though it clearly reproduces capitalism as well."

Hartmann's (1979) critique was part of a broader attempt by feminist analysts at the time to develop a theory of gender, which was integrated into and informed by the general analysis of changes in the global economy yet avoided crude analyses of gender relation exclusively in terms of their function for capital and "the reproduction of capitalist relations of production" (Pearson, Whitehead, and Young 1981, x). The objective was to look beyond the capital–labor relation and the capitalist workplace to a larger analysis of production and reproduction as an integrated system that took the relations between women and men seriously.

A somewhat different set of challenges confronts us today. In the context of neoliberal restructuring and pervasive commodification[3] of the past three decades, there has been again growing scholarly interest in the noncommodified sphere (Vail 2010; van der Ploeg 2010). The latter is understood to include a very broad range of processes and initiatives—new consumption movements, gift economy, social economy, nonprofit enterprises, welfare policies, the provision of public goods, associational activities, and so on. Some authors (Vail 2010) have paid explicit attention to unpaid care work and included it as one component of these alternative economic circuits that are grounded in a logic predicated on social needs rather than profit. However, while useful in drawing attention to the importance of the nonmarket sphere for the proper functioning of a market system and in underlining its sheer size, there is insufficient problematization of the hierarchies, exclusions, and oppressions that characterize the noncommodified sphere. If in the 1960s and 1970s housework was seen as perpetuating capitalism and oppressing women, today the noncommodified sphere is romanticized by some, seen as a space of liberation from capitalist relations of production—a "haven in a heartless world."

Feminists tend to have a more ambivalent view of the noncommodified domain, given the significant gender inequalities that it embodies (see also the chapter by Sainsbury in this volume). The literature on the family tells us that freedom from capital, the profit motive, or even private property does not necessarily mean freedom from oppression. Patriarchal control over women's fertility and sexuality, labor, and progeny probably predated private property, even though the institution of private property may have strengthened such control (Mackintosh 1977, 126).

To say that a large part of reproductive work in all societies is provided on an unpaid basis does not mean that its provision is voluntary and costless. In fact, it imposes substantial costs on those who provide it, in the form of financial obligations, lost opportunities, and foregone earnings—which is not to deny that it also generates intrinsic rewards for those who provide it as well as stronger family and social ties and good quality services for dependents (Folbre 1994). The costs, however, are unequally borne. Women in general carry out a disproportionate share of the work, while many of the benefits go to society more broadly. The cost is also unequally born across the social hierarchy, given the generally higher rates of fertility among lower-income households who also find it more difficult to outsource care or purchase time-saving substitutes. As we will see later, these large gender gaps in the unpaid sphere may be contributing to women's decisions in some contexts not to marry and not to have children.

If in the 1960s and 1970s feminists were joined by Marxists who exposed the links between housework and capitalist accumulation, today's allies are a more mixed set of actors, including both social democrats and neoliberals. The former advocate for the adaptation of welfare regimes to women's new roles (Esping-Andersen 2009); they seek to expand and adjust the welfare state to the real changes that have taken place in women's roles and aspirations, mandating the state to take on some of the burden and cost of reproduction historically assumed by the family (read: women). They have been relatively effective in getting their perspective adopted by some national governments in Europe and some global institutions such as the European Union and the Organisation for Economic Co-operation and Development (OECD). However, in the enthusiasm for pushing unpaid work into the public domain, the extent to which it is possible, or desirable, to outsource all unpaid work has been overestimated, and women's own choices and preferences sidelined.

The neoliberal establishment, on the other hand, does not by any means advocate for anything like the social democratic welfare regime. Fearing too much government, they advocate for "more market integration" and, in some quarters, for gender roles change within the family. Women's deeper integration into the market is seen as a blessing, ignoring concerns about the manner in which such integration takes place and the perpetuation of gender hierarchies within markets. More recently, there has also been some advocacy within the World Bank (Bedford 2007) for getting more men to do unpaid work, thereby allowing women to take on more paid work. The aim is to adjust gender within the family because, after all, the family, understood very narrowly as a privatized heterosexual couple in a nuclear unit, is the key informal institution necessary to achieve poverty reduction within a largely neoliberal world. A similar thrust has been evident in the World Bank's work on sub-Saharan Africa, where the failure of liberalization policies to produce (agricultural) growth has been blamed on unequal gender roles within African households. Here again the policy message has been to adjust gender at the household level to enable the process of economic liberalization (O'Laughlin 2007).

These two approaches are very different in many respects. The social democratic attempt to reform capitalism through extensive welfare policies would allow the socialization of some of the costs of reproduction and hence reduce class and gender inequalities, while the neoliberal position endorses the abstract market that is likely to reinforce both inequalities. Nevertheless, what both approaches share is a fairly narrow and conventional view of the family. The ideal family remains the heterosexual nuclear couple, which is to be imbued with a more gender-egalitarian ethos so that women's more masculine life-course behavior can be paralleled with thoroughgoing "feminization" on the part of men (Esping-Andersen 2009, 99). The ideal heterosexual nuclear couple, however, is increasingly out of kilter with the diverse family landscape in many contexts.

FAMILY CHANGE AND CONTINUITY: GLIMPSES FROM WESTERN EUROPE, SOUTHERN AFRICA, AND EAST ASIA

Functionalist anthropologists predicted that industrialization and urbanization, as powerful social forces, would usher in a shift to nuclear family forms based on monogamous marriage. Instead what we find is the great variability of domestic institutions, as opposed to the commonality, singularity, and one-way direction of change (Therborn 2004). It is useful to begin this discussion by noting some of the changes that have swept through the advanced industrialized countries of Western Europe and North America before turning to some other regional contexts.

In the United States, for example, the idealized breadwinner–homemaker family that dominated the family landscape from the turn of the century until the middle of the twentieth century was challenged by the rapid entry of women into the labor force between 1940 and 2000[4] and the rising share of women who were unmarried, owing to divorce or nonmarriage. The percentage of women who were never married rose from 6 to 17 percent between 1963 and 1997, and the percentage previously married (mostly divorced) doubled from 10 to 19 percent (Gornick and Meyers 2003). During these same years the rise in divorce and nonmarriage meant that the percentage of children living with an unmarried parent rose from 9 to 28 percent. Given the necessity of employment for single parents, in 2000 a larger share of single mothers with children was in the labor force (71 percent) than married mothers with children of the same age (63 percent) (ibid.). Racism and class–education cleavages have been formidable problems in this context, fueling resistance to redistributive family policies, especially assistance to single-parent (very often, single-mother) families who continue to be portrayed in racialized terms.

While class and racial–ethnic inequalities are less accentuated in Europe compared with the United States, lone motherhood is nevertheless biased toward the bottom of society, while high-earning dual-career couples are concentrated in the upper half of the income distribution (Sobotka 2008; Esping-Andersen 2009). In Europe too there is a decline in marriage among women, the phenomenon being far more concentrated among less educated women; the same applies to divorce and single motherhood. As a general rule, the old convention of marriage followed by childbearing has been replaced by a proliferation of alternative paths, including cohabitation and births outside wedlock. In Scandinavia, for example, nearly half of all children are born to unmarried, but usually cohabiting, couples (Esping-Andersen 2009). While starting at a lower level, out-of-wedlock births have also more than doubled in other countries of Europe.

It is important, however, not to let comparisons with the early post-1945 period distort our understanding of the longer-term changes in family life (Oppenheimer 1997). As Esping-Andersen (2009) reminds us, in the late 1800s the average age of marriage was high and the share of lone mothers and child-less women was also substantial, just as now. So the post-1945 decades were the historically exceptional period in many respects: "people suddenly began to marry and have (more) children at younger ages," and the proportion of never-married women also dropped, while partnerships became unusually stable (Esping-Andersen 2009, 27). This was also the era of the male breadwinner family. The apparent similarities across centuries, however, disguise the different causes. To give one example, many women did not marry because a significant proportion were domestic workers and nannies and were therefore prevented from marrying and having children, and single motherhood was often caused by the death or disappearance of the father. Today the typical causes are found in divorce and in the deliberate decision to have children outside a union (ibid.).

An emerging divide in Europe to which many scholars draw attention is across education–class divides, which have become major sources of stratification: among higher educated women, nonmarital childbearing usually takes place in the context of stable cohabiting unions, whereas those with lower levels of education often experience lone motherhood or childbearing within unstable partnerships (Sobotka 2008). These rising divergences in type of partnership, childbearing, and work trajectories of lower-educated and higher-educated women are seen as contributing to the increasingly disadvantaged economic position of the former group (Sobotka 2008; Esping-Andersen 2009). Another trend to which researchers have drawn attention relates to fertility patterns: in most countries ultimate family size and childlessness seem to be clearly differentiated by education, with higher-educated women having the highest levels of childlessness and the lowest levels of fertility. Apart from this within-country differentiation, some have argued that the persistence of gender inequalities and difficulties in reconciling career and childrearing is probably the single best explanation of low fertility across countries, with Germany and Southern European countries, which are known as "non-caring" states, falling into the low fertility category (total fertility rate of 1.3 for Germany and 1.2 for Italy), while many Scandinavian countries and France, known for their caring states, exhibit near or above replacement fertility level (total fertility rate of 1.7 and above) (McDonald 2000; Gornick and Meyers 2008; Esping-Andersen 2009).

Some of the trends documented for the advanced industrialized countries—such as falling rates of marriage, increasing numbers of children born out of wedlock, and rising numbers of women supporting their children without assistance from the fathers of those children—prefigure trends in other regions. However, as the following subsection will suggest, the forces driving these trends can be very different from those that characterize the advanced industrialized countries.

Family Change in the Global Periphery

Therborn (2004), like others who have attempted to analyze family and householding arrangements across the world, begins with broad *geocultural* groupings before proceeding with various subdivisions. For Therborn, treating family systems as geocultures means "treating them as institutions or structures taking their colouring from customs and traditions, from the history of a particular area, a cultural wrapping which may remain after structural, institutional change, leaving imprints on the new institution" (11). In other words, while family systems are subject to structural and institutional change, the fact that they are also cultural systems means that they are likely to exhibit considerable path dependency.

Within the gender and development literature, Esther Boserup's (1970) analysis of *male and female farming systems* has inspired classifications that partially overlap with Therborn's and that are based on two organizational principles: (1) the degree of corporateness of the conjugal unit around which the boundaries of the household economy are organized; and (2) the degree of public mobility and hence opportunities for economic participation in the public sphere allowed to women (Kandiyoti 1988; Kabeer 1996). In both these classification systems, countries in the belt of *strong* or *classic patriarchy* of North Africa, West Asia, Confucian East Asia, and the northern plains of South Asia are distinguished from the *weaker patriarchies* of south India and southeast Asia (Kabeer 1996), where inheritance may be bilateral, household location upon marriage may be bifocal, and there is more leeway for young couples, whether through late marriage or the legitimacy of divorce (Therborn, 123). It is, however, in the sub-Saharan African and the Afro-Caribbean regions, where the clearest instances of noncorporateness of the conjugal family both in ideology and practice can be found (Kandiyoti 1988, 277).

The prevalence of less corporate forms of householding involving the relative autonomy of mother–child units in sub-Saharan Africa, especially West Africa, has attracted a great deal of attention in feminist scholarship—in good part because it raises difficult questions about the unitary household model.

Research suggests that women's and men's access to resources (including land), for example, has been symmetrical in form, even if men's access and effective possession has been far more extensive than women's (Whitehead 1990, 438). Furthermore, women have a dual productive role: working both independently of other members of the household and also contributing to household production as unremunerated family labor (ibid.). The other distinctive feature is that resources of husbands and wives are not merged into a single conjugal fund (Whitehead 1981). The responsibilities for providing for children's well-being are also often divided between father and mother—a feature that requires women to be economically independent to some degree and that has also been structurally linked to polygyny (Whitehead 1990).

These features of smallholder agricultural households had their roots in the precommodity economies and societies of the nineteenth century. While there are some elements of continuity between these historical antecedents and modern gender relations, the transformation of rural production systems and the commodification and individualization of productive resources were experienced very differently by women and men. As agrarian economies were commercialized and rural class differentiation was intensified, women's independent farming, for example, came under increasing pressure, while many men were able to solidify their command over land, labor, and capital.

Southern Africa: Missing Men and Disrupted Families?

These broad regional patterns inevitably obscure particular histories and trajectories of family and household organization and disorganization. Here we focus on some of the literature that analyses family formation in Southern Africa because of the ways the broader political economy has produced disruptive effects on family formation. It thus helps illustrate the key point raised by Elson (1998), namely, that domestic structures depend on the flow of goods, services, and values from other sectors and that when these inputs are not sufficiently forthcoming, then human capacities will be depleted and provisioning values destroyed.

In Southern Africa, or Africa of the labour reserves (Amin 1972), over several generations families were systematically divided as colonial and postcolonial governments recruited young able-bodied men from rural areas for wage work in mines and plantations, leaving women, children, and the elderly men to carry out subsistence farming and household reproduction in poorly resourced areas (O'Laughlin 1998). In South Africa where mining underpinned the economy for much of the twentieth century, men were recruited for wage work into the mines and housed in single-sex compounds. This is believed to have had a disruptive effect on marital patterns and men's engagement with their children (Niehaus 1994; Budlender and Lund 2011). Based on his research among urban residents in a South African "homeland" in the mid-1980s, Niehaus, for example, drew attention not only to conjugal instability and marital dissolution in a context where men were facing difficulties in finding paid work but also the emergence of sibling ties as the basis for domestic reorganization and household formation.

Twenty years on, some of these patterns of family disruption seem to have changed very little. There are ongoing debates, for example, about the low and declining marriage rates among the African population in South Africa and the reasons for it, which are believed to include the migrant labor system and the high cost of *lobolo* (or bridewealth) associated with marriage. One thing that seems to be clear is that low and declining marriage rates among both women and men are not recent postapartheid phenomena but ones that can be traced back at least to the 1960s, if not before (Mhongo and Budlender forthcoming). Yet the low rates of marriage do not necessarily affect fertility rates in this context, given that a large number of women have children outside of marriage. The national level statistical evidence cited by Budlender and Lund (2011) suggests further that the majority of children in South Africa today live apart from their biological fathers. In 2008, only just over a third (35 percent) of children (0–17 years) lived with both their biological parents, while close to 40 percent were living with their mother but not their father, and one in five (23 percent) were not residing with either biological parent. The fact that fathers are often absent probably means that many of the mothers must try to combine their caregiving roles with income earning, which is challenging in a context where unemployment rates are notoriously high. Grandmothers are likely to provide assistance with the care of the children (as they are likely to face even more difficulty finding paid work) while their daughters seek paid work.

The persistence of extensive structural unemployment—not only of men among whom unemployment stands at 23 percent but also of women where it reaches a staggering 31 percent—raises fundamental questions about the development model that despite respectable levels of economic growth has failed to provide jobs and livelihoods. In her detailed analysis of livelihoods in Botswana—another country of southern Africa—O'Laughlin (1998) refers to the recurrence throughout Southern Africa of a number of persistent structural commonalities: "the dependence of rural livelihoods on disposable cash income, the sharpening polarisation of agrarian production, structural unemployment, the erosion of social support from kin and community, and the corresponding dependence on social transfers" (38). In Botswana the outflow of young men (and to a lesser extent young women) from rural areas into urban centers is reflected in the persistence of large numbers of households maintained by women. The fact that many women and men do not marry and establish common households, she insists, "is because they cannot, and not because they do not wish to do so" (24).

Yet, despite high rates of structural unemployment among women, mothers do not seem to renege on their responsibility vis-à-vis their children with the ease with which men do, even if sustaining their households requires engagement in income-generating activities that are low return and do not provide a living wage for themselves and their dependents. Here, as in some other regions, informal sexual relationships among those who are located at the lower end of the class structure may give women some degree of independence. But it also means little support for mothers and their children, who suffer from both class and racial oppression. A similar phenomenon is observed by Chant (2010) based on her research in the Philippines, the Gambia, and Costa Rica. She refers to a tendency over time toward the feminization of responsibility or obligation, whereby women with young children are having to assume an increasing share of the responsibility for meeting household needs with little or no support from the fathers of their children.

Marriage in East and Southeast Asia: Delayed and Avoided

As was noted already, in comparative analyses of the family, East Asian family patterns are frequently depicted for their patriarchal character, reinforced through the Confucian ethic, with its supreme norm of "filial piety" (Therborn 2004, 119). Patriarchal norms tend to be reflected in the relative prevalence, even if significantly diminished, of stem or extended family forms, the near universality of marriage, the strong sense of filial obligation, and entrenched stratifications by gender and age within households—this region, along with South Asia, being home to some of the most skewed sex ratios in the world that are indicative of strong son preference.

While marriage may still be close to universal in many parts of South Asia, over the past two to three decades nonmarriage for women has become much more common in Southeast and East Asia, especially in the big cities (Jones 2005). Between 1970 and 1990, the percentage of women remaining single at the age of 30–34 rose from 2 to 11 percent in Taiwan; from 8 to 14 percent in Thailand; from 6 to 15 percent in Peninsular Malaysia; from 9 to 19 percent in Myanmar; the figure for the Philippines in 1990 (13 percent) was one of the highest in the region (Jones 2005). The rates of nonmarriage among men in most of these countries have tended to be lower than for women, with evidence of males rushing into marriage once they reach their late 30s (ibid., 102). What is also worth noting is that while rates of nonmarriage have tended to be higher among those with tertiary education, there is nevertheless a steady rise in the proportions never married even among those with no education or only primary education (ibid.).

Given that these are all countries where until recently marriage was close to universal and nonmarriage an aberration, there is considerable scholarly debate as to the reasons for this change (Kabeer 2007). There is also considerable public and policy concern regarding the consequences of low marriage and nonmarriage for the family and for fertility rates, which have plummeted to very low levels in some of these countries.

East and Southeast Asia have seen remarkable rates of economic growth in recent decades (the 1997 economic crisis and its aftermath notwithstanding) alongside significant improvements in education and employment opportunities. Some have argued that the high rates of nonmarriage among women reflect the failure of certain groups of women and men to find suitable partners (Quah 1998, cited in Kabeer 2007). In a context where attitudes about what makes a suitable wife and mother have been slow to change, women who are highly educated and reluctant to marry down and men who are less educated and reluctant to marry up face particular difficulties in finding suitable partners. Moreover, while historically families were actively involved in seeking partners for their offspring, this is no longer the case. Hence, nonmarriage has been hypothesized to be nonvolitional, caused by a lack of potential partners or a lack of opportunity to meet potential partners.

While a marriage squeeze is likely, especially in cities where the pool of educated women is augmented by migration leading to a shortage of potential spouses, a more convincing explanation draws attention to a number of institutional factors that may have made marriage less attractive to women. In a context where gender divisions of unpaid work within the family remain highly unfavorable to women who have to shoulder most of the responsibility with little participation from their husbands, some women may be choosing to postpone or forego marriage altogether (Jones 2005).

Women in particular have seen their employment prospects improve steadily in many of these economies, whether through employment in export-oriented manufacturing sectors or in teaching, nursing, and clerical occupations. Even though women face significant gender-based discriminations in pay and working conditions, their participation in the paid workforce may nevertheless have reduced their financial dependence on men through marriage. The contributions that daughters often make to their parents' household budgets may have also given parents an incentive for abandoning the system of arranged marriage (Salaff 1976; Jones 2005). These alternative explanations suggest that delaying both marriage and nonmarriage may be life options chosen by some women in the face of gender-inegalitarian norms and practices that continue to shape marriage and family life.

Some of the same institutional factors have been identified as contributing factors to the low fertility rates in the region—a related development that has stimulated considerable debate in recent years, both scholarly and policy oriented. McDonald (2000), for example, argues that very low fertility rates in some of the East Asian countries today can be explained by the institutional incoherence that exists with respect to gender equality. His hypothesis is that when high levels of gender equity in individual-oriented institutions (e.g., education, political rights, employment) are contradicted by low levels of gender equality in family-oriented institutions (e.g., gender division of unpaid work), fertility levels are likely to fall to very low levels. Such institutional incongruity then forces women to choose between marrying and having children and labor force participation, but not both.

While issue can be taken with McDonald's (2000) description of labor markets in East Asia as gender equitable—countries like Korea and Taiwan have some of the largest gender wage gaps in the world—access to the labor market and an individual source of income is likely nevertheless to have given women some degree of financial independence and hence an exit option out of marriages that have remained so stubbornly "traditional" despite changing social and economic conditions (Peng 2012).

These East and Southeast Asian debates on low rates of marriage, nonmarriage, and low fertility make frequent references to Japan, given that it has one of the most advanced economic structures in the region, the longest history of low fertility, and the highest proportion of never-married females in their thirties (Retherford, Ogawa, and Matsukura 2001; Jones 2005). While Japanese cultural patterns are said to be unique, certain factors affecting the (un)desirability of marriage from a woman's point of view are shared by other countries in the region: for example, the lack of intimacy in marriage; the accepted male patterns of keeping mistresses and resorting to commercialized sex; the social norms and practices that define all domestic and care work as women's work; and the rising rate of divorce (starting from a low base). The structural changes in the economy and improved educational attainments have over time improved the employment prospects of women, while conjugal and marital relations seem to have been frozen in time.

Moreover, despite rapid economic change a considerable amount of parental weight has remained in the Japanese family, as a modified stem family: close to one-fifth of all married couples were living with parents and almost a third of the 40–44-year-olds did so in 1995 (Japanese Statistics Bureau 2000, cited in Therborn 2004, 123). The rate of coresidence with parents, around 10 percent, is lower among Korean couples compared with their Japanese counterparts. The fact that many men in low-fertility East Asian countries like Japan and Korea are likely to be the only son, and hence under pressure either to cohabit with their parents or assume responsibility for their welfare, means that the prospective daughter-in-law has to assume a considerable share of the care work for her elderly parents-in-law as well, even if she and her husband do not cohabit with them. Such expectations may reinforce women's hesitations about marriage.

These societies are, however, undergoing significant cultural and normative change. Attitude surveys in Korea suggest changing expectations regarding parental care and support, over a very short period of time (Peng 2012). While in 2002 a clear majority (close to 71 percent) of respondents thought that sons and daughters should support their ageing parents financially, a much smaller percentage (nearly 41 percent) expressed such a view in 2008; similar changes were evident with regard to children's duties in caring for their elderly parents. Interestingly, women were consistently less likely than men to agree with the statement that elderly parents should be supported by the family and more likely to agree that they should be supported by family, government, and community (Peng 2012).

Over the past decade or so the Japanese and Korean governments have put in place parental leave, publicly subsidized childcare programs, and universal long-term care insurance schemes to support families in providing care for the young and the old and to encourage women to have more children (Abe 2010; Peng 2012). These are widely seen as necessary measures to reverse the tide of falling fertility rates and rapid population aging that threaten the solvency of pension systems and social insurance programs as well as the long-term prospects of economic prosperity and growth (especially since immigration is neither an obvious nor a popular option).

The Japanese long-term care insurance system, which has been in place for a longer period, seems to have reduced somewhat the burden of care carried by family carers, especially women (Abe 2010). Fertility rates, however, remain stubbornly low (in both Japan and Korea) and may require more fundamental changes both in families as well as in employment practices. In the case of Korea, for example, as Peng (2012) shows, the increased parental leave take-up masks the fact that the total take-up rate still represents less than 5 percent of eligible mothers and less than 1 percent of eligible fathers. The main reason for the low take-up is persistent workplace discrimination against workers who take the leave, by both employers and workers themselves who see these paid leaves as a net burden and profit loss. What this suggests is that institutional and social norms take a much longer time to change, especially when the government is not able to withstand pressure from employers. Noncompliance to gender equality legislations and social care policies may very well frustrate the desired outcomes that these reforms are trying to achieve.

FAMILY POLICIES: SUBSTITUTING FOR MEN?

States support families and children in a multitude of ways, including maternity and parental leaves and child-care benefits, cash transfers or tax exemptions, and child-care and elderly care services, to name a few. While family allowances vary widely, a common characteristic is that they "defray only a small percentage of the cost of children, and fail to protect women adequately from the increased risk of poverty that motherhood imposes" (Folbre 1994, 122–123). Moreover, while concern for the well-being of families and children is often the stated aim of these provisions, what states do and the conditions on which benefits are made available carry other implicit objectives and consequences, supporting particular types of families.

Public spending on family policy in the advanced industrialized countries has increased in recent years, but there are still significant variations
across countries. The Nordic countries and France, sometimes referred to as
caring states, tend to allocate a relatively higher percentage of gross domestic
product (more than 3 percent) to family policy and have placed the accent
on the provision of care services and generous parental leaves (the latter in
the Nordic countries). By contrast, the United States, Canada, and Southern
European countries tend to spend relatively low amounts (1.3 percent in the
United States, 1.2 in Spain, and 1.1 in Canada) and have been called *noncaring
states* (see UNRISD 2010).

While family policies have historically been associated with the advanced
industrialized countries (sometime motivated by pronatalism), in recent years
they seem to have proliferated across a much more diverse rage of countries.
The recent policy interest in human capital, child poverty, and the shift to the
social investment state seem to have given child-centered programs renewed
impetus and force (Jenson 2010). Public policy attention to children may also
reflect the recognition by states of the demise of the male breadwinning role,
either because fathers are absent or unable to support their families due to
unemployment and low earnings. For example, a new generation of social
assistance programs, known as conditional cash transfer (CCT) schemes, are
specifically targeted to poor women in their capacity as mothers and household managers and made conditional on compliance with certain requirements
linked to children's well-being (such as regular health checks).

CCT schemes represent one thrust of recent policy efforts aimed at children but are not the only one. Middle-income developing countries such as
Argentina, Chile, Mexico, South Africa, and Uruguay have also been experimenting with a range of care-related social policies, including early childhood
education and care services. All of these countries are also characterized by
high levels of income and ethnic inequality. The challenge they face therefore
is not only to expand service coverage but also to do so in a way that reduces
class and regional inequalities in the quality of service accessed by children
from different socioeconomic groups. This becomes a formidable challenge
when a mix of public and private provision is used.

In fact a distinct pattern that seems to be emerging is that different kinds
of public services are being targeted to children from different socioeconomic
backgrounds. Since low-income families cannot afford private childcare, they
face long waiting lists for public crèches that are few and far between and often
rely on less professionalized community services or on the unpaid care provided
by family members (Faur 2008; Staab and Gerhard 2010). In such contexts economic inequalities tend to spill over into care inequalities, and different care
modalities in turn feed into growing income inequalities, creating what Joan
Tronto (2006, 14) calls "vicious circles of unequal care."

Moreover, supporting families is not only about building crèches and providing family allowances—although that is clearly an important part of what

is needed. It is equally, if not more, urgent to create the broader economic and social conditions that facilitate family life and caregiving. Contexts where those who are lucky to find paid work have to put in extremely long hours for a wage that can barely meet their own basic needs and that of their dependents, while many others cannot find work and face insecurity, unemployment, and loss of hope and self-respect, are not going to be conducive for parenting and caregiving. "The provision of care and discipline for children," as Elson (1998, 16) points out, "is an exacting task, and the cultivation in children of a sense of ethics and of citizenship, and an ability and desire to communicate with others, is not easily undertaken by adults who themselves feel they have been denied social justice and excluded from normal society, their aspirations to a decent job and a decent house dashed."

CONCLUDING REMARKS

What is called *economic* development is ultimately dependent on the social processes that contribute to the production and maintenance of people and communities on a daily and generational basis. Mainstream political economy has paid considerable attention to the economic and political processes of the macroeconomy while it has taken domestic institutions and their unpaid contributions to social reproduction for granted. Yet factoring in the institutions and relations of the domestic sphere is far from straightforward, for it requires the recognition of their diversity across time and place, the inequalities and conflicts that they often embody, and the ideological and symbolic systems with which they are imbued. Blood or biological relations represent one possible type of kinship on the basis of which families can form. But families can also be chosen, based on ties of friendship and community rather than those of blood. Moreover, the family is neither an isolated institution nor an autonomous one: domestic units, whatever their composition and form, are rooted in social networks that provide support and solidarity as well as being connected to the wider political economy through the flow of goods, services, and values. All of this speaks against the romanticization of the family as an autonomous sphere characterized by cooperation and sharing. Nor is the problem simply one of adjusting gender roles and enhancing partnership within the family, understood very narrowly as a privatized heterosexual couple in a static nuclear unit.

The snapshots of family change across diverse regional contexts in the second part of this chapter illustrate both the themes of diversity and change as well as continuity. As the evidence from both Southern Africa and advanced industrialized countries underlined, it is not helpful to blame families, and poor women in particular who often end up providing for their children's needs, when the broader socioeconomic structures make it difficult for them to care and provision their dependents. The East Asian scenario further suggests that it is equally important for policy frameworks to adapt to real changes in society, gender relations, and ideas and ideals about how people want to live their lives rather than clinging to a traditional model of the family that may have worked only partially even in the past. Family policies, moreover, should not be just about providing parental leaves and meager child allowances. It is equally, if not more, important to create the economic and social conditions that facilitate the democratization of family life and caregiving.

NOTES

1. The literature on this theme is truly extensive; Nancy Folbre's (1986) "Hearts and Spades" remains a classic of this genre.
2. Within neoclassical economics one strand of work that recognized the intrahousehold sphere was the New Household Economics (NHE) pioneered by Gary Becker (1981). NHE, however, had serious limitations stemming from its rational choice assumptions and its methodological individualism.
3. Commodification takes place when economic value is assigned to something not previously considered in economic terms. It refers to the expansion of market trade to previously nonmarket areas and to the treatment of things as if they were a tradable commodity. Decommodification, by contrast, is conceived as "any political, social, or cultural process that reduces the scope and influence of the market in everyday life" (Vail 2010, 310).
4. The percentage of women who were in the labor force rose sharply from 28 percent in 1940 to 38 percent in 1960 and reached 60 percent in 2000 (Gornick and Meyers 2003).

REFERENCES

Abe, Aya. 2010. "The changing shape of the care diamond: The case of child and elderly care in Japan." Gender and Development Programme Paper No. 9, Geneva, UNRISD.

Amin, Samir. 1972. "Underdevelopment and dependence in Black Africa—origins and contemporary forms." *Journal of Modern African Studies* 10(4): 503–524.

Bakker, Isabella. 2003. "Neoliberal governance and the reprivatization of social reproduction: Social provisioning and shifting gender orders." In Isabella Bakker and Stephen Gill, eds., *Power, production and social reproduction*. Basingstoke, UK: Palgrave Macmillan, 66–82.

Becker, Gary S. 1981. *A treatise on the family*. Cambridge, MA: Harvard University Press.

Bedford, Kate. 2007. "The imperative of male inclusion: How institutional context influences World Bank gender policy." *International Feminist Journal of Politics* 9(3): 289–311.

Bender, Donald R. 1967. "A refinement of the concept of household: Families, co-residence, and domestic functions." *American Anthropologist* 69: 493–504.

Bezanson, Kate, and Meg Luxton. 2006. "Social reproduction and feminist political economy." In Kate Bezanson and Meg Luxton, eds., *Social Reproduction: Feminist political economy challenges neoliberalism.* Montreal: McGill-Queen's University Press, 3–10.

Biblarz, Timothy, and Evren Savci. 2010. "Lesbian, gay, bisexual, and transgender families." *Journal of Marriage and Family* 72: 480–497.

Boserup, Esther. 1970. *Women's role in economic development.* New York: St. Martin's Press.

Budlender, Debbie, and Francie Lund. 2011. "South Africa: A legacy of family disruption." *Development and Change* 42(4): 925–946.

Chant, Sylvia. 2010. "Towards a (re)conceptualization of the 'feminization of poverty': Reflections on gender-differentiated poverty from The Gambia, Philippines and Costa Rica." In Sylvia Chant, ed., *The international handbook of gender and poverty: Concepts, research, policy.* Northampton: Edward Elgar Publishing Limited, 111–116.

Ehrenreich, Barbara, and Arlie Russell Hochschild (Eds.). 2003. *Global woman: Nannies, maids and sex workers in the new global economy.* London: Granta Books.

Elson, Diane. 1998. "The economic, the political and the domestic: Businesses, states, and households in the organisation of production." *New Political Economy* 3(2): 189–208.

Engels, Frederick. 1972. *The origin of the family, private property and the state.* New York: International Publishers.

Esping-Andersen, Gøsta. 2009. *The incomplete revolution: Adapting to women's new roles.* Cambridge, UK: Polity Press.

Faur, Eleonor. 2008. "The 'care diamond': Social policy regime, care policies and programmes in Argentina." Gender and Development, "The Social and Political Economy of Care," Research Paper 3. Geneva: UNRISD. Available athttp://www.unrisd.org/unrisd/website/document.nsf/%28httpPublications%29/695F3B781B8EA4 14C125753700562C23?OpenDocument.

Faur, Eleonor. 2011. "A widening gap? The political and social organization of childcare in Argentina", *Development and Change* 42(4): 967–994.

Folbre, Nancy. 1994. *Who pays for the kids? Gender and the structures of constraint.* London: Routledge.

Folbre, Nancy. 1986. "Hearts and spades: Paradigms of household economics." *World Development* 14(2): 245–255.

Giddens, Anthony. 1992. *The transformation of intimacy: Sexuality, love and eroticism in modern societies.* Cambridge, UK: Polity Press.

Goody, Jack. 1972. "The evolution of the family." In Peter Laslett, ed., *Household and family in past time.* London: Cambridge University Press, 103–124.

Gornick, Janet C., and Marcia K. Meyers. 2003. *Families that work: Policies for reconciling parenthood and employment.* New York: Russell Sage Foundation.

Harder, Lois. 2009. "The state and the friendships of the nation: The case of nonconjugal relationships in the United States and Canada." *Signs* 34(3): 633–658.

Hartmann, Heidi. 1979. "The unhappy marriage of Marxism and feminism: Towards a more progressive union." *Capital and Class* 3(2): 1–33.

Jelin, Elizabeth, and Ana Rita Diaz-Munoz. 2003. *Major trends affecting families: South America in perspective.* Report prepared for United Nations Department of Economic and Social Affairs, Division for Social Policy and Development, Programme on the Family, New York.

Jenson, Jane. 2010. "Diffusing ideas for after neoliberalism: The social investment perspective in Europe and Latin America." *Global Social Policy* 10(1): 59–84.

Jones, Gavin. 2005. "The 'flight from marriage' in South-East and East Asia." *Journal of Comparative Family Studies* 36(1): 93–119.

Kabeer, Naila. 1996. *Gender, demographic transition and the economics of family size.* Occasional paper for Beijing No. 7. Geneva: UNRISD.

Kabeer, Naila. 2007. "Marriage, motherhood and masculinity in the global economy: Reconfigurations of personal and economic life." Working Paper No. 290, Sussex, Institute of Development Studies.

Kandiyoti, Deniz. 1988. "Bargaining with patriarchy." *Gender and Society* 2(3): 274–290.

Lewis, Jane. 2006. "Introduction: Children in the context of changing families and welfare states." In Jane Lewis, ed., *Children, changing families and welfare states.* Cheltenham, UK: Edward Elgar Publishing, 1–24.

Mackintosh, Maureen. 1977. "Reproduction and patriarchy: A critique of Claude Meillassoux, 'Femmes, Greniers et Capitaux.'" *Capital and Class* 1(2): 119–127.

McDonald, Peter. 2000. "Gender equity in theories of fertility transition." *Population and Development Review* 26(3): 427–439.

Mhongo, Christine, and Debbie Budlender. Forthcoming. *The declining rates of marriage in South Africa: What do the numbers and analysts tell us?* http://www.lrg.uct.ac.za/publications/other/

Molyneux, Maxine. 1979. "Beyond the domestic labour debate." *New Left Review* 1(116): 3–27.

Moore, Henrietta. 1994. *Is there a crisis in the family?* Occasional Paper No.3 World Summit for Social Development. Geneva: UNRISD.

Niehaus, Isak A. 1994. "Disharmonious spouses and harmonious siblings. Conceptualising household formation among urban residents in QwaQwa." *African Studies* 53(1): 115–135.

O'Laughlin, Bridget. 1998. "Missing men? The debate over rural poverty and women-headed households in Southern Africa." *Journal of Peasant Studies* 25(2): 1–48.

O'Laughlin, Bridget. 2007. "A bigger piece of a very small pie: Intrahousehold resource allocation and poverty reduction in Africa." *Development and Change* 38(1): 21–44.

Oppenheimer, Valerie K. (1997). "Women's employment and the gain to marriage: The specialization and trading model." *Annual Review of Sociology* 23: 431–453.

Padilla, Mark B., Jennifer S. Hirsch, Miguel Munoz-Laboy, Robert E. Sember, and Richard G. Parker. "Introduction: Love and globalization: Cross-cultural reflections on an intimate intersection." In Mark B. Padilla, Jennifer S. Hirsch, Miguel Munoz-Laboy, Robert E. Sember, and Richard G. Parker, eds., *Love and globalization: Transformation of intimacy in the contemporary world*, ix–xxx Nashville: Vanderbilt University Press.

Parrenas, Rachel Salazar. 2003. "The care crisis in the Philippines: Children and transnational families in the new global economy." In Barbara Ehrenreich and Arlie Russell Hochschild, eds., *Global woman: Nannies, maids and sex workers in the new global economy*, 39–54. London: Granta Books.

Pearson, Ruth, Anne Whitehead and Kate Young. 1981."Introduction: The continuing subordination of women in the development process." In Kate Young, Carol Wolkowitz, and Roslyn McCullagh, eds., *Of marriage and the market*, ix–xix. London: CSE Books.

Peng, Ito. 2012. "The boss, the worker, his wife and no babies: South Korean political and social economy of care in a context of institutional rigidities." In Shahra Razavi and Silke Staab, eds., *Global variations in the political and social economy of care: Worlds apart*, 80–100. New York: Routledge.

Pine, Frances. 2002. "Family." In Alan Barnard and Jonathan Spencer, eds., *Encyclopedia of social and cultural anthropology*, 339–346. New York: Routledge.

Quah, Stella R. 1998. *Family in Singapore: A sociological perspective*, Singapore: Times Academic Press.

Rapp, Rayna. 1991. "Family and class in contemporary America: Notes towards an understanding of ideology." In Elizabeth Jelin, ed., *Family, household and gender relations in Latin America*, 180–196. London: Kegan Paul International/UNESCO.

Retherford, Robert D., Naohiro Ogawa, and Rikiya Matsukura. 2001. "Late marriage and less marriage in Japan." *Population and Development Review* 27(1): 65–102.

Roseneil, Sasha. 2004. "Why we should care about friends: An argument for queering the care imaginary in social policy." *Social Policy and Society* 3(4): 409–419.

Salaff, Janet. 1976. "The status of unmarried Hong Kong Women and the social factors contributing to their delayed marriage." *Population Studies* 30(3): 391–412.

Sobotka, Tomas. 2008. "Overview chapter 6: The diverse faces of the second demographic transition in Europe." *Demographic Research* 19: 171–224. Available at http://www.demographic-research.org.

Sobotka, Tomas, and Laurent Toulemon. 2008. "Overview chapter 4. Changing family and partnership behaviour: Common trends and persistent diversity across Europe." *Demographic Research* 19: 85–138.Available at http://www.demographic-research.org.

Staab, Silke, and Roberto Gerhard. 2010. *Childcare service expansion in Chile and Mexico: For women or children or both?* GD Programme Paper No.10. Geneva: UNRISD.

Therborn, Göran. 2004. *Between sex and power: Family in the world, 1900–2000*. London: Routledge.

Tronto, Joan. 2006. "Vicious circles of unequal care." In M. Hamington and D. C. Miller, *Socializing care*, 3–25. Lanham, MD: Rowman & Littlefield Publishers, Inc.

UNRISD. 2010. *Combating poverty and inequality*. Geneva: Author.

Vail, John. 2010. "Decommodification and egalitarian political economy." *Politics and Society* 38(3): 310–346.

Van der Ploeg, Jan Douwe. 2010. "The peasantries of the twenty-first century: The commoditization debate revisited." *Journal of Peasant Studies* 37(1): 1–30.

Weston, Kath. 1991. *Families we choose: Lesbians gays kinship*. New York: Columbia University Press.

Whitehead, Anne. 1981. "'I'm hungry mum': The politics of domestic budgeting." In Kate Young, Carol Wolkowitz, and Roslyn McCullagh, eds., *Of marriage and the market*, 91–116. London: CSE Books.

Whitehead, Anne. 1990. "Rural women and food production in sub-Saharan Africa." In Jean Dreze and Amartya Sen, eds., *The political economy of hunger. Volume I: Entitlement and well-being*, 425–473. Oxford: Clarendon Press.

CHAPTER 12

GENDER, CARE, AND WELFARE

DIANE SAINSBURY

CARE is a highly gendered and contested concept. Contrary to many concepts that have implicitly assumed the male as norm, care has been a woman-centered concept. The importance of care to women has made it a major concern of feminist thinking. Its significance has been heightened because of the embedded nature of care in the gender division of labor in the family and society. Accordingly, care has been central to the feminist project of ending women's subordination and achieving gender equality. Furthermore, feminist scholars have theorized care, developing the concept of care and advancing care and the care economy as fields of academic research. Equally important, they have used this theorizing to challenge gender-blind research on the welfare state and the economy. In rethinking care, feminists have enlarged its relevance, converting care from an invisible activity within the home into a foundation of society and wider welfare.

This enterprise has involved much controversy. Many feminists have argued that reproductive labor, unpaid care work, and the ideology of domesticity are at the heart of women's oppression, while other feminists have emphasized the value of care and its significance to individuals, families, and societies—that caring involves ethical commitment and agency. These two perspectives have informed the gendering of welfare policies, but the perspectives have generated divisions concerning priorities and strategies among women. How care has intersected with gender, class, race, and ethnicity has also led to contestation. National contexts have further influenced conceptions of care and what is politically desirable and possible, creating additional differences.

Despite divisions, care has been a focus of women's mobilization and their engagement in welfare state politics. By putting care issues on the agenda, women contributed to setting in motion a gradual process of welfare state change that has consisted of greater state involvement in the provision of care on all levels. Historically, engagement in care issues was a vital facet of women's entering the public sphere, and the politics of care have continued to be a source of women's activism and controversy among them. Currently care issues and research on care engage women across nations and globally.

This chapter begins by defining care, discussing conceptions of care and the concept of care. The second part of the chapter deals with the care dimension of welfare states and the variety of policy responses. The third part examines explanations of the policy responses, concentrating on gender relations, the economics of care, and the politics of care. The final section of the chapter moves beyond nation states to examine care across borders, specifically looking at the European Union (EU), international organizations, and global migration. The focus of my discussion is primarily the industrialized countries with established welfare states. It is in these countries that feminist theorizing initially gendered the analysis of welfare states, and a major facet of this endeavor was to underline the importance of care and its consequences.

CONCEPTIONS OF CARE AND
THE CONCEPT OF CARE

Vying conceptions underpin the theorization of care, and major differences are reflected in definitions of care, what activities are included in care, and the implications of care for the feminist project. Two broad approaches to defining care are represented in the literature (Duffy 2005). One approach emphasizes the interpersonal nature of care, conceiving of caring as a process involving the carerand the person cared for. In an influential discussion, Berenice Fisher and Joan Tronto (1990) break the process down into four phases: (1) *caring about* (recognizing that there is a need for care); (2) *caring for* (assuming responsibility for meeting the need); (3) *caregiving* (the actual process and work of caring); and (4) *care receiving* (the interaction between carers and those receiving care). For each phase they identify a value, and the values are attentiveness, responsibility, competence, and responsiveness. These values primarily have to do with the caregiver, while other definitions put more emphasis on the recipients of care (Folbre 2006), noting that care develops the capacities of the recipients.

The second approach is rooted in the notion of social reproduction, defined as "the array of activities and relationships involved in maintaining people on a daily basis and intergenerationally" (Glenn 1992, 1) (for further discussion of this concept see chapters by Rai and Razavi in this volume). Importantly, this conceptualization includes domestic chores, such as cleaning and food preparation, and it provides a better handle for bringing class, race and ethnicity into the analysis of care. Historically, the division of domestic work among women involved class. Working-class women had no choice but to engage in paid work, frequently as household help in middle- or upper-class families. In multiracial societies, class has often intersected with race and ethnicity (Glenn 1992; Hondagneu-Sotelo 2000). As pointed out by Mignon Duffy (2005), defining care as nurturant or face-to-face services excludes very low-paid workers, obfuscating class and racial hierarchies of gendered care activities.

An additional dividing line among feminists has concerned the elevation of care versus its potential to reinforce the traditional division of labor between women and men in the family and society. Feminists have also been divided over strategies involving care, that is, to upgrade care or to redistribute caring tasks among women and men. Although both strategies seek to promote gender equality, there is a tension between the two. Public measures that support care to improve the position of carers run the risk of strengthening women's role as primary caregiver and thus counteracting a redistribution of care among the sexes. Just as important, measures supporting care can also inhibit women's entry into the labor market, and many feminists view women's access to paid employment as their chief route to financial independence.

Feminist theorizing has stressed the moral dimension of care and care as analytical concept, and both have relevance for the analysis of welfare and welfare policies. The moral discussion of care has centered on notions of moral responsibility and obligation, and it highlights interdependence and relationality. A major point is that the relational nature of care underlines that all human beings require care at times during the life course and that care is necessary for the sustenance of all societies and the general welfare. Thus, in defining the good society, the values of caring need to be taken seriously. In Tronto's (1993, 2–3) view, this involves the values of responsibility, nurturance, compassion, and meeting others' needs (see also Glenn 2000).

Care theorists have also reenvisioned citizenship, concentrating on the rights dimension of citizenship (see also the chapter by Siim in this volume). In redefining citizenship, they have stressed two aspects of the gendered nature of rights. The first is the contradiction between care, which involves dependency and interdependency, and the liberal notion of citizenship that independence and autonomy are preconditions for exercising rights. Feminists have challenged the idea of independent and autonomous human beings, pointing out that all humans are dependent upon care. The second aspect of gendered rights is the prominence of paid work as the basis of social rights. Feminists have refashioned the social rights of citizenship, emphasizing that they include the right to receive care, the right to give care, and the right to not give care. With more far-reaching consequences, they have argued that care should be the basis of social rights and entitlements. The latter in turn calls for conceiving of welfare states as caring states (Knijn and Kremer 1997; Lister 1997; Meyer 2000; Kittay 2001; Tronto 2001; Kremer 2007; Lister et al. 2007).

CARE AS AN ANALYTICAL CONCEPT AND THE CARE DIMENSION OF WELFARE STATES

The construction of care as an analytical concept is a major academic achievement of feminist theorists and scholars (Daly and Lewis 1998; Leira and Saraceno 2002; England 2005), and an important facet of gendering the analysis of welfare states and social policies has been the development of care as an analytical concept.

The first efforts to bring care into the comparative analysis of welfare grew out of a critique of the standard analytical frameworks that focused on male production workers (e.g., Esping-Andersen 1990). Feminist scholars criticized the frameworks on two counts. First, women only entered the analysis as paid workers. Second, the lack of attention to unpaid work and care not only resulted in the exclusion of women from much of the analysis, it also obscured the gendered differentiation in women's and men's social entitlements (Langan and Ostner 1991; Lewis 1992). The critique focused on the nexus between care as unpaid work, paid work and welfare and its gendered consequences. A drawback of this critique was that it equated care with unpaid work. As emphasized by Jane Jenson (1997), care involves much more than unpaid domestic work. Equating care with unpaid work also made it difficult, if not impossible, to detect the transformation of welfare states through provision of care services and care-related cash transfers.

To rectify the weaknesses of mainstream frameworks, feminist scholars began to specify gender relevant dimensions of variation of welfare state policies. Although not limited to care, these dimensions highlighted care in a variety of ways. The most important aspects related to care were gender and familial ideologies, the inclusion of the private/domestic sphere, rethinking the bases of entitlement, considering the degree that caring work was paid or unpaid, and the public provision of care (Langan and Ostner 1991; Lewis 1992; Orloff 1993; Sainsbury 1994a, 1996; O'Connor 1996).

More specifically, mainstream frameworks had focused on ideologies of redistribution and state intervention in shaping welfare policies. By contrast, feminists pointed to the importance of gender ideologies prescribing the tasks, obligations, and rights of the two sexes, and care has been among the tasks and obligations. Likewise, feminist proposals to incorporate the private–domestic sphere into the analysis made caring activities a major component. In rethinking the bases of entitlement that underpinned mainstream scholarship—need,

work performance, and citizenship—feminists added the principle of maintenance (the obligation to provide for one's family), dependent status within the
family, motherhood, and the principle of care. The principle of maintenance
generally has enhanced the social rights of the family provider and indirectly
also affected the rights of family members, including those of married women
whose rights derived from her husband's. By contrast, rights based on motherhood and caring responsibilities, embodying the principle of care, have usually
been direct rights, which have strengthened women's social rights. (Exceptions
have been maternity benefits and child allowances based on the father's work
record in social insurance schemes.) Mainstream welfare state analysis emphasized work-related benefits, whereas feminist scholars insisted on including
care-related benefits. The focus on care-related benefits also drew attention to
the state paying for care work in the home as a dimension of variation across
welfare states. A final dimension of variation, identified by feminist scholars,
was public provision of care services both in terms of the scope and the types
of services provided.

Subsequent theorizing emphasized the centrality of care for analyzing welfare states. Feminist scholars devised care regimes; they specified the prereq-
uisites for analyzing the care dimension of welfare states, recast the purpose
of welfare state policies, and constructed new frameworks. The formulation of
care regimes or caring regimes was seen as a corrective to the earlier emphasis
on the male breadwinner model of social policy, which conceived of married
women's social rights on the basis of their status as dependents in the family
and that their rights were derived from their husband's rights. This conceptualization obscured rights based on the principle of care and the provision of care
for dependents—children and the frail elderly, which are important dimensions
of caring regimes. Other crucial dimensions were how unpaid work is valued
and how care is shared among women and men (Lewis 1997, 169–173). Trudie
Knijn and Monique Kremer (1997) emphasize the right to care, to receive care,
and not to care as the foundation of caring regimes.

In attempting to clarify the types of social policies required to analyze
the care dimension of welfare states, Mary Daly (2001; Daly and Rake 2003,
50–51) presented a fourfold model of policies: (1) *monetary benefits* for providing care, which include care allowances, care credits in public pension schemes,
and tax benefits; (2) *employment-related measures* to enable caring, such as paid
or unpaid leave, flexible working hours, reduced working hours, and severance
pay; (3) *services in kind*, for example, child-care places, home helps or Meals on
Wheels, and places in residential care; and (4) *public incentives* for provision
of nonstate care, exemplified by subsidies for private care, exemption of social
security contributions (taxes), or tax reductions for employing domestic help.

Policy analysts have also stressed the need to rethink the welfare state in
terms of its central purposes, arguing that access to care was equally as important as protection against unemployment (Jenson 1997; Jenson and Sineau 2001).
According to Jane Jenson, this reorientation would entail an analysis of "the

gender division of labor among caregivers, gender differences in the capacity or need to pay, and the gender consequences of different institutionalized arrangements for provision" (Jenson, 187).

Perhaps the most elaborate framework centering on care is that presented by Mary Daly and Jane Lewis (2000, see also 1998). They formulate a framework of analysis based on social care, as distinguished from care or caring. Social care is a wider notion of the societal division of care than care or caring, which has focused on the relationships of the caregivers and the persons receiving care. Importantly, social care incorporates macrolevel relations and systemic properties. Among the merits of their framework is that it links care to the political economy of the welfare state; it includes both the micro- and macrolevel and thus bridges the private and public spheres. At the macrolevel the framework interrogates the division of care labor, responsibilities, and costs between the family, market, and the state and the voluntary–community sector and how these vary across welfare states. They also note that the core idea approximates the concept of the welfare mix. In examining state provision they emphasize both cash benefits and care services. An additional advantage of the framework is its potential for analyzing welfare state change and restructuring. The framework can be used to examine shifts in the public–private mixes of care provision over time.

In sum, Daly and Lewis's (2000) ambitious framework seeks to capture and consolidate the varieties of caring activities and their relationships to the family, state, market, and the voluntary–community sector. A problematic feature of the framework, however, is its exclusive focus on care, which only indirectly addresses the importance of women's paid employment in altering gender relations and women's welfare entitlements. In this respect the framework is incomplete in analyzing the gender dimension of welfare states (Daly and Rake 2003).

Comparative Research on the Care Dimension

Components of the framework, most notably the notion of the welfare mix and changes in public–private mixes of care provision, have been used in the comparative analysis of established welfare states during the past decade. The changing nature of public–private mixes of care during welfare state restructuring has been a major focus of comparative research on the European countries (Lewis 1998; Da Roit, Bihan, and Österle 2007; Morel 2007) and other industrial countries (O'Connor, Orloff, and Shaver 1999; Michel and Mahon 2002).

Comparative research on the care dimension of welfare states focusing on childcare has proliferated in Europe during the past decade. This probably reflects the refashioning of family policies as family–work policies, the high priority among decision makers to increase women's labor market participation, along with a concern about low birthrates in some countries, and the feminist agenda to transform the gender division of labor in the family. The growth of maternal employment in many countries necessitates policies to care for the children of working mothers.

The rise of family–work policies has also entailed a broader definition of childcare policies that includes care services, parental leaves, and allowances or tax credits for care of the child at home. The major studies represent different slants, focusing on child-care services in postindustrial societies across the world (Michel and Mahon 2002), *care arrangements* in European countries (Pfau-Effinger 2005), and child-care policy packages in similar countries such as the Scandinavian countries (Ellingsaeter and Leira 2006) or in European countries representing different types of welfare states or gender policy models (Kremer 2007; Lewis 2009). Finally, Mary Daly (2010) revisits the interrelationships between the family, state, and market to analyze change in child-care policies since the mid 1990s in Australia, France, Germany, Sweden, the United Kingdom, and the United States. Many of the studies share two common denominators: they seek to chart the development of policies in different countries and to understand the implications of the policies for gender relations.

Policies for the care of the elderly have been less in the limelight, but they too have become a major concern of decision makers in countries with aging populations. Feminist research has centered on two trends and their implications for gender relations and women: the shift to home care; and the *commodification* of care (understood as payments for care or marketization, for-profit care services provided by the market). These trends represent efforts to contain costs, but simultaneously legislation has provided new entitlements, such as long-term care insurance and care allowances for persons requiring care and for those providing care. These new entitlements have spurred the development of care markets and the growth of care providers and employees.

The design of Ungerson and Yeandle's (2007) study of cash-for-care schemes for the elderly in Europe and the United States centers on two dimensions of variation: (1) regulation of care delivery and care work, and (2) care by family members or by the labor market. The study explores the impact of these elements in the cash-for-care schemes on care relationships and the situation of the carer in terms of working conditions and social protection. It concludes there is a dualization in the working conditions of carers who are unskilled or accredited. A parallel cross-national project has examined the dynamics between care regimes and national employment models in creating and shaping the care labor market (Simonazzi 2009). Both studies point to the importance of the division of responsibilities for the care of elderly people between the family, state, and market and the degree of regulation.

Thus, contrary to the goal of Daly and Lewis's framework (2000) to overcome the fragmentation in the analysis of care, a division in cross-national care studies has continued. Most studies have focused on either childcare or care of the elderly, which largely reflects a trend toward specialization in welfare state research that has concentrated on individual policies (Castles et al. 2010, 333–508). Child-care research has predominated compared with care for the elderly, but some studies have combined childcare and elder care (Dahl and Eriksen 2005; Morel 2007; Pfau-Effinger and Rostgaard 2011). A bridge between the two has been the importance of the labor market (Morgan 2005; Ungerson and Yeandle 2007; Simonazzi 2009).

Increasingly, feminists have analyzed the public–private mixes of care provision in emergent welfare states and the developing countries, and the most ambitious cross-country research has been spearheaded by the United Nations Research Institute on Social Development (UNRISD), especially its project The Political and Social Economy of Care in a Development Context. The analytical framework of the project highlights the public–private mixes of care presented as the care diamond—provision by the family, state, market, and community (Pijl 1994, 4; Peng 2005, 2008; Razavi 2007; Ochiai 2009; ILR 2010). The project has assigned equal importance to the care of children, the sick, and the elderly, and its definition of care work includes cleaning and preparing meals, arguing that these activities are preconditions for personal caregiving. It has surveyed the policy responses of established welfare states to glean useful lessons for latecomers in the area of care policies. Simultaneously, the project has the potential to reveal ethnocentric assumptions when they are applied to a broader range of countries, as witnessed in Budig and Misra's (2010) study on the effect of care employment on earnings.

Asian feminist scholars have also used the notion of the welfare mix and the care diamond to analyze the similarities and differences in the care regimes in South Korea, China, Taiwan, Thailand, Singapore, and Japan (Ochiai and Molony 2008; Ochiai 2009). Although the most prevalent mix combines a large role for family and relatives with a large market sector, important variations exist, and they caution against viewing these countries as representing the same type of care regime.

Outcomes of Care Policies

Another development has been to theorize and empirically analyze the outcomes of care policies. A very influential theoretical contribution here is Nancy Fraser's (1994) gender equity models. She presents three ideal models, in which care arrangements are a key feature, and outlines the pros and cons of each model in achieving gender equity. The first is the universal breadwinner model where women and men enjoy equal status as earners. Universal public provision or measures to promote universal provision of care services for children and the elderly are crucial. The second is the caregiver parity model that aims at equalizing the rewards and deservingness of the role of carer and the role of earner, and policies concentrate on upgrading informal and unpaid care. In the third, the universal caregiving model or carer–earner model, the goal is to enable both women and men to combine caring and earning so that they are equally shared. In terms of care policies, this involves universal provision of services and measures to subsidize informal care targeted to both sexes.

Fraser's (1994) models have informed the construction of analytical frameworks and further efforts to develop criteria for assessing care policy outcomes

(Gornick, Meyers, and Wright 2009). Her models have underpinned the construction of care regimes in analyzing the situation of single mothers (Lewis with Hobson 1997) and later child-care regimes (Lister et al. 2007). The models have also served as the basis for a general evaluation of policies and strategies to achieve gender equality (Sainsbury 1999).

In evaluating a series of care policies, such as cash payments to the carer and to the cared-for person, leave, employment measures, incentives for market-based care, Daly (2001) expands the criteria for assessing policies. Besides gender equity, her scheme includes choice, quality of care, validating care, creation of a welfare mix, and cost considerations (51). In a similar vein, Lewis (2009) stresses agency and choice in the evaluation of care policies. Borrowing from Martha Nussbaum (1999, 39–47), who argues that human capabilities should be the goal of public policies, Lewis notes that real choice involves policies providing a wide range of options to minimize the constraints on choice (18–19).

The empirical evaluation of care policies has centered on outcomes that reconcile care and work and promote gender equality in caring responsibilities. Child-care services have been shown to increase maternal employment cross-nationally and in single country studies, while the evidence on the effects of leave policies is mixed, especially in the case of leaves of long duration. Leaves of short to moderate duration raise mothers' employment rates, increase the likelihood of returning to work, and reduce the maternal wage penalty, that is, the wage differential between mothers and nonmothers. Long leave schemes affect mothers' pay and possibilities of promotion, strengthen gender differentials in wages and earnings, but make exit from the labor market less likely (Gornick and Meyers 2003, 2009; Lewis 2009; Pfau-Effinger and Rostgaard 2011). Furthermore, it is necessary to distinguish between leave schemes and care allowances. Leave schemes usually offer some form of job protection, while care allowances remunerate caring for an infant or toddler without necessarily taking into account the carer's past or future attachment to the labor market. Turning to gender equality in caring, a recent study focused on the design of parental leave policies in twenty-one affluent countries to establish the extent that they encourage both women and men to engage in caregiving (Ray, Gornick, and Schmitt 2010). A limitation of these policy evaluation studies is that they have largely been confined the gender division of labor in the family.

EXPLAINING CARE POLICIES

Much feminist scholarship has assumed that gender relations and gender ideologies were a major explanation of policies and policy variations across welfare states. Feminist scholars sought to map out the dynamics between

gender relations and policies, that is, how gender relations and gender ideologies have shaped policies but also how policies either reinforced or could
alter gender relations (Sainsbury 1994b; Orloff 2010). A variation has been
to stress culture and family values as a determinant of policies but also as
a factor limiting the impact of policies on gender relations (Pfau-Effinger
2005; Kremer 2007). A drawback of this focus has been its lack of attention
to economic or political factors.

The Economics of Care

Feminist economists have criticized mainstream economics for its treatment of
care, which considers only paid care work and ignores unpaid care work and
its economic consequences. The failure to consider unpaid care work creates
problems in estimating economic growth as well as distortions in the costs of
care. As remedies, feminist economists have suggested new measures of care
and indices of gender differences related to care, and they have analyzed the
costs of care in terms of carers' foregone earnings, lower pay, and economic
and time poverty. The marginal position of care in mainstream economics has prompted feminist economists to propose studying the care economy
or the other economy, which is concerned with the direct production and
maintenance of human beings as an end in itself (Donath 2000; Folbre 2006;
Himmelweit 2007).

Socioeconomic developments have figured prominently as explanations
of welfare state change in the mainstream literature. Economic explanations, combined with sociodemographic change, have much relevance for care
policies. Feminists have called attention to the care crisis or the *care deficit*
(Hochschild 1995, 332; Daly 2001), the contraction in the supply of care and
the expansion in the need for care. The supply of care has shrunken as women
joined the work force. Welfare state retrenchment has further reduced the public provision of care in several countries. In the established welfare states the
demand for care has simultaneously increased on three fronts. The growth
of the aging population (both as a rising share of the population and greater
numbers of the very elderly aged 80+) has added to the demand for care provision. Senior citizens are large consumers of health care, and they often need
personal services. Second, the higher labor market participation rates of mothers have enlarged the demand of childcare. Third, an increased demand for
childcare has also resulted from shifts in family structure, especially the rise
of solo-mother families.

These processes are further linked as governments seek to reverse unfavorable dependency ratios, that is, the growth of the dependent (nonworking)
population in relation to the working population. Unfavorable dependency
ratios create an economic strain of welfare states since a declining share
of the population must finance an ever-increasing number of beneficiaries.

A solution has been to encourage women's labor market participation, which requires improving the availability of childcare. A final demographic challenge has been the falling birthrate in several countries. A long-term consequence is a further worsening of dependency ratios and labor shortages in these countries.

The growing demand for care, technological advances in medicine, and new welfare state commitments involving care, such as the introduction of long-term care insurance and better day-care provision, have accelerated the costs of care provision. Coping with higher expenditures for care has produced two somewhat contradictory trends. Ironically, the accelerating costs of public services have prompted the introduction of care-related benefits to compensate for care in the home since this is cheaper than institutional care. Welfare state restructuring has often entailed a privatization of the provision of care that has transferred more responsibilities to the family, the market, and the voluntary sector.

The established welfare states face similar economic challenges related to care, and cost containment of care has been a shared concern, yet how to achieve cost containment is clearly a matter of politics. This can be seen in the huge cross-national differences in public spending on services and care, which reflect dissimilar political priorities and goals.

The Politics of Care

Both historical and contemporary studies have emphasized gender relations as a crucial determinant of care policies, but explanatory frameworks have expanded to include the identities, goals, and motivations of key actors within and outside the state, policy coalitions, institutional arrangements, religion, and the partisan composition of governments. Many scholars have also wrestled with the issue of women's agency and their influence on care policies, often coming up with different answers.

In seeking to explain why national social insurance schemes for working men were delayed until the 1930s in the United States but benefits for mothers and children were adopted much earlier, Theda Skocpol (1992) constructs an encompassing framework involving four processes: (1) the transformation of state and party organizations; (2) the impact of political institutions on the identities, goals, and resources of groups seeking to influence policy; (3) the "fit" between group capacities and political institutions; and (4) the ways policies transform politics (41). In unlocking the puzzle, she highlights the differences between the labor movement and the women's movement in the fit between their organizing and political institutions. Unions were unevenly organized with regional strongholds, while women's organizations were mapped on to the federal structure of government, which enhanced their access to policy makers across the country and at various levels of

government. Rhetorically women's organizations gained leverage by emphasizing motherhood and domesticity.

Another strategy has been to refashion the power resources approach, which
has emphasized the partisan composition of government, working-class mobilization, and cross-class alliances (Korpi 1980; Esping-Andersen 1990). One variant
has been to reconceptualize power resources in terms of discursive and organizational resources and to explore their importance for the women's movement
in influencing policies (Hobson and Lindholm 1997). Julia S. O'Connor, Ann
Orloff, and Sheila Shaver's (1999) framework focuses on the strength of women'
movements and their strategies, particularly vis-à-vis the state; the existence
of counter movements, the relative strength of left, center, and right political
parties; the opportunity structure (mainly access to government policy makers and their receptivity to movement demands); and institutional context and
policy legacy. They find a split in policies supporting carers, with British and
Australian policies being more supportive than those of the United States and
Canada. Their analysis of movement demands shows priority to other demands
than care in the United States and Canada, such as equal rights, pay equity,
antidiscrimination legislation, and abortion on demand. A strength of their
framework is consideration of counter movements, but by focusing on gender
equality movements they pay less attention to feminist movements stressing
gender differences and wanting to upgrade care tasks to achieve parity between
the sexes. In discussing the women's movement in the United Kingdom, they
concentrate on the failed campaign for public childcare in the 1980s and 1990s
rather than on feminist endeavors to establish the deservingness of care.

In explaining the diversity of work–family policies, primarily child care,
parental leave, and work time arrangements in France, the Netherlands, Sweden,
and the United States, Kimberly J. Morgan (2006) emphasizes the interplay
between religion as a political force, gender and familial ideologies, the constellation of political parties and the nature of partisan competition, women's
movements, policy legacies, and social structural changes. Morgan concludes
that women's movements have had an important agenda setting effect but that
there was no clear effect of feminist organizing inside or outside political parties and the introduction of policies (19). Her conclusions are based on their
importance across all four cases.

A different comparative strategy is employed by Joya Misra (2003) in a
cross-national study of the adoption of child or family allowances in eighteen
industrialized welfare states. She examines the combination of certain factors
to establish *when* women's movements played a particularly important role.
The factors are state structures, left party strength, union strength, Catholic
party strength and the women's component of the left party. Her analysis
identifies several paths combining the factors with women influencing family allowance adoption during the post-WWII period in Australia, Finland,
Ireland, Denmark, Norway, Sweden, the United Kingdom, Germany, Italy, and

Australia but not in Canada or Switzerland—and not in France, Belgium, or the Netherlands during the interwar period. She concludes that both strong working-class movements and women's participation in left parties were necessary to family allowance adoption in countries without large Catholic populations.

Looking at cross-national research and case studies on women's movement politics and its influence on care policies in countries with established welfare states, we can make three observations. The first is variability in the role of women's movements, and the variability stems from movement factors—its goals, strategies, and discursive and organizational resources—institutional factors in a broad sense, and the strength of oppositional forces, including counter movements. As we saw already, not all women's movements have assigned priority to care policies. Access to the policy process is shaped by institutional factors affecting its openness. The receptivity of policy makers to movement demands is related to the policy preferences and strategic calculations of decision makers.

The second point is the importance of the movement's articulation of demands for care policies or agenda setting (Morgan 2006, 19). In several instances, women have presented new demands or innovative policy recommendations that have changed the terms of the debate and in some instances altered the universe of political discourse. However, it is not just getting the issue on the agenda; framing the issue is just as important. How an issue is framed contributes to leverage with decision makers and building alliances of support. Attention to agenda setting needs to be complemented by a consideration of alliance building, including cross-class, cross-gender, and cross-party alliances (Skocpol 1992; Hobson and Lindholm 1997).

Third, a problem in assessing women's influence results from of a preoccupation with movement politics that has caused analysts to overlook other sites and modes of influence. To illustrate, a major change in the German welfare state has been the expansion of the principle of care as a basis of entitlement in the pension system. In discussing the politics behind this change, the role of the women's movement and women's organizations in the main governing party has largely been dismissed despite the policy being in accord with their demands for upgrading care. Instead, rulings of the Constitution Court have been decisive in extending social rights based on care, but it was mothers who brought their case to the court. Women in the bureaucracy, or femocrats (Haussman and Sauer 2007), and increasingly women in parliament and the government have also exerted decisive influence. The politicization of care can spur women in a variety of sites to act. A growing body of research shows that the analysis of women's agency and policy influence should not be limited to movement politics but should also examine women's institutional presence (Bergqvist 2005; Anderson and Meyer 2006; Beyeler and Annesley 2010).

Care across Borders

Care has moved across borders in two respects. First, care policies have become transnational as they have come onto the agenda of the EU and intergovernmental organizations, such as the Organisation for Economic Co-operation and Development (OECD) and the United Nations. Women in elite positions and episteme communities, together with transnational movements and networks, have contributed to placing care issues on the international agenda. Second, global migration has altered care work, as women from developing countries move to fill domestic jobs in richer countries and this has widely different consequences for the transnational families of migrant care workers and the families paying care workers. In effect, global hierarchies of gender, class, and race and ethnicity have developed in addition to such hierarchies in national settings (Glenn 1992; Zimmerman, Litt, and Bose 2006).

Emerging Transnational Care Policies

The European Union represents an interesting case because it has the potential to develop transnational care policies that go beyond guidelines or recommendations. It also illuminates major obstacles in adopting such policies. In the EU the consideration of care issues has been influenced by its bias toward workers' rights and by the diversity of care policies of the member-states. The bias toward workers' rights is clearly manifested in the differential treatment of maternity and parental leave and child-care provision. The EU has issued directives on leave but has not been able to reach agreement on directives concerning childcare. The goals of the directives are binding on the member-states, but member-states have considerable leeway in interpretation and thus the actual content when translated or transposed into national legislation. The 1992 Pregnant Workers Directive required that working mothers be granted at least fourteen weeks of maternity leave, and the 1996 Parental Leave Directive required that all workers be granted an individual right to parental leave for at least three months. The directives provide a floor for the leave policies of the member-states, but the huge differences in their policies a decade and a half after the adoption of the directives illustrate the importance of national policy legacies. Childcare has mainly come onto the EU agenda as a facet of employment policy, and national policy legacies reflecting preferred gender relations have made agreement on child-care policies difficult. The 1992 recommendation on childcare had no binding effect, and childcare was broadly defined; it included child-care services, leave schemes for working parents, workplace measures to meet the needs of parents, and measures to encourage men's involvement in childcare. However, the 2002 Spanish presidency resulted in two EU child-care targets: (1) provision for 33 percent of children under three; and (2) for 90 percent of children between the age of three and school age. Still these are only targets, and the type of provision was not stipulated. The designation of targets came at a time when the EU assigned priority to policies reconciling work and care (Ostner and Lewis 1995; Hoskyns 1996; Hantrais 2000; Roth 2008; Lewis 2009; Kantola 2010).

To sum up, the dynamics shaping care politics in the EU involve factors pushing and preventing the adoption of care policies. Factors working for the adoption of care policies have been the goal of the EU that no member-state should have a competitive advantage or disadvantage because of its social policies, which called for a harmonization of policies. Additional factors have been EU employment goals and policies, along with the ascendancy of policies to reconcile family and work responsibilities, gender equality, and gender mainstreaming. Factors militating against the adoption of care policies have been the marginalized position of care in the EU project, the Commission's reluctance to intervene in family policies, which were long left to the member-states, and most significantly the diversity of care policies in the member-states. The diversity in policies has led to agreement around the lowest common policy denominator as reflected in the directives on leave and to a prolonged stalemate as witnessed in the 2010 deliberations on leave policies.

Care has also moved onto the agenda of intergovernmental organizations, such as the OECD and the United Nations. The OECD has centered on women's employment to promote economic development, and it eventually recognized the role of child-care policies to increase mothers' labor market participation (OECD 2002–2007). By contrast, the United Nations and its agencies have increasingly placed care in a developmental context, linking care to education and health policies. As distinct from the OECD, the United Nations agencies have also contributed to the globalization of research on care, moving the boundaries beyond the established welfare states of the original OECD countries. Equally important, researchers have sought to incorporate gender into the analysis (Daly 2001; Razavi and Hassim 2006; Razavi 2007), thus challenging the gender-blind orientation of the growing welfare state literature on the developing countries and the newly industrializing countries (e.g., Gough and Wood 2004; Rudra 2008).

Global Migration and Care

Care has crossed borders as immigrant workers have provided care both in the home and in the service sector. In analyzing the globalization of care, the focus has shifted from productive labor to reproductive labor in the international division of labor in the global economy (see the chapters by Fergsuon and Razavi in this volume). A key concept has been the global care chain, that is, "a series of personal links between people across the globe based on the paid or unpaid work of caring" where each careworker depends upon another for carework (Hochschild 2000, 131). In an important study on Filipina domestic workers in the United States (Los Angeles) and Italy (Rome), Rhacel Salazar Parreñas (2001) states that the international transfer of caretaking "refers to the three-tier transfer of reproductive labor among women in sending and receiving countries of migration" (62). The global care chain offers a broader lens that focuses on transnational care rather than limiting the consideration of care to single countries or the national level. Parreñas also examines the migration process from the level of the subject. This level of analysis taps into "narratives of displacement" that focus on the thoughts and emotions of the individual immigrant, her sense of self, and understandings of her relations to the world (31). Several other analyses of the globalization of care have followed suit, giving voice to the views and experiences of immigrant carers and domestic workers (Zimmerman et al. 2006; Lister et al. 2007; Lutz 2008; Williams and Gavanas 2008).

Despite several merits, the notion of a global care chain has its drawbacks (Zimmerman et al. 2006). A major difficulty of the global care chain was its initial narrow focus on childcare and domestic work in household settings. Nicola Yeates (2004, 2009) proposes to expand the utility of the global care chain so that it can be used to analyze a wider spectrum of immigrant careworkers. She recommends including different skill levels, care work in different settings, different types of care, and expanding the time frame to include a historical perspective. Broadening the notion in this way enables the analysis of immigrant workers in the care service sector, such as nurses. More generally, the broader notion provides a tool for studying the role of immigration in supplying a workforce in the welfare sector in receiving countries and how this recruitment affects the provision of medical care and other care services of the sending countries.

A further difficulty of the global care chain, as noted by Eleonore Kofman (2010), is that it pays little attention to the importance of national contexts and polices and how differences pattern outcomes. She argues that care regimes and migration regimes must be included in the analysis. This also opens the way for a consideration of the welfare and rights of immigrant careworkers.

European comparative studies focusing on childcare and elder care have shown the importance of variations in care regimes for the expansion of an informal care market where immigrant workers are a growing supply of care labor. A comparison of Spain, Sweden, and the United Kingdom—three countries with contrasting child-care regimes—found major differences in the settings where female immigrant workers were caring for children. The child-care policies of Spain and Sweden are polar opposites, and those of the United Kingdom fall somewhere in between. In Spain immigrant careworkers have been employed in households often in the informal economy, with low pay, no employment security, and no social rights. The lack of child-care services combined with a subsidy for working mothers has encouraged hiring a carer in the home. In Sweden public provision has largely crowded out private household solutions to childcare. Immigrants are employed as workers in public child-care centers or subsidized child-care centers catering to their ethnic community. They are part of the formal economy with job security, standard pay, and social entitlements. In the United Kingdom, the picture is more mixed, but until the 2000s several policies promoted informal care solutions with the childminder in the home as the preferred arrangement. A major lesson of the analysis is that it is not simply the lack of public provision that shapes the demand for child-care leading to an informal care market. Both Spain and the United Kingdom have been poor providers of day-care services. Still, a very small proportion of immigrant women in the United Kingdom are employed as domestic workers in households compared with Spain. Fiona Williams and Anna Gavanas (2008, 14, italics in original) argue that it is *the very nature of state support that is available*" that influences the informal sector. Spain and the United Kingdom provide some form of benefit to assist in buying childcare in the home, but in the British case these benefits (tax credits) apply for the use of registered nannies, while in Spain there is no such requirement (Lister et al. 2007; Williams and Gavanas).

Looking at elder care sheds further light on the U.K. case. Although the United Kingdom has only recently embarked on a policy of supporting care arrangements for small children, its care regime for the elderly has shared features with the Scandinavian countries (Anttonen and Sipilä 1996; Simonazzi 2009), and many immigrant women in the United Kingdom are employed in health care and personal services. Among the crucial variations are how care is organized and funded (Simonazzi 2009). Care regimes characterized by provision in kind and regulated care benefits tend to create a formal care market, whereas unregulated care benefits encourage an informal market. In addition, regulated versus unregulated labor markets reinforce the development of a formal or informal care market. In the Mediterranean countries where families are responsible for elder care and an unregulated labor market with a large gray economy, immigrant careworkers are the carers whom families hire. A much higher percentage of immigrant women are employed in household services in the three countries with the poorest public provision of care services—Spain, Italy, and Greece—than elsewhere in Europe (Kofman 2010, 123), giving rise to the term the *migrant carer model* (Simonazzi, 229). Still, the work of Emiko Ochiai (2009) and her research colleagues reveals that the migrant carer model is not solely a Mediterranean phenomenon. In East Asian countries where the market plays a major role in care provision, such as Taiwan and Singapore, there has also been a substantial transfer of domestic care work to female immigrant workers. The immigrant carer model has been on the rise across a broad spectrum of affluent countries, including the oil-rich Gulf states and the newly industrializing countries (Zimmerman et al., 2006).

A shared conclusion is the importance of regulatory policies. In other words, it is necessary to add this sort of policy to Daly's (2001) list of policies that need to be included in analyzing the care dimension of welfare states. The analysis of care further underlines the point that welfare state policies structure employment opportunities and labor markets (Esping-Andersen 1990; Morgan 2005), in this case the employment and the working conditions of careworkers.

Conclusions and Reflections

Feminist theorizing on care during the past two decades has vastly expanded the analytic tools for studying the care dimension in welfare state policies, the varieties of societal arrangements in the care provision, and their implications for gender relations and the division of labor between the sexes. Importantly, feminist scholars—both moral theorists and policy analysts—have transformed the conceptualization of care from a marginal activity into a central process crucial to human well-being and welfare (Tronto 1993, 2001; Fraser 1994; Jenson 1997; Glenn 2000; Jenson and Sineau 2001; Sevenhuijsen 2003). Furthermore, Fraser's (1994) gender equity models sought to breach the differences in feminist approaches that emphasized different paths toward women's economic emancipation—paid work versus remuneration for caring tasks—by proposing the reorganization of care work so that it would be equally shared by women and men. The sharing of care also has the potential to elevate its status.

More sobering are two trends—the globalization of care and the commodification of care—and their implications for the gender division of labor in society. The globalization of domestic carework has generally reaffirmed the home as the site of caring and family responsibilities for care. It has perpetuated the gendered nature of care since caring tasks as well as household chores remain in women's hands. In this way it counteracts a redistribution of care work among women and men. However, the transfer of care to domestic workers offers mothers, wives, and daughters the possibility of entering the labor market, altering the gender division of labor in the family to the extent that women become earners. The globalization of domestic work also has important class implications and stratifying effects. It has primarily benefited class-privileged families, men, and women. As long as hiring immigrant careworkers in the home remains a low-priced solution, it can erode the demand for child-care services outside the home. The lack of affordable day care heightens the difficulties faced by low-income mothers who must work to make ends meet. From the perspective of immigrant careworkers, migration provides the opportunity to improve earnings; however, those in the informal economy run the risk of exploitation, and their access to welfare benefits is impaired because they are often outside the social protection system. The vulnerability of immigrant careworkers is indicative of a cycle of devaluation of care work. As Evelyn Nakano Glenn (2000) notes, as long as care is devalued and poorly paid, it is more likely to be done by those who lack resources and status (women, minorities, and immigrants), and if care work is disproportionately performed by these groups their caring activities are further devalued (see the chapters by Ferguson and Rai in this volume). The commodification of care, that is, its conversion to paid work in both the private and public sectors, has not altered the gender division of labor in society, but it has changed the site of care so that more care work is done in the market and the state. An exception has been cash-for-care schemes that have generally had the home as the setting and in some cases relatives have been the providers. The commodification of care may have even intensified gender segregation of the labor market, but in some instances this has been accompanied by an elevation in status as women increasingly join the care professions. To the extent that care and reproduction work have become paid work outside the home performed by women, the traditional gender division of labor in the family has been influenced.

The analysis of care and gender has moved from single-country studies to comparative research of the established welfare states and then to the emerging welfare states, and finally it has included a global perspective. Comparative studies reveal both cross-national differences in care arrangements and conceptions of care but also underlying similarities, such as the continued devaluation of care, women's greater involvement in care work, and the lower earnings of mothers compared with fathers because mothers provide care. The devaluation of care has been reflected not only in low pay but also in the lower benefit levels of care-related benefits compared with work-related benefits across countries. Cross-national research has pointed to two solutions in expanding men's involvement in caregiving: tying care-related benefits to work-related benefits with high replacement rates; and designing parental leave so that fathers have an assigned portion that cannot be transferred to the mother. Another important cross-national difference is the availability of affordable quality day care (Jenson and Sineau 2001; Michel and Mahon 2002; Ellingsaeter and Leira 2006). In sum, welfare policies privilege certain types of families in relation to care, and this affects the gender division of labor in the family and the welfare mix of care arrangements.

Lastly, the globalization of research on care has broadened the perspectives and understandings of care, enriching the dialogue and analysis of care. This wider dialogue reveals how national contexts have shaped and limited our understandings of care, just as an earlier dialogue between European researchers revealed country and regional specificities (Ungerson 1990). This new, more encompassing dialogue promises to invigorate theorizing and empirical studies on gender, care, and welfare.

References

Anderson, Karen M., and Traute Meyer. 2006. "New social risks and pension reform in Germany and Sweden: The politics of pension rights for child care." In Klaus Armingeon and Giuliano Bonoli, eds., *The politics of post-industrial welfare states.* New York: Routledge, 171–191.

Anttonen, Anneli, and Jorma Sipilä. 1996. "European social care services: Is it possible to identify models?" *Journal of European Social Policy* 6(2): 87–100.

Bergqvist, Christina. 2005. "Gender equality politics: Ideas and strategies." In PerOla Öberg and Torsten Svensson, eds., *Power and institutions in industrial relation regimes.* Stockholm: National Institute for Working Life, 57–76.

Beyeler, Michelle, and Claire Annesley. 2010. "Gendering the institutional reform of the welfare state: Germany, the United Kingdom, and Switzerland." In Mona Lena Krook and Fiona Mackay, eds., *Gender, politics and institutions*. Basingstoke, UK: Palgrave Macmillan, 79–94.

Budig, Michelle J., and Joya Misra. 2010. "How care-work employment shapes earnings in cross-national perspective." *International Labour Review* 149(4): 441–460.

Castles, Francis G., Stephan Leibfried, Jane Lewis, Herbert Obinger, and Christopher Pierson (Eds.). 2010. *The Oxford handbook of the welfare state*. Oxford: Oxford University Press.

Dahl, Hanne Marlene, and Tine Rask Eriksen (Eds.). 2005. *Dilemmas of care in the Nordic welfare state*. Aldershot, UK: Ashgate.

Daly, Mary (Ed.). 2001. *Care work: A quest for security*. Geneva: International Labour Organisation.

Daly, Mary. 2010. "Families versus states and markets." In Francis G. Castles, Stephan Leibfried, Jane Lewis, Herbert Obinger, and Christopher Pierson, eds., *The Oxford handbook of the welfare state*. Oxford: Oxford University Press, 139–151.

Daly, Mary, and Jane Lewis. 1998. "Introduction: Conceptualising social care in the context of welfare state restructuring." In Jane Lewis, ed., *Gender, social care and welfare state restructuring in Europe*. Aldershot, UK: Ashgate, 1–24.

Daly, Mary, and Jane Lewis. 2000. "The concept of social care and the analysis of contemporary welfare states." *British Journal of Sociology* 51(2): 261–298.

Daly, Mary, and Katherine Rake. 2003. *Gender and the welfare state*. Cambridge, UK: Polity.

Da Roit, Barbara, Blanche Le Bihan, and August Österle. 2007. "Long-term care policies in Italy, Austria and France: Variations in cash-for-care schemes."*Social Policy & Administration* 41(6): 653–671.

Donath, Susan. 2000. "The other economy: A suggestion for a distinctively feminist economics." *Feminist Economics* 6(1): 115–123.

Duffy, Mignon. 2005. "Reproducing labor inequalities: Challenges for feminists conceptualizing care at the intersections of gender, race and class." *Gender and Society* 19(1): 66–82.

Ellingsaeter, Anne Lise, and Arnlaug Leira (Eds.). 2006. *Politicising parenthood in Scandinavia: Gender relations in welfare states*. Bristol: Policy Press.

England, Paula. 2005. "Emerging theories of care work." *Annual Review of Sociology* 31: 381–399.

Esping-Andersen, Gøsta. 1990. *The three worlds of welfare capitalism*. Princeton, NJ: Princeton University Press.

Fisher, Berenice, and Joan Tronto. 1990. "Toward a feminist theory of caring." In Emily K. Abel and Margaret K. Nelson, eds., *Circles of care: Work and identity in women's lives*. Albany: State University of New York Press, 35–62.

Folbre, Nancy. 2006. "Measuring care: Gender, empowerment and the care economy." *Journal of Human Development* 7(2): 183–199.

Fraser, Nancy. 1994. "After the family wage: Gender equity and the welfare state." *Political Theory* 22(4): 591–618.

Glenn, Evelyn Nakano. 1992. "From servitude to service: Historical continuities in the racial division of paid reproduction work." *Signs* 18(1): 1–43.

Glenn, Evelyn Nakano. 2000. "Creating a caring society." *Contemporary Sociology* 29(1): 84–94.

Gornick, Janet, and Marcia K. Meyers. 2003. *Families that work: Policies for reconciling parenthood and employment.* New York: Russell Sage Foundation.

Gornick, Janet, Marcia K. Meyers, and Erik Olin Wright (Eds.). 2009. *Gender equality: Transforming family divisions of labor.* London: Verso.

Gough, Ian, and Geoff Wood. 2004. *Insecurity and welfare regimes in Asia, Africa and Latin America: Social policy in development context.* Cambridge, UK: Cambridge University Press.

Hantrais, Linda (Ed.). 2000. *Gendered policies in Europe: Reconciling employment and family life.* Basingstoke, UK: Macmillan.

Haussman, Melissa, and Birgit Sauer (Eds.). 2007. *Gendering the state in the age of globalization: Women's movements and state feminism in postindustrial democracies.* Lanham, MD: Rowman & Littlefield.

Himmelweit, Susan. 2007. "The prospects for caring: Economic theory and policy analysis." *Cambridge Journal of Economics* 31(3): 581–599.

Hobson, Barbara, and Marika Lindholm. 1997. "Collective identities, women's power resources, and the making of welfare states." *Theory and Society* 26(4): 475–508.

Hochschild, Arlie Russell. 1995. "The culture of politics: Traditional, postmodern, cold-modern, and warm-modern ideals of care." *Social Politics* 2(3): 331–346.

Hochschild, Arlie Russell. 2000. "Global care chains and emotional surplus value." In Will Hutton and Anthony Giddens, eds., *On the edge: Living with global capitalism.* London: Jonathan Cape, 130–146.

Hondagneu-Sotelo, Pierrette. 2000. *Doméstica: Immigrant workers cleaning and caring in the shadows of affluence.* Berkeley: University of California Press.

Hoskyns, Catherine. 1996. *Integrating gender: Women, law and politics in the European Union.* London: Verso.

International Labour Review. (ILR). 2010. "Special issue: Workers in the care economy." *International Labour Review* 149(4).

Jenson, Jane. 1997. "Who cares? Gender and welfare regimes." *Social Politics* 4(2): 182–187.

Jenson, Jane, and Mariette Sineau. 2001. *Who cares? Women's work, childcare and welfare state design.* Toronto: University of Toronto Press.

Kantola, Johanna. 2010. *Gender and the European Union.* Basingstoke, UK: Palgrave Macmillan.

Kittay, Eva Feder. 2001. "From welfare to a public ethic of care." In Nancy J. Hirschmann and Ulrike Liebert, eds., *Women and welfare: Theory and practice in the United States and Europe.* New Brunswick, NJ: Rutgers University Press, 38–64.

Knijn, Trudie, and Monique Kremer. 1997. "Gender and the caring dimension of welfare states: Toward inclusive citizenship." *Social Politics* 4(3): 328–361.

Kofman, Eleonore. 2010. "Gendered migrations and globalisation of social reproduction and care." In Marlou Schrover and Eileen Janes Yeo, eds., *Gender, migration and the public sphere, 1850–2005.* New York: Routledge, 118–139.

Korpi, Walter. 1980. "Social policy and distributional conflicts in capitalist democracies." *West European Politics* 3(3): 296–316.

Kremer, Monique. 2007. *How welfare states care: Culture, gender and parenting in Europe.* Amsterdam: University of Amsterdam Press.

Langan, Mary, and Ilona Ostner. 1991. "Gender and welfare." In Graham Room, ed., *Towards a European welfare state?* Bristol: SAUS Publications, 127–150.

Leira, Arnlaug, and Chiara Saraceno. 2002. "Care: actors, relationships and contexts." In Barbara Hobson, Jane Lewis, and Birte Siim, eds., *Contested concepts in gender and social politics*. Cheltenham, UK: Edward Elgar, 55–83.

Lewis, Jane. 1992. "Gender and the development of welfare regimes." *Journal of European Social Policy* 2(3): 159–173.

Lewis, Jane. 1997. "Gender and welfare regimes: Further thoughts." *Social Politics* 4(2): 160–174.

Lewis, Jane (Ed.). 1998. *Gender, social care and welfare state restructuring in Europe*. Aldershot, UK: Ashgate.

Lewis, Jane. 2009. *Work–family balance, gender and policy*. Cheltenham, UK: Edward Elgar.

Lewis, Jane, with Barbara Hobson. 1997. "Introduction." In Jane Lewis, ed., *Lone mothers in European welfare regimes*. London: Jessica Kingsley Publishers, 1–20.

Lister, Ruth. 1997. *Citizenship: Feminist perspectives*. Basingstoke, UK: Macmillan.

Lister, Ruth, Fiona Williams, Anneli Anttonen, Jet Bussemaker, Ute Gerhard, Jacqueline Heinen, Stina Johansson, Arnlaug Leira, Birte Siim, and Constanza Tobio, with Anna Gavanas. 2007. *Gendering citizenship in Western Europe: New challenges for citizenship research in a cross-national context*. Bristol: Policy Press.

Lutz, Helma (Ed.). 2008. *Migration and domestic work: A European perspective on a global theme*. Farnham, UK: Ashgate.

Meyer, Madonna Harrington (Ed.). 2000. *Care work: Gender, labor and the welfare state*. London: Routledge.

Michel, Sonya, and Rianne Mahon (Eds.). 2002. *Child care policy at the crossroads: Gender and welfare state restructuring*. New York: Routledge.

Misra, Joya. 2003. "Women as agents in welfare state development: a cross-national analysis of family allowance adoption." *Socio-economic Review* 1(2): 185–214.

Morel, Nathalie. 2007. "From subsidarity to 'free choice.' Child- and elder-care policy reforms in France, Belgium, Germany and the Netherlands." *Social Policy & Administration* 41(6): 618–637.

Morgan, Kimberly J. 2005. "The 'production' of child care: How labor markets shape social policy and vice versa." *Social Politics* 12(2): 243–263.

Morgan, Kimberly J. 2006. *Working mothers and the welfare state: Religion and the politics of work-family policies in Western Europe and the United States*. Stanford, CA: Stanford University Press.

Nussbaum, Martha C. 1999. *Sex and social justice*. New York: Oxford University Press.

Ochiai, Emiko. 2009. "Care diamonds and welfare regimes in east and south-east Asian societies: Bridging family and welfare sociology." *International Journal of Japanese Sociology* 18(1): 60–78.

Ochiai, Emiko, and Barbara Molony (Eds.). 2008. *Asia's new mothers: Crafting gender roles and childcare networks in East and Southeast Asian societies*. Folkestone, UK: Global Oriental.

O'Connor, Julia S. 1996. "From women in the welfare state to gendering welfare state regimes." *Current Sociology* 44(2): 1–130.

O'Connor, Julia S., Ann Shola Orloff, and Sheila Shaver. 1999. *States, markets, families: Gender, liberalism and social policy in Australia, Canada, Great Britain and the United States*. Cambridge, UK: Cambridge University Press.

Organisation for Economic Co-operation and Development. (OECD). 2002–2007. *Babies and bosses: Reconciling work and family life*, vols. 1–7. Paris: OECD.

Orloff, Ann Shola. 1993. "Gender and the social rights of citizenship: The comparative analysis of gender relations and welfare states." *American Sociological Review* 58(3): 303–328.

Orloff, Ann Shola. 2010. "Gender." In Francis G. Castles, Stephan Leibfried, Jane Lewis, Herbert Obinger, and Christopher Pierson, eds., *The Oxford handbook of the welfare state*. Oxford: Oxford University Press, 252–264.

Ostner, Ilona, and Jane Lewis. 1995. "Gender and the evolution of European social policy." In Stephan Leibfried and Paul Pierson, eds., *European social policy: Between fragmentation and integration*. Washington, DC: Brookings Institution, 159–193.

Parreñas, Rhacel Salazar. 2001. *Servants of globalization: Women, migration and domestic work*. Stanford, CA: Stanford University Press.

Peng, Ito. 2005. "The new politics of the welfare state in a developmental context: Explaining the 1990s social care expansion in Japan." In Huck-ju, Kwon ed., *Transforming the developmental welfare state in East-Asia*. Basingstoke, UK: Palgrave Macmillan, 73–97.

Peng, Ito. 2008. *The political and social economy of care: South Korea*. Research report 3. Geneva: United Nations Research Institute for Social Development.

Pfau-Effinger, Birgit. 2005. "Welfare state policies and the development of care arrangements." *European Societies* 7(2): 321–347.

Pfau-Effinger, Birgit, and Tine Rostgaard (Eds.). 2011. *Care between work and welfare in European societies*. Basingstoke, UK: Palgrave Macmillan.

Pijl, Marja. 1994. "When private care goes public: An analysis of concepts and principles concerning payments for care." In Adalbert Evers, Marja Pijl, and Clare Ungerson, eds., *Payments for care: A comparative overview*. Aldershot, UK: Avebury, 3–18.

Ray, Rebecca, Janet C. Gornick, and John Schmitt. 2010. "Who cares? Assessing generosity and gender equality in parental leave policy designs in 21 countries." *Journal of European Social Policy* 20(3): 196–216.

Razavi, Shahra. 2007. *The political and social economy of care in a development context: conceptual issues, research questions and policy options*. Geneva: United Nations Research Institute for Social Development.

Razavi, Shahra, and Shireen Hassim (Eds.). 2006. *Gender and social policy in a global context*. Basingstoke, UK: Palgrave Macmillan.

Roth, Silke (Ed.). 2008. *Gender politics in the expanding European Union*. New York: Berghahn Books.

Rudra, Nita. 2008. *Globalization and the race to the bottom in developing countries*. New York: Cambridge University Press.

Sainsbury, Diane. 1994a. Women's and men's social rights: Gendering dimensions of welfare states. In Diane Sainsbury, *Gendering welfare states*. London: SAGE, 150–169.

Sainsbury, Diane (Ed.). 1994b. *Gendering welfare states*. London: SAGE.

Sainsbury, Diane. 1996. *Gender, equality and welfare states*. Cambridge, UK: Cambridge University Press.

Sainsbury, Diane. 1999. "Gender, policy regimes, and politics." In Diane Sainsbury, ed., *Gender and welfare state regimes*. Oxford: Oxford University Press, 245–275.

Sevenhuijsen, Selma. 2003. "The place of care: The relevance of the feminist ethic of care for social policy." *Feminist Theory* 4(2): 179–197.

Simonazzi, Annamaria. 2009. "Care regimes and national employment models."
    Cambridge Journal of Economics 33(2): 211–232.

Skocpol, Theda. 1992. *Protecting soldiers and mothers: The political origins of social
    policy in the United States.* Cambridge, MA: Belknap Press of Harvard University
    Press.

Tronto, Joan. 1993. *Moral boundaries: A political argument for an ethic of care.* New
    York: Routledge.

Tronto, Joan. 2001. "Who cares? Public and private caring and the rethinking of
    citizenship." In Nancy J. Hirschmann and Ulrike Liebert, eds., *Women and
    welfare: Theory and practice in the United States and Europe.* New Brunswick, NJ:
    Rutgers University Press, 65–83.

Ungerson, Clare (Ed.). 1990. *Gender and caring: Work and welfare in Britain and
    Scandinavia.* New York: Harvester Wheatsheaf.

Ungerson, Clare, and Sue Yeandle (Eds.). 2007. *Cash for care in developed welfare
    states.* Basingstoke: Palgrave Macmillan.

Williams, Fiona, and Anna Gavanas. 2008. "The intersection of childcare regimes
    and migration regimes: A three-country study." In Helma Lutz, ed., *Migration
    and domestic work: A European perspective on a global theme.* Aldershot, UK:
    Ashgate, 13–28.

Yeates, Nicola. 2004. "Global care chains." *International Feminist Journal of Politics*
    6(3): 369–391.

Yeates, Nicola. 2009. *Globalizing care economies and migrant workers.* Basingstoke,
    UK: Palgrave Macmillan.

Zimmerman, Mary K., Jacqueline S. Litt, and Christine E. Bose (Eds.). 2006. *Global
    dimensions of gender and carework.* Stanford, CA: Stanford University Press.

CHAPTER 13

GENDER, WORK, AND THE SEXUAL DIVISION OF LABOR

LUCY FERGUSON

INTRODUCTION

The study of work is central to any gendered analysis of political economy as it allows for a more detailed exploration of the relationship between production and social reproduction. More broadly, work is one of the key processes through which gender relations are played out in contemporary societies, influencing and disciplining the ways different actors and social groups interact between *public* and *private* spheres. This chapter sets out to demonstrate how work is gendered, both in the ways it is constructed and how this plays out in labor markets. Although work is often used as a synonym for employment in mainstream literature, here we acknowledge the importance of unpaid work—in particular, care and domestic work—and how this interacts in gendered ways with the sphere of paid employment. At the same time, it is important to recognize that not all unpaid work is care or domestic work and that not all paid work can be considered as employment. The very definition of employment itself relies on the delimitation of a public and private sphere, a gendered construction that has served to establish the borders of what is considered work, based on assumptions about whether work is considered *productive* (men's paid work in the market) or *unproductive* (women's unpaid work in the household) (Young 2003, 107). However, these assumptions obscure the ways unpaid work is vital to the functioning of any economy (Waring 1988;

Elson 2000; England and Folbre 2003). As shown in the other chapters in this section (Razavi, Sainsbury, and Rai), the separation between productive and "non-productive" work marginalizes, undermines, and privatizes non-product work such as caring and domestic labor, putting these tasks outside of the productive sphere and, consequently, the realm of work.

This chapter explores how the gender dynamics of paid work worldwide have been radically restructured over the last fifty years and the extent to which this has altered the sexual or gendered division of unpaid labor in the household and vice versa. To do this, it draws on a number of key analytical concepts and insights from a wide range of literatures—namely, (feminist) economics, sociology, and gendered political economy and development—and a global level of analysis. The concept of the sexual division of labor is employed throughout the chapter. This draws on socialist feminist approaches of the 1970s and 1980s, which argued that inequalities created by patriarchal social relations were exploited by capital-ism to create hierarchical working practices (Kuhn and Wolpe 1978; Hartmann 1983). A further key concept is the male breadwinner model—which means that labor markets have been constructed around assumptions about a primary male worker with a housewife who takes care of all domestic work in the household, supported by the male wage (Brodie 2003, 54). While traditionally the literature on gender and work has tended to focus predominantly on paid women workers, here we aim to broaden the focus to explore the gendered ways labor markets intersect with a wide range of inequalities, such as class, ethnicity, sexuality, and nationality. Throughout the chapter, an argument is developed that gender is not always the most salient inequality—for example, women are not always in a worse position than men in every context—but that labor markets are always gendered. These analytical arguments are complemented with labor market statistics from the International Labour Organization (ILO) to give a global perspective on the phenomenon being discussed. Where ILO statistics are not available, occasionally statistics from the Organisation for Economic Co-operation and Development (OECD) are used, and, where possible, global-level statistics are broken down by world regions to offer a comparative perspective.

While the gender dynamics of employment have changed, the sexual divi-sion of labor remains, and in all world regions women perform more than half of all unpaid household tasks, which, in turn, influences the ways women and men engage with labor markets. The chapter proceeds in four main sections to demonstrate the impact of the sexual division of labor on gender and work. First, it analyzes the restructuring of global production—in particular the *femi-nization of employment*—and argues that recruitment and employment practices are based on gendered assumptions about women's "natural" capacities, lead-ing to the classification of such work as low skill and low paid. The process of feminization in the three main employment sectors of agriculture, industry and services is outlined here to illustrate the interplay between the sexual division of labor and the gender dynamics of employment in more detail. Second, we look at two further contemporary phenomena in gendered employment—informalization and labor migration. Both of these processes, it is argued, draw on the sexual division of labor and discipline women's and men's interactions with global labor markets. In particular, an overview of the *global care chains* debate demonstrates the links between the convergence of male and female employment rates and the growing need for migrant labor to provide care and domestic services. The chapter then explores gender segregation in employment, setting out the ways the sexual division of labor disciplines women's and men's ideas about appropriate and accessible work options. Drawing on literature from economics and sociology, we explore the implications of, and explanations for, gender segregation in labor markets, arguing that segregation both draws on and perpetuates gender and other inequalities. Finally, the chapter analyzes in more detail how women's unpaid labor influences the ways men and women engage with the labor market. It argues that while labor markets and households have been restructured along profoundly gendered lines, assumptions about the sexual division of labor remain largely untouched; thus, the consequences of this are examined. In the conclusions, we draw together the links between feminization, migration, gender segregation, and unpaid work.

The Global Feminization of Employment

The restructuring of production and employment since the 1970s has been a profoundly gendered process. To explore this, it is useful to take a global perspective and sketch an overview of these changes and their gendered implications. The emergence of the *new international division of labor* in the 1970s—often referred to as the beginning of the era of *globalization*—involved a decentralization of manufacturing production away from industrialized nations to less developed countries, which were able to provide lower labor costs and less strict regulations. In more recent years, this process of restructuring has extended beyond manufacturing to the service and agricultural sectors (Perrons 2004, 89). Many aspects of these processes have both shaped, and been shaped by, gender relations, in particular assumptions about women's responsibilities and capacity for care and the sexual division of labor. The *feminization* of employment refers to an increase not only in women's integration into the paid workforce worldwide but also in the kinds and conditions of work that have tended to be associated with women, forcing many men as well as women into more flexible and precarious forms of labor.

Three broad trends in the feminization of employment can be identified (Standing 1989, 1999). First, the types of employment traditionally associated with women have been growing relative to those associated with men—for example, insecure and low paid as opposed to unionized and stable. Globally, the share of women who are in vulnerable employment was 52.7 percent in 2007 compared with 49.1 percent for men.[1] However, the gender gap in the share of vulnerable employment in total employment for males and females shows a diverse picture by region. For example, in the developed economies and the European Union, central and southeastern Europe (non-EU), the Commonwealth of Independent States (CIS), and Latin America, and the Caribbean, this gap was negative in 2007, meaning that women are proportionately less likely to be in vulnerable jobs than men. This is an important point to highlight, as it suggests that gender is not always the determining factor of inequality in contemporary labor markets in all contexts. Second, there has been a continuing increase in the numbers of women entering, reentering, and remaining in the paid workforce. In 2008, for example, women made up 40.5 percent of the global labor force in 2008, up from 39.9 percent in 1998.[2] In OECD countries, women's employment rates have markedly increased.[3] While in 1970 less than half (45 percent) of all women (aged fifteen to sixty-four) in OECD countries participated in the labor market, in 2008 this proportion had increased to 58 percent (OECD 2010). A third and related phenomenon is the increasing convergence of male and female labor force participation rates. In contrast to the increase in women's labor force participation worldwide from 1998 to 2008 already outlined, during the same period male participation rates fell slightly from 79.2 to 77.5 percent (ILO 2009). This convergence is also reflected in unemployment rates. In 2008, the unemployment rate for women was 6.3 percent, compared with a rate of 5.9 percent for men. While the global unemployment rate increased for both men (0.4 percentage points) and women (0.3 percentage points) between 2007 and 2008, the lower growth in women's unemployment has slightly reduced the gender gap in unemployment rates worldwide (ibid.). These illustrative statistics demonstrate the extent of the feminization of employment worldwide. However, while the concept of feminization is useful to framing the gender dimensions of global restructuring, it is important not to equate feminization with greater gender equality in labor markets. Rather, as Caraway (2007, 2) argues, "Massive inflows of women into the workforce result rarely in a seamless integration of women into men's jobs but rather in a redrawing or reconfiguration of the gender divisions of labor that separate men's work from women's work."

Feminization in Different Employment Sectors

The feminization of employment is therefore a useful guiding concept for understanding changes over time and a starting point for exploring gender and other inequalities in labor markets. This process of feminization can be observed in all three main sectors of employment—agriculture, industry, and

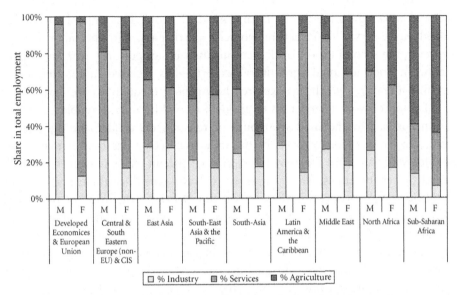

Figure 13.1 Distribution of employment by sector (sectoral employment as percentage of total employment), by sex and region, 2008.

services—and we now trace the contours of this feminization in each sector. Figure 13.1 shows the share of female and male employment in the three main sectors by geographical region.

Women remain overrepresented in the agricultural sector. Globally, the share of women employed in agriculture stands at 35.4 percent compared with 32.2 percent for men, but this proportion rises to almost half of all female employment, at 48.4 percent, if the more industrialized regions are excluded. In sub-Saharan Africa and South Asia, the agricultural sector makes up more than 60 percent of all female employment (ILO 2009). In most regions of the Global South, women who are employed are more likely than men to work in agriculture, with the exception of Latin America (United Nations 2010). A key feature of agricultural employment is that women are concentrated in seasonal, part-time and low-paid employment compared with men working in agriculture (FAO 2011). The feminization of agricultural employment is occurring in two keys ways: women are taking over more of the agricultural tasks once performed by men in smallholder cash-crop production; and are increasingly conducting wage work in nontraditional agricultural exports (Lastarria-Cornhiel 2008). Compared with industry and services, the gender dimensions of smallholder cash-crop production have received relatively little attention from feminist researchers in recent years. The limited contemporary research available has highlighted that much of women's work in agriculture is not considered by policy makers to be economic activity (Ransom and Bain 2011), despite the fact that women play a vital role in food production (Bunch and Mehra 2008). Women's unpaid work in agriculture involves not just caring and other domestic activities but often incorporates responsibilities such as collecting water and fuel and working on the family farm (FAO-ILO 2009). This unpaid and under-valued work serves to structure women's participation in the labor market. However, the second aspect of the feminization of agriculture—women's partic-ipation in nontraditional agricultural exports—has received more attention in feminist literature, which has explored how gender inequalities are perpetuated in this kind of work (Barrientos et al. 1999; Korovkin 2002; Raynolds 2002).

In contrast to the modest amount of research on gender and agricultural work, the feminization of parts of the industrial sector has been a major con-cern for feminists since the early 1980s, in particular in terms of women's work in export processing zones, which increased with the growth of the export industry worldwide (Pearson 1998). Early work on the global restructuring of production highlighted the ways gendered assumptions were central to the decentralization of manufacturing for multinational firms (Safa 1981; Fernández-Kelly 1983; Lim 1985). They revealed how ideas about women's—in particular "third-world" women's—supposed natural capacities and qualities, such as "nimble fingers", were embed-ded in the recruitment practices of such companies (Elson and Pearson 1981). In the 1990s, feminist research demonstrated the endurance of the sexual division of labor on women's employment in industry, suggesting that assumptions about the male breadwinner and women's secondary earning role have a lasting impact regardless of the actual circumstances of female employees (Wolf 1992; Lee 1998). These assumptions have created gendered discourses of work that, as Caraway (2007) argues, have come to play an even more important part in gendering the workplaces of global factories than the payment of low wages to women workers.

One limitation of the majority of the literature on the feminization of industry is its focus on predominantly female workers, with some excep-tions (for example, Elias 2008). However, it should be noted that in terms of the sectors in which women and men work worldwide, only a small propor-tion of employed women work in industry—18.3 percent in 2008, compared with 26.6 percent of men. Salzinger's concept of *productive femininity* is useful here, as it explains how feminization operates as a "discursive proc-ess which operates on both male and female bodies" (Salzinger 2003, 11). Likewise, Melissa Wright's (2006) *myth of disposability*—in which employers construct a discourse that employees can be easily and quickly replaced—is historically contingent and may be mapped on to males and females at dif-ferent times. Indeed, as Wright argues, in the contemporary dynamics of employment in industry other axes of inequality, such as ethnicity, sexu-ality, and class, may be more closely linked to *disposability* than gender. These concepts help us move away from static assumptions about women's labor in employment and toward a more gendered understanding of differ-ent types of employment.

While in general the industrial sector of employment is male dominated, the services sector is predominantly female. Worldwide, the services sector accounted for 46.3 percent of all female employment in 2008 compared with 41.2 percent of male employment, making it the largest sector for global employment by a significant amount (ILO 2009). In OECD countries, the service sector accounts for 70 percent of all employment (Perrons 2010, 168). This sector is highly gendered, as women tend to be concentrated in areas "traditionally associated with their gender roles," in contrast to the better-paid jobs in financial and business services in the private sector that are dominated by men (ILO 2007, 8). At the same time, much "services" work worldwide is informal and informalized, a highly gendered aspect of contemporary labor markets. Feminist economists have highlighted this gender segregation in the service sector, arguing that it is polarized between higher-paid information and communications technology (ICT)-enabled "knowledge work" and lower-paid catering, cleaning, and care work (Howcroft and Richardson 2010; Webster 2010), demonstrating again the influence of the sexual division of labor on employment. Women also tend to be more concentrated in public or state service sector employment than men.

A distinction between feminized and masculinized service sector work is useful here. For example, the catering, cleaning, and care work that makes up the majority of women's work in the service sector (in both the state and the private sector) is often reliant on the "embodied attributes of the worker, and his/her ability to perform emotional labor" (Webster 2010, 188). Traditionally, the notion of emotional labor has been more relevant in the Global North, but the concept has gained importance in the Global South through the rapid expansion of sectors such as tourism and call centers. As Perrons (2010, 177) argues, "(Women's) comparatively low pay is often attributed to vocation, the idea that people in this work are using their natural talents rather than formal skills, such that they do not require commensurate monetary recompense." This emphasizes how contemporary employment practices and patterns are still fundamentally shaped by women's role in the sexual division of labor. It also relates back to the previous discussion of productive femininity and demonstrates how gendered assumptions function in contemporary recruitment and employment practices in all sectors of work.

On the other hand, the masculinized aspects of some specific parts of the service sector, such as finance and information technology (IT), are overwhelmingly male dominated, with men making up 75 percent of the global IT workforce (D'Mello 2010). In spite of this, women's increasing participation in the IT and informatics fields in the Global South has lead to the emergence of "pink-collar workers" in the case of Barbados (Freeman 2010), generating a different set of expectations to the traditional notions of productive femininity valued in the agricultural and industrial sectors. This gender segregation between different service sector occupations is significant because even highly qualified employees in the care sector earn considerably less than equivalently qualified people working in more masculinized sectors. This brief overview of feminization in the three main sectors demonstrates how the sexual division of labor structures women's and men's participation in employment in the both the state and private sectors of different economies. However, it also highlights the importance of taking a global approach, as the gendered contours of inequality play out differently in different sectors and in different geographical locations.

INFORMALIZATION AND GENDERED LABOR MIGRATIONS

Another key feature of the restructuring of global production is the *informalization* of employment, a process that is feminized in a number of key ways and relates to the broader feminization of employment previously outlined. It is important to distinguish here between the informal *sector* or *economy* and the increasing prevalence of "informal characteristics" of many jobs in all sectors, such as "more outworking, contract labor, casual labor, part-time labor, homework and other forms of labor unprotected by labor regulations" (Standing 1999, 585–587). These informal features of employment have relevance beyond the traditional informal sector or economy and are features of many aspects of global production. Debates around informality and informalization in global labor markets greatly add to our understanding of the ways global restructuring affects women and men differently. In many ways, the upward trend in the female share of the labor force is, in part, due to the expansion of more flexible and informal employment, which involves a disproportionate number of women and migrant workers across the globe. Feminist research on global production networks and global value chains has analyzed how these processes of informalization are intimately linked to labor regimes in consumer countries and explores the ways the gender inputs and outputs at each node of global production are both structured by, and structure, gender relations (Barrientos 2001). At the same time, new gendered categories of cheap and informalized labor are emerging in global production, such as male and female migrant labor in Western European agriculture and young men working in export sectors, such as sports footwear, in Mexico (Pearson 2007, 206).

In addition to looking at the gender dimensions of the informalization of employment, it is also useful to explore how this process blurs the line between the formal and informal sectors of the global economy. For example, while work in export processing zones has been promoted for its ability to generate formal work for women, in reality it is very rare for women working in these factories to access the full range of benefits of formal employment (Pearson 2007, 203). Highlighting the informal sector makes a large amount of women's work in the global economy visible, as the "bulk of the female workforce in the majority world do not do labor in the formal economy regulated by national laws on pay, working hours and social protection" (ibid., 202), though a dearth of literature highlights the relative invisibility and underremuneration of informal sector work (Howcroft and Richardson 2010, 4). Benería (2010) notes that traditional conceptualizations of the formal sector have limited applicability beyond welfare state societies, because of the much higher levels of informality that define women's work in the Global South. It is therefore important to understand the processes of the informalization of employment and "degrees of informality" (Benería 2010, 149) and the ways these are gendered, as explored in the following analysis of gender segregation of the labor market.

A further aspect of global restructuring that is essential for any analysis of gender and work is migration. The total migrant labor force was approximately 175 million people in 2005 (Arat-Koç 2006, 76). Between 1965 and 1990, the number of international migrants increased by forty five million—an annual growth rate of about 2.1 percent, which has increased in recent years to approximately 2.9 percent.[4] Labor migration by men and women follows very different patterns. While migration in the post-Second World War period was dominated by men, in more recent years there has been a "feminization of international labor migration," with half the world's legal and documented migrants and refugees believed to be women (Ehrenreich and Hochschild 2003, 5). In fact, it is probable that women make up the greatest percentage of migrant workers from some regions. However, much research on migration has tended to focus on the male experience as the norm, assuming that women were either passive followers or remained at home with the rest of the family. Where women are addressed in mainstream migration discourses, they tend to be presented either as a "beautiful victim" of trafficking into the sex trade or a "sacrificing heroine" sending home remittances that contribute to development in the home country (Schwenken 2008, 771–772). The implications of this narrow presentation of female migration are that men's forced labor through trafficking is largely neglected and that assumptions about women's natural caregiving qualities are reinforced.

As a partial correction to these assumptions, feminist research on migration has focused more explicitly on the experiences of migrant women in the global economy, in particular on those migrating for care and domestic work (Ehrenreich and Hochschild 2003). The now widely used concept of the *global care chain* (Yeates 2004) evokes a "series of personal links between people across the globe based on the paid or unpaid work of caring" (Hochschild 2000,131). Women's migration for domestic work foregrounds the intersecting nature of gendered inequalities with nationality, class, and ethnicity. Feminists have highlighted the ways women perform reproductive roles for the "host" society by carrying out "women's work' as maids, nannies, caregivers for the elderly or persons with disabilities, and sex work (Arat-Koç 2006, 77; see also the chapters by Razavi and Sainsbury in this volume). This has set up global care chains, which "embed(s) women in an international political economy that reinforces, rather than weakens, class and race stratification, and in some cases can lead to serious shortages of women professionals in their home countries" (Bach 2011, 135). In these global care chains, women perform gendered labor, which is associated with women's "natural" aptitudes and, as such, is considered unskilled, reflecting arguments constructed about female employees in export processing zones (Katz 2001; Ehrenreich and Hochschild 2003; Barber 2011). A more post-structuralist analysis by Chang and Ling (2011) evokes "regimes of labor intimacy" as a counterpart to what they call "technomuscular capitalism"—which is "more explicitly sexualized, racialized and class-based than TMC [technomuscular capitalism] and concentrated on low-wage, low-skilled menial service provided by mostly female migrant workers" (30).

Highlighting women's migrant labor for domestic and care work increases the visibility of migrant women's labor in the global economy (Jones 2008, 767). However, it does little to challenge assumptions about "female marginalized migrants" (Kofman and Raghuram 2006, 295), ignoring the complex intersections of gender, class, and race at work in labor migration. In particular, it obscures the increasing migration of skilled female migrant labor for professional and managerial positions, often as contributors to social reproduction provided by the state in organized, formalized ways (Bruegel 1999; Crompton 2000).[5] Acknowledging the skilled dimensions of female migration demonstrates how at some skill levels women's experiences of migration are closer to men's. Recent studies such as that on male migrants working as "handymen" in the United Kingdom allow us to think through the ways gendered work patterns affect not only women but also men (Perrons, Plomien, and Kilkey 2010). Other research exploring male and female migrants in care work—such as McGregor's (2007) study of Zimbabwean migrants in the United Kingdom—helps to demonstrate the ways gendered migrations are mediated by relations of class and nationality. This serves as a useful counterpoint to the large body of research on female migration and opens up the debate to include discussions of men's paid work in domestic and care work. Collectively, this research demonstrates that global migration is shaped and driven by the global sexual division of labor—not just for women but also for men. Having set out the contemporary global contours of the feminization of employment, we now move on to look at the phenomenon of gender segregation in the labor force.

GENDER SEGREGATION: IMPLICATIONS AND EXPLANATIONS

Gender segregation in employment is an important analytical concept for the study of gender and work. Here we explore how gender segregation plays out in contemporary labor markets, explanations from economics and sociology, and the implications of gender segregation in employment. Since the 1960s, the term *gender segregation of employment* has been used to describe the gendered division of labor in employment. While this segregation is now less dramatic than in the past, these gendered divisions have remained resilient, in spite of substantive gendered changes in the labor market as previously outlined. A number of key concepts refine the analysis of gender segregation in employment. Horizontal or overall segregation refers to the under- or overrepresentation of men or women in a particular occupation or sector. Vertical segregation, by contrast, describes under- or overrepresentation in a particular occupation in terms of particular conditions such as income and job stability. Third, hierarchical segregation addresses the group at the top of the career ladder of specific occupations (European Commission 2009). Across the European Union, for example, in spite of equality legislation in employment, gender segregation remains high, at 25.3 percent for occupational segregation.[6] However, this varies widely between countries, with gaps as wide as ten percentage points between the most (Greece, Romania, Malta, and Italy) and least (Estonia, Slovakia, Latvia, and Finland) segregated countries (European Commission 2009, 7). Table 13.1 provides an

Table 13.1 Top ten "gender-biased" occupations on average in Europe and the United States

Many more women than men work as	Many more men than women work as
Preschool education teaching associate professionals (14.5)	Miners, shot firers, stone clutters, and carvers (80.2)
Nursing and midwifery professionals (10.1)	Building frame and related trades workers (64.8)
Secretaries and keyboard-operating clerks (9.8)	Ships' deck crews and related workers (52.9)
Nursing and midwifery associate professionals (9.5)	Building finishers and related trades workers (35.4)
Personal care and related workers (9.3)	Mining and construction laborers (35.3)
Primary education teaching associate professionals (6.2)	Agricultural and other mobile plant operators (30.5)
Shop, stall, and market salespersons and demonstrators (5.8)	Mining and mineral-processing-plant operators (24.5)
Special education teaching professionals (5.6)	Metal moulders, welders, sheet-metal workers, structural-metal preparers, and related trades workers (23.1)
Domestic and related helpers, cleaners and launderers (5.4)	Machinery mechanics and fitters (21.7)
Primary and preschool education teaching (5.3)	Power-production and related plant operators (15.9)

Notes: In the first column, the numbers in brackets are the ratios of women to men in these occupations. For example, 14.5 times more women than men work as preschool teaching associate professionals. In the second column, the genders are reversed so that, for example, there are just over 80 men working as miners, shot-firers, stone cutters, and carvers for each woman in this occupation.

Source: European Labour Force Survey and March Current Population Survey for the United States.

illustrative example of the top six jobs for women and for men in the European Union and the United States.

In global terms, there has been an overall decrease in sex-based occupational segregation in most parts of the world. However, it should be noted that this may be due to the global feminization of labor previously discussed, reflecting the deteriorating position of men rather than a substantive improvement in women's occupational status (Standing 1999, 600).

Implications

Gender segregation in employment is one of the key factors generating and perpetuating gender inequality in labor markets. Looking at gender differences in working conditions and contracts—or employment status—reveals strong divisions at the global level. Gender segregation in employment status is most pronounced in the most and least secure positions—or those considered decent and vulnerable, respectively, for clarification by the ILO—and also varies significantly by world region. For example, although employers make up the smallest category of employment worldwide, in most regions rates are twice as high for men as for women, ranging from 1 to 8 percent of the workforce. Only in Finland, Germany, and Sweden are 5 percent of employed women employers, and this proportion does not constitute more than 3 percent of the female workforce in any other region worldwide. By contrast, the majority of men and women in the global workforce are employed as wage and salaried workers, with 46 percent of female workers in this category in 2007, an increase of 3.7 percent from 1997. In some regions—OECD countries, Eastern Asia, Western Asia, and the Caribbean—employed women are more likely than men to be in wage employment, and at least 80 percent of female workers are in this category. In other regions, such as Eastern and Western Africa and Southern Asia, wage and salaried workers (both women and men) make up less than fifty percent of the workforce. Figure 13.2 shows the distribution in female status in employment.

In terms of vulnerable employment—own-account and contributing family workers—the picture is again highly varied by geographical region. In 2007, 28 percent of women workers worldwide were considered own-account workers, and 24 percent contributing family workers. From 1997, the proportion of own-account workers increased by 5.4 percent, while contributing family workers decreased by 9.3 percent, suggesting that women moved from the most vulnerable employment category into own-account, wage and salaried employment over this period. In the majority of regions, however, men are still more likely to be own-account workers, with the exception of the CIS in Asia, Central America, and South America. However, in the category of contributing family workers, high levels of gender segregation reappear, as women are more than twice as likely to be in this kind of employment compared with men in most regions. Contributing family workers are considered self-employed in a family

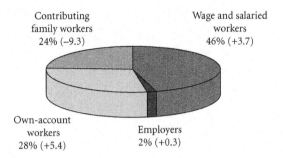

Contributing
family workers
24% (−9.3)

Wage and salaried
workers
46% (+3.7)

Own-account
workers
28% (+5.4)

Employers
2% (+0.3)

Figure 13.2 Distribution of female status in employment, 2007 (percentage point change from 1997 in parentheses). The ILO does not provide a similar breakdown for male status in employment. (From ILO 2009. With permission.)

business or enterprise, but are unpaid. This category accounts for a third of all female workers in Southern Asia, Northern Africa, and Eastern and Western Africa. This category is especially important for analyzing gender segregation, as it often entails conducting care and domestic work, replicating the sexual division of labor, and reinforcing the undervaluation of women's labor.

A further implication of gender segregation in labor markets is the *gender pay gap*. Throughout most regions and many occupations, women are paid less than men for equivalent work. In a majority of countries, women's wages represent between 70 and 90 percent of men's wages, with even lower ratios in some Asian and Latin American countries. In the EU, for example, women earn an average of 15 percent less than men for every hour worked (ILO 2009). In the OECD, gender wage gaps have decreased over time in most countries, and in the majority thereof the gap is larger for high earners. In all OECD countries, median earnings of men are higher than those of women, with an average difference of around 18 percent (OECD 2010). As Perrons (2010) notes, at the current rate it would be well into next century before the gender pay gap in OECD countries disappears. She also argues that the pay gap is much more likely to be understated than overstated, as statistics exclude the top 10 percent of earners, in which men dominate. At the same time, as outlined already, women are likely to be in very low-paid, informal jobs that may not enter into formal statistics (171). However, these national-level statistics are not able to tell us about pay gaps between different social groups. In the case of Brazil, ethnicity is a key factor influencing wages. In 1998, the average income for nonwhite Brazilian men was 46 percent of white men's, while black women earned 40 percent of the income earned by white males. In the same year, the wage gap for white Brazilian women was 79 percent, which had closed from 68 percent in 1987. In 1998, black women earned 39 percent less than white women (Young 2003, 121). In the United Kingdom, the gender pay gap declined between 1998 and 2008. However, this can partly be accounted for by widening of class differentials in UK society. While the gender pay gap is small at the lower end of the distribution, at the upper end women's pay has moved further away from that of women without qualifications and closer to that of men with qualifications (Perrons 2010, 170). Although these data are representative only of Brazil and the United Kingdom, they nevertheless point to the importance of not focusing solely on gender inequalities and highlight the complexities that are revealed by taking ethnicity and class into account.

Explanations

In terms of explanations of the causes of gender segregation in employment, the most dominant and influential have tended to come from the field of neoclassical economics, which focuses primarily on the preferences and choices of individuals in labor markets. Based on Becker's (1965) work on the allocation of time in households, human capital theory argues that "the goal of the individual is to select the utility-maximizing combination of market goods and nonmarket time" (Blau, Ferber, and Winkler 2002, 963). Using this model, economists argue that women are paid less than men because they have less skill and labor market experience and fewer qualifications as a consequence of decisions as to the allocation of the time of men and women in households (Mincer 1962; Mincer and Polachek 1974). More recently, human capital theorists have argued that women's underinvestment in education and their overrepresentation in arts and humanities disciplines in higher education reflects their expectations of prejudice in the labor market (Coate and Loury 1993). However, in terms of formal education, women in the EU outperform men all the way up to the first level of tertiary education, invalidating this argument. Indeed, in recent years, there has been a rapid gender desegregation in higher education, with the exception of mathematics and computer science.[7]

Human capital approaches to labor market theory have been strongly criticized by feminist economists, who point out that the unit of decision making is in fact assumed to be the household rather than the individual within the household (Walby 1990, 29–31). Folbre (1986) observed that neoclassical economics treated the household as a black box ruled by a benevolent dictator. Mainstream economic explanations are thus regarded as unable to explain gender segregation, as they fail to address the relationship between women's and men's labor market participation and the unequal division of care provision in the household. Through occupational segregation women tend to be concentrated in lower-paid jobs that incorporate the feminized dimensions of labor outlined already. As a consequence of widespread gendered assumptions about care roles and responsibilities, employers are able to pay men more and women less, further devaluing the specific skills required by so-called women's jobs (Bettio 1988; England 2004). In this reading, women's concentration in flexible, lower-paid work may not be a preference but rather a direct result of the unequal burden of care. Mainstream economic explanations emphasize gender deficits rather than exploring how "the work environment, the labor market and the wider economy are shaped by gendered norms and assumptions that operate to women's disadvantage" (Perrons

2010, 175). From a gender perspective, therefore, feminist economics has more to offer our analysis than mainstream theories.

The second substantive contribution to explaining gender segregation in employment comes from research in sociology. Early studies showed how attitudes to family responsibilities for women and men in the workplace differed strongly. For example, while women's fertility is seen as a liability by organizations, often a man's marriage and family plans are seen as a mark of stability. In addition, senior management ethic was identified as highly masculine, creating further barriers to women's participation in such structures (Kanter 1977). Building on this work, the sociological concept of the *cultural division of labor* describes how women and men are channeled into different occupational roles, reinforced for women by an assumption that women carry primary responsibility for child care and housework (Parcel 1999). This cultural division of labor has led to a process of *gender typing* of employment, in which women are overwhelmingly concentrated in secretarial work, nursing, and primary school teaching (Hodson and Sullivan 2008). These in turn tend to be poorly paid occupations, partly because they are predominantly filled by women (Charles and Grusky 2004).

In addition to these insights, sociological analysis also offers tools for understanding how gender interacts with class and ethnicity in the labor market—for example, the limitations imposed by the cultural division of labor for women members of minority ethnic groups may be even more restrictive (Smith 2002; Browne and Misra 2003). A further process of "occupational steering" channels women or minorities into jobs considered appropriate under the cultural division of labor (Hodson and Sullivan 2008, 87). Another useful concept developed by sociologists is the *glass ceiling*, referring to the lack of women in senior management positions. Research on the glass ceiling has shown the gendered practices that prevent women from reaching the top positions in both the private and (to a lesser extent) public sector, such as cultural capital, networking, gender stereotyping, and the characteristics of organizations (Purcell, MacArthur, and Samblanet 2010). Sociology offers tools for analyzing not just the gendered foundations of work but also the ways inequality is sustained in organizational cultures. This overview of the gender segregation of employment demonstrates the salience of the impact of the sexual division of labor on the global workforce.

THE ENDURING IMPACT OF THE SEXUAL DIVISION OF LABOR AND UNPAID WORK

Labor markets have changed. The processes of feminization, informalization, migration, and the changing contours of gender segregation demonstrate how the gender dynamics of employment have changed over time and in different geographical locations. Households too have changed. There is very little evidence to suggest that the "breadwinner" model is universally the norm, with female-headed households on the rise worldwide (see, for example, Chant 2008; see also the chapter by Razavi in this volume). The diversity of global households is reflected in the convergence of male and female labor force participation rates and growing prevalence of unemployment among men. However, in spite of the decline in the breadwinner model in concrete terms, this concept continues to shape the gendered discourse and practice of labor markets. There is evidence to suggest that macroeconomic analysis of labor markets is beginning to take into account changing household dynamics. For example, new economic models offer an "updated, 'modern' ideal of a sharing heterosexual partnership in the home" (Bergeron 2011, 75). However, this model is still premised on an assumption of a traditional nuclear family and as such fails to recognize the diversity of household arrangements and unpaid work that is done worldwide. Moreover, such models are still unable to move beyond the autonomous individual as the model economic actor and fundamentally "ignore the inexorable interdependency of human life and the importance for human well-being of connection" (England and Folbre 2003, 34).

The sexual division of labor is an enduring structure of gender inequality worldwide. As the UN's latest *Progress of the World's Women* reports:

> In spite of the changes that have occurred in women's participation in the labor market, women continue to bear most of the responsibilities for the home: caring for children and other dependent household members, preparing meals and doing other housework. In all regions, women spend at least twice as much time as men on unpaid domestic work. Women who are employed spend an inordinate amount of time on the double burden of paid work and family responsibilities; when unpaid work is taken into account, women's total work hours are longer than men's in all regions (UN 2010).

There is now a broad range of methodological tools for comparing women's and men's work in this area. Figures 13.3, 13.4, and 13.5 offer detailed statistics on women and men's unpaid domestic work in Asia, OECD countries, and globally. They reveal that the differences between Asia and the OECD are not vastly different in terms of the inequality in the allocation of time to household tasks. Variations between countries are significant. For example, the proportion of total time spent on care work by women with two children or more varies from 9 percent in Canada to 23 percent in Mexico. The largest differences are recorded for Japan and Turkey, where women spend on average four and six times more time on care work than men, respectively (OECD 2010). We can see that in all countries for which data are included, women work twice as many hours as men in all household tasks except shopping. The largest imbalances are in preparing meals and cleaning.

In addition to time spent on household caring and domestic tasks, OECD statistics show that men universally report spending more time in activities classified as *leisure* than women.[8] Gender differences in leisure time are wide across OECD countries. While Norwegian men spend just a few minutes more

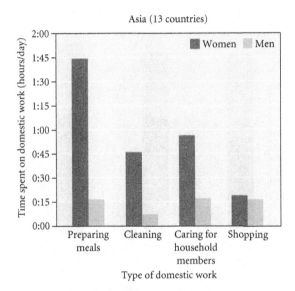

Figure 13.3 Time spent on household tasks by sex, 1999–2008, Asia. Computed by the United Nations Statistics Division based on country-level data from Statistics Sweden, UNECE, and national statistical offices (as of December 2009). Unweighted averages.

a day on leisure activities than women, Italian men spend nearly 80 minutes a day more than women on these kinds of activities (OECD 2010).

These divisions of labor in unpaid work matter because they discipline women's and men's interaction in the labor market. In addition to the previously

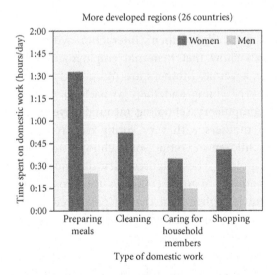

Figure 13.4 Time spent on household tasks by sex, 1999–2008, more developed regions. Computed by the United Nations Statistics Division based on country-level data from Statistics Sweden, UNECE, and national statistical offices (as of December 2009). Unweighted averages.

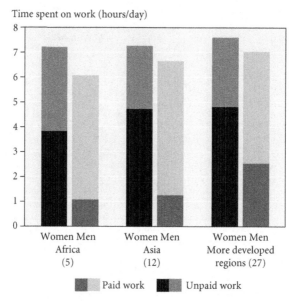

Figure 13.5 Time spent on paid and unpaid work by region and sex, 1999–2008,
Asia. Computed by the United Nations Statistics Division based on country-level
data from Statistics Sweden, UNECE, and national statistical offices (as of December
2009). Unweighted averages; the numbers in brackets indicate the number of
countries averaged.

addressed issues such as women's assumed natural capacity for care and their
overwhelming concentration in care work and care-related activities, it is interesting to look specifically at some instances of how one aspect of unpaid work—
parenting—affects women's and men's interaction with the labor market. Data
for OECD countries show that maternal employment rates tend to be lower
than for women as a whole. Mothers are more likely to be out of work when
their children are very young and then go back to work when their children
reach the age of compulsory schooling (around 6 years of age). The employment gap between mothers with very young children (less than 3 years old)
and mothers with children in compulsory school (6 to 15 years old) is, on average, 25 percentage points. These figures vary depending on women's relationship status. For example, in most countries the proportion of single mothers
in paid employment is higher than that of partnered mothers, particularly in
Greece, Italy, and Spain, where differences are around 20 percentage points. By
contrast, in countries where income support for sole parents is substantial and
where—at least until recently—there has been little expectation of them being
in work, employment rates among sole mothers are much lower than those of
partnered mothers, as, for example, in Ireland and the United Kingdom (OECD
2010). These illustrative figures demonstrate clearly how women's employment
prospects are directly affected by their continued responsibilities for child care
in the sexual division of labor.

To explore these inequalities in greater detail, we now turn briefly to a contemporary debate in gender and work—whether accounting for unpaid work has the potential to redress inequalities in the labor market. Addressing the economic value of (women's) unpaid work has long been a concern of those in the socialist feminist tradition. The wages for housework campaign of the 1970s argued that women's domestic and care work was work like any other and, as such, should be paid a salary (Dalla Costa and James 1973). This highlights the complexity of any discussion of remuneration for domestic and care work. For example, as Ehrenreich (1992) asks, to what extent is it possible to define all such activities as work? Where, for example, does an activity such as kissing children goodnight fall in our analysis of what is work (143)? In spite of these tensions, in contemporary debates feminists economists and feminist political economists have presented a case for assessing the contribution to the gross domestic product of women's unpaid labor (Hoskyns and Rai 2007). Attempts to integrate the economic contribution of unpaid work are currently under way at the Systems of National Accounting at the UN and in the United Kingdom. This is collected using methodological tools such as time use studies and other methods derived from feminist economics.

To a certain extent, therefore, it can be argued that (women's) unpaid care and domestic work is being taken seriously and taken into account in policy analyses of work and employment. Indeed, a "crisis of care" has been identified in the EU through the mass entry of women into the paid labor force along with low fertility rates and high life expectancy (Benería 2010, 143). At the global level, specific policies—in particular from the World Bank—have been designed to tackle this perceived crisis. These involve addressing men's contribution to unpaid work and funding income-generation projects that encourage women to work from home. However, such strategies have been highly criticized by feminists working on development issues, who argue that these projects serve to reinforce assumptions about the sexual division of labor and the heterosexual nuclear family rather than working to transform the basis of such inequalities (Bedford 2007; Ferguson 2010). As such, in some ways it can be argued that unpaid care work has been made visible in employment statistics and labor market analysis. However, in general this process has been carried out to the detriment of concerns for redressing inequalities in labor markets, in particular intersecting inequalities such as class, ethnicity, and sexuality. In order to draw these points together, we now turn to some final conclusions.

CONCLUSIONS

This brief overview of gender and work demonstrates that the gender dynamics of employment are neither static nor fixed. Nevertheless, by looking at the occupations in which women and men work, the gender pay gap, and unpaid care and domestic work, we can see clearly that gender inequality persists in all dimensions of labor markets, the EU, and the OECD and at the global level. As Suzanne Bair (2010, 205) argues, research shows that "*how* gender matters in a particular location on the global assembly line is variable and contingent; *that* gender matters is not." Women are not always in a worse position than men in labor markets. Indeed, in some places and at some times women's position is better than that of men's. Some of the recent analyses of the impact of the global economic crisis on developed economies initially identified it as a "man-cession", since male unemployment rose disproportionately as male-dominated private-sector jobs, for example, in heavy manufacturing and finance, went first, only to be followed by large increases in female unemployment as state-sector employees, predominantly women working in lower-level caring and clerical posts, lost their jobs as a consequence of public spending cuts.

But broad generalizations about gender inequality in employment need to take into account other axes of inequality such as class, ethnicity, national-ity, and sexuality. This moves away from an assumption that gender is always the primary inequality in every context but rather explores the ways gendered labor markets draw on and reinforce inequalities based on ethnicity, class, and nationality. However, in contrast to data on women and men's labor force par-ticipation, such information is not really counted in any substantive way. Also, it is very difficult to move beyond an analysis of *men* and *women* in employ-ment because there is currently little acknowledgment of gender diversity in statistics. This should be highlighted as an area in which research is lacking.

By weaving together statistics and analysis from different geographical and analytical levels, the chapter has shown how different literatures can productively feed into each other. For example, a focus on global care chains and gendered labor migrations demonstrates the necessity of taking a global approach to labor markets, as a national focus obscures the complexity of work in gendered ways. A global analysis also allows for a more comprehensive reflection on the ways different inequalities intersect in labor markets, in particular when nationality is brought into the picture. In addition, a wide range of literatures can be brought to bear on the analysis of gender and work. The chapter has integrated contri-butions from sociology, economics, political economy, and development studies, with the aim of teasing out some of the key contributions to this broad field of study and addressing as wide a range of themes as possible.

The multiple processes of the feminization of employment, informalization, and labor migrations have been explored here to demonstrate how the gender dynamics of labor markets and household arrangements have been restruc-tured. As argued throughout the chapter, these gendered restructurings have had little impact on increasing gender equality either in employment or unpaid work. Rather, the sexual division of labor and associated gendered myths, such as the male breadwinner model, mean that women still perform more than twice the unpaid work that men do. In turn, this disciplines labor markets in highly gendered ways, leading to gender segregation, the gender pay gap, and the concentration of women in vulnerable employment. Gender matters in the analysis of work, since without a gender analysis the unequal dynamics of employment and unpaid work are rendered invisible and the complexity of these inequalities is obscured. At the same time, work matters in the analysis of gender and politics, as both employment and unpaid work structure and discipline the ways women and men interact with the "public" sphere of informal and formal politics.

NOTES

1. The ILO defines vulnerable employment as those who fall into the categories of *unpaid family worker* and *own-account worker.*
2. 2008 is the latest year for which this data is available at the time of writing.
3. OECD countries: Australia, Austria, Belgium, Canada, Chile, Czech Republic, Denmark, Estonia, Finland, France, Germany, Greece, Hungary, Iceland, Ireland, Israel, Italy, Japan, Korea, Luxembourg, Mexico, Netherlands, New Zealand, Norway, Poland, Portugal, Slovak Republic, Slovenia, Spain, Sweden, Switzerland, Turkey, United Kingdom, United States.
4. http://www.iom.int/jahia/Jahia/about-migration/lang/en
5. For a detailed definition of social reproduction, see the other chapters on political economy in this volume.
6. Based on the IP index, which represents the share of the employed population that would need to change occupation (sector) to bring about an even distribution of men and women among occupations or sectors.
7. Eurostat (2008, Table A.20)
8. These detailed statistics are not provided by ILO. As such, OECD data has been used here instead.

REFERENCES

Arat-Koç, S. 2006. "Whose social reproduction? Transnational motherhood and challenges to feminist political economy." In K. Bezanson and M. Luxton, eds., *Social reproduction: Feminist political economy challenges neo-liberalism.* Montreal: McGill-Queens University Press, 75–92.

Bach, Jonathan. 2011. "Remittances, gender and development." In Marianne H. Marchand and Anne Sisson Runyan, eds., *Gender and global restructuring: Sightings, sites and resistances.* London: Routledge, 129–142.

Bair, Jennifer. 2010. "On difference and capital: Gender and the globalization of production." *Signs* 36(1): 203–226.

Barber, Pauline Gardiner. 2011. "Women's work *unbound*: Philippine development and global restructuring."In Marianne Marchand and Anne Sisson Runyan, eds., *Gender and global restructuring: Sightings, sites, and resistances.* New York: Routledge, 143–162.

Barrientos, Stephanie, Anna Bee, Ann Matear and Isabel Vogel. 1999. *Women and agribusiness working miracles in the chilean fruit export sector*. New York: Macmillan, Basingstoke and St Martin's Press.

Barrientos, Stephanie. 2001. "Gender, flexibility and global value chains." *IDS Bulletin* 32(3): 83–93.

Becker, Gary S. 1965. "A theory of the allocation of time." *Economic Journal* 75(299): 493–517.

Bedford, Kate. 2007. "The imperative of male inclusion: How institutional context influences World Bank gender policy." *International Feminist Journal of Politics* 9(3): 289–311.

Benería, Lourdes. 2010. "The crisis of care, international migration, and public policy." In Debra Howcroft and Helen Richardson, eds., *Work and life in the global economy: A gendered analysis of service work*. London: Palgrave Macmillan, 142–164.

Bergeron, Suzanne. 2011. "Governing gender in neoliberal restructuring: economics, performativity, and social reproduction." In Marianne H. Marchand and Anne Sisson Runyan, eds., *Gender and global restructuring: sightings, sites and resistances*. London: Routledge, 66–78.

Bettio, F. 1988. *The sexual division of labor: the Italian case*. Oxford: Clarendon Press.

Blau, Francine, Marianne Ferber, and Anne Winkler. 2002. *The economics of women, men, and work*, 6th ed.. Upper Saddle River, NJ: Prentice Hall.

Brodie, Janine. 2003. "Globalization, in/security, and the paradoxes of the social." In Isabella Bakker and Stephen Gill, eds., *Power production and social reproduction*. Houndmills: Palgrave Macmillan, 47–66.

Browne, Irene, and Joya Misra. 2003. "The intersection of gender and race in the labor market." *Annual Review of Sociology* 29: 487–513.

Bruegel, Irene. 1999. "Who gets on the escalator? Migration, social mobility and gender in Britain." In Paul Boyle and Keith Halfacree, eds., *Migration and gender in the developed world*. London: Routledge, 86–101.

Bunch, S., and R. Mehra. 2008. "Women help solve hunger: Why is the world still waiting?" Washington: International Center for Research on Women (ICRW).

Caraway, Teri. 2007. *Assembling women: The feminization of global manufacturing*. Ithaca, NY: Cornell University Press.

Chang, Kimberly A., and L. H. M. Ling. 2011. "Globalization and its intimate other." In Marianne H. Marchand and Anne Sisson Runyan, eds., *Gender and global restructuring: sightings, sites and resistances*. London: Routledge, 30–48.

Chant, Sylvia. 2008. "Dangerous equations? How female-headed households became the poorest of the poor: Causes, consequences and cautions." In Janet Momsen, ed., *Gender and development: Critical concepts in development studies*, London: Routledge, 397–409.

Charles, Maria, and David B. Grusky. 2004. *Occupational ghettos: The worldwide segregation of women and men*. Stanford, CA: Stanford University Press.

Coate, S., and G. Loury. 1993. "Will affirmative action policies eliminate negative stereotypes?" *American Economic Review* 83(5): 1220–1240.

Crompton, Rosemary. 2000. "The gendered restructuring of the middle classes: Employment and caring." In Rosemary Crompton, Flora Devine, Mike Savage and John Scott, eds., *Renewing class analysis*. Oxford: Blackwell and The Sociological Review.

Dalla Costa, Mariarosa, and Selma James. 1973. *The power of women and the subversion of the community*. Bristol: Falling Wall Press.

D'Mello, Mariza. 2010. "Are you married? Exploring gender in a global workplace in India." In Debra Howcroft and Helen Richardson, eds., *Work and life in the global economy: A gendered analysis of service work.* Basingstoke, UK: Palgrave Macmillan, 52–77.

Ehrenreich, Barbara. 1992. "Life without father: reconsidering socialist-feminist theory." In Linda McDowell and Rosemary Pringle, eds., *Defining women: Social institutions and gender divisions.* Milton Keynes: Polity Press, 140–148.

Ehrenreich, Barbara, and Arlie Russell Hochschild. 2003. *Global woman: Nannies, maids, and sex workers in the new economy.* London: Granta.

Elias, Juanita. 2008. "Hegemonic masculinities, the multinational corporation, and the developmental state: Constructing gender in 'progressive' firms." *Men and Masculinities* 10(4): 405–421.

Elson, Diane. 2000. "Gender at the macroeconomic level." In Joanne Cook, Jennifer Roberts, and Georgina Waylen, eds., *Towards a gendered political economy.* Basingstoke: Macmillan Press, 77–97.

Elson, Diane, and Ruth Pearson. 1981. "Nimble fingers make cheap workers: An analysis of women's employment in third world manufacturing." *Feminist Review* 7: 87–107.

England, P. 2004. "Does bad pay cause occupations to feminize, does feminization reduce pay, and how can we tell with longitudinal data?" Mimeo, Department of Sociology, Stanford University, Stanford, CA.

England, Paula, and Nancy Folbre. 2003. "Contracting for care." In Marianne A. Ferber and Julie A. Nelson, eds., *Feminist economics today: Beyond economic man.* Chicago: University of Chicago Press.

European Commission. 2009. "Gender segregation in the labor market: Root causes, implications and policy responses in the EU." Available online at http://ec.europa.eu/social/main.jsp?catId=738&langId=es&pubId=364&furtherPubs=yes.

FAO. 2011. *The State of Food and Agriculture 2010–11, Women in Agriculture: Closing the gender gap for development.* Rome: Food and Agriculture Organization of the United Nations.

FAO-ILO. 2009. *Gender dimensions of rural and agricultural employment: Differentiated pathways out of poverty, a global perspective.* Available online at http://www.fao.org/docrep/013/i1638e/i1638e.pdf.

Ferguson, Lucy. 2010. "Tourism development and the restructuring of social reproduction in Central America." *Review of International Political Economy* 17(5): 860–888.

Fernández-Kelly, Maria Patricia. 1983. *For we are sold, I and my people: Women and industry in Mexico's frontier.* Albany: State University of New York Press.

Folbre, Nancy. 1986. "Hearts *and* spades: Paradigms of household economics." *World Development* 14(2): 245–255.

Freeman, Carla. 2010. "Respectability and flexibility in the neoliberal service economy." In Debra Howcroft and Helen Richardson, eds., *Work and life in the global economy: A gendered analysis of service work.* London: Palgrave Macmillan, 33–51.

Hartmann, Heidi. 1983. "Capitalism, patriarchy, and job segregation by sex." In E. Abel and E. K. Abel, eds., *The signs reader: Women, gender and scholarship.* Chicago: University of Chicago Press.

Hochschild, Arlie. 2000. "Global care chains and emotional surplus value." In Will Hutton and Anothony Giddens, eds., *On the edge: Living with global capitalism.* London: Jonathan Cape, 130–146.

Hodson, Randy, and Teresa A. Sullivan. 2008. *The social organization of work*. Belmont, CA: Thomson Wadsworth.

Hoskyns, Catherine, and Shirin Rai. 2007. "Recasting the global political economy: Counting women's unpaid work." *New Political Economy* 12(3): 297–317.

Howcroft, Debra, and Helen Richardson. 2010. "Introduction." In Debra Howcroft and Helen Richardson, eds., *Work and life in the global economy: A gendered analysis of service work*. London: Palgrave Macmillan, 1–14.

ILO. 2007. *Global employment trends for women*. Geneva: ILO.

ILO. 2009. *Global employment trends for women*. Geneva: ILO.

Jones, Adele. 2008. "A silent but mighty river: The costs of women's economic migration." *Signs* 33(4): 761–769.

Kanter, Rosabeth Moss. 1977. *Men and women of the corporation*. New York: Basic Books.

Katz, Cindi. 2001. "Vagabond capitalism and the necessity of social reproduction." *Antipode* 33(4): 708–727.

Kofman, Eleonore, and Parvati Raghuram. 2006. "Gender and global labor migrations: Incorporating skilled workers." *Antipode* 38(2): 282–303.

Korovkin, Tanya. 2002. "Cut flower exports, female labour and community participation in highland Ecuador." *Latin American Perspectives* 30(4): 18–42.

Kuhn, Annette, and AnnMarie Wolpe. 1978. "Feminism and materialism." In Annette Kuhn and AnnMarie Wolpe, eds., *Feminism and materialism: Women and modes of production*. London: Routledge, 1–11.

Lastarria-Cornhiel, Susana. 2008. *Feminization of agriculture: Trends and driving forces*. Available online at http://siteresources.worldbank.org/INTWDR2008/Resources/2795087-1191427986785/LastarriaCornhiel_FeminizationOfAgri.pdf.

Lee, Ching Kwan. 1998. *Gender and the South China miracle: Two worlds of factory women*. Berkley: University of California Press.

Lim, Linda Y. C. 1985. *Women workers in multinational enterprizes in developing countries*. Geneva: ILO.

McGregor, Joann. "Joining the BBC (British Bottom Cleaners): Zimbabwean migrants and the UK care industry." *Journal of Ethnic and Migration Studies* 33(5): 801–824.

Mincer, J. 1962. Labor force participation of married women: A study of labor supply. In H. Gregg and H.G. Lewis (Eds.), *Aspects of labor economics*. Princeton, NJ: Princeton University Press, 63–97.

Mincer, Jacob, and Solomon Polachek. 1974. "Family investments in human capital: Earnings of women." *Journal of Political Economy* 82(2): 76–108.

Organisation for Economic Co-operation and Development (OECD). 2010. *Gender Brief March 2010*. Paris: OECD.

Parcel, Toby (Ed.). 1999. *Work and family: Research in the sociology of work*, vol. 7. Greenwich, CT: JAI Press.

Pearson, Ruth. 1998. "'Nimble fingers' revisited. Reflections on women and Third World industrialization in the late twentieth century." In Cecile Jackson and Ruth Pearson, eds., *Feminist visions of development: Gender, analysis and policy*. London: Routledge, 171–188.

Pearson, Ruth. 2007. "Reassessing paid work and women's empowerment: lessons from the global economy." In Andrea Cornwall, Elizabeth Harrison and Ann Whitehead, eds., *Feminisms in development: Contradictions, contestations and challenges*. London: Zed Books, 201–213.

Perrons, Diane. 2004. *Globalization and social change: People and places in a divided world*. London: Routledge.

Perrons, Diane. 2010. "Reflections on gender and pay inequalities in the contemporary service economy." In Debra Howcroft and Helen Richardson, eds., *Work and life in the global economy: A gendered analysis of service work*. London: Palgrave Macmillan, 165–184.

Perrons, Diane, Ania Plomien, and Majella Kilkey. 2010. "Migration and uneven development within and enlarged European Union: Fathering, gender divisions and male migrant domestic services." *European Urban and Regional Studies* 17(2): 197–215.

Purcell, David, Kelly Rhea MacArthur, and Sarah Samblanet. 2010. "Gender and the glass ceiling at work." *Sociology Compass* 4(9): 705–717.

Ransom, Elizabeth, and Carmen Bain. 2011. "Gendering agricultural aid: An analysis of whether international development assistance targets women and gender." *Gender & Society* 25: 48–73.

Raynolds, Laura T. 2002. "Wages for wives: Renegotiating gender and production relations in contract farming in the Dominican Republic." *World Development* 30(5): 783–798.

Safa, Helen I. 1981. "Runaway shops and female employment: The search for cheap labor." *Signs* 7(2): 418–433.

Salzinger, L. 2003. *Genders in production: Making workers in Mexico's global factories*. Berkley: University of California Press, 2003.

Schwenken, Helen. 2008. "Beautiful victims and sacrificing heroines: Exploring the role of gender knowledge in migration policies." *Signs* 33(4): 770–776.

Smith, Ryan A. (2002). "Race, gender and authority in the workplace: theory and research." *Annual Review of Sociology* 28: 509–542.

Standing, Guy. 1989. "Global feminization through flexible labor." *World Development* 17(7): 1077–1095.

Standing, Guy. 1999. "Global feminization through flexible labor: A theme revisited." *World Development* 27(3): 583–602.

United Nations. 2010. *The world's women 2010: Trends and statistics*. New York: United Nations.

Walby, Sylvia. 1990. *Theorizing patriarchy*. Oxford: Blackwell.

Waring, Marilyn. 1988. *If women counted: A new feminist economics*. San Francisco: Harper & Row.

Webster, Juliet. 2010. "Clerks, Cashiers, Customer Carers: Women's Work in European Services." In Debra Howcroft and Helen Richardson, eds., *Work and life in the global economy: A gendered analysis of service work*. London: Palgrave Macmillan, 185–208.

Wolf, Diane Lauren. 1992. *Factory daughters: Gender, household dynamics, and rural industrialization in Java*. Berkeley: University of California Press.

Wright, Melissa. 2006. *Disposable women and other myths of global capitalism*. London: Routledge.

Yeates, Nicola. 2004. "Global care chains." *International Feminist Journal of Politics* 6(3): 369–391.

Young, Brigitte. 2003. "Financial crises and social reproduction: Asia, Argentina and Brazil." In Isabella Bakker and Stephen Gill, eds., *Power production and social reproduction*. Houndmills: Palgrave Macmillan, 103–124.

PART IV

....

CIVIL SOCIETY

....

THIS section includes essays on the burgeoning literature on gender politics in civil society, that is, gender politics involving the "soft power" of voluntary action, organization, and persuasion rather than the coercive power of the state. The scope and dimensions of civil society are contested: some argue civil society should include everything outside the state, including the market, while others argue that such corporate and economic activities are the antithesis of the idea of civil society. Others wonder whether activists who move onto the terrain of the state count as civil society actors. Some have argued that civil society is a type of activity, not a physical location, and that the key feature of such activity is that it is voluntary and not subject to system imperatives such as bureaucratic rules or profit imperatives.

However it is defined, though, nearly all definitions include social movements and voluntary organizations, and these sorts of activities are the focus of this section. Discussion of civil society across these essays includes general efforts to organize (in interest groups, nongovernmental organizations [NGOs], think tanks, lobby groups) and mobilize (in movements, coalitions and campaigns) pressure and persuade governments and other citizens on matters of policy but also on matters of justice in areas often thought of as *private* or *apolitical* (e.g., the family, schools, sexuality). This includes not only women's organizing in feminist movements and organizations but also the way that gender structures men's efforts to mobilize and organize. It also includes women and men's gendered participation in nongender-focused movements (e.g., labor movements, antiracist movements, peace, environmental, conservative and racist movements).

The chapters deal with the ways that gendered identities undergird all forms of civil society organizing and the challenges (as well as advantages) that group differences present to efforts to build solidarity in women's movements and feminist movements. This literature likely has important implications for efforts to organize all forms of social movements. In addition, the essays examine the relationships between different kinds of organizing in terms of forms (for example, different types of organizations) and level, location, or context (for example, local or global, national or transnational). These essays also show how the political opportunity structure, and the political environment more generally, is gendered and how that shapes women and men's organizing. This organizing, of course, also transforms the political opportunity structure, for example, sometimes producing institutional reforms such as gender and mainstreaming and changing the public mood and cultural attitudes about gender, among other effects. As such, social movements change the relationship between state and civil society.

The first chapter by Dara Strolovitch and Erica Townsend-Bell discusses the way gender structures civil society more generally, considering a wider range of civil society organizations. The essay begins with definitional questions, explaining the meaning of civil society and how it is related to gender, both empirically and conceptually, paying particular attention to the implicit assumptions about race, class, and sexuality that undergird different conceptualizations of civil society (for example, conceptualizations of civil society as a public sphere). The question of the autonomy of civil society, and the importance of this concept for gender, is also considered. The authors also point to the contradictory impact of civil society on gender—involving as it does the capacity to simultaneously empower women while also reproducing gendered norms of inequality. This chapter asks how these definitions and relationships apply in varying ways over time and context, focusing in particular on the United States and Latin America, and highlights areas of research on civil society that require further investigation.

The second chapter examines gender in movements, focusing not so much on feminism or women's movements as on social movements more generally. The chapter examines the ways that gendered identities shape movements and also the ways that movements work in gendered environments. Kelsy Kretschmer and David S. Meyer distinguish and consider feminist, antifeminist, and nonfeminist movements and examine the role of gender in each. The chapter discusses a wide range of movements from terrorist, radical, and racist contestations to labor and peace movements.

The third chapter, titled "The Comparative Study of Women's Movements," reviews definitions of women's movements in the recent comparative and social movement scholarship on women's movements. Karen Beckwith offers distinctions between women's movements, feminist movements, and women in movements, discussing different approaches to women's activism in and support for political movements (including movements that are not women's movements). The chapter points to the distinctive advantages of taking a comparative approach to the analysis of women's movements, their similarities and differences, and their successes and failures, particularly in terms of understandings intersectionality.

The fourth chapter, by Christina Ewig and Myra Marx Ferree, examines feminist organizing from the nineteenth century to the present. Moving away from the *waves* imagery, Ewig and Ferree see feminist organizing as following a less unified logic, as cresting and falling in different parts of the world at different times. This overview explores how solidarity is constructed, given the intersectionality of feminist claims making. It also examines the changing organizational forms of feminist mobilization and links these to the changing political opportunity structure. The essay takes issue with the idea that feminist organizing is in decline.

The fifth chapter, "Local—Global—Local: Women's Global Organizing," by Jutta Joachim examines women's global and transnational organizing and connections to local action. The chapter discusses definitions and debates about the meaning of the terms global, transnational, international, local, and grassroots, especially as they apply to gender politics. Drawing on the social movement literature, the chapter explores the relations and interdependencies that exist between the local and global, showing how women's personal and local experiences have been sources of both global cooperation and solidarity as well as of conflict. The chapter examines the conceptual basis for studying transnational activist networks, especially considering the idea of cosmopolitanism, and offers an overview of the history of women's transnational campaigns. Turning to contemporary politics, Joachim examines the ways that international organizations such as the United Nations and international institutions related to human rights, for example, shape local politics, arguing that women's global activism involves filtering processes and layers of interpretations and that the initiators of campaigns do not always control the ways that their issues and problems are defined.

CHAPTER 14

SEX, GENDER, AND CIVIL SOCIETY

DARA Z. STROLOVITCH AND ERICA TOWNSEND-BELL

"FRAZZLED Moms Push Back against Volunteering" read a headline on the first page of the December 2, 2010, "Home" section of the *New York Times* (Stout 2010). "It was last spring," the article began, "somewhere between overseeing Teacher Appreciation Week and planning the fifth-grade graduation party, when Jamie Lentzner, mother of two in Foster City, Calif., reached her breaking point." Today, however, "Ms. Lentzner is a new woman. She has yet to attend a PTA meeting or decorate so much as a classroom doorknob. When she saw her name listed as chairwoman of the annual Donuts for Dads Day...she whipped out a Sharpie and crossed it out. 'No, I'm not,' she wrote. Since then, her children's room décor business has improved, and she now has time 'to play with the children.'" The article continued:

> Around the country there are a number of altruistic, devoted and totally burned-out mothers just like Ms. Lentzner who are becoming emboldened to push back against the relentless requests from their children's schools for their time...Under the headline "Just Say NO to Volunteering," Sarah Auerswald, a former PTA president in Los Angeles, wrote [on her blog] in June, "What I am about to say is not very PC, so get ready: Moms, stop volunteering so much."

If PTA meetings and graduation parties are prototypical women's voluntary activities, images of *burned-out mothers* who try to balance these activities with parenting and their paid employment have become stereotypes of twenty-first-century middle-class, heteronormative womanhood.

As such, although the *New York Times* article purported to address public schools' increasing demands for parental volunteers both male and female, its title, its placement in the "Home" section, and, most centrally, its focus on volunteerism's particular burdens for women provide a lens into some of the central issues at the nexus of the evolving relationships among sex, gender, and civil society in contemporary politics. First, the article highlights definitional questions. What is civil society and how is it related to gender, both empirically and conceptually, as well as in its capacity as an object of study? Second, the article raises questions about the implications of these definitions and relationships for understanding gender politics. Finally, do the answers to these questions vary across time or location? If so, why and to what effect?

This chapter addresses each of these three broad sets of questions about the relationships among gender, and civil society, focusing in particular on the United States and Latin America. We begin by exploring the history and evolution of the definition and meanings of civil society as they implicate women and gender, particularly as they relate to assumptions about race, class, and sexuality. We then examine women's historical and contemporary presence in civil society, reflecting on the gendered assumptions that underlie civil society's conceptualization as a public sphere. We move on to consider whether civil society functions conceptually and practically as an autonomous sphere, as well as the repercussions of autonomy, or the lack thereof, for women's involvement and for civil society's attention to gender issues. Next, we explore civil society's contradictory capacity to simultaneously empower women while also reproducing gendered norms of inequality. The essay concludes with a discussion about the implications of our discussion for contemporary gender politics and about some areas that would benefit from additional research.

These topics do not, by any means, represent an exhaustive list of the many important questions about the relationship among sex, gender, and civil society. Taken together, however, they draw attention to several constellations of questions and concepts that simultaneously illuminate key aspects of gender and civil society while also suggesting some issues that stand to benefit from further inquiry. They highlight three topics in particular: gendered spheres in civil society; the gendered impact of limited civil society autonomy; and the recreation of gendered norms in civil society. These topics make clear that examining the shifting ways in which, and the extent to which, women and gender figure into definitions of discussions about *civil society* provides a Rorschach test for discerning prevailing attitudes and normative assumptions about women and gender, particularly as these gendered norms and assumptions intersect with and help to construct race, class, and sexuality in particular locations and at particular moments in history.

CIVIL SOCIETY: SHIFTING DEFINITIONS, EVOLVING IMPLICATIONS

Spurred, in part, by its deployment by Eastern European activists and scholars, the last three decades have witnessed renewed interest in—and critiques of—civil society (Howell 2005a; Edwards 2009). Perhaps because of this renewed attention, understandings and definitions of civil society vary widely. At a general level, civil society is typically defined as the realm of public life that is distinct from the state, the economy, and the private sphere of family and the home. Yet, like many concepts in the social sciences and humanities, *civil society* is chameleon-like, encompassing broadly ranging interpretations that have been deployed "to justify...radically different viewpoints" (Edwards, 3). Among conservatives, for example, the term civil society often references efforts to reduce the "role of politics in society by expanding free markets and individual liberty" (2). Others, especially on the left, see civil society "as the seedbed for radical social movements...'the single most viable alternative to the authoritarian state and tyrannical market'" (3). As Jude Howell argues, "Politicians, activists, government bureaucrats, and intellectuals across the globe continue to embrace the discourse of civil society to explain and justify their differing visions of the world and their course of action" (38).

Definitions of civil society have also evolved over time and have done so in ways that overlap with changing ideas about women, gender, and sexuality—particularly as they intersect with other categories of oppression and marginalization such as race and class. Although civil society is typically treated as separate from the state, it was, in fact (with apologies to John Kerry), considered "of the state before it was opposed to it." That is, as anthropologist Susan Gal notes, in antiquity, civil society was more typically equated with the state, before being reconceptualized in the late eighteenth century as "not only separate from, but even opposed to, the state and its laws, on the one hand, and economic (market) relations on the other" (Gal 1997, 30). As Michael Edwards (2009, 7) explains, these Enlightenment ideas about civil society were responses to "the breakdown of traditional paradigms of authority as a consequence of the French and American revolutions." In contrast to Aristotle, Plato, and Hobbes, he writes, these thinkers tended to view civil society as a defense against unwarranted intrusions by the state on "newly realized individual rights and freedoms, organized through...a self-regulating universe of associations...that needed...to be protected from the state in order to preserve its role in resisting despotism" (ibid.).

In addition to ideological differences and variations over time, civil society theorists also note that the meaning of civil society varies geographically, by political system, and by regime type and that such variations bring with them differences in the extent to which civil society is truly autonomous from the state (Howard 2003; Oxhorn 2006). This variation is captured by the distinctions between two major conceptions of civil society's proper relationship to the state, which Foley and Edwards (1996) label *liberal* and *revolutionary* approaches to civil society. In the liberal conception, civil society is thought to be necessary to democracy because of its "ability to foster civility in the actions of citizens in a democratic polity" (38). This conceptualization, exemplified by the work of Robert Putnam (2000), contends that the fabric of democracy is upheld in large part by strong networks of association among citizens. Critics have noted, however, that the connection between civil society and politics in the liberal conception is ambiguous, as proponents of this approach typically do not distinguish among the types of associations to which one might belong. As Iris Marion Young observes, for example, Putnam's conception of civil society equates membership in bowling leagues with participation in more formal civic or political associations (Young 2000).

In contrast to such liberal schema, revolutionary notions of civil society treat it as a potentially democratizing mechanism. Liberal conceptions of civil society assume the existence of democratic states and look favorably on state–civil society interaction, whereas revolutionary models conceive of civil society as "a sphere of action that is independent of the state and that is capable—precisely for this reason—of energizing resistance to a tyrannical regime" (Foley and Edwards 1996, 38). Thus, civil society acts "as a counterweight to the state," whether authoritarian or democratic. While the two approaches are distinct, however, they are neither static nor mutually exclusive. So, for example, the civil societies of many developing democracies that once took revolutionary forms soon came to resemble liberal configurations (Diamond 1994). In some cases, such transformations take place because civil society activists gain material benefits from a more conciliatory role. In other cases, the change is due to the difficulty of maintaining the degree of autonomy necessary to sustain a revolutionary approach. Because this is particularly true of authoritarian, quasi-, or developing democratic settings, revolutionary civil society is typically more tenuous in some of the locations where it might be most beneficial (Einhorn and Sever 2001; Foley and Edwards 1996). Even where authoritarian vestiges are successfully eradicated and citizens have meaningful freedom of voice, assembly, and information, variations in the degree to which civil society organizations rely on funding from international sources as well as financial support from state and other institutions within their own countries have implications for the extent to which civil society is truly autonomous from the state. And, as we discuss at greater length in this chapter, such variations in autonomy have implications for the extent of women's empowerment.

Finally, scholars have long disagreed about whether civil society encompasses or excludes the *family*. While theorists including Jean-Jacques Rousseau, Adam Ferguson, Thomas Paine, Alexis de Tocqueville, Georg Wilhelm Friedrich Hegel, and Jürgen Habermas have distinguished civil society not only from the state but also from the private realm of family and domestic life, contemporary theorists such as Jean Cohen and Andrew Arato treat the family as part of civil society (Howell 2005b, 2).[1]

Such ambiguities and disagreements over questions such as the place of the family might seem to suggest that women and gender have been central issues among theorists of civil society, and feminist theorists have indeed begun to explore their far-reaching implications for understanding the relationship between them. As Gal (1997, 30) argues, for example, "the 'civil' or 'civilized' society of public action—whether equated with or opposed to the state—is already implicitly contrasted to a 'natural' and domestic, 'private' realm of family life and procreation, to which women were assigned." Moreover, she notes, "in the West, the 'public,' the 'private,' and 'nature' are ideas that have been variously linked together in a dynamic discourse about political power and the relation of men and women to it" (ibid.). However, many theorists of civil society have not meaningfully engaged several key questions about gender that are involved in such discourses, including feminist critiques about the gendered implications of the public–private dichotomy that constructs politics as taking place only within political institutions. As a consequence, dominant debates about, and conceptualizations of, civil society have paid scant attention to the ways in which power and subordination are manifest within civil society in ways that call into questions its characterization "as the realm of the benign, virtuous and harmonious, in contrast to the venal, oppressive state" (Howell 2005a).

Dominant theories of civil society have elided these and other important questions about women, sex, and gender. Nonetheless, in all of its meanings and across almost every historical, regime, or geographic context, examining variations among, and the evolution of ideas about, civil society consequently serves as a useful barometer for measuring shifting understandings about women, sex, and gender.

CIVIL SOCIETY AND GENDERED SPHERES

Occupying as it does the space between the state and the family that itself depends on presumptions about the existence of *separate spheres* of public and private life, the very concept of civil society might, in fact, be viewed as a product of gendered constructions of social, political, and economic life. Feminist theorists disagree, of course, about many aspects of the relationship between gender and civil society—whether the family is a part of civil society, whether civil society is more or less welcoming of women than the state or the market, and about the meaning of civil society as it relates to women and gender (Howell 2005b, 48). However, feminist scholars have long argued that, of the three traditional spheres of public society, civil society may be the most open to women's participation and leadership. Some scholars argue that the existence and persistence of civil society have, in fact, *depended on* women's participation (Pateman 1988; Ryan 1996). Scholars such as Howell (2005a, 39) go so far as to argue that this link between women and civil society is global and that women have key civil society actors in countries across the world. "Often excluded from state institutions and male dominated politics," she writes, women in different historical and cultural contexts "have found it easier to become active at the local level through, for example, community organizations, self-help groups, traders' associations, faith-based organizations, mothers' groups, or campaigning."

Civil society's relative openness to women's participation has been due, in part, to the fact that some aspects of civil society are viewed as closely aligned with what are constructed as women's "roles" and "interests," particularly those aspects of civil society that involve caretaking, such as education and health (Cosgrove 2010). Indeed, gendered assumptions about women's association with such aspects of the private sphere may be precisely what have allowed them to not only participate in civil society but also to be among its most prominent leaders.

Gendered Civil Society in the United States

In the American context, the understanding of civil society as a realm protected from the state was popularized by, among others, de Tocqueville. In his nineteenth-century classic *Democracy in America*, de Tocqueville ([1835] 2001) noted the ubiquity of what he called "associations" in the United States, arguing that nowhere had they been more "successfully used or applied to a greater multitude of objects" (95). Made possible by American Constitutional protections of free speech, assembly, and the right to petition government, he wrote, "There is no end which the human will despairs of attaining through the combined power of individuals united into a society" (ibid.).

And, without a doubt, in an era during which almost all American women, of all races and classes, lacked formal political rights as either voters or elected representatives, civil society provided some of the only opportunities for women's public roles and activities. During this period, organizations such as the National American Woman Suffrage Association (formed in 1890) and the National Woman's Party (formed in 1913) mobilized women and lobbied legislators on their behalf. Women also "came together in organizations devoted to good works: caring for the sick, teaching the young, housing orphans, and the like. Later on, their organizational purposes grew to encompass agitation on behalf of social causes...and self-improvement through intellectual and literary pursuits" (Burns, Schlozman, and Verba 2001, 73). These broadly ranging civil society activities allowed women—particularly educated, white, and middle-class women—to develop skills and "exercise public influence otherwise denied them" (Burns, Schlozman, and Verba 2001, 74). "In a sense," writes historian Anne Scott, "they provided an alternative career ladder, one that was open to women when few others were" (Scott 1991, 177; see also Lerner 1979; Baker 1984; Giddings 1984; Cott 1987; Kunzel 1991; Burns, Schlozman, and Verba 2001).

While civil society's nonpolitical, nonmarket "in-between-ness" afforded educated, white, and middle-class women opportunities not available to them within "the political party, the bench, the bar, the Congress, the city council, the university, the pulpit" (Scott 1991, 177), the valorization of civil society on the part of de Tocqueville and his intellectual descendants relied in large part on, and provides a lens into, deeply gendered, racialized, and classed premises about power, politics, and proper roles in the United States—premises that have ongoing implications for contemporary considerations about the relationship among women, gender, and civil society. In particular, de Tocqueville's (2001) sanguine view of American associations was intertwined with his assessment of American politics more broadly, which, in his description, was characterized by egalitarianism, universal, suffrage and a "shared ideology" of liberalism. Because, in his account, "everyone" could vote and "differences of opinion are mere differences of hue" (de Tocqueville, 2001, 99), he argued, everyone has a voice and the right of association could consequently "remain unrestrained without evil consequences (ibid.)" Although de Tocqueville was deeply disturbed by slavery, his assessment of nineteenth-century America as liberal, consensual, and egalitarian was possible only by bracketing and exceptionalizing issues such as women's exclusion from political life, segregation, racial violence, and the enslavement of and lack of voting rights for most African Americans (Smith 1993; Frymer, Strolovitch, and Warren 2006). The implications of de Tocqueville's views of American civil society are further evident if they are contrasted with his assessment of their European counterparts. While political associations in the United States are "peaceable in their intentions and strictly legal in the means which they employ," in Europe they are formed, "not to convince, but to fight" (de Tocqueville, 2001, 99). (This last point also illustrates another that we address: that defining civil society—particularly articulating its relationships to women and gender—is further complicated by trying to do so cross-nationally.)

De Tocqueville's treatment of women underscores and lays the groundwork for the double-edged nature of civil society for women in the United States. His discussion about political institutions did not address women's lack of political rights or equality and treated their dependence in the domestic sphere as natural. While he took these "clearly distinct spheres of action for the two sexes" as a given, however, he saw great promise in "what, for him, was their proper place...[within] civil society" (Smith 1993, 552). As Rogers Smith argues, he "presented their status [in civil society] as an expression of democracy's tendency to destroy or modify 'those various inequalities which are in origin social,' including...a tendency to make women 'more nearly equal to men'" (552).

Following de Tocqueville, scholars and political observers have argued that civil society organizations, including everything from unions to social movements to bowling leagues, "promote democratic values such as freedom of speech and association, social capital, civic participation, leadership skills, trust in government, and cross-class alliances" (Strolovitch 2007, 3; see also Verba, Schlozman, and Brady 1995; Dionne 1998; Putnam 2000; M. E. Warren 2001; M. R. Warren 2001; Skocpol 2003). As we have already begun to discuss, although civil society institutions often exclude women, and while many contemporary proponents and analysts of civil society pay scant attention to its relationships with women, gender, and sexuality, civil society is nonetheless often seen as the best hope for women's emancipation and for many democracy movements.

It is within civil society movements and organizations, Howell argues (2005a), that feminists and other women activists in the United States and internationally have so often and successfully "articulated their demands, mobilised around issues such as the right to vote, dowry, land rights and domestic violence, and created networks of solidarity" (39). Laurel Weldon (2002), for example, finds evidence that the varied associations of civil society may have more of an effect than formal legislative representation on women's equality. In particular, she finds that strong and autonomous women's movements are more important than the number of female elected officials in predicting governments' efforts to reduce violence against women. In other work, Weldon (2011) finds that the presence of separate minority women's organizations strengthens the women's movement as a whole and that those states with strong women's movements also manifest stronger policy responsiveness to violence against women, both in general terms and with regard to women of color in particular. These findings are suggestive about the progressive possibilities of civil society and its capacity to influence or even change policy and to incorporate diverse sets of actors across a variety of developing and industrialized cases. Thus, civil society can be used for transformative as well as less laudable ends. As such, one might treat civil society as a continuous political opportunity ripe for interpretation and manipulation of various types.

International Varieties of Civil Society

The widespread Western conception of civil society as a gender-neutral public sphere means that women's participation in locations such as the United Sates, indeed their centrality to a functioning civil society, has often gone unremarked (Fraser 1990; Young 2000; Howell 2005b). In contrast, in newer and developing democracies and in some authoritarian regimes, women have become a more easily tapped and better recognized resource for promotion of civil society. Some of this mobilization has been stimulated by top-down encouragement from international institutions. During the mid-1980s and 1990s, the citizen-influenced collapse of the Soviet Union, and other authoritarian regimes, rekindled faith in the capacity of civil society to topple authoritarian regimes and to bring about democratic rule. Foreign donors and aid agencies, Western states, international financial institutions, and large NGOs and intergovernmental organizations all focused on increasing the numbers of women in civil society (Einhorn and Sever 2001). Their emphasis on women was undergirded by arguments that women are more reliable participants in civil society, that they are more likely to see projects through, and that gender equality is necessary to civil society, and to all arenas of public life, for a state to make genuine claims about democratization (Alvarez 2009). This push for women's participation has created a feedback effect in which large numbers of women are directly recruited or favored by international actors and in which women's use of these political opportunities to promote attention to issues within both single- and mixed-gender organizations (Schild 1997; Hemment 2007).

Another important source of women's increased activism in civil society has been a phenomenon that might be labeled *self-mobilization*. That is, women have used the openness of civil society to mobilize in a variety of forms, and with a great diversity of participants, often as part of national struggles to oust authoritarian leaders, to enhance democracy, and to make claims for greater gender equality (Basu 1995; Baldez 2002). This bottom-up mobilization has made use of novel governing forms and mechanisms to create opportunities for more democratic inclusion and has taken the form of feminist reading circles, community kitchens, street protests, insider advocacy, feminist organizations, insurgent participation, and much more, resulting in a swelling in the numbers of female civil society participants. Though widespread across many regions, increases in women's activism are more notable in some parts of the world than others. For example, rates of women's activism are typically lower in the Middle East and Eastern Europe, where civil society's conception as a nonautonomous, even subordinate, *part* of the state, has served to dampen participation among men and women alike. Lower overall participation, combined with patriarchal gender norms and narrow understandings of what constitutes participation in civil society, has led to both fewer female participants and to a greater likelihood that women's activities will be discounted as private rather than public in nature (Einhorn and Sever 2001; Al-Ali 2005). Yet, even in locations such as the Middle East, where religious and cultural norms might be seen as preventing women from forming a majority of civil society members, their numbers have increased over time, exemplified by the broadly-based participation of women in the recent uprisings in Egypt and other countries in the region (Martin 2011).

A common feature across locations in which women's participation is very high and ones in which it is lower is that women in all of these locations have tended to mobilize as women, particularly as mothers and as caretakers. Swidler (1986) argues that this maternalist mobilization is one of the most powerful tools in their limited toolkit to create space for themselves within the public sphere of civil society. Mobilization on the basis of motherhood has been popular because it reflects conventional understandings of women's roles and interests. Women have used their customary roles to organize in protest against missing children and grandchildren, against economic choices that make it harder for them to manage their household, and against equal rights or other gender equity proposals that they argue would upset the balance of the family and thus society as a whole. In some cases, such as preauthoritarian and authoritarian Chile, women have mobilized in protest across all of these issues, with some concerns galvanizing conservative women and others motivating progressive women to emerge into the public sphere (Baldez 2002). In all of these cases women's basis for mobilization is related to traditional gender expectations, thus creating a powerful justification for gendered organizing, particularly in otherwise closed or repressive societies that limit women's public expression.

Because mobilizing as mothers conforms to traditional expectations, this "militant motherhood" (Craske 1999, 17) has frequently allowed women to mobilize in protest and to do so in a fashion that subjects them, to some degree, to less harm from the state or other antagonists. For example, because of their role as elder mothers responsible for the well-being of the community, Cameroonian women were licensed to use naked protests as a potent form of objection to government privatization of water in their communities. Notably, the protests were successful where others had not been; the shock of a naked protest convinced state actors of the seriousness of the community's opposition to water privatization. "The next day the government's water engineers fled town, and they haven't returned since" (Page 2005, 54).

While some scholars argue that such mobilization reinforces traditional or conservative societal mores such as caring for children and households, others such as Nikki Craske (1999) maintain that militant motherhood has transformative potential and that it consequently need not result in circumscribed activism limited to traditional and maternalist appeals. "Motherhood is a starting point for mobilization but can change over time...women's participation has to be understood within multiple political processes which offer ever-changing opportunities and constraints" (18; see also Perelli 1994). Indeed, it is frequently the case that mobilization based on maternal protest evolves into contestation of patriarchy and other forms of systemic injustice, as has been the case for the Association of the Mothers of the Plaza de Mayo. These Argentine women originally organized in demonstrations against the disappearance of their children, wearing white shawls instead of protest placards, so as not to anger the government. Though they maintain a focus on the recovery of disappeared children, they soon adopted a broader human rights approach in response to the political liberalization signaled by the demise of the authoritarian regime (Gúzman Bouvard 1994). Moreover, motherhood and caretaking appeals have other important benefits, namely, that they can "provide a common identity for many women that can cut across race, ethnicity, and nationality," as well as class divisions (Henderson and Jeydel 2010, 46; see also Craske 1999).

Thus, while women's participation in civil society often reflects gendered norms, it can also serve to broaden and transform them. The dramatic increase in women's mobilization within the broad associational network of civil society is important, as is the recognition that the diversity of these women has increased as well. The most visible aspects of civil society were traditionally dominated by relatively elite women with the time, resources, and social standing to participate in civil society. No doubt this understanding is informed by the recognition that elite women were more likely to leave written records of their associations. Consequently, mobilization among working-class and minority women is very likely underestimated, unless we consider various components of civil society, including representative public figures such as Sojourner Truth, mutual aid societies, resistance societies, interest groups, and other variations (Clemens 1993; Ehrick 2005). Still, one effect of the broad push from above and below that characterizes the contemporary era is the increased participation of women from nondominant groups, particularly in societies where political opportunities for collective action have grown. Because civil society organizations encompass broadly ranging goals and mandates—from development goals to strategic feminist interests to subsistence issues, among other things—women of all stripes, including rural women, working-class and poor women, indigenous women, middle-class women, lesbians and gender-nonconforming women, are now recognized as substantial contributors. In the best cases, women from these varied backgrounds come together to form stronger local, regional, and national organizations than they could by organizing across separatist lines, as is the case for many Ugandan women's groups (Tripp 2005).

As such, while men have historically been more likely than women to participate in civil society, this gendered imbalance appears to be evolving in ways that reflect changing gender norms. Indeed, as a result of greater activism among women, traditional notions of masculinity that resist voluntary labor, and global shifts in state resource provision requiring greater civil society action within the areas of health, education, and basic service and resource delivery, men are increasingly unlikely to form a major portion of civil society's participants, with the tradition most pronounced in Latin America and parts of sub-Saharan Africa (Tripp 2005; Cosgrove 2010). In many such cases men are opting out of civil society or are confining themselves to ostensibly more "masculine" forms of association, such as overtly political or labor-oriented associations; traditional male associations such as fraternal and religious orders; violent, ethnic, nationalist, or separatist organizations; and, in some cases, alternative men's organizations such as men's antiviolence groups (Einhorn and Sever 2001; Stevenson 2005). Thus, as civil society has come to reflect women's increased presence, its gendered connotations have begun to shift; whereas civil society was once a putatively gender-neutral and empirically unmarked male sphere, in many countries it is now increasingly marked as a female sphere.

While conceptions of civil society may be increasingly gendered female, this has not necessarily altered power structures in ways that equalize women's and men's voices within it. Women's participation in civil society might be said to simultaneously trouble and uphold traditional gender divides. On one hand, through civil society women have become more active participants in the public sphere. On the other hand, as traditional state responsibilities are increasingly privatized or outsourced, reliance on women's volunteerism has increased as well, such that unremunerated and unacknowledged or under acknowledged labor retains a heavily female composition. One potential implication of women's increased labor force participation, then, is the shrinking of civil society, due to women's, particularly middle-class women's, decreased availability or unwillingness to volunteer. Yet it seems that women's—especially majority, heteronormative, middle-class women's—growing workload is finally bringing about patterns of shared responsibilities between women and men. These patterns are most notable in the private sphere, particularly in the arenas of child rearing and domestic work, and they may be increasingly reflected in the public sphere (Oláh and Bernhardt 2008).

Either way, the result is that the voices of some women are better represented than others, such that the preferences and interests of minority women who are included are not necessarily as well represented as their middle-class and elite counterparts (Strolovitch 2007; Townsend-Bell 2011). Dara Strolovitch (2007) finds, for example, not only that women's organizations devote less advocacy to issues affecting low-income women but also that organizations that represent low-income people and people of color devote little attention to issues intersect gender and class or gender and race. As David Hirschmann (1998, 236) argues, while civil society opens up opportunities for women's participation "many of the same constraints, formal and informal, that limit women's empowerment in other political spheres are to be found in this one as well." As a consequence, those with power "will be in a position to manipulate opportunities for influence far more effectively than the powerless, most of whom are unlikely to have the information, or the ability to participate" (ibid.). An increasingly broad array of women now participates in a larger number and wider variety of roles within civil society organizations. Yet given the uneasy relationship among civil society, states, and international institutions, particularly in the developing world, the extent of their influence in this sphere varies widely and is often unclear, particularly regarding women who are poorer, isolated, and less formally trained.

Reinforcing Gendered Norms?

While civil society's in-between-ness has made it a realm of opportunity for women in many contexts, the idea that it should be protected from the state also brings with it risks and costs. In particular, a lack of regulation leaves civil society open to violence and other kinds of harm. More generally, civil society is not immune from the gendered norms apparent in other spheres of society. As Howell (2005a) asserts, for all of its potential for solidarity, respect, and equality, civil society can also be "an arena where gendered behaviours, norms and practices are acted out and reproduced" (40). There are numerous reasons for the recreation of such norms, not least among them what feminist theorists such as Carol Pateman (1988, 181) refers to as the patriarchal nature of civil society. Feminist theorists argue that the supposedly neutral sphere of civil society is decidedly not neutral but is instead an arena that privileges individual majority male actors in particular and, more generally, majority cultural traits, such as, in the West, the use of reason, logic, and restraint, as commonly understood by the majority population as the only valid basis for politics (Dean 1996; Young 2000). Cohen and Arato (1992, 23–24) contend that such requirements have exclusionary effects, similar to those promoted by increasingly widespread "neoconservative" models of civil society, which, they argue, "shore up (or worse, re-create) the 'traditional' hierarchical, patriarchal or exclusionary character of many of the institutions of civil society."

Indeed, as we discussed earlier, part of what makes civil society so attractive to so many is its malleability. It is consequently not surprising that some feminist scholars have been cautious about celebrating it or that some are concerned about the ease with which discourses of civil society can be appropriated and deployed for un-or antifeminist purposes. Howell (2005a) argues, for example, that the language of civil society can be used to advance neoliberal agendas in debates about "state deregulation, user choice and community provision of welfare services" or deployed as an "ideological device for justifying a particular vision of the state, which entails the return of welfare services to the family, and in practice to the unpaid and undervalued female career" (41). In addition to promoting anti-feminist and neo-liberal goals, such conservative practices also underestimate, and at times even foreclose, women's participation, as well as the participation of other social groups that do not fit dominant cultural norms. These practices also ignore and undervalue attempts on the part of nondominant groups to create counterpublics and alternative spheres that better reflect their presence and participation (Dean 1996; Young 2000).[2]

A related short-sightedness about the imperfections of civil society can obscure the presence of violence in its midst. Dean (1996, 92) argues that violence against women negatively affects their levels of self-esteem, self-confidence, and trust in others, thus limiting their participation in civil society. While violence as an actual tool is certainly more widespread than publicly recognized or addressed, threats of violence or harm, including nonphysical forms, may be just as intimidating and effective at preventing women, lesbian, gay, bisexual, and transgender (LGBT) people, low-income people, racialized minorities, or members of other marginalized social group from full participation in civil society. As such, civil society is not immune to many of the gender imbalances present in other arenas of public and private life. In fact, because civil society is the public sphere least subject to regulation many argue that it may be even more susceptible to such imbalances (Fraser 1990).

Indeed, the associations of civil society are relatively unregulated when compared with the state and therefore vulnerable to sexist and other discriminatory practices (Howell 2005b). As a consequence, although some aspects of civil society have great emancipatory potential that can serve to foster egalitarian ideologies for women and for LGBT people, other aspects preserve and even encourage conservative ideologies that foster women's dependency. As Howell (2005a, 40) notes, civil society offers "fertile soil not only to liberal, socialist and radical feminists, gay and lesbian movements, and progressive men's groups, but also to conservative women activists, anti-gay lobbies and patriarchal and misogynistic male groups."

CIVIL SOCIETY: DOES IT TRAVEL?

In addition to concerns about whether civil society is progressive or conservative with regard to women, gender, and sexuality, there are questions about its universality that are, in many ways, at the root of the concerns we raised earlier about regional and regime-based variation in women's participation and influence in civil society. In particular, scholars and civil society actors question the extent to which civil society's characterization as "a sphere of articulation and organisation separate from the state" "travels" outside of a Western context (Hall 2005, 53). As we have already begun to discuss, this conception, which originated in eighteenth-century Western Europe and North America, has also prompted questions about civil society's universality, particularly about the gendered implications of ascribing it to non-Western contexts (Howell 2005a, 53). These concerns stem in part from a lack of clarity about whether associations that are included under the formal label of civil society actually operate independently of state and international influence (Seligman 1992). Howell (2005a) indicates, for example, that these issues require much more attention, particularly as they are informed by gendered analyses. "Why have global movements around social justice, anti-capitalism, and antiglobalisation been so resistant to gender justice? How do global institutions, international development agencies and international NGOs shape debates around gender and civil society" (Howell, 53)? We address these concerns through discussions about three issues: (1) the lack of attention to gender by nongender-specific organizations; (2) the influence of external ideas and actors on the priorities and practices of civil society associations; and (3) the impact of global networks created by local–global linkages and internationally targeted rights campaigns (Howell).

The extent to which civil society organizations that are not focused on women or to LGBT people are committed to issues of gender and sexuality varies widely (Weldon 2006; Strolovitch 2007). On the one hand, a number of organizations appear unwilling to take up intersectional issues that would seem to fall directly within their purview (Strolovitch; Townsend-Bell 2011). On the other hand, however, many broad human rights organizations recreate the exclusionary tendencies that push marginalized groups and their issues to the sidelines, leaving them to organize within specific "niche" organizations such as women's or LGBT rights organizations. Some human rights groups remain hesitant to take up women's rights or LGBT issues for fear of appearing insensitive to cultural practices or traditions, while others are directly opposed to "Western" conceptions of gender equality (Otto 1996). In both cases, gendered human rights are marginalized, and, as Maruja Barrig (2006) affirms, in both cases human rights groups may argue "that they are simply respecting local culture" (110; See also Song 2007). Yet, as Barrig also notes, neglecting gender can be a two-way street, and in many cases such inattention is made possible by a number of actors, including many feminist actors who are equally willing to use tradition or culture as an excuse for evading gender issues where they pertain to minority groups and women's groups who are interested in maintaining the status quo (ibid.).

Yet civil society actors do not bear sole responsibility for the "unintersectional" approaches of many human rights and women's organizations. The priorities of external actors also influence which issues local associations emphasize, and these priorities often ignore, minimize, or distort attention to gender and gender equality in civil society. Even when associations are attentive to gender equality, whether because of external mandates or organic concern, they report that is can be difficult to assess what it really means to implement attention to gender. As an NGO activist quoted in Barrig (2006, 130) noted:

> We tried in everything we did, in every project we designed, to introduce a gender approach. Then we analyzed it, we asked, 'What is this gender focus?' It's not so easy. At times it meant highlighting the fact that women also participate in projects—but women always participate. Then, as it wasn't clear what gender really meant in practice, at times we just wrote it in the report.

As Barrig argues, the problem with this example is twofold. On one hand, the individual organization is not fully committed to incorporating a gender analysis. But the repercussions for its sleight of hand are minimal because some donor agencies are equally unconcerned with gender analyses. She writes, "Gender conditionality is sometimes supported by women staff members, but their concerns about what they see in the field do not get support from the top. The view that the gender focus is 'just on paper' clearly distorts and depoliticizes the issue" (130).

Many human rights organizations are guilty of ignoring gender equality of their own accord. But if it is true that the organizations that fund them are similarly likely to ignore gender equality as a central priority, then it is all the more unsurprising that local organizations might do so themselves. External preferences do not foreclose free choice among individual civil society organizations, but they can certainly encourage or discourage them. When international donors or domestic actors provide major sources of funding, the question of civil society autonomy is an open one, as is the question of donor intentions and how those shape gendered patterns within civil society.

There are other reasons to suspect that the concept of an autonomous civil society may not travel well. In many cases, civil society has grown because it is fulfilling service provision and redistributive roles that have historically been the responsibility of the state (Banaszak, Beckwith, and Rucht 2003). Sangeeta Kamat (2003), for example, tells the story of a civil society activist approached by the state of Maharashtra, India, to run the all of its primary health care centers (PHCs). "Please! She is urged. You will be fully in-charge of running the PHCs. You can weed out corruption of the doctors, and the poor will truly benefit. The government, she is told, cannot do as good a job as her organization would. Far from feeling flattered, Sunita reacts angrily. Why don't you hand over the management of the forests, the water works, and the police to us as well?! Then we will gladly accept your offer to manage the PHCs" (88).

Scholars also report that external control over the origination and funding of projects has both distorted the goals of women in civil society and favored middle-class women and those with more training and resources (Alvarez 1999; Einhorn and Sever 2001, Murdock 2008). In addition, increasing requirements for formalization and professionalization have closed off space for poor and minority women who have less access to these tools and skills, such as budgeting knowledge, computer access and skills, formal office space, and command of English (Hirschmann 1998). Ironically, when poor and minority women do achieve access to such tools and skills, their authenticity as representatives of these communities, and the strength of their relationships to the underrepresented group that they allegedly serve are often challenged by members of *dominant* groups. For example, many of the Costa Rican indigenous leaders interviewed by Erica Townsend-Bell admit frustration with attempts on the part of legislators to limit indigenous voices via arguments that indigenous leaders do not really represent the indigenous people, and thus are not competent to speak for them. "Some deputies [members of parliament] question why the Indigenous Board [a national indigenous association spearheading the fight for an indigenous autonomy law] is based in San José [Costa Rica] when the majority of the [indigenous] people do not live there. Rather than try to prove our authenticity we started the National Front of Indigenous Leaders which represents all of the leaders [of the local indigenous populations]" (personal interview with SERPAJ director by Townsend-Bell, July 2009).[3]

Yet while these external constraints are serious, they are not absolute. As Alvarez (2009) confirms in a reassessment of her foundational article about what she labels *the NGOization* of the Latin American feminist movement, the processes of formalization, professionalization, and organizational compromise may be very real, long-term, and perhaps permanent, but they have not prevented civil society organizations in Latin America and elsewhere from finding ways to continue to emphasize local priorities.

The influence of global networks is particularly illustrative of the double-edged impact of NGOs. That is, while international influence over civil society has resulted in important constraints it has also opened up myriad opportunities. Women have both benefited from and been responsible for the creation of global–local linkages and support networks that work to their benefit. International preferences explain a part of the notable increase in women's participation, although this increase has also come about as a result of women themselves carving out spaces within the previously masculine sphere of civil society (Towns 2010). International priorities have also helped to open or expand political opportunities for women, regardless of how they were first mobilized, to create not just local associations but also regional and international groups and to engage in international exchange of ideas and strategies for enhancing women's rights (Ferree and Martin 1995). These priorities have manifested in two central ways. First, international events such as the UN-sponsored conferences on women (1975–1995) have given women's activists stronger grounding for appeals to nation-states to implement or enforce policies that were previously unviable. In addition, the simultaneous increase in global–local linkages has meant that ideas and strategies that began at local levels can flow up to become common international approaches, such as was the case with gender quotas (Krook 2009).

CONCLUSION

As our opening vignette about overburdened mothers rebelling against "Donuts for Dads Day" suggests, the nexus of relationships among women, gender, sexuality, and civil society is complicated, evolving, and fraught with ambiguities and contradictions that reveal a great deal about dominant assumptions about women and gender in particular locations and at particular moments in history. What are the implications of the complex and shifting ways in which women, gender, and sexuality figure into discussions about civil society, particularly when it comes to understanding the contemporary politics of gender and sexuality?

First, as we have argued in this chapter, civil society has long served as both a constraining and empowering arena of action for women. On one hand, women have, historically, had more influence in and through the "third sector" than they have achieved through either the economy or the state. On the other hand, the extent and nature of this influence has been uneven, it has often been limited to middle-class and elite women, and its applicability outside the United States and Europe remains unclear. Moreover, women's civil society activities have often perpetuated, and at times perhaps even licensed, assumptions about separate spheres and gendered ideas about caregiving.

Second, as the *New York Times* article quoted at the outset of this chapter makes clear, women's increased labor force participation has forced some of the gendered contradictions about civil society to the surface in ways that illuminate a great deal about evolving norms regarding sex and gender, particularly as they overlap with race, class, and sexuality. As heterosexual, reproductive, middle-class women participate in the paid labor force in ever greater numbers, the extent to which their unpaid labor had previously supplemented and sustained civil society institutions such as schools, churches, and charities has become increasingly clear. Because women's civil society activities in these realms—in the United States and internationally—are often unremunerated, women's civil society volunteerism has also often served to justify a lack of state responsibility for resources for things like health care, child care, and education. In addition, as middle class women strive to balance their paid labor with parenting and volunteering, it has also become clearer that low-income women, women of color, and nonheteronormative and queer women have long juggled these many roles. Indeed, privatization and outsourcing will likely have a particularly deleterious effect on both men and women of color as well as on low-income men and women as they step into outsourced positions that are increasingly divorced from social and economic guarantees. However, broader and more democratic versions of civil society have also expanded in recent decades, providing a crucial source of political and social inclusion for historically marginalized groups. Strolovitch (2007) finds, for example, that while many advocacy organizations fall short of providing "intersectional representation," others engage in a prefigurative politics whereby civil society groups can promote and embody inclusive and egalitarian practices within their varied structures. Such prefigurative practices – one component of what Strolovitch calls "affirmative advocacy" – are especially common among civil society associations formed by marginalized groups and the majority associations with which they interact (Weldon 2011; Townsend-Bell 2012).

Third, conceptions of civil society's boundaries, roles, and value simultaneously reflect and construct prevailing ideas about women, sex, gender, and sexuality. Indeed, the relationship between civil society autonomy and women's presence is complex. On one hand, external influence over civil society has helped to increase the number, diversity, and influence of female participants in civil society and society in general, even if their participation is not stimulated by concerns about gender equality. On the other hand, external influence over civil society has sometimes served to limit or constrain women's capacity to act independently and to create forms of civil society that best suit their needs and interests. But while the independence that is characteristic of unregulated and autonomous civil society may allow for greater expressions of women's agency—including those of lesbian, bisexual, and transgender women, women of color, and other women whose right to mobilize on the basis of non-normative identities has historically been unrecognized—it may leave unaddressed, and at times even perpetuate or promote, violence against women.

Finally, while this chapter makes clear that civil society and gender scholars are engaged in productive conversation, it also suggests several avenues for future examinations of gender and civil society that promise to reveal a great deal about each one. For example, there remains much to be said about the gendered nature of civil society, such as whether gendered norms regarding power and authority produce differences among men and women's organizations and organizing more generally, and about whether and how such differences might, in turn, serve to constitute gender. Similarly, the relationships among local, national, and international forms and modes of civil society warrant much greater scrutiny, as does the influence and impact of conceptions of "the family" on conceptions of civil society, its operating modes, and its characteristics. Scholars should also continue to examine whether civil society furthers emancipatory goals for groups marginalized by gender, sex, and sexuality. Similarly, scholars should investigate the circumstances under which civil society organizations address the intersections among these axes of oppression and other forms of discrimination and marginalization, including, but by no means limited to, race, ethnicity, class, and disability. Exploring these and other questions will illuminate much about the roles of women, gender, sexuality, and civil society in the always evolving relationships among them and among the state, the family, the economy, and community.

NOTES

1. Although we revisit some questions about whether the *family* is inside or outside of civil society discussed here, space constraints prohibit a more extensive discussion about these debates. For an excellent overview of these debate and discussions, see Jude Howell (2005a, 40–41). Howell argues that in their discussion of Hegel's exclusion of the family from civil society:

   Cohen and Arato argue that the family should be included in civil society as "its first association". By being conceived of in egalitarian terms, the family then offers a primary experience of the principles of "horizontal solidarity, collective identity and equal participation" that form the basis of other forms of civil society association and, more broadly, political life. Such a portrayal of the family, however, ignores the power relations and hierarchies prevalent within families, often along gender and inter-generational lines, and overlooks the problems of exploitation, violence and abuse within families...Taking the family as crucial calls for a gender analysis of civil society and state institutions. It thus strengthens the idea that civil society discourses, spaces and organisations as well as state organisations and practices are shaped by, and in turn reproduce, particular configurations of gender relations...Keeping the family out of civil society, however, reifies the family as a distinct sphere with clear boundaries between the state and civil society. By implying that the family is independent from state and civil society, it removes the question of how the engendering of male and female bodies shapes these other spheres and contributes to the false impression that state and civil society are free of gender relations.

2. Notably, such alternate spheres are also attractive to numerous marginalized social groups, including men seeking to contest both narrowly circumscribed notions of hegemonic masculinity and to expand ideas about valid forms of male association beyond the traditional masculinist, formal political, or explicitly violent, nationalist, or other extremist associations mentioned earlier.

3. The Indigenous Board also includes members from all eight local indigenous populations.

References

Al-Ali, N. S. 2005. "Gender and civil society in the Middle East." In J. Howell and D. Mulligan, eds., *Gender and civil society: Transcending boundaries*. New York: Routledge, 101–116.

Alvarez, S. 1999. "Advocating feminism: The Latin American feminist NGO 'boom.'" *International Feminist Journal of Politics* 2: 181–209.

Alvarez, S. 2009. "Beyond NGOization? Reflections from Latin America." *Development*. 52: 175–184.

Baker, P. 1984. "The domestication of politics: Women and American political society, 1780–1920." *American Historical Review* 89: 620–647.

Baldez, L. 2002. *Why women protest: Women's movements in Chile*. New York: Cambridge University Press.

Banaszak, L., K. Beckwith, and D. Rucht. 2003. "When power relocates: Interactive changes in women's movements and states." In L. Banaszak, K. Beckwith, and D. Rucht, *Women's movements facing the reconfigured state*. New York: Cambridge University Press, 1–29.

Barrig, M. 2006. "What is justice? Indigenous women in Andean development projects." In J. S. Jaquette and G. Summerfield, eds., *Women and gender equity in development theory and practice*. Durham, NC: Duke University Press, 107–133.

Basu, A. 1995. *The challenge of local feminisms: Women's movements in global perspective*. Boulder, CO: Westview Press.

Burns, N., K. Schlozman, and S. Verba. 2001. *The private roots of public action: Gender, equality, and political participation*. Cambridge, MA: Harvard University Press.

Clemens, E. S. 1993. "Organizational repertoires and institutional change: Women's groups and the transformation of U.S. Politics, 1890–1920." *American Journal of Sociology* 98: 755–798.

Cosgrove, S. 2010. *Leadership from the margins: Women and civil society organizations in Argentina, Chile, and El Salvador*. New Brunswick, NJ: Rutgers University Press.

Cott, Nancy. 1987. *The grounding of modern feminism*. New Haven, CT: Yale University Press.

Craske, N. 1999. *Women and politics in Latin America*. New Brunswick, NJ: Rutgers University Press.

Dean, J. 1996. *Solidarity of strangers*. Berkeley: University of California Press.

de Tocqueville, Alexis. [1835] 2001. *Democracy in America*. New York: Signet Classics.

Diamond, L. J. 1994. "Toward democratic consolidation." *Journal of Democracy* 5: 4–17.

Dionne, E. J. 1998. *Community works*. Washington, DC: Brookings Institution Press.

Edwards, M. 2009. *Civil society*. Malden, MA: Polity.

Ehrick, C. 2005. *The shield of the weak: Feminism and the state in Uruguay, 1903–1933*. Albuquerque: University of New Mexico Press.

Einhorn, B., and C. Sever. 2001. "Gender and civil society in Central and Eastern Europe." *International Feminist Journal of Politics* 5: 163–190.

Ferree, M. M., and P. Y. Martin. 1995. "Doing the work of the movement: Feminist organizations." In M. Ferree and P. Martin, eds., *Feminist organizations: Harvest of the new women's movement*. Philadelphia: Temple University Press, 3–24.

Foley, M. W., and B. Edwards. 1996. "The paradox of civil society." *Journal of Democracy* 7: 38–52.

Fraser, N. 1990. "Rethinking the public sphere." *Social Text* 25–26: 56–80.

Frymer, P., D. Z. Strolovitch, and D. Warren 2006. "New Orleans is not the exception." *Du Bois Review* 3: 37–57.

Gal, S. 1997. "Feminism and civil society." In J. Scott, C. Kaplan, and D. Keats, eds., *Transitions, environments, translations: Feminisms in international politics*. New York: Routledge, 30–45.

Giddings, P. 1984. *When and where I enter: The impact of black women on race and sex in America*. New York: Morrow.

Gúzman Bouvard, M. 1994. *Revolutionizing motherhood: The mothers of the Plaza de Mayo*. Lanham, MD: Rowman and Littlefield.

Hemment, J. 2007. *Empowering women in Russia: activism, aid and NGOs*. Bloomington: Indiana University Press.

Henderson, S., and A. S. Jeydel. 2010. *Women and politics in a global world*. New York: Oxford University Press.

Hirschmann, D. 1998. "Civil society in South Africa: Learning from gender themes." *World Development* 26: 227–238.

Howard, M. M. 2003. *The weakness of civil society in post-communist Europe*. New York: Cambridge University Press.

Howell, J. 2005a. "Gender and civil society." In M. Glasius, M. Kaldor, and H. Anheir, eds., *Global civil society 2005/2006*. New York: SAGE, 38–63.

Howell, J. 2005b. "Introduction." In J. Howell and D. Mulligan, eds., *Gender and civil society: Transcending boundaries*. New York: Routledge, 1–22.

Kamat, S. 2003. "The NGO phenomenon and political culture in the third world." *Development* 46: 88–93.

Krook, M. L. 2009. *Quotas for women in politics: Gender and candidate selection reform worldwide*. New York: Oxford University Press.

Kunzel, R. G. 1991. *Problem women, fallen girls: Unmarried mothers and the professionalization of social work, 1980–1945*. New Haven, CT: Yale University Press.

Lerner, G. 1979. *The majority finds its past: Placing women in history*. New York: Oxford University Press.

Martin, M. 2011. "Women play vital role on Egypt's uprising." Available at http://www.npr.org/2011/02/04/133497422/Women-Play-Vital-Role-In-Egypts-Uprising.

Murdock, D. F. 2008. *When women have wings: Feminism and development in Medillín, Colombia.* Ann Arbor: University of Michigan Press.

Oláh, L. S., and E. Bernhardt. 2008. "Sweden: Combining childbearing and gender equality." *Demographic Research* 19: 1105–1144.

Otto, Dianne. 1996. "Nongovernmental organizations in the United Nations system: The emerging role of international civil society." *Human Rights Quarterly* 18(1): 107–141.

Oxhorn, P. 2006. "Conceptualizing civil society from the bottom up: A political economy perspective." In R. Feinberg, C. H. Waisman, and L. Zamosc, eds., *Civil society and democracy in Latin America.* New York: Palgrave Macmillan, 59–84.

Page, B. 2005. "Naked power: Women and the social production of water in anglophone Cameroon." In A. Coles and T. Wallace, eds., *Gender, water, and development.* Oxford: Berg, 57–74.

Pateman, Carole. 1988. *The sexual contract.* Stanford: Stanford University Press.

Perelli, C. 1994. "The uses of conservatism: Women's democratic politics in Uruguay." In J. S. Jaquette, ed., *The women's movement in Latin America: Participation and democracy.* Boulder, CO: Westview Press, 131–150.

Putnam R. D. 2000. *Bowling alone.* New York: Simon and Schuster.

Ryan, M. P. 1996. "Gender and public access: Women's politics in nineteenth century America." In C. Calhoun, ed., *Habermas and the public sphere.* Cambridge, MA: MIT Press, 259–288.

Schild, V. 1997. "New subjects of rights? Gendered citizenship and the contradictory legacies of social movements in Latin America." *Organization* 4: 604–619.

Scott, A. 1991. *Natural allies: Women's associations in American history.* Urbana: University of Illinois Press.

Seligman, A. B. 1992. *The idea of civil society.* New York: The Free Press.

Skocpol, T. 2003. *Diminished democracy.* Norman: University of Oklahoma Press.

Smith, R. M. 1993. "Beyond Tocqueville, Myrdal, and Hartz: The multiple traditions in America." *American Political Science Review* 87: 549–566.

Song, S. 2007. *Justice, gender, and the politics of multiculturalism.* New York: Cambridge University Press.

Stevenson, L. S. 2005. "The impact of feminist civil society and political alliances on gender policies in Mexico." In J. Howell and D. Mulligan, eds., *Gender and civil society: Transcending boundaries.* New York: Routledge, 163–195.

Stout, H. 2010. "Frazzled moms push back against volunteering." *New York Times,* December 2, D1.

Strolovitch, D. Z. 2007. *Affirmative advocacy: Race, class, and gender in interest group politics.* Chicago: University of Chicago Press.

Swidler, A. 1986. "Culture in action: Symbols and strategies." *American Sociological Review* 51: 273–286.

Towns, A. E. 2010. *Women and states: Norms and hierarchies in international society.* New York: Cambridge University Press.

Townsend-Bell, E. 2011. "What is relevance: Defining intersectional praxis in Uruguay." *Political Research Quarterly* 64: 187–199.

Townsend-Bell, E. 2012. "Writing the way to feminism." *Signs: Journal of Women and Culture in Society* 38(1),127–151..

Tripp, A. M. 2005. "Women in movement: transformations in African political landscapes." In J. Howell and D. Mulligan, eds., *Gender and civil society: Transcending boundaries.* New York: Routledge, 78–100.

Verba, S., K. L. Schlozman, and H. Brady. 1995. *Voice and equality.* Cambridge, MA: Harvard University Press.

Warren, M. E. 2001. *Democracy and association.* Princeton, NJ: Princeton University Press.

Warren, M. R. 2001. *Dry bones rattling: Community building to revitalize American democracy.* Princeton, NJ: Princeton University Press.

Weldon, S. L. 2002. "Beyond bodies: Institutional sources of representation for women in democratic policymaking." *Journal of Politics* 64(4): 1153–1174.

Weldon, S. L. 2006. "The structure of intersectionality: A comparative politics of gender." *Politics & Gender* 2(2): 235–248.

Weldon, S. L. 2011. *When protest makes policy.* Ann Arbor: University of Michigan Press.

Young, I. M. 2000. *Inclusion and democracy.* New York: Oxford University Press.

CHAPTER 15

ORGANIZING AROUND GENDER IDENTITIES

KELSY KRETSCHMER AND DAVID S. MEYER

INTRODUCTION

Throughout this futile war, we women held our peace.
Propriety (and husbands) permitted no peep
To escape our mouths. But we weren't exactly pleased.
We did hear how things were going. When you had passed
Some subnormally thought-out, doom-lade decree,
We'd say, aching, but on the surface simpering,
"What rider to the treaty did you decide on
Today at the Assembly?" "That's not your affair!
Shut up." And lo, I did shut up...
Because ineptitude's a shield against advice?
It got so you were yakking in the streets yourselves:
"We've got no men left in the country." "Yeah, no fake."
Hearing stuff like that, we decided women would
Muster and deliver Greece. Why piddle around?
We've got some useful things to tell you. If you stay
Quiet the way *we* always did, we'll set you straight.

(Aristophanes 2003, 31–32)

Lysistrata, the title character in Aristophanes' comedy, explains in the opening speech the reasons she and other women have decided to take the politics of war and peace into their own hands. The play is a good place to start in thinking about women and social movements. It traces the development of a social movement against the Peloponnesian Wars. Lysistrata's campaign comprises a *women's movement*, in that the activists, their concerns, and their tactics are shaped by their gendered place in various Greek city-states. Her campaign is also a *peace movement*, in that its policy concerns are explicitly about the politics of war and peace.

Lysistrata organized the women in Athens and their sisters in warring states to stand up for their interests: keeping their sons, husbands, and money out of war. The women agree to abstain from sex until the men stop fighting and to plot to use perfumes and cosmetics to bring the warriors to frustration quickly. They also pledge to stop child care and housework. But it's not just traditionally feminine roles that animate their efforts. The also seize the treasury to stop their money from funding war. The cast of activist women includes those who employ traditionally feminine wiles but also others who prove their capacity to fight with the best of the men.

Lysistrata and the women create a social movement because they are excluded from any other way to exercise political influence, and they've lost faith that those who have access to political power will be looking out for them. Both their political exclusion and the levers of influence they can exercise are gendered. Absent conventional political access, they find other ways to make claims, trying to persuade and pressure authorities to respond to their concerns. Social movements are the province of those who cannot win through conventional politics alone. Although some people are committed enough to a cause to engage in often risky politics without prospect of influence, most join movements when they believe protest is necessary—and at least potentially effective. Social movements unite people with diverse concerns and employ a range of tactics for making claims, generally including both conventional and nonconventional political strategies. Even as they seek to influence authorities, they also try to change the values of the culture in which that government operates. They build organizations and connections among activists that can exercise influence over a longer period of time (Meyer 2007).

We look at gender as effecting influence on both the inside and outside of social movements. Because social structures are gendered, the opportunities and identities available to activists are likewise gendered. The experience of gender affects the concerns of individuals who engage (or not) in both conventional politics and social movement politics. The larger social structures of gender within a society affect the routes available to individuals and organizations who seek to make claims. And we consider the influence of gendered movements on the development of politics and policies. We begin by considering the influence of gender on the way people think about their interests and their political opportunities.

Gender ideology is a ubiquitous and coercive force that shapes both our intentional decisions and our unconscious, seemingly "natural" behavior. It also exists outside of the individual—in organizations and institutions and in interpersonal interactions, where it shapes what we expect from each other and our assessments of others' capabilities and intentions. Because gender exists both in the individual and in the environment around individuals, it is worthwhile to think about how gender works to shape the operation and outcomes of social movements. After all, gender ideology and gendered structures are often targets of social movement activism, and gender also shapes the way social movements are carried out and what political and cultural social movement outcomes are conceivable at any given point.

Much of the research on gender and social movements has focused on women organizing movements of women about issues affecting women in particular (and explicitly feminist movements), but gender plays an important part in structuring women and men's participation beyond gender-specific movements. A growing body of work has begun to shine a light on this important but underdeveloped area of movement scholarship. This new research on the role of gender in social movements beyond feminist movements includes two different strands, which we can think of as gendered activism and gendered movements.

The first focuses on how gender ideology and expectations shape individual women's and men's movement experiences in different ways. Much research has treated the political process, including movement politics, as rational and calculable, viewing gender as a status that might affect interests but not an individual's perceptions of possibilities and politics (Tilly 1978; McAdam 1982; Habermas 1991; Tarrow 1998). By treating political action as what one exclusively does in the public sphere and outside of the local community, these approaches effectively ignore how gender shapes activism and universalize men's experiences as "normal." Our cultural belief that women should be constrained to the private sphere means the work they do to build social movements at the local level is undervalued and often considered nonpolitical (Robnett 1996; Stall and Stoecker 1998; Ferree and Mueller 2004).

Increasingly, however, we have seen important gender differences affecting politics and movements, including how men and women become involved in movements, what opportunities they are given in their organizations and activist communities, what tools and strategies they adopt, and how activism transforms their concept of their identities and agency. For example, Rachel Rinaldo (2008) highlights how gender and religion intersect in creating unique opportunities for women to influence the development of the Indonesian state. Building on their religious and gender identities, women organize around their political interests and construct themselves as legitimate public actors by capitalizing on the diverse interpretations of Islamic texts and laws. More generally, this work highlights that any activism reflects and takes a stance on gender politics; activism grows out of multiple social identities and is deeply gendered for both men and women.

The second strand of research emphasizes how the environment around social movements is gendered and how this affects the choices of activists and organizations. Social movement scholars have developed a range of theories to understand how social movements are mobilized, politically structured, and framed, but few of these studies address how the different social locations of men and women affect their abilities to participate and capitalize in these gendered contexts (Navarro 1989; Bouvard 1994; Sharoni 1998; Lemish and Barzel 2000; Kuumba 2001; Caiazza 2002; Viterna and Fallon 2008). A gendered environment also matters for the kinds of outcomes movement activists strive for and can realistically expect. We will discuss new perspectives on how women must make different choices and compromises when interacting with this gendered environment.

These two strands of research frequently overlap; individuals make choices based on the gendered environment, and the environment around movements sometimes shift because individual activists are working to change its gendered nature. In the following sections, we treat these strands as separate phenomena while noting the points where they speak to each other. Our discussion will focus primarily on women's experiences in movements, but we will devote some space to the way gender ideology shapes men's activism.

In thinking about social movements as gendered phenomena, we conceptualize activism as falling into three categories, including feminist movements, antifeminist movements, and ostensibly nongender-specific movements. In the first and most frequently studied category, activists have formed movements devoted to the reform of gender ideology and structures in society. The clearest examples of these movements are feminist movements, both global and national, of the past two centuries. These movements attract and recruit primarily women, and they engage directly in the work of changing how gender is conceived and carried out to open greater opportunities for women in politics, business, and education, among many other institutions. The importance of gender ideology is manifest in these movements, as its meaning is addressed and targeted at every level of feminism. Explicitly feminist movements are extensively covered elsewhere in this volume.

Here we will focus greater attention on the role of gender in the other two categories: antifeminist movements; and seemingly nongender-specific movements. Antifeminist movements are those meant to counter the claims and gains of feminist movements, protecting or restoring traditional gender norms. They are, understandably, generally conservative in nature, defending traditional gender roles of both men and women. While we might expect women to be less attracted to movements that seek to reclaim social power for men from women, many women do participate, and even lead, in these movements. In discussing these movements, we seek to understand how conservative women conceive of and use gender in carrying out their movements, and we discuss the overlap between conservative women and their more liberal counterparts in the feminist movements in terms of their relationships to men and beliefs about the role of women in the broader society. We devote special attention to women's participation in antifeminist movements because of the paradox they represent: their participation is critically important in legitimizing a movement that seeks to control women and to limit their participation in the political realm.

Unsurprisingly, the role of gender in feminist and antifeminist movements is explicit, with gender politics front and center. It is less obvious how gender ideology shapes movements that seem to not be about gender at all. But because gender is a ubiquitous phenomenon that shapes all social interactions, even movements that appear to be nongendered are gendered in very particular ways. A variety of research has been done to substantiate this claim, and we discuss much of this work.

GENDERED ACTIVISM AND ACTIVISTS

Gendered Bases of Mobilization

Gender influences the way activists participate in social movements in several important ways. Rachel L. Einwohner and her colleagues (Einwohner, Hollander, and Olson 2000) argue that movements are gendered in their composition, goals, tactics, identities, and attributions, in more or less obvious ways. Gender ideology and structures affect potential activists' availability and preferences for participation, leading to differences in how and where women and men initially become involved. Movements that focus on explicitly gendered issues, like women's employment or legal access to abortion, are likely to draw more heavily from one gender than another, which skews the gender composition of these movements from their initial organizing phase. For example, organizers of the Million Man March and the Promise Keepers, efforts devoted to promoting traditional male responsibilities among African Americans and Christians, respectively, recruited men exclusively.

Movements not based explicitly on gender may also accumulate more of one gender than another. While not obviously gendered in the issues they address, the animal rights movement and the toxic waste movement have both attracted more female than male participants. There are various reasons one gender more than another will be attracted to ostensibly nongendered issues, including stereotypes about the issues as gendered, recruitment strategies that use gendered structures (like existing friendship or occupational networks), and even the way the group is structured (centralized vs. diffuse leadership). Kuumba (2001) finds that women are more likely to be involved in the early emergent periods of movements. As they become more formalized and organized, women become less involved, especially at the leadership level (ibid.; Robnett 1996).

Movement goals are also gendered, as when a movement explicitly targets some gender hierarchies or attempts to protect traditional gender norms. Even movements that seem not to be gendered can often have implicitly gendered goals (Einwohner et al. 2000; Robnett 1997). Robnett, for example, argues that while the explicit goal of the American civil rights movement was directed at ending racial discrimination against African Americans, the subtext was often about black men gaining access to white men's power. African American women's interests were often subjugated to those who would benefit African American men.

Because activists make decisions about how to carry out their movement in a gendered system, each decision they make about goals, tactics, and alliances reflects the gendered world around them. They may do this unintentionally because gendered tactics feel more "natural" to them, and such decisions have consequences (McCammon 2012). But they also can choose gender appropriate tactics because they assess that they are the strategies that will be most effective. For instance, Equal Rights Amendment (ERA) activists were broadly painted as unladylike and family-hating women who wanted to resist their "natural" roles as mothers and wives. To counter these perceptions and to make the issue less threatening, ERA activists gave baked goods and flowers to state legislators to show that they were feminine and profamily (Marshall 1985; Einwohner et al. 2000). As this example suggests, activists use gendered coded tactics so that their messages will make sense and be persuasive to a broader public. They can use these gendered tactics even when their ultimate goals are meant to undermine the gendered political system.

In creating a campaign to promote change within any institution, activists need to define their identities in ways that address the values of that institution. Mary Katzenstein's (1998) classic study of American women's activism in the military and the Roman Catholic Church identifies distinct ways of representing gender. Church women who sought equality, explicitly insulated from any political power, projected a vision of women's religious participation that was distinct and different from what was offered by men—even as they sought clerical roles. In contrast, servicewomen who sought access to advancement within the military downplayed gender differences, using political authority to pressure the military to respond.

In similar ways, male protestors can draw on traditional ideas about masculinity by using threatening tactics or by suggesting the lack of strength in their opponents. For example, Ferber and Kimmel (2008) argue that men draw from cultural scripts about masculinity in militia movements, terrorist movements, and far-right hate groups by using military language and symbolism. Often in these movements, what it means to be a man is defined by a willingness to carry out violent acts and sacrifice one's own life in service of an abstract higher goal. Ferber and Kimmel (2008, 874) write:

> Terrorism is about the restoration of a damaged masculinity. After all, shame (and humiliation) are already coded as feminine emotions. The terrorist feels

emasculated, "feminized", and seeks through the application of rational, strategic political action, yoked to a sense of aggrieved entitlement to seek retaliatory revenge against one's perceived enemies, to restore that damaged masculinity.

Ferber and Kimmel argue that the most motivating belief in American hate movements is that white men should be naturally at the top of the global social order. Because this position is challenged, it is white men's duty to fight for its restoration. In this way, the hate movement, which is not primarily directed at gender issues, is in fact deeply gendered, and gender ideology shapes the motivations and tactics of activists.

The facile binary suggested here, that men are aggressive and use force and that women are pacific and use persuasion breaks down quickly in actual practice. Most movements dominated by men, of course, do not defend a racist patriarchy. Those who have begun to examine masculinity in social movements owe a debt to feminist mobilization and the ways this new feminism creates new possibilities for male collective identity. For example, Michael Kimmel and Thomas E. Mosmiller (1992) and Michael Messner (1997) examine profeminist men's movements. Messner (41) argues that progressive men organized in support of feminist movements because they understood it as a move "toward human liberation"; presumably, men also benefit from a world free of narrowly constructed and ultimately confining gender roles. Having men organize on behalf of women's interests is particularly useful to feminist activists. It provides their movement with a useful ally and makes opponents less able to claim that all feminists are against all men. Rather, male feminists help female feminists portray their work as seeking equal relationships, not special rights. And we must acknowledge that women can participate actively in movements that employ not only coercion but also violence (see Kampwirth 2002). In both cases, activists stretch and redefine gender identities to legitimate both their participation and their cause, drawing attention to contrasts with conventional notions of appropriate behavior.

Recognizing gender as a motivation does not just emerge from the activists themselves but is also ascribed to activists and movements by friends and foes. Movement opponents and bystanders can also bring their own gender frames when interpreting a movement. For example, Einwohner (1999) found that animal rights opponents often constructed animal rights activists negatively as rich housewives or old ladies with nothing better to do with their time. In contrast, hunters were seen as scientifically justified wildlife managers. In this way, gender is used to frame actions, and to provide credibility to one's own actions and to discredit one's opponents.

Different Stages of Participation

Men and women do not just experience gendered motivations for participating in social movements. The ways they are recruited to social movements are also structured along gender lines. Women are more likely to be recruited through informal and friendship networks, and men are more likely to be recruited through participation in already established organizations and through institutional ties (Platt and Fraser 1998; Kuumba 2001). But even when women and men are recruited to movement participation in similar ways, their social location continues to structure the meaning of their activism. For example, in her study of striking hospital workers, Maggard (1998) found that because the strikers were mostly women and because their jobs involved caretaking, the larger community struggled to view them as workers staging a legitimate strike; instead, their hospital work was seen as an extension of their natural role and their role as striking workers inappropriate.

Gendered Division of Labor within Social Movements

Preexisting gender ideology also influences the division of labor and responsibilities within and between activist organizations. Across social movements, even those organized for progressive social change, women have generally been relegated to auxiliary and stereotypically female roles, including clerical and administrative work (Zemlinskaya 2010). This is true even in movements where women played an active role in initiating and leading the grassroots effort that built the movement (Lawson and Barton 1980). For this reason, some activists have insisted on maintaining women-dominated organizations within larger multiorganization movements. Note, for example, the development of the Women's International League for Peace and Freedom and Women Strike for Peace, pacifist social justice organizations that projected a distinct gender identity within broader social movement campaigns (e.g., Swerdlow 1993).

The general pattern of the gendered division of labor appears within many social movements, including those that express the most egalitarian ideologies, including the American civil rights movement (McAdam 1992; Robnett 1996) and the antidraft movement during the Vietnam War (Thorne 1975). Indeed, it is the second-class citizenship within the social movements of the 1960s that impelled one strand of activists to take up feminism by the end of the decade (Freeman 1973; Evans 1980). Still, it is important to recognize that those whose interests are placed on the back burner in political life often find those same interests neglected within organizations expressly committed to equality (Strolovich 2007).

Even when women make up a clear majority of the participants of a movement, they are often pushed to the sidelines as men take over leadership positions. Lawson and Barton's (1980) case study of the New York Tenant Movement in New York exemplifies this pattern. Men were able to take over the movement's leadership roles in this case because the movement was compelled to interact with other sexist institutions. Activists argued, with some cause, that male leadership was more likely to win the campaign serious attention from authorities and thus to improve the prospects for success.

Women were sometimes pushed out of central movement organizations altogether and were forced to form auxiliary organizations to support a political struggle. (Think, for example, of Woody Guthrie's classic labor anthem "Union Maid," whose hero urges other women to find a union man and join the ladies auxiliary.) The outcome of this larger process of segregation is that women were less likely to be seen as central or important players in the contest and were more easily disregarded by male activists and the authority they were engaged with. Beckwith (1996) found this pattern in a study of women's participation in an antipit closure campaign in Great Britain. Women had to find ways to acquire *standing* to make claims and exercise influence, both in the larger political world and in the movement itself. When women are blocked from leadership roles or are pushed out of the organizations altogether, it is easier to ignore them, their contributions, and their larger concerns.

The flip side of exclusion, however, is autonomy. Gender inequality, while often blocking women from leadership positions, can also create specialized leadership niches for women, where they play a critical role in linking individuals to larger organizations. Belinda Robnett's (1996) study of the American civil rights movement revealed that the dominant gender ideology led male activists to block women from leadership positions, but the movement relied heavily on women to use their community ties and relationships to bring new people into the movement. In effect, exclusion from positions of national prominence within civil rights organizations pressed talented and committed female activists to the grassroots, with felicitous consequences for the development of the movement. The women's education and organizational skills, along with their community ties, were critical to the continuation of the movement. Male leaders in the movement rarely recognized this role as important, but without the particular social location of women who served as "bridge leaders" between individuals and organizations the movement would have declined as the social costs of participation began to rise.

An alternative to taking subsidiary roles in male-dominated organizations is forming single-sex or expressly women-led groups. When organizations are composed primarily of feminists, or for that matter women, the composition of the group and the ideals it expresses will constrain the issues the group embraces, the processes by which it makes decisions, and the tactics it employs. Feminism, in particular, with a concern for the systematic exclusion of certain voices, valorizes a process that ensures democratic participation. Ironically, this can impeded the political efficacy of an expressly "feminist" organization (Staggenborg 1995). Additionally, when an organization serves both idealistic expressive goals and instrumental pragmatic ones, debates within about balancing those concerns are likely to create organizational dilemmas—and often schism (Kretschmer 2009, 2010).

Taken together, this research demonstrates how gender influences the experiences and choices of individual activists. Men and women experience movements differently, starting with how they are recruited. Women come to movements in different ways, pushed into some movement work and regularly blocked from doing other work. They must make different kinds of claims to be understood and to garner attention and support from both the broader public and powerful political elites. However, gender can also be a useful tool for movement activists. As we will see in the following section, because of the gendered nature of political institutions, gendered claims and strategies can help to keep a movement alive and growing when it seems that opportunity structures are closing. As with individual activists, gendered structures provide different incentives and opportunities for men and women, and they also mean different gendered constraints on claims and tactics.

Gendering the Environment: Political Opportunities, Resource Mobilization, and Framing

The dominant theoretical perspectives for studying social movements—political opportunities, resource mobilization, and framing (see McAdam, McCarthy, and Zald 1996)developed without explicit attention to gender. As a result, theorists working within these perspectives have been slow to attend to the ways gender influences the development and influence of social movements. Some critics (e.g., Kuumba 2001; Zemlinskaya 2010) argue that gender ideologies are implicitly built into these theoretical perspectives, which tend to emphasize formal power structures and hierarchical organizations. Putting gender into consideration of opportunities, resources, and frames allows for a fuller and more variegated approach to understanding all kinds of social movements,

Political opportunities refer to the structure of incentives and sanctions, as well as routes to influence, offered potential claimants. Such opportunities affect the salience of issues and the choice of influence strategies that activists choose (Meyer 2004). Operationally, political opportunity theorists generally argue that social movements emerge and are more likely to be successful when there are (1) political opportunities in the form of shifting power relations; (2) organized and resource-rich insurgents; and (3) movement actors feeling efficacious and believing their struggle will be successful (McAdam 1982; Costain 1994; Kuumba 2001). For the most part, analysts focus on general characteristics of states or other institutions, neglecting the ways these characteristics differentially affect particular claims and particular claimants (Meyer and Minkoff 2004). Of course, each of these elements is critical for social movements to have an effect, but they are also gendered. Men and women experience them differently because women inhabit different economic, political, and social locations.

Analyses of women's movements have effectively focused on the structural characteristics of the states in which they emerge, comparing similar movements in different contexts (e.g., Banaszak 1996; Kuumba 2001; McCammon et al. 2001; Weldon 2002, 2011) or over an extended period of time (Costain 1994). The point is that the opportunities for *women* or *feminists* to organize, mobilize, advance *particular* claims, and effect influence, vary across contexts and over time, in ways that do not necessarily align with opportunities for other constituencies or claims to advance. Although most of the work focuses on women's mobilization in relatively stable contexts, gender strictures often remain even in transitional societies and states (Viterna & Fallon 2008).

Banaszak's (1996) comparison of suffrage movements in the United States and Switzerland, demonstrates the paradoxical character of Swiss democracy, which was exceptionally open on most measures of access, but still denied women, as a group, the right to vote until 1971. McCammon et al. (2001), in a study of suffrage campaigns in the United States, effectively show that opportunities are not only issue specific but also constituency specific and expressly gendered. Routes to political influence, fungible resources, and even available cultural frames that women's rights activists could employ, vary across contexts in ways that are distinct from opportunities for others. Elsewhere, McCammon (2012) argues that women's rights activists do best when they tailor their claims and tactics to the particular constellations of opportunities, resources, and cultural frames available in a particular context. Women seeking to gain the right (and obligation to serve on juries) employed a range of different arguments whose resonance varied depending upon the context for women at a particular time and place.

Scholars need to look for the particular locations in which women have safe spaces to mobilize. The analyst seeking women's movement organizations in the Arab world, for example, failing to find organized suffrage demands, for example, or politically oriented women's groups, might conclude that no women's movements exist. This would be a mistake. Tétreault (1993) shows that in Kuwait the *diwanyya* offered a protective space for women to meet and organize, building networks and ties that would be useful when opportunities for political mobilization appeared. But the importance of this space was hardly universal, applicable only to a certain class of women. Putting gender into the analysis necessitates a search for broader sets of meaningful opportunities.

Likewise, in her comparative analysis of the American civil rights movement and the South African antiapartheid movement, Kuumba (2001) argues that women have different opportunities and incentives to participate in social movements. When scholars ignore gender, they fail to understand basic differences in motivations for becoming involved. For example, sex segregation in industrial housing and the apartheid policies in South Africa often meant that African women and their children were forced into squatters' camps. Because

South African law recognized only male workers and restricted urban migration to those with worker permits, women fleeing rural poverty, unemployment, and hunger were forced to find temporary and unofficial urban housing. The increasing presence of women in the cities, and the loss of their labor in farming communities, was particularly threatening to the South African government. To bring the situation back under hand, the government extended pass requirements to women for the first time in the 1950s and began a vicious relocation program to force women back into rural areas. Kuumba argues that the changing gender composition in the cities and the particular socioeconomic and political status of women turned the antirelocation and squatter's rights movement from informal and sporadic episodes to a formal and sustained effort. Women had different incentives for mobilizing than did the men because they lacked the "worker status" that gave African men a modicum of additional security.

Recognizing gender as an axis of power imbalance leads analysts to develop a more nuanced approach to opportunities. For example, women's social and economic power, and their cultural acceptance, affects the reception context for the claims they might proffer (Rupp and Taylor 1987; Taylor 1989; McCammon 2012). Additionally, the development of opportunities in politics and commerce affect the pool of experienced leaders available as activists and organizers.

Similarly, scholars looking for mobilizable resources who focus exclusively on formal organizations will miss the often submerged networks that are critical to the initial emergence of social movements (Rupp and Taylor 1987). Underground networks that helped women find and access providers of abortions, for example, were not explicitly political, but the connections forged among participants in those networks were critical to the emergence of the abortion rights movement in the United States—and other movements as well (Staggenborg 1991). Because of the gendered division of labor and women's greater connection to the domestic sphere, their activism often takes root in local community environments. Men may come to dominate as movements grow and begin institutionalizing (West and Blumberg 1990; Ferree and Mueller 2004). This more masculine style of movement organizing is seen as more explicitly political and so has gotten the lion's share of attention from social movement theorists.

These gender constructs affect mainstream political movements as well as more radical movements. Radical movements and actions are more often associated with men and with masculine behaviors, so men have been the primary focus of studies of radical politics (Blee 1998a). By radical, we mean those movements and activists who seek fundamental restructuring of society and go far beyond reforming the existing policies and practices. Radical activists operate on both sides of the political spectrum, and women have been involved in the vast majority of these radical efforts. However, women have been neglected in these studies because radicalism has been defined as inherently male. In addition to this blind spot for women's participation in radical movements, there is often a male bias in how radical actions are perceived by both scholars and organizers. Radical actions taken by men are seen as rational and purposive, and those same actions when taken up by women are constructed as irrational and hysterical. Although radical protest exists outside of the political norm, this gendered distinction fits closely with our ideas about men existing in the political and the public, and women primarily behaving in personal and private realms (ibid.).

Finally, where political theorists discuss the cognitive liberation necessary for activists to understand new opportunities for mobilization they have largely ignored the ways that gender influences, as Kuumba (2001, 52) puts it, the "perception and definition of political opportunities." Because of shifting political opportunities and structures, gendered organizing styles can help keep movements alive after initial organizing strategies have become futile.

For example, in relatively open political environments like the United States, activists are able to keep their movements viable by institutionalizing their organizations and maintaining a highly visible and political presence in Washington, DC (Zald and McCarthy 1987; Gamson 1990; Staggenborg 1991). In more repressive environments, the less explicitly political organizing styles associated with women may be the only avenue for continuous mobilization (Rupp and Taylor 1987; Tétreault 1993). In other words, when governments crack down on explicit political dissent, women are able to draw on the gendered ideas of motherhood and domesticity to continue pressing for change. Noonan (1995) argues that this style of protest can protect female activists in times when political protesting is particularly dangerous for men. For example, women in various repressive regimes have deployed a maternal frame to justify their social movement activism against the state and other political actors. Chilean women were able to continue protesting Pinochet's brutal military government by framing their activity in terms of motherhood and their domestic responsibilities (Noonan 1995). A similar strategy has been used by women in Israel (Sharoni 1998), Argentina (Navarro 1989; Bouvard 1994), and Russia (Caiazza 2002). These frames can help translate the movement demands into easily recognizable and sympathetic cultural terms that the broader public already understands. This research is particularly important for demonstrating that political structures can be gendered, giving women different opportunities than men to push for change.

Once activated by any claim or movement, people often continue to engage in movement activism—sometimes on different issues. We saw that women mobilized on civil rights or against the Vietnam War in the 1960s often turned to feminist mobilization as those movements wound down. Indeed, Betty Friedan, cofounder of the National Organization for Women, had gained political experience as a labor journalist and activist in the 1940s and 1950. Activists who started in feminism also turned to other issues as political opportunities shifted. Meyer and Whittier (1994) note the presence of feminist activists and norms in the antinuclear movement of the 1980s. And Banaszak (2010) convincingly shows that women who came of political age as feminist activists who entered government service were able to maintain not only their values but also their activism over long periods of time and across numerous issue areas.

But activist engagement isn't always sustained, and continued participation has a great deal to do with the initial experience of mobilization (Corrigall-Brown 2011). While some people report greater feeling greater agency and autonomy following periods of activism, women who base their movement participation in their traditional identities as mothers and wives do not always seem to experience the same kind of transformation. For example, Julia Wrigley (1998) found that the working-class women who participated in the 1974 Boston antibusing campaign Restore Our Alienated Rights (ROAR) did not experience identity transformations because their movement was in defense of the status quo and required no challenge to male authority. Despite being dominated by women, the movement did not lead to women questioning their secondary status because their motivations were based in their roles as mothers. On the other hand, treatments of antiequal rights (Mansbridge 1986) and antigay movements (Fetner 2008) show that socially conservative causes can be every bit as effective at producing feelings of efficacy and long-term activism as their progressive counterparts.

The sorts of experiences that cultivate identity transformation and sustained engagement remain an area for new research. Even when movement engagement is directly related to women's unfair treatment, female activists may not experience significant identity transformation if their participation is justified and structured by traditional gender ideology. Sally Ward Maggard (1998, 289) found that women "working as 'housekeepers, nurses' aides, cooks, cooks' helpers, dietary aides, and clerical workers" who engaged in a hospital strike for back pay (successful) and union representation (unsuccessful) were not significantly changed by the experience because their jobs were seen as extensions of their natural caretaking roles. While striking, the women were instructed to behave in ladylike ways, and while on the picket line the women passed the time by "quilting, sewing, waving, reading Harlequin novels, [and] cooking over barrels" (Maggard 1998, 294). Men who supported the strike served as picket line stand-ins and bodyguards for their female relatives on the line. They also chopped firewood and built shelters close to the line for women to rest in. Men took the more dangerous night shifts on the picket line to protect the women from violence. This male involvement helped the women to continue their protest activity by making it no more demanding their regular work schedules. By enacting the protest in gendered ways, the strikers made it easier for the larger public to support the picket line, but this gendered division of work meant that none of the strikers or male supporters needed to question or restructure the existing gender arrangements. The strike did not require the women to think of themselves in new or more agentic ways.

This suggests that it is not movement participation itself that leads to women question sexism; there likely also needs to be an element of reform or restructuring that allows female activists to imagine that gender relations can

also be reformed and that their efforts may be meaningful. Basing their activism in their authority as mothers might cement, rather than subvert, the existing gender regime in their own minds.

Deploying the gendered frame of motherhood may lead to more successful
outcomes for movements (Zemlinskaya 2009), but it can also hurt the cause
for women who draw from it too heavily. Einwohner et al. (2000) describe the
double bind for women who deploy heavily gendered activism: they are less
successful in getting their message across without the motherhood frame, but
this frame also cues stereotypes about women's emotionality and irrationality
compared with men. These stereotypes, once cued by the gender frame, work
to discredit women's activism as a legitimate political voice.

Some activists attempt to sidestep this double bind by using the motherhood frame to argue that women are doing essential work for society but also
that this work does not come naturally and so women should be recognized and
supported for their critical efforts. This is demonstrated by Verta Taylor (1999)
in her work on the postpartum depression self-help movement. The women
involved promoted the idea that women needed to be respected for their roles
and to receive greater help from men in their families and communities. In
this way, motherhood is both the reason for organizing and what provides the
activists with the authority to make claims, but mobilization does not rely on
essentialized gender differences between men and women.

Ironically, it was the success of feminist movements generally that inspired
many women to join explicitly antifeminist conservative movements (Meyer
and Staggenborg 1996; Fetner 2008). For right-wing political movements, the
motherhood frame is not just a convenient sidestep around otherwise closed
political opportunities. Instead, women's traditional roles are explicitly used to
further a broader political agenda and the very reason conservative women join
a movement.

Antifeminist Movements

In response to the emergence of the feminist movement of the late 1960s and
1970s, many women became activists in defense of traditional gender roles
(Petchesky 1981; Luker 1984; Mansbridge 1986; Marshall 1986; Himmelstein
1990; Blee 1991, 1997; de Hart 1991). The most vociferous of these counter activists have been women who seek to protect the traditional female roles of wife
and mother. Paradoxically, this countermovement owes a debt to the very
feminist movement it protests. Susan Marshall (1998) argues that the feminist
activists of the 1960s made women's political activity and voice acceptable by
"erod[ing] taboos against female protest" (158). Their activism also made the
"personal political," making sexuality, family, and reproductive issues socially
and politically salient. The increasing importance of these issues created an
opportunity for women on the right to begin organizing and speaking publicly.

Importantly, the feminist movement also increased the need for the male leaders of the growing conservative movement to include women,and to women's highlight their contributions to conservative thought. Schreiber (2008) contends that the most powerful counterarguments to feminists came from conservative women. Politically active conservative women ostensibly showed that feminists were not representing all women.

Because both more extreme and moderate right-wing groups commonly hold a more traditional gender ideology, many create separate organizations for women, which focus on areas in which women are believed to naturally specialize: education, family, and children. For example, Kathleen Blee has shown that white women's participation in far-right hate movements is based in their ability to bear children for the white race. Thus, in the literature produced by these hate groups, women are rarely shown in any other capacity than as mothers (Blee 1998a). It seems unlikely that this kind of movement participation would lead women to feel more personally empowered by their activism. Rather, it likely entrenches their views of themselves as subservient to men. One possible exception is the young skinhead groups, which Blee reports, feature a number of female leaders. This has created greater gender conflict within the groups and, in some cases, has led to skinhead women to form their own groups based on the dual ideas of white power and woman power (Blee 1998b).

Likewise, Marshall (1998) argued that, while right-wing women's organizations were initially constructed to counter left-leaning feminist movements and the Equal Rights Amendment, they also provided opportunities to use women's traditional authority in education and social welfare issues to further broad conservative agenda. Specifically, Marshall found that there was a gendered division of labor among the conservative organizations, where male-dominated organizations, like the Christian Coalition presented an ostensibly more positive public image and female-dominated organizations engaged in the "dirty work" of the conservative movement. For example, while the Christian Coalition publicly called for reconciliation with African Americans, the antifeminist women's organizations mounted campaigns against "educational integration, affirmative action, and federal welfare policy that used gender as a proxy for race" (174). That is, conservative women's organizations were better able to attack programs that helped women or were the domain of women; because these programs also helped minorities in the United States, the conservative movement was able to use gender traditionalism as a shield while attacking a broad range of progressive policies.

Politically active conservative women also draw on the language and imagery developed by feminists to make their claims to the broader public, including the rhetoric of choice and valuing women's work. For example, the Independent Women's Forum (IWF), an organization of economically conservative, well-connected professional women, argues for women's greater representation in economic and political institutions while criticizing policies designed to increase gender equality. IWF has clearly benefited from feminist language on the rights and capacity of women to participate in critical social decisions, but their conservative politics mean deploying this language against the very programs feminists fought for, including Title IX programs, violence against women laws, and federal funding for day care subsidies (Schreiber 2008; Blee and Creasap 2010). Moreover, IWF's position that women are not a distinct group needing special protections often creates tension with other antifeminist groups, which emphasize the importance of traditional gender roles. While antifeminist movements seek to attack the very premise of the feminism, they are also operating in a political and social world fundamentally changed by the feminist movement (Schreiber 2008). The larger point is that challenges predicated on gender cleavages are likely to provoke or inspire countermovements that seek to preserve the status quo—or roll back norms to some imagined past.

The majority of research on gender in social movements has focused on the experience, concerns, and movements of women. While this approach is laudable in making women's contributions more visible, the emphasis on women's differentness works to make the male experience "normal" or neutral. In reality, men's participation is also gendered, and the cultural expectations about what it means to be a man in different contexts affects the way they structure organizations and the larger movements they participate in. The study of women in social movements, and the ways they can use cultural understanding of womanhood to mobilize, has turned our attention to the similar processes at work for men. Men's movements receive far less attention from researchers, with some important exceptions (see Ferber and Kimmel 2008). This is an important, if not unexpected, exclusion. *Gender analysis* is often code for the inclusion of women's perspectives. More rarely does it reflect the recognition that gender can refer to the ways that social movements construct or carry out masculinity. Men have organized social movements to defend their traditional authority over women as husbands and fathers (Schwalbe 1996). (For a review of these movements, see Zemlinskaya 2010).

CONCLUSION

Social movements form in response to cleavages in society, as people use unconventional mobilization when they believe they might get some of what they want by doing so—and will not do so otherwise. Gender is a fundamental cleavage in all the societies we know about that divides at the individual, organization, and political level. The character of the divisions and the values and meanings ascribed to people on either side of those divisions shape the nature of political conflict.

Lysistrata provides an excellent example of how social cleavages affect the claims, tactics, and constituencies gender creates. Gender shapes how we think of ourselves and our capacities to affect change in the world around us. It also shapes our access to social institutions and to the tactics we might choose in our activism. However, as in *Lysistrata*, gender is not ultimately determinative; women and men often use gender in surprising ways to justify and facilitate their political action, even if those actions violate our gendered expectations. The women in *Lysistrata* ultimately engaged in multiple kinds of social protest; some of their actions fell within the bounds of their constrained social position. But the women also flagrantly ignored the social expectation that they would submit to the authority of men in the political realm by seizing the treasury and refusing to fund the wars. Activists in the real world also face this kind of delicate balance—to use gender in the ways that will help extend and amplify a movement's goals while also challenging gender expectations when it restricts their voice and ability to affect change. The play misleads, however, in that it ends in resolution: the war ends and everyone has sex. In real life, struggles are iterative and ongoing, with each momentary resolution setting the terms of the next set of challenges.

References

Aristophanes. 2003. *Lysistrata*. Trans. Sarah Ruden. Indianapolis: Hackett Publishing.

Banaszak, Lee Ann. 1996. *Why movements succeed or fail: Opportunity, culture, and the struggle for woman suffrage*. Princeton, NJ: Princeton University Press.

Banaszak, Lee Ann. 2010. *The women's movement inside and outside the state*. New York: Cambridge University Press.

Beckwith, Karen. 1996. "Lancashire women against pit closures: Women's standing in a men's movement." *Signs* 21(4): 1034–1068.

Blee, Kathleen M. 1991. *Women of the Klan: Racism and gender in the 1920s*. Berkeley: University of California Press.

Blee, Kathleen M. 1997. "Mothers in race-hate movements." In Alexis Jetter, Anneliese Orleck and Diana Taylor, eds., *The politics of motherhood: Activist voices from left to right*. Hanover, NH: University Press of New England, 247–256.

Blee, Kathleen M. 1998a. *No middle ground: Women and radical protest*. New York: New York University Press.

Blee, Kathleen M. 1998b. "Reading racism: Women in the modern hate movement." In Kathleen M. Blee, ed., *No middle ground: Women and radical protest*, New York: New York University Press, 180–189.

Blee, Kathleen M., and Kimberly A. Creasap. 2010. "Conservative and right-wing movements." *Annual Review of Sociology* 36: 269–286.

Bouvard, G. Marguerite. 1994. *Revolutionizing motherhood: The mothers of the Plaza de Mayo*. Oxford: Rowman & Littlefield Publishers.

Caiazza, Amy. 2002. *Mothers and soldiers: Gender, citizenship, and civil society in contemporary Russia*. New York: Routledge.

Corrigall-Brown, Catherine. 2011. *Patterns of protest: Trajectories of participation in social movements*. Stanford, CA: Stanford University Press.

Costain, Anne N. 1994. *Inviting women's rebellion: A political process interpretation of the women's movement.* Baltimore: Johns Hopkins University Press.

de Hart, Jane Sherron. 1991. "Gender on the right: Meanings behind the existential scream." *Gender and History* 3: 246–260.

Einwohner, Rachel L. 1999. "Gender, class, and social movement outcomes." *Gender & Society* 13(1): 56–76.

Einwohner, Rachel L., Jocelyn A. Hollander, and Toska Olson. 2000. "Engendering social movements: Cultural images and movement dynamics." *Gender & Society* 14(5): 679–699.

Evans, Sara. 1980. *Personal politics: The roots of women's liberation in the civil rights movement and the new left.* New York: Vintage Press.

Ferber, Abby L., and Michael S. Kimmel. 2008. "The gendered face of terrorism." *Sociology Compass* 2(3): 870–887.

Ferree, Myra Marx, and Carol McClurg Mueller. 2004. "Feminism and the women's movement: A global perspective." In David A. Snow, Sarah A. Soule and Hanspeter Kriesi, eds., *The Blackwell companion to social movements.* Oxford: Blackwell, 576–607.

Fetner, Tina. 2008. *How the religious right shaped lesbian and gay activism.* Minneapolis: University of Minnesota Press.

Freeman, Jo. 1973. "The origins of the women's liberation movement." *American Journal of Sociology* 78(4): 792–811.

Gamson, William A. 1990. *The strategy of social protest,* 2nd ed. Homewood, IL: Dorsey.

Habermas, Jurgen. 1991. *The structural transformations of the public sphere: An inquiry into a category of bourgeois society.* Cambridge, MA: MIT Press.

Himmelstein, Jerome L. 1990. *To the right: The transformation of American conservatism.* Berkeley: University of California Press.

Kampwirth, Karen. 2002. *Women and guerilla movements.* University Park: Penn State University Press.

Katzenstein, Mary Fainsod. 1998. *Faithful and fearless: Moving feminist protest inside the church and military.* Princeton, NJ: Princeton University Press.

Kimmel, Michael S., and Thomas E. Mosmiller. 1992. *Against the tide: Pro-feminist men in the United States, 1776–1990: A documentary history, men and masculinity.* Boston: Beacon Press.

Kretschmer, Kelsy. 2009. "Contested loyalties: Dissident identity organizations, institutions, and social movements." *Sociological Perspectives* 52(4): 433–454.

Kretschmer, Kelsy. 2010. "Children of NOW: Pathways and consequences of breakaway organizations from the National Organization for Women." PhD dissertation, Department of Sociology, University of California, Irvine.

Kuumba, M. Bahati. 2001. *Gender and social movements.* Walnut Creek, CA: Alta Mira Press.

Lawson, Ronald, and Stefan E. Barton. 1980. "Sex roles in social movements: A case study of the tenant movement in New York City." *Signs* 6(2): 230–247.

Lemish, Dafna, and Inbal Barzel. 2000. "'Four mothers': The womb in the public sphere." *European Journal of Communication* 15(2): 147–169.

Luker, Kristin. 1984. *Abortion and the politics of motherhood.* Los Angeles: University of California.

Maggard, Sally Ward. 1998. "'We're fighting millionaires!': The clash of gender and class in Appalachian women's union organizing." In Kathleen M. Blee, ed., *No middle ground: Women and radical protest.* New York: New York University, 289–306.

Mansbridge, Jane J. 1986. *Why we lost the ERA*. Chicago: University of Chicago Press.

Marshall, Susan. 1985. "Ladies against women: Mobilization dilemmas of antifeminist movements." *Social Problems* 32: 348–362.

Marshall, Susan. 1986. "In defense of separate spheres: Class and status politics in the anti-suffrage movement." *Social Forces* 65: 327–351.

Marshall, Susan E. 1998. "Rattle on the right: Bridge labor in antifeminist organizations." In Kathleen M. Blee, ed., *No middle ground: Women and radical protest*. New York: New York University Press, 155–175.

McAdam, Doug. 1982. *Political process and the development of black insurgency, 1930–1970*. Chicago: University of Chicago Press.

McAdam, Doug. 1992. "Gender as a mediator of the activist experience: The case of Freedom Summer." *American Journal of Sociology* 97: 1211–1249.

McAdam, Doug, John D. McCarthy, and Mayer N. Zald. 1996. *Comparative perspectives on social movements: political opportunities, mobilizing structures, and cultural framings*. Cambridge, UK: Cambridge University Press.

McCammon, Holly J. 2012. *The U.S. women's jury movements and strategic adaptation: A more just verdict:* New York: Cambridge University Press.

McCammon, Holly J., Karen E. Campbell, Ellen M. Granberg, and Christine Mowery. 2001. "How movements win: Gendered opportunity structures and the state: Women's suffrage movements, 1866–1919." *American Sociological Review* 66: 49–70.

Messner, Michael A. 1997. *Politics of masculinities: Men in movements, gender lens series in sociology, v. 3*. Lanham, MD: Rowan & Littlefield.

Meyer, David S. 2004. "Protest and political opportunities." *Annual Review of Sociology* 30(1): 125–145. doi: 10.1146/annurev.soc.30.012703.110545.

Meyer, David S. 2007. *The politics of protest: Social movements in America*.

Meyer, David S., and Debra C. Minkoff. 2004. "Conceptualizing political opportunity." *Social Forces* 82: 1457–1492.

Meyer, David S., and Suzanne Staggenborg. 1996. "Movements, countermovements, and the structure of political opportunity." *American Journal of Sociology* 101: 1628–1660.

Meyer, David S., and Nancy Whittier. 1994. "Social movement spillover." *Social Problems* 41: 277–298.

Navarro, Marysa. 1989. "The personal is political: Las Madres de Plaza de Mayo." In Susan Eckstein, ed., *Power and popular protest: Latin American social movements*. Berkeley: University of California Press, 241–258.

Noonan, Rita K. 1995. "Women against the state: Political opportunities and collective action frames in Chile's transition to democracy." *Sociological Forum* 10(1): 81–111.

Petchesky, Rosalind Pollack. 1981. "Antiabortion, antifeminism, and the rise of the New Right." *Feminist Studies* 7: 206–246.

Platt, Gerald M., and Michael R. Fraser. 1998. "Race and gender discourse strategies: Creating solidarity and framing the civil rights movement." *Social Problems* 45(2): 160–179.

Rinaldo, Rachel. 2008. "Envisioning the nation: Women activists, religion and the public sphere in Indonesia." *Social Forces* 86(4): 1781–1804.

Robnett, Belinda. 1996. "African-American women in the civil rights movement, 1954–1965: Gender, leadership, and micromobilization." *American Journal of Sociology* 101(6): 1661–1693.

Robnett, Belinda. 1997. *How long? How long? African American women in the civil rights movement*. New York: Oxford University Press.

Rupp, Leila J., and Verta A. Taylor. 1987. *Survival in the doldrums: the American women's rights movement, 1945 to the 1960s*. New York: Oxford University Press.

Schreiber, Ronnee. 2008. *Righting feminism: conservative women and American politics*. Oxford: Oxford University Press.

Schwalbe, Michael. 1996. *Unlocking the iron cage: The men's movement, gender politics, and American culture*. New York: Oxford University Press.

Sharoni, Simona. 1998. "The myth of gender equality and the limits of women's political dissent in Israel." *Middle East Report* 27(3): 24–28.

Staggenborg, Suzanne. 1991. *The pro-choice movement: Organization and activism in the abortion conflict*. New York: Oxford University Press.

Staggenborg, Suzanne. 1995. "Can feminist organizations be effective?" In Myra Marx Ferree and Patricia Yancey Martin, eds., *Feminist organizations: Harvest of the women's movement*. Philadelphia: Temple University Press, 339–355.

Stall, Susan, and Randy Stoecker. 1998. "Community organizing or organizing community? Gender and the crafts of empowerment." *Gender & Society* 12(6): 729–756. doi: 10.1177/089124398012006008.

Strolovich, Dara Z. 2007. *Affirmative advocacy: Race, class, and gender in interest group politics*. Chicago: University of Chicago Press.

Swerdlow, Amy. 1993. *Women strike for peace*. Chicago: University of Chicago Press.

Tarrow, Sidney. 1998. *Power in movement*, 2d ed. New York: Cambridge University Press.

Taylor, Verta. 1989. "Social movement continuity: The women's movement in abeyance." *American Sociological Review* 54: 761–775.

Taylor, Verta. 1999. "Gender and social movements: Gender processes in women's self-help movements." *Gender and Society* 13(1): 8–33.

Tétreault, Mary Ann. 1993. "Civil society in Kuwait: Protected spaces and women's rights." *Middle East Journal* 47(2): 275–291.

Thorne, Barrie. 1975. "Women in the draft resistance movement." *Sex Roles* 1(2): 179–195.

Tilly, Charles. 1978. *From mobilization to revolution*. Reading, MA: Addison-Wesley.

Viterna, Jocelyn, and Kathleen M. Fallon. 2008. "Democratization, women's movements, and gender-equitable states: A framework for comparison." *American Sociological Review* 73: 668–689.

Weldon, S. Laurel. 2002. *Protest, policy, and the problem of violence against women: a cross-national comparison*. Pittsburgh, PA: University of Pittsburgh Press.

Weldon, S. Laurel. 2011. *When protest makes policy: How social movements represent disadvantaged groups*. Ann Arbor: University of Michigan Press.

West, Guida, and Rhoda Lois Blumberg. 1990. "Reconstructing social protest from feminist perspective." In Guida West and Rhoda Lois Blumberg, eds., *Women and social protest*. Oxford: Oxford University Press, 3–36.

Wrigley, Julia. 1998. "From housewives to activists: Women and the division of political labor in the Boston antibusing movement." In Kathleen M. Blee, *No middle ground: Women and radical protest*. New York: New York University Press, 251–288.

Zald, Mayer N., and John D. McCarthy. 1987. *Social movements in an organizational society: Collected essays*. New Brunswick, NJ: Transaction Books.

Zemlinskaya, Yulia. 2009. "Cultural context and social movement outcomes: Conscientious objection and draft-resistance in Israel." *Mobilization* 14(4): 449–466.

Zemlinskaya, Yulia. 2010. "Social movements through the gender lens." *Sociology Compass* 4(8): 628–641.

CHAPTER 16

THE COMPARATIVE STUDY OF WOMEN'S MOVEMENTS

KAREN BECKWITH

INTRODUCTION

More than a decade ago, Ray and Korteweg (1999, 48) issued a call for "systematic comparative work" on women's movements. Research on women's movements by comparative political scientists has since proliferated, to the extent that it now constitutes a major body of work, informing comparative politics, social movements analysis, democratization scholarship, gender and politics research, and feminist theory.

Common questions in the study of comparative women's movements include women's movements' strategic preferences, their alliances with political parties and others, their relationship to democracy and democratization, their policy goals and initiatives, and their success in achieving their ends. Questions to be explored further include research on women's movements' emergence, the trajectories of women's movements, the sequencing of women's movements with other movements, the impact of specific state structures on women's movements' policy outcomes, and how women's movements intersect with other forms of women's politics (e.g., movement-party, mass-elite relations, as well as feminist and nonfeminist movement alliances). The presentation of the full range of comparative research on women's movements—as well as those relationships yet to be studied—is beyond the scope of this chapter.

Women's movement scholars have also been converging on definitional consensus on *women's movement* as a concept. The emphasis on definition emerges specifically from comparative political research, as scholars working outside North American and Northern European boundaries found initial conceptions of women's movements confining and overly reliant on specific cases. In the following pages, I review definitions of women's movements in the recent scholarship. I investigate the utility of various definitions, with reference to comparative women's movements, and discuss the analytical advantages of some rather than other definitions. I differentiate among women's movements, feminist movements, and women in movements, discussing different approaches to women's activism in and support for political movements,[1] some of which will be women's movements and others of which cannot be so defined. Second, I ask what it means to study women's movements in comparative perspective and argue that a comparative politics of gender is a major useful means for analyzing women's movements, their similarities and differences, and their successes and failures. In the third section, I develop this argument further, considering the analytical leverage gained from a comparative analysis of women's movements, in terms of understandings of gender, politics, and intersection.[2]

DEFINING WOMEN'S MOVEMENTS

The general terminology of *women's movements* has been employed for decades, particularly since the 1980s, in the response of scholarship to the second-wave women's liberation activism in West Europe and North America of the 1960s and 1970s.[3] The proliferation of women's rights and women's liberation groups, methodologies of consciousness raising, mass demonstrations and marches, blossoming of feminist cultural phenomena (bookstores, publications, music, and artistic festivals), and the emergence and eventual institutionalization of women's studies, as well as the interaction of second-wave feminists studying at universities outside their own countries and the international diffusion of second-wave feminism, led quickly to scholarly attention to women's movements. International Women's Year world conferences, the collapse of the Soviet Union, and the splintering of its former East European satellite countries, and the third wave of democratization (Norris 2008) produced a range of women's mobilizations and activism worldwide. The subsequent burgeoning research on women's activism beyond North American and European borders quickly led to the problematization of the concept of women's movement and challenges to the limitations of a comparative women's movements scholarship focused on (and derived from) the North American and West European experience.

Terminologies reflecting differences in women's activism in social movements, advocating for themselves or others, emerged in scholarship on women in Latin America (e.g., Molyneux 1985; Alvarez 1990; Jaquette 1994; Baldez 2002), in research on southern European women's movements (Threlfall 1996; della Porta 2003; Valiente 2009, 2003), and in research on women's activism and organizing in the post-Soviet transitions of Central and East Europe (Wolchik 1998; Matland and Montgomery 2003). Cross-national analysis of "local feminisms" (Basu 2010b, 14–15) focused on women's organizing around specific issues in local or national contexts, much of which could not in the first instance be categorized as feminist. Finally, "the increased visibility of women in right wing movements in many parts of the world...force[d] a rethinking and redefinition" of women's interests and women's movements (Ray and Korteweg 1999, 51–52).

Research that acknowledged women's agency as women identified female activists from the right of the ideological spectrum whose activism was manifested in social movement (e.g., Ray and Korteweg 1999: 51; Bacchetta and Power 2002; Baldez 2002; Kampwirth 2006; Rippeyoung 2007; Blee 2008; Schreiber 2008). Such activism, however, could not be encompassed within an understanding of women's movements as feminist. Furthermore, scholars working from local contexts where women were organizing in communities around local issues drew attention to women's activism that constituted women's movement that was not necessarily feminist (Molyneux 1985; Basu 2010b) or that rejected *feminist* as a label but nonetheless explicitly advanced feminist issues (Tripp et al. 2009, 1415). Finally, movements opposing women's constitutional rights and liberalization of divorce and abortion (Luker 1984; Htun 2003, 168–171), women's mobilization inside and outside rightwing political parties, and women's organizing in countermovements opposing feminism put paid to uncritical and underspecified use of the term women's movement, especially those conflating women's movements and feminist movements.

These definitional debates further underscored the importance of intersectional analysis. Female activists organized in women's movements around intersectional interests of race, class, ethnicity, sexuality, nationality, and religion, which often were explicitly feminist or that articulated their interests and issues *as women* or insisted upon their identity as part of a larger women's movement (see Tripp et al. 2009; Basu 2010a; Smooth 2011). The challenge of intersectional analysis helped to encourage women's movements scholars to think through the issue of defining women's movements and to recognize women's movements that were conservative, right-wing, or nationalist.

Women's Movements Defined

Growing definitional agreement among scholars of women's movements has focused on three components of women's movements: (1) who the actors are; (2) what the actors present as their identities and interests; and (3) how the actors organize.

The most recent comparative scholarship on women's movements includes the explicit statement that women's movements are identified by their actors: women. Women's movements are those "where women are the majors actors and leaders" (Beckwith 2005, 585; see also McBride and Mazur 2008, 226; Lovenduski 2009, 175; Tripp et al. 2009, 14; Beckwith 2000; Beckwith 2001, 372). This emphasis on women's primacy as leaders and actors allows three conceptual distinctions for research. First, it distinguishes between women's movements and women in movements. This allows scholars to study social movements in which large numbers of women are active but that cannot be identified specifically as women's movements (such as the peace movement, nationalist or revolutionary movements; see, e.g., Kampwirth 2002, 2004), to investigate conditions of women's involvement in multiple movements (see Meyer and Whittier 1994), and to analyze strategic differences for female activists and leaders in women's versus other movements. Second, it encompasses women's movements that are rightly identified as feminist movements without limiting the overarching definition or excluding, by definitional fiat, women's movements that cannot be identified as feminist. Finally, the definition positions scholars to ask questions about women's movements as distinct from other political movements (see, e.g., Rucht 2003; Grey 2010; Weldon 2011).

Furthermore, women's movements are self-consciously "distinguished by [women's] gendered identity claims that serve as the basis for activism" and mobilization (Beckwith 2005, 585), "the common thread of which [is] the politicization of their lived experience *as women*" (Alvarez 1990, 56, emphasis in original). Tripp et al. (2009, 14), for example, identify African women's movements as movements that "have named women as the primary constituency that they are mobilizing, [building] organizational and/or political strategies around the concerns of women" (see also Ray and Korteweg 1999; Ferree and Mueller 2007, 577; McBride and Mazur 2008, 226; Sawer 2010, 605).

Women organize in *women's* movements around their expressed identities as women, even as the content of those identities may be different and context-pecific. Note that this is not to claim that all women everywhere have the same identities or interests, nor is it an assertion of any fundamental essential sameness of women everywhere. The content of women's identity as women and interests that derive from that recognized, politicized identity are a matter for empirical investigation rather than definitional fiat.

Finally, women's movements are part of a larger category of social movements. A wide range of research in sociology and political science grapples with the definitional boundaries of *social movement*. As Banaszak (2008, 80) observes:

> Social movements are usually defined as a mixture of informal networks and organizations that make "claims" for fundamental changes in the political, economic or social system, *and* are "outside" conventional politics, *and* utilize unconventional or protest tactics....Women's movements are therefore not clearly defined groups but a diffuse and complex set of individuals, organizations, and informal groups...The diffuse nature of movements makes defining their boundaries difficult.

Scholars have grappled with the definition of *women's* movements; they have also raised issues of what is meant by women's *movements*. Current research has led women's movements scholars to critique definitions of political movements that employ particular sets of tactics as definitional. Increasingly, women's movement scholars have rejected definitions that rely on protest behavior as failing to recognize protest as a tactic of specific movements under specific conditions rather than as an integral component of political movements (see, most recently, Sawer 2010, 604; see especially Rucht 2003, 255–260; Ferree and Mueller 2007, 595; McBride and Mazur 2008, 232–234). Furthermore, scholars have critiqued requirements of widespread public visibility as criteria for defining movements, pointing to instances of movement persistence in abeyance (Taylor 1989), of unobtrusive mobilization (Katzenstein 1998), of insider networks (Banaszak 2010), and of movement activism that is not directed at the state, including cultural phenomena that constitute major challenges to patriarchal arrangements, such as music festivals and art installations (Sawer 2010, 606), and autonomous institution-building and service provision, such as *consultori* (Ergas 1982; see also Al-Ali 2003), pregnancy counseling services, and rape crisis centers that are then taken on by state agencies (Elman 2003; Kantola 2006). "The range of locations in which activist women have mobilized...indicates the extent to which women's movements are excellent cases for integrating citizen challenges to states and societies...[such] that conventional distinctions between governments, parties, interest groups, and movements are less useful than a continuum of activist locations/targets that unifies them" (Beckwith 2001, 383).

What makes women's movements *movements*? A social movement can be defined as individuals with shared collective identity and identified grievances, linked and organized in social networks, who mount organized and sustained challenges "against powerful targets" (Tarrow 1998, 2). Such challenges may manifest themselves in fairly conventional ways—or in more contentious and transgressive means or even in unobtrusive modes (Katzenstein 1998; Valiente 2009). Nonetheless, movements are marked by activism that is both collective and challenging, in response to political structural opportunities (or discouragements or threats), new issues, and unanticipated events (Beckwith 2005, 591). Challenging, transgressive collective action distinguishes political movements from, for example, interest groups and political parties; even as movements, interest groups and political parties may share a subset of actors and may work in concert around subsets of issues. Identifying women's movements by how they move—collectively, in challenge—rather than with any particular subset of tactics, leaves strategic choices, tactical innovation, and organizational forms as empirical questions for investigation (see Rucht 2003; Bagguley 2010).

Women's movements, like political movements more generally, persist across time, in sustained interaction. Single-issue campaigns or short-lived interest groups that dissolve at the point of policy success (or defeat) do not by themselves constitute political movements. For women's movements, "there has been a continuity of gendered claims making over the last century or so, providing historical resonance to such claims" (Sawer 2010, 605).

Finally, like all social movements, women's movements rely on social networks for diffusion of information (Soule 2007), mobilization purposes, and coordination of efforts in social movement campaigns (Banaszak 2008, 79–80; Banaszak 2010; Sawer 2010, 604–605; see also della Porta and Rucht 2002). Social networks consist of similarly situated actors who know each other, recognize that they have shared interests, and communicate around those interests. Banaszak (2010, 57) analyzed insider networks of feminists in U.S. government employment, consisting of "professional women in the bureaucracy" who would occasionally meet, whose formal organizational memberships overlapped, and who were linked to other like-minded women through these connections. Networked within and outside the U.S. government, these feminist activists were key in providing information, in alerting colleagues to changing circumstances, and in militating, in coordination with others, for policy advances for women. Social networks have been key to women's historical organizing in social movement around issues of suffrage (Banaszak 1996), violence against women (Elman 1996; Weldon 2002), and women's political representation (Lovenduski 2005; Dahlerup 2006; Krook 2009), among other issues.

In sum, there is agreement (although not perfect agreement) on the definition of women's movements: women's movements are political movements characterized by the primacy of women's gendered experiences, women's issues, and women's leadership and decision making. The relationship of women to these movements is direct and immediate; movement definition, issue articulation, and issue resolution are specific to women, developed and organized by them with reference to their gender identity.

This definition encompasses nonfeminist as well as feminist movements. As suggested earlier, women's movement scholarship often conflated women's movement and feminist movement, if not in explicit terminology then in implicit analysis. Comparative women's movements research has asserted the necessity of the distinction between feminist movements and more general women's movements, identifying feminist movements as one—but not the only—form of women's movement (Alvarez 1990; Katzenstein 1998; Valiente 2003; Tripp et al. 2009). Feminist movements involve challenges to women's subordination to men (Ferree and Mueller 2007, 577) "by a gendered power analysis of women's subordination [which contests] political, social and other power arrangements of domination and subordination on the basis of gender" (Beckwith 2001, 372). Feminist movements are distinguished as "women's movements with a specific feminist discourse, and feminist movement actors present the ideas" (Lovenduski 2009, 175).

The broad definition of women's movements encompasses feminist movements as one type of women's movement but also recognizes movement organizing by nonfeminist women and by women on the right as well as on the left. It is sufficiently precise to distinguish women's movements from other political forms, such as interest groups and political campaigns, and to delin-eate the conceptual difference between women's movements and women in political movements. Although some scholars assert additional requirements for categorizing a movement as a women's movement, the definitional consen-sus has provided a foundation for comparative political analysis of women's movements.[4]

Definitional Utility

Definitions of women's movements have developed to emphasize the distinc-tiveness of the actors, *women*, and the distinctiveness of the action or mobili-zation, *movement*. The emphasis on women as primary leaders and actors and the focus on social movement (as distinct from public opinion, vote choice, or organization membership) have positioned scholars to raise new questions for empirical investigation and to modify theory for empirical testing. Arenas of extended inquiry include (but are hardly limited to) the following:

1. Distinguishing among different types of women's movements (e.g., fem-inist movements, rightwing women's movements, lesbian movements)
2. Distinguishing women's *movements* from the *campaigns* they undertake
3. Identifying the conditions under which separate women's movements work in concert or in coalition
4. Identifying the conditions under which women's movements employ similar strategies and tactics
5. Investigating women's movements as transnational actors (Keck and Sikkink 1998; Basu 2000; Weldon 2002; Moghadam 2005)
6. Examining "the extent to which collective action undertaken in defense of traditional identities spills over into feminist consciousness or con-sciousness of gender subordination" (Ray and Korteweg 1999, 51; see also Kaplan 1982; Ortbals 2007; Banaszak 2010)
7. Identifying "the conditions under which particular identities are mobi-lized" (Ray and Korteweg 1999, 52)
8. Mapping the sequencing of women's movements, including feminist movements and gay and lesbian movements
9. Examining the politics of women in movements other than women's movements (e.g., workers' movements, nationalist movements)
10. Theorizing and analyzing the intersection of women's movements with other movements (intersectionality) and of women's movement activists who are also activists in other political movements (double militancy)

The analytical leverage that these definitions permit, by distinguishing between women's movements, feminist movements, and women in political movements, is best revealed in comparative political research. Scholars of wom-en's movements working from a comparative perspective forced the issue of definitions of women's movements, and the definitional starting point of comparative women's movements can be powerfully directive, for good or ill.

WOMEN'S MOVEMENTS IN COMPARATIVE PERSPECTIVE

How have scholars conceptualized comparison and what are the comparative categories across and against which women's movements have been studied? An analysis of syllabi for courses in comparative women's movements found three major sets of comparisons: cross-national, cross-movement, and cross-time (Beckwith 2005). A more recent essay on comparative gender and institutions (Chappell 2010, 185) suggests a multidirectional research agenda that employs vertical and horizontal comparisons that are cross-national, international, and cross-time. A wide range of published research evidences a sophisticated range of comparison, combining focus on key variables and careful case selection to construct controls and variation to provide comparisons across movements, structures, and policy arenas by time and space. As comparative women's movement research has proliferated, its research questions have driven the subfield toward a range of comparative strategies.

Women's Movements and Categories of Comparison

The development of women's movements scholarship has produced multiple research strategies that identify distinct categories of comparison. Some research has employed a single comparative strategy, while other research has relied on a subset of strategies for comparison in response to the research questions.

First, scholars employ a research strategy *comparing similar women's movements within a single region*, with a primary focus on feminist movements. This has been the most common comparative strategy, holding type of movement and region constant, and investigating variation in mobilization opportunities, strategies, state responses, and policy outcomes (see, e.g., Katzenstein and Mueller 1987; Stetson and Mazur 1995; Tripp et al. 2009). The control of region, as a constant, has often but not always served as a surrogate for political system or political development, where similar systems map to a single region (e.g., presidential systems in democracies emerging from dictatorship; see Jaquette 1994; Htun 2003; e.g., democratizing parliamentary systems emerging from post-Soviet bloc dictatorship; see Matland and Montgomery 2003). This comparative analytical choice is apparent across a range of regions and movements. Several omnibus studies of women's movements group single-country chapter studies by region into sections, emphasizing region and regional similarities as key to the comparative strategy employed by the authors and/or volume editors (see, e.g., Iglitzin and Ross 1976; Basu 2010b). The emphasis on region was especially useful in the early research where research proposals focused on a single region directed to funding agencies with specific regional concerns, where languages might be the same or similar, where the data excavation project needed to be undertaken (e.g., post-Soviet Central and Eastern Europe), or where multiple scholars could work together on a common project, with assumptions of key similarities across countries within region (e.g., RNGS Project; see also Mazur 2012, Table 16.1). The comparison of the same women's movement, usually, across different countries, continues to be the most common strategy of the comparative study of women's movements.

A second comparative strategy has been to focus on *the same women's movement across different state structural arrangements*. This research identifies political system arrangements, policy regimes, or political structures as central to the research question. Cases are selected by presence of a feminist movement and by structures, regimes, or systems to assess the impact of feminist movement organizing on public policy or "the role of institutions in shaping feminist strategies" (Chappell 2002, 4). An example of this research is Bashevkin's (1998) research on conservative political regimes in Britain, Canada, and the United States, selecting cases by presence of conservative government and analyzing women's movements' success in policy initiative and defense. Gelb (1989) relies on a similar strategy, identifying state structures, party systems, and the role of organized labor as key factors shaping feminist public policy in Britain, Sweden, and the United States. This strategy has generally been employed in the study of feminist or women's rights movements or women's movements targeting the state for specific policy purposes.

A relatively new version of this second comparative strategy has been to employ a most-different-case selection rationale, with work focusing on a limited number of relatively unlikely cases, the selection of which cannot be easily reconciled with simple regional similarity. The selection of *different state structural arrangements to investigate women's movements*, in terms of their emergence, mobilization, and ultimate policy success, for examples, emphasizes the state and state structural differences. For example, Kantola (2006), in her study of British and Finnish feminism, focuses on feminist movements in three policy arenas, emphasizing feminist discourse differences in each movement's approach to the state, even as British and Finnish state structures and party systems are substantially different. Gelb (2003) compares women's movements in Japan and the United States to analyze their mobilization and to assess their subsequent impact upon public policies; Briskin and Eliasson (1999) use the cases of Canada and Sweden to investigate the impact of women's organizing on public policy. Banaszak, Beckwith, and Rucht (2003) examine women's movements in West Europe and North America in their interaction with states that varied not only in their structures and party systems but also in their patterns of state reconfiguration, asking how changes in state structures were both effected by and affected women's movements. Jennifer Disney (2008) employs a case selection strategy of dissimilarity in her work on women's movements in Mozambique and Nicaragua.

Regardless of whether the case selection identifies most-similar or most-different cases, the comparative study of women's movements reflects comparative political analysis more generally in its reference to the state as a key actor or variable. Such comparisons have focused on how women's movements mobilize and influence policy outcomes in federal (rather than unitary) state systems (see Banaszak 1996; Chappell 2002; Dobrowolsky 2003; Gamkhar and Vickers 2010; Haussman, Sawer, and Vickers 2010; Vickers 2010), in constitutional monarchies or political systems with a monarchical tradition (rather than republics; see McDonagh 2009); in states with various levels of feminist institutionalism (Andrew 2010), including state feminist arrangements (Stetson and Mazur 1995); and in states with different state structures and patterns of state reconfiguration (Banaszak et al. 2003). Recent work by Htun and Weldon (2010) examines the impact of state capacity and states' power to effect whether (and which) women's groups will mobilize for policy change. The authors argue that state capacity is, in part, an antecedent variable that conditions women's movements' activism and policy demands; they hypothesize that the higher the state capacity, the likelier it is that women's groups will mobilize around policies that require state support and enforcement than will be the case in states with low state capacity (211–212). In their study of policies against violence against women, Weldon and Htun (2010) found variation by early versus later adopter states but concluded that, for the issue of violence against women, "women's organizing in feminist movements on their own behalf is a critical and consistent catalyst of government action" (18). This was particularly the case for democratic political systems, especially under conditions where feminist movements were able to leverage international influence upon the domestic policy process. This explicitly comparative, and large-N, research that asks how women's movements succeed or fail in specific policy initiatives is a major advance in the comparative study of women's movements and in the comparative political analysis of public policy initiatives.

A substantial and related body of work focuses on gender and the social welfare state, although this scholarship is less concerned with the role of women's movements than on the gendered nature of social welfare policy regimes and policy variations across states (see Lewis 1992; Sainsbury 1999; Pascall and Manning 2000). There is still insufficient work on the relationship between women's movements and the state political economic arrangements, in terms of women's movements' impact on policy outcomes (although see Weldon 2011). Beyond the focus on state arrangements and women's movements' policy impacts, there is still little comparative research on how party *systems* condition the possibilities of women's movements' impact upon state policy making (see, however, Bashevkin 1998; see also the chapter by Kittilson in this volume). Research on women's movements' efforts to influence specific political parties and on the impact of party *types* (e.g., right-wing v. left-wing, confessional v. secular) in advancing women-friendly public policy, presents mixed findings. Although women's movements, and particularly feminist movements, appear to target left-wing parties for policy change, the impact of party type in effecting women's movements' policy demands appears to vary by policy issue (see, e.g., Beckwith 1987; Htun 2003; Teghtsoonian and Chappell 2008; Htun and Weldon 2010; Weldon and Htun 2010).

The Issue of Women's Interests

The range of comparative women's movements research reveals a common core of interests around which women's movements have organized, consistently and persistently, across time and space. For Htun and Weldon (2010, 207), the question is not whether there are common interests around which women mobilize; rather, they ask how we can explain "the global variation in gender-equality policies" and identify two dimensions of women's policy interests: status policies and doctrinal jurisdictional policies.[5] In their comprehensive study of forty-three countries, Nelson and Chowdhury (1994, 11) find four common women's policy clusters: (1) personal safety, security, and autonomy; (2) reproductive and maternal rights; (3) equal access to public power; and (4) "remaking the political and legal rules of the game." Recent comparative women's movements research has found similar common policy subsets targeted by women's movements across a wide range of countries. These policy subsets include women's political and civil rights and political representation (Banaszak 1996; Baldez 2004; Childs 2004; Diaz 2005; Lovenduski 2005; Tremblay 2007; Childs and Krook 2008; Murray 2008; Krook 2009); violence against women (Beckwith 1987; Weldon 2002; Elman 2003; Kantola 2006; Weldon and Htun 2010); child care (Mahon 1997; Collier 2001; Kantola 2006); civil divorce (Halper 1985; Beckwith 1987; Htun 2003; Revillard 2005; Osanloo 2009); and reproductive rights (Luker 1984; Beckwith 1987; Staggenborg 1991; Norgren 2001; Stetson 2001; Htun 2003).

The conditions under which women's movements target policy interests, selected by movement activists in specific state contexts, and the means by which women's movements bring influence on the state and other actors vary. However, the range and content of interests addressed by women's movements and feminist movements are remarkably similar. As Nelson and Chowdhury (1994, 11) concluded, on the basis of their comprehensive study of forty-three countries, "no [women's] issues are tied solely to one political context or economic condition." Nearly two decades later, comparative women's movement scholars find that, cross-nationally, the same interests, issues, and policy concerns emerge in the visible efforts of women's movements—if not always in the same country or at the same time and not always with success. These core women's policy subsets, consistent as interests across time and space, underscore the importance of the role of women's movements in informing the larger scholarship on representation, inclusion, and policy making and tie women's movements to the operationalization of women's interests in terms of policy representation (see also Hill and Chappell 2006; Vickers 2006).

Logics of Comparative Women's Movements across Movements

Two additional comparative logics have been employed in the study of women's movements. These strategies are less common, but they offer considerable analytical leverage, depending upon the research question. The first is a *cross-time comparison of the same women's movement in a single country*. Sonia Alvarez's (1990) work on the Brazilian women's movement and its contributions to Brazilian democracy is one example. Banaszak's (1996) work on the Swiss and U.S. women's suffrage movements is a second example. Banaszak employs two comparative strategies: a cross-national focus on two similar movements; and an additional longitudinal analysis of each movement in evaluating its successes and failures. Mansbridge (1986), in her study of the campaign for an Equal Rights Amendment, follows the U.S. feminist movement from the early 1970s to 1982, the point of Equal Rights Amendment (ERA) ratification failure. Beckwith (1987) uses a similar comparative strategy in her study of the efforts of the Italian feminist movement across a decade of three policy attempts, from 1974 to 1983, in regard to divorce, abortion, and sexual violence. The cross-time comparative strategy is perhaps less common in the comparative study of women's movements, but it provides strong analytical leverage for deciphering points of state resistance or compliance and for mapping the chronology of success and failure, as the same women's movement challenges the same state on the same or similar policy issues.[6]

The second additional, and underrepresented, research strategy is the *cross-sectional comparison of different women's movements in a single country*. Lisa Baldez's (2002) *Why Women Protest* is the exemplar of this strategy. Baldez examines Chilean women's movement activism in support of and opposition to the Allende regime, focusing on the efforts of conservative women to mobilize in movement to protest and to assist in the overthrow of the Allende government. The author further scrutinizes the role of the Chilean women's movement in protesting and helping to bring down the Pinochet regime and to revive Chilean democracy. Baldez's book was also a major factor in influencing women's movements scholars to recognize the presence of nonfeminist and antifeminist women's movements and to relinquish their synonymous use of the terms feminist movement and women's movement.

These two strategies, although relatively uncommon, permit scholars to ask important questions about women's movements that cannot easily be answered from other comparative analytical perspectives. A cross-time comparative analysis of the same women's movement affords insight into the complexities of innovation, interaction, mobilization, and outcomes, including:

- Internal transformation of a women's movement's issue framing
- The process by which a nonfeminist women's movement and its actors become feminist (or not; Kaplan 1982; Banaszak 2010)
- Strategic innovation in a women's movement
- How and under what conditions women's movements make mistakes or miss opportunities (Sawyers and Meyer 1999)
- Paths of political learning by a women's movement
- Episodes of internal and external cross-generational conflict or solidarity
- Conditions under which a women's movement enjoys success (or faces defeat)
- The waxing and waning of a women's movement's mobilization, activism, and visibility, among others

Similarly, a cross-movement strategy that focuses on different women's movements in the same country offers analytical advantages. Such a strategy allows scholars to see women's movements in interaction and to apprehend and to investigate conflict between organized women. It can also illuminate how the state responds to *which actors*, underscoring how *who the actors are* and not just *how they act* can elicit different state response, even within the same state at the same point in time. Furthermore, a cross-movement strategy can provide insights into state-movement interactions based on the same state institutional structures and similar movement identity bases, as well as illuminating:

- Gendered arrangements of institutions and practices in response to different women's movements
- Variations in state response to different women's movements
- Political opportunities available to some women's movements rather than others
- "The consequences of organizing on the basis of a shared gender identity" (Baldez 2002, 207)
- Gendered framing congruencies or contests (Goss and Heaney 2010)
- Cross-movement collaboration, coalitions, and campaigns; among others

Finally, these two strategies offer potentially powerful insights into issues of intersectionality in women's movements. Working with specific, limited cases—that is, comparative within a single state or within a single moment—permits focused and primarily qualitative analysis, including process-tracing, helping the scholar to determine "how to isolate, measure and encapsulate the complexities of identity across the various institutional levels, sites, and time frames... [a task that requires] careful thought, planning and patience" (Chappell 2010, 187).

Comparative Women's Movements and Intersectionality

Although women arguably have shared interests (Hill and Chappell 2006; Vickers 2006; Schwindt-Bayer and Taylor-Robinson 2011), not all women organize around the same interests in the same movement. For women's movements, issues of intersectionality are heightened; that is, the distinctive factors of women as a political relevant demographic majority means that women also bring with them interests and identities from (potentially) all other politically relevant demographic groups.

Intersectionality—as a political issue, a life experience, and a research methodology[7]—arose from a women's movement. The U.S. feminist movement, and the tensions around race and gender felt by committed feminists, produced the moment in which black feminists insisted upon voice as women within the movement as well as the opportunity for white feminists to reflect and to respond (see also the chapter by Hill Collins and Chepp in this volume). Intersectionality as a concept and as an analytical perspective[8] emerged in the writings and politics of African American women and from African American women's political and life experiences as those experiences informed their actual politics (Crenshaw 1991; Collins 1998, 2000, 2005; Hancock 2007a, 2007b; Jordan-Zachery 2007; Simien 2007).[9] "The [predominantly white US] feminist movement was criticized for its homogenizing and totalizing presupposition, and for silencing black women in particular, by presuming an exclusionary (white, middle-class) concept of 'woman'" (Gressgård 2008).

Intersectionality emerged as the analysis of the convergence and mutual constitution of collective identity and political structures, recognizing inequalities in political power that were not individually located but that were hegemonic social constructions of dominance and subordination that played out differently across and within gender, class, and race (among other identities). In intersectional analysis, "systems of race, social class, gender, sexuality, ethnicity, nation and age" are seen to "form mutually constructive features of social organization, which shape Black women's experiences and, in turn, are shaped by Black women" (Collins 2000, 299) and to represent "a specific constellation of social practices that demonstrate how oppressions converge" (Collins 2005, 11; see also Crenshaw 1991; Collins 1998, especially ch. 6; McCall 2005; Weldon 2006). Scholars working with politicized categories of class, sexuality, and nationality extended the more specific, original emphasis on race and sex to additional politically relevant categories. As intersectionality has moved from its historical foundations in the writings of U.S. women of color, it has become abstracted across these additional categories, potentially including intersections of categories of identities of power—for example, in the United States, sex (male) and race (white). As Crenshaw (1991, 1245) writes, a "focus on the intersections of race and gender only highlights the need to account for multiple grounds of identity when considering how the social world is constructed."

The development of intersectionality beyond its initial categories of gender and race risks losing the politicized emphasis of its origins and the political needs and demands of its original constituency: black women in the United States. The abstraction necessary for the extension of intersectionality beyond the original categories poses a similar challenge. For the purposes of this chapter, however, the emphasis on gender, and its intersectional position in comparative women's movements, lessens the likelihood that the political nature of intersectionality will be devalued or rendered invisible. Women's movements in and of themselves are political, and the challenges of attracting, recruiting, and mobilizing activists keep issues of intersectionality in the forefront: which women are available for mobilization and which issues women are mobilizing to advance, are explicit intersectionality questions. Furthermore, although most comparative women's movement research is not explicit in addressing intersectionality, insofar as the terminology of intersection is not employed, comparative political research forces the issue of how some differences (citizenship, ethnicity, class) play out in women's mobilization and activism in political movement.

By intersectionality, I mean experiences and relations of domination and subordination and contestation, embodied in individuals and structured by institutional arrangements, cultural understandings, and political practices. These power relationships constitute cleavages that may cut across each other but that may also reinforce each other (García Bedolla 2007). These cleavages are located within and experienced by individuals; such cleavages also shape institutional arrangements, political structures, and cultural norms and practices. Politically relevant identities, marking power relationships, intersect with each other, in individuals and in the political structural arrangements that reflect those power relationships. Intersectionality reflects "relationships of inequality among social groups and changing configurations of inequality along multiple and conflicting dimensions" (McCall 2005, 1773).

Intersectionality can be understood both as embodied and as structured. First, intersectionality is embodied; that is, the complexity and diversity of female experience inheres in individual women, in terms of gender and other politically inscribed identities (Baldez 2007; García Bedolla 2007). These identities develop through experience, sometimes concurrently and sometimes stepwise, as coconstitutive; they coexist, if uneasily, and are often evoked by political action, where mobilization around issues pertinent to one identity positions the individual in internal conflict with another identity or other identities. This version of intersectionality, in political action, has been termed *double militancy* in comparative research on women's movements (see, e.g., Valiente 2003).[10] Where feminists have been active in nonfeminist social movements or in nonfeminist organizations (e.g., feminists in left-wing political parties), feminists' commitments on the basis of gender and class identities create a unique positionality within the movement or organization and cause felt tensions, within individuals, in regard to their identities. How, for example, can one be a good feminist while devoting one's efforts to advance a sexist left-wing political party (Hellman 1987)? How can one be a good socialist without supporting a left-wing party, no matter how sexist? How can one speak in a meeting, as a worker, and not be dismissed as a woman? Jordan-Zachery (2007, 254) asks a similar question for African American women's politics: "am I a Black Woman or a Woman who Is Black?" More specifically, for comparative feminist movement activism, how does a black feminist position herself in a wide-ranging feminist movement dominated and directed by white women? How can a black feminist not support a feminist movement? These examples suggest that intersectionality in identity results in spoken and recognized internal tensions and in intramovement conflicts in the face of explicit calls to political activism, particularly in social movements or campaigns that implicate multiple identities. That is, although intersectionality of identities need not necessarily create internal conflict, the call to action politicizes identities and raises specific challenges to social movements. Again, because women as a politically relevant group are everywhere, whose gender identities intersect with and are mutually constructive of all other politically relevant identities—either in reinforcing or cross-cutting cleavage—intersectionality issues are heightened for women's movements. As a result, intersectionality research should provide strong leverage in the comparative analysis of women's movements.

In the comparative study of women's movements, intersectionality asks specific questions. How do women mobilize across difference (Collins 1998)? How do common interests, experienced differently, give rise to specific, collective issue agendas? Under what conditions do (some) women organize separately, and what conditions serve to mobilize nearly all women in a common campaign? Does the selection of some movement targets—for example, the state, violent husbands—remove some women from potential involvement in a movement but activate others? Does the participation of some women—but not others—improve chances for movement success in specific policy arenas (Al-Ali 2003; Banaszak 2010)?

Second, intersectionality is structured. As Weldon (2006, 238) writes, "The critique of gender analysis advanced by many women of color focuses on differences in structural position, not just differences in identity or agency." Intersectionality is reflected in and constructs political arrangements and women's movements. Intersectionality is manifested in structures as well as in individuals, as systems of inequality impinge differently across women and gender. "Categories of difference are conceptualized as dynamic productions of individual and institutional factors" (Hancock 2007b, 251). This is not to argue that intersectional identity and structure are separate; rather, identity is located in and experienced only by individuals, who are subject to the effects of structures but also form and shape institutions and practices, even if only in reaction to them (see, e.g., Young 2000, 133–141; Connell 2001). The structure of intersectionality (Weldon 2006) constructs and locates disadvantage (and advantage), imposes oppression (and offers privilege), and it channels policy outcomes.

In general, questions about the structural outcomes of intersectionality have focused on policy issues, on how policies vary across states and gender regimes (Sainsbury 1999, 2008; Connell 2001; Htun and Weldon 2010), and on how women's movements have succeeded in influencing state policy (Stetson and Mazur 1995; Briskin and Eliasson 1999; Htun 2003; Rai 2003).

A comparative politics of gender, placing gender as a central concern, points scholars to all women, in all their diversity and difference, underscoring intersectionality in comparative political analysis. It can guide research in regard to the identification of categories of political relevance for the comparative study of women's movements, alerting scholars to points in time when collective identity across difference in movement poses mobilization and solidarity challenges as well as moments when some difference is submerged in deference to a more constrained but more all-encompassing collective identity. Moreover, "axes of disadvantage...are defined differently in different national contexts, and so examining variation across national borders illuminates the variety of social arrangements that are consistent with human biology" (Weldon 2006, 237), "denaturalizing" and de-essentializing gender and gender relations. These moments should be evidenced in comparative cases of women *in* movements, such as women in the black civil rights movement and women in nationalist and anticolonial liberation movements, as well as in comparative cases of women's movements' campaigns, where intersectional issues may be heightened in efforts at collaboration and coordination, but also where a women's movement campaign may face opposition from similarly organized women.

CONCLUSION

Comparative women's movement research has proliferated across the past two decades, employing a range of comparative political analytical strategies. What have we learned from the comparative study of women's movements? Consistently, cross-nationally and cross-time, the comparative study of women's movements has shown women's movements to be the signature (if not sole) mobilizing structure for women's political influence, feminist or otherwise. Women's movements play a key role *for women* in advancing or defending women's rights and status, effecting women's public policies, and increasing women's access to political office.[11] The distinctive role of women's movements, as the signature political organizational form for women, places women more firmly in civil society than in the state (insofar as women are so overwhelmingly underrepresented in the state) and more exclusively in civil society than may be the case for many other movements. Women, and women's movements, also face a countervailing dominant state strategy, across states, of political marginalization or exclusion. The comparative study of women's movements requires, therefore, extending the boundaries of political science beyond the borders of the state and of conventional political organizational forms such as political parties and interest groups.

Comparative women's movements research identifies a range of strategic and tactical choices by women's movements facing the state. We know that women's movements can have success in a range of political institutional arrangements (unitary v. federal states) and under conservative as well as social democratic regimes (Bashevkin 1998) but, again, that women's movements are generally most successful when they can ally with or leverage left political parties in democratic political systems—but not exclusively or universally and not across all policy issues. Women's movements may have their greatest leverage when they are able to convince democratic regimes that organized women hold the key to electoral success in specific elections, but the research is not yet sufficiently developed to draw this conclusion. Women's movements have generally similar strategies in the face of the state: women do not use organized violence, and they launch a variety of sortis against states, employing separatist, autonomous, state-involved, and other strategies as they attempt to advance their goals.

Women's movements target the state for change, and they require state action in regard to initiating and implementing women-friendly public policy. Democratic states appear to be more responsive to women's movements' influence than do nondemocracies, given formal mechanisms of accountability and representation; the more democratic the regime, the wider the range of tactics employed by women's movements (Henderson and Jeydel 2007, 55). Political women also appear to have their best chances of reaching elective office when women's movements insist upon women's inclusion in representative political institutions, including political parties (see Kittilson 2006). States also appear to be most susceptible to women's movements when states are moving toward democracy. In democratic transitions, when women's movements are prepared for transition—that is, when women's movements inhabit civil society, succeed in organizing in advance of the transition, and construct alliances with other democratic actors, those movements are well positioned to gender new institutions favorably at the point of their instauration. Where women's movements serve to effect democratic transitions, they construct the conditions that have "enhanced women's citizenship in terms of women's access not only to civil and political rights but to various social and economic ones as well" (Waylen 2007, 199). This is not to claim that democratic transitions produce uniform and universal women-friendly policy outcomes; rather, research on democratic transitions suggests that political opportunities are greatest for women's movements under these conditions.

The comparative study of women's movements employs the full range of comparative political analytical tools. It places gender and women centrally in its analysis; it foregrounds sex as a major political cross-cutting axis that undergirds women's organizing in women's movements. It moves us from drawing false and inaccurate conclusions based on a single nation, and it informs and transforms our understandings of political movements more generally. Across two decades, the comparative study of women's movements has produced substantial findings about processes of democratization and modernization, about citizen initiative and resistance, and about the role of the state in responding to, facilitating, and resisting women's movements. Women's movements have been crucial for securing women's political rights, representation, and policy outcomes. The conditions under which women's movements emerge, mobilize, contest, and succeed vary, but the absence of women's movements almost thoroughly guarantees women's marginalization, exploitation, and oppression. The comparative study of women's movements makes clear where the opportunities for success might lie and how to seize them, and has revealed new insights and concerns about power and about gender. There is still much to be discovered about women's movements and about women in political movements, which can best by provided by a continuing comparative analysis and a comparative politics of gender.

NOTES

1. In this chapter, I treat *social movement* and *political movement* as synonyms; the conceptual distinction between the two is beyond the purpose of this chapter.
2. The editors requested that I focus this chapter on "the comparative study of women's movements (and issues in defining women's movements versus feminist movements)... [as] a theoretical essay covering how to define women's movements, how to operationalize or study movements, and how to deal with intersectionality in social movements." This chapter draws in part from my previous work (Beckwith 2000, 2001, 2005).
3. Movements that had labeled themselves as women's liberation movements (*emancipazione della donna; mouvement de libération des femmes*) were subsumed under the general category of women's movements, a terminology that treated *women's movements* and *feminist movements* as synonymous.
4. Ray and Korteweg (1999, 52) reject employing feminism or movement strategy as definitional components of women's movements, writing, "The literature shows that rigid distinctions such as feminine versus feminist or strategic versus practical interests limit our understanding of gender."
5. Htun and Weldon (2010, 213, n. 9) rely on Young's categories of "the sexual division of labor, hierarchies of power, and normative heterosexuality."
6. This is not to suggest that women's movements and states are static across time. Clearly the same movement adapts to challenges, opportunities, successes and failures across time; similarly, the same state makes adjustments in response to challenges and demands from women's movements.
7. For a discussion of intersectionality in comparative political field research and issues of data richness and challenge of access, see Ortbals and Rinker (2009).
8. For intersectionality as a strategy of analysis, see Bassel and Emejulu (2010) and Simien (2007), although see also McCall (2005, 1771, n. 1).
9. See also McCall (2005, 1771, n. 1) for an extended list of early writings on intersectionality.

10. Double militancy addresses only two dimensions of intersectionality (primarily gender and class), reflecting its origins.
11. There are occasional examples of women-friendly public policy enactment in the absence of a visible organized mass women's movement, but these are rare (see, e.g., Beckwith 1987 for the Italian divorce referendum of 1973; Htun 2003 for the experience of military-directed public policy regarding women; Hatem 1992, 2005 on women's political equality in Egypt in the 1950s and 1960s).

REFERENCES

Al-Ali, Nadje S. 2003. "Gender and civil society in the Middle East." *International Feminist Journal of Politics* 5(2): 216–232.

Alvarez, Sonia. 1990. *Engendering democracy in Brazil: Women's movements in transitional politics.* Princeton, NJ: Princeton University Press.

Andrew, Merrindahl. 2010. "Women's movement institutionalization: The need for new approaches." *Politics & Gender* 6(4): 609–616.

Bacchetta, Paola, and Margaret Power (Eds.). 2002. *Right-wing women: From conservatives to extremists around the world.* New York: Routledge.

Bagguley, Paul. 2010. "The limits of protest events data and repertoires for the analysis of contemporary feminism." *Politics & Gender* 6(4): 616–622.

Baldez, Lisa. 2002. *Why women protest.* Cambridge, UK: Cambridge University Press.

Baldez, Lisa. 2004. "Elected bodies: Gender quotas for female legislative candidates in Mexico." *Legislative Studies Quarterly* 29(2): 231–258.

Baldez, Lisa. 2007. "Intersectionality." *Politics & Gender* 3(2): 229–231.

Banaszak, Lee Ann. 1996. *Why movements succeed or fail: Opportunity, culture, and the struggle for woman suffrage.* Princeton, NJ: Princeton University Press.

Banaszak, Lee Ann. 2008. "Women's movements and women in movements: Influencing American democracy from the outside." In Christina Wolbrecht, Karen Beckwith and Lisa Baldez, eds., *Political women and American democracy.* Cambridge, UK: Cambridge University Press, 79–95.

Banaszak, Lee Ann. 2010. *The women's movement inside and outside the state.* Cambridge, UK: Cambridge University Press.

Banaszak, Lee Ann, Karen Beckwith, and Dieter Rucht (Eds.). 2003. *Women's movements facing the reconfigured state.* Cambridge, UK: Cambridge University Press.

Bashevkin, Sylvia. 1998. *Women on the defensive: Living through conservative times.* Chicago: University of Chicago Press.

Bassel, Leah, and Akwugo Emejulu. 2010. "Struggles for institutional space in France and the United Kingdom: Intersectionality and the politics of policy." *Politics & Gender* 6(4): 517–544.

Basu, Amrita. 2000. "Globalization of the local, localization of the global: Mapping transnational women's movements." *Meridians: Feminism, Race, Transnationalism* 1(1): 68–84.

Basu, Amrita. 2010a. "Introduction." In Amrita Basu, ed., *Women's movements in the global era: The power of local feminisms.* Boulder, CO: Westview, 1–28.

Basu, Amrita (Ed.) 2010b. *Women's movements in the global era: The power of local feminisms.* Boulder, CO: Westview.

Beckwith, Karen. 1987. "Response to feminism in the Italian parliament: Divorce, abortion, and sexual violence legislation." In Mary Fainsod Katzenstein and Carol McClurg Mueller, eds., *The women's movements of Western Europe and the United States: Consciousness, political opportunity and public policy*. Philadelphia: Temple University Press, 153–171.

Beckwith, Karen. 2000. "Beyond compare? Women's movements in comparative perspective," *European Journal of Political Research* 37(4): 431–468.

Beckwith, Karen. 2001. "Women's movements at century's end: Excavation and advance in political science." *Annual Review of Political Science* 4: 371–390.

Beckwith, Karen. 2005. "The comparative politics of women's movements." *Perspectives on Politics* 3(3): 583–596.

Blee, Kathleen M. 2008. *Women of the Klan: Racism and gender in the 1920s*. Berkeley: University of California Press.

Briskin, Linda, and Mona Eliasson (Eds.). 1999. *Women's organizing and public policy in Canada and Sweden*. Montreal: McGill-Queen's University Press.

Chappell, Louise. 2002. *Gendering government: Feminist engagement with the state in Australia and Canada*. Vancouver: University of British Columbia Press.

Chappell, Louise. 2010. "Comparative gender and institutions: Directions for research." *Perspectives on Politics* 8(1): 183–189.

Childs, Sarah. 2004. *New Labour's women MPs: Women representing women*. Abingdon, UK: Routledge.

Childs, Sarah, and Mona Lena Krook. 2008. "Critical mass theory and women's political representation." *Political Studies* 56(3): 725–736.

Collier, Cheryl. 2001. "Working with parties: Success and failure of child care advocates in British Columbia and Ontario in the 1990s." In Susan Prentice, ed., *Changing child care: Five decades of child care advocacy and policy in Canada*. Halifax: Fernwood Publishing, 117–131.

Collins, Patricia Hill. 1998. *Fighting words: Black women and the search for justice*. Minneapolis: University of Minnesota Press.

Collins, Patricia Hill. 2000. *Black feminist thought: Knowledge, consciousness, and the politics of empowerment*. New York: Routledge.

Collins, Patricia Hill. 2005. *Black sexual politics: African Americans, gender and the new racism*. New York: Routledge.

Connell, R. W. 2001. "Gender and the state." In Kate Nash and Alan Scott, eds., *Blackwell companion to political sociology*. Malden, MA: Blackwell Publishers, 117–126.

Crenshaw, Kimberle. 1991. "Mapping the margins: Intersectionality, identity politics, and violence against women of color." *Stanford Law Review* 43(6): 1241–1299.

Dahlerup, Drude (Ed.). 2006. *Women, quotas and politics*. New York: Routledge.

Della Porta, Donatella. 2003. "The women's movements, the left and the state: Continuities and changes in the Italian case." In Lee Ann Banaszak, Karen Beckwith, and Dieter Rucht, eds., *Women's movements facing the reconfigured state*. Cambridge, UK: Cambridge University Press, 48–68.

Della Porta, Donatella, and Dieter Rucht. 2002. "The dynamics of environmental campaigns." *Mobilization* 7(1): 1–14.

Diaz, Mercedes Mateo. 2005. *Representing women? Female legislators in West European parliaments*. Colchester: ECPR Press.

Disney, Jennifer. 2008. *Women's activism and feminist agency in Mozambique and Nicaragua*. Philadelphia: Temple University Press.

Dobrowolsky, Alexandra. 2003. "Shifting states: Women's constitutional organizing across space and time." In Lee Ann Banaszak, Karen Beckwith, and Dieter Rucht, eds., *Women's movements facing the reconfigured state*. Cambridge, UK: Cambridge University Press, 114–140.

Elman, Amy. 1996. *Sexual subordination and state intervention: Comparing Sweden and the United States*. Oxford: Berghahn Books.

Elman, Amy. 2003. "Refuge in reconfigured states: Shelter movements in the United States, Britain and Sweden." In Lee Ann Banaszak, Karen Beckwith and Dieter Rucht, eds., *Women's movements facing the reconfigured state*. Cambridge, UK: Cambridge University Press, 94–113.

Ergas, Yasmine. 1982. "1968–79. Feminism and the Italian party system: Women's politics in a decade of turmoil." *Comparative Politics* 14(3): 253–279.

Ferree, Myra Marx, and Carol McClurg Mueller. 2007. "Feminism and the women's movement: A global perspective." In David A. Snow, Sarah A. Soule, and Hanspeter Kriesi, eds., *The Blackwell companion to social movements*. Malden, MA: Blackwell, 576–607.

Gamkhar, Shama, and Jill Vickers. 2010. "Comparing federations: Lessons from comparing Canada and the United States." *Publius* 40(3): 351–356.

García Bedolla, Lisa. 2007. "Intersections of inequality: Understanding marginalization and privilege in the post civil-rights era." *Politics & Gender* 3(2): 232–248.

Gelb, Joyce. 1989. *Feminism and politics: A comparative perspective*. Berkeley: University of California Press.

Gelb, Joyce. 2003. *Gender policies in Japan and the United States: Comparing women's movements, rights, and politics*. New York: Palgrave Macmillan.

Goss, Kristin A., and Michael T. Heaney. 2010. "Organizing women as women: Hybridity and grassroots collective action in the 21st century." *Perspectives on Politics* 8(1): 27–52.

Gressgård, Randi. 2008. "Mind the gap: Intersectionality, complexity and 'the event.'" *Theory and Science* 10(1). Available from http://theoryandscience.icaap.org/content/vol10.1/Gressgard.html.

Grey, Sandra J. 2010. "When no 'official record' exists?" *Politics & Gender* 6(4): 622–629.

Halper, Louise. 1985. "Law and women's agency in post-revolutionary Iran." *Harvard Journal of Law and Gender* 28: 85–142.

Hancock, Ange-Marie. 2007a. "When multiplication doesn't equal quick addition: Examining intersectionality as a research paradigm." *Perspectives on Politics* 5(1): 63–79.

Hancock, Ange-Marie. 2007b. "Intersectionality as a normative and empirical paradigm." *Politics & Gender* 3(2): 248–254.

Hatem, Mervat F. 1992. "Economic and political liberation in Egypt and the demise of state feminism." *International Journal of Middle East Studies* 24: 231–251.

Hatem, Mervat F. 2005. "Secularist and Islamist discourses on modernity in Egypt and the evolution of the post-colonial nation-state." In Haideh Moghissi, ed., *Women and Islam: Images and realities*. Abingdon: Routledge, 263–294.

Haussman, Melissa, Marian Sawer, and Jill Vickers (Eds.). 2010. *Federalism, feminism and multilevel governance*. Farnham, UK: Ashgate.

Hellman, Judith Adler. 1987. *Journeys among women: Feminism in five Italian cities*. New York: Oxford.

Henderson, Sarah L., and Alana S. Jeydel. 2007. *Participation and protest: Women and politics in a global world*. New York: Oxford University Press.

Hill, Lisa, and Louise Chappell. 2006. "Introduction: The politics of women's interests." In Louise Chappell and Lisa Hill, eds., *The politics of women's interests: New comparative perspectives*. Abingdon, UK: Routledge, 1–4.

Htun, Mala. 2003. *Sex and the state: Abortion, divorce, and the family under Latin American dictatorships and democracies*. Cambridge, UK: Cambridge University Press.

Htun, Mala, and S. Laurel Weldon. 2010. "When do governments promote women's rights? A framework for the comparative analysis of sex equality policy." *Perspectives on Politics* 8(1): 207–216.

Iglitzin, Lynne B., and Ruth Ross (Eds.). 1976. *Women in the world: A comparative study*. Santa Barbara, CA: ABC/Clio Press.

Jaquette, Jane S. (Ed.). 1994. *The women's movement in Latin America: Participation and democracy*. Boulder, CO: Westview.

Jordan-Zachery, Julia S. 2007. "Am I a Black woman or a woman who is Black? A few through on the meaning of intersectionality." *Politics & Gender* 3(2): 254–263.

Kampwirth, Karen. 2002. *Women and guerrilla movements: Nicaragua, El Salvador, Chiapas, Cuba*. University Park: The Pennsylvania State University Press.

Kampwirth, Karen. 2004. *Feminism and the legacy of revolution: Nicaragua, El Salvador, Chiapas*. Athens: Ohio University Press.

Kampwirth, Karen. 2006. "Resisting the feminist threat: Antifeminist politics in post-Sandinista Nicaragua." *NWSA Journal* 18(2): 73–100.

Kantola, Johanna. 2006. *Feminists theorize the state*. Basingstoke, UK: Palgrave Macmillan.

Kaplan, Temma. 1982. "Female consciousness and collective action: The case of Barcelona, 1910–1918." *Signs* 7(3): 545–566.

Katzenstein, Mary Fainsod. 1998. *Faithful and fearless: Moving feminist protest inside the church and military*. Princeton, NJ: Princeton University Press.

Katzenstein, Mary Fainsod, and Carol McClurg Mueller (Eds.). 1987. *The women's movements of the United States and Western Europe: Changing theoretical perspectives*. Philadelphia: Temple University Press.

Keck, Margaret E., and Kathryn Sikkink. 1998. *Activists beyond borders: Advocacy networks in international politics*. Ithaca, NY: Cornell University Press.

Kittilson, Miki Caul. 2006. *Challenging parties, changing parliaments: Women and elected office in contemporary Western Europe*. Columbus: Ohio State University Press.

Krook, Mona Lena. 2009. *Quotas for women in politics: Gender and candidate selection reform worldwide*. Oxford: Oxford University Press.

Lewis, Jane. 1992. "Gender and the development of welfare regimes." *Journal of European Social Policy* 2(3): 159–173.

Lovenduski, Joni (Ed.). 2005. *State feminism and political representation*. Cambridge, UK: Cambridge University Press.

Lovenduski, Joni. 2009. "State feminism and women's movements." In Klaus H. Goetz, Peter Mair, and Gordon Smith, eds., *European politics: Pasts, presents, futures*. London: Routledge, 169–194.

Luker, Kristin. 1984. *Abortion and the politics of motherhood*. Berkeley: University of California Press.

Mahon, Rianne. 1997. "Child care in Canada and Sweden: Policy and politics." *Social Politics* 4(3): 382–418.

Mansbridge, Jane. 1986. *Why we lost the ERA*. Chicago: University of Chicago Press.

Matland, Richard E., and Kathleen A. Montgomery (Eds.). 2003. *Women's access to political power in post-communist Europe*. Oxford: Oxford University Press.

Mazur, Amy G. 2012. "A feminist empirical and integrative approach in political science: Breaking down the glass wall?" In Harold Kinkaid, ed., *The Oxford Handbook of Philosophy of Social Science*. Oxford: Oxford University Press, 533–558.

McBride, Dorothy E., and Amy G. Mazur. 2008. "Women's movements, feminism, and feminist movements." In Gary Goertz and Amy G. Mazur, eds., *Politics, gender and concepts: Theory and methodology*. Cambridge, UK: Cambridge University Press, 219–243.

McCall, Leslie. 2005. "The complexity of intersectionality." *Signs* 30(3): 1771–1800.

McDonagh, Eileen. 2009. *The motherless state: Women's political leadership and American democracy*. Chicago: University of Chicago Press.

Meyer, David S., and Nancy Whittier. 1994. "Social movement spillover." *Social Problems* 41(2): 277–298.

Moghadam, Valentine M. 2005. *Globalizing women: Transnational feminist networks*. Baltimore, MD: John Hopkins University Press.

Molyneux, Maxine. 1985. "Mobilization without emancipation? Women's interests, the state, and revolution in Nicaragua." *Feminist Studies* 2(2): 227–254.

Murray, Rainbow. 2008. "The power of sex and incumbency: A longitudinal study of electoral performance in France." *Party Politics* 14(5): 539–554.

Nelson, Barbara J., and Najma Chowdhury (Eds.). 1994. *Women and politics worldwide*. Princeton, NJ: Princeton University Press.

Norgren, Tiana. 2001. *Abortion before birth control: The politics of reproduction in postwar Japan*. Princeton, NJ: Princeton University Press.

Norris, Pippa. 2008. *Driving democracy: Do power-sharing institutions work?* Cambridge, UK: Cambridge University Press.

Ortbals, Candice. 2007. "Jumbled women's activism: Subnational and international influences on Galician equality politics." *International Feminist Journal of Politics* 9(3): 359–378.

Ortbals, Candice D., and Meg E. Rincker. 2009. "Symposium: Fieldwork, identities, and intersectionality: Negotiating gender, race, class, religion, nationality, and age in the research field abroad." *PS: Political Science and Politics*, 42(2): 287–328.

Osanloo, Arzoo. 2009. *The politics of women's rights in Iran*. Princeton, NJ: Princeton University Press.

Pascall, Gillian, and Nick Manning. 2000. "Gender and social policy: Comparing welfare states in Central and Eastern Europe and the former Soviet Union." *Journal of European Social Policy* 10(3): 240–266.

Rai, Shirin M. (Ed.). 2003. *Mainstreaming gender, democratizing the state?* Manchester: Manchester University Press.

Ray, R., and A. C. Korteweg. 1999. "Women's movements in the third world: Identity, mobilization and autonomy." *Annual Review of Sociology* 25: 47–71.

Revillard, Anne. 2005. "Women's movements and divorce legislation in France and Quebec." Paper presented at the Law and Society Association Meetings, Las Vegas, NV, June 2–5.

Rippeyoung, Phyllis L. F. 2007. "When women are right: The influence of gender, work and values on European far-right party support." *International Feminist Journal of Politics* 9(3): 379–397.

Rucht, Dieter. 2003. "Interactions between social movements and states in comparative perspective." In Lee Ann Banaszak, Karen Beckwith, and Dieter Rucht, eds., *Women's movements facing the reconfigured states*. Cambridge, UK: Cambridge University Press, 242–274.

Sainsbury, Diane (Ed.). 1999. *Gender and welfare state regimes*. Oxford: Oxford University Press.

Sainsbury, Diane. 2008. "Gendering the welfare state." In Gary Goertz and Amy G. Mazur, eds., *Politics, gender and concepts: Theory and methodology*. Cambridge, UK: Cambridge University Press.

Sawer, Marian. 2010. "Premature obituaries: How can we tell if the women's movement is over?" *Politics & Gender* 6(4): 602–609.

Sawyers, Traci M., and David S. Meyer. 1999. "Missed opportunities: Social movement abeyance and public policy." *Social Problems* May: 187–206.

Schreiber, Ronnee. 2008. *Righting feminism: Conservative women and American politics*. Oxford: Oxford University Press.

Schwindt-Bayer, Leslie, and Michelle Taylor-Robinson. 2011. "The meaning and measurement of women's interests: Introduction." *Politics & Gender* 7(3): 417–418.

Simien, Evelyn M. 2007. "Doing intersectionality research: From conceptual issues to practical examples." *Politics & Gender* 3(2): 264–271.

Smooth, Wendy. 2011. "Standing for women-which women? The substantive representation of women's interests and the research imperative of intersectionality." *Politics & Gender* 7(3): 436–441.

Soule, Sarah A. 2007. "Diffusion processes within and across movements." In David A. Snow, Sarah A. Soule, and Hanspeter Kriesi, eds., *The Blackwell companion to social movements*. Malden, MA: Blackwell, 294–310.

Staggenborg, Suzanne. 1991. *The pro-choice movement: Organization and activism in the abortion conflict*. Oxford: Oxford University Press.

Stetson, Dorothy McBride (Ed.). 2001. *Abortion politics, women's movements, and the democratic state: A comparative study of state feminism*. Oxford: Oxford University Press.

Stetson, Dorothy McBride, and Amy Mazur (Eds.). 1995. *Comparative state feminism*. Thousand Oaks, CA: SAGE.

Tarrow, Sidney. 1998. *Power in movement*, 2nd ed. Cambridge, UK: Cambridge University Press.

Taylor, Verta. 1989. "Social movement continuity: The women's movement in abeyance." *American Sociological Review* 54(5): 761–775.

Teghtsoonian, Katherine, and Louise Chappell. 2008. "The rise and decline of women's policy machinery in British Columbia and New South Wales: A cautionary tale." *International Political Science Review* 29(1): 29–51.

Threlfall, Monica. 1996. "Feminist politics and social change in Spain." In Monica Threlfall, ed., *Mapping the women's movement: Feminist politics and social transformation in the North*. London: Verso, 115–151.

Tremblay, Manon (Ed.). 2007. *Women and legislative representation: Electoral systems, political parties and sex quotas*. Basingstoke, UK: Palgrave Macmillan.

Tripp, Aili Mari, Isabel Casimiro, Joy Kwesiga, and Alice Mungwa. 2009. *African women's movements: Transforming political landscapes*. Cambridge, UK: Cambridge University Press.

Valiente, Celia. 2003. "The feminist movement and the reconfigured state in Spain (1970s-2000)." In Lee Ann Banaszak, Karen Beckwith, and Dieter Rucht, eds., *Women's movements facing the reconfigured state*. Cambridge, UK: Cambridge University Press, 30–47.

Valiente, Celia. 2009. "Political regimes matter in 'abeyance' times: Feminist organizing in Franco's Spain (1930–1975)." Paper presented at the annual meetings of the American Political Science Association, Toronto, September 3–9.

Vickers, Jill. 2006. "The problem with interests: Making political claims for 'women.'" In Louise Chappell and Lisa Hill, eds., *The politics of women's interests: New comparative perspectives*. Abingdon, UK: Routledge, 5–38.

Vickers, Jill. 2010. "A two-way street: Federalism and women's politics in Canada and the United States." *Publius* 40(3): 412–435.

Waylen, Georgina. 2007. *Engendering transitions: Women's mobilization, institutions and gender outcomes*. Oxford: Oxford University Press.

Weldon, S. Laurel. 2002. *Protest, policy and the problem of violence against women: A cross-nation analysis*. Pittsburgh: University of Pittsburgh Press.

Weldon, S. Laurel. 2006. "The structure of intersectionality: A comparative politics of gender." *Politics & Gender* 2(2): 235–248.

Weldon, S. Laurel. 2011. *When protest makes policy: How social movements represent disadvantaged groups*. Ann Arbor: University of Michigan Press.

Weldon, S. Laurel, and Mala Htun. 2010. "Violence against women: A comparative analysis of progress on women's human rights." Paper presented at the annual meetings of the American Political Science Association, Washington, DC.

Wolchik, Sharon. 1998. "Gender and the politics of transition in the Czech Republic and Slovakia." In Jane S. Jaquette and Sharon L. Wolchik, eds., *Women and democracy: Latin America and Central and Eastern Europe*. Baltimore, MD: Johns Hopkins University Press, 153–185.

Young, Iris Marion. 2000. *Inclusion and democracy*. Oxford: Oxford University Press.

CHAPTER 17

....

FEMINIST ORGANIZING: WHAT'S OLD, WHAT'S NEW? HISTORY, TRENDS, AND ISSUES

....

CHRISTINA EWIG AND
MYRA MARX FERREE

FEMINIST organizing is a moving target. Not only are feminists individually on the move, in and out of institutions, offices, and political engagements, but also their collective mobilizations change in character over time. By *feminist organizing* we mean efforts led by women explicitly challenging women's subordination to men. This differs from two broader terms: *women's movements* (movements composed of women seeking social change but not necessarily addressing women's subordination); and *feminism* (concern with women's empowerment, not necessarily collectively organized) (Ferree and Mueller 2004, 577; McBride and Mazur 2010).[1] We do not locate feminist organizing only within women's movements but rather seek to understand shifts in where organizing occurs, the factors behind these shifts, and their consequences for feminist objectives.

We begin by sketching the contours of feminist organizing from the nineteenth century to the present. Borrowing an image from historian Leila Rupp, we see global feminist organizing less like waves and more akin to "choppy seas," with feminist organizing cresting and falling in different parts of the world at different times (Rupp 1997, 48). This sketch highlights two critical issues in feminist organizing from its earliest periods to the present: how solidarity is constructed, given the intersectionality of feminist claims making; and how the organizational form of feminist mobilization varies as political opportunities change. Taking these processes into account, we end by challenging claims that feminism is demobilized and in decline (see also the chapter by Dhamoon in this volume).

A History of Global Feminist Organizing

Once feminist organizing is recognized as global, it becomes harder to see feminist movements as two historical waves (Rupp 1997; Offen 2010a). Instead, local feminist claims—such as Mary Wollstonecraft's *Vindication of the Rights of Women*—arise in the crucible of revolutionary change, create new collective understandings, and travel as discourses over time and space to be taken up in other sites by women who challenge their own status quo: a process of "vernacularization" (Leavitt and Merry 2009). Feminist organizing is connected globally with other revolutionary movements such as abolitionist, socialist, nationalist, prodemocracy, antiwar, and sexual liberation struggles. These efforts, in which both women and men participate, typically included deliberate change in gender relations. Many were transnational already in the nineteenth century, since anarchists, socialists, and other radicals were deported or emigrated and built new networks in their destinations. For example, "utopian socialists" attempted gender-equalizing communal settlements in the United States in the 1840s and in Spain in the 1930s (Kanter 1972; Ackelsberg 1991), "1848ers" from the failed bourgeois revolutions in Europe fled to North and South America with liberal ideals of civic betterment and democratic participation (Lavrin 1995; Offen 2000; Hewitt 2010a), and deported Italian anarchist women brought their working-class feminism to New Jersey and Buenos Aires in the 1890s (Molyneux 1986; Guglielmo 2010). Many radical movements spawned feminist organizing, benefited from feminist participation, and engaged in struggles over priorities that eventually changed both sides.

Transnational from the Start: From Chattel to Citizen

Historical research has changed the conventional story of women's suffrage as the first transnational women's movement, to one among many feminist efforts. Focusing on elite women's suffrage organizing creates a one-sided story of limited goals (Chafetz, Dworkin, and Swanson 1986; Zimmerman 2010).

But organizers such as Lucretia Mott (a Quaker antislavery campaigner in the United States), Flora Tristán (a French–Peruvian who organized working-class women), and Clara Zetkin (a German who led the International Women's Socialist Association) challenged the class-based politics of suffrage-centered organizations. They believed that "to truly transform society meant rooting out oppression in all its forms...emancipation of any group—slaves, for instance—was inextricably linked with emancipation for all groups—workers, women, prisoners, and other subjugated peoples" (Hewitt 2010b, 21).

Still, the international women's suffrage movement played a critical role in early feminist organizing because its organizers were concerned with freeing women from being the property of fathers and husbands and securing for women the rights of free citizens in democratic states. Organizationally, suffrage campaigns developed first where discourses of individual rights offered them the most legitimacy, and early victories came at the periphery (e.g., in New Zealand, Finland, the American West), where institutional authorities had less power (Ramirez, Soyosal, and Shanahan 1997, 737). Suffragists embraced multi-issue visions of social change and developed their skills in other movements, often religious, for education, prison reform, or temperance (Grimshaw 2010; Hammar 2010). Some connected their cause with a wider imperial project of "civilization," campaigning against indigenous customs defined as barbaric, such as polygamy, foot binding, or women's uncovered breasts (Burton 1994; Sneider 2008). Feminist antislavery advocates also moved into women-led campaigns against the "white-slave trade," the trafficking in women's bodies for prostitution (Offen 2000).

Olive Banks (1981) describes three threads of feminism that emerge in this period: a *moral reform* thread concerned about sexuality and violence against women; a bourgeois *liberal democratic* vision; and a working-class-centered *socialist* ideal. All three threads remain evident in contemporary feminist organizing, although moral reform feminists today often include both secular and religious activists (Smith 2000).

That feminist concerns for social justice in this period crisscross other political agendas is unsurprising. Feminist organizers tried to address the variety of women's concerns, leading to debates about inclusivity (Taylor 1983). Working-class, African-descent, and Jewish women as well as women of colonized and formerly colonized areas (such as Egypt, India, Latin America) insisted on being heard and forged important transnational networks (Jayawardena 1986; Miller 1991; DuBois 1994; Badran 1995; Rupp 1997). Some groups sought cross-class, cross-race, and cross-cultural understanding, but inclusion remained problematic (Rupp 1996; Offen 2010b). African American women faced recurrent racist insults, as when Susan B. Anthony asked black women activists to stand at the back of suffrage marches (Giddings 1984, 128). Some white Europeans mistakenly thought they needed to save Eastern women (especially Muslims) from oppressive practices such as the harem (Ahmed 1982), part of a broader feminist orientalism, in which U.S. and European women considered themselves more civilized than other women (Rupp 1996). These tensions remain contemporary issues for feminism.

Early struggles also highlight the vexed relation among sexuality, gender relations, and reproduction. In some countries and classes, suffragists participated in radical sexual reform movements that claimed women's sexual citizenship. Some feminists such as Ellen Keys and Helene Stöcker insisted on women's right to refuse sex in marriage and to engage in sex outside of marriage ("free love movements") (Allen 2005; Hammar 2010). In the 1920s, thousands of protestors in German cities protested for legal abortion (Ferree et al. 2002) and radical women in Greenwich Village asserted their rights to equality in marriage and sex without a wedding (Trimberger 1983).

Yet other suffragists embraced the idea of women's sexual morality being higher than men's. Feminists in temperance and home economics movements aimed to protect mothers and wives by elevating the status of domestic work and encouraging men's sexual faithfulness (Laslett and Brenner 1989). Suffragists sometimes made gains when they embraced domesticity, for example, through claims to moral uplift and municipal housekeeping (Gullett 2000; McCammon, Hewitt, and Smith 2004). Feminist claims to recognition of maternal contributions to the public good helped create welfare states (Skocpol 1992; Koven and Michel 1993; Guy 2009), but incorporation in state projects was always controversial among feminists (Cott 1987).

Feminist politics spread and changed in the decades between 1920 and 1960, often seen in the United States and Europe as the "doldrums" for feminist organizing (Taylor and Rupp 1990). Suffrage victories came late in Latin America (1949 in Chile and 1957 in Colombia). In Chile, women's energies then scattered into political parties (Lavrin 1995; Baldez and Kirk 2006), but they sustained cross-class unity in Colombia (Gonzalez 2000). Women's transnational organizing continued after suffrage to fight throughout the twentieth century for labor legislation (Berkovitch 1999), married women's citizenship (DuBois 2010), divorce and child custody (Allen 2005), and jury service (McCammon et al. 2007). Many feminist organizers also turned from suffrage to peace activism in the League of Nations and the Women's International League for Peace and Freedom (Foster 1989; Rupp 1997). African American women drew inspiration from campaigns linking domestic and global oppressions (Foster 2002). By the 1950s, feminist claims to citizenship succeeded in bringing women's views on issues of war and peace, social welfare, and the economy into public forums.

Embedded or Autonomous? From Citizenship to Self-Determination

In addition to claiming citizenship, women created organizations to challenge gendered power. Their struggles highlight the question of alliances: whether feminist organizing should be primarily autonomous (that is, exclusively via women's movements) or also should use government and other organizations.

Feminist experiences of solidarity and exclusion in social justice movements shaped what today are called theories of intersectionality.

For many feminists, solidarity meant organizing women as women to help themselves, their families, and other women. "Lifting as we climb" was the phrase popularized by the black women's club movement in the United States for this strategy (Giddings 1984, 97–98); these clubs proliferated in the Jim Crow South and were undeniably feminist in their labors (Gray White 1999, 36). Self-help is a grassroots feminist strategy for empowerment that is neither angry and antimale nor necessarily radical (Purkayastha and Subramaniam 2004). It emerged not only in the 1960s battered women's shelters and antirape hotlines but also was always a vital means of organizing (Cott 1987).

When women organized in mixed sex groups, they often discovered the political significance of gender and then looked for solidarity with other women in a struggle for feminist objectives (Ferree and Mueller 2004). From the 1950s to the 1970s, feminist organizing was both *embedded* in movements (such as labor unions, anticolonial rebellions, and racial liberation struggles) and *autonomous*, as women split from these multipurpose groups to work in feminist women's movements. *Autonomous* feminist groups are independently led but often work with other movements, state agencies, and nongovernmental organizations (NGOs) at scales from the local to the transnational. Autonomous feminist organizing includes formal organizations of and for women and grassroots, women-only collectives (Ferree and Hess 2000). Autonomous feminist organizers are often more controversial than embedded ones, but autonomous women's movements are never the only focus of feminist organizing (Jakobsen 1998).

Many of feminism's thinkers and organizers, both the reformers and the more radical, emerged from class-based or race-based political organizations of the Left. In the United States and Europe, labor feminists gained organizing experience in union activities (Kaplan 1992; Cobble 2004; DuPlessis and Snitow 2007). In Europe, women in postwar youth movements were radicalized by their fellow activist men, who were unwilling to fully include them (Katzenstein and Mueller 1987; Boxer 2010). In the United States, not only African American and white but also Latina, Asian American, and Native American women found their efforts to place women's liberation on the agenda of their movements stymied by men's indifference or resistance and established their own organizations (Evans 1979; Thompson 2002; Roth 2004). White feminist radicals might have given sexism more weight than racism, but most women of color resisted the claim that one or the other had to take first place (Ladner 1971; Hull, Scott, and Smith 1982).

In the 1970s and 1980s, contestation over sexuality grew. Lesbians challenged the heteronormative assumptions of straight women, creating new opportunities for alliances and conflicts around issues of male power in and over women's sexuality (such as prostitution, pornography, rape, and harassment) (Dworkin 1987; MacKinnon 1993). The underlying social networks among lesbians often made these communities the backbone of feminist autonomous organizing

(Rupp and Taylor 1993; Enke 2007) but made autonomous groups more vulnerable to stereotyping. The more clearly autonomous the women's organization, the more it was "suspected" of being by and for lesbians only (Echols 1989; Rupp and Taylor 1993). In contexts where same-sex relationships are strongly and violently repressed (e.g., the American South and many African countries), this association of feminism with lesbianism feeds antifeminist movements. But even in more tolerant contexts, stigmatizing feminism as lesbian or "man-hating" makes it difficult to use "the f-word" (Rowe-Finkbeiner 2004, 6).

In the movement organizing in the late 1960s and 1970s in the United States, with its tensions regarding race, class, sex, and sexuality, theorizing these intersectional concerns emerged as significant, first in the writings and actions of African American women (e.g., Beal 1970; Combahee River Collective 1981) and then further elaborated by other feminist women of color (such as Patricia Hill Collins, Evelyn Nakano Glenn, and Gloria Anzaldúa). Intersectionality, the term coined by African American lawyer Kimberlé Crenshaw (1988), means that race, class, sexual orientation, nationality, and gender are not discrete markers of difference but rather intersecting social structures of inequality experienced by individuals in specific social locations (McCall 2005; Hancock 2007).

The concept of intersectionality has traveled widely and become vernacularized, becoming an explicit norm for feminist organizers in the United States, Latin America, Africa, the Balkans and other ethnically divided contexts (Yuval-Davis 2006). In Latin America, intersectionality became important after confrontations over differences at the regional feminist *encuentros* in the 1980s, when feminists across the region sought to frame a common agenda (Alvarez et al. 2002; Sternbach et al. 1992). Emphasizing commonalities across differences was more important for feminist organizers who sought to mediate violent conflicts (Tripp 2000; Bagic 2006). However, U.S. and European feminists' attempted solidarity across religious and national lines has sometimes exacerbated controversy in women's rights struggles in other countries (Narayan 1997; Tripp 2006).

In sum, feminist organizing in the 1960s and 1970s, unlike its stereotype, was not only white and middle class and emerged other places besides the West. Tensions due to race and class differences were neither trivial nor overlooked. Intersectional feminist organizing came to mean several things. First, it made the divergent positions and interests among women *visible* rather than advancing an essentializing view of women. Second, it implied *choosing priorities* politically with an eye toward inclusive solidarity, seeking common ground against the background of acknowledged differences. Third, it assumed *organizational variability* in strategies and priorities, since women's goals vary across structural locations and organizational strategies differ in their effects. Rather than identifying universal strategic interests theoretically and representing them through a single movement (Molyneux 1985), feminist intersectionality theories affirm local eclecticism as their method (Jakobsen 1998; Twine and Blee 2001; Wiegman 2008). The actual diversity of feminist practices reflects this.

Political Opportunity Structures

Autonomous strategies vary in appeal and effectiveness depending on the *political opportunity structure* (Della Porta and Diani 1999; McAdam, McCarthy, and Zald 1996). Political opportunity changes as various political projects succeed or fail at levels from the global (like the cold war or globalization) to the regional (democratization in Eastern Europe and Latin America), national (state–party relations, depth of democratic institutions), and local (distributions of income, media control).

The United Nations (UN) offered a global opportunity structure that responded to feminists and spurred transnational feminist organizing.[2] After declaring 1975–1985 the decade for women, the UN sponsored four global conferences on women (in Mexico City, Copenhagen, Nairobi, and Beijing). Under UN auspices, the Cairo International Conference on Population and Development and the Vienna Conference on Human Rights also increased global feminist opportunities. All these conferences served as an inspiration for national and regional organizing, fostered more transnational networking (Cummings, Dam, and Valk 1999; Zinsser 2002; Friedman 2003), and gave feminists the opportunity to frame women's rights and empowerment as national and transnational priorities. Feminist organizers successfully placed women's right to be free of violence on the international human rights agenda, reproductive rights on the international population agenda, and women's education and poverty on the global development agenda (Petchesky 1995; Bunch 2001; Snyder 2006). These gains provided a lever to push national governments to adopt policies to realize such goals.

The conferences also served as forums where divisions based on race and class, in and between the Global North and the Global South, resurfaced. At the first UN conference in Mexico City in 1975, divisions reflected economic hegemony by the North over the South; in Copenhagen in 1980, Zionism and apartheid were acrimoniously debated (Winslow 1995; Zinsser 2002). By the 1985 Nairobi meeting a constructive global dialogue began, partly because Southern feminists had now created their own transnational feminist organizations (Snyder 2006). The Beijing Conference in 1995 marked a watershed, with strong feminist consensus in creating a Platform for Action endorsed by most participating governments (Helly 1996; Snyder 2006). Follow-up conferences since Beijing have been smaller and weaker, in part because the United States is pushing against, rather than for, implementation and in part due to backlash from the right-wing factions of Catholicism and Islam.

Political opportunities for regional feminist organizing also vary over time. Some feminist groups emerged in the 1960s and 1970s as part of anticolonial or revolutionary struggles; others hit their peak only in the 1980s and 1990s as part of democratization movements. The variation suggests both global and regional dynamics at work (Runyan and Peterson 2000; Bose and Kim 2009); historical time also matters. Groups coming later in countries as diverse as South Korea, Poland, and Argentina built on theories developed elsewhere and drew resources from transnational feminist advocacy networks (Moghadam 2005; Rai 2008). The legitimacy created by the UN conferences and nearly every country's endorsement of the Convention on the Elimination of all forms of Discrimination Against Women (CEDAW) provided transnational leverage for later-developing feminist movements (Schöpp-Schilling and Flinterman 2007).

In Africa, nationalist movements, democratic movements, and violent conflicts had mixed effects on feminist organizing. In Zimbabwe, women took up arms for liberation, some thinking this was the beginning of a struggle for women's equality (Geisler 1995). Their efforts initially failed but later found support in democratization movements (Ranchod-Nillson 2006). In South Africa, feminist organizers used the transition from apartheid to organize autonomously across racial lines, take on roles in government, and construct a women's policy machinery responsive to rural black women's needs (Seidman 1993, 1999; Hassim 2006). In Ghana, women successfully drew on pre-colonial women's institutions to challenge nondemocratic governments (Fallon 2008). In Uganda, the end of conflict was the critical door opening the way for cross-ethnic feminist organizing in the 1990s and 2000s (Tripp 1999). Feminism was once a term African women rejected as a Western import, but in recent years ever more women's organizations have embraced it (Tripp et al. 2009, 14).

Central American women became feminist activists through their involvement with revolutionary movements in the 1970s and 1980s. In Nicaragua and El Salvador, feminist consciousness grew when women revolutionaries saw gender issues being marginalized. In the immediate postrevolutionary periods in Nicaragua, El Salvador, and to a lesser extent Guatemala, feminist movements flourished, as women took the organizing skills they learned as revolutionaries and applied them to feminist organizing (Hipsher 2001; Luciak 2001; Kampwirth 2004; Shayne 2004). The later revolutionary movement in Chiapas, Mexico in the 1990s learned from them and explicitly included feminism in its platform and feminists on its revolutionary team (Kampwirth 2002). In the long run, the outcomes for feminists were mixed: in Nicaragua, for example, while the revolutionary government embraced women's issues in the 1980s, the state subsequently turned away from women and toward the Catholic Church (Kampwirth 2008; Heumann 2010).

Across South America in the 1980s, transitions from military dictatorships to democracy provided a favorable political opportunity structure for feminist organizing. Feminists joined human rights activists and poor women's survival-oriented groups to confront dictatorships. Sometimes, these alliances created the tipping point for a democratic transition, as in Brazil and Chile (Alvarez 1990; Jaquette 1994; Baldez 2002). In many countries, feminist organizers succeeded in getting the advancement of women on the democratic agenda through creating women's ministries and reforming family law (Htun 2003; Franceschet 2005; Blofield 2006; Haas 2010).

As in South America, democratization in South Korea served as an opportunity for greater feminist organizing. Women activists in the prodemocracy movement brought an explicitly feminist agenda to it, opposing the sexual violence of the regime and supporting the rights of women workers (Nam 2000; Moon 2002). In India, the suspension of democratic rights in the "state of emergency" of the 1970s mobilized feminists as part of the prodemocracy resistance; when martial law ended in 1977, these groups turned their attention to other abuses, such as judicial insensitivity to rape and domestic violence (Subramaniam 2006). Ray (1999) highlights how opportunities for Indian feminists varied by the politics of their state government; where a single party dominated, women's organizing was constrained by its priorities, but when parties contended, feminists raised more diverse issues.

Socialism offers complex political opportunities for feminist organizing, sometimes providing a radicalizing revolutionary experience, sometimes a smothering hegemony. In Eastern Europe, the control of communist governments over civil society and claims that communism had solved the "woman question" undermined women's organizing efforts in the 1990s (Einhorn 1993; Funk and Mueller 1993; Jaquette and Wolchik 1998; Waylen 2007). Postsocialist Eastern European states emphasized a politics of reproduction, often to women's disadvantage (Gal and Kligman 2000). More recently, their gradual accession to membership in the European Union (EU) has offered these feminists opportunities to use the EU's declared commitment to gender equality to pressure local governments, playing a policy ping-pong across levels (Zippel 2004, 59; Roth 2008). The story is similar in China, where the UN Fourth World Conference on Women in 1994 provided opportunity for Chinese feminists to legitimize their own organizing (Liu 2006; Zheng and Zhang 2010).

In sum, particular opportunity structures at the global, regional, national, and local levels shape feminist organizing. Across all continents, the power of women's grassroots organizations was joined to nongender-specific movements toward democracy or political liberalization, often with stunning effect and sometimes in tension with socialist orthodoxy.

CHANGING CHALLENGES

The present moment is rife with contradictions for feminist organizers. Vibrant value-based networks at global and regional levels have characterized feminist organizing for over a century, and reflexivity about the challenges of intersectionality has increased inclusive solidarity in many feminist organizational contexts. Feminists have arguably been the pioneers in organizing transnational advocacy networks and using the power of global norms to shift local practices of oppression (Keck and Sikkink 1998; Berkovitch 1999;

True and Mintrom 2001; Moghadam 2005; Towns 2010). Still, debates continue about feminist organizing strategies and their relative success or failure in improving women's lives.

Strategic Decisions: Inside Out or Outside In?

Feminist organizing is always happening from the outside in (by autonomous groups) and from the inside out (as embedded feminists work within organizations to activate them on women's behalf). Yet cooperation has been controversial, since "standing outside and throwing stones" seems to be a more radical position than "moving inside and occupying space" (Martin 2005, 102–104). In Australia in the 1980s, feminists purposely infiltrated the state to change policy from within—and their "femocrat" strategy was echoed by feminist activists elsewhere (Eisenstein 1996).

Embedded feminist organizing reflects the institutional structures in which it occurs; for example, in the United States, Catholic feminists became radically antihierarchal due to their powerlessness within this structure, while military feminists narrowed their goals and became more identified with their hierarchy as antidiscrimination laws gave them leverage on it (Katzenstein 1999). In the 1990s, Latin American feminists were bitterly divided between those seeking to pursue change as outsiders and those willing to collaborate with or even to work within the state; the latter were viewed by the former as "selling out" (Sternbach et al. 1992; Vargas 1992; Franceschet 2005). Differences in resources and access help explain which groups choose embedded or autonomous strategies, the ones most often dubbed "radical."

Working with or within the state encourages an organizational style that is more formalized and relies on expertise, not numbers, a style often criticized as "NGOization" (Lang 1997; Alvarez 1999). NGOization can be driven by donors; financial contributions to feminist causes bring a need for fiscal accountability (Bagic 2006; Thayer 2010). Fiscal austerity commonly produced more NGOs, too, as states used feminist organizations to do some of their work in poor communities. Institutional isomorphism—groups copying each other to have structures and activities that seem appropriate—is also likely a factor (Clemens and Cook 1999). Finally, the UN conferences and parallel NGO forums spurred NGOization by offering more access to formally organized groups (Markovitz and Tice 2002; Alvarez 2009).

NGOs typically participate in "transnational advocacy networks" (Keck and Sikkink 1998), mixes of individuals and groups with shared values, high levels of expertise, and direct engagement with policy makers, connected across national boundaries. Organizing such networks facilitates feminist influence on government policy. In the early 1990s, this was true in cases as diverse as European Union development of sexual harassment policies (Zippel 2006), Canadian asylum policy for battered women (Alfredson

2008), and South Korean revisions in family law (Maddison and Jung 2008). NGOs serve as sites for developing feminist knowledge (Zippel 2006; Alvarez 2009), for building support for feminist positions (Markovitz and Tice 2002; Alvarez 2009), and for facilitating subsequent mobilizations (Ferree and Mueller 2004).

However, critics of NGOization point to the tendency of such groups to prefer the contributions of highly educated women (who can offer expertise) to grassroots protest and community engagement (Lang 1997; Naples 1998; Alvarez 1999; Hemment 2007). Moreover, professionalization fosters hierarchy among women's organizations, since those judged more expert receive more financial support (Ewig 1999; Murdock 2008; Thayer 2010). Feminists critical of NGOization stress the contributions grassroots groups make to building a culture of empowerment, habits of protest, and counterhegemonic identity as a radical activist (Ryan 1992; Hercus 2005; Dufour, Masson, and Caouette 2010). They value the emotional ties created through protest activities (Staggenborg and Taylor 2005). Negative and positive assessments of NGOization reflect context: Chinese feminists embraced the UN push toward NGO development as creating opportunities to organize, while Indian feminists saw the same process as threatening their grassroots organizations and diluting their radical claims (Liu 2006).

In addition to feminist NGOs, the 1990s witnessed the flourishing of "state feminism": women's policy machineries inside the state, including women's caucuses in legislative and executive offices (McBride and Mazur 2010). Time and again, across national contexts, the "jaw" strategy of combining feminist efforts within government with an autonomous base outside it has proved the most effective (Lycklama à Nijeholt, Sweibel, and Vargas 1998; Woodward 2004; Ewig 2006). Shirin Rai (2008, 74) describes this position as being "in and against the state."

In sum, feminist organizations have moved toward professionalization, but not without controversy. Despite organizers' success in creating advocacy networks and having influence on and through state policies, opinion remains divided on the extent of substantive feminist gains. Some analysts see insider feminism as winning a feminist struggle for women's access to state power that began in suffrage campaigns (Walby 2011); others view the consolidation of feminist politics in institutions as potentially coopting feminist objectives (Cornwall and Molyneux 2008).

Generational Conflict?

In the 1990s and 2000s, younger feminists claimed to do third-wave feminist politics (Walker 2006), contrasting themselves and their issues with those of earlier generations. The third-wave argument appears mostly in Western Europe and the United States, where the so-called second wave crested earlier;

in many parts of the world, surges of feminist organizing began only in the 1980s or 1990s, and generational succession is moot (Graff 2004). This generation, born between 1961 and 1981 or about thirty years after the blossoming of these countries' autonomous feminist movements, encountered feminism differently. They may have had feminist mothers; feminist analyses had considerable cultural legitimacy; organized antifeminism was growing; and a pervasive consumer culture proclaimed feminism had succeeded, died, and been replaced by commodities symbolizing freedom (Walker 1995; Baumgardner and Richards 2000; Henry 2004; Walby 2011).

Relationships between younger and older U.S. feminists are complicated by a media culture that presents earlier feminists as dowdy, asexual, insufficiently radical, and exclusively white, stereotypes from which younger feminists would like to distance themselves (Henry 2004; Scanlon 2009, 127; Showden 2009, 180). Weigman (2008) also identifies an *idiom of failure* used to distinguish the present righteous radicalism from the limited and luckless feminism of the past. Yet many younger feminists in advanced industrial societies do recognize that their foremothers made controversial, transformative demands that became the common sense of their lives and are aware that gender equality has not actually been realized (Baumgardner and Richards 2000; Henry 2004; Heywood 2006).

While claims of postfeminism gained currency in the United States in the 1990s, these were part of the mobilization against feminism, not a part of it. Postfeminists stress that women should assert themselves individually (rather than turn to collective action) and should renounce overblown claims to victimhood (Schreiber 2008; Showden 2009). Their stance relates to the family values agenda, which accepts what conservatives call *equity feminism* (access on men's terms) and resists any fundamental rethinking of gender (Buss and Herman 2003).

Young feminists and nonfeminists alike appreciate *grrrl power*, their ability to exercise greater sexual self-assertion than their mothers' generation could, but feminists place more value on collective action, intersectional justice, and an inclusive vision of sexuality, one that embraces queer sexuality's many forms (Snyder 2008; Scanlon 2009; Showden 2009). Some warn that young feminists' orientation to consumer culture may obscure their own imbrications with global inequalities and lead to a reprise of Global North–South misunderstandings (Woodhull 2004).

Dangers of Co-optation?

Today feminist organizers are concerned about varieties of co-optation: by neoliberalism; by neoeugenic concerns about declining birth rates in Western Europe and population growth in emerging economies; by militarized conflicts between advanced industrial nations and their Islamic (rather than communist) "others." Feminist organizing successes and failures sometimes do reflect less on their strategic choices than on how their demands resonate with larger forces that they do not control. Certainly neoliberalism is a major force restructuring global relations today, as colonialism once was. Some feminists even attribute the gains of neoliberalism in part to feminist organizing, however unwittingly (Bumiller 2008; Eisenstein 2009). Nancy Fraser (2009) writes that feminism's critique of the family wage opened doors to low-wage employment of women globally, because neoliberal capitalism used this feminist rhetoric to justify access to the poorest paid and most precarious jobs. Similarly, in Bolivia, women's activists aligned with its recent Left government look askance at the primarily middle-class feminists whose NGOs flourished with the outsourcing of social service work to them under neoliberal governments of the 1990s and early 2000s (Monasterios 2007). Other feminists warn that abandoning rights rhetoric will again sideline women and enable a socialist politics unwilling to take seriously issues of sexuality, reproductive rights, or violence against women (Wiegman 2008; Boxer 2010; Walby 2011).

The instrumentalization of feminist rhetoric for state purposes is also not new and has been widely critiqued by Russian, Chinese, and Eastern European feminists. They found their communist governments cynically wrapped themselves in feminist rhetoric without necessarily advancing feminist projects (Funk and Mueller 1993; Sperling 1999; Liu 2006). Neoeugenic concerns seem to be the most recent iteration. In the 1990s, the Fujimori government of Peru "hijacked" global feminist discourse of reproductive rights for Malthusian ends (Ewig 2006). In the 2000s the EU paid attention to bringing men into childcare and women into paid employment as part of a welfare state agenda defined not as women's emancipation but as "human capital development" (Jenson 2008).

Feminist organizers today debate how much success feminism has really had. Do the benefits of state adoption of feminist rhetoric outweigh the costs of instrumentalizing feminist demands? Sometimes feminist anger over state misappropriation of their claims dominates, for example, condemning how concern for women's freedom was used as a ploy to gain support for U.S. military interventions in Iraq and Afghanistan (Abu-Lughod 2002; Cloud 2004; Sjoberg 2006). Feminists are sincerely divided about whether the state is acting in women's best interests by supporting microenterprises (Keating, Rasmussen, and Rishi 2010), banning Islamic head covering for women in schools (whether in Turkey or in France) (Ertürk 2006), or legalizing prostitution (Outshoorn 2004; Agustin 2007). Others are cynical about the state's reasons but still see a policy as good for women, as with the German restructuring of child care leaves to make them shorter, better paid, and partially shared with fathers (von Wahl 2008). As feminist discourse has become more acceptable, it has become crucial to distinguish this rhetoric from the actual effects on society that are being legitimated by using it.

Conclusion:
Against Feminist Decline

After this survey of global feminist organizing it may seem odd to think that feminism may be past its peak, in abeyance, or finally over. The frequent observation that feminism is in decline does capture the loss of centrality of autonomous women's movements for feminist organizing. Paradoxically, the increasing legitimacy of feminism makes autonomous women's movements not feminists' preferred way to direct political attention to gender issues. Confusing autonomous women's movements—just one strategy—with all feminist organizing obscures the continuing vitality of feminism.

First, feminist organizers work within a wide variety of movements for social justice, as they have always done. Embedded organizers may not be counted when the vitality of feminist activism is assessed, but the opportunity structure increasingly encourages embedded over autonomous feminist organizing. Economic crises brought on by neoliberal globalization, democratic openings in political systems, and changing willingness among male activists to acknowledge gender issues all draw contemporary feminist organizers to work within multi-issue groups (Jakobsen 1998; Naples 1998; Thayer 2010). For example, in the 1980s, the devastation of the HIV/AIDS epidemic increased solidarity between lesbians and gay men, which not only contributed to the rise of the lesbian, gay, bisexual, transgender (LGBT) and queer movement (Bernstein 1997) but also made LGBT, intersex, queer, and transgender organizing much more significant for U.S. feminists today than it was in the 1970s (Barclay, Bernstein, and Marshal 2009; Gould 2009). Multi-issue movements critical of globalization, such as the World Social Forum, also tap feminist energies, but when these campaigns fail to prioritize gender issues feminists may return from embedded to autonomous strategies (Marchand 2003; Desai 2009).

Second, the shift toward a higher proportion of insider to outsider strategies produces fewer feminist rallies on the streets and more feminist "dinner parties" (Baumgardner and Richards 2000, 15), more feminists in parliaments, and more feminists doing the work of the movement for pay in professional jobs—in academia, government, and business. Third, the very pervasiveness of feminism sometimes makes it less noticeable. From women's ministries to the girl power rhetoric in marketing consumer goods, feminism is active, but "like fluoride" in the water "we scarcely notice that we have it" (Baumgardner and Richards 2000, 17).

Finally, feminist organizing is often hidden in plain sight. Across all regions, feminism remains a contested, often stigmatized, term, so feminist organizing is paradoxically a global force that rarely names itself as such. Around the world, transnational organizations focused on feminist issues are less likely to use the word *feminist* than to describe their concerns as *women's rights, gender policy,* or *social justice* (Ferree and Pudrovska 2004; Walby 2011).

In sum, feminist organizing responds to both the inherent intersectionality among race, class, gender, and sexualities and the priorities of its social context. Feminist organizing strategies shift between autonomy and embeddedness, emphasizing autonomy when gender concerns are ignored or trivialized by other movements and embeddedness when their participation is welcomed. Inclusive solidarity (seeking common ground across difference) represents a political choice, but variation in the extent to which feminist organizers have sought exclusive solidarity (likeness as a basis for common efforts) or pursued autonomous women's movement organizing as strategies should not be confused with feminist vitality.

Placing the heyday of feminism in the 1970s is a dangerous myth. It ignores change, limits feminism to only some places in the globe, and celebrates a time when there were so few feminists (and so much ridicule) that nearly all were driven to the streets. Feminist organizing today is more global, more vital, and more transformative. It builds on what has been accomplished but also stimulates important debates over strategies, allies, and effectiveness. It varies in timing and emphasis by region and appreciates the plurality of local feminist paths. It rests on the commitment of many more individual feminists and organizational resources than feminists of the 1920s or 1970s could have imagined. Feminist organizing continues; its heyday may yet come but certainly has not yet passed.

NOTES

1. On women's movements, see the chapters by Beckwith, Joachim, and Kretschmer and Meyer in this volume.
2. For more on global–local interactions, see the chapter by Joachim in this volume.

REFERENCES

Abu-Lughod, Lila. 2002. "Do Muslim women really need saving? Anthropological reflections on cultural relativism and its others." *American Anthropologist* 104(3): 783–790.

Ackelsberg, Martha A. 1991. *Free women of Spain: Anarchism and the struggle for the emancipation of women.* Bloomington: Indiana University Press.

Agustin, Laura 2007. *Sex at the margins: Migration, labour markets and the rescue industry.* London: Zed Books.

Ahmed, Leila. 1982. "Western ethnocentrism and perceptions of the harem." *Feminist Studies* 8(3): 521–534.

Alfredson, Lisa S. 2008. *Creating human rights: How noncitizens made sex persecution matter to the world.* Philadelphia: University of Pennsylvania Press.

Allen, Ann Taylor. 2005. *Feminism and motherhood in Western Europe, 1890–1970.* New York: Palgrave Macmillan.

Alvarez, Sonia E. 1990. *Engendering democracy in Brazil: Women's movements in transition politics.* Princeton, NJ: Princeton University Press.

Alvarez, Sonia E. 1999 "Advocating feminism: The Latin American feminist NGO 'boom.'" *International Feminist Journal of Politics* 1(2): 181–209.

Alvarez, Sonia E. 2009. "Beyond NGOization? Reflections from Latin America." *Development* 52(2): 175–184.

Alvarez, Sonia E., Elizabeth Jay Friedman, Ericka Beckman, Maylei Blackwell, Norma Stoltz Chinchilla, Nathalie Lebon, Marysa Navarro, and Marcela Ríos Tobar. 2002. "Encountering Latin American and Caribbean feminisms." *Signs: Journal of Women, Culture and Society* 28(2): 537–579.

Badran, Margot. 1995. *Feminists, Islam and nation: Gender and the making of modern Egypt.* Princeton, NJ: Princeton University Press.

Bagic, Aida. 2006. "Women's organizing in Post-Yugoslav countries: Talking about donors." In Myra Marx Ferree and Aili Mari Tripp, eds., *Global feminism: Women's organizing, activism and human rights.* New York: New York University Press, 141–165.

Baldez, Lisa. 2002. *Why women protest: Women's movements in Chile.* Cambridge, UK: Cambridge University Press.

Baldez, Lisa, and Celeste M. Kirk. 2006. "Gendered opportunities: The formation of the women's movement in the United States and Chile." In Lee Ann Banaszak, ed., *U.S. women's movements in global perspective.* Lanham, MD: Rowman & Littlefield, 133–150.

Banks, Olive. 1981. *Faces of feminism: A study of feminism as a social movement.* New York: St. Martin's Press.

Barclay, Scott, Mary Bernstein, and Anna-Maria Marshall. 2009. *Queer mobilizations: LGBT activists confront the law.* New York: New York University Press.

Baumgardner, Jennifer, and Amy Richards. 2000. *Manifesta: Young women, feminism and the future.* New York: Farrar, Straus and Giroux.

Beal, Frances. 1970. "Double jeopardy: To be black and female." In Toni Cade Bambara, ed., *The black woman: An anthology.* New York: New American Library, 109–122.

Berkovitch, Nitza. 1999. *From motherhood to citizenship: Women's rights and international organizations.* Baltimore, MD: Johns Hopkins University Press.

Bernstein, Mary. 1997. "Celebration and suppression: The strategic uses of identity by the lesbian and gay movement." *American Journal of Sociology* 103(3): 531–565.

Blofield, Merike. 2006. *The politics of moral sin: Abortion and divorce in Spain, Chile and Argentina.* New York: Routledge.

Bose, Christine, and Minjeong Kim. 2009. *Global gender research: Transnational perspectives.* New York: Routledge.

Boxer, Marilyn J. 2010. "Rethinking the socialist construction and international career of the concept 'bourgeois feminism.'" In Karen Offen, ed., *Globalizing feminisms, 1789–1945.* New York: Routledge, 286–301.

Bumiller, Kristen. 2008. *In an abusive state: How neoliberalism appropriated the feminist movement against sexual violence.* Durham, NC: Duke University Press.

Bunch, Charlotte. 2001. "International networking for women's human rights." In Michael Edwards and John Gaventa, eds., *Global citizen action.* Boulder, CO: Lynn Reinner Publishers, 217–229.

Burton, Antoinette. 1994. *Burdens of history: British feminists, Indian women, and Imperial culture, 1865-1915*. Chapel Hill: University of North Carolina Press.

Buss, Doris, and Didi Herman. 2003. *Globalizing family values: The Christian Right in international politics*. Minneapolis: University of Minnesota Press.

Chafetz, Janet S., Anthony G. Dworkin, and Stephanie Swanson. 1986. *Female revolt: Women's movements in world and historical perspectives*. Totowa: Rowman & Allanheld.

Clemens, Elisabeth S., and James M. Cook. 1999. "Politics and institutionalism: Explaining durability and change." *Annual Review of Sociology* 25(1): 441–466.

Cloud, Dana. 2004. "To veil the threat of terror: Afghan women and the 'clash of civilizations' in the imagery of the US war on terrorism." *Quarterly Journal of Speech* 90(3): 285–306.

Cobble, Dorothy Sue. 2004. *The other women's movement: Workplace justice and social rights in modern America*. Princeton, NJ: Princeton University Press.

Combahee River Collective. 1981. "A black feminist statement." In Cherríe Moraga and Gloria Anzaldua, eds., *This bridge called my back: Writings by radical women of color*. Watertown, MA: Persephone Press, 210–218.

Cornwall, Andrea C., and Maxine Molyneux. 2008. *The politics of rights: Dilemmas for feminist praxis*. New York: Routledge.

Cott, Nancy F. 1987. *Grounding of modern feminism*. New Haven, CT: Yale University Press.

Crenshaw, Kimberlé. 1988. "Race, reform and retrenchment, transformation and legitimation in antidiscrimination law." *Harvard Law Review* 101(7): 1331–1387.

Cummings, Sarah, Henk Van Dam, and Minte Valk. 1999. *Women's information services and networks: A global source book*. Oxford: Oxfam Publishing.

Della Porta, Donatella, and Mario Diani. 1999. *Social movements: An introduction*. Malden, MA: Blackwell Publishing.

Desai, Manisha. 2009. *Gender and the politics of possibilities: Rethinking globalization*. Lanham, MD: Rowman and Littlefield.

Dubois, Ellen Carol. 1994. "Woman suffrage around the world: Three phases of suffragist internationalism." In Caroline Daley and Melanie Nolan, eds., *Suffrage and beyond: International feminist perspectives*. New York: New York University Press, 252–274.

Dubois, Ellen Carol. 2010. "Internationalizing married women's nationality: The Hague campaign of 1930." In Karen Offen, ed., *Globalizing feminisms, 1789–1945*. New York: Routledge, 204–216.

Dufour, Pascale D., Dominique Masson, and Dominique Caouette. 2010. *Solidarities beyond borders: Transnationalizing women's movements*. Vancouver: University of British Columbia Press.

DuPlessis, Rachel Blau, and Ann Snitow. 2007. *The feminist memoir project: Voices from women's liberation*. New Brunswick, NJ: Rutgers University Press.

Dworkin, Andrea. 1987. *Intercourse*. New York: Free Press.

Echols, Alice. 1989. *Daring to be bad: Radical feminism in America 1967–1975*. Minneapolis: University of Minnesota Press.

Einhorn, Barbara. 1993. *Cinderella goes to market: Citizenship, gender and women's movements in East Central Europe*. New York: Verso.

Eisenstein, Hester. 1996. *Inside agitators: Australian femocrats and the state*. Philadelphia, PA: Temple University Press.

Eisenstein, Hester. 2009. *Feminism seduced: How global elites use women's labor and ideas to exploit the world*. Boulder, CO: Paradigm Publishers.

Enke, Anne. 2007. *Finding a movement: Sexuality, contested space and feminist activism.* Durham, NC: Duke University Press.

Ertürk, Yakin. 2006. "Turkey's modern paradoxes: Identity politics, women's agency and universal rights." In Myra Marx Ferree and Aili Tripp, eds., *Global feminism: Transnational women's activism, organizing and human rights.* New York: New York University Press, 79–109.

Evans, Sara M. 1979. *Personal politics: The roots of women's liberation in the civil rights movement and the New Left.* New York: Vintage.

Ewig, Christina. 1999. "The strengths and limits of the NGO women's movement model: Shaping Nicaragua's democratic institutions." *Latin American Research Review* 34(3): 75–102.

Ewig, Christina. 2006. "Hijacking global feminism: Feminists, the Catholic Church and the family planning debacle in Peru." *Feminist Studies* 32(3): 632–659.

Fallon, Kathleen M. 2008. *Democracy and the rise of women's movements in sub-Saharan Africa.* Baltimore, MD: Johns Hopkins University Press.

Ferree, Myra Marx, and Beth Hess. 2000. *Controversy & coalition: The new women's movement,* 3d ed. New York: Routledge.

Ferree, Myra Marx, and Carol Mueller. 2004. "Feminism and the women's movement: A global perspective." In David Snow, Sarah Soule, and Hans-Peter Kriesi, eds., *The Blackwell companion to social movements.* New York: Blackwell Publishers, 576–607.

Ferree, Myra Marx, and Tetyana Pudrovska. 2004. " Global activism in 'virtual space': The European women's lobby in the network of transnational women's NGOs on the web." *Social Politics* 11(1): 117–143.

Ferree, Myra Marx, Dieter Rucht, William Gamson, and Jürgen Gerhards. 2002. *Shaping abortion discourse: Democracy and the public sphere in Germany and the United States.* New York: Cambridge University Press.

Foster, Carrie A. 2002. "Challenges to U.S. economic imperialism, 1915–1930: The case of the Women's International League for Peace and Freedom." In Virginia M. Bouvier, ed., *The globalization of U.S.-Latin American relations: Democracy, intervention, and human rights.* Westport, CT: Praeger, 65–82.

Foster, Catherine. 1989. *Women for all seasons: The story of the women's International League for Peace and Freedom.* Athens: University of Georgia Press.

Franceschet, Susan. 2005. *Women and politics in Chile.* Boulder, CO: Lynne Rienner.

Fraser, Nancy. 2009. "Feminism, capitalism and the cunning of history." *New Left Review* 56: 97–117.

Friedman, Elisabeth Jay. 2003. "Gendering the agenda: The impact of the transnational women's rights movement at the UN conferences of the 1990s." *Women's Studies International Forum* 26(4): 313–331.

Funk, Nannette, and Magda Mueller. 1993. *Gender politics and post-communism: Reflections from Eastern Europe and the former Soviet Union.* New York: Routledge.

Gal, Susan, and Gail Kligman. 2000. *The politics of gender after socialism.* Princeton, NJ: Princeton University Press.

Geisler, Gisela. 1995. "Troubled sisterhood: Women and politics in Southern Africa: Case studies from Zambia, Zimbabwe and Botswana." *African Affairs* 94(377): 545–578.

Giddings, Paula. 1984. *When and where I enter: The impact of black women on race and sex in America.* New York: Bantam.

Gonzalez, Charity Coker. 2000. "Agitating for their rights: The Colombian Women's movement, 1930–1957." *Pacific Historical Review* 69(4): 689–706.

Gould, Deborah B. 2009. *Moving politics: Emotion and ACT UP's fight against AIDS.* Chicago: University of Chicago Press.

Graff, Agnieszka. 2004. "A different chronology: Reflections on feminism in contemporary Poland." In Stacy Gillis, Gillian Howies and Rebecca Munford, eds., *Third wave feminism: A critical exploration*, 2nd ed. New York: Palgrave, 142–155.

Gray White, Deborah. 1999. *Too heavy a load: Black women in defense of themselves, 1894–1994.* New York: W.W. Norton.

Grimshaw, Patricia. 2010. "Settler anxieties, indigenous peoples, and women's suffrage in the colonies of Australia, New Zealand, and Hawai'i, 1888 to 1902." In Karen Offen, ed., *Globalizing feminisms, 1789–1945.* New York: Routledge, 111–121.

Guglielmo, Jennifer. 2010. "Transnational feminism's radical past: Lessons from Italian immigrant women anarchists in industrializing America." *Journal of Women's History* 22(1): 10–33.

Gullett, Gayle. 2000. "Constructing the woman citizen and struggling for the vote in California: 1896–1911." *Pacific Historical Review* 69(4): 573–593.

Guy, Donna. 2009. *Women build the welfare state: Performing charity and creating rights in Argentina, 1880–1955.* Durham, NC: Duke University Press.

Haas, Liesl. 2010. *Feminist policy making in Chile.* University Park: Pennsylvania State University Press.

Hammar, Inger. 2010. "From Fredrika Bremer to Ellen Key: Calling, gender and the emancipation debate in Sweden, c. 1830–1900." In Karen Offen, ed., *Globalizing feminisms, 1789–1945.* New York: Routledge, 78–95.

Hancock, Ange-Marie. 2007. "When multiplication doesn't equal quick addition: Examining intersectionality as a research paradigm." *Perspectives on Politics* 5(1): 63–79.

Hassim, Shireen. 2006. *Women's organizations and democracy in South Africa: Contesting authority.* Madison: University of Wisconsin Press.

Helly, Dorothy. 1996. "Beijing '95: The Fourth World Conference on Women." *NWSA Journal* 8(1): 171–178.

Hemment, Julie. 2007. *Empowering women in Russia: Activism, aid and NGOs.* Bloomington: Indiana University Press.

Henry, Astrid. 2004. *Not my mother's sister: Generational conflict and third wave feminism.* Bloomington: Indiana University Press.

Hercus, Cheryl. 2005. *Stepping out of line: Becoming and being feminist.* New York: Routledge.

Heumann, Silke. 2010. *Sexual politics and regime transition: Understanding the struggle around gender and sexuality in post-revolutionary Nicaragua.* Amsterdam: University of Amsterdam.

Hewitt, Nancy A. (Ed.). 2010a. *No permanent waves: Recasting histories of U.S. feminism.* New Brunswick, CT: Rutgers University Press.

Hewitt, Nancy A. (Ed.). 2010b. "Re-rooting American women's activism: Global perspectives on 1848." In Karen Offen, ed., *Globalizing feminisms, 1789–1945.* New York: Routledge, 18–25.

Heywood, Leslie L. (Ed.). 2006. *The women's movement today: An encyclopedia of third-wave feminism*, vol. 1, A–Z. Westport, CT: Greenwood.

Hipsher, Patricia. 2001. "Right and left wing women in post-revolutionary El Salvador: Feminist autonomy and cross-political alliance building for gender equality." In Victoria González and Karen Kampwirth, eds., *Radical women in Latin America: Left and right*. University Park: Pennsylvania State University Press, 133–164.

Htun, Mala. 2003. *Sex and the state: Abortion, divorce and the family under Latin American dictatorships and democracy*. Cambridge, UK: Cambridge University Press.

Hull, Gloria, Patricia Scott, and Barbara Smith. 1982. *All the women are white, and all the blacks are men, but some of us are brave: Black women's studies*. Old Westbury: Feminist Press.

Jakobsen, Janet. 1998. *Working alliances and the politics of difference: Diversity and feminist ethics*. Bloomington: Indiana University Press.

Jaquette, Jane S. (Ed.). 1994. *The women's movement in Latin America: Participation and democracy*. Boulder, CO: Westview Press.

Jaquette, Jane S., and Sharon L. Wolchik. 1998. "Women and democratization in Latin America and Central and Eastern Europe: A comparative introduction." In Jane S. Jaquette and Sharon L. Wolchik, eds., *Women and Democracy: Latin America and Central and Eastern Europe*. Baltimore, MD: Johns Hopkins University Press, 1–28.

Jayawardena, Kumari. 1986. *Feminism and nationalism in the third world*. London: Zed Books.

Jenson, Jane. 2008. "Writing women out, folding gender in: The European Union 'modernizes' social policy." *Social Politics* 15(2): 131–153.

Kampwirth, Karen. 2002. *Women and guerrilla movements: Nicaragua, El Salvador, Chiapas, Cuba*. University Park: Pennsylvania University State Press.

Kampwirth, Karen. 2004. *Feminism and the legacy of revolution: Nicaragua, El Salvador, Chiapas*. Athens: Ohio University Press.

Kampwirth, Karen. 2008. "Neither left nor right: Sandinismo in the anti-feminist era." *NACLA Report on the Americas* 41(1): 30–34.

Kanter, Rosabeth Moss. 1972. *Commitment and community: Communes and utopias in sociological perspective*. Cambridge, MA: Harvard University Press.

Kaplan, Gisela. 1992. *Contemporary Western European feminism*. New York: New York University Press.

Katzenstein, Mary F. 1999. *Faithful and fearless: Moving feminist protest inside the church and military*. Princeton, NJ: Princeton University Press.

Katzenstein, Mary F., and Carol Mueller (Eds.). 1987. *The women's movements of the United States and Western Europe: Consciousness, political opportunity, and public policy*. Philadelphia: Temple University Press.

Keating, Christine, Claire Rasmussen, and Pooja Rishi. 2010. "The rationality of empowerment: Microcredit, accumulation by dispossession and the gendered economy." *Signs: Journal of Women in Culture and Society* 36(1): 153–176.

Keck, Margaret E., and Kathryn Sikkink. 1998. *Activists beyond borders: Advocacy networks in international politics*. Ithaca, NY: Cornell University Press.

Koven, Seth, and Sonya Michel (Eds.). 1993. *Mothers of a new world: Maternalist politics and the origins of welfare states*. New York: Routledge.

Ladner, Joyce. 1971. *Tomorrow's tomorrow: The black woman*. New York: Doubleday Books.

Lang, Sabine. 1997. "The NGOization of feminism." In J. W. Scott, C. Kaplan, and D. Keates, eds., *Transitions, environments, translations: Feminisms in international politics*. New York: Routledge, 101–120.

Laslett, Barbara, and Johanna Brenner. 1989. "Gender and social reproduction: Historical perspectives." *Annual Review of Sociology* 15: 381–404.

Lavrin, Asunción. 1995. *Women, feminism and social change in Argentina, Chile and Uruguay, 1890–1940*. Lincoln: University of Nebraska Press.

Leavitt, Peggy, and Sally Merry. 2009. "Vernacularization on the ground: Local uses of global women's rights in Peru, China, India and the United States." *Global Networks* 9(4): 441–461.

Liu, Dongxiao. 2006. "When do national movements adopt or reject international agendas? A comparative analysis of the Chinese and Indian women's movements." *American Sociological Review* 71(6): 921–942.

Luciak, Ilja. 2001. *After the revolution: Gender and democracy in El Salvador, Nicaragua and Guatemala*. Baltimore: Johns Hopkins University Press.

Lycklama à Nijeholt, Geertje, Joke Sweibel, and Virginia Vargas. 1998. "The global institutional framework: The long march to Beijing." In Geertje Lycklama à Nijeholt, Virginia Vargas, and Saskia Wieringa, eds., *Women's movements and public policy in Europe, Latin America, and the Caribbean*. New York: Garland Publishing, 25–48.

MacKinnon, Catherine. 1993. *Only words*. Cambridge, MA: Harvard University Press.

Maddison, Sarah, and Kyungja Jung. 2008. "Autonomy and engagement: Women's movements in Australia and South Korea." In Marian Sawer and Sandra Grey, eds., *Women's movements- flourishing or in abeyance?* New York: Routledge, 33–48.

Marchand, Marianne. 2003. "Challenging globalization: Toward a feminist understanding of resistance." *Journal of International Studies* 29(S1): 129–150.

Markovitz, Lisa, and Karen Tice. 2002. "Paradoxes of professionalization: Parallel dilemmas in women's organizations in the Americas." *Gender & Society* 16(6): 941–948.

Martin, Patricia Yancey. 2005. *Rape work: Victims, gender and emotions in organization and community context*. New York: Routledge.

McAdam, Doug, John McCarthy, and Mayer Zald 1996. *Comparative perspectives on social movements*. New York: Cambridge University Press.

McBride, Dorothy, and Amy Mazur. 2010. *The politics of state feminism: Innovation in comparative research*. Philadelphia: Temple University Press.

McCall, Leslie. 2005. "The complexity of intersectionality." *Signs: Journal of Women in Culture and Society* 30(3): 1771–1800.

McCammon, Holly J., Lyndi Hewitt, and Sandy Smith. 2004. "'No weapon save argument': Strategic frame amplification in the U. S. woman suffrage movements." *Sociological Quarterly* 45: 529–556.

McCammon, Holly J., Courtney Sanders Muse, Harmony D. Newman, and Teresa M. Terrell. 2007. "Movement framing and discursive opportunity structures: The political successes of the U.S. women's jury movements." *American Sociological Review* 72: 725–749.

Miller, Francesca. 1991. *Latin American women and the search for social justice*. Hanover: University Press of New England.

Moghadam, Valentine. 2005. *Globalizing women: Transnational feminist networks*. Baltimore: Johns Hopkins University Press.

Molyneux, Maxine. 1985. "Mobilization without emancipation? Women's interests, the state and revolution in Nicaragua." *Feminist Studies* 11(2): 227–254.

Molyneux, Maxine. 1986. "No god, no boss, no husband: Anarchist feminism in nineteenth century Argentina." *Latin American Perspectives* 13(1): 119–145.

Monasterios P., Karin. 2007. "Bolivian women's organizations in the MAS era." *NACLA Report on the Americas* 40(2): 33–37.

Moon, Seungsook. 2002. "Carving out a space: Civil society and the women's movement in South Korea." *Journal of Asian Studies* 61(2): 473–500.

Murdock, Donna F. 2008. *When women have wings: Feminism and development in Medellín, Colombia.* Ann Arbor: University of Michigan Press.

Nam, Jeong-Lim. 2000. "Gender politics in the Korean transition to democracy." *Korean Studies* 24: 94–112.

Naples, Nancy. 1998. *Community activism and feminist politics: Organizing across race, class and gender.* New York: Routledge.

Narayan, Uma. 1997. *Dislocating cultures: Identities, traditions and third world feminism.* New York: Routledge.

Offen, Karen M. 2000. *European feminisms, 1700–1950: A political history.* Stanford, CA: Stanford University Press.

Offen, Karen M. 2010a. "Surveying European women's history since the millennium: A comparative review." *Journal of Women's History* 22(1): 154–177.

Offen, Karen M., ed. 2010b. *Globalizing feminisms 1789–1945.* New York: Routledge.

Outshoorn, Joyce. 2004. *The politics of prostitution: Women's movements, democratic states and the politics of sex commerce.* New York: Cambridge University Press.

Petchesky, Rosalind. 1995. "From population control to reproductive rights: Feminist fault lines." *Reproductive Health Matters* 3(6): 152–161.

Purkayastha, Bandana, and Mangala Subramaniam. 2004. *The power of women's informal networks: Lessons in social change from South Asia and West Africa.* Lanham, MD: Lexington Books.

Rai, Shirin. 2008. *The gender politics of development.* London: Zed Books.

Ramirez, Francisco O., Yasemin Soyosal, and Suzanne Shanahan. 1997. "The changing logic of political citizenship: Cross-national acquisition of women's suffrage rights, 1890 to 1990." *American Sociological Review* 62: 735–745.

Ranchod-Nilsson, Sita. 2006. "Gender politics and the pendulum of political and social transformation in Zimbabwe." *Journal of Southern African Studies* 32(1): 49–67.

Ray, Raka. 1999. *Fields of protest; Women's movements in India.* Minneapolis: University of Minnesota Press.

Roth, Benita. 2004. *Separate roads to feminism: Black Chicana and White feminist movements in America's second wave.* Cambridge, UK: Cambridge University Press.

Roth, Silke. 2008. *Gender politics in the expanding European Union: Mobilization, inclusion, exclusion.* New York: Berghahn Books.

Rowe-Finkbeiner, Kristin. 2004. *The F-word: Feminism in jeopardy: Women, politics and the future.* Emeryville: Seal Press.

Runyan, Anne Sisson, and V. Spike Peterson. 2000. "The radical future of realism: Feminist subversions of IR theory." In Andrew Linklater, *International relations: Critical concepts, volume 4.* London: Routledge, 1693–1730.

Rupp, Leila J. 1996. "Challenging imperialism in international women's organizations 1888–1945." *NWSA Journal* 8(1): 8–27.

Rupp, Leila J. 1997. *Worlds of women: The making of an international women's movement.* Princeton, NJ: Princeton University Press.

Rupp, Leila J., and Verta Taylor. 1993. "Women's culture and lesbian feminist activism: A reconsideration of cultural feminism." *Signs: Journal of Women, Culture and Society* 19(1): 32–61.

Ryan, Barbara. 1992. *Feminism and the women's movement: Dynamics of change in social movement.* New York: Routledge.

Scanlon, Jennifer. 2009. "Sexy from the start: Anticipatory elements of second wave feminism." *Women's Studies* 38: 127–150.

Schöpp-Schilling, Hanna Beate, and Cees Flinterman. 2007. *The circle of empowerment: 25 years of the UN Committee on the Elimination of Discrimination Against Women.* New York: Feminist Press.

Schreiber, Ronnee. 2008. *Righting feminism: Conservative women in American politics.* New York: Oxford University Press.

Seidman, Gay W. 1993. "'No freedom without the women': Mobilization and gender in South Africa, 1970–1992." *Signs: Journal of Women in Culture and Society* 18(2): 291–320.

Seidman, Gay W. 1999. "Gendered citizenship: South Africa's democratic transition and the construction of a gendered state." *Gender & Society* 13(3): 287–307.

Shayne, Julie. 2004. *The revolution question: Feminisms in El Salvador, Chile and Cuba.* New Brunswick, NJ: Rutgers University Press.

Showden, Carisa. 2009. "What's political about new feminisms?" *Frontiers* 30(2): 166–198.

Sjoberg, Laura. 2006. *Gender justice and the wars in Iraq: A feminist reformulation of just war theory.* Lanham, MD: Lexington Books.

Skocpol, Theda. 1992. *Protecting soldiers and mothers: The political origins of social policy in the United States.* Cambridge, MA: Belknap Press of Harvard University Press.

Smith, Bonnie G. 2000. *Global feminism since 1945: A survey of issues and controversies.* New York: Routledge.

Sneider, Allison L. 2008. *Suffragist in an Imperial Age: U.S. expansion and the woman question, 1870–1929.* New York: Oxford University Press.

Snyder, Margaret. 2006. "Unlikely godmother: the UN and the global women's movement" In Myra Marx Ferree and Aili Mari Tripp, eds., *Global feminism: Transnational women's activism, organizing and human rights.* New York: New York University Press, 24–50.

Snyder, R. Claire 2008. "What is third wave feminism? A new directions essay." *Signs: Journal of Women in Culture and Society* 34(1): 175–196.

Sperling, Valerie 1999. *Organizing women in contemporary Russia: Engendering transition.* New York. Cambridge University Press.

Staggenborg, Suzanne, and Verta Taylor. 2005. "Whatever happened to the women's movement?" *Mobilization* 10(1): 37–52.

Sternbach, Nancy Saporta, Marysa Navarro-Aranguren, Patricia Chuchryk, and Sonia E. Alvarez. 1992. "Feminisms in Latin America: From Bogotá to San Bernardo." *Signs: Journal of Women, Culture and Society* 17(2): 393–434.

Subramaniam, Mangala. 2006. *The power of women's organizing: Gender, class and caste in India.* Lanham, MD: Rowman and Littlefield.

Taylor, Barbara. 1983. *Eve and the New Jerusalem: Socialism and feminism in the nineteenth century.* London: Virago Press.

Taylor, Verta, and Leila Rupp. 1990. *Survival in the doldrums: The American women's rights movement, 1945 to the 1960s.* Columbus: The Ohio State University Press.

Thayer, Millie. 2010. *Making transnational feminism: Rural women, NGO activists, and northern donors in Brazil.* New York: Routledge.

Thompson, Becky. 2002. "Multiracial feminism: Recasting the chronology of second wave feminism." *Feminist Studies* 28(2): 336–360.

Towns, Ann. 2010. *Women and states: Norms and hierarchies in international society.* Cambridge: Cambridge University Press.

Trimberger, Ellen Kay. 1983. "Greenwich Village, 1900–1925." In Ann Snitow, Christine Stansell, and Sharon Thompson, eds., *Powers of desire: the politics of sexuality.* New York: Monthly Review Press.

Tripp, Aili. 1999. *Women and politics in Uganda.* Madison: University of Wisconsin Press.

Tripp, Aili. 2000. "Rethinking difference: Comparative perspectives from Africa." *Signs: Journal of Women in Culture and Society* 25(3): 649–675.

Tripp, Aili. 2006. "The evolution of transnational feminisms: Consensus, conflict and new dynamics." In Myra Marx Ferree and Aili Mari Tripp, eds., *Global feminism: Transnational women's activism, organizing and human rights.* New York: New York University Press, 51–75.

Tripp, Aili, Isabel Casimiro, Joy Kwesiga, and Alice Mungwa. 2009. *African women's movements: Changing political landscapes.* Cambridge, UK: Cambridge University Press.

True, Jacqui, and Michael Mintrom. 2001. "Transnational networks and policy diffusion: The case of gender mainstreaming." *International Studies Quarterly* 45: 27–57.

Twine, France Winddance, and Kathleen Blee. 2001. *Feminism and antiracism: International struggles for justice.* New York: New York University Press.

Vargas, Virginia. 1992. *Como Cambiar el Mundo sin Perdernos: El Movimiento de Mujeres en el Perú y América Latina.* Lima: Centro de la Mujer Flora Tristán.

von Wahl, Angelika. 2008. "From family to reconciliation policy: How the grand coalition reforms the German welfare state." *German Politics & Society* 26(3): 25–49.

Walby, Sylvia. 2011. *The future of feminism.* Cambridge, UK: Polity.

Walker, Rebecca (Ed.). 1995. *To be real: Telling the truth and changing the face of feminism.* New York: Anchor.

Walker, Rebecca (Ed.). 2006. "'Becoming the third wave' from *Ms.* Magazine." In Leslie Heywood, ed., *The women's movement today: An encyclopedia of third-wave feminism, vol. 1.* Westport, CT: Greenwood Press, 3–5.

Waylen, Georgina. 2007. *Engendering transitions: Women's mobilization, institutions and gender outcomes.* Oxford: Oxford University Press.

Wiegman, Robin. 2008. "Feminism, institutionalism and the idiom of failure." In Joan Scott, ed., *Women's studies on the edge.* Durham, NC: Duke University Press, 39–68.

Winslow, Anne. 1995. *Women, politics and the United Nations.* Westport, CT: Greenwood Press.

Woodhull, Winifred. 2004. "Global feminisms, transnational political economies, third world cultural production." In Stacy Gillis, Gillian Howies, and Rebecca Munford, eds., *Third wave feminism: A critical exploration*, 2d ed. New York: Palgrave, 156–167.

Woodward, Alison. 2004. "Building velvet triangles: Gender and informal governance." In Thomas Christiansen and Simona Piattoni, eds., *Informal governance in the European Union.* Cheltenham, UK: Edward Elgar, 76–93.

Yuval-Davis, Nira. 2006. "Intersectionality and feminist politics." *European Journal of Women's Studies* 13(3): 193–209.

Zheng, Wang, and Ying Zhang. 2010. "Global concepts, local practices: Chinese feminism since the Fourth World Conference on Women." *Feminist Studies* 36(1): 40–70.

Zimmerman, Susan. 2010. "The challenge of multinational empire for the international women's movement: The Habsburg Monarchy and the development of feminist inter/national politics." In Karen Offen, ed., *Globalizing feminisms 1789–1945*. New York: Routledge, 153–169.

Zinsser, Judith P. 2002. "From Mexico to Copenhagen to Nairobi: The United Nations decade for women 1975–1985." *Journal of World History* 13(1): 139–168.

Zippel, Kathrin. 2004. "Transnational advocacy networks and policy cycles in the European Union: The case of sexual harassment." *Social Politics* 11(1): 57–85.

Zippel, Kathrin. 2006. *The politics of sexual harassment: A comparative study of the United States, the European Union and Germany.* Cambridge, UK: Cambridge University Press.

CHAPTER 18

LOCAL—GLOBAL—LOCAL: WOMEN'S GLOBAL ORGANIZING

JUTTA JOACHIM

IN the age of globalization, slogans such as, "Local is global" or "Global is local" have become popular mobilizing tools for social movements either to draw attention to the effects that, for example, decisions by international institutions, such as the International Monetary Fund or the World Trade Organization have on farmers in African countries or to illustrate that local problems are no longer only the exclusive affair of the state but should be of concern to the international community. Gender and feminist studies have long been attuned to problems associated with dichotomies, such as the local and the global. Rather than fixed and separate, scholars have pointed out that distinctions such as these are socially constructed and artificial. Nor are the effects of globalization far from uniform, but instead contradictory, creating opportunities for some and more hardship for others (Prügl and Meyer 1999).

In this chapter on women's global organizing, I will take a closer look at the relations and interdependencies that exist between the local and global. Drawing on the social movement literature and more precisely Sidney Tarrow's (2005) concept of the *rooted cosmopolitan*, I will first illustrate how, historically, women's personal and local experiences have not only given rise to global campaigns from early on but also have been a source of conflict. In the second part, I will then turn to more contemporary debates related to gender mainstreaming and discuss how global ideas and norms may be appropriated and tailored to fit particular circumstances at the local level but at the same time may pose problems for women's organizing. Whether the movement is upward from the local to the global or downward from the global to the local level, the examples presented here illustrate that women's global activism involves filtering processes and layers of interpretations whereby the authors of campaigns potentially lose control of how their issues and problems are defined.

Because the terms *global* and *local* as well as ones that are often used synonymously, such as *international, transnational,* or *grassroots,* remain "hotly contested among postcolonial, Third World, and international feminist scholars" (Napels 2002, 5), some discussion of them is needed before embarking on the history of women's organizing. The term global is attractive to some because it transcends sovereignty and citizen identity. It makes the "political and economic relations forged across geographical boundaries...[as] the most relevant sites of decision making and identity formation" (e.g., Booth 1998, 120). Moreover, it draws attention to political processes that go beyond the confines of intergovernmental organizations, involving also nongovernmental actors (Prügl and Meyer 1999, 4). Others, by comparison, consider the term as rather problematic since it tends "to minimize cultural and contextual differences that are valued by women's movements in different cultures and contexts, and indeed to disregard profound differences among women even within national boundaries" (Antrobus 2004, 1; see also Grewal and Kaplan 2002). The term international is equally contested. On the one hand, it highlights the continued relevance of territorial boundaries, and, on the other hand, it is viewed as being too state- and Euro-centric. Given the problems related to these terms, transnational has been considered by many a viable alternative and a corrective because it acknowledges state as well as nonstate actors and their cross-boundary work within but also outside the framework of international organizations (e.g., Grewal 1999; Alvarez 2000; Moghadam 2001) and constitutes the arena where the international and local intersect (Marx Ferree and Tripp 2006, vii).

Although the terms local and the grassroots draw attention and make visible the varied effects of globalization on people's daily lives as well as their responses to them, they too suffer from problems. According to Nancy Napels (2002, 4), local and grassroots may be subject to "romanticization" of these sites of struggle or be associated with "othering" women who are indiscriminately referred to as the disenfranchised, voiceless, and poor. Moreover, the terms fall short of "captur[ing] the politics of accountability and the extent to which so-called grassroots groups are inclusive and encourage participatory democratic practices" (ibid., 7).

Similar to the terms global, transnational, international, local, and grassroots, so are the terms *women's movement* and *feminist movement* subject to debate (see also the chapters by Beckwith and Ewig and Ferree in this volume). The former has commonly been criticized for it suggests a monolithic movement in which all women are the same and ignores the differences among women due to their race, class, ethnicity, culture, sexual orientation, or locality (e.g., Mohanty 1991). At the same time, the term women's movement has been considered valuable because it "retains a focus on women's agency" (Prügl and

Meyer 1999, 6). With respect to the term feminist, which according to Valerie Sperling, Myra Marx Ferree and Barbara Risman (2001, 1158) applies to movements in which the participants share "a principled commitment to challenging gender hierarchy" critics reject it as being Western and bourgeois or for being antimale and too radical (Moghadam 2001, 78).

When women's organizing is examined across time, the positive as well as negative implications of the various terms become apparent as well. Despite the problems associated with them, all will be applied in this chapter since they are part of the history and politics of women's (feminist) organizing across boundaries. In this regard, they are telling of the movement from an international to a more global movement; of the tensions between members and groups as result of class, race, ethnicity, and geography; of the challenges that working both globally and locally pose; and of the structures in which the actors engage and which they cannot escape entirely.

Rooted Cosmopolitans and Transnational Activism

The social movement literature is quite helpful for understanding the connections between the local level, on the one hand, and the global level, on the other hand, because it provides useful concepts. Three have thus far been applied most frequently to the international level (see, for example, Keck and Sikkink 1998; Friedman 2003; Joachim 2007): (1) the political opportunity which captures the institutional and broader environment in which activism occurs; (2) the mobilizing resources which movement organizations and their networks have at their disposal; and (3) the frames, the organizations and networks employ and which are reflective of their shared understandings of problems, solutions, and strategies. Each is suited to shed light on what appears to be characteristic for global activism today: its multiple layers.

With respect to the opportunity structure, many scholars have drawn attention to changes in response to globalization, to the growth of international institutions, and to global activism. Consequently, movements and their organizations are no longer confined to the national level but can engage in what some refer to as *venue shopping* (Baumgartner and Jones 1991). They are able to move into an opportunity space in "which they encounter others like themselves, and form coalitions that transcend their borders" (Tarrow 2005, 25). Whether activists make use of these spaces hinges on and is mediated by developments and opportunities at the domestic level (see, for example, Cram 2001). Movements and nongovernmental organizations (NGOs) are, according to Kathryn Sikkink (2005), more likely to reach out to allies at the international level if they encounter resistance at the local and domestic level or if decision-making with respect to different policy areas is uploaded to international or regional institutions, as for example has been the case in the European Union. But even then, the respective actors remain nationally grounded and pursue what some refer to as an *insider-outsider strategy*, viewing the international level as a complementary and compensatory option to the national level (ibid.). The actors and their mobilizing resources, similar to the opportunity structures, reflect interdependencies between the local and the global level.

Sidney Tarrow (2005, 29) refers to them as rooted cosmopolitans and defines them as "people and groups who are rooted in specific national contexts, but who engage in contentious political activities that involve them in transnational networks of contacts and conflicts." The biographies of those spearheading international campaigns, NGOs, and their networks are telling in this respect. Many of these leaders have gained experience and been involved in national activism before moving to the international level. Bella Abzug, former president of the Women, Environment, and Development Organization (WEDO) and leading figure of women's international organizations during the special conferences organized by the United Nations in the early 1990s, is an illustrative example of this. Her activism at the international level was informed by her experiences as member of the U.S. Congress and a local activist. To make women's lobbying activities during the UN conferences more effective, she introduced the caucus system, which women had used as a vehicle for organizing in the Congress. The caucus provided a forum for women from different regions of the world to discuss events at the conferences and coordinate their strategies in turn.

As Valentine Moghadam (2001, 106, 144) illustrates in her book on transnational feminist networks, Devaki Jain, the founder of Development Alternatives with Women for a New Era (DAWN), or Marieme Hélie-Lucas of Women Living Under Muslim Law (WLUML) also support Tarrow's (2005) thesis regarding the rooted cosmopolitans. Both played a decisive role for the formation of the transnational networks to which they belong. They were visionary and highly educated, and their entrepreneurial work at the global level was informed by local ideas, norms, histories, experiences, and strategies. While the focus in the literature has often been on such visible individuals or their organizations, they are only the tip of the iceberg of what might be called a politics of rooted cosmopolitanism and be defined as the attempt to engage in advocacy and networking at both the national and local level as well as global and transnationally sometimes simultaneously, sometimes separate from each other, sometimes involving the same and at other times different individuals, and having various, contradictory effects.

The framing concept is useful in this respect. It draws attention to the intersubjective context in which new ideas and norms emerge and which forms the backdrop against which these ideas and norms are then interpreted, accepted, or contested. It "render[s] events or occurrences meaningful" and "function[s] to organize experience and guide action, whether individual or collective" (Snow et al. 1986, 464). However, the framing concept makes apparent that while activ-ists are motivated by moral causes, they also behave strategically to mobilize sup-port. They "fashion shared understandings of the world and of themselves that legitimate and motivate collective action" (McAdam, McCarthy, and Zald 1996, 6). International relations scholars have illustrated how ideas promoted by differ-ent groups originated at the national or local level and were framed and modi-fied as they traveled up to the international level. Margaret Keck and Kathryn Sikkink (1998), for example, illustrate this process with respect to testimonies of individuals who have been victims of violence at the local level and how they are "discovered and presented normally involves several layers of prior translation." They are filtered "through expatriates, through travelling scholars like ourselves, or through media," which is why there is "frequently a huge gap between the sto-ry's original telling and the retellings—in its sociocultural context, its instrumen-tal meaning, and even in its language. Local people, in other words, sometimes lose control over their stories in a transnational campaign" (ibid.).

Just as experiences and ideas are framed to gain acceptance at the inter-national level, so are international norms tailored and appropriated in differ-ent ways when they are applied at the national level. Although studies on the implementation of international norms convey the impression that international norms are either taken over as such or are opposed, more recent work illus-trates that the case is rarely that clear-cut. Instead, "local agents reconstruct foreign norms to ensure the norms fit with the agent's cognitive priors and identities" (Acharya 2004, 239), a process Acharya refers to as *norm localization* and Alvarez (2000) as *transnationalism reversed*.

In the following section, I will illustrate how the theoretical concepts help us understand and bring to the fore the linkages between the local and global level in the case of women's international organizing.

From the Local to the Global: Women's Global Organizing

Women's global organizing dates back to the early nineteenth century. Within the framework of the UN, women's organizations and groups successfully lob-bied for the establishment of the Commission on the Status of Women (CSW) in 1946, a policy-making body tasked with the promotion of gender equal-ity and the advancement of women's rights, the adoption of a gender-based treaty; for the Convention on the Elimination of All Forms of Discrimination against Women in 1979; and for the Declaration on the Elimination of Violence against Women in 1993. Most recently, they have made inroads in the Security Council (SC), which has adopted several resolutions with respect to gender and peacekeeping. Despite these milestones, the longevity of the women's movement is also indicative that even today gender constitutes a basis for discrimination, marginalization, and oppression. In this section, I will look at women's transnational activism historically, illustrating not only how women's organizing has changed but also how the connections between the local and national levels have both engendered global and international activism and have been a source of conflict.

Women's Organizing at the Turn of the Century— Women's Rights as Equal Rights (1900–1950s)

The turn of the century is generally associated with the first wave of what may be referred to as women's international organizing, bringing women of mostly Europe and North America together around issues related to peace and political and civil rights, including suffrage, labor issues, and equal nationality rights. The First International Women's Congress that women organized in The Hague in 1915 illustrates not only the linkages between the three different issues but also how women's activism was influenced by international events and local circumstances. Sparked by the devastating effects of World War II, the congress attracted from both belligerent and neutral countries women who advanced a series of proposals of how to bring about world peace. Though often assumed, struggles for political and civil rights, including suffrage, were however not limited to the Northern Hemisphere. Instead, partly inspired by and appealing to universal principles and partly through solely national campaigns, women around the globe began to demand more participation and by doing so planted the seeds for first transnational and later global movements.

The women who initiated meetings such as the First International Women's Congress but also those who took part come close to what Tarrow (2005, 43) conceives of as a subgroup of rooted cosmopolitans, that is, transnational activists, and defines as "individuals and groups who mobilize domestic and international resources and opportunities to advance claims on behalf of external actors, against external opponents, or in favour of goals they hold in common with transnational allies." First, women's activism at the international level at the time, "emerged from [their] domestic political or social activities" (ibid.). Many of those traveling to The Hague had been, at the national level, at the forefront of social reform movements such as the temperance, antislavery, prostitution, and penal reform movements in the United States and later the suffrage movements. Second, women who engaged in transboundary campaigns were often of bourgeois or aristocratic decent, "with leisure time and sufficient resources to engage in international travel and communication" (Stienstra 1994, 48; see also Rupp 1994). Given their resources, they were able to "shift their activities among levels, taking advantage of the expanded nodes of opportunity of a complex international society" (Tarrow, 43).

Women either created these opportunities on their own or worked through existing international institutions. With respect to the former, the Seneca Falls Conventions held in the United States in 1848, for example, constituted an important symbolic event regarding the formation of an international women's movement. Over three hundred women gathered and adopted the Declaration of Sentiments drafted by Elizabeth Cady Stanton, Lucretia Mott, and others. Resembling the U.S. Declaration of Independence in structure and language, the declaration identified all men as responsible for women's oppression and compiled a list of grievances about the ways women were denied their rights. The conventions paved the grounds for the first international women's organizations—the International Congress of Women (ICW), the Socialist Women's Alliance (SWA), and the International Alliance of Women (IAW)—which were established in 1888, 1907, and 1904, respectively. They too are indicative of the local–global connection since national organizations provided the template for transnational activities. Nevertheless, at the time neither of these organizations was truly global. According to Rupp and Taylor (1999, 367), "Women from the United States, Great Britain, western and northern Europe constituted the original membership of international [women's] organizations and also dominated their leadership" (see also Rupp 1994). Yet there were also exceptions. As Ellen Dubois (2000, 547) documents in her study on the women's suffrage movement in the Pacific, women from India took part in the founding meeting of the International Congress of Women in 1888, and among the chapters of the Women's Christian Temperance Union were ones from China, Japan, Korea, and Burma. In addition to these organizations, Aili Tripp (2006, 56) cites other examples that attest to transnational organizing in other parts of the world, including the International Women's Congress in Buenos Aires in 1910 with delegates from Peru, Paraguay, Uruguay, and Argentina or a meeting of women from Pacific Rim countries in 1928 in Honolulu, which paved the way for the Pan-Pacific Women's Association in 1930 (ibid., 57).

Apart from organizing meetings on their own, women's activists seized opportunities created by international institutions based on the assumption that "the advancement of women in different countries required governmental policies and democratic opportunities for women to influence" (Pietilä 2007, 1). Women were present at the Paris Peace Conference in 1919, where the League of Nations and the International Labor Organization (ILO) were founded, asking governments, among other things, to promote universal suffrage and to work for both the abolishment of trafficking in women as well as state-supported prostitution (Pietilä 2007). According to Miller (1994), women's engagement with the League of Nations was not only key to women's equality but also engendered international politics in two other important respects. First, women demanded access to intergovernmental meetings, which until then had been the exclusive realm of heads of states, foreign ministers, and diplomats. Second, through their well-prepared proposals, they placed on the international agenda what had previously been perceived as exclusively domestic issues (ibid.). Finally, governmental meetings provided also a platform for transnational networking and exchanges. Activists from the United States marched together with women from Latin America in the streets of Havana in 1928 during the Sixth Pan-American Conference calling for justice and equal rights for women (Stienstra 1994, 71). And a smaller group of women carried that demand inside governmental halls and through their lobbying contributed to the establishment of the first intergovernmental body to deal with women's issues, the Inter-American Commission on Women (Comisión de Interamericano Mujere, or CIM), which collected data on the civil and political status of women in the Americas. Moreover, the pressure that activists exerted contributed to the adoption of two treaties at the Pan-American Conference in Montevideo in 1933: the Convention on the Nationality of Women; and the Treaty on the Equality of Rights between Men and Women (Berkovitch 1999, 81–82; Joachim 2007, 59–65). Both not only were "the first two official international conventions that explicitly set sexual equality as a principle to be incorporated into national legislation" (Berkovitch 1999, 81) but also became important reference points for women's activism in the League of Nations and later the United Nations (Tripp 2006, 59).

Although women were often viewed of and portrayed as a monolithic bloc, differences existed already back then between activists. The equal rights frame, for example, divided women engaged in the League of Nations into reformers who aimed for equal political rights but protective legislation in all other areas and others who conceived of themselves as egalitarians and struggled for women's equality in all areas. Organizations belonging to the two groups fought over not only what constituted appropriate solutions for improving women's status or strategies but also who was more or less feminist (Pfeffer 1985, 462). As a leading equalitarian, Lady Margaret Rohnda of the National Women's Party, stated in 1926: "One may divide the women in the woman movement into two groups, the feminists and the reformers who are not in the least feminist, who do not care tuppence about equality for itself... But your organization is one of the very few in the world today which is purely feminist" (ibid.).

Furthermore, conflicts erupted between North American and Latin American activists over who could represent and speak for women in the Inter-American Commission on Women (Tripp 2006, 57; Joachim 2007, 64). Finally, racial identity politics divided women even at the turn of the century, which highlights that transnational initiatives do not take place in a vacuum but instead "were frequently closely entwined with the colonial project of modernization and the missionary project of promoting Christian beliefs, values, and lifestyle" (Tripp 2006, 58). As Christina Ewig and Myra Marx Ferree illustrate in their chapter in this volume, suffragist in the North sometimes considered themselves as more civilized than other women whom they attempted to educate. However, according to Tripp (2006), this posture was far from uniform. While "some colonial feminists thoroughly supported the imperial project and were bent on carrying out their civilizing mission," others neither actively supported nor challenged it. Few, according to Aili Tripp, favored the independence of women in developing countries (Tripp 2006, 59). The responses of women living in colonized countries also varied ranging from welcoming the support of Northern women to indifference and resistance (ibid.).

Women's Organizing during the 1970s and 1980s

The second wave of women's organizing at the international level spans from the 1970s to the 1980s. Similar to the first, it had many local roots. Student protests in Europe and the civil rights movements in the United States were incubators for women's movements that started to mobilize around issues including equal pay and abortion rights. In the third world, by comparison, women had become disillusioned with the largely male leaderships of political parties and developed a feminist political consciousness. In Latin America, left feminists reacted to authoritarianism and initiated the *encuentros*, regional meetings between 1981 and 1996 that played an important in the democratization of the region, but also proofed an important vehicle for transnational exchanges among women and advocacy (Alvarez 1999, 3; see also Jaquette 1994). Finally, as Moghadam (2001, 86) points out, broader socioeconomic developments mobilized women, including "the internationalization of capital and global assembly line production; the growing industrial reliance on female labor; changes in the social and economic functions of the state [and] a worldwide increase in the population of educated and employed women with grievances and an emergent sense of collective identity." Together these forces contributed to the globalization of women's movement and posed new challenges.

During the 1970s and 1980s, the UN became a major focal point for women. Quite a number of international women's organizations formed prior to and following World War II. Many of these organizations obtained consultative status with the UN Economic and Social Council (UNECSOC) and as a result were able to exert pressure on both governments and UN officials to devote more attention to women's issues. They lobbied for the establishment of the CSW (see Pfeffer 1985, 468; Joachim 2007, 123) and the inclusion of an antidiscrimination clause in the Universal Declaration of Human Rights adopted in 1948. The overall climate was favorable. In the context of shifting power relations within the UN from North and West to South and East, an economic crisis triggered by rising oil prices, decolonization, and growing awareness of environmental problems the global agenda was redefined. Several so-called special conferences were organized with the intention to identify pressing issues, including ones devoted to the environment (Stockholm in 1971), population (Bucharest in 1974), and food (Rome in 1974). Unlike in the 1990s, women's issues and concerns however were treated as special and separate. In addition to designating 1975 as the International Women's Year and conducting the first UN World Conference on Women in Mexico City, the UN arranged two further meetings during the UN Decade for Women (1975–1985) in Copenhagen in 1980 and Nairobi in 1985.

The conferences inspired the establishment of women's organizations and networks throughout the world. Particularly, the end-of-decade-conference in Nairobi was a catalyst in this regard. Many prestigious foundations in the North, particularly in the United States, such as the Ford, Carnegie, or Rockefeller foundations, sponsored workshops in preparation for the governmental conference (Fraser 1987, 201–202), which resulted in more long-lasting structures, such as DAWN (ibid., 202; see also Moghadam 2001). At the same time, the conference provided a platform for cross-boundary exchanges and impetus for local and national organizing. Similar to the meetings in Mexico City and Copenhagen, an NGO forum took place prior to the governmental conference in Nairobi, though in a much looser fashion.

As much as these conferences provided opportunities for women from different parts of the world to come together, they also are reflective of the challenges with which nationally rooted activists are confronted. Based on their experiences, histories, and cultures, women had different understandings of which issues were the most pressing, what feminism meant, or whether it provided a useful tool for women's organizing at all (Stienstra 1994). Discussions and exchanges were framed by political realities pitting women from the North against participants from the South (Jaquette 1995, 47). Clashes occurred "among nationally or regionally framed feminisms, mainly due to disagreements between Western feminists, who emphasized women's need for legal equality and for sexual autonomy, and Third World feminists, who emphasized imperialism and underdevelopment as obstacles to women's advancement" (Moghadam 2005, 85). In addition, similar to the first wave of transnational activism when colonial feminists thought that third-world women needed to be civilized, there was also a tendency among activists from the North in the 1970s and 1980s to cast women in developing countries as "'the oppressed other' of their more liberated self" (Desai 2002, 28; see also Mohanty 1991). Conflicts such as these reflect, according to Peggy Antrobus (2004), that "international" still had a meaning insofar as "national and cultural differences between women were recognizable and paramount" (17).

Despite conflicts and deep rifts, single issues helped women to discover commonalities, as for example, in the case of sexual violence, and moved them "toward greater coherence and even common positions" (Antrobus 2004, 17). Moreover, teach-ins eased the tension between women's group. Intended to empower women, participants exchanged knowledge about lobbying techniques and how to obtain funding or communication with the media. Statements by observers of the Nairobi forum in 1985 provide some evidence of the effects: "Organizers, though they faced disagreements, managed to preserve an atmosphere of open debate and spirit of reconciliation. This was in noticeable contrast to Mexico City and Copenhagen, where much of the debate on peace issues had broken down into vitriolic misunderstandings. The underlying sense was that the women's movement had matured over the course of the Decade of Women" (Stephenson 1995, 149). Finally, broader developments contributed to the emergence of a collective identity. According to Moghadam (2005, 87), parallel processes like "Islamic fundamentalism, communalism, and similar forms of identity politics in the South, along with Reaganism and Thatcherism and the post-Keynesian shift in the North" alarmed women around the world and led "to a convergence of sorts and a shared vocabulary between women activists in developed and developing countries. For feminists in the South, issues of sexuality and personal autonomy assumed importance, while feminists in the North began to recognize the salience of economic factors and forces in their lives."

Although the UN conferences can be considered a watershed with respect to second-wave transnational mobilization, not all the organizations and movements that emerged were inspired by them and, thus, resulted from top-down processes. Instead, national and regional developments "impelled local movement actors to build transborder connections from the bottom-up" (Alvarez 2000, 3). Quite a number of scholars have shown in recent years (e.g., Jayawardena 1986; Lavrin 1995; Snyder 1995; DuBois 2000) that women's movements in Africa, Asia, and Latin America have also developed independently with their own intrinsic philosophy and distinct goals (Tripp 2006, 59). Moreover, there was no unanimous consent among women that working through established institutions, such as the UN, should be the preferred strategy which, according to Tarrow (2005, 29), is also characteristic of rooted cosmopolitans and, more precisely, transnational activists. Some "behave as 'insiders,' lobbying and collaborating with international elites to the point of co-optation, while others challenge international institutions' policies and, in some cases, contest their existence."

Skepticism toward the UN is reflected in both academic writing about the transnational women's movements and the actions of participants. With respect to the former, Alvarez (1999), for example, concludes in her study on transnational feminist organizing in Latin America that the influence of UN conferences is not only positive because it also diverts attention from the issues of most direct concern to local activists. Analyzing the relationship between the UN and NGOs, Diane Otto (1996, 128) raises doubts as to whether the UN, with its "state-centric world view," can rise to the challenge of reorienting its focus to be inclusive of peoples as well as states. Her uneasiness was shared by groups of activists in the 1970s and 1980s who, wary of co-optation, organized what some referred to as *counterevents* (Russell and Van de Ven 1984, 218). The international tribunal on crimes against women in Brussels in 1976 and the international tribunal concerning reproductive rights and health in Amsterdam in 1984 are examples of these. Modeled after the war tribunals in Nuremberg and Tokyo, the organizers were convinced about "the power of personal testimony to educate, politicize, and motivate" (ibid., 219). By sharing "personal experiences and problems, we come to see that these problems are not merely personal, but that they are caused or exacerbated by the way women are regarded and treated in general,…We come to see that many of our problems are externally or socially induced, and hence, widely shared by other women" (ibid., 67). The tribunal in Brussels led to the establishment of the International Feminist Network, and the one in Amsterdam gave rise to the Women's Global Network for Reproductive Rights (WGNRR), which was intended to promote solidarity between the North and South. Moreover, both stimulated national initiatives against gender violence throughout Europe and North America as well as in Latin America and Asia. In addition, the tribunals had more lasting effects. They became a master framework for women's transnational activism in the 1990s.

Given that these tribunals had been intended to empower women and were in opposition to state institutions, it is somewhat ironic that they also helped to jumpstart discussions within the UN on the issues, however, in a more confined fashion and on the basis of scientific expertise rather than personal experiences. Their effects highlight that distinctions such as those between insiders and outsiders are never as clear-cut as they may seem and lend support to the argument by Keck and Sikkink (1998, 19) that testimonies frequently engender campaigns at the international level but are also subject to a filtering processes.

Women's Transnational Activism in the 1990s and Gender Mainstreaming

The end of the cold war is frequently characterized as a symbolic event. In the case of the women's movements, it demarks the onset of the third wave of their organizing. At the national level, women's organizations were at the forefront of democratization movements in Latin America (e.g., Alvarez 1998, 1999) and Africa (e.g., Van Allen 2001; Leslie 2006; Fallon 2008). At the international level, they emerged as the most visible actors during the specialized conferences the UN had organized in the early 1990s with the intention to identify the most pressing issues in the absence of superpower rivalry, beginning with the Conference on Environment and Development in Rio de Janeiro in 1992, continuing with the World Human Rights Conference in Vienna in 1993 and the International Conference on Population and Development in Cairo in 1994, and concluding with the Fourth World Conference on Women in Beijing in 1995. Similar to other movements, the growing availability of the Internet and e-mail facilitated transboundary exchanges between women (Moghadam 2001, 91; Mastrangelo Gittler 1996, 86).

The third phase illustrates what Tarrow (2005) considers the potential of transnational organizing. It "...is producing mechanisms and processes that escape the narrow confines of international institutions and may be leading to an ultimate fusion between domestic and international activism" (29). While active in separate locations and at different levels, women profited from the fact that they were working at both domestic and international levels and were pursuing both insider and outsider strategies. With respect to the former, it was precisely the regional and local activism that was responsible for women's issues and concerns being taken seriously at the international level and included in the final conference documents. In the case of the Human Rights Conference, for example, women activists attended the regional conferences held in preparation for the official governmental meeting in Vienna. They prepared consensus documents on the basis of which they successfully lobbied the inclusion of women's human rights in the respective draft platforms of action. These achievements, in turn, gave women's groups greater leverage at the final preparatory meeting and the actual conference, because they were able to hold governments accountable to their regional and national commitments (Joachim 2007, 125). Moreover, "emboldened by IGO's discursive sanctioning of diversity" (Alvarez 2000, 14), financial support from foundations, and involvement with regional and global women's organizing coalitions, Beijing mobilized and gave greater visibility to thus far marginalized groups. For example, Afro-Latin American women gained "a new foothold within the historically predominantly white and mestiza local feminist movement" (ibid.).

The activities of women's organizations during and leading up to the Human Rights Conference are indicative of interdependencies between insider and outsider strategies. At the same time victims of gender-based violence staged an global eighteen-hour tribunal at the NGO forum modeled after those in Brussels and Amsterdam (Bunch and Reilly 1994), women's organizations and groups also lobbied governmental representatives using science backed up by reports and statistics. Prior to the governmental conference the Center for Women's Global Leadership and the International Women's Tribune Center circulated a global petition by calling on governments to among other things "comprehensively address women's human rights at every level of [the] proceedings" had been translated from an initial six into twenty-four languages and was sponsored by over a thousand groups that gathered almost half a million signatures from 124 countries (Center for Women's Global Leadership 1993, 38). While all these examples suggest a blurring of boundaries, there are also developments that speak to the contrary.

One of these is professionalization, or what Alvarez (1999) refers to as NGOization and what Clive Archer (1983, 303), in reference to international women's NGOs, describes as the change from "little old ladies in tennis shoes" to becoming professional women in business suits. Compared with decades ago, when most of the organizations were run by volunteers, women's organizations are now made up of a paid and highly educated staff, including lawyers or individuals with social science degrees. As a result of this transformation, many organizations have started to place greater emphasis on insider strategies and are also increasingly consulted by governments for advice. The growing involvement of activists in international institutions has been a source for conflict.

NGOs change roles from being "outside critical agents demanding issue recognition and action, to that of partners in developing workable frameworks and principles for implementing action" (Gough and Shackley 2001, 329; see also Alvarez 2000, 23). Moreover, professionalization also introduces and reinforces power asymmetries within networks since "international funding agencies and private foundations…tend to favour larger, already well-resourced, more professionalized feminist NGOs whose work has measurable 'policy relevance' over smaller, less formalized, typically more grass-roots or identity-solidarity-oriented movement organizations" (Alvarez 2000, 23; see also Friedman 1999). The campaign leading up to the International Conference on Population and Development (ICPD) in Cairo is particularly telling in this respect. In preparation, the International Women's Health Coalition (IWHC) in New York formed the Women's Alliance, which drafted a Women's Declaration on Population Policies titled "Women's Voices '94"(IWHC 1994) defining women's ability to control their fertility as a human right and specifying seven ethical principals that population policies and programs should honor to ensure the centrality of women's well-being (Antrobus et al. 1993). Although signed by over two thousand individuals and organizations from over 110 countries, the document was subject to criticism by women's groups from both the North and the South. In the eyes of their members, the document had been drafted by an exclusive group of women who were not representative of the entire women's movement but rather were part of its pragmatic wing, which was too accepting of population policies and the population establishment (Joachim 2007, 153–154).

Resisting professionalization, however, is not without problems either. Moghadam (2005) lists a few of the challenges volunteer organizations face, including "a tendency toward overwork on the part of a core of members," the danger of the core group "to become a kind of political elite, or the emergence of a charismatic leader who may abuse power or encounter resentment" (96). In addition, "lack of transparency and accountability in financial matters and in decision-making also could result in problems of legitimacy" (ibid.). Seen this way, nonprofessionalization can, in the eyes of Suzanne Staggenborg (1999, 129) who has studied the prochoice movement in the United States, become a liability in the realization of political goals.

Similar to their style of organizing, women's organizations engaged in international institutions have changed the way they frame their concerns. According to Elisabeth Friedman (2003), the greatest achievement of transnational women's rights movements in the 1990s came in "gendering the agenda" of the UN (313). Contrary to the first- and second-wave movements, when issues were treated as solely women's issues requiring special attention, the 1990s gave way to gender mainstreaming. "Movement participants shaped global understandings of issues from human rights to population growth, simultaneously mainstreaming gender analysis into areas formerly considered 'gender-neutral' and prioritizing women's rights as integral to the achievement of conference goals" (ibid., 314). Gender mainstreaming highlights the ways earlier framing efforts by rooted cosmopolitan lead to subsequent ones. Gender mainstreaming dates back to the 1970s and the call for the integration of women in development (Baden and

Goetz 1997, 4–5). Nevertheless, it also indicative of the conflicts generally associated with the introduction of new frames.

Particularly women from the South felt that the concept did not resonate with their local experiences. Some of their arguments are reminiscent of earlier debates but also have been echoed in scholarly analysis and feminist activists in the North (see the chapter by Lombardo, Meier, and Verloo in this volume). Critics assert that gender mainstreaming in their countries has been used as "a scheme to buy off once committed activists" (Makibaka, 1995, 5), has shifted the focus in policy circles "away from women to 'men at risk'" (Baden and Goetz 1997, 6), denies the very existence of women specific disadvantage and the need for specific measures (Kabeer 1994, xii), contributes to a preoccupation with the minutiae of procedures at all levels rather than clarity and direction about goals (Razavi and Miller 1995a, 1995b), and has resulted in depoliticization. At the same time, gender mainstreaming was also fiercely opposed by conservatives who interpreted it as the "deconstruction of women" and a mutable gender identity. According to Baden and Goetz their reactions may be attributed to the perceived greater influence and presence of feminist NGOs, the greater visibility of lesbians in NGOs, and the inclusion, for the first time in the UN conferences on women, of very open language on sexual and reproductive rights (Baden and Goetz 1997, 12). According to Friedman (2003), however, there is a further reason for the opposition that transnational activists faced: "as women's rights advocates became more successful at developing mainstreamed frames and promoting them through sophisticated repertoires of action, they 'taught' their opposition how to respond to them" (327).

Apart from the controversies that it is subject to, gender mainstreaming is also an example of how local ideas are carried upward and engender discussions in international institutions. The adoption of gender mainstreaming of security is particularly telling in this respect. According to Tripp (2006, 68), African women, who had experienced many civil conflicts, not only made peace a central issue at the Beijing conference but also were very proactive in pushing the issue in international forums more generally. Their efforts contributed in part to the adoption of UN Security Council 1325 "Women, Peace and Security" in 2000, which urges member-states to include women in peace negotiations and give them roles in peacekeeping missions around the world (Porter 2007, 11–17; Cohn 2008; Sheperd 2008).

From the Global to the Local

Once accepted at the global level, frames are often carried back to the local level by rooted cosmopolitans, with the aim most frequently to bring about and stimulate domestic change. This transnationalism reversed (Friedman 1999) can have and has had, as illustrated already, positive effects and can be a catalyst for the formation of women's movements and the establishment of women's agencies within governments, which in turn can push for new laws or changes in existing institutions. Nevertheless, transnationalism reversed also brings with it its own set of problems for both the actors involved and the norms or ideas at stake.

Studying the implementation of the CEDAW in Finland and Chile, adopted in 1979 by the General Assembly of the United Nations as the first international treaty to define all forms of discrimination against women as human rights violations, Susanne Zwingel (2005) identifies three factors that determine whether and to what extent global norms will be implemented: "first, the degree to which political institutions enable the representation of women's interests within public policy formation; second, the existence of transnational governmental or non-governmental activism that supports the appropriation and implementation of international norms, and third, the level of cultural affinity with the Convention" (408; see also the chapter by Lombardo et al. in this volume). With respect to the first factor, Zwingel finds that women's organizations in democratic systems appear to have a better chance to build coalitions and mobilize support in favor of legal changes than in ones where women's interests are unrepresented.

While transnational links help to reinforce and lend legitimacy to the claims of norm advocates, their effects are far from uniform, nor are the links that exist always productive. Studying the impact of transnational activism in Venezuela, Friedman (1999) suggests that while the existence of women's movements is important, it is also critical to ask what stage they are in. Drawing on her insights from the Nairobi and Beijing women's conferences, she posits that links with other actors across state boundaries may be more beneficial in the early stages of a movement when it still lacks infrastructure than later on when a movement is preoccupied with internal problems (32). Furthermore, the impact of transnational links of norm advocates may be weakened or even neutralized through similar links by norm opponents. In the case of CEDAW, the efforts of women's groups in favor of the convention in Chile were counteracted by powerful transnational church-related networks promoting values opposing the convention (Zwingel 2005, 409–410). Finally, external funding might be counterproductive. While it provides a basis for transnational organization in many cases, it also introduces power asymmetries between groups, "exacerbates power and resource imbalances among activist organizations on the home front" (Alvarez 2000, 23), leads to dependencies and undermines autonomy, creates elites and externally selected representatives of a movement (Friedman 1999, 10, 32), and, due to the competition for funding, may ultimately also weaken solidarity among women (Vargas and Olea Mauleon 1998, 56).

In addition to transnational links or support and the stage of the movement, implementation and the acceptance of global norms also hinge on their resonance and affinity with norms and ideas in the national setting or the ideologies of the administration in power. According to Grewal (1999, 339), the patriarchal nature of legal systems in many nation-states in Asia, Africa, or

Latin America into which global norms are introduced and that constitutes the ground on which new laws are to be discussed is a "hostile context." Because it is "so profoundly hegemonic and unfriendly to the interests of women," it prevents the proper implementation of human rights instruments for women (ibid.). Also, even if new laws are adopted, the misogyny of the legal systems prevents that they are administered (Singh 1994, 377). Even worse, the laws can be used as a tool by the political leadership to solidify their power and serve as a means "to punish those who are marginal to various societies" (Grewal 1999, 339). While ideological factors play an important role with respect to the resonance of global norms, based on her study of the impact of the Nairobi and Beijing women's conferences in Venezuela Friedman (1999, 33) concludes that they "alone [are] not determinative." Instead, gender relations may be yet one more sphere of competition for parties to ensure their power (ibid.). Nevertheless, the (mis-)fit between global norms and local norms and ideas seems to play an important role as to why the efforts of transnational women's rights activists either crepitate or result in institutional or legal changes.

According to Zwingel (2005, 411), norm advocacy is more difficult when discrepancies exists since, on the one hand, opposed groups can "construct national normative settings as unchangeable due to 'cultural traditions,'" and, on the other hand, differences among norm advocates may come to the fore. In the Chilean case, for example, Zwingel attributes different view points and noncooperative strategies among women's groups with respect to reproductive rights to the negative connotations of the issue in public discourses where it is equated with the ultimate goal of legalizing abortion rather than reproductive health and self-determination (ibid., 409). What appears to be crucial in assessing the degree of (mis-)fit is the content of global norms and how deeply they are rooted in local contexts.

With respect to the women's rights as human rights frame that has been used as a mobilizing tool by women's groups following the UN World Conference on Human Rights in Vienna in 1993, Grewal (1999, 337), for example, asserts that it sustains and reinforces established hierarchies between "the geopolitical context of human rights internationalism and the nationalisms." Although presented as a universal norm by primarily Northern women's NGOs, it is essentially Euro-centric. It refers to a normative European or "'American' subject gendered, as woman, who is white and heterosexual" (ibid., 351). Ilumoka (1994, 320) makes a similar claim, arguing that "the international women's rights movement, like the international human rights movement, largely projects the concerns of privileged women who are able to make their voices heard. The voices of middle-class European and American women ...." The women's human rights frame presumes a self-conscious, coherent group of persons that cuts across class and cultural lines and has identity of interests and thus ignores the complexity and multiplicity of women's experiences, subject positions, and "localized specificities of gender inequalities" (Grewal 1999, 340). In the eyes of Miller (2004), the frame has a further weakness. Because it has primarily been associated with gender-based violence, it also reinforces traditional beliefs about women (ibid.).

While the negative consequences of transnationalism reversed have been more vividly discussed in the literature with respect to developing countries, some of the same problems also apply to industrialized ones. A recent study examining the implementation of Security Council Resolution 1325 in Sweden, Great Britain, and Germany, for example, finds that quite often a gap exists between what is officially labeled as gender mainstreaming and what it means in practice. What is portrayed as a progressive instrument is based upon a closer look at traditional interpretations of gender equality. Rarely do the designed instruments attempt more than adding women in or even attempt to target men or boys (Joachim and Schneiker 2012). Nonetheless, governmental actors hail their domestic actions and the leadership they exercise at the international level "as a transformatory triumph" while using the resolution "as a means of coopting gender dynamics in order to preserve the existing gender status quo" (Puechguirbal 2010, 184). Observations such as these raise doubts about how norm implementation has thus far been discussed in the literature, whereby norms are envisioned to spiral down (Risse and Sikkink 1995) to the national level. Instead, they suggest that we need to pay more attention to the messages they carry; how they are appropriated, interpreted, and tailored to local conditions; and how they may reinforce rather than undo existing power structures both nationally as well as internationally. Moreover, the work of Alvarez (2000) with respect to women's transnational organizing in the Latin American context shows that we also need to reflect more on what impact transnationalism reversed has on movement dynamics as she finds contradictory effects. While on one hand transnational activism has provided advocates with "new, internationally sanctioned political scripts they can deploy locally, which unlike the shared feminist movement signifiers...have greater potential political 'resonance' vis-à-vis local policy makers" (16), it has, on the other hand, fueled the growing rift between insiders and outsiders, that is, those who are willing to work and engage with government and international institutions and those who are opposed to it (ibid., 24).

CONCLUSION

Boundaries are hardly as firm and exclusive as they are made out to be. This overview of women's global organizing across time provides ample examples of that. Faced with resistance and opposition in their own countries, activists have seized the opportunities created by international events and through international institutions to mobilize support for their concerns. At the same, they have used global norms and ideas to pry open spaces in their own localities.

Throughout time, linking the global and local has, however, been a source of conflict over how to reconcile different identities or ideas about strategy. Looking back in time therefore not only offers insights as to how the global women's movement has evolved but also may provide useful lessons for current campaigns as to how to negotiate the different levels and how to be cosmopolitan while staying locally rooted.

REFERENCES

Acharya, Amitav. 2004. "How ideas spread: Whose norms matter? Norm localization and institutional change in Asian regionalism."*International Organization* 58: 239–275.

Alvarez, Sonia E. 1998. "Latin American feminisms 'go global': Trends of the 1990s and challenges for the new millenium." In Sonia E. Alvarez, E. Dagnino, and A. Escobar, eds., *Cultures of politics/politics of cultures: Re-visioning Latin American social movements.* Boulder, CO: Westview Press, 294–324.

Alvarez, Sonia E. 1999. "Advocating feminism: the Latin American feminist NGO 'boom.'" *International Feminist Journal of Politics* 1: 181–209.

Alvarez, Sonia E. 2000. "Translating the global: Effects of transnational organizing on local feminist discourses and practices in Latin America." *Meridians* 1: 1–27.

Antrobus, Peggy. 2004. *The global women's movement: Origins, issues and strategies.* London: Zed Books.

Antrobus, Peggy, Sonia Correa, M. de la Fuente, Adrienne Germain, Lois Keysers, B. Madunagu, and Jacqueline Pitanguy. 1993. International Conference on Population and Development (ICPD-Cairo '94): History and process of some initiatives. Buzios, Brazil.

Archer, Clive. 1983. *International Organizations.* London and Boston: Allen and Unwin.

Baden, Sally, and Anne Marie Goetz. 1997. "Who needs [sex] when you can have [gender]?"*Feminist Review* 56: 3–25.

Baumgartner, Frank R., and Bryan D. Jones. 1991. "Agenda dynamics and policy subsystems." *British Journal of Political Science* 53: 1044–1074.

Beckwith, Karen. 2013. "The comparative study of women's movements." In Karen Celis, J. Kantola, L. Weldon and G. Waylen, eds., *Oxford handbook on gender and politics.* Oxford: Oxford University Press.

Berkovitch, Nitza. 1999. *From motherhood to citizenship: Women's rights and international organizations.* Baltimore: The John Hopkins University Press.

Booth, Karen M. "National mother, global whore, and transnational femocrats: The politics of AIDS and the construction of women at the World Health Organization." *Feminist Studies* 24 (1998): 115–139.

Bunch, Charlotte, and Niamh Reilly. 1994. *Demanding accountability: The global campaign and Vienna tribunal for women's human rights.* New Brunswick, NJ: Center for Women's Global Leadership and United Nations Development Fund for Women.

Center for Women's Global Leadership. 1993. *International Campaign for Women's Human Rights, 1992–1992 Report.* New Brunswick, NJ: Center for Women's Global Leadership.

Cohn, Carol. 2008. "Mainstreaming gender in UN Security Policy: A path to political transformation." In Shirin M. Rai and G. Waylen, eds., *Global governance, feminist perspectives*. Basingstoke, UK: Palgrave Macmillan, 185–206.

Cram, Laura. 2001. "Governance 'to go': Domestic actors, institutions and the boundaries of the possible." *Journal of Common Market Studies* 39: 595–618.

Desai, Manisha. 2002. "Transnational solidarity: Women's agency, structural adjustment, and globalization." In Nancy A. Napels and M. Desai, eds., *Women's activism and globalization*. New York: Routledge Press, 15–34.

DuBois, Ellen. 2000. "Woman suffrage: The view from the Pacific." *Pacific Historcal Review* 69: 539–551.

Ewig, Christina, and Myra Marx Ferree. 2013. "Organizing: What's old, what's new? History, trend and issues." In Karen Celis, J. Kantola, L. Weldon and G. Waylen, eds., *Oxford handbook on gender and politics*. Oxford: Oxford University Press.

Fallon, Kathleen M. 2008. *Democracy and the rise of women's movements in sub-Saharan Africa*. Baltimore: John Hopkins University Press.

Fraser, Arvonne. 1987. *The U.N. decade for women: Documents and dialogue*. Boulder, CO: Westview Press.

Friedman, Elisabeth. 1999. "The effects of 'transnationalism reversed' in Venezuela: Assessing the impact of UN global conferences on the women's movement." *International Feminist Journal of Politics* 1: 357–381.

Friedman, Elisabeth J. 2003. "Gendering the agenda: The impact of the transnational women's rights movement at the UN conferences in the 1990s." *Women's Studies International Forum* 26: 313–331.

Gough, Clair, and Simon Shackley. 2001. "The respectable politics of climate change: The epistemic communities and NGOs." *International Affairs* 77: 329–345.

Grewal, Inderpal. 1999. "Women's rights as human rights: Feminist practices, global feminism, and human rights regimes in transnationality." *Citizenship Studies* 3: 337–354.

Grewal, Inderpal, and Caren Kaplan. 2002. *Scattered hegemonies: Postmodernity and transnational feminist practices*. Minneapolis: University of Minneapolis Press.

Ilumoka, Adetoun. 1994. "African women's economic, social and cultural rights— Toward a relevant theory and practice." In Rebecca Cook, *Human rights of women: National and international perspectives*. Philadelphia: University of Pennsylvania Press, 307–325.

International Women's Health Coalition. (IWHC). 1994. *Women's voices 1994. Women's Declaration on Population Policies (In Preparation for the 1994 International Conference on Population and Development)*. New York: International Women's Health Coalition.

Jaquette, Jane S. 1994. *The women's movement in Latin America: Participation and democracy*. Boulder, CO: Westview Press.

Jaquette, Jane S. 1995. "Losing the battle/winning the war: International politics, women's issues, and the 1980 mid-decade conference." In Anne Winslow, ed., *Women, politics and the United Nations*. Westport, CT: Greenwood Press, 45–60.

Jayawardena, Kumari. 1986. *Feminism and nationalism in the third world*. London: Zed Books.

Joachim, Jutta. 2007. *Agenda setting, the UN, and NGOs: Gender violence and reproductive rights*. Washington, DC: Georgetown University Press.

Joachim, Jutta, and Andrea Schneiker. 2012. "Changing discourses, changing practices? Gender mainstreaming and security." *Comparative European Politics* doi:10.1057/cep.2011.35 (23 January 2012).

Kabeer, Naila. 1994. *Reversed realities: Gender hierarchies in development thought.* London: Zed Press.

Keck, Margaret E., and Kathryn Sikkink. 1998. *Activists beyond borders: Advocacy networks in international politics.* Ithaca, NY: Cornell University Press.

Lavrin, Asuncion. 1995. *Women, feminism, and social change in Argentina, Chile, and Uruguay, 1890–1940.* Lincoln: University of Nebraska Press.

Leslie, Agnes Ngoma. 2006. *Social movements and democracy in Africa: The impact of women's struggle for equal rights in Botswana.* London and New York: Routledge.

Lombardo, Emanuela, Petra Meier and Mieke Verloo. 2013. "Policy making." In Karen Celis, J. Kantola, L. Weldon and G. Waylen, eds., *Oxford handbook on gender and politics.* Oxford: Oxford University Press.

Makibaka. 1995. *The gender trap: An imperialist scheme for co-opting the world's women: A critique by the Revolutionary Women of the Philippines of the U.N. draft platform of action, Beijing 1995.* Luzon, Philippines: Makibaka.

Marx Ferree, Myra, and Aili Mari Tripp. 2006. "Preface." In Myra Marx Ferree and A. M. Tripp, eds., *Recognizing transnational feminism.* New York: New York University Press, vii–ix.

Mastrangelo Gittler, Alice. 1996. "Taking hold of electronic communication." *Journal of International Communication* 3: 85–101.

McAdam, Doug, John D. McCarthy, and Mayer N. Zald. 1996. "Introduction: Opportunities, mobilizing structures, and framing processes—Toward a synthetic, comparative perspective on social movements." In Doug McAdam, J. D. McCarthy, and M. N. Zald, eds., *Comparative perspectives on social movements: political opportunities, mobilizing structures, and cultural framings.* New York: Cambridge University Press, 1–22.

Miller, Alice M. 2004. "Sexuality, violence against women and human rights: Women make demands and ladies get protection." *Health and Human Rights* 7: 16–47.

Miller, Carol. 1994. "Geneva—The key to equality: Inter-war feminists and the League of Nations." *Women's History Review* 3: 219–245..

Moghadam, Valentine M. 2005. *Globalizing women: Transnational feminist networks.* Baltimore: Johns Hopkins University Press.

Mohanty, Chandra Talpade. 1991. "Under Western eyes: Feminist scholarship and colonial discourses." In Chandra Talpade Mohanty, A. Russo, and T. Lourdes, eds., *Third world women and the politics of feminism.* Bloomington: Indiana University Press, 51–80.

Napels, Nancy. 2002 "Changing terms of community activism, globalization and the dilemmas of transnational feminist practice." In Nancy A. Naples and M. Desai, eds., *Women's Activism and Globalization: Linking Local Struggles and Transnational Politics.* New York: Routledge, 3–14.

Otto, Dianne. 1996. Non-governmental organizations in the United Nations system: The emerging role of international civil society. *Human Rights Quarterly* 18: 107–141.

Pfeffer, Paula F. 1985. "A whisper in the Assembly of Nations: United States's participation in the international movement of women's rights from the League of Nations to the United Nations." *Women's Studies International Forum* 8: 459–471.

Pietilä, Hilkka. 2007. *The unfinished story of women and the United Nations.* New York: UN Non-Governmental Liason Service.

Porter, Elisabeth J. 2007. *Peacebuilding: Women in international perspective.* London: Routledge.

Prügl, Elisabeth, and Meyer, Mary K. 1999. "Gender in global governance." In Mary K. Meyer and E. Prügl, eds., *Gender politics in global governance.* Lanham, MD: Rowman and Littlefield, 3–16.

Puechguirbal, Nadine. 2010. "Discourses on gender, partriarchy and Resolution 1325: A textual analysis of UN documents." *International Peacekeeping* 17: 172–187.

Razavi, Shahra, and Carol Miller. 1995a. *Gender mainstreaming: A study of efforts by the UNDP, the World Bank and the ILO to institutionalise gender issues.* Geneva: UNRISD.

Razavi, Shara, and Carol Miller. 1995b. "From WID to GAD: Conceptual shifts in the women in development discourse." Geneva: UNRISD/UNDP.

Risse, Thomas, and Kathryn Sikkink. 1995. "The socialization of international human rights norms into domestic practices: Introduction." In Thomas Risse, S. C. Ropp and K. Sikkink, eds., *The power of human rights: International norms and domestic change.* Cambridge: Cambridge University Press, 1–38.

Rupp, Leila J. 1994. "Constructing internationalism: The case of transnational women's organizations, 1888–1945." *American Historical Review* 99: 1571–1600.

Rupp, Leila J., and Verta Taylor. 1999. "Forging feminist identity in an international movement: A collective identity approach to feminism." *Signs: Journal of Women in Culture and Society* 24: 363–386.

Russell, Diana E. H., and Nicole Van de Ven. 1984. *Crimes against women: The Proceedings of the International Tribunal on Crimes Against Women.* East Palo Alto, CA: Frog in the Well.

Sheperd, Laura J. 2008. "Power and authority in the production of United Nations Security Council Resolution 1325." *International Studies Quarterly* 52: 383–404.

Sikkink, Kathryn. 2005. "Patterns of dynamic multilevel governance and the insider-outsider coalition." In Donatella della Porta and S. Tarrow, eds., *Transnational protest and global activism: People, passion, and power.* Lanham, MD: Rowman and Littlefield, 151–174.

Singh, Kirti. 1994. "Obstacles to Women's Rights in India." In Rebecca Cook, ed., *Human rights of women: National and international perspectives.* Philadelphia: University of Pennsylvania Press, 375–396.

Snow, David, E. Burke Rochford, Steven K. Worden, and Robert D. Benford. 1986. "Frame alignment processes, micromobilization and movement participation." *American Sociological Review* 51: 464–481.

Snyder, Margaret. 1995. "The politics of women and development." In Anne Winslow, ed., *Women, politics and the United Nations.* Westport, CT: Greenwood Press, 95–116.

Sperling, Valerie, Myra Marx Ferree and Barbara Risman. 2001 "Constructing Global Feminism: Transnational Advocacy Networks and Russian Women's Activism." *Signs: Journal of Women in Culture and Society* 26: 1155–1186.

Staggenborg, Suzanne. 1999. "The consequences of professionalization and formalization in the pro-choice movement." In Jo Freeman and V. Johnson, eds., *Waves of protest: Social movements in the sixties.* Lanham: Rowman and Littlefield, 99–134.

Stephenson, Caroly M. 1995. "Women's international nongovernmental organizations at the United Nations." In Anne Winslow, ed., *Women, politics and the United Nations.* Westport, CT: Greenwood Press, 135–154.

Stienstra, Deborah. 1994. *Women's movements and international organizations.* New York: St. Martin's Press.

Tarrow, Sidney. 2005. *The new transnational activism.* Cambridge, UK: Cambridge University Press.

Tripp, Aili Mari. 2006. "The evolution of transnational feminisms: Consensus, conflict, and new dynamics." In Myra Marx Ferree and A. M. Tripp, eds., *Global feminism: Transnational women's activism, organizing, and human rights.* New York: New York University Press, 51–75.

Van Allen, Judith. 2001. "Women's rights movements as a measure of African Democracy." *Journal of African and Asian Studies* 36: 63.

Vargas Valente, Virginia, and Cecilia Olea Mauleón. 1998. "El proceso hacia Beijing: reflexiones desde adentro." Virginia Vargas Valente, eds., *Caminos a Beijing: IV Conferencia Mundial de la Mujer en América Latina y el Caribe.* Lima: UNICEF, Ediciones Flora Tristan, UNIFEM, 13–33.

Zwingel, Susanne. 2005. "From intergovernmental negotiations to (sub-) national change." *International Feminist Journal of Politics* 7: 400–424.

PART V

....

PARTICIPATION AND
REPRESENTATION

....

THIS section looks at participation and representation, key aspects of democratic politics and the focus for many feminist demands for equality, empowerment, and inclusion. Although it does not limit its scope of study to Western, liberal, representative democracies, to date much of the gender and politics scholarship has displayed a marked normative preference for what are commonly regarded as democratic values. It is concerned with the fair distribution of decision-making power between both sexes. The main aim of the gender and politics scholarship in this domain of political science is to understand— theoretically and empirically—the processes that lead to exclusion from and inclusion in democratic rights, practices, and institutions. At its core has been a focus on the inclusion of women and gendered issues and interests in governance for, by, and in the name of the people. Moreover, the potential future research agendas that the essays in this section outline require a further expansion of the concept of women with democratic inclusion involving a plurality of subgroups of women.

Given that the usual starting point for thinking about women in the gender and politics scholarship is underrepresentation in participative and representative processes, it is also focused on the study of processes of change. But this approach dichotomizes between women and women's movements as agents of change and political decision-making institutions—like legislatures, governments, political parties, electoral systems, constitutions, and courts—as tools and targets of change. Many studies conclude that institutional change is possible and that in most cases agency and pressure from below are a necessary condition for change. Nevertheless, it is widely recognized that institutions determine to a great extent the route, shape, and scope of such change. As such, many of the most recent studies of gendered patterns of political participation and representation have some sympathy with new institutionalist approaches. Furthermore, many have broadened their focus from women alone to understanding how participation and representation are gendered. So, for example, they also include more analysis of men and men's interests, which hitherto had been somewhat neglected given the dominant focus on women's representation and participation.

An important development in this scholarly field concerns theories and empirical concepts of change: the indicators of improved women's representation and participation and how to measure effectiveness of women's strategies for inclusion and the quality of the representational relationship. A general trend seems to be to move away from one-dimensional indicators like numbers of women in elected assemblies or gender equality clauses in constitutions for measuring change toward more sophisticated concerns with "real-life" political and socioeconomic status and conditions in general. However, this feminist concern with assessing the gendered dimensions of representation and participation poses many challenges that, according to the authors of this section, future research needs to engage with.

The section opens with a wide-ranging chapter on political representation that provides an overall frame for the essays that follow. It situates the issues and challenges that are dealt with in more depth by the essays on different political systems, political parties, electoral systems and courts, law and constitutions. In this essay Sarah Childs and Joni Lovenduski deal with authorized, symbolic, descriptive, and substantive representation but focus on the latter two. It starts with the reasons for the presence of women in representative institutions and the explanations for their underrepresentation, pointing to the importance of party organization, rules, and ideology and introducing the critical mass (and critical acts) debate. Next the chapter discusses differences among women due to party affiliation and intersectionality. Tying into long-standing debates about the concept of *women's interests,* it discusses whether and how differences among women distort the descriptive argument for the representation of women. Childs and Lovenduski point to the importance of institutions "designed with either democracy or women in mind" as sites where representation occurs. These are moreover not limited to elected legislatures and that poses challenging questions about accountability to women (and the women's movement) and contestation by them.

In "Political Systems and Gender," Aili Mari Tripp asks whether the type of political system—democratic, authoritarian, socialist, or hybrid—and within-system diversity matter in promoting gender equality, and, if so, how. In contrast to studies that limit investigating the impact of regime type to the political representation of women in national legislatures, this chapter also considers gender equality outcomes in the economic, social welfare, and cultural arena. Explanations for the importance of regime types and regime change include culture and ideology and capacity of women's organizations to operate politically. Important puzzles for future cross-country comparative research include the need to reach a consensus on patterns of gender equality policies and outcomes to enhance and to obtain a better understanding of why some nondemocratic states enhance gender equality in the absence of popular pressures.

Next, "Party Politics" by Miki Caul Kittilson deals with political parties, which the other chapters in the section all indicate are a key to women's political representation and participation. The first issue dealt with in the chapter is the gender gap in party support, and it draws attention to the exogenous factors influencing women's and men's partisan preferences. Second, the chapter focuses on gendered party organizational structures. It discusses the effectiveness of integration into mainstream party channels, as opposed to the strategy of establishing women's parties or party women's organizations that lobby the party from within for more women candidates, leadership, and substantive issues of concern to women. Also the reasons why and when parties include women and women's issues are discussed pointing to the importance of, among others, parties as a complex set of formal institutions (selection and the importance of networks, ideology, nomination rules, centralization, and fractionalization), as well as to informal institutions. Rightfully reminding the reader that parties (and women) are strategic actors, the chapter discusses party change in favor of women, which, although slow, uneven, and incomplete, is occurring as a complex bottom-up and top-down process with important interparty dimensions (the contagion effect).

The chapter "Electoral Politics" by Mona Lena Krook and Leslie Schwindt-Bayer provides an overview of the gendered impacts of electoral systems. It begins with an account of how electoral systems impact upon candidate emergence, discussing the supply-and-demand model of candidates and how formal and informal institutions shape these in gendered ways. It outlines the empirical studies on the gendered effects of electoral formulas, district and party magnitude, and the ballot structure. Next the chapter deals extensively with electoral gender quotas as a demand-side strategy to increase the number of women in political office, what types exist, why they get adopted, and what effect they have. The effect of quotas and of women's descriptive representation on female legislators' behavior is also discussed with regard to representing women's interests, citizens' attitudes toward political participation, including feelings of trust and legitimacy, and the effect on gender stereotypes.

The final essay in this section is "Judicial Politics and the Courts" by Rachel Cichowski. It deals with feminist jurisprudence, gender and courts, and constitutionalism and human rights. The key question is to what extent is the law a process that enables institutional and real change as opposed to the law as fostering oppression of women. In clarifying first what type of change has been sought, she draws our attention to the developments in feminist theories and jurisprudence, including recent gay and lesbian jurisprudence and gay and lesbian and third-world feminism. The practical implications of these approaches are illustrated for the cases of equality and harm. Next the chapter moves onto law in action and discusses litigation (before national as well as international courts) as a process of change empowering women as well as the limits of litigation. The question of how to bring about change in terms of more gender equality is also posed in relation to constitutions and international human rights. The chapter points at the discrepancy between the widespread feminist mobilization for constitutional reform and the paucity of research on gender and constitutions.

CHAPTER 19

POLITICAL REPRESENTATION

SARAH CHILDS AND
JONI LOVENDUSKI

INTRODUCTION

To understand how and why political representation is so central to feminist politics we first discuss traditional theories of representation. We follow this discussion with a consideration of how gender and politics scholars (most of whom would identify themselves as feminist) have used the term, paying particular attention to continuing debates and controversies. We then briefly summarize the state of scholarship on women's political representation before turning our attention to women's substantive representation—the dimension of representation that has been the focus of attention over the last decade or so. Eight questions that are central to the contemporary research agenda on substantive representation are identified and then discussed in turn.

We contend that the very notion of *representation* tells us that the represented is not present. Prevailing conceptual definitions in any period are shaped by their advocates, who are themselves formed by their political context and priorities. Thus, the meaning of the term political representation is both contingent and contested, a complex combination of elements ill-suited to simple definition or application. The concept has a lengthy pedigree among theorists and practitioners of politics. It became a significant focus of debate in arguments about diversity and identity politics in the late 1980s and 1990s. This followed a couple of decades in which much more was made of participatory democracy (Urbinati and Warren 2008, 393). Traditional political theory makes clear that political representation is paradoxical.

For advocates of democracy, the transition from the ideal of the Athenian city state assemblies to large and populous nations created a problem of democratic participation (Dahl 1989). Above a certain size and territory, there was little possibility that all citizens could participate in their self-government. Political representation solves this problem through its practice of delegating or entrusting the advocacy of citizen interests to a smaller number of individuals who gather in assemblies and make decisions. Most theorists of political representation try to identify its component elements and to specify its core characteristics. They focus on the activities of elected representatives. There are long-standing controversies about the practice of representation, notably over whether elected representatives are delegates of their constituents or their trustees.

The process of understanding the components of political representation led inevitably to an industry of taxonomy construction (Birch 1971; McLean 1991; Rao 1998; Mansbridge 2003). The most influential was Hanna Pitkin's (1967) *The Concept of Representation*. Her four types of representation are (1) authorized, where a representative is legally empowered to act for another; (2) descriptive representation, where the representative stands for a group by virtue of sharing similar characteristics such as race, sex, ethnicity, or residence; (3) symbolic representation, where a leader stands for national ideas; and (4) substantive representation, where the representative seeks to advance a group's policy preferences and interests. Pitkin finds that each has ambiguity and complexity and hence must be accompanied by caveats. Most notable in light of subsequent feminist scholarship is Pitkin's dismissal of descriptive representation. She rejects its key assumption of a link between characteristics and action and believes that a focus on descriptive representation leads to a focus on the characteristics at the expense of attention to the action of representatives. This is of course a logical possibility, but most observers of political representation are all too aware of possible discrepancies between the characteristics of representatives and their actions.

In common with most theorists of her day, Pitkin (1967) did not take up issues of gender. Until fairly recently the assumed political actors, both represented and representative, were implicitly male (Pateman 1988). Only with the emergence of gender and politics scholarship toward the end of the twentieth century were issues of women's representation addressed by political theorists and political scientists. Those who did so were mostly feminists. The subsequent feminist study of political representation has both theoretical and empirical strands. In terms of theory, two books dominate this research: Pitkin's, which was not explicitly gendered; and Anne Phillips's (1995) *The Politics of Presence* which was. The work of these two influential scholars marks a critical shift in the theorization of political representation in the academy. Arguably, after Pitkin no one regarded descriptive representation as important, while after Phillips no one regarded it as unimportant. A considerable scholarship grew around Phillips's idea of a politics of presence (Mansbridge 1999; Young

2002) whereby political deliberation is said to require the participation of key groups if democratically representative decisions are to be made.

Feminist Development of Concepts of Representation

The relative importance, indeed the practical applications and interactions, of two of Pitkin's (1967) concepts of substantive and descriptive have come under close feminist scrutiny. There is relatively little feminist scholarship, theoretical or empirical, on authorized representation. Conceptual and, to a lesser extent, empirical research on symbolic representation is also somewhat limited. For Pitkin, symbols are often arbitrary with no resemblance to the represented. Assessing the adequacy of symbolic representation relies on whether the representative is believed in, a criterion Pitkin found wanting. For feminists the notion that women are symbolically represented when they believe they are, even if all the representatives are men, is intuitively unsatisfactory (Childs 2007, 78; see also Meier and Lombardo 2010, 7). As Phillips (1995) writes, the presence of the formerly excluded signals their political equality (40, 45).

Empirical studies of women's symbolic representation usually take one of three forms. First, and most common, are studies that conceive of symbolic representation in terms of the media representation of women politicians. These examine the amount of coverage women politicians receive relative to men, the dominance of stereotypical representations, and sex-specific narratives that frame women politicians, for example, the *first-woman* or *newcomer* frames (Childs 2008). Second are studies that investigate the role model effect of women politicians. These empirical studies to date offer mixed findings both for women's psychological engagement, levels of political interest, attention, and efficacy and political activism such as joining a party or campaigning (Campbell and Wolbrecht 2006). Recent research has found that the presence of high-profile and viable women politicians positively affects younger women's expectations that they will participate in politics, not least through girls' enhanced discussion of politics, and to increased discussion of politics among women of all ages (ibid; Wolbrecht and Campbell 2007). Yet other studies find no association. Zetterberg's (2008) research on Latin America, for example, finds little relationship between sex quotas and women's levels of political interest, trust in politicians or political parties, and perceptions of political knowledge. It appears, then, that the relationship between symbolic and descriptive representation (the relationship between the presence of women in politics and women at the mass level) is more complicated than feminists may have wished. Finally, the least developed work on symbolic representation is research that subjects political symbols to gendered analysis and considers women as political symbols. Calling for a discursive turn, Meier and Lombardo (2010) hold that symbols are not merely visual. Hence, scholars should examine the ways women and men are symbolically represented (in their terms, *constructed* and *ranked*) through metaphors, stereotypes, frames, and underlying norms and values in constitutions, laws, judicial decisions, treaties, administrative regulations, and public policies as well as in more traditional symbols such as national flags, images, public buildings, public spaces, and statues.

Of the two dimensions of representation most extensively explored by feminists, the research agenda has gradually shifted from a focus on descriptive representation (counting the numbers of women present) to considerations of substantive representation and the relationship between the two. Descriptive representation was a central interest for gender and politics scholars so long as there was not very much of it to examine. But as the numbers of women in elected legislatures grew it became possible to ask other questions, not least about what women representatives did once they were present. For many feminists the claim that women's political presence will engender women's substantive representation, even if accompanied by qualifications and caveats, is appealing. They reason that gendered experiences will underpin women representatives' greater tendency to act for women. Over time empirical studies have become more sophisticated, reflecting a change in the central research question from "when women make a difference" to "how the substantive representation of women occurs" (Childs and Krook 2008).

In addition to developments in gender and politics research on substantive representation political theorists, both feminist and mainstream, began to talk about representation in terms of claims making. Representatives—who may or may not be elected—are regarded as making claims to know what constitutes the interests of those they seek to represent (Saward 2006; Squires 2008; Urbinati and Warren 2008). Feminist reactions to these and other constitutive theories of representation (Mansbridge 2003; Celis et al. 2008; Disch 2011) have been largely favorable, although debates and questions remain. For example, does claims making constitute substantive representation in and of itself? Is a representative who claims to act for women, really acting for women? How might one evaluate between competing claims to act for women? (Celis 2008; Severs 2010; Celis and Childs 2011). Do such notions of representation, taken to the extreme, accord with Pitkin's (1967) concerns over fascist theories of representation—where "the leader must force his followers to adjust themselves to what he does" (107).

Gender and politics scholarship is characterized not only by its dominant feminism but also its common concern to conceptualize representation in such a way that its practice can be systematically assessed. The extensive body of work highlights and attempts to correct the neglected interconnections among all of Pitkin's (1967) categories (Schwindt-Bayer and Mischler 2005) focuses on the relationships between substantive and descriptive representation (Lovenduski 2005a; Bratton and Ray 2002), reformulates Pitkin's categories in the light of feminist theories of representation and the requirements for research on the United States (Dovi 2007), and proposes new categories to take into account the requirements of deliberative democracy (Mansbridge

2003). Arguably iterative, the tensions in the relationships between theoretical and empirical gender and politics research have been remarkably productive. And while to some extent feminist empirical and theoretical work on representation proceeds along separate paths, both strands are sites of considerable debate about the significance of descriptive representation and its connections to substantive representation and more recently of symbolic representation (Meier and Lombardo 2010). For example, if women are symbolically represented as marginal to politics, or lacking legitimacy or effectiveness (the "woman-politician-pretender" juxtaposed to the "male-politician-norm"), then this may negatively affect both their chances of being present in our political institutions (descriptive representation), as well as their abilities to act for women (substantive representation) once there (Meier and Lombardo 2010). As Celis (2008, 71) writes, feminist scholars reject any clear-cut separation between, or hierarchy of, the various dimensions of representation. For her, representation refers to the making present of women, in at least one sense: formally, descriptively, symbolically, or substantively (Celis 2008, 80).

In the remainder of this essay we consider the interplay and relative importance of substantive and descriptive representation. We draw on a set of linked questions developed by various scholars as they operationalized the concept of political representation for empirical research (Celis et al. 2008; Lovenduski and Gaudagnini 2010; Dovi 2007, 2010). There are eight questions:

1. Why should women be represented?
2. Who are the representatives of women?
3. Which women are represented?
4. Where does the representation of women occur?
5. How is the substantive representation of women done?
6. When does the representation take place?
7. To whom are representatives accountable?
8. How effective is the (claimed) representation?

Why Should Women Be Represented?

There are three main arguments for why women should be representatives in our elected political institutions. The powerful justice argument is mobilized wherever women claim political representation and contends that it is simply unfair for men to dominate descriptive representation, a claim that is especially telling in countries that purport to be democratic, or modern. Pragmatic arguments stress the electoral advantage of increasing the numbers of women representatives, namely, that political parties will be perceived as more women friendly and, as a result, attract women's votes. Difference arguments are of two kinds: (1) that women will bring a different style and approach to politics than men; (2) that women are a heterogeneous group who require equal descriptive representation if their diversity is to be reflected in decision making. Only the justice argument makes no claims about substantive representation. The pragmatic and difference arguments both imply that women's presence will improve their substantive representation.

Despite reservations about a researchable concept of women's interests and the complexities of constructing a "women's" policy agenda (question 3 below), most feminist political scientists are attracted to the potential of descriptive representation to deliver at least a measure of substantive representation and make (highly qualified) arguments to support this belief. For example, the "transformative" argument predicts that increasing the presence of women will change politics by improving the democratic functioning of legislatures (Phillips 1998). This approach assumes that women representatives will behave in a more democratic fashion and will pay more attention to political inequalities than men. The "overlooked interests" argument is that "male representatives are not always aware of how pubic policies affect female citizens" (Dovi 2007, 307–309). In a similar vein Jane Mansbridge (1999) argues that descriptive representation can be justified in four contexts: contexts of mistrust; uncrystallized, not fully articulated interests; historical political subordination; and low de facto legitimacy. The implication of her first two arguments is that some kind of a link exists between substantive and descriptive representation. Since Phillips (1995) argued so effectively for a politics of presence, feminists have contended that a necessary condition of the representation of women's interests (however these might be defined) is the presence of women in our political institutions and other places where decisions are made. Phillips reasons that interests are realized in the course of deliberation and decision making as various options, implementation strategies, and competing concerns are discussed. Only when present may women benefit from such realization and insert their interests. While the logic of Phillips's claim is inescapable it has proved more difficult to demonstrate that the representation of women's interests necessarily follows from the presence of women representatives in a particular institution, although a great deal of circumstantial evidence that this is the case has been assembled and presented. Laurel Weldon (2002, 1156) points out that the presence of individual women is insufficient to guarantee the substantive representation of women because "individuals can rarely provide a complete account or analysis of the obstacles confronting the group without interacting with others from the group."

Who Are the Representatives of Women?

The short answer to this question is men. In most of the world's legislatures the overwhelming majority of elected representatives are men. The average percentage of women in lower houses of Parliament, as of 2010, is a mere 19.3 percent (http://www.ipu.org/wmn-e/world.htm). In only one country—Rwanda—do

Table 19.1 Women's Representation in National Parliaments, 1997 and 2010

Region	Lower House, 1997	Lower House, 2010	% Increase
Nordic Countries	35.9%	42.1%	6
Europe—OSCE member including Nordic	14.3%	22.0%	6
Americas	13.5%	22.5%	8
Asia	9.7%	18.6%	9
Europe, excluding Nordic	12.3%	20.1%	8
Sub-Saharan Africa	10.8%	18.3%	7
Pacific	12.8%	13.2%	0
Arab States	3.7%	9.2%	5

Source: http://www.IPU.org.

women constitute more than half of the members, even though women constitute more than half of the world's population. Fewer than twenty-five countries worldwide meet the United Nations (UN) criterion that a minimum of 30 percent women should be present in the legislature.[1] Moreover, women's descriptive representation is not universal. Women are absent from the legislatures of nine countries: Belize, Micronesia, Nauru, Palau, Oman, Qatar, Saudi Arabia, Solomon Islands, and Tuvalu.

The overall global trend for women's descriptive representation in national parliaments is upward, despite widely reported falls in postcommunist countries, individual fluctuations within particular countries, and stagnation in others. But recent increases are neither large nor decisive. Over the last decade the global average has increased by just 6 percent. Table 19.1 shows the regional increases between 1997 and 2010, at best the increase is 9 percent over more than a decade and in the Pacific region there has been little change. Global and regional averages mask significant intraregional differences. The top ten ranking countries, as of December 2010, are as follows: Rwanda, 56.3 percent; Sweden, 46.4 percent; South Africa, 44.5 percent; Cuba, 43.2 percent; Iceland, 42.9 percent; Netherlands, 40.7 percent; Finland, 40 percent; Norway, 39.6 percent; Belgium, 39.3 percent; Mozambique, 39.2 percent.[2]

Analyses that focus on the total number of women in a particular legislature have been criticized for failing to acknowledge within-country differences (Kittilson 2006). Different political parties within the same country may well return different proportions of women representatives. In the United Kingdom, for example, women's descriptive representation is asymmetric as the Labour Party returns most of the women Members of Parliament (MPs).

What explains low numbers of women in politics? Various cultural, socio-economic, and political factors and conditions have been identified in analysis of advanced Western democracies. More egalitarian cultures, greater secularization, and early women's enfranchisement are said to be positively correlated with higher numbers of women representatives (cultural factors). Other predictors are the level of women's participation in the public sphere, in the pipeline professions from which politicians are recruited, and a strong social democratic tradition (socioeconomic factors). Finally, the presence of majoritarian electoral systems is thought to hinder, whereas proportional electoral systems, especially those with higher district magnitude, favor greater numbers of women (political factors). All of these explanations find some empirical support, but none appears to be either a necessary or sufficient condition of women's representation (Dahlerup and Freidenvall 2010). The use of sex quotas is positively correlated with, but not a guarantee of, higher levels of women representation (see also the chapter by Mona Lena Krook and Leslie Schwindt-bayer in this volume).

The geographic and temporal specificity of many explanatory factors has also been shown to be significant. Mona Lena Krook's (2010) analysis of women's descriptive representation in Western democracies and in sub-Saharan Africa concludes that women's descriptive representation reflects different combinations of conditions and that the effect of individual conditions may be mediated by or dependent upon the presence or absence of others. For example, in sub-Saharan Africa, higher levels of women's descriptive representation are not affected by the type of electoral system but are associated with (1) the presence of quotas and postconflict situations, (2) women's high status and postconflict situations, or (3) quotas, women's low status, and high levels of development (Krook 2010, 902). Low levels of representation are associated with (1) no quotas and women's low status, (2) women's high status and nonpostconflict societies, or (3) low levels of development and nonpostconflict societies (Lovenduski 2005a; Krook 2010, 903).

Within countries political party organization, rules and ideology can variously determine the rules of the game including the legal, electoral, and party systems (Norris and Lovenduski 1995; Kenny and Mackay 2009) (see also the chapter by Miki Kittilson in this volume). In simple language, the numbers of women selected as legislative candidates will be determined by the interaction between the *supply* of applicants wishing to pursue a political career and the *demands* of selectors who choose candidates on the basis of their preferences and perceptions of abilities, qualifications, and perceived electability (Norris and Lovenduski 1995). The supply-and-demand model assessment of sex and gender differences indicates first that women's resources will be fewer, smaller, and different from men's, thereby reducing the number of women in the supply pool for candidate selection Second, women may experience negative discrimination when they seek selection. Accordingly, the political marketplace is distorted and unlikely to produce an equilibrium solution (Krook 2009, 4).

While the requirements of descriptive representation are at least superficially straightforward in that only women can descriptively represent women, those of substantive representation are more complicated. Much feminist theory (Phillips 1995; Mansbridge 1999; Dovi 2002) suggests that women's substantive representation is much more likely to be undertaken by the (relatively few) women representatives present in legislatures. Two concepts are used to predict substantive representation: critical mass and critical acts. Critical mass is a term borrowed from physics by Rosabeth Moss Kanter (1977) to assess change in organizations. The term is usually understood to hold that, once women constitute a particular proportion of a parliament, politics will be transformed because a tipping point of some kind is reached (Studlar and McAllister 2002). But this reading does not capture the subtleties of feminist treatment of the concept. Dahlerup's (1988) classic (and often misquoted) article argues that it is not critical mass or the numbers of women who are present but critical acts that are important. Her insight shifts the focus of the argument from an emphasis on presence to scrutiny of what happens when women are present to what else happens when the numbers of women change. It is an argument for the consideration of substantive representation that does not deny the significance of presence.

Recent scholarship suggests that critical actors may, even when the numbers are small, undertake critical acts for women (Dahlerup 1988; Childs and Krook 2006, 2008). What distinguishes a critical actor from other representatives is their relatively low threshold for action. They are motivated, possibly by their feminism, possibly by a looser less explicit gendered experience, to initiate the substantive representation of women (Childs and Krook 2006). This understanding does not rule out the possibility that individual male representatives might well have acted for women in the past and may well do so today. But it does require feminist researchers to consider fully the contexts in which representation takes place. Representatives who act for or claim to act for women are not limited to our elected legislatures. Representation takes place in a variety of other fora, either separate from or in addition to political ones (Celis et al. 2008). Future research should explore the interactions between these different kinds of representatives.

Which Women Are Represented?

This complex question is closely related to the who (2) and the what (4) questions. The central issues are both descriptive and substantive. Here we ask what kind of women our elected representatives are, and we acknowledge the contested nature of the concept of women's interests (which we address in the next section). The case for descriptive representation weakens when we consider which women become elected representatives. They rarely share social backgrounds with women in the electorate; this is a pattern that also holds for men but one that is not often problematized. European women elected representatives are more likely to be highly educated, middle-class, elite women (Mateo Diaz 2005). Yet the politically salient differences among women are as substantial as those among men and include class, ethnicity, race, religion, age, group memberships, party affiliations, marital status, children at home, school, other dependents, employment status, right- and left-wing women, and feminist and antifeminist women.

Feminist scholars frequently capture difference by framing in terms of the concept of intersectionality (Weldon 2006), according to which various bases of oppression interact in multiple forms of discrimination against women (see also the chapter by Patricia Hill Collins and Valerie Chepp in this volume). Although women's heterogeneity, and how it might affect conceptions of representation, is quite well theorized (see Phillips 1995; Young 2002; Dovi 2007), there is relatively little data on the representation of the various social categories of women, and what there is tends to reflect the political culture of the country in which the data are collected. Political party differences have generally received the greatest attention. Thus, we have good information on the presence of women from different political parties in most countries, on race and ethnicity in the United States, on race and class in the United Kingdom, and on caste in India, but relatively poor information on other aspects of difference. Difference itself can be politically sensitive, sometimes too sensitive to be officially recorded. In post-genocide Rwanda, for example, the election of a majority of women to the legislature is held to be an indication that tribal divisions are being healed, but it is illegal to ascribe tribal identity to anyone.

Demographic distortions in the mirror of representation have been used against claims for women's political presence. In the Anglo-American democracies divisions of both race and class inform the counter argument that women's descriptive representation means effectively the presence only of white, middle-class, elite women. Historically, European socialist men opposed women's suffrage and women's movements for much the same reason (Lovenduski 1986). In India the movement for women's political representation was criticized for the failure of its middle-class leaders to form alliances with lower-caste women. Htun (2004) takes up this point when she argues that candidate quotas are the suitable solution for women's descriptive underrepresentation while reserved places are best for minority ethnic groups. Thus, when reserved places are used to promote women they risk division in minority communities. Indeed, during the Indian movement for women's political representation a prominent politician said the relevant bill was for *balkati auraten,* or short-haired women, a reference to upper-class urban feminists (448). In short, difference continues to be a huge problem for feminists who deny the unitary category of *women* as essentialist and aim to represent women's diversity in politics, a condition that has yet to be achieved by men. In summary, if different groups of women experience inequality differently, they may well have different interests to be represented. Thus, it is only when at least the salient differences among women are mirrored by their elected representatives that there is real purchase in the descriptive argument.

Shifting our attention from descriptive to substantive representation, we find charges that, in practice, substantive representation is merely the representation of elite women's interests. But the concept of *women's interests* has proved contentious for gender and politics scholars. Feminists have variously sought to identify women's objective and subjective interests (Sapiro 1998), have rejected the concept in favor of need (Diamond and Hartsock 1998), have tried to avoid the opposition of need and interest by favoring being present (Jonasdottir 1990), or have preferred the term *women's concerns* (Cockburn 1996) or *women's perspectives* (Lovenduski 2005a). As Celis (2005, 2008) helpfully notes, these terms capture the private distribution of labor, for example, women's roles in giving birth and caring for children (Sapiro 1998), and emphasize the role of the gendered division of productive labor (Diamond and Hartsock 1998) or refer to perspectives that derive from women's structural position in society (Phillips 1995; Young 2002; Lovenduski 2005). A recent four-country comparison suggests drawing a distinction between women's issues (the broad policy category such as the reconciliation of work and family life) and women's interests (the specific content given to this category by various actors). Although there was some agreement over what constitutes women's issues across the United Kingdom, Finland, Belgium, and the United States—equal pay and violence against women, for example—others were more country specific, such as women's access to sport in the United States. Celis et al. (2009) concluded therefore that, in addition to the contested nature of women's interests, what constitutes women's issues varies over time and between different countries.

In empirical studies two main approaches to operationalizing women's interests are found (Celis 2005, 2008). In the first, women's interests are subjectively defined by the researcher as either those traditionally associated with women (such as child caring and the family) or those with a feminist accent (such as abortion or domestic violence). This approach suffers according to Celis from a tendency to essentialize women, which is theoretically untenable and undermines feminist concerns about heterogeneity and intersectionality. It risks both ignoring differences between women at a particular place and time as well as failing to recognize that women's interests may vary significantly across spaces and time. The second approach looks to the demands of the contemporary women's movement to identify women's interests (Celis 2005, 2008; McBride and Mazur 2010). This approach can be challenged on the grounds that it privileges women's movement, that is, feminist, concerns. It also assumes that women's movements are free to articulate their demands. For these reasons Celis et al. (2008) contend that we would do better to acknowledge that women's concerns are a priori undefined, context related, and subject to evolution. Another danger of the vexed problem of understanding women's interests is the temptation to conflate women's interests with feminists' understanding of women's interests (Schreiber 2008). Only more recently have gender and politics scholars begun to address explicitly the challenge posed by conservative and antifeminist representatives who claim to act for women (Celis and Childs 2011).

The difficulties of establishing a nonessentialist set of women's concerns have not in practice prevented feminists from advocating specific policies for women. A feminist policy agenda can be constructed by reviewing research that proceeds from feminist definitions. This agenda includes equal pay and equal treatment at work, reproductive rights including abortion, child care and domestic labor, sexual freedom, violence against women, prostitution and trafficking, female genital mutilation, and political representation.[3] The Research Network on Gender and the State (RNGS), an international network of feminist scholars researching state feminism and feminist policy in Western democracies, analyzed five policy areas: job training; prostitution; abortion; political representation; and the gendering of a major issues. The gendering of a key contemporary issue was included in recognition of the fact that women have interests in mainstream policies.[4] Franceschet and Piscopo's (2008) study of substantive representation in Argentina argues that promoting gender quotas, penalizing sexual harassment, and combating violence against women are matters of women's interests. One reason for such common policy concerns across countries may be the transmission of collective women's issues via international women's movements and feminist activists and international actors such as the UN. The Convention on the Elimination of All Forms of Discrimination against Women (CEDAW), adopted in 1979 by the UN General Assembly, and the Beijing Platform for Action (1995) stand out in this respect.[5] CEDAW addresses, inter alia, prostitution (Article 6), political representation, (Article 7), education (Article 10), employment (Article 11), women's health (Article 12), women's economic and social benefits (Article 13), and marriage and family life (Article 16). Beijing 1995 addressed, inter alia, women's poverty, education, health, violence against women, conflict, economic inequality, power sharing and politics, women's human rights, and the rights of the girl child.[6] Another important qualification to presence effects is found in the interplay between party and sex. Many studies have found that party affiliation explains more than sex (Norris 1986; Norris and Lovenduski 1995; Lovenduski and Norris 2003 Dodson 2006; Kittilson 2006), particularly in highly visible, confrontational and partisan settings. Moreover, it is very often women members of left-leaning parties rather than women representatives from the rest of the political spectrum who make the most effort to raise women's issues and concerns.

Where Does the Representation of Women Take Place?

Representation occurs in institutions. Institutions, defined as rules and processes, shape debate and decision making not least by determining who is and is not a representative and how, where, and when decisions are made. These institutions may or may not have been designed with either democracy or women in mind. Feminist institutionalist research has specifically explored the place of women and women's advocates in political institutions. The work considers the configurations of systemic (electoral and party systems), practical (formal and informal criteria for candidate selection and method of ballot composition), and normative institutions (norms of equality and representation) to establish whether they facilitate or hinder women's descriptive representation (Krook 2009; see also Kenny and Mackay 2009) and if they affect women's substantive representation (Wängnerud 2000; Lovenduski 2005; Dodson 2006; Mackay et al. 2008; Lovenduski and Guadagnini 2010; McBride and Mazur 2010).

To date most studies emphasize the role of elected legislatures, which often confirm decisions made elsewhere and not necessarily by electorally accountable officials. Appointed government and other public bodies, political parties, economic organizations such as trade unions, professional and employer organizations, firms, nongovernmental organizations (NGOs), social movements, the print, broadcasting, and electronic media have been shown to play a part in political decision making and are arenas in which women have sought presence. Only a fraction of these positions are directly elected, many are appointed, and some are self-selected. A number of feminist scholars have attempted to research representation beyond legislatures and have looked at executives, agencies, parties, and social organizations of various kinds (Breitenbach 1981; Karvonnen and Selle 1995; Bergqvist 1999; Annesley 2010; McBride and Mazur 2010). The composition of their corporate bodies, the committees that exercise decision making power over most aspects of political life, were a huge concern for Nordic scholars and activists who identified gender gaps in representation and operated to implement various kinds of quotas policies in public appointments to correct such imbalances (Hernes and Vole 1980; Karvonnen and Selle 1995; Bergqvist 1999). Note that as we write (summer 2012) Belgium has introduced quotas for women on boards and commissions.[7] The most sustained research on state appointments and agencies has concentrated on the established democracies of the political West, but there is a growing literature on other political systems (Weldon 2002; Waylen 2007; Goetz 2009) (see also the chapter by Aili Mari Tripp in this volume).

The political system or country in which the debate takes place, the institutional sites (especially their proximity to power) on which it is conducted and the bases from which its participants operate all affect representation. In Western and Northern European democratic systems research finds a consistent relationship between citizenship type and the percentage of women in the lower house, a predictable effect of tendency for corporatist and quasi-corporatist systems to have relatively high numbers of women in parliament and a positive association of citizenship model, legislator presence, and the tendency for women legislators to intervene in debates on selected women's issues (Krook, Lovenduski, and Squires 2009; Lovenduski and Guadagnini 2010). Theories of public policy suggest that influence varies according to the policy sector under consideration, a finding that holds for women's advocacy. Access to the policy subsystem is a crucial group resource. Research on the old democracies indicates considerable variation in both institutionalization and the effectiveness of the actors who are present (Lovenduski and Guadagnini 2010; McBride and Mazur 2010).

Where policy systems are closed, women's advocates are especially dependent on interventions by legislators (Lovenduski and Guadagnini 2010). In terms of constitutional arrangements it is clear that important decisions are eventually, at least formally, decided in the legislature. Legislators are constrained by party discipline and party manifestos, institutions that historically are dominated by men and male concerns. In such systems women's movements and officials appointed to represent women may actually have more scope to represent women than elected legislators bound by party discipline (Lovenduski and Norris 1993; Cowley and Childs 2003; Guadagnini 2007).

Even so, in party democracies the activism and effectiveness of women's advocates in political parties is one of the crucial determinants of the quality of their representatives (Lovenduski 2005; Kittilson 2006; Childs 2008). Research on women's advocates in executives and governments is a relatively new subfield, but there is scattered evidence that women's advocates at least attempt to intervene. Recent British examples include interventions in cabinet by Clare Short, Patricia Hewitt, Harriet Harman, and Yvette Cooper, all of whom are reported to have acted to raise women's issues (Childs 2008; Annesley 2010).

How Is Substantive Representation Done?

What are the processes through which women's claims are formulated, refined, and advanced? A central question is what happens when women's presence is achieved. How, if at all, do representatives claim and act for women? There are problems in researching this question. Beyond analyses of roll-call voting, much of the process of representing an interest in our elected political institutions and other institutions may be hidden from view, a matter of behind-the-scenes organizing and influence and hence expensive and difficult to research in any systematic way. Given concerns about the limits of using roll-call voting, in which party tends to explain more than sex, investigations of the attitudes, policy priorities, and initiatives made by women legislators have become common. This work generally finds that women legislators are more likely to act for women than men (Bratton and Haynie 1999; Ayata and Tutuncu 2008; Wängnerud 2000; Swers 2002, 2005; Taylor-Robinson and Heath 2003) but that women may be marginalized into certain soft policy areas including women's committees. Hence, there is considerable recognition that women must change the institutions they enter (Heath, Schwindt-Bayer, and Taylor-Robinson 2005). While it is impossible to disagree with such conclusions they place a huge, and additional, burden on women representatives (Lovenduski 2005)—downplaying the fact that any "parliament has a strong regulating capacity, its own logic, a strong inertia, very little room for innovation, and many ways to socialise or assimilate 'dissidents'" (Mateo Diaz 2005, 225).

Within decision-making processes, one of the most common techniques used by women's advocates is framing (see also the chapter by Emanuela Lombardo, Petra Meier and Mieke Verloo in this volume). Women's representatives put forward explicitly gendered ideas in attempts to frame or reframe a debate so that its discourse is gendered or regendered in line with women's interests. These gendered frames may be, but are not necessarily, feminist. Most issues have gender dimensions as they implicitly or explicitly reflect some notion of relations between women and men and masculinity and femininity. The strategy of framing exposes the biases of debates by drawing attention to their gendered content or offering a regendering of an already explicitly gendered frame. Women's representatives have become skilled at these processes, which are central to their political repertoires. In addition, movement actors engage in and frequently initiate consultative relationships with political institutions that may establish consultative groups that include movement actors. Contribution to policy research by expert movement actors is one of several forms of lobbying and a major site of framing. It feeds into deliberation in terms of content and discourse hence is an attempt to gender subsequent debate (Skjeie 1993; Mazur 2001; Stetson 2001; Outshoorn 2004; McBride and Mazur 2010; Sauer 2010).

Finally, women's advocates go into coalition with other actors, making alliances both within movements and between movements, civil society, and the state. Feminist research reveals policy cooperation between women's policy agencies and movement advocates located in different arena such as autonomous women's movements, the media, political parties, trade unions, legislatures, government, and public administration. The literature includes discussions of strategic partnerships between women's movements and women's policy machinery (Holli and Kantola 2005) (see also the chapter by Dorothy E. McBride and Amy Mazur in this volume). A common metaphor is that of the triangle, capturing the idea of an alliance between movements, state, and some other entity. Although there is no agreement on the definition of the triangle, its components or its strategic location, most include state actors, legislators, and women's movement actors who are linked to each other through different organizations and political processes (Vargas and Wieringa 1998; Halsaa 1999; Mazur 2002; Woodward 2003).

Thus, for the most part women's advocates use the standard operating procedures of the political system in which they are acting. Arguably they are operating through most of the known channels of influence and using the full range of techniques. But despite some evidence of institutional change, they do so from a disadvantaged position in relation to established (usually masculine) actors.

When Does the Representation Take Place?

Although very little attention has been paid to this question to date, it deserves a place on the research agenda. Political memoires and biographies often include accounts of the importance of time and timing in terms of both strategy and tactics. Yet representation scholars rarely give time systematic attention, although some researchers advocate and employ research designs that arguably better capture the processes of substantive representation (Dodson 2006; Celis et al. 2008). Political time is complex. We know, for example, that time is a resource for elected politicians and that women, on average, have less of it than men. This facet of time is most frequently addressed in respect of women's descriptive representation, as a supply side barrier to women's equal presence (Norris and Lovenduski 1995). In respect of substantive representation, two dimensions of timing look to be particularly important and worthy of subsequent research: (1) *juxtaposition,* examples of which include connection to other issues, proximity to election years, the phases of the world and national economy, the public opinion cycle, and the timetable of the decision process; and (2) *sequence,* for example, whether an attempt to act on a particular issue is followed by victory or defeat for women's advocates or if a claim is an obvious extension of a previously enacted policy. A classic example of juxtaposition is the insertion of a ban on sex discrimination in the U.S. 1964 Civil Rights Act in which an amendment extending rights for women was added to the bill by southern Democrat Virginian congressman Judge Howard Smith who hoped (wrongly) that this would sufficiently increase opposition to the bill to prevent its enactment (Meehan 1985). Sequence is illustrated by the extension of the public sector duty, previously limited to racial minorities and disabled people, to promote sex equality in the British Equal Rights Act of 2010 and the successive Equality and Anti Discrimination Directives of the European Union that extended the rights of women (and other groups) over a period of three decades.

To Whom Are the Representatives Accountable?

For Pitkin (1967, 11), accountability is "the holding to account of the representative for his actions." Here we confront another contradiction of a representative democracy. On one hand, representatives must be able to act; on the other, they must account for those actions. In short, accountability theory claims that genuine representation exists only where there are effective, transparent controls that make the representative responsible to the represented (57). Accountability theory may be used to falsify claims that even those who are not allowed to vote are virtually represented (for example, that prefranchise women were represented by male heads of household).

In democracies, regular, fair and free elections are a crucial form of accountability and the nonnegotiable component of democracy. Yet the problem of how best to institutionalize accountability into a modern democratic political structure in which elections are crucial but do not yield detailed policy mandates remains. At the system level, accountability is a function of the institution in which representatives act. So, where movement actors are in the legislature they are accountable to their electorate, their parties, and their constituencies; where they are in trade unions to their members and co-workers; in parties to their fellow members, but also more indirectly to the electorate and to the interests that are the basis of party support.

While particular elected representatives may be accountable to women's movements at the level of ideas, constitutions do not normally provide for direct accountability of elected or appointed representatives to women's movements, even where they may have been influential in getting women selected and elected and appointed to positions in the executive or getting agencies established and are often involved in the formal or informal nomination of leaders. There are exceptions. Some equality agencies are committees of movement representatives or included designated places for some movement representatives (Guadagnini and Donà 2007). Even so, many elected women representatives feel an obligation to represent women (Childs 2004; Mateo Diaz 2005). When they intervene on issues that are women's movement priorities and make claims that are congruent with feminist or women's movement demands, representatives are trying to represent women by forwarding movement ideas to decision makers. But are they accountable to women even though crucial elements of accountability are missing? We think not.

Accountability is a largely unexplored dimension of feminist representation research, some of which can be read as a catalogue of justifications for demands for the accountability of state actors to women's movements. But that is not how democratic political systems are constructed. Accountability is normally provided for by imperfect formally democratic processes in which movement voices are absorbed into aggregating electoral politics that were not designed to take account of the interests of women. Women's movements aim to correct the resulting imbalances, but their effectiveness is limited by the nature of the systems in which they operate (Lovenduski and Guadagnini 2010). There is very little feminist political representation theory that acknowledges this problem in real political systems. Mansbridge's (2003) discussion is a rare exception but one that presupposes a system of loose party discipline. Hence, it is not applicable to the cases of party government in which voters have little choice of candidate and legislators are subject to party discipline that are characteristic of European democracies or where legislator deliberation is not decisive. Even where there is provision for accountability of officials to women's movements, it is rarely direct. The provision for accountability in most political systems depends upon channels that predate demands for women's inclusion, thus adding to the layers of institutional insulation of male elites. Perhaps, as Dodson (2006, 22) argues, feminists have been (too) content to accept the actions of women representatives because for the most part they have been "consistent with what feminist scholars believe is the appropriate direction policy should take." Unfortunately, that is no longer, if it ever was, a sustainable position, particularly when conservative and antifeminist women are present in political institutions.

How Effective Is the (Claimed) Women's Representation?

Good representation requires that the represented are made present. As we write there is some agreement that women's representation is effective when they are sufficiently present in institutions and when attempts at substantive representation are made. Good representation exists along a continuum from "non-representation—[to]—representation" (Celis 2008, 82). It is, however, difficult to specify much further. It cannot satisfactorily be argued that certain interests are women's interests a priori. And even if it could, we cannot yet tell exactly how increasing the numbers of women affects their representation. Counting the number of women in a particular institution at a particular time establishes the level of women's descriptive representation and permits comparison over time and place.[8] Data on the sex of political representatives are readily available (http://www.ipu.org). Low numbers of women are a common basis for claims for minimum requirements or quotas of women's presence. Parity of women and men should be the standard. Any figure below that is arbitrary and risks the unintended consequence of creating a glass ceiling (Trimble and Arscott 2003). Accordingly the demands for *greater representation* have changed to demands for *parity* or sex *balance* with provision for intersectionality.

While the measurement of descriptive representation is relatively straightforward, its relationship with substantive representation is more opaque. Numerous mediating factors, identified in a range of studies, are found to affect representatives' actions (see Dodson 2006). Often identified in the very same literature that finds some presence effects, they include the external political environment, institutional norms, the impact of party affiliation, ideology and cohesion, differences among women representatives, representatives' newness, institutional position, including front- and back-bench and government or opposition membership, committee appointment and leadership, women's caucus presence, the existence of a women's policy machinery, and the vagaries of policy making.[9] The attitudes and behavior of women and men may converge (Swers 2002, 10), as gender roles alter, or because women's presence within legislatures causes men to act for women (Reingold 2000, 50; Mateo Diaz 2005). Contemporary gender and politics scholarship also acknowledges the multiple sites and actors involved in women's substantive representation (see Weldon 2002) and argues that the substantive representation of women is likely to take place at different and interacting levels of political institutions and in a variety of political and other fora (Celis et al. 2008). In sum, representatives are increasingly regarded as acting in complicated institutional settings and wider political contexts that must themselves be subject to analysis (Lovenduski 2005; *Politics & Gender* 2009).

Institutional analysis may also further qualify conclusions about the achievements of substantive representation. What looks like not very much substantive representation may, in fact, be quite considerable given the effort needed to achieve feminized change in a particular setting (Childs 2008, 170; Dodson 2006, 29).

For some scholars, substantive representation is confirmed when representatives *routinely* act for women and bring women's perspectives to political debate; for others the inclusion of a *diversity* of women's interests is required (Trimble 1993, 1997, 2000; Celis 2008, 83). Yet others look to notions of congruency between the represented and the representatives (Severs 2010). Recent work on representative claims (Saward 2006; Squires 2008) adds another layer of complication: any simple understanding of congruency between the interests of the represented and subsequent action by representatives appears incompatible with more creative or anticipatory (Mansbridge 2003) understandings of representation. In this respect, Severs (2010, 416) draws our attention once again to the possibility that one can "feel" represented while not "being represented" when she writes of the need to be able to "differentiate between symbolic and policy responsiveness." The legitimacy of certain claims to represent women may not also be as easily determined as the notion of an economy of claims suggests (Dodson 2006; Saward 2006). If some claims makers are advantaged over others, if the represented are not able to contest claims (Severs 2010; Disch 2011), or if the system lacks sufficient institutionalized processes, or other means, of accountability (Urbinati and Warren 2008), we might wish to withhold our judgment that women are being represented.

Conclusions

If there is a single conclusion to be drawn from our account of the political representation of women, it is that their exclusion from politics is ubiquitous, operated through layer upon layer of established male dominated institutions (not least political parties) that are insulated by layer upon layer of formal and informal rules of exclusion. The tasks involved in achieving sex parity in political institutions are enormous. There is no single reason for women's underrepresentation—and hence no single or simple solution. Moreover, it is not enough to secure simple parity of presence in legislatures; the institutions themselves must be regendered, must be feminized.

Both the theory and the practice of representation are in a complex process of change that poses huge challenges. At least four broad themes are still to be explored in empirical research on women's substantive representation and may constitute the research agenda of the next decade or so. First, scholars must consider competing interpretations of what constitutes *good* substantive representation as articulated by different representatives both inside and outside of legislatures. Second, the contestation of particular claims and actions by those who are being represented demand consideration. For example, socialist, conservative, liberal feminist, black, or poor women may disagree about whether they are being well represented by particular representative claims and acts. Third, the quality of the representational relationship deserves greater attention. In other words, to what extent are our representatives examples of Dovi's (2002) "preferable descriptive representatives" who have a sense of belonging to women, share their aims, and have strong mutual relationships with those they represent? What is the quality of the communication and connections between the represented and the representative (Dodson 2006, 25)? Fourth, in all this, accountability—too often the poor relation of representation—will need to come very much more to the fore.

NOTES

1. We see no reason it should be set at this level.
2. Source: IPU, Quota Project (http://www.quotaproject.org/).
3. Celis, Childs, Kantola and Krook (2010), citing Dodson and Carroll (1995), Swers (1998), Reingold (2000), O'Regan (2000), Taylor-Robinson and Heath (2003), Wolbrecht (2002), Bratton (2005), and Dodson (2006).
4. http://libarts.wsu.edu/polisci/rngs/; McBride and Mazur (2010).
5. Currently, 186 countries have ratified or acceded to CEDAW, although the United States is notable for only have signed it. http://treaties.un.org/Pages/ViewDetails.aspx?src=TREATY&mtdsg_no=IV-8&chapter=4&lang=en
6. http://www.un.org/womenwatch/daw/beijing/platform/plat1.htm
7. http://www.time.com/time/world/article/0,8599,2108607,00.html
8. Notwithstanding the tendency to refer to *gender* quotas, what is to be represented when we talk of descriptive representation is sex—the biological males and females whose presence as elected representatives in our political institutions can be counted. Measurement of women's participation in civil society and women's movement groups is less straightforward.
9. Hawkesworth (2003), Kathlene (1995), Carroll (2001), Trimble and Arscott (2003), Gotell and Brodie (1991), Dodson (2001), Chaney (2006), Thomas (1994), Weldon (2002), Reingold (2000), Swers (2002), Childs and Withey (2006), Childs (2008), Bratton and Ray (2002), Reingold (2008), Dodson (2006), Lovenduski (2005b), Mateo Diaz (2005), and Bratton and Ray (2002).

REFERENCES

Annesley, Claire. 2010. "Gender, politics and policy change: The case of welfare reform under New Labour." *Government and Opposition* 45(1): 50–72.
Ayata, Ayse Gunes, and Fatma Tutuncu. 2008. "Critical acts without a critical mass." *Parliamentary Affairs* 61(3): 461–75.

Bergqvist, Christina. 1999. *Equal democracies? Gender and power in the Nordic Countries*. Oslo: Scandinavian University Press.

Birch, Anthony. H. 1971. *Representation*. Basingstoke, UK: Macmillan.

Bratton, Kathleen. 2005. "Critical mass theory revisited: The behavior and success of token women in state legislatures." *Politics & Gender* 1(1): 97–125.

Bratton, Kathleen A., and Leonard P. Ray. 2002. "Descriptive representation, policy outcomes, and municipal day-care coverage in Norway." *American Journal of Political Science* 46(2): 428–437.

Breitenbach, E. 1981. "A comparative study of the women's trade union conference and the Scottish women's trade union conference." *Feminist Review* 7: 65–86.

Campbell, David. E., and Christina Wolbrecht. 2006. "See Jane run: Women politicians as role models for adolescents." *Journal of Politics* 68(2): 233–247.

Carroll, Susan J. 2001. *The impact of women in public office*. Bloomington: Indiana University Press.

Celis, Karen. 2005. "Reconciling theory and empirical research: Methodological reflections on women MP's representing women's interests." Paper presented at the Annual Meeting of the American Political Science Association, Washington, DC.

Celis, Karen. 2008. "Gendering representation." In Gary Goertz and Amy Mazur, eds., *Politics, gender, and concepts*, 71–93. Cambridge, UK: Cambridge University Press.

Celis, Karen, and Sarah Childs. 2011. "The substantive representation of women: What to do with conservative claims?" *Political Studies* 60(1): 213–225.

Celis, Karen, Sarah Childs, Johanna Kantola, and Mona Lena Krook. 2008. "Rethinking women's substantive representation." *Representation* 44(2): 99–110.

Celis, Karen, Sarah Childs, Johanna Kantola, and Mona Lena Krook. 2009. "Constituting women's interests through representative claims." Paper presented at the Annual Meeting of the American Political Science Association, Toronto, Canada, September 3–6.

Chaney, Paul. 2006. "Critical mass, deliberation, and the substantive representation of women: Evidence from the UK's devolution programme." *Political Studies* 54(4): 691–714.

Childs, Sarah. 2004. *New Labour's women MPs*. London: Routledge.

Childs, Sarah. 2007. "Representation." In Georgina Blakeley and Valerie Bryson, eds., *The impact of feminism on political concepts and debates*. Manchester: Manchester University Press, 73–91.

Childs, Sarah. 2008. *Women and British party politics*. London: Routledge.

Childs, Sarah, and Mona Lena Krook. 2006. "Should feminists give up on critical mass? A contingent yes." *Politics and Gender* 2(4): 203–205.

Childs, Sarah, and Mona Lena Krook. 2008. "Critical mass theory and women's political representation." *Political Studies* 56(3): 725–736.

Childs, Sarah, and Julie Withey. 2006. "The substantive representation of women: The case of the reduction of VAT on sanitary products." *Parliamentary Affairs* 59(1): 10–23.

Cockburn, Cynthia. 1996. "Strategies for gender democracy." *European Journal of Women's Studies* 3: 7–26.

Cowley, Philip, and Sarah Childs. 2003. "Too spineless too rebel." *British Journal of Political Science* 33(3): 345–365.

Dahl, Robert. 1989. *Democracy and its critics*. New Haven, CT: Yale University Press.

Dahlerup, Drude. 1988. "From a small to a large minority: Women in Scandinavian politics." *Scandinavian Political Studies* 11(4): 275–298.

Dahlerup, Drude, and Lenita Freidenvall. 2001. "Judging gender quotas—Predictions and results." *Policy & Politics* 38(3): 407–425.

Diamond, Irene, and Nancy Hartsock. 1998. "Beyond interests in politics." In Anne Phillips, ed., *Feminism and politics*. Oxford: Oxford University Press, 193–223.

Disch, Lisa. 2011. "Toward a mobilization conception of democratic representation." *APSR* 105(1): 100–113.

Dodson, D. L. 2001. "Acting for women." In Susan J. Carroll, ed., *The Impact of Women in Public Office*. Bloomington: Indiana University Press, 225–242.

Dodson, Debra. L. 2006. *The impact of women in Congress*. Oxford: Oxford University Press.

Dodson, Debra, and Susan J. Carroll. 1995. *Voices, views, votes*. New Brunswick, NJ: Rutgers University.

Dovi, Suzanne. 2002. "Preferable descriptive representatives: Will just any woman, Black or Latino do?" *APSR* 96(4): 729–743.

Dovi, Suzanne. 2007. *The good representative*. Malden, MA: Blackwell.

Dovi, Suzanne. 2010. "Measuring representation: Rethinking the role of exclusion." Paper presented at the American Political Science Association annual meeting, Washington, DC, September 2–5..

Franceschet, Susan, and Jennifer M. Piscopo. 2008. "Gender quotas and women's substantive representation: Lessons from Argentina." *Politics & Gender* 4(3): 393–425.

Goetz, Anne Marie. 2009. *Progress of the world's women in 2008/9. Who Answers to Women?* www.unifem.org/progress/2008.

Gotell, Lise, and Janine Brodie. 1991. "Women and parties: More than an issue of numbers." In Hugh G. Thorburn, ed., *Party politics in Canada*. Scarborough: Prentice-Hall Canada, 53–67.

Guadagnini Marila and Alessia Donà. 2007. "Women's policy machinery in Italy between European pressure and domestic constraints." In Joyce Outshoorn and Johanna Kantola, eds., *Changing state feminism*. New York: Palgrave Macmillan, 164–181.

Guadagnini, Marila. 2007. "The reform of the state in Italy." In Melissa Haussmann and Birgit Sauer, eds., *Gendering the state in an age of globalisation*. Lanham, MD: Rowman and Littlefield, 169–181.

Halsaa Beatrice. 1999. "A strategic partnership for women's policies in Norway." In Geertije Lyclama, ed., *Women's movements and public policy in Europe, Latin America and the Caribbean*.New York: Garland, 157–169.

Hawkesworth, Mary. 2003. "Congressional enactments of race-gender: Toward a theory of raced-gendered institutions." *American Political Science Review* 97(4): 529–550.

Heath, R. M., Leslie A. Schwindt-Bayer, and M. M. Taylor-Robinson. 2005. "Women on the sidelines: Women's representation on committees in Latin American legislatures." *American Journal of Political Science* 49: 420–436.

Hernes, Helga Maria, and Kirsten Voje. 1980. "Women in the corporate channel: A process of natural exclusion." *Scandinavian Political Studies* 3(2): 163–186.

Holli, Anne Maria, and Johanna Kantola. 2005. A politics for presence: State feminism, women's movements and political representation in Finland. In Joni Lovenduski, ed., *State Feminism and Political Representation of Women in Europe and North America*. Cambridge: Cambridge University Press, 62–84.

Htun, M. 2004. "Is gender like ethnicity? The political representation of identity groups." *Perspectives on Politics* 2(3): 439–458.

Jonasdottir, Anna. G. 1990. "On the concept of interest, women's interests, and the limitations of interest theory." In Kathleen B. Jones and Anna G. Jonasdottir, eds., *The political interests of gender, developing theory and research with a feminist face*. London: SAGE, 33–65.

Kanter, Rosabeth Moss. 1977. "Some effects of proportions on group life." *American Journal of Sociology* 82(5): 965–990.

Kathlene, Lyn. 1995. "Position power versus gender power: Who holds the floor?" In Georgia Duerst-Lahti and Rita Mae Kelly, eds., *Gender power, leadership, and governance*. Ann Arbor: University of Michigan Press, 167–194.

Karvonnen, L., and P. Selle (Eds.). 1995. *Women in Nordic politics: Closing the gap*. Hants: Dartmouth.

Kenny, Meryl, and Fiona Mackay. 2009. "Already doin' it for ourselves? Skeptical notes on feminism and institutionalism." *Politics & Gender* 5(2): 271–280.

Kittilson, Miki Caul. 2006. *Challenging parties, changing parliaments*. Columbus: Ohio State University Press.

Krook, Mona Lena. 2009. *Quotas for women in politics: Gender and candidate selection reform worldwide*. New York: Oxford University Press.

Krook, Mona Lena. 2010. "Women's representation in parliament: A qualitative comparative analysis." *Political Studies* 58(5): 886–908.

Krook, Mona Lena, Lovenduski, Joni. And Squires, Judith. 2009. "Gender Quotas and Models of Citizenship." *British Journal of Political Science* 39(4): 781–803.

Lovenduski, Joni. 1986. *Women and European politics*. Brighton: Harvester.

Lovenduski, Joni. 2005a. *Feminizing politics*. Cambridge, UK: Polity.

Lovenduski, Joni. 2005b. *State feminism and the political representation of women*. Cambridge, UK: Cambridge University Press.

Lovenduski, Joni, and Marila Guadagnini. 2010. "Political representation." In Dorothy McBride and Amy Mazur, eds., *The politics of state feminism*. Philadelphia: Temple University Press, 164–192.

Lovenduski, Joni, and Pippa Norris (Eds.). 1993. *Gender and party politics*. London: SAGE.

Lovenduski, Joni, and Pippa Norris. 2003. Westminster women: The politics of presence. *Political Studies* 2003: 84–102.

Mackay, Fiona, Georgina Waylen, Susan Franceschet, and Jennifer Piscopo. 2008. Feminism and Institutionalism International Nework. Available at http://www.femfiin.com/

Mansbridge, Jane. 1999. "Should blacks represent blacks and women represent women? A contingent 'yes.'" *Journal of Politics* 61(3): 628–657.

Mansbridge, Jane. 2003. "Rethinking representation." *American Political Science Review* 97(4): 515–528.

Mateo Diaz, Mercedes. 2005. *Representing women: Female legislators in West European parliaments*. Essex: ECPR.

Mazur, Amy. 2002. *Theorizing Feminist Policy*. Oxford: OUP.

Mazur, Amy. 2001. *State feminism, women's movements and job training: Making democracy work in the global economy*. New York: Routledge.

McBride, Dorothy, and Amy Mazur. 2010 *The politics of state feminism: Innovation in comparative research*. Philadelphia: Temple University Press.

McLean, Ian. 1991. "Forms of representation and systems of voting." In David Held, ed., *Political theory today*. Cambridge, UK: Polity, 172–196.

Meehan, Elizabeth. 1985. *Women's Rights at Work: Campaigns and Policy in Britain and the United States*. Basingstoke: Macmillan.

Meier, Petra, and Emanuela Lombardo. 2010. "Towards a new theory on the symbolic representation of women." Paper presented at the American Political Science Association annual meeting, Washington, DC, September, 2–5.

Norris, Pippa, and Joni Lovenduski. 1995. *Political recruitment.* Cambridge, UK: Cambridge University Press.

O'Regan, Valerie. 2000. *Gender matters. Female policymakers' influence in industrialized nations.* Westport, CT: Praeger.

Outshoorn, Joyce. 2004. *The politics of prostitution: women's movements, prostitution and the globalization of sex commerce.* New York: Palgrave Macmillan.

Pateman, Carole. 1988. *The sexual contract.* Cambridge, UK: Polity.

Phillips, Anne. 1995. *The politics of presence.* Oxford: Clarendon Press.

Phillips, Anne. 1998. "Democracy and representation: Or, why should it matter who our representatives are?" In Anne Phillips, ed., *Feminism and politics.* Oxford: Oxford University Press, 224–241.

Pitkin, Hanna F. 1967. *The concept of representation.* Berkeley: University of California Press.

Politics & Gender. 2009. "Critical perspectives on gender and politics section." *Politics & Gender* 5(2): 237–280.

Rao, Nirmala. 1998. Representation in local politics: A reconsideration and some new evidence. *Political Studies* 66: 19–35.

Reingold, Beth. 2000. *Representing women.* Chapel Hill: University of North Carolina Press.

Reingold, Beth. 2008. *Legislative women, getting elected, getting ahead.* Boulder, CO: Reiner.

Sapiro, Virginia. 1998. "When are interests interesting." In Anne Phillips, ed., *Feminism and politics.* Oxford: Oxford University Press, 161–192.

Saward, Michael. 2006. "The representative claim." *Contemporary Political Theory* 5: 297–318.

Sauer Birgit. 2010. "Framing and gendering." In Dorothy McBride and Amy Mazur, eds., *The politics of state feminism.* Philadelphia: Temple University Press, 193–216.

Schreiber, Ronnee. 2008. *Righting feminism.* New York: Oxford University Press.

Schwindt-Bayer, Leslie A., and William Mischler. 2005. "An integrated model of women's representation." *Journal of Politics* 67(2): 407–428.

Severs, Eline. 2010. "Representation as claims making: Quid responsiveness." *Representation* 46(4): 411–423.

Skjeie, Hege. 1993. "Ending the male political hegemony: The Norwegian experience." In Joni Lovenduski and Pippa Norris, eds., *Gender and party politics.* London: SAGE, 231–262.

Squires, Judith. 2008. "The constitutive representation of gender." *Representation* 44(2): 187–204.

Stetson, Dorothy McBride. 2001. "Welfare reform: America's hot issue." In Melissa Haussmann and Birgit Sauer, eds., *Gendering the State in an Age of Globalisation.* Lanham, Boulder: Rowman and Littlefield, New York: Plymouth, 281–300.

Studlar, Donley T., and Ian McAllister. 2002. "Does a critical mass exist?" *European Journal of Political Research* 41(2): 233–253.

Swers, Michele L. 1998. "Are women more likely to vote for women's issue bills than their male colleagues?" *Legislative Studies Quarterly* 23(3): 435–448.

Swers, Michele L. 2002. *The difference women make: The policy impact of women in Congress.* Chicago: University of Chicago Press.

Taylor-Robinson, Michelle M., and Roseanna M. Heath. 2003. "Do women legislators have different policy priorities than their male colleagues? A critical case test." *Women and Politics* 24(4): 77–100.

Thomas, Sue. 1994. *How women legislate.* New York: Oxford University Press.

Trimble, Linda. 1993. "A few good women: Female legislators in Alberta, 1972–1991." In Cathy Cavanaugh and Randy Warne, eds., *Standing on new ground: Women in Alberta.* Edmonton: University of Alberta Press, 87–118.

Trimble, Linda. 1997. Feminist Policies in the Alberta Legislature, 1972–1994. In: Jane Arscott en Linda Trimble, eds., *In the Presence of Women: Representation and Canadian Governments.* Toronto: Harcourt Brace, 128–154.

Trimble, Linda. 2000. "Who's represented? Gender and diversity in the Alberta legislature." In Manon Tremblay and Caroline Andrew, eds., *Women and political representation in Canada.* Women's Studies Series 2. Ottawa: University of Ottawa Press, 257–289.

Trimble, Linda, and Jane Arscott. 2003. *Still counting: Women in politics across Canada.* Canada: Broadview.

Urbinati, Nadia, and Mark. E. Warren. 2008. "The concept of representation in contemporary democratic theory." *Annual Review of Political Science* 11: 387–412.

Vargas, Virginia, and Saskia Wieringa. 1998. "The triangle of empowerment: Processes and actors in the making of public policy for women." In Geertije Lyclama à Nijeholt, Virginia Vargas, Saskia Wieringa, eds., *Women's Movements and Public Policy in Europe, Latin America and the Caribbean.* New York/London: Garland Publishing, 3–23.

Wängnerud, Lena. 2000. "Testing the politics of presence: Women's representation in the Swedish Riksdag." *Scandinavian Political Studies* 23(1): 67–91.

Waylen, Georgina. 2007. *Engendering transitions.* Oxford University Press: Oxford.

Weldon, Laurel S. 2002. "Beyond bodies: Institutional sources of representation for women in democratic policymaking." *Journal of Politics* 64(4): 1153–1174.

Weldon, Laurel S. 2006. "Moving to a comparative politics of gender?" *Politics & Gender* 2: 221–263.

Wolbrecht, Christina. 2002. "Female legislators and the women's rights agenda." In Cindy Simon Rosenthal, ed., *Women transforming congress.* Norman: University of Oklahoma Press, 170–239.

Wolbrecht, Christina, and David E. Campbell. 2007. "Leading by example: Female members of Parliament as political role models." *AJPS* 51(4): 921–939.

Woodward Alison E. 2003. "Building velvet triangles: Gender and informal governance." In Thomas Christiansson and Simona Piattoni, eds., *Informal governance in the European Union.* Cheltenham, UK: Edward Elgar, 76–93.

Young, Iris Marion. 2002. *Inclusion and democracy.* Oxford: Oxford University Press.

Zetterberg, Pär. 2008. "Do gender quotas foster women's political engagement? Lessons from Latin America." *Political Research Quarterly* 62: 715–730.

CHAPTER 20

POLITICAL SYSTEMS AND GENDER

AILI MARI TRIPP

INTRODUCTION

Two central questions have dominated the literature on regime type and gender: does the political system matter in promoting gender equality, and if so, how? This chapter explores the debates on these topics, first by looking at general cross-national studies and then by examining more closely the patterns found in democracies, authoritarian regimes, socialist states, and hybrid regimes with respect to gender equality. The chapter takes a look at the impact of transitions to democracy on gender equality and discusses new directions for research in the area of political systems and women's status. It also briefly compares various political formations within regime types and their impacts on gender policy and outcomes, contrasting, for example, better-off welfare states with poor welfare states; postcolonial countries by former colonizers; established democracies with emerging or newer democracies; and socialist with postsocialist countries.

Cross-national research has produced varying findings on the importance of political systems, depending on the measures and methodologies employed. One of the most studied questions with respect to regime type has been in relation to women's political representation in national legislatures. However, this bias in the literature may have limited a fuller understanding of the relationship between regime type and women's status, which needs to be studied by looking over time at a combination of factors that include first and foremost gender inequalities across a wide range of outcomes beyond formal representation, such as in economic, social welfare, and cultural arenas as well as in a variety of political arenas. In addition, one also needs to include an under-standing of the attitudes toward gender equality; gender policies adopted by governments; extent of women's rights activism to bring about change; and the broader international environment of gender norms and institutional changes in the adoption of treaties and conventions. However, policies, attitudes, activ-ism, even international pressures—while important—do not tell us enough about outcomes for equality. Negative cultural attitudes toward gender equality, for example, can be circumvented by policies, such as the use of parliamentary reserved seats for women. Policies can be diluted or not implemented. Women's movements and international pressures can be ignored and counter-movements can undermine their efforts. Moreover, even the adoption of policies does not tell us enough about how they are framed and whether women's interests and welfare are at the core of the intervention. Thus, gender equality outcomes are key to any comparison of regimes.

By introducing a broader range of measures of gender equality beyond women's representation in parliaments, the relationship between regime type and women's status becomes clearer. This is because representation of women in legislatures cannot be taken as a sole measure of women's advancement since so many nondemocratic countries have introduced quotas to improve women's representation in parliaments without always adopting other more far-reaching policies (see also the chapter by Mona Lena Krook and Leslie Schwindt-Bayer in this volume). They have adopted quotas for reasons that range from conformity to changing international norms; response to institutional pressures from the United Nations (UN) system, Inter-Parliamentary Union, and other regional bodies; and as a result of lobbying by women's movements (Tripp and Kang 2008). Socialist countries in Eastern Europe and the former Soviet Union had quotas as part of their ethos of equality within a generally undemocratic order. Quotas may also serve symbolic purposes for the state or signal a modernist stance of the establishment or ruling party in the face of a populist Islamicist challenge. In other cases, quotas have been used to obtain women's votes, to create new patronage networks, or to cultivate national legitimacy on a world stage. Because quotas are not always introduced with the goal of promoting gender equality, the popular measure of women's representation in parliaments provides only a partial measure of women's overall status.

For this reason, some cross sectional studies have found an inverse rela-tionship between women's representation and democracy (Paxton 1997; Kunovich and Paxton 2005; Tripp and Kang 2008), while some earlier studies by Kenworthy and Malami (1999) and Reynolds (1999) did not find any correla-tion. Most recently, Paxton, Hughes, and Painter (2012) found in a longitudinal study that democracy does not influence *levels* of women's political represen-tation at the start of political liberalization, but it does affect the *growth* of women's representation over time by creating conditions under which women can mobilize to improve their status by increasing representation. They found that the growth in civil liberties, in particular, results in the growth of female legislative representation, suggesting that political opening allows for greater mobilization of women for representation. Tripp and Hughes (2010) were able to replicate these findings in a more detailed longitudinal study of women's legislative representation in Africa, where the women's movement has played an especially important role in bringing about gender reforms after the 1990s, when political liberalization took hold across the continent.

Htun and Weldon (2010) seek to explain global variation in gender equality policies to explain how and why regime type matters. They find that the priorities, strategies, and effectiveness of advocates and opponents of advancing women's rights are influenced by state capacity, policy legacies, international vulnerability, and the degree of democracy. They find considerable variability in policies adopted and found that regime type was not always an automatic predictor of support for, or opposition to, particular reforms. Variation depended on (1) whether the policies in question were "status policies" that challenged practices and policies that kept women in a subordinate position (e.g., policies and laws regarding the family, violence against women, reproductive freedoms, and gender quotas), (2) class-based policies that targeted women's position in the sexual division of labor (e.g., maternity or paternal leave and child care), and (3) policies that challenged religious, traditional, or customary institutions. Their study found that democratic countries had more developed civil societies, which allowed women's organizations to have greater influence, whereas authoritarian regimes tended to suppress civil society. At the same time, democracy also empowered religious institutions and other institutions resistant to change.

Research in the area of attitudes has sought to explain why regime type matters. Inglehart and Norris (2003) find that attitudes toward women's leadership are more egalitarian in democracies. Examining seventy countries that account for 80 percent of the world population, Inglehart, Norris, and Welzel (2002, 322) find that democracies create citizens who are more supportive of gender equality. But the relationship is mediated by culture and the changes in attitudes that accompany democratization. While in the past, the existence of democratic institutions preceded the expansion of citizenship rights (like granting women the right to vote), support for gender equality today is a consequence of democratization, and at the same time it is fostering greater democracy and support for democratic institutions. Modernization, economic development, and the emergence of a postindustrial society leads to cultural change, which in turn transforms gender roles and fosters greater political representation of women along with the development of democratic institutions. Inglehart et al. argue that democratic societies usually have more women in parliament than undemocratic societies because economic development leads to social and cultural transformations, which simultaneously allow for gender equality and make it more likely for democratic institutions to flourish.

They also use culture to explain variation among democracies. For example, they argue that women in the Nordic countries have advanced in terms of political leadership faster than women in France and Belgium, even though all are postindustrial countries. Culture matters more than economic development in determining women's political leadership. Cultural change creates an atmosphere of tolerance, trust, and political moderation. It leads to values of gender equality; to tolerance of foreigners, gays, and lesbians; to societies that value self-expression and individual freedom; and to activist political orientations—all values that are crucial to their definition of democracy.

While much of the literature has focused on political systems in relation to attitudes, policy adoption, and the one measure of female legislative representation, the big gap in the literature remains in the area of outcomes. Simple cross-national bivariate regressions between regime type and broader measures of women's status reveal a strong correlation between democracy and women's status, even when controlling for economic growth (gross domestic product) (see Table 20.1).[1] This is evident from bivariate correlations using data from 134 countries, including Freedom House[2] data, to capture levels of civil liberties and political rights and the Global Gender Gap Index of the World Economic Forum to measure economic participation, political empowerment, educational attainment, and health and survival (see Table 20.1). The findings are similar using Polity Data in lieu of Freedom House data. Further multivariate analysis would be required to refine these findings, but the correlations between these measures the gender gap and levels civil liberties and political rights are strong and statistically significant.[3]

Thus, adopting a broad range of measures, particularly outcomes in gender gaps in political, economic, education, and health arenas, would strengthen existing work that has found correlations in policy adoption in a variety of fields and in attitudinal orientations in examining the importance

Table 20.1 Democracy and Gender Gap Index

	Correlation with Level of Democracy	Correlation with Level of Democracy Controlling for GDP Per Capita
Overall Equality Composite	0.61***	0.54***
Economic Opportunity	0.45***	0.44***
Educational Attainment	0.40***	0.28***
Health and Survival	0.34***	0.35***
Political Empowerment	0.44***	0.37***
% Women in Parliaments	0.32***	0.25***

*p < .10.
**p < .05.
***p < .01.
Source: Freedom House (http://www.freedomhouse.org) 2010 data on regime type; The Global Gender Gap index from World Economic Forum 2010 data on Economic Opportunity, Educational Attainment, Health and Survival and Political Empowerment (http://www3.weforum.org/docs/WEF_GenderGap_Report_2010.pdf); UN Human Development Report for 2010 GDP per capita.

of regime type in advancing women's rights. However, more fine-grained existing studies of particular regime types show that, while these general patterns hold, there is still considerable variation across issue area, regions, and time.

For example, there are differences in gender equality when one contrasts democracies in advanced postindustrial countries with democracies in emerging economies like India, Mexico, Chile, and Indonesia. There are similarly differences between authoritarian regimes, with socialist states adopting policies more akin to the welfare states than to bureaucratic authoritarian regimes in Latin America or the colonial state. Postconflict countries in Africa have adopted more legislation and made more constitutional changes regarding women's rights and political representation than nonpostconflict countries (Tripp 2011, Tripp and Hughes 2010). Oil-producing countries in the Middle East are particularly slow to adopt gender reforms relative to others (Ross 2008). Countries where women's rights have been framed in collective terms as parallel to class or as collective maternal rights (in contrast to more individualistic liberal frames) have often found it easier to adopt certain policies that treat women as a group, such as adopting electoral quotas, welfare policies providing generous child care, maternity leave, and other incentives for mothers to enter the labor force.

DELINEATING REGIME TYPES

For the purposes of this chapter, I delineate regimes into three basic types: democracies; hybrid regimes; and authoritarian regimes. In *democracies,* civil liberties and political rights are generally protected. Elections allow for a regular changeover of leadership. Even with all their flaws, democracies have mechanisms in place to ensure transparency and accountability. Civil society can operate independently of the state, can serve as a watchdog of the state, and can pressure the state for change.

In contrast, *hybrid* regimes range across a spectrum from *semidemocracies* to *semiauthoritarian* regimes.[4] Semidemocracies (sometimes referred to as electoral democracies) hold regularly contested, closed-ballot, multiparty elections in which political parties have free access to the electorate through media and campaigning and in which there is not massive voter fraud. They allow for changes in party dominance and the alternation of the head of state. However, there are inconsistencies in the extent to which they ensure civil liberties and political rights.

Semiauthoritarian regimes hold regular competitive elections; however, it is not clear that the rulers in these countries are interested in fully opening up the political process and relinquishing power. Ruling parties dominate the legislature and dominate over the course of repeated elections. Semiauthoritarian regimes do not allow for genuinely competitive elections. Frequently, massive voter fraud occurs, and opposition parties do not always have either free access to the electorate through the media or the same advantages as incumbents when campaigning—for instance, state resources. Incumbents invariably return to power, and the dominant party remains dominant over long periods of time. They lack consistency in guaranteeing civil liberties and political rights. Thus, they combine characteristics of both democracies and authoritarian states.

Unlike semiauthoritarian regimes, *authoritarian regimes* make little pretense of incorporating democratic institutions beyond holding elections. Civil liberties and political rights are limited. Challenges to executive dominance are suppressed and have almost no impact in autocratic settings. Authoritarian regimes may also hold regular elections, but they are often ruled by a monarch, oligarch, military junta, or other type of autocrat. These systems encompass totalitarian–socialist regimes, fascist regimes, as well as the autocratic systems found, for example, in Latin America in the 1970s and into the 1980s or in postindependence Africa from the 1960s through the 1980s.

DEMOCRACIES

Research, primarily in Europe, has focused on the ways gender policy has evolved in a variety of democracies based on different conceptions of citizenship, gender regimes, and different welfare state arrangements. Siim's (2000) *Gender and Citizenship*, for example, contrasts both the ideology and practice of citizenship as it affects women's status in three countries. She critically examines republican citizenship in France, liberal citizenship in Britain, and social citizenship in Denmark. Not only does she look at the relationship between ideologies of citizenship and state policy regarding gender, but she also shows the ways women have influenced and engaged these policies. She explores the limitations of France's pronatalist policies deriving from notions of republican citizenship, the dilemmas posed by Britain's male breadwinner model for social policy, and some of the limitations of the Danish social citizenship model with respect to globalization and migration and restructuring of the welfare state.

Walby (2004) examines the impact of different gender regimes on advancing gender equality. She argues that there is a transformation taking place worldwide that is bringing gender relations into the public realm away from a domestic-based gender regime. These regime transformations take different forms in different parts of the world. Focusing on democracies, she identifies the Nordic social democratic public service route, which provided services like child care that facilitated women entering into the paid labor force. A second regime is the U.S. market-led route, where the mechanisms that permit women to enter the labor force come from the market itself. The third regime is the regulatory route, adopted by the European Union (EU), which promotes women's employment by removing discrimination, regulating work hours to be compatible with care work, and promoting policies of social inclusion. These gender regimes differ based on the extent to which policy is driven by the state rather than the market, their capacity for allowing historically excluded groups into the decision-making process, and their attentiveness to inequality. Since the mid-1970s the focus in the EU has been on social inclusion as expressed through a new employment-based set of regulations.

There has also been research into cross-national variations in the impact of welfare state policies on gender relations and, in particular, differences based on the strength of organized labor, state capacity, the character of labor markets, forms of women's mobilization, nature of discourses and ideologies within various countries, and race relations (Orloff 1996, 74). According to Orloff (2009, 330), some have looked for coherent clusters of countries, or "gendered welfare regimes," based on the logic of the male breadwinner (Lewis 1992); others have focused on motherhood models (Leira 1992, 2002; Bergqvist et al. 1999; Borchorst and Siim 2002; Ellingsæter and Leira 2006); and still others on support for personal female autonomy (Saraceno 2007; González et al. 2000). Yet another approach examines the role of liberalism, which relies on equal opportunity legal and regulatory frameworks (O'Connor, Orloff, and Shaver 1999; Orloff 2009).

Some scholars have argued that the differences within democracies fall along lines of difference versus equality feminism (see also the chapter by Judith Squires in this volume). O'Connor et al. (1999), in examining social welfare policies, employment regulation, service provision, and abortion rights, found that Australia and Britain adopted more gender-differentiated policies, while Canada and the United States adopted an equality approach. They linked this to differences between the countries, such as the greater strength of organized labor in Britain and Australia, and the greater feminist mobilization around women's rights in North America. According to Orloff (2009), the gendered dimensions of welfare states are partially independent of class related features and differ from typologies based on other aspects of power, difference, and inequality.

Among the most common approaches have been those that link differences in gender policies to family policy models adopted by different political parties (Korpi 2000, Korpi, Ferrarini and Englund 2009). The family policy models promote care arrangements in a variety of ways, ranging from the dual-earner model (Denmark, Finland, Norway, and Sweden) to traditional arrangements (Austria, Belgium, France, Germany, Italy, and the Netherlands), with a large group outside of either model (Australia, Canada, Ireland, Japan, New Zealand, Switzerland, United Kingdom, and United States). Social democratic parties, for example, have often embraced the dual-earner model supported by public care services (Hobson and Lindholm 1997; Huber and Stephens 2000). Similarly, the socialist countries in the Eastern bloc adopted a version of this latter model with respect to gender equality but without the political freedoms enjoyed by the advanced welfare states.

If one adopts a narrower definition of gender equality that focuses on women's access to employment and child care, then countries with left-leaning parties in power appear to be more amenable to promoting women's rights, while conservative parties have been less supportive of women's rights or have been supportive in ways that strengthened the breadwinner–caregiver model while limiting personal autonomy (Korpi 2000). However, according to Orloff (2009), some researchers have argued for more expansive definitions of equality that also account for participation, political freedom and equal opportunity (Ferree and Martin 1995).

Finally, important cross-national research has shown the importance of state feminism in promoting gender equality, especially when linked to women's movements. State machineries to advance women's rights are not necessary for women's movements to have policy impact, but they increase the likelihood that the state will respond. Moreover, they can be crucial when the conditions for movement success are absent (McBride and Mazur 2010) (see also the chapter by Dorothy McBride and Amy Mazur in this volume).

AUTHORITARIANISM

A wide range of regime types would fall into the category of authoritarian: fascist, socialist, autocratic military juntas, some monarchies, and most theocracies. This makes it difficult to generalize about such regimes types. The following section looks at three examples of authoritarian regimes that illustrate some of the variance: bureaucratic authoritarian regimes in Latin America (c. 1960s–1980s); single-party autocracies in Africa (c. 1960s–1980s); and state socialism in the former Soviet Union (1917–1991) and Eastern Europe (1940s–1980s).

Bureaucratic Authoritarian Regimes in Latin America

Bureaucratic authoritarian regimes in Latin America from the 1960s to the 1980s generally restricted divorce and reproductive rights, especially abortion; they upheld discriminatory marriage and divorce laws and did little to fight violence against women (Waylen 2007a, 145). Some authoritarian regimes, like Brazil, were more inclined to reform than others like Argentina and Chile. Moreover, there is variation over time as well: the authoritarian regime in Argentina in the 1960s was more socially liberal than later governments.

In Latin America, the Catholic Church was instrumental in shaping and constraining the extent to which women's movements were able to advance women's rights during periods of authoritarianism. Htun's (2003) *Sex and the State: Abortion, Divorce, and the Family under Latin American Dictatorships and Democracies* examines these dynamics. She shows how between 1960 and 1990, conservative military governments in Latin America sometimes introduced woman-friendly policies, while democratization did not always herald changes in old laws pertaining to women, especially in the area of abortion. Divorce was legalized in authoritarian Brazil in 1978, but not in Chile (until much later in 2004) where church–state relations were much stronger. Modernization was associated with women's rights, and, by introducing limited reforms for women, the military leaders of Argentina, Chile, and Brazil believed they were modernizing in a way that would buy them political legitimacy. During the transition to democracy, elite coalitions of lawyers, feminist activists, transnational activists, doctors, legislators, and state officials brought about social change, depending on how well these elite coalitions were able to link up with state institutions. However, as the case of Chile shows, church–state relations acted as a constraint on the introduction of woman-friendly norms. Thus, according to Htun, the particular configurations of state–society alliances were more important than simply whether a country was democratic or authoritarian in bringing about changes affecting women's status.

Postindependence Autocracies in Africa

The postindependence period in Africa after the late 1950s was marked by authoritarian rule. After independence, women found their organizational efforts curtailed once again; only this time the constraints came not from colonial powers but from the newly independent single-party and military regimes, which increasingly limited autonomous associational activity. National women's activities were to be channeled through a single women's organization, usually linked to the ruling party, which used it as a source of funds, votes, and entertainment (Steady 1975; Staudt 1985). Moreover, even though these organizations claimed to represent the interests of all women in their respective countries, especially rural women, they often served as more of a mechanism of generating votes and support for the country's single party. Ruling parties and regimes sought to bring women into state-related clientelism by controlling women's associations through various strategies, including the creation of women's wings tied to the ruling party; suppressing or controlling independent associations by banning, co-opting, and absorbing them; mandating registration of autonomous associations in state-run umbrella organizations; and infiltrating associations with patronage networks. These forms of control parallel attempts to control other forms of associational life, including trade unions, cooperatives, student and youth organizations, market traders, and other societal interests that could potentially threaten the state (Wallerstein 1964; Wunsch 1991).

The net effect of these efforts to control women's mobilization was to depoliticize women and to keep their political activities circumscribed within their organizations rather than to give them political roles within the political parties. It kept women focused on *developmental* or welfare-type activities, handicrafts, income-generating projects, entertainment, and social concerns rather than on pushing an independent women's rights agenda. To the extent that these organizations did mobilize around women's rights concerns in this period, they could do so only as long as they did not challenge the ruling party (Tripp et al. 2009).

The relationship between the ruling party and women's organizations was sometimes solidified by placing an association under the control of the wife of the head of state or under the leadership of other female relatives of party and state leaders, a phenomenon described as a *femocracy* by Mama (Mama 1995; Ibrahim 2000). First ladies frequently headed the larger national women's organizations: Nana Agyeman Rawlings, wife of Ghanaian president Jerry Rawlings, chaired the 31st December Women's Movement in Ghana; Maryam Babangida, wife of Nigerian president Ibrahim Babangida, headed the Better Life for Rural Women Programme; while Betty Kaunda, wife of Zambia's Kenneth Kaunda, was affiliated with the Women's League in Zambia. These dynamics changed with the emergence of autonomous women's movements as political space opened up in the 1990s. These new movements had their own leaders, agendas, and funding sources independent of the ruling party and government.

State Socialism in the Former Soviet Union and Eastern Europe

State socialist countries generally have had an ideological commitment to gender equality, emerging from an interest in the *woman question* in which women were to be emancipated through their involvement in the labor force and through the abolition of class relations (Waylen 2007b, 141). In socialist Soviet Union and after the late 1940s in Eastern Europe, women's rights were advanced primarily by the state and ruling party, without impetus from an independent women's movement. Molyneux (1985) argues that women's rights and equality were subsumed under the objectives of economic development and social stability and that the roles of women were seen as symmetrical and complementary to those of men while emancipation referred to liberation from a traditional social order.

With the 1917 Bolshevik Revolution, the Soviet regime introduced reforms to improve women's status and encourage full political and economic participation. The right to vote had been won a few months prior to the revolution in 1917. Marriage, abortion, and property laws were changed to improve the status of women. Initially these policies had been influenced by Bolshevik feminists, although it was not long before their aspirations took the back seat

to other goals of establishing a socialist state and accommodating the changing goals and national production needs. The Bolsheviks drew on the Marxist
rationalization that women's emancipation lay with their participation in social
production. Women were to work full time both inside and outside the home,
carrying a double burden that was not shared by men (Sperling 1999). The
family was seen as a bastion of tradition and backwardness that needed to be
undermined so that people's energies could be redirected to the public domain
and toward building up the economy to create a socialist state. Women economically engaged in the workforce were critical to this shift, but to bring this
equality about, the functions of household needed to be oriented toward serving the public domain (Lapidus 1993).

Although there were important differences between the Eastern European
countries that became socialist in the late 1940s, they all sought to bring women
into the paid workforce, reaching some of the highest rates of female employment in the world: women made up as much as 90 percent of the workforce
in the Soviet Union and almost 80 percent in Poland. Unusually large numbers of these women were of child-bearing age. They were generally employed
in lower-level positions at lower wages and faced considerable gender-based
job segregation in the retail trades, education, medicine, and light industry
(Wolchik 1995). Women were underrepresented in top economic and other
white-collar positions (Fodor 2002, 371). As in the Soviet Union, they were
integral to the labor-intensive strategy of economic development. Pay structures necessitated the dual-worker household and, together with reproductive
policies, facilitated the high levels of female employment found in these countries (Wolchik 1995).

While increasing their involvement in the labor force, women shouldered
most of the care of the home and children. In spite of occasional party rhetoric
about husbands and wives sharing responsibilities in the home, in reality gender roles in the home changed little. According to Fodor (2002, 371):

> Food shortages required that women spend hours standing in line waiting
> for produce to arrive at a store, nursery schools were often understaffed and
> inadequate, laundry facilities far away, precooked meals in the supermarket
> proved to be expensive for most people, and hot lunches provided in the
> workplace lacked nutritional value as well as taste.

Policies were introduced that gave women greater access to education, particularly at the secondary level, in teachers' training colleges and technical education schools (Wolchik 1995). By the 1970s, women had parity with men in
educational institutions (Fodor 2002, 371). They had extensive maternity and
child-care leaves. Women were granted child-care allowances, were guaranteed
their jobs after maternity leave, had access to child care, and enjoyed other
social provisions. There were protections for single mothers. Women had the
right to abortion and contraceptives except for Romania, where abortion was
criminalized and contraceptives were unavailable (Gal and Kligman 2000a).

Women were better represented in legislatures than in most parts of the world, but their real political power was limited. In the Soviet Union women were almost completely excluded from the key policy-making institutions like the All-Union Central Committees and state Councils of Ministers (Moses 1977). Thus, women's impressively high levels of representation in the Soviet era were somewhat illusory in that they did not reflect the real nature and extent of women's political involvement. Until the late 1980s, women held on average 31 percent of the legislative seats in Eastern Europe and the Soviet Union, which was the highest for any region of the world at the time.

HYBRIDS

The largest expansion of hybrid regimes in the past two decades has taken place in Africa. Between 1975 and 2005, the proportion of democracies in the world increased by 19 percent, based on Freedom House figures. The proportion of hybrid countries did not change much globally. However, in Africa, although one saw the same 19 percent increase in new democracies in this period (1975–2005), much of the liberalization that occurred, especially after 1990, involved the softening of authoritarian regimes themselves and a movement away from politically closed autocratic systems. Thus, hybrid states in Africa increased by 17 percent, while authoritarian countries decreased by 36 percent (Tripp 2010).

Uganda was one such hybrid semiauthoritarian regime. It was also one of the first countries in Africa to significantly increase the presence of women within the legislature and government. Uganda adopted legislative quotas for women as early as 1989, thus increasing the number of women in parliament from claiming one seat in 1980 to 18 percent of the seats in 1989 and 37 percent of the seats by 2011. Women hold key cabinet positions (28 percent of cabinet seats are held by women); Uganda had a woman vice president, the first in Africa, for ten years, and in 2011 got a female speaker of the house. The 1995 constitution had an extraordinary number of clauses addressing women's rights. Thus, at the outset, the regime won the approval of large numbers of women who were convinced that this government was committed to improving the status of women.

Women's organizations were prominent within the emerging civil society in Uganda after the 1990s. As long as they avoided activities that were deemed too political, they were able to operate. Those engaged in advocacy faced restrictions and the government attempted to pass legislation restricting nongovernmental organization (NGO) activities, but these efforts were met with resistance. Some women's organizations had their workshops closed down; others experienced difficulties registering or were threatened with closure. While not pervasive, the restrictions were enough to keep them wary of what they said and did publicly. Some civil society actors were explicitly warned against becoming too political. Nevertheless, the women's movement managed to operate within the unpredictability of these constraints that are typical of hybrid regimes.

In addition to the aforementioned involvement in politics and constitution making, the women's movement was able to get an affirmative action policy in place at the most prestigious Makerere University. It also influenced school curricula to include gender concerns in sex education classes, which was important given the high rates of HIV infection. In 2006, women's organizations were instrumental in the passage of the Disability Act, which was moved as a private member bill to provide for equal opportunities in education and employment for people with disabilities. The movement around disabilities in Uganda was an offshoot of, and has been closely related to, the women's movement. Women's rights activists have also been vocal around a number of other major pieces of legislation. Their lobbying led to legislative and policy changes regarding issues of inheritance and property rights, land rights, domestic violence, trafficking, female genital cutting, sexual exploitation during conflict, an increase in maternity leave days from forty-five to sixty days in 2007, and numerous other issues affecting women and other politically marginalized people. An active Gender and Growth Assessment Coalition is at the forefront of a lobbying and advocacy initiative around issues of women's access to land and finance, the reform of labor laws, and commercial justice. In 2011 an Equal Opportunities Commission was formed to tackle laws, policies, customs, and traditions that discriminate against women. In 2007, a constitutional court struck down key provisions of the Succession Act regarding women's right to inherit property. It also issued a ruling that decriminalized adultery for women.

Although some of these issues brought the women's movement into conflict with the regime, one might argue that a high level of interest group activity by women has been tolerated because women as a group have for a long time been among the staunchest supporters of the Museveni government. Many women initially endorsed the regime because of its antisectarian stance, believing that sectarianism would lead to the return of civil conflict. They also were encouraged by the government's support of women's advancement politically, economically, educationally, and in other areas.

It is widely acknowledged that women voted heavily in support of Museveni in the 1996 presidential elections; however, that support has been waning since then, especially after the government withdrew support of an amendment to the 1998 Land Act that would have provided the right to spousal co-ownership of land. In 2006, the government finally shelved a Domestic Relations Act, which had been in the works for more than two decades. As a result of these policies and general constraints on political rights and civil liberties, some disaffected women leaders began aligning themselves with opposition parties.

Both the progress and limitations on improving women's status speak to the priorities of a hybrid regime. The goal of remaining in power supersedes concerns for freedom of speech, freedom of association, political freedoms, human rights, and women's rights. All democratization measures are controlled by the regime, which has been limiting political space and centralizing power since the mid-1990s, both within the movement itself and within the country. The system that has resulted has kept one person in power for more than twenty-six years and limited the possibilities for the development of a truly competitive electoral system and loyal opposition. While it has allowed women to advance themselves in ways they could not have envisioned under previous authoritarian regimes, the constraints on further democratization present real challenges to further advancing a women's rights agenda.

REGIME CHANGE

With the surge of the third wave of democratization, scholars began to evaluate its impact on gender equality. They found that the democratic transitions from Latin America to East Europe were fairly disappointing in terms of their gender outcomes. Waylen's (2007a, 2007b) comparative study is supported by much of the literature on transitions in Latin America (Htun 2003; Tobar 2003; Franceschet 2005) and Eastern Europe (Einhorn 1993; Buckley 1997; Jaquette and Wolchik 1998; Gal and Kligman 2000a, 2000b; True 2003). The literature on transitions in Latin America found that democratic consolidation led to the weakening of women's movements and their autonomy as political processes became institutionalized and women's organizations were coopted by political parties (Alvarez 1989; Jaquette 1994; Waylen 1994).

The political and economic reforms in Eastern Europe and the former Soviet republics left women without their past net of social security provisions, low-cost child care, job security, and relatively high levels of political representation due to the abolition of legislative quotas for women. According to a major UNICEF (1999) report on the region, by the end of the 1990s Russia had one of the region's largest gender gaps in wages with women making about 40 percent of men's wage. In Ukraine women made one-third of the men's wages. Prior to the 1990s, Soviet women enjoyed one of the highest rates of labor force participation in the world with job security. By the end of the 1990s there were growing rates of female unemployment in all the former Soviet republics. In Russia, Ukraine, and many of the other republics women made up over 70 percent of the unemployed.

With the disintegration of the centrally planned economy in the Soviet Union, the earlier notion of woman as worker–mother was replaced by a stay-at-home mother image to allow women to "rest from production work" (Posadskaya 1993). Women, who constituted the majority of the unemployed, even among the well educated, were to be devoted to the responsibilities of caring for the family as women were among the first to lose their jobs (Racioppi and O'Sullivan 1995, 88).

One of the consequences of women's unemployment and lack of job security was the growing problem of sex trafficking in the former Soviet Union and Eastern Europe. Criminal groups lured young women with the promise of working as waitresses and barmaids overseas and then confiscated their passports, sometimes raping and beating them into submission and forcing them to work as prostitutes. The numbers of women trafficked from Ukraine, Russia, and other former Soviet republics were among the largest in the world, matching or even surpassing the numbers being trafficked from Asia and Latin America.

Economic uncertainty has also contributed to the precipitous drops in the number of births and marriage rates throughout the former Soviet Union. In the Baltic states of Latvia, Lithuania, and Estonia, for example, fertility rates dropped by 40 percent between 1989 and 1997 and marriage rates similarly dropped by 52 percent in the same period.

Changes in women's political status were also stark. In the 1990s, Eastern Europe and the former Soviet Union experienced some of the sharpest drops in female legislative representation in the world as quotas that had guaranteed women seats in parliament were eliminated. According to Inter-Parliamentary Union statistics, the percentage of seats occupied by women in the legislature dropped in the region from a high of 31 percent in 1980 to 9 percent in 1990, rising back to 15 percent by 2005. In contrast, the Nordic countries experienced an increase from 32 percent in 1990 to 40 percent in 2005, reflecting the overall improvement of the status of women in this part of Europe. Rates of female representation for the rest of Europe rose as women increased their number of seats from 11 percent in 1990 to 17 percent in 2005.

After the fall of communism in East Europe, religious and conservative political groups proposed new laws to restrict women's access to abortion in Hungary, Poland, Serbia, Slovenia, and Croatia, even though there were no popular demands for such restrictions. During the transition, Gal and Kligman (2000a) argue, political legitimacy needed to be reconstituted and reproductive rights became one of the arenas in which states sought power by attempting to shape and limit reproductive practices and sexuality through legislation. Reproductive rights became, in effect, a code for political legitimacy, morality, and nationalist concerns. In Romania, for example, extreme unhappiness with Ceausescu's reproductive policies, led to the legalization of abortion, which lent greater legitimacy to the new regime. In Poland, the government banned abortions, signaling its alliance with the Catholic Church. Gal and Kligman (2000a) show how public discussion about reproductive issues redefined state–society relations and notions of nationhood. Thus, they show how state power became preoccupied with the legal enforcement of normative reproductive heterosexuality, the surveillance of women's bodies, and other attempts to control women's bodies.

It should be noted that not all countries experienced this backlash following a political opening. In Africa, for example, democratization accompanied the expansion of women's rights, in part because it opened up political space that gave women new possibilities for demanding political rights (Fallon 2003; Lindberg 2004; Yoon 2004; Bauer and Britton 2006; Tripp et al. 2009). Similarly in East Asia, democratization opened up possibilities for Taiwanese women to gain greater political representation and for South Korean women activists to make strides in the area of legislation affecting women (Clark and Lee 2000; Lee 2000a, 2000b). Women's organizations were important in pushing for democratic political opening, and when it occurred they emerged as leading participants. They had earned legitimacy as contributors to the democratic process (Lee 2000a, 124). Lee found that democratic consolidation brought about the adoption of increased woman-friendly policies in the areas of child care, education, and employment in South Korea. Women's organizations expanded and increasingly put pressure on parties to ensure that women's rights legislation was passed, including the Basic Law for Women's Development. Women, in fact, became the most vocal interest group in Korea.

Conclusion: New Directions

By contrasting regime types, it becomes apparent that there is considerable variation within them with respect to gender equality. However, in general, the factors that have made democratic regimes more likely to be successful in achieving higher levels of gender equality in contrast to authoritarian and hybrid regimes have to do with (1) their higher levels economic growth, which have given rise to class forces that have pushed for greater equality; (2) stronger egalitarian attitudes; (3) more political space, which has allowed for the expansion of women's movements to press for change; (4) the presence of femocrats within the state to push for equality; (5) the allocation of greater state resources to proequality measures as a result of higher levels of growth; (6) stronger, less corruptible, courts to enforce gender equality; and (7) for some countries, the need to comply with regional pressures (from the European Union) and international pressures for gender equality. The political dominance of left-leaning parties may also contribute to and reflect stronger egalitarian attitudes; however, their influence on positive gender policy cuts across regime type and is not specific to democracies.

Some hybrid regimes have made gains in key areas, particularly when they have had active autonomous women's movements; when they have been influenced by international norms, donors, and women's organizations; and when there has been political will on the part of the government.

While the cross-national and comparative perspectives on political formation and women's rights have helped refine many of the assumptions about regime type, there is still much that is not known about how regimes influence gender equality. There still seems to be a lack of agreement on how best to identify patterns of gender equality policies and outcomes between countries. Moreover, many studies have focused on policies adopted and attitudes but few on actual outcomes and on how regime type influences those outcomes.

There has been growing interest in why authoritarian and semiauthoritarian states adopt female-friendly policies, even when there are no popular pressures to adopt such policies. More attention needs to be paid to why nondemocratic countries adopt gender equality policies when they are not especially interested in promoting other civil, political, and human rights. There is considerable ferment, for example, at this time in the Middle East. We are seeing the beginnings of change in countries where there has historically been little to show with respect to women's rights even prior to the "Arab spring" in Tunisia, Bahrain, Kuwait, Oman, Libya, and Yemen. Several younger Western-educated reformist monarchs in Morocco, Jordan, and Qatar see women's advancement as critical to the advancement of their countries (not just in terms of trade and relations with the European Union). They have been gradually moving their countries to adopt reforms in women's rights. What is the significance of these efforts? Why are some policies easier to change than others in semi-authoritarian and authoritarian regimes? Why are some policies easier to change in authoritarian regimes and harder to change in democracies?

How do we interpret the use of women's rights for purposes other than those of gender equality? For example, in some cases women's rights have become the battleground between secularist and Islamicist visions of national identity (Brand 1998; Charrad 2001). In many authoritarian African states women's rights have become an arena for the distribution of state patronage and the emergence of clientelistic networks. Women's rights policies and treaties are adopted to show a modern face to the world. Many countries feel pressure to comply with changing international norms regarding women and to placate donors in some cases. Historically, part of the socialist ethos in Eastern Europe and the former Soviet Union was the need to create conditions for the female labor force to serve national needs. What are the implications for women's rights when they are harnessed for these other ends where women's interests are not placed at the center of the policies? These are just a few of the questions that arise from new work in the area of political formation and women's rights.

NOTES

1. The Global Gender Gap index (1) measures gaps rather than levels of equality, (2) measures outcomes rather than inputs, and (3) ranks countries according to gender equality rather than women's empowerment. Economic participation and opportunity captures differences in labor force participation, earned income, and ratio of women to male legislators, managers, and technical and professional workers. Political empowerment measures the ratio of women to men in minister-level positions, parliamentary positions, and executive office. Educational

attainment looks at the gender gap in primary-, secondary-, and tertiary-level education and literacy rates. Health and survival measures include sex ratio at birth and gender gap in life expectancy survival.

2. http://www.freedomhouse.org.

3. The correlation using Inter-Parliamentary Union data and Freedom House data for 2010 reveals a correlation of .061 that is not significant. Controlling for gross domestic product (GDP) the correlation remains not significant at .136.

4. Hybrid regimes are characterized by different scholars in a variety of ways that are not entirely compatible. They are variously referred to as *pseudo-democracies* (Diamond 1996), *illiberal democracies* (Huntington 1997; Zakaria 1997, 2004), *electoral democracies* (Diamond 2002), *electoral authoritarian regimes* (Schedler 2006), *competitive authoritarian regimes* (Levitsky and Way 2001, 2002), *electoral hegemonic authoritarian regimes* (Diamond 2002), *contested autocracies* (van de Walle 2002), and *virtual democracies* (Joseph 1998). Further complicating matters is the fact that not everyone means the same thing by these categories, and insufficient research has been carried out to fully elaborate the political systems.

REFERENCES

Alvarez, Sonia. 1989. Politicizing gender and engendering democracy. In A. Stepan, ed., *Democratizing Brazil: Problems of transition and consolidation.* New York: Oxford University Press, 252–296.

Bauer, Gretchen, and Hannah Evelyn Britton. 2006. *Women in African parliaments.* Boulder, CO: Lynne Rienner Publishers.

Bergqvist, C., Borchorst, A., Christensen, A., Ramstedt-Silén, V., Raaum, NC and Styrkársdóttir, A. 1999. *Equal democracies: Gender and politics in the Nordic countries.* Aschehoug: Scandinavian University Press.

Borchorst, Anne, and Birte Siim. 2002. "The women-friendly welfare states revisited." *NORA: Nordic Journal of Women's Studies* 10(2): 90–98.

Brand, Laurie A. 1998. *Women, the state, and political liberalization: Middle Eastern and North African experiences.* New York: Columbia University Press.

Buckley, Mary. 1997. *Post-Soviet women: From the Baltic to Central Asia.* Cambridge, UK: Cambridge University Press.

Charrad, Mounira. 2001. *States and women's rights: The making of postcolonial Tunisia, Algeria, and Morocco.* New York: Cambridge University Press.

Clark, Cal, and Rose J. Lee. 2000. "Democracy and 'softening' society." In R. J. Lee and C. Clark, eds., *Democracy and the status of women in East Asia.* Boulder, CO: Lynne Rienner, 185–192.

Diamond, Larry. 1996. "Is the third wave over?" *Journal of Democracy* 7(3): 20–37.

Diamond, Larry. 2002. "Thinking about hybrid regimes." *Journal of Democracy* 13(2): 21–35.

Einhorn, Barbara. 1993. *Cinderella goes to the market: Citizenship, gender, and women's movements in East Central Europe.* London: Verso.

Ellingsæter, A. L., and A. Leira. 2006. *Politicising parenthood in Scandinavia: Gender relations in welfare states.* Bristol, UK: Policy Press.

Fallon, Kathleen. 2003. "The status of women in Ghana." In A. M. Tripp, *Sub-Saharan Africa: The Greenwood encyclopedia of women's issues worldwide.* Westport, CT: Greenwood Press, 72–91.

Ferree, M. M., and P. Y. Martin. 1995. *Feminist organizations: Harvest of the new women's movement.* Philadelphia: Temple University Press.

Fodor, Eva. 2002. "Gender and the experience of poverty in Eastern Europe and Russia after 1989." *Communist and Post-Communist Studies* 35: 369–382.

Franceschet, Susan. 2005. *Women and politics in Chile.* Boulder, CO: Lynne Rienner Publishers.

Gal, Susan, and Gail Kligman. 2000a. *Politics of gender after socialism: A comparative-historical essay.* Princeton, NJ: Princeton University Press.

Gal, Susan, and Gail Kligman. 2000b. *Reproducing gender: politics, publics, and everyday life after socialism.* Princeton, NJ: Princeton University Press.

González, L., M. José, T. Jurado, and M. Naldini. 2000. *Gender inequalities in Southern Europe: Women, work, and welfare in the 1990s.* London: Cass.

Hobson, B., and M. Lindholm. 1997. "Collective identities, women's power resources, and the making of welfare states." *Theory and Society* 26(4): 475–508.

Htun, Mala. 2003. *Sex and the state: Abortion, divorce, and the family under Latin American dictatorships and democracies.* New York: Cambridge University Press.

Htun, Mala, and S. Laurel Weldon. 2010. "When do governments promote women's rights? A framework for the comparative analysis of sex equality policy." *Perspectives on Politics* 8(1): 207–216.

Huber, E., and J. D. Stephens. 2000. "Partisan governance, women's employment, and the social democratic service state." *American Sociological Review* 65(3): 323–342.

Huntington, Samuel P. 1997. "After twenty years: The future of the third wave." *Journal of Democracy* 8(4): 3–12.

Ibrahim, F. A. 2000. "Sudanese women under repression, and the shortest way to equality." In M. R. Waller and J. Rycenga, eds., *Frontline feminisms: women, war, and resistance.* New York: Garland Publishing, 129–139.

Inglehart, Ronald, and Pippa Norris. 2003. *Rising tide: gender equality and cultural change around the world.* Cambridge, UK: Cambridge University Press.

Inglehart, Ronald, Pippa Norris, and Chris Welzel. 2002. "Gender equality and democracy." *Comparative Sociology* 1(3–4): 321–345.

Jaquette, Jane. 1994. *The Women's Movement In Latin America: Participation And Democracy,* second edition. Thematic Studies in Latin America. Boulder, CO: Westview Press.

Jaquette, Jane S., and Sharon L. Wolchik. 1998. *Women and democracy: Latin America and Central and Eastern Europe.* Baltimore: Johns Hopkins University Press.

Joseph, Richard. 1998. "Africa, 1990–1997: From Abertura to closure." *Journal of Democracy* 9(2): 3–17.

Kenworthy, L., and M. Malami. 1999. "Gender inequality in political representation: A worldwide comparative analysis." *Social Forces* 78(1): 235–268.

Korpi, W. 2000. "Faces of inequality: Gender, class, and patterns of inequalities in different types of welfare states." *Social Politics: International Studies in Gender, State and Society* 7(2): 127–91.

Korpi, W., T. Ferrarini, and S. Englund. 2009. "Egalitarian gender paradise lost? Re-examining gender inequalities in different types of welfare states." Presented at EMPLOY/FAMNET Workshop, Berlin, May 11–12, 2009.

Kunovich, Sheri, and Pamela Paxton. 2005. "Pathways to power: the role of political parties in women's national political representation." *American Journal of Sociology* 111: 505–552.

Lapidus, Gail Warshofsky. 1993. "Gender and restructuring: The impact of perestroika and its aftermath on Soviet women." In V. M. Moghadam, ed., *Democratic reform and the position of women in transitional economies*. Oxford: Clarendon Press, 137–161.

Lee, Rose J. 2000a. "Democratic consolidation and gender politics in South Korea." In R. J. Lee and C. Clark, eds., *Democracy and the status of women in East Asia*. Boulder, CO: Lynne Rienner, 123–141.

Lee, Rose J. 2000b. "Electoral reform and women's empowerment: Taiwan and South Korea." In R. J. Lee and C. Clark, eds., *Democracy and the status of women in East Asia*. Boulder, CO: Lynne Rienner, 47–59.

Leira, A. 1992. *Welfare states and working mothers: The Scandinavian experience*. New York: Cambridge University Press.

Leira, A. 2002. "Updating the 'gender contract'? Childcare reforms in the Nordic countries in the 1990s." *NORA: Nordic Journal of Women's Studies* 10(2): 81–89.

Levitsky, Steven, and Lucan Way. 2001. *Competitive authoritarianism: Hybrid regime change in Peru and Ukraine in comparative perspective*. Glasgow: Centre for the Study of Public Policy, University of Strathclyde.

Levitsky, Steven, and Lucan A. Way. 2002. "The rise of competitive authoritarianism." *Journal of Democracy* 13(2): 51–65.

Lewis, Jane. 1992. "Gender and the development of welfare regimes." *Journal of European Social Policy* 2(3): 159–73.

Lindberg, Staffan I. 2004. "Women's empowerment and democratization: The effects of electoral systems, participation and experience in Africa." *Studies in Comparative International Development* 39(1): 28–53.

Mama, Amina. 1995. "Feminism or femocracy? State feminism and democratisation in Nigeria." *Africa Development* 20(1): 37–58.

McBride, Dorothy, and Amy Mazur (Eds.). 2010. *The politics of state feminism: Innovation in comparative research*. Philadelphia: Temple University Press.

Molyneux, Maxine. 1985. "Mobilization without emancipation? Women's interests, the state, and revolution in Nicaragua." *Feminist Studies* 11(2): 227–254.

Moses, Joel. 1977. "Women in political roles." In D. Atkinson, A. Alexander Dallin, and G. W. Lapidus, eds., *Women in Russia*. Stanford, CA: Stanford University Press.

O'Connor, J. S., A. S. Orloff, and A. Shaver. 1999. *States, markets, families: Gender, liberalism, and social policy in Australia, Canada, Great Britain, and the United States*. Cambridge, UK: Cambridge University Press.

Orloff, Ann. 1996. "Gender in the welfare state." *American Review of Sociology* 22: 51–78.

Orloff, Anna Shola. 2009. "Gendering the comparative analysis of welfare states: An unfinished agenda." *Sociological Theory* 27(3): 317–343.

Paxton, Pamela. 1997. "Women in national legislatures: A cross-national analysis." *Social Science Research* 26: 442–464.

Paxton, Pamela, Melanie M. Hughes, and Matthew Painter. 2012. "The difference time makes: Latent growth curve models of women's political representation." *European Journal of Political Research* 49(1): 25–52.

Posadskaya, Anastasia. 1993. "Changes in gender discourses and policies in the Former Soviet Union." In V. M. Moghadam, eds., *Democratic reform and the position of women in transitional economies*. Oxford: Clarendon Press, 162–179.

Racioppi, Linda, and Katherine O'Sullivan. 1995. "The 'woman question' and national identity: Soviet and post-Soviet Russia." In R. S. and A. F. a. J. H. Gallin, eds., *The women and international development annual*. Boulder, CO: Westview Press, 173–202.

Reynolds, Andrew. 1999. "Women in the legislatures and executives of the world: Knocking at the highest glass ceiling." *World Politics* 51(4): 547–572.

Ross, Michael. 2008. "Oil, Islam, and women." *American Political Science Review* 102(1): 107–123.

Saraceno, C. 2007. "Family change, family policies and the restructuring of welfare." In *Family, market and community: Equity and efficiency in social policy.* Paris: Organisation for Economic Co-operation and Development, 81–100.

Schedler, Andreas. 2006. *Electoral authoritarianism: The dynamics of unfree competition.* Boulder, CO: Lynne Rienner Publishers, Inc.

Siim, Birte. 2000. *Gender and citizenship: Politics and agency in France, Britain and Denmark.* New York: Cambridge University Press.

Sperling, Valerie. 1999. *Organizing women in contemporary Russia: Engendering transition.* Cambridge, UK: Cambridge University Press.

Staudt, Kathleen. 1985. "Women's political consciousness in Africa: A framework for analysis." In J. Monson and M. Kalb, eds., *Women as food producers in developing countries.* Los Angeles: University of California African Studies Centre, 71–84.

Steady, Filomina. 1975. *Female power in African politics: The national congress of Sierre Leone women.* Pasadena: Munger Africana Library, California Institute of Technology.

Tobar, Marcela Ríos. 2003. "Paradoxes of an unfinished revolution." *International Feminist Journal of Politics* 5(2): 256–280.

Tripp, Aili. 2010. *Museveni's Uganda: Paradoxes of power in a hybrid regime.* Boulder, CO: Lynne Rienner.

Tripp, Aili Mari. 2011. "Legislating gender based violence in post-conflict Africa." *Journal of Peacebuilding and Development* 6(1): 7–20.

Tripp, Aili, Isabel Casimiro, Joy Kwesiga, and Alice Mungwa. 2009. *African women's movements: Transforming political landscapes.* New York: Cambridge University Press.

Tripp, Aili Mari, and Melanie Hughes. 2010. *Armed conflict, democratization, and women's legislative representation in Africa, 1980–2008.* Washington, DC: American Political Science Association.

Tripp, Aili Mari, and Alice Kang. 2008. "The global impact of quotas: On the fast track to increased female legislative representation." *Comparative Political Studies* 41(3): 338–361.

True, Jacqui. 2003. *Gender, globalization, and postsocialism: The Czech Republic after communism.* New York: Columbia University Press.

UNICEF, *Women in Transition*, The Monee Project, CEE/CIS/Baltics, Regional Monitoring Report, No. 6, 1999.

Van de Walle, Nicolas. 2002. "Africa's range of regimes." *Journal of Democracy* 13(2): 66–80.

Walby, Sylvia. 2004. "The European Union and gender equality: Emergent varieties of gender regime." *Social Politics: International Studies in Gender, State and Society* 11(1): 4–29.

Wallerstein, Immanuel. 1964. "Voluntary associations." In J. Coleman and C. Rosberg, eds., *Political parties and national integration in tropical Africa.* Berkeley: University of California Press, 318–338.

Waylen, Georgina. 1994. "Women and democratisation: Conceptualising gender relations in transition politics." *World Politics* 46(3): 327–354.

Waylen, Georgina. 2007a. *Engendering transitions: Women's mobilization, institutions, and gender outcomes.* Oxford: Oxford University Press.

Waylen, Georgina. 2007b. "Women's mobilization and gender outcomes in transitions to democracy—The case of South Africa." *Comparative Political Studies* 40(5): 521–546.

Wolchik, Sharon. 1995. *Democratization in central and Eastern Europe: progress or regression for women?* New York: Atlantic Council of the United States.

Wunsch, J. S. 1991. "Centralization and development in post-independence Africa." In J. S. Wunsch and D. Olowu, eds., *The failure of the centralized state: Institutions and self-governance in Africa.* Boulder, CO: Westview Press.

Yoon, Mi Yung. 2001. "Democratization and women's legislative representation in sub-Saharan Africa." *Democratization* 8(2): 169–190.

Yoon, Mi Yung. 2004. "Explaining women's legislative representation in sub-Saharan Africa." *Legislative Studies Quarterly* 29(3): 447–468.

Zakaria, Fareed. 1997. "The rise of illiberal democracy." *Foreign Affairs* 76(6): 22–43.

Zakaria, Fareed. 2004. *The future of freedom: Illiberal democracy at home and abroad.* New York: W.W. Norton & Co.

CHAPTER 21

··

PARTY POLITICS

··

MIKI CAUL KITTILSON

INTRODUCTION

··

Political parties are central actors in the democratic process, linking citizen interests with policy making. Therefore, parties are integral to feminist activists and gender politics. Since the 1970s, women across many democracies stepped up efforts to gain voice in party politics (Lovenduski and Hills 1981; Randall 1987; Bashevkin 1991; Kaplan 1992; Lovenduski and Randall 1993). In turn, women are integral to party politics, and gender is sewn up in party competition, formal rules, and norms. Yet political parties long ignored women's demands for representation, and this pattern holds for countries around the world (Lovenduski and Norris 1993; Harvey 1998; Sanbonmatsu 2001). Without women's voice in the debate, parties will often overlook the gendered nature of policy alternatives.

Since the 1970s, scholarship on gender and party politics has grown from questions of whether women can make inroads in party politics toward the conditions under which women achieve the strongest gains (Childs and Krook 2006). Research that focuses solely on women and men's political activities may place the onus for remedying gender inequalities solely on women themselves rather than on existing institutions and practices. Both women's activities and the gendered nature of the opportunity structure are integral to a theoretical framework. This agency–structure dichotomy is rooted in Joni Lovenduski and Pippa Norris's (1993) seminal edited volume on gender and party politics. The most promising new research highlights a web of gendered structures and institutions within parties. Attention to the gendered and dynamic nature of opportunities within parties is key to advancing research on gender and party politics.

How then does a party's opportunity structure mediate women's efforts to gain influence? Only comparative studies—whether over time, across parties, or across countries—can illuminate how party rules and processes amplify or mute voices (and thus representation) in party politics. Some party structures have proven more permeable at certain points in time. The opportunity structure is both exogenous and endogenous to the party itself (Kittilson 2006). In this sense, gender exists outside parties in social structures and is also constructed inside party politics (Sanbonmatsu 2010). Importantly, revealing the gendered opportunity structure sheds light on the role of informal institutions in creating opportunities. Rather than often studied legal barriers, evidence points toward a complex web of shared practices and norms that have differential effects for men and women (Lovenduski 1998).

The nexus of party and gender can be examined at multiple sites within party politics, and this chapter focuses on the electorate and party organization. In the electorate, women and men participate as party supporters and voters. Group differences are often dubbed a *gender gap*. How then does the opportunity structure shape the ways men and women connect to party politics? Women's activities inside parties are numerous, as party activists, party elites, and candidates and members of their party's parliamentary delegation. How can the opportunity structure influence women's strategies for inclusion inside parties? These research questions necessitate attention to party change. By taking a longitudinal approach, we can enhance our understanding of women and politics and party politics theory (Kittilson 2006; Hughes and Paxton 2008).

Past research has most often focused on women in party politics, and cutting-edge research takes stock of men and women, and the gendered nature of parties. In addition, many established studies have focused on the United States and Western Europe, and built upon studies written in English, although the scope has broadened considerably in recent decades. This chapter reflects some of those biases in the state of research on gender, women, and party politics and highlights the trajectory of future research that pays careful attention to gender and to a variety of political contexts.

GENDER IN THE ELECTORATE: SOCIAL FORCES STRUCTURE MEN AND WOMEN'S PARTY ATTACHMENTS

The importance of the party in the electorate is to link individuals to the democratic process, and men and women may connect with party politics in different ways. Given that the overriding objective of most parties is to win votes and gain office (Downs 1957; Ware 1996), party competition serves as a foundation for both the gendered nature of contemporary parties and for the strides women have taken.

In most democracies, men and women tend to support different parties, and this gap is meaningful in many instances. Since enfranchisement, women were traditionally more likely to support rightist parties due in part to women's higher levels of religiosity (Duverger 1955; Lipset 1960). In recent decades, however, women have increasingly shifted support toward leftist parties, especially as more women move into the paid workforce (Mueller 1988; Oskarson 1995; Inglehart and Norris 2000). In the United States, the gender gap intensified around 1980, rooted in the movement of more men toward the Republican Party and away from parties altogether as political independents (Kaufmann and Petrocik 1999; Norrander 1999). The partisan gender gap takes shape in the formative years of political socialization, as Fridkin and Kenney (2007) find differences between junior high age boys and girls.

Importantly, Rosie Campbell (2006) points out the dangers in treating women and men as monolithic blocks of voters. Instead, subgroup differences among men and among women are essential to understanding the forces shaping partisan attachments. Some of these intragroup distinctions may be based on age, education, income, race, ethnicity, marital, and parental status. For example, younger women are more likely to support the more leftist Labour Party in Britain and to prioritize healthcare and education (Campbell 2006). At the same time, younger women tend to have more education and are more likely to be employed. In addition, men and women's partisanship varies across regions in the United States (Norrander 1999).

How then does the opportunity structure affect men and women's partisan attachments? In the electorate, conditional forces are exogenous to political party organizations: forces are broadly social and political, with gendered implications at the individual level. First, the political climate conditions the direction and size of differences among men and women. In one of the most careful and thorough analyses of gender differences in partisanship, Box-Steffensmeier, De Boef, and Lin (2004) investigate the dynamics of the gender gap in the United States from 1979 to 2000. When the electorate overall moves in a conservative direction, gender differences widen as women's relatively more leftist position shifts further from the center. In addition, changes in the economy affect men and women differently. Because women are disproportionately affected by social spending cuts, relative to their male counterparts, women are less likely to support the party pushing for the cuts (Cheney, Alvarez, and Nagler 1998).

Cross-national studies of the gender gap in partisan support point toward similar fundamental social and economic mediating forces with differential effects for men and women. In recent decades in postindustrial societies, women's steady entrance into the paid labor force coupled with declining attendance at religious services has eroded traditional conservative values and gender roles, weakening the ties that once linked women with more conservative parties

(Inglehart and Norris 2000). Iversen and Rosenbluth (2006) suggest that rising levels of women in the workforce are not alone in driving gender differences in party support but also increases in women's autonomy through rising divorce rates, which heighten the chances that women may use welfare state benefits. Increased dependence on these benefits means women will be less likely to support the more conservative parties advocating spending cuts. Further, across countries and over time, men and women tend to have different labor market opportunities, and women's higher levels of employment in the public sector also increase their support for social spending and leftist parties.

Gendered Party Organizational Structures

From Scandinavia to Latin America, in nearly every country where party membership rolls are recorded by gender, women make up nearly half of party members (Sundberg 1995; Htun 2005). However, like most organizations, the higher up the ladder one goes, the fewer women one encounters. Across democracies, we find the fewest women at the highest echelons of the party structure (Putnam 1976; Bashevkin 1993). Certainly men and women's qualifications, resources and years of service within the party organization contribute toward their chances for election to party leadership positions. Thus, even as women work within the party ranks and accumulate political capital at ever higher rates, women are still woefully underrepresented among party leadership. Although no formal rules barring women exist in the parties of democracies today, women's opportunities within parties are relatively more closed than those of their male counterparts.

Inside the Party Organization: To Women's Section, or Not to Women's Section?

In most democracies around the world, parties play an essential gatekeeping role in the recruitment of women for office, including the United States (Gibson et al. 1983; Herrnson 1988; Lovenduski and Norris 1993; Aldrich 2000; Norris 2006; Sanbonmatsu 2006). Despite persistent underrepresentation, in recent decades women's numbers within the party hierarchy and as party candidates have grown substantially. Parties vary greatly in the gender composition of their leadership, candidates, and parliamentary delegations (Lovenduski and Norris 1993; Norris and Lovenduski 1995). For example, in South Africa the Democratic Party sends a delegation of 20 percent women to parliament, while the African

National Congress sends nearly double that percentage. Similarly, the percentage of women in the Bundestag from the German Christian Democratic Party grew from almost 7 percent in 1983 to 22 percent by 2009.

Women's movements differ over whether to pursue electoral and party politics or to instead seek change solely through the movement itself and protest-based forms of participation. By the 1980s, most democracies witnessed a resurgence of women's activity in party politics (Lovenduski and Norris 1993). Party women sought greater gender equality in parties and programmatic policy changes. In Sweden, Norway, and Finland, women chose the party politics avenue early on and as a consequence made sizeable gains in electoral politics decades before women in most other democracies (Gelb 1989; Sainsbury 1993; Kittilson 2006).

Historically, women's recruitment as party supporters and members often occurred through parties' internal women's organizations, sometimes known as auxiliaries or sections. In fact, women's party organizations were sometimes established before women had the right to vote (Sundberg 1995) and eventually served as mechanisms to elicit women's support but traditionally relegated women to positions of coffee servers and helpers within the party. However, the era of the large women's organization is over for most parties, and many contemporary women's organizations lobby for power over policy making (Dahlerup and Gulli 1985). Women's wings within Latin American and European parties, increasingly built upon their functions to mobilize women to vote, moved to advocating for women's power within the party and as candidates for office (Dahlerup and Gulli 1985; Htun 2005). Today's looser and more streamlined women's organizations lobby party leaders and participate in party decision-making processes.

Are women more effective in integrating into mainstream party channels or organizing a women's organization within mainstream parties or in forming their own separate women's parties? One line of reasoning suggests a separate women's organization within the party facilitates women's gains. Women's party organizations have proven important forces for promoting more women for office (Lovenduski and Norris 1993; Leyenaar 2004, 110–112; Kittilson 2006; Wiliarty 2010). These sections can channel and articulate women's demands for greater representation, both in substance and in women's presence among decision makers. By fostering repeated interactions among party women, party women's organizations encourage a sense of group consciousness and provide a launching pad for campaigns to influence party leaders to address gender inequality.

In contrast, others theorize that women's sections within parties hinder women's integration into mainstream party channels by isolating women, keeping them from the centers of real power (Appleton and Mazur 1993). For example, this very concern motivated a set of young women within the Danish parties and the Dutch Labor Party to shut down their women's sections around 1970, much to the chagrin of senior women in the party who had worked hard to build up the women's sections (Dahlerup and Gulli 1985; Leyenaar 2004). However, Dutch Labor women reversed course in 2000 with a reinvigorated women's network, revving up their pursuit of gender equality policies.

Taken together, the evidence from party women's organizations suggests they can be important forces for change, depending upon the prevailing patterns of representation within parties (Wiliarty 2010). It is likely that a two-pronged strategy is most effective. That is, women in parties may maximize their gains when they simultaneously pursue both women's organizations and mainstream party channels.

While women's parties have formed in some rare instances, women's participation in party politics most often occurs through established parties, replete with traditions of exclusion and gendered opportunity structures. At different points in time and varying degrees of success, women's parties have emerged in countries such as Russia, Armenia, Belarus, Bulgaria, Georgia, Kyrgystan, Moldova, Ukraine, Lithuania, and Iceland. More women in the workforce and women's rising education levels in part explain the demand for women's parties. John Ishiyama (2003) examines the rise of a set of women's parties in postcommunist countries and points toward the political opportunity structure in providing windows of opportunity for women's parties to gain momentum. Specifically, presidential systems and candidate-centered elections enhance the likelihood that these small parties will have some electoral success.

Connections hold tight between women on the inside of parties and in parliaments. Women's presence among party elites is a key predictor of the adoption of gender quota policies and of the election of women to parliamentary office (Tremblay and Pelletier 2001; Kittilson 2006) (see the chapter by Mona Lena Krook and Leslie Schwindt-Bayer in this volume). More women at all levels of the party, and especially women as party elites (e.g., on the party's National Executive Committee) who are willing to let down the ladder, can benefit women's efforts for nomination, contingent upon the electoral and nomination rules (Kunovich and Paxton 2005; Kittilson 2006). Women among the party elite similarly work to expand the scope of policy agendas. In more cohesive parties, women's power among the party leadership proves especially important. Systematic analysis of 142 parties in twenty-four democracies from 1990 to 2003 shows that women's rising numbers among a party's parliamentary delegation and among its leadership contribute to greater emphasis on social justice issues (Kittilson 2011). In addition, more women within the top-party ranks improve the likelihood that a party will adopt gender quotas for party offices and for parliamentary candidates (Caul 1999; Kittilson 2006).

Gender in Party Organizations:
Competition and Institutions

Women candidates fare as well as male contenders across democracies (Darcy and Schramm 1977; Welch and Studlar 1986; Rule 1987; Darcy, Welch, and Clark 1994; Htun 2005; Fieldhouse 2008; Murray 2008) The key is getting more women to run for office, and as gatekeepers to elected office, parties' opportunity structures can facilitate and hinder women's gains as party elites and party members of parliament (MPs).

How then does party competition shape women's opportunities inside parties? Party competition may spur parties to run more women for office or to adopt policies to promote women such as gender quotas or to offer policy changes. In a comparison of American and Canadian parties from the 1970s to 1990s, Lisa Young (2000, 10) notes that women and women's movements are "most able to influence political parties when they are able to offer crucial resources—either money or votes—to the parties." Karen Beckwith (2007) contends that opportunities for women peak after a scandal or major electoral failure that topples a male party leader, which taints the group in power. Having fewer women leaders in place when scandal hits means fewer women are tainted by scandal or electoral failure. Supporting this relationship, Sylvia Bashevkin's (2010) study of party leaders in Canada from 1975 to 2009 finds women tend to win top posts when electoral competition is weaker, and especially among parties with little chance of assuming government. Evidence from Britain shows that the British Labour Party's promotion of women for office followed after years of Labour defeat at the polls. Eventually, party leaders acknowledged that women's votes were key to winning government and that promoting women for office might help gain women's electoral support (Perrigo 1996). Thus, not only is women's presence important among the set of party leaders, but also the activities of these women in convincing other key actors that promoting women for office and gender-related policies will be electorally advantageous.

Competition often shapes party efforts to promote women and new policies through a process of contagion. Matland and Studlar (1996) find evidence for processes of contagion across the party systems of Canada and Norway. When one party runs more women for office, rival parties feel pressure to follow suit to attract women's votes. Across Western European parties, the presence of a party with quotas is linked with other parties in the system following their lead (Caul 2001). This process is especially evident in Belgium, where parties have been keen to outpace one another on gender quotas and national level quota law has coincided with party measures (Meier 2004). In South Africa, the adoption of a gender quota by the African National Congress substantially increased the number of women in their parliamentary delegation. At first, rival parties balked, citing the discriminatory nature of quotas. Yet competition among parties for women's votes eventually led other South African parties to follow suit, adopting quotas (Britton 2008).

Party organizations also present women with a complex set of institutions. Institutions include the rules of the game, standard practices, and shared norms (North 1990; Thelen 1999; Helmke and Levitsky 2004). Political institutions are rarely gender neutral but rather reinforce the power of dominant players in politics, who have traditionally been men (Kenney 1996; Lovenduski 1998, 2005). Formal institutions are codified, while informal institutions often operate as uncodified rules perpetuated outside of the official legal arena (Helmke and Levitsky 2004). Czudnowski (1975) theorizes formal institutions make it easier for new challengers to enter party politics. Because formal institutions are transparent to all aspirants, they are not limited to those already on the inside. Where and when women and men can similarly discern these institutions, women's opportunities for advancement are enhanced (Lovenduski and Norris 1993).

In contrast, parties also operate on less explicit (yet still routinized, institutionalized) practices and norms. And some parties rely on these informal institutions more than other parties. Common practices within parties may constrain women while bolstering men's traditional lock on power. Importantly, the routine practices and standards of party gatekeepers shape men and women's chances for advancement among the party ranks. Parties approach men to run for office more frequently than women in the United States (Lawless and Fox 2005). Further, party selectorates often value a common set of qualifications for potential candidates, such as prior office holding and a service to the party. While some qualifications are less gendered than others, many embody traditionally masculine traits (Tremblay and Pelletier 2001). Lovenduski (2005, 75) reports that across the British parties women reported being held to different standards than their male counterparts. For example, women candidates often report being questioned over who will look after their children or whether a spouse is supportive of candidacy.

Elin Bjarnegård (2010) traces the consequences of informal institutions for men and for women in Thai party politics. In Thailand, parties are less institutionalized and frequently rely on informal institutional practices. Specifically, gendered political networks among the pool of potential candidates advantage men in the nomination process. Male aspirants tend to network with other men, while women tend to network with other women. Thus, women are largely excluded from male centers of power, rendering less support for women's burgeoning political careers within party circles (ibid.).

Beyond the degree of formalization, four additional sets of institutions condition men and women's opportunities in party politics: party ideology; nomination rules; degree of centralization; and factionalization. Party ideology is the most often cited party characteristic to affect women's fortunes. Connections between women's movements and parties have been tighter with leftist parties compared with centrist and rightist parties (Jenson 1982; Katzenstein and Mueller 1987, 6). Further, feminist organizations have typically maintained tighter relationships with leftist parties than centrist or rightist parties, and the connections between women's organizations and parties appear integral to parties prioritizing gender-related issues (Mazur 2002).

Leftist parties are often more likely to nominate women to winnable positions and thus send more women to parliament than rightist parties (Duverger 1955; Beckwith 1986, 1992; Randall 1987, 108; Erickson 1993; Matland 1993; Matland and Studlar 1996; Caul 1999; Craske 1999; Kittilson 2006). In addition, leftist parties have promoted more women to their top echelons. In a study of 135 provincial and federal party leadership contests in Canada from 1980 to 2005, major parties and rightist parties elected fewer women as leaders (O'Neill and Stewart 2009).

However, party ideology may matter less today than in recent years as rightist parties have often made strides in promoting women for office. Childs and Webb (2011) document changes taken by the British Conservative Party to promote women MPs as part of a campaign to modernize the party's image under David Cameron's leadership. The Conservative leadership recommended that particular constituencies consider a set of priority candidates who come from underrepresented groups such as women, when drawing up their shortlist of nominees (Childs 2008). Across Latin America, Htun (2005) suggests a similar trend, as major right-wing parties have gained ground in promoting women for office. Similarly, Wiliarty (2010) examines women's numerous achievements in the German Christian Democratic Party, from the adoption of candidate gender quotas to more liberal abortion policies.

Candidate nomination procedures within parties directly filter women's efforts to achieve office, and these processes are intimately linked with the degree of centralization within parties. Candidate selection procedures vary considerably from one party to the next, even within the same country. Greater centralization means party leadership has more control over who is nominated to run for the party. Past studies are divided over whether central party control aids or inhibits women. On one hand, Kira Sanbonmatsu (2006) finds that in the American context party leaders often underestimate women's ability to win votes and are less supportive of women's candidacies. Evidence from Sweden offers a similar conclusion. Women's swift and considerable gains as parliamentarians across the Swedish parties resulted from their nominations at the local and constituency level, and the national party organizations rarely intervened (Sainsbury 1993). On the other hand, both widely comparative and studies of the United States suggest that party leaderships can promote women for office, under the right circumstances (Burrell 2006; Kittilson 2006).

In addition, parties' candidate selection procedures offer a direct mechanism to increase the number of women candidates (Hinojosa 2009). Gender quotas can deliver a fast track to more women in office (Dahlerup 2006). Party-level and national-level candidate gender quotas alike often bring gains for women, although the amount of change varies across countries, parties, and types of quota policies (Htun and Jones 2002; Meier 2004; Tripp and Kang 2008; Krook 2010). Increasingly, parties have set targets and more formal quotas for gender equality in the number of candidates on the party list, and often for women's placement on the list. The Quota Database shows that as of 2010 nearly sixty countries around the world had at least one party with a gender quota policy (http://www.quotaproject.org). These policies represent an explicit acknowledgment by parties that having more women candidates is desirable and that direct action must be taken to level the playing field. Whether gender quotas are part of party's electoral strategy, the outcome is most often gains for women in parliament (Tripp and Kang 2008). In Argentina, Franceschet and Piscopo (2008) find compelling evidence that new policies such as gender quotas can introduce complications in the process of substantive representation—quotas can both represent a new mandate for women and reinforce older gender stereotypes. If elected women are tagged *quota women* as a consequence of this policy, negative connotations can hinder women's ability to raise new issues and to lobby the party leadership for new pieces of legislation.

Finally, factionalization within parties can open up windows of opportunity for women. Jo Freeman (1987) notes that the Democratic Party in the United States operates on the basis of group claims, while the Republican Party is more oriented toward the power of individuals within the party. Thus, organized groups such as the women's movement have found greater representation in the Democratic Party. In an important book on gender in the German Christian Democratic Party (CDU), Sarah Wiliarty (2010) credits women's achievements to the power of the CDU's Women's Union. Importantly, the CDU routinely represents group interests by recognizing organized factions, and privileging those who form alliances. Since the 1960s, the Women's Union shifted from largely a social group into a power player in CDU policy making. When the Women's Union gained power as part of the party's dominant coalition, gains in party and parliamentary power followed suit. In a similar fashion, within the British Labour Party, as the powerful trade union faction saw its organizational strength decline, unionists increasingly sought women's support within the party, bolstering women's representation (Perrigo 1996).

Factionalism is reported to work differently in Islamist parties in Jordan and Yemen in the 1990s. In a study of women in the Islamic Action Front, and Yemeni Reform Group, Clark and Schwedler (2003) document women's limited but surprising gains despite a hostile patriarchal culture and attribute the timing of women's success to divisive splits between the dominant party factions, which opened up short-term opportunities for individual women to gain party leadership positions. Importantly, these women were not formally organized as a power-seeking group within the party.

Party Change: A Gendered Lens

Existing party and institutional theories fall short in explaining change over time. Theories of party change are often characterized by evolutionary adaptation, suggesting party convergence toward a similar model (Katz and Mair

1995). However, on gender-related issues and women's candidacies, parties diverge significantly. Indeed, party-level differences trump national-level differences. By taking stock of women's gains in party politics, it is clear that parties do not automatically reflect changes in their surroundings, nor do they adapt in some passive, evolutionary process. Instead, both parties and women are strategic actors, who respond and lead change the institutional structures they face (Lovenduski and Norris 1993). Women's activities and pressure from the bottom up appear to be a necessary force for party change but not a sufficient force. Often the impetus for visible policy changes is led by the party leadership and sparked by party competition for votes. Party leaders may promote new issues when those efforts appear to benefit the party on Election Day (Wolbrecht 2000). Visible rule and policy changes on gender-related issues are often part of a party strategy to court women voters and thus exemplify party change led from the top down.

Women seek equality inside party organization and as party nominees for elected office. In addition, women seek to expand party policy profiles to include gender-related issues and to highlight the gendered implications of policy alternatives more generally. As women make gains, parties' formal and informal institutions shift over time—some parties adopt gender quotas for candidates, and some parties emphasize new gender-related issues, while other parties reinvigorate sex-segregated organizational vehicles, such as women's sections. By taking dynamics into perspective, we can better understand the reciprocal relationship between women's strategies and goals on one hand and the institutional opportunity structure on the other. To maximize their efforts, women in parties take into account the existing and often masculine institutions that shape opportunities. Likewise, in an effort to achieve gender equality and to introduce new issues into party politics, women have and will transform party rules, processes, norms, and goals. It is, in part, through wholesale shifts in formal rules and through incremental changes in informal institutions that parties change.

Party competition is integral to both party change and realizing women's and feminist gains alike. An environment in which parties vie for women's votes is conducive to women's nomination for elected office, often through a process of contagion of gender policies and strategies across parties (Costain 1992; Kolinsky 1993; Matland and Studlar 1996; Norris 1999; Baldez 2003). Similarly, party competition leads parties to highlight new issues, and in some instances those previously neglected issues are related to gender equality or traditionally private concerns such as parental leave.

Women's achievements in party politics defy the notion that parties are roadblocks to women's political power. Women's progress in party politics exemplifies a process of democratic inclusion, albeit a contested, slow, uneven, and incomplete process. Increasingly, women participate at higher rates as party activists, leaders, and elected officials. At the electoral level, parties attempt to court women's votes by prioritizing new issues and running more women for office. As women have brought claims for greater representation to parties, parties as organizations have altered internal institutions such as candidate selection procedures (Lovenduski and Norris 1993; Tremblay and Pelletier 2001). And women's efforts have led to policy achievements—from candidate gender quotas and reserved seats for women to greater emphasis on new issues such as parental leave policies. Similar processes of party change have of course been exemplified by, for example, trade unions and blue-collar workers. More recent shifts related to women and gender remind party scholars that parties do more than adapt to changing circumstances, they continue to incorporate new issues and new groups in an effort to expand their bases of support.

Conclusions

Women's activities may be aimed at altering the party organization or the party's profile in government. Women within parties, both individually and as organized groups, have played an instrumental role in expanding the scope of the policy agenda in party politics. For example, women within American parties have worked to raise new issues (Freeman 1987; Wolbrecht 2000; Sanbonmatsu 2008). The American women's movement pushed the Democratic Party to adopt more feminist policy positions, aligning the Democrats with women's rights, while the more conservative Republican Party moved toward opposing these policies (Wolbrecht 2000). Both feminist and antifeminist women's groups have been active at the Democratic and Republican conventions for decades (Freeman 1987, 1993). And women within these parties have frequently invoked the gender gap in the vote to lobby party leaders for policy change or greater attention to gender-related issues (Mueller 1988).

Despite women's recent strides in historically male-dominated party politics, party scholarship dedicates scant attention to the role of women and gender (Childs 2008; Sanbonmatsu 2008). What does a gendered lens teach us about party politics? A focus on gender highlights some important lessons: parties are still important to representation because they can and do change over time, and both formal and informal party institutions (the party opportunity structure) impact different sets of people in different ways.

Part of the opportunity structure for men and women is exogenous to parties. Party competition and political scandals can open up windows of opportunity for newcomers such as women. However, it is integral to have women with established track records inside the party to take advantage of these power shifts. In this way, the party's role in the electorate connects with its organizational face.

Other parts of the opportunity structure are endogenous to parties, and this web of formal and informal rules is especially relevant to mediating change in the party organization and in party policy profiles. Where party institutions are formalized and transparent, outsiders such as women find it easier to discern the rules in the first place. Beyond often-cited quota policies, it is clear that intraparty women's organizations can play an active role in advancing women's candidacies and policy goals. Comparing studies of the United States with other democracies, women's sections within parties appear most effective in more centralized and cohesive parties. Further, top-down electoral strategies to appeal to women voters through symbolic policies and women's candidacies are most often realized in centralized party structures. Where social networks are important to recruitment, circles of established power holders are often male and thus favor the entrance of men. Further, reliance on masculine characteristics and qualities implicitly favors male contenders for nomination.

Pioneering research has tended to focus on women as a group. Women as a group are quite diverse, and women's interests are continually redefined over time and around the world (Celis et al. 2009). A renewed focus on intersectionality reminds us that women have very different interests based upon their age, socioeconomic background, ethnicity, family ties, and occupation. Nuanced future research will open the doors to the circumstances under which formal and informal institutions benefit differently situated women. Further, greater attention to party strategy will allow us to better understand how and why parties target certain sets of men and women alike and how the context of a given election augments the power of a given group. As we seek to understand how and why parties respond to gender-related issues, it is imperative to consider not only issues that disproportionately affect women at a certain juncture in time (such as gender equality) but also the gendered implications of party policies more generally.

REFERENCES

Aldrich, John H. 2000. "Southern parties in the state and nation." *Journal of Politics* 63: 643–670.

Appleton, Andrew, and Amy Mazur. 1993. "Transformation or modernization: The rhetoric and reality of gender and party politics in France." In Joni Lovenduski and Pippa Norris, eds., *Gender and party politic.* London: SAGE, 86–112.

Baldez, Lisa. 2003. "Elected bodies: The gender quota law for legislative candidates in Mexico." *Legislative Studies Quarterly* 29(2): 231–258.

Bashevkin, Sylvia. 1991. "Women's participation in political parties." In Kathy Megyery, ed., *Women in Canadian politics.* Research Studies of the Royal Commission on Electoral Reform, vol. 6. Toronto: Dundern Press, 124–156.

Bashevkin, Sylvia. 1993. *Toeing the lines: Women and party politics in English Canada.* Toronto: Oxford University Press.

Bashevkin, Sylvia. 2010. "When do outsiders break in? Institutional circumstances of party leadership victories by women in Canada." *Commonwealth & Comparative Politics* 48(1): 72–90.

Beckwith, Karen. 1986. *American women and political participation*. Westport, CT: Greenwood Press.

Beckwith, Karen. 1992. "Comparative research and electoral systems: Lessons from France and Italy." *Women & Politics* 2: 1–33.

Beckwith, Karen. 2007. "Numbers and newness: The descriptive and substantive representation of women." *Canadian Journal of Political Science* 40(1): 27–49.

Bjarnegård, Elin. 2010. "Men in politics: Revisiting patterns of gendered parliamentary representation in Thailand and beyond," Ph.D. dissertation, Uppsala Universitet.

Box-Steffensmeier, Janet M., Suzanna De Boef, and Tse-Min Lin. 2004. "The dynamics of the partisan gender gap." *American Political Science Review* 98(3): 515–528.

Britton, Hannah E. 2008. "Challenging traditional thinking on electoral systems." In Manon Tremblay, ed., *Women and legislative representation*. New York: Palgrave Macmillan, 111–122.

Burrell, Barbara. 2006. "Political parties, women's organizations and efforts to recruit women candidates." In Susan J. Carroll and Richard L. Fox, ed., *Gender and elections: Change and continuity*. New York: Cambridge University Press, 184–202.

Campbell, Rosie. 2006. *Gender and the vote in Britain*. Colchester, UK: ECPR Press Monographs.

Caul, Miki L. 1999. "Women's representation in parliament: The role of political parties." *Party Politics* 5(1): 79–98.

Caul, Miki L. 2001. "Political parties and candidate gender policies: A cross-national study." *Journal of Politics* 63(4): 1214–1229.

Celis, K., S. Childs, J. Kantola, and M. L. Krook. 2009. "Constituting women's interests through representative claims." Paper presented at the annual meeting of the American Political Science Association, Toronto, Canada, September 3–6.

Cheney, Carol Kennedy, R. Michael Alvarez, and Jonathan Nagler. 1998. "Explaining the gender gap in U.S. presidential elections." *Political Research Quarterly* 51(2): 311–339.

Childs, Sarah. 2008. *Women and British party politics*. London: Routledge.

Childs, Sarah, and Mona Lena Krook. 2006. "Should feminists give up on critical mass? A contingent yes." *Politics & Gender* 2: 522–530.

Childs, Sarah, and Paul Webb. 2011. Sex, gender *and the conservative party*. Basingstoke, UK: Palgrave.

Clark, Janine Astrid, and Jillian Schwedler. 2003. Who opened the window? Women's activism in Islamist parties. *Comparative Politics* 35(3): 293–312.

Costain, Anne N. 1992. *Inviting women's rebellion: A political process interpretation of the women's movement*. Baltimore: Johns Hopkins University Press.

Craske, Nikki. 1999. *Women and politics in Latin America*. New Brunswick, NJ: Rutgers University Press.

Czudnowski, Moshe M. 1975. Political recruitment. In Fred Greenstein and Nelson Polsby, eds., *Handbook of political science: Micropolitical theory*, vol. 2. Reading, MA: Addison Wesley, 52–73.

Dahlerup, Drude. 2006. *Women, quotas and politics*. London: Routledge.

Dahlerup, Drude, and Brita Gulli. 1985. "Women's organizations in the Nordic Countries: Lack of force or counterforce?" In Elina Haavio-Mannila and T. Skard., eds., *Unfinished democracy*. Oxford: Pergamon Press, 59–78.

Darcy, Robert, and Sarah Slavin Schramm. 1977. "When women run against men." *Public Opinion Quarterly* 41: 1–12.

Darcy, Robert, Susan Welch, and Janet Clark. 1994. *Women, elections and representation*. Lincoln: University of Nebraska Press.

Downs, Anthony. 1957. *An economic theory of democracy*. New York: Wiley.

Duverger, Maurice. 1955. *The political role of women*. Paris: UNESCO.

Erickson, Lynda. 1993. "Making her way in: Women, parties and candidacies in Canada." In Joni Lovenduski and Pippa Norris, eds., *Gender and party politics*. London: SAGE.

Franceschet, Susan, and Jennifer M. Piscopo. 2008. "Gender quotas and women's substantive representation: Lessons from Argentina." *Politics & Gender* 4: 393–425.

Freeman, Jo. 1987. "Whom you know versus whom you represent: Feminist influence in the Democratic and Republican parties." In Mary Fainsod Katzenstein and Carole McClurg Mueller, eds., *The women's movements of the United States and Western Europe: Consciousness, opportunity and public policy*. Philadelphia: Temple University Press, 215–244.

Freeman, Jo. 1993. "Feminism versus family values: Women at the 1992 Democratic and Republican Conventions." *PS: Political Science and Politics* 26: 21–27.

Fridkin, Kim, and Patrick Kenney. 2007. "Examining the gender gap in children's attitudes towards politics." *Sex Roles* 56(3–4): 133–140.

Gelb, Joyce. 1989. *Feminism and politics*. Berkeley: University of California Press.

Gibson, James L., Cornelius P. Cotter, John F. Bibby, and Robert Huckshorn. 1983. "Assessing party organizational strength." *American Journal of Political Science* 27: 193–222.

Harvey, Anna. 1998. *Votes without leverage: Women in American electoral politics, 1920–1970*. New York: Cambridge University Press.

Helmke, Gretchen, and Steven Levitsky. 2004. "Informal institutions and comparative politics: A research agenda." *Perspectives on Politics* 2(4): 725–737.

Herrnson, Paul S. 1988. *Party campaigning in the 1980s*. Cambridge, MA: Harvard University Press.

Hinojosa, Magda. 2009. "Whatever the party asks of me: Women's political representation in Chile's Union Democrata Independiente." *Politics & Gender* 5(3): 377–408.

Htun, Mala. 2005. "Women, political parties and electoral systems in Latin America." In Julie Ballington and Azza Karam, eds. *Women in Parliament: Beyond Numbers*. Stockholm: International IDEA, 122–143.

Htun, Mala, and Mark Jones. 2002. "Engendering the right to participate in decision-making: Electoral quotas and women's leadership in Latin America." In Nikki Craske and Maxine Molineux, eds., *Gender and the politics of rights in Latin America*. London: Palgrave, 32–56.

Hughes, Melanie, and Pamela Paxton. 2008. "Continuous change, episodes, and critical periods." *Politics & Gender* 4(2): 233–264.

Inglehart, Ronald, and Pippa Norris. 2000. "The developmental theory of the gender gap: Women's and men's voting behavior in global perspective." *International Political Science Review* 21(4): 441–463.

Ishiyama, John. 2003. "Women's parties in post-communist politics." *Eastern European Politics and Societies* 17: 266–304.

Iversen, Torben, and Frances Rosenbluth. 2006. "The political economy of gender: Explaining cross-national variation in the gender division of labor and the voting gap." *American Journal of Political Science* 50(1): 1–19.

Jenson, Jane. 1982. "The modern women's movement in Italy, France and Great Britain: Differences in life cycles." *Comparative Social Research* 5: 341.

Kaplan, Gisela. 1992. *Contemporary Western European feminism.* New York: New York University Press.

Katz, Richard, and Peter Mair. 1995. "Changing models of party organization and party democracy: The emergence of the Cartel Party." *Party Politics* 1: 5–28.

Katzenstein, Mary, and Carole McClurg Mueller. 1987. *The women's movements of the U.S. and Western Europe.* Philadelphia: Temple University Press.

Kaufmann, Karen M., and John R. Petrocik. 1999. "The changing politics of American men: Understanding the sources of the gender gap." *American Journal of Political Science* 43(3): 864–887.

Kenney, Sally J. 1996. "New research on gendered political institutions." *Political Research Quarterly* 49(2): 445–466.

Kittilson, Miki Caul. 2006. *Challenging parties, changing parliaments: Women and elected office in contemporary Western Europe.* Columbus: The Ohio State University Press.

Kittilson, Miki Caul. 2011. Women, parties and platforms in post-industrial democracies. *Party Politics* 17(1): 66–92.

Kolinsky, Eva. 1993. *Women in contemporary Germany.* Oxford: Berg.

Krook, Mona Lena. 2010. *Quotas for women in politics: Gender and candidate selection reform worldwide.* Oxford: Oxford University Press.

Kunovich, Sheri, and Pamela Paxton. 2005. "Pathways to power: The role of political parties in women's national political representation." *American Journal of Sociology* 111: 505–552.

Lawless, Jennifer, and Richard L. Fox. 2005. *It takes a candidate: Why women don't run for office.* Cambridge, UK: Cambridge University Press.

Leyenaar, Monique. 2004. *Political empowerment of women: The Netherlands and other countries.* Amsterdam: Martinus Nijhoff Publishers.

Lipset, Seymour Martin. 1960. *Political man.* Garden City, NY: Doubleday Anchor Books.

Lovenduski, Joni. 1998. "Gendering research in political science." *Annual Review of Political Science* 1: 333–356.

Lovenduski, Joni. 2005. *State feminism and political representation.* London: Cambridge University Press.

Lovenduski, Joni, and Jill Hills. 1981. *The politics of the second electorate.* New York: Routledge.

Lovenduski, Joni, and Pippa Norris. 1993. *Gender and party politics.* London: SAGE.

Lovenduski, Joni, and Vicky Randall. 1993. *Contemporary feminist politics.* Oxford: Oxford University Press.

Matland, Richard E. 1993. "Institutional variables affecting female representation in national legislatures: The case of Norway." *Journal of Politics* 55: 737–755.

Matland, Richard E., and Donley T. Studlar. 1996. "The contagion of women candidates in single-member district and proportional representation electoral systems: Canada and Norway." *Journal of Politics* 58(3): 707–733.

Mazur, Amy. 2002. *Theorizing feminist politics*. Oxford: Oxford University Press.

Meier, Petra. 2004. "The mutual contagion effect of legal and party quotas: A Belgian perspective." *Party Politics* 10(5): 583–600.

Mueller, Carole. 1988. *The politics of the gender gap*. Beverly Hills, CA: SAGE.

Murray, Rainbow. 2008. "The power of sex and incumbency: A longitudinal study of electoral performance in France." *Party Politics* 14(5): 539–554.

Norrander, Barbara. 1999. "The evolution of the gap." *Public Opinion Quarterly* 63: 566–576.

Norris, Pippa. 1999. "A gender-generation gap?" In Geoffrey Evans and Pippa Norris, eds., *Critical elections: British parties and voters in long-term perspective*. London: SAGE, 65–79.

Norris, Pippa. 2006. "Recruitment." In Richard S. Katz and William Crotty, eds., *Handbook on political parties*. London: SAGE, 89–108.

Norris, Pippa, and Joni Lovenduski. 1995. *Political recruitment: Gender, race and class in the British parliament*. Cambridge, UK: Cambridge University Press.

North, Douglass C. 1990. *Institutions, institutional change, and economic performance*. New York: Cambridge University Press.

O'Neill, Brenda, and David K. Stewart. 2009. "Gender and political party leadership in Canada." *Party Politics* 15(6): 737–757.

Oskarson, Maria. 1995. "Gender gaps in Nordic voting behavior." In Lauri Karvonen and Per Selle, eds., *Women in Nordic politics*. Aldershot: Dartmouth, 59–81.

Perrigo, Sarah. 1996. "Women and change in the Labour Party, 1979-1995." *Parliamentary Affairs* 49(1): 116–129.

Putnam, Robert. 1976. *The comparative study of political elites*. Englewood Cliffs, NJ: Prentice Hall.

Randall, Vicky. 1987. *Women and politics: An international perspective*. Chicago: University of Chicago Press.

Rule, Wilma. 1987. "Electoral systems, contextual factors and women's opportunity for election to parliament in twenty-three democracies." *Western Political Quarterly* 40(3): 477–498.

Sainsbury, Diane. 1993. "The politics of increased women's representation: The Swedish case." In Joni Lovenduski and Pippa Norris, eds., *Gender and party politics*. London: SAGE, 263–290.

Sanbonmatsu, Kira. 2001. *Democrats, Republicans and the politics of women's place*. Ann Arbor: University of Michigan Press.

Sanbonmatsu, Kira. 2006. "The legislative party and candidate recruitment in the American states." *Party Politics* 12(2): 233–256.

Sanbonmatsu, Kira. 2008. "Representation by gender and parties." In Christina Wolbrecht, Karen Beckwith and Lisa Baldez, eds., *Political women and American democracy*. Cambridge, UK: Cambridge University Press, 96–109.

Sanbonmatsu, Kira. 2010. "Organizing American politics, organizing gender." In Jan Leighley, ed., *Oxford handbook of American elections and political behavior*. New York: Oxford University Press, 415–432.

Sundberg, Jan. 1995. "Women in Scandinavian party organizations." In Lauri Karvonen and Per Selle, eds., *Women in Nordic politics*. Aldershot: Dartmouth, 83–111.

Thelen, Kathleen. 1999. "Historical institutionalism in comparative politics." *American Review of Political Science* 2: 369–404.

Tremblay, Manon, and Rejean Pelletier. 2001. "More women constituency party presidents." *Party Politics* 7(2): 157–190.

Tripp, Aili Mari, and Alice Kang. 2008. "The global impact of quotas." *Comparative Political Studies* 41(3): 338–361.

Ware, Alan. 1996. *Political parties and party systems.* Oxford: Oxford University Press.

Welch, Susan, and Donley Studlar. 1986. "British public opinion toward women in politics." *Western Political Quarterly* 39(1): 138–154.

Wiliarty, Sarah Elise. 2010. *The CDU and the politics of gender in Germany.* Cambridge, UK: Cambridge University Press.

Wolbrecht, Christina. 2000. *The politics of women's rights: Parties, positions and change.* Princeton, NJ: Princeton University Press.

Young, Lisa. 2000. *Feminists and party politics.* Vancouver: UBC Press.

CHAPTER 22

....

ELECTORAL INSTITUTIONS

....

MONA LENA KROOK AND
LESLIE SCHWINDT-BAYER

INTRODUCTION
....

Political scientists have long recognized that electoral institutions—the formal and informal rules governing the electoral process—play a crucial role in structuring the dynamics of political life. The vast majority of studies have examined electoral institutions as explanations for a wide range of political phenomena, such as the nature of political party systems, patterns of political representation, and trends in political participation. A smaller subset of research has focused on explaining the emergence of electoral institutions and why countries change their electoral rules. A third subset of the literature emphasizes the gendered nature of electoral institutions, asking questions about how electoral rules and norms affect men and women in politics differently, how gender influences the adoption of electoral rules, and, of particular interest in recent years, why countries adopt women-friendly electoral institutions, such as gender quotas, and what the consequences of those rules are for politics.

In this chapter, we review the research in this third area, focusing on how electoral institutions shape the *emergence of candidates*, the *outcomes of elections*, and the dynamics of *democratic politics*. First, both formal and informal institutions influence opportunities for women and men to be nominated as candidates to elected office. A host of studies reveal that men have long been advantaged by electoral institutions, whereas women have long been disadvantaged. Institutions, such as electoral rules, party practices, and the recent introduction of new institutions in the form of electoral gender quotas, can improve gender equality in the emergence of candidates by increasing the representation of women on party ballots. Second, a variety of formal rules, including electoral formulas, district magnitudes, and ballot structures, are central in determining gender equality among elected representatives, once they have been nominated. For example, research shows that proportional representation electoral systems and higher district and party magnitudes increase the numbers of women who win seats in legislatures. Third, electoral institutions have important implications for democracy, affecting the status and behavior of legislators as well as the views that citizens have vis-à-vis the political process. Electoral institutions can have gendered effects in these areas, shaping women's and men's attitudes and behavior differently. Research in all three areas, therefore, demonstrates the need to consider how electoral institutions are gendered. It highlights the political advantages that men have long received from male-designed electoral institutions and elucidates ways that women contribute to—and benefit from—the basic frameworks of electoral politics.

Research on electoral institutions is but one of many dimensions of research on gender and politics. It fits most clearly into the broader area of work on gender and political institutions. Adopting a broad definition of *institutions*, this literature investigates the formal and informal rules, practices, and norms shaping gendered patterns of political access, behavior, and outputs (among others, see Lovenduski 1998; Kittilson and Schwindt-Bayer 2010, 2012; Krook and Mackay 2011).[1] A great deal of this research focuses on institutions as a target and instigator of political change, tracking the efforts of women's movements to engage with state and party actors (see essays in Part 4) as well as the degree of state responsiveness to women's political demands (see essays in Part 6). However, the literature that most extensively and explicitly explores the role of institutions across their many facets is research on gender and electoral politics, which we explore in detail here. Most of this literature to date treats women and women's interests as fairly homogenous and does not disaggregate by class, race, or sexuality. We retain this approach but discuss the importance and challenges of incorporating questions of intersectionality into this research agenda in the chapter's conclusion.

CANDIDATE EMERGENCE

The starting point of many studies of gender and politics has been the observation that, in countries around the globe, men are overrepresented in politics, whereas women constitute a small minority of elected officials. To answer the question of why fewer women than men occupy political office, scholars have pursued two main approaches. One is to focus on dynamics of candidate selection, analyzing how trends in political recruitment in general lead women to be less likely than men to come forward and be selected as candidates. A second involves exploring cross-national variations to identify factors associated with higher and lower levels of female representation. These two areas of research have come together explicitly in recent years, through analyses of the introduction and impact of electoral gender quotas.

Dynamics of Candidate Selection

Microlevel studies have been inspired by what has come to be known as the supply and demand model of candidate selection (Randall 1982; Norris and Lovenduski 1995). This model can be understood in terms of a sequential model of political recruitment progressing from (1) those who are *eligible* to run to (2) those who *aspire* to run, (3) those who are *nominated*, and (4) those who are eventually *elected* (Norris 1997). If no mechanisms of distortion are at work, the characteristics of the individuals present at each of these four stages should be roughly the same. Yet this is far from being the case: women often "fall away" at greater rates in the transition from each stage to the next, leaving men overrepresented. To understand why, researchers have asked whether women's underrepresentation stems from gender differences in political ambition causing fewer women than men to consider running (the *supply* of female aspirants), biases in the recruitment practices of male elites leading them to select fewer women than men (the *demand* for certain types of candidates), or prejudices on the part of voters preferring to elect men over women (the *outcomes* of elections).

Because voter bias has been found to be a weak explanation, research has focused primarily on the role of supply- and demand-side factors to explain why women are underrepresented in electoral politics (for more discussion of the role of political parties and party leaders in candidate recruitment, see the chapter by Kittilson in this volume). According to Norris and Lovenduski (1995), the two key factors that shape the supply of aspirants are (1) resources, such as time, money, and experience, and (2) motivation, such as drive, ambition, and interest in politics. This explanation focuses on the strategic calculations of potential candidates, seeking to understand why women are much less likely than men to believe that they are qualified to run for political office (Fox and Lawless 2004; Lawless and Fox 2005). Once aspirants emerge, their selection as candidates largely hinges on elite perceptions of their abilities, qualifications, and experience. Although elites generally frame their decisions as being based on merit, there is substantial evidence that many employ information shortcuts associating group characteristics as a proxy for abilities (Norris and Lovenduski 1995, 14; cf. Niven 1998).

While relying on an economic metaphor that implies efficient operation of the political market, this literature highlights—albeit implicitly—a range of formal and informal institutions shaping both the supply of and demand for female candidates (Krook 2010b; Krook 2010d). These institutions are clearly gendered, creating distinct opportunities for women and men to be chosen as potential candidates. They include formal institutions such as electoral laws, which influence the availability of seats and therefore inform party nomination strategies, as well as rules governing the candidate selection process within parties themselves, such as the presence or absence of primaries and the formal powers of individuals and groups within parties to choose or veto potential candidates (Franceschet 2005; Macaulay 2006). However, they also extend to more informal institutions, such as party practices regarding political apprenticeships, group memberships, spheres of recruitment, and beliefs about female candidates as liabilities or assets in the competition for electoral seats (Kolinsky 1991; Lovenduski and Norris 1993; Opello 2006; Sanbonmatsu 2006). Additional formal and informal considerations include broader legal and social norms, such as perceptions regarding the legitimacy of affirmative action and broader traditions of group representation (Inhetveen 1999; Meier 2000; Krook 2009).

Electoral Gender Quotas

The low numbers of women in elected office has inspired a number of campaigns around the globe to increase women's political representation. In some countries, like the United States, the focus has mainly been on supply-side strategies: raising money, talent spotting, and training women to wage effective political campaigns (Wolbrecht, Beckwith, and Baldez 2008). In most cases, however, the emphasis has been on demand-side explanations. Evidence from a variety of countries indicates that women's representation increases as the proportion of female party elites grows (Kunovich and Paxton 2005; Kittilson 2006), as well as when changes in the electoral and national landscape create opportunities for women's groups in civil society and political parties to lobby successfully for the increased selection of female candidates (Lovenduski and Norris 1993; Bauer and Britton 2006; Opello 2006; Wiliarty 2010). The introduction of electoral gender quotas, in particular, has played an important role in forcing elites to rethink the existing battery of "qualifications" for political office.

Gender quotas have now been adopted in more than one hundred countries, almost all within the last fifteen years (Dahlerup 2008; Krook 2009).[2] These policies vary in terms of where they appear, when they have been introduced, and how they attempt to alter candidate selection processes. In the language of electoral institutions, the adoption of gender quotas represents an instance of electoral reform (Celis, Krook, and Meier 2011). Although few studies conceptualize quota introduction in this way (see, however, Schwindt-Bayer and Palmer 2007; Krook 2009), doing so highlights the importance of considering gender inequality as a motivation for institutional change. This perspective also elucidates the need to consider a wide array of actors involved in electoral change and strategies for pursuing it.

Reserved seats are found in Africa, Asia, and the Middle East. They first emerged in the 1930s and were the main type of quota adopted through the 1970s, but a new wave of these measures has appeared since the year 2000. They involve setting aside seats for women that men are not eligible to contest. The proportion they mandate varies widely, from 3 percent to 30 percent. These policies are typically established through constitutional reforms and occasionally through changes to electoral laws, creating special electoral rolls for women, designating separate districts for female candidates, or distributing seats for women to parties based on their proportion of the popular vote (Howard-Merriam 1990; Nanivadekar 2006; Tripp 2006; Norris 2007;).

Party quotas were first adopted in the early 1970s by a small number of socialist and social democratic parties in Western Europe. Over the course of the 1980s and 1990s, however, they began to appear in a diverse array of political parties in all regions of the world. They are adopted voluntarily by individual parties that commit the party to aim for a certain proportion of women among its candidates to political office, usually between 25 percent and 50 percent. The particular phrasing of this requirement varies, however; some policies identify women as the group to be promoted by the quota (Durrieu 1999; Goetz and Hassim 2003; Valiente 2005), while others set out a more gender-neutral formulation, referring to a maximum or minimum percentage of candidates of one sex (Guadagnini 2005; Freidenvall, Dahlerup, and Skjeie 2006). In countries with proportional representation (PR) electoral systems, party quotas govern the composition of party lists; in countries with majoritarian arrangements, they are directed at a collection of single-member districts (Russell 2005; Opello 2006).

Legislative quotas, finally, tend to be found in developing countries, especially Latin America, and postconflict societies, primarily in Africa, the Middle East, and Southeastern Europe. Appearing in the 1990s, they are enacted through reforms to electoral laws or constitutions and are mandatory provisions applying to all parties. They generally call for women to form between 25 percent and 50 percent of all candidates. While their language is usually gender neutral, these policies vary in terms of how strictly their goals are articulated; some speak vaguely about facilitating access (Giraud and Jensen 2001), whereas others offer concrete guidelines regarding the selection and placement of female candidates (Jones 2004; Meier 2005). They are also implemented in different ways depending on the electoral system, applying to party lists (Meier 2004) or a group of single-member districts (Murray 2004). However, given their status as law, a distinctive feature of these measures is that they may contain sanctions for noncompliance and be subject to oversight from external bodies (Jones 1998; Baldez 2004).

Scholars have offered at least four explanations for the widespread and rapid adoption of quota policies. One focuses on the role of women's mobilization, which may involve women's organizations inside political parties, women's movements in civil society, women's groups in other countries, and even individual women close to powerful men (Bruhn 2003; Kittilson 2006), as women come to realize that change is likely to occur only through specific, targeted actions to promote female candidates (Krook 2006). A second account suggests that elites adopt quotas for strategic reasons, related to competition with other parties (Caul 2001; Meier 2004; Davidson-Schmich 2006) or opportunities to maintain control over rivals within or outside the party (Chowdhury 2002; Baldez 2004). A third is that quotas are introduced when they mesh with party- or country-specific values of equality and representation (Inhetveen 1999; Meier 2000; Opello 2006). A final explanation is that quotas spread through the efforts of international and transnational actors (Krook 2006; Norris 2007; Bush 2011).

As a result of these various processes, quotas have now been adopted in countries with a broad range of institutional, social, economic, and cultural characteristics. Yet the mere advent of gender quotas has not resulted in uniform increases in the percentage of women in parliament. Rather, some countries have witnessed dramatic increases following quota adoption (Bauer and Britton 2006; Kittilson 2006; Nanivadekar 2006), whereas others have seen more modest changes (Murray 2004; Siregar 2006) or even setbacks (Htun 2002; Verge 2008) in numbers of women elected. Reasons for variations include differences in policy details, related to wording (Htun 2002), requirements (Chama 2001; Meier 2004), sanctions (Murray 2004; Schmidt and Saunders 2004), and perceived legitimacy (Yoon 2001). They also depend on interactions between quotas and other political institutions, like electoral systems, district magnitudes, and ballot structures (Htun and Jones 2002; Tremblay 2008b; Schwindt-Bayer 2009) as well as party structures (Davidson-Schmich 2006; Kittilson 2006) and broader legal frameworks (Baines and Rubio-Marin 2005). A final factor, more difficult to quantify, is the political will to implement or resist quota provisions (Krook 2009). Quotas thus do not simply lead to numerical gains proportional to the quota policy but interact in important ways with features of the broader political context.

ELECTION OUTCOMES

An extensive literature in political science demonstrates that electoral institutions are critical to determining election outcomes. Electoral arrangements, for example, help to explain why some countries have two-party systems whereas others have multiparty systems (Duverger 1954). They also influence how legislators behave once elected, specifically whether they are responsive to their political parties and party leaders or cultivate personalistic followings (Cain, Ferejohn, and Fiorina 1987; Carey and Shugart 1995). Along similar lines, gender and politics scholars have long recognized that electoral rules are an important—if not *the* most important—variable affecting why women are underrepresented in legislatures. Duverger (1955, 148) may have been the first to note that proportional representation (PR) electoral systems are more favorable to female candidates than majoritarian systems.[3] In the five countries he studied, the three with PR electoral rules (France, Norway, and the Netherlands) had more women in office than the two countries with single-member district plurality (SMDP) systems (Great Britain and the United States). Since then, numerous studies have confirmed this pattern across a large number of countries and elections, and researchers have begun to delve more deeply into the differences among electoral systems to elaborate the nuanced ways electoral rules shape women's representation. This work has focused on electoral formulas, district and party magnitude, and ballot structure.[4]

Electoral Formulas

In their broadest conceptualization, electoral formulas refer to whether an electoral system allocates seats in proportion to votes that are received (PR) or based on the candidates or parties winning at least a plurality of votes (majoritarian or plurality systems). More nuanced work delves into specific differences within and across proportional and majoritarian systems, focusing on the mathematical formulas used to allocate seats. It distinguishes between quota formulas (such as Hare, Droop, Imperiali, and Reinforced Imperiali) and divisor formulas (such as d'Hondt, Sainte-Laguë, and modified Sainte-Laguë) in PR systems and majority rules and reduced-threshold or plurality rules in majoritarian systems. While the former has received significant attention in the gender literature, the latter has received very little.

Empirically, numerous studies have shown that countries with PR systems have significantly more women in office, all else equal (Duverger 1955; Rule 1981, 1987, 1994; Norris 1985; Darcy, Welch, and Clark 1994; Matland and Studlar 1996; Paxton 1997; Caul 1999; Kenworthy and Malami 1999; Reynolds 1999; Yoon 2004; Tremblay 2008b). In two of the earliest analyses, Norris (1985) and Rule (1987) present cross-national statistical studies of the effect of the type of electoral system in the context of other possible explanations for the varying levels of women's representation in national legislatures. Studying more than twenty advanced industrial or Western European states in the early 1980s, their studies find that the type of electoral system is the most significant predictor of varying levels of women's representation. A large amount of research following these studies has confirmed this trend (Matland and Studlar 1996; Yoon 2004; Tremblay 2008b; Tripp and Kang 2008; Paxton, Hughes, and Painter 2010).

Scholars have offered a number of reasons PR systems produce more women in office than majoritarian systems. Some emphasize links between

PR rules and party voting, arguing that PR systems allow party leaders to put women on ballots and be assured that voters will not counter their efforts to get women into office (Castles 1981; Rule 1987). Others have highlighted the fact that PR systems have higher rates of legislative turnover than plurality systems (Matland and Studlar 2004), making it easier for women to run for and win office because they are not competing as newcomers against incumbents (Schwindt-Bayer 2005; Tremblay 2007). However, the most popular explanation focuses on the differences in district magnitudes in PR and majoritarian systems. Whereas the availability of multiple seats per district in PR systems allows parties to "balance the ticket" in terms of gender representation (Matland 1998; Stockemer 2008), the single seats contested in most types of majoritarian systems create a zero-sum game, requiring a man to be excluded if a woman is chosen. These structural differences mean that the "contagion effect" witnessed in some PR systems, whereby competition for voters leads larger and more centrist parties to respond to efforts by small leftist parties to promote women's election (Matland and Studlar 1996), is less likely to occur in majoritarian systems.

Although controlling for the type of electoral system in comparative research on women and politics has become routine, recent work suggests that electoral system effects may vary across political and economic contexts. For example, women in some regions of the world benefit from PR rules whereas they do not in other regions (cf. Krook 2010c). Yoon (2004) finds that sub-Saharan African countries that use PR electoral rules elect more women to office than those that use SMDP or mixed electoral systems. In contrast, Stockemer (2008) notes that electoral rules have differential effects: the distinction between PR and SMDP affects women's election in Europe, but it plays no role in explaining variations among Latin American and Caribbean countries. Matland (1998) observes a similar pattern. He argues that the effect of electoral rules may depend on levels of economic development: below a particular threshold, women simply do not have a sufficient level of resources to get elected.

The mixed empirical evidence necessitates a closer look at the theoretical underpinnings of the connection between the type of electoral system and women's representation. This reveals that the logic behind the expected relationship is not very sound: all of the theories for why PR should lead to more women in office rely on intervening variables that are theoretically and empirically distinct from the electoral formula. They rely on the size of the district magnitude, legislative turnover, party rules for candidate selection procedures, and the strategies employed by parties at election time. These factors may correlate with PR systems or majoritarian systems, but they are fundamentally distinct from a dichotomous classification of electoral formulas. This suggests that grouping electoral systems into the broad categories of PR, majoritarian, and mixed systems is inappropriate, given that causal effects appear to be linked more to other factors that vary quite widely within each type of system (Moser 2001).

District and Party Magnitude

One more nuanced measure of electoral systems is the size of the electoral district, or district magnitude. As alluded to already, higher district magnitudes increase incentives for parties to balance their tickets. In an SMDP system, for example, winning a legislative seat is a zero-sum game where a candidate from only one sex can win the election. Since women have long been excluded from the political process, parties have little incentive to fill the one position they could win with female newcomers. As district magnitude increases, the likelihood of winning a seat increases because the game is no longer zero-sum. Multiple candidates can be elected from each district. Larger districts are more favorable to the election of women because they make room for female newcomers without displacing male candidates. Parties thus have incentives to nominate both men and women to their ballots.

Empirical research has linked district magnitude to the election of more women in many countries (Schwindt-Bayer 2005; Tremblay 2008b). Engstrom (1987), for example, examines the election of women in Ireland where district magnitude varies from three to five and observes that more women get elected from the four- and five-member districts than from the three-member districts. Along similar lines, Matland and Brown (1992) find that multimember districts elect more women than single-member districts in two U.S. states. Rule (1987) confirms these conclusions in a study of twenty-three advanced industrial states, finding that PR systems with larger district magnitudes have more women in office than those with smaller district magnitudes. At the same time, however, the effects of district magnitude on women's election are not necessarily linear (Schwindt-Bayer 2005). Instead, there appears to be a diminishing returns effect whereby increases in district magnitude at lower levels, from one to two or three to four, for example, are likely to lead to larger increases in the election of women than increases in district magnitude at higher levels, from seventy-five to seventy-six, for example. Consequently, logging district magnitude offers a more appropriate specification of this variable in large-N cross sectional statistical analyses (Rule 1987; Schwindt-Bayer 2005).

Yet, while numerous studies have found a link between district magnitude and women's election to office, others have also found little to no relationship (Welch and Studlar 1990; Studlar and Welch 1991; Matland 1993; Matland and Taylor 1997; Kittilson 2006; Schmidt 2008a, 2008b). Matland (1993) and Matland and Taylor (1997) suggest that, instead of district magnitude, *party magnitude* determines the proportion of seats won by women because it measures the number of seats that each party is likely to win in a district rather than the overall number of seats that are available. Because it is rare for one party to win every seat in a district, parties make calculations about whether to include women and where to put them on the ballot based on the number of seats that they expect to win rather than the number of seats in the entire district. Empirical studies on the effect of party magnitude on women's election lend support to this line of thinking (Matland 1993; Matland and Taylor 1997; Jones 2004, 2009; Schmidt and Saunders 2004; Schwindt-Bayer, Malecki, and Crisp 2010).

Ballot Structure

In addition to noting differences in women's rates of election under PR and SMDP, Duverger (1955) suggests that female candidates may be more successful under electoral rules that give voters less choice. He reports that in the first half of the twentieth century in Norway voters were more likely to cross women off of the ballot in municipal elections where voters could express preference votes (89). This led later scholars to consider the role of ballot structure in the election of women. At its simplest, *ballot structure* refers to whether party ballots are closed to preference voting or whether rules permit open or flexible ballots whereby voters can indicate the particular candidates they prefer. It is unclear, however, just what effect differences in the openness of the ballot to preference voting has on the election of women (Tremblay 2007). On one hand, closed-list ballots could help women's election in systems where voters may discriminate against female candidates. Party leaders can ensure greater representation of women by putting women on their ballots. On the other hand, preference voting could lead to more women in office than would party voting in societies that are supportive of gender balance (Kittilson 2005; Schmidt 2008b; Tremblay 2008a).

Empirical work does not offer a clear answer. Analysis of voter bias is ambivalent as to its nature and effects. Although some early research found that the public was reluctant to vote for female candidates (Ekstrand and Eckert 1981) and a recent study discovers that bias against women remains a factor in voter choice (Lawless 2004), the vast majority find that—when seat, region, and incumbency are factored in as controls—voters not only elect male and female candidates at equal rates (Studlar and McAllister 1991; Norris, Vallance, and Lovenduski 1992), but may even vote in greater numbers for women over men (Milyo and Schosberg 2000; Black and Erickson 2003; Brians 2005). Schwindt-Bayer et al. (2010) find that in open-list systems the effect of ballot structure depends on cultural predispositions toward women's equality in society. In Ireland, where political attitudes toward gender inequality persist, women won fewer preference votes than men, all else equal. In the Australian Senate, however, women won more preference votes than men, likely reflecting cultural attitudes that favor gender equality. In countries like Finland and Denmark, these patterns may also stem from "vote for women" campaigns (Bergqvist 1999; Haavio-Mannila 1979).

The recent adoption of gender quotas has caused the debate over ballot structure to become more one-sided. Most analyses emphasize the benefits of closed-list systems for the election of women because they facilitate quota implementation (Archenti and Tula 2008; Baldez 2004; Htun and Jones 2002). In closed systems, voters vote for the list as it was constructed by the party.

If the quota requires women to be in winnable positions on the party ballot, then the presence of women on ballots will translate directly into their election. In open-list systems, quotas are far less effective because voters can disturb the party's ranking of candidates and can choose men over women (Jones and Navia 1999; Miguel 2008; Schmidt 2008a; Jones 2009; Wauters, Weekers, and Maddens 2010). Consequently, while research has historically focused on the distinction between PR and majoritarian systems, this means of conceptualizing electoral rules overlooks the role of other structures like district (and party) magnitude, gender quotas, and ballot structure in helping or hindering the election of women to political office.

DEMOCRATIC POLITICS

Early research on gender and electoral institutions focused primarily on how political structures shape women's emergence as candidates and ultimately their election to office. More recent work, however, has begun to explore the broader effects of these institutions on gendered dynamics of democratic politics. Some studies focus on how female legislators represent their constituents, both female and male (Schwindt-Bayer 2006, 2010). Others emphasize gender differences in how citizens view the political process and participate in it (Sanbonmatsu 2003; Karp and Banducci 2008; Kittilson and Schwindt-Bayer 2010, 2012). This focus has become particularly important with the introduction of gender quotas to the political scene because quotas may exacerbate and potentially alter prevailing trends (cf. Franceschet, Krook, and Piscopo 2012). Concerns with how electoral institutions shape the gendered nature of democratic politics are rooted in normative arguments that women's presence in politics is good for democracy. Phillips (1995), among others (Williams 1998; Mansbridge 1999; Young 2000; Dovi 2002), argues that an increase in the proportion of female policy makers is necessary for a number of reasons: to represent women's interests, draw on women's resources for the good of society, enhance justice, and provide role models. This has led to significant empirical interest in the consequences of greater gender equality in politics for the representation of a diversity of issues and the views of constituents toward the political process, as well as growing interest in how electoral institutions may directly and indirectly mediate these dynamics.

Legislator Behavior

A large body of work theorizes and analyzes the effects of gender on policy making, seeking to understand when, how, and why female legislators act on behalf of women as a group and whether male legislators represent women's interests (see the chapter by Sarah Childs and Joni Lovenduski in this section). Recent studies aim to nuance this focus by acknowledging that individuals may navigate this process in different ways (Childs and Withey 2006; Childs and Krook 2009), as well as by pinpointing various institutional constraints on legislative behavior. The latter do so by highlighting the masculine nature of parliamentary institutions, in terms of biases and assumptions that take the "male" experience as the norm and by emphasizing the ways male legislators and party leaders use formal and informal institutions to exclude women. These may include working hours, policy negotiation practices, and debating styles that exclude women or lead them to feel like outsiders in the policy-making process (Rosenthal 1997; Carroll 2001; Ross 2002; Puwar 2004; Mackay 2008). This literature also extends to new work on further institutional obstacles to efforts to substantively represent women's concerns, such as the importance of party discipline (Childs 2004; Htun and Power 2006; Macaulay 2006; Tripp 2006; Beckwith and Cowell-Meyers 2007), the strength and quality of democracy (Goetz and Hassim 2003; Creevey 2006; Longman 2006; Tremblay 2007), the selection of parliamentary leadership posts and committee assignments (Heath, Taylor-Robinson, and Schwindt-Bayer 2005; Schwindt-Bayer 2010), as well as opportunities presented by the creation of women's caucuses (Thomas 1994; Reingold 2000).

The introduction of gender quotas has been accompanied by a paradoxical set of effects, influencing prospects for representing women's interests (Franceschet and Piscopo 2008). On one hand, claims that politics will change as a result of women's inclusion may contribute to a "mandate effect," leading citizens, as well as legislators, to anticipate that the women elected through quotas will promote women's concerns, perhaps to an even greater degree than women elected before quotas. On the other hand, negative publicity surrounding gender quotas can also generate a "label effect" that stigmatizes female legislators, reducing their willingness and ability to pursue feminist policies. This may additionally empower men who can marginalize women into certain areas of legislative activity.

Initial research provides evidence for both effects: women elected via quotas in some countries have reported feeling especially obligated to act for women as a group, based on the fact that they have been elected because they are women (Skjeie 1991; Schwartz 2004), whereas those in other countries have tried to disassociate themselves from women's issues in an effort to show that they are "serious" politicians (Childs 2004). The fact that many quotas are not rooted in processes of constituency formation may prevent quota women from acting independently from party leaders (Cornwall and Goetz 2005; Pupavac 2005; Burnet 2008; Hassim 2009). Consequently, some scholars suggest that women might be more effective in nonquota environments (Archenti and Johnson 2006), although others view these dynamics as problems faced by female MPs more generally, not related to quota provisions (Zetterberg 2008).

Citizen Effects

A related literature focuses on gender and citizen attitudes toward and participation in democracy. The most prominent line of research examines how the increased presence of women in office affects the political preferences and behavior of women and men in society (Hansen 1997; Sapiro and Conover 1997; High-Pippert and Comer 1998; Atkeson 2003; Atkeson and Carrillo 2007; Wolbrecht and Campbell 2007; Karp and Banducci 2008; Desposato and Norrander 2009; Reingold and Harrell 2010). However, a new wave of research has begun to identify electoral rules themselves as important explanations for the varying views of politics that women hold in countries around the world. Comparatively, wide variation exists in gender gaps, with men being more supportive of democracy than women in some states while women are more satisfied with democracy than men in others (Sanbonmatsu 2003; Karp and Banducci 2008). Although some scholars suggest that political factors, social dynamics, and historical contexts can have important conditioning effects on men's and women's attitudes toward and involvement in politics (Sapiro and Conover 1997; Morgan, Espinal, and Hartlyn 2008), there are good reasons to believe that electoral rules may play a role.

Specifically, particular electoral institutions, such as PR, large district magnitudes, or preference voting, are designed to maximize representativeness and give the electorate a say in the individuals who represent them. Consequently, some scholars suggest that the use of these institutions could send signals to the electorate that the government is both representative and inclusive, psychologically triggering positive feelings toward government among the citizenry, especially women (Schwindt-Bayer and Mishler 2005; Kittilson and Schwindt-Bayer 2010, 2012). These findings are consistent with studies of mass attitudes and behavior that have not focused specifically on the gender dimension, showing that electoral rules, such as PR electoral systems, consensus democracies, multiparty and parliamentary systems, and preferential voting rules are important, and often overlooked, explanations of civic engagement (Anderson and Guillory 1997; Banducci, Donovan, and Karp 1999; Lijphart 1999; Norris 1999; Anderson et al. 2005; Farrell and McAllister 2006; Aarts and Thomassen 2008).

Recent work on gender quotas adds further insights regarding potential links between electoral institutions and patterns in women's political engagement and participation. Although quotas are designed to increase women's numbers in office, they can also enhance perceptions of democratic justice and legitimacy as well as provide new role models for female citizens. Belief in the first is corroborated in many case studies showing that a common motivation for adopting quotas on the part of governments and political parties is to gain domestic or international legitimacy (Htun and Jones 2002; Araújo and García 2006; Krook 2006b). Most of the evidence of symbolic effects, however, focuses on how citizens interpret and respond to the introduction of gender quota policies, which are theorized to have two major effects.

On one hand, quotas can serve as symbols that generate feelings of support for the political system, sending signals to women that they are accepted as citizens and that the political sphere is open to them (Kittilson 2005, 2010; McDonagh 2010). Various case studies indicate, for example, that quotas increase the rate at which female voters contact their representatives (Kudva 2003; Childs 2004). Others find that quota adoption has the effect of encouraging women to begin a political career, to acquire political skills, and to develop sustained political ambitions (Geissel and Hust 2005; Bhavnani 2009) while also building support for women's movement organizing (Sacchet 2008). However, some observe that quotas have little or no effect on women's political activities, such as their willingness to sign petitions or participate in protests (Zetterberg 2009) or their levels of political ambition (Davidson-Schmich 2009).

On the other hand, quotas may contribute to a breakdown of traditional gender norms. Some scholars suggest that quotas pose a radical challenge to politics-as-usual because they involve fundamentally renegotiating the gendered nature of the public sphere (Sgier 2004). A study of India supports this claim by showing that exposure to female leaders as a result of quotas can weaken gender stereotypes as well as can eliminate negative bias in how the performance of female leaders is perceived among male constituents (Beaman et al. 2009). Other work reveals, however, that outward acceptance of the legitimacy of quotas often masks continued resistance. This is especially true among male elites, many of whom attribute women's underrepresentation to choices made by individual women rather than to structural patterns of discrimination (Meier 2008; cf. Holli, Luhtakallio, and Raevaara 2006). The effects of quotas may thus be mediated in important ways by gender identities.

DIRECTIONS FOR FUTURE RESEARCH

The literature on gender and electoral institutions thus makes important contributions to political analysis by highlighting how gender norms and identities affect three major facets of the electoral process: the emergence of candidates; the outcomes of elections; and the dynamics of democratic politics. The available research, however, does not yet explore the full spectrum of possibilities related to questions of gender or electoral institutions. With respect to gender, there is little work as of yet that analyzes the role of men or masculinities in electoral politics, beyond studies observing the masculine nature of the public sphere (Lovenduski 1998; Krook 2010a). Yet appreciating how gender works in elections requires attending to the fate of both women and men, as marginalized and privileged categories of political actors. Both formal and informal electoral institutions shape how men experience candidate selection processes

(Childs and Cowley 2011), as well as the outcomes and effects of elections. For example, research in this area might highlight the role of men as both protagonists and antagonists in the adoption of gender-specific electoral institutions, such as gender quotas. Much of the work on quota adoption emphasizes women's movements and female legislators as actors critical to the passage of quota policies, but men too have played important, but often underresearched, roles. Similarly, literature on electoral rules and legislator behavior might also examine how men represent women's issues and whether this varies across systems that prioritize legislator responsiveness to male party elites rather than the masses.

Understanding how gender operates also necessitates greater attention to diversity among women. Although a wave of theoretical contributions argue that it is vital to incorporate questions of intersectionality into political research (Weldon 2006; Hancock 2007; see essays in Part 1), relatively few scholars have empirically studied how the interaction of multiple identities affects what kinds of women are selected as candidates, are elected to office and respond to different kinds of political cues (see, however, Hughes 2011). Part of the reason for this is the empirical challenges the concept of intersectionality poses. It is most often understood to refer to the experiences of minority women—but formulated differently, might refer to comparisons among groups to better understand how the effects of different identities interact among, for example, majority men, minority men, majority women, and minority women (McCall 2005). Studies of the first have grown dramatically in recent years (see among others Philpot and Walton 2007; Hughes 2011; Holmsten, Moser, and Slosar 2010). Those on the second have been fewer but have yielded important new insights regarding combined effects (Scola 2007; Hancock 2009).

A challenge for future research on intersectionality, if the focus remains largely on minority women, is to devise ways of overcoming the problem of small sample sizes. Qualitative research methods could prove especially useful, focusing on women's views of their different identities and how they play out in their own political lives, which would lend important insight into how those women were selected as candidates, elected to office, and how they behaved in office. Another strategy might be to examine the complicated effects that more inclusive electoral rules have on diverse groups of women in the population—minority women, lower-class women, and less politically mobilized women. Comparing this to men with multiple identities would clarify the complexities of gender as just one of many political identities.

Along similar lines, existing research has analyzed many aspects of electoral institutions but has not yet considered all of their potential effects on gendered patterns of election and political engagement. Research on the effect of electoral rules has focused on broad distinctions between PR and majoritarian systems and examined nuances in district magnitude and ballot structure, but it has often overlooked other important parts of electoral systems, such as specific electoral formulas with PR and majoritarian systems, electoral thresholds, compulsory voting, or enfranchisement, that could also have gendered effects on citizen views of government and political participation. Work on candidate selection processes has focused heavily on the new phenomenon of gender quotas but has not to the same extent delved into the consequences of centralized versus decentralized nomination procedures or who controls the selection process within parties. Work on all of these topics would help better nuance scholarly understanding of the gendered dimensions of electoral institutions.

A final overlooked area of exploration is how electoral rules directly affect women's legislative behavior. A large literature on legislative politics argues that electoral institutions provide important incentives to elected representatives to behave in certain ways. Cain, Ferejohn, and Fiorina (1987) emphasize the personal vote in British politics, and Carey and Shugart (1995) argue that party control over party ballots, vote pooling, and the type of vote interact with district magnitude to provide incentives for cultivating a personal vote. Yet very little research has examined how electoral rules may affect the representation of women's issues and the behavior of male versus female legislators (see, however, Tremblay 2003; Schwindt-Bayer 2010). Similarly, much remains to be done with respect to how electoral institutions shape how men and women view their democracies and how the presence of women in politics directly affects female citizens' political engagement and participation, an effect that may be filtered through the broader electoral context. Despite the many important and useful insights of existing studies, therefore, future research will be critical for fully understanding the interplay between electoral institutions and gendered political trends.

Notes

1. For an overview of formal and informal institutions, and relations between them, see Helmke and Levitsky (2004).
2. Similar measures have been introduced for minority groups in nearly forty countries (Krook and O'Brien 2010).
3. Much of the literature distinguishes between PR and single-member district plurality (SMDP) electoral rules, but SMDP is just one of several majoritarian systems. In many cases, the effects produced by SMDP also appear under the other majoritarian formulas. Thus, we use the broader term *majoritarian* in this essay when distinguishing between the effects of PR and majoritarian systems generally and refer to *SMDP* when referencing effects specific to SMDP systems.
4. Research on women in the executive branch has developed significantly in recent years (Escobar-Lemmon and Taylor-Robinson 2005, 2009; Jalalzai 2004, 2008). Yet very little of it has emphasized electoral rules, in large part due to the small number of women elected, as opposed to appointed, to posts in the executive. We thus focus here on legislative electoral institutions.

References

Aarts, Kees, and Jacques Thomassen. 2008. "Satisfaction with democracy: Do institutions matter?" *Electoral Studies* 27(1): 5–18.

Anderson, Christopher J., André Blais, Shaun Bowler, Todd Donovan, and Ola Listhaug. 2005. *Losers' consent: Elections and democratic legitimacy.* New York: Oxford University Press.

Anderson, Christopher J., and Christine Guillory. 1997. "Political institutions and satisfaction with democracy: A cross-national analysis of consensus and majoritarian systems." *American Political Science Review* 91(1): 66–81.

Araújo, Clara, and Ana Isabel García. 2006. "Latin America: The experience and the impact of quotas in Latin America." In Drude Dahlerup, ed., *Women, quotas, and politics.* New York: Routledge, 83–111.

Archenti, Nélida, and Niki Johnson. 2006. "Engendering the legislative agenda with and without the quota." *Sociologia* 52: 133–153.

Archenti, Nélida, and María Inés Tula. 2008. "Algunas Cuestiones Iniciales sobre las Leyes de Cuotas." In Nélida Archenti and María Inés Tula, eds., *Mujeres y Política en América Latina: Sistemas Electorales y Cuotas de Género.* Buenos Aires: Heliasta, 9–29.

Atkeson, Lonna Rae. 2003. "Not all cues are created equal: The conditional impact of female candidates on political engagement." *Journal of Politics* 65(4): 1040–1061.

Atkeson, Lonna Rae, and Nancy Carrillo. 2007. "More is better: The influence of collective female descriptive representation on external efficacy." *Politics & Gender* 3(1): 79–101.

Baines, Beverley, and Ruth Rubio-Marin (Eds.). 2005. *The gender of constitutional jurisprudence.* New York: Cambridge University Press.

Baldez, Lisa. 2004. "Elected Bodies: The gender quota law for legislative candidates in Mexico." *Legislative Studies Quarterly* 24(2): 231–258.

Banducci, Susan A., Todd Donovan, and Jeffrey A. Karp. 1999. "Proportional representation and attitudes about politics: Evidence from New Zealand." *Electoral Studies* 18(4): 533–555.

Bauer, Gretchen, and Hannah E. Britton (Eds.). 2006. *Women in African parliaments.* Boulder, CO: Lynne Rienner.

Beaman, Lori, Raghabendra Chattopadhyay, Esther Duflo, Rohini Pande, and Petia Topalova. 2009. "Powerful women: Does exposure reduce bias?" *Quarterly Journal of Economics* 124(4): 1497–1540.

Beckwith, Karen, and Kimberly Cowell-Meyers. 2007. "Sheer numbers: Critical representation thresholds and women's political representation." *Perspectives on Politics* 5(3): 553–565.

Bergqvist, Christina (Ed.). 1999. *Equal democracies? Gender and politics in the Nordic countries.* Oslo: Scandinavian University Press.

Bhavnani, Rikhil. 2009. "Do electoral quotas work after they are withdrawn? Evidence from a natural experiment in India." *American Political Science Review* 103(1): 23–35.

Black, Jerome H., and Lynda Erickson. 2003. "Women candidates and voter bias: Do women politicians need to be better?" *Electoral Studies* 22(1): 81–100.

Brians, Craig Leonard. 2005. "Women for women? Gender and party bias in voting for female candidates." *American Politics Research* 33(3): 357–375.

Bruhn, Kathleen. 2003. "Whores and lesbians: Political activism, party strategies, and gender quotas in Mexico." *Electoral Studies* 22(1): 101–119.

Burnet, Jennie E. 2008. "Gender balance and the meanings of women in governance in post-genocide Rwanda." *African Affairs* 107(248): 361–386.

Bush, Sarah N. 2011. "International politics and the spread of quotas for women in legislatures." *International Organization* 65(1): 103–137.

Cain, Bruce E., John A. Ferejohn, and Morris P. Fiorina. 1987. *The personal vote.* Cambridge, MA: Harvard University Press.

Carey, John M., and Matthew Soberg Shugart. 1995. "Incentives to cultivate a personal vote." *Electoral Studies* 14(4): 417–439.

Carroll, Susan J. (Ed.). 2001. *The impact of women in public office.* Bloomington: Indiana University Press.

Castles, Francis. 1981. "Female legislative representation and the electoral system." *Politics* 1(2): 21–27.

Caul, Miki. 1999. "Women's representation in parliament: The role of political parties." *Party Politics* 5(1): 79–98.

Caul, Miki. 2001. "Political parties and the adoption of candidate gender quotas: A cross-national analysis." *Journal of Politics* 63(4): 1214–1229.

Celis, Karen, Mona Lena Krook, and Petra Meier. 2011. "The rise of gender quota laws: Expanding the spectrum of determinants for electoral reform." *West European Politics* 34(3): 514–530.

Chama, Mónica. 2001. *Las mujeres y el poder.* Buenos Aires: Ciudad Argentina.

Childs, Sarah. 2004. *New Labour's women MPs.* New York: Routledge.

Childs, Sarah, and Philip Cowley. 2011. "The politics of local presence: Is there a case for descriptive representation?" *Political Studies* 59(1): 1–19.

Childs, Sarah, and Mona Lena Krook. 2009. "Analysing women's substantive representation: From critical mass to critical actors." *Government and Opposition* 44(2): 125–145.

Childs, Sarah, and Julie Withey. 2006. "The substantive representation of women: The case of the reduction of VAT on sanitary products." *Parliamentary Affairs* 59(1): 10–23.

Chowdhury, Najma. 2002. "The implementation of quotas: Bangladesh experience." Paper presented at the IDEA Workshop, Jakarta, Indonesia, September 25.

Cornwall, Andrea, and Anne Marie Goetz. 2005. "Democratizing democracy: Feminist perspectives." *Democratization* 12(5): 783–800.

Creevey, Lucy. 2006. "Senegal: Contending with religious constraints." In Gretchen Bauer and Hannah E. Britton, eds., *Women in African parliaments.* Boulder, CO: Lynne Rienner, 215–245.

Dahlerup, Drude. 2008. "Gender quotas—Controversial but trendy." *International Feminist Journal of Politics* 10(3): 322–328.

Darcy, Robert, Susan Welch, and Janet Clark. 1994. *Women, elections, and representation,* 2d ed. Lincoln: University of Nebraska Press.

Davidson-Schmich, Louise K. 2006. "Implementation of political party gender quotas: Evidence from the German Lander 1990–2000." *Party Politics* 12(2): 211–232.

Davidson-Schmich, Louise K. 2009. "Who wants to run for office from which party?" Paper presented at the Annual Meeting of the American Political Science Association, Toronto, Canada, September 3–6.

Desposato, Scott W., and Barbara Norrander. 2009. "The gender gap in Latin America: Contextual and individual influences on gender and political participation." *British Journal of Political Science* 39(1): 141–162.

Dovi, Suzanne. 2002. "Preferable group representatives: Will just any woman, black, or Latino do?" *American Political Science Review* 96(4): 729–743.

Durrieu, Marcela. 1999. *Se dice de nosotras*. Buenos Aires: Catálogos Editora.

Duverger, Maurice. 1954. *Political Parties*. New York: Wiley.

Duverger, Maurice. 1955. *The political role of women*. Paris: UNESCO.

Escobar-Lemmon, Maria, and Michelle M. Taylor-Robinson. 2009. Getting to the top. *Political Research Quarterly* 62(4): 685–699.

Ekstrand, Laurie E., and William A. Eckert. 1981. "The impact of candidate's sex on voter choice." *Western Political Quarterly* 34(1): 78–87.

Engstrom, Richard L. 1987. "District magnitude and the election of women to the Irish Dail." *Electoral Studies* 6(2): 123–132.

Escobar-Lemmon, Maria C., and Michelle M. Taylor-Robinson. 2005. "Women ministers in Latin American government: When, where, and why?" *American Journal of Political Science* 49(4): 829–844.

Farrell, David M., and Ian McAllister. 2006. "Voter satisfaction and electoral systems: Does preferential voting in candidate-centred systems make a difference?" *European Journal of Political Research* 45(5): 723–749.

Fox, Richard L., and Jennifer L. Lawless. 2004. "Entering the arena? Gender and the decision to run for office." *American Journal of Political Science* 48(2): 264–280.

Franceschet, Susan. 2005. *Women and politics in Chile*. Boulder: Lynne Rienner.

Franceschet, Susan, Mona Lena Krook, and Jennifer M. Piscopo (Eds.). 2012. *The impact of gender quotas: Women's descriptive, substantive, and symbolic representation*. New York: Oxford University Press.

Franceschet, Susan, and Jennifer M. Piscopo. 2008. "Gender quotas and women's substantive representation: Lessons from Argentina." *Politics & Gender* 4(3): 393–425.

Freidenvall, Lenita, Drude Dahlerup, and Hege Skjeie. 2006. "The Nordic countries: An incremental model." In Drude Dahlerup, ed., *Women, quotas and politics*. New York: Routledge, 55–82.

Geissel, Brigitte, and Evelin Hust. 2005. "Democratic mobilisation through quotas: Experiences in India and Germany." *Commonwealth & Comparative Politics* 43(2): 222–244.

Giraud, Isabelle, and Jane Jenson. 2001. "Constitutionalizing equal access: High hopes, dashed hopes?" In Jytte Klausen and Charles S. Maier, eds., *Has liberalism failed women? Assuring equal representation in Europe and the United States*. New York: Palgrave, 69–88.

Goetz, Anne Marie, and Shireen Hassim (Eds.). 2003. *No shortcuts to power: African women in politics and policy making*. New York: Zed Books.

Guadagnini, Marila. 2005. "Gendering the debate on political representation in Italy: A difficult challenge." In Joni Lovenduski, ed., *State feminism and political representation*. New York: Cambridge University Press, 130–152.

Haavio-Mannila, Elina. 1979. "How women became political actors: Female candidates in Finnish elections." *Scandinavian Political Studies* 2(4): 351–371.

Hancock, Ange-Marie. 2007. "When multiplication doesn't equal quick addition: Examining intersectionality as a research paradigm." *Perspectives on Politics* 5(1): 63–79.

Hancock, Ange-Marie. 2009. "An untraditional intersectional analysis of the 2008 election." *Politics & Gender* 5(1): 96–105.

Hansen, Susan B. 1997. "Talking about politics: Gender and contextual effects on political proselytizing." *Journal of Politics* 59(1): 73–103.

Hassim, Shireen. 2009. "Perverse consequences? The impact of quotas for women on democratisation in Africa." In Ian Shapiro, Susan C. Stokes, Elisabeth Jean Wood, and Alexander S. Kirshner, eds., *Political representation*. New York: Cambridge University Press, 211–235.

Heath, Roseanna M., Leslie A. Schwindt-Bayer, and Michelle M. Taylor-Robinson. 2005. "Women on the sidelines: Women's representation on committees in Latin American legislatures." *American Journal of Political Science* 49(2): 420–436.

Helmke, Gretchen, and Steven Levitsky. 2004. "Informal institutions and comparative politics: A research agenda." *Perspectives on Politics* 2(4): 725–740.

High-Pippert, Angela, and John Comer. 1998. "Female empowerment: The influence of women representing women." *Women & Politics* 19(4): 53–66.

Holli, Anne Maria, Eeva Luhtakallio, and Eeva Raevaara. 2006. "Quota trouble: Talking about gender quotas in Finnish local politics." *International Feminist Journal of Politics* 8(2): 169–193.

Holmsten, Stephanie S., Robert G. Moser, and Mary C. Slosar. 2010. "Do ethnic parties exclude women?" *Comparative Political Studies* 43(10): 1179–1201.

Howard-Merriam, Kathleen. 1990. "Guaranteed seats for political representation of women: The Egyptian example." *Women and Politics* 10(1): 17–42.

Htun, Mala. 2002. "Puzzles of women's rights in Brazil." *Social Research* 69(3): 733–751.

Htun, Mala N., and Mark P. Jones. 2002. "Engendering the right to participate in decision-making: Electoral quotas and women's leadership in Latin America." In Nikki Craske and Maxine Molyneux, eds., *Gender and the politics of rights and democracy in Latin America*. New York: Palgrave Publishers, 32–56.

Htun, Mala, and Timothy J. Power. 2006. "Gender, parties, and support for equal rights in the Brazilian congress." *Latin America Politics and Society* 48(4): 83–104.

Hughes, Melanie M. 2011. Intersectionality, quotas, and minority women's political representation worldwide. *American Political Science Review* 105(03): 604–620.

Inhetveen, Katharina. 1999. "Can gender equality be institutionalized? The role of launching values in institutional innovation." *International Sociology* 14(4): 403–422.

Jalalzai, Farida. 2004. "Women political leaders: Past and present." *Women & Politics* 26(3–4): 85–108.

Jalalzai, Farida. 2008. "Women rule: Shattering the executive glass ceiling." *Politics & Gender* 4(2): 1–27.

Jones, Mark P. 1998. "Gender quotas, electoral laws, and the election of women: Lessons from the Argentine provinces." *Comparative Political Studies* 31(1): 3–21.

Jones, Mark P. 2004. "Quota legislation and the election of women: Learning from the Costa Rican experience." *Journal of Politics* 66(4): 1203–1223.

Jones, Mark P. 2009. "Gender quotas, electoral laws, and the election of women: Evidence from the Latin American vanguard." *Comparative Political Studies* 42(1): 56–81.

Jones, Mark P., and Patricio Navia. 1999. "Assessing the effectiveness of gender quotas in open-list proportional representation electoral systems." *Social Science Quarterly* 80(2): 341–355.

Karp, Jeffrey A., and Susan A. Banducci. 2008. "When politics is not just a man's game: Women's representation and political engagement." *Electoral Studies* 27(1): 105–115.

Kenworthy, Lane, and Melissa Malami. 1999. "Gender inequality in political representation: A worldwide comparative analysis." *Social Forces* 78(1): 235–269.

Kittilson, Miki Caul. 2005. "In support of gender quotas: Setting new standards, bringing visible gains." *Politics & Gender* 1(4): 638–644.

Kittilson, Miki Caul. 2006. *Challenging parties, changing parliaments.* Columbus: Ohio State University Press.

Kittilson, Miki Caul. 2010. "Comparing gender, institutions, and political behavior: Toward an integrated framework." *Perspectives on Politics* 8(1): 217–222.

Kittilson, Miki Caul, and Leslie A. Schwindt-Bayer. 2010. "Engaging citizens: The role of power-sharing institutions." *Journal of Politics* 72(4): 990–1002.

Kittilson, Miki Caul, and Leslie A. Schwindt-Bayer. 2012. *The gendered effects of electoral institutions: Political engagement and participation.* Oxford, UK: Oxford University Press.

Kolinsky, Eva. 1991. "Political participation and parliamentary careers: Women's quotas in West Germany." *West European Politics* 14(1): 56–72.

Krook, Mona Lena. 2006. "Reforming representation: The diffusion of candidate gender quotas worldwide." *Politics & Gender* 2(3): 303–327.

Krook, Mona Lena. 2009. *Quotas for women in politics: Gender and candidate selection reform worldwide.* New York: Oxford University Press.

Krook, Mona Lena. 2010a. "Studying political representation: A comparative-gendered approach." *Perspectives on Politics* 8(1): 233–240.

Krook, Mona Lena. 2010b. "Why are fewer women than men elected? Gender and the dynamics of candidate selection." *Political Studies Review* 8(2): 155–168.

Krook, Mona Lena. 2010c. "Women's representation in parliament: A qualitative-comparative analysis." *Political Studies* 58(5): 886–908.

Krook, Mona Lena. 2010d. "Beyond supply and demand: A feminist-institutionalist theory of candidate selection." *Political Research Quarterly* 63(4): 707–720.

Krook, Mona Lena, and Fiona Mackay (Eds.). 2011. *Gender, politics, and institutions: Towards a feminist institutionalism.* New York: Palgrave.

Krook, Mona Lena, and Diana Z. O'Brien. 2010. "The politics of group representation: Quotas for women and minorities worldwide." *Comparative Politics* 42(3): 253–272.

Kudva, Neema. 2003. "Engineering elections: The experiences of women in Panchayati Raj in Karnataka, India." *International Journal of Politics, Culture and Society* 16(3): 445–463.

Kunovich, Sheri, and Pamela Paxton. 2005. "Pathways to power: The role of political parties in women's national representation." *American Journal of Sociology* 111(2): 505–552.

Lawless, Jennifer L. 2004. "Politics of presence? Congresswomen and symbolic representation." *Political Research Quarterly* 57(1): 81–99.

Lawless, Jennifer L., and Richard L. Fox. 2005. *It takes a candidate: Why women don't run for office.* New York: Cambridge University Press.

Lijphart, Arend. 1999. *Patterns of democracy: Government forms and performance in thirty-six countries.* New Haven, CT: Yale University Press.

Longman, Timothy. 2006. "Rwanda: Achieving equality or serving an authoritarian state?" In Gretchen Bauer and Hannah E. Britton, eds., *Women in African parliaments.* Boulder, CO: Lynne Rienner, 133–150.

Lovenduski, Joni. 1998. "Gendering research in political science." *Annual Review of Political Science* 1: 333–356.

Lovenduski, Joni, and Pippa Norris (Eds.). 1993. *Gender and party politics.* Thousand Oaks, CA: SAGE.

Macaulay, Fiona. 2006. *Gender politics in Brazil and Chile: The role of parties in national and local policymaking.* New York: Palgrave Macmillan.

Mackay, Fiona. 2008. "'Thick' conceptions of substantive representation: Women, gender, and political institutions." *Representation* 44(2): 125–140.

Mansbridge, Jane. 1999. "Should blacks represent blacks and women represent women? A contingent 'yes.'" *Journal of Politics* 61(3): 628–657.

Matland, Richard E. 1993. "Institutional variables affecting female representation in national legislatures: The case of Norway." *Journal of Politics* 55(3): 737–755.

Matland, Richard E. 1998. "Women's representation in national legislatures: Developed and developing countries." *Legislative Studies Quarterly* 23(1): 109–125.

Matland, Richard E., and Deborah Dwight Brown. 1992. "District magnitude's effect on female representation in U.S. state legislatures." *Legislative Studies Quarterly* 17(4): 469–492.

Matland, Richard E., and Donley T. Studlar. 1996. "The contagion of women candidates in SMD and PR electoral systems: Canada and Norway." *Journal of Politics* 58(3): 707–733.

Matland, Richard E., and Donley T. Studlar. 2004. "Determinants of legislative turnover: A cross-national analysis." *British Journal of Political Science* 34(1): 87–108.

Matland, Richard E., and Michelle M. Taylor. 1997. "Electoral system effects on women's representation: Theoretical arguments and evidence from Costa Rica." *Comparative Political Studies* 30(2): 186–210.

McCall, Leslie. 2005. "The complexity of intersectionality." *Signs* 30(3): 1771–1800.

McDonagh, Eileen. 2010. "It takes a state: A policy feedback model of women's political representation." *Perspectives on Politics* 8(1): 69–91.

Meier, Petra. 2000. "The evidence of being present: Guarantees of representation and the Belgian example." *Acta Politica* 35(1): 64–85.

Meier, Petra. 2004. "The mutual contagion effect of legal and party quotas: A Belgian perspective." *Party Politics* 10(5): 583–600.

Meier, Petra. 2005. "The Belgian paradox: Inclusion and exclusion of gender issues." In Joni Lovenduski, ed., *State feminism and political representation*. New York: Cambridge University Press, 41–61.

Meier, Petra. 2008. "A gender gap not closed by quotas: The renegotiation of the public sphere." *International Feminist Journal of Politics* 10(3): 329–347.

Miguel, Luis F. 2008. "Political representation and gender in Brazil: Quotas for women and their impact." *Bulletin of Latin American Research* 27(2): 197–214.

Milyo, Jeffrey, and Samantha Schosberg. 2000. "Gender bias and selection bias in house elections." *Public Choice* 105(1–2): 41–59.

Morgan, Jana, Rosario Espinal, and Jonathan Hartlyn. 2008. "Gender politics in the Dominican Republic: Advances for women, ambivalence from men." *Politics & Gender* 4(1): 35–63.

Moser, Robert G. 2001. "The effects of electoral systems on women's representation in post-communist states." *Electoral Studies* 20: 353–369.

Murray, Rainbow. 2004. "Why didn't parity work?" *French Politics* 2(4): 347–362.

Nanivadekar, Medha. 2006. "Are quotas a good idea?" *Politics & Gender* 2(1): 119–128.

Niven, David. 1998. "Party elites and women candidates: The shape of bias." *Women & Politics* 19(2): 57–80.

Norris, Pippa. 1985. "Women's legislative participation in Western Europe." *West European Politics* 8(4): 90–101.

Norris, Pippa. 1999. "Institutional explanations for political support." In Pippa Norris, ed., *Critical citizens: Global support for democratic governance*. New York: Oxford University Press, 217–235.

Norris, Pippa. 2007. "Opening the door: Women leaders and constitution building in Iraq and Afghanistan." In Barbara Kellerman, ed., *Women who lead*. New York: Jossey-Bass, 197–226.

Norris, Pippa (Ed.). 1997. *Passages to power*. New York: Cambridge University Press.

Norris, Pippa, and Joni Lovenduski. 1995. *Political recruitment: Gender, race, and class in the British Parliament*. New York: Cambridge University Press.

Norris, Pippa, Elizabeth Vallance, and Joni Lovenduski. 1992. Do candidates make a difference? Race, gender, ideology, and incumbency. *Parliamentary Affairs* 45(4): 496–547.

Opello, Katherine A. R. 2006. *Gender quotas, parity reform and political parties in France*. New York: Lexington Books.

Paxton, Pamela. 1997. "Women in national legislatures: A Cross-national analysis." *Social Science Research* 26: 442–464.

Paxton, Pamela, Melanie M. Hughes, and Matthew A. Painter. 2010. "Growth in women's political representation: A longitudinal exploration of democracy, electoral system, and gender quotas." *European Journal of Political Research* 49(1): 25–52.

Phillips, Anne. 1995. *The politics of presence*. New York: Oxford University Press.

Philpot, Tasha S., and Hanes Walton, Jr. 2007. "One of our own: Black female candidates and the voters who support them." *American Journal of Political Science* 51(1): 49–62.

Pupavac, Vanessa. 2005. "Empowering women? An assessment of international gender policies in Bosnia." *International Peacekeeping* 12(3): 391–405.

Puwar, Nirmal. 2004. "Thinking about making a difference." *British Journal of Politics and International Relations* 6(1): 65–80.

Randall, Vicky. 1982. *Women and politics*. London: Macmillan.

Reingold, Beth. 2000. *Representing women: Sex, gender, and legislative behavior in Arizona and California*. Chapel Hill: University of North Carolina Press.

Reingold, Beth, and Jessica Harrell. 2010. "The impact of descriptive representation on women's political engagement: Does party matter?" *Political Research Quarterly* 63(2): 280–294.

Reynolds, Andrew. 1999. "Women in the legislatures and executives of the world: Knocking at the highest glass ceiling." *World Politics* 51(4): 547–572.

Rosenthal, Cindy Simon. 1997. "A view of their own: Women's committee leadership styles and state legislatures." *Policy Studies Journal* 25(4): 585–600.

Ross, Karen. 2002. "Women's place in "male" space: Gender and effect in parliamentary contexts." *Parliamentary Affairs* 55(1): 189–201.

Rule, Wilma. 1981. "Why women don't run: The critical contextual factors in women's legislative recruitment." *Western Political Quarterly* 34(1): 60–77.

Rule, Wilma. 1987. "Electoral systems, contextual factors and women's opportunity for election to parliament in twenty-three democracies." *Western Political Quarterly* 40(3): 477–498.

Rule, Wilma. 1994. "Parliaments of, by, and for the people: Except for women?" In Joseph Zimmerman and Wilma Rule, eds., *Electoral systems in comparative perspective: Their impact on women and minorities*. Westport, CT: Greenwood Press, 15–30.

Russell, Meg. 2005. *Building New Labour: The politics of party organisation*. London: Palgrave.

Sacchet, Teresa. 2008. "Beyond numbers: The impact of gender quotas in Latin America." *International Feminist Journal of Politics* 10(3): 369–386.

Sanbonmatsu, Kira. 2003. "Gender-related political knowledge and the descriptive representation of women." *Political Behavior* 25(4): 367–388.

Sanbonmatsu, Kira. 2006. *When women run: Gender and party in the American states*. Ann Arbor: University of Michigan Press.

Sapiro, Virginia, and Pamela Johnston Conover. 1997. "The variable gender basis of electoral politics: Gender and context in the 1992 U.S. election." *British Journal of Political Science* 27(4): 497–523.

Schmidt, Gregory D. 2008a. "The election of women in list PR systems: Testing the conventional wisdom." *Electoral Studies* 28(2): 190–203.

Schmidt, Gregory D. 2008b. "Success under Open List PR: The election of women to congress." In Manon Tremblay, ed., *Women and legislative representation: Electoral systems, political parties, and sex quotas*. New York: Palgrave Macmillan, 161–172.

Schmidt, Gregory D., and Kyle L. Saunders. 2004. "Effective quotas, relative party magnitude, and the success of female candidates: Peruvian municipal elections in comparative perspective." *Comparative Political Studies* 37(6): 704–724.

Schwartz, Helle. 2004. "Women's representation in the Rwandan parliament," M.A. thesis, University of Gothenburg, Sweden.

Schwindt-Bayer, Leslie A. 2005. "The incumbency disadvantage and women's election to legislative office." *Electoral Studies* 24(2): 227–244.

Schwindt-Bayer, Leslie A. 2006. Still supermadres? Gender and the policy priorities of Latin American legislators. *American Journal of Political Science* 50(3): 570–585.

Schwindt-Bayer, Leslie A. 2009. "Making quotas work: The effect of gender quota laws on the election of women." *Legislative Studies Quarterly* 34(1): 5–28.

Schwindt-Bayer, Leslie A. 2010. *Political power and women's representation in Latin America*. New York: Oxford University Press.

Schwindt-Bayer, Leslie A., and William Mishler. 2005. "An integrated model of women's representation." *Journal of Politics* 67(2): 407–428.

Schwindt-Bayer, Leslie A., Michael Malecki, and Brian F. Crisp. 2010. "Candidate gender and electoral success in single transferable vote systems." *British Journal of Political Science* 40(3): 693–709.

Schwindt-Bayer, Leslie A., and Harvey D. Palmer. 2007. "Democratic legitimacy or electoral gain? Why countries adopt gender quotas." Paper presented at the annual meeting of the Midwest Political Science Association, Chicago, IL, April 12–15.

Scola, Becki. 2007. "Women of color in state legislatures: Gender, race, ethnicity and legislative office holding." *Journal of Women, Politics & Policy* 28(3–4): 43–70.

Sgier, Lea. 2004. "Discourses of gender quotas." *European Political Science* 3(3): 67–72.

Siregar, Wahidah Zein Br. 2006. "Women and the failure to achieve the 30 percent quota in the 2004–2009 Indonesian parliaments: The role of the electoral system." Paper presented at the International Political Science Association World Congress, Fukuoka, Japan.

Skjeie, Hege. 1991. "The rhetoric of difference: On women's inclusion into political elites." *Politics & Society* 19(2): 233–263.

Stockemer, Daniel. 2008. "Women's representation: A comparison between Europe and the Americas." *Politics* 28(2): 65–73.

Studlar, Donley T., and Ian McAllister. 1991. "Political recruitment to the Australian legislature: Toward an explanation of women's electoral disadvantages." *Western Political Quarterly* 44(2): 467–485.

Studlar, Donley T., and Susan Welch. 1991. "Does district magnitude matter? Women candidates in London local elections." *Western Political Quarterly* 44(2): 457–467.

Thomas, Sue. 1994. *How women legislate*. New York: Oxford University Press.

Tremblay, Manon. 2003. "Women's representational role in Australia and Canada: The impact of political context." *Australian Journal of Political Science* 38(2): 215–239.

Tremblay, Manon. 2007. "Democracy, representation, and women: A comparative analysis." *Democratization* 14(4): 533–553.

Tremblay, Manon. 2008a. "Conclusion." In Manon Tremblay, ed., *Women and legislative representation*. New York: Palgrave Macmillan, 233–247.

Tremblay, Manon (Ed.). 2008b. *Women and legislative representation: Electoral systems, political parties, and sex quotas*. New York: Palgrave Macmillan.

Tripp, Aili, and Alice Kang. 2008. "The global impact of quotas: On the fast track to increased female legislative representation." *Comparative Political Studies* 41(3): 338–361.

Tripp, Aili Mari. 2006. "Uganda: Agents of change for women's advancement?" In Gretchen Bauer and Hannah E. Britton, eds., *Women in African parliaments*. Boulder, CO: Lynne Rienner, 111–132.

Valiente, Celia. 2005. "The women's movement, gender equality agencies and central-state debates on political representation in Spain." In Joni Lovenduski, ed., *State feminism and political representation*. New York: Cambridge University Press, 174–194.

Verge, Tania. 2008. "Cuotas voluntarias y legales en España: La paridad a examen." *Revista Española de Investigaciones Sociológicas* 123: 123–150.

Wauters, Bram, Karolien Weekers, and Bart Maddens. 2010. "Explaining the number of preferential votes for women in an open-list PR system: An investigation of the 2003 federal elections in Flanders (Belgium)." *Acta Politica* 45(4): 468–490.

Welch, Susan, and Donley T. Studlar. 1990. "Multimember districts and the representation of women." *Journal of Politics* 52(2): 391–412.

Weldon, S. Laurel. 2006. "The structure of intersectionality." *Politics & Gender* 2(2): 235–248.

Wiliarty, Sarah Elise. 2010. *The CDU and the politics of gender in Germany: Bringing women to the party*. New York: Cambridge University Press.

Williams, Melissa S. 1998. *Voice, trust, and memory: Marginalized groups and the failings of liberal representation*. Princeton, NJ: Princeton University Press.

Wolbrecht, Christina, Karen Beckwith, and Lisa Baldez (Eds.). 2008. *Political women and American democracy*. New York: Cambridge University Press.

Wolbrecht, Christina, and David E. Campbell. 2007. "Leading by example: Female members of parliament as political role models." *American Journal of Political Science* 51(4): 921–939.

Yoon, Mi Yung. 2001. "Democratization and women's legislative representation in sub Saharan Africa." *Democratization* 8(2): 169–190.

Yoon, Mi Yung. 2004. "Explaining women's legislative representation in sub-Saharan Africa." *Legislative Studies Quarterly* 29(3): 447–468.

Young, Iris Marion. 2000. *Inclusion and democracy*. New York: Oxford University Press.

Zetterberg, Pär. 2008. "The downside of gender quotas? Institutional constraints on women in Mexican state legislatures." *Parliamentary Affairs* 61(3): 442–460.

Zetterberg, Pär. 2009. "Do gender quotas foster women's political engagement? Lessons from Latin America." *Political Research Quarterly* 62(4): 715–730.

CHAPTER 23

JUDICIAL POLITICS AND THE COURTS

RACHEL CICHOWSKI

INTRODUCTION

This chapter focuses on law, courts, and constitutionalism from a gendered perspective. Today the forces of legalization are proceeding at unparalleled rates around the globe. Traditional local norms and legal institutions are increasingly subject to these global pressures, substituting diverse local settings with a general law. Women are critically interconnected with these transformations both as the innovators and subjects of legal change. Dense networks of transnational activists have led to new international women's human rights provisions such as the 1979 Convention on the Elimination of all Forms of Discrimination Against Women (CEDAW). Likewise, new international legal instruments and institutions including the International Criminal Court and its founding treaty led to innovations in domestic protection of women's rights. Similarly, enhanced constitutional power is a hallmark of new democracies, changing the domestic legal context in which women both understand and claim their rights. This trend changes how we come to use the law, practice the law, and study the law. The long-term effect of this transformation remains a pressing empirical and normative question for those scholars interested in law and courts.

Gender and politics scholars are particularly well situated to understand these new global challenges. Feminist legal perspectives privilege diversity of experience and thus can examine these new harmonizing global structures through the lens of difference. This chapter focuses on law, courts, and constitutions from a gendered perspective. The chapter will provide key debates and developments in this field of study and does so explicitly through a lens that understands the ways legal processes are mutually constitutive of gendered social organization. The chapter will begin by briefly elaborating a conceptual framework for a gendered perspective of law and courts. Next, it will focus on three main areas that define the scholarship in this field that are of particular interest to gender and politics scholars: feminist jurisprudence; gender and the courts; and gender, constitutionalism, and human rights. Together this overview provides a template to examine the global challenges facing law and courts scholars today.

Feminist work in the area of law and courts adopts a dynamic understanding of law and the legal processes. Law is not static but gains meaning and is redefined through use (by individuals, social groups, legislators, judges). Further, the law embodies both power and interests that are also dynamic. Thus, in any system of governance, mobilization and litigation present avenues for institutional change and are particularly fruitful for exposing the many processes through which governance can evolve in a way that both changes and is shaped by gendered social organization. Mobilization processes involve the strategic action of individuals and groups to promote or resist change in a given policy arena. Litigation enables actors to question existing rules and procedures. And the court's judicial rule making can lead to the creation of new rules and procedures that can serve as new opportunities for action.

Understanding the law as a process rather than a static institution provides us with a rich foundation to elaborate how feminist scholarship contributes to our theoretical and practical understandings of law, judicial politics, and constitutionalism.

Gender and the Law: Evolving Feminist Jurisprudence

This section provides an historical overview of the main developments in feminist jurisprudence as an approach to the study of law and politics. This approach began in the 1960s and today has come to define and inform many substantive areas of law such as divorce, domestic violence, and sexual harassment to name just a few. Feminist jurisprudence offered a major critique to mainstream understandings of the law—including the way the law is defined, adjudicated, and enforced. Drawing from the previously discussed general framework, the chapter highlights how this scholarship exposed the ways law fosters the oppression of women vis-à-vis the state and society yet also reveals how legal developments can lead to the improvement of women's status. The first part focuses on the development of feminist jurisprudence as an approach to gender and the law. Then the practical application of these approaches is discussed in two areas of law: equality and harm. A few of the key questions that will be raised are: Are legal institutions capable of protecting women? How does the law intersect with women's experiences and what is its role in perpetuating gendered social, economic, legal, and political systems? These questions touch on central debates engaged by feminist approaches to the law.

Beginning in the late 1960s and 1970s, feminist jurisprudence developed in waves that parallel the main fields of feminist theory: liberal theory, dominance theory, cultural theory, socialist theory, and postmodern theory. Classic feminist legal theory focused on women's inequality under the law. Using liberal theory—that women and men were equal persons—feminist legal theorists and jurists brought attention to women's unequal status under the law. In particular, they highlighted the ways the legal system was discriminatory, unjust, and gendered by treating women as different. It moved beyond identifying the historical reality that the law is constructed by elite men, to the practical effect of this bias. Justice Ruth Bader Ginsburg (1978) and Wendy Williams (1981, 1984, 1992) called for the elimination of laws that treat women and men differently. Liberal theory offered a challenge to laws that embodied differences based on stereotypes about women's mental, emotional, or physical characteristics. It was through the action of these scholars, lawyers, and jurists that the concept of equal treatment was fully developed and applied within equal protection discourse.

Despite the importance of this early work, the shortcomings of this "sameness" approach soon became apparent and led to the development of feminist legal theory that focused on women's differences. This theoretical approach is commonly referred to as *cultural* or *difference* feminism and it refocused the cause by arguing that equal treatment protections failed to value the real differences associated with women's lives due to its harmonizing sameness approach. Psychologist Carol Gilligan (1982) was crucial to the development of cultural feminism more generally by studying how cultural and social norms shape the psychological behavior of men and women. The differences in turn affect gender identity and social roles. So in stark contrast to the sameness approach, for cultural feminists, equality in the law came from valuing, acknowledging, and accommodating those differences associated with women—many focusing on women's role in child bearing and economic disadvantage vis-à-vis men (Kay 1985; Finley 1986; Littleton 1987; West 1997; Williams 2000).

The sameness versus difference debate initiated a subsequent development in feminist legal theory put forth by theorists and activists arguing that a focus on difference masks the real key to women's inequality: dominance. Thus, the aptly named *dominance* theorists assert that inequality in the law is a direct result of women's lack of power, or dominance by patriarchal structures, particularly as expressed in the concepts of sex and sexuality. Catherine MacKinnon's (1989) scholarship developed this radical approach and was directly consequential to the expansion of legal protections for women in such areas as sexual harassment law. Two final classic feminist perspectives to the law came from socialist feminists and postmodernists. The former privileging class and economic relationships in understanding inequality before the law (Eisenstein 1988; Hartmann 1979, while the latter sought to question the very category and boundaries presented by the law as expressed in legal theory, be it conventional or feminist (see Norrie 1993). Together, these classical theorists—from the early work grounded in liberal theory to their postmodern counterparts—offered a critical first step in unveiling the inequalities experienced by women before and under the law.

The next stage of feminist jurisprudence evolved in the late 1980s and 1990s when feminist scholars challenged this earlier work for being essentialist. That is, assuming a universal, static homogeneous category of woman and one that was based on a white, middle-class heterosexual model. Antiessentialist theorists provided a critical challenge raising the importance of race, class, and sexual orientation in constructing a more nuanced understanding of gender and the law. Crenshaw's (1989) work exposed the ways in which discrimination law in effect was erasing black women due to the requirements under the law. Doctrinal requirements dictated that discrimination be identified as either racial or sexual. Thus, discrimination that was unique to women of color went unrecognized. Interestingly, her work also illustrates that black women were perceived as different enough to not be strong candidates for class-action suits on grounds of either sex or race—bringing into stark relief critical problems with discrimination law: a male norm in racial cases and a white norm in gender equality claims.

Angela Harris (1990) similarly critiqued feminist legal theorists for singularly focusing on gender disadvantage rather than the reality of black women who experience discrimination at the intersection of racial and sexual inequalities. Her research on rape law identified the limitations of work by feminist theorists, in particular MacKinnon (1978) and West (1988), which focused implicitly on the perspective and experience of white women. Critical race theorists were not calling for discrimination to be examined in light of two separate areas of oppression: race and gender. Instead, this scholarship illustrates how race and gender were interconnected in complex ways highlighting the significance of intersectionalities when examining discrimination and inequality. Mari Matsuda (1992) examines this complexity as one of multiple consciousness. She argues that women have multiple consciousnesses, and these can play out very differently depending on identity characteristics that have a direct impact on how the discrimination is then lived.

Similar to critical race theorists, classic feminist legal theory was further challenged by the development of gay and lesbian jurisprudence (Cain 1989; Robson 1990; Eaton 1993; Majury 1994). This scholarship highlighted the heterosexual assumptions of classic legal theorists and called for a vision of gender that was not limited to the heterosexual experience. Finally, feminist jurisprudence evolved to reflect challenges arising from globalization and the differential status of women around the globe. In particular, this scholarship challenges the American dominance and imperialist assumptions embedded in feminist legal theory that did not adequately reflect the culture, perspective, and lives expressed by third-world feminists (see Brems 1997). Together, these strands of feminist jurisprudence—classical feminist theory, critical race theory, gay and lesbian jurisprudence, and third-world feminism—define the ways scholars examine the intersection between gender and the law.

What is the practical application of these gendered theoretical approaches? The areas of equality and harm are central examples. Feminist legal theory raises significant questions regarding the application of the principle of equality. What approach to equality will provide an adequate balance between a woman's right to individual liberty and her identity as a woman? In employment settings, questions arise such as if women are equal, how might this be expressed in workplace regulations? Does equality demand respect for difference given variation in life experiences, or does equity hinge on sameness treatment with men? Further, should women be dealt with as individuals or a class?

Pregnancy is an area of law where you see a clear tension between the sameness versus difference debate in equality law. The sameness perspective states any difference in treatment between men and women should be erased as it is at the root of discrimination. Difference theorists would argue that pregnancy involves practical differences, and these should be acknowledged within the law. What meaning is equality given in this case? Does equality mean women should be treated exactly the same as men, or does it call for women to be treated differently, such that their differences prevent equity being achieved from equal treatment? Thus, one feminist approach calls for legal reform to recognize the differences of women as a class (Kay 1985).

Other approaches to equality include the acceptance model (Littleton 1987), which shares an affinity to the difference approaches. This approach argues that the law should focus on remedying the effects of differences rather than the differences themselves. Equality functions to make these differences costless, such that equality should require that women receive maternity leave and security to return to their job after birthing. Feminist critique of equality rights also challenges traditional understanding of rights that purposefully exclude women's needs. To attain equality, rights must then be informed by the experiences of women and others who are excluded. Both MacKinnon (1987) and Williams (1992) argue that equality rights must be distributed in a way that recognizes how they empower those to whom they are granted.

Alongside equality, harm is another area of the law that gained greater clarity due to a gendered approach. Feminist jurisprudence is critical to integrating diverse perspectives as a necessary component to the definition of harm. Feminist legal scholars illuminate the patriarchal bias in the law and rethought basic assumptions regarding harm: how is harm identified? What is harm? What counts as harm in our legal system? What actions are excluded from definitions of harm? What is the effect on women and how can the law be reformed?

Three areas of law form the foundation of feminist research on harm: rape, sexual harassment, and domestic violence. Feminist scholars argue that harm was erroneously being defined within a historical legal framework that understood women as property belonging to men. Thus, this scholarship led the way for incremental legal reform in expanding the definition of harm, which ultimately led to an increase in prosecutions (Schulhofer 1998). Here too we see the difference between scholars working from a reformist (similar to many sameness perspectives) approach and dominance or radical approaches. For example, reformist scholars argue for the treatment of rape to be similar to other nonconsent crimes (such as theft) (Estrich 1987) or how the current law could be applied to harms such as date rape (Fellows and Balos 1991). Radical or dominance feminists raise questions with the ability of masculine courts to understand harm in a way that is consistent with how women are conditioned to react to violence (such that consent in rape cases is often misunderstood) (West 1988). Similarly, MacKinnon's (1989) work on sexual harassment identifies women's empowerment and involvement in constructing how harm is understood. Despite these variations in approaches, the practical application of feminist jurisprudence across areas of law is both increased prosecution and greater protections for women under the law.

GENDER AND THE COURTS

Following this historical overview of feminist jurisprudence approaches to the law, we now examine the law in action. This section elaborates how gender approaches provide a more nuanced understanding of judicial politics and courts. The scholarship raises a key paradox. On one hand, feminist critics of courts highlight their limitations for offering women effective protection arguing they are oppressive patriarchal institutions, while at the same time legal activists successfully use litigation to bring substantive and procedural reform widening the net of protection for women.

Again, drawing from the general framework discussed in the introduction, this section focuses on adjudication of the law as a dynamic process. Gender scholarship illustrates how litigation or rights claiming as a process can both shape and be shaped by gendered social structures. The section first examines processes of litigation and rights claiming at the domestic, transnational, and international levels. Then it focuses on the role of gender in judging. Key questions that define this scholarship and area of study are: Does litigation and rights claiming as a process hinder or empower women? How can courts be used for reform? In what ways does a gendered approach give us a more nuanced understanding of the consequences (both intended and unintended) of litigation and rights claiming? If, how and why do female judges affect judicial decision making?

Gender scholarship privileging the reform potential of litigation is consistent with the basic assumptions of comparative judicial politics research. That is, through litigation, a court's resolution of societal questions or disputes can lead to the clarification, expansion, and creation of rules and procedures (Shapiro 1981, 35–37). Thus, in any system of governance with an independent judiciary possessing judicial review powers, the judicial decision provides a potential avenue for reform: for the clarification and expansion of laws. The court's rule-making capacity operates within the institutional framework of an existing body of rules and procedures (e.g., a constitution, statute, or international treaty), yet a court's jurisprudence can subsequently lead to reform of these laws (Shapiro 1981; Stone Sweet 2000).

Yet courts do not act on their own initiative. Instead, they need to be activated by an individual or group. The choice to mobilize the law begins as a result of action by individuals (or a group acting on behalf of individuals) that are either disadvantaged or advantaged by an available set of laws. In general, feminist activists and women's movements experience relative success at using courts as an avenue to pressure for political reform and do so by using an explicit or implied set of rights. In the United States, there is a long tradition of marginalized groups using the courts as an opportunity to challenge existing governance structures and exclusionary policies (McCann 1994). Most notable are the activities of the early civil rights movement on issues such as school segregation (for example, the *Brown v. Board of Education* decision; see Morris 1984) and also a host of other social movements including the American labor movement (Forbath 1991), the welfare movement (Piven and Cloward 1979), and the animal rights movement (Silverstein 1996).

Scholars examine the ways the American women's movement uses similar litigation strategies in a host of substantive areas of law from employment discrimination to sexual harassment (O'Connor 1980; Costain 1992; Strebeigh 2009). In the 1970s, law clinics such as the one founded by now U.S. Supreme Court Justice Ruth Bader Ginsburg, the Rutgers–Newark Women's Rights Litigation Clinic, were essential for not only training lawyers to critically understand the needs of women but also to support strategic litigation that aimed to reform law (Taub 1999). MacKinnon's (1978, 1989) theoretical and practical work on sexual harassment served as the basis by which sexual harassment claims were litigated in the United States and then subsequently codified in statute. Various nongovernmental organizations including the American Civil Liberties Union (ACLU) and the Center for Constitutional Rights are key players both in representing claimants and also filing amicus briefs in a wide variety of sex discrimination areas. Today, one cannot understand the evolution of women's rights in the United States without a thorough examination of the courts—developments that expand far beyond the equality claims of the 1970s and today include issues such as same sex marriage and asylum laws (Stetson 2004; Cushman 2010).

Another common law country example is Canada. With the passage of the Canadian Charter of Fundamental Rights in 1982, women's groups and strategic legal activists looked to the Canadian Supreme Court as a viable avenue for bringing reform. Groups such as the Women's Legal Education and Action Fund (LEAF) were critical by providing the legal expertise and funding. Feminist activists founding the organization saw litigation strategies as an effective mechanism to make the charter rights meaningful and reflect the reality of women (Manfredi 2005). It was a campaign to move the rights in a direction from formal equality to substantive equality in the pursuit of women's social, political, and economic equality.

This type of litigation requires and remains tied to a hospitable legal environment: a set of rights; courts with judicial review powers; and mobilized activists with resources (Cichowski and Stone Sweet 2003). Yet increasingly these conditions are met, even in civil law countries, as we find these general patterns of legal mobilization spreading around the globe (Cichowski and Stone Sweet 2003; Kelemen 2011). Nongovernmental organizations in Latin America and Southeast Asia, to name a few, are increasingly turning to courts to demand accountability in protecting women's rights in a range of areas including reproductive rights, maternal health, and divorce law (Feld 2002; Subramanian 2008; Arellano 2010). The courtrooms of Europe are also increasingly home to women's rights activists. Often seemingly individual litigation in reality benefits from strategic organized interests and activists (Harlow and Rawlings 1992; Hoskyns 1996; Cichowski 2004, 2007). In the case of the United Kingdom, the implementation of the Human Rights Act of 1998 incorporated the European Convention on Human Rights into the domestic legal system giving the judiciary added power to protect rights. While this clearly has opened the door for greater legal mobilization in U.K. courts, feminist scholars continue to scrutinize the effects (Conaghan and Millns 2005; Grabham and Hunter 2008).

Litigation in the United Kingdom also brings attention to the growing significance of transnational and international law for the domestic protection of women's rights. In Europe, individual activists and women's rights organizations successfully use the Court of Justice of the European Union (ECJ) to push for and attain reforms in domestic employment policies—from equal pay to maternity policies (Hoskyns 1996; Alter and Vargas 2000; Cichowski 2004, 2007; Ellis 2005). Women's rights activists in the 1960s and 1970s saw the Treaty of Rome (the treaties governing the European Community, today the European Union, or EU) as a stepping-stone to expanding women's labor rights. A series of ECJ cases, *Defrenne* decisions (ECJ 1971, 1976, 1978) resulting from test cases brought by a Belgian activist lawyer are now famous for expanding both EU and domestic gender equality laws (Cichowski 2007). It is widely accepted that over the last fifty years, the ECJ's case law, which at times is initiated by strategic activists, plays an integral role in the development of EU antidiscrimination law and in effect continues to bring domestic level reforms across the twenty-seven member-states (Ellis 2005).

Interestingly, litigation before the other European regional court, the European Court of Human Rights (ECtHR) reveals a similar dynamic with examples covering a host of substantive areas of law from reproductive rights to transgender rights (Cichowski 2006). Likewise, there is a global expansion in international and domestic women's rights organizations looking to international legal institutions to enhance and enforce domestic protection of women's rights. Scholars discuss the potential and realized success of litigation and legal complaints brought before the Intra-American Court of Human Rights (Robinson 2005), the African Commission on Human and People's Rights (Wing and Smith 2003), and the United Nations Committee on the Elimination of All Forms of Discrimination Against Women (Hoq 2001). Beyond the work of international courts, international law also shapes domestic litigation in areas such as wartime sexual violence (MacKinnon 2006; Baylis 2009). Even international courts with no private party access such as the international criminal court affect how gender justice is realized at the domestic level (e.g., Chappell 2008, 2011).

Together this scholarship illustrates that feminist activism not only shapes litigation and contributes to reforms but also may present limitations for women's right protections (Cahn 1991; Williams 1992). Feminists are quick to point out the potential limitation of turning rights protection over to the judiciary, which is a comparatively new phenomenon in many civil law countries (McColgan 2000). Regardless of the jurisdiction or location, the assumption of neutrality both of the law and those engaged in developing, protecting, and enforcing the law (e.g., judges, lawyers, law enforcement) is a central issue challenged by feminist scholars (Baer 1999). Further, litigation may continue to reveal greater success in attaining formal equality rather than bringing reforms in areas of substantive equality (Smart 1989). Scholars argue that accepting the law, and litigation process as neutral masks the masculine view—which is often portrayed as universal—that is embedded in the judicial structure. The use of precedent (judicial reasoning relying on past case law) in the American system, but also increasingly observed in European and international courts, is problematic from a feminist perspective as its path dependence can make reform of discriminatory laws particularly challenging. For example, in the area of labor law, scholars (both feminist and nonfeminist) highlight the misapplication of past case law to current situations (Becker et al. 2007). A male norm of the past is wrongfully applied to a very different experience of women workers today. Thus, courts also present the potential to undermine progress. We see a similar challenge at the international level. While the ECJ clearly expanded EU equality rights, its case law also at times has created greater conflicts between progressive domestic equality laws and narrower EU level interpretations—leading to further domestic versus supranational conflicts over the application of equality law (e.g., *Kalanke* decision, ECJ 1995).

Beyond litigation, an important area of research for gender and the courts involves judging. Do female judges decide cases differently? Does the presence of female judges on the bench cause their male counterparts to engage in decision making differently? What explains cross-national variation in the number of female judges? The research includes both nonfeminist approaches as well as those engaged in feminist critique. Nonfeminist research is primarily carried out by judicial behavior scholars, most who are American political scientists examining the effects of judicial behavior on decision making throughout the American judiciary (e.g., Boyd, Epstein, and Martin 2010). This research generally can be understood as the "add women and stir" research approach, where sex becomes a critical variable under examination in a large-*N* analysis of judicial behavior. The research tests four main explanations of the effects of sex on judicial decision making: difference; representational; informational; and organization.

The *difference* approach draws heavily from the early work of feminists (Gilligan 1982). They argue that women are connected in society differently and hold an alternate worldview than men, and, thus, we would expect this female perspective to carry across areas of the law and lead to varying general patterns of judging (Sherry 1986; Steffensmeier and Herbert 1999). The *representational* approach posits that women judges will represent women's interests as a class, such that women judges rule progressively for women in areas such as sex discrimination and sexual harassment (Carroll 1984). The *informational* approach is similar in effects but argues that these pro-women decisions are not due to female judges representing women as a class per se but instead come from first hand information gathered through shared personal and professional experiences (Peresie 2005). Finally, the *organization* approach expects little variation in judging across sex given the way the judiciary is organized with men and women receiving a similar education, same procedures, and same constraints on the bench (Sisk, Heise, and Moriss 1998).

Beyond the judicial behavior approaches, feminist scholars are examining the effects of female judging. Sally Kenney's (2008a, 2013) research on judges in the United Kingdom poses the question why was the first woman appointed to its highest appellate court almost twenty-five years after the United States and Canada? Kenney (2008a) adopts a policy agenda setting approach to understand the forces that led up to the appointment of Lady Brenda Hale in 2003. Importantly, she argues that agenda setting theories previously failed to consider the explanatory power of feminist discourse in instituting policy change. British feminists used the discourse of representation, equality in employment, and legitimacy to successfully attain reform in equality on the bench. Notably her work raises a critical voice and warning to gender and judging scholars to be careful of the "trap of essentialism" (Kenney 2008b, 88) and the importance of discursive change (Kenney 2004). When studying judging, she calls for a more nuanced understanding of gender effects in such important ways as recognizing that gender consciousness is acquired not automatic; that, similar to women, men may have experiences that affect how they rule on women's issues; and finally that these effects must not be assumed but instead continue to be the subject of empirical analysis (Kenney 2013).

GENDER, CONSTITUTIONALISM, AND HUMAN RIGHTS

This final section examines feminist approaches in the area of constitutionalism and women's human rights; both are higher-order norms either within domestic or international law. This builds from the previous two sections as the interaction between law and courts is at the center of constitutionalism and human rights. Constitutionalism is a booming industry with over one hundred new or revised constitutions being adopted over the last twenty years. Interestingly, gender equality provisions are widespread, along with mechanisms to promote gender equality (see Dobrowolsky and Hart 2003). Similarly, there is a global expansion in international legal instruments specifically affecting the status of women's rights (e.g., CEDAW 1979; establishment of rape as a war crime under international law; *Akayesu* decision ICTR in 1998; UN Resolution 1820 on women, peace, and security in 2008). The effects of these constitutional designs and new international reforms are far from uniform and provide avenues for future research. For example, the EU's adoption of soft law measures, such as gender mainstreaming and the open method of coordination processes, may introduce innovative European-wide solutions to gender equality yet do little to minimize conflicts arising between domestic and EU-level constitutional rights (Beveridge 2008; Beveridge and Velluti 2008). Similarly, Merry (2006) argues for the importance of international legal instruments such as CEDAW for protecting women's rights but links its regulatory strength to domestic legal consciousness and local cultures.

How can feminist approaches inform comparative constitutional analysis? Scholarship in this area focuses on the role of women as movement activists, legal experts, government officials, and judges in constitutionalism processes. Research also examines the consequences of constitutional provisions for the status of women. Feminist scholarship is important not only for critically reflecting on the effects of gender equality rights in new constitutions but also for raising the need to examine the gendered effects of certain structural constitutional designs. For example, constitutional provisions mandating a certain type of electoral system can have a direct effect on the inclusion of women in politics. A central question raised by this research is how does gendered analysis provide a more complex and complete picture of the process of constitutionalism?

Despite the growing theoretical and practical significance of comparative constitutional research there is a relative paucity of research examining gender and constitutions. Yet feminist activists have a long history of mobilizing for constitutional change. Scholars show the role of feminist activists in the drafting and adoption of the Canadian Charter of Rights and Freedoms (Green 2003; Murphy 2003), the Nicaraguan Constitution (Morgan 1990), and constitutional changes in Uganda and Brazil (Verucci 1991; Furley and Katalikawe 1997). This research stands out from more general work on constitutionalism by explicitly examining the role of gender in these processes. For example, research on the United Kingdom highlights the nuanced ways women sought to engage the processes of constitutional change for their ends on varying levels—regionally in Scotland (Mackay, Myers, and Brown 2003) and supranationally with European institutions (Hart 2003). Women throughout Europe use the constitutional process driven by the ECJ to enable the expansion of EU and domestic sex equality protections (Cichowski 2007).

Feminist scholarship is quick to point out the setbacks that accompany these "one step forward, two steps back" advancements in constitutionalism. For example, seven years after the adoption of the Canadian Charter, few women were bringing discrimination cases and instead men were using the charter to undo previously created protections and benefits for women. Likewise, Aboriginal or first-nations women, refugees, and immigrants all do not necessarily enjoy the protection that the Canadian Charter in theory provides to all women (Broadbent 2001; Green 2003). Time and time again, constitutionalism is often characterized by some formal equality change, yet substantive equality remains a distant aspiration (Baines and Rubio-Marin 2005).

Recent scholarship moves the analysis away from a focus only on constitutional rights and instead scrutinizes the effects of other constitutional provisions on women's equality (Williams 2009). Structural elements can directly affect the status of women such that proportional representation electoral systems have a greater impact on women's representation than do first past the post systems (Dahlerup and Freidenvall 2009). Federalism versus unitary systems and presidential versus parliamentary systems are constitutional mechanisms often put into place to accommodate cultural, religious, or ethnic divisions, yet they can have real impacts on women. Similarly, Albertyn's (2003a; 2003b) research on South Africa illustrates how greater equality in practice was directly related to constitutional mechanisms ensuring parity for women in parliament. Further, she argues that while this presence might be important at a particular historic moment, many of the contemporary challenges facing South African women (poverty, violence, and AIDS/HIV) is going to take more than parliamentary action to bring change in day-to-day lives.

Irving's (2008) research provides a book-length template for how states could achieve gender equity and agency through the constitution. Her design goes beyond equality and rights: "Both equity and agency involve more than rights or prohibition on discrimination. Both are implicated in the architecture and design of a constitution: in the way power is structured, the way the arms of government relate to each other, the demarcation between political/public and private, the separation of powers...they involve questions of jurisdiction, representation, and citizenship, among other" (3). Gendering a constitution means scrutinizing the whole document from constitutional language to citizenship to reproductive rights to mechanisms for incorporating international and customary law. This feminist scholarship pushes constitution designers to move beyond the box of equality rights.

Contemporary constitutionalism in the area of gender is also intricately linked to human rights. Increasingly domestic constitutions come under the scrutiny of international human rights instruments. Yet feminist scholars raise questions whether these general human rights are a real solution to ending gender oppression and subsequently call for the development of women's human rights. Feminists acting as movement organizers, policy makers, and international lawyers attained considerable gains over the last half-century building on the general expansion in international human rights to construct these women's human rights instruments, such as mentioned already, CEDAW and rape as a war crime (Robinson 2005). These gains result from scholars and practitioners questioning the neutrality and genderless nature of international law (Charlesworth, Chinkin, and Wright 1991; Charlesworth and Chinkin 1993; Charlesworth 1994; Romany 1994). The development of women's human rights as a movement and approach to international constitutionalism did not evolve without challenges and serious debate amongst feminist scholars. This does not undermine the real gains but instead poses a set of challenges for developments in the future.

A key debate surrounding the utility of a women's human rights approach focuses on the tensions between the particular and universal. Cultural relativists argue women's human rights frameworks embody a universal assumption that fails to take into account culture—thus misunderstanding gender implications, as gender structures emerge from cultural norms (Brems 1997) (see also the chapter by Judith Squires in this volume). Subsequently, universalistic rights (e.g., CEDAW) are developed as diametrically opposed to the establishment of group or cultural rights. On the other hand, scholars defending a universal approach to human rights embrace the power of the language of rights to challenge gender structures and injustice while at the same time acknowledging difference and diversity (Donnelly 1993; Steans 2007). Women's human rights are viewed as a useful political tool that transnational feminist scholars and practitioners use to challenge injustices and discrimination around the world.

Others attempt to bridge the gap between the particular and the universal. Lloyd (2007) argues that human rights discourses are most progressive for women when they can lead to the reconfiguration of what is meant by human and transform limiting norms. This approach requires accepting that the processes by which the rights are constructed are historically and culturally meaningful. Similarly, others argue that what might appear as particular in one context might be universal in another and that it is the clash between these particular universals that fosters growth and ongoing political reform (Laclau 1996). This is consistent with and revisits the general critique of human rights as embodying masculine, imperialist, and Western frames (Lloyd 2007).

These debates lead scholars to grapple with a larger question that comes with the development of international constitutionalism: are women's human rights approaches more effective at abating women's oppression and violations than a more general body of human rights? Grewal (1988) argues no, in that women's human rights treat the violation as one experienced by an individual woman and in doing so masks the larger political and economic structures that produce the conditions for the violation in the first place. Practitioners such as Obando (1994) argues to the contrary, stating that instruments such as CEDAW don't individualize women's experience but instead make them the focus of collective concern: experiences that governments have the duty to attend to, even if law enforcement fails. By making certain criminal acts (rape and domestic violence) punishable by courts, this gives greater visibility to the oppression that women experience. Another response to this question is a concern that by invoking rights specifically for women there is the fear that states can use these in a way that maintains their power over female populations: it may resubordinate certain categories of identity (e.g., as mother–caregiver, more vulnerable) (Lloyd 2007). Together this scholarship illustrates the complexity at both the domestic and international level of processes developing and defining how constitutions, constitutional rights, and human rights can embrace and incorporate gender.

Conclusions

From the early work of feminist legal theorists to women human rights activists, gender research significantly changed not only the way we conceptualize the legal process but also how it is implemented in practice. The gains are many: domestic equality laws; expanded opportunities for bringing discrimination claims; and international norms demanding state accountability in protecting women's rights. The chapter highlights that the challenges also abound. Past inequalities were the catalyst for change, which led to a more nuanced and gendered understanding of law, courts, and constitutionalism and suggests how they may serve as a foundation for theoretical and empirical work in the future. We need scholarship that continues to scrutinize the global disparities in access to the law, courts, and constitutional rights and highlights the stark variation that characterizes the real life of women around the globe. Approaches privileging the significance of intersectionalities—across race, class, and sexual orientation—will be integral to this research trajectory. However, this may call on scholars and practitioners to rethink the very foundations upon which inclusive legal processes sit. Rather than focusing on an elaborate system of gendered laws, courts, and constitutional rights, increasingly gendered political and legal advancements may hinge on the fulfillment of basic societal needs (education, health, water, economic stability)—areas that continue to disproportionately affect women and remain at the center of gender and politics.

REFERENCES

Albertyn, Catherine. 2003a. "Towards substantive representation: Women and politics in South Africa." In A. Dobrowolsky and V. Hart, eds., *Women making constitutions: New politics and comparative perspectives*. New York: Palgrave Macmillian, 99–117.

Albertyn, Catherine. 2003b. "Contesting democracy: HIV/AIDS and the achievement of gender equality in South Africa." *Feminist Studies* 29(3): 595–615.

Alter, Karen, and Jeannette Vargas. 2000. "Explaining variation in the use of European litigation strategies: European community law and British gender equality policy." *Comparative Political Studies* 33: 452–482.

Arellano, Maria de Jesus Medina. 2010. "The need for balancing the reproductive rights of women and the unborn in the Mexican courtroom." *Medical Law Review* 18(3): 417–426.

Baer, Judith. 1999. *Our lives before the law: Constructing a feminist jurisprudence*. Princeton, NJ: Princeton University Press.

Baines, Beverly, and Ruth Rubio-Marin. 2005. "The gender of constitutional jurisprudence." New York: Cambridge Unviersity Press.

Baylis, Elena. 2009. "Reassessing the role of international criminal law: Rebuilding national courts through transnational networks." *Boston College Law Review* 50: 1–85.

Becker, Mary, Cynthia Grant Bowman, Victoria F. Nourse, and Kimberly A. Yuracko. 2007. *Feminist jurisprudence: Taking women seriously*. St. Paul, MN: West Publishing Company.

Beveridge, Fiona. 2008. "Implementing gender equality and mainstreaming in an enlarged European Union." In F. Beveridge and S. Velluti, eds., *Gender and the open method coordination and perspectives on law, governance and equality in the EU*. London: Aldershot Ashgate, 11–34.

Beveridge, Fiona, and S. Velluti. 2008. "Gender and the OMC: Introduction and perspectives." In F. Beveridge and S. Velluti, eds., *Gender and the open method coordination and perspectives on law, governance and equality in the EU*. London: Aldershot Ashgate, 191–208.

Boyd, Christina L., Lee Epstein, and Andrew Martin. 2010. "Untangling the causal effects of sex on judging." *American Journal of Political Science* 54(2): 389–411.

Brems, Eva. 1997. "Enemies or allies? Feminism and cultural relativism as dissident voices in human rights discourse." *Human Rights Quarterly* 19: 136–164.

Broadbent, E. 2001. *Democratic equality: What went wrong?* Toronto: University of Toronto Press.

Cain, Patricia A. 1989. "Feminist jurisprudence: Grounding the theories." *Berkeley Women's Law Journal* 4: 191–14.

Cahn, Naomi. 1991. "Defining feminist litigation." *Harvard Women's Law Journal* 14: 1–20..

Carroll, Susan J. 1984. Woman candidates and support for feminist concerns. *Western Political Quarterly* 37(2): 307–323.

Chappell, Louise. 2008. "Governing international law through the international criminal court: A new site for gender justice?" In S. Rai and G. Waylen, eds., *Global governance: Feminist perspectives*. London: Palgrave Macmillan, 160–184.

Chappell, Louise. 2011. "Nested newness and institutional innovation: Expanding gender justice in the international criminal court." In M. L. Krook and F. Mackay, eds., *Gender, politics and institutions: Toward a feminist institutionalism.* London: Palgrave Macmillan, 163–180.

Charlesworth, Hilary. 1994. "What are women's international human rights?" In R. Cook, ed., *Human rights of women: National and international perspectives.* Cambridge, UK: Cambridge University Press, 57–84.

Charlesworth, Hilary, and Christine Chinkin. 1993. "The gender of Jus Cogens." *Human Rights Quarterly* 15: 63–76.

Charlesworth, Hilary, Christine Chinkin, and Shelley Wright. 1991. "Feminist approaches to international law." *American Journal of International Law* 85: 613–635.

Cichowski, Rachel A. 2004. "Women's rights, the European Court and supranational constitutionalism." *Law & Society Review* 38: 489–512.

Cichowski, Rachel A. 2006. "Courts, rights and democratic participation." *Comparative Political Studies* 39: 50–75.

Cichowski, Rachel A. 2007. *The European court and civil society.* Cambridge, UK: Cambridge University Press.

Cichowski, Rachel A., and Alec Stone Sweet. 2003. "Participation, representative democracy and the courts." In R. Dalton, B. Cain, and S. Scarrow, eds., *New forms of democracy? Reform and transformation of democratic institutions.* Oxford: Oxford University Press, 192–222.

Conaghan, Joanne, and Susan Millns. 2005. "Gender, sexuality and human rights." *Feminist Legal Studies* 13(1): 1–14.

Costain, Anne N. 1992. *Inviting women's rebellion: A political process interpretation of the women's movement.* Baltimore: Johns Hopkins University Press.

Crenshaw, Kimberlé. 1989. "Demarginalizing the intersection of race and sex: A black feminist critique of antidiscrimination doctrine, feminist theory and antiracist politics." *University of Chicago Legal Forum,* 139–168.

Cushman, Clare. 2010. *Supreme court decisions and women's rights.* Washington, DC: CQ Press.

Dahlerup, Drude, and Leniat Freidenvall. 2009. "Gender quotas in politics—A constitutional challenge." In S. Williams, ed., *Constituting equality: Comparative constitutional law and gender equality.* Cambridge, UK: Cambridge University Press, 29–52.

Dobrowolsky, Alexandra, and Vivien Hart (Eds.). 2003. *Women making constitutions.* New York: Palgrave Macmillan.

Donnelly, Jack. 1993. *International human rights.* Boulder, CO: Westview Press.

Eaton, Mary. 1993. "At the intersection of gender and sexual orientation: Toward lesbian jurisprudence." *Southern California Review of Law and Women's Studies* 3: 183–218.

ECJ (Court of Justice of the European Union). 1971. *Defrenne I,* Case 80/70, ECR 1971: 445.

ECJ (Court of Justice of the European Union). 1976. *Defrenne II,* Case 43/75, ECR 1976: 455.

ECJ (Court of Justice of the European Union). 1978. *Defrenne III,* Case 149/77, ECR 1978: 1365.

ECJ (Court of Justice of the European Union). 1995. *Kalanke,* Case C-450/93, ECR 1995: 3051.

Eisenstein, Zillah. 1988. *The female body and the law.* Berkeley: University of California Press.

Ellis, Evelyn. 2005. *EU Anti-discrimination law.* Oxford: Oxford University Press.

Estrich, Susan. 1987. *Real rape.* Cambridge, MA: Harvard University Press.

Feld, Louise. 2002. "Along the spectrum of women's rights advocacy: A cross-cultural comparison of sexual harassment law in the United States and India." *Fordham International Law Journal* 25(5): 1205–1281.

Fellows, Mary Louise, and Beverly Balos. 1991. "Guilty of the crime of trust: Nonstranger rape." *Minnesota Law Review* 75: 599.

Finley, L. 1986. "Transcending equality theory: A way out of the maternity and the workplace debate." *Columbia Law Review* 86: 1118–1182.

Forbath, William E. 1991. *Law and the shaping of the American labor movement.* Cambridge, MA: Harvard University Press.

Furley, O., and Katalikawe J. 1997. "Constitutional reform in Uganda: The new approach." *African Affairs* 96: 243–260.

Gilligan, Carol. 1982. *In a different voice: Psychological theory and women's development.* Cambridge: Harvard University Press.

Ginsburg, Ruth Bader. 1978. "Sex equality and the constitution." *Tulane Law Review* 52: 451–453.

Grabham, Emily, and Rosemary Hunter. 2008. "Encountering human rights: Gender/sexuality, activism and the promise of the law." *Feminist Legal Studies* 16: 1–7.

Green, Joyce. 2003. *Balancing strategies: Aboriginal women and constitutional rights in Canada.* In A. Dobrowolsky and V. Hart, eds., *Women making constitutions: New politics and comparative perspectives.* New York: Palgrave Macmillian, 36–51.

Grewal, Inderpal. 1988. "On the new global feminism and the family of nations: Dilemmas of transnational feminist practice." In Ella Shohat, ed., *Talking visions: Multicultural feminism in a transnational age.* Cambridge, MA: MIT Press, 501–532.

Harlow, Carol, and Richard Rawlings. 1992. *Pressure through law.* London: Routledge.

Harris, Angela. 1990. "Race and essentialism in feminist legal theory." *Stanford Law Review* 42: 581.

Hart, Vivien. 2003. "Redesigning the polity: Europe, women and constitutional politics in the UK." In A. Dobrowolsky and V. Hart, eds., *Women making constitutions: New politics and comparative perspectives.* New York: Palgrave Macmillian, 118–131.

Hartmann, Heidi. 1979. "The unhappy marriage of Marxism and feminism: Towards a more progressive union." *Capital and Class* 3(2): 1–33.

Hoq, Laboni Amena. 2001. The women's convention and its optional protocol: Empowering women to claim their internationally protected rights. *Columbia Human Rights Law Review,* 32: 677–726.

Hoskyns, Catherine. 1996. *Integrating gender: Women, law and politics in the European Union.* London: Verso.

Irving, Helen. 2008. *Gender and the constitution: Equity and agency in comparative constitutional design.* New York: Cambridge University Press.

Kay, Herma Hill. 1985. "Equality and difference: The case of pregnancy." *Berkeley Women's Law Journal* 1: 1–37.

Kelemen, R. Daniel. 2011. *Eurolegalism: The rise of adversarial legalism in the European Union.* Cambridge, MA: Harvard University Press.

Kenney, Sally J. 2004. "Equal Employment Opportunity and representation: Extending the frame to courts." *Social Politics* 11: 86–116.

Kenney, Sally J. 2008a. "Gender on the agenda: How the paucity of women judges became an issue." *Journal of Politics* 70(3): 717–735.

Kenney, Sally J. 2008b. "Thinking of gender and judging." *International Journal of the Legal Profession* 15(1–2): 87–110.

Kenney, Sally J. 2013. *Gender and justice: Why women in the judiciary really matter.* New York, NY: Routledge.

Laclau, Ernesto. 1996. *Emancipation(s).* London: Verso.

Littleton, Christine A. 1987. "Reconstructing sexual equality." *California Law Review* 75: 1279–1337.

Lloyd, Moya. 2007. "(Women's) human rights: Paradoxes and possibilities." *Review of International Studies* 33: 91–103.

Mackay, Fiona, Fiona Myers, and Alice Brown. 2003. "Towards a new politics? Women and the constitutional change in Scotland." In A. Dobrowolsky and V. Hart, eds., *Women making constitutions.* New York: Palgrave Macmillan, 84–98.

MacKinnon, Catherine. 1978. *The sexual harassment of working women: A case of sex discrimination.* New Haven, CT: Yale University Press.

MacKinnon, Catherine. 1987. *Feminism unmodified: Discourses in life and law.* Cambridge, MA: Harvard University Press.

MacKinnon, Catherine. 1989. *Towards a feminist theory of the state.* Cambridge, MA: Harvard University Press.

MacKinnon, Catherine. 2006. *Are women human? And other international dialogues.* Cambridge, MA: Harvard University Press.

Majury, Diana. 1994. "Refashioning the unfashionable: Claiming lesbian identities in the legal context." *Canadian Journal of Women & Law* 7: 286–317.

Manfredi, Christopher P. 2005. *Feminist activism in the supreme court: Legal mobilization and the women's legal education and action fund.* Vancouver: University of British Columbia Press.

Matsuda, Mari J. 1992. "When the first quail calls: Multiple consciousnesses as jurisprudential method." *Women's Rights Law Reporter* 14: 297–300.

McCann, Michael W. 1994. *Rights at work: Pay equity reform and the politics of legal mobilization.* Chicago: University of Chicago Press.

McColgan, Aileen. 2000. *Women under the law: the false promise of human rights.* London: Addison, Welsey, Longman.

Merry, Sally Engle. 2006. *Human rights and gender violence.* Princeton, NJ: Princeton University Press.

Morgan, M. I. 1990. "Founding mothers: Women's voices and stories in the 1987 Nicaraguan constitution." *Boston University Law Review* 70(1): 1–110.

Morris, Aldon. 1984. *The origins of the civil rights movement.* New York: Free Press.

Murphy, Ronalda. 2003. "Constitutional rights discourse: Canadian and South African femininst engagement." In A. Dobrowolsky and V. Hart, eds., *Women making constitutions.* New York: Palgrave Macmillan, 20–35.

Norrie, A. (Ed.). 1993. *Closure or critique: New directions in legal theory.* Edinburgh: Edinburgh University Press.

Obando, Ana Elena. 1994. "How effective is a human rights framework in addressing gender-based violence." Available at http://www.awid.org/Library/How-Effective-is-a-Human-Rights-framework-in-addressing-Gender-based-Violence.

O'Connor, Karen. 1980. *Women's organizations' use of the courts.* Lexington, MA: Lexington Books.

Peresie, Jennifer L. 2005. "Female judges matter: Gender and collegial decision making in the federal appellate courts." *Yale Law Journal* 114(7): 1759–1790.

Piven, Frances F., and Richard A. Cloward. 1979. *Poor people's movements: Why they succeed, how they fail.* New York: Vintage.

Robinson, Joan. 2005. "Another women's body found outside Juarez." *Wisconsin Women's Law Journal* 20: 167–188.

Robson, Ruthann. 1990. "Lesbian jurisprudence." *Law and Inequality Journal* 8: 443–468.

Romany, Celina. 1994. "State responsibility goes private: A feminist critique of the public/private distinction in international human rights law." In R. Cook, ed., *Human rights of women: National and international perspectives.* Cambridge, UK: Cambridge University Press, 85–115.

Schulhofer, Stephan J. 1998. *Unwanted sex: The culture of intimidation and the failure of law.* Cambridge, UK: Cambridge University Press.

Shapiro, Martin. 1981. *Courts: A comparative and political analysis.* Chicago: University of Chicago Press.

Sherry, Suzanna. 1986. "Civic virtue and the feminine voice in constitutional adjudication." *Virginia Law Review* 72(3): 543–616.

Silverstein, Helen. 1996. *Unleashing Rights: Law, meaning, and the animal rights movement.* Ann Arbor: University of Michigan Press.

Sisk, Gregory C., Michael Heise, and Andrew P. Morriss. 1998. "Charting the influence on the judicial mind: An empirical study of judicial reasoning." *NYU Law Review* 73(5): 1377–1500.

Smart, Carol. 1989. *Feminism and the power of law.* London: Routledge.

Steans, Jill. 2007. "Debating women's human rights as a universal feminist project: Defending women's human rights as a political tool." *Review of International Studies* 33: 11–27.

Steffensmeier, Darrell, and Chris Herbert. 1999. "Women and men policymakers: Does the Judge's gender affect the sentencing of criminal defendants?" *Social Forces* 77(3): 1163–1196.

Stetson, Dorothy McBride. 2004. *Women's rights in the USA.* New York: Routledge.

Stone Sweet, Alec. 2000. *Governing with judges.* Oxford: Oxford University Press.

Strebeigh, Fred. 2009. *Equal: women reshape American law.* New York: W.W. Norton.

Subramanian, Narendra. 2008. "Legal change and gender inequality: Changes in Muslim family law in India." *Law and Social Inquiry* 33(3): 631–642.

Taub, Nadine. 1999. "The Rutgers–Newark Women's Rights Litigation Clinic: An old and new story?" *Rutgers Law Review* 51: 1023–1030.

Verucci, F. 1991. "Women and the new Brazilian constitution." Trans. and intro. D. Patai. *Feminist Studies* 17(3): 557–569.

West, Robin. 1988. Jurisprudence and gender. *University of Chicago Law Review* 55(1): 1–72..

West, Robin. 1997. *Caring for justice.* New York: New York University Press.

Williams, J. 2000. *Unbending gender: Why families and work conflict and what to do about it.* New York: Oxford University Press.

Williams, Patricia. 1991. *The alchemy of race and rights.* Cambridge, MA: Harvard University Press.

Williams, Susan (Ed.). 2009. *Constituting equality: Comparative constitutional law and gender equality.* Cambridge, UK: Cambridge University Press.

Williams, Wendy. 1981. "Firing the woman to protect the fetus: The reconciliation of fetal protection with equal opportunity goals under Title VII." *Georgetown Law Journal* 69: 641–704.

Williams, Wendy. 1984. "Equality's riddle: Pregnancy and equal treatment." *New York University Review of Law and Social Change* 13: 325–380.

Williams, Wendy. 1992. "The equality crisis: Some reflections on culture, courts and feminism." *Women's Rights Law Report* 14: 151–170.

Wing, Adrien Katherine, and Tyler Murray Smith. 2003. "The new African Union and women's rights." *Transnational Law Journal & Contemporary Problems* 33: 33–82.

PART VI

....

THE STATE,
GOVERNANCE, AND
POLICY MAKING

....

In contrast to some of the other sections in this handbook, understanding the state, governance, and policy making has always been seen as a central part of political science. Until the rise of the broader concept of governance, which facilitated the incorporation of a more diverse range of actors and activities, much of the conventional scholarship in this area traditionally relied on quite narrow and rather conventional understandings and definitions of politics, policy making, and the state. And again, most of this work has been gender blind (although as part of its broader vision, some recent discussions of governance have recognized women's organizations as part of the policy networks that are increasingly important in diffused and diverse polities in which power is more dispersed and states more fractured).

Despite some early ambivalence about the state, gender scholars too have long recognized the importance of the state and policy-making processes, and they have studied them in a variety of ways since the 1970s. They have considered, using a range of different theoretical approaches and perspectives, the ways the state is gendered and, in particular, focused on the nature of gender institutions and the making of gender policy within the state, whether under the guise of state feminism, women's policy agencies, (WPAs), or more generally. More recently, as we have seen in the handbook introduction, there has been an institutional turn within some of the gender and politics scholarship as well as in much of political science, as an increasing amount of work has been influenced by some variants of new institutionalist thinking.

The chapters in this section consider how the institutions associated with the state and governance operate, what they do, and how policy-making processes and their outputs are gendered. The authors provide both an overview of the key debates in their area but they are also writing informed by a range of perspectives—whether this is, for example, a feminist institutionalist or a feminist critical political economy one. A number of common themes stand out (as well as commonalities with other parts of the handbook). First, feminism as a political project, and feminist theory and analysis as a way of understanding the state, governance, and policy making, are both central. The question of whether the state and institutions of governance can be used to achieve change and in particular to further gender equality has been of key importance to many feminist activists and scholars alike. A range of views have been promulgated—some have argued that state institutions can be used for this purpose while others have been more skeptical about the potential for positive institutional change and policies and policy making that promotes gender equality. Various different strategies to advance gender equality—such as the creation of women's policy agencies and gender mainstreaming initiatives—have also been attempted, again with varying assessments of their effectiveness.

Second, many of the chapters touch on the relationship between institutions and actors, both actors within institutions—whether they are femocrats or other policy makers inside institutions—or feminist and other activists outside of institutions trying to effect change. The key role that can be played by both and the potential for effective alliances forming between the two also recurs in many of the chapters. What is the room for agency, and how far are actors constrained by the institutions that they are operating within? Finally, the move to governance also ties in with an increasing emphasis on the importance of looking at different levels and their interaction, namely, not just the national but also the local, regional, and international, both for feminist strategy and understanding how institutions operate and policies are made and implemented. The use of broader notions of governance also helps the integration of a political economy perspective into the analysis of institutions and policy making. A number of the chapters end by suggesting that, as part of using broader definitions of institutions and understandings of how they are gendered and operate in gendered ways, one way forward would be to move away from a very explicit focus on gender policy and policy making and gender-specific institutions and look more generally at institutions and policy making even if they do not explicitly have an overt gender brief.

The section begins with an overview chapter on the state and governance by Louise Chappell. In this she explores developments in feminist thinking in three areas related to the state. She gives us a survey of the competing feminist theories of the state, outlining, as she sees it, a shift from the more monolithic conceptions of the state (some of which, for example, saw the state as patriarchal) to ones that understand the state as much more differentiated and as gendered, informed variously by notions of governance, poststructuralism, and intersectionality. Chappell ends her survey of how feminist understandings of the state and governance have changed by examining how gender operates within the state and how the state constitutes gender relations within society. In the final part of the chapter she considers feminist engagements with the state touching on a range of different institutional arenas such as the constitutional and judicial sphere.

Kate Bedford broadens out the scope to provide us with an introduction to the debates about multilevel governance (MLG) as they have been engaged in by and affected gender scholars. She aims to show that there is no agreement about what attention to MLG might tell those scholars interested in gender and institutions, but productive debates have occurred about the potentially democracy enhancing effects of MLG networks. She begins by outlining the impact of the shifts in institutional mandates and design on gender equality projects at various levels—local, national, regional, and international. She brings in a political economy focus by examining a key theme of the current literature on gender and MLG, namely, the relationship between neoliberalism and the rescaling of political authority arguing for example that feminists need to extend critical scrutiny to the political production of the family as a level of governance. She then touches on the impact of MLG on feminist mobilizing, showing how different types of feminist activism are affected differently by MLG trends ending by discussing the implications of the *forum shopping* that MLG facilitates and considering its implications for the affective dimensions of activism.

In their chapter, Dorothy McBride and Amy Mazur look directly at gender specific institutions and initiatives within the state by considering WPAs and state feminism. Drawing on the now large literature in this area, they describe the phenomenon of women's policy agencies and outline some of the major issues and emerging research agendas that dominate the field. After describing the development of and central assumptions underlying WPAs, the main body of the chapter describes the framework, methods, research results, and theory of state feminism in Western postindustrial democracies as it has been elaborated by the Research Network on Gender Politics and the State (RNGS), as the group of scholars who have done most work in this area. The chapter ends by describing how the RNGS research challenges conventional wisdom about the effectiveness of agencies and the possibilities for state feminism to change gender policy and policy making and to help us gender the broader study of democracies.

After three chapters that delineate different aspects of the institutional terrain that feminist and other actors inhabit and interact with, the final two chapters in this section look more specifically at policy making and its outcomes. Emanuela Lombardo, Petra Meier, and Mieke Verloo focus on policy making. They expand and build on feminist policy studies and use scholarship from a range of disciplines to analyze how policy making can (re)produce gender inequality or counteract it. Loosely following the development of feminist policy studies, they begin by charting how women were brought into the analysis of policy making, particularly in development studies, before the focus moved to how gender bias is constructed in policy making using more discursive approaches, and the advent of gender mainstreaming. Throughout the chapter they emphasize the importance of recognizing multiple inequalities using the language of intersectionality as well as the importance of a wide range of institutional approaches.

In the final chapter in this section, Merike Blofield and Liesl Haas focus on policy outputs on gender equality, asking what do policies on gender equality look like—both ideally and in practice? They do this through an overview of the literature that attempts to categorize gender equality policies and to spell out the different stages of the policy process. They draw on examples from three issue areas that have been identified by feminists as ones where gender inequalities are particularly embedded: reproductive capacities; gender-based violence; and the work–family nexus. Their empirical material comes primarily from Europe and Latin America.

CHAPTER 24

THE STATE AND GOVERNANCE

LOUISE CHAPPELL

Is the state patriarchal? Does it produce and reproduce gender? If so, how? What are the implications of gendered state and governance structures for those seeking to challenge the gender status quo? These questions are at the heart of feminist research on the state and governance. Scholars have provided vastly different and more highly sophisticated responses to these questions. The aim of chapter is to explore developments in feminist thinking on the state in three areas. It starts with an overview of competing feminist theories in these areas and charts the shift from a monolithic and patriarchal conception of the state to one that is differentiated and gendered. It then discusses how gender operates within the state and how the state constitutes gender relations within society. The final section addresses feminist engagement with the state, including the venues, strategies, orientation, and the outcomes of this interaction. There is an extensive literature in each of these three areas. While this chapter cannot cover the full breadth of work in this area, it does offer a guide to the major debates and some of the key contributors to the field.

FEMINIST THEORIES OF THE STATE AND GOVERNANCE

Feminists have adopted very different approaches to the state. For many years the fault lines in debate existed between those who adopted either a radical or socialist or liberal position. More recently, scholars working within poststructuralist, institutionalist, and postcolonial paradigms have critiqued these positions for being overly deterministic or simplistic and have offered a more differentiated view of the state where patriarchy is replaced by gender as defining the relations between and among men and women (for another outline of these debates see Waylen 1998). As we shall see, these recent interpretations have opened new avenues for exploring feminist engagement with the state, and an alternative to the inevitable co-option trap that is often the end point of radical and socialist feminist interpretations. The following discussion examines earlier interpretations of the state before exploring the differentiated state positions and the link between theories of the state and of governance.

The Monolithic State

Initial Western feminist theories of the state grew out of radical and socialist/ Marxist and liberal traditions. The first two positions share much in common, not the least of which is that the state operates as a capitalist and a monolithic patriarchal structure that has a universal effect on all women: it operates to keep all women everywhere oppressed. One of the most important scholars using a radical feminist perspective is Catharine MacKinnon, whose book *Towards a Feminist Theory of the State* (1989) still remains an influential text. For MacKinnon the state is male in a feminist sense. That is, the law (though which the liberal state is constituted) "sees and treats women the way men see and treat women. The liberal state coercively and authoritatively constitutes the social order in the interests of men as a gender—through its legitimating norms, forms, relation to society, and substantive policies" (161–162).

MacKinnon (1989) argues the state has no capacity to function autonomously of male interests. In her view, "However autonomous of class the liberal state may appear, it is not autonomous of sex. Male power is systemic. Coercive, legitimated, and epistemic, it *is* the regime" (170; for discussion, see Heath 1997, 50). When women engage with the state, they are treated as liberal individuals, which, MacKinnon argues, means being treated as men. Where women's needs align with those of men, such as in employment, then they can achieve a degree of formal equality, but where they don't, such as in the case reproductive rights or family violence, the state treats them differently (see McDonagh 2009, 231). In the latter case, this means that the state either fails to take action or, when it does act, reinforces gender stereotypes, such the view that women are weak and dependent, leaving them vulnerable to further discrimination and violence. Some feminists working in non-Western contexts have also advanced a view of the state and its laws as patriarchal. Indian scholars have suggested that in South Asia "the outcome of trials and the unwillingness of the police to probe violence against women at home and in society has led to a situation in which the law as a whole can easily be taken to be an instrument of patriarchal oppression" (Gonsalves 1993, 126 in Kapur 2007).

Feminists operating within a Marxist and socialist tradition supplement this view of a male state with one that envisions it as having a capitalist base and the "dual system" of capitalism and patriarchy operate to achieve a similar effect: male domination and female subordination (see, for example, Barrett 1980; for a discussion see Acker 1989; Walby 2007). For both radical and socialist and Marxist feminists, male dominance is not inherent within the state as such but exists outside it and has become embedded within it. Family and capitalist relations, "the private sphere," is the crucible for male dominance and acts as the foundation upon which state operates (see Acker 1989).

These theories of the state have attracted criticism for various reasons. One problem is that they "approac[h] a conspiracy theory. One is left searching for Patriarchal Headquarters to explain what goes on" (Franzway, Connell, and Court 1989, 29). For Joan Acker (1989), the problem is that the notion of patriarchy used in these approaches leaves other social theories—such as class relations—untouched, treating them as seemingly gender neutral (237). The universalist assumptions underpinning these theories have also been roundly criticized, both by black feminists from within Western liberal states (see Mirza 1997) who reject the view that women and men share a unified set of interests and by non-Western feminist scholars who see it as having relevance only in democratic and Western contexts not where there are significant variations in state capacity and the use of state violence (see Rai 1996). Writing about the application of patriarchal theories in India and Pakistan, Ratna Kapur (2007) argues these approaches are problematic because they are "ahistorical, decontextualized and universalistic" and also because they establish an "essentialist construction of women only as victims, rather than as agents of resistance and change" (128). Feminists across a variety of contexts also feel uncomfortable with the end point of such theories: that is, despite their efforts to bring about significant legislative and policy reforms—in areas including reproductive rights, equal pay, and protection from violence—activists are conceived as little more than co-opted patriarchal pawns, suffering from false consciousness. A major limitation of these theories is that they cannot account for challenges to and changes within the gender order of the state over time, especially changes that benefit (some groups of) women.

In contrast to the radical and socialist interpretations of the state are those that treat it as a neutral or even a positive entity for women. Liberal feminists working within a pluralist paradigm—which sees state power as widely dispersed and where a wide spectrum of interests are reflected within the state—tend toward the former position, assuming that the state can be a neutral arbiter and that women can overcome male domination by entering state institutions in significant numbers (see, for example, Kanter 1977). In the view of sociologists Mike Savage and Anne Witz (1992), such a position assumes that "...*power wipes out sex*. In other words, once women have organizational power, their gender pales into insignificance" (15, emphasis in original). Liberal feminists along with those from radical and socialist positions view the state as a coherent entity, albeit one that strives to protect individual liberties, rather than capitalist and patriarchal interests. Critics reject this position both because it does not account for the complexities of the state and because improving the nominal representation of women does not address the state's gender bias. Further, the liberal view presumes all women are committed to a gender equality project, which clearly they are not (see Duerst-Lahti 2002, 375), and fails to account for the deeply embedded gender norms or the "masculine logic" (Watson 1990, 9) upon which the state operates.

An even more positive interpretation of the state is reflected in some Nordic feminist welfare state approaches (see Hernes 1988), which stem from a social democratic tradition and see the state as a potentially "benign instrument for social change enabling women to avoid dependence on individual men" (Waylen 2008a, 125). Here state social policy is seen as a way to empower women and potentially institutionalize gender equality (Kantola 2006, 10). However, even scholars working in this tradition acknowledge the catch in their position: that the shift from women's private dependence on men to a public dependence on the welfare state can make the women the objects rather than the subjects of policy making unless they have power within the apparatus of the state (for a discussion see Kantola 2006, 10–11). This position is also critiqued for its overemphasis on social rights, such as access to paid employment. This emphasis has been seen to come at the expense of the protection of women's civil rights, including bodily integrity issues. According to Kantola, this orientation helps explain the slow response to addressing violence against women in Nordic states (2006).

These various perspectives on the state cast the relationship between gender interests and the state in either–or terms—that is, between those who see the state *either* as patriarchal (or capitalist) and oppressive of women *or* as gender neutral or positive and potentially enhancing women's emancipation. In the first reading, patriarchy and the state are fused and intertwined; in the second, they are only loosely related and easily untangled. In recent years this binary thinking has been challenged by a number of alternative approaches to the state including poststructuralist/discursive, institutionalist, and postcolonialist approaches.

The Differentiated State

The poststructuralist/discursive approach has been articulated by scholars working in the Australian context who were interested in developing theories that better reflected feminist interactions with and in the state. In this view, states are not patriarchal as such, but the different institutions of the state are "culturally marked as masculine" and operate largely as the "institutionalisation of the power of men" (Franzway et al. 1989, 41). Critically important here is the notion of discourse and the ways the state is involved in constructing and reproducing frameworks of meaning through dominant ideas and language (Pringle and Watson 1990, 230). In Pringle and Watson's view, "Power relations are actively constituted in and through discourse: they do not reflect economic or sexual power" (232). Unlike radical and socialist accounts of the state, this position privileges gender over patriarchy, a set of relations constituted discursively through the state. Instead of conceiving of the state as a coherent entity with a predictable effect, this perspective emphasizes its incoherence, instability, and varying effects on both men's and women's interests (230). Wendy Brown's (1995) analysis of the state follows similar lines. In her view, the state "is not a thing, system or subject, but a significantly unbounded terrain of powers and techniques, and ensemble of discourses, rules and practices, cohabitating...in contradictory relation to each other" (31). For Brown, male power operates through the state, but it is neither predictable nor complete.

While this differentiated view of the state has had a significant impact on the field, some view it as making the state seem overly complex (Hoffman 2001) or critique it for leaving the notion of structures behind. An alternative to the discursive approach to the state can be found in work that (re)introduces political institutions to explain state structures and outcomes (Kantola 2006, 32). A burgeoning feminist institutionalist literature uses some of the concepts to emerge from the poststructuralist approach to the state, such as an emphasis on gender, including an understanding of hegemonic masculinity. At the same time, some of the tools of "mainstream" institutionalism are adopted, including a focus on formal and informal institutions—the rules of the game—and attention to institutional change and stasis, but a critical gender dimension is added (for an introduction see Kenney 1996; Lovenduski 1998; Mackay and Waylen 2009; Krook and Mackay 2011). The value of this approach is that it highlights the way taken-for-granted masculine norms have become embedded within state institutions through rules, processes, ideologies, and discourses and in ways that shape their operation and outcomes (Duerst-Lahti 2002; Mackay 2011). It then takes this critique further by seeking to identify openings and opportunities for challenging what appear to be locked-in features of the state—male-dominated legislatures, gender-exclusionary constitutions, gendered policy making processes, and so on. The feminist institutionalist approach to the state eschews the usual normative debate about whether the state is "good" or "bad" for women's equality to consider what effect political institutions have on shaping gender relations and, in turn, the extent to which these relations can be (re)gendered through new rules, policies, and discourses to better reflect the differences and complexities of the lives of both men and women.

Feminist institutionalists unpack the state so that it is treated as a variety of separate institutions (Chappell 2002; Duerst-Lahiti 2002), each of which operates along its own gender codes and provides different obstacles and opportunities for unsettling the existing gender order. As Hester Eisenstein (1996, xvii) notes:

> ...To speak of "the state" is misleading. "The state" means the entire apparatus of government, from parliaments, cabinets, and bureaucracies administering programs for health, welfare, education, and commerce to the judicial system, the army and the police...Each has a different relation to women.

Feminist institutionalists also pay attention to informal institutions—the less codified but no less important rules and norms—that operate within and through the state (see Mackay, Kenny, and Chappell 2010, Chappell and Waylen 2013). The comparative scholarship emerging in the field of feminist institutionalism is sensitive to differences between state institutions within and between polities and demonstrates the ways different institutional configurations constrain, and at times enhance, attempts to change to the existing gender order. Such comparative work has considered institutional effects on feminist movements in Australia and Canada (Chappell 2002); on gender and transitions to democracy in states such as Chile, South Africa, and Hungary (Waylen 2007); on female representation in parliaments and parties within Latin America and the United Kingdom (Franceschet 2011; Kenny 2011); and on policy developments and debates across Western liberal states (Weldon 2002; Kantola 2006; McBride and Mazur 2010). Demonstrating the importance of institutional legacies and new design features can influence the operation of gender within the state is also a feature of this work; for example, Fiona Mackay's (2009) research demonstrates how the rules of the new Scottish Parliament opened up opportunities for feminist engagement for a time, before old practices and past gendered institutional legacies reasserted themselves and closed off some of these different ways of doing politics.

Feminists working within a postcolonial paradigm have added another more complex reading of the state. Drawing on experiences in postcolonial contexts in Asia, Africa, and Latin America, this work challenges, if not the central preoccupation with the state found in Western feminist political thought, then at least the degree of influence attributed to it (Manji 1999, 439; Goetz 2007). This work suggests that the state is closely bound up with societal relations—especially those based on tribal, kin, and religious foundations—and that these are at least as important as the state in regulating women's lives (Mukhopadhyay 2007). This work demonstrates how colonial rule often left family law including rights around marriage and divorce, property, and custody of children in the hands of nonstate actors such as religious institutions and tribal authorities, which meant matters essential to women's equality and citizenship were outside the purview of the state. Through the period of decolonization and modern state building, which is continuing in some parts of the world, many states maintain this dual legal system. As a result, "despite the existence of equality clauses in constitutions, unequal treatment sanctioned by custom, kinship and religious regulations continues to hold sway" (ibid., 272). Of course, as feminist research has demonstrated, colonialism in practice varied between states, and these variations have mattered greatly in terms of women's access to state (rather than religious or community sanctioned) legal arrangements (see Charrad 2001; Htun and Weldon 2011). As Charrad's study on North Africa demonstrates, the extent to which kin relations were enshrined in postcolonial state building made a significant difference to women's citizenship. For instance, in Morocco "women's citizenship rights were curtailed in favour of male-dominated patrilineages. By contrast, in Tunisia, where kin-based formations exerted much less social and political influence in the modern state, women gained significant individual rights, even though many aspects of gender inequality persisted" (Charrad 2007). Kapur's (2007) work on South Asia points to similar outcomes and also highlights how women experienced different relations with the state depending upon their community and religious ties—for example, between Muslim and Hindu women in India. This work reinforces the view that women's relationship with the state cannot be understood in monolithic terms. Colonial legacies matter greatly to women's opportunities to engage with the state, but how they matter differs with each context and between different groups of women.

Gender and Governance

The trend toward a more diffused notion of the state has led feminist scholars to turn their attention to theories of governance. Governance has become a catchall phrase under which many different concepts have been grouped. As pioneer feminist scholar in this area Georgina Waylen (2008a, 118) contends, governance covers both an understanding of the changing *structures* of government and market interactions and changing *processes* of governing, including the place of society and markets as alternatives to the state. Scholars working across the subfields of public administration, international relations and international political economy, and comparative politics have applied the concept of governance but without any analysis of its gender dimensions (ibid.). It is necessary to address each dimension of *governance*—including the market, public–private relations, and networks—to assess how gender, as well as *race* and *class* (see Rai 2008), operates and intersects with each of them (Waylen 2008a). Waylen argues that the turn to governance does not mean that feminist conceptions of the state should be left behind; indeed the reverse is the case (ibid., 125). The state remains a key aspect of governance; its regulatory role in particular is more important than ever. As a result, feminists need to interrogate the position and influence of the state within shifting state, market, and society dynamics and consider the ways the gender dimensions of each element of the governance framework is (re)shaped and (re)constituted through their interaction.

A key analysis of developments in governance structures, and the place of the state within these, is provided in Lee Ann Banazsak, Karen Beckwith, and Dieter Rucht's (2003) collection *Women's Movement Facing a Reconfigured State*. The authors demonstrate how changes wrought by globalization and other forces have led to a restructuring of the state so that there has been a relocation of formal state power. State authority has been relocated in three directions: (1) uploaded to regional and international governance bodies (such as the

European Union [EU] or United Nations [UN] bodies or through free trade agreements); (2) downloaded to provincial institutional structures including state and local governments; and (3) laterally loaded, especially away from representative to quasi-governmental or nongovernmental (i.e., market-based) arenas (3–6).

In Banazsak, Beckwith and Rucht (2003), and in other recent scholarship, feminists have examined the gender dimensions of these directional shifts (for further discussion of the gendered implications of multilevel governance see the chapter by Bedford in this volume). The effect downloading of state power on gender relations is discussed in an emerging literature on multilevel govern-ance and federalism including studies on devolution in the United Kingdom (Mackay 2010) and a range of federations (see Haussman, Sawer, and Vickers 2010; Vickers 2011). These studies show how divisions of responsibilities between local-, meso-, and national-level governments are being reconfigured in ways that directly impact policy areas related to women's lives including violence, reproduction, child-care, and welfare provisions. The lateral loading aspect has also interested feminist researchers, who have sketched out the implications of the marketization of traditional areas of state responsibility, especially core aspects of the welfare state, on gender relations within the public and private realms (see, for example, Brennan 2010).

Understanding the implications of the uploading of governance arrange-ments on gender relations has also been an area where feminists have started to make a significant impact. Collections by Mary Meyer and Elisabeth Prugl (1999) and Shirin Rai and Georgina Waylen (2008) (see also the chapter by Bedford in this volume) demonstrate the critical importance of including a gen-der perspective in any analysis of the operation of institutions outside nation states including the UN, EU, World Bank, International Monetary Fund, and International Criminal Court (ICC). These analyses are important for a number of reasons. They show that gender norms operate equally within state and extr-astate institutions, and, as with states, there is a great deal of heterogeneity across institutions of global governance in terms of how gender relations are configured (Waylen 2008b, 256). Variations are apparent between legal, eco-nomic, and bureaucratic arenas as well as between old and new institutions of global governance.

In summary, feminist theorizing about the state has come a long way in the past three decades. Few feminists still subscribe to a monolithic view of the state that operates according only to male interests. Instead, due to the influ-ence of poststructuralism, most gender scholars now work with a differentiated view of the state. Some feminist scholars do not go as far as others to conceive of the state only or even primarily as a discursive arena but prefer to uphold the notion of the state as a single entity, albeit made up of a complex array of institutional sites and structures and one that reflects its past. Nevertheless, there is general agreement across the various approaches, influenced by femi-nists operating outside a white, middle-class, and heterosexual framework, that the state does not have a consistent impact on all women and men. Indeed, as the following discussion shows, contemporary feminist state theory is more interested in understanding the way the state and society are together involved in constituting gender relations than in viewing them as predetermined. The governance literature, as it becomes gendered, adds another important dimension to feminist understandings of the state, highlighting the way the state operates within a complex set of relations and processes—each of which has its own gender foundations. As this research illustrates, a focus on the state takes us only so far in understanding regulation, power, and authority. The impact of the state can only now be understood as operating in a web of relationships that captures global and local arenas as well as market and other nonstate institutions.

THE STATE AND THE CONSTRUCTION OF GENDER

The development of more complex theories of the state has also changed and refined the way feminists understand the operation of gender relations within it. Feminists see the state as gendered but also as reproducing gender (Randall and Waylen 1998). Moreover, as a range of scholars has pointed out, the gender hierarchies constituted through the state are not the only ones that count. The intersection between gender and other structures of power including race, class, and sexuality is critical to understanding the lived realities of women and men's lives (see also the chapters by Hawkesworth and Hill Collins and Chepp in this volume).

What do we mean when we say the state is gendered? First, it infers that the state is inhabited by men in (often vastly) greater numbers than women: this is what Savage and Witz (1992) define as the state's *nominal* gender dimension. The historic absence of women within state institutions raises issues about the nature of democratic citizenship, equality, and justice. Women's absence from positions of power in the state has also had a further gendering effect: without women's input, laws and policy decisions made at the highest level have tended to disregard the unequal political, economic, and social position of the two sexes as well as reinforce stereotypical assumptions about male and female behavior (see Acker 1992, 567).

Although the most obvious, the nominal gender dimension of the state is a relatively weak expression of gender relations and is largely overcome by the entry into the state of women, and particularly feminists, who work to challenge gender stereotypes and assumptions. But state institutions also have a more deeply embedded *substantive* gender dimension (Savage and Witz 1992).

That is, they operate on a logic of appropriateness based on masculine norms, expectations, and practices (Chappell 2006b). As Lovenduski (1998, 339) notes:

> ...The public world was designed to accommodate activity according to the codes of masculinity. The value cluster found in the masculine code inscribes the most influential vision of what it means to "act in public." In human terms the vision is incomplete, ruling out intimacy, emotion and affection from public institutions.

Masculine codes shape both the behavior of individuals within state institutions (regardless of their sex) and institutional outcomes, such as laws, policies, ideas, and discourses.

This identification of the substantive gender dimensions of the state has shifted attention away from individuals within the state and toward the practices and process of the state that produce and reproduce relations between men and women as well as between groups of men and groups of women. As Htun (2005) notes, studying gender and the state is not about studying the behavior of individual men or women. Rather, it requires us to explore how "through its laws and policies, symbolic power, the statements and behavior of officials, and subtle patterning of society," the state upholds the large-scale social structures and processes, including the sexual division of labor, normative heterosexuality, and war and militarism (162).

Through her gender regimes theory, Raewyn Connell (2005) makes an important contribution to understanding gender as a structure. In Connell's view, every institution has its own gender regime, reflecting the patterning of, and interaction between, each dimension of gender relations. These dimensions include the gender relations of power; the gender division of labor; the gender dimension of emotion and human relations; and the gender dimension of culture and symbolism (7). Although analytically distinct, in practice these dimensions of the gender structure "are found interwoven in actual relationships and transactions" (ibid.). This regime operates within the institutions of the state, but not in predictable or stable patterns. Rather, the state and gender are dynamic because there exist "crisis tendencies" within the gender regime that, when triggered, enable new political possibilities (1990, 532, for more on the notion of gender see the chapter by Hawkesworth in this volume).

In her work, Connell (2002) also challenges the dominant dichotomous reading of gender that sees it as "the cultural difference of women from men, based on the biological difference of male and female" (8)—an account that can see gender only where it exists *between* men and women. Although Connell agrees gender operates between men and women, she is equally interested in identifying the gender dimensions that exist *among* women and *among* men. This includes the operation of gender relations between heterosexual and homosexual women or between working-class and middle-class men. Here her concept of *hegemonic masculinity* (Connell 1995) is useful for exploring the various ways masculinity is constructed between different groups of men, for instance between those who act in violent and nonviolent ways (also see Carver 1998 on masculinity).

Connell (1987) suggests that there are hierarchies within the gender order of the state, with various forms of hegemonic masculinity at work across different state institutions. This masculinity is demonstrated in different ways in different parts of the state and includes, for instance, "the physical aggression of front line troops or police, the authoritative masculinity of commanders and the calculative rationality of bureaucrats" (128–129). These forms of hegemonic masculinity have been shown to be both heterosexual and racist, with nonwhite men either feminized or treated as uncivilized through discursive practices (Hooper 2001, 56). In this reading of the state, different displays of femininity are also evident across the different state arenas—the caring nurse, the competent secretary, and the domineering school headmistress. As social constructions, gender norms do not determine that women will act in a feminine way or men the reverse. However, political actors, traditionally men, have acted *as if* sex and gender are mapped onto each other (Carver 1998). Men, operating within a hegemonic normative code, have been thought to possess the appropriate skills, knowledge, and temperament to design and maintain the institutions of the state, while most women—assumed to be irrational, fragile, and dependent—have tended to be relegated to supporting roles (Lovenduski 2005; for a further discussion on masculinities also see Hooper 2001, ch. 3).

Not only does gender involve the personal characteristics of women and men, but, more vitally, it also is "a matter of the social relations within which individuals and groups act" (Connell 2002, 9). With such a perspective we are able to think about gender as operating through institutions, including different areas of the state, such as the bureaucracy, the judiciary, and the legislature without linking it to specific individuals.

Along with Htun (2005) and Connell (1990), Karen Beckwith (2005) also shifts the emphasis from individuals to the ways gender operates as a *process* within institutions. For Beckwith, this process operates at two levels: "1) as the differential effects of structures and policies upon women and men, and 2) as the means by which masculine and feminine actors (often men and women, but not perfectly congruent, and often individuals but also structures) actively work to produce favorable gendered outcomes" (132). Very often, as Beckwith and others have pointed out, gender processes appear as gender neutral but in fact have distinct impact on women and men's lives (132; see also Duerst-Lahti 2002; Stivers 1993). These seemingly gender-neutral processes are not the outcome of a conscious strategy on behalf of all men to dominate all women. Rather, they have arisen because male privilege has been normalized within the state, through organizational rules, routines, and policies and through masculinist ideology (Duerst-Lahti, 373) and discourses such that they have rendered "women, along with their needs and interests, invisible" (Hawkesworth 2005, 147).

Feminist scholars have exposed the gendered foundations of seemingly neutral practices across an array of institutions. This includes the recruitment practices of political parties (Kenny 2011); bureaucratic norms in Westminster systems that privilege full-time workers and expect them to be supported by stay-at-home wives (Chappell 2002); legal and constitutional arrangements that protect male perpetrators of violence and leave women vulnerable and without access to legal avenues (MacKinnon 1989; Kenney 2010; Dobrowolsky and Hart, 2004; Kapur 2007); and welfare state provisions which maintain women's dependence if not on male breadwinners, then on the state (Orloff 1996), just to name a few. What these diverse studies show is that, although gender processes operate across the state, their influence differs. Building on the differentiated notion of the state, key feminist scholars such as Joni Lovenduski (1998) pay careful attention to the "distinctively gendered cultures" across state institutions and identify and account for the various kinds of "masculinities and femininities that are performed" (348).

Gender does not merely exist in the state, but it is also reproduced through it. The products of institutions—laws, policies, and rules—are imbued with these internal values and come to shape societal norms and expectations, which are then reflected onto institutions; in this sense gender and institutional outcomes can be seen as coconstitutive and mutually reinforcing. Eileen McDonagh (2009) provides an analysis of how this process operates in the United States in her engaging book *The Motherless State*. Here McDonagh suggests the identity of public policies in the United States have been masculine in nature, both in terms of the emphasis on militarism and on individualism, which treats men as the norm. What is not reflected in these public policies are women's duties as mothers and carers, in other words, a maternalist discourse. In comparable states, welfare policies, gender quotas, and, in some cases, the operation of a heredity monarchy where women can assume leadership provide a strong maternalist foundation to the state (51). Without such policies and institutions, the U.S. state reflects onto society the view that women are not suitable political leaders. McDonagh concludes that addressing gender inequalities and opening the state to women requires a hybrid state—capable of embracing liberal individualism (where women are treated the same as men) with maternalism (which recognizes women's differences to men) (55).

Two criticisms are often mounted against much of the existing research on the production and reproduction of gender and the state. The first is that gender is often taken as a synonym for studying women and the ways state practices shape women's relations with men, but not the reverse. With some exceptions (see, for example, Connell 1995; Carver 1999; Beckwith 2001), the emphasis on gender research is overly focused on the ways women are disadvantaged by existing gender hierarchies but not the way men are privileged (and some men are disadvantaged) or the myriad ways seeming neutral processes and norms operate to uphold or naturalize certain forms of masculinity.

A second critique focuses on the limited extent to which scholars have identified linkages between gender processes and other power relations, especially those related to race, class, sexuality, and religious background. This critique first emerged in the work of African American feminists, who argued that the unique experiences of black women could not be added onto white women's analyses of gender oppression (see hooks 1981; Collins 1990). Similarly, lesbians, disabled women, and poor women have also been critical of the ways gender research has focused on the experiences of middle-class, white, heterosexual, able-bodied women and has not considered how class and sexuality are also produced through the state in ways that impact men's and women's lives as equally as gender does (see, for example, Johnson 2003). As noted earlier, feminist scholars in postcolonial contexts have also mounted a strong and convincing critique along these lines. Scholars and activists from these various positions have not argued for these other identities to be added to dominant feminists analyses of gender so that women from nonmainstream backgrounds are seen as carrying a double or triple burden. Rather, they have called for a reconceptualization of the intersection between different social structures where "every social position is defined by an interaction between…hierarchical systems" (Weldon 2008, 195; also see Hawkesworth 2003; Walby 2007; for a detailed discussion see the chapter by Hill Collins and Chepp in this volume).

As with feminist efforts to denaturalize male privilege in the state, the intersectional approach brings to light hidden class, race, and other social structures and demonstrates how these structures combine to situate certain groups of women and men in positions of advantage and disadvantage. As Laurel Weldon (2008), a leading scholar in this area, notes, intersectionality is not a concept that applies only to marginalized groups. It "is an aspect of social organization that shapes all of our lives: gender structures shape the lives of both women and men, and everyone has a race/gender identity…." (195). Mary Hawkesworth's (2003) study of black women in the U.S. Congress is an excellent example of these hierarchical relationships and shows how race and gender operate as a compound to silence, stereotype and challenge their authority compared with other men and women in this specific political institution.

The state is gendered in terms of its personnel but more importantly in its structures and processes. This situates both men and women in particular positions in relation to the state, toward each other, and between each other. As intersectionality theorists remind us, the state is also raced, classed, and heterosexist. Unlike earlier approaches to the state that treated these attributes as permanent, most recent approaches to gender and the state consider its gender power base to have a normative foundation or view it as a regime that is prone to crises and change. Contemporary feminist theorizing that conceptualizes the state as differentiated and gender as an unstable regime or dynamic process has had a significant impact on the way feminist scholars and activists now think about engaging with the state. Over time they have shifted their focus from normative questions about whether feminists *should* engage with the state—radical and socialist feminists arguing no and liberals arguing yes—to empirical questions about the how, when, and where gender equality seekers can work in and through the state to bring about structural, policy, and discursive changes that challenge gendered power relations. In the final section, we consider the range of venues, strategies, and actors involved in regendering the state.

FEMINIST ENGAGEMENT WITH THE STATE

Current feminist thinking about engagement with the state is influenced in part by a recognition that the state is unavoidable if changes to the gender order are to occur. Moreover, more recent theorizing also shows that feminists also need to look beyond the state to governance structures above and below it to disrupt these relations of power. No feminist would argue that bringing about changes in these arenas is a straightforward or simple process due to the embedded masculinist (and racist and classist) logics of the state and governance as well as the contested and often conflicting goals of different groups of feminist actors operating in different institutional environments. However, the critical point is that these logics are open to challenge: because the state is differentiated, complex, and unstable, there are opportunities for feminist activists to unsettle the gender order. As Beckwith (2005) puts it, state institutions and politics are not only gendered but also can be gendered: "that is, that activist feminists...can work to instate practices and rules that recast the gendered nature of the political" (132–133). Such a position takes contemporary feminist understandings of engagement with the state much further than earlier interpretations that saw it as leading inevitably to co-option and any perceived progress representing a false consciousness on the part of activists.

In investigating feminist engagement with the state, electoral and bureaucratic arenas have attracted particular attention. Electoral institutions research has investigated how legislatures, electoral rules, and political parties are gendered such that they preclude or limit women (and feminists) participation in these institutions as well as the masculine nature of the laws and norms to emerge from these institutions (see the chapter by Krook and Schwindt-Bayer in this volume). This research has, however, also demonstrated how women have been able to work within and outside the state to open up new opportunities for advancing women's presence in the state.

In terms of the administrative arm of the state, the entry of women's activists to work as femocrats in the state has been given significant attention. This research first arose in the Australia context (Franzway et al. 1989; Sawer 1990; Eisenstein 1996; Chappell 2002) but has become a focus of study across Western liberal states and in non-Western settings (McBride and Mazur 2010 Rai 2002; Weldon 2002; Tripp et al. 2009). Research on what has come to be known as *state feminism* and the relationship between feminist movements and WPAs have been scrutinized in detail through the RNGS network and by others (see the chapter by McBride and Mazur in this volume; also Outshoorn and Kantola 2007; Tripp et al. 2009). Other important work in this area includes Lee Ann Banaszak's (2010) study, that investigates the opportunities and constraints for feminist activists working outside designated women's agencies in the U.S. bureaucracy. Her work demonstrates the importance of looking across all areas of the bureaucracy to get a complete picture of feminist engagement and influence in the state. Comparative research on state feminism has drawn attention to the importance of the specific features of the institutional environment to the success or failure of this form of engagement. For instance, work in the Latin American context has emphasized significant role powerful executives have played in frustrating or furthering the work of feminist policy makers (Franceschet 2011).

In each of these venues, feminists have employed a range of strategies with varying degrees of success. The use of gender quotas (Tripp and Kang 2008; Krook 2009) to increase the number of women in the parliamentary arena—based on the expectation that women's presence will influence gender equality outcomes—has been a widespread strategy. The push by women's groups to secure reserved seats for women in India and Pakistan and to introduce quotas in many other parts of the world, with some outstanding success, such as in Rwanda, are cases in point (see Krook 2009; Tripp et al. 2009), However, as Htun and Jones (2002) demonstrate, in the Latin American context such reforms alone often do not overcome normative or substantive gender discrimination. Another internationally popular strategy has been to encourage states and governance bodies such as the UN, EU, and ICC to adopt gender mainstreaming practices in their law and policy development and implementation processes (see True and Mintrom 2001; Rai and Waylen 2008). Research has shown that the success of both gender specific and gender mainstreaming policy initiatives require the presence of strong political commitment and other power and financial resources. These resources are often difficult to amass—especially in developing states (see Goetz and Hassim 2002 on Uganda and South Africa)—but are even more difficult to hold onto over time (Outshoorn and Kantola 2007).

Other forms of feminist engagement with the state have also been evaluated. Feminist efforts in the constitutional and judicial realm for example is a growing area of study for political scientists interested in evaluating the role of feminist judges, prosecutors, and legal advocates to the development of legal institutions and jurisprudence as well as feminist activists influence on constitutional creation and reform (see the chapter by Cichowski in this volume; also Kenney 2010; Dobrowolsky and Hart 2004). One successful legal strategy is discussed by Eturk (2006, 96), who describes how women successfully challenged the Turkish Supreme Court's use of the notion of respectability to determine a sentence in a rape case against a prostitute. The increasing importance of governance structures and processes has highlighted new venues through which feminist engagement takes place. While feminist action within local- and meso-levels of government has always been evident, the pressures on this level of government have been reinforced in recent years, making them an essential site for those seeking gender equality (Mackay 2010; Vickers 2011). The importance and success of feminist engagements at the state and provincial levels of government has been examined in recent comparative studies across North and South America, Africa, and Australia (see Haussman et al. 2010; Molyneux

2007; Chappell and Vickers 2011) and demonstrates the importance of sympathetic political parties, in combination with multilevel government, to bring about policy advancements for women.

International institutions, especially regional bodies such as the EU and Asia Pacific Economic Cooperation (APEC) that directly influence state policies, have also become targets for gender-equality seekers (see Rai and Waylen 2008). Arguments about the need for gender justice, including women's access to political power and the recognition of the private realm, have had some impact internationally, such as through Convention on the Elimination of Discrimination Against Women (CEDAW), the Beijing Platform, and the Rome Statute to the ICC. Such international developments offer important tools to gender actors within nation states to challenge government's to implement their commitments and reflect international norms (see Keck and Sikkink 1998; Ferree and Tripp 2006). However, they do not automatically result in states removing discriminatory laws from their books, introducing new law and changing policies in areas related to women's citizenships rights. Achieving such commitments are always easier said than done, especially in the area of family law (Weldon and Htun 2011). Nonetheless, the "uploading" of particular issues, especially related to human rights, has paved the way for new global debates and a shared language that is especially important to actors in non-Western states where women's rights are often poorly protected (see, for instance, Paidar 2002, 246 on the importance of CEDAW in Iran; Eturk 2006 on Turkey).

Initially, these strategies were construed in dichotomous insider–outsider terms with feminists seen to either enter the state to become insiders (and at high risk of co-option) or remain outside the state in activist, advocate, and service delivery positions within the women's movement. In her important book on gender equality activists' entry into the U.S. military and Catholic Church Mary Katzenstein (1998) makes an important contribution to rethinking this relationship. Rejecting the long-standing insider–outsider dichotomy, Katzenstein encourages scholars to think about activism as operating along a continuum. In her view, different actors will see themselves more or less as insiders or outsiders depending upon their accountability to an institution in a financial, organizational, and discursive sense (39–40). The more actors see themselves as accountable to an institution along each of these axes, the stronger their insider status will be. A common situation for women's activists who enter political institutions is that they feel financially and organizationally accountable to the institution but continue to identify themselves with, and seek to be accountable to, external women's organizations and ideals. The term *outsiders within*, coined by African American feminist scholar Patricia Hill Collins, nicely sums up the position of women who have multiple accountabilities within a particular institutional setting (Collins 1998 in Roth 2006, 158).

Katzenstein's (1998, 40) analysis highlights the limitation of the insider–outsider dichotomy for understanding not only the position of insiders but also outsiders' relationship to the state. Often, outsiders are able to maintain their organizational and discursive autonomy but rely upon the state for financial assistance and thus enter into an accountability relationship with it. The rules that condition the financial ties between institutions and external groups can vary significantly; the extent of the financial accountability will determine on which end of the insider–outside continuum external actors sit. Women's health, refuge, child-care, prochoice, and other organizations have each had to grapple with the dilemma of wanting to maintain their independence yet also needing state financial resources to provide services for their members. In her work on women's activists inside the United States, Banaszak (2010, 85–89) also makes an important contribution to rethinking the insider–outsider distinction by reversing the arrow; she demonstrates that feminist engagement with the state doesn't always work from the outside in, but in her study she shows how many women converted to feminism while in bureaucratic jobs within the state and then left to take up activist jobs in the feminist movement. Identifying insiders and outsiders is further complicated when governance structures are taken into account. The downloading, uploading, and marketization of traditional state functions and lines of authority blurs any distinction that might ever have existed about feminists' insider or outsider status in relation to the state. For example, the contracting out of welfare services entangles feminists in new relationships with the state as well as with the market.

The scholarship on feminist engagement with the state indicates mixed results in terms of activists' ability to challenge its gender foundations. Studies have shown that feminist efforts to recast the underlying norms, discourses, processes, and policies of state institutions are often met with marginalization, trivialization, and outright hostility (see Katzenstein 1998, 9; Hawkesworth 2003; Roth 2006). Feminists have also had trouble institutionalizing changes within the state. As work on WPAs has demonstrated, even when it looks like gender policy analysis has become an integral activity of the state, unsympathetic governments can swiftly dismantle these agencies and drastically devalue femocrats skills (Kantola and Outshoorn 2007; Teghtsoonian and Chappell 2008). Given the hazardous terrain (Katzenstein 1998, 9) feminist state activists are operating on, such outcomes are hardly surprising, but nor are they the whole story.

A vast body of empirical research now demonstrates that, acting on their own, feminist activists are not able to challenge the gender status quo within the state. However, it does show that important changes to the gender order can be achieved when institutional and political factors are in alignment, such as when a sympathetic government is in office; a feminist judge is on the bench; porous policy processes are open to new actors; or new institutions are created (see Lovenduski 1998; Kantola 2006; Eturk 2006; McBride and Mazur 2010). Institution building that occurs in the aftermath of conflict or a major upheaval, such as in the situations of Rwanda and South Africa (Goetz and Hassim 2002) or in other periods of transition, can, as Waylen (2007) reminds us, provide opportunities for positive gender outcomes. Changes can sometimes be dramatic, such as the creation of a new constitution that recognizes women or new political parties, legislatures, or gender policy machinery, or subtle, such as a shift in the framing of a policy, but the changes are nonetheless real and (very often) cumulative.

Recent research has also demonstrated that such shifts are possible not only within nation-states but also within global institutions. Recent work on transnational feminist activism has clearly demonstrated that while these actors must contend with counter movements and are never guaranteed success (Chappell 2006a), they have been able to recast gender assumptions, norms, and practices at the international level—such as in relation to the recognition of women's civil, political, and economic rights including their specific experiences violence, education, and health-care needs. Moreover, once these shifts are recognized internationally, the potential exists for them to be diffused back to states in ways that alter local gender practices (see Keck and Sikkink 1998; Friedman 2003; Zwingel 2005).

Accepting the dynamism of state institutions and the ability for activists to "reinscribe" their gender foundations is not to suggest that will always be successful or are on an unswerving trajectory toward progress (however that may be interpreted). As activists know only too well, such alignments are not only rare but are also rarely permanent. The election of a different government or changes in personnel in the public sector can lead to a retreat back to an earlier logic of appropriateness or to the creation of a new but equally restrictive one from the point of view of relaxing gender codes. A major contribution made by feminist scholars of the state is to better identify when, where, and how such political opportunities arise and the sorts of strategies that best take advantage of them. A priority for future research is to identify how best to preserve the hard-won gains once they are in place.

CONCLUSION

Feminist conceptions of the state have evolved markedly in the past three decades. An important shift has been from a patriarchal to a gendered view of the state. This has involved a rejection of the view of the state as male to one that sees the state as a complex array of gendered institutions and discourses. Increasingly, it is also conceived as operating within a wider set of processes and relations, understood as the system of governance. Rather than seeing the state in patriarchal terms, it is now understood as a constellation of gender relations that are constituted through it. Identifying the gender dimensions of the state and governance has been a critical contribution of feminist scholarship; it has exposed as politically constructed and gender biased seemingly natural and neutral norms and processes. Moreover, this scholarship has shown that such norms and processes—which are reflected in state laws, policies, and discourses—have differential effects on men and women and between different groups of men and women. A complex account of the state, and an understanding of the constitutive nature of gender relations have led to a reconceptualization of feminist engagement with the state. No longer conceived as an arena either to be entirely avoided or wholeheartedly embraced, the state is seen as unavoidable but also as alterable. While recasting state practices and policies is not easy, feminist scholarship has demonstrated that under the right conditions it is possible.

The feminist project in relation to the state is nowhere near complete. The development of an intersectionality approach to understanding the state requires more detailed comparative work to be undertaken within and between states to better understand how gender relates to other structures of power and how these might be simultaneously unsettled to bring about greater equality between men and women and among groups of men and women. Further, related to this point is the need to continue to explore how different sorts of states and institutions operate in different contexts. Much work to date has focused on democratic states in the West, but as the emerging feminist postcolonial literature suggests we also need to further explore the operation of gender in different types of states, not only to understand the operation of these states but also to better reflect on the assumptions and biases inherent in the dominant work in the field (on this point see Tripp 2006).

One thing that has remained constant over the course of the past three decades has been the feminist lament that their contribution to understanding the state has not been taken seriously by the 'mainstream.' The importance of gender and other relations of power to the operation of the state has been documented empirically and defended theoretically, but very little of it is reflected in nonfeminist work. This is frustrating for scholars working in this field, but it also provides an important insight into an ongoing weakness in the discipline. As Mary Hawkesworth (2005, 152) argues, "When political scientists ignore the operations of gender power documented by feminist scholars, their omissions...perpetuate distorted accounts of the political world." The challenge remains to have standard conceptions of the state, which remain focused on force and power, acknowledge its gender and relational power dimensions.

REFERENCES

Acker, Joan. 1989. "The problem with patriarchy." *Sociology* 23(2): 235–240.

Acker, Joan. 1992. "From sex roles to gendered institutions." *Contemporary Sociology* 21(5): 565–69.

Banaszak, Lee Ann. 2010. *The women's movement inside and outside the state.* Cambridge, UK: Cambridge University Press.

Barrett, Michele. 1980. *Women's oppression today: Problems in Marxist feminist analysis*. London: Verso.

Beckwith, Karen. 2001. "Gender frames and collective action: Configurations of masculinity in the Pittston Coal Strike." *Politics & Society* 29(2): 297–330.

Beckwith, Karen. 2005. "A common language of gender?" *Politics & Gender* 1(1): 128–137.

Brennan, Deborah. 2010. "Federalism, childcare and multi-level governance in Australia." In Melissa Haussman, Marian Sawer, and Jill Vickers, eds., *Federalism, feminism and multilevel governance*. Surrey: Ashgate, 37–50.

Brown, Wendy. 1995. *States of injury: Power and freedom in late modernity*. Princeton, NJ: Princeton University Press.

Carver, Terrell. 1998. "A political theory of gender: perspectives on the 'universal subject.'" In Vicky Randall and Georgina Waylen, eds., *Gender, politics and the state*. London: Routledge, 18–28.

Chappell, Louise. 2002. *Gendering government: Feminist engagement with the state in Australia and Canada*. Vancouver: University of British Columbia.

Chappell, Louise. 2006a. "Comparing political institutions: Revealing the gendered logic of appropriateness." *Politics & Gender* 2(2): 223–234.

Chappell, Louise. 2006b. "Contesting women's rights: Charting the emergence of a transnational conservative counter-network." *Global Society* 20(4): 491–520.

Chappell, Louise, and Georgina Waylen. 2013. "Gender and the hidden life of institutions." *Public Administration* forthcoming.

Chappell, Louise, and Jill Vickers. 2011. "Gender, politics and state architecture." *Politics & Gender* 7, (2) 251–254

Charrad, Mounira. 2001. *States and women's rights: The making of postcolonial Tunisia, Algeria, and Morocco*. Berkeley: University of California Press.

Charrard, Mounira. 2007. Unequal Citizenship: Gender Justice in the Middle East and North Africa. In M. Mukhopadhyay and N. Singh, eds., *Gender justice, citizenship and development*. New Delhi: Zubaan 233–262.

Collins, Patricia Hill. 1990. *Black feminist thought: Knowledge, consciousness and the politics of empowerment*. Boston: Unwin Hyman.

Connell, Raewyn. 1990. "The state, gender, and sexual politics: Theory and appraisal." *Theory and Society* 19(5): 507–544.

Connell, Raewyn. 1995. *Masculinities*. Cambridge, UK: Polity.

Connell, Raewyn. 2002. *Gender*. Cambridge, UK: Polity.

Connell, Raewyn. 2005. "Advancing gender reform in large-scale organisations: A new approach for practitioners and researchers." *Policy and Society* 24(2): 5–24.

Dobrowolsky, Alexandra, and Vivien Hart (Eds.). 2004. *Women making constitutions: New politics and comparative perspectives*. Basingstoke, UK: Palgrave Macmillan.

Duerst-Lahti, Georgia. 2002. "Governing institutions, ideologies, and gender: Toward the possibility of equal political representation." *Sex Role* 47(7–8): 371–388.

Eisenstein, Hester. 1996. *Inside agitators: Australian femocrats and the state*. Sydney: Allen and Unwin.

Eturk, Yakin. 2006. "Turkey's modern paradoxes: Identity politics, women's agency and universal rights." In M. Ferree and A. Tripp, eds., *Global feminism: Transnational women's activism, organizing, and human rights*. New York: New York University Press, 79–109.

Ferree, Myra Marx, and Aili Mari Tripp (Eds.). 2006. *Global feminism: Transnational women's activism, organizing, and human rights*. New York: New York University Press.

Franceschet, Susan. 2011. "Gendered institutions and women's substantive representation: Female legislators in Argentina and Chile." In Mona Lena Krook and Fiona Mackay, eds., *Gender, politics and institutions*. Basingstoke, UK: Palgrave Macmillan, 58–78.

Franzway, Suzanne, R. W. Connell, and Dianne Court. 1989. *Staking a claim: feminism, bureaucracy and the state*. Sydney: Allen and Unwin.

Friedman, Elisabeth Jay. 2003. "Gendering the agenda: The impact of the transnational women's rights movement at the UN conferences of the 1990s." *Women's Studies International Forum* 26(4): 313–331.

Goetz, Anne Marie. 2007. "Gender justice, citizenship and entitlements: Core concepts, central debates and new directions for research." In M. Mukhopadhyay and N. Singh, eds., *Gender justice, citizenship and development*. New Delhi: Zubaan, 15–57.

Goetz, Anne Marie, and Shireen Hassim. 2002. "In and against the party: Women's representation and constituency building in Uganda and South Africa." In M. Molyneux and S. Razavi, eds., *Gender justice, development, and rights*. Oxford University Press, 306–337.

Haussman, Melissa, Marian Sawer, and Jill Vickers. 2010. *Federalism, feminism and multilevel governance*. Surrey: Ashgate.

Hawkesworth, Mary. 2003. "Congressional enactments of race-gender: Toward a theory of raced-gendered institutions." *American Political Science Review* 97(4): 529–550.

Hawkesworth, Mary. 2005. "Engendering political science: An immodest proposal." *Politics and Gender* 1(1): 141–156.

Heath, Mary. 1997. "Catharine MacKinnon: Toward a feminist theory of the state?" *Australian Feminist Law Journal* 9: 45–63.

Hernes, Helga Maria. 1988. "Scandinavian citizenship." *Acta Sociologica* 31(3): 199–125.

Hoffman, John. 2001. *Gender, sovereignty and the state: Feminism, the state and international relations*. Basingstoke, UK: Palgrave MacMillan.

hooks, bell. 1981. *Ain't I a woman? Black women and feminism*. Boston: South End Press.

Hooper, C. 2001. *Manly States: Masculinities, International Relations and Gender Politics*. New York: Columbia University Press.

Htun, Mala. 2005. "What it means to study gender and the state." *Politics and Gender* 1(1): 157–166.

Htun, Mala, and Mark P. Jones. 2002. "Engendering the right to participate in decision making: Electoral quotas and women's leadership in Latin America." In N. Craske and M. Molyneaux, eds., *Gender and the politics of rights and democracy in Latin America*. New York: Palgrave, 32–56.

Htun, Mala, and S. Laurel Weldon. 2011. "Comparative perspectives on women's rights in family law: A global overview." *Indiana Journal of Global Legal Studies*, 18 (1): 145–165.

Johnson, Carol. 2003. "Heteronormative citizenship: The Howard Government's views on gay and lesbian issues." *Australian Journal of Political Science* 38(1): 45–62.

Kanter, Rosabeth M. 1977. *Men and women of the corporation*. New York: Basic Books.

Kantola, Johanna. 2006. *Feminists theorize the state*. Basingstoke, UK: Palgrave MacMillan.

Kapur, Ratna. 2007. "Challenging the liberal subject: Law and gender justice in South Asia." In M. Mukhopadhyay and N. Singh, eds., *Gender justice, citizenship and development*. New Delhi: Zubaan, 116–170.

Katzenstein, Mary Fainsod. 1998. *Faithful and fearless: Moving feminist protest inside the church and military.* Princeton, NJ: Princeton University Press.

Keck, Margaret, and Kathryn Sikkink. 1998. *Activists beyond borders: Advocacy networks in international politics.* Ithaca, NY: Cornell University Press.

Kenney, Sally. 2010. "Critical perspectives on gender and judging." *Politics & Gender* 6(3): 433–441.

Kenney, Sally J. 1996. "New research on gendered political institutions." *Political Research Quarterly* 49(2): 445–466.

Kenny, Meryl. 2011. "Gender and institutions of political recruitment: Candidate selection in post-devolution Scotland." In Mona Lena Krook and Fiona Mackay, eds., *Gender, politics and institutions.* Basingstoke, UK: Palgrave Macmillan, 21–41.

Krook, Mona Lena. 2009. *Quotas for women in politics: Gender and candidate selection reform worldwide.* New York: Oxford University Press.

Krook, Mona Lena, and Fiona Mackay (Eds.). 2011. *Gender, politics, and institutions: Towards a feminist institutionalism.* Basingstoke, UK: Palgrave Macmillan.

Lovenduski, Joni. 1998. "Gendering research in political science." *Annual Review of Political Science* 1: 333–356.

Lovenduski, J. 2005. *Feminizing Politics.* Cambridge: Polity Press.

Mackay, Fiona. 2009. "Institutionalising "new politics" in post devolution Scotland: 'Nested newness' and the gendered limits of change." Paper presented at the European Conference on Politics and Gender, Queen's University Belfast, January 21–23.

Mackay, Fiona. 2010. "Devolution and the multilevel politics of gender in the UK: The case of Scotland." In M. Haussman, M. Sawer, and J. Vickers, eds., *Federalism, feminism and multilevel governance.* Surrey: Ashgate, 155–168.

Mackay, Fiona. 2011. "Conclusion: Towards institutionalism?" In Mona Lena Krook and Fiona Mackay, eds., *Gender, politics, and institutions: Towards a feminist institutionalism.* Basingstoke, UK: Palgrave Macmillan, 181–193.

Mackay, Fiona, Meryl Kenny, and Louise Chappell. 2010. "New institutionalism through a gender lens: towards a feminist institutionalism?" *International Political Science Quarterly* 31(5): 578–588.

Mackay, Fiona, and Georgina Waylen. 2009. "Critical perspectives on feminist institutionalism." *Politics and Gender* 5(2): 237–280.

MacKinnon, Catharine. 1989. *Toward a feminist theory of the state.* Cambridge, MA: Harvard University Press.

Manji, Ambreena. 1999. "Imagining women's 'legal world': Towards a feminist theory of legal pluralism in Africa." *Social and Legal Studies* 8(4): 435–455.

McBride, Dorothy, and Amy Mazur. 2010. *The politics of state feminism: Innovations in comparative research.* Philadelphia: Temple University Press.

McDonagh, Eileen. 2009. *The motherless state: Women's political leadership and American democracy.* Chicago: University of Chicago Press.

Meyer, Mary K., and Elisabeth Prugl (Eds.). 1999. *Gender politics in global governance.* Lanham, MD: Rowman and Littlefield.

Mirza, Heidi Safia. 1997. *Black British feminisms: A reader.* London: Routledge.

Molyneux, Maxine. 2007. "Refiguring Citizenship: Research perspectives on gender justice in the Latin American and Caribbean region." In M. Mukhopadhyay and N. Singh, eds., *Gender justice, citizenship and development.* New Delhi: Zubaan, 58–115.

Mukhopadhyay, Maitrayee. 2007. "Situating gender and citizenship in development debates: Towards a strategy.". In M. Mukhopadhyay and N. Singh, eds., *Gender justice, citizenship and development*. New Delhi: Zubaan, 263–314.

Orloff, Ann. 1996. "Gender in the welfare state." *Annual Review of Sociology* 22: 51–78.

Outshoorn, Joyce, and Johanna Kantola (Eds.). 2007. *Changing state feminism*. Basingstoke, UK: Palgrave Macmillan.

Paidar, Parvin. 2002. "Encounters between feminism, democracy and reformism in contemporary Iran." In M. Molyneux and S. Razavi, eds., *Gender justice, development, and rights*. Oxford: Oxford University Press, 241–272.

Pringle, Rosemary, and Sophie Watson. 1990. "Father, brothers, mates: The fraternal state in Australia." In Sophie Watson, ed., *Playing the state: Australian feminist interventions*. Sydney: Allen and Unwin, 229–242.

Rai, Shirin. 1996. Women and the state in the third world: Some issues for debate. In Shirin Rai and Geraldine Lievesly, eds., *Women and the state: International perspectives*. London: Taylor and Francis, 5–22.

Rai, Shirin. 2002. *Mainstreaming gender, democratising the state? National machineries for the advancement of women*. Manchester: Manchester University Press.

Rai, Shirin. 2008. "Analyzing global governance." In Shirin Rai and Georgina Waylen, eds., *Global governance: Feminist perspectives*. Basingstoke: Palgrave, 19–42.

Rai, Shirin, and Georgina Waylen (Eds.). 2008. *Global governance: Feminist perspectives*. Basingstoke, UK: Palgrave.

Randall, Vicky, and Georgina Walyen (Eds.). 1998. *Gender, politics and the state*. London: Routledge.

Roth, Benita. 2006. "Gender inequality and feminist activism in institutions: Challenges of marginalization and feminist fading." In Louise Chappell and Lisa Hill, eds., *The politics of women's interests: New comparative perspectives*. London: Routledge Press, 157–174.

Savage, Mike, and Anne Witz. 1992. Theoretical introduction: Gender in organizations. In *Gender and bureaucracy*, ed. Mike Savage and Anne Witz, Oxford: Blackwell Publishers, 3–62.

Sawer, Marian. 1990. *Sisters in suits: Women and public policy in Australia*. Sydney: Allen and Unwin.

Stivers, Camilla. 1993. *Gender images in public administration: Legitimacy and the administrative state*. Newbury Park, CA: SAGE.

Teghtsoonian, Katherine, and Louise Chappell. 2008. "The rise and decline of women's policy machinery in British Columbia and New South Wales: A cautionary tale." *International Political Science Review* 29(1): 29–51.

Tripp, Aili Mari, Isabel Casimiro, Joy Kwesiga, and Alice Mungwa. 2009. *African women's movements: Changing political landscapes*. Cambridge, UK: Cambridge University Press.

Tripp, Aili Mari, and Alice Kang. 2008. "The global impact of quotas: On the fast track to increased female legislative representation." *Comparative Political Studies* 41(3): 338–361.

Tripp, Aili Mari. 2006. Why so slow? The challenges of gendering comparative politics. *Politics & Gender* 2(2): 249–264.

True, Jacqui, and Michael Mintrom. 2001. "Transnational networks and policy diffusion: The case of gender mainstreaming." *International Studies Quarterly* 45: 27–57.

Vickers, Jill. 2011. "Gendering federalism: Institutions of decentralization and power-sharing." In Mona Lena Krook and Fiona Mackay, eds., *Gender, politics and institutions*. Basingstoke, UK: Palgrave Macmillan, 129–146.

Walby, Syliva. 2007. "Complexity theory, systems theory and multiple intersecting social inequalities." *Philosophy of the Social Sciences* 37(4): 449–470.

Watson, Sophie. 1990. "The state of play." In Sophie Watson, ed., *Playing the state: Australian feminist interventions*. Sydney: Allen and Unwin. 3–19.

Waylen, Georgina. 1998. "Gender, feminism and the state: An overview." In Vicky Randall and Georgina Waylen, eds., *Gender, politics and the state*. London: Routledge, 1–17.

Waylen, Georgina. 2007. *Engendering transitions: Women's mobilization, institutions and gender outcomes*. Oxford: Oxford University Press.

Waylen, Georgina. 2008a. "Gendering governance." In Gary Goertz and Amy Mazur, eds., *Politics, gender and concepts: Theory and methodology*. Cambridge, UK: Cambridge University Press, 114–135.

Waylen, Georgina. 2008b. Transforming global governance: Challenges and opportunities. In *Global governance: Feminist perspectives*, eds. Shirin Rai and Georgina Waylen. Basingstoke, UK: Palgrave.

Weldon, Laurel S. 2002. *Protest, policy and the problem of violence against women: A cross national comparison*. Pittsburgh: Pittsburgh University Press.

Weldon, Laurel S. 2008. "Intersectionality." In Gary Goertz and Amy Mazur, eds., *Politics, gender and concepts: Theory and methodology*. Cambridge, UK: Cambridge University Press, 193–218.

Zwingel, Susanne. 2005. "From intergovernmental negotiations to (sub)national change." *International Feminist Journal of Politics* 7(3): 400–424.

CHAPTER 25

....

GENDER, INSTITUTIONS, AND MULTILEVEL GOVERNANCE

....

KATE BEDFORD

INTRODUCTION

....

This chapter provides a broad introduction to debates about multilevel governance (MLG) trends as they relate to gender and politics. Following a brief explanation of MLG, I examine the debates that gender scholars and activists are having about the topic. Feminists have had immensely productive conversations about the impact of shifts in institutional mandates and design on gender equality projects, at the transnational, national, and subnational level. I seek to foreground some of these in arguing that MLG is a significant, and gendered, topic for concern. I highlight five themes in this regard: (1) the diverse effects that rearrangements of legal and political architecture have on gender policy making, especially regarding feminist work within international institutions; (2) MLG and feminist political economy; (3) the impact of MLG on feminist mobilizing; (4) the gendered politics of scale attribution; and (5) the affective attachments associated with different levels of governance by various feminist actors.

My intention in addressing these topics is not to describe a consensus on what attention to gender, institutions, and MLG might tell politics scholars. There is no consensus. In contrast, there are intense disagreements about issues such as the democracy-enhancing effects of MLG networks or the impact of international institutions on gender equality. I intend, rather, to establish these five topics as especially interesting moments of conversation about MLG, institutions, and gender, to the extent that they aid us in identifying some significant questions being raised by feminist researchers.

Based on this partial overview of debates, I argue that rearrangements of political architecture have had varied, diverse effects on gender policy making. Some women's groups have benefited, especially from consolidation of the transnational tier of policy making, but others have struggled to gain inclusion into new governance networks or have been disappointed by the limited gains achieved. No general theory of the relationship between MLG trends and women's ability to achieve equality goals has thus far emerged, and more research is crucial.

Greater consensus is evident in feminist critiques of how MLG trends are linked to neoliberalism and in work on MLG and feminist mobilizing. Although the key debates here—over, for example, the political economy of 'NGOization' or the impacts of 'inclusion' on feminist politics—remain unresolved, they are highlighted in a range of research as among the core questions of the political present. This confirms the centrality of MLG concerns to studies of gender and politics.

Moreover, by including the final two topics (on the need for attentiveness to the politics of scale attribution and to the affective dimensions of forum shopping) I seek to expand the disciplinary ground upon which our conversations about MLG rest. I contend that our discussions of MLG would benefit enormously from more systematic integration of insights from other fields, including political geography and affective politics. This is not an unusual position: after all, James Scott (2010) is fond of telling U.S. politics scholars that they risk extinction unless at least half of their reading is outside the discipline. However, I suggest that interdisciplinarity is especially important for feminists working on institutions and MLG, whether they are concerned with empirical puzzles, theoretical development, or a mixture of the two.

AN OVERVIEW OF
MULTILEVEL GOVERNANCE AND ITS
RELEVANCE TO GENDER SCHOLARS

The concept of MLG emerged from scholarship on changes in the European Union (EU) during the 1980s. The term "initially described a 'system of continuous negotiation among nested governments at several territorial tiers—supranational, national, regional and local'" (Hooghe and Marks 2003, 234), and it was used in debates about EU federalism. However, MLG debates were subsequently extended to analyze how responsibilities and political participation avenues were being redirected downward and sideways in the enlarging EU, including away from governments altogether (at whatever level), to encompass civil society groups, firms, and so on. An illustrative example is the development of the EU's Open Method of Coordination, a mode of governance used in areas such as employment and social policy. Policy competence rests largely with member-states, but EU institutions aim to play a coordinating role and to include the voices of civil society, employers, and trade unions. Intensive work is devoted to defining a shared view of a policy problem that extends beyond traditional state actors (Beveridge and Velluti 2008, 3).

Significantly, the term MLG is now applied beyond EU debates, referring broadly to an interlinked cluster of political shifts. These include the growing importance of transnational governing institutions; the growing interdependence of governments at different levels and the growing interdependence between governments and nongovernmental actors; and proliferating jurisdictions, rule systems, and centers of authority (Marcussen and Torfing 2007, 4–5). Global trends toward decentralization and devolution are also important (Bache and Flinders 2004), as are informal networks and soft rules in new regulatory arrangements. Overall, MLG scholars emphasize the multicentered, complex, interwoven, and dispersed nature of power, politics, and policy making (Hedmo and Sahlin-Andersson 2007, 199) and are attentive to the ways multiple actors interact in a range of formal and informal policy networks. Social movement scholars have also turned to MLG to test theories about how political opportunity structures (POS) are affected by changes in political architecture or to see how movements are adapting protest strategies (e.g., Imig and Tarrow 2001; Joachim and Locher 2009).

MLG is understood to be a normatively superior mode of allocating authority by many observers, although for differing reasons (Bache and Flinders 2004; Andrew 2010). Some wish to shrink the state and increase the ability of individuals to resolve problems (ideally using market mechanisms). Others favor MLG because of its perceived potential to take decision making closer to people or offer new access points to social movements if central governments are unresponsive (Keck and Sikkink 1998; Solanki 2010). Some have seen in MLG the seeds of a more cooperative, consensus-based approach to politics, where stronger actors are forced to take into account the views of partners and compromise and deliberative problem-solving become key features of decision making (Marcussen and Torfing 2007). In this view MLG networks contribute to the production of public purpose, generalized trust, and common values.

Critics (or skeptics) dispute (or qualify) these tendencies. As Peters and Pierre (2004) put it, MLG can appear a cozy, consensus-based, nonconflictual process, yet serious concerns about accountability, transparency, and inclusion lurk beneath the surface (77). For example, the supranational bodies playing key roles in global governance may lack standard mechanisms of liberal democratic political accountability (Bache and Flinders 2004; Torfing 2007), since there may be no free and equal access to appoint the decision makers and voting power may be unfairly distributed.[1] Moreover, it can be hard to hold actors accountable within dense, interlinked networks where decisions emerge from complex regulatory knots, since it is unclear who is responsible for what (Hedmo and Sahlin-Andersson 2007, 213; Torfing 2007; Beveridge and Velluti 2008). Reliance on informal negotiations and few formal rules can also be a problem, in part because consensus agreements can be dictated by stronger players (Peters and Pierre 2004, 87). A number of case studies have confirmed that apparently consensus-based networks can suffer serious democratic deficits whereby, for example, opponents are barred from participating, or state administrators exert considerable power.[2] Other scholars have focused on how the POS characteristic of MLG networks may channel activism in particular directions, with implications for social movement accountability and legitimacy. For example, Doug Imig and Sidney Tarrow (2001, 8) suggest that Europe's authorities encourage the expression of claims through lobbying and other routine forms to contain more contentious forms of collective action (see also Hooghe 2008; Joachim and Locher 2009).

Bob Jessop has been especially critical of the tendency to strip power and hierarchy from some discussions of MLG and to exaggerate the reduced power of the state when celebrating the democratizing potential of networks. He argues, in contrast, that states have taken on increasingly important roles as metasteerers of capitalist development (Jessop 2004, 49). They play new roles in calibrating the activities of different actors, in providing the ground rules for governance, in organizing dialogue among different policy communities, in serving as a "court of appeal" for disputes, and in trying to shape the identities and tactics of different actors.[3] Different forms of coordination and self-organization take place here "in the shadow of hierarchy" (65). Such concerns about accountability, unequal power, and the limits of inclusion within new governing arrangements continue to generate considerable debate.

However, generally MLG scholars have failed to consider gender to any significant degree. The communitarian faith in shared values characteristic of some MLG literature is rarely tempered by findings from feminist work; neither is the metasteering debate extended beyond discussion of the state's unitary interest in perpetuating capitalism. The field also rests on claims about government (and its difference from governance) that are remarkably inattentive to feminist scholarship on power.[4]

Nonetheless, the concept of MLG is an attractive one for many feminists, for a number of reasons. Most obviously, in its focus on multiple sources of authority MLG work overlaps with feminist work on legal and political pluralism. Feminist scholarship has generated compelling findings on the interconnection between social or private institutions, such as the family, and political or state institutions in constituting gender inequalities (Mackay and Meier 2003). We thus share obvious affinities with a scholarly perspective that also uses a multicentered approach to power. In addition, many gender and politics scholars are interested in how gender fits into new governing arrangements, asking questions such as how gender policies forged in transnational institutions have impacted other levels, how POSs shift for feminist organizing when governance forms change, whether a move to local decision making will benefit women, and how accountability in gendered terms is to be secured in networks (Rai 2003; Beveridge and Velluti 2008; Sawer and Vickers 2010; Prügl 2011). As international organizations have taken a growing interest in gender, feminists have also turned to examine gender policy entrepreneurship in transnational sites. Simultaneously, local-level women's NGOs play increasingly institutionalized roles within many communities and nations. The role of state feminism, and of the state within feminist mobilizing, has also been reinterrogated as gender scholars respond to altered governance arrangements across the globe.

In the following discussion I cover a number of these distinct areas by foregrounding the five themes outlined at the outset of the chapter. In this way I consider both what research on gender and politics can add to MLG literature and what feminist studies (more broadly) might learn from greater attentiveness to the multiple scales of political activism around gender.

MULTILEVEL GOVERNANCE, POLITICAL ARCHITECTURE, AND GENDER EQUALITY POLITICS

A number of scholars have examined the impact of governance reform on gender politics (see overview in Rai and Waylen 2008; Gray 2010; Prügl 2011; see also the chapter by Chappell in this volume). An early collection by Banaszak, Beckwith, and Rucht (2003) on state reconfiguration and women's movements in Western Europe and North America is a key example. State reconfiguration referred to shifts of authority upward or downward, the weakening power of elected state spheres, and the growing reliance on other, partly nonelected bodies to make polices. This can occur via moving policies upward to supranational bodies, via lateral loading (the horizon redistribution of responsibilities away from parliamentary bodies to, for example, quasi-autonomous NGOs or courts), or through off-loading state responsibilities onto the family, the community, and the market (5–6).

In particular, there has been considerable debate about gender politics in international organizations, in part because feminists seized the opportunities provided by the uploading of responsibilities. For example, MLG reforms associated with Europeanization have provided new opportunities for women's activism via mechanisms such as Article 119 of the Treaty of Rome (on equal pay),[5] directives on equal treatment in areas such as social security and pensions, and European Court of Human Rights rulings (Kantola and Outshoorn 2007). U.K. feminists turned to the EU level (and local government; see Cooper 1995) when the national level was closed to their influence under Margaret Thatcher, trying to use the European courts to force the strengthening of domestic equal pay and sex discrimination legislation (Sawer and Vickers 2010, 11). In Spain, the EU supported women's policy agencies and provided leverage for feminists seeking to influence both central and regional governments (Bustelo and Ortbals 2007, 213). Such EU-focused research confirms that women's groups can gain from MLG through the ability to forum shop, pragmatically targeting different levels of government in response to new configurations of power.[6]

The UN has also been a key site for research on gender and MLG. UN support was pivotal to the creation of national gender equality policy machineries in many countries (Rai 2003), and Outshoorn and Kantola (2007) found that all twelve countries in their study of women's policy agencies in Western democracies experienced positive effects from the UN (269). UN-level gender policy has also provided new leverage for social movement actors to pressure states. For example, an Austrian law against marital rape was passed only after urgent recommendations from the committee that monitors state signatories to the UN Convention on the Elimination of All Forms of Discrimination Against Women (CEDAW; Sauer 2007, 55), while Nepali feminists secured improvements in domestic violence provision using CEDAW's optional protocol provisions.[7]

Other transnational sites have provided similar evidence of what Keck and Sikkink (1998) term the *boomerang effect*, where domestic actors can use transnational venues to win concessions from their governments. After the Indian parliament blocked a homeworker protection bill, the Self Employed Women's Association moved its activism to the International Labour Organization (ILO) level, for example, lobbying for enforcement of Convention 177 on Home Work (Prügl 1999). Likewise, Mexican feminists secured an important ruling from the Inter American Court of Human Rights regarding women's rights to medical attention in cases of legal abortion (Macdonald and Mills 2010).

With international organizations like the EU and UN playing increasingly important roles as sites for gender equality policy, several new themes have emerged in gender research. First, feminists have transnationalized their debates about the dilemmas of gender work inside mainstream institutions. Transnational institutions are now commonly studied as gender policy-making bodies in their own right, with their own distinctive bureaucratic cultures, gender policy frames, and so on. Moreover, in line with efforts to mainstream gender into the heart of an organization's activities, a range of international institutions now frame gender equality as a core component of their mandates, whether to reduce poverty, to ensure human rights, or to protect the environment. Thus, scholars and practitioners are increasingly focusing on how gender equality can be framed to fit existing transnational organizational mandates and how such mandates may constrain feminist policy output (Rai 2003;

Prügl and Lustagarten 2006; Beveridge and Velluti 2008; Rai and Waylen 2008; Lombardo, Meier, and the Verloo 2009; Prügl 2011).

For example, Ostner and Lewis (1995) note that work of the European Commission and the European Court of Justice (ECJ) on gender has been heavily influenced by the fact that the key opening for policy entrepreneurship was created by Article 119 of the Treaty of Rome, establishing the right of equal pay for equal work. Thus, EU gender policy had to be cast as employment related, limiting the potential for this new tier of governance to affect issues such as violence or the gender division of labor in the household. Clavero and Galligan (2009) concur that the creation and development of the EU involves the creation and development of a European gender order distinctly shaped by the EU's institutional identity.

Within the World Bank (the world's largest and most influential development institution), feminist bureaucrats face different hurdles (Bedford 2009). The Bank's charter forbids it from engaging in activities that do not have economic development as their objective, and furthermore the institution's internal culture is technocratic, economistic, and statistics driven. This context results in well-known pressures for efficiency framings of gender policy, focused on how attentiveness to gender enhances productivity and growth. The Bank's gender regime is also heavily influenced by its commitments to loving partnership between men and women as key to development success. Hence, policy initiatives that target men as carers and women as labor force participants are especially likely to succeed within the institution. As is evident here, hegemonic gender policy frames within transnational institutions may promise inclusion to some actors, with specified visions of gender harmony, and exclude others.[8]

A second key theme in literature on gender policy making in shifting political architectures concerns the extent to which successes at the transnational level filter down into concrete changes in gender relations. Many have examined the complex processes of translation, norm diffusion, and vernacularization as gender rights move from transnational institutions to other levels of governance (e.g., Merry 2007; Krook and True 2010; Zwingel 2010; Prügl 2011; see also the chapters by Lombardo, Meier, and Verloo and Blofield and Haas in this volume). Key concerns here include the enormous gap separating formal rights provisions from implementation, and the ever-present problem of ensuring compliance. Most transnational gender rights instruments rely on soft law mechanisms that lack enforcement power, so it is hard to hold states to account for violations. For example, scholars writing on the EU have tracked uneven compliance with gender-equality directives and varied evidence on whether member-states are converging on one set of EU-inspired gender norms and practices (Ostner and Lewis 1995; Beveridge and Velluti 2008; Clavero and Galligan 2009). National-level implementation is influenced by preexisting policy and cultural frames, such as the dominant national vision of gender equality and the willingness to litigate as a way of achieving social movement successes.[9] However, large variations in compliance behavior remain even when such factors are taken into account, leading Clavero and Galligan to suggest a rethink of what is needed to translate transnational rights achievements into grounded enforcement (109).

Third, much of the work on transnational institutions troubles a top-down, linear policy narrative about governance, instead emphasizing the increasing complexity of governance structures and the intertwining of responsibilities at multiple levels. Shifts in transnational governance arrangements cannot be viewed in isolation: they have to be studied alongside changes at other levels, particularly in relation to the new role of states, regions, and communities in gender politics. For example, some possibilities have opened up for feminists through EU-led decentralization. Celis and Meier (2007, 67) highlight the value of regional women's policy agencies in Belgium, and Amy Mazur (2007) notes the opportunities created for French feminists through the EU-influenced dispersal of Paris-based governing to regions. Writing of the multilevel organizing undertaken by German feminists as they navigated the 1996 EU directive on parental leave, MacRae (2010, 128) shows that Europeanization and localization have blurred distinctions between levels, leading to fluid configurations of power wherein scalar hierarchies can no longer be assumed. Actors and spaces merge together, in a system of unstable power relations: a given policy outcome is due to the interaction, since the levels are linked and mutually constitutive (138–139; see also Kantola and Outshoorn 2007, 9; Prügl 2011). As a result, it is essential that scholars pay comprehensive attention to multiple scales and to how shifts in one governance tier impact others.

In this regard, much research highlights the difficulty of attributing a fixed, permanent status to any political system and the value of reexamining standard assumptions about polities from gendered perspectives. In a recent collection, Haussman, Sawer, and Vickers (2010) explore the gendered impact of federalist decentralization, examining how changes in national-level political architecture have altered women's citizenship and the extent to which women's groups participated in and benefited from governance reform. One of their key insights is that political systems look very different when explored from the perspective of different actors. As Miriam Smith (2010) demonstrates, for example, Canada is typically seen as more decentralized than the United States by federalism scholars, but in lesbian and gay rights the opposite is true: Canada's federal government has more power to effect change than its U.S. counterpart (99).

The same system can also be assessed divergently by different women's movements located within the same territory. For example, Kiera Ladner (2010) argues that MLG is a mixed bag for indigenous women in Canada for reasons different from those highlighted by Anglo or Francophone feminists. Ladner is highly critical of federal government intervention into indigenous sovereignty on gender grounds (such as via federal efforts to establish matrimonial property law on reserve land), seeing the state not as a guarantor of women's rights but as "the obstacle to achieving women-friendly policy because it disallowed and destroyed indigenous political and legal orders and institutionalised patriarchy"

(77). Mary Katzenstein (2003) likewise fleshes out the divergent effects of state reconfiguration on U.S. women. The rights that wealthier women have to equal pay, to merit-based employment and promotion, to reproductive choice, and to credit "are fundamentally unaltered" (209). However, poor women's rights have been sabotaged, via the abolition of welfare benefits and attacks on their access to abortion. Women's citizenship is thus bifurcated on class and race lines (205), confirming that governance reorganization processes do not have uniform effects on women's equality-seeking politics.

The ability of feminist civil society groups to pressure national governments using transnational venues also varies. As Marian Sawer (2007) notes, in the past Australian women's organizations were able to use international norms to embarrass their government, but this space shrunk as the state prioritized its relationship with the United States and distanced itself from the UN human rights system (26). Thus, a "bleak" national picture under the John Howard Parliament was left mostly untouched by appeals to transnational institutions (31). Such work confirms that a boomerang politics of shame is not always effective in gender equality politics, in part because it may provoke a populist backlash in the name of sovereignty (Sawer and Laycock 2009, 145–146).

In addition, countermovements can also take advantage of the tendencies within MLG systems to provide multiple entry points—and they usually have more money so can do it better than feminists. For example, Christian Right opponents of the UN's gender machinery have used it for their own ends, trying (sometimes successfully) to get antiabortion and antigay initiatives onto the Commission on the Status of Women's agenda (Bedford 2010). In her examination of reproductive rights in the United States, Haussman (2010) also shows that prolife actors have proved skilled forum shoppers, turning variously to federal governments, state governments, or individual medical practitioners to block women's access to abortion depending on the POS. Haussman notes bluntly that prolife forces have won contests with prochoice advocates at multiple levels because they have more money, returning our attention to questions of power and resources and the ways these interact with political architecture (111).

National-level research has also elucidated the complex cost–benefit interplay of MLG for women's organizing and the key role of other variables. Political architecture clearly matters, but the extent and the how, why, and to whom vary considerably. For example, Fiona Mackay (2010) argues that key differences between the domestic violence policies of Scotland and England can be explained by devolution and the possibilities it provided for Scottish women's strategic engagement in a new political architecture. They were able to secure support for women-only services, for ring-fenced funding, and for mainstreaming of an explicitly feminist analysis of violence (163). Provincial-level organizing also provided a relatively supportive site for women's groups in Quebec (Dobrowolsky 1998; Mahon and Collier 2010), where feminists allied with left-leaning nationalists to achieve policy gains. However, governments based on ethnonationalist, territorial distinctions have harmed women's interests in Nigeria, leading feminists to call on the central government, the courts, and transnational institutions to defend the constitutional rights of women (and ethnic minorities) from incursions by state governments (Obiora and Toomey 2010, 219).

Celis and Meier (2007) also highlight the "asymmetric structure of women's policy agencies" in Europe, wherein some regions flourish but there is a vacuum on gender equality initiatives elsewhere (70). Canadian women in provinces without left-leaning administrations or strong women's movements connected to governing bodies have feared *losing* ground when federal-level action on women's issues is localized (Andrew 2010; Sawer and Vickers 2010). Processes of state decentralization have proved similarly uneven for Mexican women. Feminists in Mexico City were able to take advantage of decentralization when they expanded abortion rights in 2007 as a result of their alliance with the left-leaning PRD party. However, since then thirteen other states have reversed previously existing reproductive rights, leading Macdonald and Mills (2010) to conclude that the "new federalism" has "permitted the entrenchment of anti-democratic, masculinist domains at the subnational level" (188). Such research confirms that while *the local* can be a productive site for feminists in some countries and regions, moving gender equality struggles to this level can lead to an increasingly uneven, fragmented political landscape (Bustelo and Ortbals 2007, 220–222).

Indeed, in some cases the demand to take decision making closer to the people can be perilous for progressive politics, especially when gender and sexuality are involved. As Miriam Smith (2010) notes, the fact that the U.S. system has provided so many direct democracy opportunities to undermine lesbian and gay rights claims has proved extremely damaging (especially since the opponents of those rights are so wealthy). Muslim women face similar threats from referenda in Switzerland. This issue is not, of course, reserved to federal systems, since unitary states can also put minority rights up for public ballot, but it is an issue of MLG in that it confirms the dangers posed to feminist politics of local-level mechanisms that can override rights secured at other levels.

For all of these reasons, gender and politics scholars generally support the need for more context-specific analyses of the impacts of MLG trends on gender equality politics while noting that this will not necessarily add up to a universal theory. Overall, as Mahon and Collier (2010) conclude, the complexity of POS in a MLG system provides multiple entry points for gender equality politics, and women's movements can benefit if they are flexible and able to shift the scale of their operations to take advantage, especially if they can access new transnational opportunity structures (65). Similarly, Sawer and Vickers (2010) argue that, on balance, "although multilevel...organizing presents challenges, a worse option in terms of political architecture may be for policy power to be concentrated in the hands of just one government," since this leaves women vulnerable to being frozen out by conservatives, with no recourse to overlapping jurisdictions (12). Outshoorn and Kantola (2007) found that MLG was also a key factor in the success of some women's policy agencies, since it enabled them to both "use supra-national regulation as a lever at the state level, and decentralization as an opening to set the agenda with gender issues at regional and local levels" (284).

However, as Gray (2010) concludes in her overview of the literature, institutional structure is only one among many variables shaping a POS, and findings about it are mixed and indeterminate (28). Indeed in some cases it is unclear whether governance arrangements are an independent or a dependent variable (i.e., whether political architectures determine political outcomes, are the result of them, or both; see Chandler 2010, 141). In this regard there is a clear need for more research on the way institutional structure interacts with other variables, such as the ability of feminists to influence the framing of the gender policy problem, the effectiveness of compliance mechanisms, the presence of left-leaning administrations, the newness of the architecture, the strength of local and municipal government structures, the distribution of resources, and the extent to which minority rights can be undercut by referenda.

The Political Economy of Multilevel Governance

A second key theme of current literature on gender and MLG is the relationship between neoliberalism and the rescaling of political authority. As many observers have noted, MLG can be a cloak for neoliberal cuts in social programs, with responsibilities for what were once state services dumped onto underresourced entities at the provincial, municipal, local, or community level. For example, Holli and Kantola (2007) link the Finnish recession of the early 1990s to the intensification of MLG trends and the rollback of redistributive policies (84). Municipalities got increased autonomy and decision-making powers in a context of spending cuts, such that local solutions often involved privatization or delegation of responsibilities to the third sector (85; see also Dobrowolsky 2003 on Canada).

While numerous critics have addressed this issue, feminist scholars and activists are especially attuned to the interplay between MLG and political economy (see the chapter by Rai in this volume). This is partly because the responsibilities being downloaded are often cast off on women as volunteers and partly because the services being chosen for rescaling are typically those associated with carework. For example, Latin Americanists have identified that government policies to decentralize and download social responsibilities have clearly gendered effects. Women's groups are increasingly invited to participate in development projects, and poor women often see their roles of securing community and family survival instrumentalized (Alvarez 1999). MLG can thus represent the circumvention of women's demands for state provision of services (Lind 2005, 94), and the successful enlisting of "female altruism at the service of the state" (Molyneux 2006, 437).

North American scholars and activists have also grappled with the interactions between MLG and neoliberal trends toward privatization and state retrenchment. For example, Rebecca Dolhinow (2010) examines the relations of governance involved in *colonias* in the U.S.–Mexico border region. *Colonias* are unincorporated communities in the United States established, illegally, by developers and usually sold to migrant workers. They often lack key infrastructure. Rather than provide this infrastructure directly, state and local governments typically support NGO interventions that require inhabitants to offer voluntary labor. As Dolhinow highlights, women are targeted by NGOs as leaders in this process. In this way they become conduits for new forms of neoliberal governmentality (4), unintentionally serving projects that supplant the radical potential of community organizing and replace it with a demobilized, depoliticized variant focused on infrastructural provision (19). She summarizes a key tension over the role of MLG within feminist political economy thus (49):

> The greatest contradiction of women's activism in colonias is that if they do nothing, nothing will improve. But if they do something, they become the perfect working poor, as they are willing to create their own infrastructure and demand next to nothing from the state, not even what the state requires be provided for others.

Ruth Wilson Gilmore (2007, 47) offers another compelling account of this dynamic in her description of the emergence of an "anti-state state" in the United States, where nonprofit organizations take responsibility for people who are "in the throes of abandonment" by governments at all levels (45). When viewed in this light, MLG trends in the U.S. both stem from and reinforce the idea "that piecemeal voluntary efforts can somehow replace a systematic public approach to eliminating poverty" (Ahn 2007, 63), a position that few feminists (if any) would support.

Deborah Brennan (2010) explores different links between MLG and political economy in her research on Australian child care. Recent changes in child-care policy have given more power (and government funding) to corporate providers while reducing the power of nonprofit providers and parents. Privatization need not be channeled through localizing voluntarism then: in this case distant corporate interests benefited, as when a Boston-based consulting group won the tender to develop the Rudd government's child-care policy framework (Brennan 2010, 49). This marketized model:

> ...has increased the power of private interests and reduced the effectiveness of traditional avenues of advocacy aimed at governments. It has positioned parents as "consumers" rather than citizens and created a more individualised,

consumer-oriented, politics of childcare, thus intensifying the need for feminists to attend to multiple sites, or scales, of government and private sector governance. (50)

Such findings confirm the value of examining what Kantola and Outshoorn (2007, 12) term the context-specific particularities of neoliberalism when studying the relationship between MLG and political economy (see also Prügl 2011, 87). In Europe the feminist relationship to the welfare state was never unequivocally positive, and hence its restructuring should trigger complex and specific analysis rather than generalized melancholic investment in loss. Or, as Solanki (2010, 175) notes, in India there is a particularly "uneasy coexistence" between neoliberal and socially progressive visions of MLG, given the importance placed by social movements on challenging top-down, centralized development planning. Thus, activists are in especially difficult positions as they navigate tensions between participation and privatization, off-loading of services, and community ownership. Such tensions are, as noted already, inherent to debates about MLG as a Janus-faced project, but they play out differently depending on the relationship between private, public, and movement actors involved in governance networks.

THE IMPACT OF MULTILEVEL GOVERNANCE ON FEMINIST MOBILIZING

A third, connected theme in debates about the democratizing impact of new governance arrangements centers on the complex ways MLG has affected feminist mobilizing. This relates to important critiques of the NGOization and professionalization of feminism, particularly regarding the way organized women have been demobilized as protest agents and remobilized as service providers and consultants. They have also been drawn into closer relationships with governing institutions via new imperatives toward inclusion and participation. At issue here is the specific way MLG networks influence the autonomy of feminist organizing and also the general, older, debate about how feminists should interact with the state, transnational institutions, or private foundations (see also the chapters by Ewig and Marx Ferree, Chappell, and Joachim in this volume).

Feminist work within politics generally regards the state as a dynamic, shifting site for struggle rather than as a fixed entity with predetermined gender interests. Specific configurations of state power in specific places and their interactions with specific feminist movements are understood to matter (Cooper 1995; Prügl 2011). For example, in a comparative analysis of domestic violence activism in countries with different political architectures, Elman (2003) shows that when U.K. and U.S. feminists turned to the state for money, having at first relied on provision of services within their own activist communities, the women's movement became increasingly professionalized, with growing distinctions between staff and clients. In both cases violence against women shifted from being a political issue to a clinical one, where therapy or criminalization supplanted activism. However institutionalization, professionalization, and deradicalization were *less* comprehensive in the United Kingdom than the United States, because survivors in the former had greater access to established social services and affordable public housing due to previous social movement successes.

Different types of feminist activism are also differently affected by MLG trends. In a European-wide analysis of how MLG affects social movements, Helfferich and Kolb (2001) find that the European Women's Lobby has "succeeded handsomely" in using EU structures to advance women's goals (143; see also Clavero and Galligan 2009). However, activism is directed toward expert-led, professionalized groups rather than mass-based mobilization. Celia Valiente (2003) offers a similar account of the way MLG arrangements have encouraged Spanish feminists to become more involved in state-funded service provision. While the POS has not been positive or negative as a whole (because the opportunities opened up or closed down depend on the aims of different feminist groups), Valiente concludes that the women's movement has lost some autonomy from the state: "groups have been busier managing their subsidized projects and less active in protesting against authorities" (46).

The Revolution Will Not Be Funded provides another sustained, critical treatment of the impacts that MLG arrangements have on radical organizing (INCITE! 2007). This collection explores the impact of both state and foundation funding on a variety of social movements, including that to stop violence against women. A key point here is that private foundations are increasingly important actors, given the growing role of philanthropy in filling funding gaps left by the restructuring state. This trend raises concerns about foundation accountability (Ahn 2007) and about the metagovernance projects being pursued. Dylan Rodríguez (2007) argues that progressive foundation funders— upon which U.S. gender work often relies—"exer(t) a disciplinary or repressive force on contemporary social movement organizations while nurturing a particular ideological and structural *allegiance* to state authority that preempts political radicalisms" (29, emphasis in original). Spaces of resistance and radical political experimentation are thus less and less likely to be found within NGO structures; rather, they "disappear and disperse into places unheard, unseen, and untouched by the presumed audiences of the non-profit industrial complex" (31).

MLG networks—which can be usefully thought of as a prime manifestation of the non-profit industrial complex—are seen here primarily through the lens of co-optation. Writing of INCITE!'s experiences of working with foundation funders on antiviolence organizing among women of color, Andrea Smith (2007) argues that capitalist interests and the state use nonprofits to monitor and control social justice movements, to redirect activist energies into career-based modes of organizing, and to encourage movements to model themselves after capitalist structures, with a focus on competition and developing leadership skills to become policy makers and bureaucrats (3–8). In response, several authors urge movements to seek out spaces of resistance beyond those identified by funding streams and to revitalize their own activist cultures by going against the formalizing, professionalizing imperatives inculcated by MLG networks.

Such work is useful in part because it productively reopens debates about the feminist relationship to formal political structures. This is a vital act in a MLG era of mainstreamed equality talk, where women's empowerment is espoused by most states and transnational institutions and where opportunities for feminist civil society groups to get included in governance networks can be extensive. In addition, diverse accounts of how feminists organize in the current era of Big Society institutionalized volunteerism and service contracts allow us to think more expansively about where feminist politics is located. As Outshoorn and Oldersma (2007) note, many politically active feminists in Europe resist formal organizations entirely, opting instead for informal (often virtual) networks, cultural interventions, or confrontational protest events that do not seek legitimacy with any formal political actors, state or otherwise. Few are interested in gaining influence in traditional politics via mechanisms such as lobbying. Their mobilizations come into view once scholars look beyond institutionally recognized MLG networks for activism located elsewhere, to see possibilities of feminist politics done differently.

THE POLITICS OF SCALE ATTRIBUTION

Having examined how MLG literature returns feminist politics scholars to core questions regarding the nature of counterhegemonic mobilization, in this section I broaden conversations further to explore the value of greater attentiveness to the *spatial* dynamics of governance and to the ways new MLG practices produce scale differently. Here I take the lead from scholars who link MLG work to a scalar approach to politics. This conceives scales as products of economic, political, and social activities and relationships (Mahon and Keil 2009, 4). As Larner, Lewis, and Le Heron (2010, 177) note, new spaces of governance such as networks, sectors, clusters, and communities "are not pre-given—they are constantly in-the-making and under review." Likewise, Dolhinow (2010) examines how *colonia* spaces are produced through the interaction of state and federal (in)action, developer profit seeking, the culture of self-reliance and resistance to private property regulation characteristic of the U.S. Southwest, and immigrants' desire for community (7). A key insight here is to recognize the different

levels of governance being brought together in networks as constructions, produced via economic and political processes (Mahon and Keil 2009, 8), rather
than seeing the level as predetermined, natural, or outside of politics.

Denaturalizing scales of governance is in many respects a staple feature of
feminist analysis, which has long been marked by critical interrogation into why
and how certain issues are framed as private or public concerns. The gendered
politics of scale attribution has always been a key concern of those asking, for
example, why and how so much violence against women came to be excluded
from the criminal law, and defined within the realm of family. Likewise, what
explains Caroline Andrew's (2010) pithy observation that in Canada "provinces
have education, health and social services and thus, in a sense, 'have' women"
(87)? Put differently, what are the historical and political factors that explain
why those issues have been institutionalized as rightly belonging to the substate
scale—a question that needs addressing before debating what effect this scale
attribution has on women's organizing?

Careful attention to conflicts over scale attribution and designation are crucial in this regard. As Ladner (2010) points out, many indigenous political actors
see themselves as involved in a nation to nation relationship with Canada (69).
Misrecognition (or violent colonial redesignation) of scale may lead to indigenous issues being reassigned and driven far lower down the political scale.
Critical attention to this political process of scale assignment is, for Ladner,
part of the move to decolonize our understanding of MLG (67). Likewise, attention must be paid to the historical uses of customary rule, local government,
and native administration under colonialism, whereby colonial powers often
constructed lower levels of government for the purposes of imperialism (Obiora
and Toomey 2010, 211). Indeed feminists in many nations continue to grapple
with the gendered colonial legacy of who, and what, got designated as legitimately belonging to customary authorities; unless MLG literature can address
the gendered and racialized political production of scale in these cases, it is
unlikely to be effective in theorizing postcolonial governance.

Judith Resnick (2001–2002) made a particularly important intervention
into this debate about contested scale attribution in her analysis of the 2000
Supreme Court decision in *United States v. Morrison* [529 U.S. 598] holding
unconstitutional a civil rights remedy for victims of gender-based violence. The
remedy, contained in the 1994 Violence Against Women Act, was struck down
on the grounds that the issue of violence was "truly local" (619). The ruling
was grounded in the assumption that a particular rule of law rightly regulates
a single aspect of human action and that certain issues properly, and perma-
nently, belong to certain scales within a given political architecture. Resnick
notes the fallacy of this reasoning. Category mistakes are common—such as
holding that the protection of wolves is an activity sufficiently commercial in
character to permit federal law making but that measures to secure payment
of child support are not (629–630)—and permanent categorization is itself a
mistake. After all, the areas identified as local in this litigation—family life and

criminal law—have long been subjected to federal lawmaking (622). She suggests an alternative approach, involving a questioning of categorization and a recognition that any assignment of jurisdiction is likely to be transitory (622–623). There are risks and anxieties stemming from this position, both for those attached to the federal or the transnational as sites of protection for women's rights and for those who understand the local as "inevitably a site of participatory democracy" (664). However, risks notwithstanding, it is important to extend the same critical scrutiny to all the scales being generated through contemporary politics: none can be taken for granted, naturalized, or assumed to be democratically accountable. As Resnick argues, neither "'the national' (n)or 'the local' has an intrinsically rosy glow" (676).

In closing I would suggest that it is especially important to extend critical scrutiny to political production of the family as a level of governance at present, given its central role in new MLG frameworks (see also Prügl 2011, chapter 2; and the chapters by Razavi and Lind in this volume for further discussion of the family and heteronormativity). Some observers have argued that state restructuring can involve efforts to revitalize the family as the nucleus of society,[10] and transnational actors have also become involved in attempts to govern interpersonal relations in a range of ways. For example, World Bank gender staff have noted the problem posed by "absent fathers and unstable family environments" in their work on the Dominican Republic, Haiti, and Jamaica (World Bank 2002, x); the gender policy review for these countries praised legislation put in place in the Dominican Republic to introduce "penalties for desertion of family" (7), and it foregrounded NGOs dealing with fatherhood in discussions of civil society interventions on gender issues (60). In postcrisis Argentina the Bank supported a family-strengthening initiative, funding NGOs to help "strengthen family cohesion (and) solidarity between male and female members" of households (World Bank 2000, 1) to "test the hypothesis that the promotion of a more cohesive and less segregated family life will positively impact the ability of families to face challenges posed by poverty" (3).[11] Levels of governance are interacting in extremely complex ways here, with multilateral lenders seeking to bolster certain intimate attachments as part of new, more inclusive development agendas and acting in alliance with states, feminists, and religious actors. But one lesson is clear: it is not simply that states or transnational institutions are dumping responsibilities downward, onto families that are always already configured, but that the production and regulation of certain kinds of interpersonal intimate attachments has increasingly become part of the business of new governance actors. Our understanding of what responsibilities rightly belong to the family, versus other levels, and of what conjugal attachments should mean politically and economically is thus shifting as the family becomes increasingly relevant to, and the object of, governance. While feminists are always well placed to trouble assumptions that the family "has an intrinsically rosy glow" (Resnick 2001–2002, 676), then, their critical accounts of how politics produces this scale seem particularly important at present.

THE AFFECTIVE DIMENSIONS OF
FORUM SHOPPING

Finally, it is worth briefly considering another key contribution that feminist scholarship can make to debates about MLG, via its attention to the emotive, affective dimensions of forum shopping. While considerable emphasis has been rightly placed on the strategic, pragmatic tactics used by feminist activists when confronted with a multilevel POS, other work has probed the political production and circulation of attachment to (or repulsion from) various scales of governance. Space is hereby provided to critically interrogate the deeply felt and politically salient affective relations that activists have to various spacially arranged nodes in MLG networks, whether these be the state, the family, the community, the region, or the transnational.

At issue here is our ability to explain the sometimes visceral responses of different feminist actors to political strategies grounded in bolstering certain levels of governance and to understand those responses as produced collectively and politically rather than as just reflecting individual preference for strategy. Without that ability, it is hard to understand what is at stake in conflicts over whether feminists should take World Bank money or whether they should work with state security forces as part of their antiviolence initiatives. Moreover, without a comprehensive interest in why different feminist political projects seek to settle where they do (e.g., in the state, the community, counterculture), affective attachments are in effect organized out of our inquiries about feminist politics. Rather, the general tendency is to assess political architectures based on cost–benefit, pragmatic reasoning, with orientations to levels understood to be flexible and strategic and perhaps equally cynical.

Yet, as a number of scholars have demonstrated, the affective dimensions of activist cultures can tell us a lot about politics. Elisabeth Wood (2003, 253) found that *campesinos* in El Salvador supported insurgents during the civil war not because they calculated the tangible costs and benefits of so doing but because they were motivated by affective bonds. People helped insurgents because of their deepening conviction—reinforced by growing state violence—that the government no longer merited their loyalty or acquiescence (120). Facing high costs, they nonetheless got involved because of emotional and moral commitments: out of loyalty to the dead, such that they did not suffer in vain; as a way to express outrage; out of a desire to be "part of the making of history" (18–19); and to assert dignity and personhood in the face of repression. There was pleasure in agency and pride in defiance (18).

In a very different context, Ann Cvetkovich (2003, 10) also argues that "affective life pervades public life." She uses the framework of trauma to understand this pervasion, seeing trauma not as a medicalized, pathologized site of individual experience but as "a name for experiences of socially situated political violence" (3). Cvetkovich uses this lens to forge overt connections between politics and emotion, foregrounding public articulations of trauma that do not look to the state for resolution. For Cvetkovich, trauma can be a foundation for creating counterpublic spheres, and she celebrates the unpredictable forms of politics that emerge when trauma is kept in view rather than contained within an institutional project at any level (16). She also highlights political mobilizations that intervene against the use of trauma to reinforce U.S. nationalism and that instead use histories of genocide, slavery, colonialism, and diaspora to insist on the foundational violence of the postcolonial settler state (see also Ladner 2010).

Such work suggests that the choice of level not only is restricted by resource constraints[12] but also is significantly shaped by sedimented histories of emotive attachment (or repulsion), themselves the products of politics. As several authors note, for example, feminist distrust of the state informs much of the debate about MLG (e.g., Della Porta 2003; MacRae 2010; Solanki 2010), and this distrust stems from varied politicized responses to collective trauma, including past and ongoing state violence, and state complicity in repression at other levels.[13] There have been multiple feminist, antiracist, and queer acts of defiance against political projects seeking to generate allegiance to various nation-states in the post-September 11 context, including through attempts to stop gender and sexuality rights struggles being used in ways that justify war.[14] These acts of defiance are, in part, born of disgust with the state. Simultaneously, emotional attachment to the welfare state can be keenly felt and political salient in some countries, with feminists defending state institutions that have provided them and their loved ones with free health care or good education. While some activists desire localized politics in part out of horror at violent state institutions, then, others feel angry and betrayed that the anti-state state has abandoned them and their communities (Gilmore 2007).

Still others fear projects to bolster community or family, as sites associated with tyrannous majorities, violence, intolerance, and superexploitation of women's labor. These negative associations are, in turn, in part the result of feminist politics—they are an outcome of political, activist labor. They reflect a collective commitment to puncture the illusion of affective fulfillment in assimilation, or domestic contentment (Cvetkovich 2003, 11–12), and to make visible the unequal power relations and harms so often occluded in celebrations of happy homes and contented localities. Those who insist on cultivating attachments in other ways may take agentic pride in resisting political strategies (or academic literatures) that seek to produce affective allegiance to family and community; they have certainly used that resistance to craft immensely rich theoretical alternatives (e.g., Joseph 2002).

Attention to the affective dimensions of MLG debates does not, then, tell us whether we should take state money or ally with the police when we are participating in new governance networks. Rather, it allows us to understand better what is at stake in our conflicts over these issues and to ponder how our attachments to various levels of governance are politically produced, both by ourselves in feminist community and by others who may seek our allegiance.

CONCLUSION

Interest in MLG is part of a long durée conversation about the nature of power and the practice of politics. It relates to core questions about the overlapping scales through which governing is made possible, what type of institutional arrangements are best placed to secure democracy, what role the state should and does play within an increasingly global polity, what form of government is best placed to secure minority interests against majoritarian tyranny, and whether radical change can be pursued through inclusion in formal politics. It is unsurprising that feminists addressing such questions disagree about the answers. Nonetheless, gender scholars have been having an immensely productive conversation about the topic (sometimes decades before MLG was coined as a term) and I hope that the preceding pages have pointed to some particularly fruitful ongoing debates.

Taking the five themes addressed in this chapter together, two conclusions appear particularly salient. First, MLG trends have such diverse effects that a general theory about which political architectures benefit *women* is unlikely to emerge. In fact, we already know that governance reorganization processes have nonuniform effects on women's equality-seeking politics. Professionalized women able to position themselves as gender policy experts will assess the possibilities of MLG very differently from women positioned as clients in governance networks or from women whose care services are being dismantled in the name of community ownership. Transnational institutions can be double-edged swords, as can community-level inclusion initiatives: in both cases the desire and ability of different feminist groups to mobilize effectively within new governing structures is highly contingent, both on external factors (e.g., the framing of gender equality required to secure progress in a given institution, the presence of left-leaning allies at a given governance tier, or the compliance mechanisms in place to translate rights gains into grounded enforcement) and on internal factors specific to each group (e.g., the aim of the mobilization and how various tiers of governance are collectively understood and experienced). It would thus seem crucial to foreground such diverse experiences of MLG and to explore variations in feminist mobilizing vis-à-vis governance arrangements more systematically and comprehensively, including by seeking out feminist protest politics conducted outside the purview of formal governance networks and funding streams.

Second, while research on gender, institutions, and MLG has proved enormously fruitful when conducted within politics departments, expanded interdisciplinarity would yield significant results. Here I have argued for the value of greater attentiveness to the politics of scale attribution and to the affective dimensions of forum shopping, requiring openness to literatures in geography, history, law, cultural studies, and postcolonial theory. There are no doubt other, maybe better, examples of how debates from other disciplines and interdisciplines might add to and reframe feminist conversations about governance arrangements. But suffice it to say that politics scholarship on gender, institutions, and MLG would benefit from more systematic integration of insights from other fields. Pace Scott (2010), we might not be facing extinction without this, but with it our research paradigms will evolve in some exciting new directions.

ACKNOWLEDGMENT

Thanks to Emily Grabham, Helen Kinsella, Debora Lopriete, Rianne Mahon, Lisa Mills, Shirin Rai, Georgina Waylen, and an anonymous reviewer for comments on an earlier draft.

NOTES

1. See for example, voting weight depends on economic contribution in the World Bank.
2. For example, Sørensen (2007) on Denmark and Borrás (2007) on the EC's exclusion of some participants from debates about genetically modified food.
3. See also Marcussen and Torfing (2007, 13) on state attempts to influence the processes and outcomes of MLG networks.
4. For example, government is typically defined as formal state institutions unified by a joint monopoly of legitimate, coercive power (Marcussen and Torfing 2007, 2–3), absent attention to the fact that "legitimate" gender violence has never been the sole preserve of the state.
5. Subsequently amended by Article 141 of the Treaty of Amsterdam.
6. On forum shopping see Brennan (2010), Chappell (2002), and Dobrowolsky (1998).
7. The Optional Protocol allows for individual complaints and independent inquiries accusing a state of violating its responsibilities under the convention (see Zwingel 2010).
8. See Lombardo, Meier, and Verloo (2009), especially the contributions from Marx Ferree and Bacchi.
9. See also Prügl (2011) on sub-national variation in gender regimes, and the relevance this has for the outcomes of gender mainstreaming initiatives in European rural development policy.

10. On family revitalization in Austria see Sauer (2007).
11. See Bedford (2009) for further analysis of this new approach to heteronormativity in development and the importance of assessing multiple scales (the family, the national, the regional, and global) in gender and development scholarship.
12. On women as less able to *physically* move jurisdictions due to family ties and resource constraints see Sawer and Vickers (2010, 7).
13. These include, for example, genocidal violence of colonial settlement (Ladner 2010); the experiences of violent policing that shape protest cultures in Florence (della Porta 2003, 49–50); and the structural violence of poverty and racism (and the way in which those harms are subsequently normalized) (Merry 2007, 41–45).
14. See, for example, the activities documented at http://nohomonationalism.blogspot.com/

REFERENCES

Ahn, Christine. 2007. "Democratizing American philanthropy." In INCITE!, ed., *The revolution will not be funded.* Boston: South End Press, 63–76.
Alvarez, Sonia. 1999. "Advocating feminism: The Latin American feminist NGO 'boom.'" *International Feminist Journal of Politics* 1(2): 181–209.
Andrew, Caroline. 2010. Federalism and feminism: The Canadian challenge for women's urban safety. In *Federalism, feminism and multilevel governance*, ed. Melissa Haussman, Marian Sawer and Jill Vickers, 83–96. Farnham: Ashgate.
Bache, Ian, and Matthew Flinders (Eds.). 2004. *Multi-level governance.* Oxford: Oxford University Press.
Banaszak, Lee Ann, Karen Beckwith, and Dieter Rucht. 2003. "When power relocates: interactive changes in women's movements and states." In *Women's movements facing the reconfigured state.* Cambridge, UK: Cambridge University Press, 1–29.
Bedford, Kate. 2009. *Developing partnerships: gender, sexuality, and the reformed World Bank.* Minneapolis: University of Minnesota Press.
Bedford, Kate. 2010. *Harmonizing global care policy? Care and the Commission on the Status of Women.* Geneva: UNRISD.
Beveridge, Fiona, and Samantha Velluti. 2008. "Introduction." In *Gender and the open method of coordination*, ed. Fiona Beveridge and Samantha Velluti. Farnham: Ashgate, 1–9.
Borrás, Susana. 2007. "Governance networks in the EU: the case of GMO policy." In Martin Marcussen and Jacob Torfing, eds., *Democratic network governance in Europe.* Basingstoke, UK: Palgrave, 232–251.
Brennan, Deborah. 2010. "Federalism, childcare and MLG in Australia." In Melissa Haussman, Marian Sawer and Jill Vickers, eds., *Federalism, feminism and multilevel governance.* Farnham: Ashgate, 37–50.
Bustelo, María, and Candice Ortbals. 2007. "The evolution of Spanish state feminism: A fragmented landscape." In Joyce Outshoorn and Johanna Kantola, eds., *Changing state feminism.* Basingstoke: Palgrave, 201–223.
Celis, Karen, and Petra Meier. 2007. "State feminism and women's movements in Belgium." In Joyce Outshoorn and Johanna Kantola, eds., *Changing state feminism.* Basingstoke: Palgrave, 62–81.

Chandler, Andrea. 2010. "Women, gender and federalism in Russia: A deafening silence." In Melissa Haussman, Marian Sawer, and Jill Vickers, eds., *Federalism, feminism and multilevel governance*. Farnham: Ashgate, 141–154.

Chappell, Louise. 2002. *Gendering government: Feminist engagement with the state in Australia and Canada*. Vancouver: University of British Columbia Press.

Clavero, Sara, and Yvonne Galligan. 2009. "Constituting and reconstituting the gender order in Europe." *Perspectives on European Politics and Society* 10(1): 101–117.

Cooper, Davina. 1995. *Power in struggle: Feminism, sexuality and the state*. Buckingham: Open University Press.

Cvetkovich, Ann. 2003. *An archive of feelings: Trauma, sexuality, and lesbian public cultures*. London: Duke University Press.

Della Porta, Donatella. 2003. "The women's movement, the left, and the state: continuities and changes in the Italian case." In Lee Ann Banaszak, Karen Beckwith, and Dieter Rucht, eds., *Women's movements facing the reconfigured state*. Cambridge, UK: Cambridge University Press, 48–68.

Dobrowolsky, Alexandra. 1998. "Of "Special Interest": Interest, Identity and Feminist Constitutional Activism in Canada." *Canadian Journal of Political Science* 31: 707–742.

Dobrowolsky, Alexandra. 2003. "Shifting states: women's constitutional organizing across time and space." In Lee Ann Banaszak, Karen Beckwith, and Dieter Rucht, eds., *Women's movements facing the reconfigured state*. Cambridge, UK: Cambridge University Press, 114–140.

Dolhinow, Rebecca. 2010. *A jumble of needs: women's activism and neoliberalism in the colonias of the southwest*. London: University of Minnesota Press.

Elman, R. Amy. 2003. "Refuge in reconfigured states: shelter movements in the US, Britain, and Sweden." In Lee Ann Banaszak, Karen Beckwith, and Dieter Rucht, eds., *Women's movements facing the reconfigured state*. Cambridge, UK: Cambridge University Press, 94–113.

Gilmore, Ruth Wilson. 2007. "In the shadow of the shadow state." In ed. INCITE!, ed., *The revolution will not be funded*. Boston: South End Press, 41–52.

Gray, Gwendolyn. 2010. "Federalism, feminism and multi-level governance: The elusive search for theory?" In Melissa Haussman, Marian Sawer, and Jill Vickers, eds., *Federalism, feminism and multilevel governance*. Farnham: Ashgate, 19–33.

Haussman, Melissa, Marian Sawer, and Jill Vickers, eds. 2010. *Federalism, feminism and multilevel governance*. Farnham: Ashgate.

Haussman, Melissa. 2010. "Caught in a bind: the US pro-choice movement and federalism." In Melissa Haussman, Marian Sawer, and Jill Vickers, eds., *Federalism, feminism and multilevel governance*. Farnham: Ashgate, 111–124.

Hedmo, Tina, and Kerstin Sahlin-Andersson. 2007. "The evolution of a European governance network of management education." In Martin Marcussen and Jacob Torfing, eds., *Democratic network governance in Europe*. Basingstoke: Palgrave, 195–213.

Helfferich, Barbara, and Felix Kolb. 2001. "Multilevel action coordination in European contentious politics: the case of the European Women's Lobby." In Doug Imig and Sidney Tarrow, eds., *Contentious Europeans: Protest and politics in an emerging polity*. Oxford: Rowman and Littlefield, 143–161.

Holli, Anne Maria, and Johanna Kantola. 2007. "State feminism Finnish style: strong policies clash with implementation problems." In Joyce Outshoorn and Johanna Kantola, eds., *Changing state feminism*. Basingstoke, UK: Palgrave, 82–101.

Hooghe, Liesbet, and Gary Marks. 2003. "Unraveling the central state, but how? Types of multi-level governance." *American Political Science Review* 97(2): 233–243.

Hooghe, Marc. 2008. "The POS for civil society organisations in a multilevel context." In William Maloney and Jan W. van Deth, eds., *Civil society and governance in Europe: From national to international linkages.* Cheltenham, UK: Edward Elgar, 71–90.

Imig, Doug, and Sidney Tarrow. 2001. "Studying contention in an emerging polity." In Doug Imig and Sidney Tarrow, eds., *Contentious Europeans: Protest and politics in an emerging polity.* Oxford: Rowman and Littlefield, 3–26.

INCITE! (Eds.). 2007. *The revolution will not be funded.* Boston: South End Press.

Jessop, Bob. 2004. "Multi-level governance and multi-level metagovernance." In Ian Bache and Matthew Flinders, eds., *Multi-level governance.* Oxford: Oxford University Press, 49–74.

Joachim, Jutta, and Birgit Locher. 2009. "Introduction." In Jutta Joachim and Birgit Locher, eds., *Transnational activism in the UN and the EU: A comparative study,* London: Routledge, 3–18.

Joseph, Miranda. 2002. *Against the romance of community.* Minneapolis: University of Minnesota Press.

Kantola, Johanna, and Joyce Outshoorn. 2007. "Introduction." In Joyce Outshoorn and Johanna Kantola, eds., *Changing state feminism.* Basingstoke, UK: Palgrave, 1–19.

Katzenstein, Mary Fainsod. 2003. "Re-dividing citizens—Divided feminisms: The reconfigured US state and women's citizenship." In Lee Ann Banaszak, Karen Beckwith, and Dieter Rucht, eds., *Women's movements facing the reconfigured state.* Cambridge, UK: Cambridge University Press, 203–218.

Keck, Margaret, and Kathryn Sikkink. 1998. *Activists beyond borders: Advocacy networks in international politics.* Ithaca, NY: Cornell University Press.

Krook, Mona Lena, and Jacqui True. 2010. "Rethinking the life cycles of international norms: The United Nations and the global promotion of gender equality." *European Journal of International Relations* 20(10): 1–25.

Ladner, Kiera. 2010. "Colonialism isn't the only answer: Indigenous peoples and MLG in Canada." In Melissa Haussman, Marian Sawer, and Jill Vickers, eds., *Federalism, feminism and multilevel governance.* Farnham: Ashgate, 67–82.

Larner, Wendy, Nick Lewis, and Richard Le Heron. 2010. "State spaces of 'after neoliberalism': Co-constituting the New Zealand designer fashion industry." In Roger Keil and Rianne Mahon, eds., *Leviathan Undone? Towards a political economy of scale.* Toronto: University of British Columbia Press, 177–194.

Lind, Amy. 2005. *Gendered paradoxes: Women's movements, state restructuring, and global development in Ecuador.* University Park: Pennsylvania State University Press.

Lombardo, Emanuela, Petra Meier, and Mieke Verloo (Eds). 2009. *The discursive politics of gender equality: Stretching, bending and policymaking.* London: Routledge.

Macdonald, Laura, and Lisa Mills. 2010. "Gender, democracy and federalism in Mexico: Implications for reproductive rights and social policy." In Melissa Haussman, Marian Sawer, and Jill Vickers, eds., *Federalism, feminism and multilevel governance.* Farnham: Ashgate, 187–198.

Mackay, Fiona, and Petra Meir. 2003. *Institutions, Change and Gender Relations: Towards a Feminist New Institutionalism.* Prepared for the Joint Sessions of the European Consortium of Political Research, workshop 23 (Changing constitutions, building institutions and (re)defining gender relations). On file with author.

Mackay, Fiona. 2010. "Devolution and the multilevel politics of gender in the UK: the case of Scotland." In Melissa Haussman, Marian Sawer, and Jill Vickers, eds., *Federalism, feminism and multilevel governance*. Farnham: Ashgate, 155–168.

MacRae, Heather. 2010. Multiple policy scales and the development of parental leave policy in Germany. In *Federalism, feminism and multilevel governance*, ed. Melissa Haussman, Marian Sawer and Jill Vickers, 127–139. Farnham: Ashgate.

Mahon, Rianne, and Cheryl Collier. 2010. "Navigating the shoals of Canadian federalism: Childcare advocacy." In Melissa Haussman, Marian Sawer, and Jill Vickers, eds., *Federalism, feminism and multilevel governance*. Farnham: Ashgate, 51–66.

Mahon, Rianne, and Roger Keil. 2009. "Introduction." In Roger Keil and Rianne Mahon, eds., *Leviathan undone? Towards a political economy of scale*. Toronto: University of British Columbia Press, 3–23.

Marcussen, Martin, and Jacob Torfing. 2007. "Introduction." In Martin Marcussen and Jacob Torfing, eds., *Democratic network governance in Europe*. Basingstoke, UK: Palgrave, 1–22.

Mazur, Amy. 2007. "Women's policy agencies, women's movements and a shifting political context: Towards a gendered republic in France?" In Joyce Outshoorn and Johanna Kantola, eds., *Changing state feminism*. Basingstoke, UK: Palgrave Macmillan, 103–123.

Merry, Sally Engle. 2007. "Introduction: States of violence." In Mark Goodale and Sally Engle Merry, eds., *The practice of human rights: tracking law between the global and the local*. Cambridge, UK: Cambridge University Press, 41–48.

Molyneux, Maxine. 2006. "Mothers at the service of the new poverty agenda: Progresa/Oportunidades, Mexico's Conditional Transfer Programme." *Social Policy Administration* 40(4): 425–449.

Obiora, L. Amede, and Sarah Toomey. 2010. "Federalism and gender politics in Nigeria." In Melissa Haussman, Marian Sawer, and Jill Vickers, eds., *Federalism, feminism and multilevel governance*. Farnham: Ashgate, 211–225.

Ostner, Ilona, and Jane Lewis. 1995. "Gender and the evolution of social policies." In Stephan Leibfried and Paul Pierson, eds., *European social policy: Between fragmentation and integration*. Washington DC: Brookings Institution, 159–193.

Outshoorn, Joyce, and Johanna Kantola. 2007. "Assessing changes in state feminism over the last decade." In Joyce Outshoorn and Johanna Kantola, eds., *Changing state feminism*. Basingstoke, UK: Palgrave, 266–285.

Outshoorn, Joyce, and Jantine Oldersma. 2007. "Dutch decay: the dismantling of the women's policy network in the Netherlands." In Joyce Outshoorn and Johanna Kantola, eds., *Changing state feminism*. Basingstoke, UK: Palgrave, 182–200.

Peters, B. Guy, and Jon Pierre. 2004. "MLG and democracy: A Faustian bargain?" In Ian Bache and Matthew Flinders, eds., *Multi-level governance*. Oxford: Oxford University Press, 75–91.

Prügl, Elisabeth. 1999. *The global construction of gender*. New York: Columbia University Press.

Prügl, Elisabeth. 2011. *Transforming masculine rule: Agriculture and rural development in the European Union*. Ann Arbor: University of of Michigan Press.

Prügl, Elisabeth, and Audrey Lustagarten. 2006. "Mainstreaming gender in international organizations." In Jane Jacquette and Gale Summerfield, eds., *Women and gender equity in development theory and practice: Institutions, resources, and mobilization.* Durham, NC: Duke University Press, 53–70.

Rai, Shirin (Ed.). 2003. *Mainstreaming gender, democratising the state? Institutional mechanisms for the advancement of women.* Manchester: United Nations/ Manchester University Press.

Rai, Shirin, and Georgina Waylen (Eds.). 2008. *Global governance: Feminist perspectives.* Basingstoke, UK: Palgrave.

Resnick, Judith. 2001–2002. "Categorical federalism: Jurisdiction, gender, and the globe." *Yale Law Journal* 111: 619–680.

Rodríguez, Dylan. 2007. "The political logic of the non-profit industrial complex." In INCITE!, ed., *The revolution will not be funded.* Boston: South End Press, 21–40.

Sauer, Birgit. 2007. "What happened to the model student? Austrian state feminism since the 1990s." In Joyce Outshoorn and Johanna Kantola, eds., *Changing state feminism.* Basingstoke: Palgrave, 41–61.

Sawer, Marian. 2007. "Australia: The fall of the femocrat." In Joyce Outshoorn and Johanna Kantola, eds., *Changing state feminism.* Basingstoke, UK: Palgrave, 20–40.

Sawer, Marian, and David Laycock. 2009. Down with elites and up with inequality: Market populism in Australia and Canada. *Commonwealth & Comparative Politics* 47.2: 133–150.

Sawer, Marian, and Jill Vickers. 2010. "Introduction: Political architecture and its gender impact." In Melissa Haussman, Marian Sawer, and Jill Vickers, eds., *Federalism, feminism and multilevel governance.* Farnham: Ashgate, 3–18.

Scott, James. 2010. *Theory talk #38: James Scott on agriculture as politics, the dangers of standardization and not being governed,* May 15. Available at http://www. theory-talks.org/2010/05/theory-talk-38.html.

Smith, Andrea. 2007. "Introduction." In INCITE!, ed., *The revolution will not be funded.* Boston: South End Press, 1–18.

Smith, Miriam. 2010. "Federalism and LGBT rights in the US and Canada: A comparative policy analysis." In Melissa Haussman, Marian Sawer, and Jill Vickers, eds., *Federalism, feminism and multilevel governance.* Farnham: Ashgate, 97–109.

Solanki, Gopika. 2010. "A fine balance? MLG and women's organising in India." In Melissa Haussman, Marian Sawer, and Jill Vickers, eds., *Federalism, feminism and multilevel governance.* Farnham: Ashgate, 171–185.

Sørensen, Eva. 2007. "Local politicians and administrators as metagovernors." In Martin Marcussen and Jacob Torfing, eds., *Democratic network governance in Europe.* Basingstoke, UK: Palgrave, 89–108.

Torfing, Jacob. 2007. "Discursive governance networks in Danish activation policy." In Martin Marcussen and Jacob Torfing, eds., *Democratic network governance in Europe.* Basingstoke, UK: Palgrave, 111–129.

Valiente, Celia. 2003. "The feminist movement and the reconfigured state in Spain." In Lee Ann Banaszak Karen Beckwith, and Dieter Rucht, eds., *Women's movements facing the reconfigured state.* Cambridge, UK: Cambridge University Press, 30–47.

Wood, Elisabeth Jean. 2003. *Insurgent collective action and civil war in El Salvador.* Cambridge, UK: Cambridge University Press.

World Bank. 2000. *Argentina—Family Strengthening and Social Capital Promotion Project—PROFAM (LIL)*. Project Information Document (Report No. PID9623; Project Id. ARPE70374) (July 31). Washington, DC: World Bank.

World Bank. 2002. *A review of gender issues in the Dominican Republic, Haiti, and Jamaica*. Report 21866-LAC. Washington, DC: World Bank.

Zwingel, Susanne. 2010. "Translating international women's rights: CEDAW in context." Paper presented at the conference on Gender and Global Governance, Geneva, October.

CHAPTER 26

WOMEN'S POLICY AGENCIES AND STATE FEMINISM

DOROTHY E. MCBRIDE AND AMY G. MAZUR

WHEN a government creates a Ministry for Women's Affairs, a Commission on Gender Equality, or a Bureau for Women and Work, it could be an act of subversion against male-dominated politics: a legitimate center for gender equality within the state. The Platform of Action adopted at the United Nations Fourth World Conference on Women in Beijing in 1995 certainly recognized such a potential: agencies would be mechanisms "... to support government-wide mainstreaming of a gender equality perspective in all policy areas" (United Nations 1996). Agencies also have the potential to promote increased women's representation and to develop and implement meaningful and authoritative policies on their behalf. Given their promise, the study of the extent to which these structures successfully promote women's claims and gender equality is the study of the extent to which there is state feminism.[1]

Feminist researchers from across the globe have looked at women's policy agencies and the prospects for state feminism. With increasing dialogue and collaboration, these scholars today form a community that has the capacity to sustain a global research agenda. This chapter draws from their work to describe the phenomenon of women's policy agencies and to set forth some major questions, issues, findings, and emerging research agendas. The first part of the chapter maps out the development and proliferation of agencies over the twentieth century. The second section addresses three assumptions central to the study of agencies and state feminism. The third and main part of the chapter describes the framework, methods, research results, and theory of state feminism in Western postindustrial democracies based on the work of the Research Network on Gender Politics and the State (RNGS). It then shows how RNGS research results challenge conventional wisdom—in fact, myths—about the effectiveness of agencies. The conclusion returns to the implications of the research findings and agendas for understanding state feminism and gendering the broader study of democratization.

Women's Policy Agencies Worldwide[2]

The Three Waves of Women's Policy Agencies

In this chapter we define women's policy agencies as state-based structures at all levels and across all formal government arenas assigned to promote the rights, status, and condition of women or strike down gender-based hierarchies.[3] Such agencies appeared in the early twentieth century, but it was the United Nations (UN) Commission on the Status of Women in 1947 and the International Women's Year (IWY) Conference process in the 1970s that provided a template for adoption. At the same time, agencies were a product of the efforts of national governments to address women's movement demands from the 1960s to the present. Looking at the establishment of agencies, scholars identify three stages that followed the initiative of the UN women's policy process and the ebbs and flows of women's movements (Rai 2003a; Squires 2007).

In the first wave, prior to the 1970s, a handful of women's policy agencies were set up in Western democracies, for example, the Women's Bureau in the United States, created in 1920, the Women's Bureau in Canada created in 1954, and the Study Group on Women's Work in France created in 1965. Such offices were always focused on the status or condition of women and women's issues, most often in the area of employment. Following the first UN conference in Mexico City in 1975, which called for countries to establish women's policy machinery, and the explosion of women's movements in Western countries governments responded by systematically setting up more agencies. By the mid-1980s all Western countries and by the mid-1990s 127 countries across the globe had national offices (Rai 2003a). This second wave of women's policy agency growth coincided with a trend toward focusing on gender equality rather than women's condition alone. A part of this second stage of agency development was the pursuit of gender mainstreaming—incorporating a gender perspective into all areas of policy—a charge usually, but not always, given to the women's policy agencies.[4] The link between gender mainstreaming and women's policy agencies, once again, clearly came from the international arena—the United Nations as well as other international organizations (True and Mintrom 2001; Staudt 2003).

In the final phase, beginning in the late 1990s and particularly in Western European countries, agencies shifted from a focus on women and gender toward diversity goals with responsibility for inequalities due to race, ethnicity, sexual orientation, age, and disability. The trend toward diversity agencies has also coincided with a scholarly shift toward assessing intersectionality, that is, how different systems of oppression intersect to produce variation in effects for groups of women from different ethnic backgrounds and with various socioeconomic characteristics (e.g., Weldon 2008; see also the chapter by Hill Collins and Chepp in this volume). As Lovenduski (2007) and Squires (2007) show in the case of the U.K. agencies, this trend provides both opportunities and challenges for addressing issues of gender equality. In the United States, for example, the women's movement benefited from the wide reach of the Equal Employment Opportunities Commission because it could base its claims for gender equality on effective legal arguments for race equality. In the French case, on the other hand, the establishment of a new authority that incorporates all forms of discrimination coincided with the downgrading of developed women's policy machinery at the national and subnational levels (Lépinard and Mazur 2009). It remains to be seen the degree to which the development of the new diversity agencies will contribute to the disappearance of women's policy machineries altogether—a question of keen interest on the state feminist research agenda.[5]

Issues in Studying Women's Policy Agencies and State Feminism

The special focus of RNGS scholars on women's policy agencies and state feminism has provided many lessons of use to others interested in the topic. In this section we address three of them. These pertain to assumptions that some of us in the network had believed, a but subsequently found were not only incorrect but also barriers to a clear understanding of the role of agencies and the phenomenon of state feminism. The first pertains to the importance of rigor in conceptualization of state feminism; the second addresses assumptions about Western bias; and the third cautions against the expectation that countries in the same geographical region will have similar experiences with agencies.

Assumption 1: State Feminism Is a Synonym for Women's Policy Agencies

It is important not to assume that the existence of agencies is proof of feminist outcomes. While the terms *state feminism* and *women's policy agencies* are often used interchangeably, there is a difference between the structures themselves and the process of state feminism in which the women's policy agencies are a central player. The relationship between the two concepts is part of the genesis of their use by those international researchers who, for the most part, have studied agencies in Western postindustrial countries where the concept of state feminism moved from "a loose notion to an operationalized concept" (McBride and Mazur 2007, 501).

To summarize this shift in the idea of state feminism, beginning in the 1980s the term was associated with the presence of women's policy agencies themselves. Later in the 1990s, when the RNGS network took on a systematic study of women's policy agencies we sharpened the concept of state feminism to assess what agencies did: the degree to which women's policy machineries effectively promoted women's interests within the state, through advancing women's movements actors' ideas and claims in policy debates and content and helping the actors that forwarded those claims to gain access to state governing arenas. Although some researchers continue to use the loose notion of state feminism as a synonym for women's policy agencies, the more precise idea that agencies are separate from the process of state feminism permits empirical research into the activities, effectiveness, and impacts of agencies. It sets the stage to study the extent to which agencies do, in fact, promote the status of women and gender equality.

Assumption 2: Western Bias Prevents Global Research

A more controversial issue in state feminism research is the question of Western bias (Valiente 2007). The idea of creating a government structure for women's interests is based on ideas of specialized bureaucracies that fit democratic and comparative wealthy and economically developed societies.[6] For non-Western observers, there is a question of whether such a mechanism could be transposed to societies outside the West, especially to nondemocratic, authoritarian settings or unstable and economically challenged countries. In the final analysis, it is thus possible that these agencies are only a by-product of the level of political and economic development of postindustrial democracies and will always be irrelevant in other contexts.

Historically, women's policy machineries are associated with Western notions of government and specific levels of postindustrial democratic development. Nevertheless, the United Nations beginning in the 1970s systematically placed the establishment of women's policy agencies at the center of its campaign to

promote gender equality worldwide. National agencies became important players at the international policy conferences as potential instruments for promoting gender equality in the context of democratic and economic development.
Also, other international organizations have made the establishment of women's
policy agencies a criterion for a host of economic related aid, trade status, and
membership. The European Union, for example, requires that postcommunist
states in Central Eastern Europe include a women's policy agency in their transitional governments before being considered for EU membership. Having a
gender equality mechanism is seen today as an essential feature of a democratic
state. Thus, it was not a big leap to make these agencies the linchpin of gender
mainstreaming for developing non-Western countries.

The focus on Western postindustrial democracies played out in the scholarly community that emerged in the 1990s around the study of women's policy
agencies and state feminism. It was scholars interested in gender politics in the
Western democracies that developed the concept of state feminism to study the
new phenomena of women's policy agencies in the West. From the beginning they
were careful to tailor their research to that context. The concepts and theories
did not assume a global reach or apply automatically to non-Western contexts.

It is up to experts in non-Western gender politics to decide whether the
tools to study state feminism—concepts, theories, and findings—can travel for
research outside of the west. Some scholars have already suggested topics that
are especially important in this regard. As Rai and others (2003a) show in a
study of women's policy agencies conducted for the UN, some factors that help
agencies achieve real change in the developing countries were not important
in Western countries, for example, state capacity, the nature of civil society,
availability of resources, and, perhaps most important, whether there was a stable democracy. "Democratization processes are therefore crucial for embedding
national machineries in the architecture of government" (38). Similarly, Valiente
(2007) identified the deep differences between the contexts in Western postindustrial democracies and other parts of the world, including the different ways
state and society interrelate, the absence of certain sectors of policy, and the
absence of well-organized women's movements. What the proliferation of wom-
en's policy agencies in non-Western parts of the world means for the condition
of women and gender equality is not self-evident, nor can it be assumed; it is
a question for study and must be carefully examined by experts of the various
countries and regions.

Assumption 3: Regional Patterns of Women's
Policy Agencies

Given the range, diversity, and complexity of governments, politics, and societies, many find it helps to generalize about regions of the world. Even the previous discussion of West and non-Western countries falls into that convenient

approach. However, we caution against the tendency to assume regional patterns and group agencies in, for example, Latin America, South Asia, or the Middle East. One of the major findings of the RNGS study of the characteristics of women's policy agencies in Western postindustrial democracies is that there are virtually no structural patterns by region, whether geographically or in terms of state–society relations. Rather than common trends in state feminism by regional grouping of country, we found that women's policy agencies' impact and influence varied more by the policy context in which they operated within a given country.

So far, there has not been systematic study of women's policy agencies and state feminism outside the West. There are numerous individual case studies in a broad range of national contexts, some of which provide a great deal of detail, but there is little effort to analyze trends across countries or regions. Rai (2003a) is one of the few studies that examine state feminism across more than one region. Goetz (2003) and Kardam and Acuner (2003) compare agencies in more than one country, and many other studies examine agencies within single countries without making any regional generalizations.[7] Thus, evidence for regional or national patterns is limited. At the same time, analyses suggest that there is a similar diversity of structures and effectiveness that may have less to do with specific national or regional contexts than with levels of economic or political development. For example, in authoritarian systems women's policy agencies tend to have few links to women's movements and are highly symbolic being used by the ruling regime to legitimize power (Robinson 1995; Zheng 2005).

Still, any conclusions about women's policy agencies outside of the West must await a more systematic analysis of the monographs in the secondary literature and in turn the development of systematic studies that compare with the findings about women's policy agencies and state feminism in the West.

Agencies, Movements, and State Feminism in Postindustrial Democracies: The RNGS Study

The Evolution of the Concept of State Feminism

RNGS connects the development of the concept of state feminism to the changing relationships between women's movements and states beginning in the 1960s. At first, movements mobilized women through autonomous, informal groups engaged in spontaneous protest; they often viewed the state as the enemy—the embodiment of patriarchal dominance.[8] After the decline of these grassroots autonomous movements in many countries after the 1970s, movement actors and analysts began to look to the state as a means to overcome social and economic inequality (for more discussion of the state see the chapter by Chappell in this volume). This process was closely tied to growing interest in studying women's policy agencies and the idea of state feminism (see Mazur and McBride 2008).

Pioneers in this area were in Scandinavian countries whose women's movements had been less from the grassroots and whose attitudes toward the state were generally positive. Helga Hernes (1987) favored the term in her book *Welfare States and Woman Power: Essays in State Feminism*. Her view was comprehensive: state feminism included a range of public policies and rules but also "the interplay between agitation from below and integration from above" that would lead to a "woman-friendly polity" (15). Siim (1991) called Hernes's idea *feminism from above*, a term that meant not only favorable policies but also the presence of feminist women in government offices. "The expression then referred to both feminists employed as administrators and bureaucrats in positions of power and to women politicians advocating gender equality policies" (189). While most Scandinavian scholars used the term to label some type of interaction between activists outside the state and sympathetic feminists inside the state, a few focused on women's policy agencies (Nielsen 1983; Dahlerup 1986), but none offered a definition of feminism. A woman-friendly polity usually meant the smooth relationship for women between their family, working and public life. Was that feminist?

Unlike the Scandinavian scholars, Australians had an active tradition of feminist skepticism of the patriarchal state. However, in the late 1980s, Australian researchers observed the growing number and relevance of women's policy agencies in their own country and directed their work to understanding what these offices did for women. This led to new theorizing about feminism and the state (Sawer 1990; Eisenstein 1996). Work of Australian scholars Pringle and Watson (1992) and Franzway, Court, and Connell (1989) challenged the claim of the monolithic patriarchal state by observing that states, in fact, comprise many different arenas for political and administrative action. This more complex view of states opened the way for many scholars to see them not as enemies but as a means by which feminist activists could challenge the male-dominated way of doing things and be successful. Rather than focus on the complex array of agencies they found at all levels of government, however, Australian researchers were primarily interested in the individuals—called *femocrats*—who worked in those agencies and elsewhere and who promoted a feminist agenda through those structures. They called this system a *femocracy* and therefore did not embrace the concept of state feminism in their work.

Origins of the RNGS State Feminism Framework

While scholars and activists were reconsidering the relationships between women's movement demands and states between the 1970s and 1990s, the United

Nations elevated the importance of institutional machineries for gender equality through its IWY Policy Conferences. Each conference produced a detailed plan of action for women's rights and gender equality to be followed by member-states.[9] Government-based women's policy machineries charged with implementing policies to achieve the goals for improving conditions for women were a central component of these plans. Thus, in this period there was a rapid spread of agencies throughout the world; these initiatives attracted the attention of more and more scholars and activists who were mostly interested in the activities of agencies in their own countries.

A group of these scholars contributed case studies of agencies in a range of countries from Australia to Scandinavia, United States and Canada to Spain and Italy, Great Britain to Poland for the edited volume *Comparative State Feminism* (McBride Stetson and Mazur 1995). This book, which included a comparative analysis of the cases, was the first to use the concept of state feminism to mean women's policy agencies as structures, their origins, resources, relation to women's movements, and effects. Despite its contribution to recognizing the importance of the growing phenomena of women's policy machineries, both the conceptualization and research design for the book were weak, casting doubt on the comparative analysis. It was clear to the contributors that more work needed to be done. Thus, in 1995, the RNGS was formed and set to work developing a coherent and rigorous research design and refining the concept of state feminism to facilitate carrying out the design. We settled on this initial nominal definition: state feminism occurs when women's policy agencies acting as allies of women's movement actors achieve policy goals and procedural access to policy-making arenas.

To carry out the RNGS research design, more than forty experts on gender policy signed up to study individual policy debates between the 1960s and 2000s on abortion, job training, political representation, and prostitution and debates on priority topics of the 1990s (called hot issues) in one of thirteen postindustrial democracies.[10] To complete the debates and report the results for each of the issues in the study took over ten years.[11] These studies of separate issues used methods of process tracing and descriptive statistics. As the case studies were completed, the concept of state feminism was refined and the state feminism theoretical framework began to take shape. The framework thus combines features of the initial RNGS research design and research model with ongoing comparative analysis of policy debates as well as insights from four bodies of theory: representation; social movements; institutionalization; and framing and policy making. The framework proposes that women's movements are more likely to receive favorable responses from the state when they ally with women's policy agencies. That alliance is observed first by looking for the extent to which there is agreement between actors and agencies on motivational and strategic frames expressed on the issue under consideration in a debate. Second, looking at the extent to which agencies gender the issue frames used by policy actors reveals the success of the agency as an ally. The success of the women's movement actors is found when the policy content at the end of the debate coincides with movement goals (a substantive outcome) and when movement actors are included as part of the policy subsystem at the end of the debate (a procedural outcome).

When agency–movement alliances achieve these movement procedural and substantive goals, the result is movement state feminism; when agency–movement alliances achieve feminist movement procedural and substantive goals, the result is transformative state feminism. This delineation of two types of state feminism—movement and transformative—arises from the conceptualization of women's movement and feminism in the framework. This conceptualization is, for many, one of the most important contributions of the RNGS state feminism framework: it offers, for the first time in comparative gender politics research, a tool to study women's and feminist movements cross-nationally and over time (see the full description in McBride and Mazur 2008). Briefly, for the state feminism framework, women's movement is defined as having two components: the discourse developed by women as they contemplate their own gender consciousness in relation to society; and the actors who present that discourse in public life. The actors—such as organizations, individuals, and groups—are the focus of empirical research; they are identified as part of the women's movement by their discourse.

Women's movement discourse has three essential components: identity with women as a group; language that is explicitly gendered; and ideas that are expressed as women representing women. Feminist discourse has the same components but is a subcategory that includes other features: the goal of changing the status of women in society and politics and the challenge to gender-based hierarchies and structures of subordination of women. Just as the women's movement actors are those who express movement discourse, the feminist movement actors are those who express feminist discourse; thus, the feminist movement is a subcategory of the women's movement.

To summarize, the state feminism framework delineates two types of agency movement alliances: movement state feminism where agencies help movement actors gain procedural and substantive responses; and transformative state feminism where agencies successfully aid feminist movement actors achieve feminist substantive and procedural responses. With the accumulation of both kinds of substantive and procedural success over time, governments become more democratic. State feminism is a continuous concept; that is, there are degrees of state feminism in terms of the extent to which agencies represent movement frames, whether agencies are successful in gendering the issue frame of the debate, and whether agencies help movement actors achieve substantive or procedural success or both. The state feminism framework looks for explanations for patterns of state feminism in terms of combinations of agency resources and structural characteristics, women's movement characteristics, policy environment characteristics, and elements of left-wing support.

Theoretical Foundations for the State Feminism Framework

The framework benefits from the insights of four strands of theory: institutionalism and state; social movement; democracy and representation; and policy and framing. Here we briefly summarize the contributions of each.

Institutionalism and the State

The growing interest in the 1980s in women's policy agencies coincided with the rise in attention more generally to studying the state as an entity as set forth in Skocpol's (1985) introduction to *Bringing the State Back In*. Two themes in this "return to the state" informed the development of the state feminism framework. First was attention to the capacity of the state to have an impact on society generally. Second was the assumption that rather than being only the object of interest groups, state processes themselves had effects on the organization of political groups; for example, interest groups and social movements were affected by interaction with state structures.

Other scholars identified with *new institutionalism* also challenged the notion that the state was a monolith and called for attention to specific structures and their effects. This fit nicely with Australian feminist critiques of traditional state theory. The message of this work was that the meaning of the state is relative to specific cultures. Since there was no consensus on a definition of the state, authors were free to adapt the meaning to the needs of the particular research context. Conceiving of the postindustrial democratic state as a set of arenas opened opportunities to explore these arenas through different policy subsystems instead of the government as a whole. It then became reasonable to assume that interest groups and social movements face an array of opportunities—some more accessible than others—to enter state arenas and be heard. For RNGS, this meant that one could look among the policy subsystems and debates for those contexts where agencies and women's movement and feminist movement actors might form alliances and seek positive state responses. At last, there would be a way to answer Dahlerup's (1986) call for more attention to the question of whether the state or state agencies have helped or hurt women.

Social Movements and Women's Movements

Who speaks for women? Can there be agreement about whether specific state actions help or hurt women? Social and women's movement theory helped RNGS address this controversial question. No entity speaks for all women, but since the 1960s the mobilization of women has spread second-wave movements across countries of Europe and North America. Knowing what women's movement actors want comes closer than any other indicator of knowing what women want from the state. The question becomes, then, to what extent have movement actors been effective in achieving their goals? In other words, what is the outcome of movement mobilization?

Rather that looking at outcomes, however, most social movement theory has focused on understanding and explaining the formation and development of movements. An exception was the work of William Gamson (1975), who studied the impact of social movement organizations on the state in the United States. Years later, Giugni (1995, 1998) and Diani (1997) pushed for more attention to the impact of social movements. Despite their interest there were problems in defining and measuring outcomes and being able to say convincingly that whatever happened was due to the activities of movement actors. To solve the problem, RNGS took another look at Gamson's typology. He offered two kinds of responses to movement demands: (1) procedural, or the recognition of movement activists within policy-making institutions; and (2) substantive, or gaining new advantages through policy change. RNGS was able to adapt this framework to assess the outcomes of movement activism. The most successful outcome was called dual response, both substantive policy and procedural access; the least successful was no response.

Movement theory suggested explanations or drivers of movement success with the state that have been used for explaining both the development and outcomes of movements (McAdam, McCarthy, and Zald 1996). Most can be grouped under two types: (1) *resource mobilization*, where one examines the internal features of movements, their membership, activities and protests, organizations and mobilization; and (2) *political opportunity structure*, which concentrates on external factors such as state organization, political parties, legislative process, points of access, and cultural compatibility. From this approach the state feminism framework proposed and adapted explanations grouped according to characteristics of women's movement actors (resource mobilization) and characteristics of the policy environment at the time of each debate (political opportunity structure). In addition, studies of movements have often mentioned left-wing support, that is, close ideological and organizational relations with leftist political parties and trade unions, as particularly important in movement success. They argue that, since left-wing parties and unions typically include change and equality as part of their ideologies, it seems likely that when those parties are in power, the state will be more favorable to demands from social movements for equality. And, when those movements are close to the left-wing parties and unions, movement actors will take leadership positions and provide direct links. Such left-wing support is also likely to favor an active role for women's policy agencies in assisting movement actors in achieving their goals.

Democracy and Representation

Both feminist and nonfeminist assessments of democracy and representation suggest ways that state feminism may have an effect on enhancing representativeness and thus democratization of established Western democracies. Following Hanna Pitkin's (1967) framework, there is the widespread recognition of two types of representation pertaining to women and the state: descriptive and substantive. These coincide with those indicators of movement success offered by Gamson (1975) and adapted to the state feminism framework. Descriptive representation refers to the presence in government of people who share similar characteristics with groups in the citizenry. So with respect to women's movements, descriptive representation is achieved for women when movement actors are included in decision-making arenas, what Gamson labeled *procedural access*. Substantive representation refers to advancing the policy preferences of a group, that is, when movement goals are included in policy content. Thus, according to the framework, state feminism increases both these types of representation. It follows, then that the more instances of state feminism found, the greater the democratization.

Policy Conflict and Framing

Frames—definitions of issues that set forth the policy problem and desired solution—are the language of policy conflict. Framing theory connects many parts of the state feminism framework: comparing frames is a means of locating alliances between agencies and movement actors; the influence of agencies in policy debates comes by their ability to influence issue frames, or definitions of alternatives, used by policy actors; and the assessment of whether substantive or procedural success is achieved is shown by comparing frames expressed by actors in the subsystem and the content of policy outputs with women's movement actor frames.

Policy conflict theory connects frames to policy processes. At the core of the conflict is the distribution of power: "The *definition of alternatives is the supreme instrument of power* (Schattschneider 1960, 66, emphasis in original). The definition of alternatives in a particular debate is an issue frame. Issue frames determine who has influence and who is permitted to sit at the table where policy is made. If the issue frame is about women or gender, for example, this invites women's representatives to have a say. Thus a goal of women's movement actors is to influence the issue frame of the debate to reflect their perspectives, either directly or with the help of other state actors such as women's policy agencies.

Theory of State Feminism

The state feminism framework served as the basis for the analysis of data from policy debates studied by RNGS researchers. There were several propositions, including the following: (1) women's movement actors have been successful in getting positive responses from the state over the years from 1960s to early 2000s; (2) women's policy agencies formed alliances with movement actors; (3) movement actors were more likely to be successful when they allied with agencies; and (4) explanations for both movement success and women's policy agency effectiveness in aiding movement actors were found among characteristics of the movement generally, favorable characteristics of the policy environment, favorable characteristics of the agencies, and support from left-wing parties, trade unions, and governments. To examine these propositions we used an integrative mixed methods approach—qualitative comparative analysis (crisp set) (csQCA); bivariate correlation and ordinal regression; and case studies tracing causal mechanisms. Each of these methods offered a different angle on the data. CsQCA permitted us to examine the way the presence or absence of various explanatory conditions combined to produce outcomes. Correlations and ordinal regression made use of the RNGS quantitative data set (nominative and ordinal measures) to assess the influence of single variables on the outcomes. The case studies analysis looked in detail at the descriptive data on each policy debate.

The results of this mixed-methods analysis made it possible to offer a new set of theoretically powerful and empirically robust propositions that move the framework to the status of a theory. Building from the state feminism framework, this theory of state feminism presents a more complex picture of the movement agency relations and their effects than the framework offered and also recognizes the subtle effects of various policy contexts. In addition, the theory rejects single-variable and global generalizations in favor a more complex picture of causation, that is, the many configurations of conditions that produce particular outcomes of interest—the success of women's movement actors and the effectiveness of agencies in that success.

Here we offer the description of the theory abridged from the capstone book for the state feminism project, *The Politics of State Feminism: Innovation in Comparative Research* (McBride and Mazur 2010, 258–260):[12]

> Women's policy agencies can and do form alliances with women's movement actors to achieve procedural access and policy change in favor of movement goals. Agencies can facilitate movement success by adopting microframes that are compatible with or match women's movement actors' frames: Gendering issue definitions used by policy actors with those frames brings about access, policy success, and political cultural change in specific policy subsystems and in the state, more broadly speaking. The degree of activism of agencies is a significant cause of more favorable state responses to movement demands. The most effective agencies—Insiders—play a necessary backup role in gaining complete movement success, Dual Responses, if usually favorable conditions are not present.[13] Agencies also may form partial alliances or fail completely when movements are still successful in achieving their goals. The result is women's movement success, but not state feminism.
> The patterns of successful agency-movement alliances are patterns of state feminism. Alliances that achieve specifically feminist goals are cases of Transformative State Feminism; those that achieve movement goals more broadly are Movement State Feminism. There is limited ability of

feminist movement actors to gain complete success in debates, but the likelihood is greater when agencies gender policy debates in feminist terms that match movement actor claims. With the accumulation of women's movement success over time in a given country, democratic governments become more democratic through increased substantive and descriptive representation of advocates for women, a previously excluded constituency.

Women's policy agencies on their own are not a cause of expanded inclusiveness of women in democracies in this broad sense. Instead, agencies tend to be effective allies when women's movement actors confront conditions that are unfavorable to their success in particular debates, but are not a continuing influence over time—once again a backup role.

The most promising explanations for movement success are combinations of agency activities and characteristics of movement, policy environments, agencies, and Left support. These features include the type of agency and its leadership, the priority of the debate issue to the movement as a whole, the support of women members of Parliament, the degree of openness of the policy subsystem, and the degree to which the issue frame at the beginning of the debate fits with women's movement microframes. Agency effectiveness may also be affected in a path-dependent manner by characteristics of previous debates on the issue and of previous coalitions with women's movement actors.

Patterns of state feminism vary by types of policy sectors. Any path-dependent effects occur by sector and not by country or by regional groupings of countries. Country patterns in state feminism may exist but will not be as important as patterns within different policy sectors that transcend national or regional contexts.

DEBATES: DEBUNKING CONVENTIONAL WISDOM

It is easy to be skeptical of the assertions made by state feminism theory. After all, looking at politics in most postindustrial democracies, rarely are any agencies in the news; they seem to be small and insignificant in relation to the vastness of contemporary governments and bureaucracies, and they are not part of the central business of government—defense, finance, justice, immigration, foreign affairs, or environment. Further, agencies devoted to women or gender may seem old-fashioned in the age of diversity or quite limited with respect to the more fashionable broad goals of gender mainstreaming.

Such skepticism is not new. From the beginning feminist critics and other critics considered agencies to be instruments of the political classes—little more than lame attempts to appease newly mobilized women's movements. As the UN Plans of Action rolled out, they called for more agencies. As seen in Action 296 in the 1995 Platform, this admonition from the UN seemed to involve writing a report to the UN that would have little internal effect:

> In order for the Platform for Action to be implemented, it will be necessary for Governments to establish or improve the effectiveness of national machineries for the advancement of women at the highest political level, appropriate intra- and inter-ministerial procedures and staffing, and other institutions with the mandate and capacity to broaden women's participation and integrate gender analysis into policies and programmes. The first step in this process for all institutions should be to review their objectives, programmes and operational procedures in terms of the actions called for in the Platform. A key activity should be to promote public awareness and support for the goals of the Platform for Action, inter alia, through the mass media and public education. (United Nations 1996, 120)

In fact, it is not surprising that many see agencies as having to do more with the requirements of international bodies like the EU and the UN than with the interests of women and activists for women internally.

The last section of this chapter takes on some of the criticisms of agencies and shows that based on our empirical findings they are, for the most part, myths. This list comes from no single published source but rather from the scholarly and movement discourse we, as researchers, have observed. The integrative mixed methods analysis of over one hundred policy debates across the issues and countries in the RNGS study offers concrete and empirically replicable results that counter some of the sweeping generalizations. With this discussion, we encourage more systematic research using concepts and methods that further refine these nuanced findings about the potential of agencies to be allies of women's movements and the conditions for their success.

Myth 1: Agencies are mostly just symbolic as far as women's movements are concerned. They really don't make any difference

To determine whether agencies make any difference, the RNGS research measured the degree of movement state feminism in two ways. One was a typology that classified the agencies in terms of whether the microframes they offered in each debate were compatible with women's movement microframes and whether they were effective in gendering the issue frame of the policy debate with those movement-friendly microframes. The result was four types: insiders (agencies did both); marginals (agencies had movement-friendly microframes but were not effective in the debate); antimovement agencies (agencies were effective but did not support movement goals); and symbolics (agencies did not take a position and did not gender the debate). In 108 debates studied in thirteen countries across issues of abortion, job training, political representation, prostitution, and priority issues of the 1990s, agencies were symbolic in only 27 percent, or twenty-nine debates. They took up movement goals in 66 percent, or seventy-two debates, and were effective insiders on behalf of the movement in 35 percent, or thirty-eight debates. There was issue variation: agencies were most effective in political representation debates and least on priority issues and job training. The highest level of symbolic agencies was in priority issue or hot issues (41 percent) and abortion (30 percent). By no means were the agencies mostly symbolic.

The other way of looking at movement state feminism was an ordinal measure of the degree of activity of agencies, from doing nothing or working against the movement to matching movement demands and gendering the issue frame. Running a bivariate analysis, we found a significant correlation between the degree of agency activity and the degree of state response.[14] Using ordinal regression, with models that included agency activity with other explanatory variables such as the policy environment model, women's movement strength model and left support model, the analysis confirmed the significant independent influence of agencies on state response to movement demands.

Myth 2: Agencies and their leaders are susceptible to becoming tools of patriarchy. The state would never allow institutions that undermine the system

According to the state feminism framework, cases of transformative state feminism show the extent to which the state accepts feminist demands from movement actors and agencies to challenge gender hierarchies and the subordination of women. In these cases, feminist insider agencies bring about feminist state responses (either procedural or substantive or both). Looking at the achievements of feminist movement actors, overall they have been less successful than the more general movement actors in gaining policy change along feminist lines, although they have been quite successful in penetrating policy subsystems. Agencies have not been reluctant to promote feminist microframes, however. In the debates where agencies took a position (excluding symbolic agencies), a majority (62 percent) advanced a feminist microframe. Among the insider agencies, half were feminist; that is, they were effective in gendering the issue frame with those feminist ideas. Further, feminist insiders were always successful in getting a feminist outcome, either procedural, policy content, or both. This means that, by accepting feminist policies and procedural inputs, the states in postindustrial democracies have made legitimate those ideas that challenge the traditional gender hierarchies. Over time, these have the potential to undermine the male dominated policy subsystems across the issues. There are, however, no trends across time that suggest transformative state feminism is on the increase, nor are there any countries that are consistently more feminist that others.

Myth 3: Agencies can't do anything unless they have feminist leaders who are responsible to the women's movement rather than to the political bosses

There are many policy debates where feminist leaders made the difference between success and failure for the movement–agency alliances. At the same time, feminist leaders have been at the head of symbolic agencies. Their presence seems to be most important in explaining cases of transformative state feminism: the most feminist insiders—both presenting feminist movement goals and gendering debates with those feminist ideas—tend to be ministries close to power, led by leaders with ties to feminist movement actors and in a position to propose policies. But feminist ties do not negate the need for agency heads to be responsible to the political bosses. Among the agencies that took an anti-movement stand, and there were relatively few, the feminist heads of ministries followed the lead of the government bosses, not the proposals of feminist movement actors. In other debates on other issues at other times, a feminist minister could push the agency to full effectiveness on behalf of movement goals.

With respect to movement state feminism, comparing the effective agency allies (insiders) with the ineffective allies (marginals) we found the effective ones were, in fact, less likely to have leaders with experience in the women's movement or feminist movement. Feminist leadership did not show up as part of any consistently winning combination of conditions that led to positive outcomes for movement actors (using csQCA). As with many of the conclusions of the study, the specific context of the policy arena affects the value of feminist expertise on the effectiveness of the agency. Some debates are already gendered at the beginning, leaving less for agencies to do in gendering debates. In other cases, the feminist leader almost singlehandedly has pushed the movement demands through parliamentary processes.

Myth 4: Governments never give agencies enough resources to do any good. They are too small and buried to be effective allies of women's movements. It's better to address the parliament directly

Agencies may be small and weak in comparison with parliaments and conventional ministries, but they can be effective allies all the same. Sometimes, parliaments, due to tight party control, may be closed to outside organizations. In those cases, working through an executive commission, for example, that is in proximity to cabinet offices or through a quasi-women's policy agency in a dominant political party is the only way for women's movement actors to be heard.

Although generally small, agencies vary in the number and extent of resources granted by the government. Some governments endow agencies with resources, and these have remained in place or even increased over time. We have found that administrative capacity—staff, budget, divisions, field offices—is often a condition, along with others, for agency effectiveness in gendering debates. But big does not always mean better. Placement in the political hierarchy can be key; executive commissions typically have small staffs, no divisions or field offices, yet they are close to the power brokers and may be headed by a powerbroker herself. At the same time, some agencies have lots of resources but little influence over policy making (for example, the Institute for Women in Spain). These may remain in an advisory or policy recommending role, dependent on others to refer proposals for response. The findings from causal mechanism case studies remind us that it is wise to assess the importance of administrative resources and structural characteristics in relation to subsystems when decisions are made and, consequently, to expect this to vary with the issue and topic for debate. These lessons remind us to avoid the sweeping generalizations often represented by conventional wisdom. Close and rigorous observation shows the complexity of agencies as they operate in dynamic policy environments.

Myth 5: The era of agencies is over; they have disappeared along with the feminist movement

Neither feminist movements nor gender machineries are a thing of the past. Movement actors continue to work with agencies to influence policy debates. And while agencies may not be essential for movement success, they often make the difference when usually favorable conditions for movement success are not present. This is the back-up role we have already talked about. These agencies are not on the wane either. On the contrary, looking at the agencies that appeared in policy debates in this study, we see that the trend over time is for agencies to persist and to grow in number, power, and resources from the 1960s to early 2000s. Another trend is that offices have moved closer to centers of decision-making power. At the same time, although the majority of machineries are well established and not in decline, we also find agencies that are weak or have disappeared.

The role of women's policy agencies in promoting women's movement goals has remained important since the end of the period covered by these debates (early 2000s). Activists continue to turn to agencies as allies and state feminism continues to be found. Similarly, women's movements and, specifically, feminist movements are not dying away and as long as they persist women's policy agencies will be resources for them. Agencies are resilient, and although a change in political leadership may temporarily decrease their resources and access (e.g., the United States under Republican domination in the early 2000s) they are revived with a change in administration, for example, under the Barack Obama administration in the United States. As long as the idea of the disaggregated state remains a useful approach to the study of politics, policy, and influence, we will continue to find the place of agencies, and movement influence will vary according to the issue being considered and the resulting policy subsystems and arenas. Some arenas are open to movement access, but others are not; in that case, often an agency that is located inside the policy subsystem, such as advisory bureaus and councils, can bring the movement perspective to the policy makers.

Conclusions

This chapter has shown the various ways women's policy agencies through state feminism are important sites of representation, policy change, and ultimately democratization. The theory of state feminism in the Western context indicates the importance of women's policy agencies as a back-up for women's movements when all else fails. The RNGS analysis clearly shows the complexity of the determinants and dynamics of state feminism. The absence of national and regional patterns makes the analyst drill down to the sectoral level. It is not clear how women's policy agencies and state feminism are going to weather the diversity–intersectional moment or the prospective of serious economic decline. If the past predicts the future, then women's policy agencies will find a niche and fill the cracks left by nonfeminist actors and perhaps even bring a feminist perspective into diversity politics. But this is a question for ongoing and future state feminism research.[15]

Given the nascent nature of research on women's policy agencies and state feminism outside of the West, there is much work to be done. First and foremost, the new scholars who have conducted the deep descriptive studies of agencies need to assess what can be done with state feminism theory and approaches developed for studying the West. Expanding dialogue between the various research communities seems to be the most productive way forward. But resources must be marshaled to help support the time-consuming and labor-intensive studies that are necessary to examine issues of agencies and state feminism systematically across the entire globe. The investment of time and effort will be worth it, in the final analysis, given the degree of new insight and systematic understanding such a gendered analysis of the state will bring to democracies—struggling, emerging, and consolidating—and their critical processes.

NOTES

1. This idea of state feminism—the effectiveness and impact of women's policy agencies as allies of advocates for women and equality—has been developed through the research of the Research Network on Gender Politics and the State (RNGS). For more on RNGS go to libarts.wsu.edu/pppa/rngs/index.html

2. The use of the term of *worldwide* makes references to the international comparative study of women and politics published in 1994 and coedited by Barbara Nelson and Najma Chowdhury. This monumental work brought together scholars to write on gender and politics in forty-three countries of the world using a common analytical framework. In each case, experts from the particular country wrote about gender and politics issues.

3. RNGS discovered a form of agency similar to these but not fully located within the state; these are called quasi-women's policy agencies (QUAWPA). Examples include women's commissions in political parties and certain women's parliamentary commissions without formal statutory authority.

4. In the RNGS study of seventy-five women's policy agencies in thirteen Western postindustrial democracies from the 1960s to the 2000s, only 10 percent had mandates that sought to systematically promote gender across all policy areas; 75 percent had mandates to promote gender equality over several but not all policy areas.

5. For more on women's policy agencies and intersectionality also see the forthcoming special issue in *Social Politics*, "Intersectionality in the Equality Architecture," edited by Sylvia Walby and Mieke Verloo.

6. These ideas are associated with the work of Max Weber, who set forth the elements of rational government organization appropriate to industrialized societies.

7. Rai (2003a) and Ugalde (2003); Honculada and Ofreneo (2003) Lycklama à; and Kwesiga (2003) and Rai (2003b) examine agencies in single countries. Nijeholt, Vargas, and Wieringa (1998) take on agencies in Latin American and the Caribbean, but in single-country studies on Peru (Anderson 1998), Jamaica (McKenzie 1998), Brazil (Pitanguy 1998), Mexico (Lamas 1998), and Chile (Molina 1998). Okeke-Ihejirika and Franceschet (2002) compare state feminism in Africa and Latin America. There have been quite a few monographs of state feminism in certain but not all Latin American countries (see, e.g., Alvarez 1990; Baldez 1991, 2001; Matear 1995; Schild 1995; Lievesley 1996; Waylen 1996; Friedman 2000a, 2000b; Franceschet 2003; Richards 2003, 2004) and some recent work on sub-Saharan African countries (Ghana—Madsen 2010; Cameroon, Mozambique, and Uganda—Tripp, Casimiro, and Kwesiga 2009).

8. An exception in the 1960s was liberal feminism, a component of women's movements in the United States and Great Britain. From the beginning of the second wave, these feminists sought to work with government believing that by changing state laws, equality could be advanced.

9. IWY conferences were held in Mexico City (1975); Copenhagen (1980); Nairobi (1985); and Beijing (1995).

10. At the beginning, sixteen countries and the European Union were sites for study and analysis. By the end RNGS had coverage of three to five issues in thirteen countries, the basis for the findings discussed in this paper: Austria; Belgium;

Canada; Finland; France; Germany; Great Britain; Ireland; Italy; Netherlands; Spain; Sweden; and the United States.

11. There are books that cover each of the issues published during this period: abortion (McBride Stetson 2001); job training (Mazur 2001); prostitution (Outshoorn 2004); political representation (Lovenduski 2005); hot issue (Haussman and Sauer 2007).

12. This section includes only the theory based on findings of the integrated mixed methods analysis of the policy debates, using the state feminism framework. The book also includes additions to the theory based on the work of contributing authors. These authors focused on contributions of the RNGS studies to the four founding theories of social movement, representation, framing, and new institutionalism: Joyce Outshoorn, Joni Lovenduski and Marila Guadagnini, Birgit Sauer, and Dorothy McBride and Amy Mazur. Their chapters provided some information that permitted deepening and broadening the state feminism theory but did not change the central elements.

13. Insiders are those agencies that gender the issue frame of a debate with ideas that are congruent with women's movement claims.

14. Spearman's rho of .279 ($p < .003$). These ordinal measures were:
    State Response
    0. State does nothing
    1. WMA policy change or procedural access
    2. WMA policy change and procedural access
    WPA Activity
    0. WPA does nothing or has anti WM microframe
    1. WPA compatible/mixed with WMA
    2. WPA matches WMA
    3. WPA compatible/mixed and gender issue frame
    4. WPA matches and gender issue frame

15. The forthcoming special issue of *Social Politics* edited by Verloo and Walby, with national case studies of how gender equality machineries have integrated issues of ethnic diversity and intersectionality, will be an important source of information and analyis.

REFERENCES

Alvarez, Sonia E. 1990. "Contradictions of a 'women's space' in a male-dominant state: The political role of the Commissions on the Status of Women in Post-authoritarian Brazil." In Kathleen Staudt, ed., *Women, international development, and politics: The bureaucratic mire*. Philadelphia: Temple University Press, 37–78.

Anderson, Jeanine. 1998. "Peruvian women and the Peruvian state." In G. Lycklama à Nijeholt, V. Vargas, and S. Wieringa, eds., *Women's movements and public policy in Europe, Latin America, and the Caribbean*. New York: Garland, 77–96.

Baldez, Lisa. 1991. "Coalition politics and the limits of state feminism in Chile." *Women and Politics* 22(4): 1–28.

Baldez, Lisa. 2001. "Coalition politics and the limits of state feminism in Chile." *Women & Politics* 22(4): 1–28.

Dahlerup, Drude. 1986. "Introduction." In D. Dahlerup, ed., *The new women's movement*. Bristol: SAGE, 1–26.

Diani, Mario. 1997. "Social movements and social capital: A network perspective on movement outcomes." *Mobilization: an International Journal* 2(2): 129–47.

Eisenstein, Hester. 1996. *Inside agitators: Australian femocrats and the state*. Philadelphia: Temple University Press.

Franceschet, Susan. 2003. "'State feminism' and women's movements: The impact of Chile's Servicio Nacional de la Mujer on women's activism." *Latin American Research Review* 38(1): 9–41.

Franzway, S., D. Court, and R. W. Connell. 1989. *Staking a claim: Feminism, bureaucracy and the state*. Sydney: Allen & Unwin.

Friedman, Elisabeth. 2000a. "State-based advocacy for gender equality in the developing world: Assessing the Venezuelan National Women's Agency." *Women & Politics* 21(2): 47–80.

Friedman, Elisabeth. 2000b. *Unfinished transitions: Women and the gendered development of democracy in Venezuela, 1936–1996*. University Park: Pennsylvania State University Press.

Gamson, William A. 1975. *The strategy of social protest*. Homewood, IL: Dorsey Press.

Goetz, A. 2003. "National women's machinery: State-based institutions to advocate gender equality." In S. Rai, ed., *Mainstreaming gender, democratizing the state? Institutional mechanisms for the advancement of women*. Manchester: Manchester University Press, 96–114.

Giugni, Marco G. 1995. "Outcomes of new social movements." In Hanspeter Kriesi, Ruud Koopmans, Jan Willem Duyvendak, and Marco Giugni, eds., *New social movements in Western Europe: A comparative analysis*. Minneapolis: University of Minnesota Press, 207–237.

Giugni, Marco G. 1998. "Was it worth the effort? The outcomes and consequences of social movements." *Annual Review of Sociology* 98: 371–393.

Haussman, Melissa, and Birgit Sauer (Eds.). 2007. *Gendering the state in the age of globalization. Women's movements and state feminism in postindustrial democracies*, Lanham, MD: Rowman and Littlefield.

Hernes, Helga Maria. 1987. *Welfare state and woman power: Essays in state feminism*. Oslo: Norwegian University Press.

Honculada, J., and Ofreneo, R. P. 2003. "The National Commission on the Role of Filipino Women, the Women's Movement and Gender Mainstreaming in the Phillippines." In Shirin Rai, ed., *Mainstreaming gender, democratizing the state?* Manchester: Manchester University Press, 131–145.

Kardam, Nüket, and Selma Acuner. 2003. "National women's machineries: Structures and spaces." In Shirin Rai, ed., *Mainstreaming gender, democratizing the state? Institutional mechanisms for the advancement of women*. Manchester: Manchester University Press, 96–114.

Kwesiga, J. 2003. "The national machinery for gender equality in Uganda: Instutionalised gesture politics?" In Shirin Rai, ed., *Mainstreaming gender, democratizing the state? Institutional mechanisms for the advancement of women*. Manchester: Manchester University Press, 203–222.

Lamas, Marta. 1998. "The Mexican feminist movement and public policy making." In G. Lycklama à Nijeholt, V. Vargas, and S. Wieringa, eds., *Women's movements and public policy in Europe, Latin America, and the Caribbean*. New York: Garland, 113–126.

Lépinard, Eléonore, and Amy G. Mazur. 2009. "Republican universalism faces the feminist challenge: The continuing struggle for gender equality." In Syvlain Brouard, Andrew Appleton, and Amy Mazur, eds., *The French Fifth Republic at fifty: Beyond stereotypes.* Palgrave/Macmillan, 247–266.

Lievesley, Geraldine. 1996. "Stages of growth? Women dealing with the state and each other in Peru." In Shirin M. Rai and Geraldine Lievesley, eds., *Women and the state: International perspectives.* London: Francis & Taylor, 45–60.

Lovenduski, Joni (Ed.). 2005. With contributions by Diane Sainsbury, Claudie Baudino, Marila Guadagnini and Petra Meier. *State feminism and the political representation.* Cambridge, UK: Cambridge University Press.

Lovenduski, Joni. 2007. "The UK: Reforming the House of Lords." In M. Haussman and B. Sauer, eds., *Gendering the state in the age of globalization: Women's movements and state feminism in postindustrial democracies.* Lanham, MD: Rowman and Littlefield, 263–280.

Lycklama à Nijeholt, G., V. Vargas, and S. Wieringa (Eds.). 1998. *Women's movements and public policy in Europe, Latin America, and the Caribbean.* New York: Garland.

Madsen, Diana. 2010. "Getting the institutions right for gender mainstreaming—The strategy of gender mainstreaming revisited in a Ghanaian context." Ph.D. diss.,. Roskilde University, Denmark.

Matear, Ann. 1995. "The Servicio Nacional de la Mujer (SERNAM): Women and the process of democratic transition in Chile 1990–94." In David E. Hojman, ed., *Neo-liberalism with a human face? The politics and economics of the Chilean model.* Liverpool: Institute of Latin American Studies, The University of Liverpool, 93–117.

Mazur, Amy G. (Ed.). 2001. *State feminism, women's movements, and job training: Making democracies work in the global economy.* New York: Routledge.

Mazur, Amy G., and Dorothy E. McBride. 2008. "State feminism." In Gary Goertz and Amy G. Mazur, eds., *Politics, gender and concepts: Theory and methodology.* Cambridge, UK: Cambridge University Press, 244–269.

McAdam, Doug, John D. McCarthy, and Mayer N. Zald. 1996. *Comparative perspectives on social movements: Political opportunities, mobilizing structures, and cultural framings.* Cambridge, UK: Cambridge University Press.

McBride Stetson, Dorothy (Ed.). 2001. *Abortion politics, women's movements and the democratic state: A comparative study of state feminism.* Oxford: Oxford University Press.

McBride, Dorothy, and Amy G. Mazur. 2007. "State feminism since the 1980s: From loose notion to operationalized concept." *Politics & Gender* 3(4): 501–512.

McBride, Dorothy E., and Amy G. Mazur. 2008. "Women's movements, feminism and feminist movements." In Gary Goertz and Amy G. Mazur, eds., *Politics, gender and concepts: Theory and methodology.* Cambridge, UK: Cambridge University Press, 219–243.

McBride, Dorothy E., and Amy G. Mazur. 2010. *The politics of state feminism: Innovation in comparative research.* Philadelphia: Temple University Press.

McBride Stetson, Dorothy, and Amy G. Mazur (Eds.). 1995. *Comparative state feminism.* Thousand Oaks, CA: SAGE.

McKenzie, Hermione. 1998. "The women's movement and public policy in Jamaica." In G. Lycklama à Nijeholt, V. Vargas, and S. Wieringa, eds., *Women's movements and public policy in Europe, Latin America, and the Caribbean.* New York: Garland, 49–76.

Molina, Natacha G. 1998. "Women's struggle for equality and citizenship in Chile." In G. Lycklama à Nijeholt, V. Vargas, and S. Wieringa, eds., *Women's movements and public policy in Europe, Latin America, and the Caribbean*. New York: Garland, 127–142.

Nelson, Barbara, and Najma Chowdhury. 1994. *Women and politics worldwide*. New Haven, CT: Yale University Press.

Nielsen, Ruth. 1983. *Equality legislation in comparative perspective: Towards state feminism*. Copenhagen: Women's Research Center in Social Sciences.

Okeke-Ihejirika, Philomina E., and Susan Franceschet. 2002. "Democratization and state feminism: Gender politics in Africa and Latin America." *Development and Change* 33(3): 439–466.

Outshoorn, Joyce (Ed.). 2004. *The politics of prostitution: Women's movements, democratic states, and the globalization of sex commerce*. Cambridge, UK: Cambridge University Press.

Pitanguy, Jacqueline. 1998. "The women's movements and public policy in Brazil." In G. Lycklama à Nijeholt, V. Vargas, and S. Wieringa, eds., *Women's movements and public policy in Europe, Latin America, and the Caribbean*. New York: Garland, 97–112.

Pitkin, Hanna Fenichel. 1967. *The concept of representation*. Berkeley: University of California Press.

Pringle, Rosemary, and S. Watson. 1992. "Women's interests and the post structuralist state." In M. Barrett and A. Phillips, eds., *Destabilizing theory: Contemporary feminist debates*. Cambridge, UK: Polity Press, 53–73.

Rai, Shirin (Ed.). 2003a. *Mainstreaming gender, democratizing the state? Institutional mechanisms for the advancement of women*. Manchester: Manchester University Press.

Rai, Shirin. 2003b. "The National Commission for Women: The Indian experience." In Shirin Rai, ed., *Mainstreaming gender, democratizing the state? Institutional mechanisms for the advancement of women*. Manchester: Manchester University Press, 223–243.

Richards, Patricia. 2003. "Expanding women's citizenship? Mapuche women and Chile's National Women's Service." *Latin American Perspectives* 30(2): 41–65.

Richards, Patricia. 2004. "Pobladoras, Indígenas, and the state: Conflicts over women's rights in Chile." New Brunswick, NJ: Rutgers University Press.

Robinson, Jean. 1995. " Women, the state and the need for civil society: The Liga Kobiet in Poland." In Dorothy McBride Stetson and Amy Mazur, eds., *Comparative state feminism*. Thousand Oaks, CA: SAGE, 203–220.

Sawer, Marian. 1990. *Sisters in suits, women and public policy in Australia*. Sydney: Allen & Unwin.

Schattschneider, E. E. 1960. *The semisovereign people: A realist's view of democracy in America*. New York: Holt, Rinehart & Winston.

Schild, Veronica. 1995. "NGOs, feminist politics and neo-liberal Latin American state formations: Some lessons from Chile." *Canadian Journal of Developmental Studies*, 16(4): 123–147.

Siim, Birte. 1991. "Welfare state, gender politics and equality policies: Women's citizenship in the Scandinavian welfare states." In Elizabeth Meehan and Selma Sevenhuijsen, eds., *Equality politics and gender*. London: SAGE, 175–192.

Skocpol, Theda. 1985. "Bringing the state back in: Strategies of analysis in current research." In Peter B. Evans, Dietrich Rueschemeyer, and Theda Skocpol, eds., *Bringing the state back in*. Cambridge, UK: Cambridge University Press, 3–37.

Squires, Judith. 2007. "The challenge of diversity: The evolution of women's policy agencies in Great Britain." *Politics and Gender* 3(4): 513–530.

Staudt, Kathleen, 2003. "Gender mainstreaming: Conceptual links to institutional machineries." In Shirin Rai, ed., *Mainstreaming gender, democratizing the state? Institutional mechanisms for the advancement of women*. Manchester: Manchester University Press, 40–66.

Tripp, Aili Mari, Isabel Casimiro, and Joy Kwesiga. 2009. *African women's movements: Transforming political landscapes*. Cambridge, UK: Cambridge University Press.

True, J., and M. Mintrom. 2001. "Transnational networks and policy diffusion: The case of gender mainstreaming." *International Studies Quarterly* 45: 27–57.

Ugalde, Silvia Vega. 2003. "The role of women's movements in institutionalizing a gender focus in public policy: The Ecuadorian experience." In Shirin Rai, ed., *Mainstreaming gender, democratizing the state? Institutional mechanisms for the advancement of women*. Manchester: Manchester University Press, 117–130.

United Nations. 1996. "The Beijing Declaration and the platform of action." Fourth World Conference on Women, Beijing, China, Department of Public Information, UN New York, September 14–15.

Valiente, Celia. 2007. "Developing countries and new democracies matter: An overview of research on state feminism worldwide." *Politics and Gender* 3(4): 530–541.

Waylen, Georgina. 1996. "Democratization, feminism and the state in Chile: The establishment of SERNAM." In Shirin M. Rai and Geraldine Lievesley, eds., *Women and the state: International perspectives*. London: Taylor & Francis, 103–117.

Weldon, Laurel. 2008. "Intersectionality." In G. Goertz and A. G. Mazur, eds., *Politics, gender and concepts: Theory and methodology*. Cambridge, UK: Cambridge University Press, 193–218.

Zheng, Wang. 2005. "State feminism? Gender and socialist state formation in Maoist China." *Feminist Studies* 31(3): 519–544.

CHAPTER 27

....

POLICY MAKING

....

EMANUELA LOMBARDO,
PETRA MEIER, AND
MIEKE VERLOO

INTRODUCTION

....

Policy-making is an ongoing process of planning, executing, and evaluating interventions by states, at different levels of government, including the establishment
of institutions, to define the rules steering society. As a result of these interventions or attempts at it, existing inequalities across all domains are affected in
their nature or degree. As such, policy making can (re)produce gender+[1] inequality or counteract it, through a reactive diagnosis or a proactive prescription.

Starting with feminist activists and scholars challenging a lack of attention for sex and gender in policy initiatives and in policy-making literature,
and accompanied by attempts at bringing women in and addressing the genderedness of policy making and the broader context thereof, a field evolved
that contains both elements of diagnosis and prescription. More recently, similarly to policy praxis, this academic field focuses more broadly on the design,
implementation, and evaluation of policies and strategies furthering gender+
equality. A growing number of gender+ scholars coming from a broad range of
disciplines such as politics, anthropology, economics, geography, history, law,
or social science studies specific policy fields such as child care, domestic violence, healthcare, labor market policies, reproductive rights policies, social policies more broadly, or the welfare state as such.

While similarly to Mazur (2002) we opt to call this field feminist policy
studies, we recognize the diversity of foci the various scholars have, ranging

from an eye on women, their concerns, needs and position, through a gender perspective, to an outspoken normatively founded feminist position, whereby not all feminists share the same normative assumptions on how the (societal) position of (men and) women should look. Similarly, there are different usages of the concept of gender, sometimes being simply a synonym of the socio-demographic variable of sex, while others build on the heritage of scholars such as Joan Scott who treat gender as a socially and historically constructed relation. Gendering might stand for policy contexts, processes or initiatives containing a male bias as much as for the insertion of a more gender equal perspective. What much of this research misses, though, is a focus on masculinity, making this chapter look rather blank on this issue.[2] Like other research with a women, gender, or feminist focus, this scholarship is to a large extent ignored by the mainstream of the discipline, in this case public policy studies.[3]

In this chapter we expand and build on earlier overviews of feminist policy studies (Hawkesworth 1994; Mazey 2000; Mazur 2002; Mazur and Pollack 2009; Orloff and Palier 2009) and further link the knowledge from various subdisciplines. The chapter is organized around a number of topics, thereby loosely following the chronological development of the field of feminist policy studies. The next section looks into early—mainly development—studies on the analysis of the absence of women in the policy-making process and its impact for the gender-biased normative frameworks underlying policies. The following two sections look at the broader context and process of policy making: on how political goals or interests that originate in various feminist movements fare in the policy-making process and under which conditions and in which circumstances the state responds to them; and at the genderedness of the policy-making context and process itself. The other sections look into the making of policies more specifically: first by analyzing the unpacking of the construction of policy problems and thereby the needs and interests as related to feminist goals; then looking into new strategies and policies for overcoming a gender bias in the making of policies; and outlining some recent developments in research on furthering gender+ equality. The chapter concludes by summing up the findings.

Bringing Women In

A gender analysis of policy making can be drawn back to the 1970s, when feminist practitioners and scholars from a broad variety of disciplines started criticizing the absence of women in development planning. They tackled the presumed unitary character of the household, the gender roles within it, and the unilateral focus on the formal economy. Boserup (1970, 2007), in her seminal work on women's role in economic development, documented extensively how women assure the nutrition of the family by being food producers and suppliers, also for the local market, and the growing female involvement (in low paid unskilled jobs) in the industry. Others analyzed the role women play in rural development (Benería 1982), the informal sector or industrial homework (Benería and Roldán 1987), or their and men's income patterns (Dwyer and Bruce 1988). Women in development issues traditionally focused on family needs and were directed toward welfare policies (Kabeer 1994), often having an adverse impact upon women and children (Tinker and Bramsen 1976; Lycklama à Nijeholt 1987), ignoring the productive role of women, or even redistributing (the control over) production means, such as land, water, or equipment, from women to men (Agarwal 1981; Shiva 1989), thereby worsening the power balance between the sexes (Rao, Anderson, and Overholt 1991). Emphasis was put on the blindness of development planning for the relation between gender and class (Benería and Roldán 1987; Sen and Grown 1988) or poverty (Buvinic, Lycette, and McGreevey 1983), ignoring the specific interests women have (Molyneux 1985).

This literature pointed at the failures in the design, implementation, evaluation, and ultimate effects of development policies, due to its male bias (Elson 1995b; Jahan 1995) and the role international and development organizations (should) play in these matters (Staudt 1990; Goetz 1997; Miller and Razavi 1998). Consequently, it underlined the need to decompose household patterns and to consider the roles and positions of women beyond stereotypes (Benería 2003; Jaquette and Summerfield 2006). Only so could these programs foster development, but—especially—empower women (Tinker 1990; Molyneux and Razavi 2003). Feminist scholars and policy makers in international organizations or development nongovernmental organizations (NGOs) suggested alternative planning and evaluation frameworks as well as management strategies that were sensitive to gender as a factor in development processes (Jain 1983). For instance, Overholt et al. (1985) developed frameworks analyzing the general project objectives, assessing how these relate to both men's and women's needs, anticipating the project's effects on the life and social position of women, and looking at their involvement with the project. This literature also underlined the need to consider women as actors to be involved in the development process, among others because of the roles they traditionally played in community management (Sen and Grown 1988; Moser 1993), in that this literature not only made a diagnosis of what went wrong in development planning but also put forward a prognosis of what to do. This prescriptive component is especially interesting since it is one of the pillars of later important trends in feminist policy studies such as gender impact assessment, gender budgeting, gender evaluations, and gender mainstreaming more broadly.

FEMINIST ISSUES AND STATE POLITICS

A significant proportion of the feminist policy literature looks into the responsiveness of political systems to feminist requests, studying the extent to which feminist ideas, needs, and interests make it to the political agenda and into policies. Important in this literature are critical success factors, the reasons and the conditions under which states and institutions adopt and pursue women-friendly, gender-balanced or feminist policies (Stetson and Mazur 1995; Outshoorn and Kantola 2007) (see also the chapter by McBride and Mazur in this volume). In this respect much of this literature is prescriptive, in that it looks for the ideal setting for women's organizations and feminist activists to act and achieve their goals.

Hawkesworth (1994), in her early review of feminist policy studies, discusses some of the main American works that study the extent to which feminist ideas, needs, and interests make it to the political agenda. Many of these studies find that the creation of feminist policy networks of grassroots and organized women and the use of a nondiscrimination strategy had been crucial (Freeman 1975; Boneparth 1982; Gelb and Palley 1996; Stetson 2004). Yet they diverge in the assessment of equality strategies to gender policy making. Freeman (1975) criticizes the limitations of the reformist nondiscrimination strategy in challenging male-entrenched privileges, while Gelb and Palley (1996), Boneparth (1982), and Stetson (2004) praise the advantage of a reformist policy that might achieve some results precisely because it is not explicitly threatening male power.

The Research Network on Gender Politics and the State (RNGS) was the first major project that explored comparatively the extent to which women's policy agencies (Stetson and Mazur 1995) in Western postindustrial democracies are successful both in promoting women's representation in policy-making spheres and in bringing women's interests and gender issues into the political agenda (Mazur 2002; Outshoorn 2004; Lovenduski 2005; Haussman and Sauer 2007; McBride and Mazur 2010). These studies center on the agenda-setting and adoption stages of the policy-making process, analyzing the role, position, and scope of women's policy agencies and women's movements. Employing a comparative methodology for a longitudinal analysis of selected policy debates across countries, RNGS studied the interactions between the women's movement and the state. Success is defined in relation to the effectiveness of the women's policy agency in representing women's movement concerns and in advancing their claims in policy debates about for instance abortion, job training, prostitution, political representation, and other issues (Squires 2007). McBride and Mazur's (2010) study shows that women's policy agencies matter to the success of the women's movement, since the more active the agencies are the more likely the state responses reflect the women's movement goals. Although women's policy agencies are not a necessary and sufficient condition for the women's movement to achieve their goals, these insiders in the state can nonetheless be allies for the movement, particularly when contextual conditions are not favorable.

European Union (EU) policy processes offer a good case to observe how and why feminist ideas are incorporated in policy making, since the multitiered dimension of EU governance creates opportunities and constraints at different levels and for a variety of institutional and civil society actors. Van der Vleuten's (2007) pincers' model explains the adoption and implementation of EU gender equality policies in the member-states thank to the action of actors that squeeze unwilling states from below and from within, through the mobilization of domestic feminist and nonfeminist actors, and from above, through the action of supranational institutions such as the European Commission and the European Court of Justice. The model provides analytical tools that enrich the discussion by Ostner and Lewis (1995) on the needles' eyes the EU gender equality policy needs to pass through at the EU and national levels to be adopted and implemented; by Hoskyns (1996), who links success in the implementation of EU gender policy with the EU responsiveness to the demands of the women's movements at the domestic level; or by Zippel (2004, 2009), who looks at the importance of gender equality transnational networks in raising the issue of sexual harassment in the EU.

Similarly, feminist federalism scholars analyze to what extent federal or multilevel systems create windows of opportunity as compared to unitary states by the extent to which they allow for venue shopping (Chappell 2000, 2002a, 2002b; Gray 1998) or, rather, throw up multiple veto points (Vickers 1994; Sawer and Vickers 2001; Haussman, Sawer, and Vickers 2010) and turn women into second-order citizens (Mettler 1998). More recently, this literature focuses on a conditional approach (Vickers 2010), examining more precisely under which conditions federal state architectures and other multilevel settings allow for promoting women's or feminist policies. Beveridge, Nott, and Stephen (2000) showed how government decentralization in Scotland, Wales, and Northern Ireland opened up opportunities for implementing gender mainstreaming; Hudson and Rönnblom (2007) look into the effects of regionalization on the development of gender equality policies (see also the chapter by Bedford in this volume).

Other scholars look at systems more broadly, such as Walby (2009), who has reflected on success factors in gendering policy making by developing a model that pays attention to the complexity and intersectionality of inequality regimes, such as gender, class, and ethnicity within institutional domains such as the economy, polity, violence, and civil society. Change in the systems is caused not only by negative feedback loops but also by positive ones "in a mechanism that drives small changes in a system onwards, escalating change" (85). For example, in line with the previous discussion, Walby argues that the early Swedish success in gendering policy making began when the percentage of women in decision making reached more than 40 percent, as this change destabilized the system and caused the incorporation of women's needs in the political agenda.

Still other scholars look into broader structural and contextual features, such as the role of macrolevel institutional features and more contingent political factors (Zippel 2006; Franceschet 2010; Htun and Weldon 2010), dictatorships and democracies (Htun 2003), processes of democratization (Waylen 2007; Rai 2008; Walby 2009), or legacies of former communist regimes (Saxonberg and Sirovatka 2006). In the EU context, attention is especially paid to consequences of processes of Europeanization (Liebert 2003; Schmidt and Radaelli 2004; Woll and Jacquot 2010; Lombardo and Forest 2012), the enlargement to Central and Eastern European countries (Bretherton 2001; Roth 2008; Krizsan and Popa 2010), and the constitution-making process (León et al. 2003; Lombardo 2005; Millns 2007; Kantola 2010). Others focus on economic parameters and ideological factors (the ideology of the political system and of organized religion) as hindering feminist success (Kaplan 1992), promoting care policies (Morgan and Zippel 2003), or copying policies from other contexts (Gornick and Meyers 2003). They reveal how processes of economic liberalization have led to structural adjustment policies that have provoked cuts in state spending on welfare, health, and education, which have negatively affected women and girls while increasing the care burden for women due to the reduction of state provisions (Elson 1995a; Mahon and Michel 2002; Dobrowolsky 2009; Fraser 2009). Of relevance in this context is also the feminist literature on the role of the welfare state in shaping women's lives and promoting or hammering gender equality (Orloff 1996, 2009) or on citizenship regimes more specifically (Lister 2003; Siim 2000 and in this volume).

THE MALE BIAS OF THE POLICY CONTEXT AND PROCESS

In addition to looking into critical success factors for promoting women's issues, gender equality, and a feminist agenda, feminist policy scholars also pay attention to the male bias present in the policy context and process. Institutions, such as parliaments and governments, are pervaded by a "deeply embedded culture of masculinity" (Lovenduski 2005, 48; Rai 2010). Feminist scholars uncovered androcentric biases hidden in social practices and concepts that were formerly considered *gender-neutral* (Jones and Jonasdottir 1988). They point at the fact that organizational processes and political and bureaucratic practices are gendered and thereby contain a male bias (Savage and Witz 1992). Newman (1995) shows that gender structures administrative practices and operational routines of state agencies by creating different routines depending on whether agencies are male or female dominated. In particular, gender scholars have shown that public policies, law, organizational processes within public administrations, and broader political and economic processes of change, far from being gender neutral, tend to reproduce the male norm masqueraded as "neutral" and to systematically disadvantage women (Rees 1998; Shaw 2000). The androcentrism of policy making suggests that institutions, their processes, and policies are not only based upon but also reinforce male power advantage (Hawkesworth 1994, 105; Inhetveen 1999). Broader processes of policy change, from democratization to economic or institutional reforms, have also been criticized by feminist scholars for their consequences, as has been underlined in the previous section.

Examples of gender-biased public policies and their gendered implications abound. Literature is profuse, especially on the effects of labor market policies, policies reconciling paid work and care work, family policies, and welfare policies more broadly speaking (see also the chapters by Blofield and Haas and Sainsbury in this volume). For example, employment policies have been criticized by gender scholars for their gender bias, as when they place the emphasis on higher employment rates for women but not on the quality of the work available to women (Rubery 2005; Rubery, Smith, and Fagan 1999). Welfare policies that differentiate the type of benefits for employed and nonemployed people, granting pension rights only to the former or penalizing interruptions in the participation in the labor market or part-time schemes, tend to perpetuate a male breadwinner–female caregiver model that increases women's dependence from the male partner and promotes the feminization of poverty (Hawkesworth 1985; Sapiro 1986; Fraser 1989; Orloff 1996; Sainsbury 1996; Orloff, O'Connor, and Shaver 1999; Meyers, Gornick, and Peck 2001; Johnson, Duerst-Lahti, and Norton 2007). Lower-class, often migrant, women, working in the care (frequently informal) economy are especially penalized by welfare policies that tend to protect employed people and that end up perpetuating hierarchical relations not only between men and women but also among women (Ehrenreich and Hochschild 2002). Public child-care and parental leave policies may have adverse effects on the employment patterns of women (Gornick 2006, 2007; Gornick, Meyers, and Ross 1998).

THE CONSTRUCTION OF A GENDER
BIAS IN POLICY MAKING

While the literature discussed so far pays attention to women's interests and needs but sees them as more or less given, more recent discursive literature suggests that such needs and interests are constructed in policy processes. It has thereby been very helpful for studying the content of the policies designed and implemented and for designing more gender balanced policies. This paradigmatic shift can be attributed to Carol Bacchi's (1999, 66) "what's the problem? represented to be approach." In this approach (gender equality) policies assume particular interpretations of what is the problem at stake. Policy proposals have "in-built problem representations," as for instance measures to increase women's representation in managerial positions that emphasize training programs for women create the problem as women's (not men's) lack of training (ibid.). Important in this approach is the focus on gaps and absences in policy discourse by asking "what is left unproblematized," thereby uncovering the norms embedded in particular constructions, which reflect non-neutral taken-for-granted beliefs and hegemonic assumptions. This has contributed to an understanding of how there can be slow progress or even unintended consequences in policies that are designed to foster gender+ equality because there are deeper mechanisms that reproduce male power.

Drawing on Bacchi's (1999) approach, the discursive feminist policy literature has especially developed within European comparative research projects such as Mainstreaming Gender Equality in Europe (MAGEEQ) and Quality in Gender+ Equality Policies (QUING). The development of a specific methodology of critical frame analysis has enabled researchers to make the interpretative and normative content of policy documents more explicit, by identifying the diagnosis of the problem, the solutions proposed, the roles assigned to various actors, the gender and intersectional dimensions of texts, and the norms and mechanisms involved in the construction of a particular policy issue. Research has discussed the framing of a variety of policy issues in Europe (Roggeband and Verloo 2007; Verloo 2007; Lombardo and Verloo 2009; Lombardo and Meier 2009).

This scholarship has contributed to the development of a discursive approach to explore processes of contestation and attribution of meanings to gender equality, during which the concept can be *stretched* to incorporate new meanings (for instance, when gender equality is conceived as intersecting with other inequalities), *shrunk* (into antidiscrimination in a strictly legal sense), or *bent* to other goals than that of gender equality (such as economic growth) to fit into existing policy frames (Lombardo, Meier, and Verloo 2009). Further developments in discursive politics analyses (Ferree et al. 2002; Ferree 2009a, 2009b) have shown that different meanings of gender+ equality policies are rooted in different historical understandings of inequality and have developed frameworks to understand why policies are framed the way they are (Verloo and Walby 2010). Some discursive analyses have also allowed for grasping the shifts in the meaning/content of gender policies through the years, such as EU (Stratigaki 2004; Lewis 2006; Lombardo and Meier 2008; Knijn and Smit 2009) or the Organisation for Economic Co-operation and Development (OECD; Mahon 2009) discourses on reconciliation policies.

Other constructivist approaches to policy making, often from international relations, have focused on processes of norms making, legitimating, and diffusion by looking at the different levels of governance (Elgstrom 2000; True and Mintrom 2001). The increasing EU governance through soft instruments as the open method of coordination in the area of gender+ policy has attracted scholarly attention due to the facilitation of norm diffusion through social learning that it encloses (Beveridge and Velluti 2008).

More recently this literature connects to the literature discussed in the previous section, analyzing how discursive and material opportunities and political dynamics are linked to gender+ equality progress in policy making (Bacchi 2004; Ferree 2009b; Hafner-Burton and Pollack 2000; Krizsan and Popa 2010; Lombardo and Forest 2012; Verloo and Walby 2010).

Mainstreaming Gender into Policy Making

Against the logic of a false gender neutrality of policy making, feminists have devised strategies to mainstream gender equality into policy making. Gender mainstreaming, or the incorporation of a gender perspective into policy making, has generated a variety of "productive tensions in theory and practice," as Walby (2005, 321) argues. It has been conceptualized according to different quality criteria (Lombardo 2005; Lombardo and Meier 2006) and different visions of equality, such as *inclusion* (connected to the strategy of equal treatment), *difference* (linked to positive actions), and *transformation* of existing gender roles and policy practices, that mainstreaming has been especially expected to deliver (Rees 1998; Verloo 2001; Squires 2005; Walby 2005).

Borrowing concepts and tools from development studies, where mainstreaming first emerged, feminist scholars have identified different political approaches. Jahan (1995), in the development studies context, distinguishes between *integrationist* and *agenda-setting* approaches. Integrationist approaches to gender mainstreaming introduce a gender perspective into existing policy paradigms without questioning them (ibid.). This has been associated with more technocratic applications of mainstreaming (Verloo 2005). This expert-bureaucratic model, based on the inclusion of gender experts in policy machineries, has been adopted in a number of European countries, Australia, New Zealand, and Canada (Barnett-Donaghy 2004a; Rees 2005). Agenda-setting approaches imply a transformation and reorientation of existing policy paradigms, by changing decision-making structures and processes, prioritizing gender objectives among competing issues, reorienting the mainstream political agenda, and rethinking and rearticulating policy ends and means from a gender perspective. In this approach "women not only become part of the mainstream, they also reorient the nature of the mainstream" (Jahan 1995, 13). This has been associated with more participatory forms of mainstreaming, as in the case of Northern Ireland (Barnett-Donaghy 2004b).

To reorganize policy processes and mechanisms from a gender perspective, gender experts and practitioners have devised a variety of policy tools, many of which were already in use in development planning. They have designed methods of gender impact assessment (Verloo and Roggeband 1996; Woodward and Meier 1998) to make visible the effect of public policies on gender inequalities, for instance, giving visibility to the gender impact of economic policy that is based on the existence not only of the paid economy, the one usually targeted by economic policy, but also on the unpaid economy of care predominantly performed by women (Himmelweit 2002). Feminist economists have elaborated tools to analyze budgets from a gender perspective (Elson 1997, 1999, 2004; Budlender, Sharp, and Allen 1998). The rising use of gender budgeting (Rubin and Bartle 2005) and experiences as the Women's Budget Initiative in South Africa (Budlender 2000; Budlender et al. 2002), which have brought together feminist activists, academics, NGOs, policy makers, and legislators, reveal the importance of institutional/civil society collaboration to ensure that women's needs are adequately "counted" and "valued" in government budgets (Waring 1988). Another rising practice is the training of civil servants and politicians. Reflections on how to improve such training as part of wider strategies to gender policy making are growing among the community of trainers, consultants, development, and policy experts (Frey et al. 2006; UN INSTRAW community of practice[4]; QUING and TARGET research projects[5]). Within the EU, attention is also paid to the promises and pitfalls of the open method of coordination (O'Connor 2005; Beveridge and Velluti 2008; Hafner-Burton and Pollack 2009).

More recently, there has been attention for the weakening of the support for gender mainstreaming across Europe, at the level of the rhetorical support for this strategy as well as in standstills in the development of accountability measures and sanctions connected to existing promises to deploy the strategy, and a breaking down of institutional arrangements (Smith and Villa 2010). Also, studies showed that the introduction of gender mainstreaming risked the dilution of gender expertise and dismantling of the infrastructures created to support women's policies, based on the mistaken assumption that gender equality is already in the mainstream (Hafner-Burton and Pollack 2000; Mazey 2002). One major feature of gender mainstreaming that has been studied is the slow development of this strategy and its ineffective implementation. Many different reasons are given for this. Competing definitions and multiple meanings of gender mainstreaming coexist, which meant that the way gender mainstreaming could be achieved in practice was far from clear and that it is more difficult to assess what it is that is actually implemented (Rees 1998; Mazey 2000; Verloo 2005). The strategy is also based on voluntaristic efforts rather than binding commitments (Behning and Serrano 2001; Verloo 2005; Walby 2005) so that it becomes "everybody's—and nobody's-—responsibility" (Mazey 2002, 228).

A key weakness of the implementation of gender mainstreaming is the lack of specific bodies or units within governmental departments holding a responsibility for monitoring the application of the mainstreaming initiatives introduced (Beveridge et al. 2000). The consolidation of femocrats and the participation of gender experts in the policy process (Woodward 2003) is key to ensure that policy making is based on "gendered" knowledge (Beveridge and Nott 2002; Squires 2005). The creation of gender units in all governmental departments could favor the implementation and monitoring of mainstreaming initiatives, as is argued for the Spanish case (Bustelo and Ortbals 2007). Elite expertise, however, is not enough for ensuring an effective implementation of gender mainstreaming. A favorable context for a successful implementation of gender mainstreaming seems to require a high level of gender equality awareness among policy makers who are not gender experts (Verloo 2001; Woodward 2003; Walby 2005). Roggeband and Verloo (2006, 629) show that the mainstreaming and gender impact assessment paradox is that the "actors trapped in gender discourses [gender-blind civil servants] are held responsible for transforming these discourses." The voluntary basis of the instrument and the limited resources and power of gender experts and NGOs who support the implementation of gender impact assessment can do little to contrast civil servants' resistance to apply the gender tool.

The organizational characteristics affecting public policy implementation in general promote a more integrationist and expert-bureaucratic type of mainstreaming (McGauran 2009). It seems therefore that gender mainstreaming, too, cannot "escape the genderedness of organizations," as the case of the Human Resources of a Belgian Ministry shows (Benschop and Verloo 2006, 20), due to the fact that power differences between the business and the feminist agendas determine compromises that hinder the transformative potential of mainstreaming. Experiences of mainstreaming gender into different sectors, from agriculture (Pruegl 2009) to development (Subrahmanian 2004), reveal mechanisms of cooptation of feminist goals by policy makers due to power mechanisms (Stratigaki 2005). As Mazey (2000, 343) states, since gendering policy making requires a critical review of policy makers' conceptualization of policy problems, "change will entail questioning of deeply embedded cultural values and policy frames, supported by institutions and powerful advocacy coalitions."

Recent Feminist Approaches to Policy Making

Although gender targets, tools, and data developed as part of the mainstreaming strategy are indeed crucial for the promotion of gender equality (Villagómez 2004), scholars have also denounced the pitfalls of the "gender tools business" for the depoliticization of a feminist project. The governmental use of gender impact assessment, statistical data, benchmarks, targets, and indicators might involve a normalization of the political project of gender equality into a technical and apolitical one where it is assumed that gender equality will be achieved through the compliance of procedures. This toolkit approach might lose the power dimension of the gender struggle (Currie 1999) and leave the prevailing unequal gender relations untouched (Mukhopadhyay 2004). The increasing governmental reliance on technical solutions to the problem of gender inequality is judged as unlikely to transform mainstream political and organizational processes, power hierarchies, and unequal gender relations (Tiessen 2005; Verloo 2005).

A reason suggested for this technicalization of gender is that it is easier for gender advocates to sell and for policy makers to accept a view of gender mainstreaming based on a neutral toolkit rather than on feminist premises, such as the challenging of power hierarchies and a radical questioning of policy processes and actors (Lombardo and Meier 2006). Stratigaki (2005) similarly claims that barriers to gender mainstreaming in the EU are due to the patriarchal opposition to feminist goals implied in the strategy. The diffusion of a technocratic model of gender mainstreaming where bureaucrats, and sometimes experts, are the main actors helps to understand the prevalent spreading of the toolkit model (Verloo 2005). Other approaches focus on the intentionality and rationality inherent in the definition of gender mainstreaming as contributing to a toolkit model (Meier and Celis 2011). This literature on the politicization of the strategy of mainstreaming contributes to an understanding of policy making as essentially political.

A new development in equal treatment policies, which has not been much reflected in gender mainstreaming literature, is the growing attention to multiple discrimination and the legal institutionalization of equal treatment across a wider range of inequality axes, combined with shifts in the institutional architecture of antidiscrimination bodies toward integrated bodies addressing multiple discrimination (Kantola and Nouisiainen 2009; Krizsan, Skeje, and Squires 2012). These developments are studied as part of gender equality policies, establishing them as "gender+" equality policies, which can work toward gender equality only if intersectionality of gender with other axes of inequality is integrated. This is, for instance, the case of studies that criticize policies, as in Sweden, that give access to assisted reproduction to both homosexual and heterosexual couples, but deny this right to single people, be they hetero or homosexuals (Kvist, Carbin, and Harjunen 2009).

Variations on the political process approach are among the most powerful set of theoretical notions, often combining elements of political opportunity structures, mobilizing networks, and framing dynamics, including strategic framing that explain the success or failure of policy making that promotes gender+ equality. The impulse to this has been given by Hafner-Burton and Pollack (2000), who apply a social movement theory approach to analyze the application of gender mainstreaming in five areas of EU policy. They argue that three factors can explain the implementation of gender mainstreaming—political opportunities opened by EU institutions; networks of gender advocates; and the strategic framing of gender mainstreaming (emphasizing gains in terms of efficiency) to make it fit with the dominant frame of a given directorate general (e.g., competition)—to avoid potential resistance from policy makers that are more market oriented and less familiar with gender issues. Other scholars have used such frameworks in studies on the impact of shifts in political opportunities on the strength and nature of gender mainstreaming.

Alliances and forums have been suggested as ways to successfully mainstream gender into policy making. Despite the dangers of co-option of feminist agendas by the state, the collaboration of feminist activists and experts with state actors has been key to further gender equality goals (Subrahmanian 2004; Woodward 2004) but also difficult to implement (Meier 2007). Scholars in politics and development tend to agree that, to repoliticize gender, this collaboration needs to work toward the creation of spaces for the empowerment of the most marginalized so that they can express their voices (Fraser 1989; Mukhopadhyay 2004; Verloo 2005). Scholars show the relevance of velvet triangles of feminist bureaucrats, trusted academics, and the women's movement for implementing gender mainstreaming into policy making (Lycklama à Nijeholt et al. 1988; Woodward 2004). There is also prototheorizing that centers on concepts of social and policy learning, thereby shifting the focus away from political dynamics to socialization or knowledge transfer (Beveridge and Velluti 2008).

CONCLUSION

Policy making is the process of planning, implementing, and evaluating state interventions, that can challenge or reproduce inequalities. Although the borders of feminist policy research are not as neatly defined, there is a lot of research on gender+ and policy making from different fields and approaches. Whether the focus is placed more on the process or the content of policy making, feminists have criticized the androcentric character of policy making, showing that the way policies are made is not gender+ neutral but rather based on the male (heterosexual, white, or other) norm. Androcentric policy making creates gendered categories of privileged and unprivileged people in which women (and other groups) are systematically disadvantaged. If the existence of male biases and norms is, broadly speaking, represented as the main problem with policy making, feminists have suggested different ways for tackling the problem by enhancing gender+ equal processes and policies.

Development planning has been identified as the field where a gender+ analysis of policy making first emerged, criticizing the absence of women in policy making and proposing ways to gender development policies. The study of critical success factors that favor the entry of women's ideas into politics has been undertaken by numerous approaches, exemplified by the RNGS works, that have explored the gendering of policy making at the agenda-setting, adoption, and implementation stages. If the former field has mostly analyzed the process and actors of policy making, discursive politics approaches, exemplified by the MAGEEQ and QUING research, have studied the construction of gender bias in the content of policy making, thus focusing on the "making" of gender+ policies at the design and formulation stages of the process. At the level of policy strategies the challenging of gender+ biases in policy making was more explicitly placed on the agenda through gender mainstreaming. The prescriptive part of the work on gender and policy making on how policies should be done was then particularly developed through works on gender mainstreaming, gender impact assessment, or gender budgeting, thereby borrowing and further developing concepts and tools from development studies.

Recent research on gender and policy making has evolved in several directions, mainly focusing on the implementation of gender mainstreaming, with some works criticizing the pitfalls of a technocratic approach to mainstreaming and suggesting ways to empower women, while other works try to explain the successful or unsuccessful implementation of mainstreaming. While recent research explores the institutionalization of multiple inequalities and political intersectionality, the prominence given in the literature to mainstreaming gender has yet to shift to an analysis of mainstreaming "gender+," thereby joining the efforts of the intersectionality and the mainstreaming literatures in fruitful analyses of policy making. Though, as yet, there have been a few encounters between the intersectionality and the mainstreaming literatures (see for instance Barnett-Donaghy 2004b; Squires 2005), theoretical and empirical analyses of the mainstreaming of intersectionality in policy making deserve more attention.

Moreover, other dimensions of the unequal character of policy making could be further explored. Except for development planning, there are few feminist works addressing policy making in areas that are not explicitly considered as gender-related areas, such as transport or agriculture. Evaluating policy making from a gender perspective requires more attention (Bustelo 2003). More research is also needed to explain why and to what extent there is progress in gender+ equal policy making. Some studies set benchmarks and targets to assess progress in gender-equal policy making or discuss how specific developments in gender+ equality such as women's inclusion in the labor market or in political representation can be considered as signs of progress (Walby 2009). Other scholars (Ferree 2009b) have shown how assessing progress in gender+ equality policies is context related and dependent on the specific institutional and discursive opportunities structure so that what appears as quality policy making in Europe for instance does not necessarily apply to the U.S. context. In other studies (Rai 2008; Fraser 2009) the focus is placed on how processes such as neoliberalism and globalization not only can have negative implications on gender+ equal policy making but also are complexly intertwined with them.

Yet more reflexive and empirical works on the quality criteria to assess progress in policy making from a gender+ perspective would help to identify what are the chances for success of policy strategies that aim at furthering gender+ equal policy making.

The analysis of the different scholarly strands that focus more on the process or on the content of gender+ equality policies has also shown that connections between both approaches could be strengthened to the benefit of a more complex and complete understanding of gender+ and policy making. In theoretical and methodological terms this means that there is room for studies that will adopt new discursive institutionalist and sociological approaches (Schmidt 2010) for studying the discursive, institutional, and actors' dynamics of policy making in gender+ equality.

In terms of the work on intersectional policy making, more empirical research is needed on the privileged gender+ groups (e.g., middle-class, heterosexuals, white men and women). That is, while gender+ theorizing has highlighted power inequalities that policy making creates, reproduces, or challenges and has pointed at the existence of privileged subjects that are set as the norm, there is a need for empirical works that target such intersecting privileged groups and their role in policy-making processes.

Finally, the gendered character of policy making has been studied without a substantial challenge to the use of fixed gender categories so that, for instance, transgender issues become part of the gender+ literature and political agenda rather than part of the sexuality literature and agenda. Thus, one area for future research would be to study the degree to which policy making is gender+ equal and constructs gender+ categories of women and men that exclude issues of gender identities and expression. Scholars on gender+ equality and policy making will need to dedicate more effort to exploring how to challenge and go beyond the use of the categories of men and women.

NOTES

1. The concept of *gender+* equality refers to gender as always intersected by other axes of inequality.
2. An exception is Orloff and Monson (2002) on men in the history of U.S. social policy.
3. See, for instance, Kenney (2003) on the absence of gender (research) in mainstream agenda setting scholarship or Rixecker (1994) on its absence in policy design studies. This absence is also reflected in the lack of any allusion to such research or gender tout court in most public policy handbooks (an exception being Parsons 1995).
4. See http://www.un-instraw.org/gtcop/index.php?lang=en
5. See Madrid Declaration on Advancing Gender+ Training at http://www.quing.eu/files/madrid_declaration.pdf

References

Agarwal, Bina. 1981. *Water resources development and rural women.* New Delhi: Ford Foundation.

Bacchi, Carol. 1999. *Women, politics and policies: The construction of policy problems.* London: SAGE.

Bacchi, Carol. 2004. "Policy and discourse: challenging the construction of affirmative action as preferential treatment." *Journal of European Public Policy* 11(1): 128–146.

Barnett-Donaghy, Tahnya. 2004a. "Applications of mainstreaming in Australia and Northern Ireland." *International Political Science Review* 25(4): 393–410.

Barnett-Donaghy, Tahnya. 2004b. "Mainstreaming: Northern Ireland's participative-democratic approach." *Policy and Politics* 32(1): 49–62.

Behning, Ute, and Amparo Serrano. 2001. *Gender mainstreaming in the European employment strategy.* Brussels: ETUI.

Benería, Lourdes (Ed.). 1982. *Women and rural development.* New York: Praeger.

Benería, Lourdes. 2003. *Gender, development and globalization: Economics as if all people mattered.* New York: Routledge.

Benería, Lourdes, and Martha Roldán. 1987. *The crossroads of class and gender: Industrial homework, subcontracting, and household dynamics in Mexico City.* Chicago: University of Chicago Press.

Benschop, Yvonne, and Mieke Verloo. 2006. "Sisyphus' sisters: Can gender mainstreaming escape the genderedness of organizations?" *Journal of Gender Studies* 15(1): 19–33.

Beveridge, Fiona, and Sue Nott. 2002. "Mainstreaming: A case for optimism and cynicism. *Feminist Legal Studies* 10(3–4): 299–311.

Beveridge, Fiona, Sue Nott, and Kylie Stephen. 2000. "Mainstreaming and engendering of policy-making: A means to an end?" *Journal of European Public Policy* 7(3): 385–405.

Beveridge, Fiona, and Samantha Velluti (Eds.). 2008. *Gender and the open method of coordination: Perspectives on law, governance and equality in the EU.* Aldershot: Ashgate.

Boneparth, Ellen (Ed.). 1982. *Women, power and policy.* New York: Pergamon.

Boserup, Ester. 1970. *Woman's role in economic development.* London: Allen and Unwin.

Boserup, Ester. 2007. *Woman's role in economic development.* Intro. Nazneen Kanji, Su Fei Tan, and Camilla Toulmin. London: Earthscan.

Bretherton, Charlotte. 2001. "Gender mainstreaming and EU enlargement: swimming against the tide?" *Journal of European Public Policy* 8(1): 60–81.

Budlender, Debbie. 2000. "The political economy of women's budgets in the South." *World Development* 28(7): 1365–1378.

Budlender, Debbie, Diane Elson, Guy Hewitt, and Tanni Mukhopadhyay. 2002. *Gender Budgets make cents: Understanding gender responsive budgets.* London: Commonwealth Secretariat.

Budlender, Debbie, Rhonda Sharp, and Kerry Allen. 1998. *How to do a gender-sensitive budget analysis: Contemporary research and practice.* London: Australian Agency for International Development and Commonwealth Secretariat.

Bustelo, Maria. 2003. "Evaluation of gender mainstreaming: Ideas from a metaevaluation study." *Evaluation* 9(4): 383–403.

Bustelo, María, and Candice Ortbals. 2007. "The evolution of Spanish state feminism: A fragmented landscape." In Joyce Outshoorn and Johanna Kantola, eds., *Changing state feminism*. Basingstoke, UK: Palgrave, 201–223.

Buvinic, Mayra, Margaret A. Lycette, and William Paul McGreevey (Eds.). 1983. *Women and poverty in the third world*. Baltimore: John Hopkins University Press.

Chappell, Louise. 2000. "Interacting with the state: feminist strategies and political opportunities." *International Feminist Journal of Politics* 2(2): 244–275.

Chappell, Louise. 2002a. *Gendering government: Feminist engagement with the state in Australia and Canada*. Vancouver: University of British Columbia Press.

Chappell, Louise. 2002b. The femocrat strategy: Expanding the repertoire of feminist activists. *Parliamentary Affairs* 55(1): 85–98.

Currie, Dawn H. 1999. "Gender analysis from the standpoint of women: The radical potential of women's studies in development." *Asian Journal of Women's Studies* 5(3): 9–44.

Dobrowolsky, Alexandra. 2009. *Neoliberalism and after? Women and public policy in Canada: Continuity and change*. Oxford: Oxford University Press.

Dwyer, Daisy, and Judith Bruce (Eds.). 1988. *A home divided: Women and income in the third world*. Stanford, CA: Stanford University Press.

Ehrenreich, Barbara, and Arlie Russel Hochschild (Eds.). 2002. *Global woman: Nannies, maids and sex workers in the new economy*. London: Granta books.

Elgstrom, Ole. 2000. "Norm negotiations: The construction of new norms regarding gender and development in EU foreign aid policy." *Journal of European Public Policy* 7(3): 457–476.

Elson, Diane. 1995a. "Gender awareness in modeling structural adjustment. *World Development* 23(11): 1851–1868.

Elson, Diane (Ed.). 1995b. *Male bias in the development process*. Manchester: Manchester University Press.

Elson, Diane. 1997. *Gender-neutral, gender-blind, or gender-sensitive budget?: Changing the conceptual framework to include women's empowerment and the economy of care*. London: Commonwealth Secretariat.

Elson, Diane. 1999. *Gender budget initiative*. London: Commonwealth Secretariat.

Elson, Diane. 2004. "Engendering government budgets in the context of globalization(s)." *International Feminist Journal of Politics* 6(4): 623–642.

Ferree, Myra Marx. 2009a. "An American roadmap to equality? Framing feminist goals in a liberal landscape." In Janet Gornick and Marcia Meyers, eds., *Gender equality: Transforming family divisions*. New York: Polity Press, 283–315.

Ferree, Myra Marx. 2009b. "Inequality, intersectionality and the politics of discourse. Framing feminist alliances." In Emanuela Lombardo, Petra Meier, and Mieke Verloo, eds., *The discursive politics of gender equality: Stretching, bending and policy-making*. London: Routledge, 86–104.

Ferree, Myra Marx, William Gamson, Jürgen Gerhards, and Dieter Rucht. 2002. *Shaping abortion discourse: Democracy and the public sphere in Germany and the United States*. Cambridge, UK: Cambridge University Press.

Franceschet, Susan. 2010. "Explaining domestic violence policy outcomes in Chile and Argentina." *Latin American Politics and Society* 52(3): 1–29.

Fraser, Nancy. 1989. *Unruly practices: power, discourse and gender in contemporary social theory*. Cambridge, UK: Polity Press.

Fraser, Nancy. 2009. "Feminism, capitalism and the cunning of history." *New Left Review* 56: 97–117.

Freeman, Jo. 1975. *Women: A feminist perspective.* Palo Alto, CA: Mayfield Publishing.

Frey, Regina, Jutta Hartmann, Andreas Heilmann, Thomas Kugler, Stephanie Nordt, and Sandra Smykalla. 2006. *Gender manifesto: A call for critical reflection on Gender-oriented capacity building and consultancy.* Available at http://www. gender.de/mainstreaming/GenderManifesto_engl.pdf.

Gelb, Joyce, and Marian Lief Palley. 1996. *Women and public policies: Reassessing gender politics.* Charlottesville: University of Virginia Press.

Goetz, Anne Marie (Ed.). 1997. *Getting institutions right for women in development.* London: Zed.

Gornick, Janet C. (Ed.). 2006. "Special issue on work–family reconciliation policies: Theory and practice." *Journal of Comparative Policy Analysis: Research and Practice* 8(2): 99–205.

Gornick, Janet C. (Ed.). 2007. "Special issue on does policy matter? The impact of work-family reconciliation policies on workers and their families." *Journal of Comparative Policy Analysis: Research and Practice* 9(2): 111–214.

Gornick, Janet C., and Marcia K. Meyers. 2003. *Families that work: Policies for reconciling parenthood and employment.* New York: Russell Sage Foundation.

Gornick, Janet C., Marcia K. Meyers, and Katherin E. Ross. 1998. "Public policies and the employment of mothers: A cross-national study." *Social Science Quarterly* 79(1): 35–54.

Gray, Gwen. 1998. "Access to Medicare under strain: New pressures in Canada and Australia." *Journal of Health Politics, Policy and Law* 23(6): 905–947.

Hafner-Burton, Emilie, and Mark Pollack. 2000. "Mainstreaming gender in the European Union." *Journal of European Public Policy* 7(3): 432–456.

Hafner-Burton, Emilie, and Mark Pollack. 2009. "Mainstreaming gender in the European Union: Getting the incentives right." *Comparative European Politics* 7(1): 114–138.

Haussman, Melissa, and Birgit Sauer (Eds.). 2007. *Gendering the state in the age of globalization.* Lanham, MD: Rowman & Littlefield.

Haussman, Melissa, Marian Sawer, and Jill Vickers (Eds.). 2010. *Federalism, feminism and multilevel governance.* Aldershot, UK: Ashgate.

Hawkesworth, Mary. 1985. "Workfare and the imposition of discipline." *Social Theory and Practice* 11(2)" 163–181.

Hawkesworth, Mary. 1994. "Policy studies within a feminist frame." *Policy Sciences* 27(2–3): 97–118.

Himmelweit, Susan. 2002. "Making visible the hidden economy: The case for gender-impact analysis of economic policy." *Feminist Economics* 8(1): 49–70.

Hoskyns, Catherine. 1996. *Integrating gender: Women, law and politics in the European Union.* London: Verso.

Hudson, Christine, and Malin Rönnblom. 2007. "Regional development policies and the constructions of gender equality—The Swedish case." *European Journal of Political Research* 46(1): 47–68.

Htun, Mala. 2003. *Sex and the state: Abortion, divorce and the family under Latin American dictatorships and democracies.* New York: Cambridge University Press.

Htun, Mala, and Laurel Weldon. 2010. "When do governments promote women's rights? A framework for the comparative analysis of sex equality policies." *Perspectives on Politics* 8(1): 207–216.

Inhetveen, Katharina. 1999. "Can gender equality be institutionalized? The role of launching values in institutional innovation." *International Sociology* 14(4): 403–422.

Jahan, Rounaq. 1995. *The elusive agenda: Mainstreaming women in development.* London: Zed Books.

Jain, Devaki. 1983. *Development as if women mattered or can women build a new paradigm?* New Dehli: Institute of Social Studies Trust.

Jaquette, Jane, and Gale Summerfield (Eds.). 2006. *Women and gender equity in development theory and practice.* Durham, NC: Duke University Press.

Johnson, Cathy Marie, Georgia Duerst-Lahti, and Noelle H. Norton. 2007. *Creating gender: The sexual politics of welfare policy.* Boulder: Lynne Rienner Publishers.

Jones, Kathleen B., and Anna Jonasdottir (Eds.). 1988. *The political interests of gender: Developing theory and research with a feminist face.* London: SAGE.

Kabeer, Naila. 1994. *Reversed realities: Gender hierarchies in development thought.* London: Verso.

Kantola, Johanna. 2010. *Gender and the European Union.* Basingstoke, UK: Palgrave.

Kantola, Johanna, and Kevät Nousiainen (Eds.). 2009. "Special issue on institutionalizing intersectionality in Europe." *International Feminist Journal of Politics* 11(4): 459–609.

Kaplan, Gisela. 1992. *Contemporary Western European feminism.* New York: New York University Press.

Kenney, Sally. 2003. "Where is gender in agenda setting?" *Women & Politics* 25(1–2): 179–207.

Knijn, Trudie, and Arnoud Smit. 2009. "Investing, facilitating, or individualizing the reconciliation of work and family life: Three paradigms and ambivalent policies." *Social Politics* 16(4): 484–518.

Krizsan, Andrea, and Raluca Popa. 2010. "Europeanization in making policies against domestic violence in Central and Eastern Europe." *Social Politics* 17(3): 379–406.

Krizsan, Andrea, Hege Skeje, and Judith Squires (Eds.). 2012. *Institutionalizing intersectionality.* Basingstoke, UK: Palgrave.

Kvist, Elin, Maria Carbin, and Hannele Harjunen. 2009. "Domestic services or maid? Discourses on gender equality, work and integration in Nordic policy debate." Vienna: QUING Project. Available at http://www.quing.eu/files/WHY/kvist_carbin_harjunen.pdf.

León, Margarita, Mercedes Mateo Diaz, and Susan Millns. 2003. "Engendering the Convention: Women and the future of the European Union." Available at http://www.eui.eu/RSCAS/WP-Texts/03_01p.pdf.

Lewis, Jane. 2006. "Work/family reconciliation, equal opportunities and social policies: The interpretation of policy trajectories at the EU level and the meaning of gender equality." *Journal of European Public Policy* 13(3): 420–437.

Liebert, Ulrike (Ed.). 2003. *Gendering Europeanization.* Brussels: Peter Lang.

Lister, Ruth. 2003. *Citizenship: feminist perspectives.* New York: New York University Press.

Lombardo, Emanuela. 2005. "Integrating or setting the agenda? Gender mainstreaming in the European constitution-making process." *Social Politics* 12(3): 412–432.

Lombardo, Emanuela, and Maxime Forest. 2012. *The Europeanization of gender equality policies: A discursive-sociological approach.* Basingstoke, UK: Palgrave.

Lombardo, Emanuela, and Mieke Verloo. 2009. "Stretching gender equality to other inequalities: Political intersectionality in European gender equality policies." In Emanuela Lombardo, Petra Meier, and Mieke Verloo, eds., *The discursive politics of gender equality: Stretching, bending and policy-making.* London: Routledge, 68–85.

Lombardo, Emanuela, and Petra Meier. 2006. "Gender mainstreaming in the EU: Incorporating a feminist reading?" *European Journal of Women's Studies* 13(2): 151–166.

Lombardo, Emanuela, and Petra Meier. 2008. "Framing gender equality in the European Union discourse." *Social Politics* 15(1): 101–129.

Lombardo, Emanuela, and Petra Meier. 2009. "Stretching, bending and inconsistency in policy frames on gender equality: Discursive windows of opportunity?" In Emanuela Lombardo, Petra Meier, and Mieke Verloo, eds., *The discursive politics of gender equality: Stretching, bending and policy-making.* London: Routledge, 138–152.

Lombardo, Emanuela, Petra Meier, and Mieke Verloo (Eds.). 2009. *The discursive politics of gender equality: Stretching, bending and policy-making.* London: Routledge.

Lycklama à Nijeholt, Geertje. 1987. "The fallacy of integration: the UN strategy of integrating women into development revisited." *Netherlands Review of Development Studies* 1(1): 23–37.

Lycklama à Nijeholt, Geertje, Virginia Vargas, and Saskia Wieringa (Eds.). 1988. *Women's movements and public policy in Europe, Latin America and the Caribbean.* New York: Garland.

Lovenduski, Joni (Ed.). 2005. *State feminism and political representation.* Cambridge, UK: Cambridge University Press.

Mahon, Rianne. 2009. "The OECD's discourse on the reconciliation of work and family life." *Global Social Policy* 9(2): 183–204.

Mahon, Rianne, and Sonya Michel (Eds.). 2002. *Child care policy at the crossroads: Gender and welfare state restructurings.* New York: Routledge.

Mazey, Sonia (Ed.). 2000. "Introduction: Integrating gender." Intellectual and 'real world' mainstreaming." *Journal of European Public Policy* 7(3): 333–345.

Mazey, Sonia. 2002. "Gender mainstreaming in the EU: Delivering on an agenda?" *Feminist Legal Studies* 10(3–4): 227–240.

Mazur, Amy. 2002. *Theorizing feminist policy.* Oxford: Oxford University Press.

Mazur, Amy, and Mark Pollack. 2009. "Gender and public policy in Europe: An introduction." *Comparative European Politics* 7(1): 1–11.

McBride, Dorothy, and Amy Mazur, (Eds.). 2010. *The politics of state feminism: Innovation in comparative research.* Philadelphia: Temple University Press.

McGauran, Anne-Marie. 2009. "Gender mainstreaming and the public policy implementation process: Round pegs in square holes?" *Policy and Politics* 37(2): 215–233.

Meier, Petra. 2007. "Involving private actors in policy-making: Reflections on gender mainstreaming and governance." In Kris Deschouwer and Theo Jans, eds., *Politics beyond the state." Actors and policies in complex institutional settings.* Brussels: VUB press, 217–234.

Meier, Petra, and Karen Celis. 2011. "Sowing the seeds of its own failure. Implementing the concept of gender mainstreaming." *Social Politics* 18(4): 469–489.

Mettler, Suzanne. 1998. *Dividing citizens: Gender and federalism in new deal public policy.* Ithaca, NY: Cornell University Press.

Meyers, Marcia K., Janet C. Gornick, and Laura R. Peck. 2001. "Packaging support for low income families: Policy variation across the U.S. states. *Journal of Policy Analysis and Management* 20(3): 457–486.

Miller, Carol, and Shahra Razavi (Eds.). 1998. *Missionaries and Mandarins: Feminist engagement with development institutions.* London: Intermediate Technologies, with UNRISD.

Millns, Susan. 2007. "Gender equality, citizenship and the EU's constitutional future." *European Law Journal* 13(2): 218–237.

Molyneux, Maxine. 1985. "Mobilisation without emancipation: Women's interests, state and revolution in Nicaragua." *Feminist Studies* 11(2): 227–254.

Molyneux, Maxine, and Shahra Razavi. 2003. *Gender justice, development and rights.* Oxford: Oxford University Press.

Morgan, Kimberly J., and Kathrin Zippel. 2003. "Paid to care: The origins and effects of care leave policies in Western Europe." *Social Politics* 10(1): 49–85.

Moser, Caroline. 1993. *Gender planning and development: Theory, practice and training.* New York: Routledge.

Mukhopadhyay, Maitrayee. 2004. "Mainstreaming gender or 'streaming' gender away: Feminists marooned in the development business." *Institute of Development Studies* 35(4): 95–103.

Newman, Meredith Ann. 1995. "The gendered nature of Lowi's typology: Or who would guess you could find gender here?" In Georgia Duerst-Lahti and Rita Mae Kelly, eds., *Gender, power, leadership, and governance.* Ann Arbor: University of Michigan Press, 141–164.

O'Connor, Julia S. 2005. "Employment-anchored social policy, gender equality and the open method of policy coordination in the European Union." *European Societies* 7(1): 27–52.

Orloff, Ann. 1996. "Gender in the welfare state." *Annual Review of Sociology* 22: 1–28.

Orloff, Ann. 2009. "Gendering the comparative analysis of welfare states: An unfinished agenda." *Sociological Theory* 27(4): 317–343.

Orloff, Ann, and Renée Monson. 2002. "Citizens, workers or fathers? Men in the history of U.S. social policy." In Barbara Hobson, ed., *Making men into fathers.* New York: Cambridge University Press, 61–91.

Orloff, Ann, Julia O'Connor, and Sheila Shaver. 1999. *States, markets, families: Gender, liberalism and social policy in Australia, Canada, Great Britain and the United States.* New York: Cambridge University Press.

Orloff, Ann, and Bruno Palier. 2009. "The power of gender perspectives: Feminist influence on policy paradigms, social science, and social politics." *Social Politics* 16(4): 405–412.

Ostner, Ilona, and Jane Lewis. 1995. "Gender and the evolution of European social policies." In Stephan Leibfried and Paul Pierson, eds., *European social policy: Between fragmentation and integration.* Washington, DC: Brookings Institution, 159–193.

Outshoorn, Joyce (Ed.). 2004. *The politics of prostitution.* Cambridge, UK: Cambridge University Press.

Outshoorn, Joyce, and Johanna Kantola (Eds.). 2007. *Changing state feminism.* Basingstoke, UK: Palgrave.

Overholt, Catherine, Mary B. Anderson, Kathleen Cloud, and James E. Austin. 1985. *Gender roles in development projects: A case book.* West Hartford, CT: Kumarian Press.

Parsons. Wayne. 1995. *Public policy: An introduction to theory and practice to policy analysis.* Cheltenham, UK: Edward Elgar.

Pruegl, Elisabeth. 2009. "Does gender mainstreaming work? Feminist engagements with the German agricultural state." *International Feminist Journal of Politics* 11(2): 174–195.

Rai, Shirin. 2008. *The gender politics of development: Essays in hope and despair.* London: Zed books.

Rai, Shirin (Ed.). 2010. "Special issue on ceremony and ritual in parliament." *Journal of Legislative Studies* 16(3): 201–409.

Rao, Aruna, Mary B. Anderson, and Catherine A. Overholt. 1991. *Gender analysis in development planning: A case book.* West Hartfort, CT: Kumarian Press.

Rees, Teresa. 2005. "Reflections on the uneven development of gender mainstreaming in Europe." *International Feminist Journal of Politics* 7(4): 555–574.

Rees, Teresa. 1998. *Mainstreaming equality in the European Union: Education, training and Labour Market policies.* London: Routledge.

Rixecker, Stefanie. 1994. "Expanding the discursive context of policy design: A matter of feminist standpoint epistemology." *Policy Sciences* 27(2–3): 119–142.

Roggeband, Conny, and Mieke Verloo. 2006. "Evaluating gender impact assessment in the Netherlands (1994–2004): A political process approach." *Policy and Politics* 34(4): 615–632.

Roggeband, Conny, and Mieke Verloo. 2007. "Dutch women are liberated, migrant women are a problem." *Social Policy and Administration* 41(3): 271–288.

Roth, Silke (Ed.). 2008. *Gender politics in the expanding European Union. Mobilization, inclusion, exclusion.* New York: Berghahn Books.

Rubery, Jill. 2005. "Reflections on gender mainstreaming: An example of feminist economics in action?" *Feminist Economics* 11(3): 1–26.

Rubery, Jill, Mark Smith, and Colette Fagan. 1999. *Women's employment in Europe. Trends and prospects.* London: Routledge.

Rubin, Marilyn, and John Bartle. 2005. "Integrating gender into government budgets: A new perspective." *Public Administration Review* 65(3): 259–272.

Sainsbury, Diane. 1996. *Gender, equality and welfare states.* Cambridge, UK: Cambridge University Press.

Sapiro, Virginia. 1986. "The gender basis of American social policy." *Political Science Quarterly* 101(2): 221–238.

Savage, Michael, and Anne Witz. 1992. *Gender and bureaucracy.* Oxford: Blackwell.

Sawer, Marian, and Jill Vickers. 2001. "Women's constitutional activism in Australia and Canada." *Canadian Journal of Women and the Law* 13(1): 1–36.

Saxonberg, Steven, and Tomas Sirovatka. 2006. "Failing family policy in post-communist Central Europe." *Journal of Comparative Policy Analysis: Research and Practice* 8(2): 185–202.

Schmidt, Vivien. 2010. "Taking ideas and discourse seriously: Explaining change through discursive institutionalism as the fourth 'new institutionalism.'" *European Political Science Review* 2(1): 1–25.

Schmidt, Vivien, and Claudio Radaelli. 2004. "Policy change and discourse in Europe: Conceptual and methodological issues." *West European Politics* 27(2): 183–210.

Sen, Gita, and Caren Grown. 1988. *Development, crises and alternative visions: Third world women's perspectives.* London: Earthscan.

Shaw, Jo. 2000. "Importing gender: The challenge of feminism and the analysis of the EU legal order." *Journal of European Public Policy* 7(3): 406–431.

Shiva, Vandana. 1989. *Staying alive: Women, ecology and development.* London: Zed Books.

Siim, Birte. 2000. *Gender and citizenship. Politics and agency in France, Britain and Denmark.* Cambridge, UK: Cambridge University Press.'

Smith, Mark, and Paola Villa. 2010. "The ever-declining role of gender equality in the European Employment Strategy." *Industrial Relations Journal* 41(6): 526–543.

Squires, Judith. 2005. "Is mainstreaming transformative? Theorising mainstreaming in the context of diversity and deliberation." *Social Politics* 12(3): 366–388.

Squires, Judith. 2007. *The new politics of gender equality.* Basingstoke, UK: Palgrave.

Stetson, Dorothy McBride. 2004. *Women's rights in the U.S.A.: Policy conflict and gender roles,* 3d ed. New York: Garland/Routledge.

Stetson, Dorothy McBride, and Amy Mazur. 1995. *Comparative state feminism.* Thousand Oaks, CA: SAGE.

Stratigaki, Maria. 2004. "The cooptation of gender concepts in EU policies: The case of 'reconciliation of work and family.'" *Social Politics* 11(1): 30–56.

Stratigaki, Maria. 2005. "Gender mainstreaming vs positive action: An on-going conflict in EU gender equality policy." *European Journal of Women's Studies* 12(2): 165–186.

Staudt, Kathleen. 1990. *Managing development: State, society, and international contexts.* Newbury Park, CA: SAGE.

Subrahmanian, Ramya. 2004. "Making sense of gender in shifting institutional contexts: Some reflections on gender mainstreaming." *Institute of Development Studies* 35(4): 89–94.

Tiessen, Rebecca. 2005. "What's new about gender mainstreaming? Three decades of policy creation and development strategies." *Canadian Journal of Development Studies* 26: 705–720.

Tinker, Irene (Ed.). 1990. *Persistent inequalities: Women and world development.* New York: Oxford University Press.

Tinker, Irene, and Michele Bo Bramsen. 1976. *Women and world development.* Washington, DC: Overseas Development Council.

True, Jacqui, and Michael Mintrom. 2001. "Transnational networks and policy diffusion: The case of gender mainstreaming." *International Studies Quarterly* 43(1): 27–57.

Van der Vleuten, Anna. 2007. *The price of gender equality: Member states and governance in the European Union.* Aldershot, UK: Ashgate.

Verloo, Mieke. 2001. "Another velvet revolution? Gender mainstreaming and the politics of implementation." IWM Working Paper 5/2001, IWM, Vienna.

Verloo, Mieke. 2005. "Reflections on the concept and practice of the Council of Europe approach to gender mainstreaming." *Social Politics* 12(3): 344–365.

Verloo, Mieke (Ed.). 2007. *Multiple meanings of gender equality: A critical frame analysis of gender policies in Europe.* Budapest: CPS Books.

Verloo, Mieke, and Conny Roggeband. 1996. "Gender impact assessment: the development of a new instrument in the Netherlands." *Impact Assessment* 14(1): 3–21.

Verloo, Mieke, and Sylvia Walby. 2010. "Deliverable No. 71: Final WHY Report." Vienna: QUING Project. Available at http://www.quing.eu/files/deliverables/D71.pdf.

Vickers, Jill. 1994. "Why should women care about federalism?" In Douglas M. Brown and Janet Hiebert, eds., *Canada: The state of the federation.* Kingston: Institute of Intergovernmental Relations, Queen's University, 135–151.

Vickers, Jill. 2010. "A two-way street: Federalism and women's politics in Canada and the United States." *Publius: The Journal of Federalism* 40(3): 412–435.

Villagómez, Elisabeth. 2004. "Gender responsive budgets: issues, good pratices and policy options." Paper presented at the regional symposium on mainstreaming gender into economic policies, Geneva, UN Economic Commission for Europe, January 28–30.

Walby, Sylvia. 2005. "Gender mainstreaming: Productive tensions in theory and practice." *Social Politics* 12(3): 321–343.

Walby, Sylvia. 2009. *Globalization and inequalities: Complexity and contested modernities*. London: SAGE.

Waring, Marilyn. 1988. *If women counted*. New York: Harper and Row.

Waylen, Georgina. 2007. *Engendering transitions: Women's mobilization, institutions and gender outcomes*. Oxford: Oxford University Press.

Woll, Cornelia, and Sophie Jacquot. 2010. "Using Europe: Strategic action in multi-level politics." *Comparative European Politics* 8(1): 110–126.

Woodward, Alison. 2003. "European gender mainstreaming: Promises and pitfalls of transformative policy making." *Review of Policy Research* 20(1): 65–88.

Woodward, Alison. 2004. "Building velvet triangles: Gender and informal governance." In Thomas Christiansen and Simona Piattoni, eds., *Informal governance in the European Union*. Cheltenham, UK: Edward Elgar, 76–93.

Woodward, Alison, and Petra Meier. 1998. "Gender impact assessment: A new approach to changing policies and contents of citizenship?" In Virginia Ferreira, Teresa Tavares, and Sílvia Portugal, eds., *Shifting bonds, shifting bounds: Women, mobility and citizenship in Europe*. Oeiras: Celta Editora, 95–105.

Zippel, Kathrin. 2004. "Transnational advocacy networks and policy cycles in the European Union: The case of sexual harassment." *Social Politics* 11(1): 57–85.

Zippel, Kathrin. 2006. *The politics of sexual harassment: A comparative study of the United States, the European Union and Germany*. Cambridge, UK: Cambridge University Press.

Zippel, Kathrin. 2009. "The European Union 2002 Directive on Sexual Harassment: A feminist success?" *Comparative European Politics* 7(1): 139–157.

CHAPTER 28

....

POLICY OUTPUTS

....

MERIKE BLOFIELD AND
LIESL HAAS

DESPITE the efforts of feminist movements, progressive political parties, and even government agencies devoted to women's rights, gender inequality remains entrenched in the socioeconomic structures that govern women's lives. From the struggle to balance work and family, to control their sexuality and reproductive lives, and to live free from gender-based violence, women across the globe face a host of obstacles to full equality.

Under the best of circumstances, the culmination of forces that influence policy making in democratic societies, from social movement mobilization to effective negotiations within the state, can result in the creation of public policies that address gender equality. The preceding chapter focused on causal factors; in this chapter, we focus on policy outputs on gender equality. What should such policies on gender equality look like? What do they look like in practice? Debates about the shape and purpose of policies on gender equality take place not only between feminists and their opposition but also among feminists themselves, as they struggle to design and implement policies that will impact the myriad forms of gender inequality that exist in daily life. These debates are fundamental: What is, and where do we see gender inequality? Which policies promote or reduce gender equality in its various manifestations? And how can policies be designed and implemented in ways that address gender inequalities most effectively? We address these questions through an overview of the literature that attempts to categorize these policies and an overview of the different stages of the policy process, broadly defined as policy outputs. We do so by drawing on illustrative examples from three broad issue areas, identified by feminists as areas where inequalities between women and men are particularly embedded: women's reproductive capacities; the work–family nexus; and violence against women, or, gender-based violence.[1]

The existence of gender inequality is a global phenomenon, but it manifests with tremendous variation across countries and on different issues. Before public policies can be created to address gender inequality, we must first identify and measure its prevalence and degree. We begin this chapter with an overview of the most significant existing indices that cross-nationally measure gender inequality in society.

Even when there is agreement about the existence of a particular form of gender inequality, disagreements inevitably arise over the appropriateness and feasibility of possible policy solutions. This is the case, in part, because gender inequality is a complex issue that potentially impacts any area of life. But beliefs about gender equality are also rooted in larger cultural, economic, and ideological debates about women's roles in society. In this sense it is important to recognize that debates about gender are never "just" about gender. When we attempt to understand and evaluate public policies in this area, we must recognize the ways that these policies touch on other issues that are politically contested in a particular society. Policies to address gender inequality therefore do so through a particular socioeconomic and political lens. We discuss the efforts of scholars to make visible these larger dynamics, and we analyze the major typologies that have been developed to categorize policies on gender equality. Finally, policy outputs encompass a dynamic process consisting of several distinct, but interrelated, stages. We focus here on policy outputs in their broadest sense, covering issue framing, policy adoption, implementation, and policy outcomes. We examine the variation that exists in policy outputs in each of these stages. The geographical scope of this chapter includes advanced industrialized countries and Latin America.

MEASURING GENDER EQUALITY

How do we conceptualize gender inequality in practice, and how can we measure it? A good place to start when evaluating gender equality is with outcome measures of women's status vis-à-vis men and the gender gap in practice. These gaps need to, of course, be contextualized within the dramatic global socioeconomic differences. For example, women in a poor country may have a low standard of living relative to women elsewhere but be relatively equal (for example, in literacy rates or health) with the men in their society. On the other hand, gender inequality may be higher in a given rich country despite women in that country being better off in an absolute sense than women elsewhere.

In an attempt to evaluate gender equality more systematically across states and regions, international organizations have developed a number of different indices that attempt to measure the socioeconomic gender gap on a wide variety of factors cross-regionally. Well-known indices are the World Economic Forum Gender Gap, and the United Nations (UN) Gender-Related Development Index (GDI) and the Gender Empowerment Measure (GEM), included in the annual UN Human Development Reports until 2009, and since 2010, the Gender Inequality Index (GII). The Organisation for Economic Co-operation and Development's (OECD's) Gender, Institutions and Development Database (GID-DB 2009; http://www.oecd.org/document/16/0,3343,en_2649_33935_39323280_ 1_1_1_1,00.html) includes 160 countries and sixty indicators mostly on outcome measures on women's status in different social and economic areas, although some indicators combine legal rights with actual outcomes. The United Nations and World Bank collect sociodemographic and economic data, and Social Watch has produced a gender equity index that includes cross-national data on economic activity, empowerment, and education.[2] Numerous indicators have been developed within regions.[3] These indices develop a set of measurements to compare the gender gap in health, education, employment/income, and, in some cases, political participation, factors they identify as critical to gender equality. However, for many issues we lack data and what we have often has serious validity and reliability concerns, and for this reason these indices should be used with caution.[4]

Tackling Gender Inequality through Public Policy

Despite their weaknesses, these indices do direct our attention to the tremendous cross-national variation we see in women's status and gender equality, the recognition of which can form the basis of government action and of scholarly efforts to understand the causes of such variation. For example, if occupational data indicate that women drop out of the labor force after having children in some countries and not in others, we can then examine whether there is a relationship to parental leave and child-care policies. If we see high rates of hospitalizations for abortion complications in some countries and not in others, it directs our attention to the extent to which legal abortion and contraception is available.

Within this context, we also see extensive variation across countries and regions in the degree to which governments acknowledge gender inequality, how this inequality is defined, what types of policies are adopted in each case, and to what extent these policies are enforced. In practice, policies to address gender inequality usually focus rather narrowly on particular areas of inequality[5], for example, employment discrimination, access to reproductive rights, or domestic violence.[6]

However, particularly since the Beijing Conference on Women in 1995, more scholars and practitioners have argued for the "mainstreaming" of gender analysis into all issue areas and public policies, claiming that gender inequalities may affect any and all issue areas and that policies must address gender inequality in a more holistic and integrated way. For example, women's employment may be impacted both by their degree of access to reproductive rights and their vulnerability to gender-based violence as well as by factors that may seem ostensibly gender neutral, such as access to public transportation. Policies that can address the interactions among these issues will be more effective in addressing each of them. Overall, policies that may not explicitly address gender can also aggravate, maintain, or reduce gender inequalities, and the goal of gender mainstreaming is to evaluate all public policies from a gendered perspective.

There have been many attempts to simplify the complex reality of gender inequalities and to categorize policies that address them. Here we are using the standard definitions of each, where *sex* refers to biological differences between men and women and *gender* refers to the socially constructed norms of behavior to which men and women are expected to conform.[7] These typologies focus on the varying assumptions about gender and gender inequality at the root of different government policies, and they attempt to unpack the cross-cutting cleavages, such as class or culture, that intersect with gender across specific policy areas.

TYPOLOGIES ON GENDER EQUALITY

One of the most basic distinctions we can identify in gender equality policies is between policies that make distinctions based on sex, and policies focused more broadly on gender. Sex discrimination occurs when an individual is "treated less favourably on grounds of sex than another is, has been or would be in a comparable situation" (Prechal and Burri 2009, 4). EU gender equality law refers to this as *direct discrimination*. Direct, or de jure, discrimination against women can occur over a wide range of issues, including, for example, unequal pay, access to land, employment, or education. Discrimination against women on the basis of sexual orientation, or discrimination against pregnant women, for example in employment, housing, or services, represent additional examples of sex discrimination.

Sex discrimination occurs in multiple forms across countries. In over one-third of countries around the world women are banned from certain types of paid work, such as work in traditionally male fields or night work, or from work that might be considered dangerous for a pregnant woman or her fetus regardless of whether a woman is pregnant (United Nations Women 2011, 28–29). Married women in particular may be restricted in their ability to make decisions independently. For example, until 1977, married women in West Germany officially needed their husband's permission to work outside the home. In Chile, until 1994, husbands had disproportionate control over marital property as well as complete legal authority over children. Women may not be able to file for divorce or may be much more limited than men in the circumstances where divorce is allowed. In Brazil, prior to 1998, a husband was allowed to file for an annulment claiming that his wife was not a virgin at marriage while the wife did not have that right. Where such discrimination is explicitly prohibited (in treaties such as Convention on the Elimination of Discrimination Against Women [CEDAW], constitutions, or by the EU) policies would seek to eliminate these discrepancies.

These policies are predicated on a notion of "sameness" between women and men. Verloo and Lombardo (2007, 23) explain that this policy approach uses "strategies of equal opportunities" to eliminate the explicit barriers to women's socioeconomic and political participation. This type of inequality is relatively straightforward (if often politically charged) to remedy through policy because policy makers can simply overturn the discriminatory statute or law or outlaw directly discriminatory behavior.[8]

However, feminists have long argued that, even where direct discrimination in a given area has been legally prohibited, because women have historically been subject to a multitude of economic, political, and cultural restrictions, merely eliminating explicit sex discrimination will not eliminate inequalities between women and men. Much of this inequality stems from gender roles in what has traditionally been considered the *private sphere* of the family. Even in the absence of explicit discrimination, lack of regulation of some aspects of the private sphere (for example, of domestic violence), is likely to harm women more than men (United Nations Women 2011, 31). Relatedly, traditional gender roles create de facto inequalities that affect women and men differently. Even with explicit legal equality between women and men in the public sphere (which has already been achieved at this point in most Western democracies), we can still see gender inequalities in policy outcomes and in society. In all countries, albeit to different degrees, women earn less than men as a group, women are more likely to be victims of domestic violence and sexual assault, women's participation in the labor market is more likely to be affected by having children, women end up doing significantly more unpaid care work than men, and women are much more likely to end up as single parents than men. When government policy fails to recognize the gender inequalities entrenched in societal norms and institutions, it amounts to what EU gender equality law refers to as "indirect discrimination" (Prechal and Burri 2009, 4). In other words, women face discrimination not only on account of their sex but on account of their gender roles. Because of this, simply lifting restrictions on the type of employment open to women, for example, is unlikely to enable women to participate on an equal footing in the labor force, as long as women are also primarily responsible for child care. Another way to talk about this is to use the language of gender *equity*. The World Health Organization defines gender equity as "fairness and justice in the distribution of benefits, power, resources and responsibilities between women and men. The concept recognizes that women and men have different needs, power and access to resources, and that these differences should be identified and addressed in a manner that rectifies the imbalance between the sexes" (Payne 2009, 3).

In some cases, discrimination based on gender roles can be quite obvious. For example, many countries do not accord paid domestic workers equal labor rights with other workers. While this discrimination, strictly speaking, is based on occupation, not sex, and legally applies to both women and men in this sector, it stems from gendered views of "women's work" in the household, and indeed the vast majority of workers in this sector are female (United Nations Women 2011: 36–37; Blofield 2012). Some issues relevant to gender equity may not be as obvious and seem ostensibly gender neutral (at least to policy makers), yet the consequences of state action or inaction on the issue impact women and men differently. For example, laws that limit benefits to part-time workers can disproportionately impact women, as they are more likely than men to be employed part-time (Prechal and Burri 2009, 4). Pension laws that base retirement income on years in the formal labor market also discriminate indirectly against women, who, as a group, accrue fewer years of formal employment because of the time spent outside the labor market raising children.

On the other hand, women can be the primary beneficiaries of policies that are not focused exclusively on women. Both men and women benefit from sex education, but since women disproportionately bear the costs of unwanted pregnancy, sex education and access to contraception make a greater impact on women's status than on men's. Both women and men benefit from the availability of day care for their children, and in individual cases this service may be just as important for the father as for the mother. However, since women as a group tend to take on more child-rearing tasks and other care work, they will on average benefit more from increased access to day care, as it will allow women to participate more competitively with men in the labor market.

In attempting to rectify inequalities based on gender roles, policies can approach the problem of gender equity from two potentially contradictory directions. On one hand, policies can be developed that would recognize and reward the type of work that women are more likely to do, by, for example, subsidizing unpaid care work through a wage for the homemaker. The goal of such policies can be to enhance women's status by "affirm[ing] difference from the male norm" (Verloo and Lombardo 2007, 23). Fraser (1997) refers to this as the recognition-based claim, which would aim to affirm group differentiation by, for example, revaluing femininity. On the other hand, policies could support women's efforts to participate equally in public life with men, for instance, by providing day care to working mothers. *Positive actions*, such as quotas or affirmative action in hiring, education, or representation in government also seek this goal, as such policies aim to counteract historical obstacles to women's participation in public life.

Along this vein, a vast literature has developed to address the way states promote or discourage traditional gender roles within the household and labor force in the more developed welfare states in particular (for more discussion of gender, care, and welfare see the chapter by Sainsbury in this volume). In response to Esping-Andersen's (1990) famous *Three Worlds of Welfare Capitalism*, many authors have sought to construct parallel gender-based typologies, based on whether government policies encourage traditional gender roles and stay-at-home mothers, or encourage the entry of women into the workforce. These typologies include Lewis's (1992) *strong male breadwinner* and *weak male breadwinner* types, Sainsbury's (1994) *universal breadwinner* and *individual* model, Fraser's (1994) breadwinner versus caregiver model, Gornick and Meyers' (2003) "dual-earner/dual-carer model," and "maternalism" (Orloff 2006), among others. At the same time, other scholars have sought to incorporate gender "into the core concepts of research on the welfare state" (Orloff 1993, 306). Orloff includes "the capacity [specifically of women] to form and maintain an autonomous household" (319) as a key dimension of analysis on the welfare state. More broadly, much of the literature centers on theorizing how states address the public–private dimension and the "social care" dimension, given their importance to gender equality (see, for example, Fraser 1994; Jenson 1997; Lewis 1997; Esping-Anderen 1999, 2002, 2009; O'Connor, Orloff, and Shaver 1999; Daly and Lewis 2000; Sainsbury 2008; Morgan 2009;).

While most scholars argue that policies that promote mothers' employment and provide public child-care services promote gender equality more than promoting traditional families or paying women caregiving wages to stay at home, there is a broad recognition that neither model, or set of policies, is sufficient to promote more gender equality in the household. For this, many feminists call for more "transformative" policies seeking to change "all established norms and standards of what is/should be female and male" (Verloo and Lombardo 2007, 23), Esping-Andersen (2009, 99) calls for the "feminization of the male life cycle." This parallels Fraser's (1997) redistribution-based claim, the thrust of which is to dedifferentiate social groups by undermining group differences (for example, by abolishing the gendered division of labor).

Another strand of policy typologies, developed largely independently of the welfare state literature and focusing more closely on the policy process itself, also seeks to distinguish policies according to the degree to which they challenge traditional gender roles in a given society. For example, Molyneux (1985) distinguishes between *practical* and *strategic* gender interests, arguing that "practical interests are usually a response to an immediate perceived need, and they do not generally entail a strategic goal such as women's emancipation or gender equality" (233). An example would be advocating for better nutrition for children. Strategic interests, on the other hand, seek to overcome and transcend these roles. In a similar vein, Gelb and Palley (1996) distinguish between policies based on *role maintenance* (such as access to education) and *role change* (such as abortion rights). Pickup, Williams, and Sweetman's (2001) global study of domestic violence legislation distinguishes between rights-based laws, which view women as individuals, and laws based on traditional conceptions of women's social roles. Blofield and Haas (2005) distinguish between rights-based and role-based claims, where "role-based framing seeks to better women's situation in a way that does not threaten a woman's role as wife and mother in a traditional conception of the family" and "a rights-based framing seeks to extend individual rights to women" (38–39). An example of the former is a policy that allows working women to take breaks to nurse their infants or ensures homemakers access to health insurance through their husbands' employment, and an example of the latter is a policy that seeks to equalize the property rights of women and men in marriage or guarantees legal abortion as a woman's right to control her body (ibid.).

Not surprisingly, scholars have found that policies that do not fundamentally challenge existing gender roles in a given society are more easily adopted and implemented. Blofield and Haas (2011) argue that in Latin America policies that contradict Catholic doctrine on women and family life face more resistance. Htun and Weldon (2010b), writing on sex equality policies worldwide, find a similar religious cleavage at work behind successful and unsuccessful policies. Whether an issue confronts religious opposition depends, of course, on the religion, on the denomination, and on place and time, as religions can change doctrine and shift priorities over time.

Finally, policy debates about gender inequality are often inseparable from economic considerations. For instance, establishing a system of child care for working parents or providing support for care work requires significant budgetary outlays by the government. Other policies, such as the legalization of divorce or the decriminalization of abortion, do not, in and of themselves, involve redistributive measures by the state. Blofield and Haas (2011, drawing on Fraser 1997), contrast redistributive with regulatory policies. For Blofield and Haas, the redistributive dimension encompasses two dynamics: whether the policy area requires redistribution of resources across classes; and whether the policy area requires significant outlays on the part of the state. Similarly, Htun and Weldon (2010b) differentiate between status-based and class-based policies. This class component is an important distinction because policy outputs with a clear economic component may be viewed as threatening to class privileges and will face a different set of political obstacles than other policies. In political discussions of policy options, economic concerns may be a sincere concern of policy makers, or the economic costs of policies could be used as a maneuver to avoid addressing contentious issues of gender inequality.

Even issues that do not at first appear tightly linked to economic debates, such as sanctioning domestic violence or decriminalizing abortion, are likely to incur costs at the implementation stage. In the case of domestic violence, this can involve establishing a system of support for victims of violence that may include shelters and other immediate services, in addition to the costs of prosecuting offenders. In the case of abortion, providing broad access to all women to abortion and reproductive health-care services requires a clear economic investment by the government. Similarly, we may see differential gender effects from socioeconomic policies that do not at first appear linked to gender, for example, cutbacks in public services that low-income mothers in particular rely on. For this reason, to understand policy outputs we must examine these issues at each output stage.

Gender Mainstreaming

Gender mainstreaming represents an attempt to move our thinking about gender inequality and policy making beyond the sameness–difference dichotomy that dominates earlier research on the subject as well as beyond a narrow issue-based focus (for more discussion of mainstreaming see the chapter by Lombardo, Meier, and Verloo in this volume). Gender mainstreaming is a contested subject, but the most commonly cited definition was devised by Mieke Verloo, as chair of the Council of Europe Group of Experts: "Gender mainstreaming is the (re)organization, improvement, development and evaluation of policy processes, so that a gender equality perspective is incorporated in all policies at all levels at all stages, by the actors normally involved in policy making" (Council of Europe 1998, 15). Gender mainstreaming is both a theoretical approach, which seeks to understand and challenge the gendered assumptions of policy, and a policy tool itself, which attempts to redesign policy outputs to reduce gender inequality. Although gender mainstreaming has only been used on a comprehensive scale as a policy tool in advanced industrialized countries, especially Europe, the theoretical insights it offers travel well to other regions of the world. The preceding chapter deals with this concept at length; we briefly outline it here.

As with policies on gender equality overall, a chief tension within gender mainstreaming concerns the degree to which it aims to incorporate a gender perspective into the existing policy structure or whether it seeks a more radical transformation of existing policy paradigms. The first approach is often termed *integrationist* and the second *agenda-setting* (see Jahan 1995; Lombardo 2005; Walby 2005). A number of theorists contrast the transformative goal of gender mainstreaming from earlier approaches focused on either equal opportunities (sameness), which corresponds to sex discrimination, or special programs and positive action (difference), which would attempt to address gender discrimination. In this sense, gender mainstreaming offers "neither the assimilation of women into men's ways, nor the maintenance of a dualism between women and men, but rather something new, a positive form of melding, in which the outsiders, feminists, changed the mainstream" (Walby 2005, 323). Squires (1999,

2005) uses the terms *inclusion, reversal,* and *displacement* to distinguish between policies focused on antidiscrimination and sameness, positive difference, and gender mainstreaming. Different approaches predominate at certain time periods, on particular policy issues, and also evolve over time (Daly 2005).

A consideration of inequality in its broadest sense demands additional attention to issues of race–ethnicity, class, and sexuality. Intersectionality starts from the premise that women—or men—are not a uniform group and that gender inequalities interact with other forms of inequality.[9] Squires (2005) emphasizes the need for an intersectional approach to gender mainstreaming that takes account of multiple forms of inequality beyond gender, notably race and ethnicity, class, sexual orientation, and disability while recognizing that "the move to consider equality and diversity rather than simply gender equality renders the process of mainstreaming infinitely more complex" (382). In this regard, intersectionality remains a critical theoretical lens through which to analyze policy outputs, but its incorporation into the various stages of policy making faces significant challenges.

While the responsibility for gender mainstreaming in Europe especially, to various degrees across countries, now spreads across government ministries as well as levels of government (Daly 2005; Walby 2005), concerted efforts to promote gender mainstreaming in policy are often centered in "women's policy machineries,"[10] which are "state-based mechanisms charged formally with furthering women's status and gender equality" (Mazur and McBride 2008, 244). By the end of the 1990s, 127 countries had set up women's policy agencies (WPAs), although many remained quite weak (see Rai 2003).

THE STAGES OF THE POLICY PROCESS

It is useful to examine policies that address gender equality—in different ways, as discussed already—at the various stages of the policy process, all of which present specific challenges. This section examines four distinct, but interconnected, phases of policy outputs on gender equality: issue framing; policy adoption; policy implementation; and policy outcomes.

Issue Framing

Before an issue can be formulated into policy, it must first be defined as a political problem. The groups or institutions best positioned to define the scope of the problem will have tremendous impact on the type of policy that is adopted as well as its implementation and outcomes. Feminist researchers emphasize the ways that issues of gender equality are problematized in dramatically different ways, depending on which groups are able to determine the *policy discourse* (Verloo and Lombardo 2007) or *policy debate* (Mazur and McBride 2008) surrounding particular issues. Another way to conceptualize this is in terms of policy frames. Ferree et al. (2002,193) explain that "framing organizes perceptions of social and political problems and gives meaning to specific situations and issues." Sauer (2010), drawing on the Research Network on Gender Politics and the State (RNGS) data,[11] distinguishes between general frames, issue frames, and microframes. General frames refer to a universe of political discourse (Jenson 1989). These can either promote, be neutral on, or discourage gender equality, explicitly or implicitly. Gender equality, or traditional values, are examples of a general frame. Issue frames reference specific policy areas, such as health, human rights, or crime. Finally, microframes refer to the arguments of individuals or groups attempting to influence the policy debate. Sauer draws on Squires (2005) to identify three primary microframes: a frame focused on equality and rights; difference framing; and a transformative frame (197). Quality in Gender+ Equality Studies (QUING 2011), a multi-authored cross-country project, uses inclusive, transformative, rejective, and neutral frames to classify policy discourse on gender equality in Europe.

The way an issue is framed has a tremendous effect on the way it is translated into policies and the way those policies are implemented (see, for example, Smith 2007). As discussed already, gender equality can be framed primarily as a problem of direct, sex-based discrimination or as one of more far-reaching gender equity. With the latter, conceptions of gender roles will have a significant impact on what specific policies are proposed to deal with the problem. For example, as the welfare state literature has shown, women can be framed primarily as mothers and caregivers, as workers, or as citizens, with implications for the type of policies that are proposed, adopted, and implemented.

Given how controversial abortion is in many countries, framing on this issue is particularly contested. Most of the frames in support of abortion rights focus on sex discrimination, with the idea that women deserve the same individual rights, control over their bodies, and access to health care as men. The dominant contesting frame does not tend to explicitly reject gender equality but rather portrays abortion as homicide. More recently, opponents of abortion have also framed abortion as a human rights violation and as harmful to a woman's health, in an attempt to co-opt the major frames used to defend the practice (see, for example, Morgan 2011).

Framing is a strategic choice and depends on the time, the country, and the political dynamics. For example, in Finland in 1970, when abortion was liberalized, it was framed as a medical need.[12] In Germany, where the procedure has remained controversial over decades, Ferree et al. (2002) find that a *fetal life* frame dominates abortion discourse, while the less prevalent woman's right to self-determination frame tends to be viewed as a right that must be balanced with the fetal right to life (105–130). At the other end of the spectrum within Europe, in Ireland and Poland the political influence of the Catholic

Church creates greater space for conservative discourses that frame abortion as akin to murder.[13] We see also competing frames between the EU and individual member states. For example, a recent ruling by the European Court of Human Rights condemned Ireland's restrictive abortion law as endangering women's lives and violating women's rights (McKittrick 2010). In the United States, abortion has been framed by two opposed camps primarily in terms of either individual rights (a woman's right to privacy and to control of her body) or homicide (Ferree et al.).

In Latin America, the Catholic Church is a major political player, and moral frames that equate abortion with murder dominate public debate (and are reflected in most of the region's laws). In Chile, a 1991 failed bill to decriminalize therapeutic abortion portrayed women seeking abortion as already mothers who needed access to safe abortion so that they could continue to care for their families, framing support for abortion rights in role maintenance terms (Blofield and Haas 2005; Haas 2010). Increasingly, proponents of abortion rights in the region are framing abortion as a human right and a public health issue for poor women in particular, drawing on international treaties, sometimes successfully as in the Constitutional Court of Colombia (AWID 2005).

Violence against women (VAW) includes a wide range of issues from rape, sexual assault, and domestic violence to trafficking, genital mutilation, and workplace harassment. In contrast to abortion, where individuals may fall on opposite sides of the policy debate, all sides tend to condemn violence in public. What differs are the diagnostics of the problem and the proposed solutions. For example, competing domestic violence frames focus on the definition of the problem, its origins, and the appropriate government response. These can range from encompassing, transformative frames (linking it to broader socioeconomic, structural inequalities) to narrow responses that focus on the criminalization of physical violence.

In most EU documents, domestic violence is framed as a public matter. EU texts may also frame domestic violence as a reflection of male dominance and gender inequality. Drawing on QUING data, Hadjiyanni and Kamoutsi (2005) find that often domestic violence is framed in a degendered way, either as a health problem or as a human rights problem, creating what they consider quite strong limitations to efforts at mainstreaming the fight against sexual violence. This can end up minimizing the "transformative gender equality elements" in the policy (Krizsán and Popa 2013). Rejective frames are less common. In some Central and East European countries, frames classified as rejective by the authors link the problem to individual deviance and alcoholism rather than social structures (Dabrowska 2011—also using QUING).

Overall, in the case of both abortion and violence against women, human rights and public health frames have increased in political debate. Degendering the issues in this way could be seen as an example of strategic framing, for example, as a way to sell the issue to a public and a government where gender equality is not an influential theme.

Policy Adoption

When we consider the wide range of ways that policies delineate the problem of gender inequality, even within a particular region, we see the clear impact that framing by different stakeholders can have on the policies adopted and implemented (a discussion of broader causal factors is outside the scope of this chapter).

Policies can stem from the executive, the legislature, or the judiciary and include laws, constitutional changes, court rulings, as well as other forms of policies, such as executive decisions or decrees, which may not have the force of law but form part of government policies. Policy adoption can also take place at different levels of a political system; central or federal government, state or provincial government, and local government or, in the European Union, at the EU level.

We can see significant reforms toward gender equality around the world in the past few decades at this stage of the policy process, particularly on sex-based discrimination but also on promoting gender equity, attesting to the success of feminists in influencing framing, and agenda-setting on women's rights (Htun and Weldon 2010b, 2010c). Virtually all countries have ratified the CEDAW, and many have, often relatedly, revised national laws. For example, today 173 countries guarantee paid maternity leave, 125 countries outlaw domestic violence, while 117 countries have equal pay laws and outlaw sexual harassment (United Nations Women 2011, 24). On the other hand, explicit discrimination remains in many of the almost two hundred countries of the world. In fifty countries, for example, the minimum legal age for marriage is lower for females (ibid., 28–29).

This policy stage has received the most attention and is also probably the easiest to examine cross-nationally, particularly with regard to the more visible indicators of government policy, such as laws.[14] Overall, reform on a global level appears to have been more widespread on laws that prohibit direct sex-based discrimination and on policies that do not directly challenge traditional gender roles, for example, laws to combat domestic violence. On the other hand, direct sex-based discrimination continues to be more prevalent on issues where traditional gender roles are challenged (often tied to religious doctrine), for example, on access to legal abortion or equal rights in the family (Blofield and Haas 2005, 2011; Htun and Weldon 2010a, 2010b, 2010c).

Even on issue areas where an international consensus on prohibiting sex discrimination is emerging, actual laws and policies vary dramatically. In the EU, where all member countries are subject to EU directives prohibiting pay discrimination between the sexes, these directives may be interpreted differently in national laws. In the United Kingdom, for example, it is harder to prove discrimination on equal pay compared with many other EU countries (Prechal and Burri 2009, 5). Although 125 countries have outlawed domestic violence, here, too, the specific policies vary considerably. For example, while spousal rape is illegal across Europe and Latin America, in Argentina the law requires

clear proof of physical injury or the testimony of witnesses. In Cyprus a con-
viction for spousal rape carries a maximum penalty of life in prison, but in
Greece the law stipulates few penalties for first-time offenders (Hague Domestic
Violence Project, http://www.haguedv.org/).

In other areas, there is less consensus on the goal of the law altogether.
On abortion, laws can span from the right to abortion on demand (within a
certain time period) as is the case for example in Sweden, Norway, Denmark,
and many former Soviet Bloc countries, to a prohibition and criminalization of
abortion under all circumstances, even when the life of the mother is at risk,
as is the case for example in Chile, Nicaragua, El Salvador, and the Dominican
Republic (Center for Reproductive Rights 2008). Between these two opposite
legal regimes, many countries maintain certain restrictions on the legal right to
abortion by establishing conditions under which abortion is permissible (e.g.,
rape or incest, fetal deformity, woman's physical or mental health, socioeconomic factors) or through other legal restrictions such as waiting periods, mandatory counseling, parental consent clauses, or control over time periods for
the procedure (ibid.; Outshoorn 1996). Such restrictions are tied to the dominant frames in policy adoption; for example, in Germany, to get an abortion on
request the woman must see a counselor, whose goal is to dissuade her from an
abortion, reflecting an attempt to balance the competing frames of a woman's
right and fetal life (Outshoorn, 147).

On gender equity, particularly policies on work and the family, we see
broad variation as well. Within more developed welfare states, in countries
where dominant frames have historically viewed women as primarily mothers
and caregivers, government policies also tended to restrict the ability of married women and mothers to participate in the workforce, earlier with marriage
bans, and more recently with joint tax policies and scant provision of subsidized childcare. On the other hand, in states where the dominant frame has
viewed women and mothers as workers, policies have promoted public daycare
and individual taxation to encourage labor force participation rates of mothers.[15] Such policy differences are also relevant outside advanced industrialized
countries, for example in Latin America, although the welfare states are less
developed.[16]

The variation we see in policy adoption reflects different framings of the
original policy problem, as expressed by the dominant political groups in each
society. The shape of particular policies, in terms of the definition and scope of
the policy, as well as the legal form the policy takes, influences the way these
policies are implemented on the ground.

Policy Implementation

Laws and policy directives that guarantee sex equality and promote gender
equity are necessary but not sufficient to actually achieve either. Effective

implementation, which "starts after the decision to adopt a particular course of action is made" (Quade 1992, 338), is crucial. Some scholars refer to this as "policy effort."

How can we measure implementation? Implementation is a dynamic process that takes place over time. We can assess implementation via government outputs, as they are referred to in the public administration literature and which can be defined as "visible measures of government activity" (Dye 1992, 354).[17] A measure of government output could be the number of public daycare spots; a measure of policy effort could be the increase in service provision following a legal reform or policy mandate to extend coverage. For example, in Denmark, almost half, while in Spain, only 3 percent, of zero- to three-year-olds were in public daycare in the 1990s, reflecting clear differences in dominant frames of motherhood and in policy effort to integrate mothers into the labor force (Esping-Andersen et al. 2002, 74). In 2006, the Spanish government committed itself to extending public funding to 20 percent of under-three-year-olds; by 2009, 12 percent of this age group was in public daycare and another 13 percent in private daycare (Aguilar, Escobedo, and Montagut 2010, 23–24). In Denmark, on the other hand, by the 2000s, coverage of one- to two-year-old children was 85 percent (Esping-Andersen 2009, 94).

Countries may rank order quite differently on legal equality and implementation or enforcement, due to many factors affecting this stage of the policy process. The type of law or policy adopted influences implementation. For example, a law prohibiting sex discrimination in the workplace will involve legal mechanisms of enforcement, while an equity-based policy that guarantees access to free daycare will require significant public outlays in service provision if carried through. Similarly, the framing and content of the policy, its mandate, scope, and specificity (e.g., whether budgetary outlays are written into the policy) all influence how the policy is likely to be implemented (Luciano et al. 2003; Walby 2005, 325). For example, in Spain early childhood education and care was framed as a child's right to education by the Socialist government in the 1990s, leading to a policy with universal reach for older preschoolers but, when implemented, limited opening hours, given that concerns regarding access to daycare for working parents, especially mothers, were not part of the framing of the law (Valiente 2001a). In Latin America, most countries define *family violence* as a civil rather than criminal matter. As a result, enforcement of the law falls to family tribunals or civil courts, where the "penalties for domestic violence are seldom severe enough to send a strong message that such acts are unacceptable" (Franceschet 2008, 5–6, drawing on Rioseco Ortega 2005).

Laws, and even more so constitutional guarantees, can be enforced through the courts and also have more staying power than executive policies, which, without the force of law, are subject to potential changes in executive priorities and, especially over time, changes in executive leadership.[18] On the other hand, even laws are often not adequately enforced. State capacity is crucial; if the state does not have a functioning bureaucracy, even the most transformative laws promising complete gender equity will make little difference to the lives of most people. Ministries and courts can suffer from inadequate infrastructure and budgets as well as lack of qualified staff. For example, Bolivia's law on domestic workers' rights is more egalitarian on paper than Chile's, but implementation by the Ministry of Labor is so weak that in practice extant rights are more strongly enforced in Chile (Blofield 2012). On domestic violence, inadequate budgets is cited as one of the biggest obstacles to the enforcement of laws in Latin America (Luciano et al. 2003; Franceschet 2008). In addition, the nature of the judicial system, as well as the mandate of labor inspectorates and equality bodies, will play an important role in how a law is actually enforced (Prechal and Burri 2009, 24–30; United Nations Women 2011). Executive agencies and courts can also be dominated by biased attitudes. For example, judges who do not believe domestic violence to be a serious crime can apply lenient sentences to offenders. This is a significant problem in Greece, for example (United Nations Women; Hague Domestic Violence Project). On the other hand, lack of legal enforcement is not always bad for gender equity, if the laws are inequitable to begin with. In Latin America, while most abortions are criminalized with prison sentences both for women and accomplices, in practice states do little to go after the high proportion of women in the region who have committed the crime of abortion.

An executive commitment to gender mainstreaming and the existence of strong women's policy agencies with oversight are likely to enhance more gender equitable implementation. For example, while Spain and Portugal had nearly identical laws on abortion between the mid-1980s and late 2000s (allowing for abortion in cases of threat to life and physical or mental health, rape or incest, and fetal deformity), interpretation and implementation of these laws were very different. In Spain, the Women's Institute within the socialist government had pushed for a liberal interpretation of the mental health clause, and by the late 1990s over 90 percent of the over sixty thousand annual legal abortions were performed under this clause (Valiente 2001b, 243). However, in Portugal the executive implemented a highly restrictive interpretation of the same clause, granting authority to hospital committees, and in 1995 Portugal had only 256 legal abortions while the estimated actual clandestine abortion rate was about thirty thousand annually (see Blofield 2008, 404). Franceschet (2010) shows how the Chilean women's ministry played a crucial role in enforcing its domestic violence laws more effectively than Argentina, where a weak women's policy agency had little effect.

While many organizations and scholars have collected data on government outputs such as expenditures on different policies on gender equality (see, for example, OECD Family Database and UN Statistics), more in-depth research on implementation is time-consuming and tends to be hindered by limitations on access to data. Even for the European Union, Mazur (2009, 7) notes that "the resource demands of engaging in comparative studies of implementation and impacts of public policies on gender relations are enormous", arguing that this "should be the focus of the next generation of large, publicly funded, cross-national research projects." Such resource constraints, not to mention lack of access to data, are of course even more stark for academics doing research on developing countries.

Policy Outcomes

Policy outcomes are the consequences of the policy-making process and beyond the direct control of the policy makers (Biggs and Helmes 400). The cross-national indices mentioned at the beginning of the chapter are often used as outcome measures. In Dye's (1992) words, outcomes are "changes in society that are associated with measures of government activity" (35). For example, while the number of public daycare spaces is a measure of government output, the level of unmet demand for such spaces (harder to measure) and, more broadly, the labor force participation rate of mothers with under school age children (easier to measure), are examples of policy outcomes. While policy outcomes can be caused by a number of factors beyond state action, government policies clearly play an important role. On gender and welfare state policies, for instance, despite similar employment rates, differences in government policies led to poverty rates among lone mothers of 4 percent in Sweden versus 56 percent in the United States in the 1990s (Kilkey and Bradshaw 1999, 158–161). Similarly, in Denmark and Germany, two neighboring countries with similar gross domestic products, different family and child-care policies led to an employment rate of mothers with two or more children under the age of twelve years of 60 percent in Denmark and 19 percent in Germany in the 1990s (Esping-Andersen 2002, 78). In the United Kingdom, where equal pay discrimination is harder to prove, the gender wage gap among full-time workers in industry and services in 2002 was the highest among fifteen OECD countries at 30 percent (Gupta, Smith, and Verner 2006, 48).

The issue of abortion illustrates the importance of examining each stage of the policy process—framing, laws, implementation, and outcomes—to assess their impact on gender equality. Were we to derive conclusions about the practice of abortion in a country simply by looking at abortion laws and how they are framed or even their implementation, we would likely be significantly off the mark. In democratic Latin America, where legal abortions are rare due to restrictive framing, laws and implementation, it has been estimated that in practice 28 percent of pregnancies actually end in clandestine abortions, translating to over four million abortions per year (Alan Guttmacher Institute 2012). The extensive physical effects of clandestine abortions, including high hospitalization rates and inflated maternal mortality (ibid; Blofield 2008, Cohen 2009) are largely borne by lower-income women who cannot afford expensive but safe, private illegal abortions (Blofield 2006, 2008; Blofield and Haas 2011). On the other hand, in many

European countries with much higher legal abortion rates, the actual abortion rates are much lower, due in large part to comprehensive access to prevention.

Similarly, in the case of violence against women, there is a clear gap between the passage of laws and effective implementation, which in turn limits the impact of the policies on actual rates of violence. For example, in the last two decades domestic violence policies have been passed throughout Latin America, but enforcement of the laws remains a serious regional problem, due both to the persistence of social norms that normalize violence against women and to the economic challenges Latin American countries face in implementing domestic violence laws (Luciano et al. 2003), and rates of domestic violence remain high across the region. Data from the United States indicates that proper implementation of domestic violence laws—from the training of police to the establishment of shelters—is a critical step in reducing rates of domestic violence (Roel et al. 2005).

CONCLUSIONS

This chapter has overviewed typologies on gender equality as well as outputs at various stages of the policy process. While scholars have identified distinct patterns in types of government policies, more research is needed that links different policy frames to their adoption, implementation, and outcomes. Many of the constraints of more systematic, cross-national analysis of the stages of policy outputs are resource based, given the careful analysis examining these links requires. The dearth of reliable data, particularly in developing countries, and inconsistencies in definitions and measurements of gender inequality make cross-country comparison challenging. Nevertheless, such research can help us clarify the connections between the stages of the policy process, particularly the impact of policies on outcomes. For example, is there a relationship between policies that frame gender inequality in role maintenance terms with government commitment to enforce those policies? How does degendering a particular policy in favor of a focus on health, or human rights, or the family impact concrete indicators of gender inequality on that issue? Does framing policy from an intersectional perspective improve outcome rates, or does it complicate coordination across government agencies and hamper implementation? Furthermore, we need to explore more thoroughly the unintended consequences of policy choices, a concern central to gender mainstreaming.

Of course, at the root of all of these debates are larger questions about the meaning of gender and what it means to create a society free from gender inequalities. Should policy strive to eliminate gender differences or to find ways to accommodate them? What would transformative policies look like in practice? Addressing these questions requires more theoretical and empirical analysis as well as coordination between practitioners of both.

Notes

1. Of course, these are not exhaustive, and other areas such as sexual orientation are crucial as well.
2. See the United Nations, 2012, "Statistics and indicators on women and men", available at http://unstats.un.org/unsd/demographic/products/indwm/statistics.htm#families; Genderstats; http://web.worldbank.org/WBSITE/EXTERNAL/TOPICS/EXTGENDER/EXTANATOOLS/EXTSTATINDDATA/EXTGENDERST ATS/0,,menuPK:3237391~pagePK:64168427~piPK:64168435~theSitePK:3237336,00.html), and Social Watch, a nongovernmental organization (NGO) (2008, http://www.socialwatch.org/node/9269).
3. See Walby (2005) for outcome indicators by the European Union. Some databases include laws and policies as well as outcomes. See the OECD Family Database (2010) (http://www.oecd.org/document/4/0,3746,en_2649_34819_37836996_1_1_1_1, 00.html) on family-related sociodemographic and economic indicators, laws, and policies for OECD countries. ECLAC/CEPAL has a gender indicators database for Latin America and the Caribbean. The Institute for Women's Policy Research's (IWPR 2002–2009; http://www.iwpr.org/initiatives/states/the-status-of-women-in-the-states-state-reports) index collects data on women's social, economic, and political status in the fifty U.S. states.
4. See Beer (2010) and Walby (2005).
5. Discrimination based on sexual identity and orientation can also be included here (for more on this point, see, for example, Squires 2005; Verloo and Lombardo 2007).
6. Domestic violence is increasingly referred to as *intimate partner violence.*
7. Verloo and Lombardo (2007), for example, refuse to define gender inequality because the term remains so contested and amorphous.
8. Implementation, as discussed later, requires mechanisms of enforcement.
9. See Weldon (2008) for an overview.
10. More recently, most analysts refer to gender equality machineries.
11. See McBride and Mazur (2010).
12. *Helsingin Sanomat,* March 20, 1970.
13. For an analysis of Polish discourse, see Walsh (2011).
14. The ILO collects data on employment laws around the world (ILO Database, http://www.ilo.org/dyn/travail), and the OECD collects data on parental leave laws for OECD countries (OECD Family Database). UN Women (2011) publishes annual reports on women's rights around the world.
15. See discussion of welfare state typologies for references.
16. See Martínez Franzoni (2008) and Pribble (2006).
17. See Biggs and Helms (2007) and Dye (1992). Our chapter uses a broader definition of *outputs* to encompass all stages of the policy process.

18. On the other hand, especially in presidential systems, a policy initiated by the executive (rather than a nongoverning legislature), is more likely to be implemented, given that the tools of implementation—ministries, bureaucracies—are in executive control.

REFERENCES

Aguilar, Manuel, Anna Escobedo, and Teresa Montagut. 2010. "Local welfare policies in Spain: Employment, housing and child care." WILCO Publication 06. Available at http://www.wilcoproject.eu/public/assets/img/uploads/WILCO_WP2_Report_06_ES.pdf.

Alan Guttmacher Institute. 2012. "Facts on induced abortion worldwide." In Brief, January.

Association for Women's Rights in Development. (AWID). 2005. "Challenging abortion law in Colombia: An interview with Monica Roa." July. Available at http://www.awid.org/Library/Challenging-abortion-law-in-Colombia2.

Beer, Caroline. 2010. "Measuring and comparing gender equality policy across the Mexican states." Paper presented at the gender equality policies workshop of the Conference of the American Political Science Association, Washington DC, September 1–4.

Biggs, Selden, and Lelia Helms. 2007. *The practice of American public policymaking.* Armonk, NY: M.E. Sharpe.

Blofield, Merike. 2006. *The politics of moral sin: Abortion and divorce in Spain, Chile and Argentina.* New York: Routledge.

Blofield, Merike. 2008. "Women's choices in comparative perspective: Abortion policies in late-developing Catholic countries." *Comparative Politics* 41: 4.

Blofield. Merike. 2012. *Care work and class: Domestic workers' struggle for equal rights in Latin America.* University Park: Pennsylvania State University Press.

Blofield, Merike, and Liesl Haas. 2005. "Defining a democracy: Reforming the laws on women's rights in Chile, 1990–2002." *Latin American Politics and Society* 47(3): 35–68.

Blofield, Merike, and Liesl Haas. 2011. "Gender equality policies in Latin America." In Merike Blofield, ed., *The great gap: Inequality and the politics of redistribution in Latin America.* University Park: Pennsylvania State University Press, 278–309.

Center for Reproductive Rights. 2008. *The world's abortion laws: Factsheet.* New York: Center for Reproductive Rights.

Cohen, Susan. 2009. "Facts and consequences: Legality and safety of abortion worldwide." *Guttmacher Policy Review* 12(4): 2–6.

Council of Europe. 1998. "Gender mainstreaming: Conceptual framework, methodology and presentation of good practices." Council of Europe EG-S-MS. Strasbourg, France. Available at http://www.coe.int/t/dghl/standardsetting/equality/03themes/gender-mainstreaming/EG_S_MS_98_2_rev_en.pdf.

Dabrowska, Magdalena. 2011. "Getting less patriarchal and more European? Discourses on domestic violence in Poland." Paper presented at the QUING symposium on gender-based violence policies in the EU, Lancaster, UK, April 12–13.

Daly, Mary E. 2005. "Gender mainstreaming in theory and practice." *Social Politics: International Studies in Gender, State and Society* 12(3): 433–450.

Daly, Mary, and Jane Lewis. 2000. "The concept of social care and the analysis of contemporary welfare states." *British Journal of Sociology* 51(2): 281–298.

Dye, Thomas R. 1992. *Understanding public policy*. Englewood Cliffs, NJ: Prentice Hall.

Esping-Andersen, Gøsta. 1990. *The three worlds of welfare capitalism*. Cambridge, UK: Polity Press.

Esping-Andersen, Gøsta. 1999. *The social foundations of postindustrial economies*. Oxford: Oxford University Press.

Esping-Andersen, Gøsta. 2009. *The incomplete revolution: Adapting to women's new roles*. Cambridge, UK: Polity Press.

Esping-Andersen, Gøsta, with Duncan Gallie, Anton Hemerijck, and John Myles. 2002. *Why we need a new welfare state*. New York: Oxford University Press.

Ferree, Myra Marx, William A. Gamson, Jürgen Gerhards, and Dieter Rucht. 2002. *Shaping abortion discourse: Democracy and the public sphere in Germany and the United States*. Cambridge, UK: Cambridge University Press.

Franceschet, Susan. 2008. "The politics of domestic violence policy in Latin America." IAPR Technical Paper Series, TP 08001, January. Available at http://www.iapr.ca/files/iapr/iapr-tp-08001_0.pdf.

Franceschet, Susan. 2010. "Explaining domestic violence policy outcomes in Chile and Argentina." *Latin American Politics and Society* 52(2): 1–29.

Fraser, Nancy. 1994. "After the family wage: gender equity and the welfare state." *Political Theory* 22: 591–618.

Fraser, Nancy. 1997. *Justice interruptus: Critical reflections on the "post-socialist" condition*. New York: Routledge.

Gelb, Joyce, and Marian Lief Palley. 1996. *Women and public policies: Reassessing gender politics*. Charlottesville: University Press of Virginia.

Gornick, Janet C. and Marcia K. Meyers. 2003. *Families that work*. New York: Russell Sage Foundation.

Gupta, Nabanita Datta, Nina Smith, and Mette Verner. 2006. "Child care and parental leave in the Nordic Countries: A model to aspire to?" Discussion Paper 2014, Institute for the Study of Labor (IZA), Bonn.

Haas, Liesl. 2010. *Feminist policymaking in Chile*. University Park: Pennsylvania State University Press.

Hadjiyanni, Andromachi, and Fray Kamoutsi. 2005. "Dimensions of public debate on sexual violence against women: Similarities and differences between Greece and EU policy framing." *Greek Review of Social Research* 117: 189–220.

Htun, Mala N., and Laurel Weldon. 2010a. "Comparative Perspectives on Women's Rights in Family Law: A Global Overview." *Indiana Journal of Global Legal Studies* 18(1): 145–165.

Htun, Mala N., and Laurel Weldon. 2010b. "When do governments promote women's rights? A framework for the comparative analysis of sex equality policy." *Perspectives on Politics* 8(1): 207–216.

Htun, Mala N., and Laurel Weldon. 2010c. "International norms on women's human rights: the personal becomes the international." Paper presented to the American Political Science Association 2010 Conference, Washington DC, August 20.

Jahan, Rounaq. 1995. *The elusive agenda: Mainstreaming women in development*. London: Zed.

Jenson, Jane. 1989. "Paradigms and political discourse: Protective legislation in France and the United States before 1919." *Canadian Journal of Political Science* 2: 235–258.

Jenson, Jane. 1997. "Who cares? Gender and welfare regimes." *Social Politics* 4(2): 182–187.

Kilkey, Majella, and Jonathan Bradshaw. 1999. "Lone mothers, economic wellbeing, and policies." In Diane Sainsbury, ed., *Gender and welfare state regimes*. Oxford: Oxford University Press, 147–184.

Krizsán, Andrea, and Raluca Popa (forthcoming, 2013). ""Frames in Contestation: Gendering Domestic Violence Policies in Five Countries of Central and Eastern Europe." *Violence Against Women*. Sage Publications.

Lewis, Jane. 1992. "Gender and the development of welfare regimes." *Journal of European Social Policy* 2: 159–173.

Lewis, Jane. 1997. "Gender and welfare regimes: Further thoughts." *Social Politics* 4: 160–177.

Lombardo, Emanuela. 2005. "Integrating of setting the agenda? Gender mainstreaming in the European constitution-making process." *Social Politics: International Studies in Gender, State and Society* 12(3): 412–432.

Luciano, Dinys, Simel Esim, and Nata Duvvury. 2003. *How to make the law work? Budgetary implications of domestic violence policies in Latin America*. Washington DC: International Center for Research on Women (ICRW).

Martínez Franzoni, Juliana. 2008. "Welfare regimes in Latin America: Capturing constellations of markets, families and policies." *Latin American Politics and Society* 50(2): 67–100.

Mazur, Amy G. 2009. "Comparative gender and policy projects in Europe: Current trends in theory, method and research." *Comparative European Politics* 7(10): 12–36.

Mazur, Amy G., and Dorothy E. McBride. 2008. "State feminism." In Gary Goertz and Amy G. Mazur, eds., *Politics, gender and concepts: Theory and methodology*. Cambridge, UK: Cambridge University Press, 244–269.

McBride, Dorothy E., and Amy G. Mazur. 2010. *The politics of state feminism: Innovation in comparative research*. Philadelphia: Temple University Press.

McKittrick, David. 2010. "Ireland's abortion law 'violated women's rights'." *The Independent*, December 17. Available at http://www.independent.co.uk/news/world/europe/irelands-abortion-law-violated-womans-rights-2162658.html.

Molyneux, Maxine. 1985. "Mobilization without emancipation? Women's interests, the state, and revolution in Nicaragua." *Feminist Studies* 1(1–2): 227–254.

Morgan, Kimberly J. 2009. "Caring time policies in Western Europe: Trends and implications." *Comparative European Politics* 7(1): 37–55.

Morgan, Lynn M. 2011. "Claiming Rosa Parks: Strategic secularism and human rights in Latin America." Paper presented at the conference on global flows, human rights, sexual and reproductive health, University of Sussex, July. Available at http://www.sxpolitics.org/wp-content/uploads/2009/02/morgan-claiming-rosa-parks-sussex-short-version.pdf.

O'Connor, Julia S., Ann Shola Orloff, and Sheila Shaver. 1999. *States, markets, families: Gender, liberalism and social policy in Australia, Canada, Great Britain and the United States*. Cambridge, UK: Cambridge University Press.

OECD. 2011. OECD Family Database. OECD, Paris.

Orloff, Ann Shola. 2006. "From maternalism to 'Employment for All': State policies to promote women's employment in the affluent democracies." In Jonah D. Levy, ed., *The state after statism: New state activities in the age of liberalization*. Harvard University Press, 230–269.

Orloff, Ann Shola. 1993. "Gender and the social rights of citizenship: The comparative analysis of state policies and gender relations." *American Sociological Review* 58: 303–328.

Outshoorn, Joyce. 1996. "The stability of compromise: Abortion politics in Western Europe." In Marianne Githens and Dorothy McBride Stetson, eds., *Abortion politics: Public policy in cross-cultural perspective.* New York: Routldge, 145–162.

Payne, Sarah. 2009. "How can gender equity be addressed through health systems?" World Health Organization Policy Brief 12, Copenhagen.

Pickup, Francine, Suzanne Williams, and Caroline Sweetman. 2001. *Ending violence against women: A challenge for development and humanitarian work.* London: Oxfam.

Prechal, Sacha, and Susanne Burri. 2009. "EU rules on gender equality: How are the transposed into national law?" European Commission Directorate General for Employment, Social Affairs and Equal Opportunities. Unit G.2, Publications Office of the European Union, Luxembourg.

Pribble, Jennifer. 2006. "The politics of women's welfare in Chile and Uruguay." *Latin American Research Review* 41(2): 84–111.

Quade, E. S. 1989. *Analysis for public decisions,* 3d ed. Englewood Cliffs, NJ: Prentice Hall.

Quality in Gender+ Equality Policies (QUING). 2011. "Framing gender equality in the European Union and its current and future member states." European Commission Sixth framework Programme Integrated Project, Deliverable 61, Final LARG Report, Vienna, Institut für die Wissenschaften vom Menschen (IWM).

Rai, Shirin (Ed.). 2003. *Mainstreaming gender, democratizing the state? Institutional mechanisms for the advancement of women.* Manchester: Manchester University Press.

Rioseco Ortega, Luz. 2005. *Buenas Prácticas para la Erradicación de la Violencia Doméstica en la Región de América Latina y el Caribe.* Santiago de Chile: CEPAL, Unidad Mujer y Desarrollo.

Roel, Janice, Chris O'Sullivan, Daniel Webster, and Jacquelyn Campbell. 2005. *Intimate Partner Violence Risk Assessment Validation Study: The RAVE Study Practitioner Summary and Recommendations: Validation of tools for assessing risk from violent intimate partners.* Washington, DC: Department of Justice Grant Document 209732. Available at https://www.ncjrs.gov/pdffiles1/nij/grants/209732.pdf.

Sainsbury, Diane (Ed.). 1994. *Gendering welfare states.* London: SAGE.

Sainsbury, Diane (Ed.). 2008. "Gendering the welfare state." In Gary Goertz and Amy G. Mazur, eds., *Politics, gender and concepts: Theory and methodology.* Cambridge, UK: Cambridge University Press, 94–113.

Sauer, Birgit. 2010. "Framing and gendering." In Dorothy E. McBride and Amy G. Mazur, eds., *The politics of state feminism: Innovation in comparative research.* Philadelphia: Temple University Press, 193–2015.

Smith, Anna Marie. 2007. *Welfare reform and sexual regulation.* New York: Cambridge University Press.

Squires, Judith. 1999. *Gender in political theory.* Malden, MA: Blackwell.

Squires, Judith. 2005. "Is mainstreaming transformative? Theorizing mainstreaming in the context of diversity and deliberation." *Social Politics: International Studies in Gender, State and Society* 12(3): 366–388.

United Nations. 2012. "Statistics and indicators on women and men." Available at
    http://unstats.un.org/unsd/demographic/products/indwm/statistics.htm#families.
United Nations Women. 2011. "Progress of the world's women, 2011–2012: In pursuit
    of justice." Available at http://progress.unwomen.org.
Valiente, Celia. 2001a. "Do political parties matter? Do Spanish parties make a
    difference in childcare policies?" In Tricia David, ed., *Promoting evidence-based
    practice in early childhood education: Research and its implications*, vol. 1. New
    York: Elsevier Science, 97–114.
Valiente, Celia. 2001b. "Gendering abortion debates: State feminism in Spain." In
    Dorothy McBride Stetson, ed., *Abortion politics, women's movements, and
    the democratic state: A comparative study of state feminism*. Oxford: Oxford
    University Press.
Verloo, Mieke. 2005. "Displacement and empowerment: Reflections on the concept
    and practice of the Council of Europe approach to gender mainstreaming and
    gender equality." *Social Politics: International Studies in Gender, State and Society*
    12(3): 344–365.
Verloo, Mieke, and Emanuela Lombardo. 2007. "Contested gender equality and policy
    variety in Europe: Introducing a critical frame analysis approach." In Mieke
    Verloo, ed., *Multiple meanings of gender equality: A critical frame analysis of
    gender policies in Europe*. Budapest: CPS Books, 21–49.
Walby, Sylvia. 2005. Measuring women's progress in a global era. *International Social
    Science Journal,*. 184: 371–387.
Walsh, Denise. 2010. *Women's rights in democratizing states: Just debate and gender
    justice in the public sphere*. Cambridge, MA: Cambridge University Press.
Weldon, S. Laurel. 2008. "Intersectionality." In Gary Goertz and Amy G. Mazur,
    eds., *Politics, gender and concepts: Theory and methodology*. Cambridge, UK:
    Cambridge University Press, 193–218.

PART VII

....

EQUALITY, CITIZENSHIP, AND NATION

....

PROCESSES of globalization, migration, and multilevel governance brought major challenges to feminist theories and activism. Migration and globalization reinforced questions about the universal character of the feminist project. Equality was increasingly considered a white Western women's cause that was imposed on women of non-Western cultures—in Judith Squires's words, particularity masquerading as universalism. Models of equality and citizenship and women's identity were challenged to come to terms with intersectionality and difference particularly with regard to women of non-Western and nonliberal and illiberal cultures. The debate about equality versus difference that marked feminist thinking about equality, citizenship, and identity was further complicated by the feminism versus multiculturalism puzzle, as epitomized by Susan Moller Okin's critical question, Is multiculturalism bad for women? Intersectionality imposed yet another layer of complexity on to the feminist thinking about equality, citizenship, and identity, again heightening the salience of acknowledging diversity.

In addition to the renegotiation of equality with diversity within the nation-state, processes like globalization, Europeanization, and multilevel governance also encouraged feminist scholarship to move beyond the state and to develop postnational notions of citizenship and to deal with nonnational arenas. *Nation* and *citizenship* are powerful concepts that construct (and are constructed by) gender. While some postcolonial theory rejects the constructive power of nations and proclaims a cosmopolitan citizenship, other scholars still see these as powerful constructions that secure the biological and cultural reproduction of the nation and the stability of states by distributing civil rights and duties. Issues of security and the protection of the nation in times of war and conflict (militarization) are tightly interwoven into these. However, women are not only passive subjects of the construction of nations and citizenship but also participate actively in nationalist and postnationalist struggles and in (re) defining citizenship and security. As nations and states are constantly evolving, the gendered inclusion and exclusion of women in the nation and the citizenry are central foci of gender and politics scholars.

The five chapters in this section map the old and new debates and the puzzles surrounding equality, citizenship, identity, nations, and security. They provide some signposts through the impasses and tensions created by diversity and intersectionality. Indeed, they give suggestions about how to avoid cultural relativism and hold onto feminist moral judgments regarding equality and fairness while accepting that cultures are hybrid and also how to continue gendering citizenship models while accepting that—in Birte Siim's words—vocabularies of citizenship are shaped by spaces and places. Moreover, there is a remarkable coherence in the solutions and third ways proposed in these chapters. Equality, citizenship, identity, nations, and security are recognized as unfinished projects that need inclusive dialogue and deliberation, which establishes strong links with processes of participation and representation. Only a contextualized, contingent, situated approach, as opposed to a dogmatic theoretical stance, can meet the ambitious expectation to do all and do it at the same time, that is, to take diversity and intersectionality seriously and at the same time address subnational, national, and transnational arenas. Taken together, these chapters appear to move away from grand theories about equality, citizenship, identity, nations, and security—except, of course, unless the new grand theory is accepted as being procedural in nature, which is a retreat to the process of determining equality and citizenship and away from universal theoretical claims about their substance.

The key contributions of the feminist scholarship presented in this section to political science concern, first, revealing the gendered nature and implications of these universal and neutral values and concepts. Feminist critical scholarship, for instance, showed that liberal notions of equality resulted in inequality and that classic citizenship, multicultural, nation building, and national security models and notions were tailored to male citizens and were gender-blind. Second, the solutions to deal with the complexity of identities and values in the multicultural and postnational era proposed by gender and politics scholars have added value that travels beyond gendered analyses and feminist concerns.

The first essay, "Universalism and Equality," by Judith Squires, explores the theoretical and normative contents of the concept of equality. It covers the feminist debates on equality as sameness and difference and as socioeconomic redistribution, cultural recognition, and political representation. The essay also discusses the shift toward diverse groups and multiple equality considerations, and the implications of the feminism versus multiculturalism debate for equality as a universal value. Squires then points to the dangers of the emergence of the concept of multiple equality strands and intersectionality—whereby equality for one group can conflict with and erode equality of other strands—but at the same time asserts that they provide an important theoretical resource with which to negotiate the debates between feminism and multiculturalism. Principles about (gender) equality need to be arrived at through inclusive deliberative processes based on specific and contextual knowledge. This can be seen as a middle way between idealistic theory on equality that increasingly loses legitimacy and an ethical relativism.

The second essay, "Citizenship," by Birte Siim, deals with the dual challenge posed by globalization, migration, and multilevel governance to renegotiate citizenship within and beyond the nation state. It describes the classic national citizenship models, the differentiation in citizenship rights in multicultural societies, and the extension of rights as defined by recent citizenship scholarship. Next the chapter analyzes the gendering of citizenship, describing how the equality versus difference debate gave rise to alternative citizenship models and how the renegotiation of equality with diversity within citizenship models foregrounded contextual approaches and deliberative perspectives. The chapter discusses citizenship in a global age where global governance and cosmopolitanism begged postnational and multilevel citizenship models. In that respect, attention is paid to European integration and to the politics of human rights and the implications gendering these, examining, for instance, global care chains, a moral cosmopolitanism that stresses women's rights as human rights, and the role of the European Union (EU) in fostering equality.

The third essay, "Multiculturalism and Identity," by Baukje Prins and Sawitri Saharso, discusses liberal and critical multiculturalism and the gender dilemmas between universalism and relativism and questions regarding the subject and individual autonomy they pose. The chapter extensively engages with the multiculturalism versus feminism debate, discussing four liberal answers to the question about how to deal with the universalism–relativism issue and the problem of individual autonomy. The authors point to the significant contributions of feminists to critical multiculturalism with regard to the importance given to standpoints and intersections, hegemonic discourses constructing identities and counterhegemonic discourses, and how diversity is experienced and lived in the flesh. A third position, both within the liberal and the critical discourse of multiculturalism, is also elaborated, stressing contextual reasoning and understanding of liberal and cultural values and narrative identity.

The fourth chapter, "Gender, Nations, and Nationalisms," by Suruchi Thapar-Björkert, presents an overview of the evolution of the scholarship on nation and nationalism and provides an explanation for the gender blindness of this literature. It then presents and discusses the key feminist contributions on women and the nation and women's integration in the project of modern nationhood. These review sections are followed by two substantive discussions of the interrelatedness of gendered and national identities at the symbolic level and the politicization of women's lives within the private as well as the public sphere. In nationalist discourses women have been the symbols of nationalist culture, but the discourse of the nation is also implicated in particular elaborations of masculinity. Drawing on the Indian case, the chapters further asserts that women not only have been co-opted in nationalist agendas but also have used nationalism to strategically carve political spaces and recognition in the postcolonial context. Finally, the chapter explores the linkage between nationalism, religion, and violence on behalf of the nations and reflects on the recent new Arab Nationalism.

The final chapter of this section, "Security, Militarization, and Conflict," by Lene Hansen, follows the chapter on nationalism as issues of security were traditionally defined as national security. The first part of the chapter, however, discusses how what is seen as a security issues was broadened and also gendered by framing gender issues as important to the survival of the community. The chapter gives an account of how states and international institutions have, over recent decades, moved to acknowledge gendered security problems. This involves a number of cases, for example in terms of the more traditional security sector, to look at how women are involved in conflicts, as combatants as well as peace activists; how women are made gendered targets, especially through the adoption of mass rape as a weapon of war; but also how the international community has moved to prosecute war time rape as a crime against humanity. The chapter also discusses the view of women as peaceful subjects and masculinity in relation to security.

CHAPTER 29

EQUALITY AND UNIVERSALISM

JUDITH SQUIRES

INTRODUCTION

The pursuit of gender equality has been widely endorsed as a central policy goal by governments and international organizations around the world. Yet the meaning of gender equality, and its centrality to feminist aims, has been a source of significant debate. The demand for equality between the sexes has frequently been countered by a competing demand that gender difference be recognized and women's specificity valued. For some, the idea that women are different has been used to exclude women from valued and fulfilling social engagement: the notion that women might not be capable of the rational, abstract, universalizing form of reasoning needed to engage in public arenas of work and politics needs—from this perspective—to be countered with an assertion of women's similarity to men. For others, the articulation of a woman's voice, or a feminist standpoint, is needed to counter the false impartiality of patriarchal reasoning. This tension between equality and difference remains one of the fundamental features of feminist theory and practice.

One of the central theoretical legacies of this debate has been the broadening of the understanding of equality: the earlier focus on economic and class inequalities has been supplemented, and at times displaced, by a preoccupation with cultural identity and group hierarchies. Equality has come to be viewed as requiring not only redistribution of material goods or income but also recognition of cultural identities and representation of particular standpoints. This theoretical challenge has created greater conceptual space for mainstream consideration of gender equality—leading to widespread policy changes across the globe, from the introduction of gender quotas to ensure women's increased participation in political decision making and the creation of women's policy agencies to facilitate the inclusion of women's voices in political debate to the introduction of gender mainstreaming to allow for a gendered perspective to be adopted in the formulation of policy proposals.

Yet the same theoretical insight also led to heightened awareness of cultural identity more broadly, with other identity groups making related claims for recognition and representation. Minority ethnic groups have made similar demands for recognition and inclusion, generating a politics of multiculturalism that echoed aspects of feminist equality politics but that represented a new challenge for gender equality advocates. Concern about the "perils of multicultural accommodation" (Shachar 1998, 287), viewed as potentially entailing the reinscription of structures of masculine domination, led some to argue that multiculturalism was bad for women (Okin 1999). Feminists were therefore confronted with the dilemma of either embracing a global ethical discourse grounded in universal principles of justice (Nussbaum 2000) or of opting for a more grounded, interpretive understanding of local cultural norms (Mohanty 1991). The tension between feminism and multiculturalism was, in effect, heightened by the "culturalist tendency to interpret the universal appeal at abstract moral principle as the replay of Western hegemonic imperialism" coupled with the "universalist tendency to interpret the cultural feminist suspicion of regulative normative ideals as the equivalent of a nihilistic, radical relativism" (Dietz 2003, 418–419).

This apparent tension between the claims of gender and cultural equality was complicated by the demand—made initially by black feminists—that equality policies needed to be formulated in a manner that is sensitive to intersectionality (for further discussion of intersectionality see the chapter by Hill Collins and Chepp in this volume). Recognition of the fact that discrete forms of oppression shape and are shaped by one another lead for a call to theorize the intersections of race, class, and gender. The emergence of the concept of *intersectionality*, attentive as it is to the cross-cutting nature of structures of oppression and the overlapping nature of groups, offers an important theoretical resource with which to negotiate the debates between feminism and multiculturalism. Meanwhile, the growing challenges posed by global interdependence heightened concern about global justice but also addressed the presumption of universalism embedded within earlier egalitarianism. As the obstacles to achieving equality in the real-world circumstances faced by those who are subjected to inequality across the globe are confronted, so the claims to universality made by liberal egalitarians look increasingly like particularity masquerading as universalism. In this context feminist critical theory suggests that what is needed is the production of specific and contextual knowledge via dialogue rather than the abstract thought experiments more typical of liberal egalitarianism. The challenge that continues to preoccupy feminist debate is whether this represents an abandonment of universalism and an embrace of ethical relativism or whether what is in fact required is a modified universalism.

This chapter starts by surveying recent debates about the concept of equality, first outlining the liberal egalitarian focus on questions of redistribution and then introducing the critique of this redistributive focus as articulated by advocates of a politics of recognition, who emphasize the importance of not only maldistribution but also cultural oppression. This broader understanding of equality is then augmented by a consideration of the need to also focus on issues of political participation and democratic inclusion. The chapter then turns its attention to gender equality in particular, arguing that the embrace of the broader conceptualizations of equality as entailing recognition and representation as well as redistribution enabled gender equality to gain a global prominence. The pursuit of the active participation of women in decision making as an essential component of gender equality was manifest in relation to a range of influential strategies, including candidate quotas, women's policy agencies, and gender mainstreaming, which have been adopted internationally as part of a global campaign to promote gender equality. The third section of the chapter then turns its attention to the emergence of a multiple inequalities agenda, which has further complicated the way equality is conceptualized and promoted by acknowledging that the identity groups that seek recognition and inclusion are themselves diverse and that their equality claims may conflict. The debate between feminism and multiculturalism focused on the tensions between equality considerations pertaining to gender and ethnic identity, with some feminists opting for universalist assertions of the importance gender equality and others embracing a more culturally relativist acceptance of different cultural practices. If the feminism–multiculturalism debate raised a question about the universality of gender equality considerations, the equality demands made on the grounds of sexuality, disability, and age further complicate matters for gender equality advocates. By highlighting the cross-cutting and intersectional nature of discriminatory practices, the multiple inequalities framework that is now dominant leads to a sense that indicators of inequality are themselves diverse and culturally specific. The final section of the chapter therefore focuses directly on the question of universalism, exploring the pros and cons of attempting to hold onto some universal measures of gender inequality to avoid ethical relativism, and surveys abstract philosophical defenses of universalism and more grounded discursive attempts to do so. The chapter concludes by suggesting that feminist debates about equality and universalism generally lead to a sense that the challenge posed by global interdependence makes it increasingly difficult to defend the legitimacy of conceptions of equality claiming to derive from ideal theory, which increasingly appear as particularity masquerading as universalism.

THE CONCEPT OF EQUALITY

Modern citizenship has been widely understood to entail civil, political, and social rights: equality before the law, equal access to parliamentary institutions, and a guarantee of economic and social well-being. While liberal polities are generally grounded on their commitment to civil and political equality, the pursuit of social equality has been more fraught and contested, particularly given the empirical existence of extensive inequality of wealth and income in capitalist societies. Debates about equality among contemporary political theorists—and liberal egalitarians in particular—have as a result tended, until recently, to focus on social equality (implicitly assuming that civil and political equality have been assured and therefore no longer require scrutiny). The tension between the principled liberal–democratic commitment to egalitarian citizenship and the continued material inequality of economic and social well-being has generated a substantial theoretical literature, which attempts to explain and justify the place of social inequality from an egalitarian perspective, reflecting upon which material distributions are just.

Redistribution

The first thing of note within this literature is that very few people indeed argue for a distribution of wealth and income that is equal in the sense of being the same for all. Ronald Dworkin (2002, 2), for instance, states categorically that no one would now seriously propose equality of outcome as a political ideal. Perhaps because equalizing outcomes has come to be viewed as a politics of envy that denies choice (see Phillips 2004, 2), the liberal egalitarian literature is characterized, with a very few exceptions, not by a debate between equality of opportunities and outcomes but by debate on different sorts of equality of opportunity. On a minimal conception of equality of opportunity, "a person's race or gender or religion should not be allowed to affect their changes of being selected for a job, of getting and good education, and so on" (Swift 2001, 99). What matters are their skills and talents. Even socialist egalitarians such as Gerry Cohen advocate "equal access to advantage" (Cohen 1989, 907).

The assumption that inequality is perfectly acceptable as long as it is based on talent has been criticized by more radical liberal egalitarians on the basis that such a meritocratic system is compatible with, and indeed may generate, a society with huge disparities in income and status in which a talented elite dominate while the disadvantaged are deemed to have failed as a result of their own personal deficiencies. John Rawls (1971, 108) describes this approach to equality as an "equal chance to leave the less fortunate behind in a personal quest for influence and social position." In its place, he famously proposed a theory of justice that entails a principle of equal basic liberties and a second principle in which "social and economic inequalities are to be arranged so that they are a) to the greatest benefit of the least advantaged, and b) attached to offices and positions open to all under conditions of fair equality of opportunity" (302). Other liberal egalitarians moved to base their defense of equal opportunities not on talent but on effort and ambition (Dworkin 2002, 199). Equality here becomes something individuals must earn—and whether they earn it will depend upon their choices (Armstrong 2003, 415). A key concern for these egalitarians is which part of individuals' lives is the result of their choices and which part is not.

Authors working within the framework of gender justice have criticized liberal–egalitarian theories of distributive justice as gender blind and androcentric. For example, many theories of egalitarian justice assume that the concept of justice applies only to the public sphere, taking distributions within the family as given. Feminist political theorists have argued that analyses of social justice that are sensitive to gender need to include the private sphere and consider the gendered division of labor within it (Okin 1989; Phillips 1997). They have also challenged the individualism inherent within much mainstream egalitarian theorizing, which marginalizes the impact of social structures, ignores the significance of social groups, and fails to identify structural inequalities (Young 2000). Ingrid Robeyns (2003, 541), for example, suggests that liberal egalitarianism is "structurally unable to account for the cultural aspects of gender, race, and other dimensions of human diversity that create unjust inequalities between people." For this reason, advocates of equality increasingly turned their attention to issues of not only redistribution but also recognition.

Recognition

Critics of the liberal egalitarian focus on equality of opportunity argue that these liberal theories of equality tend to lack a theory of inequality: they don't analyze the origins of the forms of inequality that they want to eradicate. As Iris Young (1990, 22) notes, "Many discussions of social justice often presuppose specific institutional structures whose justice they fail to bring under evaluation." Perhaps as a result, liberal egalitarians tend to advocate the free market as the surest route to egalitarian justice, which means that they maintain a concern with material and financial distributions rather than distributions of power or status (focusing on distribution rather than recognition).

However, following the civil rights movement in the United States, movements across the globe have focused attention on racism, sexism, ageism, discrimination in relation disability, and sexual orientation, complicating prior equality discourses that had focused primarily on economic inequalities (Baker et al. 2004, 10). The demands of these egalitarian movements challenged not only elite policy discourse but also academic conceptions of inequality. The old equality discourse, which had focused on the distribution of material goods, was increasingly cast by radical social movements as overly reductive and by political elites as unrealistically utopian. These combined critiques ushered in the new politics of equality (Kantola and Squires 2010).

Influentially, Young (1990, 19) argues that while there were pressing reasons to attend to the issues of the distribution of wealth and resources, "many public appeals to justice do not concern primarily the distribution of material goods" but focus on stereotyping and negative cultural representations. To pursue these wider goals of equality, one needs to engage with and eradicate oppression—which, she suggested, "consists in systematic institutional processes which inhibit people's ability to play and communicate with others or to express their feelings and perspectives on social life in context where others can listen" (38)—and domination, which "consists in institutional conditions which inhibit or prevent people from participating in determining their actions" (ibid.). This challenge to the politics of distribution brought the issue of recognition to the forefront of theoretical debate (Taylor 1992) and suggested that formal antidiscrimination laws needed to be supplemented by positive action measures to ensure greater social inclusion for marginalized groups.

Focusing on the nondistributive issues of social structures, feminist theorists have noted that in the context of a patriarchal society the pursuit of gender equality is constantly entrapped by exaggeration and denial. Two distinct strategies have consistently emerged, for example, when considering how employment legislation ought to be drafted to deal with the fact that women may require pregnancy leave and benefits. The first approach proposes that pregnancy should be included within general gender-neutral leave and benefit policies. Such policies would be relevant to any physical condition that renders anyone, male or female, unable to work. The second approach suggests that this does not actually constitute the pursuit of gender neutrality because it takes male lives as the norm and so disadvantages women (Williams 1983). From this perspective, the problem is not only that policies claiming to be neutral are actually partial but also that the distinctiveness of women's contribution is not positively recognized. By contrast, some feminists propose a gender-differentiated approach that might positively recognize, and give public confirmation of, the social contribution of childbearing. This entails the recommendation of positive action strategies, based on women's differences from men. Although some gender-equality advocates argued that this strategy served to reinforce feminine stereotypes rather than feminist principles (Rhode 1992, 154), the idea of sexual difference continued to underpin a significant strand of feminist thought (see, for example, Braidotti 1991; Grosz 1994). The campaign to increase the numbers of women in the French legislature was, for example, based on the argument that 50 percent representation of both women and men in all decision-making bodies was needed because humanity was divided into two essentially different parts— women and men—and both sexes have a right to represent their sexual difference in the same proportion (Agacinski 2001).

Similar concerns about the significance of cultural identity were also raised by theories concerned about ethnic, linguistic, and religious group identities. Advocates of a politics of recognition, or difference theorists, insist that liberal egalitarianism has privatized cultural, religious, and other differences, which the state should recognize and take into account in its laws, institutions, practices, and policies. Treating citizens as equals does not entail treating them equally: laws may legitimately grant exemptions to some groups and not to others, and public policies may focus on those groups whose cultures are under threat (Kymlicka 1995). From this perspective a politics of redistribution defines justice too narrowly and fails to focus on the importance of the diversity of ways of thought, of life, tastes, and moral perspectives.

One of the most influential theorists of a politics of recognition is Charles Taylor, who explains that treating people equally will entail distributive concerns but treating them as equals need not, because this entails recognizing what is different and distinctive about them. Treating people as equals will require giving due acknowledgment to each person's identity, and this entails recognition of what is peculiar to each (Taylor 1992, 39). Accordingly, recognizing the unique identity of everyone requires not an identical set of rights for all but public acknowledgment of the particular worth of each.

The argument that each individual's unique identity ought to be recognized to grant that person dignity frequently slips into a correlative—but distinct— claim that *group* identities require recognition. These two claims are linked by the assumption that the expression of one's unique identity will take the form of a group identity—that groups portray an authentic expression of one's individuality (Benhabib 2002, 53). This second assertion of the importance of group difference challenges the individualism of liberal egalitarianism, emphasizing instead the culturally embedded nature of people. While liberal egalitarians do of course acknowledge that individuals differ culturally and religiously, they tend to view these differences as contingent and politically nonpertinent. From the perspective of a politics of recognition, this move is suspect: far from abstracting from differences, liberal polities and policies have more frequently institutionalized the values and norms of the dominant culture. Difference theorists therefore suggest that, rather than denying the significance of these cultural norms, the state should acknowledge the diversity of cultures within the polity, grant laws that exempt some groups from laws and not others, create political institutions that give special group representation rights to marginalized groups, and modify cultural symbols in recognition of the presence of diverse groups. Even some theorists working within the distributive paradigm have come to acknowledge the importance of cultural recognition to the pursuit of equality. Will Kymlicka (1995), for example, argues that genuine equality requires group-specific rights for ethnic and national minorities (see also the chapter by Baukje Prins and Sawitri Saharso in this volume). Arguing against those who suggest that equality requires equal rights for each individual regardless of race or ethnicity, he suggests that some minority claims may eliminate inequalities and are therefore just. Group-differentiated rights—such as territorial autonomy, veto powers, guaranteed representation in central institutions, land claims, and language rights—are argued to help rectify disadvantages associated with being outvoted by the majority group: these demands for increased powers or resources are necessary to ensure the same opportunity to live and work in one's culture (110). So, although some advocates of a politics of difference are critical of the distributive paradigm, Kymlicka's defense of group-differentiated land rights is based on a theory of distributive justice in that the claims are based on what groups need now to sustain themselves as distinct societies.

Taken as a whole, these debates indicate that cultural recognition was introduced squarely onto the egalitarian agenda, eclipsing the primary status previously given to issues of redistribution. In this way the shift in concern from economic to cultural inequalities was accompanied by a shift in focus from sameness to difference. Equality now appeared to require a respect for difference rather than a search for similarities. It also tended to focus on the importance of equality between groups rather than between individuals, incorporating analyses of the systems and structures that constitute and perpetuate the inequalities under consideration in the first place.

Although this move to theorize equality as entailing the recognition of difference has been extremely influential in recent years, there are critics of this trend. Two concerns have emerged as particularly pressing: the first focuses on the degree to which the tendency to privilege groups leads to fragmentation of the wider polity; the second focuses on the extent to which the preoccupation with cultural recognition and political inclusion results in the marginalization of issues of economic distribution. These concerns might be thought of as the problems of reification and displacement, respectively (Fraser 2000).

In relation to the first of these, many liberal egalitarians have argued that the politics of recognition formalizes and freezes identities that are actually subject to constant change and thereby undermines solidarity across groups. As one critic notes, a "focus on affirming identity produces debilitating political fragmentation, diverts attention from widening material inequality, and leads to a fetishism of identity groups, reinforcing the tendency of such groups to become exclusionary to outsiders and coercive to insiders" (Kiss 1999, 194). Others have argued that the retribalization inherent in group-specific claims erodes a sense of public spiritedness (Elshtain 1995, 74) and endangers national identity (Miller 1995, 132). Given the controversial status of groups, and group rights, within the equality–difference debates, it is worth focusing on the place of groups in the various articulations of a politics of recognition and difference and noting that the move from making the ontological claim regarding the importance of recognition to the dialogical self to the advocacy claim regarding the importance of group rights to a just society is highly contested.

Benhabib (2002, 53), for instance, argues that it is "theoretically wrong and politically dangerous' to assume that the individual's search for authentic selfhood should be subordinated to the struggles of groups." This is an interesting challenge, because unlike many of the critics of group rights Benhabib embraces certain aspects of a politics of difference. She challenges the view of the moral self as a disembedded and disembodied being and rejects universalistic moral theories that are restricted to the standpoint of the "generalized other" (Benhabib 1992, 159l). She also suggests that the abstraction inherent in this mode of theorizing leads to the denial of difference. Yet she nonetheless claims that Taylor makes an "illicit move" from the right of the individual to pursue an authentic form of life, to the claim that groups pursuing a politics of difference would accommodate the realization of such individual authenticity (Benhabib 2002, 65). For Benhabib, the conception of groups entailed within the latter claim is too unitary to be sensitive to the contradictions and antagonisms within as well as between groups.

Anxieties about "the problem of reification" (Fraser 2000, 108) have led advocates of a politics of difference to argue that groups can best be viewed in relational rather than substantial terms. Groups should be conceptualized "not as substances or things or entities or organisms or collective individuals—as the imagery of discrete, concrete, tangible, bounded, and enduring 'groups' encourages us to do—but rather in relational, processual, dynamic, eventful, and disaggregated terms" (Brubaker 2004, 53). In this way they hope to "retain a description of social group differentiation, but without fixing or reifying groups…" (Young 2000, 89–90). The question remains, however, how this reconceptualization of groups impacts on the actual political strategies advocated in the name of these groups. Barry (2001), for instance, maintains that—notwithstanding this relational notion of social groups—Young continues to assume that the possession of a distinctive culture is what defines somebody as a member of a group. In so doing, she misdiagnoses the problem and therefore develops inappropriate cures.

Indeed, Barry (2001) suggests in his "egalitarian critique of multiculturalism" that the proposed group-based cures are not only inappropriate but also counterproductive. All policies aimed at achieving group recognition can actually achieve, he suggests, is "a minor reshuffling of the characteristics of the individuals occupying different locations in an unchanged structure that creates grossly unequal incomes and opportunities" (326). He argues that the politics of difference is mistaken in its assertion that equality requires recognition of citizens' identity-related differences (305–317) and suggests that the problems addressed by difference theorists can all ultimately be reduced to problems of formal economic inequality (319). Accordingly, traditional liberal legal policies can address the problem. Moreover, the preoccupation with difference undermines the solidarity necessary for the politics of redistribution (325).

This last claim links the two broad critiques of the politics of difference: the problem of reification and the problem of displacement. The former, which relates to the inappropriate preoccupation with groups, is argued to contribute to the latter, which relates to the declining concern with economic inequality, both theoretically and practically. In this way, liberal egalitarians argue that the emergence of a politics of difference not only diverts theoretical attention from issues of redistribution to those of recognition but also informs diverse policy initiatives that further erode the conditions required to pursue a redistributive politics. For the claim implicit in a politics of recognition—that groups have differences that require state recognition—shifts attention away from the structures that create inequalities and onto the characteristics of the claimant. One of the limitations of focusing on group rights therefore lies in the fact that depicting the problem of inequality as a problem relating to the group as an entity serves to obfuscate the problem of inequality as a problem of systematic structures of oppression and domination. In other words, the reification of group identities contributes to the displacement of struggles to address economic inequality.

While more sympathetic to the concerns of difference theorists, Anne Phillips (1999, 1) also interrogates the "parting of the ways between political and economic concerns." Her argument, which is that there has been a shift of attention from the class inequalities that undermine democracy to the gender, racial, or cultural hierarchies that subvert equal citizenship (14), grapples with the problem of displacement. She notes that this shift has resulted in a polarization between economic and political approaches to inequalities, with political approaches appearing to jettison concern with economic issues altogether (15). Similarly, Fraser (1995) argues that the preoccupation with cultural domination works to marginalize concerns about economic injustices. Accordingly, she proposes a theoretical framework that addresses both the political economy and culture, and considers both redistribution and recognition as appropriate responses to inequality but ones that stand in tension to one another: the affirmative politics of recognition conflicts with the transformative politics of redistribution, in that the former affirms group identity whereas the latter aims to eliminate the group as a group (Fraser 2000).

Representation

The lengthy debate about recognition and redistribution signals the extent to which concerns about both maldistribution and cultural oppression now frame attempts to theorize equality. Yet the binary construction of this debate has perhaps obfuscated the importance of domination in relation to theorizing equality. The neat dichotomy between recognition and redistribution appears to allow no place for specifically political issues, pertaining to political participation and citizenship. It pits economic maldistribution against cultural oppression and thereby allows no conceptual space for considerations of democratic inclusion.

While equality theorists have focused on economic maldistribution and difference theorists have focused on cultural oppression, recent feminist political theorists have tended to be both critical of the economic individualism of liberal egalitarians and concerned about the essentialism of recognition theorists. Their emphasis on democratic inclusion shifts attention from the perennial equality of what? question (resources or dignity?) to the wider issue of who partakes in this very debate. Centrally, it focuses attention on the legitimacy of the actual process by which the norms of equivalence are derived. In this way a concern with democratic participation is emphasized as central to equality considerations.

Whereas Taylor's politics of recognition focuses on oppression, Young's politics of difference aims to challenge both oppression and domination, focusing attention on democratic inclusion as well as cultural recognition. Accordingly, Young (2000) proposes that mechanisms for the effective representation of all citizens should entail institutional and financial support for the self-organization of oppressed groups, group generation of policy proposals, and group veto power regarding specific policies that affect a group directly (141–142). These proposals have been echoed practically in international campaigns to introduce candidate quotas for women, reserved seats for ethnic minorities, and group representation on a wide array of governing bodies.

Overall, the recognition–redistribution debate set up something of a false dichotomy in suggesting that one needs to decide whether to pursue redistributive or recognition remedies. For, as Isin and Wood (1999, 154) note, the question that faces us is not whether to engage in cultural recognition, economic struggle, or democratic activity "but how to do all and at the same time."

GENDER EQUALITY

The reconceptualization of equality as including recognition and representation considerations underpinned to emergence of gender equality as a widely accepted political goal, with the pursuit of gender equality widely endorsed as a central policy goal by governments and international organizations around the world (Inglehart and Norris 2003). Of course, the growing global concern with gender equality does not mean that there has been universal agreement as to its nature. The meaning of gender equality has been "hotly contested" as it has traveled "across different national borders, amidst different policy actors, both at institutional and non-institutional levels, and across a variety of national and international organisations" (Lombardo, Meier, and Verloo 2009, 1). Gender equality can be understood in a range of ways, variously focusing attention on life expectancy and income distribution (Sen 1992), welfare regimes and employment rates (Sainsbury 1996), or political participation (Kenworthy and Malami 1999). Nonetheless, its role as a bon mot in political discourse generally rested on a presumption that the equality in question was formal equality of opportunity between women and men, particularly within the political arena. Influentially, the United Nations Platform for Action stated that "without the active participation of women and the incorporation of women's perspectives at all levels of decision making, the goals of equality, development and peace cannot be achieved" (United Nations 1995, 181).

The active participation of women in decision-making has frequently been pursued via three central strategies: candidate quotas; women's policy agencies; and gender mainstreaming (Squires 2007). Candidate gender quotas have been adopted in more than one hundred countries, leading to the suggestion that quota fever has affected the world (Dahlerup and Freidenvall 2004, 32). Gender mainstreaming was adopted by the United Nations at the 1995 conference on women in Beijing and then taken up by the European Union, its member-states, and international development agencies and is now "an international phenomenon" (True 2003; Walby 2005). These soft-law tools complemented the wide-spread creation of women's policy agencies, which had been recommended by the earlier Unitied National World Conference on Women in Mexico City 1975.

Quotas

Candidate gender quotas have been adopted in more than one hundred countries, either in the form of reserved seats, which are designated places for women in political assemblies that men are not eligible to contest (in Africa, Asia, and the Middle East), party quotas that aim to increase the proportion of party candidates that are women (in Western Europe, Australia, and New Zealand), or legislative quotas that require political parties to nominate a certain percentage of women among their candidates (in Latin America and Southeastern Europe) (Krook 2009) (see also the chapter by Mona Lena Krook and Leslie Schwindt-Bayer in this volume). Scholars offer differing explanations for quota adoption, ranging from women's mobilization and transnational norm dissemination to the strategic incentives of political elites (Krook 2004). There is also significant divergence in relation to evaluations of their impact, including arguments that the adoption of quotas has led to increases, stagnation, and even decreases in the numbers of women elected. Nonetheless, the widespread adoption of candidate quotas is a clear manifestation the growing commitment to the use of positive action measures to promote the political equality of women. Candidate quotas aim primarily to recognize women's political under-representation and to secure their improved social inclusion; they aim to counteract institutional processes that reinforce cultural domination rather than to redistribute material resources that perpetuate economic inequality. The resulting policies focus on levels of descriptive rather than substantive representation: with the number of women present in decision-making arenas rather than the nature of the decisions made and their impact on the female electorate (Celis et al. 2008).

Mainstreaming

A second key strategy that emerged during this period to address gender equality was gender mainstreaming (see also the chapter by Emanuela Lombardo, Petra Meier, and Mieke Verloo in this volume). Best understood as a set of tools and processes that help to integrate a gender perspective into all policies at the planning stage, mainstreaming operates by requiring those involved in the policy process to consider the likely effects of policies on the respective situation of women and men and then revising proposed policies if necessary such that they promote gender equality rather than reproduce gender inequality. While the theoretical potential of gender mainstreaming was initially thought to be significant, evaluations of its practical implementation to date have been somewhat more circumspect (Bacchi and Eveline 2004; Teghtsoonian 2004). Critics worry that organizations are adopting some of the mainstreaming tools in the absence of an overall gender framework, focusing on the effective implementation of specific techniques of policy praxis and bracketing larger questions about social transformation (Daly 2005, 436). In line with the general features of the new equality politics, there is a targeting of tools here rather than of equality itself. Given that equality of opportunity is so difficult to measure and hence monitor, techniques tend to stand in for outputs as measures of effectiveness. As a result, legitimacy increasingly resides with being seen to adopt the appropriate techniques rather than actually generating greater equality.

Policy Agencies

Following the United Nations World Conference on Women in Mexico City in 1975, which recommended that governments establish agencies dedicated to promoting gender equality and improving the status and conditions of women, women's policy agencies were actively promoted by trans-national women's groups and widely adopted by national governments throughout the late 1970s and 1980s

(Chappell 2002, see also the chapter by Dorothy E. McBride and Amy G. Mazur in this volume). By 2004, 165 countries had women's policy agencies (DAW 2004), representing a "rapid global diffusion" of a state-level bureaucratic innovation that is "unprecedented in the post-war era" (True and Mintrom 2001, 30). Although the form and remit of these policy agencies differed across countries, research indicates that they have generally been successful in advancing women's concerns both substantively and descriptively (McBride Stetson and Mazur 1995; Rai 2003; Squires 2007). They have done so by establishing effective links between women's movements and the state and facilitating women's access into decision-making processes (Mazur 2001; Lovenduski 2005).

All of this indicates that gender equality has become widely accepted as a political goal over the last few decades, with many countries and transnational institutions committing themselves to gender equality; conventions have been signed, special bureaucracies and new political and administrative positions created, new policy and legal instruments developed and installed, and progress monitored in newly produced indices and rankings.

EQUALITY AND MULTICULTURALISM

Yet it is not only gender equality that has grown in public significance; while state institutions have been created to promote greater gender equality, multicultural policies have been adopted to respond to the challenges of cultural diversity (Kymlicka 1995; Parekh 2000; Modood 2007), and the demands of other identity groups, including disability (Albert 2004), religious belief (Bader 2003), sexuality (Richardson 2000), and age (Fredman and Spencer 2003) have all emerged a key political concerns (see also the chapter by Baukje Prins and Sawitri Saharso in this volume). This is symptomatic of the degree to which contemporary equality policies and theories now tend to focus on issues of cultural and political inequality rather than inequalities in distributional goods. Those who are considered to be unequal are increasingly seen to be ethnic minorities, disabled, the elderly, gays and lesbians, religious minorities, and so on rather than the poor. Poverty is no longer the focus for the new politics of equality, notwithstanding the fact that many of the minority groups are differentially exposed to poverty. This is particularly evident in the EU's framing of equality, due in large measure to the specific nature of the EU's powers, which led it to focus on equal treatment in employment (Walby 2005).

While the issue of multiple inequalities is not new, significant attention is currently paid to the tensions between the various equality strands, with particular theoretical focus on the relation between feminism and multiculturalism (Shachar 1998; Okin 1999; Phillips 2009). This generates an emerging discussion relating to the differences between inequalities, which may necessitate specific institutional mechanisms for tackling specific discriminations (Verloo 2006). Scholars have argued that the current emphasis on multiple discrimination, however, assumes that the categories can be treated similarly and does not address difficult political and normative issues about which category should be privileged at times of conflict (Squires 2009).

It is therefore particularly significant that a concern with gender equality has frequently been pitted against the promotion of multiculturalism. Indeed, opponents of multiculturalism often tend to focus on gender inequality in their attempts to discredit the multicultural project, deploying principles of gender equality and claims about the maltreatment of women as part of a demonization of minority cultural groups. Feminists have argued that multicultural measures can shore up the power base of the powerful members within minority communities and encourage the public authorities to tolerate practices that undermine women's equality (Okin 1999). They have focused attention on the tensions that arise when culturally diverse democratic states seek to pursue both justice for religious and cultural minorities and gender equality, frequently reinforcing gender inequality within minority communities (Song 2009). The debate about feminism and multiculturalism has, as a result, generally been framed in a manner that depicts the value of gender equality as an important limit on cultural accommodation, with some feminists allowing that there are circumstances under which egalitarian justice requires special accommodations for cultural minorities and others focusing on the dangers of so doing. The universalist claims of gender equality are here pitted against the more particularist multicultural claims for recognition.

It is in this context that Phillips (2009) insists multiculturalism per se is not the problem but rather the uncomplicated use of culture that is found within much of the discourse on multiculturalism, on both sides of the debate, that presents a reified notion of culture that exaggerates its unity and solidity (8). In her theoretical defense of a nonessentialized multiculturalism, Phillips gives a compelling account of how one can underpin the introduction of mechanisms for addressing the under-representation of ethnocultural minorities without appealing to an essentialized notion of culture. Phillips's challenge is to those discourses of culture that deny human agency by defining individuals through their culture, promoting cultural stereotypes, and exaggerating the extent of cultural difference. She highlights the way the preoccupation with the equality of women in minority groups plays a central role in this depiction of minority groups as profoundly different. Cases in which culture is inappropriately invoked to justify violence against women have rightly given rise to concerns about how the claims of culture can sustain inequalities against women. However, critics of multiculturalism often accept highly contested cultural interpretations and describe oppressive practices as definitively cultural in ways that lead to a perception of minority cultures as inherently oppressive and coercive and present multiculturalism as innately polarized to the interests of women. In this, culture is employed in highly selective ways, in which the behavior of individuals from ethnocultural minority groups is explained through appeal to their culture whereas the behavior of others is seen as reflecting their personal choice (29).

Thus, in Phillips's (2009) version of multiculturalism, the particular is continually illuminated by the universal. Both feminism and the political theory of multiculturalism have unwittingly played a part in encouraging this overemphasis on difference: theorists of multiculturalism have for their part deliberately emphasized the scale, significance, and legitimacy of cultural diversity to illuminate inequalities along ethnic and cultural lines and have tended to focus on examples such as female genital cutting and child marriages, which have contributed to the representation of peoples and cultures as profoundly different in their practices, values, and beliefs (23–25). Feminism meanwhile has also played its part in generating strong binaries between liberal and illiberal groups, as with Okin's (1999) asymmetrical treatment of cultures in her essay titled "Is Multiculturalism Bad for Women?" Okin's focus on alien practices, which are highly contested, provides the grounds for arguing that other cultures might need to be eradicated. Meanwhile, any abuse of women's rights in Western liberal cultures are judged to be an "aberration" because the "norm of gender equality…is at least formally endorsed" by liberal cultures (9, 16–17). In failing to contextualize practices, Okin can be seen to reproduce what Uma Narayan (1997) terms a *colonialist stance* toward other cultures, that is, the drawing of implicit contrasts between the culture existing outside of history that is irrational and unchanging and a culture that is rationalist, enlightened, and liberal.

Yet in acknowledging the difficulties of the colonialist stance, feminist critics have disarmed themselves of many of the tools with which to make normative judgments and evaluate oppressive practices. The central issue becomes that of how to act effectively against abuses of women without simultaneously promoting cultural stereotypes (Dustin and Phillips 2008, 420). Phillips's (2009) multiculturalism without culture attempts to negotiate this challenge, beginning from the point of "an unashamed normative commitment" to the principle of equality (ibid., 2), insisting that in developing a case for multiculturalism it is the rights of individuals and not the rights of groups that matter (ibid., 165). However, other theorists have opted to take a more structural approach to the challenge of competing equality demands, focusing not on individuals but on the intersections between groups.

INTERSECTIONALITY

The concept of intersectionality emerged in response to the inability of various singular analyses of structural inequality to recognize the complex interrelation between forms of oppression (see also the chapter by Patricia Hill Collins and

Valerie Chepp in this volume). While multicultural advocates of racial equality may fail to adequately acknowledge the gendered inequalities within their
own minority groups, feminist advocates of gender equality may similarly fail
to appreciate the ways racial stereotyping impacts different women's experiences of gendered inequality differently. Theories of intersectionality hold that
discrete forms of oppression shape, and are shaped by, one another (Crenshaw
1991). The concept was developed within black feminism, emerging as a tool for
theorizing the intersections of race, class, and gender and used initially to show
that the insertion of gender as a category of analysis transformed the understanding of race and class in traditional African American scholarship (Brewer
1999). Advocates of intersectionality argue that failure to recognize the significance of these intersections results in both simplistic analyses and ill-conceived
policy interventions. This approach still retains a notion of structural inequalities and operates with groups as the subject of equality policies rather than
individuals; however, it is attentive to the cross-cutting nature of structures of
oppression and the overlapping nature of groups.

One approach to the formulation of equality policies that are sensitive to
intersectionality is additive. Here each axis of discrimination remains distinct,
and equality advocates remain attentive to the distinctive nature of each inequality strand, avoiding an oversimplistic assumption that all inequalities are
of the same order and therefore amenable to the same sort of policy response.
The emphasis remains on groups as the subjects of equality, but attention is
focused on the contradictions and antagonisms within as well as between
groups (Benhabib 2002, 53). Contradictions between groups take many forms,
but most make the pursuit of an integrated equality agenda, which embraces
multiple equality strands equally, rather fraught. For instance, many feminists
have argued that the recognition of ethnic minority and religious group rights
may limit and erode the pursuit of gender equality (Okin 1999, 7–24). It has
been suggested that the cultural minorities claiming group rights in the name
of equality are frequently more patriarchal in their practices and beliefs than
are majority cultures. The granting of ethnic or religious group exemptions in
the name of identity-based equality may therefore work against the promotion
of gender equality. Similarly, affirming the identity of religious groups may conflict with ensuring full participation of gay, lesbian, and bisexual people, while
a commitment to retaining older workers may hinder strategies to increase
employment participation rates among ethnic minorities (Fredman 2003, 29).
Promoting equality with respect to one equality strand may therefore conflict
with, or even erode, the equality of another. For instance, assertions of gender
equality can be used to critique minority cultural groups—"said to keep their
women indoors, marry their girls off young to unknown and unwanted partners, and force their daughters and wives to wear veils." (Phillips 2009, 2)—in a
manner that magnifies apparent cultural differences and does little to promote
ethnic equality. All of this suggests that, where multiple equality strands compete for moral support and financial resources, the creation of an integrated

equality agenda that embraces each of these equality strands equally will not be straightforward.

One response to this has been to focus attention on complexity within groups. Unsettling the apparent unity within equality strands, much intersectional analysis has emphasized the extent to which static notions of groups work to the disadvantage of minorities within the minorities, hiding the oppression of groups' internal minorities (which might variously include women, children, the poor). As one critic recently noted, "Well-meaning accommodations aimed at mitigating power inequalities between groups may end up reinforcing power hierarchies within them" (Shachar 2001, 4).

Another response from those who seek to hold onto the notion of intersectionality as productive while acknowledging the difficulties surrounding the additive form of intersectionality has been to advocate a more discursive or "transversal" approach to intersectionality (Yuval-Davis 2006, 193–209). Seeking to offer an alternative to the additive model, Yuval-Davis emphasizes communication rather than identity, dialogue rather than essences. This approach accepts that the world is seen differently from different standpoints but stresses that any one standpoint will be unfinished and that dialogue between those with different standpoints will produce a fuller knowledge, will allow participants to negotiate a common political position, and will enable them to mutually reconstruct themselves in the process. From this perspective solutions to the problems of inequality will always require discussion and dialogue. As Benhabib (1992, 163) notes, every procedure of universalizability presupposes that "like cases ought to be treated alike": the difficulty lies in knowing what constitutes a "like" situation. Similarly, Monica Mookherjee (2001) argues that rectification of unequal circumstances "cannot be achieved by applying preconceived interpretations of the term equality itself. This is because a necessary, if not sufficient, condition of equality is the enabling of excluded groups to unsettle and destabilize meanings and interpretations which the institutional culture has hitherto taken as universal and complete" (69). Enabling excluded groups to unsettle institutionally accepted conceptions of equality will require parity of participation, which makes democratic inclusion central to both the meaning and realization of equality.

EQUALITY AND UNIVERSALISM

Given what has already been outlined, there is a genuine debate as to whether equality remains a universal value for feminism and multicultural democracies today. There is a growing recognition that indicators of inequality are themselves diverse, including life expectancy and physical health, bodily integrity and safety, educational access and attainment, access to paid work, rates of pay, political empowerment, and being treated with dignity (Robeyns 2003a, 76–86). As Sen (1992, xi) argues, human diversity "is no secondary complication (to be ignored, or to be introduced 'later on'); it is a fundamental aspect of our interest in equality."

Sen's (1999) "capability approach" to equality focuses on "what people are actually able to do and to be" (18). He has criticized the inequality literature in welfare economics for its exclusive focus on income and broadens this focus out to include the real freedoms that people have for leading a valuable life. This introduces the notion of people's capacities to undertake activities of value and focuses attention on what people are able to be and to do, not on what they can consume or on their incomes. He suggests that "the question of gender inequality...can be understood much better by comparing those things that intrinsically matter (such as functionings and capabilities), rather than just the means [to achieve them] life...resources. This issue of gender inequality is ultimately one of disparate freedoms" (Sen 1992, 125). Capabilities are people's potential functionings, which are "beings and doings" such as taking part in a community, caring for others, being healthy, and being sheltered (Robeyns 2003a, 63). Resources are a means to enhance people's well-being, and people differ in their abilities to convert these resources into capabilities due to a variety of personal, social, and environmental factors. Inequalities in resources can therefore be significant causes of inequalities of capabilities, but so can other factors including human diversity, which has a central place in this approach. An advantage of this approach is that it is not limited to the market but includes nonmarket dimensions of well-being.

While recognizing the value of pluralizing the measure of inequality, some scholars specify a list of human capabilities that might be measured when trying to establish degrees of gender inequality. Most influentially, Nussbaum (2003) offers a cross-national basis for claims to social justice and equality by providing a philosophical justification for a universal account of human capabilities. She parts company with Sen (2004) in his refusal to endorse a specific list of central human capabilities and his focus on interactive processes of public reasoning. Although Sen does not speak directly to this point, his reticence to construct a list unsettles support for grand universalism. Ingrid Robeyns (2005) draws this point out, arguing for "sensitivity to context" and urging us to "pay due attention to the discursive and deliberative aspects of our philosophical or academic projects" (11). Nussbaum's commitment to a universal list is aimed to guarantee a "minimal conception of social justice" (40) that can challenge paternalism. Yet, while she insists that human capabilities be specific in an abstract manner, to "leave room for the activities of specifying and deliberating by citizens and their legislatures and courts" (42), the derivation of this list marginalizes the political struggles that are involved

in their formulation and institutionalization. Critics suggest that her modi-
fied universalism remains ethnocentric (Charusheela 2008). As Okin (2003, 296) notes, Nussbaum's "highly intellectualised conception of a fully human life and some of the capacities central to living it seem to derive far more from an Aristotelian ideal than from any deep or broad familiarity with the lives of women in the less-developed world." Robeyns (2003a), by contrast, takes issue not with the content of the list but with the process by which it is derived, emphasizing the importance of the procedural aspects of democratic practice (69).

The idea that theorists must proceed by first establishing what equality or justice requires under ideal conditions and only then consider local applica-tions is rendered increasingly problematic in light of the growing challenges posed by global interdependence. The impact of discourses of globalization has generated a burgeoning literature on global justice, in which contextual considerations are inevitably given a more prominent role than has been the case within earlier debates about equality when confined to a presumed liber-al–democratic nation-state. One consequence of the fact that the nation-state has ceased to be assumed to be the site within which claims of equality are articulated is that discussions about theories of justice have shifted to the glo-bal arena, and as a result "it becomes harder to sustain the myth of the politi-cal theorist as a monological source of authority on the meaning of justice" (Hutchings 2010, 231).

The abstracted approach employed by liberal egalitarians looks too abstracted to function as an adequate guide for collective action. As Colin Farrelly (2007, 859) argues, "Armchair theorizing about justice in ideal theory severely limits the practical insights of liberal egalitarianism as such theoriz-ing often brackets the complex and contentious issues that make the struggle for justice in real societies difficult." In addition, the claims to universality made by liberal egalitarians look increasingly like particularity masquerading as universalism.

The significant point here is that feminist critical theory "shifts the tradi-tional division of labour between political theory, political science and political action" (Hutchings 2010, 246). It is not simply that feminist normative politi-cal theory has traditionally been more attentive to empirical inquiry than its mainstream equivalent. Rather, feminist critical theory affirms that theories of justice "require specific and contextual knowledge about what is unjust to whom and how" (ibid.). The attempt to arrive at moral norms through the isolated thought experiments of the theorist are, on this view, seen as much a part of the problem as the solution to addressing various patterns of ine-quality. The pursuit of impartiality and a single set of principles to govern the public realm necessarily represses complex difference, paradoxically creating dichotomy rather than unity. If the citizen is understood to be a universal rea-soner, detached and impartial, he or she must abstract from the "particularity of affiliation, of social or group perspective, that constitutes concrete subjects" (Young 1990, 100). Given these concerns about impartiality feminist theorists have thus tended to assert the need for substantive principles of justice to be arrived at through actual deliberative processes in which all affected parties participate, either directly or through representatives.

Conclusion

There are a large number of equality philosophies that dispute both how we ought to measure equality (whether it is equality of opportunity or outcome that ought to be of concern) and what it is we ought to be measuring (resources, status, capabilities). There are many possible norms against which we might measure equality, and the process by which we determine these is of vital importance. The norms of equality are not universal and cannot be derived from abstract philosophical reasoning but rather are contextual and can legitimately be understood only as the product of democratic deliberation. Recent strategies that have emerged to secure women's political equality entail working assumptions about the nature of gender equality and about indicators of gender inequality. The promotion and adoption of these strategies therefore not only works to address pre-existing inequalities but also promotes particular understandings of what gender equality comprises and how we ought to measure it. These understandings will inevitably privilege some people's conceptions of equality and fail to do justice to others. The more inclusive the process by which the criteria of gender equality are determined, the more people are likely to find that the pursuit of gender equality policies addresses their own concerns. Participation in political decision-making is a constitutive part of gender equality and not just a means to it.

References

Albert, Bill. 2004. "Is disability really on the development agenda? A review of official disability policies of the major governmental and international development agencies." Disability Knowledge and Research. Available at http://94.126.106.9/r4d/PDF/Outputs/Disability/RedPov_disability_on_the_agenda.pdf.

Agacinski, Sylvaine. 2001. *Parity of the sexes*. Trans. L. Walsh. New York: Columbia University Press.

Armstrong, Christopher. 2003. "Opportunity, responsibility and the market: Interrogating liberal equality." *Economy and Society* 32(3): 410–427.

Bacchi, Carol, and Joan Eveline. 2004. "Mainstreaming and neoliberalism: A contested relationship." *Policy and Society: Journal of Public, Foreign and Global Policy* 22(2): 98–118.

Bader, V. 2003. "Taking religious pluralism seriously." *Ethical Theory and Moral Practice* 5(1): 3–22.

Baker, John, Kathleen Lynch, Sara Cantillon, and Judy Walsh. 2004. *Equality.* Basingstoke, UK: Palgrave.

Barry, Brian. 2001. *Culture and equality.* Cambridge: Polity Press.

Benhabib, Seyla. 1992. *Situating the self.* Cambridge: Polity Press.

Benhabib, Seyla. 2002. *The claims of culture: Equality and diversity in the global era.* Princeton, NJ: Princeton University Press.

Braidotti, Rosi. 1991. *Patterns of dissonance: An essay on women in contemporary French philosophy.* Cambridge, UK: Cambridge University Press.

Brewer, Rose. 1999. "Theorizing race, class and gender: The new scholarship of Black feminist intellectuals and black women's labor." In Stanlie M. James and Abena P. A. Busia, eds., *Theorizing black feminisms: The visionary pragmatism of black women.* New York: Routledge, 13–30.

Brubaker, Rogers. 2004. "Ethnicity without groups." In Steve May, Tariq Modood, and Judith Squires, eds., *Ethnicity, nationalism and minority rights.* Cambridge, UK: Cambridge University Press, 50–77.

Celis, Karen, Sarah Childs, Johanna Kantola, and Mona-Lena Krook. 2008. "Rethinking women's substantive representation." *Representation* 42(2): 99–110.

Chappell, Louise. 2002. *Gendering government: Feminist engagement with the state.* Vancouver: University of British Columbia Press.

Charusheela, S. 2008. "Social analysis and the capabilities approach: A limit to Martha Nussbaum's universalist ethics." *Cambridge Journal of Economics* 33(6): 1135–1152.

Cohen, Gerry. 1989. "On the currency of egalitarian justice." *Ethics* 4: 906–944.

Crenshaw Williams, Kimberle. 1991. "Mapping the margins: Intersectionality, identity politics, and violence against women of color." *Stanford Law Review* 43(6): 1241–1299.

Dahlerup, Drude, and Lenita Freidenvall. 2004. "Quotas as a 'fast track' to equal representation for women: Why Scandinavia is no longer the model." *International Feminist Journal of Politics* 7(1): 26–48.

Daly, Mary. 2005. "Gender mainstreaming in theory and practice." *Social Politics* 12(3): 433–450.

Division for the Advancement of Women. (DAW). (2004). "Commission on the Status of Women," March 1–12. Available at http://www.un.org/womenwatch/daw/csw/48sess.htm.

Dietz, Mary. 2003. "Current controversies in feminist theory." *American Review of Political Science* 6: 399–431.

Dustin, Moira, and Anne Phillips. 2008. "Whose agenda is it?: Abuses of women and abuses of 'culture' in Britain." *Ethnicities* 8(3): 405–424.

Dworkin, Ronald. 2002. *Sovereign virtue.* Cambridge, MA: Harvard University Press.

Elshtain, Jean-Bethke. 1995. *Democracy on trial.* New York: Basic Books.

Farrelly, Colin. 2007. *Justice, democracy and reasonable agreement.* Basingstoke, UK: Palgrave Macmillan.

Fraser, Nancy. 1995. "Recognition or redistribution? A critical reading of Iris Young's 'Justice and the politics of difference.'" *Journal of Political Philosophy* 3(2): 166–180.

Fraser, Nancy. 2000. "Rethinking recognition." *New Left Review*, 3: 3107–3120.

Fredman, Sandra. 2003. "The age of equality." In S. Fredman and S. Spencer, eds., *Age as an equality issue*. Oxford: Hart, 21–69.

Fredman, Sandra, and S. Spencer. (Eds.). 2003. *Age as an equality issue*. Oxford: Hart.

Grosz, Elisabeth. 1994. *Volatile bodies: Toward a corporeal feminism*. Bloomington: Indiana University Press.

Hutchings, Kimberly. 2010. "Global justice." In Colin Hay, ed., *New directions in political science: responding to the challenges of an interdependent world*. Basingstoke, UK: Palgrave Macmillan, 231–249.

Inglehart, Ronald, and Pippa Norris. 2003. *Rising tide: Gender equality and cultural change around the world*. Cambridge, UK: Cambridge University Press.

Isin, Engin, and Patricia Wood. 1999. *Citizenship and identity*. London: SAGE.

Kantola, Johanna, and Judith Squires. 2010. "The new politics of equality." In Colin Hay, ed., *New directions in political science*. Basingstoke, UK: Palgrave, 88–108.

Kenworthy, L., and M. Malami. 1999. "Gender inequality in political representation: A Worldwide comparative analysis." *Social Forces* 78(1): 235–269.

Kiss, Elizabeth 1999. "Democracy and the politics of recognition." In Ian Shapiro and Casiano Hacker-Cordon, eds., *Democracy's edges*. Cambridge, UK: Cambridge University Press, 193–209.

Krook, Mona Lena. 2004. "Gender quotas as a global phenomenon: Actors and strategies in quota adoption." *European Political Science* 3(3): 59–65.

Krook, Mona Lena. 2009. *Quotas for women in politics: Gender and candidate selection reform worldwide*. Oxford: Oxford University Press.

Kymlicka, Will. 1995. *Multicultural citizenship*. Oxford: Clarendon Press.

Lombardo, Emanuela, Petra Meier, and Mieke Verloo (Eds.). 2009. *The discursive politics of gender equality: Stretching, bending and policymaking*. London: Routledge.

Lovenduski, Joni (Ed). 2005. *State feminism and political representation*. Cambridge, UK: Cambridge University Press.

Mazur, Amy (Ed.). 2001. *State feminism, women's movements and job training: Making democracies work*. London: Routledge.

McBride Stetson, Dorothy, and Amy Mazur. 1995. *Comparative state feminism*. London: SAGE.

Miller, David. 1995. *On nationality*. Oxford: Oxford University Press.

Modood, Tariq. 2007. *Multiculturalism*. Cambridge, UK: Polity Press.

Mohanty, Chandra. 1991. "Cartographies of struggle: Third world women and the politics of feminism." In C. Mohanty, Ann Rosso, and Lourdes Torres, eds., *Third world women and the politics of feminism*. Bloomington: Indiana University Press, 1–47.

Mookherjee, Monica. 2001. "Justice as provisionality: An account of contrastive hard cases." *Critical Review of International Social and Political Philosophy* 4(3): 67–100.

Narayan, Uma. 1997. *Dislocating cultures—Identities, traditions and third world feminism*. London: Routledge.

Nussbaum, Martha. 2000. *Women and human development: The capabilities approach*. Cambridge, UK: Cambridge University Press.

Nussbaum, Martha. 2003. "Capabilities as fundamental entitlements: Sen and social justice." *Feminist Economics* 9(2–3): 33–59.

Okin, Susan Moller. 1989. *Justice, gender and the family*. New York: Basic Books.

Okin, Susan Moller. 1999. "Is multiculturalism bad for women?" In Joshua Cohen, Matthew Howard, and Martha Nussbaum, eds., *Is multiculturalism bad for women?* Princeton, NJ: Princeton University Press, 7–26.

Okin, Susan Moller. 2003. "Poverty, well-being and gender: What counts, who's heard." *Philosophy and Public Affairs* 31(3): 280–316.

Parekh, Bhikhu. 2000. *Rethinking multiculturalism: Cultural diversity and political theory.* Basingstoke, UK: Macmillan.

Phillips, Anne. 1995. *The politics of presence.* Oxford: Clarendon Press.

Phillips, Anne. 1997. "What has socialism to do with sexual equality?" In Jane Franklin, ed., *Equality.* London: Institute for Public Policy Research, 102–121.

Phillips, Anne. 1999. *Which equalities matter?* Cambridge, UK: Polity Press.

Phillips, Anne. 2004. *Defending Equality of Outcome* (online). London: LSE Research online. Available at: http://eprints.lse.ac.uk/533/1/equality_of_outcome.pdf.

Phillips, Anne. 2009. *Multiculturalism without culture.* Princeton, NJ: Princeton University Press.

Rawls, John. 1971. *A theory of justice.* Cambridge, MA: Harvard University Press.

Rai, Shirin (Ed.). 2003. *Mainstreaming gender, democratizing the state: Institutional mechanisms for the advancement of women.* Manchester: Manchester University Press.

Rhode, Deborah. 1992. "The politics of paradigms: Gender difference and gender disadvantage." In Gisela Bock and Susan James, eds., *Beyond equality and difference: Citizenship, feminist politics and female subjectivity.* London: Routledge, 149–192.

Richardson, Diane. 2000. "Constructing sexual citizenship: Theorising sexual rights" *Critical Social Policy* 20(1): 105–135.

Robeyns, Ingrid. 2003. "Is Nancy Fraser's critique of theories of distributive justice justified?" *Constellations* 10(4): 538–553.

Robeyns, Ingrid. 2003. "Sen's capability approach and gender inequality: Selecting relevant capabilities." *Feminist Economics* 9(2–3): 61–92.

Robeyns, Ingrid. 2005. "The capability approach: A theoretical survey." *Journal of Human Development* 6(1): 93–114.

Sainsbury, Diane. 1996. *Gender equality and welfare states.* Cambridge, UK: Cambridge University Press.

Sen, Amartya. 1992. *Inequality re-examined.* Oxford: Clarendon Press.

Sen, Amartya. 1999. *Development as freedom.* New York: Anchor Books.

Sen, Amartya. 2004. "Dialogue capabilities, lists and public reason." *Feminist Economics* 10(3): 77–80.

Shachar, Ayelet. 1998. "Group identity and women's rights in family law: The perils of multicultural accommodation." *Journal of Political Philosophy* 6(3): 285–305.

Shachar, Ayelet. 2001. *Multicultural jurisdictions: Cultural differences and women's rights.* Cambridge, UK: Cambridge University Press.

Song, Sarah. 2009. *Justice, gender and the politics of multiculturalism.* Cambridge, UK: Cambridge University Press.

Squires, Judith. 2007. *The new politics of gender equality.* Basingstoke, UK: Palgrave.

Squires, Judith. 2009. "Intersecting inequality: Britain's equality review." *International Feminist Journal of Politics* 11(4): 496–512.

Swift, Adam. 2001. "Equality." In Adam Swift, *Political philosophy.* Cambridge, UK: Polity, 91–131.

Taylor, Charles. 1992. "The politics of recognition." in Charles Taylor and Amy Gutmann, eds., *Multiculturalism and "the politics of recognition."* Princeton, NJ: Princeton University Press, 25–74.

Teghtsoonian, Kathleen. 2004. "Neoliberalism and gender analysis mainstreaming in Aotearoa/New Zealand." *Australian Journal of Political Science* 39(2): 267–284.

True, Jacqui. 2003. "Mainstreaming gender in global public policy." *International Feminist Journal of Politics* 5(3): 368–396.

True, Jacqui, and Michael Mintrom. 2001. "Transnational networks and policy diffusion: The case of gender mainstreaming." *International Studies Quarterly* 45: 27–57.

United Nations. 1995. *Platform for action and the Beijing declaration*. New York: Author.

Verloo, Mieke. 2006. "Multiple inequalities, intersectionality and the European Union." *European Journal of Women's Studies* 13(3): 211–228.

Walby, Sylvia. 2005. "Comparative gender mainstreaming in a global era." *International Feminist Journal of Politics* 7(4): 453–471.

Williams, Wendy. 1983. "Equality's riddle: Pregnancy and the equal treatment/special treatment debate." *New York University Review of Law and Social Change* 13: 325–380.

Young, Iris Marion. 1990. *Justice and the politics of difference*. Princeton: Princeton University Press.

Young, Iris Marion. 2000. *Inclusion and democracy*. Oxford: Oxford University Press.

Yuval-Davis, Nira. 2006. "Intersectionality and feminist politics." *European Journal of Women's Studies* 13(3): 193–209.

CHAPTER 30

....

CITIZENSHIP

....

BIRTE SIIM

INTRODUCTION

....

Globalization and migration have inspired new ideas about multilevel, transnational, and postnational citizenship. Mobility across and within national borders has challenged the nation-state, and citizenship, migration, and politics of belonging have become contested issues in liberal democracies. Migration has been followed by growing concerns about integration of immigrant and refugees in the national communities and by accommodation of cultural and religious diversity of minorities. Multilevel governance has raised issues about relations between rights and obligations on the subnational, (trans)national, and global levels.

These developments have challenged the classical citizenship models attached to the nation-state. Scholars have started to criticize what has been labeled methodological nationalism, that is, "the assumption that the nation/ state/society is the natural social form of the modern world" (Wimmer and Glick-Schiller 2002, 301; see also Beck 2002), and have proposed new postnational citizenship models. This chapter aims to discuss the challenges to rethink the citizenship frame within and beyond the nation-state from a gender and diversity perspective. The focus is on two contested themes: to renegotiate equality with diversity within the nation-states; and to develop a postnational notion of citizenship beyond the nation-state (Delanty 2000; Faist 2007). Arguably the renegotiation of equality and diversity raises contested questions for citizenship theory and research about overcoming the "us–them" division within, across, and beyond the nation-states.

The chapter suggests that these citizenship issues can contribute to illuminate peoples' real-life experiences, because they concern multiple and intersecting inequalities, which is the basis for claims for full and equal citizenship. They thus concern claims for citizenship rights and cultural recognition not only by a diversity of women's groups but also by minorities living within one country and immigrants and refugees moving across the nation-state borders. Examples are Muslim women's problems with accommodation of headscarves within liberal democracies (Rosenberger and Sauer forthcoming) and the struggles for access to democratic citizenship rights and the right to family unification for immigrants and refugee groups who live and work legally in a country (Lister et al. 2007, 77–109).

The first part gives a brief overview of the classical national citizenship model and the main citizenship traditions following T. H. Marshall's seminal work. It then reviews the rethinking of citizenship from historical and comparative perspectives and discusses the feminist proposals to gender citizenship since Carole Pateman's classical analysis of Mary Wollstonecraft's dilemma. The second most substantive part explores recent challenges to citizenship from globalization and migration and discusses postnational, cosmopolitan, and multicultural citizenship frames. The final section discusses proposals for a reconfiguration of citizenship, which address the dual challenges from diversity and globalization. It argues that future research should develop an intersectional and situated approach to citizenship able to explore the contextual meanings of equality and diversity and speak to interrelations between the subnational, national, and transnational arenas.

The Classical National Citizenship Models

Citizenship has become a key concept at the center of policy debates within and across national borders. Citizenship is an essentially contested concept in social and political theory and research and refers to the relations of individuals' and social groups' to public life. The notion of citizenship can be traced to the Greek polis that tied rights to membership of the city, excluding women and slaves. The modern version of citizenship is connected to the twin processes of nation building and industrialization following the American and French revolutions. Freedom of contract and protection of property rights were important elements, and the growth of markets contributed to break down traditional hierarchies and to foster equality and opportunity.

Marshall ([1950]2002), in the essay "Citizenship and Social Class," first developed a modern framework for the notion of citizenship based upon principles of freedom, equality, and solidarity. In Marshall's seminal work citizenship was defined as "a status bestowed on all those who are full members of a community" (1950, 18). This notion of citizenship refers to equal civil, political, and social rights. All citizens should have the same rights but also the same duties to pay taxes and do military duty. His work was based on a vision of equal rights for the working class in capitalist society inspired by the evolution of civil, political, and social rights in Britain from the eighteenth to the twentieth century.

Following Marshall, citizenship has a double focus: it is both a normative vision about equal rights and respect and a tool for analyzing the social and political developments of modern societies. Citizenship is an analytical frame, which conceptualizes who is included and who is excluded in the national communities—who is defined as being inside and who is outside society. Citizenship thus has a dual nature as both "internally inclusive" and "externally exclusive" (Lister et al. 2007, 11).

The classical concept of citizenship is connected to the two major political traditions of civic republicanism and liberalism. Liberalism has been preoccupied with the defense of the freedom of individuals and civil rights vis-à-vis the state and has given priority to the private virtues of individuals over public virtues. The liberal understanding has been criticized, because it tends to underestimate the need for an active state to defend political liberty and for creation of a political community that can defend individual freedom (Kymlicka 2002).

Civic republicanism has been preoccupied with the creation of a just society, and this tradition has given priority to the creation of solidarity between citizens tied together in a political community. The republican understanding has been criticized because it underestimates civil rights and tends to subsume individuals under the needs of the political community (Kymlicka 2002). Communitarianism is a form of civic republicanism that in both its liberal and conservative versions have emphasized participation and belongings to the political community (Delanty 2000, 35).

The three main European traditions (the German, the French, and the British) correspond to some extent to the three legal citizenship traditions—the ethnocultural definition of nationality (*jus sanguinis*), the republican definition of nationality (*jus solis*), and the English tradition rooted in the common law. Since the 1990s European integration and political developments in relation to immigration and asylum have moved the three closer together. The Nordic social democratic version of citizenship represents a mix of these traditions and is sometimes conceptualized as a separate approach, which links equal social and economic rights with the development of the welfare state (Siim 2000; Lister et al. 2007; Melby, Ravn, and Carlsson-Wetterberg 2008).

Marshall's framework has become a key reference for analysis of contemporary citizenship and has also been taken up by marginalized social groups. It has been criticized for its Anglo-and Euro-centric bias as well as for its male bias, because it was premised upon the reality and vision of a British model and on the second-class citizenship of women and minorities (Pateman 1988; Lister 1997; Siim 2000). Marshall's focus was on the inclusion of the working class in industrial societies. Since then new problems have emerged with the inclusion of other marginalized groups in postindustrialized societies (Bottomore 1992), especially women, ethnonational and religious minorities, immigrants, and refugees. Gender and marginalized social groups represent a major challenge for the universal framework of citizenship, which cannot acknowledge the diversity of peoples' real-life experiences, for example, the accommodation of the rights of cultural and religious minorities. This tension between equality and diversity has inspired alternative frameworks, models, and designs (Lister et al. 2007).

Scholars often distinguish between three analytical dimensions of citizenship: (1) equal status, rights, and obligations[1]; (2) political participation and citizens' voice; and (3) identities and belonging (Siim 2000; Bellamy, Castiglione, and Santoro 2003; Lister et al. 2007). Migration research distinguishes between national and postnational citizenship models and has added a fourth supranational/external dimension to national policies, which conceptualizes access to the country (Soysal 1994; Lister et al. 2007, 78). Post-Marshallian frameworks have raised new issues and debates, for example, about contextualizing and gendering the main citizenship traditions.

Contextualizing Citizenship Regimes

Comparative research has explored the contextual nature and various historical routes to citizenship. Scholars have identified a number of citizenship (migration) and welfare regimes with specific political opportunity structures, welfare, migration and integration policies, and discursive framings of rights and responsibilities of equality and diversity (e.g., Koopmans and Stratham 2000; Bellamy et al. 2003). These variations in citizenship traditions, political institutions, and understandings have created national path dependencies (e.g., Koopmans and Stratham 2000; Bellamy et al. 2003). Research has explored the institutional variations and cultural meanings of gender, race–ethnicity, and class (in)equalities according to processes of inclusion and exclusion cross-nationally (Lister et al. 2007).

One example is Bryan S. Turner (1993), who in the article "Outline of a Theory of Citizenship" introduced a model with two dimensions that aims to identify political dynamics as well as variations in citizenship regimes:

- *An active–passive dimension,* which expresses how citizenship rights became institutionalized in modern democracies from above by the involvement of the monarchy or from below through revolutionary movements.
- *A public–private dimension,* which expresses whether citizenship rights and norms are associated with the public or private arena

The first dimension differentiates between an active, participatory republican model and a model with institutionalization from above. The second dimension differentiates between a liberal model, with an emphasis on private, individual rights and a passive state, and a republican model, which emphasizes public virtues and an active state.

Another example is Richard Bellamy et al.'s (2003) study "Lineages of Citizenship: Rights, Belongings and Participation." This comparative study gives an overview of the different legal traditions and historical contexts, which have contributed to create various liberalisms and republicanisms. This approach differentiates between a *polity dimension*, which specifies the territorial and functional spheres (i.e., seeing the subjects either as passive or active), and a *regime dimension*, which refers to the political arrangements and styles of governance, the scope of intervention in private life.

In the move toward multicultural societies ethnicity tends to become an independent factor explaining differentiation in citizenship rights. Ruud Koopman and Paul Stratham (2000) introduce an institutional model with two dimensions that is used to distinguish between variations in ethnicity–migration regimes. One is the *formal and legal basis* for citizenship (i.e., the vertical dimension) that places a regime between an ethnocultural (*jus sanguinis*) and a territorial (*jus solis*) pole. The other is a *political–cultural* horizontal dimension, which places a regime between cultural monism (assimilation) and cultural pluralism. This model has been influential in comparative discussions about migration regimes.

One recent example is Karen Borevi's (2010) study of the Swedish migration and integration policies. In her revised model *the horizontal axis* ranges from passive to active state approaches to ethnocultural diversity, and *the vertical axis* represents conceptions of the national community, from ethnos to demos. The aim is to capture the tensions in European integration policies between ethnos and demos (23).

Citizenship research has recently proposed a plethora of new rights, for example, cultural rights (Turner 1993), reproductive rights, sexual and bodily rights, ethnic and religious rights, and ecological rights (Lister [1997]2003). Scholars have also been concerned with the interrelations between national regimes and political institutions on the one hand and citizens' identities and practice in their daily lives on the other hand. It has become increasingly important to study how individual citizens and social groups understand and negotiate their rights, responsibilities, and belongings on different sites and localities and how policies and discourses affect citizens' individual and collective identities and belongings as well as their practice. One example is the notion of lived citizenship, which refers to peoples' practice and identities conceptualizing "the meaning that citizenship has in peoples' lives and how peoples' social and cultural backgrounds affect their lives as citizens" (Lister et al. 2007, 168).

Gendering Citizenship

Feminist research has criticized the gendered meanings and effects of Marshall's citizenship model and has contributed to politicize the public–private divide

(Pateman 1988; Siim 2000; Lister 2003; Lister et al. 2007). One of the first feminist approaches to citizenship was presented by Pateman (1988) in the path-breaking book *The Sexual Contract*. Pateman criticized the false universalism of the liberal social contract, with economic and legal independency as criteria for citizenship, which excluded married women from political citizenship. She revealed the contradiction in liberal theory between the public and private arena: between free and equal individuals in public life and the social inequality of men and women in the family. Her analysis of Wollstonecraft's dilemma—that married women are confined to the domestic sphere as mothers while men are associated with the public sphere as workers and citizens—illustrates that women in modern patriarchal societies are still caught between equality in the public sphere and gender difference in the private families, between universalism and particularism. It followed that there are two different roads to women's equal citizenship. One strategy focuses on universal equality and inclusion of women as equal citizens but tends to deny their particularity as women. The other strategy focuses on inclusion of women's difference and particularity but tends to reproduce inequality. Pateman proposes a differentiated citizenship model as a means to include women both as equal citizens and as women in their difference.

Pateman's (1988) work became the inspiration for a number of feminist citizenship approaches that introduced democratic models based upon the inclusion and empowerment of women and other marginal social groups. One influential example is Iris M. Young (1990, 2000) who, in *Justice and the Political Difference*, and *Inclusion and Democracy* proposes a deliberative model, which aims to include and empower women and marginalized social groups in democracy from below. Another example is Anne Phillips (1995), who in *The Politics of Presence* proposed a revised model of representation emphasizing inclusion of women in democracy from above through a temporary quota system, which would change the institutional design of the polity.

During the 1980s American scholars often followed Pateman's (1988) emphasis on the patriarchal character of the welfare state focusing on women's exclusion from democratic citizenship. During the same time Scandinavian feminist research started to conceptualize the women-friendly Scandinavian welfare states and the linkage between social, economic, and political rights (Hernes 1987; Siim 2000; Melby et al. 2008). The most influential example of this Scandinavian exceptionalism is Helga M. Hernes's work on Scandinavian citizenship, which she argues is based upon a combination of citizens' inclusion from below (through the labor and other social movements) and their incorporation from above in political institutions. Hernes's perception of the Scandinavian welfare states as potentially woman friendly—"a state where injustice on the basis of gender would be largely eliminated without an increase in other forms of inequality, such as among groups of women" (15)—and Scandinavian state feminism[2] is based upon the synergy between women's political and social citizenship became an inspiration for feminist approaches to citizenship (Lister [1997]2003; Borchorst and Siim 2008).

In the influential book *Citizenship: Feminist Perspectives*, Ruth Lister ([1997]2003) reformulated Pateman's (1988) dilemma between universalism and particularism as a tension between the universalistic ethic of justice and the particularistic ethic of care, which gives equal status to women and men in their diversity. Lister ([1997]2003) argued that this is a creative tension to be overcome by a new citizenship model, which she calls "differentiated universalism" (90). She suggests that this model could become a tool for overcoming the conflicts between formal (civil and political) and substantive (social and economic) rights. Lister's critical synthesis thus embraces the two main traditions, liberalism and republicanism, and her emphasis on human agency "with the capacity for free choice and self-development" contributed to recast women as political actors not victims (39).

Feminist scholarship has emphasized that citizenship is a contested and contextualized concept (Siim 2000). One of the main points is that "vocabularies of citizenship" vary according to social, political and cultural contexts and reflect political and legal institutions, historical legacies and cultural traditions (Lister et al. 2007). Citizenship has been characterized as janus-faced, because it defines who is included in but also who is excluded from the national communities. From this perspective one of the challenges to citizenship research is to study the dynamic relations between citizens' inclusionary claims and its exclusionary force. Migration and integration legislation regulates access to the country and conditions for achieving citizenship rights from the local to the national and transnational arena. This has created barriers between citizens with full rights (i.e., groups who lack formal rights and often live as second-class citizens) and noncitizens, for example, irregular and illegal immigrants who are outside of society and have no formal rights.

The diversity of women's, immigrants', and minority groups' struggling for equal rights and accommodation of ethnocultural and religious diversity are shaped by spaces and places, that is, the interface between the political and discursive opportunity structures and the association of social and political actors with collective organizations. On the individual level peoples' identities, experiences, and practices in everyday life are part of their lived citizenship, which is defined as "the meaning that citizenship actually has in people's lives and the ways in which people's social and cultural backgrounds and material circumstances affect their lives as citizens" (Lister [1997]2003, 3).

Feminist research has also contributed to challenge the false universalism of the category *women* (and *man*). Black people, disabled and older people, and gays and lesbians who do not conform to the universal norm are often discriminated against and perceived as second-class citizens. Together with immigrant and refugee groups they still represent the other, whose claim to citizenship is insecure in many parts of the world. Scholars have recently explored sexual, bodily, and ecological dimensions, which illustrate new meanings of citizenship (see Lister [1997] 2003). Sexual citizenship refers to the claims for sexual autonomy by women, lesbians, and gays, and the politics of sexual citizenship promotes the citizenship status of sexual minorities and articulates new claims to sexual rights understood as "a set of rights to sexual expression and consumption." (Richardson cited from Lister 2003, 127) Ecological citizenship refers both to rights and responsibilities of citizens' and their relationship to nature and the wider environment, for example, green activism.

Feminist scholarship has during the last ten years been concerned with the intersections of gender with other forms of differences and inequalities. One of the main themes has been to analyze the theoretical, methodological, and political implications of differences among groups of women, for example, according to ethnicity–race and sexuality (Siim and Squires 2008; Verloo 2006).

Today there is a rich feminist literature with a plurality of citizenship theories and models. One main approach aims to develop a situated citizenship through contextual studies of women's citizenship from historical and comparative perspectives (Lister et al. 2007). Another approach aims to expand citizenship studies beyond Western Europe from postcolonial and poststructural perspectives (Yuval-Davis 2007; Stoltz, Sun, and Wang 2010). Finally, one strand of feminist scholarship has reconceptualized the notion of citizenship by adding new dimensions and meanings, for example, sexual and bodily citizenship or intimate citizenship[3] (see Lister 2003).

THE DUAL CHALLENGE FROM GLOBALIZATION AND MIGRATION

Globalization, European integration, and increased migration and mobility across and within borders have created problems with social cohesion and integration of immigrant and refugees within and across nation states. Claims for recognition for cultural diversity and respect for the human rights of immigrants and refugees have become contested political issues for the national and global communities. These socioeconomic and political developments linked to increasing migration and mobility across and within nation states have inspired new (post)-national models based on diversity, which challenge both the focus on equal rights (Kymlicka 1995) and criticize methodological nationalism, that is, the predominant focus on the nation state as the main model in mainstream social science[4] (Soysal 1994; Delanty 2000; Sassen 2003).

One main position aims to rethink citizenship by expanding the notion beyond the nation state through postnational models, for example, the notion of cosmopolitan citizenship that links citizenship to human rights (Linklater 2003), global citizenship with moral commitments to outsiders and global environmental concerns (Heater 2002), or multilayered European citizenship that links the national and transnational levels (Liebert 2007). Another main position aims to expand citizenship within the nation state and have proposed multicultural models, which address diversity and accommodation of cultural and religious rights of immigrants and ethnonational minorities (Kymlicka 1995; Modood 2007).

This chapter argues that the challenge to include diversity is a dual challenge to develop new meanings of citizenship, which can accommodate multiple diversities within the nation-states, as well as new postnational notions of citizenship able to address overlapping memberships and identities of citizens in a globalized world. Future research should address the new conditions for the key dimensions of citizenship: rights, duties, participation, and identities on the theoretical and analytical level. And scholars should confront theory and research and develop models, policies, and visions for multilayered citizenship models, which aim to overcome the divisions between us and them and to accommodate diversity on the subnational, national, and transnational levels.

CITIZENSHIP, MULTICULTURALISM, AND DIVERSITY

The academic debate about multicultural citizenship was sparkled by Will Kymlicka's (1995) book *Multicultural Citizenship*. The book proposed a multicultural model, which recognizes the ethnocultural, ethnonational rights and religious rights of minorities. His notion of multicultural citizenship was an important step toward accommodation of ethnocultural diversity in liberal democracies. His multicultural model has later been criticized for defending group rights, for freezing identities, and for ignoring diversities and inequalities related to gender (Okin 1999) and religion (Modood 2007).

Kymlicka (1995) presents a comprehensive multicultural approach, which introduced a strong liberal defense for the accommodation of the diversity of minority groups (see also the chapter by Baukje Prins and Sawitri Saharso in this volume). Claims for recognition of ethnonational and ethnocultural diversity have raised new issues about the state's obligation to respect the rights of old and new minorities (ibid.; Eisenberg and Spinner Halev 2005). Kymlicka's influential concept of multicultural citizenship distinguishes between three forms of group-differentiated rights that need protection by the state: (1) *self-governing rights* for national minorities and indigenous communities; (2) *polyethnic rights* for ethnic minorities, for example, immigrant groups and refugees who need special accommodations in their new countries for their religious, linguistic, or cultural differences; and (3) special *representation rights* for historically disadvantages groups or their members within government institutions, for example, cultural or religious groups or women. Issues of voice, which are linked to representation, are controversial but have become central to debates about democratic citizenship. In the original model national minorities had a strong claim for protection of their rights, while new immigrant groups have a weaker claim. Kymlicka's later notion of citizenship in diverse societies (Kymlicka and Norman 2000) proposes a comprehensive model with diverse arguments for accommodating different types of minorities.

Tariq Modood (2007) proposes an alternative multicultural model, which focuses on accommodation of religious groups in democracy. In the book *Multiculturalism* Modood criticizes Kymlicka's approach for its liberal bias and for its main emphasis on national minorities. He offers an alternative conception of *political multiculturalism*, which focuses on accommodation of religious groups in democracy, based on the idea of difference, multi, equal dignity, and equal respect (20). He emphasizes the novelty of the ethno-religious mix in European democracies and the need to include Muslims in contemporary conceptions of democratic citizenship at the level of "identities, associations, belonging, including diasporic connections; behavior, culture, religious practice etc.; and political mobilization" (50).

The theory and practice of multiculturalism has been criticized the last ten years from many sides, for example, by liberals (Joppke 2003), cosmopolitans, and feminist scholars (Okin, 1999; Shacher 2005). Anne Phillips (2007) proposes a multicultural model without culture and without groups. Rainer Bauböck (2008) proposes a defense of diversity within a framework of rights that includes cultural groups and focuses on practical public policies rather than on political ideas. This is presented as a constructivist approach, which emphasizes that cultural diversity is socially constructed rather than naturally given. Bauböck distinguishes between multiculturalism as a set of political ideas on one hand and public policies that address social facts on the other hand. The proposed model of rights in the context of diversity is premised on three basic values: (1) cultural liberties; (2) equality; and (3) the right to self-government. He emphasizes that rights can be stated in both individualist and universal terms and that group-differentiated and collective rights can be justified by both moral individualism and universalism.

Bauböck's (2008, 15) multiculturalist and egalitarian model within the framework of rights is presented as a contextualized liberal defense of multiculturalism. The focus is primarily on the accommodation of cultural diversity of minorities but claims for equality, which include exemptions, protection against discrimination, public support of recognition, and special political representation, can in principle be extended to other kinds of inequalities. This approach addresses multiple diversities and inequalities according to culture, religion, and nationality, but it does not deal with inequalities according to gender and sexuality.

The Debate between Multiculturalism and Gender Equality

Multiculturalist and feminist approaches to citizenship have been interpreted as two different paradigms and have presented models that give primacy to different equality claims (see also the chapters by Judith Squires and Baukje Prins and Sawitri Saharso in this volume). Defenders of multiculturalism have argued for state protection of ethnonational or religious rights, while feminists have focused on gender and on defending women's rights. One example is Susan Moller Okin, who claimed that there is a contradiction between multiculturalism, defined as state protection of the cultural rights of minorities, and women's rights. Okin's approach was read by many as a liberal defense of universal gender equality against cultural diversity because she criticized the defense of minority cultures from the perspective of gender equality and women's rights.

Okin's (1999) influential article "Is Multiculturalism Bad for Women?" provoked an intense debate in the United States (see Cohen 1999), which spread to Europe (Eisenberg and Spinner Halev 2005). She claimed that group rights are potentially, and in many cases also in practice, antifeminist and harmful for women, because minority groups often have patriarchal religion and family structures, exemplified by forced marriages and polygamy. First, group rights contribute to strengthen men's patriarchal control over women in minority cultures, and, second, the most powerful men often formulate the interests, values, and practices of the group.

This attack on the multicultural paradigm was sharply criticized by both feminists and liberals as being premised upon an essentialist perception of culture that would force minority women to choose between my rights and my culture. Okin (2005) later explains that her essay was not an attack on collective rights per se; her main point had been the importance of giving women a voice in all negotiations about groups rights (88–89).

In a response to Okin's (2005) criticism, Kymlicka (1999) stresses that states should protect collective rights of minorities only through *external restrictions* on the majority, for example, representation rights and language rights, but states should not defend collective rights that impose *internal restrictions* of individual rights/autonomy within the group (31–34). He argued that feminism and multiculturalism are potential allies in a struggle for a more inclusive concept of justice that combines individual and collective rights and takes account of both gender-based and ethnic diversity.

The debate inspired a growing sensitivity to "the paradox of multicultural vulnerability," that is, to the fact that vulnerable social groups' needs and interests can be undermined by group rights (Shachar 2000, 200). Okin, Shachar, and Phillips all agreed about the importance of giving women and other vulnerable groups a voice in both minority cultures and in society (see Eisenberg and Spinner Halev 2005; Modood, Triandafyllidou, and Zapata-Barrero 2006).

Feminist scholars have increasingly discussed proposals to link approaches to gender equality with concerns for minority rights (Siim and Squires 2008). Anne Phillips (2007) argues that egalitarians should be committed to both sex equality and at least some version of multiculturalism and has introduced a deliberative diversity model. She finds that rights should be attached primarily to individuals and concern discrimination: "the multicultural question is—whether existing legislation is biased towards the cultural identities or religious beliefs of particular groups. Laws and rules that enjoy majority support may reflect a cultural bias" (166).

To sum up, citizenship models have moved from a primary focus on inequality according to class and gender to an increasing focus on multiple inequalities (Hancock 2007). Arguably there is still a tension in citizenship approaches between multiculturalist models, which focus on ethnocultural, national, and religious diversities as primary categories, and feminist models, which focus on gender as the primary category.

Multiculturalism has been criticized by feminist scholars for ignoring women's rights. Okin's approach to women's rights gives primacy to gender, and Modood's approach gives primacy to religion. Both models can be characterized as *unitary approaches,*[5] which give primacy to one category, while Kymlicka's, Phillips's, and Bauböck's approaches aim to address multiple inequalities.

Multiculturalist and feminist models both aim to renegotiate equality with diversity within citizenship models, and both are critical toward the universal model but give primacy to different forms of inequalities. One promising research strategy could be to move toward contextual approaches, which address intersections between multiple inequality creating categories, where relationships between the categories is perceived not as universal but as situated and dependent on time and space (Yuval-Davis 2007; Siim and Squires 2008).

CITIZENSHIP IN A GLOBAL AGE

Globalization and increased migration and mobility of peoples across borders have created both problems and opportunities for citizenship theory and research. Research has demonstrated that there are new conditions for citizenship, which tend to undermine the classical models of citizenship based upon a unity between rights, duties, participation, and identities within the nation-state (see also the chapter by Suruchi Thapar-Björkert in this volume). Scholars have interpreted the internationalization of human rights norms and the weakening of state sovereignty both as the end of the national citizenship model (Soysal 1994) and as the potential for the reconfiguration of citizenship in a global age (Delanty 2000).

Global governance has inspired notions of postnational citizenship and cosmopolitan and global citizenship, but it is contested whether the vision of a global, cosmopolitan citizenship is feasible and desirable and what kind of model of global citizenship should indeed prevail. Defenders of cosmopolitan citizenship models have argued that the globalization of rights and responsibilities can be perceived as the essence of a globalization of citizenship (Linklater

2003). Skeptics argue that the state still has the sole power to exclude outsiders through the policing of the boundaries of citizenship and residence, that no common language and culture has emerged, that no world government exists, thus a global citizenship with duties to the human race is neither feasible nor desirable (Kymlicka 1999; Joppke 2003). Optimists like Derek Heater argues in *World Citizenship* (2002) that globalization could become the basis for a multi-layered conceptualization of citizenships that would embrace the notion of global citizenship and the use of international human rights law.

Cosmopolitanism has inspired new postnational citizenship models. The key aspect of the cosmopolitan thesis is that citizenship and nationality have today become separated, since the state is no longer the exclusive reference point of sovereignty and that there are new possibilities for participation and rights both within and beyond the state (Delanty 2000, 53). One influential strand is David Held's (1999) notion of cosmopolitan democracy, which proposes to reform international organizations like the United Nations to develop a set of binding political institutions at the global level from above. One variation is discursive democracy, which aims at forming a global civil society through which social movements and nongovernmental organizations can pursue their goals across national borders and change the dominant discourses from below (Dryzik 2000). Delanty's notion of civic cosmopolitanism rooted in civic communities is another strand, presented as a thin cosmopolitanism, which situates cosmopolitanism in real-live communities. This position aims to articulate a form of community, which mediates between nationalism and postnationalism (Delanty, 137–145).

The debate about new forms of citizenship premised on a reconfiguration of citizenship in a postnational and multileveled polity has raised key issues. One contested issue concerns the new politics of human rights, which includes rights to personal autonomy. Whether the discourse of human rights has become more appropriate once we live outside the confines of the nation-state?

Scholars like Turner (1993) argue that political globalization can be used to expand democracy and human rights through the "human rights regime"—that is, an international framework for the protection of human rights. The international social movement for women's rights as human rights is one example of an expansion of the scope of human rights to protect women (Siim 2010). In the essay "Outline of a Theory of Human Rights," Turner poses that there is a need for a sociological theory of human rights as a supplement to the theory of citizenship. A global concept of citizenship should contribute to focus the responsibilities of the more affluent nation states vis-à-vis those societies in the developing world that lacks the resources to translate the development of human rights, as defined in the UN covenant, to effective citizenship rights.

Postnationalism and transnationalism has entered the research agenda and skeptics and defenders of cosmopolitan models both use references to the European Union to support their claims. Supporters argue that the European integration proves that a transnational democratic citizenship model is both feasible and desirable, and skeptics argue that the prevailing democratic deficit in the EU institutions and the lack of popular citizens' support for the EU-project proves that a transnational citizenship model is not feasible or indeed desirable (Shapiro and Hacker Córdon 1999).

Citizenship research has started to address the specific challenges from European integration to citizenship (Delanty 2000; Faist 2007). EU citizenship is a supplementary, third form of citizenship derived from national citizenships, a form of nested citizenship based upon residence. European integration has created a dilemma between the national and transnational dimensions of EU citizenship as well as between insiders and outsiders: EU citizens' have gained new rights and EU public policies have addressed discrimination according to gender, race–ethnicity, sexuality, age, and handicap. But since migration policies have generally become more restrictive, it is increasingly difficult for third-country nationals to enter the EU legally and for immigrants to obtain citizenship and be included in the EU as equal citizens. The European Parliament has obtained more power, but there is still a democratic deficit, and citizens' political identities and belongings are mainly tied to local, regional, and national communities rather than to transnational politics.

The impact of EU citizenship is contested. It has been interpreted as a fortress Europe, which has contributed to the exclusionary side of citizenship (Lister [1997]2003, 47) as well as an example of a postnational citizenship model based upon a deterritorialized notion of person's rights (Soysal 1994). Delanty (2000) analyzes both the limitations and potentials of EU citizenship. He finds that in spite of its present limitations, it opens new institutional possibilities for democratic citizenship, because the definition of European citizenship is based upon residence rather than on birth. Citizenship is still with some exceptions equated with nationality, and to fully enfranchise immigrants from outside Europe European citizenship would have to transcend national citizenship by defining citizenship in terms of residence. At the moment citizens of member-states who are not resident in their country can vote only in local elections but not in national elections. According to Faist and Kivisto (2007) the global trend toward an increasing tolerance of dual citizenship represents a pluralization of citizens' ties across the borders of sovereign states. They notice that EU citizenship has facilitated dual citizenship in member-states, because they do not require citizens from other member-states to renounce their original citizenship upon naturalization.

FEMINIST APPROACHES TO TRANSNATIONALISM

Globalization and European integration has created a multileveled polity, which has placed relations between citizens' rights or obligations, participation, and identities on the subnational, national, and transnational arenas on the research agenda. Feminist scholarship has started to reimage the citizenship frame from a multilevel perspective and to explore what a multilayered conception of citizenship that extends from the local to the transnational level means from a gender perspective (Hobson, Carson, and Laurence 2007; Liebert 2007; Yuval-Davis 2007; Siim and Squires 2008). One example of feminist concerns with the new local–global dynamic is the debate about global-care chains (see also the chapter by Diane Sainsbury in this volume). This refers to immigrant women workers from the poor South who leaves their own countries, and often their own children, to enter as nannies, au pair, or care workers to countries in the Global North. Here they work as legal, semilegal, or illegal workers in private families contributing to the housework, taking care of children, and the elderly and disabled, thus enabling women in the Global North to enter the formal labor market (Lister et al. 2007, 137– 165). Another example is women (and men) from Eastern Europe, Russia, Africa, and Asia who enter the EU and Western Europe to work or study and end up as prostitutes or become victims of trafficking.

Nira Yuval-Davis's (1997) influential work aims to rethink nationality and the nation/nation state as an imagined community and develop transnational citizenship from a gender perspective[6] (see also the chapter by Suruchi Thapar-Björkert in this volume). She has recently proposed a multilayered citizenship model, which focuses on transnational identities and introduces the notion of belonging as a way to enrich and clarify discussions of contemporary citizenship (ibid.). The main argument is that people are no longer connected primarily to the nation-state but are simultaneously citizens in more than one political community. Contemporary citizenship is understood as the participatory membership in all political communities as a politics of belonging where peoples' citizenship in intersectional ways is linked to multilayered polity, sub-, cross-, and suprastate political communities (Yuval-Davis 2006a, 2006b). This is an ambitious model, which aims to link transnational and intersectional perspectives and also addresses the changing role of the nation-state toward a growing securitization of today's borders and boundaries (Yuval-Davis 2007, 561). Arguably this research strategy can contribute to the understanding of the use and misuse of gender equality by neonationalist forces as well as for developing new postnational approaches to citizenship.

Wendy Sarvasy's (2011) approach to cosmopolitanism, transnational democracy, and global citizenship is inspired by the historical experiences, scholarship, and activism of prominent feminists around the First World War. She has recently introduced a multilevel global citizenship based upon the lived experiences of feminist activist researchers, especially Grace Abbott and Alice Hamilton. She claims that their experiences have demonstrated how a multilevel citizenship might work in practice. Abbott's experiences were based on her commitment to the Chicago Hull-House experiment, and Hamilton's were based on her international commitments at the International Congress of Women at the Hague in 1915. Sarvasy notices that the problem of redesigning the domestic–global by introducing global citizenship persists, although the historical context may be different. One example of the new local–global dynamic is the Filipina migrant domestic workers who struggle to claim their multilevel rights within the context of the domestic worker contracts in the household and in this way uses the location of the family as a site of practicing global citizenship.

Gender, Diversity, and European Integration

Gender research has explored the contradictory logic of globalization, European integration and migration from a perspective of gender equality. Judith Squires's (2007) book *The New Politics of Equality* provides a useful overview of the global gender equality breakthrough by national governments, international organizations like the UN, and transnational structures like the EU. Today there is a global discourse about gender equality and a global feminist activism, and research that has succeeded in integrating women's rights and gender mainstreaming within the human rights regime. Feminist scholarship has started to discuss the tensions between global citizenship and human rights and has proposed various versions of cosmopolitanism (Stoltz et al. 2010).

Gould (2004) distinguishes between moral and political cosmopolitanism. Feminist scholars have been inspired by moral cosmopolitanism, which pertains to universalistic approaches to peoples' status as moral beings with various rights and duties. Political cosmopolitanism concerns theories about democracy and the global governance and has been criticized for its European bias. Feminist versions of cosmopolitanism present situated versions of cosmopolitanism based upon "women's rights as human rights," which rejects abstract forms of universalism. Lister ([1997] 2003) argues that global citizenship and human rights can offer tools to challenge citizenship's exclusionary power, for example, through international human rights law and global governance.

European integration has also put gender equality and mainstreaming policies on the political agenda (Squires 2007). Gender equality and antidiscrimination policies have become part of the EU agenda and part of transnational structures, politics, and concerns. It is contested whether European citizenship is a potential or a problem for gender equality and women's rights. Squires notices that the political strategies to institutionalize gender equality in the EU have made the contradictory logic of Europeanization visible: on one hand, feminist concerns have contributed to the transformation of institutional norms and practices; but, on the other hand, at the same time basic concerns about social rights and democratic justice have been supplanted by arguments and ideologies of women's social utility.

One position is Ulrike Liebert's (2007), whose approach represents an exception to the feminist EU skepticism. Her framework illustrates the positive perception of EU citizenship, which focuses on EU as a provider of gender and minority right. Liebert identifies the modern gender paradox, defined as the necessity to reconcile universal ideals of equality and the postmodern emphasis on diversity. The aim is to develop European citizenship to accommodate the gender paradox in the context of (multi)cultural diversity and gender the European public sphere by restructuring democratic citizenship from a deliberative perspective (14).

Liebert's (2007) approach focuses on the European citizenship paradox, which emerges as a result of the tensions between EU citizenships norms—for example, of equality and nondiscrimination—and member-state practices in the context of regional disparities and social inequalities that market integration arguably deepens. From this context she assesses the four citizenship models: (1) the liberal market citizenship; (2) the republican citizenship; (3) the cosmopolitan citizenship; and (4) the deliberative citizenship (15–19), through the lens of gender equality. According to Liebert, the deliberative citizenship model transcends the other models: (1) it counteracts the exclusionary bias of the liberal market by expanding civil society deliberation and participation in EU governance; (2) it avoids the harmonizing and homogenizing assumptions of the republican model; and (3) it leaves it to deliberating social constituencies to negotiate conflicting norms depending on places and spaces. "From a feminist perspective, a deliberative European citizenship conception promises women and feminist movements an equal voice and, thus to do better than others in reconciling claims for individual equality and the needs for the protection of gender based difference" (19).

Liebert's (2007) model has a clear deliberative bias, and it is a problem that it does not explore the unequal power relations between women citizens and EU polity or intersecting inequalities among women or between women and other social groups, but the strength is the contextual approach to EU institutions and equality policies. Proponents of EU citizenship like Liebert's view the antidiscrimination agenda as a crucial part of EU citizenship rights and norms.

Squires's (2007) participatory approach represents a somewhat different position, which emphasizes the contradictory aspects of the new European diversity agenda for gender equality. She has identified the tendency to devise institutions and laws to address multiple inequalities (160). For example, Article 13 of the Amsterdam Treaty recognizes six strands as requiring measures to combat discrimination: sex; racial and ethnic origin; disability; age; religion; and sexual orientation.[7] According to Squires, these equality strands forms the basis for a new political diversity agenda, which obliges nation-states to address multiple forms of discrimination and to consider the interaction between strands. As a result, policies to combat multiple intersecting forms of discrimination are emerging as central political priority across EU member-states (see also the chapter by Patricia Hill Collins and Valerie Chepp in this volume).

Squires (2007) is critical of EU mainstreaming processes, which she notices has not yet addressed multiple inequalities or issues of outcome (see also the chapter by Emanuela Lombardo, Petra Meier, and Mieke Verloo in this volume). She finds, however, that the diversity agenda is a potential strategy to empower women who have not been part of the dominant gender equality discourses, for example, immigrant or minority women. She proposes an alternative participative–democratic model to gender and diversity mainstreaming[8] based upon an integrated approach to gender and diversity mainstreaming (163–178): "for without inclusive deliberation as to what gender equality entails—and therefore what form gender equality policies should take—the pursuit of gender equality can itself become an exclusionary process, undertaken for considerations of utility rather than justice" (177–178).

Mieke Verloo's (2006, 214) position presents a criticism of the recent EU move from a primary focus on gender equality toward policies that address multiple inequalities. The focus is on the mainstreaming as a process and points toward three basic concerns: (1) the assumed similarities of inequalities; (2) the need for structural approaches; and (3) the political competition between inequalities. According to Verloo the one-size-fits-all approach to multiple discriminations is problematic since it "is based upon an incorrect assumption of sameness or equivalence of social categories connected to inequalities and of mechanisms and processes that constitute them" (223). Verloo's discursive approach[9] focuses on policy processes, whereas Squires's (2007) participative–democratic model discusses the participation of actors in the process, especially who has the power to define what mainstreaming is or should be.

Kantola and Nousiainen (2012) present a recent analysis of the EU gender equality regime, which emphasize EU's political–institutional aspects, that is, the specific combination of antidiscrimination law, soft law, policy agencies, and politics in the interfaces with civil society. They find that the Amsterdam Treaty of 1997 by institutionalizing different policies represents a major development in EU gender policy. The treaty made positive action an acceptable tool in states' policy making, made a new legal basis for antidiscrimination directives, and widened the basis of equality from gender and nationality to race and ethnicity, religion and belief, age, disability, and sexual orientation. According to Kantola and Nousiainen (2012) the overall result is a new focus on the issue of intersectionality in Europe. At the same time they highlight the tensions and contradictions in EU equality policies: intersectionality has, on one hand, entered strongly in the EU political discourse in the form of multiple discrimination, but the new focus has, on the other hand, not changed the legal framework or the institutional set up . They conclude that there are still many barriers to ensuring citizen's formal rights and to combat multiple and intersectional discrimination in the EU.

EU has a unique transnational institutional framework and the various approaches emphasize specific aspects of EU equality policies. From a democratic citizenship perspective one of the crucial aspects is the potential for participation and deliberation of civil society actors in the practical implementation of the new rights. Arguably the focus on intersectionality may open for what Squires (2007) calls inclusive deliberation, that is, dialogues between concerned social groups about what gender equality is and how it related to other forms of inequalities, for example, related to race end ethnicity. At the same time EU citizenship is still exclusionary toward non-EU citizens, since it is "nested citizenship," which is derivative of member-state citizenship (Faist 2007), with rights being restricted to EU citizens.[10]

The debates about the implications of the human rights regime and gender mainstreaming illustrate the tensions and conflicts between (gender) equality and ethnocultural diversity, which need to be addressed both on the level of theory and, research as well as on the level of practical politics. The global gender equality discourse and the European turn to diversity has arguably provided new conditions for giving voice and influence to diverse and marginalized social groups. It is, however, contested whether the strengthening of EU citizenship and the adoption of the antidiscrimination doctrine of the Amsterdam Treaty can become a step toward a more inclusive definition of rights and protection. The debates illustrate the dilemmas of citizenship between insiders and outsiders; the tensions in the normative visions between human rights, EU citizenship, and national rights; and tensions between norms about (gender)equality and nondiscrimination of minority groups.

Future Research Agenda: Citizenship, Diversity, and Transnationalism

This chapter has argued that in a global age it has become crucial to rethink citizenship from the dual perspective of transnationalism and diversity. The future research agenda should therefore explore the reconfiguration of the key dimensions of citizenship rights and responsibilities, participation, and identities beyond the nation-states, and it should explore tensions between equality and accommodation of diversity on the subnational, national, and transnational levels. The academic debate has identified new challenges from postnational governance and multileveled polity to the classical citizenship model linked to the nation-state, but scholars disagree about the implications.

In terms of theory, one contested question is whether and how the citizenship frame can incorporate structural inequalities, political conflicts, divisions, and citizens' emotions and passions within and beyond the nation-states (Mouffe 1992, 2000). In terms of research, one of the future challenges is overcoming the dominant Western bias, Euro-centrism, and methodological nationalism of previous citizenship research. The research agenda should start to explore the meanings, concepts, and models of citizenship from different parts of the world, from East and West, North, and South, from the developing as well as the developed countries. On the level of politics one of the future research issues is the need to develop citizenship frames capable of contributing to combating new forms of nationalisms and xenophobia and overcoming the division between them and us within and beyond the nation-states.

Cosmopolitan models have responded to the challenge from globalization and diversity by proposing alternative citizenship models premised upon post-nationalism governance and multilevel polity. Scholars have conceptualized the links between subnational, national, and transnational human rights and between the formal rights and citizens' practice in the embryonic transnational civil society through transnational social movements, networks, for example, the European Women's Lobby (EWL) and the European Network against Racism (ENAR), and International Non Government Organizations (INGOs). Transnational belongings mean reimagining community in a post-Westphalian context (Anderson 1991).

Scholars have emphasized that nation-states are still important in the global age. National histories, political institutions, and belongings affect both the meanings and interactions of the main social categories, for example, gender, race–ethnicity, and class. It is therefore important to develop a situated approach to transnationalism and cosmopolitanism rooted in civic communities. One example is Delanty's (2000) approach, which aims to construct alternative understandings of belonging to the nation that gives expression to "the discursive space within the national imaginary" (144). Arguably, this model of cosmopolitanism would be capable of addressing the challenges from nationalism and neonationalist forces, which often use references to gender equality and women's and sexual rights against minority groups.

Feminist scholarship has contributed to the rethinking of the classical citizenship approaches by adding new dimensions of citizenship and proposing new approaches and models linked both to postcolonial, postnational, and poststructural paradigms (Stoltz et al. 2010). Today feminist scholars debate what theories, models, and research strategies would be capable of addressing all dimensions of women's public and private lives, focusing not only on gender inequality but also on all forms of inequalities to combat the exclusion of women and marginalized social and cultural groups not only on the national but also on the global level.

This is an ambitious research agenda. The meanings of citizenship, equality, and diversity are contested, situated, and contextual and competing political projects and feminist visions of gender equality and women's rights exist on the national, transnational, and global level. It is debatable whether it is feasible and desirable to aim to incorporate all aspects of women's particular citizenship into one comprehensive grand theory based upon one (normative) vision (e.g., a gender-fair citizenship)[11] or whether feminist scholarship should rather aim to be pluralist and develop competing theories, which could focus on specific aspects of women's lives, explore particular forms of inequalities, and propose diverse visions of gender equality and women's rights from either poststructural, postcolonial, or postmodern perspectives? A future research agenda for a feminist reconfiguration of citizenship should first confront the various feminist citizenship theories and models. Second, feminist scholars should confront citizenship theory and research, including situating postmodern, poststructural, and postcolonial citizenship approaches. Finally, a feminist rethinking of citizenship should root citizenship praxis in normative visions about politics of solidarity in difference, a reflective solidarity based upon a (feminist) transversal politics.

To sum up, this chapter has argued that the transnational turn is a fruitful conceptual move to transcend the methodological nationalism, Euro-centrism, and Western bias of the classical citizenship models and should be interpreted as a precondition for understanding the new global and postnational forms of governance, identities, and activism. This means that the reconstruction of citizenship must be transnational and multilayered to be able to address citizens' rights and obligations, identities, and participation within the context of new multilevel political governance. It is further argued that citizenship must be situated to address multiple inequalities and combat exclusionary aspects of citizenship from various contexts linking the global with the local–regional and national arenas. Finally, it has suggested that one of the feminist contributions to citizenship research has been to insist on an intersectional approach to citizenship exploring the links between gender equality and diversity. This is a promising methodological approach for studying inclusionary and exclusionary processes and framings of citizenship, capable of focusing on the intersections of multiple inequalities within and beyond the nation-states.

NOTES

1. Marshall's classical model focused on the rights dimension, but duties and responsibilities can also been conceptualized as a separate dimension (Delanty 2000, 17).
2. Helga Maria Hernes (1987, 153) defined state feminism as "feminism from above in the form of gender equality and social policies and the feminization of welfare state relevant professions" linked to "feminization from below" through the mobilization of women in political and cultural activities.
3. One example of this research strategy is provided by the FEMCIT project "Gendered Citizenship in a Multicultural Europe: Issues, Challenges, Visions: The Impact of Contemporary Women's Movement", a European Commission funded 6. Frame Work project (http://www.femcit.org/).
4. Andreas Wimmer and Nina Glick Schiller (2002) distinguish the different modes of methodological nationalism that have characterized mainstream science and show how they have influenced research on migration arguing that the naturalization of the nation-state can be found in different disciplines and many intellectual variations. The article attempts to move beyond the Charybdis of methodological nationalism without falling into the Scylla of methodological fluidism and the rhetoric of cosmopolitanism. The ambitious goal is to develop a set of concepts for the study of migration that does more than reflect the preconditions and taken for granted assumptions of our times (327).
5. Hancock (2007) proposes a useful distinction between unitary, multiple, and intersectional approaches to diversity and difference. Unitary approaches address one primary category; multiple and intersectional approaches address more than

one category. In the multiple approaches the categories have a predetermined relationship to each other, whereas in intersectional approaches the categories matter equally and the relationship between categories is an open empirical question. See also Myra Marx Ferree's (2009) historical and dynamic approach to intersectionality.

6. Yuval-Davis's (1997) book *Gender and Nation* was inspired by Benedict Anderson's (1983) understanding of the nation as an imagined community "because the members of even the smallest nation will never know most of their fellow-members, meet them, or even hear of them, yet in the minds of each lives the image of their communion" (15). It demonstrated how gender contributes to define the nation as an imagined community—for example, via arguments of origin, kinship, culture, and religion—and it presents examples of how creation of identity politics has been used to exclude specific groups. She has recently distinguished between *belonging* and *politics of belonging*: belonging refers to emotional attachment and to feeling at home and feeling safe; politics of belonging refers to "specific political projects aimed at constructing belonging in particular ways to collectives that are, at the same time, themselves being constructed by these projects in very particular ways" (Yuval-Davis 2006a, 197).

7. Article 13 states that the "Council" may take appropriate action to combat discrimination based on sex, racial or ethnic origin, religion or belief, disability, age or sexual orientation. This was also included in the Treaty of Lisbon. For analysis of European gender equality policies, see Lombardo, Meier, and Verloo (2009).

8. Squires argues that the concept of intersectionality is more precise than the concept of diversity, because it focuses attention on the locations at which or processes by which marginalized groups experience not only multiple but also particular forms of inequalities.

9. In the introduction to the book *Discursive Politics and Gender Equality* the discursive approach to politics is defined as "the intentional and unintentional engaging of policy actors in conceptual disputes that result in the meanings attributed to the terms and concepts employed in specific contexts" (Lombardo et al. 2009, 10).

10. This contrasts to *citizenship of residence*, where citizenship is no longer rooted in the nation-state but is located in an expanding circle of ties that move from the locality through the region to the transnational level (Kivisto 2007, 276).

11. The questions are inspired by the FEMCIT project Gendered Citizenship in a Multicultural Europe and proposes a normative vision of a gender-fair citizenship. It is a European 6.FW project that aims to explore the relationship between the changing forms and relationships of gendered citizenship and women's movement in select European countries over the last forty years.

References

Anderson, Benedict. [1983] 1991. *Imagined communities: Reflections on the origin and spread of nationalism*. London: Verso.

Bauböck, Rainer. 2008. "Beyond culturalism and statism: Liberal responses to diversity." Eurosphere Working paper series 06, University of Bergen.

Beck, Ulrich. 2002. "The cosmopolitan society and its enemies." *Theory, Culture and Society* 19(1–2): 17–44.

Bellamy, Richard, Dario Castiglione, and Emilio Santoro (Eds.). 2003. *Lineages of European citizenship: Rights, belonging and participation in eleven nation-states.* Basingstoke, UK: Palgrave/Macmillan.

Borchorst, Anette, and Birte Siim. 2008. "Women-friendly policies and state feminism. Theorizing Scandinavian gender equality." *Feminist Theory* 9: 207–224.

Borevi, Karen. 2010. "Dimensions of citizenship: European integration policies from a Scandinavian perspective." In Bo Bengtsson, Per Strömblad, and Ann-Helén Bay, eds., *Diversity, inclusion and citizenship in Scandinavia.* Newcastle: Cambridge Scholars Publishing, 19–46.

Bottomore, Tom. 1992. "Citizenship and social class: Forty years on." In T. H. Marshall and Tom Bottomore, eds., *Citizenship and social class.* London: Pluto Press, 55–93.

Delanty, Gerard. 2000. *Citizenship in a global age. Society, culture, politics.* Buckingham: Open University Press.

Dryzik, John. 2000. *Deliberative democracy and beyond: Liberals, critics and contestations.* Oxford: Oxford University Press.

Eisenberg, Avigail, and Jeff Spinner Halev. 2005. "Introduction." In Avigail Eisenberg and Jeff Spinner Halev, eds., *Minorities within minorities: Equality, rights and diversity.* Cambridge: Cambridge University Press, 1–18.

Faist, Thomas. 2007. "Introduction: The shifting boundaries of the political." In Thomas Faist and Peter Kivisto, eds., *Dual citizenship in global perspective: From Unitary to multiple citizenship.* Basingstoke, UK: Palgrave/Macmillan, 1–13.

Faist, Thomas, and Peter Kivisto, eds. 2007. *Dual citizenship in global perspective: From Unitary to multiple citizenship.* Basingstoke, UK: Palgrave/Macmillan

Ferree, Myra Marx. 2009. "Inequality, intersectionality and the politics of discourse: framing feminist alliances." In Emanuela Lombardo, Petra Meier, and Mieke Verloo, eds., *The Discursive politics of gender equality.* London: Routledge, 68–85.

Gould, C. Carol. 2004. *Globalizing democracy and human rights.* Cambridge, UK: Cambridge University Press.

Hancock, Ann-Marie. 2007. "When multiplication doesn't equal quick addition: Examining intersectionality as a research paradigm." *Perspectives on Politics* 5(1): 63–79.

Heater, Deater. 2002. *World citizenship: Cosmopolitan thinking and its opponents.* London: Continuum.

Held, David. 1999. "The transformation of the political community: Rethinking democracy in the context of globalization." In Ian Shapiro and Casiano Hacker-Cordon, eds., *Democracy's edges.* Cambridge, UK: Cambridge University Press, 11–27.

Hernes, Helga M. 1987. *Welfare state and woman power: Essays in state feminism.* London: Norwegian University Press.

Hobson, Barbara, Marcus Carson, and Rebecca Laurence. 2007. "Recognition struggles in transnational arenas: Negotiating identities and framing citizenship." *Critical Review of International Social and Political Philosophy* 10: 483–470.

Joppke, Christian. 2003. "Multicultural citizenship." In Engin F. Isin and Bryan S. Turner eds., *Handbook of citizenship studies.* London: SAGE, 246–260.

Kantola, Johanna, and Kevät Nousiainen. (2012) "The European Union: Initiator of a New Anti-discrimination Regime ." In Andrea Krizan, Hege Skjeie, and Judith Squires, eds., *Institutionalizing intersectionalities in Europe.* New York: Palgrave, 33–58.

Kivisto, Peter. 2007. "Conclusion: The boudaries of citizenship in a transnational age." In Thomas Faist and Peter Kivisto, eds., *Dual citizenship in global perspective: From unitary to multiple citizenship*. New York: Palgrave/Macmillan, 272–287.

Koopmans, Ruud, and Paul Stratham (Eds.). 2000. *Challenging immigration and ethnic relations politics: Comparative European perspectives*. Oxford: Oxford University Press.

Kymlicka, Will. 1995. *Multicultural citizenship*. Oxford: Oxford University Press.

Kymlicka, Will. 1999. "Liberal complacencies." In Joshua Cohen, Matthew Howard, and Martha Nussbaum, eds., *Is multiculturalism bad for women?* Princeton, NJ: Princeton University Press, 31–34.

Kymlicka, Will. 2002. *Contemporary political philosophy: An introduction*. Oxford: Oxford University Press.

Kymlicka, Will, and Wayne Norman (Eds.). 2000. *Citizenship in diverse societies*. Oxford: Oxford University Press.

Lombardo, Emanuela, Petra Meier, and Mieke Verloo. 2009. "Stretching and bending gender equality: A discursive politics approach." In Emanuela Lombardo, Petra Meier, and Mieke Verloo, eds., *The discursive politics of gender equality: Stretching, bending and policymaking*. London: Routledge, 1–18.

Linklater, Andrew. 2003. "Cosmopolitan citizenship." In Engin F. Isin and Bryan S. Turner eds. *Handbook of citizenship studies.*London: SAGE, 318–333.

Liebert, Ulrike. 2007. "The European citizenship paradox: Renegotiating equality and diversity in the New Europe." *Critical Review of International, Social and Political Philosophy* 10: 417–442.

Lister, Ruth. [1997] 2003. *Citizenship: Feminist perspectives*. Basingstoke, UK: Palgrave/Macmillan.

Lister, Ruth, F. Williams, A. Antonnen, J. Bussemaker, U. Gerhard, J. Heinen, S. Johansson, A. Leira, and B. Siim. 2007. *Gendering citizenship in Western Europe: New challenges for citizenship research in a cross-national context*. Bristol: Policy Press.

Lombardo, Emanuela, Petra Meier, and Mieke Verloo (Eds.). 2009. *The discursive politics of gender equality: Stretching, bending and policymaking*. London: Routledge.

Marshall, T. H. [1950] 2002. "Citizenship and social class." In T. H. Marshall and Tom Bottomore, *Citizenship and social class*. London: Pluto Press, 3–49.

Melby, Kari, Anna-Birte Ravn, and Christina Carlsson-Wetterberg (Eds.). 2008. *Gender equality as a perspective on welfare: The limits of political ambition*. London: Polity Press.

Modood, Tariq. 2007. *Multiculturalism: A civic idea*. London: Polity Press.

Modood, Tariq, Anna Triandafyllidou, and Richard Zapata-Barrero (Eds.). 2006. *Multiculturalism, Muslims and citizenship: A European approach*. London: Routledge.

Mouffe, Chantal. 1992. "Democratic citizenship and the political community." In C. Mouffe, ed., *Dimensions of radical democracy*. London: Verso, 225–239.

Mouffe, Chantal. 2000. *The democratic paradox*. London: Verso.

Okin, Susan Moller. 1999. "Is multiculturalism bad for women?" In Joshua Cohen, Matthew Howard, and Martha Nussbaum, eds., *Is multiculturalism bad for women?* Princeton, NJ: Princeton University Press, 9–24.

Okin, Susan Moller. 2005. "Multiculturalism and feminism: No simple question, no simple answers." In Avigail Eisenberg and Jeff Spinner Halev, eds., *Minorities within minorities: Equality, rights and diversity*. Cambridge, UK: Cambridge University Press, 67–89.

Pateman, Carole. 1988. *The sexual contract*. Stanford, CA: Stanford University Press.

Phillips, Anne. 1995. *The Politics of Presence*. Oxford: Oxford University Press.

Phillips, Anne. 2007. *Multiculturalism without culture*. Princeton, NJ: Princeton University Press.

Rosenberger, Sieglinde, and Birgit Sauer (Eds.). 2012. *Politics, religion and gender: Framing and regulating the veil*. London: Routledge.

Sarvasy, Wendy. 2011. "Rebellious daughters: A feminist genealogy of global citizenship." Paper presented at the Western Political Association meeting, San Antonio, April 20–23.

Sassen, Saskia. 2003. "Towards post-national and de-nationalized citizenship." In Engin F. Isin and Bryan S. Turner eds. *Handbook for citizenship studies*. London: SAGE, 277–299.

Shachar, Ayelet. 2000. "Should church and state be joined at the altar? Women's rights and the multicultural dilemma." In Will Kymlicka and Wayne Norman, eds., *Citizenship in diverse societies*. Oxford: Oxford University Press, 199–223.

Shapiro, Ian, and Casiano Hacker Córdon (Eds.). 1999. *Democracy's edges*. Cambridge, UK: Cambridge University Press.

Siim, Birte. 2000. *Gender and citizenship: Politics and agency in France, Britain and Denmark*, Singapore: Cambridge University Press.

Siim, Birte. 2010. "Gender, diversity and transnational citizenship." In P. Stoltz, M. Svensson, Z. Sun, and Q. Wang, eds., *Gender equality, citizenship and human rights: Controversies and challenges in China and the Nordic countries*. London: Routledge, 74–92.

Siim, Birte, and Judith Squires. 2008. *Contesting citizenship*. London: Routledge.

Soysal, Yasemin N. 1994. *Limits of citizenship: Migrants and postnational membership in Europe*. Chicago: University of Chicago Press.

Squires, Judith. 2007. *The new politics of gender equality*. Basingstoke, UK: Palgrave/Macmillan.

Stoltz, Pauline, Cindy Sun, and Qi Wang (Eds.). *Gender equality, citizenship and human rights: Controversies and challenges in China and the Nordic countries*. London: Routledge.

Turner, Bryan S. (Ed.). 1993. *Citizenship and social theory*. London: SAGE.

Young, Iris Marion. 1990. *Justice and the politics of difference*. Princeton, NJ: Princeton University Press.

Young, Iris Marion. 2000. *Inclusion and democracy*. Oxford: Oxford University Press

Yuval-Davis, Nira. 1997. *Gender and nation*. London: SAGE.

Yuval-Davis, Nira. 2006a. "Belonging and the politics of belonging." *Pattern of Prejudice* 40(3): 197–214.

Yuval-Davis, Nira. 2006b. "Intersectionality and feminist politics." *European Journal of Women's Studies* 13: 193–209.

Yuval-Davis, Nira. 2007. "Intersectionality, citizenship and contemporary politics of belonging." *Critical Review of International, Social and Political Philosophy* 10: 561–574.

Verloo, Mieke. 2006. "Multiple inequalities, intersectionality and the European Union." *European Journal of Women's Studies* 13(3): 211–228.

Wimmer, Andreas, and Nina Glick Schiller. 2002. "Methodological nationalism and beyond: nation-state building, migration and the social sciences." *Global Networks* 2(4): 301–334.

CHAPTER 31

MULTICULTURALISM AND IDENTITY

BAUKJE PRINS AND
SAWITRI SAHARSO

INTRODUCTION

Issues of culture, identity, and difference appeared on the feminist academic and political agenda through two different discourses, those of *liberal multiculturalism* and *critical multiculturalism*. Both fully developed in the 1990s but kept a careful distance from each other.

The liberal discourse started as an exposition of the political reasoning behind the official politics of multiculturalism as it had been embraced by Western immigration countries like Canada, Australia, and the United Kingdom since the early 1970s. In these countries in response to the claims by native and immigrant minorities a practice had grown of accommodating minority cultures. Liberal multiculturalism holds that individuals have not only civil, political, and social rights but also the right to speak their own language and live according to their own culture and religion. For this reason, minority groups are entitled to equal respect for their cultural identity, and they need group rights to protect their cultural identity. As awareness grew that minority cultures may include practices that are harmful to women, feminists worried that group rights might be granted at the expense of minority women. For instance, they feared that, out of respect for minority cultures, governments would recognize polygamy or condone forced marriages. This gave rise to what is now referred to as the *multiculturalism versus feminism* or the *minorities within minorities* debate (see also the chapters by Judith Squires and by Birte Siim in this volume).

The discourse of critical multiculturalism started as an interrogation of the social and political drawbacks of liberal multiculturalism. It was inspired by (Black) feminist and poststructuralist perspectives on politics and power that challenged the individualistic bias of liberalism. People's behavior and ways of thinking should be interpreted not as the outcome of autonomous and rational deliberation but as predominantly determined by their position within a society stratified along lines of class, gender, racial, and age differences. These scholars insisted that members of minority groups did not so much need more (individual or collective) rights but a transformation of society as a whole. While discussions about the possibility and limits of liberal multiculturalism took place among social and political philosophers and scientists, critical multiculturalism was mainly developed (and disputed) within the humanities, more specifically in areas such as women's studies, African American studies, and cultural studies.

In this chapter we will describe these two discourses of multiculturalism and focus on two persistent questions that came up time and again in both discourses: questions regarding the tensions between universalism and relativism; and questions regarding the conception of the subject and individual autonomy. The first refers to the dilemma that feminists want to speak out against gender injustices, whether in our own or in another culture, yet feel hesitant to judge the lives of women in other cultural traditions. This anxiety derives from the fear of repeating the colonial and racist gesture of imposing Western values as if they were universal values. The second issue originates in the fact that criteria that determine a person's autonomy are contested. If some women defend their right to live by traditions that in the eye of others merely endorse their subordinate position, should their choice be rejected because they thereby show a lack of autonomy, or does their position suggest that dominant notions of the subject and autonomy are in need of revision? We will argue that, within both the liberal and the critical discourse of multiculturalism, interesting "third" positions have been elaborated around conceptions of democratic dialogue, contextual reasoning, and narrative identity that offer promising ways out of these intricate problems.

LIBERAL MULTICULTURALISM

One of the most influential theorists of multiculturalism is the Canadian philosopher Will Kymlicka. In *Multicultural Citizenship*, Kymlicka (1995) observed that not only in Canada but also in many countries around the world indigenous minorities were given group rights to help them preserve their culture. Kymlicka developed a framework that aimed to provide the theoretical foundation for this practice.[1] Kymlicka's central idea is that to become autonomous individuals we need culture. We decide what is important to us and how we want to lead our lives, but it is our culture that provides us with meaningful options and that defines and structures our world. This means that our culture is the inescapable context of our autonomy (83–84). Second, our culture gives us a sense of identity and a sense of natural belonging to a community (89). This aspect of autonomy and identity building is why culture is important for us.

Fairness requires that members of minority groups have an equal right to their societal culture (Kymlicka 1995, 86). One does not have an equal opportunity to choose a life of, say, a hunter-gatherer if one cannot experience that life. To be able to offer their members a rich context of choice, minority cultures sometimes need protection. The hunter-gatherer minority may need special land rights to ward off the wood-cutting industry. Or minorities may need language rights to educate their children in their own language or the right to practice their customary law. Hence, a concern for individual well-being may require certain group-differentiated rights, so claims Kymlicka, and his defense of group rights ultimately rests on the liberal values of individual autonomy and freedom. This is why his theory became a landmark: hitherto it was believed that a defense of group rights could be based only on a communitarian outlook that gives group rights priority over the rights of individuals.

Susan Moller Okin (1999),[2] however, doubts whether any politics of multiculturalism, even of Kymlicka's (1995) liberal kind, can really guarantee the rights of women while simultaneously granting a particular minority group rights to uphold its own culture or religion. Most cultures, so runs her argument, have as their principal aim the control of women's sexuality and reproductive capacities by men. This control is expressed in cultural rules that regulate the lives of women in the community. Polygamy, forced marriage, divorce systems biased against women, and culturally licensed sexual harassment (e.g., marriage through rape) are all expressions of a worldview that considers women as inferior to men and all deny women the right to decide over their own bodies and lives. Okin believes that many minority cultures are patriarchal, often more so than the surrounding majority culture. This being so, group rights might function as a license for minorities to oppress their women (and other vulnerable group members) (Okin 1999, 16–17). From a feminist perspective, Okin argues, multiculturalism is not part of the solution but part of the problem. Similar concerns were articulated in Europe by Wikan (2002), Hirsi Ali (2006), Amara (2003), and Kelek (2005) and in Canada by Manji (2005).

Is Multiculturalism Bad for Feminism?
The Accused Talk Back

Okin's (1999) essay sparked the multiculturalism versus feminism debate. How did the accused react? Kymlicka (1995) shared Okin's concerns. Group rights should in his view not be misused to oppress individual group members: "I have defended the right of national minorities to maintain themselves as culturally distinct societies, but only if, and in so far as, they are themselves governed by liberal principles" (153). To avoid misuse he made a distinction between external protections and internal restrictions. Minority rights aim to protect the minority group against the larger society, but they should not restrict the basic liberties of its own members. Kymlicka is convinced that many group rights meet this condition and that Okin's dismissal of minority group rights in general is unwarranted (Kymlicka 1999, 32).

Bhikhu Parekh (1999), another multiculturalist, responds with a question: minority cultures are asked to conform to fundamental liberal values, but what is the meaning of these values? There is among liberals no unanimity about this. Moreover, the content of values may vary according to contexts. Parekh accuses Okin (1999) of liberal fundamentalism because she suggests that there is only one and undisputed set of liberal values, and that liberalism is the better view of life. "From a multicultural perspective," he writes, "the liberal view of life is culturally specific and neither self-evident nor the only rational or true way to organize human life;...liberal relations with non-liberal cultures should be based not on dogmatically asserted liberal values but on a critical and open-minded dialogue" (74).[3] Moreover, what if the women concerned do not share the view that they are oppressed? Against the idea that these women would all suffer from false consciousness he states "We should avoid the mistaken conclusion that those who do not share our beliefs about their well-being are all misguided victims of indoctrination." (Parekh 1999: 73).

Chandran Kukathas defends the most radical position in favor of cultural diversity, not by arguing for group rights but by being against any interference by the state in the internal life of minorities (see Kukathas 2003). He agrees with Okin (1999) that there is a conflict between feminism and multiculturalism, insofar as some groups do not accord women equal dignity, neglect women's interests, and seek (multicultural) accommodation of their traditions. But in his view, in cases where the interests of women conflict with the claims of culture, the latter should prevail (Kukathas 2001).

To understand this position, we need to know Kukathas's understanding of multiculturalism. Unlike Kymlicka (1995), Kukathas's (2003) theory is grounded not in the value of individual autonomy but in freedom of association and freedom of conscience. Kukathas's idea of a multicultural society is that of an association of associations. Minority groups have to be able to survive by their own strength, without the support of cultural group rights, but also without the state intervening in case of oppression of internal minorities. This does not end up in "a formula for creating a lot of private hells" (Barry 2001, 143), because those who wish "to go it alone" (Kukathas 2003, 140) can preserve their culture only if they succeed in making it attractive enough for people to remain members of that community.

It is of crucial importance then that group members have a right to exit, so that we can be sure that those who stay do so voluntarily. He realizes that this will not form a foolproof guarantee that no woman will be coerced to lead a life she does not want to lead. Daughters may be socialized into compliance and therefore acquiescence. Yet he believes that the alternative, to use the power of the state to correct the power balance within minority families, is wrong, because there is no reason to assume that the state has superior knowledge about the good life. Likewise, he argues, if women are disempowered by their socialization into compliance, then they cannot be empowered by treating their preferences as inauthentic (Kukathas 2001, 96).

Among feminists there were also many who shared the multiculturalists' objections to Okin's (1999) essay. Okin wrongly assumes, according to Bonnie Honig (1999, 38), "that Western liberal regimes are simply and plainly 'less patriarchal' than other regimes, rather than differently so, perhaps worse in some respects and better in others." She illustrates her point with examples of women-friendly practices in non-Western cultures and sexist practices in American culture. For Azizah Y. Al-Hibri (1999, 41), Okin's essay exemplified a "Western patriarchal feminism" that would do third-world and minority women no good. Non-Western women have no need to be rescued by Western women. Moreover, "people of faith are entitled to their religious beliefs whether secular feminists approve of these beliefs or not" (44).[4]

We do not intend to further reconstruct the debate, but it undoubtedly points to real problems we encounter when we want to address minority practices that are harmful to women. Okin (1999) is correct in drawing attention to these practices, and it is relevant to ask how public agencies can intervene against cultural practices that are harmful to women. Yet if we continue along the line of argument of Parekh (1999) and Honig (1999) we easily end up on a relativistic position: all cultures have their good and bad sides, and therefore we cannot say which one is the better one. Likewise, we think Kukathas (2001) rightly signaled that if women are disempowered by their socialization into compliance, then they cannot be empowered by treating their preferences as inauthentic. And even if they may not all be "misguided victims of indoctrination" (Parekh 1999, 73), is it not a bit too simplistic to assume, as Al-Hibri (1999) does, that they are capable enough to decide for themselves? How should we understand the autonomy and moral agency of women under cultural conditions that entail severe constraints (Baum 1997, 243)?

There is now a large and growing body of feminist writing exploring how liberal democracies should deal with minority practices, now also referred to as traditional harmful practices (THPs),[5] which infringe on the rights of individuals, that is, women. How should we deal with the universalism–relativism issue and the problem of autonomy? In the following, we will discern four different liberal answers to this question.

Principle-Driven Liberalism

When confronted with the question of whether a practice should be tolerated, the principle-driven approach weighs the practice against liberal principles.

Within a true principle-driven liberal perspective, there is no a dilemma regarding universalism–relativism because liberal principles are considered as universal. This is clear, for instance, in the work of Martha Nussbaum (1999). Nussbaum's perspective is based on the capabilities approach to human development elaborated with the economist Amartya Sen (1985).[6] Given her universalism it comes as no surprise that Nussbaum is not afraid to judge other cultures. Female genital mutilation, for instance, is a practice that should be eradicated because it clearly limits women's capabilities. A typical multiculturalist objection such as, "Isn't it ethnocentric to hold one's own culture as the benchmark for the principles and practices that are appropriate for all people?" is dismissed as utterly out of place (121–129). Regarding the capacity for autonomy of the women involved, Nussbaum writes, "Can the mothers of these girls make an informed choice as to the value of female sexual pleasure? They have been immersed in traditional beliefs about women's impurity; lacking literacy and education, as a large proportion do, they have difficulty seeking out alternative paradigms....their situation is made more difficult by fear and powerlessness....they are highly likely to have experienced marriage and sexual life as a series of insults to their dignity, given the ubiquity of domestic violence and marital rape. Should they believe that [female genital mutilation] is a bad thing for their daughters...they have no power to make their choices effective" (127).

Because the mothers' capacity for autonomy is seriously harmed by their cultural upbringing and their right to autonomy is severely curtailed, it is necessary to develop policies to protect these women from cultural oppression. Yet it is precisely this type of argument that third-world feminists have criticized as a colonial discourse that represents third-world women as passive victims who need an external force, others, to bring about change (see, e.g., Njambi 2004).

A principle-driven approach that is more sensitive to the critique that Western feminists should avoid paternalism is found in the work of Marilyn Friedman (2003). Friedman wants to prevent women from being forced to lead oppressive lives yet does not want to impose liberalism on nonliberal groups. Central to her approach is the concept of personal autonomy as the central principle that should be respected, but nonliberal cultures often do not value personal autonomy. Friedman solves this problem by making a distinction between a content-neutral conception of autonomy and a substantive conception of autonomy. The substantive autonomy of a choice depends on the content of what is chosen, requiring that these contents be consistent with the value of autonomy. The content-neutral autonomy of a choice depends only on the question of whether the choice is made under conditions of autonomy. A choice to live a life of total servility manner would not, following a substantive account of autonomy, qualify as an autonomous choice because a servile life is not consistent with the value of autonomy. However, according to the content-neutral account we should accept that choice if it is made autonomously.

What is the advantage of this distinction? We usually argue that a traditional practice like female genital cutting is such a bad thing that no woman would ever voluntarily choose it. The severity of the outcome and the content of the choice determine for us whether a choice is voluntary. This contains the risk, though, of a cultural bias that leads us to assume that if people consent to a practice that is very alien to us they are not really capable of autonomy. Friedman's (2003) distinction helps to avoid this cultural trap. A critique on Friedman's approach is that it is not clear what should happen to those whose choices do not meet the standards of procedural autonomy. Should their choices be ignored? That is odd, and particularly so given Friedman's ambition to pay more respect to the choices of minority women (see Okin 2005, 79).

A Democratic Approach

In a democratic approach it is democratic deliberation that should define whether a practice is to be tolerated. The basic idea is that, after all have spoken, this public deliberation will have generated a compromise that all parties are willing to accept. If we are to decide on the toleration of oppressive practices, it is very important that those whose lives are most directly touched by it, and in particular the most vulnerable, young women, are consulted. What are their experiences? What are their views on their culture? And what are their views on possible interventions carried out on their behalf by the state in the group's internal affairs?

According to Monique Deveaux (2005), the democratic approach requires that we listen to the voices of those engaged in a practice and thus hopefully prevent their autonomy from going unrecognized. She presents the case of the South African Customary Marriage Act to illustrate her views. There are two kinds of oppression present in this case. First, apartheid had oppressed the South African peoples and their customary laws. Second, the patriarchy of most of the customary laws oppressed women. If customary law was reformed so that it no longer is oppressive to women, then there would be little customary left about it. It would amount to abolition of the law instead of recognition, which after so many decades of cultural oppression under apartheid was unwanted. Instead, representatives of a wide range of groups were consulted, and there was much frank discussion about the actual lived practices of customary marriage. This led to a partial reform; women, for instance, got the right to initiate divorce, but polygamy was not outlawed—one of the concessions made to the chiefs. Not all were happy with the outcome, but the compromise reached was seen by most as a fair and legitimate outcome. Deveaux believes that a democratic solution to conflicts of culture is likely to yield more beneficial reform, and she expects this to have greater legitimacy. But there is no guarantee that this sort of procedure will lead to liberal, nondiscriminatory outcomes. We have to accept the outcome of the democratic deliberation, irrespective of its content.

While the principle-driven approach will not allow practices that conflict with liberal principles, despite what the majority of actors believes (hence is liberal, but not necessarily democratic), the democratic approach may allow practices that conflict with liberal principles because it feels bound to accept the outcome of democratic decision making (and hence is democratic but not necessarily liberal). In fact, Okin (2005) started from a principle-driven approach but later expressed her preference for a democratic approach.

The Institutional Approach

A third approach to liberal multiculturalism proposes to resolve the tension between respecting cultural difference and protecting women's rights by developing governance systems that divide the areas over which the state or the minority group has power. Institutional systems of shared governance should, on one hand, give public recognition to minority groups, and, on the other hand (minimally and hence less extensively), they should secure the rights of minority group women. An example is Ayelet Shachar's (2001) joint governance model. Shachar starts from the assumption that minority group women have an identity as both state citizens and minority group members and may have an interest in both. Joint governance, such as in the area of family law, might mean that the group be given the right to decide who by birth or marriage is a group member (family law's demarcating function), but the state has legal authority over the distributive aspects of family law, such as, in case of divorce, ownership of matrimonial property or entitlement to child custody. Joint governance would force the state and the minority group to cooperate with each other, as neither has enough power to resolve legal disputes without cooperation from the other authority. Thus, they are both forced to make trade-offs.

Shachar (2001) argues that this would not force minority women to choose between their culture and their rights. Moreover, she expects that with the two parties relegated to each other, minority women may be in a better position to renegotiate oppressive group traditions. Thus, she aims both to respect minority women's culturally defined interests (e.g., to remain in their cultural community) and to create more space for them to increase their autonomy.

A Contextualist Approach

Finally, we can distinguish an approach that claims that both liberalism and culture must be contextually understood. The most radical deconstruction of culture yet, combined with a plea for multicultural policies, is developed by British political theorist Anne Phillips (2007). Her critique of much of multicultural theory and its feminist critics alike is that in the debate about tensions between gender equality and cultural diversity, both have reified non-Western or minority cultures as distinct and robust "things" that determine the beliefs and behavior of their members. This ignores the agency of non-Western people as if they were incapable of autonomy, for example, to choose for themselves how they want to shape their (cultural) identity. Non-Westerners are thus their (monolithic unchanging) culture, as either victims or perpetrators, while Westerners are influenced only by (plural, fluid, and changing) cultural environments. Phillips's (2010) approach is based on "respect for culturally diverse individuals," not "recognition of things called cultures" (10).

If one wants to know what measures are required as a matter of justice in the case of traditionally harmful practices, it is no use expecting that liberal principles will prescribe what to do. Liberal principles are generic, so runs the contextualist argument, and therefore too indeterminate for this task. One needs to immerse oneself in the specifics of a case and argue out how the different principles and interests at stake should be understood and balanced against each other and thus to reach a contextual sensitive judgment (see also Carens 2000).

To take an example, in the Dutch debate on sex selective abortion (SSA) the practice was discussed as an incomprehensible choice stemming from a misogynist culture. When we immerse ourselves in the background of SSA, we will find that the families involved often cannot afford the expensive dowry they are supposed to give their daughter in marriage. This is a culturally specific reason, yet it is one we can understand across cultures. We should therefore not assume too quickly that the women concerned are not capable of defining their interests.[7] This does not mean that SSA is not a moral wrong. Policies against SSA are necessary, but they should take into account the culturally shaped identities of minority women. While the Dutch debate on SSA focused on whether the abortion law should be tightened to ban SSA, a contextual analysis would point to the necessity of a policy that tackles the cultural context that gives rise to requests for SSA (see Saharso 2005).

CRITICAL MULTICULTURALISM

The liberal discourse of multiculturalism not only met with wholesale feminist rejections, as articulated by Okin (1999) and others, but also elicited feminist criticisms claiming that liberal thinkers had not sufficiently thought through the critical implications of the "multi" in multiculturalism. In a programmatic essay, Lauren Berlant and Michael Warner (1994, 108) defined critical multiculturalism as a "project of organizing a critical culture primarily against capitalism, class exploitation, and consumer passivity." Its adherents saw themselves as part of an academic movement that focused on the discursive empowerment of marginal groups (Chicago Cultural Studies Group 1994, 124–126). It initiated the development of, next to women's studies, new academic disciplines such as African American studies, Chicana–Chicano studies, Black studies, and cultural studies.

From these circles of critical scholars, at least six objections against liberal multiculturalism are brought to the fore. First, liberal espousals of human diversity ignore the actual inequalities and power differences between the dominant (white, Western) majority and racial and ethnic minorities. American Black feminist scholar bell hooks (1993), for instance, claims that sunny images such as that of the Rainbow PUSH Coalition are nothing but a "perversion of the progressive vision of cultural diversity" (238). Second, focusing on cultural and ethnic differences has a politically divisive effect: the policy of equal treatment to support all minority groups in maintaining their own identity incites them to compete with one another about funds and resources instead of fighting together against the shared predicaments of racism and discrimination (Davis 1996; Yuval-Davis 1999). Third, when adopted by big corporations as a market strategy to lure consumers into buying their products or as a human resources strategy to manage diversity, liberal celebrations of diversity have detrimental homogenizing effects. Thus, Donna Haraway (1997) resists what she calls the ever returning "Sacred Image of the Same" in advertisement campaigns by United Colors of Benetton or in a *Times* special issue proudly presenting the new multicultural America using a morphed image of a racially mixed young woman that perfectly fits the dominant ideal of female beauty (242–243, 259–261).[8] Fourth, liberal multiculturalism is accused of representing cultures as static, ahistoric, and mutually exclusive entities, which does not do justice to their actually dynamic and fluid character (Brah 1996). This essentialist approach of diversity causes a fifth problem: it leaves unchallenged the authority of traditional community leaders to define what is essential to the preservation of their culture. As a consequence, it becomes difficult to question the role traditionally ascribed to women within, for instance, fundamentalist religious movements (Anthias and Yuval-Davis 1992, 193). Finally, the conception of the autonomous and rational subject underlying liberal defenses of multiculturalism does not offer an adequate representation of the often fragmented, multilayered, and hybrid identities of the actual members of multicultural societies (Anzaldúa 1987).

Although feminists within both strands of multiculturalism share similar concerns about the inherent sexism in traditional cultural and ethnic groups, critical multiculturalists address them from a different perspective on politics and power. Liberal thinkers, we could say, start from above. Their notion of politics refers to the sphere of the (nation-)state and its institutions, and they conceive of politics as a sphere of reasonable deliberation on how legitimate state power can be used to improve the lives of citizens. Liberal multiculturalists attempt to find out which principles, laws, rules, and policies a good or just government should follow to meet the needs and interests of minority groups.

Critical multiculturalists, on the other hand, start from below. They develop ideas about the role and strategy of oppositional movements in improving the lives of citizens. For them, politics is about the struggles for hegemony between the (ethnic and religious) majority and different minorities. They discuss ways marginalized groups may achieve empowerment, challenge dominant ideas and create counterhegemonic practices. The aim of critical multiculturalism is to break through the (supposedly) homogenizing tendency of the hegemonic way of thinking and make room for the history and heritage of minority groups. Political power is located not so much in the "official-political" sphere of government and governmental institutions but in the organization of everyday life as a "discursive political' realm" (Fraser 1989, 26). Rather than explore, as liberal multiculturalists do, the possibilities and limits for the equal recognition of other cultures, critical multiculturalists question whether and to what extent forms of (liberal) multiculturalism may actually worsen rather than improve the lives of individuals, situated as they are at the intersection of axes of social inequality such as gender, race, class, ethnicity, and sexuality.[9]

Standpoints and Intersections

A line of feminist thought that made a significant contribution to the critical discourse on multiculturalism is developed by women of color and third-world women who take issue with the (Western) women's movement for its inherent racism and classism (Moraga and Anzaldúa 1981; Sandoval [1982]1990; Mohanty, Russo, and Torres 1991) (see also the chapter by Patricia Hill Collins and Valerie Chepp in this volume). Mainstream feminism, it is argued, has long mistaken the concerns of white women for those of women in general, thereby ignoring race, ethnicity, and class as axes of inequality. Some talk about a "double jeopardy" (Beale 1970) or even a "triple jeopardy" (Collins 1991), as women of color suffer not only from sexism but also from racism and poverty. To empower such marginalized women, sociologist Patricia Hill Collins (1986, 1991) develops the contours of what she calls a Black feminist standpoint. Many, however, find that such additive approaches are inadequate. In societies stratified by numerous axes of difference and equality, the lives of men and women are structured by multiple and interlocking systems of gender, race, class, and sexuality and hence are far more complex.

To grasp this complexity, Black legal scholar Kimberlé Crenshaw (1991) coined the concept of intersectionality. According to Crenshaw, women's identities are always lived in the modalities of other categories of identity, such that gender is always lived in the modalities of ethnicity and class, nationality in the modalities of gender and race, or class in the modalities of gender and nationality. The intersectional approach thus takes into account differences not only between but also within groups of women (1242).

However, by representing the social reality of intersecting axes of identity as "converging" systems of oppression (Crenshaw 1991, 1245), within these early conceptions of intersectionality women are still seen as passive bearers of the meanings of categories imposed upon them by a sexist, racist, patriarchal, or homophobic system. As such, they tend to fall back to the additive account they wished to leave behind. As in standpoint theory, the only conceivable strategy of resistance is to self-consciously reappropriate one's identity as, for instance, a Black woman or a working-class lesbian.

Hegemonic Practices

Some feminists find that identity politics is an unfortunate road to take as it is based on reified identity categories, collapses categories of personal and collective identity, takes political differences between women as mere "reflections of different stages of raised consciousness," and mistakenly believes that the basis for political action is a reality to be discovered and subsequently changed (Anthias and Yuval-Davis 1992, 191).

Inspired by the tradition of (British) cultural studies and (French) poststructuralist philosophy, these feminist scholars adopt alternative conceptions of power and politics as developed within the post-Marxist theory by Ernesto Laclau and Chantal Mouffe ([1985]2002). In their plea for radical democracy Laclau and Mouffe adopt Antonio Gramsci's notion of power as hegemony, that is, the power of a bloc of parties that have entered into a temporary alliance. Hegemonic formations are the contingent and provisional outcome of political struggle; they always have to reckon with the existence of marginalized but potentially subversive counterhegemonic discourses. From a poststructuralist perspective, identities are always constructed in and through hegemonic discursive practices. Identity categories therefore not only limit women's freedom of movement and choice but also provide narrative and enabling resources for resisting these categorizations. So critical multiculturalists question and deconstruct the detrimental effects of what Inderpal Grewal and Caren Kaplan (1994, 17) call "transnational scattered hegemonies" and also look for sites where new figurations of the (female feminist) subject are created and transformative forms of politics are practiced.[10]

New Figurations of Subjectivity

One of the central aims of critical multiculturalists is to radically interrogate the modernist and humanist notions of subjectivity and identity upon which the liberal discourse of multiculturalism is built. The ensuing challenge is to develop "analytical frames capable of addressing multiple, intersecting, axes of differentiation" (Brah 1996, 210). Such analytical frames need to be radically antiessentialist and should include marginalized discourses and forms of subjectivity and ways of thinking while simultaneously avoiding their assimilation within the hegemonic discourse. Stam and Shohat (1994), therefore, speak of polycentric multiculturalism as a project that consistently "thinks and imagines 'from the margins'" and grants epistemic advantage to those who are equipped with a "double consciousness" (300). The subject is to be seen as "a site of multiple voicings" not originating from one unitary and self-transparent subject but as constituted by "a discourse that traverse[s] consciousness" (Alarcón 1990, cited in Brah and Phoenix 2004, 78). One example is Gloria Anzaldúa's exploration of the figure of *the new mestiza*[11] who as a "a product of crossbreeding" (Anzaldúa 1987, 81) provides "hybrid progeny, a mutable, more malleable species with a rich gene pool" (77). Rather than celebrating diversity as something smooth and easy, the mestiza experience is one of living racial, cultural, and linguistic diversity "in the flesh." To cope with her body and soul being the site of a constant "clash of cultures" (81), the mestiza develops a considerable tolerance for ambiguity and ambivalence (79). Other examples of such alternatives to the modernist notion of the autonomous and rational subject are Trinh's (1989) inappropriate/d other, Sandoval's (1991) oppositional consciousness, and Haraway's (1991) cyborg.

By these new figurations critical feminist multiculturalists attempt to indicate how diversity and difference destabilize our notion of the (female feminist) subject. However, this radical decentering of the subject raises the question as to the origins of critique and resistance. If "there is no doer behind the deed," as Judith Butler (1990, 142) approvingly quotes Friedrich Nietzsche's dismantling of the illusions of autonomy and rationality, how can we then conceive of creative resistance or innovative action? Where does real change come from if the subject is no longer an autonomous source of speech and action but is simply a node in a discursive field of (counter)hegemonic forces? The difficulty to address such questions becomes particularly acute when the position of women within (fundamentalist) Islam appears on the agenda of Western feminism.

Transversal Politics

In an ethnographic study of a Muslim women's mosque movement in Cairo in the 1990s, Saba Mahmood (2005) shows how these pious women wholeheartedly subject themselves to the demands of Islam. Admittedly, they do not meet the liberal feminist criteria of autonomy, but according to Mahmood they nevertheless are active agents. Building on Butler's (1990) notion of the performativity of gender, Mahmood argues that their agency consists in their deliberate engagement in practices of self-cultivation through the performance of "repeated bodily acts" by which they train their "memory, desire and intellect to behave according to established standards of conduct" (214). The problem with this analysis is that it meets the feminist demand to respect the choice of women who self-consciously opt for a nonliberal lifestyle but that it leaves precious little room for questioning the misogynist assumptions underlying these established standards of conduct.

In the wake of the Salman Rushdie affair of 1989,[12] British sociologist Nira Yuval-Davis (1992, 285) observed that as "carriers" of religious norms and values,

Muslim women especially are expected to contribute not only to the biological but also to the cultural reproduction of their collectivity. As a consequence, they are the object of strong social control within their community. British policies of multiculturalism were at least partly responsible for the significant growth of fundamentalist movements in the United Kingdom that imposed uniformity on their members (283). From the perspective of critical multiculturalism, Yuval-Davis's critique was problematic, as it could feed into already existing racist and xenophobic sentiments toward Muslims in the United Kingdom and seems disrespectful of the autonomy of this religious minority group. Yet, against the grain, in the early 1990s there emerged an organization in London, Women Against Fundamentalism (WAF), that did question the role of women within Islamic fundamentalism without relapsing into a position of cultural imperialism. According to Yuval-Davis, WAF succeeded in finding an effective voice amid the minefield of politically correct standpoints during the Rushdie affair, because the movement practiced a form of *transversal politics*. Transversal politics, a term adopted from Italian feminists who worked with members of conflicting national groups (Yuval-Davis 1994), consists of the formation of coalitions of individuals from various backgrounds who organize on the basis of a common stance regarding a specific issue. This common stance is based on dialogues in which each participant brings in her own experiences and identity (i.e., rooting) while simultaneously attempting to put herself in a situation of exchange with other members of the coalition (i.e., shifting) without either decentering herself or homogenizing the other (Yuval-Davis 1999, 123). All feminist (and other democratic) politics can thus be seen as a form of coalition politics whose boundaries are set "not in terms of 'who' we are but in terms of what we want to achieve" (Yuval-Davis 1997, 126).[13] This poststructuralist interpretation of intersectionality neither is based on the (liberal) assumption of the feminist subject as autonomous and rational nor lapses into a relativistic position that renders each reference to hegemonic norms and values suspect.

WAF did not present itself as antitraditional or antireligious but forged a critical third position, aptly expressed in the slogan, "Our tradition—resistance, not submission!" (Yuval-Davis 1999, 114). In this respect, WAF shows a remarkable similarity with the strategy set out by the French feminist movement *Ni putes, ni soumises* (Neither whores, nor submissive) (Amara 2003) a couple of years later. Here too was a coalition of religious and secular women, who together challenged both the image upheld by fundamentalist Muslims of independent women as whores and the Islamophobic assumption that all Muslim women are oppressed.

Concrete Others and Interactive Universalism

An interesting middle ground between the discourses of liberal and critical multiculturalism is explored by Seyla Benhabib (2002). On one hand, Benhabib agrees with critical multiculturalists in their rejection of the mosaic version of multiculturalism, that is, "the view that human groups and cultures are clearly delineated and identifiable entities that coexist while maintaining firm boundaries" (8). Instead, cultures should be seen as radically hybrid and polyvocal rather than coherent and pure wholes (25). But on the other hand, with liberal multiculturalists Benhabib is adamant that feminists should take the dimension of normative deliberation seriously (7). Her critical account of cultural diversity is therefore based on two pillars: a narrative conception of identity; and an interactive account of universalism.

According to the narrative model of identity, to become a self is to insert oneself into already existing webs of narratives. We cannot freely choose the webs of signification that we are caught in, yet we have the capacity "to weave out of those narratives...a life story that makes sense for us" (Benhabib 1999, 344). This account of identity thus leaves room for the multiplicity and fragmentation of individual subjects but simultaneously acknowledges the need for a core self. It leaves room for some form of autonomy, understood not as the feature of a dislocated and isolated subject but as the ability of people to sometimes critically distance themselves from their lives and actions.[14]

To take a critical distance, Benhabib (1999) claims, involves the capacity "to take a universalistic attitude of hypothetical questioning" (354, note 13). This universalistic attitude requires us to follow a procedure whereby we truly interact with others. For this purpose we should adopt the viewpoint not only of the generalized but also of the concrete other. For example, we should put ourselves in the position of others insofar as they are like us, such as beings with the same basic needs, equal rights and duties; however, we also should take account of their position insofar as they are truly other than us, such as beings with a different history, faith, and culture (Benhabib 1992). Benhabib's theory thus brings together the conception of politics as embraced by liberal thinkers as a sphere of reasonable deliberation on the legitimate use of state power to enhance the lives of citizens and the critical view that perceives of politics as the struggle to give voice to marginalized groups. In her view, policies regarding cultural, ethnic, and religious minorities should be based on normative guidelines that emerge when we follow the truly democratic procedures of interactive universalism.

Conclusion

As we have argued, liberal and critical multiculturalism started with radically opposed conceptions of individual autonomy and different positions regarding universalism and relativism. Liberalism has long held that human rights are universal and conceives of autonomy as an innate capacity that (adult) persons all posses by virtue of their humanity. This makes the autonomous individual a presocial category, which prevents us from asking under what cultural conditions this autonomy is constituted. Poststructuralism, from which critical multiculturalism takes its inspiration, radically decentrered the subject as an historical invention or an effect of power. Since it is context that determines our identity, critical multiculturalists tend to take a relativistic outlook to questions of cultural diversity. By presenting the individual as a fully socially constituted category they likewise prevent questioning the conditions for autonomous agency. On both sides we saw attempts to amend these shortcomings by recognizing more fully (1) that we are both culturally constituted and autonomous persons and (2) that across different cultures we may share some basic ideas in our thinking about justice.

If we critically assess the feminist credentials of both approaches, it is clear that liberal multiculturalists have given more thought to the issue of government intervention on behalf of minority women. They make clear that cultural diversity and gender equality are not necessarily at odds. Policies against THP, so claim the democratic and the contextualist approaches in particular, should take into account the culturally shaped identities of minority women and be based on culturally sensitive judgment. But the exclusive focus of the liberal debate on culture and on inequalities within minority groups is unfortunate insofar as the continuation of THP often is, as the example of sex selective abortion illustrated, an effect of the interplay of both cultural and material interests. Critical multiculturalism, on the other hand, does a good job giving a voice to resistance movements in the margins but leaves us empty-handed in cases where women consent with traditional practices that we consider harmful to them. This is not so much because it is less normative than liberal multiculturalism but because its normativity has a different target, that is, the deconstruction and dismantling of hegemonic ideas and practices leading to a radical transformation of modern Western culture.

We think, however, that both liberal and critical multiculturalists still underestimate the severity and scope of the problem of THP. Their focus is on a limited amount of prototypical examples like female genital cutting or forced marriage, while other equally harmful practices go unrecognized. In many parts of Africa, for instance, women cook on wood that they collect and carry home piled up on their head. In rural South Africa this is "not just a result of the gender division of labour, but is, in itself, a key way of engendering life" (Matinga 2010, 212). Collecting firewood leads to musculoskeletal injuries, while cooking on firewood leads to chronic respiratory infections (ibid.). Yet this method of firewood energy acquisition and use is neither classified as a THP nor recognized as a problem of sustainability or risky work conditions. Likewise, we believe that many Western practices should but are as yet not recognized as THP, for instance forms of plastic surgery such as cutting the labia or narrowing the vagina based on notions of female beauty and sexual attractiveness generated by the rise of the so-called raunch culture (see Jeffreys 2005; Levy 2006).

In our view, Anne Phillips's contextual approach to liberal multiculturalism and Seyla Benhabib's deliberative understanding of critical multiculturalism offer the most promising starting points for critically addressing THP without rendering minority women as passive victims of their culture. Both Phillips's emphasis on the need for contextual understanding of liberal and cultural values and Benhabib's conception of taking account of not only the generalized but also the concrete other point to the never-ending feminist task to scrutinize situations, practices, and conditions that may be harmful to women but are as yet not recognized as such.

NOTES

1. Like Iris Marion Young (1990), Kymlicka argues for a broader notion of justice that does not merely focus on problems of (socioeconomic) distribution but also includes the issue of equal recognition of different identities and cultures. However, while Young's argument for a "politics of difference" starts from the political demands of new social movements such as the feminist and the gay movement, Kymlicka's concern is primarily with the recognition of national minority cultures.
2. It was Okin (1999) that attracted attention, but see for the fuller argument Okin (1998).
3. See Parekh (2000, particularly ch. 9) for a full account of his discussion of traditional harmful practices.
4. Okin (1998) was so widely discussed that it is impossible to list all the reactions. For interesting contributions to the feminist discussion, see also Benhabib (2002, ch. 4), Coene and Longman (2010), Sauer and Strasser (2008), and Volpp (2001).
5. See, for example, http://www.unicef.org/publications/index_26024.html or http://www.un.org/womenwatch/daw/egm/elim-disc-viol-girlchild/ExpertPapers/EP.4%20%20%20Raswork.pdf
6. The approach does not ask whether people have equal rights but whether they possess the capabilities to perform the activities that are definitive of a life that is truly human (Nussbaum 1999, 41–42).
7. On this, see also Saharso (2007).
8. Slavoj Žižek (1997, 46) speaks of multiculturalism as "the cultural logic of multinational capitalism...the problematic of multiculturalism—the hybrid coexistence of diverse cultural life-worlds—...is the form of appearance of its opposite, of the massive presence of capitalism as universal world system: it bears witness to the unprecedented homogenization of the contemporary world" (see also Žižek 2001, 238–239).
9. For an elaborate exposition of critical multiculturalism, see Gordon and Newfield (1996, 445–469).
10. In an overview of the methodological implications of the notion of intersectionality, Leslie McCall (2005) refers to early theories of intersectionality as the *intracategorical*

approach (which focuses on qualitative case studies into the position of one particular, marginalized category), while poststructualist accounts of intersectionality start from an *anticategorical* perspective (which point out the exclusionary effects of categorization and further deconstruct of existing categories of identity). To these two approaches McCalls adds (and promotes) a third approach: the *intercategorical* perspective, which strategically uses existing categories in large-scale quantitative multigroup and comparative studies to "analyze the intersection of the full set of dimensions of multiple categories" (1787). For a more in-depth discussion of early and poststructuralist theories of intersectionality, see also Prins (2006).

11. *Mestiza* is the Spanish word for a woman of mixed racial ancestry. Anzaldúa speaks specifically of the identity of Chicana women as a mix of white, Mexican, and indigenous cultures.

12. In 1989, the Iranian ayatollah Khomeini issued a fatwa on the British–Indian author Salman Rushdie for his blasphemic portrayal of the prophet Muhammad in his novel *The Satanic Verses*. This led to many violent protests against Rushdie in the Muslim world and to the murder of several translators and publishers of his book; Rushdie went into hiding for years on end. The affair triggered vehement discussions, especially in Great Britain, forcing intellectuals to rethink their hitherto quite tolerant attitude toward Islam and to consider the scope of and relation between fundamental human rights, such as the rights to free speech and self-expression, and the freedom of religion.

13. It shows similarities with Donna Haraway's poststructuralist conception of feminist politics as a politics of "cyborgs" that consists of temporary alliances based not on shared identities but on "affinity," "the appeal of one chemical nuclear group for another, avidity" (Haraway 1991, 155).

14. What Benhabib (1999) finds missing in poststructuralist accounts of the subject is the notion of intentionality. She agrees with Judith Butler (1990) that linguistic agency can be seen as the possibility to reiterate and thereby sometimes transform existing conventions and norms. But while Butler sees this as part of the subversive potential of language itself, Benhabib thinks that such processes of resignification can take place only through language in use, in other words through communication. And when people communicate, they utter a statement with the intention to raise a claim to truth, rightness, or sincerity. Hence, to make sense of linguistic utterances, we need to postulate that there indeed is "a doer behind the deed" (Benhabib 1999).

References

Alarcón, Norma. 1990. "The theoretical subject of *This bridge called my back* and Anglo-American feminism." In G. Anzaldúa, ed., *Haciendo Caras*. San Francisco: Aunt Lute, 356–369.

al-Hibri, Aziza Y. 1999. "Is Western patriarchal feminism good for third world/ minority women?" In J. Cohen, M. Howard, and M.C. Nussbaum,, eds., *Is multiculturalism bad for women?* Princeton, NJ: Princeton University Press, 41–46.

Amara, Fadela. 2003. *Ni putes, ni soumises*. Paris: La Découverte.

Anthias, Floya, and Nira Yuval-Davis. 1992. *Racialized boundaries: Race, nation, gender, colour and class and the anti-racist struggle*. New York: Routledge.

Anzaldúa, Gloria. 1987. *Borderlands. La Frontera: The new mestiza*. San Francisco: Aunt Lute Books.

Barry, Brian. 2001. *Culture and equality*. Cambridge, UK: Polity Press.

Baum, Bruce. 1997. "Feminism, liberalism and cultural pluralism: J.S. Mill on Mormon polygynie." *Journal of Political Philosophy* 5(3): 230–253.

Beale, Frances. 1970. "Double jeopardy: To be black and female." In Toni Cade, ed., *The Black Woman: an anthology*. New York: Mentor, 90–100.

Benhabib, Seyla. 1992. "The generalized and the concrete other: The Kohlberg-Gilligan controversy and moral theory." In S. Benhabib, ed., *Situating the self: Gender, community and postmodernism in contemporary ethics*. Cambridge, UK: Polity Press, 148–177.

Benhabib, Seyla. 1999. "Sexual difference and collective identities: The new global constellation." *Signs* 24(2): 335–361.

Benhabib, Seyla. 2002. *The claims of culture. equality and diversity in the global era*. Princeton, NJ: Princeton University Press.

Berlant, Lauren, and Michael Warner. 1994. "Introduction to critical multiculturalism." In David T. Goldberg, ed., *Multiculturalism: A critical reader*. Oxford: Blackwell, 107–113.

Brah, Avtar. 1996. *Cartographies of diaspora: Contesting identities*. London: Routledge.

Brah, Avtar, and Ann Phoenix. 2004. "Ain't I a woman? Revisiting intersectionality." *Journal of International Women's Studies* 5(3): 75–86.

Butler, Judith. 1990. *Gender trouble: Feminism and the subversion of identity*. New York: Routledge.

Carens, Joseph H. 2000. *Culture, citizenship and community: A contextual exploration of justice as even-handedness*. Oxford: Oxford University Press.

Chicago Cultural Studies Group. 1994. "Critical multiculturalism." In David T. Goldberg, ed., *Multiculturalism: A critical reader*. Oxford: Blackwell, 114–139.

Coene, Gily, and Chia Longman (Eds.). 2010. *Feminisme et multiculturalisme: Les paradoxes du debat*. Bruxelles: Peter Lang Editors.

Collins, Patricia Hill. 1986. "Learning from the Outsider Within: The Sociological Significance of Black Feminist Thought." *Social Problems* 33(6): S14–S32.

Collins, Patricia Hill. 1991. *Black Feminist Thought: Knowledge, Consciousness and the Politics of Empowerment*. New York: Routledge.

Crenshaw, Kimberlé Williams. 1991. "Mapping the margins: Intersectionality, identity politics, and violence against women of color." *Stanford Law Review* 43(6): 1241–1299.

Davis, Angela. 1996. "Gender, class, and multiculturalism: Rethinking 'race' politics." In Avery F. Gordon and Christopher Newfield, eds., *Mapping Multiculturalism*. Minneapolis: University of Minnesota Press, 40–48.

Deveaux, Monique. 2005. "A deliberative approach to conflicts of culture." In A. Eisenberg and J. Spinner-Halev, eds., *Minorities within minorities: Equality, rights and diversity*. Cambridge, UK: Cambridge University Press, 340–362.

Fraser, Nancy. 1989. "Foucault on modern power: Empirical insights and normative confusions." In N. Fraser, ed., *Unruly practices: Power, discourse and gender in contemporary social theory*. Cambridge, UK: Polity Press, 17–34.

Friedman, Marilyn. 2003. *Autonomy, gender, politics*. Oxford: Oxford University Press.

Gordon, Avery F., and Christopher Newfield (Eds.). 1996. *Mapping Multiculturalism*. Minneapolis: University of Minnesota Press.

Grewal, Inderpal, and Caren Kaplan (Eds.). 1994. *Scattered hegemonies: Postmodernity and transnational feminist practices*. Minneapolis: University of Minnesota Press.

Haraway, Donna. 1991. "A cyborg manifesto: Science, technology, and socialist-feminism in the late twentieth century." In D. Haraway, ed., *Simians, cyborgs, and women: The reinvention of nature.* London: Free Association Press, 149–181.

Haraway, Donna. 1997. *Modest_Witness@Second_Millennium.FemaleMan©_Meets_ OncoMouse™: Feminism and Technoscience.* New York: Routledge.

Hirsi Ali, Ayaan. 2006. *The caged virgin: A Muslim woman's cry for reason.* London: Free Press.

Honig, Bonnie. 1999. "My culture made me do it." In J. Cohen, M. Howard, and M. C. Nussbaum, eds., *Is multiculturalism bad for women?* Princeton, NJ: Princeton University Press, 35–40.

hooks, bell. 1993. "A revolution of values: The promise of multicultural change." In Simon During, ed., *The cultural studies reader,* 2d ed. London: Routledge, 233–240.

Jeffreys, Sheila. 2005. *Beauty and misogyny: Harmful traditional practices in the West.* London: Routledge.

Kelek, Nela. 2005. *Die fremde Braut: Ein Bericht aus dem Inneren des türkischen Lebens in Deutschland.* Köln: Kiepenheuer & Witsch.

Kukathas, Chandran. 2001. "Is feminism bad for multiculturalism?" *Public Affairs Quarterly* 15(2): 83–98.

Kukathas, Chandran. 2003. *The liberal archipelago: A theory of diversity and freedom.* New York: Oxford University Press.

Kymlicka, Will. 1995. *Multicultural citizenship.* Oxford: Oxford University Press.

Kymlicka, Will. 1999. Liberal complacencies. In J. Cohen, M. Howard, and M. C. Nussbaum, eds., *Is multiculturalism bad for women?* Princeton, NJ: Princeton University Press, 31–34.

Laclau, Ernesto, and Chantal Mouffe. [1985]2002. *Hegemony and socialist strategy.* London: Verso.

Levy, Ariel. 2006. *Female chauvinist pigs: Women and the rise of raunch culture.* New York: Free Press.

Mahmood, Saba. 2005. *Politics of piety. The Islamic revival and the feminist subject.* Princeton, NJ: Princeton University Press.

Manji, Irshad. 2005. *The trouble with Islam today: A wake-up call for honesty and change.* Toronto: Random House of Canada.

Matinga, Magi N. 2010. "We grow up with it: Experiences, perceptions and responses to the energy-health nexus: A multi-level grounded ethnography," Ph.D. diss., University of Enschede.

McCall, Leslie. 2005. "The complexity of intersectionality." *Signs: Journal of Women's Studies* 30(31): 1771–1800.

Mirnadé, A., and E. Enriquez (Eds.). 1979. *The birth of Chicana feminism.* Chicago: University of Chicago Press.

Mohanty, Chandra Talpade, Ann Russo, and Lourdes Torres (Eds.). 1991. *Third world women and the politics of feminism.* Bloomington: Indiana University Press.

Moraga, Cherríe, and Gloria Anzaldúa (Eds.). 1981. *This bridge called my back: Writings by radical women of color.* Watertown, MA: Persephone Press.

Njambi, W. N. 2004. "Dualisms and female bodies in representations of African female circumcision." *Feminist Theory* 5(3): 281–303.

Nussbaum, Martha C. 1999. *Sex and social justice.* Oxford: Oxford University Press.

Okin, Susan Moller. 1998. "Feminism and multiculturalism: Some tensions." *Ethics* 108: 661–684.

Okin, Susan Moller. 1999. "Is multiculturalism bad for women?" In J. Cohen, M. Howard, and M. C. Nussbaum, eds., *Is multiculturalism bad for women?* Princeton, NJ: Princeton University Press, 7–24.

Okin, Susan Moller. 2005. "Multiculturalism and feminism: No simple questions, no simple answers." In A. Eisenberg and J. Spinner-Halev, eds., *Minorities within minorities: Equality, rights and diversity.* Cambridge, UK: Cambridge University Press, 67–89.

Parekh, Bikhu. 1999. "A varied moral world." In J. Cohen, M. Howard, and M. C. Nussbaum, eds., *Is multiculturalism bad for women?* Princeton, NJ: Princeton University Press, 69–75.

Parekh, Bikhu. 2000. *Rethinking multiculturalism: Cultural diversity and political theory.* Houndmills, UK: MacMillan Press.

Phillips, Anne. 2007. *Multiculturalism without culture.* Princeton, NJ: Princeton University Press.

Phillps. Anne. 2010. *Gender and culture.* Cambridge, UK: Polity Press.

Prins, Baukje. 2006. "Narrative accounts of origins: A blind spot in the intersectional approach?" *European Journal of Women's Studies* 13(3): 277–290.

Saharso, Sawitri. 2005. "Sex selective abortion: Gender, culture and public policy in the Netherlands." *Ethnicities* 5(2): 248–266. + Sex-Selective Abortion. A Reply, 279–281.

Saharso, Sawitri. 2007. "Is freedom of the will but a Western illusion? Individual autonomy, gender and multicultural judgement." In B. Arneil, R. Dhamoon, and A. Eisenberg, eds., *Sexual justice/cultural justice.* London: Routledge, 122–138.

Sandoval, Chela. 1991. "U.S. third world feminism: The theory and method of oppositional consciousness in the postmodern world." *Genders* 10: 1–24.

Sandoval, Chela. [1982]1990. "Feminism and racism: A report on the 1981 National Women's Studies Association Conference." In G. Anzaldúa, ed., *Making Face, Making Soul/Haciendo Caras. Creative and Critical Perpsectives by Feminists of Color.* San Francisco: Aunt Lute, 55–71.

Sauer, B., and S. Strasser (Eds.). 2008. *Zwangsfreiheiten: Kulturelle Diversität, Geschlechteregalität und feministische Handlungsmöglichkeiten.* Wien: Promedia Verlag.

Sen, Amartya K. 1985. *Commodities and capabilities.* Oxford: Elsevier Science Publishers.

Shachar, Ayelet. 2001. *Multicultural jurisdictions: Cultural differences and women's rights.* Cambridge, UK: Cambridge University Press.

Smith, Barbara (Ed.). 1983. *Home girls.* New York: Kitchen Table.

Stam, Robert, and Ella Shohat. 1994. "Contested histories: Eurocentrism, multiculturalism and the media." In David T. Goldberg, ed., *Multiculturalism: A critical reader.* Oxford: Blackwell, 296–324.

Trinh, Min-ha. 1989. *Women, native, other: Writing postcoloniality and feminism.* Bloomington: Indiana University Press.

Volpp, L. 2001. "Feminism and multiculturalism." *Columbia Law Review* 101: 1181–1218.

Wikan, Unni. 2002. *Generous betrayal: Politics of culture in the new Europe.* Chicago: University of Chicago Press.

Young, Iris Marion. 1990. *Justice and the politics of difference.* Princeton, NJ: Princeton University Press.

Yuval-Davis, Nira. 1992. "Fundamentalism, multiculturalism and women in Britain."
    In James Donald and Ali Rattansi, eds., *"Race," culture and difference*. London:
    SAGE, 278–291.
Yuval-Davis, Nira. 1994. "Women, ethnicity and empowerment." *Feminism and
    Psychology* 4 (1): 179–198.
Yuval-Davis, Nira. 1997. *Gender & nation*. London: SAGE.
Yuval-Davis, Nira. 1999. "Ethnicity, gender relations and multiculturalism." In Rodolfo
    D. Torres, Louis F. Mirón, and Jonathan Xavier Inda, eds., *Race, identity, and
    citizenship: A reader*. Oxford: Blackwell, 112–125.
Žižek, Slavoj. 1997. "Multiculturalism, or, the Cultural Logic of Multinational
    Capitalism." *New Left Review* 1(225): 28–51.
Žižek, Slavoj. 2001. *Did somebody say totalitarianism?* London: Verso.

CHAPTER 32

GENDER, NATIONS, AND NATIONALISMS

SURUCHI THAPAR-BJÖRKERT

INTRODUCTION

The aim of this chapter is to explore some significant interpretive trends within the literature on gender, nations, and nationalism. First, I will outline the trajectories of research on the nation that have analyzed how the political, social, and civil spheres were constituted as well as constitutive of people's identities. So when Ernest Gellner (1983) wrote his classic text *Nations and Nationalisms*, he envisaged the nation by the following statement, "two men are of the same nation if and only if they recognize each other as belonging to the same nation...nations are the artefacts of men's convictions and loyalties and solidarities" (7). The statement raises important points about the recognizable markers that are necessary for men to align themselves with some men and distance themselves from others. However, this statement discusses nation formation in relation to only one gender, men. Feminist contributions have, thus, highlighted the marginalization of women and gender from mainstream analyses of nationalist movements and nation-state formation. In particular, these scholarly contributions have illustrated how gender relations frame nationalist demands, how nationalist ideology configures gender relations within specific geopolitical contexts, and how gender shapes relationship between nations. Second, I will analyze how historical projects shape and are in turn shaped by national and sexual stereotypes that govern differential access to power and privilege. Third, the institutionalization of gendered norms in nationalist discourse has typically meant that the costs and benefits of nationhood and national belonging fall unevenly on men and women. In exploring tensions between women's co-option, agency, and resistance within nationalist projects, I will draw on examples from India, Ireland, sub-Saharan Africa, and Latin America to illustrate these ideas. This discussion introduces the debate on the politicization of women's lives and their nationalist contributions in both public and domestic spheres. Finally, I will explore the unholy alliance between religion and nationalism and how that justifies gendered violence and ethnic cleansing on behalf of the nation and is often driven by a specific religious ideology.

HISTORICAL UNDERSTANDINGS ON NATION AND NATIONALISMS

With the collapse of the empires across Europe in 1917–1918, discussions about nationalism, nation-state, and national self-determination moved to the center of international political imagination. It was against this backdrop that scholars such as Carlton B. Hayes (1931), Hans Kohn (1944), Edward H. Carr (1945), Louis Snyder (1954), Boyd Shafer (1955), and Alfred Cobban (1969) undertook their explorations of nationalism. Together these scholars pointed toward a range of factors that could explain the rise of nationalisms: the strength of the national bourgeoisie, the emergence of the bureaucratic state, establishment of citizenship, and the growth of universal education. It was, however, Elie Kedourie's (1960) theorization that was a turning point for later theorists on nationalism, such as Ernest Gellner (1983), Anthony Smith (1998), and John Breuilly (1985). In his seminal work *Nationalism*, Kedourie argued that "nationalism is a doctrine invented in Europe at the beginning of the nineteenth century" (1). For him, nationalism was a critical response to the alienation that German and European intellectuals experienced with regard to tradition, social values, and bureaucratic absolutism. Kedourie's ideas resonated in the work of Gellner, the main exponent of the modernist approach to understanding nationalism. While Gellner agreed with Kedourie that nationalism was modern, he did not think that it was invented. Rather, it was an inevitable consequence of the transition to modernity that all societies experienced since the eighteenth century. Gellner's main thrust is that nationalism, nation, and the international order of national states are the product of modern conditions such as capitalism, bureaucracy, and industrialism. Gellner (but also Anderson 1983; Hobsbawm 1990) insisted on the idea of the impossibility of the nations in the premodern period. Thus, political, economic, and social transformation (for example, the industrial revolution) from tradition to modernity could facilitate the emergence of nationalism.

Critiquing the instrumentalist approach of the modernists, Anthony Smith (1995b) argues that the modernist fallacy fails to grasp the "continuing relevance and power of pre-modern ethnic ties and sentiments in providing a firm base for the nation-to-be" (40). Smith (1995a) points out that there are striking parallels between the premodern era and the modern idea of national identity. Two issues in relation to Smith's critique are important from the perspective of this chapter. The first relates to his idea that modernist accounts concern themselves with elite manipulation of the masses rather than the dynamics of the masses themselves. As Smith argues, no attention has been given to how social groups (for example, the poor or the powerless) have been mobilized in accordance with their own cultural and political traditions, their memories, myths, and vernacular forms of expression. The second issue for Smith (1995b) is why would people choose ethnicity and nationalism "as a vehicle for their advancement rather than class or religion. Why should so many people be prepared to fight and die for ethnic communities whose struggles seem desperate..." (39). It was in response to both the primordial[1] and modernist approaches that Smith (1999) elaborated his ethnosymbolist approach. For ethnosymbolists, what "gives nationalism its power are the myths, memories, traditions and symbols of ethnic heritage and the ways in which a popular living past has been and can be re-discovered and re-interpreted by modern nationalist intelligentsia" (9). Smith is interested in the concept of the *ethnie* (ethnic community)—collective "cultural unit(s)" that are much older than nations. Drawing a distinction with the primordialist approach, Smith argues that "ethnies are constituted not by lines of physical descent but by a sense of continuity, shared memory and collective destiny, that is, by lines of cultural affinity embodied in myths, memories, symbols and values, retained by a given cultural unit of population"(Smith 1999, 187). Thus, Smith departs from both Benedict Anderson (1983), who associates the origin of modern nations and nationalism with "print capitalism" and the role of media in creating the imaginary community, and Gellner (1983), who views it as a product of industrialism.

Connecting the past and the present was Ernest Renan's (1994) analysis of nation as "a soul, a spiritual principle' constituted by a rich legacy of memories; and present-day consent" (19). According to Renan, the nation shares not only common memories but also an amnesia, a collective forgetfulness that enables the members to forget past differences while concentrating on the things that link them together. Renan's concept of the nation owes much to Rousseau (1762), and in Renan's scheme the nation was an entity united by the same political institutions, the same rules and regulations, the same rights and obligations, which made membership in the nation more a matter of voluntary choice than a matter of birth or blood as the German romantic nationalist Johann Gottfried von Herder argued. The voluntarist understanding of the nation also incorporates the idea of a subjective identity, which to some extent can be acquired and is not a fixed identity that one is born into. The nation in this understanding moves beyond ethnic determinism and instead incorporates the idea of change, and nation forming becomes a fluid process that entails renegotiation of boundaries. Renan's overcited concept of nationalism as an "everyday plebiscite" resonates with Billig's (1995) understanding of banal nationalism. Drawing on Hannah Arendt (1963), Billig argues that banality cannot be associated with harmlessness or benignity. Instead, it is about the "ideological habits" that reproduce nations and these "habits" are embedded in everyday life. Billig argues that nationalism, "far from being an intermittent mood in established nations, is an endemic condition" reproduced in the everyday lives of citizens through "continual flagging" (6–9). Pushing these debates further Brubaker (1996) argues that nations are often understood as substantial entities, collectivities, or communities and the notion of nations as "real entities" adopts categories of practice as categories of analysis (15). Brubaker suggests that we focus on nationness "as a conceptual variable" and instead of asking the question, "What is a nation?" we should be looking at how nationhood "as a political and cultural form (is) institutionalized within and among states" (16).

There are of course some difficulties with the concept of the nation, especially when juxtaposed with the state. Arguably, some distinctions need to be maintained between the nation and the state rather than conflating them (see McCrone 1998) (Smith 2000; also see Hobsbawm 1990). A state can be constituted by ethnically and culturally heterogeneous nations; a state can be multinational; a nation may not necessarily have its own state; and a nation can exist without a state. Of specific importance to this chapter is the idea that through an ideology of nationalism the state can create a sense of internal sovereignty, foster an exclusionary majoritarian nationalism, or risk itself to the exigency of retaliatory minority nationalisms. The nationalist goal could also be to secure a state of its own for the nation. Moreover, processes that lead to the formations of national identities may not necessarily be voluntary but entail much coercion, as we have, for instance, seen during the dissolution of the former Yugoslavian state (the socialist federal republic of Yugoslavia in the 1990s). Furthermore, the most homogeneous nation-states contain within their borders people who are only partially integrated into the hegemonic construction of the nation.

Arguably, the current debates have moved forward from those of historians and international relations scholars in the 1960s and 1970s (see Thompson and Fevre 2001). However, the most determining feature missing from mainstream theories of nationalism has been the role of women and gender in political societies since the discussions on nationalism have been primarily *by men about men*. I would emphasize three reasons for this gender blindness. First, the overemphasis on nationalism as a collective process assumed that it was the same process for men and women. Second, the contribution of women to nation formation was seen as insignificant, and nations and nationalism were conceived as only about men and masculinity rather than about how nationalism constitutes and is constitutive of both men and women. Third, the separation of political and paternal power, exemplified in the writings of social contract theorists (such as John Locke and Jean-Jacques Rousseau), in the seventeenth and eighteenth centuries, laid the foundation for understanding of public and private as inevitably following from the natural characteristics of the sexes: natural subordination as opposed to free individualism (Laslett 1960; Birch 1989). Women were excluded from the status of "individuals" and from participating in the public world of equality, consent, and convention (Pateman 1989; also see Elshtain 1981; Fraser 1990).

Much of the scholarship on nationalism unconsciously reinstated the same divisions by placing women on the margins of the public-political sphere. In locating the paradoxes in national narratives and drawing on the example of Britain's emergent national narrative of post-1859, McClintock (1997, 91) argues that "the family as a metaphor offered a single genesis narrative for national history while, at the same time, the family as an institution became void of history and excluded from national power. The family became, at one and the same time, both the organising figure for national history and its antithesis." The subordination of woman to man and child to adult and "hierarchies within the nation could be depicted in familial terms to guarantee social difference as a category of nature" (ibid.). In rejecting the claim that the separation of private and public follows inevitably from the natural characteristics of the sexes (Imray and Middleton 1983), feminists have remodeled the idea of the public as a contested space by arguing that the public sphere was not the domain of propertied men only but that women participated in the discursive public sphere and in the formation of public opinion (see Mellor 2002). Unlike Habermas (1991), who argues that women could get entrance to the public domain only as readers, Mellor argues that women published their free and reasoned opinions and their views were openly circulated not only through the economic institutions of print culture (newspapers and journals, books, circulating libraries) but also through the public forums of the debating societies and the theater, in eighteenth- and nineteenth-century England (Mellor, 2–7). Furthermore, women were actors as well as spectators in those spaces defined as public in the late eighteenth-century England, and they participated in a range of strategies from leading food riots to raiding brothels, writing and publishing across a range of genres, and boycotting the shops of political opponents; toward the end of the nineteenth century they were also present within local politics (Davidoff 1995, 240).

En(gendering) Nationalism

In an important theoretical intervention *Women-Nation-State* Nira Yuval-Davis and Floya Anthias (1989) reversed the neglect of women by previous scholarship and provided a thorough analysis of how women affect and are affected by national and ethnic processes in relation to both civil society and the state. Substantiated through case studies in different geographical and political contexts—Britain, Australia, South Africa, Uganda, Israel, Iran, Turkey, Cyprus, and Italy—Yuval-Davis and Anthias identified five ways through which women participate in ethnic and national processes. First, women are the biological reproducers of members of ethnic collectivities as well as the reproducers of boundaries of ethnic–national groups. On one hand, the emphasis is on individual state and interstate policies that limit the reproduction of people born within specific ethnic groups, by controlling its women through forced sterilization or birth control campaigns. On the other hand, women can be encouraged to reproduce the "right" ethnic group orchestrated through encouragement couched as child or maternal benefits. Second, women are the main channel through which the symbolic boundaries of ethnic and national identity are reproduced. Thus, women not only shoulder the responsibility of the "transfer of cultural and ideological traditions of ethnic and national groups" but often "constitute their actual symbolic configuration" (see Yuval-Davis and Anthias 1989, 6). Often religious, customary laws, social traditions, or state legislation can dictate who will marry whom as well as serve as a pointer to how the future progeny will be incorporated in the ethnic collective.

Third, women also contribute to the ideological reproduction of the collectivity and bear the responsibility for the transmission of cultural norms. In an interesting essay in *Women-Nation-State*, Deborah Gaitskell and Elaine Unterhalter (1989) describe the construction of the Afrikaner nation and the symbol of the suffering Afrikaner motherhood in the early twentieth century. As public affairs became increasingly Anglicized, mothers encouraged Afrikaner language and cultural identity in the home. Gaitskell and Unterhalter point out that despite the different ideological content of Afrikaner and African National Congress (ANC) nationalism, the symbol of the "mother" straddled through racial boundaries. Fourth, women are the symbolic signifiers of ethnic–national differences and contribute to the construction, reproduction, and transformation of ethnic–national categories. Finally, Yuval-Davis and Anthias (1989, 7) contend that women are participants in national, economic, political, and military struggles. Women participate in national liberation struggles, in guerilla warfare, or in the military. The roles women play or are expected to play are not always imposed on them, but women actively participate in reproducing, modifying, and controlling other women. Furthermore, they have pointed out the centrality of race, class, and ethnicity for understanding nationalism, an issue that until recently has been marginalized in the discussions of white feminists (also see Yuval-Davis 1997).

Sylvia Walby (1997) questions whether these five categorizations encompass all the major ways gender and ethnic–national relations intersect. First, Walby argues that this categorization privileges the ideological or cultural level and the specificity of gendered division of labor is understated. In relation to this, there is more focus on "what women can do for nations rather than on what nations can do for women" (Walby 2000, 527). Reducing women to the "level of pawns or political symbols" leads to the "reduction in the economic content of different patterns of gender relations" (ibid.). In other words, there is very little reference to the economic costs and benefits of different national projects for women. Second, Walby claims that the "maintenance of boundaries between ethnic/national groups is also a conflict between different forms of social hierarchies, not only different cultures" (ibid.). Even the most cohesive ethnic–national group almost always entails a system of social inequality and one where the dominant groups typically exercise hegemonic control over the "culture" and the "political project of the collectivity" (Walby 1997, 177–178). Third, different genders and classes may be differentially enthusiastic about the national–ethnic project, depending on the extent to which they agree with the priorities of their political leaders. Significantly, there are differences between women themselves (on the basis of race, class, age, religion and education) that affect the nature and extent of their participation in nationalist politics (Sinha 2006). Women's contributions to nation building have been affected by their differences from men but also by differences between women (Thapar, 1993). Fourth, there are contradictions inherent in the gender agenda of nationalist projects. Some feminists have questioned whether women being a part and process of the national body politic have actually provided women with national agency. Women can be both hostages to such projects and active participants in them (Kandiyoti 1991, 431). Finally, an overemphasis on women's symbolic roles should not understate the fact that women can strategically use these symbols to carve out political spaces for themselves (Thapar-Björkert 2006).

Feminist response to the omission of women from the discussions of mainstream nationalism has led scholars to chronicle women's participation and their leadership in national and opposition politics as well as to uncover the mechanisms of women's exclusion from political organizations and decision-making bodies. However, while this has filled a critical gap in the study of nationalism, it misses "the major way in which gender shapes politics, through men and their interests, their notions of manliness, and masculine micro and macro cultures" (Nagel 1998, 243). Referring to nationalist movements as building on men's experiences and expectations and drawing on the interconnections between manhood and nationhood, Enloe (1989, 43) suggests that "nationalism has typically sprung from masculinised memory, masculinised humiliation and masculinised hope." Her insights challenge the simple correlation between *gender and women* by pointing out that nationalisms can be understood as masculine projects (also see Jayawardena 1986, 1995; Meaney 1993; Sharkey 1994; McClintock 1995). Similarly, McClintock argues that nations are historical practices through which social difference is both invented and performed. Thus, nationalism is a gendered discourse, and it cannot be understood without a "theory of gender power" (McClintock 1997, 90). Illustrating these ideas through examples from late eighteenth- and nineteenth-century Europe, Glenda Sluga (1989, 90) argues that by 1793 "the legislators of the new French Republic had defined popular national sovereignty in terms of its masculine citizenry." *Patriotism* and *national identity* advocated by the Jacobin republican government was defined in terms of orderly female behavior, and women's exclusion from the public sphere was increasingly premised on the identification of femininity with the private sphere. Any public activity of women that challenged the gender order in turn challenged the national moral order and was thus constructed as nationally subversive. Similarly, George Mosse (1985) analyzes how nationalism in nineteenth-century Europe was conditioned by the ideology of a Western bourgeois family morality with its concern for respectability, moral character, and physical beauty. This contributed to a sharp differentiation between gender roles but also to gendered stereotypes evident in the way German masculinity and morality were, for example, constructed in opposition to the loose-living French Forces in the wars against the French Revolution and Napoleon.

National and Sexual Identities

National identity can also be constructed in relation to the Other, where people "who are deemed inferior...are represented as feminised, controlled and subordinate" (Moore 1994, 145)—though who and what get defined as the non-national Other is historically contingent. Thus, gender difference can come to stand in for other forms of hierarchically organized difference, in opposition to other women and other men (Sinha 2006, 13).

With specific emphasis on "international order," Enloe (1989) examines how hierarchical relations between nations and gendered constructions of the *oriental woman* facilitated European civilization missions. The oppression of so-called native women was used in the rhetoric of colonialism to render morally justifiable its project of undermining or eradicating the cultures of colonized people. This gendering takes place on various levels. First, the *colonized nation* is gendered as female and entails a feminized subordination of the whole nation, as femininity is associated with retrogressive rather than progressive qualities. Second, the *colonized male* is gendered in ways that stress his inferiority to the colonial male. Third, the *colonized female* is represented in highly gendered ways by the colonizer for their specific political purposes (Thapar-Björkert and Ryan 2002). Furthermore, hegemonic masculinity entailed drawing a distance from racial and sexual masculine countertypes, for example, being a white man is not being a Jew or an Asian or an Indian or a black (Nagel 1998, 246).

Parallel to this process, the colonized female is represented in particular ways by nationalist projects to invert the imagery propagated by the colonizers, and since these representations are on behalf of the nation they are rendered legitimate and justifiable. This is most evident in the context of anticolonial nationalism. Tamar Mayer (2000) argues that both Indian and Caribbean nationalism developed in reaction to British imperialism's feminization and infantilization of both the colonies and the indigenous men (also see Sinha, 1995)..

Significantly, sexual identity and national identity are mutually dependent. Spike Peterson (1999, 55) argues that nationalism is not only gendered but also heterosexist and that the costs of noncompliance are high. Echoing similar sentiments, Nagel argues that "correct heterosexual behaviour constitutes gender regimes...Because of the common importance of proper gender role and sexual behaviour to ethnic community honour and respectability, a great deal of attention is paid to the sexual demeanour...and enforcement...of sexual conduct" (Nagel 2000, 113). Thus, sex and the nation intersect to produce notions, real or imagined, of other nationalities' sexual character, potential threats, and issues of virility and fecundity. It is in this context that we can understand the metaphor of the rape of the nation through the rape of the woman. Rape constitutes an instrument of militarized, masculinized nationalism, and it is on a women's body that the politics of the nation are mapped (see Enloe 2000; see also the chapter by Lene Hansen in this volume). Women's bodies become the battleground of men's wars and the violation of women "sabotages(s) the underpinnings and therefore continuity of their communities" (Peterson, 45). In critiquing the edited collection on *Nationalisms and Sexualities* by Andrew Parker et al. (1992) for its conceptual looseness, Sam Pryke (1998, 530) identifies three interconnections between nationalism and sexuality: national sexual stereotypes; sexuality in national conflict; and sexuality in nation building. National stereotypes reflect the sexual attributes of a nationality such as passion, promiscuity, or virility; the perceived threat of enemy sexuality becomes pronounced during tension between and within nations such as during conflicts and finally the nature of appropriate sexual boundaries that are deployed within nation-building processes.

The gendered response of anticolonial nationalist projects illustrated these intersections between nationalism and sexual identities.

National Symbolism—Mothers of the Nation

In popularizing the symbol of womanhood, a specific identity of the woman based on qualities such as self-sacrifice, affection, and kindness was created. Beth Baron (2005) analyzes elite Egyptian women's nationalist mobilization against the British occupation since World War I. She examines how the nationalist demands for independence galvanized women's political consciousness and feminized nationalist metaphors and symbols. Women drew an empowering parallel between family and nation and were prominent until full independence in 1952. Adopting familial and kinship idioms, the men were referred to as the sons and brothers and women as the mothers of the nation (Baron 2005, 36; see also Kandiyoti 1991; McClintock 1993; Moghadam 1994).

Women were expected to fulfill their duty to the nation through biological reproduction. For example, in the rejection of communism in the former Yugoslavia and the reassertion of the nationalist ideology, the meaning of *patriotic womanhood* shifted from a woman whose main task was to build socialism through work toward a woman who regenerated the nation through her role as a mother (see Cockburn 1998). This change in perception was seen from the mid-1980s onward with the growth of Serbian nationalism within the Yugoslav socialist system, stimulated by the fear that Serbia might lose Kosovo to Albania. In this context, the "reproductive potential" of women was emphasized, and the task of "Serbian national rebirth" was placed on women (Bracewell 1996, 28). She had not only to produce "little Serbs" but also "to bear fighters" (29). Her heroism lay in her willingness to sacrifice her children for the nation. In such contexts of demographic renewal, abortion is often projected as a threat to the nation. In 1992, the Ministry for Renewal in Croatia established a Department of Demographic Renewal, which developed strategies to raise an ethnically clean birth rate and provided incentives to women who gave birth to more than four children (Albanese 2001).

When women are accorded the symbolic roles as mothers of the nation, the intersections of sexual purity and national honor politicize both the public and domestic–familial domains—the events in one domain reflect on the other. Women as wives and mothers become the bearers of masculine honor (Nagel 1998, 255). Thus, "women's shame is the family shame, national shame and man's shame...the family, nationhood and manhood (are) all politicised and associated with national imagery" (249). Interestingly, it was the private domain in which men's honor was located and a domain in which no dilution of national identity had taken place.[2] In India, the home was the uncolonized domain that represented the spiritual quality of the national culture (Chatterjee 1986, 1989, 243; Bagchi 1990, 65). The spiritual role of the new nationalist woman represented the mark of superiority of Hindu identity with alien culture but was also a sign of women's "newly acquired freedom" (Chatterjee 1989, 245). However, so the new woman's newly acquired freedom could still be contained within the parameters set by the nationalist leaders, the *common woman* construct was created. She lacked the veneer of gentility or the attributes of middle-class docility and submissiveness (Thapar 1993, 83). This construct set moral limits on women's behavior and code of conduct. The nationalist woman as the embodiment of the nation was the nurturer of civilization and the defender of the civilization and the motherland. The symbolism was supported by religious metaphors drawn largely from Hindu religion (Sarkar 1984; Pandey 1990; Thapar 1990; Chowdhury-Sengupta 1992;).

Motherland (Bharatmata)

Indian nationalist leaders realized the significance of the concept of a unified motherland, a motherland (*Bharatmata*) stretching from the Himalayas to the Indian Ocean. This idea aligned the duties and responsibilities of the mother with the duties of a woman toward her nation. Women used the word *mata* (mother) when referring to the soil of India. Activist Narayani Dixit recited a poem written by her husband, Kalka Prasad Tripathi, a congressman, when she was released from Kanpur jail in 1943:

You have showered like the rain on the dense clouds of the enemy. You have
risen like the morning light on this dark empire Oh! *Bharatmata*, nurturer of
competent sons. (Transcript of interview with Narayani Dixit, 1994, Kanpur)

While darkness is associated with the British Empire, *Bharatmata* (mother–
nurturer–defender) is the bearer of good tidings.

The symbolic representation of the *Bharatmata* served a dual purpose.
First, it effectively controlled the feelings of resentment and disappointment felt
by women toward the nationalist leaders for encouraging their menfolk to fight
the British or when their sons, fathers, and brothers were hauled into jails or
thrown in *kala pani* (black water, or imprisonment for life). Second, the image
of one mother of the whole nation, who was pure and untouched and whose
honor had to be protected through the sacrifice of "countless citizen warriors"
(Peterson 1998, 44), aroused the national sentiments and emotions of the population as a whole. The symbolic association of the nation with the motherland
and the merging of the nation–community with the selfless mother–devout
wife evokes the obvious and necessary response to come to her defense and
protection (Chhachhi 1991, 165).

The idea of *Bharatmata* was propagated through poetry, literature, and the
cinema. The image was invariably that of a crowned and beautiful woman in
shackles, weeping tears of blood, or of the same woman holding aloft a trident and
leading her countless sons and daughters into battle. In the context of Indonesian
nationalist struggle, Saraswati Sunindyo (1998) argues that the iconography of a
suffering *Ibu Pertiwi* (motherland) was used as a trope to "rally youth to the
task of freeing and rescuing the motherland from her deepest suffering, suffering
caused by the colonial power that had taken her dignity and dispossessed her of
her wealth" (11). The suffering is depicted in nationalist songs describing "tears
[running] down her cheeks" and "the mother is suffering" (ibid.).[3]

Poets like Bal Krishna Sharma Navin (1898–1960), Harbans Rai Bachan
(1907–), and Mahadevi Verma (1907–1987) disseminated the concept of
Bharatmata. One poem by Bal Krishna Sharma, "The Song of the Morning
Breeze," highlights the idea of a mother in distress:

> May the nectar like milk of the mother turn into bitter gall. May the tears of
> her eyes dry up to leave a stream of blood behind. Hey poet, string together
> the words that will be cataclysmic. (Sharma 1989, 20)

The Indian vernacular literature, the media, and the speeches of nationalist
leaders became the most important vehicle for dissemination of these ideas.

Motherhood: Vehicle of Oppression or Emancipation?

Debates around symbolic role models have revealed the uncomfortable tensions
between feminism and nationalism, and, arguably, though women were at the
center of nationalist discussion, their individual interests were subordinate to the

collective interest of the nation (Bracewell 1996). In the context of India, Rao (1999) argues that gendered symbolism could displace women from constitutive processes of the symbolic construction within the nation since it allowed the "nation to represent itself as a woman," for example, as *Bharatmata*, whereas women "could not represent themselves, their own identity or their Indianness" (319).

However, we need to go beyond the nationalist rhetoric and analyze how women not only accepted their symbolic roles but also participated in the process of actively propagating them and encouraged other women to do the same (Jolly 1994, 44; see also Sharpley-Whiting, 1998). Einhorn (1996) argues that women can and sometimes do reject the unitary identity assigned to them by others and move beyond the restricted roles assigned to them through the nationalist agenda. In the Yugoslavian nationalist discourse women tried to use the symbolic representation of the mother to argue against the policies of the state, "to protest against the war and for peaceful negotiations in a way in which men (even fathers) could not" (Bracewell 1996, 30). But whereas Serbian nationalism privileged the biological reproducer, the nationalist movement in India privileged the symbolic category of women as mothers of the nation. The self-sacrifice of an Indian mother, nurturer, and guardian of the domestic sphere was reconfigured as national sacrifice in the public sphere, transcending the rigidity of biological reproduction to include the ideological and social reproduction and nurturance and maintenance of a specific national identity. The symbolic use of representations may not be used by women to reverse gender roles but to empower those specific roles to facilitate their political contribution and to achieve recognition of those roles (see also Passerini 1989). So motherhood is associated not necessarily with subordination but with developing a political consciousness and in the process becoming aware of their political contribution. On a different tack, Denis Kandiyoti (1988), with reference to classic patriarchy, argues that women in Asia, sub-Saharan Africa, and the Middle East have resisted new capitalist developments and new roles for women "for alternatives that are perceived in keeping with their respectable and protected domestic roles" (280).

Similarly, women in Argentina used their roles as mothers (as embodied in the construction of the *marianismo*) to claim political justice. *Marianismo* is rooted in a combination of the primitive awe (Mesopotamian culture) that adores the reproductive ability of a woman and in Catholic values that view Virgin Mary as the embodiment of spiritual and moral strength of women (Steven 1973, 94; Fisher 1993). As mothers of the disappeared, Las Madres de Plaza de Mayo claimed justice from the repressive junta between 1976 and 1983. In defiance of a regime that operated in secrecy, mothers demonstrated in Buenos Aires before the presidential palace in Plaza de Mayo, carrying pictures of their disappeared children (*desaparecidos*) and demanding their return (Bouvard 1994). Contrary to the conservative ideologies espoused by most Latin American militaries, which saw women's roles as primarily in the domestic sphere, the Madres used their traditional roles as a linchpin of the protests.

This made it harder for a government that elevated motherhood to persecute women who argued that they were fulfilling their maternal role by searching for their missing children. Most of these women were housewives, few had received an education beyond high school, and none of them had any previous political experience but still challenged state power, which disfavored any public expression of dissent and protest. Through their demonstrations, these women politicized public spaces, which were governed largely by conservative male-dominated politics (Alvarez 1990). In the context of anti-British Egyptian nationalism, Beth Baron (2005) points out that the symbolism of mothers of the nation gave women a maternal authority to engage more openly in society and politics. Interestingly, elite women recognized women as bearers and rearers of future citizens but argued that the nation would advance only with girls' education and women's progress: "only educated mothers would imbue their sons with love for the nation" (47). At the same time, stressing their commonalities as mothers helped them to forge alliances across religious and ethnic divides. In the context of African nationalism—as opposed to Afrikaans nationalism— McClintock (1997, 107) argues that "motherhood is less the universal and biological quintessence of womanhood than it is a social category under constant contest." African women transformed the ideology of motherhood to justify acts of untraditional "public militancy" (mothers of revolution) and, like their Egyptian counterparts though on a different tack, "appealed to a racially inclusive image of motherhood in their campaigns to fashion a non-racial alliance with white women" (ibid.).

Moving beyond Symbolic Repertoires: Politicization of Women's Lives

In understanding the complexity of women's engagement with nationalist movements, it is imperative to distinguish between how women have been represented in national histories and symbolic repertoires, on one hand, and how women have actually renegotiated and challenged their roles and contributions to nationalism on the other. While operating within the parameters of nationalist needs, women have recognized their own needs.

One of the enduring difficulties in analyzing women's relationship to and roles within nationalisms is that they are frequently located in the private sphere and are thus made invisible. Furthermore, academic canons have emphasized only "visible" activities in the public sphere as "nationalist" and "patriotic" (Jayawardena 1986; Rao 1994), disregarding the fact that the domestic sphere was also a site where identities were continuously negotiated. As McClintock (1995) argues, the cult of domesticity, particularly under imperialism, was not something that can be assigned to the natural domain of the family. Rather, domesticity was a "dimension of male and female identities shifting and unstable and an indispensable element both of the industrial market and the imperial enterprise" (5). Private domains were permeable and part of larger public actions. For example, and as discussed in the preceding section, women reappropriated the symbols of nationalism and in the process reconstituted and politicized motherhood. Thus, the complex relations and overlaps between the domestic and the political and the home and the public arena are of central importance in the analysis of nationalism. Women did not simply accept traditional roles or traditional gender hierarchies, but rather they played the nationalist game in ways that the male nationalist leaders had not anticipated and found difficult to challenge. Some women used their nationalist experience to carve political spaces for themselves, making themselves visible in the public domain. While these women may have constituted only a minority, their importance to the public and political discourses of the nation cannot be underestimated.

Politicization of the Domestic Sphere

One of the best examples of the politicization of domestic sphere is women's involvement during the Irish War of Independence in 1919–1921, with the British army occupying Ireland and imposing martial law on the civilian population. Branches of the Republican women's organization Cumann na mBan became affiliated to units of the Irish Republican Army and became "an army of women" (Ward 1989, 163). Originally formed in 1914, Cumann na mBan or Women's Council had established over eight hundred branches by 1921 (Conlon 1969) and is estimated to have had in excess of three thousand members (Ward 1989). Women played an active and crucial part in the Irish struggle for independence (ibid.). Most of these activities were secret, undercover, and frequently hidden within the domestic sphere and became a significant source of challenge to the British colonial rule (Thapar-Björkert and Ryan, 2002). Most Cumann na mBan activists were young, unmarried, and economically active women (Sheehan 1990). They were mainly from Catholic backgrounds and came from urban, middle-class families as well as rural farming families (ibid.). Hundreds were arrested and imprisoned (McCoole 1997). Thousands had their homes raided and searched (Conlon 1969). Many were interrogated, intimidated, and threatened (Ward 1989; Keyes McDonnell 1972; Clarke 1991).[4]

The Irish Republican Army engaged in a two-year guerrilla war and relied very heavily on female involvement at two key levels. While outside home, women were increasingly used as intelligence agents, couriers, and dispatch riders, in the domestic sphere they provided a network of safe houses across the country. With tens of thousand of British troops in Ireland, women risked the ever-present threat of attack, arrest, and imprisonment. Typical among these women was Kathleen Keyes McDonnell, a young wife and mother who provided food and shelter for the Republican guerrilla fighters. Although operating within the domestic sphere and appearing to perform traditional gender roles, she exemplifies the blurring of boundaries in nationalist warfare. An active member of the Republican women's group Cumann na mBan, Keyes McDonnell devoted her home to the war effort. Despite constant military raids, she provided a meeting place for the Irish Republican Army, a hiding place for secret documents, and a refuge for 'wanted men' (Keyes McDonnell 1972).

The domestic sphere was transformed as simultaneously a site of resistance and a site of danger. In the Irish context of a guerrilla war fought out in the countryside and isolated villages, women who remained in the privacy of the domestic sphere were easy targets for frustrated British soldiers and particularly vulnerable to attack (Conlon 1969; Clarke 1991). The militarization of the domestic sphere also meant that gender roles were challenged as men left their homes and families and women became the defenders of the domestic space and the mainstay of the guerrilla army. In relation to women's engagement in Palestinian national struggle in Lebanon (1968–1982) and in the West Bank during the Intifada in the 1990s, Julie Peteet (1997, 108) argues that "the continuous violation of the home—the violent entries, searches and demolitions...quickly cast aside notions of the home as a space distant from conflict." Instead, the blurring of boundaries between the home front and the battlefront collapsed the distinctions between feminine and masculine spaces in conflict (ibid.).

Within the Irish Republican Army there was concern about women's involvement in militancy and the transgression of gender boundaries (Ryan 2000). These concerns were to become even more pronounced, however. In July 1921, a truce was declared between the British government and the Republican forces. Later that year a treaty was negotiated that set out the partition of Ireland and the semi-independence of the southern Free State. However, the terms of the treaty proved divisive, splitting the Republican movement and leading to civil war (Blake 1986). Cumann na mBan was the first national organization to officially reject the Treaty with Britain (Ward 1989). In addition, the six women members of the Irish parliament, Dail Eireann, all supported the Republican movement and opposed the treaty. Thus, from the outset, women were very publicly associated with the Republican side. In the ten months of bitter civil war that followed, the Republicans were outnumbered by the Free State Army, which supported by Britain's military might inflicted severe casualties among their former comrades. The defeat of the Republicans ended the war in 1923. The Free State government led by William Cosgrave set about cementing its authority and asserting the legitimacy of the new nation-state.

Politicization of the Public Sphere

Some historical accounts from sub-Saharan Africa argue that "nationalist revolutions were patriarchal revolutions" (Chadya 2003, 156). With reference to Tanzania,

Nigeria, and South Africa, Joyce Chadya argues that the inequalities women experience in the postcolonial state reflect the historical hierarchies between women's movement and nationalist movements. Even where women's movements arose independently of the nationalist movements, like in Nigeria, they were not accepted as equals and were denied the opportunity to run for parliamentary elections. However, it would also be incorrect to suggest that women were merely the dupes of nationalism who were conveniently drawn into the national movement and then later quickly shunted back to a depoliticized domestic sphere or that the women's rights were marginalized. It thus becomes even more important to find ways through which their narratives can be reclaimed.

With reference to Tanzania, Susan Geiger (1996) argues that the narratives of Tanganyika African National Union (TANU) disrupt the mainstream historiographical tradition that privileges the contributions of men only. Interestingly, these women brought to TANU "an ethos of nationalism already present as trans-ethnic, trans-tribal social and cultural identity" (469). Urban women's dance groups (ngoma) were transformed into vehicles for nationalist mobilization, through exchanging information, organizing mass rallies, and fund-raising locally for TANU in the 1950s. These dance associations, considered as innocuous by colonial officials, "did not simply prepare women for nationalism...they expressed and so produced nationalism, not only through song and dance but through the relationships between and among the societies and women in them" (471). Even though nationalism in Tanzania has been criticized for its shortcomings, especially the way uneducated TANU women were excluded from government posts after independence (Chadya 2003), these "ordinary" women "constructed, reproduced and 'solidified'" Tanganyikan nationalism (Geiger, 473). Similarly, Hassim (2004) explores how the nationalist movement in South Africa, headed by the African National Congress (originally organized as South African Natives National Congress), did not reinforce women's position as secondary political subjects. From 1969 onward women in the ANC in exile, organized in a women's section and headed politically by a women's secretariat, made the transition from acting as social workers to becoming political agents in their own right. By the 1980s and with the support of then ANC president Oliver Tambo, women formulated strategies that would integrate gender equality into ANC's core principles and through the lessons learned during exile "the women's national coalition wrote gender equality into the state and constitution" (455).

NATIONALISM, RELIGION, AND VIOLENCE

The previously outlined debates in terms of women as symbolic repositories and women as agents of nationalism assume central importance when religion or ethnicity becomes a driving force for nationalist mobilization and the imagined nationalist identity is constructed partly by downplaying internal divisions such as caste and class differences (Anderson 1991, 6). Clara Connolly (1991) argues that, in the process of the rediscovery of the fundamentals, women and children are the symbolic repositories of a community's identity, with the main responsibility for upholding the honor of the community. One of the goals of the fundamentalist project is then to protect women from "unholy outsiders" (69), which could entail a continuum of violence: death by one's own kinsmen; violation by men of other community; or, in between these options, taking your own life, that is, "sublimating your vulnerability and making of it something heroic" (Menon and Bhasin 1998, 57). Ritu Menon and Kamla Bhasin (1993) argue that the link between the three decisions is the patriarchal consensus that, first, sanctions a violent resolution of women's sexuality and sexual status and, second, insists on women's silence regarding their own sexuality by attaching shame and stigma to the profound violation of the self. This is best exemplified in a well-researched example of the partition of India into two new sovereign and separate states of India and Pakistan in 1947. The partition was a specific historical juncture marked by religious hatred and unanticipated brutal massacres of Hindus, Muslims, and Sikhs who were caught in the process of mass migration between the newly created India and Pakistan. The lived experience of partition that encompasses the trauma of displacement, destruction, and death has until very recently received limited recognition in nationalist political discourse. Butalia (2000, 105) narrates the account from a book *Mool Suta Ukhde* (Torn from the Roots) in which the author mentions that "women were paraded naked in the streets, several had their breasts cut off, their bodies were tattooed with marks of the 'other' religion, in a bid to defile the so-called 'purity' of the race, women were forced to have sex with men of the other religion, many were impregnated. They bore children often only to have them taken away forcibly" (see also Butalia 1993).

For me, this issue also has a domestic genealogy. In August 1947, my mother, Dr. Kamala Seth (then fourteen years old), my maternal grandmother, Iqbalwati Seth (née Handa), and three siblings were stationed at Khanewal district of Multan division in West Punjab (undivided India). My maternal grandfather, Raghunath Lal Seth, was a police inspector serving British India and had not yet received orders from the government to move to India. Consequently, he had to stay behind. Raghunath Lal Seth asked his brother, Somnath Seth, to take the family of four siblings, of whom my mother was the eldest, and move to India. The uncle boarded the train, but the train stopped at Samasatta Station in Bahawalpur Division, 90 km from Multan. They had to spend the night at the platform in Samasatta, as they were informed that they would need a different connecting train to India. The trains that came to Pakistan from India were painted green and decorated with flowers and green flags: these refugee trains were carrying Muslims who were migrating from India to Pakistan. My mother's uncle, Somnath Seth, was scared to move out of the waiting room to get some food. They spent the night at the platform hungry and in fear of assault by the Muslims, barricading the room with large heavy tables. After they reached India, they were informed that one of the compartments of the train was found full of bodies of Hindu and Sikh men, women, and children who had been massacred en route.

Similarly, Khushwant Singh (2006, 212) narrates in his book *Train to Pakistan of* the events in a village in the Frontier called Mano Majra:

> In the height of the afternoon sun, a train stopped at Mano Majra. It approached slowly almost like a coffin bearing the dead. No one came out and hardly anyone approached it till a truckload of Army men surrounded it. An hour later, policeman came to the village and went door-to-door asking for wood, oil or even kerosene. They could not collect enough of either to cremate the bodies this train had brought to Mano Majra.

Ironically, while my mother and her family escaped unhurt, my father's life narrative, also from West Punjab in a similar time frame, unfolded in a different way, reflecting a different dimension of nationalism. My paternal grandfather, the late Amar Nath Thapar, was a government servant and worked as a stationmaster at a small railway station called Abbaspur Station, 7 km from Lyallpur District (Western Punjab) in undivided India (present-day Faisalabad). He was living in the government quarters meant for railway employees. Following the partition of the country in August 1947, there was general chaos everywhere. Though my grandfather was placed under police protection, he could not leave his post and move to India without receiving orders from the Indian government.

On August 2, 1947, my grandfather was on his way back home after his night duty. Some local Muslims were aware (through their informers) that my grandfather and his family would be leaving for India shortly. They attacked my grandfather with swords and killed him while he was on his way back to his quarters. My father, Dr. Raj Kumar Thapar, then a sixteen-year-old boy, spent the summer vacations with his father, and at the time the incident happened he was asleep on the roof *(chat)* of the house. He woke up to the sound of cries from the huge crowd that gathered. When he peeped from the rooftop, he saw his father lying dead in the middle of the road. He was terrified by what he saw but also feared that the same local Muslim men who were trying to gain entry to the house would kill him as well. Luckily, they were not successful, and my father was smuggled out of his house under the cover of night by some Sikh men, who then locked him inside the waiting room of the railway station to keep him safe from the marauding hordes.

These ethnicized nationalist politics resonate with Kaldor's (2004) formulation of *new nationalism*. In supporting the structuralist arguments made by the modernists, Kaldor argues that new nationalism, which has been constructed in the post-cold war period, "excludes others of a different nationality and has much in common with religious fundamentalism…this is not only because of the religious character of nationalism but also because many nations are defined in religious terms" (166). Interestingly, and what is perhaps understated in Kaldor's analysis is that new transnational nationalist ideologies draw on the same symbolic repertoire as the nationalisms of the nineteenth and twentieth centuries.

CONCLUSION

The resurgence of nations and nationalism as a significant political force coincides with the transformative changes in the global economy. The development of socially heterogeneous, multicultural, and multiethnic societies in Western Europe has given rise to debates on postnational citizenship. Massive immigration undermines the power and legitimacy of the traditional nation state and the emergence of denizens opens up further debates on postnational citizenship.

Paradoxically, the contradictory effects of globalization such as the rise of information-based economy, the formation of global virtual communities, and the changing nature of warfare have meant that the homogeneity of the nation-state is challenged (Kaldor 2004, 166). While the resurgence of nationalism in post-Soviet Europe, and former Yugoslavia, for example, has emphasized the power of self-determination, it has also led to new gendered patterns of inclusion and exclusion. There is an emergence of new vulnerabilities vis-à-vis the nation states and those nations that do not have states. More importantly, in specific contexts, the nation-state has been unable to fulfill its agenda for economic reforms and social justice toward marginalized social groups and subnational minority groups.

More recently, we see new forms of political articulation and political practice that challenge traditionalist understandings of the nation-state and state-building processes. The much debated new Arab Nationalism could radically alter the geopolitical landscape of the Middle East with its widespread rejection of the official ideology and increasing popular political pressure since January 2011. This new Arab nationalism is to a large extent post-Islamic, and each country in the Arab world faces a unique situation. It is, however, debatable whether this would be comparable to the old Arab nationalism of the Nasserite years of the 1950s and 1960s, when religion was pushed back into the private sphere away from the public arena of streets, schools, and universities. For example, in Tunisia, from a gender perspective, women's rights were taken care of in the constitution after independence in 1956: polygamy was abolished, and women got the right to vote and the same rights as men to divorce and were forbidden to wear veils.

State nationalist grievances in Tunisia and Egypt may have started the fire in the beginning of 2011, but the Arab identity helped to spread this process of change. Though Arab identity proved essential in spreading the unrest, the core problem around which protests were organized in each state was essentially national: jobs, freedom, and dignity. Thus, we have a dualist claim on both, an Arab identity and state nationalism. It is likely that state nationalism will strengthen now as new regimes turn their attention inward to the plethora of postrevolutionary problems they will face. Popular expectations on ongoing political transitions in both Egypt and Tunisia are far exceeding what transitional governments can deliver, particularly when it comes to quick economic benefits. Yet the awakening of the Arab youth—perhaps a more appropriate description of the momentous change in the region—is undoubtedly a powerful new force, and its ability to bring about a more democratic future will be profound.

The significance of gender in national projects has been reinstated and has opened new areas of inquiry in relation to men and women's differential experiences to power and domination in international politics. Of particular significance in the 2011 rising is the role of women who came out in many thousands on to the streets and squares of Cairo as well as provincial towns. Yet women are not reaping the benefits of a revolution that explicitly called for equality and social justice, for example, the issue of women's representation in Egypt and in the rest of the Arab world is still unaddressed. It is of utmost importance to include women during a transitional political phase or postrevolutionary period: the committee assigned to draft the new Constitution in Egypt in May 2011 did not include any women, and only one woman was appointed in the new cabinet. Also, a lot depends on whether the military is willing to embark on a process that will rid itself of its privileges and instead install a pluralistic governance based on merit rather than patronage. In particular, specific guarantees covering the political representation of women need to be written into Egypt's new constitution to ensure a significant women's parliamentary presence.

Unlike Tunisia and Egypt, in Libya political structures and state institutions need to emerge from scratch. The biggest challenge is to put together a cohesive transitional government that would be seen as legitimate by the majority of Libyans. To conclude, this postrevolution era will lead to the development of new forms of thinking on gender and nationalism, particularly the role of youth in bringing about political reforms and democratic change.

ACKNOWLEDGMENTS

This chapter is dedicated to my parents, Drs. Kamala Thapar and Raj Kumar Thapar, whose inspirational personal narratives sparked the desire to research this subject. A special thanks to Gunnel Björkert for her valuable insights on the Arab Spring and to, Dr. Santosh Kumar Thapar and Anil Thapar, for providing contextual personal information on the partition of India.

NOTES

1. The roots of primordialist thinking can be traced back to the German philosophers, especially Johann Gottfried Herder, who argued for the atavistic power of the blood and soil (*Blut und Boden*) that bound one closely with ones people (*das Volk*). Thus, the nation is founded on primordial attachments that can be rooted in biology or culture.

2. In Iranian nationalist discourse the symbolic imagery was significant even though it was not articulated around the anticolonial axis. From the late eighteenth through the first decades of the twentieth centuries, Iranian modernity was discursively shaped by concepts such as the nation, politics, and homeland (*vatan*). The *vatan* was discursively constructed as a beloved female or another complementary construction of *vatan* as the mother (Najmabadi 1997).

3. The symbolism of the *Bharatmata* was not confined to the colonial period but became an important vehicle of the Sangh Parivar (composed of the BJP, RSS, VHP, Bajrang Dal) for mobilizing anti-Muslim hatred in postcolonial India (Kishwar 1993).

4. The violence on revolutionary and guerrilla women also challenged the projected civilized masculinity of British administration. In India, the assaults on the revolutionary woman's body were perceived as an assault on the nation, and they questioned the masculine restraint of the British colonizers (Thapar 1998, 600) as well as challenged the dominant construction of femininity as passive.

REFERENCES

Albanese, Patricia. 2001. "Nationalism, war and archaization of gender relations in the Balkans." *Violence Against Women* 7(9): 999–1023.

Alvarez, E. Sonia. 1990. *Engendering democracy in Brazil: Women's movements in transition politics*. Princeton, NJ: Princeton University Press.

Anderson, Benedict. 1983. *Imagined communities: Reflection on the origin and spread of nationalism*. London: Verso.

Arendt, Hannah. 1963. *Eichmann in Jerusalem: A report on the banality of evil*. New York: Viking.

Bagchi, Jasodhara. 1990. "Representing nationalism: Ideology of motherhood in colonial Bengal." *Economic and Political Weekly* 25(42–43): 20–27.

Baron, Beth. 2005. *Egypt as a woman: Nationalism, gender and politics*. Berkeley: University of California Press.

Billig, Michael. 1995. *Banal nationalism*. London: SAGE.

Birch, Harold Anthony. 1989. *Nationalism and national integration*. London: Unwin Hyman.

Blake, Frances. 1986. *The Irish civil war*. London: Information on Ireland.

Bouvard Guzman Marguerite. 1994. *Revolutionising motherhood: The mothers of the Plaza de Mayo*, New York: Rowman and Littlefield.

Bracewell, Wendy. 1996. "Women, motherhood and contemporary Serbian nationalism." *Women's Studies International Forum* 19(1–2): 25–33.

Breuilly, John. 1985. *Nationalism and the state*. Chicago: University of Chicago Press.

Brubaker, Rogers. 1996. *Nationalism reframed: Nationhood and the national question in the New Europe.* Cambridge, UK: Cambridge University Press.

Butalia, Urvashi. 1993. "Community, state and gender: On women's agency during partition." *Economic and Political Weekly* 28(17): WS12–WS21.

Butalia, Urvashi. 2000. *The other side of silence: Voices from the partition of India.* London: C. Hurst and Co.

Carr, Edward Hallet. 1945. *Nationalism and after.* London: Macmillan.

Chadya, Joyce M. 2003. "Mother politics: Anti-colonial nationalism and the woman question in Africa." *Journal of Women's History* 15(3): 153–157.

Chatterjee, Partha. 1986. *Nationalist thought and the colonial world: A derivative discourse.* London: Zed.

Chatterjee, Partha. 1989. "The nationalist resolution of the women's question." In Kum Kum Sangari and Sudesh Vaid, eds., *Recasting women: Essays in colonial history.* New Delhi: Kali for Women, 233–254.

Chhachhi, Amrita. 1991. "Forced identities: The state, communalism, fundamentalism and women in India." In Deniz Kandiyoti, ed., *Women, Islam and the state.* London: Macmillan, 115–144.

Chowdhury-Sengupta, Indira. 1992. Mother India and Mother Victoria: Motherhood and nationalism in nineteenth-century Bengal. *South Asia Research* 12(1): 20–37.

Clarke, Kathleen. 1991. *Revolutionary woman.* Dublin: O'Brien Press.

Cobban, Alfred. 1969. *The nation-state and national self-determination.* London: Collins.

Cockburn, Cynthia. 1998. *The space between us: Negotiating gender and national identities in conflict.* London: Zed.

Conlon, Lil. 1969. *Cumann na mBan and the women of Ireland.* Kilkenny: Kilkenny People Press.

Connolly, Clara. 1991. "Washing our linen: One year of women against fundamentalism." *Feminist Review* 37: 68–77.

Davidoff, Leonore. 1995. *Worlds between: Historical perspectives on gender and class.* New York: Routledge.

Einhorn, Barbara. 1996. "Links across difference: Gender, ethnicity and nationalism." *Women's Studies International Forum* 19(1–2): 1–3.

Elshtain, Jean Bethke. 1981. *Public man, private women: Women in social and political thought.* Princeton, NJ: Princeton University Press.

Enloe, Cynthia Maneuvers. 2000. *The international politics of militarizing women's lives.* Berkeley: University of California Press.

Enloe, Cynthia. 1989. *Bananas, beaches and bases: Making feminist sense of international politics.* Berkeley: University of California Press.

Fisher, Jo. 1993. *Out of the shadows: Women, resistance and politics in South America.* London: Latin America Bureau.

Fraser, Nancy. 1990. "Rethinking the public sphere: A contribution to the critique of actually existing democracy." *Social Text* 25–26: 56–80.

Gaitskell, Deborah, and Unterhalter, Elaine. 1989. "Mothers of the nation: A comparative analysis of nation/race and motherhood in Afrikaner nationalism and African national Congress." In Nira Yuval-Davis and Floya Anthias, eds., *Women_Nation-State,* London: Macmillan, 59–78.

Geiger, Susan. 1996. Tanganyikan nationalism as "women's work": Life histories, collective biography and changing historiography. *Journal of African History* 37: 465–478.

Gellner, Ernest. 1983. *Nations and nationalism.* Ithaca, NY: Cornell University Press.

Habermas Jürgen. 1991. *The structural transformation of the public sphere: An enquiry into a category of bourgeois society.* Cambridge, MA: MIT Press.

Hassim, Shireen. 2004. "Nationalism, feminism and autonomy: The ANC in exile and the question of women." *Journal of Southern African Studies* 30(3): 433–456.

Hayes, J. H. Carlton. 1931. *The historical evolution of modern nationalism*. New York: Richard R. Smith.

Hobsbawm, E. J. 1990. *Nations and nationalism since 1780: Programme, myth, reality.* Cambridge, UK: Cambridge University Press.

Imray, Linda, and Audrey Middleton. 1983. "Public and private: Marking the boundaries." In Eva Gamarnikow, David Morgan, June Purvis and Daphne Taylorson., eds., *The public and the private*. London: Heinemann Educational Books, 12–27.

Jayawardena, Kumari. 1986. *Feminism and nationalism in the third world*. London: Zed Press.

Jayawardena, Kumari. 1995. *The white woman's other burden*. London: Routledge.

Jolly, Margaret. 1994. "Motherlands? Some notes on women and nationalism in India and Africa." *Australian Journal of Anthropology* 5(3): 41–59.

Kaldor, Mary. 2004. "Nationalism and globalisation." *Nations and Nationalism* 10(1–2): 161–177.

Kandiyoti, Deniz. 1988. "Bargaining with patriarchy." *Gender and Society* 2(3): 274–290.

Kandiyoti, Deniz. 1991. "Identity and its discontents: Women and the nation." *Millennium: Journal of International Studies* 20(3): 429–443.

Kedourie, Elie. 1960. *Nationalism*. London: Hutchinson.

Keyes McDonnell, Kathleen. 1972. *There is a bridge at bandon: A personal account of the irish war of independence*. Cork, Ireland: Mercier Press.

Kishwar, Madhu. 1993. "Religion at the service of nationalism: An analysis of Sangh Parivar politics." *Manushi* 76: 1–20.

Kohn, Hans. 1944. *The idea of nationalism: A study in its origins and background*. New York: Macmillan.

Laslett, Peter. 1960. *John Locke: Two treatises of government*. Cambridge, UK: Cambridge University Press.

Mayer, Tamar. 2000. *Gender ironies of nationalism: Sexing the nation*. London: Routledge.

McClintock, Anne. 1993. "Family feuds: Gender, nationalism and the family." *Feminist Review* 44: 61–80.

McClintock, Anne. 1995. *Imperial leather: Race, gender and sexuality in the colonial context*. New York: Routledge.

McClintock, Anne. 1997. "No longer in a future heaven: Gender, race and nationalism." In Anne McClintock, Aamir Mufti, and Ella Shohat, eds., *Dangerous liaisons: Gender, nation and post-colonial perspectives*. Minnesota: Minnesota University Press, 89–112.

McCrone, David. 1998. *The sociology of nationalism: Tomorrow's ancestors*. London: Routledge.

McCoole, Sinead. 1997. *Guns and chiffon: Women revolutionaries and Kilmainham Gaol*. Dublin: Government of Ireland Publications.

Meaney, Gerardine. 1993. "Sex and nation: Women in Irish culture and politics." In Ailbhe Smyth, ed., *Irish women's studies reader*. Dublin: Attic Press, 230–244.

Mellor, Anne K. 2002. *Women's political writing in England, 1780–1830*. Bloomington: Indiana University Press.

Menon, Ritu, and Kamala Bhasin. 1993. "Recovery, rupture and resistance: Indian state and the abduction of women during Partition." *Economic and Political Weekly* 28(17): WS2–WS11.

Menon, Ritu, and Kamala Bhasin. 1998. *Borders and boundaries: Women in India's partition*. New Delhi: Kali for Women.

Moghadam, V. M. 1994. *Identity politics and women: Cultural assertions and feminisms in international perspectives*. Oxford: Westview.

Moore, Henrietta. 1994. "The problem of explaining violence in the social sciences." In Penelope Harvey and Peter Gow, eds., *Sex and violence: Issues in representation and experience*. London: Routledge, 130–145.

Mosse, George L. 1985. *Nationalism and sexuality: Middle- class morality and sexual norms in Modern Europe*. Madison: University of Wisconsin Press.

Nagel, Joane. 1998. "Masculinity and nationalism: Gender and sexuality in the making of nations." *Ethnic and Racial Studies* 21(2): 243–269.

Nagel, Joane. 2000. "Ethnicity and sexuality." *Annual Review Sociology* 26: 107–133.

Najmabadi, Afsaneh. 1997. "The erotic vatan (homeland) as beloved and mother: To love, to possess and to protect. *Comparative Studies in Society and History* 39(3): 442–467.

Pandey, Gyanendra. 1990. *The construction of communalism in colonial North India*. New Delhi: Viking.

Parker, Andrew, Mary Russo, Doris Sommer, and Patricia Yaeger. 1992. *Nationalisms and sexualities*. London: Routledge.

Passerini. Luisa. 1989. "Women's personal narratives: Myth, experience and emotions." In Personal Narratives Group, ed., *Interpreting women's lives: Feminist theory and personal narratives*. Bloomington: Indiana University Press, 189–198.

Pateman, Carole. 1989. *The disorder of women: Democracy, feminism and political theory*. Cambridge, UK: Polity Press.

Peteet, Julie. 1997. "Icons and militants: Mothering in the danger zone." *Signs* 23(1): 103–129.

Peterson, Spike V. 1998. "Gendered nationalism: Reproducing 'us' versus 'them.'" In Lois Ann Lorentzen and Jennifer Turpin, eds., *The woman and war reader*. New York: New York University Press, 41–49.

Peterson, Spike V. 1999. "Sexing political identities/nationalism as heterosexism." *International Feminist Journal of Politics* 1(1): 34–65.

Pryke, Sam. 1998. "Nationalism and sexuality, what are the issues." *Nations and Nationalisms* 4(4): 529–546.

Rao, Uma. 1994. "Women in the frontline: The case of UP." In Leela Kasturi and Majumdar Vina, eds., *Women and Indian nationalism*. New Delhi: Vikas, 28–52.

Rao, Shakuntla. 1999. "Woman-as-symbol: the intersections of identity politics, gender, and Indian nationalism." *Women's Studies International Forum* 22(3): 317–328.

Renan, Ernest. 1994. "What is a nation." In John Hutchinson and Anthony Smith, eds., *Nationalism*. Oxford: Oxford University Press, 17–18.

Rousseau Jean-Jacques. 1762. *Du Contrat Social, Ou Principes Du Droit Politique*. Amsterdam.

Ryan, Louise. 2000. "Drunken tans: Representations of sex and violence in the Anglo-Irish war, 1919–21." *Feminist Review* 66: 73–92.

Sarkar, Sumit. 1984. *Modern India: 1885–1947*. Delhi: South Asia Books.

Shafer, Boyd C. 1955. *Nationalism: Myth and reality*. New York: Harcourt, Brace and World.

Sharkey, Sabina. 1994. *Ireland and the iconography of rape: Colonisation, constraint and gender*. London: University of North London Press.

Sharma, Bal Krishna. 1989. *Mandakini*. New Delhi: NCERT.

Sharpley-Whiting, Denean. 1998. *Frantz Fanon: Conflicts and feminism.* Lanham, MD: Rowman and Littlefield Publishers.

Sheehan, Aideen. 1990. *Cumann na mBan: Policies and activities.* In David Fitzpatrick, ed., *Revolution? Ireland 1917–23.* Dublin: Trinity History Workshop, 88–97.

Singh, Kushwant. 2006. *Train to Pakistan.* New Delhi: Roli Books.

Sinha, Mrinalini. 1995. *Colonial masculinity: The "manly" Englishman and the "effeminate Bengali" in the late nineteenth century.* Manchester: Manchester University Press.

Sinha, Mrinalini. 2006. *Gender and nation.* Washington, DC: American Historical Association.

Sluga, Glenda. 1998. "Identity, gender and the history of European nations and nationalisms." *Nations and Nationalisms* 4(1): 87–111.

Smith, Anthony D. 1995a. *The ethnic origins of nations.* Oxford: Blackwell.

Smith, Anthony D. 1995b. *Nations and nationalism in a global era.* Cambridge, UK: Polity Press.

Smith, Anthony D. 1998. *Nationalism and modernism.* London: Routledge.

Smith, Anthony D. 1999. *Myths and memories of the nation.* Oxford: Oxford University Press.

Smith, Anthony D. 2000. "Theories of nationalism: Alternative models of nation formation." In Michael Leifer, ed., *Asian nationalism.* London: Routledge, 1–21.

Snyder, Louis Leo. 1954. *The meaning of nationalism.* New Brunswick, NJ: Rutgers University Press.

Steven, P. Evelyn. 1973. "Marianismo: The other face of machismo in Latin America." In Ann Pescatello, ed., *Female and male in Latin America.* Pittsburg: University of Pittsburg Press, 231–254.

Sunindyo, Saraswati. 1998. "When the earth is female and the nation is mother: Gender, the armed forces and nationalism in Indonesia." *Feminist Review* 58: 1–21.

Thompson, Andrew, and Ralph Fevre. 2001. "The national question: Sociological reflections on nation and nationalism." *Nations and Nationalism* 7(3): 297–315.

Thapar, Romila. 1990. "The politics of religious communities." *Seminar* 365: 1–7.

Thapar, Suruchi. 1998. "Gender, nationalism and the colonial jail: A study of women activists in India." *Women's History Review* 7(4): 583–615.

Thapar-Björkert, Suruchi. 1993. "Women as activists: Women as symbols." *Feminist Review* 44: 81–96.

Thapar-Björkert, Suruchi. 2006. *Women in the Indian national movement: Unseen faces and unheard voices, 1930–1942.* New Delhi: SAGE.

Thapar-Björkert, Suruchi, and Louise Ryan. 2002. "Mother India/Mother Ireland: Comparative gendered dialogues of colonialism and nationalism in the early twentieth century." *Women's Studies International Forum* 25(3): 301–313.

Walby, Sylvia. 1997. *Gender transformations.* London: Routledge.

Walby, Sylvia. 2000. "Gender, nations and states in the global era." *Nations and Nationalism* 6(4): 523–540.

Ward, Margaret. 1989. *Unmanageable revolutionaries: Women and Irish nationalism.* London: Pluto Press.

Yuval-Davis, Nira. 1997. *Gender and nation.* London: SAGE.

Yuval-Davis, Nira, and Floya Anthias. 1989. *Woman-nation-state.* London: Macmillan.

CHAPTER 33

....

SECURITY, CONFLICT, AND MILITARIZATION

....

LENE HANSEN

INTRODUCTION

....

Security is several things at once. It is an academic concept that stands at the center of security studies, a field that includes a range of specific approaches like feminist security studies and gender analysis. *Security* is also a word used in everyday language by politicians, the media, and activists, either on its own or by being hyphenated, such as in *cyber security, social security, food security,* or *human security.* Such diverse uses show that security is a site of political struggle: to define something as a matter of security is to claim that this is an issue that is really important. In the words of Barry Buzan, Ole Wæver, and Jaap de Wilde, security is "a special kind of politics or [as] above politics" (Buzan, Wæver, and de Wilde 1998, 23). Because security is a site of struggle, it is impossible to come to an agreement on how the concept should be defined. This, as Buzan (1991, 7) explains, does not imply that security should be abandoned but rather that it should be understood as a concept that is essentially political and ambiguous. This chapter explores how security is imbued with gender and how its analysis provides an important addition to our understanding of some key themes in gender and politics such as the public–private divide, nations and nationalism, and the uses of different constructions of masculinity and femininity.

Security's status as a site of struggle implies that feminists have had to fight to get women's security problems—and gender more broadly—onto the academic and policy agenda. Although women's security problems are far from recent, as the history of wartime rape or sex selective abortions show (Brownmiller 1975,

140–173; Hudson and den Boer 2004, 23–64), it has only been during the past twenty-five years that *gender* has begun to enter the discipline of security studies (Cohn 1987; Sylvester 1987; Tickner 1992; Buzan and Hansen 2009, 138–141). Over the same quarter-century, there has also been a heightened acceptance of gendered insecurity problem by policy makers, usually in response to feminist activism (Cockburn 2010) (see also the chapters by Emanuela Lombardo, Petra Meier, and Mieke Verloo and Merike Blofield and Liesl Haas in this volume). Some of the issues that feature more prominently on the political agenda today than twenty-five years ago are sex trafficking and honor killings, and an important milestone in terms of women's security problems was the adoption of Resolutions 1325 by the United Nations (UN) Security Council in 2000. This resolution explicitly recognizes the specific threats faced by women and children during armed conflict, and it calls attention to the contribution that women can make to conflict prevention and peace building. Some of the conflict-related themes mentioned in the resolution are mine clearance, incorporating HIV/AIDS awareness into peacekeeping training programs, and increasing women's participation in decision making. Nongovernmental organizations and feminist activists played a crucial role in preparing drafts and lobbying for the resolution's adoption (Cohn, Kinsella, and Gibbings 2004).

Those working in the field of gender and security agree that gendered insecurities should be recognized, studied, and addressed politically. Yet there is still considerable diversity in terms of how far security is expanded beyond security studies' traditional focus on the military and what in political discourse is defined as national security. One body of research is concerned with what has historically been the main domain of security studies, namely, military conflict and why states go to war. Others stretch the scope to look more closely at the local impact of war on soldiers and civilian populations, including what happens when a conflict is solved and social relations—and that include gender relations—are assumed to return to normal. A third body of research moves security from the study of conflict and militarization to issues that are said to fundamentally endanger and threaten women, including food shortage, environmental degradation, or the upsurge in conservative religious practices.

There is also diversity in terms of how gender and security are studied. Epistemologically, we find feminist and gender scholars working in the empiricist, standpoint, and poststructuralist (or postmodern) traditions identified by Sandra Harding. Empiricist conceptions ground security in objective material and measurable factors, for instance, the number of women killed by malnutrition or raped during war. Standpoint conceptions suggest that security is a subjective condition—that it is based on what people fear and what beliefs they hold. Subjective understandings of security usually examine belief systems, threat perceptions, and women and men's lived experiences. Scholars might, for instance, ask whether women and men differ in their perception of what threatens their security or how they have experienced a war coming to an end. Poststructuralists, by contrast, define security as a discursive condition; that is, whether something is a question of (in)security depends on whether there are political actors who hold that this is something which is so important that it constitutes a threat to our survival. The focus also shifts from whether women (or men) are threatened to what subject positions are available when speaking insecurity. Women who have been trafficked for sex work are, for instance, often constrained by a choice between being illegal immigrants or victims (Berman 2003). There are, of course, potential tensions between these three epistemological positions, but feminist scholars working on security and conflict have tended to speak in favor of a pluralistic field where scholars might adopt—and combine—different positions. This chapter seeks not to side with one particular feminist position, in terms of neither substantial focus nor epistemology, but to give an account of the central academic and political dynamics that come into view when we put *gender* and *security* together.

The first section elaborates on the political dynamics and ambiguities that surround security by further explaining how bringing gender and security together invoke some of the grand dichotomies of political life: between the national within the state and the international–interstate arena; between the state or collective on one hand and the individual on the other; and between the public and the private. The next sections examine the main ways gender and security have been connected in academic and policy discourse. Then I discuss the claim that women are more peaceful than men—which, if true, would imply that bringing more women into political power would produce a more secure world. A variation of this thesis is the argument that women have different, and again more peaceful, views of foreign and security policies. Then the chapter examines how gender can become a referent object for security, that is, how women can become individuals or collectives whose security is in need of defense and protection. Then the chapter turns to militarism and masculinity—not that the two are inherently linked or that women have no involvement in militant actions but because the military and militarization have been central for highlighting that gender and security is not just a women's question. The last section briefly sums up, explains how feminist security studies has contributed to the wider field of security studies, and suggests where feminist and gender analysis might move in the future.

SECURITY AND KEY POLITICAL DICHOTOMIES

To see something as a matter of security is, as noted already, to make the claim that there is an existential threat to someone or somebody that needs to be countered. This often seems most obvious when we are dealing with military conflicts between states, where state A is attacking state B, but security is applied not only to military threats or to interstate conflicts. Gender issues that have been made matters of security include sex trafficking where institutions like the European Union (EU) have taken initiatives to combat the selling of women's bodies. In such cases, there is conflict in that there is a conflict of interest between the interests of the trafficked women, the criminal networks who control them, and the sending and receiving countries (Berman 2003; Aradau 2008). But it is clearly a different form of conflict than that of military combat.

But if security is applicable to all sorts of threat beyond those of military conflict, are there then any limits to what security is? Yes, in the sense that it is impossible for all issues to be constituted as those of security at the same time—that is, in the terminology of Wæver (1995), to be securitized—but also because security issues need to be situated in a particular way in relation to three of the big dichotomies that make up our understanding of political life: the national–international; the state–individual; and the public–private. Gender is significant for how we understand these dichotomies, and these dichotomies are central for whether and how gender can become part of security.

The National–International

One of the most important distinctions in politics is that between the domestic arena and the international, or what R. B. J. Walker (1993) calls inside–outside. Political relations inside the state are fundamentally different from those between states. Inside states we have governments who make sovereign decisions; internationally there are no sovereign authorities. In terms of security, states are deemed responsible for the security of their citizens; that is, they must offer them protection against external attacks but also against attacks from other citizens and nonstate institutions. States have, in Weberian terms, the monopoly on the legitimate use of violence, but with that monopoly comes also the responsibility for ensuring that people can live in relative safety from each other. States can also be held responsible for countering threats that go beyond physical attacks. States cannot easily overlook famine, financial crashes, and climate changes that will wipe out major parts of one's territory.

This of course is not to say that states actually take good care of their citizens' security. In the real world, in many parts of the world, we find governments turning a blind eye to things that threaten their populations, including those that stem from economic structures of inequality, and in some cases states are even persecuting their own citizens. But the inside–outside distinction nevertheless works to establish two different spheres that have two different kinds of rules. The inside–outside distinction also implies that there is an inbuilt resistance toward states telling other states how they should organize themselves domestically. In international politics, this is summed up in the principle called nonintervention in domestic affairs. On one hand, this of course provides dictatorial states with room to disregard insecurity domestically; on the other hand, as a principle of international politics, it also works to prevent conflicts, as states abstain from interfering in the political arrangements of other countries. As with the idea that states are responsible for the security of their citizens, the principle of nonintervention in domestic affairs is not always upheld in practice. During the cold war there were numerous examples of the superpowers supporting or undermining the regimes of other countries, and over the past twenty years we have seen a series of humanitarian interventions undertaken, at least rhetorically, in defense of threatened populations and women (Shepherd 2006).

The national–international distinction is important for security as such, but it is also important more specifically for understanding how gender becomes part of security. For one thing, the national–international distinction has left a trace on security in that the urgency and existential nature that comes with security goes right to the heart of a collective's survival. When we speak of security, we are implying that there is a national in front of security. Security is not, in other words, social security or questions of domestic equality, unless such issues are explicitly lifted into that realm. To make gender a matter of security is thus not only to make the case for example that women's structural economic disadvantage is a threat to their status and livelihood, it requires that economic disadvantage is put into the mode of this is a radical threat to the identity and survival of our community as a whole. This is not to say that it is impossible to get women's security issues onto the political agenda, but it does mean that for such issues to become security, rather than, say, equality, they have to be articulated as linked to physical or symbolic survival.

The crucial question therefore becomes how communal survival has been defined historically in a given context and what hindrances and possibilities this implies for making women's security a part of security proper. Let me illustrate this by two examples. Wartime rape became widely recognized as a gendered security problem during and in the wake of the war in Bosnia in the 1990s. These rapes were seen as threatening the psychical security of individual women who were actual or potential victims. But they were also constituted by the Bosnian government, women's movements, nongovernmental organizations, and later by the Tribunal in the Hague as threats to the wider Bosnian community (Hansen 2001). The constitution of wartime rape as a gendered security problem thus ran through a communal survival logic where attacks on women became an attack on Bosnia.

To take another, and perhaps more complex, example, abortion has been made a security issue by activist in countries that deny women abortion on the grounds that women have a right to make reproductive choices. In the absence of legal and safe access to abortion, women are forced to rely on procedures that cost them their fertility or even their lives, and such loss of (reproductive) rights effectively constitutes a physical threat to a major part of a community's members. Such attempts to situate the right to abortion within a security logic have often, however, been defeated by counterdiscourses that hold that it is not only the unborn child who is threatened by abortion, but the community as such as it has a principled normative commitment to the unborn. To suspend with that principle is thus to compromise one's essential identity.

The national–international also leaves another trace on security, in that while it is in principle possible that issues that are exclusively domestic in kind can be the subject of security it is almost always the case that there is a connection to the international. The international comes in, of course, in cases where the threat in question has a direct interstate military conflict dimension, such as soldiers from one country raping the population of another. The international also enters gender insecurity when soldiers or peacekeepers from one country carry diseases such as HIV/AIDS to another country, thus raising questions of threats and protection, masculinity and femininity, gender and the international (Enloe 1989, 84–91; Elbe 2003). Or the international comes into view as West European governments seek to counter sex trafficking through a mixture of deportation and support projects for women back home (Aradau 2008). But the international also enters domestic security in less explicit ways. Those fighting for the recognition of women's domestic insecurities will often seek to mobilize international networks in their struggle to transform the community they live within. Such calls and mobilizations often point to the sparse, although growing, body of international resolutions and reports that call for further attention to women's security problems, most prominently perhaps Resolution 1325 (Shepherd 2008).

The Individual–Collective

Another major dichotomy, already touched on, is that between the individual and the collective, which in modern politics is predominantly that of the state. Much debate in security studies revolves around whether the individual or a larger collective should be the referent object for security. This of course is not surprising in that the relationship between the individual and the community within which he or she lives is one of the foundational aspects of social and political thought. Conventional approaches to security have taken the state to be the unproblematic referent object for security, and this has produced a blindness to the particular insecurities women have suffered. Moreover, as Cynthia Enloe (1989) points out in one of the first feminist works on gender and security, international politics, including security politics, is a masculine domain, and it has been conducted by soldiers, businessmen, diplomats, and heads of states who are by and large men. The work that women do, as diplomatic wives, prostitutes working around military bases, or domestic maids, is deemed natural and not worthy of investigation. "Only men, not women or children, have been imagined capable of the sort of public decisiveness international politics is presumed to require" (Enloe 1989, 4). In that light, unsurprising feminists have brought gender into the study of security through a bottom-up approach that analyzes "the impact of war at the microlevel" (Tickner 2001, 48) and that starts "from the perspective of individual women's lives" (Sjoberg 2010, 5; see also Hoogensen and Stuvøy 2006, 211). Yet because individual lives are always constituted in relation to larger discursive, political, and economic structures, such lives are never just about the individual. When Elina Penttinen (2008) studies the lives of female Russian prostitutes working in the clubs of Helsinki, she is also examining the economic conditions that brought these women to Helsinki in the first place. Or when peacekeepers describe their relations with local girls they navigate the cultural norms that govern sexual relations at home with those of being in the field. This becomes, in Paul Higate and Marsha Henry's (2004) study, a way of concretely embodying notions of masculinity within a political economy of peacekeeping. Put differently, the individual is always negotiating and negotiated in relations to a series of collectives, identities, and institutions. To constitute something as a gendered security problem is thus to perform a practice that is simultaneously individualizing (it defines individual women's problems as worthy of being security problems) and collectivizing (through defining a gendered problem as crucial to the collective's survival, the collective itself is being (re) produced with a particular gendered identity). Yet, as underscored by the concept of intersectionality, to formulate something as a threat to women's insecurity is almost always to invoke not just gender identity but also race, nationality, ethnicity, religion, age, and class (Cockburn 2010, 150–152).

The Public–Private

The third dichotomy that should be considered is that of the public and the private. For something to be a security problem implies that it is brought into the public: a security issue is something that is of such significance that we need to do something to counter it. Issues that are strictly speaking located within the private sphere can thus become the subject of securitization, as when the fate of Afghan women is constituted as one of the reasons the United States should fight the Taleban (Tickner 2002). The requirement that women stayed largely at home and wore the burka when outside could be seen as an extreme case of confining women to the sphere of the private. The public and the private are not spheres that have an objective and transhistorical existence; they are produced and negotiated, and their boundaries shift over time (see also the chapter by Merike Blofield and Liesl Haas in this volume). The constitution of such boundaries is thus crucial to what become matters of security and what does not. Take, for instance, the issue of sex trafficking. One might suspect that the growing concern with the security problems faced by trafficked women stems at least in part from shifting norms in the realm of sexual politics, which makes it less acceptable today than fifty years ago to see the buying of sexual services as a private choice and transaction.

The public–private is also important because the historical construction of the male patriarch as the head of both public and private privileged men over women, and it produced—or legitimated—an understanding of men as different from women: as rational, forceful, not intimidated, farsighted, and objective, whereas women were emotional, weak, timid, shortsighted, and vacillating. Men were protectors, domestically of the patriarchal family and internationally of the body politics, self-sacrificing, patriotic, brave, aggressive, and heroic. Women were supportive and, in the words of Jean Bethke Elshtain (1987), *beautiful souls*. Even in those places where men and women are today formally equal in terms of their public rights, the history of the public–private split has caused a gendering of political space, indeed of politics itself (Elshtain 1981; Pateman 1983). This means that politics is a masculine space and masculinity is associated with "power, autonomy, rationality, and public," whereas femininity is associated with "weakness, dependence, emotion, and private" (Tickner 1997, 614). As we shall see in the next section, such assumptions have implications for how women and men enter security policies as well as academic analysis.

WOMEN AS PEACEFUL SUBJECTS

As Enloe (1989, 5) points out, most feminists are "reluctant to accept explanations that rest on an assertion that men and women are inherently different." To the extent that gender differences are said to exist, they are produced through socialization. Yet the fact that men have been constituted as masculine and women as feminine for centuries and that this has taken place across the globe implies that such socially produced differences have a deeply institutionalized quality to them. The notion that women are (socialized into being) a different kind of security subject, that is a more peaceful one, is thus hard to eliminate. This notion resurfaces from time to time within feminist work itself. One of the first scholars to identify the significance of women for security, peace researcher Elise Boulding, held that women hold different values, behave more cooperatively, favor critical epistemologies, and are "more interested in identifying alternative security systems than in studying arms control" (Boulding 1984, 2–3). Such statements are less prominent today, although the view that gender decides "who is peaceful and who is not" still appears (Hoogensen and Stuvøy 2006, 212). This notion is to some extent supported by the existence of women's peace movements, which go back to Women's International League for Peace and Freedom founded during World War I (see also the chapters by Karen Beckwith and by Christina Ewig and Myra Marx Ferree in this volume). More recent examples of movements who have got the attention of the media and established political actors are the women's camp at the military base Greenham Common during the 1980s and Women in Black, a worldwide women's peace movement that started in Israel in 1988 (Cockburn 2010).

The idea that men and women differ in their understandings of war and peace is also at the center of quantitative studies of public opinion that have identified a "gender gap" in men's and women's foreign policy attitudes (Togeby 1994). Examining the support for using U.S. military force from 1990 to 2003, Richard C. Eichenberg (2003, 112–113) concludes, for instance, that women are less supportive of the use of military force and that they are relatively more sensitive to humanitarian issues. To the extent that security politics become a central theme in elections, women's attitudes might have implications for what policies states pursue. Studies of gender differences among the electorate also note, however, that one should be cautious not to attribute such variation to essential identities as women are generally poorer than men and more left-leaning and this affects views of security politics.

For most feminists what is most significant about the notion that women are more peaceful than men is to understand and study how this assumption continues to play a role in domestic and international politics. Helen Kinsella argues, for instance, that Resolution 1325 builds upon a troubling understanding of women as peacemakers (Cohn, Kinsella, and Gibbings 2004, 136; see also Shepherd 2008, 115–121, 162). Another way that the resilience of women are peaceful comes through is in the media's continued fascination with women who defy gender stereotypes. Twenty years ago, Margaret Thatcher, who was Britain's prime minister during the Falklands War against Argentine, was the woman continuously invoked to prove that women were not inherently nice, cooperative, or weak on security (Enloe 1989, 5–7). More recently, we have such prominent figures as Condoleezza Rice, who was national security advisor and secretary of state to U.S. president George W. Bush, and Angela Merkel, Germany's prime minister since 2005, or, at the lower echelons of power, the female guards at Abu Ghraib, the Iraqi prison where torture and prisoner abuse was documented by photos leaked to the press in 2004. On one hand, the actions of the female guards, of whom the most well-known was Lynndie England, could be said to undermine support for the argument that women are different and kinder enactors of security. Yet, on the other, we might read the shock and horror that women could behave this way as an indication that traditional gender stereotypes are still in place: without such assumptions, England would have been one amongst a group of guards rather than the one who became the icon of Abu Ghraib (Enloe 2004b). As Enloe (1989, 6) points out in the case of Margaret Thatcher, the way women are represented visually is also significant for understanding how such women simultaneously transgress and reaffirm conventional understandings of gender. Seeing Thatcher as the only woman in heads of states photos, "we suddenly noticed that everyone else was male" (Enloe 1989, 6). And, the picture of England holding the naked prisoner on a leash became emblematic of the way masculinity and femininity were at the heart of the humiliations at Abu Ghraib.

The significance of the idea that women are peaceful goes beyond those high-profile individual cases that disturb it. Looking to how larger groups or categories of women are involved in security practices, there are several important examples of collectives failing to perform according to standard femininity assumptions. Two such examples are those of female combatants (Alison 2004; MacKenzie 2009) and suicide bombers (Brunner 2005; Gentry 2009). As in the cases of individual transgressive women, women who perform such activities have been subject to media attention, at least when they first become known. Yet, as feminists also point out, such female security enactors are often constituted through traditional notions of gender. This implies that female combatants are overlooked during postconflict reconstruction as national and international institutions assume the combatant is male (MacKenzie 2009). In the case of suicide bombers, traditional notions of femininity are at work in explanations that hold that women become suicide bombers because they are unmarried or widows, thus deprived of men, or that they are emotional and manipulated by cunning males rather than political agents making choices about their own lives (Brunner 2005).

The notion that women are peaceful has a gendered corollary, in that it relies upon a juxtaposition to men being (more) bellicose. But, in the same way as feminists have identified the historical and socially constructed genesis of the peaceful women, they have pointed to the constructed nature of masculinity. Thus, if masculinity can be shifted from one of warrior aggression to one of empathy and negotiation, one heightens the possibility for conflict resolution and prevention (Connell 2005, 1813–1814). Institutionally, one of the key ways that masculinity has been embedded has been through the military. With a few exceptions, men have been the ones defending territory, the body politics, and women and children (Elshtain 1987). Women have in most cases not been conscripted, and men can therefore be said to have a specific gendered security problem insofar as they are more likely to die in combat. Men are, moreover, more likely to be the targets of executions and massacres aimed at civilian populations during warfare (Jones 1994). As R. Charli Carpenter (2003) holds, when women and children rather than men are evacuated from besieged territories, it is in response to norms that make women and children subjects in need of protection rather than to objective assessments of who are most likely to be at risk. So, for feminist researchers, the main point is not that women are always more insecure than men. The concern is rather with the way men and women are constituted as different forms of security subjects and that these in turn are visible in politics and analysis to different extents. To take combat deaths, these are a part of traditional security analysis insofar as military capability, including the strength of one's armed forces, is a key component in the study of war. Women's insecurity problems—wartime rape, increased domestic violence postconflict, and shortage of food, which usually affects women worse—are, on the other hand, absent as these take place outside the scope of proper conflict. Yet the way that male combat deaths are represented through added numbers and a disembodied language fail to reflect how men are impacted very differently by war depending on their socioeconomic, geographical, racial, and national identity and status (Connell 2005, 1809). Aggregated numbers also fail to mirror the complicated ways that individuals negotiate the intersection between these identities or how individual sufferings and losses make up what feminists characterize as the lived life of conflict (Cohn 1987; 2006).

Gendered Referent Objects

As noted already, it has been crucial for feminist scholars to make threats to women and their contributions to practices of security visible. Feminists have also argued that what or who becomes the subject of public policy and foreign policy is thoroughly gendered. This gendering implies that a multitude of gendered insecurities are not constituted as worthy of (sufficient) attention: women and female children suffer, for instance, disproportionately during famine; wartime rape and rape following conquest has until very recently been seen as expectable if not acceptable; and trafficked women are often either ignored or deported with little concern for their further destiny. Women and men are, in other words, not equal referent objects in front of the state and the insecurity women experience is a product of "unequal gendered structural relations" (Tickner 1997, 616). The gendered referent object is one that is both individual and collective: it foregrounds the individual woman—or man—yet this individual is given only as gendered through her or his location within a gendered economic, political, and cultural structure.

Digging deeper into what makes gender a referent object for security we should note first that to identify women as a referent object says little about the specific constitution of this object and thus about what kind of security responses should be adopted. Take the example of sex trafficking where "trafficked women" are made the referent object of security. Yet there are two very different discourses in Western Europe, one that constitutes those trafficked as victims and one that constitutes them as illegal immigrants. Victims have been tricked and are in need of protection against (usually) male criminal networks; illegal immigrants are at least partially responsible for the situation they have brought themselves in (Petersen 2001; Berman 2003). The security responses that flow from these two referent objects are thus different: illegal immigrants can simply be deported, whereas victims call for some kind of protection, be that asylum, a temporary residency, or a rehabilitation program at home. Yet, as feminist analysis points out, one problem with these two constitutions of the gendered referent object is that they lock trafficked women into binary positions—either they are victims deprived of agency or they are illegal immigrants who circumvent the law—and these fail to capture the more complex negotiations of agency and subjectivity that trafficked women articulate (Penttinen 2008).

Second, while it is important to identify women as a distinct referent object, it is also a referent object that never appears in isolation from other referent objects, be that the nation, the ethnic group, a religious community, class, or ideology. Women—and men—negotiate how these identities intersect, but as Cynthia Cockburn (2010, 150–151) stresses, intersectionality is also at work at the macrolevel as structures and institutions of power impact which kind of referent objects can be argued politically. The relationship between women and the nation is, for example, a complicated one that can take many forms (see also the chapter by Suruchi Thapar-Bjorkert in this volume). Women have been appropriated by conservative romantic projects that constitute women as the soft, vulnerable, gentle heart of the nation, but women's rights have also been invoked by postcolonial movements. Religious and gendered identities are also often intertwined. An extreme example of such intertwining is that of the Taliban regime in Afghanistan, which invoked Islamic norms in their defense of restricting women physically. We should note also that referent objects are not things or identities that exist out there as objective categories but that they are constituted and (re)produced through material and discursive practices. Such (re)productive practices can come in the form of continuous, steady, everyday activities such as referring to soldiers as he or putting on a burka. These practices might often be hard to recognize as practices precisely because they are so firmly institutionalized and feminist scholars thus encourage us to defamiliarize what looks familiar. But (re)productive practices might also be more specific, high-profile, and targeted. Take, for example, the case of wartime rape in Bosnia, which worked to humiliate not only the women who were raped but also "their" male's masculinity as they were unable to protect "their" women. Rapes were productive in that they constituted or reinforced gendered and national identities among rape victims and survivors, raping soldiers and males on the other side (Hansen 2001).

As these examples show, women is a referent object that is difficult to articulate as separate from other collective referent objects. The nation, for instance, has a much longer history of being constituted as a freestanding or privileged referent object, and this in turn implies that most of nonfeminist security studies overlook gender or hold that it can be subsumed through the study of other referent objects (Hansen 2000). Because gender usually appears in policy discourse through an intertwining with other referent objects it is open to various policy responses. Therefore, it is hard to say what the feminist response to a given security problem should be. Should feminists support military intervention in defense of women or advocate more nonviolent forms of conflict resolution? While many feminists writing on security have tended to take the latter route, there are also some who hold that there might be instances where the use of force is called for (Sylvester 2010).

Third, what we might call the politics of the referent object also raises the question of whether a gendered referent object is truly articulated or whether it is strategically mobilized to gain support for what is effectively a nongendered security agenda. The war against Afghanistan was, for instance, legitimized by the Bush Administration as being in defense of women living under the non-Western, repressive, barbaric Taliban regime (Hunt 2002; Tickner 2002; Nayak 2006; Shepherd 2006). Yet, argue feminists, this has turned out to be by and large rhetoric only as women's security problems have been overlooked or inadequately attended to (Enloe 2004a, 268–305). Such dissonance between rhetoric and action shows that one should be careful to deduce that women have become a genuine referent object for security from what heads of state or international institutions declare. Yet we might also see the invocation of women, even if just rhetorical, as an indication that securitizing actors do believe that women's rights are important to their audiences.

Fourth, as noted already, the referent object is not something that exists out there independently of (re)productive practices. Referent objects are, in other words, collectives that are imbued with a particular form of gendered meaning. We might identify referent objects as these are constituted in discourse, for example, in debates over what it means to incorporate women in postconflict reconstruction programs. But feminists also call for being attentive to the way that world politics is lived and embodied by actual human beings (Tickner 2005, 7). To take one example, Yvonne A. Braun's (2011) intersectional analysis traces the way gender, age, and class are intertwined in lived experiences of insecurity—including food insecurity—in the cases of three women adversely affected by the Lesotho Highlands Water Project. Put differently, if we study security only through what governments and big international institutions say about it, we cannot be sure to identify all the ways gendered insecurities feature in peoples' lives. This does not mean that we should see gender as an individual concept, but we should expand the number and kinds of actors and processes that is part of security analysis and incorporate methodologies that embrace an "ethnographic style of individually oriented story-telling typical of anthropology" (Tickner 1997, 615) or "hermeneutic and interpretative methodologies" that "allow subjects to document their own experiences in their own terms" (Tickner 2005, 19).

Experience thus emerges as an epistemological strategy through which to incorporate a feminist perspective. "Too often, women's experiences have been deemed trivial or only important in so far as they relate to the experiences of men and the questions they typically ask" (Tickner 2005, 7). Including women's experiences lend space to previously marginalized subjects, but experiences are not individual or exclusively agential because the subject whose experience is being conveyed is there only as he or she is constituted through gendered structures. Put differently, we cannot conceive of women's experience without a prior assumption of gender being a meaningful cultural, biological, material, and political identity. And experiences do not reside (exclusively) within the individual; they are narrated to others and hence negotiated in relations to those representations of insecurity, identities, and referent objects voiced in a given setting.

MILITARIZATION AND MASCULINITY

Feminists argue that war and conflict play an enormous role for women's—and men's—lives and that this should be thoroughly recognized and contextualized. The adoption of Resolution 1325 is thus described as an extraordinary achievement by activists as well as academics (Cohn, Kinsella, and Gibbings 2004, 137, 139). Countries that are preparing for war or that have entered a permanent state of insecurity undergo deep-seated processes of militarization. Militarization entails a prioritization of the military, economically in that more resources are devoted to weaponry and personnel, politically in that the military gets to have a higher say in decision making, and culturally in that military norms are constituted as desirable not only within the military but in society as such. There is a tendency to constitute such desirable military features and identities as hypermasculine and thus to accentuate gender differences. The preparedness for war that militarization entails also imply that more decisions can be made in secret or without public deliberation, because this is a national emergency (Wæver 1995). Take, for example, the way the prison camp in Guantanamo or the use of water boarding, where a prisoner is given the feeling of drowning, were legitimized as necessary because of the war against terror by the Bush Administration. Even for those who are not in the military or detained at Guantanamo, militarization has consequences because it changes the general political atmosphere and procedures.

War and militarization have had complex implications for women's lives. In some cases, war has brought women into traditional masculine domains and roles, as workers and heads of households, as men were at the front. At other times, militarization has reinforced traditional constructions of masculinity and femininity as men were called upon to fight and women were positioned as those to be protected (Elshtain 1987). To conventional security studies, the main focus has been on war itself or on how demilitarization after war has affected the risk of future fighting. Feminists by contrast have devoted extensive attention to what happens to women postconflict. World War II was, for example, a major case of women being mobilized as workers, only to be sent back home after war ended. This, in turn, reinstalled women's economic dependence on the male breadwinner and worked against a collective feeling of identity that women might have with other female workers. Feminists have also drawn attention to how female combatants are forgotten by international institutions and state agencies that seek to reintegrate soldiers into peacetime society (MacKenzie 2009) and how female combatants are often not readily accepted by their society (Alison 2004). This may in part be because female combatants are believed to have been sexually involved with male combatants and their reputation is compromised or because they problematize dominant constructions of women as peaceful or passive.

Conflict might also continue postconflict as incidents of domestic abuse have been shown to rise. Much of this abuse is attributable to traumatic experiences soldiers have incurred during combat, with many soldiers showing symptoms of traumatic stress. Popular culture, film in particular, has been an important medium for drawing attention to this phenomenon. The Vietnam War was emblematic in this respect with the figure of Rambo, who in the first movie *First Blood* was a lone wolf who failed to fit into an American society unable to understand its veterans' suffering. More recently, the consequences of the wars in Iraq and Afghanistan for soldiers' health and their family and friends have been critically engaged by films such as *In the Valley of Elah* (directed by Paul Haggis, 2007). Militarization also has a linguistic and gendered component in that the language used to describe warfare and weaponry tends to be patriarchal and rational–scientific (Hook 1985, 71). In an early, feminist analysis, Carol Cohn (1987) shows how the language of nuclear deterrence was gendered and sexualized—with talk of *penetration aids, big sticks,* and *soft laydowns*—while human losses were constituted through the disembodied category of *collateral damage* (Cohn 1987). As Cohn also points out, speaking the language of nuclear weaponry was fun and made one feel in control. The power of nuclear discourse was thus not simply to provide a technical, scientific language but to provide a sense of cognitive mastery over a "technology that is finally *not controllable*" (704).

Much of the early work on gender, security, and conflict was devoted to bringing attention to women's security problems. Yet, because feminists and gender scholars understand gender as a relational concept, women and femininity are inevitably constituted through juxtapositions to men and masculinity. As Elshtain (1998, 448) later puts it, her 1987 *Women and War* was misnamed because the book engaged as much with the historical construction of *men's* relationship to war as that of women's. As a consequence, this chapter has already pointed to the role of masculinity in the construction of the public–private distinction, to the specific threats that men face due to their historical responsibility for fighting on behalf of the body politics, and to the fact that men is a subject that intersects with class, race, religion, age, and other markers of identity to produce very varied male insecurity problems.

Focusing particularly on the male side of gender relationality, a body of research has incorporated insights from men's or masculinity studies and highlighted the particular significance of masculinity for conflict, peace and security often through R. W. Connell's influential concept of hegemonic masculinity. Connell adopted Gramsci's concept of hegemony to highlight, in Charlotte Hooper's formulation, that gender structures build on "moral persuasion and consent rather than brute force (although such ascendency may be backed up by force)" and that gender structures change historically (Hooper 1998, 34; Connell and Messerschmidt 2005, 831). Hegemonic masculinity, moreover, is a pattern of practices, and it refers to "the currently most honored way of being a man," which might not necessarily be the most empirically prevalent form of masculinity (Connell and Messerschmidt, 832). Connell and Messerschmidt (2005) also point to the significance of complicit masculinity and the compliance of heterosexual women for institutionalizing dominant forms of masculinity. One should also note that local gender orders interact with other local orders as well as with the global one "(Connell 2005, 1804–1805).

Scholars working on masculinity and security have explored gender dynamics at three different—often intersecting—levels of analysis. First, drawing on fieldwork and other ethnographic methods, the ways specific men negotiate their masculinity are brought out. As Higate and Henry (2004, 484) point out, the military is "the exemplary masculinized institution" which makes it an important site of research: if hegemonic masculinity is reconstituted within the military, we might have good reasons to expect it being—or becoming— reconstituted elsewhere, too. Moreover, soldiers are important practitioners of foreign and security policy. Thus, global and local forms of masculinity stand at the center of how populations experience the (gendered) encounter with one's own soldiers, enemy combatants, occupying forces, or peacekeepers. The performance of masculinities that transgress local or global norms is furthermore crucial for how warfare and postconflict reconstruction are legitimized or contested (Hansen 2001). As studies of peacekeepers by Higate and Henry and Claire Duncanson (2009) underscore, it is important to identify the ways experiences of masculinity vary. Studying the autobiographies of four British soldiers involved in peacekeeping in Bosnia in the 1990s, Duncanson (75–77) suggests for instance that seniority in age and rank might allow for the articulation of a peacekeeper masculinity that is more inclusive of traditional feminized qualities.

Second, masculinity—and femininity—is a discursive figure that is employed in the construction of countries, peoples, and continents. Hooper (1998, 36) notes, for instance, how British imperialists of the nineteenth-century "imagined the 'Orient' as an exotic, sensual, and feminized world, a kind of halfway stage between 'Europe's enlightenment' and 'African savagery.'" Within this feminized world, there were degrees of femininity, and Hooper shows that what constitutes femininity can change: from the association of doing women's work such as laundry or cooking (Chinese immigrants to the United States) to having "manipulative tendencies" (attributed to the Japanese) (ibid.). Masculinity might also be employed to construct the Other in inferior ways. Duncanson (73) shows, for example, how the dominant construction of the Balkan soldier was one who is hypermasculine, "aggressive, irrational and violent." Such constructions are important because they form the broader political terrain upon which foreign policy decisions are made. If the Orient is a feminized space, it lends itself to protection and perhaps education; if the Balkans is inhabited by aggressive and irrational males, one might question whether peacekeeping forces can facilitate any long-term solution.

Third, work on masculinity has also been concerned with whether the state itself has a gender, more specifically whether its foreign and security policies can be said to be masculine or feminine. Focusing on the international domain, J. Ann Tickner held as early as 1988 that so-called Realist assumptions about state behavior are built upon a "masculine world view" illustrated for example by nuclear strategy whose "vocabulary of power, threat, force, and deterrence, has a distinctly masculine ring" (428–429). A feminist worldview would by contrast open for an understanding of power as mutually enabling and empowering, for nonviolent conflict resolution driving by a practice of care, and for an appreciation of the Other as a human being rather than an alien enemy. Examples of female state behavior identified by Tickner included small states, the Southern African Development Co-ordination Conference, and the European Community (434). States might in short pursue masculine as well as feminine foreign policies. Cases of hypermasculine state behavior include the policies of the United States toward Iraq and Afghanistan after September 11 (Nayak 2006; Maruska 2010), while feminism might be found in Scandinavian development policies (Richey 2001). Yet as hegemonic masculinity as well as desirable femininity change across time and space, such assessments are always made in relation to a particular context (Sylvester 2001, 244).

Conclusion

This essay has provided an overview of how security—as a concept and a political and academic practice—intersects with gender. I started by explaining that security is a site of struggle that has been approached from multiple substantial and analytical angles: gender as an explanation for why states go to war, gender as it impacts upon and is impacted by armed conflict, and gender-related security problems beyond the realm of the military. Epistemologically, security has been approached from empiricist, standpoint feminist, and poststructuralist perspectives. The first section discussed in more detail how bringing gender and security together draw upon specific and often ambiguous articulations of three dichotomies: the national–international; the individual–collective; and the public–private. Central to debates over gender and security is also the question of whether women are a particular, and more peaceful, kind of subject. I discussed how few feminists would subscribe to this notion but that it continues to govern policies and media representations, particularly of women who fail to accommodate to established "peaceful" norms. Then the essay turned to a more in-depth discussion of how women can become referent objects for security—that is, those who need to be secured. To fully understand not just whether women become referent objects but also how and what implications ensue, one needs to dig deeper into the ways gendered subjectivities are constituted. One also needs to examine the intersection between gender and other referent objects, whether a gendered referent object is merely strategically and rhetorically invoked, and in what ways a referent object can be spoken into being. The last part of the essay discussed the gendered dimensions of militarization and postconflict reconstruction as well as the ways masculinity is crucial for the articulation of lived experiences, discourses about national, regional, and civilizational Selves and Others, and a possible characterization of states' foreign policies.

Situating gender analysis on the wider terrain of security studies, it has over the past twenty-five years made a series of important contributions. First, women and men have become recognized as categories worthy of academic analysis and political attention, and this has in turn shown how international relations and security evolve around embodied beings rather than abstract structures. Second, feminist security studies has played a crucial role within the larger critical security studies move, which has argued in favor of an expansion of security beyond the military–political sector and the state as the privileged referent object. Feminists have also made the important point that the goal is not to substitute the state with another privileged referent object, be that the nation, religion, or women. Most gendered security problems cannot be understood in isolation, only through the way women and men as referent objects intersect with race, age, class, nation, and religion. Third, feminist have played an important role in the critique of the West. They have drawn upon postcolonial literature and non-Western perspectives to highlight that the definition of what security entails is dependent upon time, space, and access to power. Feminists have also problematized the political and academic separation between security and development and the way colonial practices and neoliberal economic structures have impacted global gender orders. Fourth, feminists have highlighted how the wars against and in Iraq and Afghanistan have been legitimated in part as being in defense of women but that this rhetoric has been insufficiently matched by political initiatives. This in turn shows the necessity of carefully examining the intersection between language and practice, more specifically the pitfalls of strategic discourse. Five, gender analysis has been one of the key sites for examining the connections between activism, academic theorization, and policy formulation. Sixth, and finally, gender analysis and feminist security studies make up a fascinating microcosm within the wider field of security studies in that it brings together a wide-ranging pallet of ontological, epistemological, and methodological approaches. As Christine Sylvester (2007) points out, the general tendency within the discipline of International Relations—of which security studies is a part—has been that of a camp structure where individual perspectives turn inward, focusing on their own debates. Gender analysis and feminist security studies provide possibly the best example of intercamp dialogue countering this insular trend.

Looking to the future, it seems safe to say that gender and feminist analysis is now so firmly institutionalized within security studies that it is very unlikely to disappear (Buzan and Hansen 2009, 265–272). Historically, one of the main drivers of gender analysis and feminist security studies has been political events—for instance, nuclear deterrence, mass rape in the wars in Bosnia and Kosovo, and the wars in Afghanistan and Iraq—so whichever new wars or other issues that manage to manifest themselves on the global or regional agenda are likely to be picked up. How such events will impact theory building is of course impossible to say for sure, but the six ways gender and feminist analysis have impacted the field of security studies so far are likely to be important for how the subfield of feminist security studies moves forward.

REFERENCES

Alison, Miranda. 2004. "Women as agents of political violence: Gendering security." *Security Dialogue* 35(4): 447–463.

Aradau, Claudia. 2008. *Rethinking trafficking in women: Politics out of security.* Houndsmills, UK: Palgrave Macmillan.

Berman, Jacqueline. 2003. "(Un)popular strangers and crisis (un)bounded: Discourses of sex-trafficking, the European political community and the panicked state of the modern state." *European Journal of International Relations* 9(1): 37–86.

Boulding, Elise. 1984. "Focus on: The gender gap." *Journal of Peace Research* 21(1): 1–3.

Braun, Yvonne A. 2011. "Left high and dry: An intersectional analysis of gender, dams and development in Lesotho." *International Feminist Journal of Politics* 13(2): 141–162.

Brownmiller, Susan. 1975. *Against our will: Men, women and rape.* New York: Fawcett Columbine.

Brunner, Claudia. 2005. "Female suicide bombers—Male suicide bombing? Looking for gender in reporting the suicide bombings of the Israeli–Palestinian conflict." *Global Society* 19(1): 29–48.

Buzan, Barry. 1991. *People, states & fear: An agenda for international security studies in the post-cold war era.* Hemel Hempstead: Harvester Wheatsheaf.

Buzan, Barry, and Lene Hansen. 2009. *The evolution of international security studies.* Cambridge, UK: Cambridge University Press.

Buzan, Barry, Ole Wæver, and Jaap de Wilde. 1998. *Security: A new framework for analysis.* Boulder, CO: Lynne Rienner.

Carpenter, R. Charli. 2003. "'Women and children first': Gender, norms, and humanitarian evacuation in the Balkans 1991–1995." *International Organization* 57(4): 661–694.

Cockburn, Cynthia. 2010. "Gender relations as causal in militarization and war." *International Feminist Journal of Politics* 12(2): 139–157.

Cohn, Carol. 1987. "Sex and death in the rational world of defense intellectuals." *Signs: Journal of Women in Culture and Society* 12(4): 687–718.

Cohn, Carol. 2006. "Motives and methods: using multi-sited ethnography to study US national security discourses." In Brooke A. Ackerly, Maria Stern, and Jackie True, eds., *Feminist methodologies for international relations.* Cambridge, UK: Cambridge University Press, 91–107.

Cohn, Carol, Helen Kinsella, and Sheri Gibbings. 2004. "Women, peace and security: Resolution 1325." *International Feminist Journal of Politics* 6(1): 130–140.

Connell, R. W. 2005. "Change among the gatekeepers: Men, masculinities, and gender equality in the global arena." *Signs: Journal of Women in Culture and Society* 30(3): 1801–1825.

Connell, R. W., and James W. Messerschmidt. 2005. "Hegemonic masculinity: Rethinking the concept." *Gender & Society* 19(6): 829–859.

Duncanson, Claire. 2009. "Forces for good? Narratives of military masculinity in peacekeeping operations." *International Feminist Journal of Politics* 11(1): 63–80.

Eichenberg, Richard C. 2003. "Gender differences in public attitudes toward the use of force by the United States, 1990–2003." *International Security* 28(1): 110–141.

Elbe, Stefan. 2003. "HIV/AIDS and the changing landscape of war in Africa." *International Security* 24(2): 159–177.

Elshtain, Jean Bethke. 1981. *Public man, private woman: Women in social and political thought.* Princeton, NJ: Princeton University Press.

Elshtain, Jean Bethke. 1987. *Women and war.* Chicago: University of Chicago Press.

Elshtain, Jean Bethke. 1998. "Women and war: Ten years on." *Review of International Studies* 24(4): 447–460.

Enloe, Cynthia. 1989. *Making feminist sense of international relations: Bananas, beaches & bases.* Berkeley: University of California Press.

Enloe, Cynthia. 2004a. *The curious feminist: Searching for women in the new age of empire.* Berkeley: University of California Press.

Enloe, Cynthia. 2004b. "Wielding masculinity inside Abu Ghraib: Making feminist sense of an American military scandal." *AJWS* 10(3): 89–102.

Gentry, Caron E. 2009. "Twisted maternalism: From peace to violence." *International Feminist Journal of Politics* 11(2): 235–252.

Hansen, Lene. 2000. "The little mermaid's silent security dilemma and the absence of gender in the Copenhagen School." *Millennium* 29(2): 285–306.

Hansen, Lene. 2001. "Gender, nation, rape: Bosnia and the construction of security." *International Feminist Journal of Politics* 3(1): 55–75.

Higate, Paul, and Marsha Henry. 2004. "Engendering (in)security in peace support operations." *Security Dialogue* 35(4): 481–498.

Hoogensen, Gunhild, and Kirsti Stuvøy. 2006. "Gender, resistance and human security." *Security Dialogue* 37(2): 207–228.

Hook, Glenn D. 1985. "Making nuclear weapons easier to live with: The political role of language in nuclearization." *Bulletin of Peace Proposals* 16(1): 67–77.

Hooper, Charlotte. 1998. "Masculinist practices and gender politics: The operation of multiple masculinities in international relations." In Marysia Zalewski and Jane Parpart, eds., *The "man" question in international relations.* Boulder, CO: Westview, 28–53.

Hudson, Valerie M., and Andrea M. den Boer. 2004. *Bare branches: The security implications of Asia's surplus male population.* Cambridge, MA: MIT Press.

Hunt, Krista. 2002. "The strategic co-optation of women's rights: Discourse in the 'war on terrorism.'" *International Feminist Journal of Politics* 4(1): 116–121.

Jones, Adam. 1994. "Gender and ethnic conflict in ex-Yugoslavia." *Ethnic and Racial Studies* 17(1): 115–134.

MacKenzie, Megan. 2009. "Securitization and de-securitization: Female soldiers and the reconstruction of women in post-conflict Sierra Leone." *Security Studies* 18(2): 241–261.

Maruska, Jennifer Heeg. 2010. "When are states hypermasculine?" In Laura Sjoberg, ed., *Gender and international security: Feminist perspectives.* London: Routledge, 235–255.

Nayak, Meghana. 2006. "Orientalism and 'saving' US state identity after 9/11." *International Feminist Journal of Politics* 8(1): 42–61.

Pateman, Carole. 1983. "Feminist critiques of the public/private dichotomy." In Stanley I. Benn and G. F. Gaus, eds., *Public and private in social life*. London: Croom Helm, 118–140.

Penttinen, Elina. 2008. *Globalization, prostitution and sex-trafficking: Corporeal politics*. London: Routledge.

Petersen, Karen Lund. 2001. "Trafficking in women: The Danish construction of Baltic prostitution." *Cooperation and Conflict* 36(2): 213–238.

Richey, Lisa Ann. 2001. "In search of feminist foreign policy: Gender, development, and Danish state identity." *Cooperation and Conflict* 36(2): 177–212.

Shepherd, Laura J. 2006. "Veiled references: Constructions of gender in the Bush Administration discourse on the attacks on Afghanistan post-9/11." *International Feminist Journal of Politics* 8(1): 19–41.

Shepherd, Laura J. 2008. *Gender, violence and security: Discourse as practice*. London: Zed.

Sjoberg, Laura. 2010. "Introduction." In Laura Sjoberg, ed., *Gender and international security: Feminist perspectives*. London: Routledge, 1–14.

Sylvester, Christine. 1987. "Some dangers in merging feminist and peace projects." *Alternatives* 12(4): 493–509.

Sylvester, Christine. 2001. "Writing feminist International Relations from Nordic perspectives: An appreciation." *Cooperation and Conflict* 36(2): 239–247.

Sylvester, Christine. 2007. "Whither the international at the end of IR." *Millennium* 35(3): 551–573.

Sylvester, Christine. 2010. "Tensions in feminist security studies." *Security Dialogue* 41(6): 607–614.

Tickner, J. Ann. 1988. "Hans Morgenthau's principles of political realism: A feminist reformulation." *Millennium* 17(3): 429–440.

Tickner, J. Ann. 1992. *Gender in international relations: Feminist perspectives on achieving global security*. New York: Columbia University Press.

Tickner, J. Ann. 1997. "You just don't understand: Troubled engagements between feminists and IR theorists." *International Studies Quarterly* 41(4): 611–632.

Tickner, J. Ann. 2001. *Gendering world politics: Issues and approaches in the post-cold war era*. New York: Columbia University Press.

Tickner, J. Ann. 2002. "Feminist perspectives on 9/11." *International Studies Perspectives* 3(4): 333–350.

Tickner, J. Ann. 2005. "What is your research program? Some feminist answers to International Relations methodological questions." *International Studies Quarterly* 49(1): 1–22.

Togeby, Lise. 1994. "The gender gap in foreign policy attitudes." *Journal of Peace Research* 31(4): 375–392.

Wæver, Ole. 1995. "Securitization and desecuritization." In Ronnie Lipschutz, ed., *On security*. New York: Columbia University Press, 46–86.

Walker, R. B. J. 1993. *Inside/outside: International relations as political theory*. Cambridge, UK: Cambridge University Press.

INDEX

....

CPSIA information can be obtained
at www.ICGtesting.com
Printed in the USA
BVOW09s0259120617
486557BV00003B/6/P